D1505119

UNDER THE EDITORSHIP OF

Dayton D. McKean

UNIVERSITY OF COLORADO

Organizing fo

INTERNATIONAL ORGANIZATIO

HOUGHTON MIFFLIN COMPANY

The Riverside Press

LOW

Peace

IN WORLD AFFAIRS

Daniel S. Cheever
HARVARD UNIVERSITY
H. Field Haviland, Jr.
HAVERFORD COLLEGE

"STRAINING FOR EVER TO THE LIGHT
THAT FLOWS FROM REGIONS OUT OF SIGHT"

MAN

UNO

FOR

O. T. C. and *B. B. H.*

*The cartoon on the title page is by David Low.
Copyright Low all countries. Reprinted by
permission of the artist.*

PREFACE

"The United Nations Charter represents man's most determined and promising effort to save humanity from the scourge of war and to establish justice between the nations."
— JOHN FOSTER DULLES, *Secretary of State* [1]

"The United nations . . . was a fraud in its inception, a hypocrite in its operation; but for the fact that it first reddened Korean mountains with sacred American blood, it would have been a farce in its demise."
— DONALD WILSON, Past National Commander, American Legion [2]

PERCHED ON A BIT OF LAND carved out of the edge of Manhattan Island, overhanging the East River, stands the towering glass-and-steel slab of the central United Nations building. Its bold but marginal situation, in relation to its skyscraper-studded surroundings, is appropriately symbolic of its equally cramped position in the political world. It is a courageous structure reaching towards a more integrated world. At the same time, it is hemmed in by the older world of national interests and resistance to change.

The United Nations is only one of many universal and regional organizations that have sprung out of the soil of international relations in recent years and, by disturbing age-old traditions, have become the objects of intense controversy. This volume is written as an attempt to cut through the jungle of tangled issues that have entwined themselves around, and often obscured, the realities of these institutions. The authors' basic objective is to lay bare the significance of these organizations in relation to the total setting of international political, economic and social relations. The goal is to reveal them as they actually are — neither stronger nor weaker — and to analyze them not as self-contained and self-propelled entities but as a few among many channels through which governmental and nongovernmental interests operate.

A work of this scope naturally rests on the contributions of a great many people to whom the authors wish to acknowledge their great debt of gratitude. We are especially grateful to Mr. Raymond Dennett, Director of the World Peace Foundation, who, in collaboration with Professor Margaret Ball, of Wellesley College, and the present authors, planned a work that would, among other things, stress the continuing problems of international organizations and especially the fundamental unity, rather than uniqueness, of the League and UN experiences. Unfortunately, other commitments prevented Mr. Dennett and Professor Ball from continuing with the project,

---

[1] Speech before the Subcommittee of the Senate Foreign Relations Committee on the United Nations Charter, Department of State Press Release No. 19, January 18, 1954.
[2] Speech delivered on March 21, 1953, quoted in Alexander Uhl, *The Assault on the UN* (Washington: Public Affairs Institute, 1953), p. 7.

although both have been of great assistance. Mr. Dennett has read almost the entire manuscript and given us most valuable advice. Building on the original plan, the authors have also given greater attention to economic and social issues and the development of regional systems than has been usual in a book of this character.

One of our greatest debts, which all humanity shares with us, is owed to those courageous men of good will who have dared to experiment in the direction of bolder cooperation among nations, to build stronger bridges joining governments and peoples. Robert Cecil, Woodrow Wilson, Albert Thomas and Fridtjof Nansen are among the members of this small band of peaceful revolutionaries. As for those who are now in the thick of the battle, we are deeply grateful to the many national and international officials who have been so generous with their time and counsel. To name them individually would not only do an injustice to those we might neglect to mention but would risk embarrassing those we did cite by seeming to lay on their shoulders some of the burden of our own views.

Within the academic family, we have unashamedly exploited every opportunity to wring the last ounce of wisdom from many of our associates, among whom the following have been particularly helpful: Ralph Bunche, Inis L. Claude, William Y. Elliott, Clyde Eagleton, Rupert Emerson, William T. R. Fox, Carl J. Friedrich, Leland Goodrich, Arthur N. Holcombe, Philip Jacob, Joseph E. Johnson, Gertrude Leighton, L. Larry Leonard, Gerard Mangone, Warren Manshel, Dayton McKean, David Mitrany, Leo Pasvolsky, Guy Pauker, William Reitzel, Benjamin Rivlin, John Roche, Herman Somers, Robert Strausz-Hupé, Richard Swift, Ralph Townley, Richard W. Van Wagenen, Nicholas Wahl and Anne Winslow. Like all authors, however, we hasten to shield these good people from the barbs of critical readers by pointing out that the errors of fact and judgment which may be found in these pages are entirely our own.

It is also doubtful whether we could have carried this project off without the generous financial assistance given us by the Carnegie Corporation and the Harvard Foundation for Advanced Study and Research. The editors and staff of the Houghton Mifflin Company have been unfailingly patient and determinedly civil in the face of our frailties. Our research and secretarial assistants have been able and faithful partners who have made significant contributions in substance as well as form. These include Robert Hirschfield, MacAlister Brown, Richard Rosecrance and Mrs. Ray Lincoln. Not the least important is the debt we owe each other, for a work of this magnitude would have been difficult to manage single-handedly in the light of our other responsibilities. Then there are our wives, for whom the dedication of this work is grossly inadequate compensation for their constant and sympathetic understanding, encouragement and both research and editorial assistance. Finally, we thank our children — Danny, Libby, Holly, Debby and Mark — who suffered our preoccupation with only minor and restrained rebellions.

Daniel S. Cheever

H. Field Haviland, Jr.

CONTENTS

Part Three   LEAGUE AND UNITED NATIONS AT WORK

Part Four   REGIONAL AND OTHER SYSTEMS

Part Five   FUNDAMENTAL ISSUES

Appendices

Index

PART ONE

Introduction

1

Purposes, Principles and Problems

As THIS BOOK went to press, the headlines of a single number of *The New York Times* reported the following world-wide activities of various international organizations: a meeting of the allies who fought for the UN in Korea to plan the forthcoming peace conference, a tribute by Vice-President Richard Nixon to former President Harry Truman for deciding to initiate UN sanctions against North Korean aggression, an Indian query before the UN Committee on Information from Non-Self-Governing Territories regarding the status of Puerto Rico, consideration by the Security Council of the possibility of debating the French Government's difficulties in Morocco, the relation of the Trieste question to the North Atlantic Treaty Organization (NATO), the need for a more vigorous information program regarding NATO and UN treatment of Chinese prisoners in Korea. Exactly fifteen years earlier, in an equally stormy period of world history, the *Times* reported aggressive rumblings in Czechoslovakia and Japan, as well as a comforting prophecy by United States Secretary of Commerce Daniel Roper that war was "unlikely," but never a word of the League of Nations

1

or any other international organization of that unhappy era on the eve of
World War II.

The difference between these two sets of headlines is one dramatic
measure of the most important fact about today's international agencies:
that they are more ambitious, pervasive, influential and indispensable than
ever before. Every major power, including the United States and the Soviet
Union, finds it to its advantage to participate in many of these organizations — not primarily for reasons of sentiment but practical national interest. The stark truth is that no state, even the most powerful, is now capable
of surviving on the strength of its own unaided resources. In some comments to the press on May 28, 1953, President Dwight D. Eisenhower
argued that it was not only desirable, but downright essential that the
United States cooperate with the UN. "No single free nation," he said,
"can live alone in the world. . . . If you are going to try to develop a coalition . . . you have got to compromise." [1]

Nation-State Still Paramount

But it is important to take a broader look to see these agencies in the
total setting of international relations. While recognizing that they have
never been stronger, one must also recognize that they operate in a world
in which the nation-state is still king — the most powerful unit of social
organization, fortified by historical tradition and all the administrative and
technological skills of our age. The international "community" is conspicuous by its relative weakness. It lacks a common legislature, executive
and judiciary comparable to those that are at once the symptoms and
preservers of the relative integration of most national societies. International relations are still uncomfortably like the state of "warre" which the
philosopher Thomas Hobbes described in the seventeenth century:

> . . . Kings, and Persons of Soveraigne authority, because of their Inde-
> pendency, are in continuall jealousies, and in the state and posture of Gladi-
> ators; having their weapons pointing, and their eyes fixed on one another;
> that is, their Forts, Garrisons, and Guns, upon the Frontiers of their King-
> domes; and continuall Spyes upon their neighbours; which is a posture of
> War.[2]

There are, of course, some scattered rays of international collaboration
that have pierced this hostile climate. The moral goals advocated by some
men of good will have established new standards of enlightenment. Some
governments and peoples have reached across national boundaries to engage in cooperative ventures, such as the UN, that have somewhat strengthened the embryonic sense of world community. A young American aviator,
Captain Byron Dobbs, of Clio, Michigan, when questioned as to why he
had endured intense torture during his captivity in North Korea rather than

[1] *The New York Times,* May 29, 1953, p. 4.
[2] *Leviathan* (London: Dent, 1914), p. 65.

sign a confession, replied, "I am normally not a religious man. . . . But I did feel that the UN would live or die on the basis of what happened on this peninsula. I felt that I should do my part." [3] Many men have come to recognize the increasing material interdependence of mankind. On the other hand, because of continuing human tensions, whose destructive potential has been fantastically magnified by the frightening technological progress of our day, never before have so few destroyed so many of their fellowmen and so much material wealth as in this bloodiest century of them all.

In this context it becomes clear that international organizations are only one of many channels which states use to implement their national policies. They have been given almost no authority to legislate and must content themselves with recommendations. They have generally been discouraged from dealing directly with the man in the street, but have usually been compelled to speak through the screen of national governments. They have been fenced off from some of the most pressing problems of human affairs by the barrier of "domestic jurisdiction" and have received only small fractions of the sums spent by national governments. Finally, what they have accomplished, in spite of all these barriers, has stirred some hornets' nests of national xenophobia and loosed a swarm of stinging denunciations by patriotic vigilantes. Mrs. Elise Johnston, testifying before a subcommittee of the United States Senate Committee on Foreign Relations in behalf of the National Society for Constitutional Security, vehemently opposed any strengthening of the UN Charter.

> Gentlemen, we refuse to be frightened by talk of atomic warfare. Our ancestors ran the risk of roasting alive in their cabins with yelling Indians waiting outside to torture them. . . . I still live by the maxim in my first-grade copybook, "The coward dies a thousand deaths; the brave man dies but once." . . . In 1776, if the slogan "Peace at any price" had been popular, this Nation would not have been founded. We are willing to fight as our ancestors fought, but not under a world flag for a composite pattern of Asiatic and African ideologies in which we will be a minority group. . . . [4]

A Time for Thought

The stakes are too great, however, to abandon hope of progress. If ever there were a time for sober, objective and factual analysis of the problems of international organization, that time has come. Among the factors which lend special urgency to this effort are the development of hydrogen bombs in both the United States and the Soviet Union, the use of military sanctions in Korea in the name of the UN and the provision in the UN Charter for a possible constitutional review conference in 1955.

[3] *The New York Times*, September 6, 1953.

[4] *Hearings Before a Subcommittee of the Committee on Foreign Relations, United States Senate, 81st Congress, 2nd Session, on Resolutions Relative to Revision of the UN Charter* (Washington: Government Printing Office, 1950), p. 569.

Moreover, certain aspects of international organization would seem to deserve greater emphasis than they have sometimes received in the past. Hence, a conscious effort has been made in this volume to avoid discussing international organizations in a virtual vacuum with little more than perfunctory reference to outside economic and political forces. The aim here is rather to place the activities of these organizations in their proper dimension with respect to the larger setting of international relations. To counterbalance some of the more traditional preoccupation with the constitutional façade, particular emphasis is also placed on informal interpretation and process. There is less stress on organization as such and more on what organizations actually do and on the shaping of those activities by national and other interests.

Many books on international organization have been designed in terms of the agencies discussed, such as the UN Economic and Social Council or World Health Organization, rather than functional areas, such as economic development or health, in which more than one agency usually participates. The present volume is organized both structurally and functionally. Part Two concentrates on the basic organization and authority of the League and UN, including some discussion of the forces that molded their origin and subsequent evolution. Part Three explores what has actually been done in all major political, economic and social fields through the interrelated actions of various agencies. It has also been customary to discuss the League first and the UN second, in chronological order. It has seemed more useful in this study to concentrate upon parallel analysis. Hence the various aspects of the League and UN are considered side by side through all of Parts Two and Three.

Regional organizations are relative newcomers to the international scene. But their increasing role in world affairs warrants giving them equal billing in Part Four. Finally, this work tries to go beyond the usual descriptive emphasis to some extended analysis of major persistent issues, particularly in Part Five. We have felt an obligation to present our own specific conclusions on controversial questions wherever such conclusions seem justified. These are not presented as absolute or inevitable judgments handed down from Olympus, but solely as the best current evaluations of two among many observers in the field.

Underlying Questions

The overriding objective of this study is to appraise the past development of major international organizations, in terms of certain criteria discussed below, in order to help increase general understanding of that experience and improve the capacity of these bodies to meet the needs of mankind. The achievement of this end depends on the answers to a series of subsidiary questions which are the principal themes of this volume. To begin with, what have been the patterns of national and other interests that have shaped the creation of these organizations? How comprehensive has the scope of their jurisdictions been? How adequate have their functions been (ranging from research through negotiation and decision-making to action)? Have their structures (membership, plenary assemblies, executive committees, sub-bodies and staffs) been appropriate to their functional responsibilities? How satisfactory have their relationships been with international bodies, governments, nongovernmental organizations and individuals? What has been their actual impact? By asking these questions about each agency one can systematically compare them and judge their adequacy.

Running through these questions are certain persistent issues that should be kept in mind and are dealt with in some detail in Part Five of this volume. For example, some deal with various economic and social matters. Does human nature set any rigid limits on the development of international organizations? What is the relation of technology to international agencies? What is the validity of the "functional" approach to international relations? What contributions can international organizations make to the building of a sense of community? What are the implications of the "full employment" philosophy and the "welfare state?"

Then there are certain "political" and "military" issues. Is collective security possible? What are the requirements for an effective system of collective security? What is the validity of the concept of sovereignty? What problems are involved in the conflict between juridical equality and economic and political inequality? What is the validity of the concept of "domestic jurisdiction?" Are "national interests" and "international interests" necessarily antithetical? Are power politics and democracy reconcilable? What problems are involved in the relations between national governments and international agencies? How essential is it that members of international bodies observe democratic procedures domestically? How can the decisions of international organizations be more effectively implemented? Are regional and universal organizations mutually antagonistic? To what extent have international organizations developed "personalities" of their own? What are the relative merits of bilateral and multilateral diplomacy? What are and should be the character and role of international law? What is the feasibility of world government?

Imperatives of Analysis

All too frequently writers on social problems leap on polemical steeds and gallop off to tilt with beasts they never define, brandishing weapons they never explain. How often men call a thing "good" or "bad" without specifying their basic assumptions and criteria. The rest of this chapter, therefore, seeks to make clear to the reader some of the fundamental premises on which this study is based.

Definition of "International Organization"

First, it is useful to say what is meant by the term "international organization." In the briefest form possible, it can be defined as any cooperative arrangement instituted among states, usually by a basic agreement, to perform some mutually advantageous functions implemented through periodic meetings and staff activities. In thinking about the role of such organizations, it is important to avoid extremes. Some of the current "realists" are inclined to think that international agencies are quite passive instruments — meeting halls — that add nothing that would not take place without them. Many "idealists" tend to see them as independent creatures with wills and lives of their own.

Supporting the "realist" or "instrumentalist" argument, one must recognize that such organizations usually do not have the authority or the resources to rival the stronger national governments and hence are largely dominated by and dependent on the influence of the more powerful states. Thus, the term international *organization* seems preferable, at this stage, to international *government*.

On the other hand, to say that nations act the same as they would if such agencies did not exist is patently false. An international organization, by its very nature, is the token and reflection of a commitment on the part of its member states to act differently from the way they would if it did not exist. Such an agency is not buildings or murals, but a process — an agreed way of working together toward certain common ends. This process is both the effect and cause of some degree of consensus among governments and peoples. Of course, there could and would be international cooperation without organization, but it would be of a different character — more like the Concert of Europe than the League or United Nations, more susceptible to sheer balance-of-power maneuvers, involving less representative and regularized coordination of policies.

By creating an organization, states involve themselves in a pattern of collaboration which leads them to meet periodically, contribute information and money, negotiate on common problems, make some compromises, give due consideration to the consequent recommendations, and, more often than not, comply with those recommendations. Further attributes that lend weight to such organizations are their staffs, who come the closest to thinking in terms of a common interest rather than any particular national interest; and their diplomatic and legal status, which allows them, among other things, to be represented in various deliberations that affect them and to sue before national and international courts. Finally, a few organizations have been granted authority in some fields to adopt, by less than unanimity, decisions that are binding on all members. This is true of some enforcement powers of the UN Security Council and the Organization of American States as well as certain regulatory functions of the European Coal and Steel Community (Schuman Plan).

The ultimate evidence of the influence generated within these organizations is that every power, including the strongest, has had to modify its course as a result of pressures exerted through the deliberative process of such agencies, as the United States has felt compelled to do in connection with UN decisions on the Italian colonies, Indonesia and Korea.[5] It bears repeating, however, that the activities of an international organization are not the product of an organic personality nor, on the other hand, of any single state. They represent a collective body whose decisions result from an ever-shifting balance of influences weighted in favor of the stronger states. Those who say that international law is not law are also prone to say that international organizations cannot be compared with national government. It would seem more accurate, however, to say that there is a whole spectrum of infinite gradations from the strongest to the weakest organization. All national and international institutions fall somewhere between these extremes, and some of the less developed national governments, in Asia, Africa and Latin America, doubtless are more centrifugal than an international agency such as the European Coal and Steel Community.

> International organizations have exerted direct influence upon the forces of world politics. . . . It is difficult to . . . point to instances in which . . . the intrinsic weight and prestige of an international body, apart from the power of its members or the other factors, has significantly modified world politics. The important fact is that the organization has altered the configuration of world forces . . . these bodies have been able to take collective action that expresses an international will greater than the composite will of the members.[6]

"Human Nature" and Organization

"You can't change human nature." How often this and similar sentiments have been used to pass judgment on international events. Every analysis of social issues stands or falls according to the soundness of its basic assumptions regarding the roots of man's behavior. If, for example, men are inherently warlike, there is little hope for reeducation through the efforts of the UN Educational, Scientific and Cultural Organization (UNESCO). It is obviously beyond the scope of this work, however, to attempt to trace the infinitely complex pattern of man's nature.[7] All that can be done here is to make explicit certain major assumptions that underlie this study.

[5] For commentary in support of this statement by a distinguished former United States delegate to the UN, see Benjamin V. Cohen, "The Impact of the United Nations on United States Foreign Policy," *International Organization*, Vol. 5, No. 2 (May 1951), pp. 274–281; a similar line of reasoning is explored with respect to the Soviet Union in Alexander W. Rudzinski, "The Influence of the United Nations on Soviet Policy," *International Organization*, Vol. 5, No. 2 (May 1951), pp. 282–299.

[6] Charles E. Rothwell, "International Organization and World Politics," *International Organization*, Vol. 3, No. 4 (November 1949), pp. 615, 617–618.

[7] A few of the outstanding works that provide most useful background are the following: Hadley Cantril, ed., *Tensions That Cause Wars* (Urbana: University of Illinois Press, 1950); Otto Klineberg, *Tensions Affecting International Understanding* (New York: Social Science Research Council, 1950); Clyde Kluckhohn and H. A. Murray, eds., *Personality in Nature* (New York: Knopf, 1949); Gardner Murphy, ed., *Human Nature and Enduring Peace* (Boston: Houghton Mifflin Company, for Reynal and Hitchcock, 1945); Talcott Parsons and Edward A. Shils, eds., *Toward a General Theory of Action* (Cambridge: Harvard University Press, 1951).

Fundamental to this analysis is the conclusion that the aggressive attitudes which produce various forms of social conflict, including wars, are not immutable. They can be modified and redirected.[8] What is universally rather uniform is the "raw material" of personality at birth: "a mass of untutored tendencies, movements, impulses, more complicated than those which we see in kittens, puppies, or young apes, but as blind and naive and, moreover, as plastic and modifiable. . . . "[9] Subsequent development is guided chiefly by the environment of family, friends, school, church and occupation. There is no universal mold into which all men are pressed, but rather a multitude of local "norms."

Fundamental Assumptions

International organization, like national government, is the child, not of peace and prosperity, but of insecurity. Hence, the decision as to what ends and means should be prescribed for international agencies depends ultimately on one's diagnosis of the basic diseases those organizations have been created to deal with: military, political, economic and social insecurity.[10] Immediately the tremendous complexity of the problem becomes apparent.

> Peace is determined by biological, psychological, political, economic, social, cultural, ideological, metaphysical, military, institutional, technological, and probably many other factors, whose effect is modified by any number of combinations between them and their position in time and space. . . . There is no certainty regarding either the conditions of peace or the causes of war, and as a consequence there can be none regarding man's ability to produce them.[11]

No single-cause theory — such as inborn aggression, economic inequality or class warfare — is adequate. Only by appreciating the multiplicity and interrelation of the causes of insecurity can one think realistically about the role of international organization.

Military Threat. The principal threat to security that haunts most nations today and on which they spend the largest portion of their budgets is the danger of military attack. Moreover, the long-range historical trend, because of the technological revolution, has been in the direction of an ever-increasing potential to destroy. Fewer and fewer are able to destroy more and more until thoughtful men everywhere are beginning to recognize that

[8] For an account of one of many experiments, see R. Lippitt and R. White, eds., *Child Behavior and Development* (New York: McGraw-Hill, 1943), pp. 485–508.

[9] Murphy, *op. cit.*, p. 14.

[10] Among the many studies of the sources of international conflict, two that are particularly useful are: Quincy Wright, *A Study of War*, 2 Vols. (Chicago: University of Chicago Press, 1942); Luther Lee Bernard, *War and Its Causes* (New York: Henry Holt, 1944).

[11] Werner Levi, *Fundamentals of World Organization* (Minneapolis: University of Minnesota Press, 1950), pp. 45, 48.

OUR PROGRESS TOWARD DESTRUCTION

| 1 AN ARROW COULD KILL ONLY ONE | 2 A CANNON BALL COULD KILL BUT A FEW | 3 AN ARTILLERY SHELL COULD KILL DOZENS |

MOST OF THE VICTIMS WERE COMBATANTS

| 4 A BLOCKBUSTER CAN KILL HUNDREDS | 5 BUT AN A-BOMB CAN KILL TENS OF THOUSANDS | 6 AND A BACTERIAL BOMB MAY KILL MILLIONS |

MOST OF THE VICTIMS ARE CIVILIANS

Headline Series, *Foreign Policy Association*

the price of modern warfare is likely to be the annihilation of our civilization.

> War is no longer, as it once was, a rational instrument of foreign policy, the continuation of diplomacy by other means. In centuries past, resort to wars could be defended as a means to an end. . . . The total war of our age has fundamentally altered the traditional relationship between political means and military means. Today war has become an instrument of universal destruction, an instrument which destroys the victor with the vanquished.[12]

Another aspect of this evolution is that the economic base required for superiority in modern warfare has grown far beyond the capabilities of all but a handful of nations. It is this factor, more than any other, which has shrunk the number of "great powers" from five in 1815 (Britain, Russia, Austria, Prussia and France) to three in 1919 (United States, Britain and France) to two in 1953 (United States and the Soviet Union). Contrary to

[12] Hans J. Morgenthau, "The Foreign Policy of the United States," *The Political Quarterly*, Vol. 22, No. 1 (January–March 1951), p. 47. Also see Bernard Brodie, ed., *The Absolute Weapon* (New York: Harcourt, Brace, 1946); Vannevar Bush, *Modern Arms and Free Men* (New York: Simon and Schuster, 1949); Robert T. Oppenheimer, "Atomic Weapons and American Policy," *Foreign Affairs*, Vol. 31, No. 4 (July 1953).

the tradition of juridical equality in international law, there is no equality in material resources, military might and political influence. There are the "great powers" just mentioned, the "middle powers" (Western European states, Canada, Australia, Sweden, India, China, Argentina and Brazil) who range themselves along the center of the power spectrum, and the "small powers" who fall in the lowest power range.

Political Problems. Other basic sources of international tension are problems of political motivation and organization. Nationalism and the nation-state are frequently singled out as the principal purveyors of dissension. Nationalism is not a unique phenomenon. It is one manifestation of the familiar "in-group" identification, which is also expressed in other loyalties centering around lesser groups, such as the family. It is not static in intensity, but tends to rise or fall with fluctuations in internal and external insecurity. Nor is it static in the extent of community embraced, but, as demonstrated in United States experience, it can expand from Plymouth Plantation to Massachusetts to all of the forty-eight states. Hence, there is no reason why such group loyalty cannot extend to an even larger community. It has been a useful force in leading men to resolve conflicts of subordinate affiliations, to work together to solve common problems and to defend what seems just against external aggression. But to the extent that members of such national communities refuse to recognize any loyalty beyond their national boundaries and make nationalism a barrier to international cooperation, it has been a potent force for conflict. While nationalism is an obvious response to certain psychological needs, it has also been demonstrated that such emotions can be directed into other channels more conducive to human welfare.[13]

Since the nation-state is such a powerful and persistent phenomenon, some authors have recently devoted considerable effort to warning their fellowmen that it is foolish — indeed, dangerous — to expect nations to act on any basis other than their own national interest.[14] But to agree with this observation is not to deny the possibility of broad as well as narrow interpretations of national interest. The late Senator Arthur Vandenberg, for example, was able to convert his own concept of United States national interest from one of relative isolationism to one of substantial international cooperation. And the evolution of official United States policy has followed this same trend.

Another controversial question is whether international organizations must be based on the assumption that the primary objective of every state is power. The usual corollary of such a statement is that there is and must

[13] Among many studies of nationalism, those that deserve particular attention include: John Cohen, *Human Nature, War, and Society* (London: Watts, 1946), pp. 150–151; Hans Kohn, *The Idea of Nationalism* (New York: Macmillan, 1945).

[14] For example, see Hans J. Morgenthau, *In Defense of the National Interest* (New York: Knopf, 1952); for a symposium on this theme, see "The National Interest — Alone or With Others," *The Annals of the American Academy of Political and Social Science,* Vol. 282 (July 1952).

be a different standard of morality for states than for individuals and that no state will allow moral scruples to interfere with its power drive. It would seem, however, that such a corollary may rate individual morality too high and state morality too low. One must also remember that there are as great differences among states on this score as there are among individuals. No one can pretend that the United States or United Kingdom is as unscrupulously dishonest about its international obligations as were the German Nazis or Italian Fascists. At the same time, it has already been said that the absence of any strong world government leaves each state far more independent in its actions than is the case with the average individual in most national societies.

The relation between power and other objectives, including the pursuit of moral values, is as complex and interrelated in national as in personal motivation. Most governments feel that, in the present world, they must seek power if the nation is to survive. And, since the need always seems to outrun the means, the quest is never entirely satisfied. Moreover, the power drive may in extreme cases become an overriding pathological obsession, though even such extremity is often rationalized as necessary in some other terms, such as the welfare of an elite "class" or "race." On the other hand, in most states, as with individuals, power is thought of primarily as a means rather than an end. The objectives may be classified according to political, economic and social interests or the relative "extension" or "abnegation" of influence.[15]

Against this background, should one think of international organizations as a substitute for the "balance of power" process among nations, or is such balancing as much a part of the international body politic as breathing in the human body? An objective analysis of political procedure tends to support the conclusion that

> The process of so balancing and harmonizing forces and interests that none will establish an intolerable domination over all, and each will co-exist with the others in rough parity, is of the essence of all politics, at least where power is shared among equals. In this large sense a dynamic balance . . . is the presupposition of all civic order and stable government.[16]

What is so reprehensible about today's international balance of power is that it is unrestrained by bonds of common government and law comparable to those that help to keep peace in the more developed national communities. The objective, therefore, should not be to abolish the balance of power altogether — which would discard the baby along with the bath water — but to prohibit the use of warlike methods in the operation of that process.

[15] For discussion of this as well as other aspects of the issue, see Arnold Wolfers, "The Pole of Power and the Pole of Indifference," *World Politics*, Vol. 4, No. 1 (October 1951), pp. 39–63.

[16] Frederick L. Schuman, *The Commonwealth of Man* (New York: Knopf, 1952), p. 34.

Another controversial question is whether democratic governments are necessarily more conducive to international cooperation than undemocratic governments, hence making it desirable for international organizations to be composed only of democratic regimes. The truth is that democratic governments will favor a cooperative policy only if the active electorate and their leadership feel that their interests are served thereby, but this is not always the case, for a variety of reasons, as was demonstrated by the American public on the eve of the Spanish-American War.[17] Furthermore, since democratic governments must have the support of a large segment of their constituency, they are notoriously difficult to mobilize behind any positive action, for or against peace. In the final analysis, democratic procedures do not lead automatically to either cooperation or non-cooperation. But, since ultimate control by the great majority of the people seems most likely to result in the greatest satisfaction for the greatest number, it seems the best foundation for international agencies aimed at the general welfare of mankind.

Another core assumption of this book touches on the question: How extensive should the ultimate unit of political organization be? The basic premise here is that lacing two or more nations — or individuals — together in a common organization will not *guarantee* anything, but will at least increase the *potential* for material well-being and social harmony.

> An organization provides a framework for social action. It integrates the unit into the whole and orders the functions of human interrelations. . . . It permits specialization and cooperation. Through organized effort, the end product of united action grows quantitatively and qualitatively far beyond the sum total of independent, individual action by each unit, quite apart from the fact that some problems could not be solved except by organized endeavor. . . . Within nations, people have long since accepted a common, superior authority as the best guarantee of the survival of the individual and the peaceful solution of social problems. . . . The absence of these factors in the relations of individuals belonging to different nations is the crux of the discrepancy between the integrated social life of the state and the hazardous existence of international society.[18]

An important corollary of these statements is that the more extensive the organization, the greater the potential for these benefits.

One should also remember that there is nothing final about the present pattern of nation-states. All of these represent amalgamations of smaller communities that were once more independent than they are today. And the present states could, if men desired it, be merged into larger communities. There is no validity whatsoever in the legal fiction, frantically championed in some quarters, including the Soviet Union, that every state possesses absolute "sovereignty" that is as solid as Gibraltar and cannot be

[17] George Kennan, *American Diplomacy, 1900–1950* (Chicago: University of Chicago Press, 1951), Chap. 1.
[18] Levi, *op. cit.*, pp. 3, 13.

divided or delegated. In fact, no state, including the greatest, is absolutely independent — politically, economically, militarily or legally. No state is free to do as it pleases because no state is strong enough to stand alone.

There are also certain significant long-range political trends which have affected international organizations. First, the growing interdependence of modern society, the impact of various crises — chiefly wars and depressions — and changes in political and economic theory have led to an increasing role for government in the daily affairs of men. This trend has strengthened the hand of governments, as compared with nongovernmental interests, within international organizations. The growth of centralized national planning has also meant that each negotiation on a particular subject has to be coordinated with many related policy matters, a necessity which has greatly complicated and often retarded such deliberations. On the other hand, national integration has provided unified administrative channels for implementing those policies that states can agree upon.

Another important development has been the increasing use of multi-lateral, as distinguished from the more traditional bilateral, channels to deal with international problems. This trend also reflects interaction between the growth of economic interdependence and the development of an internationalist ideology. Each has affected the other. This evolution bears an interesting resemblance to the growth of central governmental coordination within nation-states. But this has not been a constant unilinear development. There have been disastrous reverses, notably two world wars in the twentieth century. Nevertheless, the long-range trend still continues. Whether this will lead to world government is problematical. It depends on which road man chooses: cooperation or conflict.

A further significant trend has been the growing status and influence of the underdeveloped countries, chiefly those with the greatest material and population resources — China, India, Pakistan, Indonesia, Turkey, Egypt and Indo-China. This movement stems from the economic development mentioned above, their increased bargaining power in the midst of conflicts among the great powers, including two world wars and the present "cold war," and the rise of various ideologies, including Western egalitarianism, democracy, anti-imperialism, nationalism and communism.

Economic and Social Problems. The struggle for worldly wealth is as old as man. States strive to better their economic condition both as an end in itself and as a source of power to gain other objectives. The growth, decline, conflict and cooperation of states have always been shaped to a very large extent by the character of their economic foundations. It is also important to keep in mind the long-range technological trend which has vastly increased productivity through improved techniques involving, among other things, greater specialization and diversity of effort. This has resulted in tremendous advances in interdependence and intercommunication. But this trend has not automatically produced cooperation. If one is partially dependent on one's neighbor's resources, there is still the choice of seeking to benefit thereby through cooperation or conquest. What does follow automatically from this technological evolution, however, is that, if one values maximum utilization of world economic resources, the development of such resources must be coordinated on a world-wide basis. No country can remain isolated from any other.

International organizations are concerned, not only with productivity, but the relationship between production and population trends. Large populations are obviously not enough in themselves to provide great economic strength. They must be supplemented by large-scale investment, technology and raw materials. China and India have tremendous human resources, but still relatively little of the other factors. Britain has a comparatively small population (only about 51 million), but her great industrial development makes her the third most powerful nation in the world. The fact that the United States and the Soviet Union are the only states that possess all the necessary factors in large measure makes them the two greatest powers today.

Population trends over the centuries reveal clearly the interaction of population and technology. World population growth was relatively sluggish until the industrial revolution began, about 1750, to bring about a remarkable increase in the ratio of material wealth per person which provided better food, housing, medical care, leisure and education. These benefits resulted in a rapid reduction in the death rate with a consequent explosive expansion of population. Subsequently the rise in individual expectations and the urbanization of society, including the increased requirements for individual training and equipment to maintain an industrial society, led to a desire to have fewer children and higher standards of living. Assisted by improved birth control education and methods, the "fertility rate" declined to achieve a new "demographic balance." [19]

While some advanced Western nations, notably England and France, have begun to experience marked declines in the rate of population growth, the major underdeveloped countries are just entering or are in the full swing of a population "explosion" similar to the earlier one of the West. This has been a central factor in the expanding influence of these "younger" nations in world politics. And to win their support in the "cold war," the older powers have given them limited aid to hasten their technological development, which will not only further accelerate the population increase in many cases, but also increase productivity. Countries which cannot seem to boost production enough to meet the needs of all of their populations have sought to export these population "surpluses." But many countries, particularly the United States, which once served as convenient "escape valves," have in recent decades closed their gates to all but a trickle.

Another significant aspect of these production-population trends, too often ignored, is the fact that the increased standard of living in the West

---

[19] Kingsley Davis, *Human Society* (New York: Macmillan, 1949); Frank Notestein and others, *The Future Population of Europe and the Soviet Union* (Geneva: League of Nations, 1944).

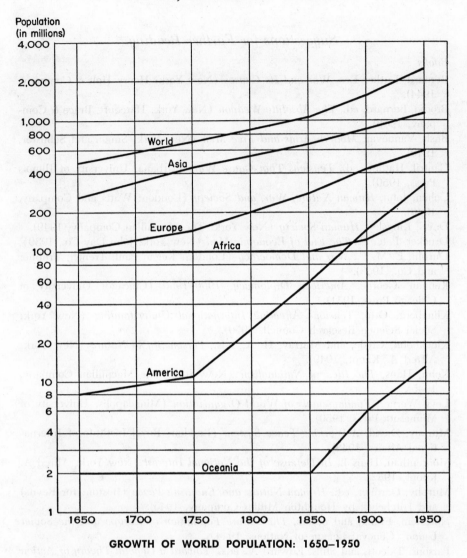

Population
(in millions)

GROWTH OF WORLD POPULATION: 1650–1950

(From *Modern World Politics*, Third Edition, by Kalijarvi and Associates, published by Thomas Y. Crowell Company, 1953)

has been an essential part of the development of democracy. It has made possible the material wealth, leisure and education to equip the "common man" to gain and maintain increased political power. And that enhanced influence has in turn been used as a lever to gain a still larger share of the wealth. Indeed, it is doubtful whether democracy can be successful, at least in Western terms, without a certain minimum of this economic development. And, given the development, it is almost certain that the man in the street will insist on a higher political, economic and social status.

Suggestions for Further Reading

Books

Bernard, Luther Lee, *War and Its Causes* (New York: Henry Holt & Company, 1944).

Brodie, Bernard, ed., *The Absolute Weapon* (New York: Harcourt, Brace & Company, 1946).

Bush, Vannevar, *Modern Arms and Free Men* (New York: Simon and Schuster, 1949).

Cantril, Hadley, ed., *Tensions That Cause Wars* (Urbana: University of Illinois Press, 1950).

Cohen, John, *Human Nature, War, and Society* (London: Watts and Company, 1946).

Davis, Kingsley, *Human Society* (New York: The Macmillan Company, 1949).

Drucker, Peter F., *The End of Economic Man* (New York: John Day Co., 1939).

Durbin, E. M. F., *War and Democracy* (London: Kegan Paul, Trench, Trubner and Co., 1938).

Kennan, George, *American Diplomacy, 1900–1950* (Chicago: University of Chicago Press, 1951).

Klineberg, Otto, *Tensions Affecting International Understanding* (New York: Social Science Research Council, 1950).

Kluckhohn, Clyde, and Murray, H. A., eds., *Personality in Nature* (New York: Alfred A. Knopf, 1949).

Kohn, Hans, *The Idea of Nationalism* (New York: The Macmillan Company, 1945).

Levi, Werner, *Fundamentals of World Organization* (Minneapolis: University of Minnesota Press, 1950).

Mitrany, David, *A Working Peace System* (London: Royal Institute of International Affairs, 1943).

Morgenthau, Hans J., *In Defense of the National Interest* (New York: Alfred A. Knopf, 1952).

Murphy, Gardner, ed., *Human Nature and Enduring Peace* (Boston: for Reynal and Hitchcock by Houghton Mifflin Company, 1945).

Notestein, Frank, and others, *The Future Population of Europe and the Soviet Union* (Geneva: League of Nations, 1944).

Parsons, Talcott, and Shils, Edward A., eds., *Toward a General Theory of Action* (Cambridge: Harvard University Press, 1951).

Royal Institute of International Affairs, *Nationalism* (London: Oxford University Press, 1939).

Schuman, Frederick L., *The Commonwealth of Man* (New York: Alfred A. Knopf, 1952).

Schwarzenberger, Georg, *Power Politics*, 2nd ed. (London: Stevens & Sons, 1951).

Van Wagenen, Richard W., *Research in the International Organization Field* (Princeton: Center for Research on World Political Institutions, 1952).

Weber, Max, *Theory of Social and Economic Organization*, tr. by A. M. Henderson and T. Parsons (New York: Oxford University Press, 1947).

Wright, Quincy, *A Study of War*, 2 Vols. (Chicago: University of Chicago Press, 1942).

Periodicals

Oppenheimer, Robert T., "Atomic Weapons and American Policy," *Foreign Affairs*, Vol. 31, No. 4 (July 1953).

Rothwell, Charles Easton, "International Organization and World Politics," *International Organization*, Vol. 3, No. 4 (November 1949).

Symposium, "The National Interest — Alone or With Others," *The Annals of the American Academy of Political and Social Science*, Vol. 282 (July 1952).

Wolfers, Arnold, "The Pole of Power and the Pole of Indifference," *World Politics*, Vol. 4, No. 1 (October 1951).

Early Development of International Organization

The Western State System

BECAUSE MEN communicate with one another more effectively than do other mammals, they are concerned with politics and the business of government. That is why Aristotle in Book I of his *Politics* declares that man is by nature a political animal.[1] Indeed, government, as we understand the term, began with literate societies. Government has arisen from the needs of society and, in different eras of history, has taken different forms. That is the basis for the maxim, *ubi societas, ibi jus* (where there is community, there is law).

The Greek City-State

Despite their political acumen, the ancient Greeks were unable to extend the rule of law beyond the confines of the small and relatively homogeneous city-state. Athens provided the most famous example of Greek democracy. Citizens participated fully in the governing process by means of highly developed procedures and institutions. Athens, at the peak of her power in the fifth century, B.C., however, was locked in mortal combat with oligarchic Sparta, in some respects the model for Plato's ideal republic.

A study of the Greek city-state system is enlightening to the student of international organization because many of the characteristics of modern international relations were exhibited. The difficulties of establishing a political community in the hearts and minds of men were amply demonstrated. To the ancient Greek the city-state was the embodiment of his entire political and social existence. It was the individual "writ large." It was the focus of his political, religious, and cultural loyalty. Government did not extend beyond the city walls. In the face of foreign invasion — Persian, Macedonian or Roman — the Greeks were unable to achieve polit-

[1] Aristotle, *Politics,* tr. by William Ellis (New York: Dutton), Everyman Edition, Book I.

ical unity. Even in Athenian democracy, moreover, the political community did not include the entire population. Only "citizens" voted. Slaves had no political rights. Non-Greeks were "barbarians."

Athens, perhaps best described as a "capitalist democracy," was inevitably an enemy of Sparta, dedicated to communal living and totalitarian discipline and planning. Relations between states were governed by the politics of the balance of power. Imperialism emerged. Lesser states fell under the influence of the greater. Athens won an empire, but did not extend her political institutions to her vassals and allies. A "bipolar" power system emerged when cities threatened by Athens gravitated to Sparta. The end was defeat for Athens and exhaustion for both.

External danger brought some measure of cooperation, as it does among allies today. The Greeks pooled their military resources sufficiently to defeat the Persian barbarians at Marathon in 490 B.C. and Thermopylae in 480 B.C. But a sufficiently firm alliance against Macedonia was not forthcoming despite the eloquence of Demosthenes. In 338 B.C. Philip of Macedonia was master of Greece. Unity was next imposed by Roman conquest completed in 146 B.C.

Although political unity was never voluntarily established among these ancient city-states, procedures to regulate interstate relations were highly developed. A network of treaties and alliances regulated matters of common concern, including defense, religious festivals and commerce. Between Greek states at least, peace came to be thought of as a normal relationship. Ambassadors were exchanged though not regularly maintained. Ways of "recognizing" states were established. Consular services grew up, and special privileges were granted both consular and diplomatic officers. There was a body of custom, similar to modern international law, governing both war and peace. Perhaps most important was the development of third-party judgment and even permanent agencies for the "peaceful settlement" of interstate disputes. Arbitration was common. Disputes might be submitted to the Delphic oracle, a third state, or tribunal picked by the disputants, or an interstate council.

Despite the brilliance of Greek civilization, which was nourished by city-state patriotism, and despite the internal stability of many cities, permanent law and order embracing all was not achieved short of conquest. The very civic pride which nourished the arts and domestic politics seems to have worked against political unity. Greek civic pride presented much the same dilemma as does nationalism today. Are patriotism and everlasting peace incompatible? How to develop in men's minds an emotional and ideological loyalty to the great community without loosening the bonds of civic pride that bind together the lesser community? Is government under law possible without intense patriotism?

Universal Empire

There have been several nearly universal empires in the course of history, but Rome afforded the example that has generally fired the imaginations of partisans of world law and order. The *Pax Romanus* left to Western civilization an ideal of unity that has never been wholly lost. Citizenship after 212 A.D. was extended to the whole empire that embraced the Mediterranean area, all of civilized Europe including England, and the Near East to the borders of India. Not all peoples in this far-flung empire shared equal political privileges, but all benefited from the protection to life and property afforded by a common rule of law. Thus, it was natural for St. Paul, speaking in Athens, to look beyond the city walls in declaring all men to be the children of God. There existed in fact a political community that lent plausibility to the moral doctrine of the brotherhood of man. Christianity, of course, was drawing heavily from Stoic doctrine that had already done much to raze the moral distinction between "citizen" and "barbarian" and to affirm a moral community of all mankind. Throughout this broad realm to be a *civus romanus* meant that one might expect the benefits of a unified system of government and law while retaining one's local cultural identity.

We look to Rome, therefore, not for a preview of modern international relations emphasizing independent units as in ancient Greece, but to catch a glimpse of legal, commercial, military and administrative methods that held together congeries of different peoples and cultures. Rules and customs common to all the peoples of the empire, for example, were gradually ascertained and embodied in the *jus gentium* which in later centuries became a fertile source of international law. To Western civilization Rome bequeathed universal law and administration, and the Christian church built on the foundations of Judaic monotheism and Stoicism. Owing largely to Stoic doctrine, it was the individual rather than his city, tribe or status that really mattered.

Feudalism

The fall of Rome marked the beginning of a long and steady decline of the spirit of universalism. Particularism, at least governmentally, became the order of the day. Yet, as the temporal power of Rome waned, the Christian church waxed strong and preserved many of the former's concepts of law and justice. New kingdoms were established by the Empire's barbarian invaders who, while destroying the old Empire, embraced its religion. At least the notion of political unity persisted in the "Holy Roman Empire," in which the control of Christendom was held to reside jointly in the Pope as spiritual sovereign and the Emperor as temporal sovereign. The latter was usually a German king who, as a descendant of Charlemagne, succeeded to the Carolingian Empire. Thus, while political fragmentation persisted for nearly a thousand years, with serfs binding themselves to a local lord for protection, a shadowy notion of political universalism persisted, reinforced by the universal spiritual authority of the Papacy.

This authority provided an early bulwark for what may be described as the spirit of internationalism. The Church restricted the horrors of incessant wars between rival medieval barons and princes. A "truce of God" restricted wars to certain days of the week and certain seasons of the year. The Pope also arbitrated disputes between rulers. Perhaps the most famous example was the division between Spain and Portugal of the lands each claimed in the New World on the basis of discovery during the fifteenth century.

Rise of the National State

The extreme decentralization of feudal society was gradually reversed in the late Middle Ages and early Renaissance. Many loosely associated or warring principalities were consolidated under a king. The growth of commerce and the rise of towns in the late Middle Ages were in some instances sources of strength for the king against the feudal barons. The national state, really a monarchical state at first, gradually emerged in Western Europe. Spain reached the peak of her power in the sixteenth century, but was soon challenged by France and England.

In Italy, however, a welter of chronically warring city-states had grown up. By the fourteenth century, no German (Holy Roman) Emperor had visited Italy for nearly half a century. This was the period of the "Babylonian Captivity," when the Popes resided at Avignon largely under the control of the French Monarchy. The spirit of universal order was doomed beyond recall despite the efforts of a few individuals crying in the wilderness. Dante Alighieri, poet, jurist and author of the *Divine Comedy*, pleaded for the restoration of the Holy Roman Empire. His *De Monarchia*, published in about 1309, constituted a moving defense of universalism. As Heaven was regulated by a single ruler, so should mankind be ruled by a single prince and one law. A prince of wide authority must prevail over lesser princes and settle disputes between them. The age of the Roman Emperor Augustus was held up as the Golden Age of Mankind.

Likewise, Pierre Dubois, a French lawyer, urged a sort of world confederation of Christian princes to maintain peace by mobilizing armed force against any ruler waging war contrary to the confederation's principles. His work, primarily a plea for a crusade in the Holy Land, was written in 1306 with the title, *De Recuperatione Terrae Sanctae*. The presumably victorious Christian princes were to form a council and a court with the Pope as principal arbitrator.

Such plans found little favor in their day. Despite Dante's plea, Italy was soon torn by strife between Guelfs and Ghibellines, supporters of the Papacy and Emperor respectively, with city-states such as Florence, Siena and Milan seeking to advance their own fortunes by shifting their support first to one side and then the other. The experience of the Italian city-states of the Renaissance, like that of the Greek states over seventeen hundred years before, provides insights for the student of modern international relations.

Principles of Interstate Relations

> "We are much beholden to Machiavel and others, that write what
> men do, and not what they ought to do." — FRANCIS BACON, *Pro-
> ficiencies and Advancement of Learning*

Reason of State

Perhaps we are most indebted to a Florentine civil servant and diplomat,
Niccolò Machiavelli, for a "scientific" analysis of international politics. A
true Renaissance figure, he analyzed with cold detachment and scant regard
for traditional ethics what actually took place in the relations between rival
states and princes. Hence Machiavelli is considered by many to be the
father of modern political science and diplomacy.[2] Not interested in European unity and frankly secular in his approach, he was passionately devoted
to the unification of Italy. His most famous work, *The Prince,* written in
1513, was a prince's handbook. Dedicated to Lorenzo de Medici, grandson
of Lorenzo the Magnificent, Florence's most famous prince, he sought to
show how a ruler, by the wise use of diplomacy and force, might increase
his power. A prince must stop at nothing to further the interests of his
own state. Otherwise he would succumb to a ruler more ruthless and
skilled than he in the wiles of statecraft. Unlike Dante's cherished universalism, the state, for all practical purposes, becomes an end in itself.

Sovereignty

Another sixteenth-century theorist, Jean Bodin, deserves mention, as he
gave to the world a theoretical formulation regarding the state that dove-
tailed with Machiavelli's "power politics." In his *De Republica,* appearing
in 1576, Bodin stated the case for the legal concept of national sovereignty.
An apologist for absolutism, he asserted that the sovereign, as the supreme
power over citizens and subjects, was unrestrained by laws. Although above
the law, however, the sovereign was not free of moral restraint as prescribed in "divine law" or "natural law," but this shadowy concept was not
spelled out in any specific detail. Bodin, like Machiavelli, justified what
seemed to be the necessary behavior of states. Without internal authority,
external relations with foreign and hostile powers could not be managed.

Other theorists added arguments in support of the doctrine of sovereignty.
Thomas Hobbes in his *Leviathan* (1651) asserted that power was the basis
of sovereignty. The sovereign's authority derived from the power at his
disposal and was itself a source of law. "Where there is no common
power, there is no law." The only limitation of the sovereign's authority
was the individual's "natural right" and instinct of self-preservation. The
bonds of allegiance melted if a sovereign could not defend his subjects.

Further restraints to a sovereign's power were soon forthcoming. To the

2 For example, Frederick L. Schuman, *International Politics,* 5th ed. (New York:
McGraw-Hill, 1953), pp. 56 ff.

laws of God and nature Johannes Althusius (*Politics Systematically Considered*, 1609) added the terms of the ruler's contract with the people. Locke and Rousseau also developed the contract notion, arguing that sovereignty rested with the people who created governments to exercise authority.[3] The concept of sovereignty has, in fact, run through several fashions. At one time or another it has been held to reside in the monarch, the people and, finally, the state and its government. It has been given several classic formulations in national courts, one of them by Chief Justice Marshall, who declared: "The jurisdiction of the nation within its own territory is necessarily exclusive and absolute." [4]

But a system of sovereign states whose external relations were entirely unregulated by law spelled chaos. This was the lesson learned by bitter experience in the bloody Thirty Years' War of the seventeenth century. It was driven home by the writings of Hugo Grotius (Huig de Groot), a Dutch jurist and diplomat, who, shocked at the license and barbarities perpetrated by rival monarchies in their nearly perpetual wars, devoted his brilliant mind to the problem of world order.

Pacta sunt servanda

Grotius, often called the "father of international law," insisted in his great work, *De Jure Belli Ac Pacis*, that sovereignty was not absolute but was limited by divine law, nature's law and the "law of nations." The latter was, of course, the forerunner of modern international law. It was defined as the "dictate of right reason" and could be found in the writings of philosophers, historians and poets. But Grotius also declared that the actual practice of states was a source of the law of nations.

A light was now beginning to pierce the gloom of international anarchy. By turning both to reason and the practice of states, Grotius and other thinkers were able to reconcile sovereignty with an interstate legal system. By the exercise of their sovereignty governments could give their consent to fulfill obligations toward one another. Consent is an essential element of any legal system. The notion that such obligations, usually specified in treaties, must be obeyed (*pacta sunt servanda*) now became a guiding principle of international relations.

Grotius, in sum, was notable for formulating and systematizing a coherent theory of international order that was derived from the emerging principles and practices of states. To Machiavelli's "power politics" an ethical element was added. Grotius insisted that there were rules by which states are or should be guided in their relations with one another. The need of restraint upon the rapacious conduct of states was so obvious that Grotius' appeal for order through reason fell upon ready ears.

Are treaty obligations an exercise of sovereignty or a limitation of sovereignty? Learned jurists and statesmen have argued both sides, depending, in many instances, on the audience being addressed. The United States

[3] See Locke's *Second Treaties on Civil Government* and Rousseau's *Social Contract*.
[4] The Schooner Exchange *v.* M'Fadden, 7 Cranch 116, 136 (1812).

EUROPEAN STATES AFTER THE PEACE OF WESTPHALIA, 1648

Senate was reassured when Senators Connally and Vandenberg and State Department officials insisted that in ratifying the Charter and forming the UN the United States was retaining its sovereign freedom of action. Others, particularly leaders of the European Movement, have insisted that treaties inevitably involve a surrender of sovereign action and that ultimately sovereignty must be yielded further if a peaceful world is to be established. The problem is obvious. To whom shall the surrender be made? Under what circumstances? The Europeans have gone far in their efforts to answer these questions. In the main, however, sovereignty remains enshrined, and international law is very largely "treaty law."

International organization is the institutional offspring of these parents. But what of states less powerful than their neighbors? Are states *equally* sovereign?

The Equality of States

An affirmative answer was an obvious requisite for the Grotian system. Reasonable men perceived that the equality of states must be accepted as a guiding principle of an orderly international system. The sovereign equality of states was incorporated in the Treaty of Westphalia (1648), which ended the holocaust of the Thirty Years' War and provided a basic law for the state system which had by then emerged. The new states were recognized as the component units of international society. They were buttressed by the twin principles of sovereignty and equality.

But even this hoary principle is yielding in the face of brute facts. States are not equal. There are enormous differences in population, area, natural resources, and in many other respects. The Charter of the United Nations bows both to sovereign equality and political inequality. A guiding principle stated in Article 2 is the "sovereign equality of all . . . Members." Yet, on the other hand, only certain big states have permanent seats on the Security Council. All but five of the most powerful UN Members may be bound legally by decisions in which they have not taken part or even oppose. A number of specialized agencies, including the International Labor Organization, the World Bank and the International Monetary Fund, give favored positions to the more influential states. Inevitably international organization has been unable to ignore the actual inequalities of states.

Characteristics of the State System

In addition to developing certain principles of conduct, the Western state system has displayed characteristics which, because they bear on the role of international organization, deserve mention. These include the politics of the balance of power, policies of imperialism, and nationalism as an ideology.

The Balance of Power

Although international relations became far more orderly after the Grotian system had become fundamental law in the Treaty of Westphalia, international politics was still vastly different from the internal politics of a state. First of all, war was not eliminated. Armies and alliances remained the order of the day. There was no central authority to enforce the law or protect the independence of states. "Self-help" guided state policy and was dignified as a legal principle. Defense and the enforcement of international obligations were not the responsibility of the international community. In these circumstances the weak allied with the strong to preserve their independence. The strong allied with the weak to counter the might of other powerful states. Peace and indeed the application of the principle of sovereign equality depended upon an equilibrium or balance of power that was uneasy and at the same time essential.

This brings us to a second point. The balance-of-power system is of necessity a universal system although it has characterized modern European politics particularly. The rival coalitions headed by Britain and France fought all over the globe in the eighteenth and early nineteenth centures, in North America, India, and at other strategic points in addition to Europe itself. There were earlier world-wide rivalries between Spain and Portugal and between Britain and Spain. Twentieth-century wars tend to be global wars. Germany's growing strength in Europe, for example, was the signal for Japan to expand her empire in the Pacific. For the United States, Britain and the Commonwealth, World War II was a two-front war fought in nearly every corner of the world. Similarly, the terms "bipolarity" and "cold war" have been used to describe international politics since 1945. The Soviet Union dominates a number of Communist powers while the United States is the most powerful member of a counter coalition of Western powers. Although a group of increasingly influential Arab-Asian countries is not identified with either side, the policy of each coalition is to insure that, at the very least, the strength of these neutrals shall not be added to that of its rival.

International organization forms, as we shall see, a focal point in the politics of the balance of power. Rivalries carry over into the debates and behavior of the United Nations. Regional organizations are very largely a higher stage in the development of alliance and coalitions. Most important, in establishing international organizations a prime object has been to make the entire international community responsible for maintaining peace and order. In no other way has it seemed possible to lessen sufficiently the dangers of balance of power politics.

Imperialism

Another characteristic of the Western state system, imperialism, should be noted. This movement had much to do with the development of international organization in the nineteenth and twentieth centuries as governments sought to substitute cooperation for rivalry in handling explosive colonial problems. We have already seen that the Greek city-states exhibited a proclivity toward colonial expansion abroad and, despite the normal assumption of peace among Greek states, expansion at home. The emerging secular states of the Renaissance embarked almost at once on policies of colonial expansion and empire. European conflicts took the form of colonial rivalries abroad. The first half of the nineteenth century, however, witnessed a declining interest in colonial expansion. The Spanish, British and French Empires in North America had already been lost. Under the tutelage of Adam Smith and the eighteenth-century "Physiocrats," "free trade" had come into vogue.

The industrial revolution was the most important factor giving rise to a renewed burst of imperialism in the second half of the nineteenth century. Populations suddenly expanded at phenomenal rates. Tariff walls were erected to protect infant industries. Increased needs for markets, raw materials and investment opportunities caused the European powers to stake out claims in the great nonindustrial and relatively weak areas of Asia and Africa. The first decade of the twentieth century marked the peak of colonial expansion. Nearly half the earth's surface and over a third of its population were under colonial rule.

Meanwhile this scramble for real estate had brought some of the major powers to blows. In certain matters such as slavery, however, these powers had found it wise to coordinate their colonial policies by rudimentary forms of international organization that will be discussed below. Meanwhile imperialism had been given considerable impetus by another force characteristic of the state system — nationalism.

Nationalism

The role of international organization and indeed the character of international relations depend heavily on the character and nature of nationalism. One observer describes it as the "most significant factor in public life today." [5] At times, the spirit of nationalism, which focuses men's loyalties on the nation-state, seems to threaten any real progress toward international cooperation. Yet nineteenth-century thinkers, such as the Italian patriot Mazzini, felt that truly self-governing nation-states could exist peaceably, side by side, in a "natural harmony of interests." He and other nineteenth-century liberals felt that a more orderly world would come about if political frontiers coincided with national frontiers. Turmoil in their view was caused by the suppression of nationalities under alien rule, a cry that was taken up by non-European peoples in the twentieth century. If the principle of "self-determination" were followed, wars might cease. People who felt they belonged together, so the argument ran, and were at the same time permitted to rule themselves would not be aggressive. Woodrow Wilson was a principal spokesman of this liberal line. Largely through his

[5] Carlton J. H. Hayes, *Essays on Nationalism* (New York: Macmillan, 1941), p. 1.

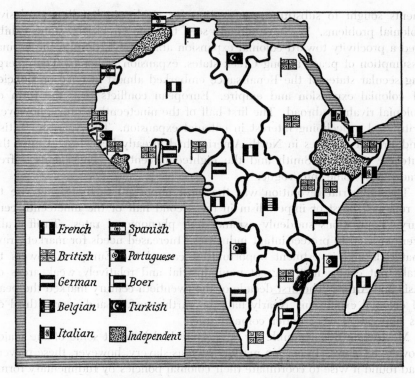

NATIONALISM CARVES UP A CONTINENT

Some national frontiers in Africa about 1900

From *World in the Making*, by James A. Joyce (Henry Schuman, Inc.)

efforts self-determination and self-government became the guiding principles of the Versailles peace system and the League of Nations.

The League's misfortunes and World War II, however, dampened the liberal faith in nationalism. Hitler showed that the national spirit could be manipulated as readily by the unscrupulous as by the scrupulous. Nationalism could fuel the engines of empire as readily as the machinery of democracy. With the addition of racism it became a "high-test" fuel that blew the machine apart. Nationalism evidently cannot be counted on to curb the extremes of power politics. Yet international organization, as it operates today, depends upon the national spirit almost as much as on loyalty to itself. Collaborative measures agreed to in the UN or NATO are of little value unless the participating states have the will and means to carry them out. And the Member's capacity depends on the loyalty and discipline of its citizens. These in turn depend heavily upon patriotism and the national spirit.

Nationalism is hard to define. Yet its moral force is very conspicuous — sometimes by its absence. We can at least be certain of a few points. Government depends upon patriotism or civic loyalty of some sort. It is doubtful whether even totalitarian governments can rule by force alone. Nationalism can be a fertile source of civic loyalty. But this particular form of loyalty has not always been with us. In the Middle Ages Europeans were primarily loyal to their spiritual authorities. As secular power first took hold in the modern state, it was often buttressed by the "divine right" of kings.

Since the French Revolution, however, loyalty to the nation-state (*la patrie* or the "fatherland") has generally been superior to any other loyalty. Monarchical states gave way to nation-states composed of people who believed they constituted a single nation which must, therefore, be free of control by alien nations. Common elements such as language, religion, custom, race, territory and political traditions all fortify this belief. But these elements exist in different proportions in different nations. Some elements may be lacking entirely. Some states are multinational in character. The belief itself is what is important in world affairs.

Meanwhile a new ideology, communism, has emerged. In some instances it has joined forces with nationalism at least temporarily, as in China and some other Asian areas, to give new vitality to peoples long subject to foreign influence. More often nationalism counters communism owing to the growing realization that the latter has become primarily an instrument of Soviet power. In these circumstances nationalism may be a bulwark, though not always a sure one, against Communist (Soviet) expansion. The interplay of these two basic forces has influenced the development of twentieth-century international organization.

Organizing International Political Relations

"An Ambassador is an honest man sent to lie abroad for the good
of his country." — SIR HENRY WOTTON, *17th century*

"Diplomacy is the application of intelligence and tact to the conduct of official relations between the governments of independent states." — SIR ERNEST SATOW, *1917* [6]

Since the dawn of history, there has been a progressive development of procedures and organizations to cope with interstate relations. Self-interest has provided the incentive. Although the conference system which characterizes international organization is sometimes described as the "new diplomacy," it does not mark any sharp break with the past. Many of the older forms of diplomacy, moreover, are very much alive. At the same time, however, many advocates of international organization have hoped to alter the character of international relations in a fundamental way. For the uncertainties of balance-of-power politics, they have sought to substitute a governmental system including rudimentary elements of the legislative,

[6] Sir Ernest Satow, *A Guide to Diplomatic Practice* (New York: Longmans, 1917), Vol. I, p. 1.

executive and judicial functions. International organization is both an instrument of diplomacy and evidence of some sense of community among nations.

Diplomatic and Consular Practice

The arts of diplomacy have long been under careful cultivation. The Greek states developed diplomatic and consular practices. Papal and Imperial Ambassadors played important roles in the Middle Ages. Machiavelli gained his political insights by serving as a Florentine diplomat. A few diplomatic landmarks should be pointed out to illustrate the main lines of development.

Negotiations leading up to the Peace of Westphalia of 1648 were impeded for several years owing to controversies over meeting places, titles and ranks of envoys. Quarrels of this sort continued for the next century and a half. The occurrence of incidents and even duels over diplomatic prerogative were recorded as late as 1768.[7] Since an affront to an ambassador is tantamount to an affront to the state, orderly international relations required the establishment of closely prescribed diplomatic rules and procedures. Diplomatic niceties reflect the inherent tension of international relations rather than the foibles of individual vanity.

For these reasons, rules were worked out at the Congress of Vienna to settle these matters of state. A hierarchy of diplomats was set up, including four ranks: ambassadors and papal legates, envoys extraordinary and ministers plenipotentiary, ministers resident and chargés d'affaires. The distinction between ministers resident and ministers plenipotentiary has been abandoned. Ambassadors and ministers are accredited to the chief of state and chargés to the minister of foreign affairs. Among the diplomatic corps as a whole in a given capital, precedence is determined by length of service. The system presupposes the equality of states, and its general acceptance greatly facilitates the conduct of international affairs.

To assist them in their work, diplomats have been granted certain privileges and immunities. A chief of mission (usually an ambassador), his family, and his servants are immune from local jurisdiction. His official residence, an embassy or legation depending on his rank, is inviolate. The right of asylum in the embassy is still claimed by some countries on the basis of the embassy's extraterritorial status. An ambassador may not be arrested, although his recall may be demanded as *persona non grata*. He is free of customs duties and other taxes and is exempt from jury duty. Some of these privileges and immunities have been extended also to the secretariats of international organizations as well as to the accredited national delegates.

Meanwhile, consular services were established almost as early as diplomatic services to expedite foreign trade and commerce. While the diplomat is concerned with the foreign policy of his government, the consul provides

[7] *Ibid.*, p. 19.

governmental assistance to individual citizens engaged in international trade.

Treaties

A treaty is a formal agreement between states. Conventions and protocols are the same as treaties for all practical purposes. Treaties are a source of international law and have been the principal means of establishing orderly international relations. They are as old as history, with the earliest known example dating from about 3000 B.C. Since states insist on their sovereign independence, there is no way of regulating matters of mutual concern save by an expression of mutual consent. Such consent may be granted by acquiescence in cutsom or by a definite act of agreement, such as signing a treaty.

The number and scope of treaties have increased enormously in modern times. While they were once concerned primarily with alliances, terms of peace and royal marriages, treaties now deal with economic, social and cultural affairs, including such matters as disease control, air facilities, navigational aids, postal arrangements and telecommunication. In the last fifty years the United States has entered into well over twice as many treaties as it did in all its previous history.

An increasing number of treaties, moreover, are multilateral in that they are entered into by several states concerned with a treaty's subject. The UN Charter is only one of many examples. With the increasing complexity of international life, the trend toward multilateralism may be expected to continue. At the international level the multilateral treaty is the closest approximation to domestic legislation that exists.

Conferences

Since many treaties, especially the multilateral variety, grow out of international conferences, the number and scope of the latter have also increased. The conference is a technique of diplomatic negotiation and, like all aspects of diplomacy, is surrounded by numerous and complicated rules of procedure. The international conference is today the principal policy organ of nearly every international organization. By 1946 the United States was a member of fifty important international agencies and several lesser ones, and in a single year participated in nearly 450 conferences.

Conferences are held only after careful advance preparation regarding the subject of negotiation, the participating nations, rules of procedure and meeting places. Until the last half of the nineteenth century most conferences dealt with the terms of peace to conclude a war. Now conferences are as varied in subject as treaties. Thus the conferences that culminated in the Peace of Westphalia rearranged the map of Europe. By the nineteenth century, however, conferences were used to reach agreements on other international problems, such as transportation, health and slavery.

Some conferences are termed *ad hoc* since they are called for a specific purpose and are disbanded once the business at hand has been completed.

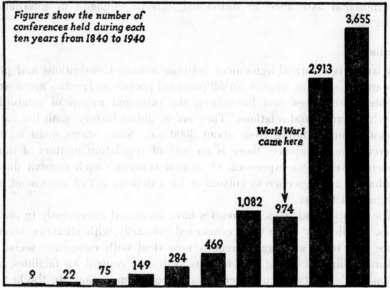

Figures show the number of conferences held during each ten years from 1840 to 1940

World War I came here

9 22 75 149 284 469 1,082 974 2,913 3,655

1840-49 1850-59 1860-69 1870-79 1880-89 1890-99 1900-09 1910-19 1920-29 1930-39

INTERNATIONAL CONFERENCES
How they have grown during a hundred years

From *World in the Making*, by James A. Joyce (Henry Schuman, Inc.)

Others are periodic with preparations made for a further meeting at the close of a particular session. The Hague Conferences of 1899 and 1907 and the conferences of the inter-American system prior to the establishment of the Organization of American States were of this type. With the establishment of international organizations such as the League, the UN and the International Labor Organization (ILO), a third type, the continuing conference, has emerged. Recurring meetings are provided for. The United Nations General Assembly must meet at least once a year. The Security Council is required to be organized so as to "function continuously." Whether continuous or recurring, such conferences are generally serviced by a permanent staff of officials comprising a secretariat that serves the organization rather than the member governments. Thus international conferences have developed from exceptional and sporadic meetings reserved for special occasions into familiar standing institutions of international organizations. Like Congress or Parliament, the General Assembly comes into regular session each year. Continuity is maintained, reports are made on past performance, and new items are included on the agenda. The conference process is a rudimentary legislative process which exists on both universal and regional levels. It may be multipurpose, as is the UN General Assembly, or be concerned with a single problem such as ocean fisheries. Some states today participate in as many as four or five hundred conferences a year, with several going on simultaneously. National existence is clearly not an isolated phenomenon.

The Congress of Vienna (1815).[8] The conference that brought the Napoleonic wars to a close deserves special mention as a forerunner of modern international organization. To rebuild the Europe of 1789 that had been brought tumbling down by the French Revolution and its Napoleonic aftermath, the crowned heads of Europe and their diplomatic retinues repaired to Vienna in brilliant pomp and circumstance. The list of notable statesmen included Metternich, of Austria; Talleyrand, of France; Castlereagh, of England; and Czar Alexander I of Russia.

The Concert of Europe. From the Congress of Vienna and other conferences of the great coalition against Napoleon emerged the Holy Alliance and the Quadruple Alliance which provided for a succession of congresses which ultimately developed into the system known as the "Concert of Europe." The inspiration for the system was the common fear that the application of balance-of-power principles was haphazard and inadequate to insure a combination of states against an aggressive power. There must be closer integration and common leadership among the powers anxious to preserve the *status quo.*

The soil had already been prepared for some sort of conference system.[9] Dante and Pierre Dubois have been mentioned already. A Frenchman, Emeric Crucé, proposed a world union of independent states. His work, entitled *Le Nouveau Cynée,* was published in 1623. Such a union was intended to foster trade and the arts and to promote tolerance and brotherhood among peoples. A permanent conference of ambassadors was to sit continuously in a neutral city in order to settle differences among states. Rulers were to be "trustees of the peace" and to enforce majority decisions by common action.

Henry IV of France had advanced at the end of the sixteenth century the "Grand Dessein" proposed by his Minister, the Duc de Sully. The map of Europe was to be redrawn so as to provide a universal Christian republic composed of fifteen equal units. There were to be a European Senate of sixty representatives, four from each state, and six local Councils. The object of the union was to preserve the *status quo.* Disputes were to be settled by arbitration, and a joint army was to enforce the agreement. Doubtless, Sully was really trying to curb Hapsburg power. Perhaps that is one reason why his proposals failed to receive serious consideration.

William Penn observed that Old World conflicts, despite ocean barriers, almost invariably had repercussions in the new. In 1693 he proposed a "Parliament of Europe" in his *Essay Toward the Present and Future Peace of Europe.* This body would make law and have compulsory jurisdiction over international disputes. Failure to abide by the parliament's decisions

---

[8] See C. K. Webster, *The Congress of Vienna* (New York: Oxford, 1919).
[9] Space permits only cursory treatment of these early proposals for a league of nations. The reader is referred to the Suggestions for Further Reading for Chap. 2.

would bring into play the combined might of states against the lawbreaker. The votes to be cast by each state would be determined by quotas based upon national wealth.

A similar proposal was advanced in 1712 by the Abbé de Saint-Pierre in his *Project to Bring Perpetual Peace in Europe.* A senate, composed of two representatives from each member, was to sit permanently at Utrecht. Its presidency was to be rotated among the members. Expenses of this union or league would be met by assessments based on the members' capacity to pay. Decisions would be made either by a majority vote or by a three-fourths vote. The union's object was security for the personal rule of sovereigns and for the independence of their states. Provisions for peaceful settlement were similar to earlier schemes. Sanctions provisions, however, including armed contingents for the union, were worked out in considerable detail. These contingents were to be of equal size and placed under the command of an over-all commander-in-chief. The philosopher Rousseau revived these thoughts in 1761 in a work entitled *Extrait du Projet de Paix Perpétuelle de M. l'Abbé de Saint-Pierre.* Rulers, however, including Frederick the Great, found practical difficulties. Cardinal Fleury is credited with the remark: "Admirable! Save for one omission; I find no provision for sending missionaries to convert the hearts of princes." [10]

In 1793 Jeremy Bentham published in England his *Principles of International Law,* which included "A Plea for an Universal and Perpetual Peace." He urged that statesmen in charge of foreign policy think in terms of the international interest as well as the national interest. War might be prevented by defensive alliances and mutual guarantees among states, disarmament and the abandonment of colonialism. A peace tribunal must have authority to enforce its decision on states disturbing the peace.

The German philosopher, Immanuel Kant, developed similar thoughts in 1795 in his *Zum ewigen Frieden* ("Toward Perpetual Peace"), which postulates that the problem of first importance for the human race is the establishment of a civil society administering justice according to law. The foreign relations of states must be regulated by an international federation. Every state, even the smallest, would rely for its safety, not on its own power or on its own judgment of right, but on the combined power of the federation and on its common will and law. To be successful, such a federation would require the establishment of representative government in all states although some might be republics and others monarchies. Despotism was the enemy of peace. The federation would not be a superstate. Its authority might be extended gradually; its purpose would be to end war forever.

Thus, by 1815 many proposals had been advanced to establish peaceful international relations. Some of them were incorporated in the concert system, and some of them were among the fundamental assumptions of the League and the UN.

[10] L. Larry Leonard, *International Organization* (New York: McGraw-Hill, 1951), p. 26.

The Holy Alliance. This scheme was proposed by Czar Alexander I. Agreed to by Russia, Austria and Prussia, it was characterized by romanticism and even mysticism. The three rulers pledged themselves "in the name of the Most Holy and Indivisible Trinity to take for their sole guide the precepts of that holy religion, namely, the precepts of justice, Christian charity, and peace. . . . " They were to "remain united by the bonds of a true and indissoluble fraternity" as "members of one and the same Christian nation." [11] Castlereagh thought this nonsense, but the English statesman was enthusiastic for a time about another development, the "congress system."

The Quadruple Alliance. At Paris, in November 1815, Austria, Russia, Prussia and Great Britain formed the Quadruple Alliance to enforce the peace settlement. In 1818 this alliance became a quintuple alliance with the addition of France, now docile under restored Bourbon rule. This development was a landmark in the history of international organization for several reasons. First, the alliance, though forged in war, was continued after hostilities to enforce the peace. Second, periodic conferences were instituted when the great powers agreed to renew their meetings at fixed periods. Third, despite the suspicions of the smaller powers, it was generally agreed that the maintenance of peace depended on this sort of big-power collaboration. These notions were carried over into both the League and the UN.

Four congresses were held between 1818 and 1822. Their chief activity was to authorize intervention by one of the great powers to put down revolts in Naples and Spain. In 1822, however, Britain abandoned this first development of the congress system when it sought the suppression of *all* revolutions in order to maintain the *status quo*. The following year Britain was supported by the United States' Monroe Doctrine opposing any extension of the Alliance's activity to suppress independence movements in the New World. Significant was the fact that the system was readily abandoned by a member when it felt that its national interest was no longer being served.

Yet, despite the demise of the original alliance, the concert system continued in other forms until 1914. While periodic congresses were abandoned, meetings of the European great powers were held from time to time. The concert operated at the Berlin Congress of 1878 dealing with Turkey and the "Eastern question"; the Berlin Conference of 1884–85 regulating certain aspects of imperial rivalry in Africa; the Algeciras Conference of 1906 on the Moroccan question; and the London Conference of 1912–13 which limited the Balkan War. The concert system was not a formal organization but a disposition on the part of the great powers to confer together. One of their first concerted actions was the recognition and neutralization of Belgium. But the system was unable to cope with the conflicting national policies that culminated in World War I. Despite the

[11] See F. L. Schuman, *op. cit.*, p. 185.

Concert of Europe, rival alliances and alignments hardened in the last quarter of the nineteenth century.

The River Commissions. The Congress of Vienna also concerned itself with the economic life of the European powers. Heavy traffic moved on the great river systems of Europe, and there was a growing demand by merchants that uniform rules and regulations be applied by all the riparian states. Territorial sovereignty yielded to mercantile interests. The Congress established the rule that international rivers, defined as rivers crossing or forming the boundary of more than one state, should be administered for the benefit of international commerce as a whole. The administration of these rules, including the maintenance of navigational aids, was left to the riparian states.[12]

To implement the new rule, a Rhine Commission was established by the Vienna Treaty. It was composed of one member from each state bordering the Rhine. Each state had one vote save for certain administrative matters, when voting strength was distributed according to the length of the river bank of each state. Also, "Rhine Courts" were established at convenient points to insure uniform interpretation of the regulations. Their decisions were binding on all states concerned. Appeals could be made both to national courts or to the international Commission itself. The latter had considerable authority. It made regulations, and only changes in the fundamental treaty required a full-scale international conference. The Commission had enough discretion to keep pace with changing circumstances.

The success of the Rhine Commission led to the establishment of the European Danube Commission by the Treaty of Paris in 1856. Several powers in the years preceding the Crimean War had been dissatisfied with Russia's control of the mouth of the Danube. Instead of giving control to Turkey, one of the Crimean War victors, the governments agreed to internationalize the river by creating a "European Commission." The Vienna principles of free navigation were applied, and, in addition, several nonriparian states with interests in Danube river traffic were included in the new Commission. Its task was to improve the river and regulate its traffic.[13] The Commission met twice annually and made decisions by both majority and unanimous rule. An Executive Committee of certain member governments carried on between sessions. The day-to-day work of licensing tugs and pilots, imposing penalties and maintaining channels was managed by a permanent staff.

The Danube Commission provided the model for other river commissions, including those on the Elbe and Oder Rivers. It functioned with conspicuous success until World War II. Its reëstablishment and the continuation of the principles first enunciated at Vienna have been thwarted by the

---

[12] J. P. Chamberlain, *The Regime of the International Rivers: Danube and Rhine, Studies in History, Economics, and Public Law* (New York: Columbia University Press, 1920), p. 43.

[13] F. B. Sayre, *Experiments in International Administration* (New York: Harper, 1923), p. 29.

descent of the "iron curtain" since the river's mouth and much of its length are under Communist control.

Slavery. The European Concert dealt also with the question of slavery. At the Congress of Vienna the antislavery movement in England led the British Government to propose the prohibition of the slave trade, including enforcement by economic boycotts and armed international police on the coast of Africa. The Congress, however, was unwilling to go beyond a mere antislavery declaration. Yet this step marked a change from the past. Like piracy, slavery was recognized as a matter of concern to all nations. National antislavery policies were gradually agreed upon. In 1890 the powers at the Brussels Conference concluded a General Act for the Repression of African Slave Trade and established two bureaus, one at Brussels and one at Zanzibar, the latter to control the liquor traffic which complicated the slavery problem.

Peaceful Settlement of Disputes

Long before the League of Nations or the UN, procedures had been developed in the state system for the settlement of disputes without recourse to war. States, however, were not legally obligated to use them. These procedures are still in use and were made obligatory to varying degrees in both the League Covenant and the UN Charter. There is still no assurance, however, that states will forego the use of force in favor of pacific settlement. The development of judicial settlement in the international community has not been unlike its development in other communities. In primitive society self-help was the principal means of redressing grievances. As confidence in neighbors increases, self-help gives way to arbitration. Ultimately, third-party judgment is accepted as binding, and judicial procedures replace self-help and arbitration. There is as yet no judicial process generally accepted in the international community for *all* classes of disputes. Only carefully defined "legal disputes" are considered "justiciable" by most governments. Yet some progress has been made toward placing the responsibility of third-party judgment on the shoulders of the international community as a whole.

Good Offices and Mediation. When two states are about to come to blows, a third party may, without offense to either party, so far as the law is concerned, offer its good offices in settling the dispute. Technically, "good offices" involves merely bringing the parties together with suggestions as to the substance of the dispute. When suggestions and solutions are advanced, "good offices" shades off into mediation. These distinctions have been embodied in treaties and decisions of international tribunals. President Theodore Roosevelt used his good offices to bring Japan and Russia to a conference table on American soil in order to halt the Russo-Japanese War. Once national pride had been sufficiently overcome so that both parties could be persuaded to negotiate, Roosevelt's role shifted to that of a mediator. Both devices are forms of diplomacy. Neither involves third-party judgment. Both aim at political compromise rather than a judicial solution.

Commissions of Inquiry. Another step forward was taken in the *Convention for the Pacific Settlement of International Disputes* drawn up by the First Hague Conference of 1899. If states were unwilling to trust third-party judgment, they might at least be willing to have an impartial investigation of the facts by a third party. As with mediation, this procedure was entirely voluntary. Moreover, states were generally unwilling to accept it until issues of "honor" and "vital interests" were excepted. Nonetheless, the procedure was blessed with an early success. When the Russian fleet during the Russo-Japanese War of 1904 mistakenly opened fire on some unsuspecting British fishing boats, Russia accepted responsibility for the damage by payment of an indemnity to the fishermen after the facts of the case had been established by a commission of inquiry. The Bryan Treaties of 1913 and 1914 went further in providing that such commissions be established by states in advance of a dispute, that no dispute be excluded from their scope, and that hostilities be prohibited until the commission had reported. Thus, further progress was made toward the obligatory features of the Covenant and the Charter.

Arbitration. Arbitration is a step closer to judicial procedure and has had a long and honorable history. Until the establishment of the Permanent Court of International Justice (PCIJ), it was, in fact, the principal means of settling disputes according to legal standards. Both the Covenant and the Charter designate arbitration as distinct from mediation or conciliation on the one hand and from diplomacy on the other.[14] Technically, the parties before arbitral tribunals are states, but in fact they are often individuals whose claims are presented by states.

Arbitration, prior to the twentieth century, required in each instance a special treaty (*compromis* or *compromis d'arbitrage*) signed by the disputing states. This treaty established: (1) the question to be answered; (2) the appointment of the arbitrators; (3) the rules of law or standard of justice to be applied; (4) the obligation of both parties to abide by the award. The shortcomings of this system were many. Most obvious was the absence of a court, a general code or any obligation to arbitrate at all. There was no presumption in advance of a dispute that arbitration would be followed. Agreement on rules and procedures had to be thrashed out in each instance. These sometimes proved as difficult to decide as the dispute itself.

Despite these difficulties, the United States and Great Britain resorted to arbitration on a number of important occasions. The Jay Treaty of 1794 provided for the arbitration of numerous disputes carrying over from the Revolutionary War. The *Alabama Award* of 1872 remains a landmark in the modern era of arbitration and provides a good illustration of arbitral

[14] For a discussion, see Clyde Eagleton, *International Government* (New York: Ronald Press, 1948), pp. 221–227.

procedures. In the Treaty of Washington of 1871 the two governments agreed upon three rules concerning the duties of a neutral state to be applied and the establishment of a tribunal of five members appointed by the Chiefs of State of the United States, Great Britain, Italy, Switzerland and Brazil, respectively. The tribunal found that Great Britain had violated the principles of international law governing neutrality in periods of civil strife by permitting the Confederate sea raider *Alabama* to fit out in British ports during the American Civil War. The tribunal decided by four votes to one that Great Britain should pay an indemnity of $15,500,000 to the United States. A considerable increase of activity in international arbitration followed the successful conclusion of this case.[15]

Many statesmen and international lawyers soon advocated two more steps, obligatory arbitration and the development of a permanent tribunal. International relations might become more orderly, it was thought, if states were obligated to settle their disputes in court.

The Permanent Court of Arbitration. When the First Hague Conference bogged down on the disarmament question, therefore, the delegates turned to the problem of settling disputes by peaceful means. The American delegation, for example, had been instructed by Secretary of State John Hay to seek the establishment of a court. The Conference finally included in its famous Convention for the Pacific Settlement of International Disputes provisions for a Permanent Court of Arbitration. This institution has remained in continuous existence since its organization in 1900, but in reality is neither permanent nor a court.

The Court consists of a panel of members, an Administrative Council, and an International Bureau. The panel includes for each signatory state a list of four individuals "of known competence in questions of international law, of the highest moral reputation, and disposed to accept the duties of arbitration." No regular Court sessions are held, and only about one-third of the total membership of about 150 has ever actually arbitrated a dispute. Members remain on the panel for six years, and serve on an arbitral tribunal only when they are specifically selected by states that have concluded a *compromis* submitting a dispute to arbitration.

The Administrative Council is headed by the Dutch Minister of Foreign Affairs and consists of the diplomatic representatives of the signatories at The Hague. It determines the budget and administrative policy. The International Bureau consists of four persons of Dutch nationality headed by a Secretary-General. It maintains the registry and archives and communicates with governments. The signatories to the Convention finance the modest expenses of the institution.

At the Second Hague Conference in 1907, the American delegation was instructed by Secretary of State Elihu Root to go even further, if possible. Root sought obligatory arbitration and "the development of The Hague

[15] Manley O. Hudson, *International Tribunals, Past and Future* (Washington: Carnegie Endowment for International Peace and Brookings Institution, 1944), p. 5.

tribunal into a permanent tribunal." This objective was not immediately attained. Despite the efforts of various Presidents, the United States Senate was unwilling to yield what it felt to be its treaty-making prerogative so that the United States could be committed in advance to arbitrate even limited classes of disputes. Not until 1908 did the Senate finally approve a series of arbitration treaties which, however, excepted "vital interests," "independence" and "national honor," and which required Senate approval of a *separate compromis for each arbitration*. This was scarcely the obligatory arbitration that orderly international relations required.

Meanwhile, France and Britain took a bolder step in 1903 by agreeing that

> differences which may arise of a legal nature . . . shall be referred to the Permanent Court of Arbitration . . . provided nevertheless that they do not affect the vital interests, the independence or the honor of the two Contracting States, and do not concern the interests of third Parties.[16]

Although this treaty seems to have left little to the arbitral process, it was the first general treaty of obligatory arbitration, and it utilized the first standing international tribunal.

The Permanent Court of Arbitration was never very active. Most of its business (seventeen cases) came before the establishment of the League and the PCIJ. One of its most famous cases was the *North Atlantic Coast Fisheries Case of 1910*, involving the rights of British (Canadian) and American fishermen off the Newfoundland coast. Perhaps its most notable achievement was to convince statesmen of the feasibility of a real world court.

Other developments included a convention drafted at The Hague in 1907 for an International Prize Court, which never came into being because the signatories could not decide on the rules to be applied in adjudicating cases. The United States, among others, also proposed at that time the establishment of a Court of Arbitral Justice "of free and easy access, composed of judges representing the various judicial systems of the world, and capable of ensuring continuity in arbitral jurisprudence." This promised to be a real court, but the project foundered when the delegates could not agree how to select its judges. As the reader may have guessed, small states insisted on equality with big states, so that the bench would have included a judge from every member country. The result would have been a congress, not a court. More successful was a Central American Court of Justice established in 1907 by Costa Rica, Honduras, Nicaragua and El Salvador, which heard several cases in its single decade of activity.

Organizing International Economic Relations

The industrial revolution resulted in a great increase in the variety and importance of trade and other activities across state frontiers. Even prior

---

[16] Quoted in Eagleton, *op. cit.*, p. 228.

to the establishment of modern industry, however, there was a great deal of what might be characterized as European economic and cultural activity. Private associations, or "private international organizations," were formed to foster activities of one sort or another all over the world. As one distinguished observer has written: "There is an International Wine Office to encourage the use of wine, and an International Bureau against Alcoholism to discourage it." [17]

More important was the development of an increasing number of official international administrative organizations, sometimes known as "public international organizations." The number of these increased steadily throughout the nineteenth century.

Public International Unions [18]

Some of the most noteworthy intergovernmental administrative organizations were the river commissions already discussed in connection with the Vienna settlement. Other "nonpolitical" organizations soon followed. Like the river commissions, they were established by treaty, had a permanent or continuing conference and bureau, and were open to all states interested in the specific activity involved. Until the League and, more particularly, the UN, these economic institutions were set apart from the primarily political activities of the concert system. Yet both these aspects of international organization had a single cause: the growing interdependence of states.

One of the earliest organizations was the Universal Postal Union, established at Berne in 1875. All powers, whether friendly with one another or not, have a mutual interest in regularizing international postal services. Its work and structure are described in Chapter 19. It continues today as one of the most successful of the UN specialized agencies.

By 1914 there were in existence thirty public international unions the policies of which were generally laid down in each instance by a congress or conference, while the daily work was managed by a bureau or commission. International problems dealt with in this fashion included transportation and communication facilities, disease control, economic problems and labor legislation.

Specific organizations included, among others, the International Bureau of Weights and Measures, the Wireless Telegraph Union, the International Sugar Union, the International Institute of Agriculture, the International Office of Public Health, the Union for the Suppression of the African Slave Trade, the International Opium Commission, and so on.

One public union, the International Sugar Union, deserves special mention because its power was more extensive than the recommendatory authority of most unions. In 1902 cutthroat competition in the production and marketing of sugar led several of the sugar-producing countries to agree to equalize competition and aid consumption through the reduction

---

[17] Eagleton, op. cit., p. 121.

[18] This is also the title of a pioneering study by Paul S. Reinsch (Boston: Ginn for the World Peace Foundation, 1911).

of taxes. A bureau to collect information was established at Brussels. Constant supervision of the agreement, however, was exercised by a commission composed of one delegate from each member which, by majority vote, could order any signatory state to change its domestic legislation to accord with the agreement. This grant of supranational authority was unique. As conditions improved, the powers withdrew from these restrictions, and the organization was formally ended by 1920.

Thus by World War I there were several types of international organization. Many statesmen and observers felt that if the several strands could be woven together a network of lasting peace might be established.

Suggestions for Further Reading

Books

Chamberlain, J. P., *The Regime of the International Rivers: Danube and Rhine, Studies in History, Economics, and Public Law* (New York: Columbia University Press, 1923).

Cresson, W. P., *The Holy Alliance* (New York: Oxford University Press, 1922).

Eagleton, Clyde, *International Government*, 2nd ed. (New York: Ronald Press, 1948).

Friedrich, C. J., *Inevitable Peace* (Cambridge: Harvard University Press, 1948).

Howard-Ellis, C., *The Origin, Structure, and Working of the League of Nations* (Boston: Houghton Mifflin Company, 1928).

Hudson, Manley O., *International Tribunals* (Washington: Carnegie Endowment for International Peace and Brookings Institution, 1944).

Kohn, Hans, *World Order in Historical Perspective* (Cambridge: Harvard University Press, 1943).

Leonard, L. Larry, *International Organization* (New York: McGraw-Hill Book Company, Inc., 1951).

Levi, Werner, *Fundamentals of World Organization* (Minneapolis: University of Minnesota Press, 1950).

Mander, L. A., *Foundations of Modern World Society* (Stanford: Stanford University Press, 1947).

Mangone, G. J., *The Idea and Practice of World Government* (New York: Columbia University Press, 1951).

Nicolson, H., *The Congress of Vienna: A Study in Allied Unity, 1812–22* (New York: Harcourt, Brace & Company, 1946).

Potter, P. B., *An Introduction to the Study of International Organization*, 5th ed. (New York: Appleton-Century-Crofts, 1948).

Ralston, J. H., *International Arbitration from Athens to Locarno* (Stanford: Stanford University Press, 1928). ·

Reinsch, P. S., *Public International Unions* (Boston: Ginn and Company, 1911).

Sayre, F. B., *Experiments in International Administration* (New York: Harper & Brothers, 1920).

Schuman, F. L., *International Politics*, 5th ed. (New York: McGraw-Hill Book Company, Inc., 1953).

Sharp, Walter R., and Kirk, Grayson C., *Contemporary International Politics* (New York: Rinehart and Company, 1940).

Webster, C. K., *The Congress of Vienna* (New York: Oxford University Press, 1919).

Woolf, L. S., *International Government* (New York: Brentano, 1916).

Documents

United States, *International Agencies in Which the United States Participates*, Department of State Publication 2699 (Washington: U.S. Government Printing Office, 1946).

————, *Participation of the United States Government in International Conferences, July 1, 1946–June 30, 1947*, Department of State Publication 3031 (Washington: U.S. Government Printing Office, 1948).

PART TWO

League and United Nations —
Structure and Authority

3

Origins and Comparison

THE GREAT DIVIDE that separates the history of international organization before and after 1919 is the creation for the first time of a permanent universal coordinating body, the League of Nations. To be sure, the bricks and mortar that went into the making of the League were far from new, but the total profile of the plan was quite a bold innovation. Never before had there been a continuing organization aimed at embracing the bulk of mankind, reinforced by regular meetings and pledged to facilitate worldwide cooperation on political, economic and social problems. The UN, on the other hand, is a more direct extension of the past. And yet, because neither the United States nor the Soviet Union was particularly friendly towards the League and because some internationalists have been prone to read greater progress into the UN Charter than it actually embodies, it has been fashionable in some quarters to speak of the UN as if it were the product of spontaneous conception.

Such a view lacks long-range perspective. The League-UN experience should be treated as two episodes of a single story, and the structure and functions of these two systems should be compared side by side. The objectives of this chapter, therefore, are to call attention to this continuity, as well as the differences, between the organizations and to analyze the general environments which produced them.

Genesis of the League

To understand the child, one must know the parents. The key to the nature of the League Covenant is the fact that it was shaped primarily by the interests of the major Allied and Associated Powers which emerged from World War I the exhausted victors over the even more exhausted Central Powers. Nor is it surprising that the two nations with the greatest economic and military resources, the United States and Great Britain, were also the most influential architects of the Covenant. The final product was a British machine guided by certain Wilsonian principles. The French and Italians, though included among the Big Four of the Peace Conference, played decidedly second fiddles. The smaller members of the wartime alliance and certain neutral countries submitted proposals and were consulted briefly, but exerted relatively little influence. The views of the enemy powers received even less attention. As to substance, the preoccupation of the Anglo-Saxons was to prevent another world war, through the limited functions of peaceful settlement of disputes and international sanctions, rather than to attempt any far-reaching surrender of national sovereignty or extensive economic and social cooperation.

Experience Before and During War

The roots of the League stretched back to the earliest peace plans discussed in Chapter 2. Naturally, the concepts that were most influential were those most familiar to the statesmen who designed the Covenant. They included the Concert of Europe, the Hague Permanent Court of Arbitration, and the various technical bodies such as the Universal Postal Union. Even as late as July 1914, however, the conciliatory British Foreign Secretary, Sir Edward Grey, had to admit that his fondest hope — an improved and organized Concert — was still "too Utopian to form the subject of definite proposals." [1] War was the stern tutor. It was the unprecedented and prolonged destruction of the world conflict, made possible by the technological revolution, that persuaded thoughtful men that some way must be found to prevent a recurrence of such devastation.

Other links in the chain were the Allied wartime organizations for military and economic cooperation. The need for coordination at the highest level first brought about occasional *ad hoc* conferences of the British and

[1] Alfred Zimmern, *The League of Nations and the Rule of Law, 1918–1935* (London: Macmillan, 1936), p. 81.

French Prime Ministers and other selected Ministers. By late 1916 there had evolved a Supreme War Council, composed of the Prime Minister and one other Minister from each country in the alliance, supported by professional advisers and a permanent staff. It was this body which finally appointed Marshal Foch as the supreme Allied Generalissimo. No comparable machinery had ever been created before, and it was a powerful administrative weapon in the struggle for survival. The initiative in this development had been taken by the British, who had had previous experience with an intergovernmental Committee of Imperial Defence, which, by 1909, had become a channel for coordinating British and Dominion policies, assisted by its own advisers and staff.[2]

The war also required machinery to coordinate the procurement, shipping, allocation and distribution of supplies, from sugar to gunpowder. This effort began with a Revictualling Commission (better known by the more awesome French title, *Commission Internationale de Revitaillement*, or simply CIR). This agency ultimately sprouted twenty boards and committees dealing with various commodity programs. Since shipping soon became the principal bottleneck, central control finally rested with an Inter-Allied Maritime Transport Council (AMTC) which during the last months of the war held the reins of 90 per cent of the world's seagoing tonnage. The permanent central "brain trust" of this body was the Transport Executive, composed of one representative apiece from Great Britain, the United States, France and Italy. Three of these men (Messrs. Salter, Monnet and Atolico) later transferred their energies to the League Secretariat.

Mr. Arthur Salter became particularly influential through his speaking and writing.[3] His principal thesis was that the secret of the AMTC success had been that it did not attempt supranational government but relied on day-to-day voluntary cooperative decisions of top-level officials who had the authority in their own governments to carry out these decisions. This is said to have spelled "the doom of the vague dreams of world government that were current in certain 'advanced' circles in the nineteenth century . . ."[4] Unfortunately, Mr. Salter failed to emphasize that what worked under the pressure of war might not (and did not) work when men relaxed after the storm had passed. During the struggle, the external threat to the Allies' survival was obvious; the objective, relatively simple; and the benefits of cooperation seemed vastly to outweigh the necessary sacrifices involved. None of these considerations remained as compelling in peacetime. Evidence of this change of climate came earlier than expected. When the British proposed in October 1918, one month before the war was to end, that the inter-Allied economic machinery be continued after the armistice to assure efficient and uninterrupted relief and reconstruction, the

[2] *Ibid.*, pp. 137–142.
[3] Arthur Salter, *Allied Shipping Control: An Experiment in International Administratior.* (New York: Oxford, 1921).
[4] Zimmern, *op. cit.*, p. 149.

United States, in the person of Mr. Herbert Hoover, rejected the plan.[5] Mr. Hoover preferred something similar to his Belgian Relief organization, the Allies being represented in proportion to their resources to support it.

Voice of the People

In democratic nations there are always those leaders of public opinion who are the major entrepreneurs of influential ideas and who condition, mobilize and interpret the views of the general public. Since internationalists in the enemy and neutral countries were scarcely free to speak publicly during the war, leadership in the movement to create an international organization had to come primarily from the Allied and Associated Powers, chiefly the United States, Great Britain and France. Among the most noteworthy groups were the League to Enforce Peace, led by former President Taft, and the British League of Nations Society, closely allied with a group headed by Lord Bryce, distinguished statesman and political philosopher.

The plans of these bodies were of what Professor Alfred Zimmern called the "fire brigade" variety. The machinery was designed to go into action only to prevent the outbreak of war. The underlying philosophy was primarily diplomatic and legalistic, relying on the traditional methods of settling disputes by conciliation or judicial procedure, sanctions against nations failing to submit disputes for such settlement and the quasi-legislative function of formulating and codifying rules of international law. But there were loopholes to allow "legal" war. Only "justiciable" disputes were to be settled by binding decisions. No provision was made for central control of sanctions or economic and social cooperation.[6] Another project called *The Framework of a Lasting Peace,* drafted principally by Mr. Leonard Woolf under the auspices of the British Fabian Society, was a far more positive and daring plan. While it followed the general pattern of the other proposals regarding the handling of disputes, it also aimed at attacking the sources of war through long-range economic and social activities following the trails blazed by such technical bodies as the Universal Postal Union. This approach was soon nicknamed "gas and water internationalism." Here was the most farsighted plan up to that time.[7]

Governmental Blueprints

The general impression one has of the trail of governmental proposals that led to the Covenant is that the Americans and British did more thorough planning than anyone else, that this effort came relatively late (not in earnest until after the fighting had stopped in November 1918), and that it was restricted to a comparatively small number of dedicated interna-

[5] *Ibid.,* pp. 151–159.

[6] Many of the private plans are published in the exhaustive collection edited by John H. Latané, *Development of the League of Nations Idea, Documents and Correspondence of Theodore Marburg,* 2 Vols. (New York: Macmillan, 1932).

[7] Leonard S. Woolf, *The Framework of a Lasting Peace* (London: Allen & Unwin, 1917).

tionalists in each country, the British making the most organized effort. The
first serious studies were initiated in the summer of 1917, when the British
created a committee under Sir Walter Phillimore, noted international lawyer; and the French, a committee under Leon Bourgeois, former Premier
and devoted internationalist. As might have been expected, the "Phillimore
Plan" was a version of the "fire brigade" type.[8] The "Bourgeois Plan" was
of the same school, but made all wars illegal. It provided for binding arbitration of *all* disputes not settled otherwise and military sanctions controlled by a council dominated by the great powers. Both of these projects
were in due course sent to Washington to nudge Wilson into revealing his
own ideas.

The President thought, however, that discussion of the details of such
plans at that stage might cause harmful dissension. Hence, he used his
influence to keep the British and French proposals secret. It was not until
July 1918, only four months before the war was to end, that he requested
his personal adviser, Colonel E. M. House, to prepare a tentative draft.
These initial ideas were strongly influenced by Wilson's earlier plans regarding the Pan-American system and House's reaction to the Phillimore
Plan. The House draft tended to follow the "fire brigade" motif, but with
several distinguishing features, including: authority to issue binding judgments in *all* disputes, mutual guarantees of territorial integrity combined
with possible revision of territorial arrangements by a three-fourths vote,
reduction of armaments, nationalization of arms manufacturing and the
right of League intervention in any war or threat of war. It was this plan
which Wilson adopted, with only a few changes, as his own first draft. But
he did not show these projects to his Secretary of State, Robert Lansing,
in whom he had little confidence.

As the armistice was being arranged in November 1918, an influential,
but nameless, draft was drawn up in the British Foreign Office — hence
the unofficial name of "Foreign Office Memorandum" — apparently with
the participation of Professor Zimmern.[9] Its purpose was to tie together
the best features of the Concert of Europe, Hague Court, Postal Union,
Woolf's Fabian plan and the Committee of Imperial Defence. It provided
for the coordination of all international, economic and social activities as
well as the more traditional political and legal functions. War was outlawed, but not all disputes were deemed appropriate for binding judgments.
Two bodies, rather than one, were proposed: an executive conference of
the great powers, meeting annually, and a larger plenary body, inspired
by the British Imperial Conference, meeting only every four or five years.
Finally, there was marked emphasis on the importance of a well-staffed
permanent secretary.

It was this plan which formed the basis of the "Cecil Draft," named for
Lord Robert Cecil, noted British statesman and internationalist, who was

[8] This and most of the other governmental proposals are published in David Hunter
Miller, *The Drafting of the Covenant,* 2 Vols. (New York: Putnam's, 1928).

[9] Zimmern, *op. cit.,* pp. 189–208.

placed in charge of the League of Nations section of the Foreign Office. The Memorandum seems also to have provided the core of the first top-level plan to be revealed to the public at large: *The League of Nations: A Practical Suggestion,* published in December 1918 by the farsighted and eloquent South African General, Jan Christiaan Smuts. But this scheme departed significantly from the Memorandum in not attempting to outlaw war entirely and in excluding from League supervision the German Pacific and African colonies. He explained that the latter were too much "barbarians" to warrant expectations of self-government. It also happened that the Dominions had a special interest in these territories and wanted control over them. Smuts also enlarged the executive council by adding two representatives of the "intermediate" powers and two representing the "minor" powers, to serve on a rotating basis. The great powers would be the only "permanent members."

Paris, 1919

Thus the stage was set as the curtain rose on the Paris Peace Conference in January 1919.[10] A great upsurge of popular hope for eternal peace burst forth in a crescendo of adulation of President Wilson — "Wilson the Just," as many men in the street called him. Professor James Shotwell later described the great demonstration in the Place de la Concorde:

> The tribute of respect which Paris paid to Wilson was one that I never saw the like of and shall never see again. As one of the papers put it, it was a "pious privilege" . . . to see the man who is in their eyes and in the eyes of most of the oppressed of Europe, the first moral force in the world today . . . guns started booming. . . . The crowds began to strain against the guards. Over the river we soon saw the bright helmets of the Garde Republicaine . . . and behind them, . . . Wilson. . . . The people cheered wildly.[11]

The pattern of interests that was to leave its imprint on the final outcome was revealed in the structure and process of the Conference. The drafting of the Covenant was to be supervised by a League of Nations Commission composed of two representatives from each of the five major powers (United States, Great Britain, France, Italy and Japan) and one representative from each of five lesser allies (Belgium, Brazil, China, Portugal and Serbia). At the first meeting, however, the smaller countries succeeded in having four more of the smaller states added — Greece, Poland, Czechoslovakia and Rumania. But the key decisions were usually made in separate meetings of the Big Three (Wilson, Lloyd George and Clemenceau).

[10] Among numerous accounts of the Conference, the major ones are David Lloyd George, *Memoirs of the Peace Conference,* 2 Vols. (New Haven: Yale University Press, 1939); Miller, *op. cit.;* and H. W. V. Temperley, ed., *A History of the Peace Conference of Paris,* 6 Vols. (London: Henry Frowde and Hodder & Stoughton, 1924).

[11] James T. Shotwell, *At the Paris Peace Conference* (New York: Macmillan, 1947), pp. 86–87. Used by permission of The Macmillan Company.

The draft used as the basis of discussion was one prepared by the Anglo-Americans: House and Cecil, advised by their legal experts, David Hunter Miller and Cecil Hurst — hence the name "Hurst–Miller Draft." A French proposal, heavily influenced by the Bourgeois Plan's emphasis on airtight collective security, was tabled and given no direct consideration. Nor did it receive any firm support from the chief French delegate, Georges Clemenceau, walrus-mustached "Tiger of France," who expressed little faith in such internationalist schemes. An Italian draft also followed the Bourgeois pattern, but with unique emphasis on a truly international legislative function and economic and social development. This, too, was filed away without serious examination. The Japanese were primarily interested in using the Covenant and League as instruments to outlaw racial discrimination, particularly regarding immigration restrictions in the United States and Australia, but outbursts of indignation in California and the intransigent opposition of the Australian Prime Minister, William Morris Hughes, blocked that effort.

A preliminary draft was completed only eleven days after the Commission's first meeting, and President Wilson presented it to a plenary session of the Conference. He then immediately sailed for home to beard the Republican opposition in its den, while others remaining in Paris consulted with Allies not represented on the Commission. The neutral nations were allowed only to present their views at a series of unofficial meetings. After Wilson returned in mid-March 1919, the Commission pressed on to finish the job. But the atmosphere was less friendly than before due to a combination of circumstances including resistance to the "reservations" which Wilson had been persuaded to propose — safeguarding the Monroe Doctrine, exempting domestic issues and the right of withdrawal — and bitter struggles with the French, Italians and Japanese over their particular objectives regarding the Covenant and general peace settlement.

During the course of the Conference, there were several major compromises that left their mark on the League. Wilson, for example, wanted a strong guarantee of territorial integrity combined with the possibility of revising territorial and other agreements ("peaceful change"), but the British succeeded in blunting these efforts, which they considered excessive invasions of national sovereignty. Wilson also began by proposing a stronger Assembly than the British wanted. The latter were primarily interested in safeguarding peace through an improved "Concert" of great powers which were to control the League via their dominance in the executive council. Related to this issue was the understandable desire of the smaller powers for stronger representation in the council. This difference was reconciled by granting the smaller nations four seats, as originally recommended by Smuts. A majority of the council — five seats — remained in the hands of the great powers, which would be the only "permanent members."

It was on April 28, 1919, that President Wilson laid the final draft of the Covenant before the entire Peace Conference. At the same time an Organizing Committee was appointed to plan the establishment of the League at Geneva, and Sir Eric Drummond was chosen as the first Secretary-General. At the last minute, however, a cruel blow was dealt the infant organization by the refusal of the United States Senate, led by Senators Henry Cabot Lodge and William E. Borah, to allow the United States to join the League. This decision removed one of the main supports on which the structure had been designed to rest.

Genesis of the United Nations

In 1945, twenty-six years after the founding of the League, a new but strikingly similar organization, the United Nations, rose out of the flames that had consumed the old. The intervening years had been full of hopes and frustrations, limited collective efforts to combat outbreaks of aggression, followed by the most catastrophic man-made destruction of all history, World War II. The damage done to the material and human foundations of our civilization and the potential for doing even greater damage were immeasurably more vast in 1945 than in 1919. But the men who planned the new world again designed it in the image and likeness of what was most familiar: the League pattern, more or less as it had evolved by the time the fighting began in 1939.

The national interests which shaped the new-old system were reminiscent of those which had dominated the negotiations of 1918–19 in that the Anglo-Americans still marched at the head of the column. But the greatly expanded industrial resources of the United States had placed it far in advance of everyone else in terms of sheer power superiority. Britain's economic position, on the other hand, had deteriorated badly, due to war damage, long-term economic trends, and considerable unrest within her empire. But, reinforced by her traditional ties with America, symbolized in the warm friendship of President Franklin Roosevelt and Prime Minister Winston Churchill, her political influence was second only to that of the United States. France's economic position was equally precarious, and her political influence had been decisively eclipsed, not only by her defeat and occupation at the hands of the Axis, but also by the quixotic leadership of General Charles de Gaulle, who soon succeeded in antagonizing President Roosevelt and others. Italy and Japan were now among the vanquished. The Soviet Union, on the other hand, which had been seething with revolutionary indigestion in 1919, had become a war partner of the democracies and a great power.

China's position in the world did not warrant a position among the strongest powers, but President Roosevelt wanted her included among the Big Five because of traditional United States relations with China and that country's long struggle against Japan. Moreover, China was represented at many of the planning conferences by the able and popular Wellington

Koo, who had also been an influential figure in the League. Several of the so-called middle powers — especially Canada, Australia, Belgium, the Netherlands and New Zealand — exerted considerable influence both because of their substantial contributions to the war effort and the quality of some of their delegates. The Latin Americans were consulted by the United States, made some contributions, but were not a major force. The Asians were in a state of turmoil and not yet in a position to speak with as strong a voice as they have more recently.

Wartime Cooperation

Once again the heat of battle had tended to melt armies and economies together — but only temporarily. The basic character of the alliance machinery was fundamentally the same as during World War I, although much more fully developed, relying on close day-to-day voluntary cooperation among top national officials rather than attempting any integrated central government. The key to the nature of the process was that decisions were effective because they were made only by unanimous consent, not because they were made by any supranational authority. The network of joint agencies was composed almost entirely of United States and United Kingdom representatives. Russia was not included in such an intimate embrace but was consulted through looser *ad hoc* arrangements.[12]

The United States–United Kingdom machinery was established far more rapidly and extensively than during World War I. Only two weeks after the bombing of Pearl Harbor, Prime Minister Churchill arrived in Washington for the so-called "Arcadia" Conference, and, ensconced on the top floor of the White House opposite Harry Hopkins' room, he agreed with President Roosevelt to a thorough pooling of the two nations' military and economic resources. A Combined Chiefs of Staff, centralized in Washington, was to integrate military strategy under the general direction of the two heads of state. It was decided not to adopt the United States State Department's plan for a Supreme War Council, including the Soviet Union and China,[13] nor a looser form of alliance first proposed by the British.[14] Unified commands under single military leaders were then and subsequently agreed upon for the Mediterranean, Europe, Southwest Pacific and Southeast Asia. As for the effectiveness of these instruments, one observer has said, "The Combined Chiefs of Staff provided leadership which was integrated, balanced, and comprehensive and gave the Allies a vast and

---

[12] Accounts of the allied organization are to be found in: J. J. Llewellin, "Machinery of Wartime Cooperation Between the British Commonwealth and the United States," *International Conciliation*, No. 398 (March 1944), p. 178; S. McKee Rosen, *Combined Boards of the Second World War: An Experiment in International Administration* (New York: Columbia University Press, 1951); *Guide to United Nations and Allied Agencies* (New York: UN Information Office, 1945).

[13] Cordell Hull, *The Memoirs of Cordell Hull* (New York: Macmillan, 1948), Vol. 2, pp. 1115–1124.

[14] Robert Sherwood, *Roosevelt and Hopkins* (New York: Harper, 1948), pp. 469–470.

UNITED NATIONS - COOPERATION IN WAR

ECONOMIC

STRATEGIC

COMBINED RAW MATERIALS BOARD

COMBINED FOOD BOARD

COMBINED PRODUCTION & RESOURCES BOARD

COMBINED SHIPPING ADJUSTMENT BOARD

COMBINED CHIEFS OF STAFF ORGANIZATION

MUNITIONS ASSIGNMENT BOARD

PACIFIC WAR COUNCIL

INTER-AMERICAN DEFENSE BOARD

We have learned that no nation, no matter how powerful and wealthy, can win the war alone

Headline Series, *Foreign Policy Association*

incalculable advantage over their enemies in the higher direction of the war." [15]

The two allies also decided in January 1942, as in World War I, to establish various joint bodies to regulate the flow of essential supplies without which the leviathans could not survive. The most crucial and controversial subject during the January negotiations was how to organize the allocation of munitions. The British thought in terms of dividing the world into two spheres under the United States and United Kingdom respectively, while the Americans wanted a more integrated procedure. Finally, the United States won British acceptance of a Combined Munitions Assignment Board "to be tried for one month," with Harry Hopkins, the only man who seemed to have the confidence of both sides, acting as Chairman.[16] Fortunately, this body continued to function throughout the war with no more than that temporary mandate.

A Combined Raw Materials Board was also created in January to plan

[15] Chester Wilmot, *The Struggle for Europe* (London: Collins, 1952), p. 100.
[16] Sherwood, *op. cit.*, pp. 470–473.

54

the optimum development and use of scarce raw materials. A Combined Shipping Adjustment Board was charged with promoting the most efficient use of available shipping space, including the chartered fleets of the Netherlands, Norway and other allied governments. A Combined Production and Resources Board, to which the Canadians gained admission in November 1942 because of their significant industrial output, was established in June 1942 to see that the production of the three countries was properly integrated and utilized to the maximum degree. A Combined Food Board, also set up in June 1942, with Canada added in October 1943, planned the supply of food, fertilizers and agricultural implements.

More specialized commodity agencies created during the war included Combined Aluminum and Magnesium, Copper, Rubber and Steel Committees; an International Cotton Advisory Committee; and an International Wheat Council. Regional bodies established to make optimum use of scarce resources in their respective areas included a Middle East Supply Center, an Anglo-American Carribean Commission, an Eastern Group Supply Council and various Inter-American agencies. This whole far-reaching network of some fifty UN wartime agencies, supported by myriad sub-bodies, represented, as General George C. Marshall wrote in 1945, "the most complete unification of military effort ever achieved by two allied nations." [17]

The Arcadia Conference also produced the term "United Nations." As former Secretary of State Cordell Hull tells it, President Roosevelt, on the morning of December 31, 1941, discussed the draft text of a joint statement of basic objectives with Winston Churchill as he was taking a bath and there suggested that it be called "Declaration by United Nations." "The distinguished bather agreed, and thus the term 'United Nations' came into being." [18]

Activating Public Opinion

Because the destruction of World War II was far more crushing than that of World War I and because the League had left a solid deposit of useful experience, influential private groups, chiefly in the major democratic countries, began early in the war to think more diligently than ever of ways to improve world organization for peace. Again most of the organized thinking was done in the Anglo-American countries. And, because of their immunity from direct war damage and their greater resources, the United States groups carried out the most intensive preparations.

American Planners. Among the more influential bodies in the United States was the Commission to Study the Organization of Peace, established at the end of 1939, under the direction of Professor James T. Shotwell, noted international scholar and official of the Carnegie Endowment for International Peace, who had played a prominent role in world affairs ever since the Paris Peace Conference of 1919. This group served as a major

[17] Quoted in Wilmot, *op. cit.*, p. 99.
[18] Hull, *op. cit.*, Vol. 2, p. 1124.

coordinator of the views of leading internationalists — including Frank Aydelotte, John Foster Dulles, Clark M. Eichelberger, Frank Graham, Philip Jessup, Charles P. Taft and Quincy Wright — many of whom were also members of other groups such as the Council on Foreign Relations, Foreign Policy Association and League of Nations Association.[19] The group which concentrated upon academic opinion was the Universities Committee on Postwar International Problems, organized during the summer of 1942, under the direction of Professor Ralph Barton Perry, distinguished Harvard philosopher, in close cooperation with the World Peace Foundation.[20]

A major cooperative effort among various religious faiths was the National Study Conference on the Churches and a Just and Durable Peace, organized by a Commission of the Federal Council of the Churches of Christ in America [21] under the Chairmanship of John Foster Dulles, leading international lawyer and statesman. The Institute of Pacific Relations held two major conferences during the war attended by delegates from many UN countries particularly interested in the Pacific area: the first in Quebec, December 1942, and the other in Virginia, January 1945.[22] The Institute also sponsored an Inquiry during 1938 and 1939 out of which emerged a provocative book by Professor Percy E. Corbett, *Postwar Worlds*.[23] The Council on Foreign Relations contributed many proposals and some staff to the State Department and sponsored the preparation of such studies as Professor Eugene Staley's *World Economy in Transition*.[24] These, of course, are only samples of some of the more influential private efforts in the United States.[25]

A rough comparative analysis of these various blueprints indicates a broad pattern of consensus. Perhaps the first central motif to note is that the large majority favored a reinforced League rather than either the isolationist extreme of nonparticipation or the internationalist extreme of world government. On the other hand, it is interesting that most of these private plans, weighted, of course, in favor of international cooperation, supported a stronger version than the United States finally proposed at the Dumbarton Oaks and San Francisco Conferences. As to structure, all groups endorsed the basic framework of the League: an assembly, council, mandates (now "trusteeship") commission, court and secretariat. The

[19] Reports of the Commission were published in *International Conciliation*, Nos. 369 (April 1941); 379 (April 1942); 389 (April 1943); 396 (January 1944); and 403 (September 1944).

[20] Summaries of the Committee's Reports were published in *International Conciliation*, Nos. 401 (June 1944); 405 (November 1944); 410 (April 1945); and 414 (October 1945).

[21] A report was published in *International Conciliation*, No. 409 (March 1945).

[22] Among the many conference documents, preliminary summary reports of these meetings have appeared in two volumes: *War and Peace in the Pacific* (New York: Institute of Pacific Relations, 1943), and *Security in the Pacific* (New York: Institute of Pacific Relations, 1945).

[23] (New York: Institute of Pacific Relations, 1942).

[24] (New York: Council on Foreign Relations, 1939).

[25] See other bibliographical references in subsequent chapters.

major change was an inclination to accept conclusions developed in the last years of the League (expressed in the 1939 "Bruce Report") [26] that economic and social activities should be expanded and their supervision transferred from the overloaded political council to a separate council under the general direction of the assembly.

Details of Proposals. Regarding political-military functions, most of these plans wanted to keep the general features of the League but to strengthen them through outlawing aggressive force, supported by binding sanctions with some attempt at a truly international police force. There was a considerable difference of views, however, as to whether all great powers, not directly involved, should have a "veto." Moreover, both the Commission to Study the Organization of Peace and the Universities Committee wanted all disputes to be settled ultimately by binding decisions, thus closing the gap that had caused so much trouble in the League. There was less emphasis than in 1919, however, on disarmament.

Most of the proposals favored much more extensive and active cooperation than under the League in postwar relief and reconstruction, reducing trade barriers, stabilizing foreign exchange, improving labor conditions, bettering health, developing cultural relations, assisting refugees and other migrants, and encouraging better food production and nutrition. There was also support for cooperative programs that represented even more marked changes in thinking, such as economic development of underdeveloped countries, full employment, international lending, securing universal human rights and promoting social security. Regarding colonialism, there was broad agreement that the League mandates system should be continued but that UN supervisory authority should be strengthened and that the colonial powers should recognize some international responsibilities with respect to all their non-self-governing territories. There was also a sizable minority that felt that all dependent territories should be placed under direct international administration.

Private planning in Britain was not as extensive nor as well financed as in America, but small circles were active and influential. These included the League of Nations Union, Royal Institute of International Affairs, as well as political, business, labor and other interests. In general, British opinion seems to have agreed with that in the United States, especially on the political-military side, but it also reflected Britain's reluctance to abandon her economic regulatory shields or lose control of her empire. Unlike the situation during World War I, there was no possibility of extensive planning in France, the Netherlands and other Axis-occupied countries. Internationalist opinion in the neutral countries was free but not strongly organized. And there could be no free expression of internationalist opinion in the Soviet sphere or enemy countries.

[26] See Chap. 8.

National Interests

Because of the balance of forces in world affairs mentioned above, the United States Government was the dominant power in the governmental planning process in even greater degree than in 1919. And at the head of the American Government, President Roosevelt and Secretary of State Cordell Hull, unlike President Wilson, were determined to start early and lay · the foundations of postwar cooperation while the wartime alliance was still firm. Within the administration, the planning initiative was seized as early as September 1939 by Secretary Hull, who had always had great faith in a general international organization — considerably more, apparently, than President Roosevelt — and was all too conscious of the way President Wilson had by-passed the State Department.[27] Secretary Hull was also a former Congressman and Senator, and, remembering the bitter executive-legislative vendetta in 1919, insisted on close coordination with Congress, especially the leading figures of Tom Connally, Democratic Chairman of the Senate Foreign Relations Commitee, and Arthur Vandenberg, ranking minority member.[28] Hence the planning process involved a balance of interests, not only among various executive agencies, but between the more internationalist administration and the less internationalist legislature.

The general trend of official United States thinking, even as early as July 1943, was that the over-all pattern of the League should be retained but that, because of the unfortunate past experience of both the United States and the U.S.S.R. with respect to the League as well as other considerations, it should be given a new name. It should also be strengthened through outlawing war, providing strong collective sanctions under the control of a council dominated by the great powers, each of whom would have a "veto" except when party to a dispute in the pacific settlement of differences, expanding economic and social cooperation through the UN and separate "specialized agencies," and reinforcing the mandates system with independence as the ultimate goal. But it was recognized from the beginning that Congress would never consent to giving the UN any binding authority over United States interests except by its own consent in each case. Hence, the veto was as strongly insisted upon by the United States as by any other power.

Far less staff, time and facilities were made available for postwar planning in the United Kingdom than in the United States. At the same time, the British and Americans consulted far more with each other than with any other country, including the Soviet Union, and it was these two powers

[27] Hull, op. cit., Vol. 2, Part 8; the detailed official account of the United States' postwar planning process is published in *Postwar Foreign Policy Preparation, 1939–1945,* Department of State Publication 3850 (Washington: Government Printing Office, 1950).

[28] Hull, op. cit., especially pp. 1259–1263, 1657–1670. *The Private Papers of Senator Vandenberg,* edited by Arthur H. Vandenberg, Jr., with the collaboration of Joe Alex Morris (Boston: Houghton Mifflin, 1952); Daniel S. Cheever and H. Field Haviland, Jr., *United States Foreign Policy and the Separation of Powers* (Cambridge: Harvard University Press, 1952), pp. 100–106.

that determined the framework of the postwar machinery. While the British generally agreed with the United States political and military plans, although Churchill began by emphasizing regional security spheres, each supervised by a great power, they were far more wary about lowering their tariff and other economic defenses and far more interested in plentiful and cheap credit to reconstruct their badly mangled economy. Also, under Conservative Party leadership until the summer of 1945, they vehemently resisted American efforts to loosen the bonds of their colonial system.

The Soviet Union seemed interested in the UN primarily as an instrument for assuring itself a place in the great-power council and, hence, a decisive share in the control of international relations. But the Russians wanted a great-power veto over all questions before the council, while the United States and United Kingdom were willing to have the veto apply to only matters involving sanctions. In the economic and social sphere, the Soviet Union seems to have been chiefly concerned with relief and reconstruction assistance. It showed little enthusiasm for general cooperation on long-range problems and began by urging that the economic and social apparatus be entirely divorced from the political structure. The Russian attitude towards UN supervision of dependent territories was divided between its desire to gain administrative control over an area, such as Tripolitania, and to use the system as a lever to break the hold of other powers over their dependencies.

France, playing a relatively insignificant role during the planning process, generally agreed with the United States and United Kingdom, but was very conservative on colonial policy. China was somewhat more influential, assisted by the close relations of Chiang Kai-shek and Wellington Koo with the American leaders, but tended to be more interested than the great powers in economic and social cooperation and a liberal colonial policy. The "middle" states, particularly Canada, Australia and New Zealand, exerted significant influence, often mediating among the giants, especially at San Francisco, and pushing hard for less great power dominance, a stronger assembly and economic and social program, and more liberal standards in colonial administration. The Latin Americans, Asians and Africans also tended to follow this line, but carried less weight.

Road to Peace

The governmental planning process was not as simple as it had been in 1918–19, centering chiefly around a single "peace conference." The determination to construct the postwar organizations before negotiating the peace treaties and to assign some major economic and social functions to semi-independent agencies, patterned after the prewar International Labor Organization (ILO), meant that there was not to be merely one conference, but a whole series of conferences.

The first official step was taken when President Roosevelt and Prime Minister Churchill met at sea, where both men were always most content, off Newfoundland aboard HMS *Prince of Wales* and the USS *Augusta* dur-

HOW THE CHARTER CAME INTO BEING

ATLANTIC CHARTER
Aug. 14, 1941

DECLARATION BY UNITED NATIONS
Jan. 1, 1942

MOSCOW DECLARATION
Oct. 30, 1943

DUMBARTON OAKS
Aug.-Oct. 1944

YALTA CONFERENCE
Feb. 1945

SAN FRANCISCO CONFERENCE
Apr. -June 1945

PREPARATORY COMMISSION
Nov.-Dec. 1945

FIRST ASSEMBLY (IN LONDON)
Jan., 1946

Headline Series, *Foreign Policy Association*

ing August 1941. There they discussed, among other things, a statement of joint objectives based on a draft prepared by Churchill. The Prime Minister wanted a firm pledge to build a new general international organization to satisfy internationalist opinion in his country, but Roosevelt resisted, both because of hostile opinion in the United States and his own view that such an organization should not be formed "until after a period of time

60

had passed and during which an international police force composed of the United States and Great Britain had had an opportunity of functioning." [29] There was also some conflict between the American desire for freer trade and Churchill's defense of the Commonwealth preferential system. The most relevant pledges of the two powers for this study were as follows:

> Fourth, . . . to further the enjoyment by all States . . . of access, on equal terms, to the trade and to the raw materials of the world which are needed for their economic prosperity. . . .
>
> Fifth, . . . to bring about the fullest collaboration between all nations in the economic field with the object of securing, for all, improved labor standards, economic adjustment, and social security.
>
> Eighth, . . . Since no future peace can be maintained if land, sea, or air armaments continue to be employed by nations which threaten, or may threaten, aggression . . . they believe, pending the establishment of a wider and permanent system of general security, that the disarmament of such nations is essential. . . . [30]

Immediately after the attack on Pearl Harbor, this commitment was extended to the Soviet Union and twenty-three other governments in the form of the United Nations Declaration proclaimed at Washington in January 1942. Shortly thereafter, in February, the United States began gathering pledges for a postwar relaxation of trade restrictions, tied to its wartime aid, as it negotiated a Lend-Lease Agreement with Britain. In May and June of the following year, all of the United Nations met for the "first postwar conference," the Food and Agriculture Conference, at Hot Springs, Virginia, to create the first new specialized agency, the Food and Agriculture Organization (FAO). Many observers also thought of this meeting as a "rehearsal" for creating the new League.

In October 1943, Secretary of State Hull, a long sufferer from claustrophobia, agreed to take the first airplane ride of his life, at the age of seventy-one, to go to Moscow to reach agreement with the Russians on a number of points of conflict. Hull had finally won President Roosevelt's consent to plan for a general international organization, and he was delighted to secure a Russian commitment for the same objective in the Moscow Declaration of the Four Nations on General Security issued on October 30:

> That they recognize the necessity of establishing at the earliest practicable date a general international organization, based on the principle of the sovereign equality of all peace-loving States, and open to membership by all such States . . . for the maintenance of international peace and security. . . . [31]

[29] Sumner Welles, *Where Are We Heading?* (New York: Harper, 1946), p. 15. For other accounts of these discussions, see Sherwood, *op. cit.;* Winston S. Churchill, *The Grand Alliance* (Boston: Houghton Mifflin, 1950), Chap. 4.

[30] Quoted in *International Conciliation*, No. 372 (September 1941), p. 596.

[31] Quoted in *International Conciliation*, No. 395 (December 1943), p. 602.

The following month, representatives of the allies gathered in Washington to sign the Agreement establishing the UN Relief and Rehabilitation Administration (UNRRA) in order to avoid the fumbling which followed World War I by preparing in advance for a truly international large-scale rehabilitation effort. The first meeting of an established specialized agency to consider postwar problems was the conference of the International Labor Organization (ILO) in Philadelphia in April 1944. In July 1944, the United Nations met at Bretton Woods, New Hampshire, to form the International Monetary Fund (IMF) and International Bank for Reconstruction and Development (IBRD).

The first Big Three meeting devoted entirely to the creation of a general international organization was held in Washington, during August and September 1944, at the lovely Dumbarton Oaks estate, former home of Robert Woods Bliss, once Ambassador to Argentina, who had donated it to Harvard University. It is scarcely surprising that the major emphasis at Dumbarton Oaks was on security rather than economic and social matters. Unlike the League, there was to be a clear division of functions between the Assembly and Security Council, with the latter "primarily responsible for the maintenance of international peace and security" and solely charged with taking "action." The Council's decisions on the employment of sanctions were to be binding, subject to the great power "veto," and to be implemented through national contingents made available in advance through special treaties. The major dispute was between the Russians, who insisted that the great powers be allowed to exercise their veto on all questions, and the British and Americans, who wanted to prohibit a party to a dispute from voting in its own case. Even President Roosevelt could not budge the Soviet Ambassador, Andrei Gromyko, in an hour-long session beginning at seven-thirty in the morning. Finally, the issue was left to the heads of state at the subsequent Yalta Conference.

The Soviet Union and United Kingdom tended to give the Assembly a less important role than the Americans but soon accepted the United States point of view. The Russians also finally agreed that economic and social activities as well as security functions should be under the UN. Accord was also reached on more extensive economic and social objectives than in the Covenant, further development of the ILO-type specialized agencies coordinated under the ECOSOC and General Assembly, and the reëstablishment of an international court similar to the prewar Permanent Court of International Justice. There was no discussion of the colonial problem, however, largely because the United States Chiefs of Staff thought the issue would breed disunity among the allies and also because they were opposed to placing the hard-won Japanese mandated islands in the Pacific under UN supervision.[32]

Since the Soviet Union insisted she could not meet with China because she was not at war with Japan, separate United States–United Kingdom–China talks were held on the Dumbarton Oaks draft during September

[32] Hull, op. cit., p. 1706.

and October 1944. The Chinese delegation, led by Wellington Koo, tended to emphasize economic and social cooperation and liberal trusteeship provisions more than security, but was not in a position to press its views.

At the favorite Russian seaside resort of Yalta, on the Black Sea, Roosevelt, Churchill and Stalin met in elaborate palaces inherited from Czarist days, during February 1945, to hammer out further compromises on various military and postwar issues. Regarding the voting question, it was decided that the Big Five, even when parties to disputes, might veto the application of sanctions but not recommendations dealing with the peaceful settlement of disputes. The Americans and British firmly opposed another Russian proposal that all sixteen of the Soviet Republics be given separate representation in the UN, but Roosevelt agreed in a private talk with Stalin to support representation for two of them: the Ukrainian and Byelorussian Republics. On the touchy colonial issue, as Secretary of State Edward Stettinius, who had taken over when Secretary Hull resigned because of illness, began reading a draft proposing a slightly reinforced mandates system, the famous Churchillian wrath erupted against what the Prime Minister alleged was mischievous meddling with the British Empire.[33] But agreement was finally reached on the basic principles of a trusteeship system.

At Chicago, in November 1944, the International Civil Aviation Organization (ICAO) was formed in spite of vehement differences between the United States and Commonwealth nations on the future sharing and development of world air traffic. Early in 1945, there was an Inter-American Conference on War and Peace, held at Mexico City, in which the Latin Americans pledged support of a general international organization but expressed considerable concern that the smaller states and regional systems, such as theirs, should be given stronger voices.

San Francisco, 1945

> "The work, my friends, is peace; more than an end of this war — an end to the beginning of all wars; yes, an end, forever, to this impractical, unrealistic settlement of the differences between governments by the mass killing of peoples. Today . . . as we go forward toward the greatest contribution that any generation of human beings can make in this world — the contribution of lasting peace — I ask you to keep up your faith. . . ."[34]

These words were part of the last address written by President Roosevelt, to be delivered on April 13, 1945, on the eve of the San Francisco Conference, which was to convene on April 25. The address was never delivered, however, since the President died on April 12. But the "work" of peace went ahead as the UN Conference on International Organization began its

[33] Edward R. Stettinius, Jr., *Roosevelt and the Russians* (Garden City: Doubleday, 1949), pp. 237–239.

[34] *International Conciliation*, No. 412 (June 1945), pp. 404–405.

meetings in the ornate Opera House during the faultless spring weather of San Francisco. Here the Big Four, acting as the Sponsoring Powers, laid the Dumbarton Oaks Draft before forty-six other states that had either signed the Declaration of the United Nations by January 1942 or had declared war on the Axis by March 1945.

The principal division of interests which underlay the negotiations was between the Big Four, pledged to defend a common set of proposals and anxious to avoid reopening old wounds, and the middle and smaller countries that, in the main, resented what they alleged was excessive domination of the UN by the great powers, especially as symbolized in the veto. Hence the smaller countries deluged the Conference with a snowstorm of amendments aimed at strengthening their hand and liberalizing the economic, social and trusteeship provisions, without, however, advocating world government any more than the great powers. There were also cleavages within each of these camps. The Soviet Union was the most intransigent exponent of great power dominance, while the United States and United Kingdom tended to be somewhat more conciliatory in meeting the complaints of their many lesser allies.

Among the other states, Australia, New Zealand and a few other "progressives" were the most ambitious in the economic and social sphere, particularly on the issue of "full employment," while others, such as Argentina, were among the most conservative. On the colonial question, there was a somewhat different line-up with the United Kingdom, France and other conservative colonial powers on one side, the U.S.S.R. and China leading the anti-colonial forces, and the United States, Australia and New Zealand (the latter two being colonial powers but under labor governments) attempting to mediate. It is also important to recognize the impact of individual personalities who sometimes increased the influence of their delegations far beyond what seemed warranted by the economic and military position of their countries. Such a figure was Herbert Vere Evatt, Australian delegate, whom one writer has called the leader of the smaller states.

> His determination that the small powers should obtain as much as they possibly could, combined with his tireless energy, knowledge, and force of personality, made him at once the detestation of the Big Five and the champion of the little forty-five. If an award had been made for the ablest and most effective delegate to the Conference, it would have gone without question to Dr. Evatt.[35]

As usual, the process of the Conference also reflected the tensions arising from the special interests of the participants. The meetings began under the cloud of intense feeling over the admission to the Conference of certain controversial countries. Finally, the gates were reluctantly opened to the Ukrainian and Byelorussian Republics, according to the Roosevelt-

[35] Eugene P. Chase, *The United Nations in Action* (New York: McGraw-Hill, 1950), pp. 56–57.

Stalin agreement at Yalta, and to Argentina, sponsored by the Latin Americans and the United States, but not to the Communist-dominated government of Poland. The bitter debate over these admissions was one of the principal harbingers of the cold war.

The organization of the Conference was somewhat more representative than in 1919, although a comparison is made difficult by the fact that the Dumbarton Oaks and San Francisco phases had previously been combined in a single conference. Unlike 1919, the drafting was not done in one Commission of fourteen governments, but in twelve Committees under four Commissions and a Steering Committee, in all of which each of the Conference's fifty governments was entitled to be represented. And these bodies did a freer and more thorough job of revision than the great powers had originally intended. Decisions were also made by the more flexible two-thirds majority rather than unanimity.[36] At the same time, one must recall that the Conference was merely revising proposals previously drafted by the great powers. Furthermore, their deliberations were subject to the guidance of a fourteen-member Executive Committee (the Big Five plus Australia, Brazil, Canada, Chile, Czechoslovakia, Iran, Mexico, the Netherlands and Yugoslavia), a Coordinating Committee (composed of expert deputies of the Executive Committee to coordinate the drafts of the main Committees), and informal meetings of the Big Five at the penthouse headquarters of the United States delegation in the Fairmont Hotel on Nob Hill. And, when the latter powers firmly resisted amendments, as in connection with the veto, the smaller powers were compelled to recognize that parliamentary equality had to bow to power inequality.

The upshot of the Conference was that the Dumbarton Oaks framework remained virtually intact, but the details were thoroughly rewritten and expanded. Among the major changes adopted were a more expansive statement of the Assembly's authority to discuss and recommend, elevation of the ECOSOC and Trusteeship Council to the status of "principal organs," and enlargement of their authority. But there was no serious breaching of the veto. The most crucial dispute on this issue, which at one point seemed about to wreck the Conference, was among the great powers themselves over whether the veto should apply even to the discussion of a problem prior to any substantive decision. This was not settled until Harry Hopkins was prevailed upon to get out of a sickbed to fly to Moscow regarding that and other issues. Only then did Stalin agree with the United States' and United Kingdom's view that the veto should not apply to such "procedural" questions as merely placing a matter on the agenda.[37] In the economic and social sphere, the United States Congress had become so alarmed over the ambitions of the progressives, particularly in connection with the "full employment" question, that the Americans succeeded in having the "domestic

[36] Records of the Conference have been published as *Documents of the United Nations Conference on International Organization, San Francisco, 1945* (London and New York: UN Information Organizations, 1945–1946), hereinafter referred to as UNCIO.

[37] Sherwood, *op. cit.*, pp. 911–912.

jurisdiction" barrier apply to all UN functions rather than just peaceful settlement of disputes, as in the League Covenant. The final text of the Charter was signed on June 26, 1945.

To blow life into the Charter and prepare for the first session of the General Assembly, the Conference created a Preparatory Commission, composed of all states attending the Conference, with headquarters in London. Its Executive Committee consisted of the same fourteen states that had served as the Conference's executive body. This Committee first met in August 1945, and the Commission's final recommendations for implementing the Charter were adopted two days before Christmas. In the meantime, the United States Senate, led by the bipartisan team of Senators Connally and Vandenberg, had approved the Charter with only two dissenting votes, and enough ratifications had been deposited to put the Charter into effect on October 24, 1945, now celebrated throughout the world as UN Day. The first session of the Assembly began in London on January 10, 1946.

Other specialized agencies were not formed until after the San Francisco Conference. The World Health Organization (WHO) was created in New York City in the summer of 1946. The proposed International Trade Organization (ITO) was planned during 1947 and early 1948, but has still not been put into effect. The World Meteorological Organization (WMO) was formed in Washington during September and October 1947. A Convention for an Inter-Governmental Maritime Consultative Organization (IMCO) was drawn up during February and March 1948, but this has not yet gone into effect.

Over-All Comparison

As a prelude to the more intensive comparison of the League and UN below, it is useful to look over the rooftops of these two systems to get some sense of their general similarities and dissimilarities. The first and most important impression one has is that there is more continuity than discontinuity between them. For all their differences, they are basically the same — voluntary associations of states established to foster cooperation among their members in certain stipulated political, economic and social areas. They were both endowed with essentially the same organizational limbs, including an assembly, council, economic and social bodies, trusteeship committee, court and secretariat. The delegations of member states were to be equal in size, with one vote apiece. In most matters, these organs were authorized only to recommend, not command. In the security sphere, their founders intended that action to extinguish threats to the peace should be left primarily to the political councils dominated by the great powers.

But the two systems are not quite as identical as Tweedledum and Tweedledee. Changes have been introduced in the UN Charter which make the newer organization stronger in its authority to maintain peace and more ambitious in its economic, social and non-self-governing territory programs. While membership in both systems was opened to any state able and willing to comply with the obligations of membership which the Assembly would approve by a two-thirds majority, the Charter also provides that the Security Council must make a prior endorsing recommendation, which is subject to the veto. For this reason, admission to membership has been snarled up in East-West differences. Unlike the Covenant, the Charter contains no authority for withdrawal from the UN, but it adds a new provision that the Covenant lacked: suspension of a Member's privileges by the General Assembly on recommendation by the Security Council.

As for voting, the League's general unanimity requirement, which was qualified by a number of formal and informal exceptions, has been replaced by various majority rules in the UN: two-thirds for substantive, and majority for procedural, recommendations in the Assembly; a special majority of seven out of eleven, for procedural, and including the five permanent members for substantive, questions in the Security Council; and simple majority for all questions in the ECOSOC and Trusteeship Council.

Reinforcing Security Organization

The most publicized alterations were carried out in the collective security wing of the new structure. While the League Assembly and Council had approximately equivalent jurisdictions, with the latter thought of as the "cabinet" of the plenary body, an effort was made to draw a much sharper distinction between the two organs in the UN. The Assembly was to concentrate upon general recommendations, leaving "action" and "primary" responsibility for the maintenance of international peace and security" to the Council, which was also relieved of its nonsecurity functions. The Council continues to be composed of two kinds of states: great powers, with permanent seats, and lesser states, with temporary seats. But the Charter provided that the latter should have a slight majority, six out of eleven, rather than a minority, as originally planned in the Covenant (in practice they usually had a majority). Nor can the composition of the Security Council be altered simply by an Assembly decision; it now requires a Charter amendment.

Regarding the United Nations' policeman duties, there is less emphasis than in the Covenant on automatic sanctions and more on compulsory sanctions triggered by decision of the Security Council, subject, of course, to the Big Five veto. Under the Covenant, all Members were committed to guarantee each other's territorial integrity and political independence, but were not explicitly bound to follow League recommendations regarding enforcement action. Under the Charter, the Security Council decides on behalf of the entire UN whether peace is threatened and whether sanctions — political, military or economic — shall be applied. Such decisions are binding on all Members, military contributions to be arranged in advance through special agreements with each nation. The General Assembly may

ORGANS OF THE UNITED NATIONS

PRINCIPAL ORGANS AND SUBSIDIARY BODIES

- TRANSPORT AND COMMUNICATIONS COMMISSION
- FISCAL COMMISSION
- STATISTICAL COMMISSION
- ECONOMIC COMMISSION FOR EUROPE
- ECONOMIC COMMISSION FOR ASIA AND THE FAR EAST
- ECONOMIC COMMISSION FOR LATIN AMERICA
- COMMISSION ON HUMAN RIGHTS
- SOCIAL COMMISSION
- COMMISSION ON THE STATUS OF WOMEN
- POPULATION COMMISSION
- COMMISSION ON NARCOTIC DRUGS

REGIONAL ECONOMIC COMMISSIONS

- UNITED NATIONS INTERNATIONAL CHILDREN'S EMERGENCY FUND
- OFFICE OF THE UNITED NATIONS HIGH COMMISSIONER FOR REFUGEES

Central organs:
- SECURITY COUNCIL
- TRUSTEESHIP COUNCIL
- GENERAL ASSEMBLY
- ECONOMIC AND SOCIAL COUNCIL
- INTERNATIONAL COURT OF JUSTICE
- SECRETARIAT

- MILITARY STAFF COMMITTEE
- DISARMAMENT COMMISSION
- INTERIM COMMITTEE OF THE GENERAL ASSEMBLY
- PEACE OBSERVATION COMMISSION
- COLLECTIVE MEASURES COMMITTEE
- UN RELIEF AND WORKS AGENCY FOR PALESTINE REFUGEES IN THE NEAR EAST
- UN KOREAN RECONSTRUCTION AGENCY
- INTERNATIONAL LAW COMMISSION
- COMMITTEE ON INFORMATION FROM NON-SELF-GOVERNING TERRITORIES
- ADVISORY COMMITTEE ON ADMINISTRATIVE AND BUDGETARY QUESTIONS
- COMMITTEE ON CONTRIBUTIONS

- TECHNICAL ASSISTANCE BOARD
- ADMINISTRATIVE COMMITTEE ON CO-ORDINATION

SPECIALIZED AGENCIES

- INTERNATIONAL LABOUR ORGANIZATION
- WORLD HEALTH ORGANIZATION
- FOOD AND AGRICULTURE ORGANIZATION OF THE UNITED NATIONS
- UNITED NATIONS EDUCATIONAL, SCIENTIFIC AND CULTURAL ORGANIZATION
- INTERNATIONAL CIVIL AVIATION ORGANIZATION
- INTERNATIONAL BANK FOR RECONSTRUCTION AND DEVELOPMENT
- INTERNATIONAL MONETARY FUND
- UNIVERSAL POSTAL UNION
- INTERNATIONAL TELECOMMUNICATION UNION
- WORLD METEOROLOGICAL ORGANIZATION
- INTER-GOVERNMENT MARITIME CONSULTATIVE ORGANIZATION (Preparatory Committee)
- INTERNATIONAL TRADE ORGANIZATION (Interim Commission)

December 1952

make no recommendation while the Council "is exercising in respect of any dispute or situation the functions assigned it . . . unless the Security Council so requests." The Covenant placed great store in the reduction of armaments. The Charter devotes less attention to this issue, and speaks of "regulation" more than "reduction."

Economic, Social, Trusteeship Changes

To attack the economic and social roots of war, the Charter's objectives are far broader and bolder than those of the Covenant. Concepts not even mentioned in the older document have become key pillars of the Charter: human rights, higher standards of living, full employment, economic development, and cultural and educational cooperation. Neither system was endowed with authority to issue binding legislation, but the Charter commits Members to "take joint and separate action in cooperation with the Organization for the achievement of the purposes" set forth in the Charter. The Assembly is now the exclusive ultimate authority, no longer sharing that role with the political council. At the same time, the new ECOSOC serves as the Assembly's agent in providing more direct supervision than the larger body can give. The Commissions under ECOSOC are similar to the League's expert committees, but their members are governmental representatives rather than independent specialists. The ideal of centralization of economic and social activities directly under the League has been replaced with a system of loose UN coordination of the programs of its own bodies with those of separate specialized agencies.

One of the major innovations with respect to the colonial question is the entirely new Chapter 11 in the Charter, which binds Members controlling non-self-governing territories to aim towards certain political, economic and social objectives, very similar to those governing the trusteeship system, and to transmit regularly to the Secretary-General information on conditions in those territories. While the companion trusteeship system is basically the same as the League mandates system, it has been reinforced. The Trusteeship Council has been elevated from being an advisory body of experts under the political council, as was the Permanent Mandates Commission, to the rank of "principal organ" composed of governmental representatives. Provision has also been made for equal representation of colonial and noncolonial powers on that body. Unlike the Covenant, the Charter allows petitions to be submitted directly, rather than through the administering power, and authorizes the Trusteeship Council to inspect the trust territories and prepare annual questionnaires which the administering countries are obliged to answer. The Charter also authorizes direct international administration of territories, but, as under the League, no area can be placed under the system except through voluntary submission. The political Security Council no longer has any supervisory authority except for "strategic trusts" and any situation involving a threat to the peace. Finally, the objectives of the new system are more liberal and explicit and are the same for all trust territories.

The major change with respect to the Secretariat is the increased emphasis on the political role of the Secretary-General. Unlike the Covenant, the Charter specifically directs him to make an annual report to the General Assembly and call to the attention of the Security Council any matter which in his opinion may threaten world peace. The new International Court of Justice is virtually a carbon copy of its predecessor, the Permanent Court of International Justice, but it has been brought into much closer relationship with the general organization. Far more attention is also devoted in the Charter to the use of regional arrangements in cooperation with the UN. The prohibition against invasion of a Member's "domestic jurisdiction" applied only to the peaceful settlement of disputes in the Covenant, while under the Charter it covers all UN functions. Amendments of the Covenant required a unanimous vote of the Assembly and ratification by two-thirds of the Members, including all members of the Council. Changes in the Charter call for a two-thirds vote of the General Assembly and ratification by two-thirds of all Members, including only the permanent members of the Security Council.

These are the broad constitutional features of the first two permanent general international organizations in the history of civilization. It is also relevant to repeat that they cannot be understood except in the context of the political, economic and social forces that have shaped them in both their original founding and later evolution. Of course, the crucial question to ask about them is: how effective have they been and can they be in meeting the needs of mankind? It is this question that is the principal theme of the rest of Parts Two and Three of this volume.

Suggestions for Further Reading

LEAGUE OF NATIONS

Books

Bailey, Thomas A., *Woodrow Wilson and the Lost Peace* (New York: The Macmillan Company, 1945).

Baker, Ray S., *Woodrow Wilson and World Settlement*, 3 Vols. (Garden City: Doubleday, Page, 1922).

Birdsall, Paul, *Versailles Twenty Years After* (New York: Reynal & Hitchcock, 1941).

House, E. M., *The Intimate Papers of Colonel House*, edited by Charles Seymour, 4 Vols. (Boston: Houghton Mifflin Company, 1926–1928).

Keynes, J. M., *The Economic Consequences of the Peace* (New York: Harcourt, Brace and Howe, 1920).

Lloyd George, David, *Memoirs of the Peace Conference*, 2 Vols. (New Haven: Yale University Press, 1939).

Marburg, Theodore, *Development of the League of Nations Idea, Documents and Correspondence of Theodore Marburg*, edited by J. H. Latané, 2 Vols. (New York: The Macmillan Company, 1932).

Miller, David Hunter, *The Drafting of the Covenant*, 2 Vols. (New York: G. P. Putnam's Sons, 1928).

Salter, Arthur, *Allied Shipping Control: An Experiment in International Administration* (New York: Oxford University Press, 1921).

Shotwell, James T., *At the Paris Peace Conference* (New York: The Macmillan Company, 1947).

Temperley, H. W. V., ed., *A History of the Peace Conference of Paris,* 6 Vols. (London: Henry Frowde and Hodder & Stoughton, 1924).

Walters, F. P., *A History of the League of Nations,* 2 Vols. (London: Oxford University Press for the Royal Institute of International Affairs, 1951).

Woolf, Leonard S., *The Framework of a Lasting Peace* (London: G. Allen & Unwin, Ltd., 1917).

Zimmern, Alfred, *The League of Nations and the Rule of Law, 1918–1935* (London: Macmillan and Co., Ltd., 1936).

Documents

United States, Department of State, *Foreign Relations of the United States: The Lansing Papers, 1914–1920,* 2 Vols. (Washington: U.S. Government Printing Office, 1939–1940).

————, Department of State, *Foreign Relations of the United States: The Paris Peace Conference,* 13 Vols. (Washington: U.S. Government Printing Office, 1942–1947).

UNITED NATIONS

Books

Bentwich, Norman, and Martin, Andrew, *A Commentary on the Charter of the United Nations* (London: Macmillan & Co., Ltd., 1950).

Byrnes, James F., *Speaking Frankly* (New York: Harper & Brothers, 1947).

Churchill, Winston S., *The Grand Alliance* (Boston: Houghton Mifflin Company, 1950) and other volumes in this series.

Corbett, Percy E., *Postwar Worlds* (New York: Institute of Pacific Relations, 1942).

Dean, Vera M., *The Four Cornerstones of Peace* (New York: Whittlesey House, 1946).

Evatt, Herbert Vere, *The United Nations* (Cambridge: Harvard University Press, 1948).

Goodrich, Leland M., and Hambro, Edvard, *Charter of the United Nations, Commentary and Documents,* 2nd ed. (Boston: World Peace Foundation, 1949).

Holborn, Louise W., ed., *War and Peace Aims of the United Nations* (Boston: World Peace Foundation, 1943).

Hull, Cordell, *The Memoirs of Cordell Hull,* 2 Vols. (New York: The Macmillan Company, 1948).

Institute of Pacific Relations, *Security in the Pacific* (New York: Institute of Pacific Relations, 1945).

————, *War and Peace in the Pacific* (New York: Institute of Pacific Relations, 1943).

Kelsen, Hans, *The Law of the United Nations* (New York: F. A. Praeger, 1951).

Rosen, S. McKee, *Combined Boards of the Second World War: An Experiment in International Administration* (New York: Columbia University Press, 1951).

Sherwood, Robert, *Roosevelt and Hopkins* (New York: Harper & Brothers, 1948).

Staley, Eugene, *World Economy in Transition* (New York: Council on Foreign Relations, 1939).

Stettinius, Edward R., Jr., *Roosevelt and the Russians* (Garden City: Doubleday & Company, Inc., 1949).

Vandenberg, Arthur H., Jr., ed., *The Private Papers of Senator Vandenberg* (Boston: Houghton Mifflin Company, 1952).

Welles, Sumner, *Where Are We Heading?* (New York and London: Harper & Brothers, 1946).

Wilmot, Chester, *The Struggle for Europe* (London: Collins, 1952).

Periodicals

Bunche, Ralph J., "Trusteeship and Non-Self-Governing Territories in the Charter of the United Nations," *Department of State Bulletin*, Vol. 13, No. 340 (December 30, 1945).

Carnegie Endowment for International Peace, *International Conciliation*; most numbers for the years 1942–1946 contain relevant information.

Eagleton, Clyde, and Wilcox, F. O., eds., "The United Nations: Peace and Security," *American Political Science Review*, Vol. 39, No. 5 (October 1945).

Goodrich, Leland M., "From League of Nations to United Nations," *International Organization*, Vol. 1, No. 1 (February 1947).

Krout, John A., ed., "World Organization — Economic, Political and Social," *Proceedings of the Academy of Political Science*, Vol. 21, No. 23 (May 1945).

Documents

United Nations, *United Nations Conference on International Organization, San Francisco, 1945* (London and New York: UN Information Organizations, 1945–1946).

———, *Guide to United Nations and Allied Agencies* (New York: UN Information Office, 1945).

United States Congress. *Hearings Before the Committee on Foreign Relations, U.S. Senate, 79th Congress, 1st Session, on the Charter of the United Nations . . . July . . . 1945.*

———, *Postwar Foreign Policy Preparation, 1939–1945*, Department of State Publication 3580, General Foreign Policy Series 15 (Washington: U.S. Government Printing Office, 1950).

———, *Report to the President on the Results of the San Francisco Conference . . .* , Department of State Publication 2349, Conference Series 71 (Washington: U.S. Government Printing Office, 1945).

4

Assemblies—"Town Meetings of the World"

> "... The Charter gives the Assembly great opportunities to make an important contribution to the cause of the maintenance of peace and security." — A. A. GROMYKO, *Soviet Union* [1]

> " ... the General Assembly occupies a central position in the Organization ... it will wield great authority ... it will be concerned with the constructive solutions of international problems ... "
> — E. R. STETTINIUS, *United States* [2]

WITH THESE ENCOURAGING WORDS the chief delegates of the two greatest world powers ushered into being in 1945 the United Nations General Assembly — newest version of an old ideal, the "Parliament of the World." The late Senator Arthur Vandenberg christened it with a more Yankee name: Town Meeting of the World. While the General Assembly is most similar to its immediate predecessor, the League Assembly, its origins go back to the first intertribal gathering of history and the more recent pre-League conferences mentioned in Chapter 2. The major problems regarding the structure and authority of the League and UN Assemblies have been very similar to those of other plenary bodies, national as well as international. There is the question of membership: what interests are to be represented and how (including the issue of weighted representation)? There is the problem of how to organize the decision-making process, including rules regarding meetings, debate and voting. There is the matter of what authority to grant the assembly, especially with respect to substantive decisions, administration and budget. Finally, there is the perennial struggle between the legislature, widely representative but administratively clumsy, and the executive, streamlined for action but not pretending to be a broadly representative body. Of course, neither the League nor UN Assembly has been given truly legislative authority. Nevertheless, they have, on occasion, been the means of generating considerable

[1] UNCIO, I, p. 664.
[2] *Report to the President* . . . , Department of State Publication 2349, Conference Series 71 (Washington: Government Printing Office, 1945), p. 65.

collective influence, as in the Korean situation. One can understand that impact, however, only by analyzing the total pattern of forces behind it.

League Assembly

Birth of an Idea

The most important fact about the creation of the League Assembly is that it was primarily the child of the great powers that had won World War I — not the smaller states nor the private crusaders for international cooperation. The second most important factor is the philosophy that motivated the larger powers: that the new international organization should not attempt to rebuild the world from top to bottom but should perform the strictly limited function of acting as a "fire brigade" to extinguish the more serious fires whenever they should break out. The emphasis was more on the pound of cure than the ounce of prevention. Only a few far-sighted planners thought in terms of long-range efforts to fireproof the world by seeking to eradicate the fundamental causes of international conflict.

Most of the influential private plans — including those of the Bryce Group, British League of Nations Society, and the American League to Enforce Peace — were of the "fire brigade" school.[3] They centered primarily around the settlement of disputes, "justiciable" questions to go to a court and "non-justiciable" ones to a conciliation council with only recommendatory authority. While these plans were very remote from the League Assembly that finally emerged, the American League to Enforce Peace came closer with a proposal for occasional conferences to formulate rules of international law which would be binding on the court unless rejected by a member state within a certain period. The Bryce and American plans suggested admitting to the League only the great powers and selected smaller states, but the British League of Nations Society was willing to open the doors to all "civilized" nations desiring to join. The special American legislative conferences were also to be opened to all states. The British Fabian Society's plan, on the other hand, envisaged far broader cooperation among nations on more long-range problems through an International Council, modeled after the conferences of the Universal Postal Union, whose membership would include forty or fifty independent states.[4] The Council was to be a "continuously existing deliberative and legislative body" composed of five representatives from the great powers and two from the smaller nations.

British Governmental Thinking. While President Wilson was the central driving force behind the Covenant, his main contribution was made in the areas of general principles and goals. It was the British who were most influential in matters of organization. The first official British draft was the cautious and legalistic Phillimore Plan of March 1918 which followed

³ See pp. 48–49.   ⁴ See p. 48.

the pattern of the two private British proposals mentioned above except that it provided for arbitration rather than judicial settlement of justiciable disputes; membership was to be restricted.[5]

The Foreign Office Memorandum of November 1918 was much more like the Fabian Society's Plan and was the first to emphasize the need for two bodies rather than one.[6] It was suggested that there be a "standing interstate conference" of only the great powers which would meet annually and act as the executive committee (shades of the British Cabinet) of a plenary conference, an adaptation of the British Imperial Conference, representing all members and meeting only every four or five years. Lord Robert Cecil later used this Memorandum as the basis for his plan, which, when married with certain American proposals, became the Hurst–Miller draft that was used as the basis for discussion at the Peace Conference. General Smuts' draft of December 1918 also followed the Memorandum and insisted that, because the Assembly's powers would be merely recommendatory, each member state should have only one vote.[7] The assembly was to have no direct control over the League's work but merely to debate and recommend, leaving the initiative as much as possible to the great power-dominated council.

American and French Ideas. American governmental planning began with Colonel House's draft of July 1918 which spoke in terms of a "meeting of ambassadors and ministers" of the great powers, in almost continuous session, to engage not only in conciliation but also in formulating plans for disarmament and deciding on "territorial modifications" by a three-fourths majority.[8] President Wilson's own first draft adopted essential features of the House plan but expanded the council membership to include small as well as great powers.[9]

The French Foreign Office Plan, prepared during the summer of 1918, suggested a plenary body to consider non-justiciable disputes but gave it powers which made the British and Americans shudder.[10] Composed not of ambassadors but of higher officials authorized to bind their governments, it was intended not only to recommend settlements but to hand down final decisions and enforce them by means of sanctions — "diplomatic, legal, economic, and military."

Paris, 1919

When the Peace Conference met in January 1918 it was the Anglo-American conception of the League — one of flexible persuasion rather than inflexible compulsion — that dominated the deliberations. Wilson's second, third and fourth drafts, all prepared in Europe during the first two months of 1919, were strongly flavored by the Smuts memorandum to the extent of providing for both a council and an assembly, endorsing firm Council guid-

5 See p. 49.　　8 See p. 49.
6 See p. 49.　　9 See p. 49.
7 See p. 50.　　10 See p. 49.

ance for the Assembly and agreeing that Assembly decisions should be no more than recommendations. Wilson was also gradually persuaded by British thinking to transfer most specific security functions from the Assembly to the Council.

The British, seasoned graduates of the Concert of Europe school, did not hide the fact that they believed, as Lord Robert Cecil put it, that "the Great Powers must run the League and that it was just as well to recognize it flatly as not." [11] The British thought of the Assembly primarily as a forum in which small as well as great powers could meet approximately every four years and debate burning international issues, but they wanted to give it precious few specific functions other than the relatively harmless one of talking. Nevertheless they did suggest allowing the Assembly to consider disputes transferred to it from the Council and to provide for the revision of obsolete treaties and the correction of other disturbing international conditions.

The French rolled in their heavily armored plan described above, calling for strong binding authority and ambitious sanctions, but it was immediately sidetracked. The Italian plan was built along similar lines, although it went farther in calling for international planning to provide the "necessary conditions" for a nation's "development." But this project received even less attention than the French.

Anatomy of the Assembly

Who Were Its Members?

Each League Member was authorized to send not more than three representatives to the Assembly, a limit intended to protect the smaller states from being overwhelmed by the larger countries' ability to send an almost unlimited number of delegates. The three representatives could be, and were, supplemented by substitutes and advisers. The larger delegations tended to number about thirty.

To give the Assembly more of a parliamentary flavor, General Smuts had suggested that, at least once every four years, "representatives of national parliaments and other bodies representative of public opinion" should be included in national delegations. The Peace Conference was unwilling, however, to bind states on this matter, but, in actual practice, France, Sweden and Denmark made a sincere effort to include in their delegations representatives of their major parties. Great Britain and most other countries, however, favored the parties in power with the result that the views of these delegations often experienced radical shifts when national leadership changed hands. As for the level of representation, about half the countries sent either prime ministers or foreign ministers, who could naturally act with considerable leeway, while the others sent top ambassa-

[11] David Hunter Miller, *My Diary at the Conference of Paris* (New York: Printed for the author by the Appeal Printing Co., 1924), Vol. 1, p. 87.

dors. On the whole these delegates seem to have been a very able and distinguished body of men.

As in any political organization, the delegations tended to coagulate into blocs according to their common interests, shaped by geographical, political and economic affinities. The most powerful and united group was that composed of Great Britain and the Dominions. France and the Little Entente (Czechoslovakia, Rumania and Yugoslavia) exerted substantial influence in the earlier years, but less as time went on. Germany, after being admitted in 1926, was frequently supported by Austria, Hungary, and later, Italy. The Scandinavian states cooperated closely, sometimes joined by the Netherlands, Belgium and Switzerland. The Latin Americans also presented a united front on many questions. All of these blocs operated with greatest solidarity on matters of group prestige, e.g., the selection of League officers, but had greater difficulty maintaining united fronts on substantive issues.

How Did They Vote?

In the hallowed tradition of most previous diplomatic conferences, all Assembly decisions, according to Article 5 of the Covenant, were to be made by unanimous vote except where otherwise provided in the Covenant or Peace Treaties. The exceptions set forth in the Covenant were largely administrative and procedural matters and included: admission of new Members (two-thirds), approval of an increase of the members of the Council (simple majority), decision on procedural matters (simple majority), appointment of the Secretary-General (simple majority), and approval of a report on disputes transferred from the Council (majority including members of the Council). Fortunately the unanimity wall was also breached in a good many places by means of such devices as: allowing absences and abstentions to be ignored in counting votes, broadening the "procedural" category through liberal interpretation (to include such matters as initiating investigations), compromising beforehand in order to avoid negative votes, and developing the concept of the *vœu* (recommendation) which could be adopted by simple majority and was used to express a sentiment or opinion having no obligatory consequences but never to decide budgetary, legislative or constitutional questions. All committee decisions, moreover, were made by simple majority. In spite of these liberalizing developments, however, the unanimity rule remained a formidable barrier that blocked Assembly action on several measures that had strong majority support and compelled many proposals to be seriously whittled down before they could be squeezed through.

When Did They Meet?

Wilson, whose idealism tended to make him partial to the Assembly, wanted more frequent meetings than the quadrennial sessions favored by the British and finally succeeded in writing into the Covenant the flexible formula: "at stated intervals." Then, during its first session, the Assembly,

with no significant dispute or fanfare, adopted as part of its rules of procedure the provision that it should meet annually, an innovation that reinforced the Assembly's influence and later was judged by one observer to
be "one of the most significant acts of any League Assembly." [12] The British and French representatives on the Council feared, however, that the
ambitious Assembly might tread on the Council's toes and thus opposed
the claim that the plenary body was a permanent organ whose officers
might continue to hold their posts until each succeeding session convened.
Instead they insisted that the Assembly was a temporary body, a recurrent ambassadorial conference, and they were instrumental in persuading
the Assembly to write into its rules the fact that each Assembly should be
summoned and opened by the Council President.

Who Were Its Officers?

The principal Assembly officials were its president, seven chairmen of
the main committees who were automatically designated as vice-presidents,
and eight elected vice-presidents who were chosen in such a way that all
the first delegates of the great powers, who were not made committee
chairmen, were included as well as one or two smaller state representatives
to fill out the number. The president was a key figure, normally the delegate of a small power, who was selected as much for his personal abilities
as for his political sponsorship. Before 1936 no formal nominations were
made before the balloting, and the Secretariat played a major role in the
backstage negotiations that led to general agreement on a single candidate.
Because of some grumbling about this unofficial caucusing, the Assembly
decided in 1936 to establish a Nomination Committee to control the
process.

Committees Did the Work

The Assembly's committees were its "work horses." A General Committee
("Bureau"), composed of the president, fifteen vice-presidents, and the
chairmen of the Agenda and Credentials Committees, was the central steering body in which the views of the principal powers carried great weight.
The Assembly's main committees, whose creation was inspired by the "four
great committees" established by the League Brussels Conference on
Finance in October 1920, consisted of: the First, constitutional and legal;
Second, technical organizations; Third, reduction of armaments; Fourth,
administrative and financial; Fifth, social and humanitarian; Sixth, political;
and, from 1938 on, Seventh, various "social" questions (health, opium, intellectual cooperation, etc.) leaving the Second to concentrate on economics,
finance and transit. There were also the three procedural committees:
Credentials, Nomination and Agenda, the latter to consider and report to
the Assembly applications for the inclusion of new questions in the agenda.
Since all League Members were entitled to be represented on every

[12] Benjamin Gerig, "The Assembly of the League of Nations," *Geneva Studies*, Vol. 1,
No. 6 (Geneva: Geneva Research Center, 1930), p. 4.

main committee, though smaller delegations frequently could not take advantage of this privilege, these bodies were far larger and less manageable than the usual committees of a national legislature. Sub-committees chosen by the main committees were, on the other hand, more similar to such legislative committees since they were smaller and more shielded from the popular gaze (no public admission and no minutes). These bodies were usually selected by the main committee chairmen with an eye to representing various blocs.

Open Diplomacy

During the Peace Conference, Norway had suggested that all Assembly deliberations, except in unusual circumstances, should be open to the public. Orlando of Italy was instrumental, however, in persuading the Conference to leave this question to the Assembly's later judgment. The smaller powers, always suspicious of great-power cloak room conspiracies, were largely responsible for writing Norway's suggestion into the rules of procedure.

Major Assembly Functions

Gulliver was never tied down more carefully than was the League Assembly. The great powers were willing to let it talk, but they were afraid that if they let it do more it would jeopardize their own freedom of action, especially as expressed through the Council. Hence, the Assembly was given no authority to issue binding orders to any other League organ, much less any member state. Both the Assembly and the Council were given identical mandates to "deal . . . with any matter within the sphere of action of the League or affecting the peace of the world." The Assembly had no power to bind its "executive." The Council, on the other hand, was a "cabinet" without constitutional responsibility to its "parliament." Underlying this delicate balance was the fact that the great powers did not feel that the Assembly provided a workable union of power and responsibility. They recognized the need, and desirability, of a forum in which all member states could meet and speak freely. But the great states had the real power, and they were unwilling to have it committed to a body over which they would have uncertain control. Obviously this sentiment was stronger in political than in economic and social matters. And, as the Assembly and Council became more firmly harnessed together in practice, there was an increasing tendency to emphasize the parliament–cabinet concept.

Steps Toward Law

When the Covenant was being planned, Colonel House, the Italian Government and several of the neutral states (Norway, Switzerland and the Netherlands) had proposed that the Assembly be given binding legislative powers. But the British shied away from such strong medicine, and no such mandate was included in the Covenant. When the Assembly began to function, however, it soon became aware of the need to go beyond limited short-range projects to formulate broad policy recommendations to deal with long-range problems affecting a large number of nations — the closest approach to a legislative function to be found in the League.

The issue was first clearly posed during the Assembly's 1921 session when the British asked the Assembly to endorse a convention on traffic in women and children which had been drafted by a special conference of experts. Ironically enough, the French, who had talked in terms of a strong League at the Paris Peace Conference, insisted that the Assembly's endorsement of a draft convention would be unconstitutional since no such authority had been included in the Covenant. It should be mentioned parenthetically that the French held some very different views from those of the British on the substantive question at issue, the regulation of prostitution. Finally a large majority (31 for, none against, 21 absent or abstaining) voted for the British view. During its entire existence, however, the Assembly drafted only four conventions directly. For the most part its quasi-legislative activity took the form of initiating special drafting conferences, reviewing and passing judgment on the drafts produced, and checking on ratification and implementation. The Assembly's reluctance to draft directly resulted from a general consensus that it was too large, too short-lived, too lacking in technical expertise, and too busy to do justice to the complex and detailed job of drafting.

Settlement of Disputes

Unlike Wilson, the British had from the beginning wanted to leave the pacific settlement function almost entirely in the hands of the Council on the grounds that that body would be smaller, more flexible, easier to assemble, and more sensitive to the views of the great powers on whose cooperation would necessarily depend the success of international police efforts. And it was this thesis which was very largely woven into the fabric of the Covenant. Nevertheless the British and Americans were willing to leave the Assembly significant powers in the political field. (1) Any Member of the League could lay before the Assembly, as well as the Council, any "circumstance whatever affecting international relations which threatens to disturb international peace or the good understanding between nations. . . ." (Art. 11, par. 2). (2) The Council or a party to a dispute might refer the matter to the Assembly (Art. 15, pars. 9, 10). (3) An Assembly report, approved by the members of the Council and a majority of the other Members, exclusive of the parties, carried the same authority as a unanimous Council report (Art. 15, par. 10).

In the very first session certain leaders of the smaller powers, always the principal champions of the Assembly as the League's sovereign body, made it clear that the plenary organ should not hesitate to oversee the Council's peaceful settlement operations and, if necessary, prod that body into more vigorous action. The issue arose over what many of the smaller powers thought was inadequate Council action on the Polish–Lithuanian dispute of 1920. Since France's close relations with Poland were one reason for the Council's caution, it is not surprising that it was M. Bourgeois of France who reminded the Assembly that it should stay in the grandstand and leave action to the Council. Nevertheless, in the wake of the Assembly's criticism, the Council decided to submit a detailed report for Assembly review.

In spite of its interest in disputes, the Assembly dealt directly with only four during its entire existence: the Sino–Japanese, Bolivian–Paraguayan, Finno–Russian and Italo–Ethiopian. For the most part, the plenary body left direct action to the Council and contented itself with comment from the sidelines.

Captain of the Team

Although the great powers, influenced particularly by the British point of view, had not been willing to make the Council constitutionally responsible to the Assembly, strong pressures were exerted by the smaller powers, as soon as the League was born, to gain recognition for the Assembly as the central and sovereign supervisory organ. This issue came to a head when the Council recommended to the first session of the Assembly that, in all matters in which both bodies were competent, neither should take independent measures with regard to a question with which the other was already dealing. After intensive debate, the Assembly agreed that both organs were independent though complementary. At the same time, it was recommended that the Council present an annual report to the Assembly, a recommendation which the Council dutifully followed. During this discussion Lord Robert Cecil voiced the opinion of the Assembly's partisans when he said that the Council would ultimately come to be regarded as the executive power responsible to the whole body of the League as represented in the Assembly.[13]

The plenary body's boldest move in this direction was its gradual assumption of full control of the League's purse strings, the heart of any organization, which had not been provided for in the Covenant. The Assembly began this development during the 1920 session simply by writing this authority into its own rules of procedure and reinforced it in 1921 by creating a Supervisory Commission to act for the Assembly both during and between sessions to analyze both past and future budgets. The Assembly's control became complete when the 1928 session decided, in spite of the great powers' opposition, that the Assembly rather than the Council should appoint the members of the Supervisory Commission.

On the question of admitting new Members to the League, great as well as small states agreed from the beginning that the Assembly should be the sole judge. To guide its decisions, the Assembly established, during the first session, certain questions to be satisfied in the case of each applicant:

> Is the application in order? Is the candidate recognized *de jure* and *de facto*,
> and by which states? Does the applicant have a stable government with

13 *Assembly Records, 1920, Plenary,* p. 287.

settled frontiers? What are its size and population? Is it fully self-governing? What has been its conduct with regard to its international obligations
and the principles of the League as to armaments? [14]

Still another channel of Assembly supervisory authority was its elective
function: to choose the non-permanent members of the Council and, with
the Council, to select the justices of the Permanent Court of International
Justice and the Secretary-General.

In its resolution of May 1920 with respect to the establishment of technical organizations, the Council proposed that such bodies be made immediately responsible to the Council but that they might ask to have a
Council decision discussed at the next meeting of the Assembly. The latter
was to be kept informed of all such matters dealt with by the Council between Assembly sessions. Furthermore the Assembly was looked to in
practice to authorize, usually on the Council's recommendation, the establishment of all technical organizations, beginning with the Economic and
Financial Organization in December 1920, and to initiate many of the
important technical conferences. The Assembly's budgetary control was
also a powerful whip held over the heads of the technical bodies, although
the plenary body was compelled to recognize the relatively independent
status of the International Labor Organization (ILO).

While the Covenant said nothing about consulting the Assembly regarding the organization of the Permanent Court of International Justice, the
Council decided to submit the draft statute to the Assembly on the ground,
as one observer put it,

> that the Council, as well as others, recognized that the Assembly's funda-
> mental force was stronger than its own, since its basis of representation was
> wider; and that it facilitated the action of the Assembly in the case in order
> to give the Court the strongest possible rootage in public life.[15]

The plenary body carefully examined the statute, recommended certain
changes and transmitted it to individual governments for their ratification
(only after a minority of states prevented the Assembly from ratifying it
directly).

While the Covenant left the appointment of the Secretary-General to the
Council, it required endorsement by a majority of the Assembly. The latter, moreover, considered itself ultimately responsible for the policies governing the Secretariat.

Looking Back

Surveying the Assembly's life history, the most striking fact that emerges
is that the weakling infant grew to be a vigorous adult almost before anyone was aware of it. A plenary forum that was expected by many to be

[14] Margaret E. Burton, *The Assembly of the League of Nations* (Chicago: University
of Chicago Press, 1941), p. 88.
[15] J. S. Bassett, *The League of Nations* (New York: Longmans, Green, 1928) pp. 105,
106.

innocuous, infrequent and inconsequential quickly became influential, frequent and important. The fundamental factor underlying this evolution was a general recognition on the part of great as well as small powers that those recommendations which depended for their effectiveness on widespread interest and cooperation could not be very successful without the Assembly's consideration and approval.

On the other hand, the Assembly continued to the end of its days to labor under several serious handicaps reflecting the atomistic international "community" which it served. There was never any clear or formal reflection in its decision-making process of the obvious differences among its members in such matters as population and industrial strength. There was no system of party organization based on the direct representation of popular views, only the representation of whole governments, usually weighted heavily in favor of the parties in power at the moment. Hence it was difficult to break the larger body into smaller sub-committees since each delegation wanted to be included. Other obstacles included the unanimity rule, brevity of the annual sessions and the difficulty of convening special meetings.

A New Assembly Is Born

In London, on the cold damp day of January 10, 1946, the twenty-sixth birthday of the League Covenant, representatives of fifty-one countries crowded into the blue and gold auditorium of the Central Hall of Westminster for the first meeting of the United Nations General Assembly. A dramatic reminder that the new was rising from the ashes of the old was the presence of two distinguished gentlemen, Viscount Cecil and Dr. V. K. Wellington Koo, who had also been present, albeit less gray, at the opening of the League Assembly.

The General Assembly, like its predecessor, is accorded much of the prestige, if not the authority, of a parliament. The most pronounced difference between the new and the old is that the General Assembly has direct and strong supervisory authority over trusteeship and economic and social activities. In the political field the Assembly's authority is very similar to that exercised by the League forum except that it is specifically excluded from the Security Council's domain of binding enforcement powers. One cannot really understand this new creature, however, unless one is familiar with the environment in which it was born.

Early Blueprints

The great majority of private planners discussed in Chapter 3 assumed that there would have to be a plenary body very much like the League Assembly, although môst of them gave it relatively little attention because it seemed so obvious.[16] They were far more concerned with what would

[16] See Suggestions for Further Reading at the end of this chapter.

actually be done in the fields of security, trusteeship, and economic and social activities.

As in 1919, the great powers were convinced that the primary function of the international organization should be to keep the peace through an enforcement apparatus administered by a council which they would dominate. Similarly they tended to be less interested in the Assembly because that body seemed a less effective instrument for dealing with security problems. And again the middle and small powers had much less influence in the planning process than their giant colleagues. Unlike 1919, however, considerable, though not primary, attention was devoted to economic and social matters.

American Plans. The United States had some difficult differences to settle within its own family circle. During 1942 and 1943 President Franklin Roosevelt, influenced particularly by Prime Minister Winston Churchill and Under Secretary of State Sumner Welles, emphasized the potential role of regional organizations that would have primary responsibility for the maintenance of peace in their respective bailiwicks. Above all, President Roosevelt was haunted by one overriding concern: "We won't get any strong international organization unless we can find the way by which the Soviet Union and the United States can work together to build it up as the years go by." [17] He never seemed to believe that a world assembly could or should play a significant role in keeping the peace.[18]

Secretary of State Cordell Hull placed more emphasis on "general international organization." When Hull asked, "Aren't you at least in favor of a world secretariat?", Roosevelt scoffingly replied, "I'll give you the Pentagon or the Empire State Building. You can put the world secretariat there." [19] The earliest State Department draft yet published outlined a plenary body remarkably like, though more authoritative than, the final version adopted at San Francisco.[20] That memorandum proposed

a "general conference," in which all member states would be represented with one vote apiece, which would meet annually and would make substantive decisions by two-thirds majority, procedural by simple majority. Its functions in the political as well as the economic and social field were extensive: (1) to "act upon any matter of concern to the international community"; (2) to "give such assistance in the application of security measures (to be initiated by the Council) as may be deemed necessary for the restraint of aggression"; (3) to provide ultimate supervision (direct administration by the Council) of a Bureau of Technical (economic and social)

[17] Sumner Welles, *Where Are We Heading?* (New York and London: Harper, 1946), pp. 29–30.

[18] *Ibid.*, p. 5.

[19] Cordell Hull, *The Memoirs of Cordell Hull* (New York: Macmillan, 1948), p. 1643. Used by permission of The Macmillan Company.

[20] *Postwar Foreign Policy Preparation 1939–45*, Department of State Publication 3580 (Washington: Government Printing Office, 1950), pp. 472–483.

Services; (4) to control the budgetary system in collaboration with the Council; (5) to discuss and recommend the settlement of disputes, recommendations approved by a three-fourths majority to be binding; and (6) to approve amendments to the constitution by a three-fourths majority including the great powers.

Three months later, in October 1943, Secretary Hull won approval by the Big Three in their Moscow Declaration of the principle of a "general international organization" with no mention of regional security systems. In July 1944, just prior to the Dumbarton Oaks Conference, another United States draft was prepared which followed the basic outlines of the earlier draft but also revealed some interesting changes in American thinking:

1. The plenary body's name was now the General Assembly.
2. Its political jurisdiction had been narrowed; there was no longer any mention of assisting the Council in the application of security measures or of issuing binding settlements by three-fourths majority. It was specifically excluded from taking "action" in matters allocated to other organs (the Council) although it remained free to take action, including pacific settlement procedures, in all other matters.
3. A separate economic and social council, rather than the security council, was to administer the economic and social program under the Assembly's general supervision.
4. Specific authority was also granted to admit "independent" states to membership, which had not been mentioned in the previous memorandum; admission was not dependent on a Security Council recommendation.
5. Voting on budgetary questions was to be weighted in accordance with the members' respective contributions. All other decisions were to be made by simple majority except for two-thirds majorities on admissions, elections to the Security Council and the Court, and apportionment of expenses among the members. Amendments passed by an Assembly majority also needed ratification by two-thirds of the members including the great powers.[21]

Other Thinking. The early views of the United Kingdom were dominated by the Churchillian penchant for a rim of regional systems joined at the hub by a council dominated by the great powers. Even after the United Kingdom had been converted to the gospel according to the State Department, the British tended to give far less attention to the Assembly than the Security Council, which was still to be the power center. The Soviet Union was even less interested in the Assembly and wanted merely to make certain that it did not get in the way of the Security Council. Nor were the Russians content to allow the Assembly to occupy its time with economic and social matters, since their initial position was that the economic and social system should be established outside the United Nations framework.

The general objective of the smaller states became one of increasing the Assembly's relative role within the United Nations as their own chosen instrument. One significant expression of this point of view was Resolution 30

21 *Ibid.*, pp. 595–606.

of the Inter-American (Chapultepec) Conference of February and March 1945 which called attention to

> the desirability of amplifying . . . the powers of the General Assembly in order that its action, as the fully representative organ of the international community, may be rendered effective, harmonizing the powers of the Security Council with such amplification.[22]

Dumbarton Oaks, 1944

During the United States–Soviet Union–United Kingdom phase of the Dumbarton Oaks Conference (August 21 to September 28, 1944), the two latter powers soon accepted the general American plan for the Assembly except that the Soviet Union did not consent until the middle of the Conference to allow the economic and social system to be incorporated in the United Nations machinery. Furthermore the startling Russian demand that all sixteen Soviet Republics be recognized as separate members of the United Nations and the General Assembly was never finally relinquished during the Conference in spite of apoplectic and uncompromising objections on the part of the United States and the United Kingdom.

On the whole the Assembly was born with far less tumult and tension than was the Security Council, which came closer to the power nerves of the Big Three. Nonetheless, the great powers were willing to endow the Assembly with significant authority in political as well as economic and social matters. The Dumbarton Oaks Proposals, published in October 1944, set forth the following Assembly functions:

> 1. to consider the general principles of cooperation in the maintenance of international peace and security, including disarmament and the regulation of armaments;
> 2. to discuss any questions relating to the maintenance of international peace and security;
> 3. to make recommendations with regard to such principles or questions. Any question on which action is necessary should be referred to the Security Council by the General Assembly either before or after discussion. The Assembly should not on its own initiative make recommendations on any matter relating to the maintenance of international peace and security which is being dealt with by the Security Council.
> 4. to admit new members to the Organization upon recommendations of the Security Council.
> 5. to initiate studies and make recommendations for the purpose of promoting international cooperation in political, economic and social fields and of adjusting situations likely to impair the general welfare.[23]

---

[22] *Report of the Delegation of the United States of America to the Inter-American Conference on Problems of War and Peace,* Department of State Publication 2497, Conference Series 85 (Washington: Government Printing Office, 1946), Appendix L, pp. 103–104.

[23] *Postwar Foreign Policy Preparation* . . . , pp. 611–619.

San Francisco, 1945

When the United Nations Conference on International Organization convened in San Francisco in April 1945, the Big Three were still far more concerned with the Security Council than the General Assembly. The states of lesser magnitude, led primarily by the important middle powers — such as Australia and Canada — submitted a considerable number of amendments calculated to reinforce the Assembly's position, especially on security questions. In the course of the skirmishes that ensued, a few strategic points were captured by the smaller states, but in the main the battle failed to dislodge the great powers from any position which they considered essential. The principal significance of the few victories which the insurgents won was more their dramatization of the spirit with which the smaller powers regarded the Assembly than their direct impact upon the letter of the Charter.

Anatomy of the General Assembly

Who Are Its Members?

Before the Dumbarton Oaks Conference, the United States position was to fix the number of each state's delegates to the Assembly at six, but the Proposals adopted by that Conference did not specify any definite number. The San Francisco Conference finally decided upon a limit of five as compared with three in the case of the League Assembly. Since members of the League were inclined to compensate for their restricted number of delegates through the liberal appointment of alternates, advisers, technical advisers and experts, the General Assembly's Rules of Procedure limit the number of alternate representatives to five and advisers and experts to those actually "required by the delegation." [24]

Measuring Political Weight. Two aspects of the voting process are of central importance: the weight of each member's vote and the size of the majority required. General international organizations, as distinguished from more specialized technical bodies, have seldom succeeded in agreeing on any formula of weighted voting because it has been so difficult to find a system of weighting that would satisfy all varieties of governments — large and small, thickly and sparsely populated, industrially developed and underdeveloped. From its earliest published plan of July 1943, the United States was prepared to give each Assembly member one vote, nor was any serious consideration given at either Dumbarton Oaks or San Francisco to the possibility of a system of weighted voting. The only storm that arose on this horizon was the Soviet Union's proposal that all sixteen of its constituent republics be given separate votes. Finally President Roosevelt agreed at Yalta, in February 1945, that the Byelorussian and Ukrainian Republics should be admitted as separate members.[25]

[24] UN Doc. A/520, Rule 25.

[25] Edward R. Stettinius, Jr., *Roosevelt and the Russians* (Garden City: Doubleday, 1949), p. 187.

STRUCTURE OF THE GENERAL ASSEMBLY
AS OF 31 DECEMBER 1952

GENERAL ASSEMBLY

PROCEDURAL COMMITTEES

- GENERAL COMMITTEE
- CREDENTIALS COMMITTEE

STANDING COMMITTEES

- ADVISORY COMMITTEE ON ADMINISTRATIVE AND BUDGETARY QUESTIONS
- COMMITTEE ON CONTRIBUTIONS

MAIN COMMITTEES

- FIRST COMMITTEE POLITICAL AND SECURITY (Including the regulation of armaments)
- SECOND COMMITTEE ECONOMIC AND FINANCIAL
- THIRD COMMITTEE SOCIAL, HUMANITARIAN AND CULTURAL
- FOURTH COMMITTEE TRUSTEESHIP (Including Non-Self-Governing Territories)
- FIFTH COMMITTEE ADMINISTRATIVE & BUDGETARY
- SIXTH COMMITTEE LEGAL

AD HOC COMMITTEE
With full Membership

- AD HOC POLITICAL COMMITTEE

Other Existing Bodies Established by the General Assembly

Interim Committee of the General Assembly
Disarmament Commission
Peace Observation Commission
Balkan Sub-Commission
Collective Measures Committee
UN Commission to Investigate Conditions for Free Elections in Germany
UN Commission for the Unification and Rehabilitation of Korea
UN Korean Reconstruction Agency
Special Committee on Admission of New Members
UN Conciliation Commission for Palestine
UN Relief and Works Agency for Palestine Refugees in the Near East
Negotiating Committee for Extra-Budgetary Funds
UN Good Offices Commission on the Question of the Treatment of People of Indian Origin in the Union of South Africa
UN Commission on the Question of Race Conflict in the Union of South Africa
UN Tribunal in Libya
UN Tribunal in Eritrea
Office of the UN High Commissioner for Refugees
Ad Hoc Commission on Prisoners of War
UN Advisory Council for Somaliland
Ad Hoc Committee on South West Africa
Committee on Information from Non-Self-Governing Territories
Ad Hoc Committee on Factors (Non-Self-Governing Territories)
Committee on Special Administrative Question
Board of Auditors
UN Administrative Tribunal
UN Staff Pension Committee
Investments Committee
International Law Commission
Committee on International Criminal Jurisdiction
Special Committee on the Question of Defining Aggression
Special Committee on Measures to Limit the Duration of Regular Sessions of the General Assembly
Headquarters Advisory Committee

UN Presentation 947.4 rev.5

Even without a formal system of weighted voting in the Assembly, there is "invisible," or informal, weighting. For example, representatives of the great powers have a way of being appointed, whenever they so desire, to serve on Assembly sub-committees and commissions. The more influential middle powers also tend to be favored, though not to the same degree as the super-powers. Votes are also weighted by "attraction"; stronger states inevitably draw into their orbits smaller countries that are in varying degrees dependent upon them. This "invisible" weighting has, moreover, a very direct bearing on the relative impact of various resolutions. It is not so much their legal character as "recommendations" which determines their effectiveness but rather the quality, quantity and intensity of community support behind them. Consequently, when a large number of nations, including most of the more influential ones, vigorously endorsed the Uniting for Peace resolution by a vote of 52 to 5 with 2 abstentions during the 1950 session, the recommendation carried great weight. But, during the same session, when another resolution was adopted reaffirming a previous decision to internationalize Jerusalem, with a feeble majority of only 38 to 14 with 7 abstentions in opposition to many of the more powerful states, the decision was dead at birth.

Blocs are another variation on the weighting theme. The formation of blocs is a development which has alarmed those who had hoped that the Assembly would help to banish "balance of power" politics. Yet the coalescence of individual units into disciplined groups in order to improve their bargaining power is an inherent part of any political process. All that an international organization can or should try to do is to limit the means and regulate the procedures by which groups seek to influence each other.

There has been no single basis thus far for the divisions among the Assembly's members; on the contrary, there have been many bases some of which have conflicted — e.g., geographical versus political considerations. Various anguished criticisms of UN blocs to the contrary, *most states have joined different combinations of states according to the issues of the moment.* The most outstanding exception is the Soviet bloc, which has experienced few deviations save for the defection of the Yugoslavs. The Arab, Asian and Latin American groups operate with considerable unity on elections and appointments. Their caucuses are less effective in maintaining unbroken fronts on substantive issues except when a matter seems to affect the entire group in the same way, e.g., the impact of the Palestine situation on the Arab bloc (and even then there were internal tensions). The least disciplined alliances are the Commonwealth, Scandinavian and Benelux groups. Neither the United Kingdom nor France has the circle of close allies it had in the League. The United States frequently receives support from many states whose interests in the present world situation require close collaboration with Uncle Sam. Yet this influence often boomerangs. Thus the United States delegation was unable to win strong Latin American support in connection with the internationalization of Jerusalem or in the final vote in the 1948 regular session on the former Italian colonies.

Certain broader groupings are based on major substantive themes which run through most Assembly sessions. The principal division of this kind is the one that separates the Soviet and non-Soviet worlds, moderated occasionally by countries which have tried to perform a mediating function, e.g., the efforts of the Arab-Asian group that collaborated during the 1950 session to seek a compromise settlement in the Korean conflict. Another significant boundary is that which divides pro-colonial from anti-colonial powers with the United States and a few other ambivalent powers wandering about uncomfortably somewhere in between.

These variations of informal weighting have, however, two basic shortcomings. They are seldom entirely predictable. And they sometimes exaggerate rather than correct the inequities of the equality rule. The potential strength of the Latin American bloc, with its twenty votes, has caused particular concern, although that influence has seldom been exerted with full unity on substantive issues. For these reasons many observers, including the present authors, believe that the Assembly would be a more realistic and more useful organ if its voting mechanism were to reflect more accurately the relative international weight of the members. In 1948 Paul-Henri Spaak, the representative of a small country, Belgium, said,

> I do not think that Belgium plays the same role in international politics as the United States. I do not think that an organization such as that of the United Nations will really be able to function well if it is based upon a system that is clearly unreal. For myself, I can quite well conceive of establishing some sort of qualified vote and quantitative vote, and of having each nation in the General Assembly and later in the Security Council vote in a manner that might be described as "weighted." [26]

John Foster Dulles, citizen of a great power, the United States, wrote in his book, *War or Peace,*

> . . . the weight of its [Assembly's] recommendations would be far greater if the votes reflected not merely numbers but also ability to contribute to the maintenance of international peace and security. . . . I would not abolish . . . an Assembly vote which, like that of our Senate, reflects the sovereign equality of all nations. . . . But there might be introduced, in addition, a system of "weighted" voting. . . . Then it should be provided that decisions on important matters would require a simple majority, rather than two-thirds, under each of the two voting procedures. [27]

Unfortunately there are a lot of technical and political road blocks in the way. Many small countries still resist any diminution of the present weight of their votes. Large industrial countries such as the United States and the United Kingdom look askance at any change that might favor the bee-

[26] Paul-Henri Spaak, "The Role of the General Assembly," *International Conciliation,* No. 445 (November 1948), p. 601.

[27] (New York: Macmillan, 1950), pp. 191–192. Used by permission of The Macmillan Company.

hive populations of China and India. The anti-Communist countries disapprove of any move that might give the Soviet bloc more strength. The Soviet minority wants no reform that will make the majority even stronger than it is at present. Many states are hesitant to propose any reform which would require amendment of the Charter for fear of opening a cage of lions that might get out of control. Others are discouraged because they believe the veto, in the present world situation, blocks all possibility of any amendment. At present, therefore, no serious official consideration is being given to the possibility of introducing a formal system of weighted voting. This is such a key problem, however, that it would seem to justify conscientious efforts in both governmental and nongovernmental circles to explore the issue further.

What Kind of Majority? Regarding the size of the majority to be required, the League experience with the unanimity rule, in spite of many modifications, resulted in early and general agreement among the authors of the United Nations Charter that a more flexible procedure should be adopted. The Dumbarton Oaks Proposals provided that all "important decisions" be determined by a two-thirds vote; procedural, including the determination of additional categories of "important decisions," by a simple majority. Important decisions were to include:

1. recommendations with respect to the maintenance of international peace and security;
2. election of members of the Security Council and Economic and Social Council;
3. admission of members, suspension of the exercise of the rights and privileges of members, and expulsion of members; and
4. budgetary questions.[28]

It was this formula which was adopted at San Francisco as part of Article 18 with no serious disagreement and only the addition to the list of "important questions" of elections to the Trusteeship Council and trusteeship questions.

The great powers' willingness to accept a two-thirds majority rather than unanimity is explained not only by the League Assembly's experience but also by the fact that they expected the plenary body to be far less important than the Security Council in the crucial political sphere. And yet the Council was to have only the same recommendatory authority as the Assembly in matters of pacific settlement, as distinguished from enforcement action. Furthermore, a recommendation that could be made in the Council only with the unanimous consent of the permanent members could be made in the Assembly by a two-thirds majority without their consent. As for the attitude of the smaller countries, they also indicated a general willingness to abandon the unanimity principle without any extended discussion of the protection which they were thereby surrendering.

In Assembly committees, the procedure is streamlined. All decisions are

[28] *Postwar Foreign Policy Preparation* . . . , p. 613.

made by simple majority except for a special two-thirds requirement when voting to reconsider a decision. This makes it relatively easy to arrive at a decision. The expectation is that, once a conclusion has been reached in committee, many states which oppose the majority up to the bitter end will reconsider and decide to jump on the bandwagon. While this has been the usual pattern, there have been occasions when a weak majority decision in committee did not win two-thirds of the votes in plenary meeting, such as the First Committee's abortive proposals on the former Italian Colonies during the second part of the third session. The obvious disadvantage of the simple majority voting procedure in committee is that it does not compel the members to formulate a compromise which is definitely known to have the support of two-thirds of the votes before going to the plenary meeting. If the committee recommendation is finally defeated in plenary it is usually too late to try for a new compromise.

When Do They Meet?

The fact that the League Assembly was originally expected to hibernate between quadrennial sessions but decided to live a vigorous life of regular annual sessions prepared the drafters of the United Nations Charter for a plenary body at least as active as its predecessor. The Dumbarton Oaks Conference urged annual sessions but provided merely that the Assembly president be elected "for each session"; the same plan was adopted at San Francisco.

Annual sessions, as compared with the continuous functioning of the Security Council, were considered sufficient on the assumption that the Assembly would be less concerned than the Council with short-run crisis situations. Since its birth, however, the Assembly has had to wrestle with one emergency after another and consequently has resorted to several devices to make its influence more continuous, especially with respect to political questions. Special sessions were convoked in 1947 and 1948 to deal primarily with the Palestine situation, and a second part of the third session was held in the spring of 1949 to deal with various matters not completed during the first part. The Uniting for Peace Resolution of the 1950 session also provided that the Assembly might meet in "emergency special session" within twenty-four hours of the request therefor as compared with a regular special session to convene within fifteen days of the Secretary-General's receipt of a request. The 1950 Assembly also set a precedent by extending its session until a few days before the sixth session convened in November 1951, primarily in order to continue to deal directly with the Korean situation. As a result of these developments, the Assembly, for all practical purposes, can be as continuous as the Security Council. This is facilitated by the fact that most member states are represented by "minute men" permanent delegates stationed in the vicinity of the United Nations Headquarters in New York City.

Another effort to make the Assembly's full membership more continuously active in the political field was the creation during the 1947 session of the Interim Committee which was renewed annually until given indefinite tenure in 1949. The major pressure which led to this innovation was the desire of the United States, the author of the plan, to compensate for the Security Council's failure to take action on several critical issues, particularly the conflict on the borders of Greece. The strongest resistance came from the Soviet Union, which accused the United States of trying to by-pass the Council altogether. Certain non-Soviet countries expressed milder doubts as to the constitutional validity and political wisdom of the move.

Contrary to the impression given by the name "Little Assembly," with which the gentlemen of the press baptized the baby, it was never intended to exercise the Assembly's full authority in the political field nor to deal with any matters outside the political arena. Its carefully restricted mandate, as approved in 1947, included the following functions:

1. to consider and make recommendations to the General Assembly on: (a) matters referred to it by the Assembly, (b) any dispute or situation proposed for inclusion in the Assembly's agenda or brought before the Assembly by the Security Council, or (c) methods to be used in consideration of general principles of cooperation in the maintenance of international peace and security including the regulation of armaments;

2. to conduct investigations and appoint commissions of inquiry within the scope of its duties (by two-thirds majority); and

3. to advise the Secretary-General on the desirability of a special session in connection with any matter under discussion.[29]

The Interim Committee has not, however, lived up to the fond hopes of its parents. It has made some useful studies, particularly with respect to procedures of peaceful settlement and the Security Council voting problem, and was able to interpret the mandate of the Temporary Commission on Korea in 1948 without calling a special session, but never on its own initiative has it considered any situation or dispute or created a commission of inquiry. There are several reasons for this inactivity. The participating members have advanced cautiously with the hope of winning the confidence of the non-participating Soviet group. Many states feel that decisions on most current problems would lack political relevance unless they were made in collaboration with the Soviet Union. Finally, the Interim Committee's personnel, largely the Members' permanent delegates, has usually not been of as high a caliber as that of a regular session.

Devices involving less than full Assembly membership which have also been used to project the plenary body's authority beyond its plenary sessions have been the following:

1. The two principal organs (the Economic and Social Council and the Trusteeship Council) which operate under the Assembly's general direction.

[29] UN Doc. A/519, p. 15.

2. Assembly standing committees which deal with continuing problems and frequently meet between sessions: the Advisory Committee on Administrative and Budgetary Questions, Committee on Contributions, Board of Auditors, International Law Commission, Investments Committee and United Nations Staff Pensions Committee.

3. *Ad hoc* Assembly committees and commissions which deal with specific problems on a temporary basis, e.g., Special Committee on the Balkans, Commission on Korea, etc.

4. The practice of Assembly presidents (anticipated by United States proposals before the Dumbarton Oaks Conference) of remaining actively in office until they are replaced by the election of successors.

Who Provides Direction?

The organization of Assembly leadership was modeled largely after the League Assembly's arrangements. As in the League, it was anticipated that the Assembly's president would be its most important and influential officer. Another tradition was continued by providing for the election of a number of vice presidents — eight in the League Assembly, seven in the General Assembly — among whom, it was understood, the five permanent members of the Security Council would always be represented. The other two vice presidents and the chairmen of the standing committees would be chosen from the smaller countries.

The president's formal duties, which were reinforced in December 1949, are:

> to direct the discussions; ensure observance of the rules; accord the right to speak; put questions; announce decisions; rule on points of order; have complete control of the proceedings and over the maintenance of order; propose limitation of the number of times each representative may speak on a question, the time to be allowed each speaker, the closure of the list of speakers or the closure of the debate; propose the suspension or the adjournment of the meeting or adjournment of the debate on the item under discussion.[30]

While the president's rulings can be challenged by any delegation and overruled by a simple majority, he has sufficient authority so that with courage, tact, and a sixth sense of what the traffic will bear at any moment, he is in a strategic position to direct the deliberations.

Even more important than his formal duties, however, are the informal functions which cannot be found in the *Rules of Procedure*. During the disarmament debate in the second part of the first session, for example, Paul-Henri Spaak exerted his influence with telling effect behind the scenes in assisting the various interests to formulate a compromise.

Committees and Commissions

The Assembly's committee structure tends to follow the League pattern, although there are some notable changes. The General Committee, which

[30] UN Doc. A/520/Rev. 1, Rule 35.

in the League Assembly was an influential steering committee dominated by the great powers, has been ground down between conflicting interests to considerably smaller proportions. The large states, which are all represented in the Committee, hoped to use it to guide the course of the Assembly, but they have been so divided among themselves that they have seldom been capable of offering concerted direction. The smaller powers, on the other hand, have feared great power domination in the Committee and consequently have insisted on tying its hands to such an extent that it is unable to do much real steering. Its authority is merely to

1. advise the Assembly regarding the agenda and closing date of a session, and
2. to assist the President and the Assembly in drawing up the agenda for each plenary meeting, in determining the priority of its items, and in coordinating the committee proceedings.[31]

It is specifically forbidden to "discuss the substance of any item" or to "decide any political question." This situation has led the Executive Assistant to the Secretary-General to develop the informal device of a weekly luncheon meeting attended by the president, committee chairmen and one or two of the Executive Assistant's staff. Fortunately this body, in which the vice presidents (including the great power delegates) are not represented, has done much to fill the vacuum left by the General Committee.

There are now six main committees rather than seven: First (Political and Security), Second (Economic and Financial), Third (Social, Humanitarian and Cultural), Fourth (Trusteeship), Fifth (Administrative and Budgetary), and Sixth (Legal). Like their League predecessors, they are fully representative of the membership and for that very reason seem unfortunately elephantine in comparison with the smaller committees of the usual national legislature. Since there is no party machinery to bind delegates together in convenient bundles, except for the unpredictable and often unrealistic effect of the blocs, there are sixty separate "parties" all of which insist on separate representation. Fortunately not all of these members try to speak on every issue, but the temptations of national and personal pride are always present and difficult to resist. The debate seems slow and disjointed since speeches are usually prepared far enough in advance to allow time for necessary governmental clearance. Consequently there can be little free give-and-take except towards the end of the discussion on a particular issue when basic governmental positions are established and only minor maneuvers are involved.

This clumsiness is compensated for to some extent through the use of smaller subcommittees wherever deemed practicable. In general there are six broad functions that are assigned to the sub-bodies: intensive study of some complex problem, screening outside requests to testify, hearing testimony from outside sources, conciliating varying views, drafting recommendations and proposing nominations. The peculiar assets of these sub-

[31] UN Doc. A/520/Rev. 1, Rules 40–42.

committees are that they provide an opportunity for more intimate, more flexible and more concentrated negotiations. Their liabilities are that they place a heavy burden on the time and manpower resources of the delegations, they compel a delicate and often controversial selection of interests to be represented in the smaller body and they often encourage excessive argumentation over drafting details. There is little doubt, however, that the judicious use of subcommittees is one of the best ways to provide extra hands for the main committees.

The commissions which operate beyond the formal Assembly sessions and often in the field have already been described as a means of expanding the plenary body's influence. These groups have been established on both an *ad hoc* basis (Commission on Korea) and a continuing basis (Peace Observation Commission) to deal with single specific situations or broad categories (International Law Commission). The Assembly has directly appointed more of these in the political-legal field than in nonpolitical areas since the Economic and Social Council and the Trusteeship Council are available to handle their respective areas between Assembly sessions. The functions performed by these commissions have included: investigation and research, pacific settlement, policy formulation and promotion of compliance.

With respect to their organizational anatomy, no problem is more crucial than the character of their membership. First, there is the question of the interests to be represented: geographic (Pacific countries strongly represented in the Commission on Korea), power (the great powers may be included or excluded) and other factors such as religious interests in connection with Palestine. There is also the matter of size. The lone Palestine Mediator seemed an admirable device for bold, unified and flexible conciliation, while larger groups, such as the Balkan Commission, have seemed preferable for observational duties. The latter type usually consists of about a dozen representatives. Then there is the matter of whether to appoint personnel as state representatives or as private individuals. Individual status has been favored where there seems to be a commonly accepted professional creed which underlies the experts' opinions and wins for them widespread respect in spite of national barriers (as in the International Law Commission). In the political field the usual attitude, especially among the great powers, has been to urge governmental status so that such persons may speak with governmental authority and formulate recommendations likely to have state support. Finally there is the question of the caliber of the personnel. Unfortunately some governments have occasionally looked upon such commissions as convenient dumping grounds for individuals who were not wanted at home. In spite of all of these problems, however, the proliferation of these commissions which have carried the flag and the influence of the United Nations to countless lands has been one of the most significant means of extending and reinforcing the Assembly's authority.

Open Diplomacy

Following the general practices of the League Assembly, the General Assembly *Rules of Procedure* provide that all meetings of the plenary body and its main committees shall be held in public unless the body concerned decides that exceptional circumstances require privacy. While League subcommittees usually met in private, General Assembly rules stipulate that such meetings shall also be open to the public unless the sub-body decides otherwise. All decisions taken at a private meeting must be announced at an early public meeting of the General Assembly. While it is clearly understood by the delegates that privacy may often be more conducive to frank and intimate negotiation, there are ample opportunities for such discussions outside the formal meetings.

Major Assembly Functions

Many of the planners in Washington and London thought that the League Assembly and Council had too frequently stepped on each other's toes. They also felt that the ungainly Assembly had sometimes attempted deeds beyond its strength and had fallen flat on its face. Consequently they wanted a clearer line drawn between the roles of the new Assembly and Council.[32]

At San Francisco, however, many of the smaller states, as well as certain nongovernmental groups within the larger states, launched a fervent crusade to strengthen the Assembly's role, especially in the political field. A major symbol of that struggle and of the token victory that was won is Article 10 of the Charter:

> The General Assembly may discuss any questions or any matters within the scope of the present Charter or relating to the powers and functions of any organs provided for in the present Charter, and, except as provided in Article 12, may make recommendations to the Members of the United Nations or to the Security Council or to both on any such questions or matters.

This Article grew directly out of the amendments which some twenty smaller states proposed in order to give the Assembly the same broad jurisdiction that the League Assembly had been given by the Covenant, i.e., to "deal . . . with any matter within the sphere of action of the League or affecting the peace of the world."

The suggestion that received the strongest support was submitted by Peter Fraser of New Zealand, firmly backed by Herbert Evatt of Australia and Padilla Nervo of Mexico: that the Assembly "have the right to consider any matter within the sphere of international relations." [33] The

[32] *Postwar Foreign Policy Preparation . . .* , pp. 597–603.
[33] UNCIO, V, p. 265.

JOBS FOR THE GENERAL ASSEMBLY

Discuss any question within scope of Charter	Make recommendations when case is not before Security Council

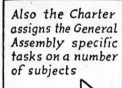  

Also the Charter assigns the General Assembly specific tasks on a number of subjects ⟹

Consider principles of arms limitation	Promote human welfare and freedom

Consider reports from other UN agencies	Supervise Trusteeship system	Elect nonperman't members of Security Council and Trusteeship Council, all members of Economic and Social Council. Also elect jointly with Security Council new UN members, Secretary Gen'l and World Court judges

Approve UN budget, apportion expenses among members	Request advisory opinions from International Court	Initiate revision of Charter

GRAPHIC ASSOCIATES

Headline Series, *Foreign Policy Association*

Soviet Union took a more conservative position, arguing that the Assembly should not have the right to deal with a question until the actions of an offending state "create a situation which represents a menace to international peace and security." While the United States and the United Kingdom fully supported the protective concept of a state's "domestic jurisdiction," they never accepted the extreme U.S.S.R. point of view, which was far more restrictive than the Dumbarton Oaks provisions. The United

States finally decided to support the smaller powers in this matter. As John Foster Dulles has told the story,

> Secretary Stettinius took a strong line, with the unanimous backing of his Delegation. On June 19th he notified the Soviet delegates and Ambassador Harriman at Moscow that unless a satisfactory solution was found by noon of the next day the United States would propose that the conference vote its own text, leaving the Soviet Union to withdraw if it wanted. Precisely at twelve o'clock the next day, June 20th, Mr. Gromyko telephoned that he had received instructions from Moscow to concur in a formula that was acceptable to the conference as a whole.[34]

Article 10 was the formula. When one studies the text, however, it becomes clear that it actually added very little to the letter of the Charter which was not already implied in the Dumbarton Oaks provisions which were incorporated in Articles 11, 13 and 14 of the Charter with relatively few changes. The significant contribution of Article 10 was the change it wrought in the spirit of the Dumbarton Oaks plan, proclaiming explicitly that the boundaries of the Assembly's authority to discuss and recommend should be as extensive as those of the entire Charter. The effect was to strengthen the prestige of the smaller powers and to ward off any attempt to narrow the scope of the Assembly.

Steps Toward Law

At San Francisco, in spite of the labors of certain private groups that urged world government, there was almost no official support, by either small or large nations, for granting the Assembly binding legislative authority. Most important of all, neither the United States nor the Soviet Union would have considered such a proposal. Nevertheless, the delegations were willing to authorize the Assembly to perform the same broad policy functions that had been performed by the League Assembly: to discuss and make recommendations, including draft conventions, regarding general problems. Moreover the General Assembly's role in trusteeship and economic and social matters was far stronger than that of the League Assembly. The enactment of recommendations into law remained with the member states.

Besides the broad grant of power set forth in Article 10, the Assembly's political functions are spelled out in further detail in Article 11(1), taken almost verbatim from the Dumbarton Oaks Proposals.

> The General Assembly may consider the general principles of cooperation in the maintenance of international peace and security, including the principles governing disarmament and the regulation of armaments, and may make recommendations with regard to such principles to the Members or to the Security Council or both.

[34] *War or Peace*, p. 38. Used by permission of The Macmillan Company.

In Article 13(1)(a), the Assembly is authorized to initiate studies and make recommendations for the purpose of "promoting international cooperation in the political field and encouraging the progressive development of international law and its codification." While China had originally proposed consideration of the "development and revision" of international law, the other sponsoring powers opposed "revision." At San Francisco the Philippines and Liberia urged that the Assembly promote codification, a concept dearer to the hearts of Roman Law states than those steeped in Common Law. The sponsoring powers finally agreed to include codification but still rejected revision. They preferred to speak of "progressive development," much to the annoyance of some of the smaller states, including Australia, Belgium and Mexico.[35]

The Philippines also proposed that the Assembly be given the authority "to enact rules of international law which should become binding upon members after such rules shall have been approved by the Security Council," but the Philippines found itself voting alone for this proposal. Belgium wanted to bestow formally upon the Assembly a function which the League Assembly had performed without specific authority: to "submit general conventions for the consideration of states . . . with a view to securing their approval. . . ." The United States argued that special conferences should do the detailed work of drafting conventions. The Soviet Union feared interference with the Security Council's prerogatives. Although twenty-five delegations finally supported Belgium, the amendment failed to win the necessary two-thirds majority.[36] Nevertheless, many delegations insisted that Article 13, reinforced by Article 10, could be interpreted to authorize Assembly recommendations in the form of draft conventions,[37] an interpretation subsequently put into effect.

The Dumbarton Oaks draft had provided that the Assembly might "initiate studies and make recommendations for the purpose of promoting international cooperation in [the] political . . . field . . . and of adjusting situations likely to impair the general welfare." Nonetheless, Senator Arthur Vandenberg wanted to add a provision, similar to Article 19 of the League Covenant, that would authorize the Assembly to make recommendations regarding various forms of peaceful change including the revision of treaties. The United States Department of State had considered this implicit in the original language, but apparently decided that it was politic to allow the Senator to make his contribution. Mr. Molotov was not so obliging, however, and firmly opposed the amendment as a potential threat to the stability of the postwar treaties which were about to be negotiated.

The compromise which seems to have paved the way for the final version of what is now Article 14 was twofold. First, it was understood that Article 107 would protect any World War II peace treaties from Assembly intervention. Second, there was to be no specific mention in the Vandenberg Amendment of treaty revision but rather the adjustment of any situation

---

[35] UNCIO, IX, pp. 177–178.   [36] *Ibid.*, p. 80.
[37] *Ibid.*, VIII, p. 208, statement by Herbert Evatt.

"regardless of origin" which might impair the general welfare "or friendly relations among nations, including situations resulting from a violation of the Purposes and Principles set forth in . . . [the] Charter." [38] The final text of Article 14 reads:

> Subject to the provisions of Article 12, the General Assembly may recommend measures for the peaceful adjustment of any situation, regardless of origin, which it deems likely to impair the general welfare or friendly relations among nations, including situations resulting from a violation of the provisions of the present Charter setting forth the Purposes and Principles of the United Nations.

Senator Vandenberg, in interpreting these provisions to the Conference, stated explicitly that he had surrendered nothing, that they clearly included the authority to recommend the revision of treaties. Mr. Molotov replied with equal ardor that such an interpretation "attacks the very basis of international law, peace, and security." [39] As for the general significance of the amendments added at San Francisco, one can only say that they made more explicit the provisions which had already been adopted at Dumbarton Oaks.

The major innovation in the Assembly's broad policy function was the decision to include responsibility for supervision of the UN economic and social program, the details of which are discussed in Chapters 8 and 9. This was the plan proposed by the United States and adopted by the Dumbarton Oaks Conference. At San Francisco many of the smaller powers strove valiantly to strengthen the economic and social provisions and succeeded in making the Economic and Social Council a "principal organ," but still left ultimate supervision in the hands of the Assembly. Article 13(1)(b) reads:

> The General Assembly shall initiate studies and make recommendations for the purpose of: . . . b) promoting international cooperation in the economic, social, cultural, educational, and health fields, and assisting in the realization of human rights and fundamental freedoms for all without distinction as to race, sex, language, or religion.

Article 60 reads:

> Responsibility for the discharge of the functions of the Organization . . . [in the economic and social field] shall be vested in the General Assembly and, under . . . [its] authority . . . , in the Economic and Social Council. . . .

Another significant innovation was the delegation to the Assembly of ultimate responsibility for guiding the trusteeship system which is considered in greater detail in Chapter 11.

[38] *Ibid.*, IX, pp. 21–22.   [39] *Ibid.*, pp. 138, 150.

Peacemaker

The great powers, including the United States, had agreed by the end of the Dumbarton Oaks Conference that the Assembly should have the same general authority as the Security Council in the field of peaceful settlement. At the same time this mandate was limited by several qualifications:

1. the Council was to exercise "primary responsibility for the maintenance of international peace and security";

2. the Assembly was not on its own initiative to make any recommendations on any matter relating to the maintenance of peace and security being dealt with by the Council; and

3. any question on which action was necessary was to be referred to the Council. (Dumbarton Oaks Proposals, Chapters V, VI, and VIII)

The provisions of the Charter on this subject (Article 11, par. 2) as finally adopted at San Francisco read:

The General Assembly may discuss any questions relating to the maintenance of international peace and security brought before it by any Member . . . , or by the Security Council, or by a state which is not a Member . . . and, except as provided in Article 12, may make recommendations with regard to any such questions to the state or states concerned or to the Security Council or to both. Any such question on which action is necessary shall be referred to the Security Council by the General Assembly either before or after the discussion.

The last sentence, taken directly from the Dumbarton Oaks draft, aroused considerable debate since the smaller powers wanted the Assembly to be more closely associated with "action" by the Council. This discussion led to a proposal that the Council submit to the Assembly reports on all measures taken to maintain international security. Since the Soviet Union insisted, however, that the plenary body must have no authority to approve or disapprove a Council report which would have the effect of placing it in a superior position, a final compromise was incorporated in Article 15:

The General Assembly shall receive and consider annual and special reports from the Security Council; these reports shall include an account of the measures that the Security Council has decided upon or taken to maintain international peace and security.

Mr. Herbert Evatt of Australia led another revolt by insisting that the Assembly should be barred from making a recommendation only so long as the "Security Council is exercising the functions assigned to it" rather than according to the Dumbarton Oaks wording which was thought to imply that the Council might block Assembly recommendations simply by keeping matters on its agenda. Mr. Evatt also wanted the plenary body to decide for itself when the Security Council was actually "exercising the functions assigned to it." Altogether fourteen countries, including France, submitted amendments along these general lines. Finally Senator Vandenberg announced a compromise draft that accepted much of the Australian thesis as the basis for Article 12:

1. While the Security Council is exercising in respect of any dispute or situation the functions assigned to it in the present Charter, the General Assembly shall not make any recommendations with regard to that dispute or situation unless the Security Council so requests.
2. The Secretary-General, with the consent of the Security Council, shall notify the General Assembly at each session of any matters relative to the maintenance of international peace and security which are being dealt with by the Security Council and shall similarly notify the General Assembly, or the Members of the United Nations if the General Assembly is not in session, immediately the Security Council ceases to deal with such matters.

General Supervisor

Over-all Role. The Assembly is armed with certain supervisory functions that are of a general nature and apply equally to all United Nations bodies. Its strongest instrument of guidance is the formulation of policy recommendations discussed above. Article 10 provides specifically that the Assembly "may discuss any questions . . . relating to the powers and functions of any organs provided for in the present Charter and . . . make recommendations . . . [on them]."

Another whip is the Assembly's authority to regulate the United Nations budget according to the provisions of Article 17 and its Rules of Procedure. The annual budget prepared by the Secretary-General is submitted, prior to each session, to an Advisory Committee on Administrative and Budgetary Questions (nine individuals, including two recognized financial experts, to serve for three-year terms). This Committee then submits to the Assembly's Fifth Committee a detailed report on the accounts of the previous year and the budget for the next. The Assembly has also created a Committee on Contributions (ten individuals to serve three-year terms) charged with the task of advising on the apportionment of United Nations expenses among the members. The 1953 scale of assessments was as follows:

Member	Per Cent	Member	Per Cent
Afghanistan	0.08	Chile	0.33
Argentina	1.45	China	5.62
Australia	1.75	Colombia	0.35
Belgium	1.37	Costa Rica	0.04
Bolivia	0.06	Cuba	0.34
Brazil	1.45	Czechoslovakia	1.05
Burma	0.13	Denmark	0.78
Byelorussian S.S.R.	0.43	Dominican Republic	0.05
Canada	3.30	Ecuador	0.04

Member	Per Cent	Member	Per Cent
Egypt	0.50	Norway	0.50
El Salvador	0.05	Pakistan	0.79
Ethiopia	0.10	Panama	0.05
France	5.75	Paraguay	0.04
Greece	0.19	Peru	0.18
Guatemala	0.06	Philippines	0.39
Haiti	0.04	Poland	1.58
Honduras	0.04	Saudi Arabia	0.07
Iceland	0.04	Sweden	1.65
India	3.45	Syria	0.08
Indonesia	0.60	Thailand	0.18
Iran	0.33	Turkey	0.65
Iraq	0.12	Ukrainian S.S.R.	1.63
Israel	0.17	Union of South Africa	0.83
Lebanon	0.05	U.S.S.R.	12.28
Liberia	0.04	United Kingdom	10.30
Luxembourg	0.05	United States	35.12
Mexico	0.70	Uruguay	0.18
Netherlands	1.25	Venezuela	0.35
New Zealand	0.48	Yemen	0.04
Nicaragua	0.04	Yugoslavia	0.44

With respect to the budgets of the specialized agencies, the agreements negotiated with those bodies have, for the most part, provided for mutual consultation in budget preparation and the submission of these budgets to the Assembly for examination and recommendations, but the agencies have jealously resisted any stronger supervision.

Another weapon in the Assembly's armory is its power (Article 108) to recommend amendments to the Charter, which must then be ratified by two-thirds of the Members, including the permanent members of the Security Council. The Assembly's role in this process caused no serious disagreement. It was the special position accorded the Big Five that disturbed most of the smaller powers who complained bitterly that this rule would merely perpetuate the veto which they had hoped would be merely a temporary expedient.

The Assembly's function of admitting new Members upon the recommendation of the Security Council gives it another means of controlling the organization. But, in this matter, it is in a far weaker position than the League Assembly which was able, also by two-thirds majority, to approve new Members, but without a Council recommendation. As for the criteria to be considered in screening applicants, Article 4(1) provides that membership is open to all "peace-loving states which accept the obligations contained in the present Charter and, in the judgment of the Organization, are able and willing to carry out these obligations."

The fundamental problem that has bedevilled the issue of membership has been the conflict between the Soviet and non-Soviet groups over the admission of their respective friends. Both sides have managed to agree jointly on the admission of only nine states since the establishment of the United Nations: Afghanistan, Iceland, Sweden, Thailand, Pakistan, Yemen, Burma, Israel and Indonesia. The Soviet bloc has prevented admission of fourteen other states: Austria, Cambodia, Ceylon, Finland, Ireland, Italy, Japan, Jordan, Laos, Libya, Nepal, Portugal, the Republic of Korea and Vietnam. And the non-Soviet group has blocked admission of seven Soviet-controlled regimes: Albania, Bulgaria, Hungary, Mongolian Peoples' Republic, North Korea, Rumania and the Vietminh regime in Vietnam.

Two International Court advisory opinions have dealt with this issue. On May 28, 1948, the Court decided by the close vote of nine to six that: (1) a member is not entitled to make its consent to admission dependent on conditions not expressly provided by Article 1(4), and (2) a member cannot make its affirmative vote subject to the admission of other states.[40] Again on March 3, 1950, the Court ruled by a vote of twelve to two that admission could not be effected by the Assembly without a Security Council recommendation.[41] In the interest of breaking the log jam on this question and admitting states of major importance such as Italy, a growing number of Members favor some "package" agreement whereby each side will agree to some of the other side's candidates in order to get its own friends into the club.

A final general supervisory authority is the Assembly's responsibility to elect the non-permanent members of the Security Council, all the members of the Economic and Social Council, and part of the members of the Trusteeship Council. Voting concurrently with the Security Council, it participates in the election of the International Court justices, and it appoints the Secretary-General upon the recommendation of the Security Council.

Special Supervisory Functions. Besides the above general functions, the Assembly was also endowed with certain special supervisory powers with respect to particular organs. Although the great states were not willing to allow their chosen instrument, the Council, to be made formally responsible to the Assembly, they did agree, albeit with occasional reluctance, to give the larger body substantial indirect guiding authority over the Council. This is implicit in the Assembly's power to make recommendations regarding both general principles and specific situations in the political field which cannot but affect the Council's "primary responsibility" for the maintenance of peace and security. And there is also Article 15:

> The General Assembly shall receive and consider annual and special reports from the Security Council; these reports shall include an account of the measures that the Security Council has decided upon or taken to maintain international peace and security.

[40] Admission of a State to the UN, Advisory Opinion, ICJ *Reports* 1948.
[41] UN Doc. A/1353.

The actual influence of an organization may overflow its formal constitutional boundaries, and so the Assembly has on occasion tried to extend its influence by hitching its wagon to the authority of the Security Council, especially with respect to enforcement action. In its 1947 Palestine resolution the Assembly recommended that the Council "determine as a threat to the peace . . . any attempt to alter by force the settlement envisaged by [that] resolution." [42] The Assembly also made its agents in Palestine, including Mediators Bernadotte and Bunche, responsible to the Security Council as well as itself, and requested the Council to support these agents, which it did after a fashion.

Because of these and other developments, one of the most significant aspects of the Assembly's evolution has been its rapid growth in influence in the political field as compared with the increasing paralysis and decline of the Security Council on many questions. There have been two major forces behind this trend. First, the great powers, Soviet as well as non-Soviet, have led the way because they have frequently preferred some kind of action in the Assembly, weak though it might be, to complete inaction in the Security Council. Second, the smaller powers have been eager to strengthen the plenary body in which they are numerically preponderant and wield far more influence than in the Council. It is not Assembly action which has weakened the Security Council, as some observers have claimed, so much as it has been Council inaction which has forced a shift to the Assembly.

Some observers consider this development a temporary detour due primarily to the current world situation. Yet the same forces were at work in the League, though far less actively than at present. These pressures are likely, in any era, to produce this same tendency to move from the inflexible to the flexible, from the less to the more representative organ on those issues which require extensive participation and support. And most crises today are world-wide in their implications and thus reinforce this trend.

To those who argue that no action in the security field should be taken without unanimity among the great powers, one can reply that such unity is desirable only to the extent that it helps to maintain peace with at least a minimum of political, economic and social justice. Unity is not the only consideration at stake and should not be purchased at too high a price. Nor does a lack of unity among the great powers necessarily block collective action, as long as a *preponderance* of power can still be mobilized against an aggressor.

On the other hand, in choosing the path that leads to the Assembly it is important to read the signposts that clearly indicate the risks involved. The greatest danger is that there is no guarantee that an Assembly resolution, although supported by at least two-thirds of the members, will have the backing of a sufficient number of powerful states to make it effective. Another danger is that as greater emphasis is placed on the use of

[42] *Official Records of the Second Session . . . Resolutions . . . ,* p. 132.

force the Assembly may neglect the more constructive nonmilitary means of easing international tensions.

With respect to the International Court, the Assembly obviously can have no direct authority over its decisions and opinions but does have the power to help elect justices, to request advisory opinions and to authorize other organs and the specialized agencies to do the same. In the case of the Secretariat, the Assembly not only exercises all of its general powers, including appointment of the Secretary-General, but also is charged with establishing regulations governing all appointments to the Secretariat (Article 101, par. 1). The Assembly's supervisory authority in the economic and social and non-self-governing territory spheres is discussed below in Chapters 8, 9 and 11.

Conclusions

If one looks back 140 years down the long avenue of history from the United Nations past the League to the Conference of Vienna and the first stirrings of the Concert of Europe, one is struck by the distance we have travelled to arrive at the General Assembly. With this perspective in mind, what seem to have been the salient trends? The international conference has developed from a discontinuous, infrequent and *ad hoc* body to a more continuous, permanent and regular channel of negotiation. The membership has gradually broadened from a handful of European powers to a more universal group, Eastern as well as Western, small and middle as well as great powers. The security function still tends to be dominated by the strong (now centered about two rather than several super-powers), but the Security Council, successor to the Concert, has gradually been drawn within the framework of the universal organization and placed very much under the influence of all rather than only a few nations, operating through the Assembly. The objectives of the plenary conference have shifted from a narrow negative concern with putting out political fires to positive long-range action to prevent them. And these latter activities have been placed increasingly under the direction of the plenary organ rather than the council. In essence, what this whole development represents is that the great powers find themselves less and less isolated from their smaller neighbors and more and more dependent on them.

Still the General Assembly which we have today is indeed a weak reed on which to depend. One cannot of course expect to see the Rome of world government built in a day, but the Assembly's structure and procedures need to be adjusted to its increasing responsibilities. Its influence must be made even more continuous on a more effective basis than at present. Its organization must be made more flexible than its cumbersome structure now allows. And its voting must be made more realistic than the anachronistic equality rule now permits. We should be encouraged, nevertheless, by the present tendency to strengthen the hand of the most representative organ of the United Nations. What is most significant is that the Assembly has proved itself during these trying years to be an instrument sensitive to the needs of the great majority of nations, large as well as small, and capable of remarkable development in order to achieve the purposes and principles espoused by that majority.

Suggestions for Further Reading

LEAGUE OF NATIONS

Books

Baker, Ray S., *Woodrow Wilson and World Settlement*, 3 Vols. (Garden City: Doubleday, Page, 1922).

Burton, Margaret E., *The Assembly of the League of Nations* (Chicago: University of Chicago Press, 1941).

House, E. M., *The Intimate Papers of Colonel House*, edited by Charles Seymour, 4 Vols. (Boston: Houghton Mifflin Company, 1926–1928).

Lloyd George, David, *Memoirs of the Peace Conference*, 2 Vols. (New Haven: Yale University Press, 1939).

Marburg, Theodore, *Development of the League of Nations Idea, Documents and Correspondence of Theodore Marburg*, edited by J. H. Latané, 2 Vols. (New York: The Macmillan Company, 1932).

Miller, David Hunter, *The Drafting of the Covenant*, 2 Vols. (New York: G. P. Putnam's Sons, 1928).

Morley, Felix, *Society of Nations* (Washington: Brookings Institution, 1932).

Temperley, H. W. V., ed., *A History of the Peace Conference of Paris*, 6 Vols. (London: Henry Frowde and Hodder & Stoughton, 1924).

Walters, F. P., *A History of the League of Nations*, 2 Vols. (London: Oxford University Press for the Royal Institute of International Affairs, 1952).

Zimmern, Alfred, *The League of Nations and the Rule of Law, 1918–1935* (London: Macmillan and Co., Ltd., 1936).

UNITED NATIONS

Books

Bentwich, Norman, and Martin, Andrew, *A Commentary on the Charter of the United Nations* (London: Macmillan and Co., Ltd., 1950).

Dulles, John Foster, *War or Peace* (New York: The Macmillan Company, 1950).

Evatt, Herbert Vere, *The United Nations* (Cambridge: Harvard University Press, 1948).

———, *The Task of Nations* (New York: Duell, Sloan and Pearce, 1949).

Goodrich, Leland M., and Hambro, Edvard, *Charter of the United Nations, Commentary and Documents*, 2nd ed. (Boston: World Peace Foundation, 1949).

Haviland, H. Field, Jr., *The Political Role of the General Assembly*, United Nations Study No. 7 (New York: Carnegie Endowment for International Peace, 1951).

Hull, Cordell, *The Memoirs of Cordell Hull*, 2 Vols. (New York: The Macmillan Company, 1948).

Kelsen, Hans, *The Law of the United Nations* (New York: F. A. Praeger, 1951).

Stettinius, Edward R., Jr., *Roosevelt and the Russians* (Garden City: Doubleday & Company, Inc., 1949).

Welles, Sumner, *Where Are We Heading?* (New York and London: Harper & Brothers, 1946).

Periodicals

Ball, M. Margaret, "Bloc Voting in the General Assembly," *International Organization*, Vol. 5, No. 1 (February 1951).

Goodrich, Leland M., "Development of the General Assembly," *International Conciliation*, No. 471 (May 1951).

Hovey, Allan, Jr., "Obstructionism and the Rules of the General Assembly," *International Organization,* Vol. 5, No. 3 (August 1951).

———, "Voting Procedure in the General Assembly," *International Organization*, Vol. 4, No. 3 (August 1950).

Spaak, Paul-Henri, "The Role of the General Assembly," *International Conciliation,* No. 445 (November 1948).

"The United Nations General Assembly: Its Expanding Role and the Issues Before the Second Session," *International Conciliation*, No. 433 (September 1947).

Wade, William, "Can Stronger General Assembly Assure World Peace?" *Foreign Policy Bulletin,* Vol. 29, No. 46 (October 6, 1950).

Documents

United Nations, *United Nations Conference on International Organization, San Francisco, 1945* (London and New York: UN Information Organizations, 1945–1946).

United States, *Postwar Foreign Policy Preparation, 1939–1945,* Department of State Publication 3580, General Foreign Policy Series 15 (Washington: U.S. Government Printing Office, 1950).

———, *Report to the President on the Results of the San Francisco Conference . . .,* Department of State Publication 2349, Conference Series 71 (Washington: U.S. Government Printing Office, 1945).

5

League Council — Great-Power Leadership

"I am proposing that all nations henceforth avoid entangling alliances which would draw them into competitions of power; catch them
in a net of intrigue and selfish rivalry, and disturb their own affairs
with influences intruded from without. There is no entangling alliance
in a concert of power. When all unite to act in the same sense and
with the same purpose all act in the common interest and are free to
live their own lives under a common protection."

— Woodrow Wilson [1]

The roots of the League Council reach back at least as far as the Concert of Europe which, as we have seen, was a big-power show. Thus the
principle that all states were sovereign and equal, legally speaking, was
balanced in the Covenant by the recognition that certain big states were
in fact more influential than others. Only a few states, it was realized, were
powerful enough to maintain order. Such states were given positions of
predominance and responsibility as permanent members of the Council
that was expected to be the most influential body of the League.

The notion of big-power responsibility was reinforced by the experience
of the World War. Victory required the closest collaboration in economic
affairs and in military strategy among the great powers in the allied camp.
By 1919, moreover, another tradition in international relations had become
firmly established. Many matters such as health, transportation and slavery,
as we have noted, were handled on a cooperative basis by public international unions. While the guiding principles were laid down by diplomatic
conferences, the actual work of such unions was often carried out by some
sort of council or commission assisted by a secretariat or bureau. Thus
the differentiation between a conference or assembly and a rudimentary
executive body was already well established. These two strands, a concert

[1] Address to the United States Senate, January 22, 1917, in Woodrow Wilson, *The
New Democracy; Presidential Messages, Addresses, and Other Papers (1913–1917)*, ed.
by Ray Stannard Baker and William E. Dodd (New York: Harper, 1926), Vol. 2,
p. 414.

of great powers and an international executive, had, moreover, already been woven together in the Danube Commission. In sum, the notion that certain big powers should form the nucleus of an executive committee of an association of nations was no novelty at Paris in 1919.

Forces Shaping the Council

An essential stepping stone to victory in World War I was the pooling of Allied military and economic resources under the control of the "principal powers," Britain, France, Italy and the United States. These powers continued their leadership after the war not only in the formulation of the Covenant at the Paris Conference, but also in the enforcement of the terms of the Armistice and the peace treaties through the Reparations Commission and the Conference of Ambassadors. The principal decisions of the Peace Conference, indeed, were made in meetings of the Big Five, the Big Four, and particularly the Big Three before presentation to the Plenary Conference.[2]

It is not surprising, therefore, that the great powers assumed for themselves a primary role in the League of Nations that arose directly from the ashes of the Concert of Europe. This development was foreshadowed in the numerous peace plans, both official and private, that emerged from both sides of the Atlantic during the four years of conflict. In addition to an assembly or conference, a court and a secretariat, such plans usually envisaged a big-power executive council with functions similar in some respects to the Concert of Europe. The American League to Enforce Peace, for example, proposed a commission of conciliation with powers of inquiry and recommendation to be bolstered by economic and military sanctions against states failing to comply with the processes of peaceful settlement. This influential proposal did not go into organizational detail. All the great powers, however, were to join the proposed league, while only certain of the lesser powers were to be included.[3]

British thinking, official and unofficial, generally emphasized the importance of a council of the big states for the maintenance of world order. Lord Grey, we have already seen, had attempted unsuccessfully to revive the corpse of the European Concert in the years between the Balkan crisis of 1912 and the incident at Sarajevo.[4] The role of the big powers was also emphasized when Colonel House was commissioned by President Wilson to revise the Phillimore Plan around the "principles of territorial guarantee and international police action against an aggressor, which were later to be embodied in Articles 10 and 16 of the League Covenant." As early as 1914 Wilson envisaged a system of peace for the Americas embodying the notion of "Mutual Guarantees of political independence under repub-

[2] Lord Maurice Hankey, *Diplomacy by Conference* (New York: Putnam, 1946), Chap. I.

[3] For details see Alfred Zimmern, *The League of Nations and the Rule of Law* (London: Macmillan, 1936), Chap. V, and J. A. Salter, *Allied Shipping Control, An Experiment in International Administration* (New York: Oxford, 1921), Parts IV and V.

[4] See Zimmern, *op. cit.*, pp. 77–81.

lican forms of government and mutual guarantees of territorial integrity." These were to be the essential principles of the League Covenant.[5] Colonel House's ideas were embodied in his *Suggestions for a Covenant of a League of Nations* and included the thought that membership in the organization be confined to the great powers.[6] Wilson's first draft Covenant of August, 1918, followed House's suggestions in many respects but laid more emphasis on sanctions.

The British Foreign Office Memorandum on "the League of Nations," of November 1918, provided that the Foreign Secretaries of the great powers, including Germany and Russia, should meet annually in an "Inter-state Conference" equipped with a permanent Secretariat to act as "a sort of executive committee of the whole body of sovereign states." The Foreign Secretaries of all the powers should also meet but at less frequent intervals. The council was to be an "improved concert" — improved in four ways:

1. by the provision of regular meetings;
2. by the establishment of a permanent secretariat;
3. by the enlargement of its area to include the whole world, and not Europe alone, as in the nineteenth century; and
4. . . . by becoming part of a world organization . . . and associated with a world-wide system of international cooperation.[7]

General Smuts was a member of the Imperial War Cabinet, and his essay, *A League of Nations; A Practical Suggestion,* of December 1918, adhered closely to the Foreign Office Memorandum. It publicized for the first time this proposed organizational structure which differentiated between a Council and an Assembly. The real work, it was expected, would be performed by the Council, a comparatively small body acting as an "executive committee." It was to "consist of the prime ministers or foreign secretaries or other authorized representatives of the Great Powers together with the representatives drawn in rotation from two panels of the middle powers and minor states respectively, in such a way that the Great Powers have a bare majority." [8] Thus the General, a representative of a small non-European power, helped lay the groundwork for both non-permanent and regional representation in the executive body which he anticipated would play the primary role in settling disputes and in carrying on the ordinary administrative work of the League including the appointment of a "permanent Secretariat and staff." As regards the proposed council, however, he omitted Russia from its membership while including Germany and suggested that the usual rule of unanimity be replaced by a heavily weighted majority vote.

[5] E. M. House, *The Intimate Papers of Colonel House,* edited by Charles Seymour (Boston: Houghton Mifflin, 1928), Vol. 4, p. 2.

[6] The House draft is included in D. H. Miller, *The Drafting of the Covenant* (New York: Putnam, 1928), Vol. 2, Doc. 2.

[7] For details on the Foreign Office Memorandum and the Smuts Plan, see Zimmern, *op. cit.,* Chaps. VII and VIII.

[8] Miller, *op. cit.,* Vol. 2, Doc. 5.

At Paris, President Wilson studied the Smuts and official British (Cecil) drafts. His second draft of January 1919 included the Smuts proposal of an "Executive Council." [9] The membership of the Council now became a point at issue between Wilson and the British. The Cecil draft had proposed that France, Great Britain, Italy, Japan and the United States constitute the Council. The British argued that membership in the Council should be limited to the great powers on the basis of the experience of the Concert of Europe in which the major states had responsibility commensurate with their power. The smaller states, the British argued, could speak in the Assembly.

President Wilson finally agreed with the British, but the French, annoyed at the Anglo-American opposition to an international police force and other French proposals, supported the small states in their vigorous campaign for Council membership. The result was a compromise in which the Council was to be composed of five permanent members noted in the British draft plus four non-permanent members to be elected by the Assembly.

Functions of the Council

Under the terms of the Covenant there was little differentiation in function between the Council and the Assembly, and the former can scarcely be compared either with the executive arm of the United States Government or with the British cabinet. To a great extent the two bodies had concurrent and complementary powers. Neither had the power to command the other. The Council as "central organ" met more frequently, was a smaller, more manageable body led by the big states and was granted certain special responsibilities in security matters such as the reduction of armaments. Yet in practice, the Assembly played an increasingly important role and in many respects came to be considered the "sovereign power" of the League.

Many factors contributed to the relative decline of the Council. The smaller powers generally sought to limit big-power hegemony. But of greater importance was the fact that the big powers pursued conflicting foreign policies that inevitably stultified the guardianship role of the Council.[10] Moreover, some of the most powerful states were not included in its membership. Finally, the Assembly, as a more representative body than the Council, proved a useful channel for mobilizing widespread support for various programs.

The Settlement of Disputes — Articles 11–15

The most important work of the Council was the settlement of disputes. Here most explicitly was a continuation of the Concert of Europe concept

---

9 The text is in Miller, *op. cit.*, Vol. 2, Doc. 7.

10 Arnold Wolfers, *Britain and France Between Two Wars* (New York: Harcourt, Brace, 1940), *passim.*

that international disputes should be settled under the guidance of the great powers. It is true that the Concert in theory now ranged over the whole globe, but in practice the League was concerned chiefly with the squabbles of European states either in Europe itself or overseas.

Article 11 formulated the principle of community interest, or "hue and cry" as Alfred Zimmern has put it, by stating that "any war or threat of war . . . is hereby declared a matter of concern to the whole League. . . ." This provision represented a bold departure from traditional practice by endeavoring to consign neutrality to the junk heap. Paragraph 2 further declared it to be

> the friendly right of each Member of the League to bring to the attention of the Assembly or the Council any circumstance whatever affecting international relations which threatens to disturb international peace or the good understanding between nations upon which peace depends.

This broad grant of authority including both the Assembly and the Council resulted in more disputes coming before the League under Article 11 than under any other article, in spite of the fact that complete unanimity was required in all such matters, since the disputants under Article 11, unlike Article 15, retained the right to vote.

Four points emerge from a consideration of Articles 11–16 dealing with the maintenance of peace. First, the Members of the League were obligated to attempt the peaceful settlement of *all* disputes, and it was assumed that "diplomacy" would take precedence over arbitration in a world of sovereign states. Secondly, the Council rather than the Assembly was expected to play the major role in settling those disputes that were brought to the League. Third, neither arbitration nor judicial settlement was compulsory, although they were presumed for certain types of disputes. Disputing nations could resort to inquiry by the Council in place of arbitration. Finally, after a "cooling off" period, war was legal under certain circumstances.

Thus Article 12 required the League Members to settle their differences by "arbitration" or "judicial settlement or enquiry by the Council," and "in no case to resort to war until three months after the award by the arbitrators or the judicial decision or the report by the Council." Judicial settlement was added as an amendment to Article 12 in September 1924. Here were set forth the traditional methods of peaceful settlement with the Council playing a diplomatic role as conciliator. Recourse to war was limited rather than prohibited, and, as on the domestic frontier, so on the international frontier a state might take the law into its own hands so long as three months had passed after an unpalatable award. As in the Bryan treaties, a "cooling off" period was felt to be an important brake on the use of force.

Article 13 specifies in detail the procedures for arbitral and judicial settlement. So concerned were the framers of the Covenant over the "vital interests" of states that arbitration or judicial settlement was not made compulsory — for even the seemingly innocuous list of items in Paragraph 2 declared to be "generally suitable for submission to arbitration or judicial settlement." Both parties had to agree to submit to the judicial process; there was no sheriff to hail them into Court. No state could get a hearing in the Permanent Court of International Justice against an obnoxious neighbor unless the latter participated voluntarily. Once arbitration or judicial settlement had been agreed upon, however, the parties were obligated to obey the award or decision, and all League Members, in turn, were required to refrain from waging "war against a Member of the League which complies therewith." If a state rejected such an award or decision, the Council was to propose the steps necessary to effect compliance. Obviously there was no assurance that compliance would in fact be obtained collectively, and war by individual League Members against the offending state might be necessary. In this case war was "legal."

Article 15 provided that "inquiry by the Council" was the means of peaceful settlement which the parties were obligated to try in the event they did not seek arbitration or adjudication. The Secretary-General was required to "make all necessary arrangements for a full investigation and consideration" of the dispute (which must be one "likely to lead to a rupture"), and the parties were to present "statements of their case" which the Council was permitted to publish in order to bring into play the sanction of world opinion. The Council's mandate was "to effect a settlement of the dispute," and it was available as an agency of mediation, conciliation or inquiry. It could of its own accord refer the matter to the Assembly and was required to do so if one of the parties so requested within fourteen days of the submission of the disputes to the Council. This was the procedure used by China in 1932 in her disputes with Japan over Manchuria. If the Council were successful in helping the parties settle the dispute, it so reported, including the facts and "the terms of settlement." If the Council failed, it reported "either unanimously or by majority vote . . . the facts of the dispute and the recommendation . . . deemed just and proper in regard thereto." If a Council report received unanimous support, not counting the votes of the parties to the disputes, the Members of the League agreed not to go to "war" with the party to the dispute complying with the recommendations. If, on the other hand, the report did not receive unanimous support (again not counting the votes of the parties), "the Members of the League reserved to themselves the right to take such action as they shall consider necessary for the maintenance of right and justice." In other words, the disputants were permitted to go to war if the Council failed to achieve a unanimous recommendation so long as they had waited three months. This was the famous "gap" of the Covenant.

There were also other gaps in the Covenant that permitted recourse to arms. Not only did there have to be unanimity in approving the Council report, but under Paragraph 2 of Article 12, that body was required to report within six months after the submission of the dispute. Failure to do so presumably permitted the parties to take whatever steps they saw fit.

Paragraph 8, Article 15, also excluded from the jurisdiction of the Council any dispute "found by the Council, to arise out of a matter which by international law is solely within the domestic jurisdiction" of one of the parties. In this case the Council simply reported its findings and could not make a recommendation of settlement. We shall see that bloody conflicts have been permitted or attempted in the name of "domestic jurisdiction" from that day to this, and that this particular gap is far wider under the United Nations Charter. Ironically enough this provision among others was insisted upon by President Wilson in the forlorn hope of winning some Republican support in the Senate for the League of Nations.[11]

Finally, Article 21 suggested to the French at least the possibility of another gap. It provided that nothing in the Covenant affected the validity of "international engagements . . . or regional understandings like the Monroe Doctrine, for securing the maintenance of peace." The reference to the Monroe Doctrine was another attempt to lure the United States Senate into supporting the League. The idea also appealed to the French who were disappointed over their failure to win approval of compulsory arbitration and an international police force, and who feared that the United States was interested in maintaining the *status quo* in the Western Hemisphere alone. As a result, France wanted authority to turn to alliances outside the League system. M. Bourgeois, one of the League's great figures, declared:

> The whole idea of obligation has now disappeared. It will, therefore, be necessary to continue and to conclude separate alliances, inasmuch as the League admits its inability to offer a formal guarantee of protection to its own members.[12]

To summarize, the Covenant did not "outlaw war" in all circumstances. It did, however, try to hobble the use of force by regularizing and developing all the known methods for peaceful settlement. Much weight was attached to the sanction of public opinion through inquiry and recommendations by the Council and "cooling-off" periods to calm hot tempers. In a world of virtual international anarchy, lacking any strong sense of community responsibility or centralized organization of force, the Covenant procedures perhaps were all that could be expected. As long as the Members adhered to the principles of the Covenant, the League was surprisingly effective. With the outbreak of aggression in the 1930's, however, it became obvious that world order required a more cohesive community and government.

Sanctions: Articles 10 and 16

In spite of many limitations, the framers of the Covenant broke new ground in 1919 in a bold effort to organize force to maintain world order.

[11] C. Howard Ellis, *The Origin, Structure, and Working of the League of Nations* (Boston: Houghton Mifflin, 1928), pp. 91–93.

[12] Felix Morley, *The Society of Nations* (Washington: Brookings Institution, 1932), p. 193.

League Members who "resorted to war" contrary to the terms of the Covenant were, under Article 16, to be coerced by sanctions. For the first time in history, collective action against offenders became the duty of every member of the "society of nations." Only economic sanctions, however, were made obligatory. The Council could merely recommend the use of military force, a stipulation that perhaps disappointed the French more than anything else in the Covenant. Ever fearful of renewed German attacks, France and other Members soon sought security arrangements outside the League system.

Paragraph 1 of Article 16 provided that any Member of the League resorting to war "in disregard of its covenants under Articles 12, 13 or 15 . . . shall *ipso facto* be deemed to have committed an act of war against all other Members of the League." The latter were at once obligated to apply nonmilitary sanctions by cutting off all trade or financial relations with the offending state including "all intercourse between their nationals and the nationals of the Covenant-breaking state." In applying financial and economic sanctions, the Members agreed to support one another; rights of passage were to be granted the forces of a Member acting in support of the Covenant. Since war was not prohibited completely, the question then arose as to when a League Member should be deemed to have committed an illegal "act of war?" An authority on the League has listed four cases when war was considered illegal under the Covenant:

1. war undertaken without recourse to arbitration, judicial settlement or inquiry by the Council (Article 12, par. 1);

2. war undertaken without waiting until three months after the award or Council recommendation (Article 12, par. 2);

3. war undertaken against a state which accepted the award or judicial decision (Article 13, par. 4) or unanimous recommendation of the Council (Article 15, par. 6); and

4. war undertaken by a non-Member who had accepted the obligations of the League under Article 17.[13]

In contrast to the requirement that nonmilitary sanctions be automatic, Paragraph 2 of Article 16 specified only that it was the "duty of the Council . . . to recommend to the several governments concerned" what armed forces each should "severally contribute to the armed forces to be used to protect the covenants of the League." This provision, calling for national contingents on an *ad hoc* basis was a far cry from the "international police force" sought by the French. Economic sanctions were applied against Italy in the Ethiopian affair, but military sanctions were never applied under the League Covenant. The fire brigade never could make up its mind to use such an extreme method.

A further weakness developed when the League Members soon diluted even the provision for economic sanctions. Who was to decide when a

---

[13] Clyde Eagleton, *International Government,* 2nd ed. (New York: Ronald Press, 1948), p. 416.

Robinson, in the London Morning Post

"L'ENFANT TERRIBLE"

Member had gone to war in disregard of the Covenant? Who was to apply sanctions? Scarcely had the League scaffolding been erected when the Second Assembly, on the advice of a Blockade Committee established to deal with these problems, adopted resolutions which interpreted the Covenant to mean that the League itself could not make economic sanctions obligatory by declaring the existence of a war. "Such a power would not be consistent with the sovereign rights of the various states." [14] In short, the automatic features of Article 16 were largely destroyed since it became the privilege of each Member to decide for itself when it was obligated to apply nonmilitary sanctions. The use of sanctions was wrecked on the rocks of state sovereignty although nonmilitary sanctions of a feeble sort were applied against Italy in 1935.

The League's enforcement machinery under Article 16 cannot properly be considered without reference to Articles 10 and 19. Under the former "The Members of the League [undertook] to respect and preserve as against external aggression the territorial integrity and existing political independence of all Members of the League." The latter attempted to make possible the revision of troublesome treaties in order to bring some means of "peaceful change" to the world community. Article 10 in the minds of Wilson and the French was the "key to the whole Covenant," although in practice its strength was soon to be diluted along with that of Article 16. These provisions made the Covenant primarily a device to freeze the *status quo* which had been dictated by the victors in World War I. Article 19 proved a weak reed so far as treaty revision was concerned. More will be said in Chapter 14 about the *status quo* and peaceful change.

[14] *Records of the Second Assembly*, p. 385.

The Council's responsibilities under Article 10 are stated in the second paragraph: "In case of any such aggression or in case of any threat or danger of such aggression, the Council shall advise upon the means by which this obligation shall be fulfilled." This provision was obviously vague and left room for equivocation. Specifically, the enforcement provision of Article 16 did not state how the Council was to "advise" on the fulfillment of the obligations of Article 10, although the French long insisted on a liberal interpretation of both articles in opposition to the British Dominions and those smaller European states who had succeeded in remaining neutral during the world war. In the words of one of the wisest commentators on the League,

> Thus the "key to the whole Covenant," so far from unlocking the riddle, became itself a cause of confusion, conveying one meaning to the French-speaking and another to the English-speaking Members of the League.[15]

We have already noted that the Second Assembly weakened the sanction provisions of Article 16. Subsequently Article 10 was similarly emasculated for all practical purposes, along with Article 16, when Persia alone opposed the adoption of a resolution submitted by Canada at the Fourth Assembly in 1923 that

> It is for the Constitutional authorities of each Member to decide, in reference to the obligations of preserving the independence and the integrity of Members, in what degree the Member is bound to assume the execution of this obligation by employment of its military forces.[16]

It became increasingly evident, therefore, that the Members of the League were far from ready to yield to the League any significant amount of their freedom of action. Incidents of this kind demonstrated in a most convincing fashion that the organization was in no way a government in the usual sense of the term. Even as a standing diplomatic conference it failed to uphold its fundamental principle of collective security. Indeed, collective security was abandoned for all practical purposes before it had been tried.

Particularly ironic was the fact that the progressive undermining of the League's authority was undertaken largely in an abortive effort to persuade the United States that it was safe to join. Equally ironic were Wilson's contrary efforts to convince the Senate of the necessity for the guar-

---

[15] Zimmern, *op. cit.*, p. 242.

[16] The Persian delegate noted that his country was surrounded by states not Members of the League such as Turkey and Russia. He unsuccessfully sought a delay of the vote in order that he might seek new instructions from Teheran. The resolution received 29 affirmative votes, 1 negative vote with 22 Members "abstaining" or "absent." The President declared the resolution as "not adopted" rather than "rejected" because the Assembly did not "pronounce in favor of the converse declaration." M. Motta of Switzerland in his capacity as rapporteur noted that "even if it were not legally valid the resolution would still be of great moral value." *Records of the Fourth Assembly, Plenary Session*, p. 86.

antees and sanctions of Articles 10 and 16 respectively as key parts of the structure since these articles came to represent little more than moral platitudes.

Supervision of Special Areas and Groups

Although the handling of international quarrels was the Council's principal concern, it had many other tasks. From Article 4 and Article 11(2) the Council derived embryonic legislative authority in economic and social matters and directed the work of the League's technical bodies discussed in Chapters 7, 17 and 20. The Council also exercised certain supervisory authority over mandated territories, other areas placed under League protection and various minority groups — all of which are discussed in Chapters 10 and 22.

Internal Administration

A number of "housekeeping" functions fell to the lot of the Council, including supervision of the personnel, organization and work of the Secretariat. Staff appointments carrying salaries of 8,000 francs or over required Council approval. With the Assembly it shared responsibility under Article 6 for the appointment of the Secretary-General and, under the Court's Statute, for the election of judges to the Permanent Court of International Justice.

It had responsibility for the care and construction of the buildings of the League and authority to determine the location of the League.

With the Assembly, the Council under Article 26 shared constituent power in amending the Covenant.

It alone determined the conditions under which states not Members of the League, but parties to a dispute, might accept the "obligations of Membership in the League for the purposes of such dispute" (Article 17), and it alone had authority to expel a Member from the League — a grant of authority under Article 16 exercised only in the case of the Soviet Union during the Finnish War of 1939. Unlike the United Nations Security Council, however, the League Council had no responsibility whatsoever in admitting states to League Membership.

Organization of the Council

Membership

Although Article 4 specified that the Council was to "consist of Representatives of the Principal Allied and Associated Powers, together with Representatives of four other Members of the League," the great powers in fact never had a numerical majority. One of them, the United States, rejected the League at once, and the Assembly in 1922 increased the number of non-permanent seats to six, in 1926 to nine, and in 1936 to eleven. One of the less edifying aspects of the League was the constant bickering over the choice of non-permanent seats resulting in jealous intrigue and maneuvering. The problem came to a head in 1926 and delayed the admission of Germany to the League for several months. When Poland, Spain and Brazil, as well as Germany, advanced claims for permanent seats, the matter was resolved by making only Germany a new permanent member. The number of non-permanent members, however, was increased from six to nine as compensation, and the Covenant was amended to give the Assembly the authority to make rules regulating both the term of office and the reëligibility of non-permanent members. As a result, certain states such as Poland and Spain obtained semi-permanent status since they, unlike most non-permanent members, were declared by the Assembly to be eligible for reëlection.

Criteria for the selection of non-permanent members were established by various League Assemblies and included "due consideration for the main geographical divisions of the world, the great ethnical groups, the different religious traditions, the various types of civilizations and the chief sources of wealth." [17] In practice, these principles meant that the various regional blocs of states such as the American states, the "Little Entente" and the Scandinavian states were usually represented on the Council. "Temporary" members were also authorized by Article 4 of the Covenant which specified that any Member of the League be invited to sit "as a member of the Council" at any meeting in which "matters specially affecting the interests of that Member" were being discussed.

Voting

The Council's voting procedures, specified in Article 5 of the Covenant, provided that decisions "on questions of substance" in both the Council and the Assembly" required "the agreement of all the Members of the League represented at the meeting." This article's second paragraph, however, authorized a majority vote on "all matters of procedure," including the "appointment of Committees to investigate particular matters." Each Member of the League represented on the Council had one vote and one representative.

The rule of unanimity was inherited from the conference procedure of the Western state system which enshrined the fundamental principle of the juridical equality of states no matter how unequal they might be in fact.

Speaking in a plenary session of the Peace Conference, Lord Cecil sought to assure the participating delegates that no superstate was in the making:

> We have laid down, and this is the great principle in all action, whether of the Executive Council or the Body of Delegates, except in very special cases . . . , all action must be unanimously agreed to in accordance with the general rule that governs international relations. That that will, to some extent

[17] D. P. Myers, *Handbook of the League of Nations* (Boston: World Peace Foundation, 1930), pp. 30–33.

. . . militate against the rapidity of action of all organs of the League is undoubted, but in my judgment, that defect is far more than compensated for
by the confidence that it will inspire that no nation whether small or great,
need fear aggression from the organs of the League.[18]

In fact, the rule of unanimity troubled the League Council surprisingly
little. Although action in the League Council was sometimes delayed or
obstructed by threatened use of the veto, unanimity was achieved with
gratifying frequency.[19] On three occasions, however, a single negative
vote prevented the Council from requesting an Advisory Opinion of the
Permanent Court on legal questions. Brazil, moreover, threatened to veto
Spain's bid for League membership in 1921 and delayed Germany's en-
trance in 1926.

The rule of unanimity was mitigated in practice primarily by finding
ways of making decisions by less than unanimous votes. Abstention, for example, was not equivalent to a veto since those members not voting were
counted as "absent." Indeed the Soviet Union was expelled from the
League in 1939 by a "unanimous" vote of seven out of fourteen members
including both abstentions and cases of actual absence. The interpretation
of "procedural questions" moreover was sufficiently broad to include the
initiation of such important functions as investigations. Also under Article
15 a disputant could not vote in its own case, although it could do so if the
dispute came before the Council under Article 11, a distinction that assumed importance in the Manchurian affair to be considered later. The
Covenant, in addition, called specifically for majority decisions in the
Council under the terms of Articles 5 and 15. Finally, the Versailles Peace
Treaties required majority decisions by the Council in certain matters.

Meetings, Officers and Subsidiary Bodies

The Council under Article 4 was required to meet "from time to time as
occasion may require and at least once a year at the Seat of the League, or
at such other place as may be decided upon." In practice it met much
more often — four times a year until 1929 and three times a year after that.
Article 11 provided that the Secretary-General must summon the Council
upon the request of any Member of the League in an emergency situation.
While most meetings were held in Geneva, the Council also met in Paris,
London, Brussels, San Sebastian, Madrid and Lugano. The President of
the Council was chosen at each session in alphabetical rotation according
to the French names of the countries represented. His role was often
crucial for the effectiveness of the Council. So diligent was M. Briand, for
example, in the pursuit of his duties in the Greco-Bulgarian dispute of
1925 and the Bolivia-Paraguay flare-up of 1928 that he was given the chair
out of turn when Japanese troops occupied Mukden in 1931.

To assist the Council in its duties, extensive use was made of *rapporteurs*,

[18] *Ibid.*, Vol. 2, p. 566.
[19] See C. A. Riches, *The Unanimity Rule and the League of Nations* (Baltimore:
Johns Hopkins Press, 1933), pp. 134–135.

who were representatives of Council members designated to assume special responsibility for particular subjects falling under the Council's jurisdiction. Lists of subjects were drawn up including the names of the states responsible for supplying the *rapporteurs*. In many instances the details of the *rapporteur's* work were attended to by the Secretariat, but the division of work depended on the competence of the individual *rapporteur* and the time he was able to devote to the task. In this way the Council shared with the Secretariat what little executive authority it had.

The procedures of the Council, in contrast to those of the Assembly, were somewhat informal. Its members sat around a curved table, the "great green horseshoe," under the gaze of the general public. Meetings were secret only in cases involving individuals or particularly delicate questions. The presence of such distinguished figures as M. Briand or Sir Austen Chamberlain, was, of course, a drawing card. The permanent members were often represented by their Foreign Ministers, but the non-permanent members were apt to be representd by diplomats of lower rank and authority. The "provisional agenda" was drawn up by the Secretary-General in consultation with the Council President and included all items requested by any League Member. Additional items were included by majority vote of the Council. While many matters were handled by the *rapporteurs,* the more important questions, including the consideration of disputes under Articles 11 or 15, were usually referred to special committees of inquiry set up by the Council to supplement the work of the *rapporteurs.* The reports and draft resolutions presented by the *rapporteurs* and the committees of inquiry normally formed the basis for the final action of the Council.[20]

On many occasions the decisions of the Council were reached after off-stage deliberations by key delegates, generally those representing the permanent members. At such times there seemed to be two bodies, the Council and an inner circle of the great powers. Formal voting was reduced to a minimum since the President in most instances simply asked the members for comment on the draft proposals. If no debate was forthcoming, the resolution was declared adopted without further comment. At all times the Secretary-General of the League sat beside the President ready to advise but without the right to vote.

Under the terms of Article 9, the Council had what proved to be the dubious benefit of one standing subsidiary body, the Permanent Advisory Commission on Armaments. It was largely superseded by the Temporary Mixed Commission established by the League Assembly.

The Council, in addition, established special minorities committees on an *ad hoc* basis to handle the minority petitions forwarded from the Minorities Section of the Secretariat.[21] Finally, of course, the Council supervised a wide range of economic, social and cultural bodies.

20 Thomas P. Conwell-Evans, *The League Council in Action* (London: Oxford University Press, 1929), Part III, Chap. 2.
21 For the Minorities problem, see Chap. 10.

The procedures of the Council were set forth both in its Rules of Procedure and in the Covenant. They were, generally speaking, admirably developed and permitted the Council to meet almost as soon as an emergency was reported to it, a great improvement over the Concert of Europe.

Later Efforts to Tighten the Covenant

The gaps and omissions that have been mentioned left the League a rather feeble policeman in the eyes of some of its Members — particularly France. The skepticism with which the League collective security system was viewed became particularly evident when steps toward disarmament were attempted as early as 1922. One problem was that in addition to constitutional deficiencies three major powers were not Members of the League at that time — Germany, the Soviet Union and the United States. Also contributory to a sense of insecurity and mutual hostility was the economic and financial chaos following in the wake of war. As we shall see in Chapter 16, no one had sufficient confidence in the League system to be willing to turn in his guns. Thus the Assembly in 1922 resolved not only that reduction of armaments could not "be fully successfull unless it is general," but that governments could not undertake "a serious reduction of armaments unless they received in exchange a satisfactory guarantee of the safety of their country." Such a guarantee might be forthcoming if all states formed "a defensive agreement . . . binding them to provide immediate and effective assistance in accordance with a pre-arranged plan in the event of one of them being attacked, provided that the obligation to render assistance to a country attacked shall be limited in principle to those countries situated in the same part of the globe." Thus everyone was to turn in weapons with the assurance that all the nearby neighbors would rally to apprehend any lawbreaker. With this bit of horse sense on the record the Members turned their attention to strengthening the fabric of the Covenant.

The Draft Treaty of Mutual Assistance, 1923

With Lord Cecil again at the helm, the Temporary Mixed Commission was founded in 1921 to consider disarmament in broader perspective than the purely military point of view of the permanent Advisory Commission. By 1923 the Mixed Commission submitted a Draft Treaty of Mutual Assistance. Its main points were that — "aggressive war was to be an international crime"; that the Council itself was to make the finding of an act of aggression within four days of the outbreak of hostilities; and that special defense arrangements would operate automatically on such a finding. The treaty combined Lord Cecil's views in favor of a general treaty of assistance with the French preoccupation with regional alliances. Thus, while the treaty "maintained the principle of general assistance," it also embodied the concept of regional security by permitting supplementary defensive arrangements so that military assistance was to be provided by states on the same continent. No definition of "aggression" was included for the obvious reason that no satisfactory one could be found by the Permanent Advisory Commission or by a committee of jurists. Thus the Council was to decide in each case whether or not aggression had occurred, as was to be the procedure under the United Nations Charter twenty-two years later. Doubtless this feature had much to do with the failure of the Members to adopt the treaty, since states were reluctant to be committed to sanctions by action of the Council alone. The treaty, in addition, raised other issues. While it received warm support from France, it got a mixed reception from France's allies as not giving them sufficient protection. In Britain, a change in government during its consideration had much to do with its rejection. The new Labor Government of Ramsay MacDonald disliked France's special treaties that were to be superimposed on the League system as too reminiscent of the prewar alliances.[22] Then as now, moreover, a fundamental question facing the "tight little isle" was whether to cast her lot with the Continent or the Commonwealth. Choosing not to complicate the management of the latter, Britain and the Dominions finally rejected the treaty, and the scheme was abandoned.

The Geneva Protocol

Perhaps the most ambitious project to close the gaps of the Covenant was the Protocol for the Pacific Settlement of Disputes endorsed by the Assembly in 1925 but never implemented by the League Members. Progress toward the reinforcement of the League seemed possible through a combination of events in 1924 that improved the political climate of Europe for a time. The governments of both Britain and France were headed by liberal leaders, MacDonald and Herriot, who were sympathetic to the League, and the Dawes reparations plan had eased the postwar financial tensions.

Many individuals had a hand in designing the Protocol. While its drafting was principally the work of Dr. Eduard Beneš, then Foreign Minister of Czechoslovakia, and M. Politis, delegate of Greece and an authority on international law, its main features owed much to other sources. An American study group headed by Professor J. T. Shotwell and a Scandinavian group, for example, had each developed the idea of utilizing the willingness to arbitrate as a test of aggression.[23]

The principal feature of the proposal was to consider a state's refusal to accept arbitration as conclusive evidence of aggression. Every signatory state was to accept the compulsory jurisdiction of the Permanent Court of International Justice over all disputes in the "optional clause" (Article 36

[22] Zimmern, op. cit., pp. 341–342; C. K. Webster and Sydney Herbert, The League of Nations in Theory and Practice (London: Allen and Unwin, 1933), p. 151.

[23] All the standard works on the League include analyses of the Protocol. For detailed information, the student should consult P. J. Noel-Baker, The Geneva Protocol (London: King, 1925); and for the legal viewpoint, D. H. Miller, The Geneva Protocol (New York: Macmillan, 1925).

of the Court Statute). The procedures of pacific settlement in Article 15 of the Covenant were supplemented with a provision that freedom of action was no longer permitted to the parties to a dispute if the Council were unable to reach a unanimous decision. In such a contingency the Council was obligated to attempt to persuade the parties to resort to arbitration or judicial settlement. If unsuccessful in this effort, the Council was obligated to select a committee of arbitrators whose decision would be binding. In this fashion the most important gap of the Covenant was to be closed.

The Protocol also sought to lessen disputes regarding questions claimed to be matters of "domestic jurisdiction" by requiring advice from the Court on such points. The Protocol recognized, however, that many matters legally under domestic jurisdiction can disturb international peace. Therefore the Council and Assembly were specifically permitted to consider such matters under the Authority of Article 11 of the Covenant, which, as we have seen, simply permitted these bodies to attempt mediation to avert war. Each Member of the League was obligated to apply sanctions under Article 16 in the event of aggression "in the degree which its geographical position and its particular situation as regards armaments allow."

As will be noted below, the Protocol was expected to be effective only on the successful conclusion of a plan of disarmament. Actually it was rejected long before a disarmament conference convened, largely owing once more to the reluctance of the British Commonwealth to become involved in collective sanctions and European quarrels. But the absence of the United States from the League was also crucial since Britain was fearful of committing her Navy in the application of sanctions while her powerful neighbor across the water insisted on "freedom of the seas" and neutrality, euphemistic terms for isolationism.

The League in general and the Geneva Protocol in particular have been criticized as perpetuating the *status quo* of the Peace Treaties.[24] The argument is that changes through "war" should not have been prohibited in the Protocol without developing more fully the process of "peaceful change." Legally speaking, however, the Protocol did not preclude changes in the *status quo* through agreement. "All that the Covenant or the Protocol of Geneva attempts to do about the *status quo* is to say that frontiers shall not be changed *as a result of aggression*." [25] Practically, however, we know that changes in the state of things are really impossible without a recognized legislative authority assisted by an executive agency able to implement its decisions. The problem of peace cannot be solved before the problem of peaceful change. The absence of sure and acceptable means of effecting changes in response to shifting circumstances is perhaps the most significant feature distinguishing the international community from most national communities. Burke, in his *Reflections on the*

[24] E. H. Carr, *International Relations Since the Peace Treaties* (New York: Macmillan, 1938), p. 91.
[25] Miller, *The Geneva Protocol*, p. 35.

Revolution in France, noted: "A State without the means of some change is without the means of its own conservation." [26]

The Locarno Treaties

In spite of the failure of the Geneva Protocol, European statesmen did not abandon their efforts to tighten the bolts of the world's security machinery. The next effort, it was logically felt, might be to apply the general principles of the Protocol on a regional basis rather than a universal basis, and the most critical area for world peace was held to be the boundary between France and Germany. Fortunately three statesmen of great capacity and genuine good will, Sir Austen Chamberlain, Aristide Briand and Gustav Stresemann, the Foreign Ministers of Britain, France and Germany, were the principal guides of Europe's destiny for the years 1925–29.[27] These years were to be the high-water mark of the League.

In rejecting the Geneva Protocol, Chamberlain had suggested to the League Council the possibility of regional security pacts by noting that the Covenant might be supplemented by special arrangements in order to meet special needs. This was the signal for Germany to repeat efforts rejected by France in 1922, to guarantee the Franco-German border and to enter a mutual pledge not to resort to war. The negotiations and all the provisions of the seven Locarno Treaties cannot be considered here in any detail. Suffice it to say that the provisions agreed upon received the approval of the Sixth Assembly of the League, incorporated to a great extent the principles of the Geneva Protocol, and made possible the entry of Germany into the League of Nations with the understanding that she would undertake League obligations to the extent that her "particular situation as regards armaments and . . . geographical position allow," a phrase salvaged directly from the abandoned Protocol.[28] The Locarno Treaties included a mutual guarantee of the Franco-Belgo-German frontiers by those three powers plus Great Britain and Italy. Both Germany and France were thus assured support in the event of aggression by the other if the Council were convinced there had been a breach of the peace. Significantly, there was no such guarantee of the *status quo* on Germany's Eastern frontier, although Germany signed arbitration treaties with Poland and Czechoslovakia. Britain was this time able to undertake a regional commitment because her Dominions were excepted unless they specifically chose to be committed. Germany, France and Belgium mutually agreed not to resort to war against each other except in "self-defence," or in support of League sanctions under Article 16 or in action "reserved" to themselves under paragraph 7 of Article 15. They were obligated to settle differences by any of the various means of pacific settlement which were more fully developed in the Treaties than under the Covenant including arbitration,

[26] Everyman Edition, p. 19.

[27] For the negotiations leading to Locarno, see C. J. Friedrich, *Foreign Policy in the Making* (New York: Norton, 1938), Chap. 7.

[28] League of Nations, *Ten Years of World Cooperation* (Geneva: League Secretariat, 1930), p. 79.

judicial procedures under the Court, conciliation by a Permanent Commission or inquiry by the Council under Article 15. The stop-gap character of the treaties was noted by the hopeful provision that they should remain in force only until the Council by two-thirds vote could certify that the League could do the job.

The Locarno system may be summarized for our purposes by saying that it sought to apply and develop further the principles of the Covenant and the Protocol on a limited (regional) basis, and that it knit together, in a single system of peace, states that had formerly been enemies in war.

The General Act of 1928

The League's final effort to improve its security system apart from disarmament was the Assembly's adoption in 1928 of the "General Act for the Pacific Settlement of International Disputes." Opinion on the best means of continuing the pursuit of peace had been divided. Some Members favored an emphasis on disarmament, while others looked primarily to arbitration. The Eighth Assembly (1927) adopted some important resolutions as a guide for action. Arbitration should be utilized "so as to extend to all countries the mutual confidence essential to the complete success of the Conference on the Limitation and Reduction of Armaments." The Council was requested to establish, in addition to the already existent Preparatory Commission on Disarmament, a Committee on Arbitration and Security to "study the principles of disarmament, security and arbitration." At last the issue of war was met head on. It was resolved that "All wars of aggression are and always shall be prohibited" and that "every pacific means must be employed to settle disputes of every description which arise between states." [29]

These steps resulted in the presentation to the Ninth Assembly (1928) of three model conventions. The first provided exclusively for conciliation procedure; the second, in addition to conciliation, provided for the compulsory jurisdiction of the Court over questions regarding the rights of states unless the parties chose arbitration; and the final convention called for the submission of all disputes to arbitration or judicial settlement by the Permanent Court. These conventions were packaged by the Assembly into one "General Act" of three separate chapters plus a fourth that combined the features of the previous three. Any state was enabled to accede to all or part of these instruments, and, in addition, the Assembly adopted three model bilateral treaties for states preferring these to multilateral undertakings. The Assembly then invited "all States, whether Members of the League . . . or not . . . to become parties to the General Act, or to conclude bilateral conventions."

The General Act came into force almost at once, but the gap was not entirely closed; by 1938 only twenty-two states had completed ratification. States now had a variety of ways in which to seek peace. Since aggression had been declared illegal by the 1927 Assembly and disputes were to be

[29] *Ibid.*, p. 85.

settled by peaceful means of some sort, the burden of armaments, it was hoped, could at last be mitigated. The failure of this effort is described in Chapter 16.

The Pact of Paris

Mention must be made of one other landmark on the tortuous trail to collective security that was not strictly the business of the League Council but gave promise of reinforcing that body's authority. After the Eighth Assembly had taken the unprecedented step in September 1927 of prohibiting "all wars *of aggression*," efforts were made to outlaw *all* wars. Interestingly enough, the approach to peace by the "outlawry" of war, rather than by the organization of force under the aegis of the Covenant, was very largely an American idea that, for a time, became widely popular. The notion was acceptable because states were more prepared to renounce war as an instrument of national policy than they were to assume the positive responsibilities of a sheriff to maintain law and order. We have seen that many states, the Commonwealth countries and the United States in particular, were "gun shy" at the thought of committing their forces in advance in behalf of a system of collective sanctions. The renunciation of war seemed the easiest way to satisfy moral scruples.

A proposal that the United States and France subscribe to a "mutual engagement tending to outlaw war" was advanced by M. Briand in a newspaper statement on April 6, 1927, the tenth anniversary of America's entry into World War I. A draft treaty soon followed for United States consideration. Six months, however, passed by before the United States was forced by public opinion to act favorably.[30] Secretary of State Kellogg then countered with the suggestion of a general pact "renouncing war as an instrument of national policy." Complicated negotiations resulted in the historic signing of a General Treaty for the Renunciation of War in Paris at the Quai d'Orsay on August 27, 1928, by the representatives of fifteen states. By 1933 sixty-five states adhered to the "Pact of Paris" (or the Kellogg-Briand Pact as it is sometimes called), which became the most nearly universal political agreement ever to come into existence.

The substance of the Pact is stated in two short articles. In the first, "The high contracting parties solemnly declare . . . that they condemn recourse to war for the solution of international controversies, and renounce it as an instrument of national policy in their relations with one another."

In the second, they agreed "that the settlement or solution of all disputes or conflicts of whatever nature or of whatever origin they may be, which may arise among them, shall never be sought except by pacific means."

The signing of the pact marked the peak of a great surge of hope and idealism, and its brief message continues to express the aspirations of man-

---

[30] See *International Conciliation*, No. 243 (October 1928), and D. P. Myers, *The Origin and Conclusion of the Paris Pact* (Boston: World Peace Foundation, 1929).

kind. But war was only "condemned and renounced" rather than out-lawed, and no enforcement machinery was provided to enforce either the prohibition against war or the obligation of pacific settlement. More important, numerous restrictions were contained in the reservations that descended upon the Pact in a flurry of diplomatic notes. Secretary Kellogg insisted that nothing in the treaty restricted or impaired in any way the right of self-defense, a right that included, for the United States, areas covered by the Monroe Doctrine. Great Britain insisted that her right of self-defense extended to "certain regions" of "vital interest" for her safety, (presumably the life line to India), while France reserved the right to act under the security obligations of her numerous European treaties.

Whatever its obvious deficiencies, the Pact has had significant influence. Its place in the law of nations was more recently strengthened by the Nuremberg trials and the United Nations Charter.[31] The Pact as an important declaration of principle would have been more useful, however, if linked to the responsibilities and procedures of the League.

Conclusions

The League Council proved to be less like a concert of great powers than its framers had anticipated. In the first place, its membership never included all the great powers at any one time. Since the League's collective security system, particularly the application of sanctions, depended upon the participation of at least all the major states, this lack proved crucial.

In the second place, the great powers that were represented on the Council failed for the most part to establish confidence or a cooperative spirit in their relations with one another. The story of the interwar period is largely the story of the conflicting foreign policies of the principal powers. Even Britain and France had widely divergent views of the League and often worked at cross purposes.[32] This could only be disastrous for a body such as the Council that depended fundamentally upon big-power teamwork. As the League security system based on arbitration, sanctions and disarmament, grew steadily more shadowy, the League shifted its attention in its second ten years to international economic cooperation.

Yet one must not sell the Council short. Unable to achieve its full capacity as guardian of the peace, it did what it could by taking a liberal rather than a strict view of its mandate under the Covenant. As a consequence, valuable contributions were made in the amelioration of disputes, and a number of potentially ugly situations were resolved under its direction.

We have also seen how nations sought to improve this system up to the

[31] For commentary, see P. C. Jessup, *A Modern Law of Nations* (New York: Macmillan, 1948), pp. 11, 134, 163–166.
[32] Wolfers, *op. cit.*

time of the Paris Pact. One must not think, however, that efforts to ensure peace stopped at this point. Aristide Briand, for example, prepared a plan for European Union in 1929. A European Union Commission was actually established by the Eleventh Assembly and began its work in 1931. Its proposals, however, were limited to economic matters and were premised on continued Franco-German rapprochement. They were doomed by the tensions of world depression and the rise of the National Socialists in Germany. Individuals and private organizations developed further schemes to remake the political map of Europe. All these developments, however, were evidence of the inadequacies of the League and its Council.

Suggestions for Further Reading

Conwell-Evans, Thomas P., *The League Council in Action* (London: Oxford University Press, 1929).

Eagleton, Clyde, *International Government*, 2nd ed. (New York: Ronald Press, 1948).

Friedrich, C. J., *Foreign Policy in the Making* (New York: W. W. Norton & Co., Inc., 1938).

Hankey, Lord Maurice, *Diplomacy by Conference* (New York: G. P. Putnam's Sons, 1946).

House, E. M., *The Intimate Papers of Colonel House*, edited by Charles Seymour, 4 Vols. (Boston: Houghton Mifflin Company, 1926–1928).

Howard-Ellis, C., *The Origin, Structure, and Working of the League of Nations* (Boston: Houghton Mifflin Company, 1928).

League of Nations, *Ten Years of Cooperation* (Geneva: League Secretariat, 1938).

Marburg, Theodore, *Development of the League of Nations Idea*, 2 Vols. (New York: The Macmillan Company, 1932).

Miller, D. H., *The Drafting of the Covenant*, 2 Vols. (New York: G. P. Putnam's Sons, 1928).

Morley, Felix, *The Society of Nations* (Washington: Brookings Institution, 1932).

Myers, D. P., *Handbook of the League of Nations* (Boston: World Peace Foundation, 1920).

Noel-Baker, P. J., *The Geneva Protocol* (London: P. S. King & Son, Ltd., 1925).

Riches, C. A., *The Unanimity Rule and the League of Nations* (Baltimore: The Johns Hopkins Press, 1933).

Salter, J. A., *Allied Shipping Control, An Experiment in International Administration* (New York: Oxford University Press, 1921).

Sharp, Walter R., and Kirk, Grayson L., *Contemporary International Politics* (New York: Rinehart and Company, 1944).

Walters, F. P., *History of the League of Nations*, 2 Vols. (London: Oxford University Press, 1952).

Webster, C. K., and Herbert S., *The League of Nations in Theory and Practice* (London: G. Allen and Unwin, Ltd., 1933).

Wolfers, Arnold, *Britain and France Between Two Wars* (New York: Harcourt, Brace & Company, 1940).

Zimmern, A., *The League of Nations and the Rule of Law* (London: Macmillan and Co., Ltd., 1936).

6

Security Council — Organization of Power

"It was taken as axiomatic at Dumbarton Oaks, and continued to be the view of the Sponsoring Powers at San Francisco, that the cornerstone of world security is the unity of those nations which formed the core of the grand alliance against the Axis. . . . Within the United Nations, the Security Council is the vehicle for continuing and developing this process of consultation [among the great powers]. In this respect, it is without precedent in international relations; it differs from the traditional alliance and is unlike the Council of the League of Nations." — EDWARD R. STETTINIUS [1]

Environment Within Which It Evolved

It is somewhat ironic to recall that the framers of the Charter insisted that big-power "unity" was the "cornerstone" of the United Nations. The experience of the war, however, suggested that the wartime collaboration of the major powers might be continued to a considerable extent and that these same powers should have authority and responsibilities commensurate with their power in a peacetime organization. These two thoughts, we have seen, had also been in the minds of the architects of the League Council, the genesis of which had foreshadowed that of the Security Council in many respects.

Policy Planning During World War II

Britain and the United States exchanged views during the war on council membership, but little was known of Soviet or Chinese thinking until just prior to the opening of the Dumbarton Oaks conversations.[2] While

---

[1] *Report to the President on the Results of the San Francisco Conference,* by the Chairman of the United States Delegation, the Secretary of State, Department of State Publication 2349, Conference Series 71 (Washington: Government Printing Office, 1945), p. 68.

[2] The Soviet proposals were not known until August 14, 1944. *Postwar Foreign Policy Preparation, 1939–1945,* Department of State Publication 3850 (Washington: Government Printing Office, 1950), p. 297.

the Big Three exhibited a common reluctance to grant much of a voice to the small powers in a postwar security organization, the Soviet Union was particularly insistent during the war and after that big-power collaboration was what really mattered. The British seeemed ready to grant a somewhat larger role to lesser powers. Churchill at one time favored a regional system capped by a World Council which was to include principally the United States, Britain and Russia, on whom would rest the "real responsibility for peace." "Certain other powers," including China, he suggested, might be included with the first three. In any event, the World Council was to have "the last word" on any matter that three proposed regional councils were unable to settle. A strong France, he went on to note, must be created "for the prospect of having no strong country between Britain and Russia was not attractive." [3]

The United States, however, seems to have been the most favorably disposed of the Big Three toward the smaller powers. In December 1943 Hull recommended to the President that a postwar international organization should have a "small executive Council" empowered to investigate matters impairing peace and security, to recommend means of settlement and to enforce its decisions taken to repress "acts or threats of aggression." Certain nations should have "indeterminate tenure" on the Council since its composition

> should be determined on the principle that certain nations have exceptional responsibilities for the maintenance of international peace . . . ; the responsibility of other states for the maintenance of security should be reflected by membership of a number of such states elected for limited periods.

Alternatively, however, Hull's memorandum noted "the Executive Council might initially be composed of the United States of America, the United Kingdom, the Union of Soviet Socialist Republics, and China solely.[4]

A draft of April 1944 provided for a total membership of eight, including China, the United Kingdom, the United States and the U.S.S.R., plus four others to be elected by an Assembly.[5] Decisions were to be taken by majority vote with the permanent members concurring on four classes of disputes. Following the acceptance of France in the deliberations of the great powers, American thinking had changed, by July 1944, to increase the Council membership to eleven, consisting of five permanent members including France and six others so that the small powers were to have a majority.[6] While the permanent members were given the right of veto, no decision could be taken by them alone since a majority of seven was required. At Dumbarton Oaks, the discussion centered on the Council's authority rather than on its membership, although Brazil was proposed by

[3] Winston S. Churchill, *The Hinge of Fate* (Boston: Houghton Mifflin, 1950), pp. 802–807, and *Postwar Foreign Policy Preparation* . . . , pp. 112 and 146.

[4] *Postwar Foreign Policy Preparation* . . . , Appendix 33, p. 576.

[5] *Ibid.*, Appendix 35, p. 582, and Hull, *The Memoirs of Cordell Hull* (New York: Macmillan, 1948), Vol. 2, p. 1652.

[6] *Ibid.*, Appendix 38, p. 595 and Hull, *op. cit.*, pp. 1674 and 1691.

the United States as a permanent member, a suggestion opposed by both the British and the Russians.[7]

Clearly it would have been difficult to exclude the smaller powers from the proposed Council. They had, after all, suffered heavily in the war and contributed to its prosecution. Some were represented in certain theater commands such as that of Southeast Asia. More important, they had actually been in a majority on the League Council. Of even greater significance was the fact that the basis for a bipartisan foreign policy in the Presidential elections of 1944 was the agreement between Hull and John Foster Dulles, a Republican spokesman, that the Dumbarton Oaks Proposals would not result in a permanent four power alliance to control the world."[8] Britain, in turn, soon gave considerable weight to the role of smaller powers owing to her associations within the Commonwealth.

Big-Power Collaboration in World War II

Teamwork between the Americans and the British during the war, though difficult at times, was simplicity itself compared with cooperation with the Soviet Union. At no time was there the close meshing of economic and military strategy that marked the partnership of the two Western powers. What coordination of strategy did exist was achieved less by standing machinery than by diplomatic conferences at the highest political level. To some observers, a partnership with the U.S.S.R., therefore, seemed a shaky foundation on which to build an edifice of peace. Ambassador Averell Harriman, for example, cited evidence to his superiors in Washington in 1944–45 that the Soviet Union might play a lone hand in the postwar world by seeking to prevent the consideration by any security organization of matters affecting her interests.[9] Yet this alleged Soviet view differed in degree rather than in kind from that of the United States and other powers. The American postwar planners, for example, concluded early in their deliberations that the United States should not seek an international organization that might limit its freedom of action in any fundamental way. This view was reinforced by the necessity of obtaining the approval of the American Senate. Both nations were preëminently powerful, and both inevitably sought national security primarily through national strength. Their interwar relations also promised difficulties for peacetime cooperation. Yet if they were both joined together in a collective security system, might they not be in a better position to resolve their differences? This clearly was an element in the hope of the postwar planners in the United States, and they had a strong argument in the fact that the League had never included both these powers. More important, the United States and Britain did collaborate sufficiently with the Soviet Union, despite many difficulties, to defeat Germany and Japan.

---

[7] Hull, *op cit.*, p. 1678.

[8] Hull, *op. cit.*, pp. 287–288, and J. F. Dulles, *War or Peace* (New York: Macmillan, 1950), pp. 123–125.

[9] *Postwar Foreign Policy Preparation* . . . , p. 346.

History repeated itself when the big powers alone assumed responsibility for the liquidation of war issues as they had in 1919. At Yalta it was agreed that permanent machinery should be set up for consultation among the three Foreign Secretaries of Britain, the United States and the U.S.S.R., who were expected to meet every three or four months. At Potsdam the group was broadened to include China and France and was designated as the Council of Foreign Ministers to meet "normally" in London and to have a "joint secretariat." Its immediate task was the drawing up of peace treaties.

Dumbarton Oaks

The functions and membership of a security council were soon agreed upon at Dumbarton Oaks. Voting procedure, however, proved a tougher nut to crack and was not finally settled until the San Francisco Conference. While the proposed Council followed the tradition of the League Council, it differed in certain important respects. First, its functions were sharply differentiated from both the Assembly and the Economic and Social Council. Second, the new Security Council was given primary responsibility for the maintenance of international peace and security with authority to determine for the whole membership of the organization the existence of an act of aggression as well as the economic, military or diplomatic sanctions necessary to meet such aggression. It was this feature of the Dumbarton Oaks Proposals which distinguished the proposed organization most sharply from previous associations of states. Here, for the first time, the great body of states agreed on an executive organ with binding authority to deal with violence.

At Yalta, Britain and the United States finally reached a meeting of minds with the U.S.S.R. on the voting procedure of the Council and were ready to face the smaller powers.

San Francisco Conference

At San Francisco, however, the newly achieved agreement of the big powers on Security Council voting was nearly dissolved when it became necessary to explain as precisely as possible to the smaller powers how the Yalta formula was to operate. Fearing that future disagreement among the Big Five would render the Council powerless to act, the smaller states sought to reduce the scope of the big-power veto. For a time Britain and the United States disagreed with the U.S.S.R. on the application of the Yalta plan. The smaller powers' efforts ceased when it became clear that no veto meant no organization. In later years, as the wartime alliance gave way to "cold war," the United States, Britain and France were to endorse some of the proposals on Security Council voting that had been advanced by the smaller powers at San Francisco. One important change was made. The "inherent right of individual or collective self-defense" was included as the famous Article 51. At Dumbarton Oaks this had been assumed to be an inherent right of states that needed no spelling out.

Senator Vandenberg and representatives of the inter-American system were anxious to make the rule explicit at San Francisco.

Functions of the Security Council

The Security Council, in distinction to the General Assembly, was intended to be world sheriff. In this respect it follows the tradition of the Concert of Europe which had policed the European community of nations. This proposition emerged unscathed at San Francisco in Article 24 of the Charter, which specifies that the Members of the organization agree that the Council is to act in "their behalf" in taking "prompt and effective action for the maintenance of international peace and security."

The Security Council, in sum, is both a more specialized body than the General Assembly and has stronger authority in the performance of its particular tasks. Unlike the League Council, it is excluded from economic and social matters except as these may be involved in the application of sanctions. Under Chapter VII of the Charter it has authority to coerce UN Members (the permanent members excepted) to cooperate in maintaining the peace. No longer do states, other than the permanent members of the Security Council, decide individually, as was the practice in the League, whether conditions require them to apply sanctions. On paper the Security Council, in terms of the authority potentially at its command, is the closest approximation in modern times to the "police power" of a national government. Practically speaking, of course, actualities have fallen far short of the potentialities suggested in the Charter.

Quasi-legislative Functions

In view of the Council's specialized role as keeper of the peace, it would be natural to expect that in comparison with the League Council it would have little legislative authority. This is precisely the case. Only in Article 26 does the Security Council share in something like a legislative function. With the assistance of the Military Staff Committee it is "responsible for formulating plans . . . to be submitted to the Membership of the United Nations for the establishment of a system for the regulation of armaments." On this matter the Security Council has a responsibility similar to that of the League Council and assists the General Assembly in this phase of the latter's legislative activity.[10]

Settlement of Disputes

The "pacific settlement of disputes" is the subject of Chapter VI of the Charter. Responsibility in this matter rests on the Security Council, the General Assembly and the signatories of the Charter themselves. For the latter, Article 33 provides that

[10] The problem of armaments and world peace is discussed in Chap. 16.

The parties to any dispute, the continuance of which is likely to endanger the maintenance of international peace and security, shall, first of all, seek a solution by negotiation, enquiry, mediation, conciliation, arbitration, judicial settlement, resort to regional agencies or arrangements, or other peaceful means of their own choice.

There is little new here. The Members of the United Nations are obligated first of all to seek the settlement of dangerous disputes by the traditional means of peaceful settlement before bothering the Security Council. Actually the Members do not always first exhaust the enumerated means of settling their disputes peacefully. The temptation to utilize the Security Council as a propaganda forum has been all too strong.

Although the parties must exhaust all possible means of resolving their disputes, the Council under Article 36 "may, at any stage of a dispute of the nature referred to in Article 33 or of a situation of like nature, recommend appropriate procedures or methods of adjustment." In so doing, however, it must take into account procedures "already adopted by the parties." Under Article 37 both the parties and the Council have further obligations. If the parties fail to settle a dispute themselves, they *must* "refer it to the Security Council." This obligation applies only to a dispute "likely to endanger international peace and security." Whether the dispute is in fact so dangerous and whether the means of settlement have failed is determined by the Council. In the case of the Berlin blockade, the United States, Britain and France argued that peaceful settlement with the Soviet Union was impossible in the situation which, in this view, constituted a "threat to international peace and security." The Council then voted to place the problem on its agenda, despite Soviet protest, in order to answer this question. When the Council decides that the continuance of a dispute is likely to endanger peace, it is obligated under Article 37 either to recommend further "procedures or methods" (Article 36) or to recommend "such terms of settlement as it may consider appropriate."

Article 38 allows the Security Council, "if all the parties to any dispute so request," to "make recommendations . . . with a view to a pacific settlement of the dispute." Such a dispute need not be of so serious a character as to endanger international peace and security.

The Council's initiative in settling disputes is set forth in Article 34. It "may investigate any disputes, or any situation which might lead to international friction or give rise to a dispute, in order to determine whether the continuance of the dispute or situation is likely to endanger the maintenance of international peace and security." The decision to "investigate" under this article is, of course, "non-procedural" and requires the support, active or passive, of the permanent members unless they are parties to a dispute. The bare bones of the Charter, however, are misleading. Many a dispute or situation has been thoroughly aired if not formally investigated before any formal decision to assume jurisdiction under this article has been taken or, as is more likely, vetoed. Such an important case as that of the Iranian complaint against the Soviet Union, for example,

1. Suggest methods of reconciliation

2. Offer specific solutions

3. Order provisional truce

4. Invoke nonmilitary sanctions

5. Invoke military sanctions

Headline Series, *Foreign Policy Association*

was never formally investigated. The procedural step of including complaints on the Council's agenda has in many instances brought out the facts and, though it is hard to prove, led to a settlement of sorts. Example of the establishment of commissions of investigation under Article 34 may be found in the Greek case and in the dispute between India and Pakistan.

The veto has sometimes been avoided when the Council by-passed Article 34 in favor of establishing mere sub-committees to ascertain the facts as in the Spanish and Corfu cases. In these instances the Soviet Union abstained, but in the Czech case the Soviet Union vetoed a similar procedure, contending that a formal investigation was involved. Certain other members of the Council have argued that there is a distinction between the work of a subcommittee that is established to gather all possible data on a matter and investigation under Article 34 to determine whether a situation or dispute allegedly endangering peaceful relations is in fact "likely to endanger the maintenance of international peace and security." The first step is procedural under Article 29, it is contended, and is necessary before the Security Council can investigate all the evidence to decide the second question under Article 34. Certainly the work of the Charter would appear to be facilitated by this view. Yet it is hard to draw a distinction between the two steps. The U.S.S.R. has maintained that the establishment of a subcommittee to gather evidence is a non-procedural matter, but, be it noted, it has used the veto in this connection only when its "vital interests" seem to be at stake as in the Czech case.

The fact is that the Council has taken a broad view of its responsibilities and relied upon the general provisions and implied powers of the Charter in performing its task. The Council is most obviously a political body. What it will and will not do depends not so much on legal hair-splitting as upon the political relations among its permanent members. Indeed, attempts to analyze the behavior of the Council in legal terms bear a certain air of unreality. Chapter VI, for example, seems to state very clearly that the Council may recommend procedures or methods of adjustment (Article 36) or terms of settlement (Article 37) only if it has decided by investigation under Article 34 that a dispute or situation is likely to endanger peace and security. In the Corfu case, however, the Council recommended reference of the case to the International Court of Justice without any finding under Article 34. One delegate had a pang of legal conscience and indicated that he thought the action was taken under Article 36. The point is obvious. Some permanent member is almost certain, for political reasons, to prevent the Council from going on record as finding a situation or dispute dangerous to the peace. Even small-power disputes, it should be remembered, are apt to involve big powers. Flexibility in Council procedures has lessened the likelihood of the veto's being exercised.

Legal technicalities, however, are tools which may be used for political ends. Article 34, for example, draws an important distinction between "situations" and "disputes." Either may be found by the Council to endanger international peace. Most matters brought to the Council have involved specifically defined disputes between two or more parties who have established claims and counter claims. But the Charter recognizes that peace may be endangered by a situation as well as by a clearly defined dispute. The character of the Franco government in Spain was held by the Polish government to be such a situation. The Council itself did not reach the same conclusion, but decided to investigate in order to find out. Many of the framers of the Charter felt during the war that peace had been shattered by situations that were not always clear disputes, such as the rise of dictators. Under Article 27, the distinction between a "dispute" and a "situation" may have important consequences so far as abstention by the permanent members is concerned. Yet the Council never seems to have decided how to determine whether a matter is a situation or dispute and after its first year has paid little attention to the distinction.

Sanctions

In the matter of sanctions, the Charter differs fundamentally from the Covenant. Under Article 39, the Security Council *alone* determines "the existence of any threat to the peace, breach of the peace or act of aggression. . . . " No attempt is made to define aggression as was the case in the Covenant, the General Protocol and the Locarno treaties. The framers felt that any attempt to define all possible acts of aggression was impossible and would only permit loopholes through which disturbers of the peace could march.[11] While the Members of the League decided for themselves when an act of war had been committed contrary to the terms of the Covenant, the Council decides for the Members of the United Nations whether peace has been broken and is empowered to act in their behalf (Article 24). Once the Council has determined the fact of aggression, it is obligated under Article 39 either to "make recommendations, or decide what measures shall be taken in accordance with Articles 41 and 42 to maintain or restore international peace and security." Article 41 specifies that economic and diplomatic measures may be employed to give effect to the Council's "decisions." Article 42 permits the Council to "take such action by air, sea or land forces as may be necessary to maintain or restore international peace and security." "Demonstrations, blockade and other operations" involving armed forces may be employed.

All of these provisions must be considered in the light of two paramount facts. First, all UN Members have agreed under Article 25 to abide by the "decisions" (not "recommendations") of the Council, and none of these measures can be set in motion without the concurrence, active or tacit, of the permanent members. Second, under Article 2, paragraph 6, the Members have undertaken to "ensure" that non-members act in accordance with the Charter's principles to the extent necessary for the maintenance of peace.

Actually, military sanctions were first applied under a Security Council recommendation when the North Koreans crossed the 38th parallel in June 1950. An expected veto was not forthcoming because the Soviet Union chose to stay away from the Council Chamber. This recommendation was followed or endorsed by the great majority of UN Members.[12]

At the same time, there is the "inherent right of individual or collective self-defense" in the event of "armed attack" specified in Article 51, a loophole that perhaps more than anything else betrays the frontier character of the international community. Like Janus, the Charter faces in two directions — forward to the organization of force on an over-all basis that is

---

[11] See comments of M. Paul-Boncour at San Francisco, UNCIO, XX, Doc. 881, III/3/46, p. 505.
[12] See discussion of the Korean case in Chap. 15.

SHORTCOMINGS OF UN PLAN

1. IT WILL NOT WORK WHEN A BIG POWER IS THE AGGRESSOR

2. IT WILL NOT WORK WHEN A SMALL AGGRESSOR IS AIDED BY A BIG POWER

3. DIFFICULTY OF ORGANIZING AN ARMY FROM DIFFERENT NATIONS

Headline Series, *Foreign Policy Association*

at least suggestive of world government, and backward to the present fragmentation of power which seems to spell international anarchy.

Although peaceful settlement and enforcement are dealt with in two separate chapters of the Charter, the finding of a threat to the peace, breach of the peace or act of aggression need not stop efforts to settle the problem peacefully. The Council, instead of calling for sanctions may, "in order to prevent an aggravation of the situation" under Article 40, "call upon the parties concerned to comply with such provisional measures as it deems necessary or desirable."

Usually the Council has hesitated to enter the dangerous territory of Chapter VII. No formal finding of a threat to the peace or act of aggression under Article 39, for example, was resorted to in the Indonesian case.

Instead, a resolution was adopted calling for a "cease fire" and the settlement of the dispute by peaceful means, without reference to any specific article. Similarly, the efforts of the Security Council to settle the Palestine issue in conjunction with the General Assembly were taken until the last moment without a formal finding of a breach of the peace. Findings under Article 39 have been arrived at only in the cases of Korea and Palestine. Most of the Council's measures under Chapter VII have involved provisional measures or the recommendation of procedures for pacific settlement. As under Chapter VI, the Council has sought to play its role under Chapter VII by interpreting the Charter fairly liberally.

Supervision of Special Areas

In connection with its primary responsibility to maintain international peace and security, the Security Council has special supervisory functions. Under the terms of Article 83 "all functions of the United Nations relating to strategic areas, including the approval of the terms of the trusteeship agreements . . . shall be exercised by the Security Council." Thus the former Japanese mandated islands, which, in 1947, were established by the United States as a trust territory, come to some extent under the supervision of the Security Council. This means, in effect, that the United States may exercise its veto to prevent any action from being taken in connection with the islands that seems contrary to American interests.

The Free Territory of Trieste was to be brought directly under the Security Council's supervision under the terms of the Italian peace treaty, but this arrangement never materialized owing to great-power differences.

Internal Administration

Since its sole substantive function is the maintenance of peace and security, the Security Council, in comparison with its League predecessor, has few "housekeeping" responsibilities. It does not supervise any international bureaus. It has no budget responsibility. It does not administer economic and social machinery and the trusteeship body as the League Council did. Nor, with the exception of the election of the Secretary-General, does it direct the Secretariat. Article 97 provides, however, that the Secretary-General is to be appointed by the General Assembly "on recommendation of the Security Council." This recommendation requires the concurrence of the permanent members and is therefore the subject of tortuous negotiations. Both the nomination and the actual appointment are conducted in private meetings. Balloting is secret. The problem, of course, is to hit on a candidate acceptable to both the Soviet Union and the Western powers.[13]

The Security Council also joins with the Assembly in electing the fifteen judges of the International Court of Justice. This procedure follows that of the League, and it is laid down in Chapter I of the Court's statute which is discussed in Chapter 12. Votes for the election of judges are "taken with-

[13] See Chap. 13.

out any distinction between permanent and non-permanent members," and "an absolute majority" of votes suffices.

The Security Council plays a crucial role in amending the Charter because, as we have seen, the permanent members must agree to such a change. The chances of amending the Charter formally in any fundamental way are therefore slight indeed. This procedure closely follows that of the League Council under Article 26 of the Covenant.

Membership in the Organization

For all practical purposes the Council, as we have noted, controls the admission of new Members to the United Nations.[14] Under Article 4 of the Charter, the General Assembly can decide to admit a new Member only "upon the recommendation of the Security Council." Unanimity of the permanent members is required for this recommendation. Resolutions of the General Assembly urging that the veto should not apply in deciding questions of membership, and noting a "general sentiment in favor of the universality of the United Nations," have fallen on deaf ears so far as the permanent members — particularly the United States — have been concerned.[15]

Organization of the Council

Membership

The Charter provides in Article 23 that China, France, the United Kingdom, the United States and the Union of Soviet Socialist Republics are to be "permanent" members of the Council, while six other states are to be elected by the General Assembly as non-permanent members for staggered two-year terms. Every year, therefore, three new Council members are elected by the General Assembly. Retiring members are not eligible for immediate reëlection. The term of non-permanent members of the League Council was three years, and certain states were eligible for reëlection.

No criteria were set forth in the Dumbarton Oaks Proposals to guide the election of non-permanent members. A basis for distinction, however, was achieved at San Francisco when some of the participating states, including Canada and the Netherlands, among others, advanced the notion that certain states possessed a degree of economic and political power that warranted a status between that of a "great power" and a "small power." As a result of their argument, certain "middle powers" have emerged with a "slightly separate constitutional position for themselves" under the terms of Article 23,[16] which was amended at San Francisco to provide that the Assembly, in electing non-permanent members of the Security Council shall "in the first instance" pay "due regard . . . to the contribution of Members of the United Nations to the maintenance of international peace

---

[14] See pp. 104–105.
[15] See Chaps. 4 and 12.
[16] G. de T. Glazebrook, "The Middle Powers in the United Nations System," *International Organization*, Vol. 1, No. 3 (June 1947), pp. 307–315.

and security and to the other purposes of the Organization, and also to equitable geographical distribution." In actual practice, the Council has always included a number of middle powers. Like the League experience, moreover, the election of non-permanent members has led to bitter wrangling in the General Assembly. It has not always been easy to reconcile the two guiding principles, the "contribution of Members" toward security and "equitable geographical distribution." Actually, the bitterest wrangles have taken place over the issue of "representation" rather than of membership. Since 1949 two governments have claimed to represent China, the Communist-dominated People's Republic and the Nationalist Government, whose real estate is limited to Formosa. As long as the Korean dispute remains unsettled, there is little likelihood that the Communist Chinese will be seated in the Security Council or in any other UN body.

The Security Council even more than the League Council continues the tradition of the Concert of Europe that certain strong states in the international community must have authority and responsibility to maintain order. This is evident in both the membership and the voting provisions of the Security Council. Whereas the Covenant provided for permanent members on the League Council, the Charter goes a step further and gives voting privileges to the Security Council's permanent members. Yet fiction became confused with fact at Dumbarton Oaks and San Francisco. Neither France nor China was a great power in the sense that the United States and the U.S.S.R. were. And Britain was greatly crippled by economic difficulties. An ordered world, however, in the view of the United Nations' architects called for centers of power in Europe and Asia to replace Germany and Japan. Perhaps the wish could be made a reality. No one was really fooled, but no one could think of a more feasible way of coping with the rapidly shifting balance of forces in the war-torn globe.

Since the Charter, moreover, cannot be amended without the concurrence of the permanent members, it is doubtful whether any of them will agree to a change in its status. How, then, will legal recognition be accorded to future change in the political situation? In this respect, the Security Council appears more rigid than the League Council, which could change its permanent membership on the approval of a majority of the Assembly. This was one of the reasons underlying the small powers' opposition to the voting procedures of the Security Council at San Francisco.

The Participation of Non-members of the Security Council

Although the formal membership of the Security Council remains fixed, Members of the United Nations that are not members of the Security Council and states not Members of the United Nations may participate without vote in the Council's discussions under certain circumstances. Under Article 31:

> Any Member of the United Nations which is not a Member of the Security Council may participate, without vote, in the discussion of any question

brought before the Security Council whenever the latter considers that the interests of that Member are specially affected.

Although such a Member participates as a matter of right, the Security Council actually retains the initiative since it decides when the interests of the Member are specially affected.[17] Under the Covenant, League Members not members of the Council were "invited to sit as a member" under similar circumstances *with the right to vote.*

Article 32 provides that any non-member of *either* the Security Council or the Organization itself, if "a party to a dispute under consideration of the Security Council, shall be invited to participate, without vote, in the discussion relating to the dispute." In contrast, Article 17 of the Covenant permitted states not Members of the League, if parties to a dispute, "to accept the obligations of membership in the League for the purposes of such dispute. . . ."

Article 32 also provides that the "Security Council shall lay down such conditions as it deems just for the participation of a state which is not a Member of the United Nations." In the Corfu Channel case, Albania was invited by the Security Council "to participate without vote in the proceedings with regard to this dispute, on condition that Albania accepts, in the present case, all the obligations which a Member of the United Nations would have to assume in a similar case."[18] On this matter, the League Council was more like a diplomatic body. It was capable of expansion to include states involved in some point at issue. The Security Council, however, remains a fixed executive agency that changes only with the prescribed elections by the General Assembly.

Voting

The framers of the Charter abandoned the traditional unanimity rule that had been observed in the Covenant, except in the case of the five permanent members of the Security Council. In so doing, they broke with precedent and recognized in law the special role played in fact by certain major powers. Article 27, Paragraph 1, provides that "each member of the Security Council shall have one vote." Thereafter the Charter breaks new ground in providing for unequal voting. Paragraph 2 states that decisions on "procedural matters shall be made by an affirmative vote of seven members." Paragraph 3 provides that

Decisions . . . on all other matters shall be made by an affirmative vote of seven members including the concurring votes of the permanent members; provided that, in decisions under Chapter VI, and under paragraph 3 of Article 52, a party to a dispute shall abstain from voting.

[17] Rules 37–39 of the Council Rules of Procedure should be read in conjunction with these provisions. *International Organization,* Vol. 1, No. 1 (February 1947), pp. 204–205.

[18] Security Council, *Official Records,* No. 7, p. 131. For a thorough discussion of Articles 31 and 32, see Goodrich and Hambro, *The Charter of the United Nations, Commentary and Documents* (Boston: World Peace Foundation, 1948), pp. 232–236.

The League Covenant, as we have noted, also made a distinction between "decisions" which required unanimity and "matters of procedure" which were decided by a majority vote. In Article 15, moreover, decisions could also be made without the participation of the parties to a dispute.

At this point similarities cease for, in the case of the Security Council, the distinction between procedural and non-procedural matters involves the right of veto by the permanent members. Although the traditional unanimity rule is drastically modified, the permanent members alone are permitted the right to veto all substantive matters. But even they cannot sit as judges in their own cause in disputes considered under Chapter VI of the Charter dealing with peaceful settlement. In the application of enforcement measures under Chapter VII, however, these powers retain the right of veto. Thus it is impossible, legally speaking, for the Security Council to declare a permanent member guilty of aggression or to impose upon that member economic, military or diplomatic sanctions without that member's consent. This implies that enforcement action on behalf of the community of nations can be taken only against a state not a permanent member of the Security Council. Even this possibility has rapidly diminished, however, for there are few international disputes that do not involve the "vital interests" of the big powers.

The veto was exercised by the Soviet Union forty-three times out of a total of forty-four instances in the Security Council's first four years. In a number of cases its use served to protect the action of "satellite" states such as Yugoslavia, Bulgaria and Rumania in the Greek case or Albania in the Corfu Channel case.[19] By 1954 the U.S.S.R. had cast sixty vetoes.

France cast the veto alone only once — in the Indonesian case to prevent the appointment of a Security Council commission to supervise cease-fire orders. Britain, China and the United States have not yet had recourse to the veto. They have, of course, usually had the support of a majority of the Council on issues of vital concern. One might almost say, however, that a tradition has been established that the Western powers do not veto, and indeed the United States now wishes to narrow the range of decisions that can be vetoed in Chapter VI. The words of Senator Connally, however, still typify the American attitude toward international organization: "Our country will have the right to exercise the veto whenever in our opinion it is wise and just to do so."[20]

The permanent members have been at odds on the implementation of their special privilege more often than not. While they agreed by the time the Dumbarton Oaks Conference was convoked that non-procedural decisions involving either peaceful settlement or enforcement action could be taken only with unanimous consent of the permanent members, they could not agree at that time on whether these members should be required to

[19] For discussion of the veto, see Dwight E. Lee, "Genesis of the Veto," and Norman Padelford, "The Use of the Veto," in *International Organization*, Vol. 1, No. 1 (February 1947), p. 33, and Vol. 2, No. 2 (June 1948), p. 227 respectively.

[20] Senate Document 58, 79th Congress, 1st Session, p. 6.

abstain if parties to a dispute. The British and Chinese delegations, arguing in terms of judicial procedure and League precedent, insisted that parties to a dispute should not be permitted to vote — that is to sit in judgment on their own case. The Russians insisted that, while the Council should make decisions by majority vote, unanimity of the permanent members should be required at *all* times except in the case of procedural questions. A compromise proposal was advanced by the Americans at Dumbarton Oaks, but not then accepted, whereby: (1) non-procedural decisions would be made by a majority of seven votes instead of a simple majority, as advocated by the Russians, or a two-thirds majority, as advocated by the British and China, and (2) parties to a dispute, including the permanent members, were to abstain *only* on decisions taken in connection with *peaceful settlement.* This compromise formula appealed at once to the British and Chinese, but not to the Soviets until the Crimea Conference, when it was decided to include it with invitations to all of the United Nations to attend the San Francisco Conference.[21] By the "Yalta Formula," in sum, a permanent member, if party to a dispute, could block only enforcement action (Chapter VII of the Charter) and not peaceful settlement (Chapter VI of the Charter).

At San Francisco leading representatives of the smaller states such as Evatt of Australia, Spaak and Rolin of Belgium, Fraser of New Zealand and Romulo of the Philippine Commonwealth, to name only a few, agreed on the necessity of big-power cooperation in the application of sanctions, but argued mightily against its use in the peaceful settlement of disputes, membership in the organization and amendment of the Charter. They found the "Yalta formula" ambiguous and specifically wanted to know if a permanent member could veto *consideration* or *discussion* of a matter. On this point, the Sponsoring Powers fell apart in a manner ominously prophetic of the future since the Russians insisted on the affirmative while the British and Americans answered in the negative.

Big-power disagreement was grist to the small-power mill, and keen leaders such as Evatt and Fraser were quick to exploit the situation in order to reduce the general authority of the sponsoring powers in the developing organization. It was evident to the great powers that they must repair the breach, and they consequently withdrew to Secretary of State Stettinius' apartment in the Fairmont Hotel atop Nob Hill. The situation was strongly reminiscent of the meetings of the Big Five and the Big Three at Paris in 1919.

Specifically, the Big Five considered a list of twenty-three questions submitted by a subcommittee of Committee III(1), to all intents and purposes a small-power questionnaire. The answers were framed in a document nearly as important as the Charter itself, "The Statement by the Delegations of the Four Sponsoring Governments on Voting Procedure in the

---

[21] *Postwar Foreign Policy Preparation* . . . , passim and especially pp. 317, 320 and Appendices 52, 53, 57.

Security Council." [22] This statement was also endorsed by France, and once more the great powers closed ranks to face the challenge of the lesser states.

All did not go smoothly in the Big Five discussions, however. All but the Soviet Union maintained that the consideration of a dispute including discussion in the Security Council was a procedural matter, therefore not subject to the veto.[23] The United States had already publicly announced that

> nothing could prevent any state from bringing to the attention of the Security Council any dispute or any situation which it believes may lead to international friction or give rise to a dispute. And, furthermore, there is nothing in these provisions which could prevent any party to such dispute or situation from receiving a hearing before the Council and having the case discussed. Nor could any other members of the Council be prevented from making such observations on the matter as they wish to make.[24]

Although the issue furnished one of the major crises of the conference, which was left sitting on its hands for several days, it was quickly settled in direct negotiations between Mr. Harry Hopkins and Marshal Stalin.[25] The relatively quick resolution of the problem caused some observers to think that overcentralized lines of command and difficulties of communications with Moscow had been factors in the Soviet attitude.[26] Of greater significance is the fact that misunderstandings of terminology and inexactitudes of phraseology seemed to lead to mutual suspicions. At one moment a delegate of the United Kingdom, in trying to explain in committee the application of the Yalta formula in specific cases, declared that a procedural vote would be sufficient to *investigate* a dispute under Chapter VI.[27] But the Sponsoring Powers had never agreed that the dispatch of committees of investigation by the Council was a procedural matter. Presumably "investigate" was here used in the sense of consideration or discussion, but the Soviet delegate soon insisted that "consideration" of a matter might commit the Security Council to a course of action leading to a decision to settle the matter and that, therefore, consideration and discussion should be subject to the big-power veto.[28] In any event, the Sponsoring Powers for

[22] For a full discussion of this document, see the *Official Records* of the Security Council, No. 32, pp. 683–684.

[23] *Report to the President* . . . , p. 73.

[24] "Operation of the Proposed Voting Procedure in the Security Council," Statement by Acting Secretary Grew on March 24, 1945, *Department of State Bulletin*, Vol. 17, No. 479.

[25] J. F. Byrnes in *Speaking Frankly* (New York: Harper, 1947), pp. 64–65, feels that Stalin had not "understood the issue involved" and was not informed "on the crucial issue of San Francisco."

[26] Yet the Soviets had a communication ship in the harbor of San Francisco, *verboten* to visitors, except for official vodka parties.

[27] This incident can be traced by studying Wellington Koo, *Voting Procedures in International Organization* (New York: Columbia University Press, 1947), p. 130; and UNCIO, XI, Doc. 417, p. 305.

[28] *Report to the President* . . . , p. 72.

a time were unable to agree on the substance of their agreement at Yalta.

In sum, two principal questions on Article 27 faced the Big Five. The first was the right of discussion in the Security Council and it embroiled principally the Big Five. The second found these powers united against the smaller powers on the application of the veto in decisions on peaceful settlement. The argument of the smaller powers, led principally by Australia, was that peaceful settlement was a matter distinct from enforcement and should not be subject to the veto. These views were strengthened by the fact that the provisions for peaceful settlement and the provisions for enforcement were set forth in separate sections of the Dumbarton Oaks Proposals.[29]

The answer to the first question was forthcoming when it was agreed in the Voting Statement that the term "procedural matters" included "discussion" and "consideration." That is, that the adoption of the Council's agenda was a procedural matter.

On the second point, the smaller powers had to choose between the breakup of the conference or yielding to the united front of the Sponsoring Powers and France. The sponsoring governments explained that the veto from their point of view must apply to all steps taken after consideration and discussion of a matter because all subsequent decisions and actions of the Security Council including investigation and recommendations might well have "major political consequences" and might "even initiate a chain of events which might, in the end, require the Council . . . to invoke measures of enforcement."[30]

The final provision of the Voting Statement that was particularly galling to the smaller powers has since become a point of friction between the Soviet Union and the other permanent members of the Security Council. The Statement provides that if there is any doubt on whether a matter is procedural, the preliminary question itself "must be taken by a vote of seven members . . . including the concurring votes of the permanent members." This provision has given rise to the "double veto," whereby first the procedural character of a question is vetoed and then the resolution itself is vetoed. The "double veto" has been exercised in several cases before the Council by the Soviet Union and once by France.[31] In the Spanish case, for example, the President ruled that a resolution [32] submitted by the British and Australian members of a subcommittee was carried by a vote of 9 to 2 with the U.S.S.R. and Poland in opposition. Mr. Gromyko insisted for the Soviet Union that "the resolution was rejected because one of the

---

[29] See comment by Koo, *op. cit.*, p. 125.

[30] Par. 4 of the Voting Statement in Goodrich and Hambro, *Charter of the United Nations, Commentary and Documents,* 2nd ed. (Boston: World Peace Foundation, 1949), pp. 216–218.

[31] See the Spanish, Greek and Czechoslovakian cases. France voted with the U.S.S.R. in the first-mentioned case.

[32] The resolution provided that the Council continue to observe the situation in Spain without prejudice to the rights of the General Assembly.

permanent members of the Council voted against it." [33] He thus forced a vote on the "preliminary question" which was decided to be "substantive" by the vote of two members of the Council against a majority of eight. The President then stated, "Here we have two of the permanent members deciding against the others that this is a question of substance."

The smaller powers have challenged the validity of the Voting Statement, arguing that it does not bind the Council or the United Nations. In this case, the Netherlands delegate noted that the ruling had no "source or foundation" in the Charter. The Australian delegate, Mr. Evatt, reiterated the views he expressed at San Francisco that the Statement was without "any authority" since it was not adapted by any official body of the San Francisco Conference. While the Statement clearly does not legally bind the non-permanent members, the fact remains that it was an authoritative expression of the views of the permanent members who have generally regulated the Council's actions under its precepts. The United States, though adhering to the Statement, is on record as holding that it is not legally binding on the organization and that the parties to it are free to explore the matter of "better" voting procedures. [34]

Meanwhile efforts to study or modify the Council's voting procedures have not been lacking. The Security Council referred the matter to its Committee of Experts in August 1947. In November of the same year, the Assembly referred the matter to its newly appointed Interim Committee which, in March 1948, established a subcommittee to consider various proposals that had been advanced to cope with the problem. A resolution introduced by all the permanent members of the Council, save the Soviet Union, embodied the recommendations of this subcommittee and was passed by the Third Assembly on April 14, 1949, despite the vigorous objections of the Soviet bloc. This resolution sought to narrow the scope of the veto by widening the range of "procedural" matters to include thirty-five kinds of decisions recommended for decision by a vote of any seven members. Among further suggestions, the resolution also specified that the permanent members should consult with one another on means of avoiding the veto before taking important decisions and that, in any event, it should not be exercised except in questions of vital importance to the organization as a whole. Here was an effort to place community interest above the particular interests of the big powers. Its effect, however, has been almost negligible. The fact remains that the Council's voting procedures cannot be changed without formal Charter amendment or an informal agreement among the permanent members. So far, the Soviet Union has remained adamant on the letter of the Four Power Voting Statement.

---

[33] Eight members supported the President ruling that the matter was procedural; Poland abstained. France and the U.S.S.R. were opposed. *Security Council Journal*, No. 41, p. 836.

[34] In the Czech case at the 303rd meeting of the Security Council, see the *Official Records*, 3rd year, No. 73, pp. 5–6. See also, first chapter of Eduardo Jiménez De Arechaga's *Voting and the Handling of Disputes in the Security Council* (New York: Carnegie Endowment for International Peace, 1951).

Abstention from Voting and Absence from Meetings

We have already seen that the third paragraph of Article 27 requires that the permanent members "abstain from voting" in non-procedural matters when they are "parties to a dispute" that is being considered under Chapter VI of the Charter dealing with peaceful settlement. At first glance it appears that the big-power veto is narrowed by these provisions. In fact, this provision can be circumvented, and abstention of a permanent member, even under Chapter VI, remains essentially voluntary.

When the Security Council first sat down to business, for example, it found in the Syria-Lebanon case of 1946 that it might be possible for a permanent member acting under the Voting Statement to deny (*a*) that it was "party" to a dispute, or (*b*) that there was a "dispute." The Charter empowers the Security Council to investigate any "situation" or "dispute" that might cause international friction or endanger peace, but it does not require the abstention of parties involved in a "situation," and the Soviet Union has refused to agree to any modification of the Charter in this respect.[35]

In stating that, with the exception of the parties to a dispute under Chapter VI, all non-procedural questions require the "concurring votes" of the permanent members, Article 27(3) seems to indicate beyond any doubt that the abstention of a permanent member not party to a dispute under Chapter VI constitutes a veto. In practice, however, something quite different has happened. Beginning with the Soviet abstention on the Spanish case in 1946, abstention by a permanent member has not been considered a veto. Though challenged by some states on occasion, the practice has become general. Yet the Soviet Union has refused to formalize it in the Council's Rules of Procedure or otherwise.

The Security Council has taken a similarly flexible view of the unanimity rule in cases where a permanent member has not been represented at the Council table when decisions have been made. In spite of the Soviet Union's "walkout" in the Iranian case in 1946, the Council went about its business including the adoption of a United States resolution that seemed to involve matters of both substance and procedure. Beginning with its resolution of June 25, 1950, however, determining the armed attack of the North Koreans as a breach of the peace and calling for a cease-fire, the Security Council has taken the gravest of substantive decisions in the absence of the Soviet Union which insisted that the Council could take no *legal* decisions as long as China was represented in the Security Council by the Nationalist Government. Military sanctions were applied for the first time under United Nations authority by a Council recommendation on June 27, 1950, with the Soviet Union officially recorded as "absent."

In sum, both procedural and substantive decisions have been taken in the absence from the Council Chamber of both permanent and non-permanent members provided the requisite majority of seven was obtained and

[35] *Security Council Journal*, No. 15, pp. 268–269.

provided the permanent members, present and voting, concurred in substantive matters. Security Council votes have been recorded as: "in favor,"
"against," "abstaining," "not voting" and "absent." In practice, neither absence nor abstention by a permanent member has constituted a veto, and
consequently the Council, for all practical purposes, has sought to coerce
one and perhaps two permanent members of the Security Council despite
protestations of the authors of the Voting Statement five years earlier that
this could not and must not happen.

We may conclude by saying that Security Council votes are weighted in
favor of certain states which, because of their power, must bear a special
responsibility for keeping the peace. In order that the permanent members' "possession of power and their use of power may be made to serve
the purpose of peace . . . they shall exercise their power only in agreement
with each other and not in disagreement." [36] Peace, it was felt, required not
the unanimity of all Members, but only those that had the capacity to
wage modern war. For this reason the law of the Charter modifies the
"sovereign equality" of states and grants special privileges to certain great
powers. Heavy responsibilities, however, are implicit in the privileges.
Yet it is scarcely an exaggeration to say that the peace system implicit
in the voting provisions of the Security Council has been discarded since
circumstances have compelled the United Nations to take measures of
peaceful settlement and enforcement against the wishes of major powers.

Meetings

Under Article 28, the Security Council is "so organized as to be able to
function continuously. Each member of the Security Council shall for this
purpose be represented at all times at the seat of the Organization." This
provision stands in contrast to the League Council which, though it met
three or four times a year for ordinary sessions, was required by the Covenant to meet only once a year. The Security Council, however, is always
in session and is presumed to be ready to function promptly on any matter
brought to its attention. When the Soviet Union insisted, in the Korean
case of June 1950, that no decision on important matters could be taken
in the absence of its delegate, some other members insisted that, under
Article 28, the Soviet delegate was obligated to remain at the Council
table. Thus, the delegate of France declared:

> The delegation of the Soviet Union, by abandoning the Council, has aban-
> doned the Charter. When it returns to the one and to the other, it will find
> again its right of speech, of criticism, of vote and veto. So long as it has not
> done so, the U.S.S.R. Government has no legal or moral basis for contesting
> the action of the United Nations.[37]

Provision is also made for "periodic meetings" in the second paragraph
of Article 28. It was intended under this Article to provide for particularly

[36] *Report to the President* . . . , p. 72.
[37] Security Council, *Official Records*, No. 17, p. 8.

important meetings at which the members might be represented by their Foreign Ministers who might be able to resolve issues of outstanding importance or particular danger. So far, no "periodic meetings" of the Council have been called, although the Secretary-General suggested such a procedure in 1950 as a means of resolving the problem of China's representation in the United Nations. Normally the members are represented by specially designated delegates, who include some of the most familiar figures of the United Nations.

The Council is permitted, under Article 28(3), to meet wherever its members feel its work will be facilitated. In practice it generally meets at the seat of the organization in New York, but its work began in London where the United Nations first opened for business, and it has met in Paris, as a matter of convenience when that city has been host to the General Assembly.

Officers

The Charter specifies only one officer for the Council, the President, a post held in turn, under the Rules of Procedure, "by the members of the Security Council in the English alphabetical order of their names." Each President holds office for one month. Under the Rules of Procedure, however, he may decide that he should not preside over the Council "during the consideration of particular questions with which the member he represents is directly connected." The Presidency then falls to the representative of the member who follows next in alphabetical rotation. Austin of the United States, for example, in the Berlin case, turned the Chair over to Bramuglia of Argentina, who not only presided but performed yeoman work in mediating the dispute.

Early in the Security Council's history, Presidents did little more than preside over the Council and administer its Rules of Procedure. Beginning in 1948, however, they have performed broader functions. It was found that private conversations at times proved more useful than public discussions in working out procedures for the settlement of a question. These conversations have taken place under the auspices of the President, who explores the points at issue and the possible procedures and terms of settlement with the parties and perhaps other Council members who wish to offer suggestions. In the India-Pakistan question when the President, who was the Belgian delegate, was about to retire from office, he was appointed by the Council to continue his function as *rapporteur*. This procedure has been followed in other instances to provide continuity. This has facilitated the handling of the Berlin, Palestine and India-Pakistan questions. The General Assembly, in turn, has recommended that the Council develop these procedures still further.[38]

The office of President attracted particular attention when Malik of the Soviet Union ended his Council boycott in August 1950 to return to the

[38] General Assembly Resolution 268 (III) B, April 28, 1949. *Official Records*, Third Session, Part II, p. 12.

Council to take his turn as President after sanctions had already been applied against the North Koreans, an action which the new President challenged as an illegality perpetrated under the prodding of the "warmongers" of the West. Under his direction during that month the Council became so entangled in procedural wrangles that little could be accomplished.

Actually the authority of the President is not very great. Many of his decisions are provisional pending action by the Council itself as in the adoption of the agenda. Meetings of the Council are called in his name, for example, but they result from the initiative of states, the General Assembly or the Secretary-General acting under Charter provisions. As the representative of a member of the Security Council he, like the other representatives, takes orders from his foreign office so far as his country's attitude on substantive issues is concerned.

Subsidiary Bodies

The Charter makes specific provision for only one subsidiary body of the Council, the Military Staff Committee which, under Article 47, consists of the Chiefs-of-Staff of the permanent members or their representatives. With the institution of this Committee the tradition of the Supreme War Council and the Combined Chiefs-of-Staff was carried over into the organization of peace.

The Military Staff Committee's functions are to "advise and assist" the Council on the military requirements for the maintenance of peace, the use of forces to be placed at the Council's disposal and the "regulation of armaments, and possible disarmament." Little has been accomplished in the meetings of the Military Staff Committee, however, save to define very specifically areas of disagreement between the Soviet Union and the other members on these matters.[39]

Other Council Committees have been established from time to time to facilitate its work. Under Article 29, the Council may, as a matter of procedure, and as noted explicitly in the Voting Statement, "establish such subsidiary organs as it deems necessary for the performance of its functions." The line between such a subsidiary organ and a committee to investigate a matter under Article 34 is, however, hard to draw. The distinction is important, of course, because a decision to investigate requires big-power unanimity. In practice, it has not always been clear whether the Council, in establishing committees and commissions, has acted under the authority of this article or under its general grant of authority. Such doubt was expressed in the establishment of the "Good Offices" Committee in the Indonesian Case.

Other subsidiary bodies have included the Atomic Energy Commission, established by the General Assembly in January 1946 but placed specifically under the Security Council's authority, and the Commission on Con-

[39] For details, see Chap. 16.

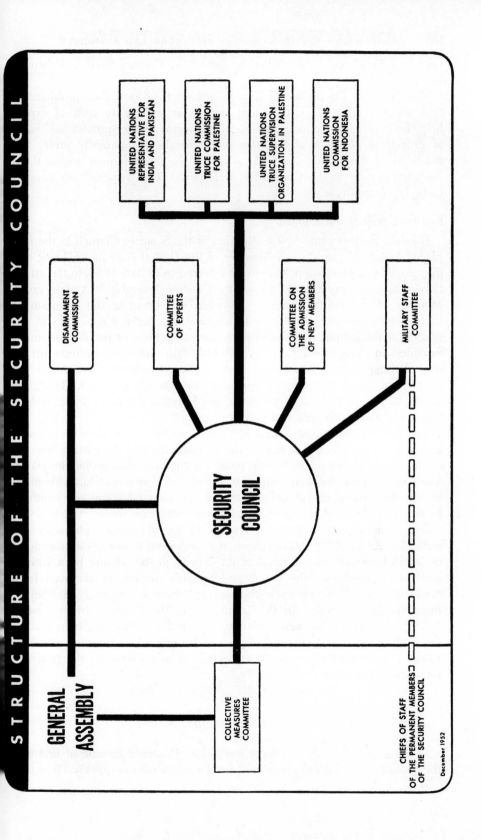

STRUCTURE OF THE SECURITY COUNCIL

GENERAL ASSEMBLY

COLLECTIVE MEASURES COMMITTEE

SECURITY COUNCIL

DISARMAMENT COMMISSION

COMMITTEE OF EXPERTS

COMMITTEE ON THE ADMISSION OF NEW MEMBERS

MILITARY STAFF COMMITTEE

CHIEFS OF STAFF of the PERMANENT MEMBERS of the SECURITY COUNCIL

UNITED NATIONS REPRESENTATIVE FOR INDIA AND PAKISTAN

UNITED NATIONS TRUCE COMMISSION FOR PALESTINE

UNITED NATIONS TRUCE SUPERVISION ORGANIZATION IN PALESTINE

UNITED NATIONS COMMISSION FOR INDONESIA

December 1952

ventional Armaments, established by act of the Council itself in February 1947.

The Council's Committee of Experts advises the Council on problems of staff and procedure including such matters as voting. In spite of expert help, however, the Council continues to operate under "provisional" rules of procedure. Certain of the permanent members apparently prefer the flexibility of this arrangement. At any rate, the diasgreement among them has carried over in the Committee of Experts. The "experts" are government representatives.

Problems Before the Council

How do matters come to the attention of the Security Council in the first place? Article 35 permits any Member of the United Nations to "bring any dispute, or any situation of the nature referred to in Article 34, to the attention of the Security Council or of the General Assembly." A state not a Member of the United Nations, however, can bring to the attention of these two bodies only a "dispute to which it is a party if it accepts in advance, for the purposes of the dispute, the obligations of pacific settlement provided in the present Charter." Usually "disputes" are brought up by one of the parties. "Situations," however, are frequently brought to the Council by states that do not appear to be directly involved. Thus, the Soviet Union, or one of its satellites, has brought situations in Indonesia, Spain and Greece before the Security Council.

The Council has insisted that it alone is in final control of its agenda. In the Iranian case, for example, the Council decided to remain "seized" of the case although Iran at one point sought to withdraw its complaint. The Council took this step, moreover, in spite of a memorandum submitted by the Secretary-General indicating that the Council could not continue to consider the case unless it voted an investigation under Article 34 or unless it actually discovered a conflict of the dangerous character described in Article 33.[40] This decision, it is important to note, is a procedural one, which permits the removal of an item from the agenda by a vote of any seven members. The Greek and Spanish cases were removed from the Council's jurisdiction in this fashion and were subsequently laid before the General Assembly. In the Iranian case, the Council, by remaining "seized" of the matter, may well have exerted a restraining influence on the parties involved. This technique can be helpful in bringing attention to the problems of quarrelsome states which may endanger the peace of the entire international community.

Conclusions

Is the Security Council a force for peace? It should be said at first that the Security Council has sometimes been written off too quickly. It is true

[40] *Security Council Journal*, No. 27, pp. 522–524.

that, plagued by the quarrels of its permanent members, it has not been able to mobilize the force of the United Nations in the manner intended by the framers of the Charter. Yet, backed by the resolute action of certain members, particularly the United States, and in the absence of the Soviet Union from its chambers, it has been able to meet the challenge of aggression in Korea. The Council has had a substantial measure of success, moreover, in ameliorating several inflammatory problems such as those involving Indonesia, Berlin, Palestine and Kashmir. Like the League Council, its principal role has been less in the realm of force than in the realm of peaceful settlement.

Yet it is true also that the General Assembly, like the League Assembly, has improvised and grown in stature while the Council has been partially paralyzed by the big-power deadlock. The Assembly, not the Council, is the organization's most influential body. Still, paradoxical though it may seem, the Council has exerted a marked influence on the foreign policies of even its most influential members. In conjunction with other organs of the United Nations, particularly the General Assembly, it has helped on occasion to curb Soviet expansion.

The Council, it should be remembered, can be evaluated properly only in the perspective of the whole United Nations system. The mitigation of many disputes including Greece and Palestine, for example, depended upon the work of the Council, the Assembly and other United Nations bodies. Peace depends increasingly in the long run on the positive functions of the Economic and Social Council, on the legislative role of the General Assembly and on the quality of the Secretariat's work. Upon these bodies and the specialized agencies falls the time-consuming process of community building upon which a rule of law must rest.

Suggestions for Further Reading

Books

Byrnes, J. F., *Speaking Frankly* (New York: Harper & Brothers, 1947).

Chase, E. P., *The United Nations in Action* (New York: McGraw-Hill Book Company, Inc., 1950).

Churchill, Winston S., *The Hinge of Fate* (Boston: Houghton Mifflin Company, 1950).

Dulles, John F., *War or Peace* (New York: The Macmillan Company, 1950).

Goodrich, Leland C., and Hambro, Edvard, *Charter of the United Nations, Commentary and Documents*, 2nd ed. (Boston: World Peace Foundation, 1949).

Hull, Cordell, *The Memoirs of Cordell Hull*, 2 Vols. (New York: The Macmillan Company, 1948).

Jiménez de Arechaga, E., *Voting and the Handling of Disputes in the Security Council* (New York: Carnegie Endowment for International Peace, 1951).

Koo, Wellington, *Voting Procedures in International Organization* (New York: Columbia University Press, 1947).

Leonard, L., *International Organization* (New York: McGraw-Hill Book Company, Inc., 1951).

Stettinius, E. R., *Roosevelt and the Russians: The Yalta Conference* (New York: Doubleday & Company, Inc., 1949).

Documents

United Nations, *Documents of the United Nations Conference on International Organization, San Francisco, 1945,* 16 Vols. (New York: United Nations Information Organizations, 1945–1946).

United States, Congress, Senate, *The Charter of the United Nations, Hearings before the Committee on Foreign Relations,* 79th Congress, 1st session, July 9–13, 1945 (Washington: U.S. Government Printing Office, 1945).

———, Department of State, *Postwar Foreign Policy Preparation, 1939–1945,* Department of State Publication 3580 (Washington: U.S. Government Printing Office, 1950).

———, Department of State, *Report to the President on the Results of the San Francisco Conference,* Department of State Publication 2349, Conference Series 71 (Washington: U.S. Government Printing Office, 1945).

Organizing for Economic and Social

Progress — The League

> "A great part of the Continent was sick and dying, its population was greatly in excess of the numbers for which a livelihood was available; its organization was destroyed, its transport system ruptured, and its food supplies terribly impaired."
>
> — JOHN MAYNARD KEYNES [1]

THIS WAS THE TRAGIC AFTERMATH of World War I which called for the most strenuous international cooperation. Yet the popular mood, especially in the United States, was to throw off the strait jacket of wartime regulatory agencies and return to the blissful state of unregulated "normalcy." When the British Government, in the person of Lord Robert Cecil, urged American governmental cooperation in the economic reconstruction of Europe, Mr. Bernard Baruch replied for the United States Government, "The salvation of the world must rest upon the initiative of individuals." [2] In spite of the wartime experience with intergovernmental cooperation, Mr. Baruch, Mr. Hoover and other American leaders preferred, once peace had been restored, to work through private channels, such as the Red Cross and other relief bodies, rather than governmental organizations. And when they felt compelled to employ governmental channels, they preferred to operate through national rather than international agencies.

Unfortunately subsequent history seems to have provided undeniable justification for the tart message that Lord Cecil sent back to Mr. Baruch:

> You think that . . . the economic situation can be solved by individual initiative. It may be so, though my own opinion is to the contrary. It may

---

[1] *The Economic Consequences of the Peace* (New York: Harcourt, Brace and Howe, 1920), pp. 22–23.

[2] H. R. G. Greaves, *The League Committees and World Order* (London: Oxford, 1931), p. 66.

be that [an economic] inquiry will show that without American assistance on a large scale nothing can be done, and it may also be that America will decline to give that assistance. If she intends to take that attitude, forgive me for saying that she ought to take it quite openly and before the face of the world. Then we in Europe shall know the extent of the problem that faces us.[3]

The United States Government insisted on the simple but scarcely constructive strategy of razing the entire structure of wartime economic agencies, including the Allied Maritime Transport Council and a host of related organs, before deciding what, if anything, to put in its place. After fumbling for three crucial months, the Allies were finally forced by a threat of famine and complete economic collapse in the conquered areas to establish, in February 1919, a Supreme Economic Council which was to become very much like the structure which had been abandoned. This Council of five representatives from each of the four major Allies was instructed to deal with the "many questions . . . arising daily . . . [concerning] finance, food, blockade control, shipping, and raw materials."[4]

Unfortunately its work was seriously impeded by many obstacles: the policy of feverish decontrol, the fact that only the Allies were represented in the organization, the absence of independent funds and the loss of precious time between the destruction of the old and the establishment of the new organs. If it had not been for this deplorable time gap,

> the German ships would have been at work in December instead of March, and food would have gone into Germany as from January instead of April with results it is not easy now to measure exactly upon the political position of Germany. . . .[5]

Planning for Economic and Social Cooperation

The great majority of the planners of the League did not believe that the League should play a very important role in economic and social affairs. The traditions of past centuries led them to believe that international organization, like castor oil, should be resorted to only in times of dire emergency. Even national governments played relatively modest roles in regulating the economic and social activities of their citizens. The proposals formulated by the Bryce Group, the American League to Enforce Peace, the British League of Nations Society, the Phillimore Committee, the French Foreign Office, Colonel House and President Wilson all emphasized judicial and military aspects and made almost no direct provision for functions in the economic and social field.

---

[3] Ibid., pp. 66–67.

[4] Ray Stannard Baker, Woodrow Wilson and World Settlement (Garden City: Doubleday, Page, 1922), Vol. 2, p. 340.

[5] Arthur Salter, Allied Shipping Control: An Experiment in International Administration (New York: Oxford, 1921), p. 222.

On the British side there were a few more courageous planners. As early as 1916 Leonard Woolf, speaking for the Fabian Society, proposed a league that would promote the "development of such joint action as is exemplified by the Universal Postal Union." [6] The British Foreign Office Memorandum, of November 1918, envisaged a league that would not only supervise and coordinate all then existing technical unions "from the Universal Postal Union to the International Seismological Association," but would also create new bodies to deal with such matters as health, industrial conditions, finance and currency, transit, conservation of resources, equality of trade, the color problem and the development of Africa. [7]

This bold draft immediately flowed into the main stream of planning by inspiring similar proposals by Robert Cecil and Jan Christiaan Smuts within a few weeks of each other in December 1918. [8] Smuts gave a classic description of the "functional" approach when he called for a league that would help satisfy

> The common economic needs of the nations belonging to the League — at any rate for the control of articles of food or raw materials or transport in respect of which there will be a shortage . . . [The League] must be an ever visible living, working organ of the polity of civilization. It must function so strongly in the ordinary peaceful intercourse of states that it becomes irresistible in their disputes; its peace activity must be the foundation and guarantee of its war power. [9]

Paris, 1919

In the marriage at the Paris Peace Conference between the Foreign Office–Cecil–Smuts positive concept and the more limited and negative Phillimore–House–Wilson approach, the former came off a weak second best. In the Hurst–Miller Draft, adopted as the basis for the League of Nations Commission discussions, only five brief articles, out of a total of twenty-two, dealt with economic and social functions. [10] The Draft called for the establishment of fair hours and humane conditions of labor, appointment of commissions to study and make recommendations on conditions of industry and labor, and provisions to secure and maintain freedom of transit and just treatment for the commerce of all members of the League. It omitted any mention of the British suggestions for commissions on economic, social and humanitarian matters, other than labor and mandates, and for placing existing international bureaus under League supervision.

Woodrow Wilson, who admitted to a friend that he was "not much inter-

[6] L. S. Woolf, *The Framework of a Lasting Peace* (London: Allen & Unwin, 1917), pp. 91–123.
[7] Alfred Zimmern, *The League of Nations and the Rule of Law, 1918–1935* (London: Macmillan, 1936), pp. 196–208.
[8] See pp. 49–50.
[9] *Ibid.*, pp. 24–25.
[10] *Ibid.*, pp. 231–237.

ested in economic questions," [11] espoused policies that were to be expected from a nation that was wealthy as well as idealistic, powerful as well as isolationist and proud of its slogans of "free trade" and "rugged individualism" as well as accustomed to many forms of oligopolistic business control. Wilson thus supported a policy of nondiscrimination in trade and freedom of the seas, although he soon realized that his earlier advocacy of "the removal, so far as is possible, of all economic barriers . . ." was quite impractical in view of America's protectionist tariffs. He displayed no active interest in long-range, positive and continuous economic and social action, nor would he agree to authorize in the Covenant any special organs to deal with such problems other than labor and the mandates.

Lloyd George represented a country far more closely linked to other nations by both trade and tradition, a nation, declining in economic power, that had suffered greater war damage in proportion to her resources than had the United States, and a nation that was vitally interested in free trade but not in freedom of the seas when it interfered with the weapon of naval blockade. Lloyd George thus favored a far-reaching and positive plan for freedom of trading and general economic and social collaboration but would not consent to any limitation of Britain's powerful instrument of naval blockade. The French plan was more like the British in calling for extensive international economic collaboration, including the establishment of permanent commissions to implement that program, but it had no significant influence on the final provisions of the Covenant. Orlando expressed Italy's desire for a League economic committee and freer access to basic raw materials which his country seriously needed, but he was scarcely listened to.

General Organizational Pattern

Necessity, more than the Covenant, was the real mother of the League economic and social system that was subsequently established. The technical organs that sprouted in the soil of Geneva during the early years arose primarily because of the obvious challenge of the world's immediate postwar ills, in spite of the absence of comprehensive provisions in the Covenant to deal with such problems. And, as the League began to cultivate these organs in 1920, it naturally copied familiar international organizations such as the Universal Postal Union and World War I agencies like the Allied Maritime Transport Council.

Following the general pattern of these models, the League established three kinds of bodies to work in each of several major functional areas: (1) plenary conferences convened by the League Assembly or Council on either an *ad hoc* or continuing basis to pass judgment on recommendations submitted by smaller bodies and to provide a center for the broadest possible cooperation under the aegis of the League; (2) smaller expert com-

[11] *Ibid.,* pp. 275–276.

mittees, meeting more frequently than the conferences, to advise both the League, usually via the Council, and other conferences; and (3) supporting staff, either League Secretariat or separate personnel.

Four sets of these three types of bodies were recognized by the League as "technical organizations": the Economic and Financial Organization, Communications and Transit Organization, Health Organization and Intellectual Cooperation Organization. Although the International Labor Organization was not established under the Covenant but under a separate section of the Peace Treaty, Chapter 13, it was somewhat comparable to the "technical organizations" and was tied to the League by several administrative bonds. As of 1939, there were also the following "advisory committees" concerned with economic and social affairs but not as part of any full-blown "organizations": the Advisory Committee on Social Questions and Advisory Committee of Experts on Slavery. The League of Nations High Commissioner for Refugees was created by the Assembly and was responsible to it but, for political reasons, was made as autonomous as possible.

There were other organizations, independently established, that were affiliated with the League under rather loose cooperative arrangements. They included several "institutes" which were placed at the League's disposal in connection with certain technical activities: the International Institute of Intellectual Cooperation, International Institute for the Unification of Private Law, International Educational Cinematographic Institute, International Center for Leprosy Research, and, under an exceptionally amorphous bond, the International Institute of Agriculture. Finally six "bureaus" were placed under the League's direction, including the International Hydrographic Bureau; this was far from the number that the Paris Peace Conference had expected to be allied with the League.

In addition to these League-affiliated bodies there were, according to the League's 1938 *Handbook of International Organizations*, approximately eight hundred public and private organizations, concerned with economic and social matters, which remained legally independent although most of them maintained some form of liaison with the League. These included many important and influential bodies whose independence often made the League's attempts at economic and social coordination extremely difficult. They resisted closer affiliation for a variety of reasons. Many feared the "political" climate of the League would damage their "technical" operations. The traditionally neutral nations wanted to remain as independent as possible. Some of these bodies were afraid that their hard-won identity would be swallowed up by the larger organizations, and many of them wanted to encourage the participation of important non-League members such as the United States.

Committees Were Directing Centers

The key bodies in this network of technical units were the rather small expert committees, whether operating as part of the "technical organizations" or alone. The plenary conferences were too large, too weighted down with the less important countries and too infrequent. The committees were appointed by the Council and consisted of about a dozen persons, usually chosen for terms of three years. Since nationals of non-League members were eligible, it was possible for United States citizens to sit on most of the committees at one time or another, even though their country was not a Member of the League.

Individuals appointed to these bodies normally had the status of private experts, rather than governmental representatives, although they were usually chosen with at least a tacit nod from their governments and often held important positions in those governments. Committee memberships were also carefully arranged so that nationals of all the major powers and a reasonable distribution of the middle and smaller states were included. While the relatively independent status of these committee members made it possible for them to act much of the time in the name of humanity as a whole, rather than of any particular nation, it was obviously impossible for them to slip the moorings of national loyalties altogether, especially in the case of representatives of the totalitarian countries.

The decisions of these technical committees were usually made by simple majority.[12] When these decisions took the form of draft conventions, they were referred to either the League Assembly or some other conference for approval, usually by unanimous decisions, before being sent to individual governments for ratification. Meetings of the main technical committees usually took place three or four times a year and lasted about a week. These bodies also appointed various subcommittees which served to bring together under the roof of the League thousands of noted experts in various specialized fields from aeronautics to zoology. Gradually a web of personal relationships was woven which seemed, at the time, to give promise of a stronger spirit of international community than had ever existed before.

A major share of the credit for the League's accomplishments in economic and social matters must also be given to the Secretariat. It was these energetic and generally competent international civil servants who stayed on the job the year 'round and provided most of the labor and ingenuity that kept the wheels turning. Although the economic and social units in the Secretariat were overshadowed in the early years by the emphasis on political problems, the economic and social staff grew rapidly in the early thirties. The number of full-time officials assigned to this technical work increased from 65 in 1923 to 143 in 1938, and the share of the Secretariat budget devoted to these activities rose from about 25 or 30 per cent in 1921 to over 50 per cent from 1930 on.[13]

Supervision and Coordination

As for the degree of control which the League intended to exert over its

[12] Cromwell Riches, *Majority Rule in International Organization* (Baltimore: Johns Hopkins Press, 1940), pp. 236–244.

[13] Egon F. Ranshofen-Wertheimer, *The International Secretariat* (Washington: Carnegie Endowment for International Peace, 1945), p. 161.

technical organs, it is interesting to note the following principles set forth in resolutions passed by the League Council in May 1920 and by the Assembly in December 1920:

1. The interior working of the various organizations should be independent.
2. Their relation with the Members of the League should be under control. Before any communication of . . . proposals . . . is made to the Members . . . the Council of the League must be immediately informed in order that they may be able to exercise their power of control if necessary. . . . The Assembly . . . should be informed of all questions dealt with in intervals between its meetings by the Council in the exercise of its power of control defined above.[14]

Legally the Council and Assembly were empowered to block, by a unanimous vote of disapproval, any communication to Member governments. In actual practice, however, the Assembly and Council granted far more freedom to the technical organs than this rigid language suggests.

The direction of this intricate machinery was assumed at first to be more the function of the Council than the Assembly because: (1) it was felt that the great powers should control such controversial and important activities in order to make them realistic and effective; (2) the Council could give more continuous supervision than the Assembly; and (3) the Council was conceived by many as the Assembly's executive arm. Practice, however, tended to place the reins more in the hands of the Assembly than originally planned because: (1) the middle and small powers insisted that Assembly guidance was more democratic than control by the Council; (2) the Assembly proved more vigorous and constructive than had been expected; and (3) the Assembly, working through its Second and Fifth Committees, had more time to devote to economic and social matters than the Council which was small in size and hard-pressed during most of its existence by a rash of political disputes.

As experience accumulated, however, there was evidence that even the Assembly was not an altogether satisfactory overseer. It, too, was harassed by political issues, especially in the black thirties. Many individuals who sat on the Second and Fifth Committees were not competent to grapple with the technical Gordian knots thrust before them, and the pressure of business frequently forced them to skim over such tangles rather superficially. These factors, plus the increasing difficulty of coordinating the fast-expanding economic and social apparatus and the desirability of facilitating the collaboration of such important non-League members as Germany, Japan, Italy and the United States, led to the League Council's creation of the Bruce Committee in May 1939 to study these problems. The Committee was named for its chairman, Mr. S. M. Bruce, Australian High Commissioner in London. The essence of that Committee's report, issued in August 1939, was that a new Central Committee

14 *Official Journal* Sup., Jan. 1921, pp. 12–13.

for Economic and Social Questions should be created to assume, under the general guidance of the Assembly, the major burden of supervising the functional bodies.[15] This Committee was to consist of twenty-four governmental representatives and not more than eight other members to be selected by the governmental representatives "on the grounds of their special competence and authority." This plan was approved by the Assembly in December 1939, and an Organizing Committee of ten governmental representatives was chosen as the core of the new body. Unfortunately the flames of war, which were already isolating Geneva, prevented any further action along these lines. Nevertheless, a seed had been sown which was to grow eventually into the United Nations Economic and Social Council.

Economic and Financial Organs

The only specific economic mandate of the Covenant was Article 23(e), which provided that "The Members of the League will make provision to secure and maintain . . . equitable treatment for the commerce of all Members of the League. . . ." This was all that was left of the third of Wilson's fourteen points of January 1918, which had called for the "removal, so far as possible, of all economic barriers and the establishment of an equality of trade conditions among all the nations consenting to the peace. . . ." The reference to the removal of economic barriers was abandoned as obviously too bitter a dose for the protectionists in both Europe and America. The objective of "equality of trade conditions" was retained but softened to "equitable treatment." When permanent organizational machinery to deal with economic and financial matters was proposed at the Peace Conference by the British, French and Italians, however, no support was forthcoming from the United States, and the plan failed of adoption. Although machinery similar to that proposed was created later, it was not established as expeditiously as it probably would have been had the Covenant explicitly provided for it.

Other interesting and prophetic ideas that were buried at the Peace Conference included: (1) Italian and Belgian plans to facilitate access to basic raw materials, a problem to be cited later by Adolf Hitler as justification for upsetting the Versailles apple cart; (2) a Belgian suggestion for an agricultural committee to improve and coordinate production in all countries; and (3) a French plan for protecting the property of foreigners, an issue which has long hampered the development of underdeveloped areas.

Economic and Financial Organization

The real initiators of the League's economic and financial machinery were the postwar famine and inflation. As a first step toward positive action,

[15] "The Development of International Cooperation in Economic and Social Affairs," *Special Supplement to the Monthly Summary of the League of Nations* (Geneva: August 1939).

Secretary-General Eric Drummond established an economic section of the Secretariat in the summer of 1919. Largely as a result of the section's studies, the League Council called a Financial Conference which met in Brussels in the fall of 1920 and recommended, among other things, the establishment of an economic and financial organization to continue the work of the Conference.

In October 1920, therefore, the League Council approved a plan for a Provisional Economic and Financial Committee consisting of two sections which soon acquired separate identities as the Economic and Financial Committees. These bodies formed the core of the Economic and Financial Organization which, in the last years of the League's life, also included a Fiscal Committee, a Committee of Statistical Experts, a Coordination Committee and supporting sections of the Secretariat.

Conferences. For most purposes, the League Assembly, especially its Second Committee, served as the guiding conference of the Economic and Financial Organization. Special conferences were also called to deal with specific issues. The first of these was the Brussels Financial Conference of 1920. Other major ones were the Geneva World Economic Conference, 1927, and the London International Monetary and Economic Conference, 1933.

Economic and Financial Committees. The Coordination Committee was established by the League Council in May 1938 to provide more continuous supervision and coordination of the Economic and Financial Organization's work than could be provided by either the Council, Assembly or occasional conferences. It consisted of a chairman appointed by the Council; the Council *rapporteurs* on economic and financial questions; representatives of the Economic, Financial, Fiscal and Statistical Committees; and a representative of the Communications and Transit Organization.

The strength of the Economic Committee lay in the fact that it brought together three or four times a year, for sessions of about a week, an international group of experts who learned to work as a team and whose far-ranging studies focused the light of world opinion on the major economic problems of the day. The fact that most of these experts also held important posts in their respective governments meant that their recommendations had considerable practical influence. On the other hand, in later years there was some feeling that the Committee was weighted too heavily on the political side and should have more direct contact with the people who would eventually determine the success or failure of its recommendations — business, labor and consumers. Furthermore, so vast was the mandate of the group that there was no single professional body of knowledge that integrated their thinking and gave them uniform standards of value as was the case, for example, with those who composed the Health Organization. Nor was there as much continuity of membership in the Economic Committee as there was in some other bodies.

The Financial Committee won a reputation for being somewhat more effective than the Economic Committee largely because of its less cosmic sphere of activity, its members' common professional banking background, its tendency to have more outstanding personnel and its greater continuity of membership.[16] Perhaps the most important accomplishment that contributed to this reputation was its surprising success, early in the League's existence, in securing desperately needed loans for Austria, Hungary and certain other destitute nations. On the other hand, the resources and authority of the Committee were hopelessly inadequate to deal with the avalanche of financial woes which descended upon the world with the advent of the depression in the early thirties.

Other Committees. In 1927, the League Assembly, on the advice of the World Economic Conference of that year, decided to establish a Consultative Committee as a more representative version of the Economic Committee. It was not to replace the latter, but to complement it by airing its work before a group composed of representatives of industry, commerce, agriculture, cooperatives, and labor. With its fifty-six members, however, this body was both too large to be manageable and too small to be sufficiently representative of all interested parties.[17]

After a succession of *ad hoc* statistical committees, a permanent Committee of Statistical Experts was authorized by an international statistical convention adopted in 1928. This body did not affect men's lives very directly and was considered neither very controversial nor very important.[18] The League Council, in December 1928, also established a permanent Fiscal Committee of twelve prominent tax experts to help achieve the coordination of separate national tax systems — e.g., to prevent overlapping taxation as well as tax evasion.

When the tragic events of the thirties began to close in on Geneva, the League made a few desperate attempts to deal with the fundamental causes of depression and its twin brother, war. In 1938, the Council appointed a Special Delegation of the Financial and Economic Committees for the Study of Economic Depressions composed of certain members of those two bodies under the chairmanship of Sir Frederick Phillips of the British Treasury. This able body continued its work through the war and produced certain studies that have been widely influential among both scholars and statesmen.[19] A similar body, the Committee of Experts for the Study of Demographic Problems, was organized by the League Council in January 1939, to suggest how best to ease the pressing tide of European population which was no longer being absorbed by the railroads and factories of the United States nor by any other nation. After the outbreak of the war, this group's studies were continued by the Office of Population Research of Princeton University.

---

[16] Greaves, *op. cit.*, pp. 64–84.   [17] *Ibid.*, pp. 47–49.
[18] Martin Hill, *The Economic and Financial Organization of the League of Nations* (Washington: Carnegie Endowment for International Peace, 1946), pp. 96–98.
[19] *Ibid.*, pp. 83–85, 131–134.

Secretariat. The small Economic and Financial Section of the Secretariat, created by Secretary-General Drummond in the summer of 1919, was soon placed under the direction of Sir Arthur Salter, who had played such an important role as chairman of the Allied Maritime Transport Executive. When Sir Arthur left the Secretariat in 1931, the single section was split into two bodies: (1) the Financial Section and Economic Intelligence Service and (2) the Economic Relations Section. The peak of this activity came in 1938 when the personnel of both sections numbered seventy. Then, in 1939, the two sections were reunited as Department II (Economic, Financial, and Transit Department). Finally, in 1940, most of this Department was moved to the Institute for Advanced Study in Princeton, New Jersey.

Communications and Transit Bodies

The British Foreign Office, Cecil, and Smuts proposals had all mentioned both communications and transport as suitable matters for League action. While a provision for commissions to deal with such subjects was included in the Cecil–Miller Draft, it failed to appear in the later Hurst–Miller version. The vague principle of "freedom of transit" was generally championed at the Peace Conference by all of the great powers, but they failed to agree on the details of any plan to make transit significantly freer. Nonetheless, the British supplied the following text of Article 23(e) of the Covenant, supplemented by Colonel House's addition of freedom of communications:

> Subject to and in accordance with the provisions of international conventions existing or hereafter to be agreed upon, the Members of the League . . . will make provision to secure and maintain freedom of communications and transit.

In addition to the Covenant, other sections of the Versailles Treaty assigned the League more specific responsibilities. Part XI stipulated conditions according to which the conquered countries should treat Allied and Associated aircraft. Part XII set forth certain provisions regarding "ports, waterways, and railways" including the following:

> 1. that Germany should allow free transit on international routes through her territories including all or part of the Elbe, Oder, Niemen, Danube, Rhine and Moselle Rivers to be administered by international commissions;
> 2. that the Allied and Associated Powers should formulate a General Convention on international waterways to be approved by the League;
> 3. that all signatories of the Peace Treaties should comply with existing Berne conventions on international railway transportation until a new convention replaced them;
> 4. that Germany should also make certain other railway concessions to the victorious powers;

5. that the League should settle disputes arising out of these provisions, might recommend their revision, and might itself actually revise certain specified articles five years after the Peace Treaties came into force.

Communications and Transit Organization

In February 1920, the League Council assumed direction of a nineteen-state committee of inquiry on transit problems which had been formed independently the previous August at the invitation of the French Government. The following month this Provisional Committee on Communications and Transit proposed the calling of the Barcelona Conference on Communications and Transit, which met from March to April 1921, and the establishment of a permanent Committee. This pioneering proposal also included an important statement of principle which was to have great influence upon all of the technical organizations:

> The members of the Committee would be considered not as representing Members of the League by whom they were nominated, but as acting in the name of the Members of the League of Nations regarded collectively.[20]

In June 1921, the League Council adopted the constitution of the Communications and Transit Organization which had been formulated at the Barcelona Conference. As the first League "technical organization" to be established, it provided the basic pattern for those that followed. It consisted of periodic General Conferences, an Advisory and Technical Committee for Communications and Transit, and the Communications and Transit Section of the Secretariat. Its scope was severely limited, however, by the fact that the responsibility for many important communications and transit fields had already been assigned to other bodies such as the Universal Postal Union, the International Telegraphic and International Radio Telegraphic Unions, the International Commission for Aerial Navigation, the Berne Central Office for Transport by Rail and various river commissions. The organization tended to concentrate, therefore, on the gaps that were left, chiefly water and road transport. As certain political and budgetary pressures developed, the Organization felt also that it was unduly restricted by the Assembly and Council and began to envy the International Labor Organization's relative independence.[21]

Conferences. The General Conferences were to be convoked by the League Council at least once every four years to examine the work of the Committee, accept or reject recommendations including draft conventions and revise the Organization's constitution whenever necessary. During the twenties, these Conferences, together with the International Labor Organization Conferences, were the most vigorous among the technical bodies and were an important supplement to the work of the Communications and Transport Committee. In the thirties, however, the General Confer-

---

[20] Greaves, *op. cit.*, p. 145.
[21] Jan Hostie, "Communications and Transit," *World Organization* (Washington: American Council on Public Affairs, 1942), pp. 158–172.

ences were supplemented by the League Assembly which was ill-equipped to supervise the Organization's work.

The Committee for Communications and Transit. The Committee for Communications and Transport was able to mobilize a remarkable group of experts — engineers, chiefs of national transport departments, directors of railways and port authorities — who, with very limited resources and authority, tried diligently to develop and coordinate the world's transport and communications systems. It is also interesting to note that the Organization's constitution explicitly provided that, unlike most other League technical committees, those states permanently represented on the League Council were "entitled as of right" to send members to the Committee. Other members were to be designated by the Assembly (before 1938, by the General Conference) according to geographic representation and interest in communications.

Secretariat. One of the first Secretariat units to be organized, the Communications and Transit Section, which numbered no more than fifteen officials, served the General Conferences as well as the Committee and its various sub-bodies. Seriously overworked, starved for funds and frequently diverted to other tasks, this Section never proved a very strong arm for the Communications and Transit Organization.

Related Organizations

The Paris Peace Conference Aeronautical Commission formulated an Air Convention, separate from the Peace Treaties, which was signed in October 1919. That Convention not only contained various substantive agreements on aviation matters but also provided for a permanent International Commission for Air Navigation to help implement and develop the terms of the Convention. The Commission, which met at least once a year, had the exceptional authority to adopt, by special majority vote, amendments to the technical annexes of the Paris Convention which then became binding upon all Commission members. While the Commission was legally placed under the League's "direction," the relationship in actual practice was little more than one of friendly cooperation.

The intensive development of radio during World War I convinced many leaders in this field that the time had come for a union of two older organizations — the International Telegraphic Union, founded in 1865, and the International Radio Telegraphic Union, founded in 1906. Because of many national differences, however, especially between the United States and France as to which of them should play host to the unification conference, the two bodies were not mated until 1932 at Madrid. The result was the International Telecommunication Union with authority over telegraphy, telephony and radio. The Union was composed of four types of bodies:

1. The Conference of plenipotentiaries was to meet only to consider revision of the basic convention and, after 1932, did not convene again during the interwar period.

2. Three "administrative conferences," of governmental delegates, dealing with telegraphy, telephony and radio respectively, were to be the supreme authorities in their special spheres and were authorized, like the Commission for Air Navigation, to revise the technical regulations adopted as part of the 1932 Madrid Convention. These met only once after 1932, in 1938 at Cairo.

3. Three "consultative committees," composed of public and private experts, were authorized to exchange information and formulate recommendations in the same three specialized fields.

4. The Bureau, inherited from the two older organizations, was the Union's permanent secretariat.

In general, the International Telecommunication Union was a substantial improvement over its two parent organizations. As time went on, however, there developed a need for some combination of the qualities of the administrative conferences and the consultative committees. The conferences tended to be too unwieldy and too infrequent. The committees were larger and more frequent but lacked the authority to revise the technical regulations.

The chief international organization concerned with the postal service remained the Universal Postal Union, established in 1874, which is discussed in Chapter 9.

International Labor Organization

Labor won a great deal for itself in the Treaty of Versailles largely because many of its more far-sighted leaders began working long before the end of the war to build an international organization that would promote the welfare of organized labor. Congresses were held, resolutions passed, petitions circulated and politicians buttonholed. Added to these efforts was the persuasion of certain threatening events — the revolution in Russia and ominous rumblings in other areas, particularly Germany and Southeastern Europe, that could be heard only too clearly at the Peace Conference in Paris. One of the Conference's first acts, therefore, was to set up a Commission on International Labor Legislation under the chairmanship of the prophet of American Labor, Samuel Gompers, to

inquire into the conditions of employment from the international aspect and to recommend the form of a permanent agency to continue such inquiry and consideration in cooperation with and under the direction of the League of Nations.[22]

The initiative in planning this labor organization was assumed from the beginning by the British, whose draft was accepted as the basis for discussion. This plan set forth the revolutionary principle of having each state send to the future labor organization one delegate representing the gov-

---

[22] Adopted Jan. 25. *Preliminary Peace Conference Protocol, No. 2* (American Commission to Negotiate Peace), Annex 4.

ernment (with two votes); one, the employers (with one vote); and one, the workers (with one vote). Mr. Gompers and Leon Jouhaux, the fiery French labor leader, wanted to give labor a stronger voice than this, but George Barnes, father of the British plan, and Emile Vandervelde, of Belgium, carried the day by arguing that governments must have half the votes as long as the organization's recommendations could not be implemented without governmental approval. It was also decided that both labor and business must be included in each state's delegation before either representative would be allowed to vote. The member states were to be guided in selecting the nongovernmental delegates by their "most representative" organizations of employers and workers. The International Labor Organization was to be composed of the familiar three principal elements:

1. a Conference, in which all the member states were to be represented, which would meet at least once a year;

2. a Governing Body composed of thirty-two persons, eight selected by the governments "of chief industrial importance" as determined by the League Council; eight, by the delegates of the other governments represented in the Labor Conference; eight, by all the employer delegates; and eight, by all the labor delegates; and

3. a Labor Office, to serve as the Organization's secretariat.

Jouhaux caused considerable consternation late in the proceedings by demanding that the organization be endowed with full legislative authority to bind member governments. The British position was that conventions passed by a two-thirds majority should become binding unless rejected by member states within a year. Both positions were too strong for American tastes, however, and Mr. Gompers, supported by Vandervelde, finally convinced the Commission that it should do no more than oblige members to submit, within twelve to eighteen months, all recommendations and draft conventions approved by a two-thirds vote to "the [national] authority or authorities within whose competence the matter lies. . . ." And, as a special concession to the United States, where most labor matters were normally handled by the states rather than the federal government, it was decided that a "federal state" might treat a "convention" as a mere "recommendation." Nevertheless, allowing a two-thirds majority to determine a conference decision was in itself revolutionary since diplomatic conferences up to that time had usually required unanimity on matters of substance and the League itself was going to continue the practice.

Sanctions and Other Attributes. There was also great hope at the Peace Conference that the Organization could be armed with effective sanctions. And it is perhaps remarkable that the Conference was able to agree on provisions that not only required annual national reports on compliance but also authorized various degrees of pressure against offending states. "Representations" by employer or worker associations and "complaints" by member states could be followed up by "commissions of inquiry," appointed by the League Secretary-General, which were authorized to make appropriate recommendations including "economic measures" to be taken against the defaulting member. If such a state did not accept the report, a final decision could be made by the Permanent Court of International Justice. If the culprit still remained obdurate, members could then resort to the recommended "measures." In spite of this formidable armory of weapons, however, the Organization in actual practice never went beyond the sanction of publicity.

Other provisions in the Peace Treaty dealt with the Organization's internal administration. Its membership was to be identical with that of the League, but a few non-League members such as Germany and the United States were subsequently welcomed to the fold. It was this infusion of major non-League members, in fact, which during the thirties made the ILO seem a more vital forum than the League itself. The Organization's expenses were to be provided by the League in accordance with a budget to be submitted annually to the League Assembly. Amendments to the ILO constitution could be made by a two-thirds majority of the Conference when ratified by the states whose representatives composed the League Council and by three-fourths of the League's Members.

Finally, towards the end of the Paris negotiations, it was decided, largely on the insistence of the French and Italians, to include in the peace treaty a "charter" of labor principles as a preamble to the ILO Constitution which became Part XIII of the Peace Treaty. These principles included "the right of association, . . . a wage adequate to maintain a reasonable standard of life, . . . an eight-hour's day or forty-eight-hours' week, . . . [and] the abolition of child labor. . . ."

Links with the League. As for the relationship between the ILO and the League, the intention of the Commission on International Labor Legislation was that the Organization should be established quite separately under an independent convention. But the Peace Conference decided that the labor provisions should be included in the Treaty of Peace. This tug-of-war between independence and integration continued over the years and tended to make the relationship somewhat vague and flexible.

On the one hand, the ILO was bound to the League by its overlapping membership, its dependence on League funds, the League Council's authority to decide which were the states of "chief industrial importance" to sit on the Governing Body, the Secretary-General's participation in the appointment of commissions of inquiry and the statement in Article 392 of the Treaty of Peace that the "International Labor Office shall be established at the seat of the League of Nations as a part of the organization of the League." On the other hand, the Organization's independence was reinforced by the crusading zeal of the first Director, Albert Thomas, a volatile French socialist whose background was that of a journalist and politician rather than civil servant. Furthermore, the ILO began to function before the League was organized. Its constitution was not included in the League Covenant, and its membership tended to be more universal than that of the League, especially after Germany, Italy and Japan had left the League, but not the ILO, and the United States had joined the ILO but not the League. The trend during the interwar years was away from a legal integration under the Peace Treaty to one of voluntary cooperation through a constant exchange of information and recommendations.

In addition to the provisions which were approved by the Peace Conference in April 1919, a companion passage was inserted in the League Covenant as Article 23(a):

> . . . the Members of the League . . . will endeavor to secure and maintain fair and humane conditions of labor for men, women, and children, both in their own countries and in all countries to which their commercial and industrial relations extend, and for that purpose will establish and maintain the necessary international organizations.

International Labor Conferences

The ILO Conference represented a marriage of the "technical" and "diplomatic" conferences which had been held separately under the auspices of the International Association for Labor Legislation before World War I. As the ILO Conference began to develop, the common views of the three interests represented — government, labor and employer — led them to organize themselves into three "groups," as they were called, that elected officers, held regular meetings and formulated common policies. This division within the Conference was markedly different from the League Assembly, with its tendency to divide into blocs of states, and made the Conference more like a true legislature since the interests of popular groups were represented directly rather than solely through their states. The governmental "group" tended to be less unified in organization and policy than either of the other two, although a majority of states tended to side with labor more than industry, partly because the governmental delegates were normally chosen from labor ministry staffs.

After its first meeting in October 1919, the Conference, until 1940, convened every year, usually in the late spring or early summer, which was far more frequently than any other technical conference met. Each session's policy discussions were set in motion by the Director's report, a tradition begun by Albert Thomas, who took full advantage of the occasion to bring to bear the leadership of the International Labor Office. The real business of the Conference was the consideration of draft recommendations and conventions which were the end products of a most thorough and painstaking procedure evolved after much criticism and experimentation during the years 1922 to 1928. (1) On a subject placed on the agenda for action the International Labor Office prepared reports on existing law and practice together with draft proposals. (2) After considering these, the Conference would adopt "conclusions." (3) The Office then used these as the basis for a questionnaire which was submitted to the member governments. (4) According to the answers received, the Office would prepare new proposals based on "an average point of view" and send these with the government replies to the member states. (5) The next year's Conference would consider that information and pass final judgment on the recommendations and conventions. Decisions in committee were made by simple majority, but ultimate approval of recommendations and draft conventions required a two-thirds majority, a procedure that foreshadowed the practice of the United Nations General Assembly.

The Governing Body

The Governing Body contained the leading figures of the Organization and was endowed with important executive functions. In contrast to the League Council's relationship to the Assembly, the Governing Body's relationship to the Conference was much more like that of a cabinet to a parliament. It was stronger than most of the League's technical committees. Unlike them, it could control the Conference's agenda, it could appoint the director of its secretariat, it had extensive enforcement authority, and it had a stronger link with the peoples of the world because it included in its membership direct representatives of labor and employers as well as governments.

In the formulation of policy, the Governing Body was buffeted by strong and conflicting winds. The labor group usually took the left position. The employer delegates normally reacted in exactly the opposite direction. And the Director and governmental group tended to try to find a "center" position. Under these pressures, perhaps the Governing Body's greatest achievement was not that it promoted this or that program but that it achieved any agreement at all.

International Labor Office

The International Labor Office was a direct descendant of the International Labor Office which had been established at Basel, Switzerland, in 1901 to serve as the permanent bureau of the International Association for Labor Legislation. Provision was made for such a secretariat in the early British plans, and it was approved at Paris without significant disagreement.

The Director of the Office, who was appointed by the Governing Body, was usually a stronger figure than the League Secretary-General. This is to be explained not so much by his constitutional authority as by the traditions established by M. Thomas. He exerted the Office's influence in two principal ways: first, by insisting that it have its own point of view on every issue and, second, by using that view as an instrument for conciliating the opposing policies of the three groups represented in the Organization.

> Thomas was little in evidence at the Conference until the conflict arose and then he was in the middle, negotiating between the customary belligerents, the employers and the workers, and pointing out one compromise after another until one was found which united the Conference.[23]

[23] Francis G. Wilson, *Labor in the League System* (Stanford: Stanford University Press, 1934), p. 111.

The size of the Office staff grew to be much larger than originally anticipated and larger than was agreeable to the employers' group. It numbered about four hundred as compared with seven hundred in the League Secretariat. Its organization was more centralized than that of the League, largely due to the tastes of M. Thomas, but administrative practices and pay scales were very similar. Constitutionally, the Office was entirely separate from the League Secretariat, except for its budget, although in practice relations between the two were cooperative. In answer to the criticism sometimes made that the two secretariats should have been combined, for the good of policy as well as administration, the majority of informed observers have said that more was accomplished for the world's workers precisely because the Office was somewhat protected from the "political" pressures of the League and its Secretariat.[24] In fact, however, the atmosphere of the Office was little less "political" than that of the League. The crucial factor in favor of a separate existence was that the activities of the Office could thereby be developed more vigorously and freely with greater world-wide attention. When war came, the Office moved to McGill University in Montreal, Canada, and activities had to be curtailed.

Conclusions

Organizations are mirrors of the environments in which they operate. The peculiar characteristics of the ILO reflected certain fundamental assumptions which were common in 1919 about relations among workers, employers and governments, and, by its very existence and work, the ILO tended to reinforce those assumptions: (1) that workers and employers should be equally concerned with the formulation of labor regulations; (2) that neither side should be allowed to dominate the other; (3) that the government should act as the principal mediator but not the sole authority; and (4) that, with private employers as well as workers represented, the basic economic system was expected to be some form of capitalism. During the interwar period, however, one or more of these assumptions were attacked by extreme individualists, capitalists, communists, fascists and even socialists. While these views gave rise to various proposals for recasting the ILO, no basic alterations were adopted.

Health Organs

Disease is no respecter of national boundaries. It had been subject to some degree of international control since 1851, and a permanent International Office of Public Health had existed in Paris since 1907. Hence, there was little doubt at the Paris Peace Conference that the League should also be concerned with health matters. While the British proposals mentioned

24 Harold Butler, *The Lost Peace* (New York: Harcourt, Brace, 1941), p. 54.

health as a matter appropriate for League action, no specific mention of it was inserted in the Covenant until late in the Conference.

The initiative was then taken by the Red Cross Society which asked that the Covenant endorse its work.[25] The British, however, did not want to relinquish to a private organization functions which they felt belonged to governments. Thus they proposed the text of Article 23(f) in order to assure the world that international health would not be neglected by the League.

> . . . the Members of the League will endeavor to take steps in matters of international concern for the prevention and control of disease.

Article 25 was also added to satisfy the Red Cross:

> The Members of the League agree to encourage and promote the establishment and cooperation of duly authorized voluntary national Red Cross organizations having as purposes the improvement of health, the prevention of disease and the mitigation of suffering throughout the world.

The British were also anxious to continue the pre-World War I regulations of opium traffic and suggested the text which was accepted as Article 23(c):

> The Members of the League . . . will entrust the League with the general supervision over the . . . traffic in opium and other dangerous drugs.

Health Organization

In February 1920 the League Council asked an international committee to draft plans for a permanent League health organization which would absorb the old International Office of Public Health in Paris, a proposal that had already been approved by the executive Committee of that Office. After such a plan had been prepared and approved by the League Council and Assembly, the United States, which was a member of the Paris Office, refused to consent to the merger. The League Council then decided, in June 1921, to create its own Health Committee without the Paris Office, and the two organizations remained separate throughout the entire interwar period.

Nevertheless, considerable coordination was achieved through an arrangement whereby the conference of the Paris Office, the so-called Permanent Committee, also acted as the conference (called the General Advisory Health Council) of the League's Health Organization. By means of this organizational overlap and through a constant exchange of information, rather effective collaboration was achieved as early as 1923. Besides the League Health Council and Committee, there were two related units in the Secretariat: the Service of Epidemiological Intelligence and Health Statis-

[25] David Hunter Miller, *The Drafting of the Covenant* (New York: Putnam's, 1928), Vol. 1, p. 400.

tics, and the Health Section. In 1923 these four components were designated the League Health Organization.

The General Advisory Health Council. This body was composed of one delegate from each of the signatories of the Rome Convention of 1907, which had created the International Office of Public Health at Paris, plus a delegate from each League member that was not a signatory of the Rome Convention. It met twice a year in Paris. Decisions were made by simple majority, and the votes of the delegates were weighted according to their governments' financial contributions to the Paris Office.

Although most of the delegates were experts assigned from their national health administrations, they attended the conferences as representatives of governments bound by governmental instructions. The link between the General Advisory Health Council and the League Health Committee meant not only that the latter's work was closely geared to the national public health departments, but also that the Health Committee tended to be more independent of the League Council and Assembly than it might have been without the Council.

The Health Committee. The Health Committee, with woefully inadequate financial resources, achieved an admirable reputation for active and disinterested service. Its dozen members, meeting two or three times a year, were for the most part renowned leaders in their field. About two-thirds of them were high officials in their national health ministries; the other third were medical professors. Two United States citizens participated from 1923 on. The common professional training of these persons tended to integrate the group in spite of the different nationalities represented.

Health Section of the Secretariat. This unit developed in response to the epidemics that were raging through Eastern Europe in 1919 and that frightened the West into positive action. Gradually the Health Section developed into one of the League's most important technical units with a peak staff of forty-eight in 1933. Early in the twenties, the Service of Epidemiological Intelligence was created with Rockefeller Foundation funds to collect and dispense information on epidemics. These units were reduced to a mere skeleton force after the outbreak of war in 1939.

League Anti-narcotic Bodies

Against the background of a series of international efforts since 1909 to control the debilitating opium traffic, the 1920 League Assembly asked the Council to establish an Opium Committee to deal with the problem. The Assembly's resolution also directed the Secretariat to promote national compliance with the Hague Convention of 1912, ratification of which had been made a condition of accepting the Treaty of Versailles. Although no conference was created to meet regularly on the drug question, special conferences were convoked in 1924, 1925, 1931 and 1936 to consider specific proposals submitted by the Opium Committee.

Advisory Committee on Traffic in Opium and Other Dangerous Drugs.
The leading figures on the Committee were individuals, like Sir Malcolm
Delevingue (Great Britain) and Sir John Campbell (India), who were sincerely interested in fighting the drug trade. Unfortunately certain interests, primarily British and Indian, which profited from the traffic were
largely successful in blocking the Committee's efforts in the early years.
Outspoken criticism of this impasse led, in 1930, to a shift in the weight
of representation from the drug-producing countries in favor of the victim-
ized drug-consuming countries and other interested nations. While this
reform broadened the Committee's membership, it did not make its task
much easier. The delegates, appointed as the representatives of governments rather than as individual experts, tended to be strait-jacketed by
national interests and were able to move no faster than the most cautious
state.

Permanent Central Opium Board. Created by a Convention of 1925,
this body was established as a kind of weak policeman to try to enforce the
provisions of the conventions of 1912 and 1925. Its specific functions were:
to act as a clearing house for certain information (quarterly import and
export statistics; annual estimates of imports and domestic consumption; annual statistics on raw material produced, manufactured drugs, and illicit
seizures) and to ask governments embarrassing questions about excessive
stocks or traffic in drugs. By a 1931 convention, the Board's muscles were
strengthened to allow it to institute embargoes against countries that exceeded their import or export quotas. The eight independent experts who
composed the Board were selected for terms of five years by the League
Council; there was also a representative of the United States which was
an important signatory of the 1925 convention.

The Drug Supervisory Body. Established by the 1931 convention, this
committee was authorized to establish narcotic manufacturing quotas on
the basis of annual governmental estimates. The four-man Body was composed of one delegate apiece from the Opium Committee, the Permanent
Central Opium Board, the Health Committee and the Paris International
Office of Public Health.

Secretariat. Until 1930, the anti-narcotic work of the Secretariat was
handled by the Social Questions Section. After that date, a separate Opium
Section was formed which served both the Opium Committee and the
Supervisory Body. Its personnel peak was seven officers in 1938. The Permanent Central Opium Board had its own secretariat, established in 1929,
which never included more than a Chief-of-Section and one or two statisticians.

Social Organs

In order to strengthen the weak international efforts that had been made before World War I to protect women and children, the British suggested the text which became Article 23(c) of the Covenant:

> ... The Members of the League ... will entrust the League with the general supervision over the execution of agreements with regard to the traffic in women and children. ...

Advisory Committee on Social Questions

Following the recommendations of the Conference on White Slave Traffic held at Geneva in 1921, the League Council, the next year, established a nine-member advisory committee to deal with the traffic in women. In 1924, as the result of Assembly recommendations, the Council established another section of the Committee to concern itself with child welfare and called the two sections the Advisory Committee on the Traffic in Women and Child Welfare. Then, in 1936, these sections were combined as a single Advisory Committee on Social Questions. With the advent of World War II, the Committee's work was brought to a virtual standstill.

This Committee, unlike most other League technical bodies, was composed of individuals who served as governmental representatives, rather than individual experts, and was not a particularly successful body. The fundamental difficulty was that the welfare of women and children was not the major concern of governments, especially in the hectic thirties. When budget allocations were made, the money tended to go to other activities.

Secretariat

The Social Questions Section of the Secretariat, established in 1919, changed names frequently during the following years as it attempted to deal with health and the drug traffic as well as the tribulations of women and children. Finally, in 1930, the Section was freed of all responsibilities other than these latter problems. Still it continued to be the weakling of the Secretariat.

Other Social Bodies

A Committee of Experts for Assistance to Indigent Foreigners was created by the League Council in 1931 to try to mitigate the poverty of foreigners, especially minors, who were suffering extraordinary hardships because of the depression. In 1937, at the request of the Assembly, the League Council appointed an expert Committee for the Study of the Legal Status of Women to prepare for publication "a comprehensive study giving full information on the legal status enjoyed by women in the various countries of the world" as a preliminary effort towards improving the condition of women. In 1932 a seven-member Advisory Committee of Experts on Slavery was created by the League Council to study and make recommendations regarding that problem.

Refugee Organs

The Russian political upheaval in 1917 set in motion a tidal wave of refugees that threatened to flood various neighboring states. Those countries, together with private charitable organizations, such as the Red Cross, urged the League to assume some of the burden. The Council finally agreed, in September 1921, to appoint Dr. Fridtjof Nansen as the League High Commissioner to deal with the problem. Here was one of those rare individuals, like Albert Thomas of the ILO, who tower above their fellowmen as great altruists and inspire extraordinary achievements in the face of the most discouraging lethargy and outright sabotage. This blue-eyed, thickly mustached Norwegian explorer and humanitarian so dominated the League's refugee effort that, when he died in May 1930, the whole program almost stalled for lack of leadership.

The High Commissioner was directly responsible to the League Council and was advised by both an intergovernmental commission of interested states and a committee of private organizations. Advice was plentiful; it was money that was scarce. Nansen received no salary and was granted only three assistants. The Red Cross furnished his field representatives until they were replaced in later years by the League's own men.

In 1924, Albert Thomas and Nansen succeeded in convincing the League Council, in spite of the unfriendly attitude of the ILO Governing Body, that the staff work of finding homes and employment for the Russian refugees should be assigned to the International Labor Office, which was then concerned with the larger problem of finding jobs on an international basis for all excess laborers. The political and legal aspects of the refugee problem were to remain with Nansen who was also to act as liaison between the League and the ILO. Unfortunately funds and national cooperation were never made available on the scale hoped for by Nansen and Thomas, and the resettlement problem was handed back to the League at the end of 1929. Nansen's death in May 1930 created a vacuum which was only partially filled by the Assembly's creation of an "autonomous" Nansen International Office for Refugees which began to function in April 1931.[26]

Two years later the rise of Hitler started new streams of persecuted people pouring into neighboring countries. To meet this emergency, the Netherlands initiated discussions in the Assembly which resulted in the cre-

[26] The Governing Body of the Office was composed of a President nominated by the League Assembly, three representatives of Nansen's Intergovernmental Advisory Commission, two persons nominated by the League Secretary-General and the ILO Director respectively, three representatives of the Consultative Committee of Private Organizations, and two persons chosen by these members of the Governing Body to represent the important international relief organizations.

ation, in October 1933, of the High Commissioner for Refugees Coming from Germany.[27] In order to avoid a veto by the German Government, which was still a Member of the League, it was decided to make the new High Commissioner as remote as possible from the League. He was to report not to the League Council, which was to appoint him, but to a separate Governing Body consisting of twelve delegates from interested governments. He was also forced to set up his office in Lausanne so that he would not be seen too often in Geneva, and his financial needs were to be met entirely by the contributions of philanthropic organizations. It was not until January 1936, after Germany had made its inglorious exit from the League, that the League Council finally consented to place the Commissioner under its own wing.

The termination of the Nansen Office's authority in 1938 in accordance with its original mandate forced the Assembly to create, at the end of that year, a new High Commissioner for Refugees who was to assume the duties of not only the Nansen Office but also the High Commissioner for Refugees Coming from Germany. Because of the Soviet Union's implacable opposition to any aid for White Russians and because of the reluctance of other countries to assume any great financial burden at a time when they were suffering from both the depression and rearmament, the new High Commissioner was also made as independent of the League as possible, and his duties were rigidly limited to political and legal functions to the exclusion of any direct economic relief.

Intellectual Cooperation

That peace depends on the state of men's minds as well as their bodies is an insight that had found expression in several pre-World War I organizations such as the Union of International Associations, a league of international nongovernmental bodies established in 1910 at Brussels. Against this background the British Foreign Office–Cecil–Smuts proposals suggested that the League also concern itself with cultural cooperation. At the Paris Peace Conference, however, no specific suggestion was put forward until the Belgians proposed an International Commission on Intellectual Relations to encourage the "development of moral, scientific and artistic international relations and . . . the formation of an international outlook." [28] Because this proposal was made late in the Conference when the tendency was to discourage any further embroidery of the Covenant, it was withdrawn without discussion.

Intellectual Cooperation Organization

During the first and second sessions of the League Assembly, M. Henri La Fontaine, a Belgian pioneer in organizing international cultural collab-

[27] James G. McDonald, "Refugees," *Pioneers in World Order* (New York: Columbia University Press, 1944), pp. 217–221.
[28] Miller, *op. cit.*, Vol. 1, p. 350.

oration, and Gilbert Murray, distinguished British scholar and educator, were largely responsible for persuading the Assembly to authorize the Council to create a Committee on Intellectual Cooperation. Since education, however, had long been jealously regarded by each state as its own private instrument for molding the minds of its citizens, it was finally decided not to mention education explicitly. Nevertheless, it was generally assumed that that subject could be dealt with within the Committee's broad jurisdiction.

In 1931 the Assembly recognized the various organs concerned with cultural cooperation as the Intellectual Cooperation Organization. These included: the International Committee on Intellectual Cooperation, International Institute of Intellectual Cooperation in Paris, International Educational Cinematographic Institute in Rome, International Bureaus and Intellectual Cooperation Section of the Secretariat, and National Committee of Intellectual Cooperation.

Conferences. From the beginning, the Committee on Intellectual Cooperation realized that if it were to grow strong it would have to sink its roots deep in the intellectual soil of each nation. For that purpose it began in 1923 to promote the establishment of "national committees of intellectual cooperation," first, to help with the immediate task of providing relief to intellectuals in Central and Eastern Europe and, later, to serve as connecting links between forty-three different countries and the main Committee on Intellectual Cooperation. These national bodies held international conferences in 1923, 1926, 1929 and 1937 which served somewhat the same purpose, though they were not composed of governmental representatives, as the conferences that supported other League technical organizations. There were also special meetings of various types of experts to deal with specific and limited problems, such as the conference on higher education at Paris in 1937. None of these conferences, however, had as close or permanent a relationship with the main Committee as, for example, the Labor Conference had with the ILO Governing Body. Thus it was suggested that the Committee make more frequent and more intensive use of the conferences of national committees, but nothing significant was ever done along those lines.

Committee on Intellectual Cooperation. The major accomplishment of the Committee on Intellectual Cooperation was to draw together the intellectual strands of many professional fields in many nations which had never before been so thoroughly coordinated. The scope of the Committee's interests was so cosmic, however, that it was always a temptation to bite off more than it could chew. And the budgetary resources allotted for intellectual chewing were always discouragingly meager. Another difficulty was the absence of any single body of knowledge or standards of value such as tended to unify the Financial and Health Committees. Furthermore the giant personalities that sat on the Committee — Bergson, Einstein, Curie and Murray — were often too high in the clouds to grapple effectively with the mundane realities of organization and administration.

International Institute of Intellectual Cooperation. Within the first few months of its existence, the Committee on Intellectual Cooperation decided that it would rather go out of business than struggle along on the starvation diet allotted to it in the League budget. Thus it made a desperate plea for external assistance which evoked an offer in 1924 from the French, who had just installed a new government eager to demonstrate its support of the League. The proposal was to establish a permanent secretariat for the Committee at Paris. Although the Assembly was somewhat reluctant to see such a staff created under the auspices of a single nation and established outside of Geneva, Gilbert Murray reminded the League Members that they themselves had forced the move by not providing the necessary funds.

The Assembly finally accepted the offer, and the International Institute of Intellectual Cooperation began to function in January 1926, in cooperation with the far smaller Intellectual Cooperation Section of the League Secretariat, as the permanent staff of the Committee on Intellectual Cooperation. The Institute consisted of a Governing Body (merely the Committee under the chairmanship of its French member), a Committee of Directors nominated by the main Committee and including five of its members, a Director and staff. The Institute's budget was donated by a few governments and was quite separate from the League's finances. Together with the League Secretariat Section, it provided a full-time staff of about one hundred.

Two similar institutes were later established, both by the Fascist Italian Government, to provide secretariats to deal with intellectual activities: the International Institute for the Unification of Private International Law, created in 1928, and the International Educational Cinematographic Institute created in 1929.

If it had not been for France's offer of the Institute, the program of the Committee on Intellectual Cooperation would have been decidedly anemic. Yet the domination of the Institute by French personnel under the direction of a French ex-minister of education and its physical separation from Geneva led critics to feel that it was too much under the thumb of France. It also suffered from a tendency to ride off in all directions at once. More careful thought about long-range objectives and a better system of priorities might have precluded much waste motion. Finally the Institute might well have unloaded many of its activities on already existing organizations rather than attempting to carry so much on its own shoulders. In spite of these shortcomings, however, the Institute made an invaluable contribution to the world's welfare by trying to organize a true league of minds.

Suggestions for Further Reading

Books

Baker, Ray Stannard, *Woodrow Wilson and World Settlement,* 3 Vols. (Garden City: Doubleday, Page, 1922).

Butler, Harold, *The Lost Peace* (New York: Harcourt, Brace & Company, 1941).

Davis, Harriet Eager, ed., *Pioneers in World Order* (New York: Columbia University Press, 1944).

Greaves, H. R. G., *The League Committees and World Order* (London: Oxford University Press, 1931).

Hill, Martin, *The Economic and Financial Organization of the League of Nations* (Washington: Carnegie Endowment for International Peace, 1946).

Keynes, John Maynard, *The Economic Consequences of the Peace* (New York: Harcourt, Brace and Howe, 1920).

McClure, Wallace, *World Prosperity* (New York: The Macmillan Company, 1933).

Miller, David Hunter, *The Drafting of the Covenant,* 2 Vols. (New York: G. P. Putnam's Sons, 1928).

Myers, Denys P., *Handbook of the League of Nations* (Boston: World Peace Foundation, 1935).

Phelan, Edward J., *Yes, and Albert Thomas* (London: The Cresset Press, 1936).

Ranshofen-Wertheimer, Egon F., *The International Secretariat* (Washington: Carnegie Endowment for International Peace, 1945).

Salter, Arthur, *Allied Shipping Control: An Experiment in International Administration* (New York: Oxford University Press, 1921).

Shotwell, James T., ed., *The Origins of the International Labor Organization,* 2 Vols. (New York: Columbia University Press, 1934).

Symposium, *World Organization* (Washington: American Council on Public Affairs, 1942).

Walters, F. P., *A History of the League of Nations,* 2 Vols. (London: Oxford University Press for the Royal Institute of International Affairs, 1952).

Wilson, Francis Graham, *Labor in the League System* (Stanford: Stanford University Press, 1934).

Zimmern, Alfred, *The League of Nations and the Rule of Law, 1918–1935* (London: Macmillan and Co., Ltd., 1936).

Periodicals

Bourquin, Maurice, "Dynamism and the Machinery of International Institutions," *Geneva Studies,* Vol. 2, No. 5 (September 1940).

Engel, S., "League Reform," *Geneva Studies,* Vol. 2, Nos. 3–4 (August 1940).

Sweetser, Arthur, "The Non-Political Achievements of the League," *Foreign Affairs,* Vol. 19, No. 1 (October 1940).

Documents

League of Nations, *Ten Years of World Cooperation* (Geneva: League Secretariat, 1930).

————, "The Development of International Cooperation in Economic and Social Affairs," *Special Supplement to the Monthly Summary of the League of Nations,* Bruce Report (Geneva: August 1939).

8

Organizing for Economic and Social Progress — The United Nations

> "Economic diseases are highly communicable. It follows, therefore, that the economic health of every country is a proper matter of concern to all its neighbors, near and distant. Only through a dynamic and soundly expanding world economy can the living standard of individual nations be advanced to levels which will permit a full realization of our hopes for the future. . . ." — FRANKLIN D. ROOSEVELT [1]

IN TINY TROPICAL HAITI, the United Nations and affiliated specialized agencies are, as this volume goes to press, providing precious penicillin to fight syphilis, teaching the people of the miserable Marbial Valley to read and write, and engaging in six other projects to help pull the poorest Haitians up to a little higher level of life. And Haiti is just one of approximately a hundred states and dependencies affected by such programs. The Haitian projects are merely a small part of a total of 723 types of programs most of which involve several different territories.[2] Thus, from the modest seeds planted before World War II, a forest of United Nations economic projects has spread across the earth.

If the League's sad experience left no other deposit, it seems to have persuaded most of the Geneva veterans that the economic and social projects were the League's most constructive and encouraging contribution to world peace. It is scarcely surprising, therefore, that one of the most striking differences between the Covenant and the Charter is the way in which the latter brings the economic and social aspect out of the shadows into the spotlight. The Charter lavishes two whole chapters (IX and X), with a total of eighteen articles, on economic and social matters as compared with the single Article 23 in the Covenant. The goals of the United Nations

---

[1] Address to the Monetary and Financial Conference, Washington, D.C., June 29, 1944. In Louise W. Holborn, ed., *War and Peace Aims of the United Nations* (Boston: World Peace Foundation, 1948), p. 288.

[2] See *United Nations Catalogue of Economic and Social Projects, 1953*, UN Doc. E/2393.

system are far more expansive than under the League. Direction of the economic and social apparatus, moreover, has been transferred from the politically harassed League Council to a specialized Economic and Social Council, and more money and staff have been provided to nurture these activities.

There are other differences the effect of which is not so clear. There is greater emphasis on organizational decentralization in the United Nations than in the League, notably in the multiplication of semi-independent specialized agencies. And individuals are appointed to the top-level bodies as governmental representatives rather than as independent experts. Some believe these changes strengthen the new system; others think they weaken it.

In spite of all these differences, however, the issues involved in creating and operating the United Nations economic and social organization are still basically the same as in the League era. There is the question of *who* is to guide the program (great powers versus middle and small, the Assembly versus ECOSOC, the United Nations versus the specialized agencies, regional versus universal bodies, etc.). There is the issue of *what* is to be done (economic, social and cultural). And there is the matter of *how* all this is to be done (research, negotiation, decision-making and implementation).

Plans for Peace

History changes course only by slow degrees. In 1945, as in 1919, the victorious great powers (now the United States more than England) once again towered above the other states in planning the economic and social apparatus, though they were compelled to bow to some of the middle powers, especially Canada and Australia, on certain issues. Once again the lessons of the prewar period guided the architects' hands. And once again the desperate allied wartime struggle for survival provided fresh, but fleeting, inspiration for postwar collaboration.

CHRONOLOGICAL PERSPECTIVE

As early as August 1941 President Roosevelt and Prime Minister Churchill devoted two of the Atlantic Declaration's eight points to the first major statement on allied postwar economic and social objectives:

> Fourth, they will endeavour, with due respect for their existing obligations, to further the enjoyment by all states, great or small, victor or vanquished, of access on equal terms, to the trade and to the raw materials of the world which are needed for their economic prosperity.
>
> Fifth, they desire to bring about the fullest collaboration between all nations in the economic field, with the object of securing for all improved labour standards, economic advancement, and social security.

This opening salvo in the allied campaign to build a better postwar world was conveniently vague and hedged noticeably, at Churchill's behest, "with due respect for their existing obligations" to protect the Commonwealth preferential system. It aimed, nonetheless, at broader and more ambitious objectives than had President Wilson's Fourteen Points and came far earlier in the struggle, in fact, four months before the United States even entered the war.

In the planning efforts that followed there was a tendency to build agencies designed to operate in a world that no longer existed. Few planners seemed to realize that they were standing on the brink of far vaster dislocations than mankind had ever previously suffered. The fundamental economic problem at the end of the war was that the leading European nations, chiefly the United Kingdom and France, as well as a host of other states in Europe and Asia, had been impoverished by the conflict to an unprecedented degree and were unable to produce enough to meet domestic needs or pay for necessary imports. On the other hand, a few fortunate countries, chiefly the United States, whose economies had not suffered direct wartime destruction, were producing and exporting more than they had before the conflict. How to prime the pumps of the devastated nations was the immediate and tremendous task which the planners tended to underestimate. A final characteristic of the wartime blueprints is that the architects began by creating separate decentralized structures and only later linked them together by means of a loose arrangement for central coordination.

First Steps, 1941–1943

The month following the Atlantic Declaration, September 1941, the British initiated the creation of the Inter-Allied Committee on Postwar Requirements which was particularly concerned with the reconstruction needs of European countries liberated from the Nazis. In February 1942 the United States signed the Lend-Lease Agreement with the British committing the latter, who consented with considerable misgivings, to

> expansion . . . of production, employment and the exchange and consumption of goods . . . , elimination of all forms of discriminatory treatment in international commerce, . . . reduction of tariffs and other trade barriers; and . . . attainment of all the economic objectives . . . in the . . . [Atlantic] Declaration. . . .

In terms of the postwar situation that was to come, however, this declaration of faith in the religion of free trade, promoted by liberals in the United States State Department and other agencies, was a very dim candle in a very dark world.

In October 1942, a British-sponsored Conference of Allied Ministers of Education began a series of meetings to plan the postwar rehabilitation and development of educational systems, the source from which UNESCO ultimately flowed.

The first major United Nations meeting on postwar problems with full United States support was the Food and Agriculture Conference which met at Hot Springs, Virginia, May to June 1943, and established an Interim Commission that later produced a draft constitution for the Food and Agricultural Organization (FAO). This was a relatively noncontroversial subject on which to launch postwar international collaboration. There was also some sentiment among the United States public that the government was being unnecessarily sluggish in preparing for peacetime cooperation among nations. Roosevelt "favored at this time the establishment of entirely separate functional agencies in the economic field and chose food and agriculture as the subject offering the best chances for immediate success in the first attempt to test the willingness and ability of the United Nations to cooperate on postwar problems."[3]

During September and October 1943, Anglo-American conversations, rising out of the Lend-Lease Agreement mentioned above, were held in Washington. Although it was not intended to reach any firm conclusions, an agenda for future discussions was formulated which anticipated an international commercial-policy organization, an international commodity-policy organization and an advisory economic staff, possibly within the framework of a general political organization, to help coordinate the efforts of the various autonomous international agencies, especially with respect to maintaining high levels of employment. The Soviet Union and China were invited to participate in similar bilateral discussions, but such talks did not materialize, except with the Canadians in January and February 1944. Instead, the postwar questions rising out of the Lend-Lease Agreements were discussed multilaterally at Bretton Woods, Dumbarton Oaks, San Francisco and later conferences.

At Moscow, in October 1943, Secretary of State Cordell Hull presented four comprehensive papers on postwar economic and social problems, the first major exchange with the Soviet Union on these matters. They dealt with surveying the requirements for repairing war damage in the Soviet Union, creating an international lending agency to supplement private and governmental lending facilities, promoting various economic and social policies most of which the United States had already examined during the Anglo-American conversations, and endorsing liberal reparations policies with respect to Germany. Hull also repeated the invitation to the Soviet Union to participate in bilateral discussions. Later Hull wrote,

> I recalled very clearly the insufficient preparation on economic matters at the time of the Versailles Conference and the incalculable harm the world suffered as a result of the inadequate treatment of economic problems after the last war. I wished to ensure that this time these questions should be considered in good time.[4]

[3] *Postwar Foreign Policy Preparation, 1939–1945*, Department of State Publication 3580 (Washington: Government Printing Office, 1950), p. 143.

[4] Cordell Hull, *The Memoirs of Cordell Hull* (New York: Macmillan, 1948), Vol. 2, p. 1304. Used by permission of The Macmillan Company.

Neither Molotov nor Eden displayed great interest at that time in postwar economic and social matters, nor did the Conference adopt any resolutions on the subject. It concentrated chiefly on security questions.

In the White House in November 1943 an agreement establishing the United Nations Relief and Rehabilitation Administration (UNRRA) was finally signed. The British first prodded the United States on this matter as early as September 1940. It came to a boil during 1942, and President Roosevelt initialed an Anglo-American draft in October of that year. Largely due to congressional opposition, however, the agreement could not be approved until more than a year later. While the British and some Americans had hoped to make UNRRA the spearhead of the whole international reconstruction effort, other United States circles, especially in Congress, were successful in limiting the agency severely in both scope and time. President Roosevelt was compelled, therefore, to make it clear that UNRRA was merely to give "first aid" in the liberated areas, "to assist in furnishing the medicine, food, clothing, and other basic necessities and essential services" but not "to solve the long-range problems of reconstruction." UNRRA was simply "to lay the foundation" for reconstruction.[5]

Last Lap, 1944–1945

The pace quickened in 1944. In April the International Labor Conference met in Philadelphia for its twenty-sixth annual session and announced its readiness to cooperate with whatever general organization was to be created. During July the Monetary and Financial Conference met at Bretton Woods, New Hampshire, and agreed to establish an International Monetary Fund (IMF) and International Bank for Reconstruction and Development (IBRD).

At the Dumbarton Oaks Conference, August to September 1944, the major dispute on the economic and social proposals arose because the U.S.S.R. wanted the economic and social system established separately from the security system, in which it showed primary interest. When the Soviet Union finally abandoned this position, midway through the Conference, all three powers approved an economic and social plan which followed the language of the United States proposals almost *verbatim*, more so than in any other section of the Dumbarton Oaks Proposals. In November fifty-two nations, minus the Soviet Union which objected at the last moment to meeting with representatives of certain "pro-fascist" countries, convened at Chicago and approved a United States-initiated plan for an International Civil Aviation Organization (ICAO).

Having devoted 1942 to 1944 to planting individual agencies wherever and whenever they seemed most needed, the allies concentrated during 1945 on building a United Nations roof that would provide some loose coverage for the whole field. At the San Francisco Conference, April to June 1945, the general blueprint of the Dumbarton Oaks plan was followed, but the whole structure was reinforced and enlarged, mainly due to the

[5] *Postwar Foreign Policy Preparation* . . . , p. 204.

liberal views pressed by the Canadian, Australian and Indian delegates, cheered on by most of the smaller states. The United States Congress reacted to this pressure by stressing the sanctity of "domestic jurisdiction."

In May 1945, with the collapse of Germany, the allies constructed three bodies to concentrate on European reconstruction: the Emergency Economic Committee for Europe (EECE), the European Central Inland Transport Organization (ECITO), and the European Coal Organization (ECO). In November 1945, a London conference approved a constitution for the UN Educational, Scientific and Cultural Organization (UNESCO). The constitution of the last major specialized agency to be formed, the World Health Organization (WHO), was approved in New York City in July 1946.

COMPLEX OF NATIONAL INTERESTS

The United States

After this brief Cook's tour of the planning process, one can look back and see the general pattern of national interests at work. Within the United States, it is interesting to recall the climate of opinion in various influential private circles (Council on Foreign Relations, Commission to Study the Organization of Peace, United States Chamber of Commerce, etc.), most of which were in close, though largely unpublicized, contact with governmental planners.[6] While these groups saw the world through United States eyes, their views showed a cautious but marked swing towards internationalism. A comparative analysis of their statements indicates that the great majority of them favored international cooperation by the United States towards the following objectives, listed in descending order of their popularity: lowering trade barriers, stabilizing and decontrolling currencies, providing postwar relief and rehabilitation, fostering long-term capital investment, promoting better food production and utilization, easing migration and fostering social security. They tended to pay less attention to organizational details, but most of those authors who considered this problem urged a considerable degree of decentralization under the loose direction of an over-all agency established as an integral part of some general organization like the League of Nations. While conservatives such as Mr. Herbert Hoover tiptoed gingerly, seeking only minimal governmental action on a very decentralized basis, enthusiastic internationalists, such as Professor Eugene Staley of the Fletcher School of Law and Diplomacy, writing for the influential Council on Foreign Relations, argued that a wide range of "concrete measures of positive economic cooperation" should be initiated under the guidance of an International Economic Organization. This Organization, modeled after the International Labor Organization, would be composed of half nongovernmental and half govern-

[6] For a few of the more influential private United States statements on postwar international economic and social problems, see Suggestions for Further Reading at the end of this chapter.

mental representatives. Operating within the framework of a "reorganized League," it would have authority not merely to recommend but to take "positive action . . . on a limited range of problems without depending always on execution by national governments." [7]

Official United States planning coincided with much of this internationalist thinking, placing great emphasis on the orthodoxy of free trade, a policy long cherished by the Roosevelt administration and appropriate for a nation with goods to export and customers eager to buy. Decentralization through the creation of various independent specialized agencies was favored, presumably because that approach made it easier to get started before the general organization was established. It also made it possible for the Russians, as well as others, to participate in some agencies but not in others, and imitated the relationship that had existed between the League and the ILO, widely considered a most successful arrangement. To coordinate this whole economic and social system the United States finally proposed, much in the spirit of the 1939 Bruce Report, a single twenty-four-member Economic and Social Council responsible to the Assembly.[8] It was this general design which was inserted in the Dumbarton Oaks draft charter with almost no alterations.

United Kingdom, Soviet Union

During the incubation stage of 1942 to 1945, when the United Kingdom was still fighting for its life amid the rubble of its war-blasted economy, those few British groups and individuals who had the time, faith and fortitude to work actively on postwar problems showed an understandable eagerness to share the burdens of reconstruction with the rest of the world, especially the croesus of North America.[9] Free trade was subordinated to planning and regulation for general economic and social welfare. Even more support was given in England than in the United States to the ILO, originally conceived by the British. Much private opinion in England also tended to look for more extensive and positive international action than was advocated in the United States.

British governmental views were cut from similar cloth but were even more conscious of the damage done by the war and consequently more aware of Britain's dependence on the United States, symbolized by the 1942 Anglo-American Lend-Lease Agreement. The United Kingdom does not seem to have devoted as much attention as the United States to planning universal coordinating machinery and was willing at Dumbarton Oaks and San Francisco to follow the United States lead on this matter. On the other hand, the United Kingdom played a very vigorous, and often initiating, role in connection with many of the specialized agencies, par-

[7] Staley, op. cit., p. 303.
[8] Postwar Foreign Policy Preparation . . . , pp. 603–604.
[9] For a few of the more influential United Kingdom sources on postwar international economic and social problems, see the Suggestions for Further Reading at the end of this chapter.

ticularly UNRRA, FAO, the International Monetary Fund, ILO and UNESCO.

The Soviet Union was the unpredictable and uncommunicative giant in the background. It is of course impossible to know what "private" Russian opinion was on the subject of international economic and social collaboration. In general, while the Soviet Union sang as loudly as anyone of the brighter world that lay ahead, it chose to seek that world by its own path.[10] In the matter of over-all coordination, we have seen that the Russians began by insisting that ECOSOC be established apart from the United Nations. After retreating on that issue, they argued that ECOSOC should have no strong or direct links with the specialized agencies. In the spirit of their own comprehensive state-directed economic and social system, they endorsed ambitious goals for the United Nations but never indicated that they would surrender any significant degree of their national freedom of action to cooperate with non-Soviet countries in achieving those goals. UNRRA was the only large-scale United Nations economic and social operation with which the Soviet Union joined forces, presumably because it stood to gain considerable material benefits and, at that early date, had not yet broken with the west. While it participated in the constitutional conferences that created some of the other specialized agencies, it actually joined none of these except the WHO, UPU, ITU and WMO. In 1949 it resigned from the WHO, but in 1953 offered to join the ILO.

Other Countries

France and China were the poor cousins, specially favored by the great powers, terribly punished by the war, and desperately dependent on their wealthier allies. Both naturally wanted the United Nations to do its utmost in the economic and social field, especially in the immediate matter of rebuilding what had been destroyed.[11] It was sadly reminiscent of the 1919 Paris Peace Conference to hear France once more place special emphasis

---

[10] The following are a few of the more noteworthy commentaries on postwar U.S.S.R. policy regarding the United Nations: Mintauts Chakste, "Soviet Concepts of the State, International Law, and Sovereignty," *American Journal of International Law*, Vol. 43, No. 1 (January 1949), pp. 21–36; Rupert Emerson and Inis L. Claude, Jr., "The Soviet Union and the United Nations: An Essay in Interpretation," *International Organization*, Vol. 6, No. 1 (February 1952), pp. 1–26; S. B. Krylov, *Materialy k Istorii Organisatsii Ob'edinennykh Natsii* (Moscow: Izdatelstvo Akademii Navk SSR, 1949) (unpublished translation); Charles Prince, "Current Views of the Soviet Union on the International Organization of Security, Economic Cooperation and International Law: A Summary," *American Journal of International Law*, Vol. 39, No. 3 (July 1945), pp. 450–485.

[11] The following are works concerning views representative of the countries discussed in this and the following paragraphs: Violet Anderson, ed., *The United Nations Today and Tomorrow* (Toronto: The Canadian Institute on Public Affairs, 1943); Herbert Vere Evatt, *The United Nations* (Cambridge: Harvard University Press, 1948); C. J. Hambro, *How to Win the Peace* (Philadelphia and New York: J. B. Lippincott Co., 1942); Holborn, ed., *War and Peace Aims of the United Nations;* Representatives of the United Nations, *The Peoples' Peace* (New York: George W. Stewart, Publisher, Inc., 1943); Jan Christiaan Smuts, *Toward A Better World* (New York: World Book Co., distributed by Duell, Sloan and Pearce, 1944).

on freer access to raw materials. China played a leading role in initiating the World Health Organization and in urging educational and other cultural cooperation.

The important and lusty middle powers, notably Canada, Australia, India and Brazil, accepted the general concept of the Dumbarton Oaks plan but, under the leadership of Canada, were successful in persuading the San Francisco Conference to take that plan apart and put it together again in an expanded and strengthened version. These nations were only too aware of the fact that they were not strong enough to stand alone. They favored extensive cooperation through the United Nations with greater emphasis on long-range and less on short-range projects than some of the more badly damaged countries advocated. Most of the smaller European and Asian states had been hard hit and were most interested in immediate relief and rehabilitation. The Latin Americans, who had been only indirectly affected by the war, placed more emphasis on long-range problems.

United Nations Economic and Social Organization

When the United Nations Economic and Social Council opened for business on January 23, 1946, its first president, India's popular and able Sir Ramaswami Mudaliar, who had been a most effective chairman of the San Francisco Conference committee that dealt with ECOSOC, said in his initial address,

> . . . on the work of this Council, on the manner in which it tackles its responsibilities, on the ability which it possesses to solve intricate economic problems of a complicated nature, depends the chance of achieving real security and peace in the world of the future. . . . [12]

In these words Sir Ramaswami concentrated the burning hope of millions that the United Nations could do something to make living on this earth less tortured than it had been during previous centuries. In pointing towards the Council he called attention to the heart of a sprawling United Nations-supervised network of agencies. This system is composed of UN-controlled and UN-affiliated bodies. This chapter deals exclusively with the first group which have been created directly under authority of the Charter: the General Assembly; the Security Council; the Economic and Social Council with its subordinate commissions, committees and other bodies; and the Secretariat.

The second group, the UN-affiliated, is composed of the so-called "specialized agencies," established by separate constitutions, and will be discussed in the next chapter.

[12] *Official Records . . . First Session . . . *, p. 7.

STRUCTURE

Over-all Direction

On the top rung of the ladder stands the General Assembly. According to Charter Article 60,

> Responsibility for the discharge of the functions of the Organization . . . [in the economic and social field] shall be vested in the General Assembly and, under the authority of the General Assembly, in the Economic and Social Council. . . .

Since the League Assembly also came to be recognized as the ultimate authority in economic and social matters, these Charter provisions represent no revolutionary break with the League system. But they provide explicit constitutional authority for a development which was not even mentioned in the Covenant. Furthermore, the Charter gives the Assembly *exclusive* final authority.

This reinforced role of the Assembly was part of the United States plan adopted at Dumbarton Oaks. At San Francisco the only friction came when Canada argued that, if the Assembly were really to be boss, it should be able to give "instructions" or "directions" to the Economic and Social Council rather than mere "recommendations." [13] The great powers did not wax enthusiastic, however, at the idea of empowering the Assembly, in which they would have no certain control, to tie the Council's hands so completely. Thus the word "recommendation" remained. But that did not alter the fact that the Council does all its business "under the authority of the . . . Assembly" and cannot perform the following functions without explicit Assembly approval:

> submitting draft conventions for governmental action (Article 62(3)), calling international conferences (Article 62(4)), making agreements with specialized agencies (Article 63), performing services at the request of Members of the United Nations and at the request of specialized agencies (Article 66(2)), and requesting the International Court of Justice for advisory opinions (Article 96(2)).

The principal bodies through which the Assembly exercises its authority are: the Second Committee (Economic and Financial), the Third Committee (Social, Humanitarian and Cultural), the Fifth Committee (Administrative and Budgetary) and the Advisory Committee on Administrative and Budgetary Questions (nine members) which reviews the Secretary-General's annual budget reports before presenting them to the Fifth Committee.

The Assembly's economic and social supervisory experience since 1946 gives one the general impression that this many-headed giant is enthu-

[13] UNCIO, X, p. 46.

siastically humanitarian but afflicted with unfortunate tendencies to be organizationally clumsy, long-winded, over-political, under-expert and ambitious beyond its means. Its efforts to juggle the bewildering array of economic and social agencies that surround it is complicated by its difficulties in coordinating its own internal machinery. It is particularly awkward to try to supervise ECOSOC, its eleven commissions and eleven affiliated specialized agencies through three main committees — the Second, Third and Fifth. One suggestion is to create a small panel of "carefully selected and informed members" drawn from these three bodies to review reports of ECOSOC, the Secretary-General, and the Assembly Committee on Administrative and Budgetary Questions and prepare recommendations to be considered briefly by the three main committees.[14] The Assembly should also reconcile itself to delegating more responsibility, including the detailed drafting of conventions, to smaller and more expert bodies, particularly ECOSOC and its commissions. At the same time, one should remember that the shift from the League pattern of strong Council control to the United Nations pattern of Assembly control has made possible the participation of a far wider circle of governments and peoples.

While the Assembly has been brought to the center of the stage, the Security Council has been relegated to the remotest corner. The only mention of the Council in the Charter's two economic and social chapters is in Article 65: "The Economic and Social Council may furnish information to the Security Council and shall assist the Security Council upon its request." Although relatively little traffic has passed between the Security Council and the Economic and Social Council thus far, the latter's role in planning the reconstruction of Korea indicates how useful a teammate it can be in connection with specific security problems.

Economic and Social Council

The General Assembly's "cabinet" in this field is the Economic and Social Council. Placing the reins of immediate supervisory authority in the hands of this body rather than the Security Council, for reasons already mentioned, is a clear break with the League system. At San Francisco, moreover, many of the smaller powers insisted that the subordinate position assigned ECOSOC at Dumbarton Oaks implied that the United Nations economic and social job was a rung below its security duties. Recalling the League experience, they were determined to correct this impression, and no fewer than seven states, including Australia, New Zealand and Mexico, submitted amendments promoting ECOSOC to the rank of "principal organ." They had no intention of removing the Council from the Assembly's supervision but merely of emphasizing its equality with the Security Council. After brief debate this change was accepted unanimously as the first San Francisco amendment regarding the economic and social system.

---

[14] *Coordination of Economic and Social Activities* (New York: Carnegie Endowment for International Peace, 1948), pp. 37–40.

STRUCTURE OF THE ECONOMIC AND SOCIAL COUNCIL

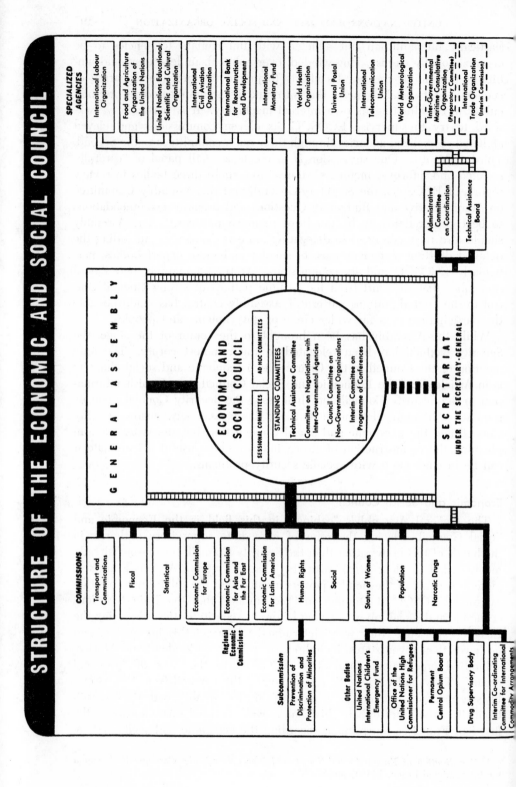

Membership. Unlike the Security Council, ECOSOC is a club with no formal admission qualifications. Charter Article 61 provides that ECOSOC shall consist of eighteen member states elected by the Assembly for three-year terms (one-third elected each year) and eligible for reëlection. Each state is allowed one representative. The Council "shall invite any Member . . . to participate, without vote, in its deliberations on any matter of particular concern to that Member." The Council may also arrange to have representatives of specialized agencies participate, without vote, and may provide for "consultation" with nongovernmental organizations.

One question involved in determining ECOSOC's composition was of course that hardy perennial: whether its members should be states or individual experts. In the League, Council members were states while most, though not all, technical committee members were appointed as individual specialists. In the ILO half the members were representatives of private employer and worker associations, while the other half represented governments. The Bruce Report looked to the private touch to neutralize the power taint of states. It recommended that eight members of the projected Central Committee for Economic and Social Questions be appointed as private experts by the twenty-four governmental members. The United States straddled this one, as it also did in the case of the Trusteeship Council, by suggesting in its plan of July 1944 that the Council consist of "qualified representatives" of twenty-four states.[15] At Dumbarton Oaks the word "qualified" was erased, presumably to leave this matter to the discretion of the individual states elected, and the number was reduced to the more manageable size of eighteen. At San Francisco these provisions were adopted without alteration.

Since not all United Nations Members could belong to ECOSOC, another fundamental issue was: should some states, because of their economic and social importance, be given priority over others. Everyone was aware of the fact, though no one said much about it, that the experts appointed to the League technical committees were usually drawn from the states of major importance in each field, which normally included our old friends, the great powers. And, in the ILO, eight of the sixteen governmental representatives on the Governing Body were required to be appointed by the member states of "chief industrial importance," as designated by the International Labor Conference. The 1944 United States plan for ECOSOC took refuge in silence on this issue, and the other great powers followed suit at Dumbarton Oaks. Their reasons for not insisting on the permanent membership which they demanded in the Security Council were undoubtedly a mixture of several ingredients. Nonsecurity questions did not seem such a direct and obvious challenge to their interests. Allowing open membership for ECOSOC would be a friendly gesture towards the smaller nations in compensation for the great powers' domination of the Security Council. Moreover, it is difficult to compare the economic, social and cultural significance of nations as a basis for weighting their representa-

[15] *Postwar Foreign Policy Preparation . . . ,* p. 604.

tion. Finally, the effectiveness of ECOSOC decisions would require world-wide support among small as well as great states.

At San Francisco, Canada and France led a drive to adopt the ILO formula: assured representation for states of chief industrial importance. For reasons just mentioned, however, this move was not successful. Nonetheless, the Conference agreed that, in practice, "important countries" should be members and inserted in the Dumbarton Oaks draft a provision that members should be eligible for reelection.

In practice, all five of the permanent members of the Security Council have invariably been members of ECOSOC, in spite of the obvious economic anemia of France and China. And certain middle powers, such as Canada, Australia and India, have been tapped more frequently than the rank and file. As for distribution of membership among geographical regions, there is virtually a gentleman's agreement that a certain pattern should generally be followed. In 1953, for example, besides the Big Five, the following areas were represented in the strength indicated: Latin America, four; Eastern Europe, two; Western Europe, one; Scandinavia, one; Middle East, two; Far East, two; and, in a class by itself, Australia. Thus, in spite of the difficulties involved in weighing nations' economic and social importance, ECOSOC membership has been commendably representative of the significant nations and regions of the world.

The Charter provision for the participation of representatives of specialized agencies in ECOSOC discussions is part of the coordinating function which is discussed below. Another window through which ECOSOC looks out upon the world is its consultation with nongovernmental organizations in accordance with Article 71. This is a new step in the old effort to link international organizations directly with the peoples of the world. The League technical committees had their "corresponding" or "associated" members connected with various nongovernmental organizations. And the ILO had its labor and employer representatives.

At the San Francisco Conference, the delegates were beseiged by swarms of dedicated associations, including fifty American groups invited to act as "consultants" to the United States delegation. Consequently Article 71, initiated by the United States, was added at San Francisco to make the UN sensitive to these nongovernmental voices. Once organized, ECOSOC immediately erected a barricade of regulations to protect itself from a possible stampede. It recognized three categories of nongovernmental organizations: "A," "B" and "Register." The "A" group was to be the most restricted, most universal in membership and interests, "most closely linked with the economic or social life of the area which they represent," and most closely associated with ECOSOC. The rules governing this system, as summarized in *Everyman's UN*,[16] are as follows:

All these organizations may send observers to public meetings of the Council and its commissions. Those in Categories A and B may submit written

16 (New York: United Nations, 1953), p. 23.

statements for circulation as documents of these UN bodies and may also present their views orally. Category A organizations may propose items for possible inclusion in the Council's provisional agenda. . . . In addition, all three groups . . . can consult with the UN Secretariat on matters of mutual concern.

The blue-ribbon "A" category included, as of December 1952:

> International Chamber of Commerce; International Confederation of Free Trade Unions; International Cooperative Alliance; International Federation of Agricultural Producers; International Federation of Christian Trade Unions; International Organization of Employers; Inter-Parliamentary Union; World Federation of Trade Unions; and World Federation of UN Associations.

Category "B," as of December 1952, contained one hundred organizations ranging alphabetically from Agudas Israel World Organization to Young Christian Workers. The third group contained more than one hundred additional organizations, registered for *ad hoc* consultations.

This consultative system has not proved very satisfactory. ECOSOC and its commissions have been so burdened with governmental problems that they have not been able to devote either extensive or intensive attention to these groups. On the other hand, some of the nongovernmental organizations have been more interested in gaining consultative status than in making a positive contribution. Others, especially the Communist-dominated World Federation of Trade Unions, have generated far more heat than light. Yet a few organizations have made outstanding contributions. Furthermore, ECOSOC has recently devoted considerable effort to improving its relations with the nongovernmental organizations.

Voting, Meetings, Officers and Publicity. Each member of ECOSOC has one vote, and decisions are made by a majority of those present and voting. Notice that this voting procedure is freer than that of the Assembly or the League Council, ECOSOC's immediate predecessor. The great powers were willing to allow this freedom not only because the economic and social area seemed less vital to national security but also because ECOSOC would operate, at least technically, under the direction of the Assembly where the two-thirds rule would apply.

ECOSOC originally planned three annual sessions, but has normally met only twice a year. These sessions come in the spring and summer for about a month to six weeks each. The second session also reconvenes briefly after each General Assembly session to plan ECOSOC's work for the coming year. A session will also be held within thirty days of a request by a majority of ECOSOC, the General Assembly or the Security Council. The Council's president, with the approval of the vice-presidents, may also call a session and fix its date.

The Council's officers are a president and a first and second vice-president, elected at the first session each year and eligible for reelection. As in the Assembly committees, but not in the Security Council, the great powers have stepped aside to give the presiding posts to the smaller countries. Thus far those elected president have been exceptionally able and respected figures, such as Sir Ramaswami Mudaliar of India, Charles Malik of the Lebanon and Hernan Santa Cruz of Chile. All meetings are held in public unless the Council decides otherwise.

Commissions. ECOSOC's sub-bodies form an extensive and somewhat bewildering network: eleven commissions (eight functional and three regional), five "standing committees," five "special bodies," and occasional *ad hoc* committees. ECOSOC's commissions are direct descendants of the League technical committees. Some of them are, in fact, obvious continuations of those bodies: for example, the Economic, Employment and Development Commission, abolished in 1951; Commission on Narcotic Drugs; Transport and Communications Commission; Statistical Commission; Social Commission; and Population Commission. On the other hand, certain other League "organizations" and "committees" have been reincarnated as independent specialized agencies, such as the WHO, UNESCO, IRO, IBRD and IMF.

The division between commissions and specialized agencies is not the result of any neat logical plan. Like Topsy, it "just growed." The first major consideration that guided this development was the fact that half the specialized agencies were already alive and kicking before the UN Charter was even signed. Many allied leaders, including President Roosevelt, were determined not to repeat the post-World War I error of providing too little too late to meet the world's reconstruction needs. Thus they began by building agencies like the FAO, IBRD and IMF for the double purpose of preparing for postwar economic requirements and rehearsing for the establishment of a general political organization. Furthermore, there was a widespread consensus that the ILO had been more successful than the League in the economic and social field and that the former should be imitated wherever practicable. Finally, by the time the San Francisco Conference convened, the six specialized agencies that had already been created had staffs and friends who urged that these bodies be allowed maximum freedom to develop independently.

At San Francisco, Charter Article 68 was adopted authorizing "commissions in economic and social fields and for the promotion of human rights, and such other commissions as may be required for the performance of its [ECOSOC's] functions." The Dumbarton Oaks version had incorporated the United States plan which mentioned only the economic and social commissions. At San Francisco, however, many groups, representative of both large and small states, sought to have their favorite causes enshrined in commissions that would be explicitly named in the Charter.

Probably the most influential force was the group of United States Republican Party leaders, especially Senator Arthur Vandenberg and Mr. John

Foster Dulles, who urged that provision be made for a human rights commission. Although the United States State Department had assumed that the Dumbarton Oaks language left ample room for a human rights body, the Department was anxious, in line with its bipartisan program on the UN, to bow to Republican suggestions wherever feasible. But other quarters were not so understanding. Brazil, supported by Uruguay and others, wondered why, if a human rights commission were to be mentioned, educational, cultural and women's rights commissions should not also be added. "The U.S. maintained that it was essential to maintain the human rights provisions. It was expected and hoped for by a great many people, and there would be profound disappointment if it were not adopted." [17] The United States held the fort, logic to the contrary, and the human rights commission was the only one specifically added to the Dumbarton Oaks draft.

Another gadfly issue, and still a source of lively contention, was the question of whether the commissions should be composed of governmental representatives or independent experts. The United States plan had favored experts, and that concept was inserted in the Dumbarton Oaks draft. At San Francisco, however, the United Kingdom delegate, in spite of the fact that his country had approved the Dumbarton Oaks language, argued that the commissions should be "leavened with experts rather than composed of them, since he wanted action." [18] Because of all that has been said about the effectiveness of League technical committees manned by experts, it is ironical that it was a League representative who "thought it would be unwise to restrict these commissions to expert bodies. The League . . . had found . . . inter-governmental . . . committee(s) . . . essential when urgent action as distinct from advice was required. . . ." [19] Finally, the problem was side-stepped by eliminating the Dumbarton Oaks mention of experts without putting anything in its place.

(1) *Functional Commissions.* In a burst of organizational energy, ECOSOC created nine commissions during its first year of operation, 1946. Two more were established in 1947; and the last, in 1948. This racing start was in marked contrast to the more hesitant and experimental pace of the League Council during the early post-World War I years.

The first nine commissions were organized on a functional basis, as distinguished from the three later regional commissions which were added as an afterthought. The organizational pattern of the functional bodies followed the recommendations of the Preparatory Commission aimed at filling squares on the organizational checkerboard not expected to be covered by specialized agencies. But the Commission was very cautious and recommended the immediate creation of only those bodies that seemed urgently necessary. And even some of those were clearly labeled "temporary": Human Rights, Economic and Employment, Social, Statistical and Narcotic Drugs. It also suggested that ECOSOC "consider the desir-

---

[17] UNCIO, X, p. 152.   [18] *Ibid.*, p. 122.   [19] *Ibid.*, p. 131.

ability of establishing at an early date" four others: Demographic, Temporary Transport and Communications, Fiscal and Coordination.[20]

More impetuous than the Preparatory Commission and more sensitive to special interests, ECOSOC created during its first year all of the above bodies except the Coordination Commission. The latter was strongly opposed by the great powers, on the grounds that coordination was primarily the job of ECOSOC itself and that such a commission would tend to be a "fifth wheel." On the other hand, ECOSOC capitulated to the militant crusade of the fair sex by elevating the Sub-Commission on the Status of Women, under the Human Rights Commission, to the level of a full-fledged Commission on the Status of Women.

(2) *Regional Commissions.* Unlike these functional bodies, which tended to follow the League pattern, the regional commissions were a new departure. League regional activities had generally been subordinated to functional committees, which were oriented primarily towards European problems. The UN experiment was initiated by European Members interested chiefly in creating machinery that would carry on the reconstruction functions of UNRRA and certain temporary European economic rehabilitation bodies. Consequently, during March 1947, ECOSOC decided to create the Economic Commission for Europe (ECE) with a mandate considerably more ambitious than that of most of the functional bodies.

Its chief responsibilities were to replace the Emergency Economic Committee for Europe (EECE), absorb the essential activities of the European Coal Organization (ECO) and the European Central Inland Transport Organization (ECITO), and take all other possible steps to get the wheels of the European economy turning. Its members included all European UN Members plus the United States. At the same ECOSOC session, the Europeans joined hands with the Asians to create a similar Economic Commission for Asia and the Far East (ECAFE) including within its membership non-Asian countries with special interests in that area: the United States, Soviet Union, United Kingdom, France, Australia and the Netherlands.

ECOSOC also requested a secretariat survey anticipating an Economic Commission for the Middle East, but friction in that part of the world, particularly between Arabs and Jews, blocked the establishment of such a body. Although the Latin Americans could not point to any direct war damage, they too wanted a commission to help make their economies bigger and better. Thus, ECOSOC agreed in February 1948 to create an Economic Commission for Latin America (ECLA), including the United States, United Kingdom, France, Canada and the Netherlands.

(3) *Functions and Membership.* In the functions they perform, the commissions are publicists, educators and salesmen rather than policemen. Like the Assembly and ECOSOC, they have no authority to command, merely to recommend. Though their functions are broadly similar, they

[20] *Report of the Preparatory Commission of the United Nations,* Doc. PC/20, December 23, 1945 (London: H. M. Stationery Office, 1946), pp. 36–39.

can be divided into four different types according to varying emphases in their work. The mildest and most scholarly are those that concentrate primarily on providing the UN with accurate facts: the Statistical and Population Commissions. Next come those that are more concerned with formulating and promoting policies in various functional fields: the Transport and Communications Commission, Social Commission, Commission on Human Rights, Commission on the Status of Women, Fiscal Commission, as well as the disbanded Economic, Employment and Development Commission. Similar functions are performed by the three regional commissions. Finally there is the body that acts most like a policeman charged with helping ECOSOC to prevent illegal traffic in drugs: the Commission on Narcotic Drugs.

In determining the membership of these commissions during the 1946 sessions, the Soviet Union took the firmest position in favor of governmental representatives to avoid the commissions' degenerating into "discussion clubs," in spite of having accepted at Dumbarton Oaks the United States plan calling for experts. The United Kingdom, France and China urged a hybrid of expert and governmental status, while the United States still favored experts. The chief argument for governmental status was that that method was most likely to assure a receptive governmental attitude towards commissions' recommendations. Those backing the experts argued that, while governmental representatives would eventually have to approve policies before they could be implemented, it was neither necessary nor desirable to make advisory bodies slaves to existing governmental attitudes. As one indignant commentator has put it, "the function of an advisory committee is to advise." [21]

Ultimately, after long and hot debate, ECOSOC decided in June 1946 that all members of commissions should be representatives of UN Members chosen by ECOSOC with the proviso that the Secretary-General consult with governments before the latter nominate their representatives. Regardless of what decision was reached on paper, it should have been apparent that actual practice was likely to be a compromise between the expert and the governmental spokesman, as it was under the League. What has changed most since League days is not the formal status of the commission members but the climate of the world in which they must operate.

While all UN Members are theoretically eligible to be honored with representation in most of the commissions, with the obvious exception of the regional bodies, the great powers are most frequently favored, with the middle powers close on their heels. Although all members of most of the commissions are, at least in principle, subject to change by election every three years, the membership of four commissions is relatively fixed. In the Narcotics Commission UN Members which are most vitally concerned as sources of or sufferers from illicit narcotics (the Big Five plus Canada, India, Peru, Turkey and Yugoslavia) were elected in August 1949 for an

[21] A. Loveday, "An Unfortunate Decision," *International Organization*, Vol. 1, No. 2 (June 1947), p. 281.

indefinite period until replaced by ECOSOC; the Commission's other five members serve the usual three-year terms. All members of the regional bodies serve indefinite terms, and the Economic Commission for Asia and the Far East enjoys the participation, under defined conditions, of certain designated non-self-governing territories as "associate" members. Even in the other commissions there has been such a marked tendency to favor the more important states that the Assembly and ECOSOC have recently begun concerted efforts to include more of the smaller nations, as much for their honor and edification as for their contribution. The size of the commissions averages between fifteen and eighteen members.

As children of ECOSOC, the Commissions' procedural rules are very similar to those of the parent body. Decisions are taken by a simple majority of those present and voting. Officers include a chairman, one or two vice-chairmen and a *rapporteur,* all elected each session. The Human Rights, Narcotic Drugs, Status of Women and Regional Commissions meet annually. The others meet once every two years. All meetings are open to the public unless decided otherwise by the commissions.

Standing Committees. Directly under the thumb of ECOSOC are its four standing committees, composed of representatives of states members of ECOSOC, which perform certain limited functions in its name. The *Technical Assistance Committee* (TAC) is a "committee of the whole," composed of all ECOSOC members, which provides broad policy direction for the technical assistance program. More detailed and continuous coordination of operations is carried out through the Technical Assistance Board (TAB), composed of the administrative heads of specialized agencies participating in the program under the direction of an Executive Chairman appointed by the UN Secretary-General.

The *Committee on Negotiations with Specialized Agencies* (eleven members under the chairmanship of ECOSOC's president) is responsible for negotiating agreements with the specialized agencies which are then presented to ECOSOC and the Assembly for approval. The *Committee on Non-Governmental Organizations* (seven members plus ECOSOC's president) advises ECOSOC on its relations with nongovernmental organizations and makes final decisions on the acceptance of items submitted by "A" organizations for the provisional agenda. The *Interim Committee on Programme of Meetings* (the president and five members) consults with the Secretary-General in planning the scheduling of conferences held under ECOSOC auspices.

Special Bodies. The five so-called "special bodies" are hybrids which exercise more independent and direct administrative authority than most of the commissions and standing committees but are under more immediate ECOSOC control than the specialized agencies. Two of these bodies are narcotics enforcement agencies inherited virtually unchanged from pre-World War II days: the *Permanent Central Opium Board* and the *Super-*

visory Body.[22] Both are based on separate treaties which were amended by a UN-formulated protocol, signed in December 1946, to transfer to the UN certain responsibilities formerly assigned to the League. These agencies have close relations with the Commission on Narcotic Drugs and are provided with staff and other administrative services by the UN. The eight members of the Permanent Central Opium Board are appointed by ECOSOC for five-year terms as independent experts without remuneration. Of the Supervisory Body's four experts, two are appointed by the WHO, and one each by the Commission on Narcotic Drugs and the Permanent Central Opium Board.

The *UN International Children's Emergency Fund* (UNICEF) was originally suggested by the UNRRA Council, at the behest of the late irrepressible Fiorello H. LaGuardia, to help fill the vacuum that was to result from that organization's untimely demise. The General Assembly established the Fund in December 1946. Its resources have been derived by passing the hat to both governments and private sources for voluntary contributions. The program is administered by an Executive Director, presently Maurice Pate, veteran United States humanitarian and Red Cross worker, under policies established by a twenty-six-nation Executive Board (eighteen members of the Social Commission plus eight other states, not necessarily UN Members, appointed by ECOSOC). Of all the "special bodies," UNICEF is most like a specialized agency and probably would be one were it not for the original determination on the part of the United States, United Kingdom and other states to lay it to rest as soon as possible. Nevertheless, the Assembly decided in 1953 to make it a permanent organization.

The *Interim Coordinating Committee for International Commodity Arrangements* (ICCICA) is the UN clearing house with respect to intergovernmental negotiations on commodity problems. Authorized by ECOSOC in March 1947, it was originally placed under ECOSOC's roof as a makeshift arrangement pending the construction of the International Trade Organization (ITO), but the latter is still little more than a blueprint. The Committee is composed of a chairman nominated by the ITO Interim Commission, a member nominated by the FAO, and a third member nominated by the Secretary-General to watch nonagricultural primary commodities. Created to worry over immediate postwar shortages, the Committee later became inactive until the rearmament of the 1950's caused new shortages.

The *Administrative Committee on Coordination* (ACC), composed of the UN Secretary-General, a chairman, and the staff heads of the specialized agencies, is the central hub joining the activities of all of these bodies. The Committee, originally suggested by the United States, was recommended to the Secretary-General by ECOSOC in the fall of 1946 after it had been decided not to create a Commission on Coordination. To facilitate its work the Committee leans heavily on a Preparatory Committee of

22 See Chapter 21 for discussion of their functions.

Deputies plus numerous sub-groups of varying degrees of activity, working on special administrative and substantive problems such as budgetary and statistical matters, public information, housing and migration. Although the early activities of the ACC were characterized by considerable fumbling and excessive concern with administrative details, it has become increasingly better organized and able to deal with substantive priorities.

Ad Hoc Committees. In order to spread the burden of its labors during its sessions, ECOSOC normally divides its work among several "sessional" committees: for example, the Economic Committee, the Social Committee and its own Coordination Committee. Other *ad hoc* committees have also been formed from time to time to deal with such problems as slavery, refugees and internal ECOSOC organization.

UN High Commissioner for Refugees. The Office of the UN High Commissioner for Refugees, a virtual carbon copy of the League refugee commissioners, was created by the General Assembly in December 1950 to begin operations in January 1951.[23] This represented a return from the large-scale UNRRA and IRO efforts to the less expensive League tradition of concentrating primarily on negotiating with governments and private agencies to protect refugees' political and economic rights. The Commissioner, at present Mr. G. J. van Heuven Goedhart (Netherlands), may engage in direct repatriation and resettlement efforts only by express Assembly direction. The UN will supply funds solely for administrative purposes, unless the Assembly decides otherwise; all other expenditures, including relief, are expected to be financed through voluntary contributions. Advised by an ECOSOC-appointed committee of fifteen nations particularly concerned with the refugee problem, the Commissioner reports annually to the Assembly through ECOSOC.

Review and Reorganization. While hopes ran high in the early years of 1946 to 1948 that ECOSOC's various sub-bodies, especially its commissions, would prove to be an effective team capable of pulling ECOSOC along at a brisk pace, the apparatus has been harrassed by a multitude of frustrations. Only a few of the commissions pulled their share of the load. Others squandered their energy by galloping in too many directions at once. Still others suffered persistent paralysis. Although dissatisfaction erupted at various times, the most concerted effort at introspection and reorganization took place during 1951 under the leadership of the United States and United Kingdom.[24] The Soviet delegation was also happy to help weed out commissions, but largely on the grounds that they were prone to meddle in "domestic" affairs.[25]

The majority of other members of ECOSOC were inclined to agree with the United States and United Kingdom that there were too many sub-bodies meeting too frequently to allow either the secretariat or govern-

[23] General Assembly Resolution 428 (V).
[24] UN Doc. E/AC.34/3, p. 1.   [25] UN Doc. E/AC.34/23.

ments to do justice to the problems discussed. And they agreed that the commission form of organization had not been altogether satisfactory.

> . . . large permanent commissions, whose members are neither entirely independent experts nor avowedly governmental representatives [though appointed by governments, they are not officially considered responsible to those governments], . . . [are] unlikely to produce . . . type of preparatory work which the Council requires. . . . The present system . . . accentuates the ever-present dangers of proliferation and overlapping . . . the commissions have come to perform . . . functions which properly belong to the Council [ECOSOC] itself; this gives rise to unnecessary repetitive debate, and overloads the Council's agenda. . . . [26]

To hammer this point home the British reminded ECOSOC that during 1949 and 1950 the plans for child welfare activities had been dragged through six separate UN bodies. Other delegations noted that persons appointed to the commissions had frequently been recruited at a rather low level of governmental rank, possessed of no great expert competence and representative of a relatively limited circle of countries. The British delegation pointed out that, "Many of the members of these commissions are members of the staffs of permanent national delegations, who are obliged by the frequency of UN meetings to become one day economists, another day experts in child welfare, the next in trusteeship questions, or human rights, or the security of the Far East." [27]

To correct this situation the majority accepted most of the British thesis except for the rigorous elimination of existing commissions. It was generally agreed that for expert advice greater reliance should be placed on the Secretariat and small groups of truly independent experts, specially selected by the Secretary-General for their individual talents. Many, including the British, cited the full employment report [28] written by just such a group as evidence of the effectiveness of that approach. For governmental consultation, ECOSOC committees or *ad hoc* political conferences could well replace commissions. It was thought "usually inadvisable to attempt to combine both those functions in a single body" as had been attempted in the commissions. This was a remarkable retreat from the position taken in 1945 and 1946, largely at the insistence of the United Kingdom and Soviet Union. It was also hoped that the meetings of subbodies could be scheduled so as to reduce conflicts and excessive peaks of activity.

When it came to the matter, however, of asking certain commissions to walk the plank to extinction, many delegations demonstrated remarkable ingenuity in justifying exceptions. ECOSOC's final decision, therefore, went no further than the original United States proposal: to eliminate only the Economic, Employment and Development Commission and three sub-

---

[26] UN Doc. E/1995, p. 10; for debate, see UN, ECOSOC, *Official Records, Thirteenth Session*, 554th to 560th meetings.
[27] UN Doc. E/AC.34/3, p. 4.   [28] See Chapter 19.

commissions: Statistical Sampling, Freedom of Information and of the Press, and Prevention of Discrimination and Protection of Minorities. The Human Rights, Narcotic Drugs and Regional Commissions were to be continued, more or less as they were, for another three years, through 1954. The other six functional commissions were also to be continued but were to meet every other year rather than annually. And increased national participation was facilitated by enlarging the membership of the Population and Status of Women Commissions. It was also decided that this reorganization should be considered tentative and be reviewed in 1954. Later the Assembly diluted these decisions further, in February 1952, by requesting ECOSOC to allow the Commission on the Status of Women to continue meeting annually and the Sub-Commission on the Prevention of Discrimination and the Protection of Minorities "to continue its work so that it may fulfill its mission." [29]

Secretariat

If the Assembly is the parliament and ECOSOC the cabinet, the Secretariat is the faithful hard-working civil service. As of 1953, there were about 1,226, of a total of 4,000 Secretariat personnel, assigned to ECOSOC affairs with a budget of $9,786,400, as compared with 110 assigned to political-military affairs with a budget of $906,600. This represents roughly a 600 per cent increase beyond the League, which had, as of 1938, only about 150 assigned to economic and social duties.[30] Nevertheless the UN staff and budget seem a pitiful drop in the bucket when one considers that the United States State Department alone had, in 1953, a staff and budget ten times those of the secretariat mentioned above merely to administer the United States international information and educational program.[31]

The largest single staff unit in this field is the Department of Economic Affairs, as was the League economic and financial staff, with a total of approximately 290 persons. Next largest is the Department of Social Affairs, with 219. The fact that the latter group is approximately 75 per cent as large as the Department of Economic Affairs gives it a more significant position in the Secretariat than that held by the League social staff, which was only about 50 per cent as large as the economic staff. It is also interesting to note that the staffs of the regional commissions, which are not part of the Headquarters staff and had no counterparts under the League,

---

[29] General Assembly Resolution 532 (VI).

[30] For UN figures see *UN Budget Estimates for . . . 1953 . . .* , General Assembly, Official Records, Seventh Session, Supplement No. 5 (A/2125). For League figures, see Egon F. Ranshofen-Wertheimer, *The International Secretariat* (Washington: Carnegie Endowment for International Peace, 1945), Chap. 10. This can be only a rough comparison due to several considerations. For example, some League personnel were supported by non-League funds; some League activities are now covered by specialized agencies which have their own independent secretariats; and in 1933–34 many clerical workers were transferred to a general pool.

[31] *Appendix to the Budget of the U.S. Government for . . . 1954* (Washington: Government Printing Office, 1953), p. 394.

number 394, about 80 per cent as large as the combined Headquarters economic and social staffs.

These industrious and largely anonymous international civil servants are among the most disinterested and vigorous champions of the UN efforts to banish economic and social insecurity. Most of them have demonstrated abilities comparable to those of the better national civil services. Some of them, such as Gunnar Myrdal, Swedish Executive Secretary of the ECE, and Ralph Bunche, Principal Director of the Department of Trusteeship and Information from Non-Self-Governing Territories, are internationally respected leaders in their fields. The chief difficulties involved in building and maintaining such staffs are the problems of prying loose top-flight personnel from their home bases, coordinating a bewildering tangle of different activities, doling out funds that are always hopelessly short of secretariat ambitions, and weaving together different philosophies and cultural backgrounds.

UN Secretariat Budget for Economic and Social Activities

UN Budget Estimates for . . . 1953

Activity	No. of Personnel	Total Expenses
Economic	289	$2,348,500
Social	219	1,776,500
Technical Assistance Administration	182	386,700
Social Activities		768,500
Economic Development Activities		479,400
Public Administration		145,000
Meetings of ECOSOC bodies		212,900
Economic and Social Services (Geneva Office)	161	1,070,200
High Commissioner for Refugees	105	673,900
ECAFE	155	1,043,800
ECLA	115	881,000
Total	1226	$9,786,400

The majority of UN members feel that the Secretariat has done a remarkably good job in view of its staggering assignments, its brief experience thus far, and its meager financial diet. In fact, we have seen that ECOSOC reached the conclusion in its 1951 self-examination that it should rely more on the Secretariat and less on its commissions for expert advice. At the same time, national delegations have regularly eclipsed their praise with certain criticisms, largely motivated by their desire to reduce the drain on their national treasuries. The major barbs aimed at the economic and social staffs have been that: headquarters personnel has not been reduced to compensate for the increase in field staff (especially the regional commissions and High Commissioner for Refugees); the Secretariat has a larger appetite for interesting projects than its pocketbook can satisfy; a fusion of the Economic and Social Departments might result in lower costs; the new Technical Assistance Administration needs tightening and better coordination with the Economic and Social Departments; the quality of personnel should be raised; turnover, lowered; and personnel should be less specialized and more flexible in assignments. Many of these suggestions, moreover, were incorporated in the Secretary-General's reorganization recommendations of 1953–54.

UN ECONOMIC AND SOCIAL OBJECTIVES

The difference between the UN Charter statement of economic and social objectives and that of the League Covenant is the difference between a general bombardment of the enemy and selective sniping. The UN goals set forth in Article 55 are both broad and bold.

> With a view to the creation of conditions of stability and well-being which are necessary for peaceful and friendly relations among nations based on respect for the principle of equal rights and self-determination of peoples, the United Nations shall promote:
>
> a. higher standards of living, full employment, and conditions of economic and social progress and development;
>
> b. solutions of international economic, social, health, and related problems; and international cultural and educational cooperation; and
>
> c. universal respect for, and observance of, human rights and fundamental freedoms for all without distinction as to race, sex, language, or religion.

The League's comparable objectives were set forth in the single Covenant Article 23, as compared with the Charter's seventeen Articles, and were restricted to eight limited and specific subjects: labor conditions; treatment of natives; "white slave," drug and arms traffic; freedom of communications and transit; equal commercial treatment; and prevention and control of disease.

"Conservatives" vs. "liberals"

The general pattern of UN objectives was established at the Dumbarton Oaks Conference on the basis of the United States plan. Nonetheless, the yeasty San Francisco mood to expand the economic and social system also had its effect upon the statement of goals. But this was not accomplished without a heated tug-of-war between the "conservatives," anchored by the United States, and the "liberals," captained chiefly by Canada and Australia, often cheered on, though with diplomatic restraint, by the United Kingdom and France. The Soviet Union showed little interest in this contest except to exploit the occasion as a rare and welcome opportunity to play the mediator.

This pulling and hauling of varying national interests is revealed most clearly in the evolution of the Charter statement regarding the Members' obligations with respect to the economic and social objectives. The Dumbarton Oaks version had said, "the Organization should facilitate solutions of" economic and social problems rather than the stronger present wording — "the United Nations shall promote" certain specific and positive objectives, such as "high standards of living" and "full employment." Even before the San Francisco Conference convened, however, some United States leaders, especially Congressmen, began to worry that perhaps the United States was exposing itself to radical outside influences on such questions as full employment and racial policies.

This opinion was largely responsible for persuading the United States Delegation, operating primarily through Senators Vandenberg and Connally, to obtain Big Four agreement during the early days of the Conference on a plan to strengthen the Dumbarton Oaks "domestic jurisdiction" clause and make it apply to the entire Charter rather than merely the section on the settlement of disputes. The Russians were willing partners in this move since they also approached San Francisco with obvious determination to protect the bastions of Soviet sovereignty.[32]   Secretary of State Edward Stettinius, in his *Report to the President on the Results of the San Francisco Conference*, put it quite plainly. The strengthening of the domestic jurisdiction clause

> seemed desirable because of the amplification of the power and authority given to the Assembly and, particularly, to the Economic and Social Council. Without this general limitation . . . , it might have been supposed that the Economic and Social Council could interfere directly in the domestic economy, social structure, or cultural or educational arrangements of the member states. Such a possibility is now definitely excluded.[33]

Pulling doggedly in the opposite direction were many of the smaller countries. As part of their general campaign to commit all UN Members to a bold program of economic and social progress, particularly a policy of "full employment," a key objective was to tie the giant United States to this program so that it would not again stumble into a depression and drag its neighbors down with it. Australia's Minister for External Affairs, Herbert Vere Evatt, later revealed this concern:

> In our view inclusion of a direct pledge by each country to carry out these purposes was desirable; the status and powers of the proposed Economic and Social Council were not adequate . . . we argued publicly and privately that too little importance had been attached in the past to the impact of domestic employment policies on international economic affairs. . . .[34]
>
> Australia is a country which depends for a significant proportion of its national income on its exports of wool, wheat and other primary products.

[32] For brief mention of these negotiations see *Postwar Foreign Policy Preparation . . .*, pp. 437, 445. Also see statement by John Foster Dulles, UNCIO, VI, pp. 507–508.

[33] Department of State Publication 2349 (Washington: Government Printing Office, 1945), p. 44.

[34] *The United Nations*, p. 30.

The depression first hit Australia through a slump overseas. . . . Consequently Australia, the Argentine, and other great exporting countries, . . . are very conscious that the inability of countries to buy one's own products has sharp and immediate repercussions on one's own economy and the economy of the rest of the world.[35]

Hence, an Australian amendment urged that, "All members of the UN pledge themselves to take action both national and international for . . . [certain specific objectives] and . . . agree to take appropriate action through" the UN, ILO and other agencies. "All members . . . undertake to report annually to the General Assembly upon the action they have taken. . . ."[36] After a lively wrestling match between these conflicting philosophies in a drafting subcommittee, the compromise language of the present Article 55 was adopted "without dissent."[37] Five days later, however, an embarrassed United States delegate, Miss Virginia Gildersleeve, was compelled, presumably by Senators Vandenberg and Connally, to request the committee to soften the language that had been adopted:

> to make it perfectly clear that there would be no interference by the Economic and Social Council in the domestic affairs of any country. She said that the purpose of the . . . [request] was to dispel fears which might arise when the Charter came up for Congressional ratification. . . .[38]

Never during the entire Conference was the United States more overwhelmingly opposed. Both the United Kingdom and Soviet Union turned against her. Australia's eloquent Herbert Evatt led the attack with a withering volley in which he insisted that the "domestic jurisdiction" clause should be sufficient protection and "referred to statements by President Roosevelt and President Truman to the effect that full employment had been adopted as an objective of the United States. He said it would be renouncing the Atlantic Charter to adopt the new proposal of the United States Delegation."[39] Consequently, at the next meeting the United States beat a hasty retreat, content with winning the committee's agreement to include in its report a statement that

> The members of [the] Committee . . . are in full agreement that nothing contained in Chapter IX can be construed as giving authority to the Organization to intervene in the domestic affairs of member states.[40]

The next skirmish took place when the drafting subcommittee reported out a compromise version of the Australian amendment calling on UN Members to pledge to take action to further the UN economic and social objectives. Although the main committee approved the draft, 34 to 0, the United States reversed its position and abstained on the grounds that the

---

[35] *The Task of Nations* (New York: Duell, Sloan and Pearce, 1949), p. 218.
[36] UNCIO, X, p. 312.   [37] *Ibid.*, pp. 39–40.
[38] *Ibid.*, pp. 52, 57–59.   [39] *Ibid.*, p. 58.   [40] *Ibid.*, p. 83.

smaller countries were trying to enmesh it in obligations which would compel it to act in spite of itself. Under American pressure, the subcommittee then went back and ground out a new draft which satisfied the United States but not the Australians who denounced it because it omitted any pledge to take "separate" as well as "joint" action. The Soviet delegate amiably offered his good offices. "He thought that the English language was rich enough to find words that would satisfy all parties, and, if that proved not to be so, he offered to draft a pledge in Russian." [41] With the Soviet delegate delighting in his role of honest broker, the United States and Australia finally brought forth the language which now appears as Article 56: "All Members pledge themselves to take joint and separate action in cooperation with the Organization for the achievement of the purposes set forth in Article 56."

Economic Objectives

Although some early United States State Department plans had spoken in terms of rather ambitious goals ("making the most effective use of the world's human and material resources," "improving . . . standards of living," and "promoting social security, economic stability, [and] general well-being," [42] the plan drafted just prior to the Dumbarton Oaks Conference spoke in muted tones of simply "the creation of conditions of stability and well-being." [43] And it was this phrase which was written into the Dumbarton Oaks Proposals.

At San Francisco, Canada, Australia and New Zealand led a drive towards the same goals as those of the early State Department thinking.[44] Finally the Conference decided to add to the Dumbarton Oaks language the objectives that now appear in Article 55: "higher standards of living, full employment, and conditions of economic and social progress and development." Mr. Evatt, the aggressive Australian laborite politician, later wrote,

> Many people were terrified of the words "full employment" at that time. When they saw that some reference was unavoidable, they tried to obtain less positive phrases such as "a high level of employment." They did not consider full employment practicable and felt that attempts to secure it might necessitate too much state interference and state planning. There may even have been some who thought that a certain measure of unemployment was desirable as a means of disciplining labour and promoting technical efficiency. However, this fight was won and the pledge was given.[45]

France also took grim pleasure in playing the same Cassandra-like role she had played at Paris in 1919. Once more, with strong support from many other countries, she urged that some specific provision be made in the

41 *Ibid.*, p. 140.   42 *Postwar Foreign Policy Preparation* . . . , p. 479.
43 *Ibid.*, p. 603.   44 UNCIO, X, p. 307.
45 *The Task of Nations*, pp. 216–217.

Charter for assuring freer and more equitable access to raw materials, such as coal, for which France was dependent, to a considerable degree, on outside sources. She argued that the power of cartels should be curbed and that the wartime Combined Boards, or something like them, should be continued. Argentina joined the chorus by expressing a similar concern regarding access to capital goods, and France sought to broaden her support by incorporating this suggestion in her own proposal.

The United Kingdom, conscious of its Commonwealth preferential system and its dependence on a strong trade position, led a vigorous counterattack. The Netherlands thought that the producers of raw materials and capital goods were as deserving of protection as the consumers. New Zealand reflected a large body of opinion, holding that modern national economic planning makes freer trade difficult, if not impossible. Others, who agreed with France, thought it wiser to leave the Charter language conveniently vague. Finally the conciliatory Soviet representative cut the Gordian knot by persuading the delegates that mention of the problem should be omitted from the Charter but be included in the Conference report. A statement was then approved which indicated that the Charter's terms were thought elastic enough to include international trade, finance, communications and transport, reconstruction, and access to raw materials and capital goods.[46]

Related to the question of access to materials was a Greek plea that the Charter be amended to provide for UN support and coordination of postwar reconstruction efforts. The United Kingdom spoke against this motion on the grounds that the problem was an immediate one that would have to be dealt with by UNRRA before the UN could be organized. But many other nations, including the Soviet Union and France, supported the Greek proposal. When it later became clear that the drafting subcommittee would not approve specific mention of reconstruction in the Charter, the Greek delegation issued a declaration urging immediate governmental action which received overwhelming Conference support.

Social Objectives

One of the more lively San Francisco debates regarding the scope of the "social" field swirled about the issue of educational–cultural–intellectual cooperation. The United States plan adopted at Dumbarton Oaks had not mentioned this matter specifically, but the Chinese, during the second phase of the Dumbarton Oaks conversations, urged explicit reference to "educational and other forms of cultural cooperation." [47] The other three powers then agreed to propose that "cultural" cooperation, presumably including education, be added to the previously adopted objectives, and this amendment was approved early in the San Francisco Conference. From the beginning of that Conference, however, there had been a strong current of opinion, backed by many American and other private groups, favoring separate mention of "educational" cooperation.

[46] UNCIO, X, p. 271.   [47] *Postwar Foreign Policy Preparation . . .*, p. 33.

The French, justly proud of the role their nation had played in developing the League Organization for Intellectual Cooperation and anxious to compensate for their reduced status at San Francisco, initiated an insistent campaign to write "intellectual" cooperation into the Charter in anticipation of the creation of a special organ to continue the prewar work in that field. Finally the United States asked for reconsideration of the statement of objectives in order to add, among other things, the word "educational" to what is now Article 55(b). When this change was subsequently adopted, the French insisted that "cultural and educational cooperation" be rendered in the official French version of the Charter as "coopération intellectuelle." Collaboration in the field of health was also added to the Dumbarton Oaks list of objectives upon the initiative of China and Brazil.

Although the Dumbarton Oaks draft had included "respect for human rights and fundamental freedoms," there was still a large body of opinion within the United States and other countries that wanted to strengthen this provision. Subsequently, at the beginning of the San Francisco Conference, the Big Four decided to recommend the addition of the fortifying phrase, "without distinction as to race, language, religion or sex." [48] The Conference not only approved this change but also added "observance of" as well as "respect for" human rights.

AVENUES TO THESE GOALS

Research, Discussion and Recommendations

History suggests that no matter how harmless an agency may seem on paper, if it can ferret out facts, expose them to the light of public scrutiny and broadcast recommendations based on those facts, it is armed with weapons that may ultimately destroy its enemies. Hence, the innocent-appearing Article 62:

> 1. The Economic and Social Council may make or initiate studies and reports with respect to international economic, social, cultural, educational, health, and related matters and may make recommendations with respect to any such matters to the General Assembly, to the Members of the UN, and to the specialized agencies. . . .
> 3. It may prepare draft conventions for submission to the General Assembly, with respect to matters falling within its competence.
> 4. It may call, in accordance with rules prescribed by the UN, international conferences on matters falling within its competence.

The abbreviated foundation on which this Article was built was the original United States version, written into the Dumbarton Oaks Proposals, which authorized ECOSOC simply "to make recommendations, on its own initiative, with respect to international, economic, social and other humanitarian matters." At San Francisco the smaller states vied with each other

[48] *Postwar Foreign Policy Preparation* . . . , p. 684.

to expand this modest structure. The Canadians, Dutch and Belgians led a successful move to continue the valuable League research efforts by specifically authorizing "studies and reports." Australia and Canada were primarily responsible for giving ECOSOC explicit authority to address its recommendations not only to the General Assembly but directly to UN Members and the specialized agencies.

Australia led the effort to authorize ECOSOC to initiate the making of conventions. Although this suggestion was first opposed by the United Kingdom delegate who claimed that that body would be too busy and too unspecialized for this task, Sir Ramaswami Mudaliar, Chairman of Committee II/3 concerned with this field, persuaded the British to withdraw their objections on the grounds that ECOSOC needed and deserved this authority and should be trusted to use its good judgment. Australia also wanted to empower ECOSOC to call conferences to deal with emergency problems. Committee II/3 finally decided that this proposal should be broadened to authorize conferences on any matter under ECOSOC jurisdiction.

Coordination

Another major function of the UN is to act as ring master, coordinating the performances of hundreds of frisky and competitive committees, commissions and organizations in the economic and social field. The Assembly and ECOSOC have relatively firm control over their own sub-bodies. But, in their relations with the constitutionally independent specialized agencies, they must rely more on the carrot than the stick. The Charter provisions regarding this latter area are rather detailed — six articles in all — as if the framers anticipated some difficulty.

The term "specialized agency" — a new expression born with the UN — is defined as an intergovernmental body with "wide international responsibilities . . . in economic, social, cultural, educational, health and related fields . . . brought into relationship with the UN. . . ." (Article 57). The UN is also empowered to initiate negotiations to create new agencies (Article 59). To coordinate these bodies ECOSOC may enter into agreements with specialized agencies, subject to General Assembly approval, defining the terms of the relationship (Article 63); may take steps to obtain reports from the agencies (Article 64); and arrange to have representatives of the agencies participate, without vote, in the deliberations of ECOSOC and its commissions, and vice versa (Article 70). Finally, while both the Assembly and ECOSOC may adopt recommendations on any aspect of the coordination process, the architects of the Charter were not willing to give the UN any binding power over the specialized agencies.

The Dumbarton Oaks version, made in the image and likeness of the July 1944 United States plan, established the distinctly anti-centralization pattern which was ultimately incorporated in the Charter.[49] At San Francisco, it was the indefatigable Canadian delegation which led the effort to reinforce the UN–specialized agency relationship by providing for re-

[49] UNCIO, III, pp. 19–22.

ports on compliance with UN recommendations, UN representation in specialized agency meetings, UN "appraisal" of the agencies' performance, UN initiation of negotiations to create new agencies, and the furnishing of UN services at the agencies' request. At the same time, Canada and other states wanted the budget review function to be placed explicitly in the hands of the Assembly rather than its underling, ECOSOC.[50] Ultimately all of these suggestions were woven into the Charter.

After San Francisco. Since San Francisco the need for coordination has become steadily more pressing, and the UN has exercised increasing ingenuity to find ways of embracing the agencies more closely without squeezing the independent life out of them. In December 1945 the Preparatory Commission set the pace by recommending the greatest possible haste in lashing the UN, just about to be launched, to those agencies that were already in existence. Among twenty matters which it listed as appropriate channels for collaboration between the organizations, it gave particular attention to representation of the agencies on a coordination commission headed by the UN Secretary-General (which later materialized as the Administrative Committee on Coordination described above).

The Commission also anticipated the possibility, not explicitly provided for in the Charter, of conferring on the Assembly the "responsibility for voting . . . [the agencies'] budgets" as part of a "consolidated budget." [51] While it was noted that the League and ILO had had such an arrangement, no mention was made of the fact that the ILO had insisted on almost complete budget autonomy except for formal Assembly review and approval. The Preparatory Commission was obviously torn between the efficiencies that might flow from such an innovation and the practical difficulties that stood in the way, such as the need for amending agency constitutions and the varying memberships of the UN and the agencies.

The actual negotiation of agreements with the specialized agencies was initiated by ECOSOC in February 1946 when it created its Committee on Negotiations. Perhaps it is unfortunate that this was the first step in the coordinating process since agencies, like most governments and individuals, are often willing to agree to more in practice than in a binding contract.[52] Thus the agencies tended to approach these negotiations like cautious wrestlers.

Pattern of Agreements. The agreements negotiated thus far can be divided into three broad categories. The first and largest group consists of agreements with those agencies that are fairly recent in origin, have far-reaching authority and have consented to a rather close relationship with the UN: ILO, FAO, ICAO, UNESCO, WHO and WMO. They have agreed to cooperate with the UN in the following matters:

50 *Ibid.*, X, pp. 21, 320, 328.
51 *Report of the Preparatory Commission of the United Nations*, p. 45.
52 See comment in *Coordination of Economic and Social Activities*, p. 13.

1. Reciprocal representation on matters of mutual concern.

2. Exchange of information and documents.

3. Reciprocal proposal of agenda items.

4. Reciprocal consideration of recommendations.

5. Regular reports by the agencies including information on compliance with recommendations.

6. Agency assistance to the Security and Trusteeship Councils as requested.

7. Furnishing of information regarding cases before the International Court of Justice.

8. Advance authorization for the agencies to request advisory opinions of the Court on legal questions within the scope of their activities and not concerned with the relationship between the UN and the agencies.

9. Cooperation on personnel procedures including "eventual development of a single unified civil service," consultation regarding possible International Civil Service Commission, exchange of personnel and common machinery for settling personnel disputes.

10. Avoidance of duplication of statistical and other services.

11. Close budgetary relations including consultation on budget preparation, transmission of annual budgets to UN and consultation "concerning appropriate arrangements for the inclusion of the [agency] budget[s] . . . within the general budget of the UN." [53]

While these agreements reflect the difficulty of trying to harness together independent agencies, they provide an ample base for collaboration. The most difficult issue was the question of the consolidated budget. Though this innovation might result in certain administrative economies, it seems of dubious practicality since it would cause great difficulties in the case of states that belonged to some of the specialized agencies but not the UN. Nor is it clear that it would be as effective an instrument as various other cooperative arrangements for coordinating the planning of UN and agency programs.

The second group of agreements consists of those with the International Bank for Reconstruction and Development (IBRD) and International Monetary Fund (IMF). The leadership of these twin agencies, heavily weighted with United States financial personnel and thinking, took the most rebellious position against UN supervision. The thesis was that these bodies were created to make decisions on the basis of strictly confidential information in accordance with pure banking principles unsullied by the profane hand of politics. While the general pattern described above was also followed here, many individual points were carefully blunted by restrictive qualifications:

1. UN representatives may attend meetings of only the Board of Governors, not Executive Directors.

2. Both agencies agree only to give "due consideration" to UN-proposed agenda items.

[53] United Nations, General Assembly, *Resolutions Adopted . . . During the Second Part of the First Session . . . .* , Doc. A/64/Add.1, p. 78.

3. The UN may make no recommendations "without reasonable prior consultation" and should refrain from such recommendations on individual loans. Nor is there any requirement to report action taken.

4. Both agencies are assured full autonomy "in deciding the form and content" of their budgets and thus are not obligated to transmit any budget to the UN.

The United States defended the full text of these agreements. The United Kingdom approved them conditionally with the hope that certain alterations could be made later. The Soviet bloc plus various liberal middle and small powers, such as Australia, New Zealand and Norway, vigorously criticized the agreements for throwing unnecessary sand in the coordination machinery. Although the skittish attitude of these two agencies is understandable, it seems excessively cautious, especially since they are bound to observe no more rigorous technical and professional standards than are such agencies as the FAO and WHO. It seems particularly unreasonable to refuse to transmit administrative budgets so that they may be part of a regular comparative analysis of costs and procedures.

The third group is comprised of the agreements with the ITU and UPU. These agencies, of old "bureau" vintage, have been in existence longer than the others, perform more limited functions of a highly specialized nature, and are less active and less closely related to the broad objectives of the UN. Consequently these agreements, though conforming to the general pattern described above, are briefer and less detailed. This is especially true of the passage regarding assistance to UN organs, personnel, budgetary arrangements, and statistical and other services.

Coordination Campaign. Since 1947, national delegations, hard-pressed by tight-fisted legislatures, have maintained a steady chorus calling for ever greater "coordination" — for the sake of efficiency, yes, but primarily to save money. This campaign has been carried on through a number of channels. On the staff side, the Administrative Committee on Coordination (ACC) (UN Secretary-General and staff directors of the specialized agencies), assisted by various sub-bodies, deal with both administrative and substantive issues involving coordination. The Technical Assistance Board (TAB) was created by ACC in 1950 to harmonize the efforts of the agencies cooperating in the Technical Assistance Program, which is undoubtedly the strongest instrument for coordination today. The Secretary-General and ACC report their efforts to ECOSOC. The Secretary-General has also published annually a *Catalogue of Economic and Social Projects* to keep everyone informed of what everyone else is doing.

The specialized agencies have been requested to submit to ECOSOC annual reports on their activities including the degree of compliance with past UN recommendations and their plans for the future. ECOSOC has also requested the specialized agencies to screen all their projects in terms of criteria developed by ACC (feasibility, significance of scope, adequacy of preparation and coordination, and significance of potential results).[54]

54 UN, Docs. E/1810 and E/1810/Corr.1; ECOSOC Resolution 324 (XI).

And the Assembly has requested them to transmit their budgets, not to ECOSOC but to the Secretary-General for incorporation as "information annexes" with his annual budget message to the Assembly. ECOSOC examines the various reports and makes appropriate recommendations to the Assembly, Secretary-General and specialized agencies. Finally, the Assembly engages in a briefer review of all relevant coordination information.

Thoughts on "Coordination." "Coordination" is perhaps the most used and least understood word in the UN economic and social vocabulary. It is also a far more central and controversial issue in ECOSOC than in any other UN organ. Why? First, the economic and social machinery is more decentralized and complex than the rest of the UN apparatus. And there is greater concern for economy, where the results are so long-range and hard to measure, which makes the Members particularly sensitive to any kind of duplication.

At the very root of the issue lies the conflict between the forces that urge unification and those that resist it. "Coordination" is the compromise that only partially satisfies each side. Nevertheless, this compromise has paid dividends that deserve frank recognition. It helped entice the Soviet Union into the UN fold. It probably resulted in squeezing a larger total of contributions out of congenitally parsimonious national treasuries than if the specialized agencies had been born part of the UN brood. And it has encouraged healthy competition among the separate staffs. But, in spite of these gains, the obvious requirements of efficiency and economy have dominated the debates since 1946 and have given rise to an overwhelming trend towards greater centralization rather than decentralization.

The present need, however, is not so much for new machinery as for a more profound and universal adoption of the habit of coordination. Governments and agencies should consult regularly and automatically not only during the execution of projects but from the earliest planning stages. They must cooperate at the bottom as well as the top where the Administrative Committee on Coordination has done a creditable job. They should think constantly in terms of pooling experience, personnel and equipment.

The concept of priorities is a useful though difficult and little understood tool. The United States has pushed it hard, while the British have been somewhat less enthusiastic. Among the obvious hurdles that stand in the way is the problem of agreeing on what is of primary importance. Some, including the British, have said the priorities are not and cannot be the result of dispassionate debate but are dictated by emergencies, such as the Korean conflict. Some have said that projects should be judged in terms of their contribution to the maintenance of peace, while others insist that they cannot and should not be measured in terms of such immediate "political" goals. Then there is the undeniable fact that agencies having different kinds of jobs (the UPU as compared with UNESCO) require different kinds of priorities. ECOSOC recognizes all of these thorns on the rose but nonetheless has gone ahead to formulate some tentative criteria.

Finally, governments themselves need to coordinate their own policies more effectively. Too frequently a state's delegate to the Second (Economic and Financial) Committee will call for a new study by the Secretariat's Economic Department, while the same country's delegate to the Fifth (Administrative and Budgetary) Committee wants to cut the Economic Department's appropriation. It is time that the right and left hands work as if they belonged to one body.

General Conclusions

Measured in terms of the most tangible and relevant yardstick available, the League experience, it is clear that the over-all UN economic and social system is fundamentally a continuation of the past. At the same time, it represents much that is significantly different. Assuming that broad, vigorous and influential international collaboration is to be desired, many of these innovations have resulted in unmistakable progress. In essence, the new system's chief strengths are its more positive and comprehensive objectives, the greater importance of these activities in relation to the UN's security functions based on a clearer recognition of the interaction of the two fields, the closer links to the full UN membership through the Assembly, the broader range of Asian and other nations participating in the system, the more thorough and competent direction furnished by a separate Economic and Social Council distinct from the Security Council and the more ample financial and personnel resources.

Yet, if this glance backwards is moderately reassuring, we have only to look ahead to see how far we have yet to travel. The all-important fact that overshadows the new system, as it did the old, is that nations are loath to relinquish any more of their freedom of action than they think absolutely essential for their well-being. Consequently the architects of the UN system, led by the major powers, have given no formal binding authority to the Assembly, ECOSOC or the Commissions, although in actual practice their policies and actions are frequently influenced by these bodies. While the Members have given larger financial contributions than they did to comparable League agencies, they still give amounts that are insignificant compared with what they devote to national programs. These are the most central and profound weaknesses which are seldom discussed in the public debates.

ASSEMBLY AND ECOSOC

The more frequently aired maladies are, in reality, more superficial — symptoms rather than causes — but nonetheless they deserve attention. First of all, the Assembly leaves much to be desired as a forum for dealing with economic and social problems. The delegates assigned to the Second and Third Committees often lack adequate competency, influence and briefing regarding the matters before them. The equal weighting of quite unequal nations is as unrealistic here as it is in the security realm. Nor is there enough time to do justice to the issues at stake. Finally, the Assembly tends to duplicate work previously done in other bodies.

ECOSOC and its sub-bodies suffer from these as well as other afflictions. While the major and middle powers enjoy more preferred positions in these agencies than in the Assembly, the weighting is entirely informal and haphazard. The deliberations frequently suffer from inadequate preparation by both staff and delegates; hasty, superficial, propagandistic and repetitive discussion; and a lack of high-level, competent and continuous representation.[55] While the matter of coordination, more complicated than in the League because of the proliferation of specialized agencies, is still a problem, informal devices centering around the Administrative Committee on Coordination and the Technical Assistance Board have greatly improved the situation.

THE COMMISSIONS

Behind the 1951 reorganization of ECOSOC Commissions lay certain fundamental considerations not likely to be apparent to the casual observer. Many of the underlying frustrations really stemmed from substantive disagreements on such difficult issues as the financing of technical assistance and the question of economic versus political human rights. Other tensions arose from the commissions' lack of authority and resources. These problems might have been met by reinforcement, not retrenchment, but none of the great powers was willing to strengthen the commissions in power or financial backing to any appreciable extent.

Regarding the administrative aches and pains, on which the United States and United Kingdom concentrated most of their fire, one of the most significant developments was the retreat from the 1945 position favoring a hybrid governmental expert over a more independent specialist. But, in spite of the more recent British enchantment with the full employment report, written by "free" experts, other expert reports have not been so pleasing to either the British or the Americans. And ultimately the experts' views require governmental support before they can be effective. This remains as essential under the new ECOSOC philosophy as under the old.

It does seem valid, nonetheless, to believe that there is somewhat greater opportunity for bold progress beyond present policies if the advice presented to governments is formulated by independent experts rather than

---

[55] For recent critical evaluations, see Henri Laugier, "Le Conseil Economique et Social," *Politique Etrangère*, Vol. 16, No. 4–5 (December 1951); A. Loveday, "Suggestions for the Reform of the United Nations Economic and Social Machinery," *International Organization*, Vol. 7, No. 3 (August 1953).

specialists tied to those same governments. Reinforcing this new philosophy is the strong vote of confidence which ECOSOC gave the Secretariat, specially selected groups of nongovernmental experts, and the more narrowly limited and professionalized commissions (Statistical, Population and Narcotic Drugs).

Another significant trend that emerges from the ECOSOC reorganization is the warm approval bestowed on the regional commissions, nonexistent in the League era, in preference to the functional commissions which were the normal League pattern. This development comes about basically because nations have felt, with justification, that the regional bodies were more sensitive to their own particular national and regional interests; the membership of these bodies is bound by stronger community ties; all nations in the area, even non-UN Members, are included in the membership; these bodies can deal with all problems in each area as a related complex rather than as isolated phenomena; they seem to have performed more positively and successfully than some of the other commissions, especially in Europe; and they have operated on a more decentralized basis close to the grass roots. Without denying the force of these arguments, one should also be aware of the possibility of an atomization of the UN economic and social program into a series of isolated regional camps.

Suggestions for Further Reading

Books

Beveridge, Sir William, *The Price of Peace* (London: Pilot Press, 1945).

British Labour Party, *Labour's Aims in War and Peace* (London: Lincolns-Prager (Publishers) Ltd., 1940).

Butler, Harold, *The Lost Peace* (London: Faber & Faber, Ltd., 1941).

Carr, Edward H., *Conditions of Peace* (New York: The Macmillan Company, 1942).

Condliffe, J. B., *Agenda For a Postwar World* (New York: W. W. Norton & Co., Inc., 1942).

Coordination of Economic and Social Activities (New York: Carnegie Endowment for International Peace, 1948).

Corbett, P. E., *Post-War Worlds* (New York: Institute of Pacific Relations, 1942).

Evatt, Herbert Vere, *The United Nations* (Cambridge: Harvard University Press, 1948).

Feis, Herbert, *The Sinews of Peace* (New York: Harper & Brothers, 1944).

Finer, Herman, *The United Nations Economic and Social Council* (Boston: World Peace Foundation, 1945).

Goodrich, Leland M., and Hambro, Edvard, *Charter of the United Nations, Commentary and Documents* (Boston: World Peace Foundation, 1949).

Hambro, C. J., *How to Win the Peace* (Philadelphia and New York: J. B. Lippincott Co., 1942).

Hansen, Alvin H., *America's Role in World Economy* (New York: W. W. Norton & Co., Inc., 1945).

Hawtrey, R. G., *Economic Destiny* (London: Longmans, Green and Co., 1944).

Hoover, Herbert, and Gibson, Hugh, *The Problems of Lasting Peace* (Garden City: Doubleday, Doran, 1942).

Hull, Cordell, *The Memoirs of Cordell Hull*, 2 Vols. (New York: The Macmillan Company, 1948).

Liberal Party, *Liberal Plan for Peace* (London: Victor Gollancz, Ltd., 1944).

Orr, Sir John, *Fighting for What?* (London: Macmillan & Co., Ltd., 1942).

Staley, Eugene, *World Economy in Transition* (New York: Council on Foreign Relations, 1939).

Viner, Jacob, and others, *The United States in a Multi-National Economy* (New York: Council on Foreign Relations, 1945).

Wells, H. G., *Guide to the New World* (London: Victor Gollancz, Ltd., 1941).

Periodicals

Commission on a Just and Durable Peace (Federal Council of the Churches of Christ in America), "Christian Standards and Current International Development," *International Conciliation*, No. 409 (March 1945).

Commission to Study the Organization of Peace, "Fourth Report . . . ," *International Conciliation*, No. 396 (January 1944). Also see reference to other Commission reports, Chap. 3.

Eagleton, Clyde and Wilcox, F. O., eds., "The United Nations: Peace and Security," *American Political Science Review*, Vol. 39, No. 5 (October 1945).

Fisher, Allan G. B., "International Economic Collaboration and the Economic and Social Council," *International Affairs*, Vol. 21, No. 4 (October 1945).

Krout, John A., ed., "World Organization — Economic, Political and Social," *Proceedings of the Academy of Political Science*, Vol. 21, No. 3 (May 1945).

Laugier, Henri, "Le Conseil Economique et Social," *Politique Etrangère*, Vol. 16, No. 4–5 (December 1951).

League of Nations Union, "Social and Economic Reconstruction," *League of Nations Union Pamphlets*, No. 432 (April 1943).

Loveday, A., "An Unfortunate Decision," *International Organization*, Vol. 1, No. 2 (June 1947).

———, "Suggestions for the Reform of the United Nations Economic and Social Machinery," *International Organization*, Vol. 7, No. 3 (August 1953).

Sharp, Walter R., "The Institutional Framework for Technical Assistance," *International Organization*, Vol. 7, No. 3 (August 1953).

Universities Committee on Post-war International Problems, "Problem V — Relief and Rehabilitation," *International Conciliation*, No. 401 (June 1944).

———, "Problems VI and VII — International Economic Collaboration; Problem VIII — Education and World Peace," *International Conciliation*, No. 405 (November 1944).

Documents

United Nations, *United Nations Conference on International Organization, San Francisco, 1945* (London and New York: UN Information Organizations, 1945–1946).

United States, *Postwar Foreign Policy Preparation, 1939–1945*, Department of State Publication 3580, General Foreign Policy Series 15 (Washington: U.S. Government Printing Office, 1950).

———, *Report to the President on the Results of the San Francisco Conference . . .*, Department of State Publication 2349, Conference Series 71 (Washington: U.S. Government Printing Office, 1945).

9

UNRRA and Specialized Agencies

United Nations Relief and Rehabilitation
Administration (UNRRA)

> "All of the United Nations agree to cooperate and share in the work of UNRRA — each nation according to its own individual resources — and to provide relief and help in rehabilitation for the victims of German and Japanese barbarism. . . . When victory comes there can certainly be no secure peace until . . . the peoples of these countries have been restored to a normal, healthy, and self-sustaining existence. . . ." — FRANKLIN D. ROOSEVELT [1]

THESE WORDS were uttered by President Roosevelt on November 9, 1943, almost two years before the guns of World War II were finally silenced, to the representatives of forty-three United and Associated Nations meeting in the ornate East Room of the White House to sign the agreement creating the first UN economic and social body to prepare the world for peace. The revolutionary significance of UNRRA was particularly apparent to those who compared it with the poorly coordinated and inadequately financed Allied efforts after World War I.[2] UNRRA was, in fact, to be the first international relief organization through which the major powers would actually merge their resources to support truly international operational programs backed by sizable funds and staff.

The motives behind UNRRA were not as simple, however, nor did that organization represent quite as much progress as President Roosevelt's optimistic eloquence seemed to suggest. Among its forty-four sponsors, UNRRA's real parents were the United States and United Kingdom, whose first interest was to bind up the world's economic and social wounds as quickly as possible, with a maximum spreading of the burden, as the best

[1] UNRRA *Journal*, First Council, pp. 1–2.   [2] See Chap. 7.

means of promoting political and economic stability. They were also interested in soaking up surpluses of commodities, chiefly wheat and wool, which might arise during the war because of the blockade or after the war because of the lack of purchasing power. Then, too, they wanted to prevent a competitive scramble for scarce relief supplies. Moreover, they used the UNRRA idea to soften the impact of the blockade and to hasten the end of the war by holding out to Axis-occupied populations the promise of relief aid as an enticing incentive. Another interest was to experiment with an international technical agency which, though never officially linked to the later United Nations organization, influenced the development of the subsequent UN-affiliated specialized agencies. And, above all, they wanted a "grand rehearsal" for the general organization which was to take the place of the League. As President Roosevelt also said in 1943, "nations will learn to work together only by actually working together. . . . It is, therefore, with a lift of hope, that we look on the signing of this agreement . . . as a means of joining . . . together still more firmly." [3]

A GREAT EXPERIMENT IS BORN

When various exile governments, such as the Netherlands, seemed to be initiating a race for relief supplies during 1941, the British called an Inter-Allied Meeting in London in September and established a cooperative program under an Inter-Allied Committee on Post-War Requirements (the "Leith–Ross Committee," named for the British head of its secretariat). The Soviet Union promptly objected that this group was too much under the thumb of Britain, too narrowly preoccupied with the needs of Europe, and too much tied to relief rather than long-range reconstruction and development.[4] The United States was not a member of the Committee but endorsed it; authorized an observer in October; and began, early in 1942, to plan a more ambitious organization under the control of the great powers with an American as director of operations (presumably to be financed chiefly by the United States).[5]

In June 1942 the five major producers of wheat (Argentina, Australia, Canada, United Kingdom and United States) established an International Wheat Council. The signatories agreed, in conjunction with a program to prevent surpluses from wrecking the wheat market, to contribute certain quotas of wheat to a pool for the relief of war-stricken countries. Also in June the British and Americans hammered out the first draft agreement to establish UNRRA, later submitted to the Russians and Chinese.[6] Further negotiations were delayed, however, due to the discouraging course of the

[3] UNRRA Journal, pp. 1–2.

[4] George Woodbridge, ed., UNRRA (New York: Columbia University Press, 1950), Vol. 1, pp. 10–11.

[5] Postwar Foreign Policy Preparation 1939–45, Department of State Publication 3580 (Washington: Government Printing Office, 1950), pp. 90–91.

[6] Ibid., pp. 515–517.

war, and a four-power draft was not released to the other forty Allied and Associated Nations until June 1943.

Then the air began to crackle with criticisms. The most threatening blast came from the United States Senate whose leadership, particularly Senator Arthur Vandenberg, insisted that the State Department incorporate provisions that would make clear the right of withdrawal, legislative approval of all financial contributions, the purely temporary character of the organization, and its limited mandate to deal with only relief and rehabilitation, not long-range reconstruction (the British had concurred on this last point in the summer of 1942).[7] The Soviet Union was equally adamant in urging that unanimity be required for all decisions but finally accepted the "Acheson compromise" reserving unanimity for only a few questions, chiefly the appointment of a Director General. Both the British and Russians favored a relatively decentralized system, presumably to safeguard their own freedom of action, while the United States insisted on centralization with ample operating authority in the hands of the Director General, always expected to be an American. Nevertheless, it remained clear at all times that the organization could not legally, though it might in practice, compel a nation to do anything against its will. The core of UNRRA's mission was decided upon by certain British and American representatives, including John Maynard Keynes and Dean Acheson, in Washington in October 1943 just before the final version was signed.

> It should be a temporary operation restricted to providing relief and rehabilitation supplies and services under the aegis of the already existing allocating agencies [the Combined Boards, dominated chiefly by the United States and United Kingdom], to nations not possessing sufficient foreign exchange resources to finance imports; observing the local distribution of these supplies and services; and attempting to secure a fair allotment of such goods and services before the Combined Boards in relation to quantities available and the just claims of competitor wealthy nations.[8]

ORGANIZATIONAL PATTERN

The structural anatomy of UNRRA, reminiscent of the pattern of the League technical "organizations" and the ILO, was composed of the three familiar elements to be incorporated in all postwar specialized agencies: a plenary assembly (in this case, called the Council), an executive body (called the Central Committee), and a staff headed by a Director General. Each member state was entitled to one representative with a single vote in the Council; decisions were made by a simple majority of the members present. The Central Committee was first composed of only the Big Four: the United States, United Kingdom, Soviet Union and China, the Director General presiding without a vote. Subsequently, in response to criticism

---

[7] *Ibid.*, pp. 203–204; Woodbridge, *op. cit.*, pp. 14–32.
[8] Woodbridge, *op. cit.*, p. 32.

of this exclusiveness, Canada and France were added in August 1945; Australia, Brazil and Yugoslavia, in March 1946.

Nonetheless, as the tempo of activities and expenditures quickened during 1945 and 1946, the Central Committee increasingly overshadowed the plenary Council, to which the Committee was constitutionally responsible. The Committee met on the average of once or twice a month, usually in Washington, while the Council met only once a year from 1943 to 1945, three times in 1946, and never thereafter. Though it was originally agreed that unanimity should be required in the Committee for only three types of questions, decisions were normally made during the initial friendly period by a "sense of the meeting" without formal vote. After friction developed between the Soviet Union and the Western powers in 1945, however, it was accepted that a decision could be reached by simple majority, though there was still some doubt about abstentions.

The Director General was nominated by a unanimous decision of the Central Committee and formally appointed by the Council. He was the chief of staff — by agreement, always a national of the United States, but, because of the character of the men appointed, never a passive "rubber stamp," often highly critical of United States policy, and always an active and influential figure who, within the budgetary limits fixed, normally held the operational initiative. At its peak, in June 1946, the total personnel numbered 27,800, the largest staff ever employed by any international agency. Total administrative expenses came to $46.8 million. Total goods and services distributed came to $3.9 billion, the largest amount ever spent by an international agency. To help guide UNRRA's policies, several regional and functional advisory committees, composed of governmental representatives, were created during the first session to advise the Council, Central Committee and Director General. Because of the pressure of events, the interests of the great powers and the ascendancy of the Director General, however, most of these committees became increasingly less influential.

CONCLUSIONS

In comparison with the tardy, loose-jointed and feeble post-World War I relief efforts under the Supreme Economic Council, UNRRA was a far bolder breed of animal. UNRRA was established long before the fighting stopped rather than after the armistice was signed. It was empowered to engage in integrated direct operations rather than merely to advise on the coordination of national programs. It had large operational funds and staff of its own, while the Supreme Economic Council had little. And its membership was far more comprehensive than that of its predecessor. Its organizational pattern not only proved adequate for the tremendous relief program it carried out but also served as an influential model for later UN bodies. And its integrated coordination of a number of related economic and social activities under a single roof afforded firmer direction than is possible in the present UN flock clustered around the Economic and Social Council. Most important of all, the United States and Soviet Union supported UNRRA as they did not support the World War I Supreme Economic Council.

On the liability side, the Council, in which all Members were equally represented, soon proved an unrealistic and unwieldy forum, while the increasing dominance of the Central Committee, in which the great powers held a virtually weighted position, evolved extra-constitutionally without general agreement. Another liability, the absence of adequate authority to supervise the implementation of aid in the various recipient countries, was due to the basic political decision underlying that organization by which all the great powers, including the United States, agreed at the outset that implementation of aid should be under the direct control of the recipient governments. Finally there was some inefficiency on the part of the staff, but evidence indicates that it was due less to the caliber of the personnel involved than the general political situation and the emergency character of the job to be done.

Food and Agriculture Organization (FAO)

"The rapidly increasing population of the world, together with the decreasing productivity of the soil, makes world famine as great a threat to our civilization as the atomic bomb." — Sir John Boyd Orr [9]

The character of FAO owes as much to the past as the present. Its chief designers were, for the most part, men who had long been active in international agricultural activities, particularly the League's nutrition program. One of the key figures was Mr. F. L. McDougall, an Australian agricultural leader who is said to have inspired the League program as part of a plan to counteract the agricultural depression of the 1930's without plowing under wheat and slaughtering pigs. Another central figure was Sir John Boyd Orr, a Scottish nutrition expert who had worked closely with the League Health Organization and was the source of much of McDougall's thinking.[10]

In the fall and winter of 1942, the darkest period of the war, McDougall and Orr were in Washington and circulated a thirty-page memorandum ("The McDougall Memorandum") calling for an ambitious postwar program to improve world nutritional conditions.[11] Discussions were held with

[9] "Science, Politics, and Hunger," *The Nation*, Vol. 169, No. 3 (July 16, 1949), p. 61.

[10] See John D. Black, "The International Food Movement," *The American Economic Review*, Vol. 23, No. 4 (December 1943), pp. 791–811.

[11] For substance of McDougall program see his article "International Aspects of Postwar Food and Agriculture," *The Annals of the American Academy of Political and Social Science*, Vol 225 (January 1943), pp. 122–127.

Department of Agriculture and other personnel, including Mr. Howard R. Tolley, then Chief of the Bureau of Agricultural Economics, and Dr. Frank G. Boudreau, Chairman of the Food and Nutrition Board and formerly an official of the League Health Organization. It was these talks which led to President Roosevelt's announcement in February 1943 that a conference would be held in the spring to explore long-range postwar food problems. As the official Department of State account has put it,

> The initiative in this move was the President's. The desirability of such a conference had been raised in the Department only a few days before, on the grounds that there was some public feeling that international discussion of postwar problems was being too long delayed and that food was a relatively noncontroversial subject on which to proceed for the first full United Nations Conference at this still exploratory stage. . . . [The President] chose food and agriculture as the subject offering the best chances for immediate success in the first attempt to test the willingness and ability of the United Nations to cooperate on postwar problems.[12]

It was at the pleasant resort of Hot Springs, Virginia, that the "first peace conference" (United Nations Conference on Food and Agriculture) met from May 18 to June 3, 1943. Unlike the Combined Food Board and other wartime organizations, the Conference was opened to all forty-four United and Associated Nations. Nonetheless, it is scarcely surprising that its decisions were shaped largely by the interests of the great powers, particularly the United States and the United Kingdom. While the Soviet Union had not played a significant role in planning the Conference, it sent a delegation which devoted most of its attention to immediate postwar relief needs. As with most postwar planning, the Conference found it easier to rebuild what had stood before than to build something new. There was general willingness to continue the familiar informational and technical advisory functions previously performed by the League and the International Institute of Agriculture in Rome.

BUFFER STOCK vs. PACT

The greatest stumbling block, which the Conference was never able to surmount, was the question closest to the pocketbooks of both producer and consumer interests: how to get more and better food into the mouths of millions of people who had inadequate purchasing power. The producers could not forget that all during the interwar years they invariably produced more than they could sell. The British, inspired chiefly by the thinking of John Maynard Keynes and John Boyd Orr (the latter was left at home presumably because of his radical ideas on governmentally managed agricultural economies), urged a "buffer stock" plan whereby an international agency would buy and sell in the open market in order to

---

[12] *Postwar Foreign Policy Preparation . . .* , p. 143.

stabilize agricultural prices and promote increased consumption at lower prices.

The United States program was patterned after the international wheat agreement, concluded in 1942 under American auspices to help soak up wheat surpluses. Andrew Cairns, Secretary of the International Wheat Council, and other United States leaders believed that the buffer stock plan, because of limited purchasing power, had proved helpless to stem the flood of serious long-run surpluses. They wanted such situations dealt with through the wheat pact type of intergovernmental commodity agreement, participated in by consumer as well as producer nations, which would seek to regulate production, stocks, and trade as well as prices. Surpluses, not sold at the prices set, would be handed to international food pools which would make them available on a loan basis, at a discount, or as a gift to deficit countries unable to pay the full price. The United States also urged that FAO wait until an over-all trade agency, later called the International Trade Organization (ITO), could coordinate all commodity agreements. The British, who were dependent on large food imports and wanted them at the lowest possible prices, resisted the American plan because they felt that such commodity agreements, based on crop restriction, direct price controls and trade quotas, had usually benefited the producer more than the consumer states.[13]

The Conference's final word on this key issue of matching supply with purchasing power was, first of all, to pass the buck to a future international full employment program that would hopefully achieve a "balanced and world-wide expansion of economic activity." The delegates then approved the principle of some kind of commodity arrangements, supported by certain vague phrases calculated to satisfy both sides, but left a specific solution of the dispute to future discussion both inside and outside FAO. As for the actual structure of FAO, the Conference created an Interim Commission on Food and Agriculture to fill in the details and present them to the individual governments for final approval. The Interim Commission set up shop in July 1943 and, by August 1944, had completed a draft constitution which was finally signed and went into effect at Quebec in October 1945.

FUNCTIONS AND STRUCTURE

The general purposes of the FAO, according to its constitution, are to improve the efficiency of agricultural production and distribution and to raise levels of nutrition and standards of living. Its weapons in this campaign are ever wider and deeper research as well as policy recommenda-

---

[13] For discussion of this debate see Jean Atherton Flexner, "Food Policies of the United Nations," *The American Economic Review*, Vol. 33, No. 4 (December 1943), pp. 812–824; "World Food Plans," *Fortune*, Vol. 28, No. 5 (November 1943), pp. 158–161; *Postwar Foreign Policy Preparation* . . . , pp. 619–621.

tions on all aspects of these matters including the provision of adequate credit and the adoption of agricultural commodity agreements. Furthermore, this early constitution contains a pioneering mandate to "furnish . . . technical assistance . . . [and] organize missions . . ." to implement the FAO's objectives in the field.

Admission to membership is authorized for those signatory states that subsequently ratified the constitution and other states approved by two-thirds of all the members. As of April 1953, sixty-eight countries had joined. The plenary assembly is the Conference in which each member state has one vote. Meetings were originally held once a year but were changed in 1949 to once every two years. Decisions are made by simple majority except that a two-thirds vote is required to make recommendations for national implementation, to submit conventions for national ratification, to admit new members, to discharge new functions assigned by governments or agreement with other public international bodies, and to recommend amendments involving new obligations (subject to ratification by two-thirds of all members and binding on only those ratifying).

The Council, established in September 1947, is the executive body which is composed of eighteen member states elected by the Conference, with one vote apiece. Previously there was an Executive Committee of fifteen experts chosen by the Conference to act for the entire membership. The Council meets twice a year and makes its decisions by simple majority. There are also various standing advisory committees appointed to deal with such matters as agriculture, economics, fisheries, forestry, nutrition, rural welfare and statistics. Regional commodity commissions have been created to study and advise on the production, distribution, conservation and consumption of certain key commodities. These include the International Rice Commission, established in January 1949, with headquarters at Bangkok, Thailand; the Indo-Pacific Fisheries Council, established in November 1948, also with headquarters in Bangkok; the European Forestry and Forest Products Commission, established in July 1948, with headquarters in Geneva, Switzerland; and the Latin American Forestry and Forest Products Commission, established in May 1949, with headquarters in Rio de Janeiro, Brazil. There are also national FAO committees in over fifty countries to serve as contacts between the FAO and various non-governmental agricultural groups. The Director-General, appointed by the Conference, supervises a staff which normally numbers approximately 1,100. The annual budget is approximately $5 million supplemented by about another $5 million furnished by the UN Expanded Technical Assistance Program beginning in 1950. FAO headquarters were moved from Washington to Rome, Italy, in April 1951. Regional offices are located in Washington, Mexico City, Rio de Janeiro, Santiago, Cairo and Bangkok.

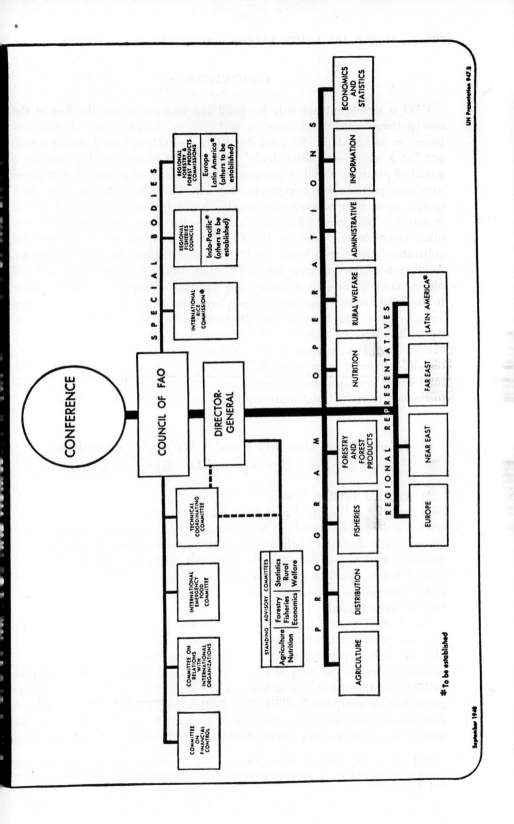

CONFERENCE

COUNCIL OF FAO

COMMITTEE ON FINANCIAL CONTROL

COMMITTEE ON RELATIONS WITH INTERNATIONAL ORGANIZATIONS

INTERNATIONAL EMERGENCY FOOD COMMITTEE

TECHNICAL COORDINATING COMMITTEE

DIRECTOR-GENERAL

SPECIAL BODIES

INTERNATIONAL RICE COMMISSION*

REGIONAL FISHERIES COUNCILS
Indo-Pacific*
(others to be established)

REGIONAL FORESTRY & FOREST PRODUCTS COMMISSIONS
Europe
Latin America*
(others to be established)

STANDING ADVISORY COMMITTEES
Agriculture Nutrition | Forestry Fisheries Economics | Statistics Rural Welfare

PROGRAM

AGRICULTURE

DISTRIBUTION

FISHERIES

FORESTRY AND FOREST PRODUCTS

OPERATIONS

NUTRITION

RURAL WELFARE

ADMINISTRATIVE

INFORMATION

ECONOMICS AND STATISTICS

REGIONAL REPRESENTATIVES

EUROPE

NEAR EAST

FAR EAST

LATIN AMERICA*

* To be established

September 1948

UN Presentation 967 B

CONCLUSIONS

FAO is significant not only for itself but because it was the first of the new postwar specialized agencies and cast its shadow upon all that followed in its footsteps. Sir John Boyd Orr and others hoped that it would not "be a mere fact-finding body" but a "great instrument for creating a world of plenty, a world of prosperity, and a world of peace." [14] His hopes were only partially and imperfectly fulfilled. The FAO is bigger, more integrated, more comprehensive in membership, more ambitious and vigorous in activities and more influential than its predecessors. Nevertheless, many other organizations, such as ECOSOC, WHO, IBRD and ILO, are also cultivating the agricultural field, and coordination is still a problem. Another fundamental step forward is that, through its missions, regional offices, commissions, conferences and national committees, FAO is closer to the "grass roots" than were its predecessors. While its staff and budget are also large, they are still pitifully inadequate. The U.S. Department of Agriculture spends about $1,205 million annually as compared with FAO's $11 million. Finally there is the shift in policy emphasis from a narrow technical interest to an appreciation of the relation of agriculture to the total world economy and a special concern regarding the problem of how to finance increased and more equitable agricultural consumption.

International Monetary Fund (IMF) and International Bank for Reconstruction and Development (IBRD)

At secluded Bretton Woods, New Hampshire, in the summer of 1944, twin agencies — the Fund and the Bank — were born to grapple with the crucial and complex problems of international lending and monetary regulation.[15] The destinies of these organizations were shaped largely by compromises worked out between the principal postwar creditor nation, the United States, and the principal debtor nation, the United Kingdom, in which process the Americans, because of their fortunate financial position, had the upper hand.

The United States, realizing that after the war it would stand in the enviable position of being not only the world's largest creditor nation but also the only great power with surplus production available for export, wanted to grease the ways of trade by stabilizing exchange rates and promoting investment but was inclined to be conservative about the conditions governing international lending. The British, compelled to live far beyond their means in fighting the war, looked forward to the bleak prospect not only of being the world's largest debtor but of being unable for some time

---

[14] "Food for All Mankind," *Survey Graphic*, Vol. 36, No. 10 (October 1947), p. 560.
[15] For major sources on planning process see Suggestions for Further Reading at the end of this chapter.

to produce enough exports to pay for even essential imports. Thus they wanted large amounts of relatively easy credit and insisted on exerting pressure on creditors as well as debtors to restore the balance of payments, a view not calculated to kindle joy in the hearts of many U.S. financial leaders.

On some issues the "White" and "Keynes" plans (named for the two major advisers involved — America's H. D. White and Britain's J. M. Keynes) looked very much like twins. They both favored: (1) exchange stabilization as a major objective; (2) a prohibition against altering exchange rates beyond narrow limits, except with international approval; (3) the use of an international currency unit defined in terms of gold (Americans called it "unitas"; the British, "bancor"); and (4) the assignment of quotas to each member nation to determine amounts that could be borrowed as well as voting strength.

BATTLE OF FINANCIAL TITANS

In other respects, the two plans looked scarcely like distant cousins. The United States proposed rather limited credit resources (originally approximately $5 billion) contributed in advance by members according to quotas and available to members to meet purely temporary (not fundamental) deficits in their balances and only by permission of the international organization. The British wanted a system, based on the pattern of their own domestic banking practices, which would exact no advance contributions but would allow a member to run a deficit in the clearing account up to the amount of its quota, limited only by the total amount of the quotas of all other members. The creditor was to receive a corresponding credit (in terms of "bancor"). The United States would thereby have assumed a potential obligation to grant credits of from $25 billion to possibly as high as $100 billion. The Union was to have authority not only to prod debtors into living within their means but also to penalize creditors whose credits rose too high on the theory that creditors as well as debtors would be to blame for balance of payments difficulties.[16]

In all of this planning, the American idea of a bank received relatively little attention until shortly before the Bretton Woods Conference. The planners tended to think of the monetary problem as the more important short-range issue, and Britain and other war-battered countries felt unable to pledge significant amounts of credit for the use of others.

In mid-June 1943 the circle of governmental consultation was widened to include seventeen other large and middle powers, including the Soviet Union, French Committee of National Liberation and China, in an informal three-day session of technical experts in Washington. Later, at the

[16] John Parke Young, "Developing Plans for an International Monetary Fund and a World Bank," *Department of State Bulletin,* Vol. 23, No. 593 (November 13, 1950), p. 782.

beginning of 1944, a group of Soviet experts went to Washington to discuss the plans and, after careful analysis of the issues, stated that they believed it would be possible for the Soviet Union to participate in the prospective organization.

In the mercifully temperate summer climate of Bretton Woods, New Hampshire, the representatives of all forty-four United and Associated Nations finally met from July 1 to 22, 1944, to complete the plans which had been so long aborning. The chief architects, the United States and United Kingdom, still had to work out a final compromise between themselves. Russia seemed primarily interested in seeing how the financial scheme could help her reconstruct and develop her war-ravaged economy. And the middle and smaller nations wanted to be certain that their needs would not be overshadowed by the interests of the great powers.

The following issues, most of them familiar since 1942, were the chief bones of contention among the delegates: (1) slicing up the quota pie so as to maximize borrowing rights under the Fund and minimize lending obligations under the Bank; (2) determining the degree of automaticity in the Fund's lending; (3) settling the argument between those favoring low and high charges for Fund lending; (4) dealing with the Soviet Union's request for lower gold contributions, special aid for postwar reconstruction and reducing the demand for information on national operations; (5) satisfying those countries, chiefly Latin American, that wanted Bank loans for development rather than reconstruction; (6) fixing limits on national restrictions aimed at fostering full employment and balancing international payments; (7) defining the transitional period during which certain restrictions would be tolerated; and (8) wrestling with various other matters such as weighted voting, withdrawal from membership and the relation of the Fund and Bank to trade and other aspects of economic policy.

The Articles of Agreement, signed at Bretton Woods, went into effect in December 1945.

ORGANIZATION OF INTERNATIONAL MONETARY FUND

Purposes and Functions

1. *General purposes:*
    a) promote international monetary cooperation;
    b) facilitate the expansion and balanced growth of trade, and contribute thereby to the promotion and maintenance of high levels of employment and real income and to the development of the productive resources of the members;
    c) promote exchange stability, maintain orderly exchange arrangements among members, and avoid competitive exchange depreciation;
    d) assist in establishing a multilateral system of payments and in eliminating foreign exchange restrictions;
    e) help members correct maladjustments in their balance of payments without resorting to measures destructive of national or international prosperity;

  f) shorten the duration and lessen the degree of disequilibrium in the international balances of payments of members.

2. *Resources available:* Each member is assigned a quota, according to the original Articles of Agreements or by a four-fifths vote plus the consent of the member. These range from $0.2 million for Panama to $3,175 million for the United States (with 33 per cent of the voting power). The four next largest are the United Kingdom (14 per cent), China (6 per cent), France (6 per cent), and India (4 per cent). Each member is required to pay 25 per cent of its quota in gold; the remainder, in its own currency.

3. *Conditions regulating access to the Fund:*

  a) Members may not alter their exchange rates more than 10 per cent from their initial par value without Fund's permission. A uniform proportionate change in all par values (i.e., changing the value of gold) requires a majority vote plus the approval of the two nations having 10 per cent of the total quotas (United States and United Kingdom).

  b) Members must maintain the gold value of their contributions to the Fund.

  c) A member may purchase, by paying an equal amount of its own currency, up to 25 per cent of its quota in some other currency or currencies in any one year, to a top limit of 125 per cent of its quota.

  d) There is a standard service charge of ¾ per cent a year and additional interest on a gradually increasing scale, as the borrower draws in excess of 25 per cent of its quota.

  e) Countries that are gaining gold and foreign exchange must use half of the amounts gained to reduce the total of their own currency previously deposited with the Fund in return for other currencies.

  f) Members may use currencies purchased from the Fund only for purposes approved by the Fund.

  g) Members pledged themselves to restore free convertibility and transfer but only after a transition period which was expected to end five years after the Fund commenced operations.

  h) The Fund may declare a currency generally scarce (most likely the United States dollar) and take steps to ration and replenish its supply of that currency. Under such circumstances members may impose temporary restrictions on payments in the scarce currency.

  i) Members may not use Fund resources to maintain large or sustained outflows of capital (flight capital) and they are authorized to control such movements.

  j) Members are pledged to furnish the Fund a vast supply of relevant information.

Structure

1. *Membership* — states attending Bretton Woods Conference who ratified Agreement before December 31, 1945, and other states admitted by Board of Governors by simple majority of total voting power; fifty-four as of April 1953.

2. *Board of Governors* — central plenary body.

  a) *Composition* — each member entitled to one Governor and one alternate with voting power according to quotas; five-year terms with eligibility for reappointment.

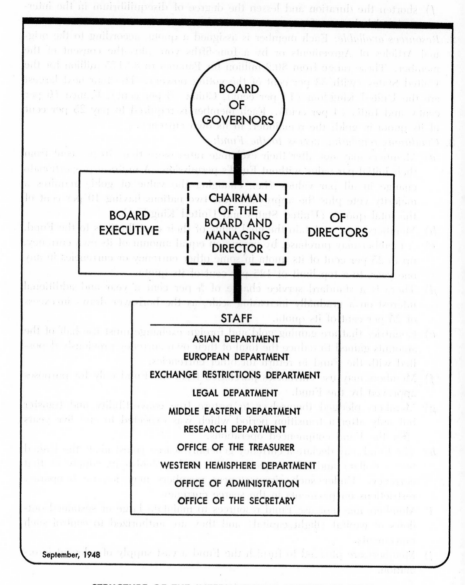

BOARD
OF
GOVERNORS

CHAIRMAN
OF THE
BOARD AND
MANAGING
DIRECTOR

BOARD
EXECUTIVE

OF
DIRECTORS

STAFF

ASIAN DEPARTMENT
EUROPEAN DEPARTMENT
EXCHANGE RESTRICTIONS DEPARTMENT
LEGAL DEPARTMENT
MIDDLE EASTERN DEPARTMENT
RESEARCH DEPARTMENT
OFFICE OF THE TREASURER
WESTERN HEMISPHERE DEPARTMENT
OFFICE OF ADMINISTRATION
OFFICE OF THE SECRETARY

September, 1948

STRUCTURE OF THE INTERNATIONAL MONETARY FUND

   b) *Meetings* — annual; additional meetings when called by five members or those with one-quarter of voting power.

   c) *Procedure* — decisions by simple majority except as otherwise provided in Articles of Agreement. Each member has 250 votes plus one additional vote for each $100,000 of its quota. Each Governor casts all the votes allotted to the member state he represents. In voting on certain matters, such as waiving conditions governing the use of the Fund's resources, voting power is adjusted to reflect members' use of the Fund's resources.

3. *Board of Executive Directors* — executive body responsible for the conduct of the Fund's general operations under authority delegated by the Board of Governors, excluding certain matters, such as revising members' quotas, which cannot be delegated.

   a) *Composition* — total of fourteen. Five Directors are appointed by the five members having the largest quotas. The remaining nine are elected by the Governors representing the other members as follows: seven by members other than the American Republics, and two by the American Republics. Terms are two years with eligibility for reappointment.

   b) *Meetings* — in continuous session.

   c) *Procedure* — decisions by simple majority except as otherwise provided in Articles of Agreement. Each Director casts as a unit the total number of votes allotted to the country which appoints him or the countries which elect him.

4. *Managing Director* — chief of the Fund's operating staff under the direction of the Executive Directors. He is appointed by the Executive Directors and serves as their chairman without a vote except a deciding vote in the case of a tie. The staff normally numbers about 440. The administrative budget is approximately $5 million a year. Headquarters: Washington, D.C.

ORGANIZATION OF INTERNATIONAL BANK FOR RECONSTRUCTION AND DEVELOPMENT

Purposes and Functions

1. *General purposes:*
   a) assist in the reconstruction and development of member territories;
   b) promote private foreign investment by guarantees or participation in loans and, when private capital is not available on reasonable terms, supplement private investment by providing finance for productive purposes out of its own capital, funds raised by it and its other resources;
   c) promote the long-range balanced growth of international trade and the maintenance of equilibrium in balances of payments by encouraging investment for development, thereby assisting in raising productivity, the standard of living and conditions of labor;
   d) coordinate its lending with other international loans so that the more useful and urgent projects will be dealt with first;
   e) have due regard for the effect of investment upon business conditions in member territories and assist in bringing about a smooth transition from a wartime to a peacetime economy.

2. *Resources available:*
   a) The Bank has an authorized capital of $10 billion divided into 100,000

shares of $100,000 each. The capital actually subscribed by the member governments as of December 1951 was $8.4 billion. The United States subscription is $3.175 billion (with 33 per cent of the voting power). The four next largest subscribers are Great Britain (with 14 per cent), China (6 per cent), France (6 per cent), and India (4 per cent).

b) The total subscription is divided into two parts: (1) 20 per cent constitutes the Bank's fund for direct lending. 2 per cent of this countries are required to pay immediately in gold or United States dollars. The remaining 18 per cent is payable in each member's own local currency upon call by the Bank. (2) 80 per cent to be paid only when the Bank needs it to make good on loans from private sources or guarantees.

3. *In implementing these objectives the Bank may:*
   a) lend funds directly, from its capital funds or from funds it may borrow in the members' investment markets;
   b) guarantee loans made by others;
   c) or participate in loans made by others.

4. *Conditions governing loans and guarantees:*
   a) Loans may be made to member countries directly, any of their political sub-divisions, or to private business or agricultural enterprises in member territories. When the member government is not the borrower, however, its central bank or some comparable agency acceptable to the Bank must guarantee the loan.
   b) The Bank must be satisfied that the borrower is unable to obtain a loan elsewhere under reasonable conditions.
   c) The Bank must be satisfied that the borrower or guarantor will be able to meet its obligations under the loan. The conditions governing liquidation of the loans are relatively flexible and subject to adjustment to meet emergency situations. The rate of interest has varied from 2 to 3½ per cent, 1 per cent of which has been the Bank's commission to cover administrative expenses.
   d) Loans are normally to be made only for specific projects of reconstruction or development.
   e) The total amount of the Bank's financial assistance is not to exceed 100 per cent of its unimpaired subscribed capital, reserves and surplus.
   f) Bank inspectors check on the "end-use" of loans with "due attention to . . . economy and efficiency and without regard to political or other non-economic considerations."
   g) Debts must be repaid at the same gold value as they were borrowed.
   h) Currencies paid to the Bank in members' own currencies and loaned directly cannot be exchanged by the borrowers for other currencies without the permission of the supplying country in each case. With loans borrowed from private sources or guarantees, the currencies can be freely exchanged after the loan or guarantee has been approved by the governments concerned.

Structure

1. *Membership* — members of the IMF which accepted membership in the Bank before December 31, 1945, and other states admitted by Board of Governors by simple majority of total voting power. Fifty-four as of April 1953.
2. *Board of Governors* — central plenary body.

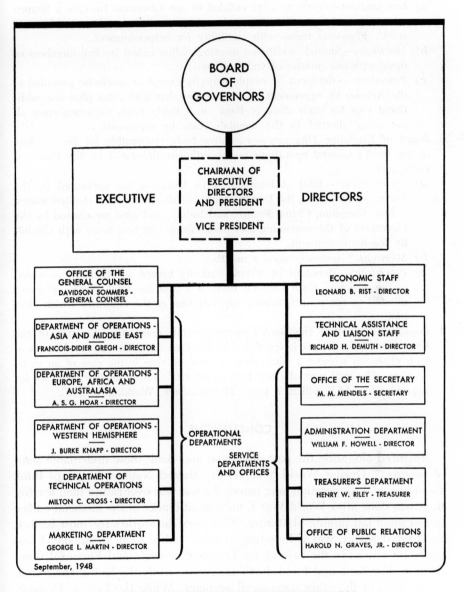

**STRUCTURE OF THE INTERNATIONAL BANK FOR
RECONSTRUCTION AND DEVELOPMENT**

a) *Composition* — each member entitled to one Governor (usually a finance minister) and one alternate, with voting power according to share of stock. Five-year terms with eligibility for reappointment.

b) *Meetings* — annual; additional meetings when called by five members or those with one-quarter of voting power.

c) *Procedure* — decisions by simple majority except as otherwise provided in the Articles of Agreement. Each member has 250 votes plus one additional vote for each share of Bank stock held. Each Governor casts all the votes allotted to the member state he represents.

3. *Board of Executive Directors* — executive body responsible for the conduct of the Bank's general operations under authority delegated by the Board of Governors.

a) *Composition* — total of fourteen. Five Directors are appointed by the five members having the largest number of shares of stock (United States, United Kingdom, China, France, and India), and nine are elected by the Governors of the remaining members. Terms are two years with eligibility for reappointment.

b) *Meetings* — normally once a month.

c) *Procedure* — decisions by simple majority except as otherwise provided in the Articles. Each Director casts as a unit the total number of votes allotted to the country which appoints him or the countries which elect him.

4. President — chief of the Bank's operating staff under the direction of the Executive Directors. He is appointed by the Executive Directors and serves as their chairman without a vote except a deciding vote in the case of an equal division. The staff normally numbers about 430. Administrative expenses are approximately $5.7 million a year. Headquarters: Washington, D.C.

CONCLUSIONS

Measured alongside the past, the Fund and Bank show undeniable signs of progress. During World War II, the United Nations began to think about financial cooperation long before the war was over rather than leaving it, as was done after World War I, until great cracks in the financial edifice forced some last minute plastering. Then, too, the world's foremost banker, the United States, was a founding member rather than an unofficial and uncertain ally as in the case of the League Economic and Financial Committees. The Bank and Fund, furthermore, are really the first of their kind, unlike most of the other specialized agencies. While the League Committees arranged a few loans and prodded national policy-makers, they never had funds of their own to lend nor as much authority, staff or administrative budget. Individual governments, it is true, had previously cooperated in lending and stabilizing operations but never through arrangements that were as permanent, integrated, authoritative or comprehensive in membership as these. Finally the Articles of Agreement reveal increased appreciation of the interaction between monetary and financial policy as well as the relation between these two areas and problems of trade, income and employment.

But these agencies are only a beginning and still very weak in the face of the tasks that confront them. The cavernous needs of nations could easily consume their resources. The major program of postwar financial assistance, the European Recovery Program, hurtled past on a separate track and quite overshadowed these two agencies. Largely because of the poverty of their bank balances, more than the inadequacy of their authority on paper, they have been relatively weak in influencing national policies. Finally, while their coordination with the UN has steadily improved, it could be tightened further.

International Trade Organization (ITO) and General Agreement on Tariffs and Trade (GATT)

What blood is to men, trade is to nations. It is scarcely surprising, therefore, that the busy planners of a better postwar world concerned themselves with machinery that would once more tackle the complex trade problems of tariffs, quotas and commodity agreements which had proved more than a match for the League. Two major schemes finally emerged. The first was the draft International Trade Organization (ITO) Charter, aimed at strengthening world trade by loosening its choking restrictions and controlling its palpitations of supply and demand in particular commodity markets. The second arrangement is called the General Agreement on Tariffs and Trade (GATT) which provided for a system of periodic conferences to engage in a vast swapping of trade concessions.

PATTERN OF INTERESTS

Of the many national interests that moulded these two plans, there can be no doubt that it was mainly the Americans who pushed them through, against some of the most tenacious and heated resistance of the whole postwar planning effort, especially on the part of the British. "Free trade" had long been a favorite battle cry of American liberals, some time after they had lost faith in domestic free trade, i.e., *laissez faire*.[17] It was also obvious to many Americans, as well as non-Americans, that, after World War II, the United States would be the only great power prosperous and efficient enough to be able to compete comfortably in a free world market. At the same time it was equally apparent that this wealthy giant was still clothed in a thick suit of tariff armor which it was unlikely to shed overnight.

During the ITO and GATT negotiations, the United States was joined in much of its free trade point of view by other nations that had traditionally depended on international trade and hoped to be able to do well in the future: Canada, Belgium, Holland and Scandinavia. The principal in-

[17] For comprehensive bibliography of private American plans see Clair Wilcox, *A Charter for World Trade* (New York: Macmillan, 1949), pp. 23–24.

gredients of the United States thesis were: (1) a desire to outlaw quantitative restrictions (chiefly import quotas) which the United States had rarely used, except in recent years, to bolster its sagging agricultural markets; (2) a willingness to engage in negotiations aimed at a cautious retreat from high tariffs; (3) insistence on special treatment for certain United States products, e.g., favoring American agricultural protectionism and discouraging foreign discrimination against United States movies; (4) a desire to muzzle cartels; (5) a preference for a code governing commodity agreements inspired by the International Wheat Agreement in opposition to the FAO-British buffer stock concept; [18] and (6) a plan to protect international investments from unreasonable expropriation and other misfortunes.

British and Other Views

When Britain had been the world's chief cornucopia of everything from nails to locomotives, she enshrined free trade as the eleventh commandment. But, as Britain looked ahead to the end of World War II, her fondness for free trade became somewhat diluted by her preoccupation with how to make ends meet. Imports had to be slashed and exports greatly boosted. During these negotiations, therefore, the British, usually supported by the French, promoted the following policies: (1) stretching the loopholes in the prohibition against quantitative restrictions (on the grounds of balance-of-payments difficulties and the maintenance of full employment); (2) whittling down the United States attack on cartels; and (3) support for the buffer stock principle of commodity control.

The middle and smaller powers stood, as usual, in the shadow of the mighty. Ever conscious of their inferior and vulnerable economic positions, they were understandably suspicious and resentful. While sharing much of this discontent, wealthy Canada had managed to carve out a special position for herself close to the two great powers. Australia and India tended to lead the "have-not" dissidents, including most of the Latin American and Asian countries. Their chief concern was defending their freedom to regulate trade as part of their effort to achieve the twin economic heavens of full employment and industrialization. The Australians had particularly fresh and bitter memories of the blow dealt their all-important wool business by the great depression which many of them considered the major United States' export during the thirties.

The argument in favor of protectionist restrictions to aid economic development was intertwined with an underlying antagonism between the small and large powers, the tension between colonial and anti-colonial states, and the popular view that the shortest road to economic development lay in the direction of forced large-scale industrialization. The interests of the Soviet Union were of relatively minor and indirect significance in these talks as compared with other UN preparatory negotiations. The Russians showed less interest in the possibility of gaining anything

[18] See pp. 232–233.

through ITO than any of the other economic specialized agencies and never attended any of the ITO or GATT meetings.

Battle of Trade Policies

The first official blow struck for freer postwar trade was the United States–inspired pledge inserted in the Atlantic Charter of August 1941 in which the United States and the United Kingdom, followed later by all the other United Nations, declared that they would

> endeavor, with due respect for their existing obligations [this qualifying phrase was added by Churchill to protect the Commonwealth preferential trade system], to further the enjoyment by all states, great or small, victor or vanquished, of access, on equal terms, to the trade and to the raw materials of the world which are needed for their economic prosperity.

Then, in February 1942, the Americans extracted, as a price of wartime aid, a British pledge, recorded in Article VII of the Anglo-American Mutual Aid Agreement, promising the "elimination of all forms of discriminatory treatment in international commerce, and . . . the reduction of tariffs and other trade barriers."

Not, however, until after the UN Charter had been drafted in the summer of 1945, did the United States and United Kingdom work out an agreement which resulted in a postwar loan of $3.75 billion to Britain at the same time that the British took the American oath of commercial liberalism, i.e., acceptance of the United States' *Proposals for the Expansion of World Trade and Employment,* published in December 1945. This cleared the way for a United States–sponsored resolution adopted by the UN Economic and Social Council at its first session in January 1946 instructing a Preparatory Committee of nineteen key countries to draft an international trade charter in preparation for an International Conference on Trade and Employment. This Committee met in London from October to November 1946 and in Geneva from May to August 1947.

At the same time, on United States initiative, the Committee agreed to sponsor tariff negotiations among its members during the Geneva session. While these negotiations took place under the umbrella of UN sponsorship, they remained legally outside the UN framework, primarily in order that the United States executive branch might adhere to the commitments as "executive agreements," rather than treaties, under the terms of the Reciprocal Trade Agreements Act of 1934.[19] The Final Act subscribed to by the governments participating in these negotiations, completed at Geneva in October 1947, was the General Agreement on Tariffs and Trade (GATT). This document incorporated certain mutual obligations aimed at reducing trade barriers, overlapping some of the provisions expected to be included in the ITO Charter, and established an administrative framework to facilitate periodic negotiations in the future.

[19] William Adams Brown, Jr., *The United States and the Restoration of World Trade* (Washington: Brookings Institution, 1950), p. 62.

The World Conference on Trade and Employment met at Havana, Cuba, from November 1947 to March 1948, one of the longest and most heated of all postwar planning conferences. This was the first trade meeting open to all nations (fifty-six attended), and the compromises tediously worked out among the elite, the nineteen members of the Preparatory Committee, now had to be defended against a chorus of complaints from the smaller and poorer nations. Approximately eight hundred amendments were proposed, two hundred of which would have knocked the props out from under the American plan. Still the most crucial and difficult crisis during the Conference was the Anglo-American conflict, chiefly over limiting import quotas. Finally an ITO Charter emerged, bloody but unbowed, and was signed by fifty-three countries on March 24, 1948. Ironically, however, the ITO has never come to life largely because of the protectionist opposition which has blocked ratification by the United States.[20] Consequently GATT has been reinforced to try to fill the vacuum.

OBLIGATIONS AND STRUCTURE

Although the ITO Charter now seems as dead as Adam Smith, it is interesting to see what that document anticipated, especially since most of its obligations have now been written into the GATT. According to the final version of the Charter, its signatories pledge to take action to:

1. achieve and maintain full and productive employment.
2. reconstruct and develop economic resources and increase productivity. Restrictions, prohibited by the ITO, may be applied, as means towards this objective, with the consent of ITO members.
3. reduce tariffs substantially on an unconditional most-favored-nation basis (i.e., make all concessions granted available to all ITO members). Should a tariff reduction result in an increase of imports so sharp as to threaten serious injury to domestic producers, a member may suspend the reduction. No new preferential arrangement may be created (aimed particularly at the sterling area) except, with ITO permission, to promote economic development or to form a customs union or free trade area.
4. relieve trade of hidden forms of protection (discriminatory internal taxes, provisions requiring a mixture of domestic with imported materials, restrictive customs procedures, etc.); afford free transit of goods moving through national territories; confine anti-dumping and retaliatory duties to cases of actual injury and limit them in amount; and publish fully and promptly all relevant trade regulations.
5. abandon, as a general principle, all quantitative restrictions on imports and exports (as the most rigid anti-competitive barrier). This rule is subject to several exceptions, including the following: (1) a member suffering serious balance of payments difficulties may use import quotas observing certain obligations, but must, in consultation with the ITO, relax them as the mem-

[20] See *Hearings Before the Committee on Foreign Affairs, House of Representatives, 81st Congress, 2nd Session on H. J. Res. 236, April and May, 1950*; also William Diebold, Jr., "The End of the ITO," *Essays in International Finance*, No. 16 (October 1952).

ber's monetary position improves and eliminate them entirely when the monetary difficulty disappears; (2) quotas on agricultural products may be used to supplement domestic production, marketing control, and surplus disposal programs if such quotas do not reduce the share of imports in the domestic market (insisted upon by United States agricultural interests); (3) discrimination in the application of quotas (aimed especially at the British) are allowed during the five-year transitional period provided for in the IMF Articles of Agreement but must be administered so as to maximize multilateral trade; after that period (ending February 28, 1952) discrimination is entirely subject to ITO or IMF control.

6. prevent exchange controls from being used to frustrate efforts of ITO; use such controls in cooperation with the IMF.

7. bring state trading monopolies into conformity with all of these objectives.

8. inform the ITO of subsidies; discuss their possible elimination; restrict export subsidies on primary commodities so as not to gain more than a fair share of world trade (subject to consultation with ITO members); and eliminate other export subsidies, with minor exceptions, after two years.

9. prevent private enterprises from fostering monopolistic control. Upon complaint, ITO may investigate and request action.

10. in general, limit intergovernmental commodity agreements to primary commodities, open to equal participation by all ITO members, subject to full publicity and regulation of production and distribution (including prices), limited in duration to periods of burdensome distress, and subject to periodic review and national action to correct conditions requiring such agreements.

11. settle all disputes under the ITO Charter by peaceful means either within or outside the ITO.

The structure of the ITO was to consist of a plenary Conference, which would make its substantive decisions by simple majority except for a two-thirds vote on waiving ITO Charter obligations and recommending draft agreements; an Executive Board of eighteen member states (eight of "chief economic importance" to be determined by a two-thirds vote of the Conference every three years and ten others to be elected by a two-thirds majority of the Conference) which would also make its decisions by simple majority; and a staff headed by a Director General nominated by the Executive Board and appointed by the Conference. Pending ratification of the ITO Charter, the signatories formed an Interim Commission for the ITO (ICITO) to prepare for the first ITO session and help administer the GATT. The organizational pattern of the ICITO followed that of the ITO with a Conference (composed of the fifty-two states that had signed the Charter), an Executive Committee (eighteen members including the major trading nations), and an Executive Secretary.

CONCLUSIONS

While the main edifice remains a dream, some of the scaffolding erected to facilitate the whole project — the GATT — still stands and is more important than ever. Although this is only a makeshift arrangement and neither as comprehensive nor as authoritative as the ITO would be, it is a very useful stopgap and is being used to accomplish much of what the ITO was intended to do.

Moreover, this whole effort, in spite of the abortive experience thus far with the ITO, indicates progress beyond what the League was able to accomplish. General recognition of the relation of trade policy to monetary and other economic considerations seems greater than under the League. The major trading power, the United States, is up to its neck in international negotiations in this field in a way that it never was during the inter-war period. And these negotiations have been more ambitious, more comprehensive in the countries involved, more truly multilateral, more frequent, and more productive, especially in tariff concessions, than before. On the other hand, the basic problems are greater because the destruction and dislocation have been greater than after World War I.

International Civil Aviation Organization (ICAO)

It was only a short while ago, in 1910, after some German balloonists plumped down unannounced on French soil, that the French government hastily called the first international civil aviation conference. But nations relinquished precious few concessions to foreign airlines during the pre-World War II period, recognized no general right of free passage over each other's territories, and demanded high prices for the few concessions they were willing to grant.[21]

Active international planning for the post-World War II period did not begin as early in this as in certain other fields but quickly came to a boil during 1944. When the International Civil Aviation Conference met at Chicago from November to December 1944, there was such a bitter row between the United States and United Kingdom factions that only part of the Conference's business was successfully completed. While the Conference was the most representative UN economic and social meeting held up to that time, with fifty-four countries represented, it was also the first UN technical meeting which the Soviet Union refused to attend, allegedly because the wartime neutrals had been invited.

The United States led a small group of nations, including the Netherlands and Sweden, which felt themselves strong enough to hold their own or better in a freely competitive development of international air transport and emphasized the economic benefits of such an approach for all countries whether they developed their own aviation systems or used those of other countries. This faction wanted an organization which would review performance, recommend standardized technical procedures and equipment, and arbitrate disputes but would not have any comprehensive binding regulatory authority. This philosophy was also supported by a group of "consuming" nations which had long been associated with United States

[21] See Chap. 17.

aviation interests, chiefly the Latin American states and China, and expressed a primary interest in the world commerce which air transport brought them.

British Commonwealth nations, led by the United Kingdom, represented the chief opposition. They argued that certain countries, especially the United States, which had continued to produce transport planes during the war while the British built fighters, had an undue competitive advantage and that the "free-for-all" approach would not necessarily result in the most desirable or efficient development of international air services. Australia and New Zealand, led by labor governments, took the most revolutionary position by advocating outright international ownership and operation of air transport services on designated trunk routes. Mr. Adolf A. Berle, Jr., then Assistant Secretary of State and head of the United States delegation, wrote a few months later,

> [the plan] was proposed by one of the greatest moral characters the present World War has produced, Peter Fraser, Prime Minister of New Zealand.... This was and is a noble conception, and one to which the world will increasingly turn as the years roll by. But it cannot be expected to become a reality until all nations are prepared to pool their interests; unhappily perhaps for all of us, this has not yet occurred.[22]

EFFORTS TO COMPROMISE DIFFERENCES

The United Kingdom, Canada and India, joined subsequently by New Zealand and Australia as well as certain European countries, wanted a strong regulatory agency, allegedly modeled after the United States Civil Aeronautics Board (CAB), with authority to allocate routes, regulate frequency of service and fix rates without going so far as to assume ownership and management. The Canadians assumed the role of the honest broker, as in several other UN planning conferences, to mediate primarily between the Americans and British, and, in this effort, developed the concepts of the five air "freedoms" around which the conference tended to revolve:

1. Flight over another country without stopping (comparable to "freedom of transit" and "innocent passage" on the earth's surface).
2. "Non-traffic landings," i.e., for refueling and overhaul without discharging or picking up passengers.
3. Carrying traffic from a plane's homeland to another country.
4. Picking up in another country traffic destined for a plane's homeland.
5. Carrying traffic between two or more countries other than a plane's homeland.

[22] "Freedoms of the Air," *Harper's Magazine*, Vol. 190, No. 1138 (March 1945), p. 331.

Finally, two optional draft agreements were formulated and opened for signature: (1) an International Air Services Transit Agreement (called the "Two Freedoms" or "Transit" Agreement) which guaranteed the first two minimal freedoms listed above which were thought to be generally acceptable; and (2) an International Air Transport Agreement (the "Five Freedoms" or "Transport" Agreement) which guaranteed all the freedoms listed above and was opposed by the Commonwealth nations. Disputes under either agreement were to be submitted to the ICAO Council, and a country failing to take suitable corrective action recommended by the Council could be suspended by a two-thirds vote of the ICAO Assembly.

The Conference also adopted a Convention on International Civil Aviation which is the constitution of ICAO. The first section sets forth certain general principles governing the nationality of aircraft, the sovereignty of each member over its air space, conditions governing flight over another nation's territory, measures to facilitate air transport, and twelve technical annexes (Appendix V of the Conference's Final Act) which could be revised by two-thirds vote of the Council, such decisions to be binding on all members unless rejected during a certain period by a majority of the members. The second part deals with the structure and authority of ICAO, described below.

The third part of the Convention deals with developing and regulating international air transport (the "five freedoms") and could do little more than refer to the two optional agreements. The fourth part includes provisions for registering all aeronautical agreements (abandoning the traditional secrecy in this area), outlawing discriminatory concessions which had long been prevalent, recognizing the Council as an arbitral body on disputes, and amending the annexes (by two-thirds vote of the Council) and the Convention itself (by two-thirds vote of the Assembly).

The Conference also adopted an Interim Agreement setting up a Provisional ICAO (PICAO), which came into being in June 1945, to operate until the Convention should be ratified by the requisite twenty-six states (which did not happen until April 1947). During 1947, ICAO also absorbed its predecessor organizations: the Comité-International Technique d'Experts Juridiques Aériens (CITEJA), as of May, and the International Commission for Air Navigation (ICAN), as of December.

PROCESS AND STRUCTURE

The basic functions of ICAO are to:

1. serve as an information clearing house. The Council is granted specific authority to request, collect, examine, and publish relevant material including costs and public subsidies, hitherto normally kept secret.

2. make recommendations on policy questions. The Assembly's role in this field is somewhat restricted by the fact that it is prohibited from dealing with any issue in a field assigned to the Council which the Council does not refer to it. The Council is granted specific and direct authority to study

"all aspects of air transport and air navigation which are of international importance . . . including the international ownership and operation of international air services . . . [and] any situation which may appear to present avoidable obstacles to the development of international air navigation. . . ."

3. exert influence to encourage compliance with ICAO policies. The Council is authorized to report directly to the contracting states, without prior reference to the Assembly, any infraction of the Convention, as well as any failure to carry out recommendations or determinations of the Council, and report to the Assembly any infraction where a contracting State has failed to take appropriate action within a reasonable time after notice of the infraction. The Assembly may authorize ICAO to enter into appropriate arrangements with any general organization set up by the nations of the world to preserve peace (reference to possible international air force).

4. amend Annexes or adopt new ones by two-thirds vote of the Council. Such decisions become effective within three months (or longer period prescribed by Council) unless in the meantime a majority of contracting states register disapproval.

5. amend the Convention by two-thirds vote of the Assembly. Such amendments become effective for those ratifying after ratification by at least two-thirds of contracting states as specified by the Assembly. The Assembly may decide that a member which does not ratify a particular amendment within a particular period shall cease to be a member of ICAO.

Membership in ICAO is open to signatory states that ratified the Convention and other states admitted by four-fifths votes of the Assembly. A plenary Assembly meets once a year and makes its decisions by simple majority with certain exceptions such as admission of new members and amendments to the Convention (two-thirds). The executive Council is composed of twenty-one states elected by the Assembly for three-year terms. The Assembly is instructed to

give adequate representation to (1) the states of chief importance in air transport; (2) the states not otherwise included which make the largest contribution to the provision of facilities for international civil air navigation; and (3) the states not otherwise included whose designation will insure that all the major geographic areas of the world are represented.

The Council is in virtually continuous session and makes its decisions by simple majority except for two-thirds when voting on Annexes.

There are also two important sub-bodies. One is the Air Transport Committee appointed by the Council from among the latter's members to study the air freedoms, international ownership, taxation, and other broad policy problems and report to the Council. The other is the Air Navigation Commission of twelve experts appointed by the Council from persons nominated by the member states to study and make recommendations to the Council regarding technical navigational problems, including revision of the Annexes. The Secretary-General, who is appointed by the Council rather than the Assembly, administers a staff which numbers about 425.

STRUCTURE OF THE INTERNATIONAL CIVIL AVIATION ORGANIZATION

ASSEMBLY

COUNCIL

FINANCE COMMITTEE

LEGAL COMMITTEE

AIR NAVIGATION COMMISSION

COMMITTEE ON JOINT SUPPORT OF AIR NAVIGATION SERVICES

AIR TRANSPORT COMMITTEE

DIVISIONS

Aerodromes, Air Routes and Ground Aids
Accident Investigation
Airworthiness
Communications
Special Radio Technical
Aeronautical Maps and Charts

Meteorological
Operations Practices
Personnel Licensing
Rules of Air and Air Traffic Control
Search and Rescue

DIVISIONS

Facilitation
Statistics

SECRETARIAT

ICAO COUNCIL

SECRETARY GENERAL

AIR NAVIGATION BUREAU
AIR TRANSPORT BUREAU
LEGAL BUREAU
ADMINISTRATION AND SERVICES BUREAU
TECHNICAL ASSISTANCE

September 1948

UN Presentation 947.10

The annual administrative budget is approximately $2.8 million. The headquarters are in Montreal, Canada.

CONCLUSIONS

The over-all impression one has of ICAO is that it is a highly centralized, efficient and active organization well suited to the limited tasks of developing and standardizing technical procedures but not equipped to deal effectively with some of the larger and more fundamental issues such as the so-called "five freedoms." Compared with the League-era organizations, chiefly ICAN and CITEJA, ICAO represents progress. It is broader in membership; more far-reaching in the range of its activities; more practical and less legalistic in its approach; equipped with stronger authority; better coordinated; directed by firmer leadership through the powerful and permanent Council, its President and Secretary-General; and served by a larger staff with funds. ICAO's Council has approximately the same authoritative position as the executive councils of the IBRD, IMF, ILO and WHO and is considerably stronger than those of FAO and UNESCO. The dangerous aspect of this organizational pattern is that the Council, which naturally tends to be dominated by the major air powers, finds it all too easy to slight the interests of the "consumer" nations. Moreover, ICAO still has no binding authority, as do many national air agencies such as the United States Civil Aeronautics Board, to control the development of air services through allocating routes and fixing rates. These matters are still left primarily to bilateral negotiations, although the ICAO headquarters are a principal center for such discussions.

Inter-Governmental Maritime Consultative Organization (IMCO)

During World War II, a United Maritime Authority controlled 90 per cent of the world's non-Axis shipping. When the fighting ceased, the immediate reaction of most shipping interests was to scrap controls and regain freedom. Nevertheless it seemed necessary to retain some minimal machinery, the United Maritime Consultative Council (UMCC), for at least a brief period, March to October 1946, chiefly to help channel relief supplies in cooperation with UNRRA. At the end of this period, under pressure from the UN ECOSOC, the UMCC prepared and adopted a draft convention which shied away from any binding controls such as those that had been endured under the stress of war but placed major emphasis upon the Adam Smithian goals of removing national restrictions to shipping and serving as an informational clearing house. Then ECOSOC convoked a special maritime conference which met during February and March 1948 and produced the present IMCO constitution. This document cannot come into effect, however, until it has been ratified by twenty-one states of which seven must each have a total tonnage of at least one million gross tons of shipping.

The anticipated functions of IMCO are aimed at improving maritime operations, including the formulation of safety regulations and removal of discriminatory and restrictive barriers. An Assembly is to meet every two years and make its decisions by simple majority, with a few exceptions such as amending the constitution by two-thirds. The Council is to be composed of the representatives of sixteen states (eight primarily concerned with furnishing shipping services and eight primarily concerned with consuming them).

World Meteorological Organization (WMO)

The weather, being immune to national frontier regulations, was an early promoter of international collaboration through the International Meteorological Organization established in 1878. Then, in 1939, the directors of the various meteorological services which were members of the IMO decided to transform the organization into an intergovernmental body in order to strengthen the position of their services with their respective governments as well as other international organizations. The convention of the new WMO was formulated and adopted by the twelfth IMO Conference of Directors in Washington, D.C., September to October 1947. The Convention came into effect in March 1950.

The general purpose of the WMO is to improve the standards and facilities of national meteorological services. Membership is open to UN Members and their territories as well as other states and territories admitted by two-thirds of the WMO members. There were seventy-nine members as of April 1953. A World Meteorological Congress meets every four years and makes its substantive decisions by two-thirds majority. An Executive Committee is composed of the presidents of regional meteorological associations, established by the Congress, and an equal number of directors of individual meteorological services elected by the Congress. This Committee meets annually and also decides policy questions by two-thirds majority. The Secretary-General is appointed by the Congress and has an annual administrative budget of approximately $190,000. The headquarters are in Lausanne, Switzerland.

Universal Postal Union (UPU)

The most widely accepted international organization is still the UPU for the simple reason that the benefits of cooperating with it are deemed by virtually all countries to far outweigh the slight sacrifices of national independence involved. While the objectives, functions and organization of the UPU have remained much the same since 1875,[23] the quickening pace

[23] See p. 41.

and volume of international postal traffic have required some reorganization, chiefly by means of the revised UPU Convention adopted by the twelfth Postal Congress in Paris, July 1947, which came into force in July 1948. The principal effect of the reorganization was to provide firmer and more continuous leadership through the new Executive and Liaison Committee.

The main functions of the UPU are to act as a research and informational center, serve as a clearing house to settle intergovernmental postal accounts, render opinions on disputes, and recommend amendments to the main Convention and the seven accessory agreements. Since accession to the main Convention is obligatory for all members, a member must either accept amendments to the Convention or resign from the UPU. Ratification of the accessory agreements, covering special services, and amendments thereto, are optional. Any state may be admitted to membership by an absolute two-thirds majority. Ninety-three states and dependent territories had joined as of April 1953.

The plenary assembly is the Universal Postal Congress which meets every five years and makes its decisions by simple majority except for important changes in the main Convention which requires two-thirds votes. The Executive and Liaison Committee is composed of representatives of nineteen member states elected on a geographic basis by each Congress to serve between Congresses. The staff Director is appointed by the Executive and Liaison Committee upon recommendation by the Swiss Supervisory Authority. The staff (called Bureau) has been placed, for reasons of administrative efficiency, under the supervision of the Swiss Postal Administration, and the employees have normally been Swiss nationals. The staff now numbers about twenty-six permanent personnel, with an annual administrative budget of $390,000. Headquarters are in Berne, Switzerland.

International Telecommunication Union (ITU)

The ITU is another veteran international organization, similar to the UPU, highly specialized in its interests and activities, and possessed of a large and comprehensive membership. Like the UPU, the ITU's basic convention was also thoroughly revised in 1947 in order to enable it to deal more effectively with the increasingly complex problems of its field. The major aims of this reorganization were to promote more continuous and intensive consideration of telecommunication problems; more effective coordination of ITU activities, chiefly through the new Administrative Council; and a stronger secretariat, apart from the Swiss Confederation.

The principal functions of the ITU are to:

1. advise allocation of the radio frequency spectrum and registration of radio frequency assignments in order to avoid harmful interference between radio stations of different countries;

2. foster collaboration with a view to the establishment of rates at levels as low as possible consistent with an efficient service and taking into account

the necessity for maintaining independent financial administration of telecommunication on a sound basis;

3. promote the adoption of measures for insuring safety of life through the cooperation of telecommunication service;

4. undertake studies, formulate recommendations, and collect and publish information on telecommunication matters for the benefit of all members and associate members.

Any state may be admitted to membership by two-thirds of the ITU members. Ninety-two states and territories had joined as of April 1953. The central plenary body is the Plenipotentiary Conference which meets every five years and reaches decisions by simple majority except for the approval of new members by two-thirds vote. There are also two specialized plenary forums: an Administrative Telegraph and Telephone Conference and an Administrative Radio Conference which meet concurrently with the Plenipotentiary Conference to deal with problems in their respective fields. The central executive body is the Administrative Council which is composed of representatives of eighteen states elected on a geographic basis by the Plenipotentiary Conference for five-year terms with eligibility for reëlection. The Council meets annually.

Among the major sub-bodies there is an International Frequency Registration Board composed of persons chosen by eleven member states, elected on a regional basis by the Administrative Radio Conference, to serve not as governmental representatives but as "custodians of an international public trust." Their functions are to advise on the most efficient allocation of radio channels and to register such assignments. There are also three other main technical advisory bodies: the Telegraph, Telephone, and Radio Consultative Committees composed of national telecommunications administrations and recognized private operating agencies which express a desire to have their experts participate. The Secretary-General is appointed by the Administrative Council and supervises a staff of about 168 with an annual administrative budget of approximately $1.3 million. The headquarters are in Geneva, Switzerland.

International Labor Organization (ILO)

As early as November 6, 1941, President Franklin Roosevelt said:

> The ILO has been tried and tested. . . . We are already engaged in surveying the immediate postwar requirements. . . . We are planning not to provide temporary remedies . . . [but] permanent cures — to help establish a sounder life . . . the ILO with its representation of labor and management, its technical knowledge and experience, will be an invaluable instrument for peace. Your organization will have an essential part to play in building up a stable international system of social justice for all peoples everywhere.[24]

[24] "Address of the President . . . ," *Department of State Bulletin*, Vol. 5, No. 124 (November 8, 1941), pp. 357–360.

These friendly words underlined the fact that the ILO was generally regarded by those who had been acquainted with the Geneva scene as the star performer of the League team and a model for future economic and social agencies. The 1939 Bruce Report was one of many public and private studies that reflected this point of view.[25] It is not surprising, therefore, that the ILO was the only League organization to pass through the war ordeal virtually unscathed except for certain minor constitutional tinkering. Consequently, the rest of this section will not repeat what has already been described in Chapter 7 but will concentrate on the reappraisal and adjustment process in which the ILO was engaged from approximately 1944 to 1946.

The exceptionally benign American attitude towards the ILO is explained not only by the general climate of opinion mentioned above but also by certain factors of special interest to the United States. The ILO was the only League organization which the United States government had officially joined. Organized American labor (primarily the AFL) had from the days of Samuel Gompers been friendly towards the ILO. "New Deal" Secretary of Labor Frances Perkins had been a strong supporter of the Organization, and an American, John G. Winant, wartime ambassador to Britain, was the ILO Director-General from 1938 to 1941 during the Montreal exile.

Britain's equally warm regard for the Organization was based on an even more intimate association with it. British labor had been the most influential force in creating the ILO in 1919; it was also particularly outspoken during World War II in urging the continuation of the Organization. The Soviet Union had, on the other hand, long and openly opposed the ILO as a carrier of the capitalist virus endangering the welfare of the world's proletariat. The Russians criticized particularly the alleged underrepresentation of labor in the ILO, the connection with the discredited League, and the admission to the ILO of certain anti-Russian governments such as Finland, Rumania and Hungary. In spite of constant ILO pleas for Russian participation during the post-World War II period, the Soviet Union made no effort to cooperate until 1953 and then only under conditions which the ILO found impossible to accept. Instead the Russians preferred to champion the Communist-dominated World Federation of Trade Unions (WFTU).

The European countries, many of which tended to follow the lead of France, thought of the ILO during the 1944–46 period primarily in terms of its usefulness with respect to their immediate concern, economic and social reconstruction. The Latin Americans, who had been some of the ILO's best customers during the war, played a vociferous role but were torn between the leftists led by Mexico's Vicente Lombardo Toledano and the rightists led by Argentina. Asian labor was still weak and largely preoccupied with the war and the liquidation of colonialism. Finally the ILO Office (the secretariat), as well as its supporters in various nations, had a

25 For discussion of Bruce Report see pp. 165–166.

strong interest in preserving and reinforcing the ILO and saw to it that that point of view was ably propounded at various UN economic and social conferences.

CONSTITUTIONAL ADJUSTMENT

The reappraisal process began officially with United States–United Kingdom agreement in the autumn of 1943 that the ILO should hold its first regular conference since 1938 during the spring of 1944. It was at Temple University, Philadelphia, that the delegates from forty-one countries met during April and May 1944. This was a dramatic gathering as many veterans in the ranks of labor, management and government were drawn together once again, after having suffered all kinds of tragedies, as the war continued to rage in many of their homelands. Although the ILO Office and some delegations had prepared suggestions for various constitutional changes, most governments, taking their cue from the British, argued that there had been too little advance consultation, that it was too early, and that the attitude of the Soviet Union was too crucial to justify any fundamental alterations at that time.

Nevertheless, the Conference adopted a ringing "Declaration of Philadelphia" which expanded the statement of objectives formulated in 1919. (An American employer representative, speaking before the ILO a few years later, confused this statement with his own country's Declaration of Independence!) The Declaration singled out for special attention the goals of expanded social security, full employment, freer migration, minimum wages and a guaranteed right of collective bargaining. At the same time that the Conference indicated its willingness to cooperate with whatever general international organization should later be established and its desire to have the Governing Body give further consideration to the proposals for constitutional reform, it also protested its determination to maintain the traditional tripartite (labor, management, government) representational system and the ILO's autonomy.[26]

The next regular ILO Conference (27th) was held at Paris, during October and November 1945, and adopted three constitutional amendments providing: (1) that any UN Member could join the ILO merely by accepting the obligations of membership; (2) that, rather than continuing its constitutional dependence on the League for its financial resources, it might make its own arrangements pending a possible subsequent agreement with the UN; and (3) that the constitution could be amended by a decision of the Conference ratified or accepted by two-thirds (rather than three-quarters) of the members, including five of the eight states of chief industrial importance (rather than all members of the League Council).

The 29th ILO Conference at Montreal, during the fall of 1946, adopted

---

[26] For accounts of this Conference, see Carol Riegelman, "Labor's Bridgehead: the ILO," *Political Science Quarterly,* Vol. 60, No. 2 (June 1945), pp. 205–221; "What is the ILO?" *Fortune,* Vol. 30, No. 3 (September 1944), pp. 160–164.

GENERAL CONFERENCE

INTERNATIONAL LABOUR OFFICE (Secretariat)

GOVERNING BODY

COMMITTEES
Finance
Staff Questions
Allocations
Employment
Standing Orders
Application of Conventions and Recommendations
On Industrial Committees
Manpower for Europe
Manpower for Asia

PERMANENT COMMITTEES
Joint Maritime Commission
Agricultural
Migration

ADVISORY COMMITTEES
On Salaried Employees and Professional Workers
Co-operation
On Juvenile Work

CORRESPONDENCE COMMITTEES
On Accident Prevention
On Industrial Hygiene
On Women's Work
On Recreation

Committee on Social Policy in Non-Metropolitan Territories
International Development Works Committee
Committee of Statistical Experts
Committee of Social Security Experts
Committee on Indigenous Labour
Sub-Committee on Automatic Coupling of Railway Vehicles

INDUSTRIAL COMMITTEES
Coal Mines
Inland Transport
Iron and Steel
Metal Trades
Textiles
Building, Civil Engineering and Public Works
Petroleum
Chemicals

JOINT COMMISSIONS WITH OTHER INTERNATIONAL ORGANIZATIONS
Industrial Hygiene
Provision for Medical Care and Health Services

[September, 1948]

other amendments which had the following effects: (1) to facilitate co-operation between the ILO and the UN; (2) to clarify and give greater recognition to the Governing Body as the executive committee of the ILO; (3) to encourage wider ratification, better implementation and improved reporting on the application of ILO conventions; (4) to require reporting on the policy of governments with respect to recommendations and unratified conventions; (5) to clarify national obligations with respect to recommendations; (6) to clarify the obligations of federal states with respect to conventions and recommendations; (7) to improve the application of conventions in nonmetropolitan territories; and (8) to empower the Governing Body to recommend to the Conference measures to secure compliance with the terms of ratified conventions.

CONCLUSIONS

Among the new adolescent specialized agencies, the ILO is a venerable sage. In this and other respects, it is unique. It is, as we have seen, the only League agency which survived the ordeal by fire practically unsinged. It is the only such agency which officiated at its own revival and vigorously promoted its own interests at the San Francisco and other UN planning conferences. Its prewar organizational experience was as important an influence as any in guiding the pattern of the new family of specialized agencies. And it began its postwar career with greater initial prestige than any other similar agency.

At the same time, the ILO itself changed character a bit during the 1944–46 adjustment period. It expanded its objectives in the direction of a more developed concept of social security and economic planning. It strengthened its leadership by reinforcing the role of the Governing Body. It adopted amendments aimed at encouraging a greater degree of governmental compliance with ILO decisions. But, with all of this restless ferment, it did not alter its fundamental organization and process.

World Health Organization (WHO)

Dr. C.-E. A. Winslow, Professor Emeritus of Yale University and sage adviser to both the League and UN health bodies, has said:

> There is no area of human activity in which it is so easy to obtain international cooperation as in the war against disease. The necessity for global organization is here most obvious since the germs of plague and yellow fever . . . ask for no passports. Furthermore, the formation of a common front in this case calls for only minor sacrifices of the attributes of sovereignty and relatively slight interference with the vested interests of individuals.[27]

[27] "The World Health Organization — Its Program and Accomplishments," *International Conciliation*, No. 439 (March 1948), p. 116.

Consequently the post-World War II planners never asked "whether" but only "how" a health agency would be organized. Within the United States there was much private support for a body that would be stronger and better integrated than the League agencies. In the United States government there was some planning as early as 1942 and 1943 within the Department of State and the Public Health Service, headed by Dr. Thomas Parran, which was beginning to steer in the direction of a unified organization (combining the League units with the Paris International Office of Public Health), universal in membership, to go beyond informational work to more operational and quasi-legislative activities.

After the United States had conducted informal talks with medical authorities in certain other countries, Brazil initiated the San Francisco Conference decision, in June 1945, to mention health specifically in appropriate sections of the UN Charter. Brazil and China also got the Conference to adopt a resolution calling for a special conference to plan a new health organization. Consequently the UN Economic and Social Council, at its first meeting early in 1946, appointed a Technical Preparatory Committee, composed of health experts from sixteen leading countries, to pave the way for such a conference. Of four draft constitutions submitted to that Committee, it was the United States version, formulated under the direction of Dr. Parran, that was chosen as the basis for discussion.

The plans formulated by this group were then considered by the International Health Conference which met in New York from June to July 1946. In addition to fifty-one UN Members, sixteen non-members were invited as well as the Allied Control Authorities for Germany, Japan and Korea. This was also one of the few postwar technical conferences attended by the Soviet Union and the Byelorussian and the Ukrainian Republics. The delegations of thirty-one of the fifty-one UN states were headed by ministers of health or chiefs of national health services or their deputies. The president of the Conference was Dr. Parran.

NEW HEALTH GOALS

While the debates were relatively harmonious, compared with some previous technical conferences (Parran referred to the delegates as a "happily married family" that "did not make news"), there were enough squabbles to indicate that the field of international health was not entirely free of controversy. Some of these differences arose in connection with the formulation of the new organization's objectives which, as finally drafted, are far bolder than those of the League Health Organization. Health was no longer to be defined as merely the absence of illness but as "a state of complete physical, mental, and social well-being," the enjoyment of which is "one of the fundamental rights of every human being without distinction of race, religion, political belief, economic or social condition." WHO's overriding objective was to be the attainment "by all peoples of the highest possible level of health."

The functions by which WHO was to pursue these objectives were to be equally ambitious. The Conference finally decided not only to continue the prewar activities but to put greater emphasis on operational work (directly engaging in research, furnishing technical assistance to national governments, etc.); expand greatly the range of interests (including modern concepts of total environmental hygiene, mental health, the improvement of teaching and training, and "administrative and social techniques affecting public health . . . including hospital services and social security"); grant the WHO the authority to recommend, by a two-thirds majority, draft conventions (which countries were to adopt or reject, giving the WHO their reasons, within eighteen months); and adopt, by simple majority, technical regulations (which are binding on all member states except those which specifically reject them within a stated period).

The procedure on conventions is very similar to that of the ILO. The provision on regulations is an even more significant innovation inspired most directly by the views of the United States delegation who had taken a hint from a suggestion made, interestingly enough, in the Senate Foreign Relations Committee that some way be found to permit the speedy application of new scientific techniques "without requiring that Committee to consider highly specialized technical matters" in the form of separate treaties.[28] Precedents cited were the procedure used to modify the International Sanitary Convention for Aerial Navigation of 1933 and comparable provisions in the Chicago Convention on International Civil Aviation. The Soviet Union and Belgium were strongly opposed to both of these quasi-legislative powers until a compromise was worked out whereby all important decisions, including the recommendation of conventions, would require two-thirds majorities.

ORGANIZATIONAL PROBLEMS

The structure of the new organization was strongly influenced by that of the League Health Organization. The WHO Assembly is reminiscent of the General Advisory Council of the Paris Office of Public Health. The Executive Board replaces the League Standing Health Committee. And the Secretariat performs the functions of the Health Section of the Geneva Secretariat.

A particularly sharp dispute flared up over the effort to merge the Pan American Sanitary Bureau (PASB) with the WHO as part of the general effort to create a more integrated international health system. The extreme centralist bloc was headed by the Soviet Union supported, in softer tones, by the United Kingdom, China and Norway. The Latin Americans, who had long received substantial subsidies from the United States via the

---

[28] *Report of the United States Delegation on the International Health Conference*, Department of State Publication 2703, Conference Series 91 (Washington: Government Printing Office, 1946), p. 17.

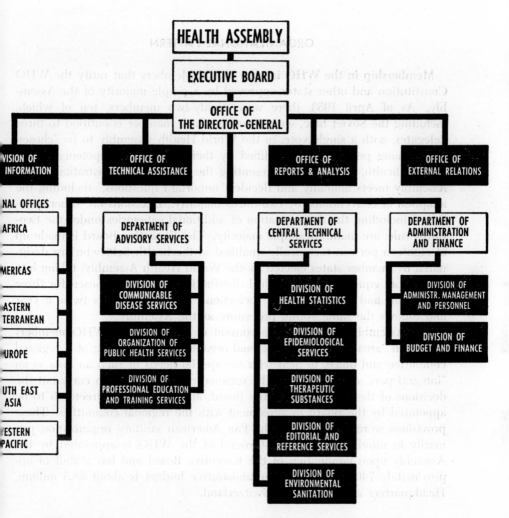

HEALTH ASSEMBLY

EXECUTIVE BOARD

OFFICE OF THE DIRECTOR-GENERAL

DIVISION OF INFORMATION

OFFICE OF TECHNICAL ASSISTANCE

OFFICE OF REPORTS & ANALYSIS

OFFICE OF EXTERNAL RELATIONS

REGIONAL OFFICES

AFRICA

AMERICAS

EASTERN MEDITERRANEAN

EUROPE

SOUTH EAST ASIA

WESTERN PACIFIC

DEPARTMENT OF ADVISORY SERVICES

DIVISION OF COMMUNICABLE DISEASE SERVICES

DIVISION OF ORGANIZATION OF PUBLIC HEALTH SERVICES

DIVISION OF PROFESSIONAL EDUCATION AND TRAINING SERVICES

DEPARTMENT OF CENTRAL TECHNICAL SERVICES

DIVISION OF HEALTH STATISTICS

DIVISION OF EPIDEMIOLOGICAL SERVICES

DIVISION OF THERAPEUTIC SUBSTANCES

DIVISION OF EDITORIAL AND REFERENCE SERVICES

DIVISION OF ENVIRONMENTAL SANITATION

DEPARTMENT OF ADMINISTRATION AND FINANCE

DIVISION OF ADMINISTR. MANAGEMENT AND PERSONNEL

DIVISION OF BUDGET AND FINANCE

ORGANIZATIONAL STRUCTURE OF THE WORLD HEALTH ORGANIZATION

PASB, favored independence. Dr. Parran finally drafted a compromise which led to the magic formula: the PASB "shall in due course be integrated with" the WHO, "to be effected as soon as possible."

In addition to the Constitution, the Conference adopted a Final Act, a Protocol providing for the absorption of the Paris Office (effected in October 1947), and an Arrangement for the immediate establishment of an Interim Commission of eighteen persons, designated by that number of states, to operate until the Constitution could be ratified by a sufficient number of countries to bring it into force. In December 1946 and January 1947 the Interim Commission assumed various UNRRA health functions. WHO itself officially came into being on September 1, 1948.

ORGANIZATIONAL PATTERN

Membership in the WHO is open to UN Members that ratify the WHO Constitution and other states approved by a simple majority of the Assembly. As of April 1953, there were eighty-two members, ten of which, including the Soviet bloc, were inactive. Each member is entitled to three delegates, with a single vote, in the World Health Assembly to be "chosen from among persons most qualified by their technical competence in the field of health, preferably representing the national administration." The Assembly meets annually and decides "important questions," including the adoption of conventions, by two-thirds majority. Decisions on "other questions," including the determination of additional categories under the two-thirds rule, are made by simple majority. The Executive Board is made up of eighteen persons technically qualified in the health field who are designated by member states elected by the World Health Assembly, taking into account an equitable geographical distribution. They are chosen for three year terms and are eligible for reelection. The Board meets twice a year and follows the same voting procedure as the Assembly.

The Assembly may, with the consent of a majority of WHO members within an "area," establish a regional organization, consisting of a regional committee and office, to deal with the special needs of such an area as an "integral part" of the WHO. The regional office is bound to carry out the decisions of the Assembly and the Board, and its regional director is to be appointed by the Board in agreement with the regional committee. These provisions were drafted with the Pan American sanitary organization primarily in mind. The Director-General of the WHO is appointed by the Assembly upon nomination of the Executive Board and has a staff of approximately 740. The annual administrative budget is about $8.5 million. Headquarters are in Geneva, Switzerland.

CONCLUSIONS

The WHO provides some of the clearest evidence of organizational progress beyond the pre-World War II era. The WHO is more integrated than the loose alliance of health agencies under the League. Its objectives are bolder and more positive. Its functions are more extensive and directly operational. Its authority to promote compliance with technical regulations and draft conventions is stronger. And its membership is more comprehensive and influential, especially with the United States pulling its full weight. But the WHO is still far from a full-blown international public health service. Its budget is woefully small, approximately $8.5 million as compared with $285 million for the U.S. Public Health Service in 1952. It has no authority to bind any state against its will, and its work can be no more effective than the individual national health ministries through which it must operate.

The major administrative headache is trying to fit everyone's pet projects into the framework of a very cramped budget. The Executive Board, with its various national as well as personal differences, is far from a unified "cabinet" as it deals with its budget. The Director-General, who must provide much of the leadership, is a "prime minister" without constituency, party or majority. Regional decentralization has further complicated the process, and the Assembly, in which the smaller nations have the most votes, often throws a monkey wrench into the Board's and Director's plans. Hence, the consideration of plans to convoke the Assembly every other year rather than annually, and the increasing emphasis on longer-range planning. Furthermore, there is often friction among the several agencies in the health field, although coordination through the TAB, strengthened in 1952, has improved considerably. Finally, it would help if the Soviet Union and its cohorts would stop shooting peas through the window and join the party.[29]

International Refugee Organization (IRO)

"Among the unpleasant realities that the Western world is trying hard to ignore is the fact that the mass migration of people has become a permanent international problem. . . . But only a few [officials] have dared tell the unpalatable truth that the 'refugee problem' cannot be wrapped up in a package and disposed of by temporary expedients or that it will not merely fade away when the money appropriated by grudging parliaments runs out." [30]

The IRO was conceived from the beginning in the anachronistic pattern of a purely emergency body, carefully handcuffed in terms of duration, power and jurisdiction. These restrictions stemmed from the same kinds of national interests which constantly hemmed in the League's refugee efforts: the antagonism of the refugees' homelands and the reluctance of other countries to accept a heavy, continuing and seemingly unproductive financial burden.

Nazi aggression, the scourge which caused the greatest outpouring of refugees just prior to and during World War II, was also the greatest blight upon the remaining League machinery responsible for dealing with the refugee problem, the Office of the High Commissioner.[31] As that agency

[29] For excellent discussion of this and other WHO issues, see Charles S. Ascher, "Current Problems in the World Health Organization's Program," *International Organization*, Vol. 6, No. 1 (February 1952), pp. 27–50.

[30] Michael L. Hoffman, "The Perpetual Refugees," *Harper's Magazine*, Vol. 201, No. 1202 (July 1950), p. 39.

[31] See pp. 182–183.

became more and more isolated, increasing use was made of the London-based Inter-Governmental Committee on Refugees (IGC).[32] But the vast job of following the liberating United Nations troops to provide millions of miserable refugees with food, clothing, shelter, medical care and transportation home was first handled by UNRRA, established in November 1943. The Inter-Governmental Committee continued to concentrate on political and legal protection (passports, property rights, etc.), while UNRRA concentrated on material needs.

After it had been decided that UNRRA should be liquidated by March 1947, the UN General Assembly, in February 1946, frantically instructed ECOSOC to study the refugee problem. An ECOSOC Special Committee on Refugees and Displaced Persons met in London from April to June 1946 and recommended a plan that served as the basis for the final IRO constitution approved by the General Assembly in December 1946. As the constitution was being drafted, the Russians insisted that only fugitives from the wartime aggressors and Franco Spain should be considered *bona fide* refugees. All others, including Poles, Balts, Yugoslavs or Russians, must be repatriated, by force if necessary. Any who resisted were obviously war criminals and were to be shipped home for prosecution. Under no circumstances should IRO engage in the resettlement of such refugees. The non-Soviet states, led by the United States and United Kingdom, were opposed to compulsory repatriation, except for actual war criminals, and favored resettlement as both a permanent solution and a means of reducing the financial drain of maintaining the temporary camps. Nonetheless, a majority of non-Soviet nations refused to commit themselves in advance either to accept refugees or support the cost of resettlement.

ORGANIZATION TAKES SHAPE

The plan finally approved by the General Assembly provided for continuing the services rendered by UNRRA: repatriation, care and assistance, legal and political protection, transportation and resettlement. This aid was to be given only to "genuine" refugees and displaced persons, as determined by the UN and IRO —not to war criminals, quislings, traitors or persons of German ethnic origin except those who fled Germany to join the UN forces. The IRO structure consisted of the usual trinity: a General Council, nine-state Executive Committee and Director-General with staff.

The temporary Preparatory Commission, created in December 1946, was soon compelled, because of laggard ratifications, to assume operational responsibility from UNRRA and the Inter-Governmental Committee in July 1947 for refugees eligible for IRO aid. IRO itself did not go into effect until August 1948, a year and a half after the constitution had been approved by the General Assembly. Then, approximately a year later, in July 1949, the major contributors, the United States, United Kingdom,

[32] See Chap. 20.

France and Canada, decided through the General Council that IRO should close its doors by June 30, 1950. Because the flood of refugees refused to recede in obedience to this timetable, however, the termination date was postponed, first to March 31, 1951, and, finally, to September 30, 1951.

Even by the latter date, however, the refugee problem was far from solved and was constantly exacerbated by new political disturbances. It was estimated in 1951 that there were still sixty to a hundred million refugees throughout the world with approximately thirteen million in Europe.[33] Nevertheless the major contributors insisted on transferring most of IRO's remaining burdens to the national governments of France, Germany, Austria and Italy in which the European IRO camps were located. The only permanent machinery which the UN created to replace IRO was the office of the High Commissioner with authority merely to provide political and legal aid and to help coordinate non-UN material assistance.[34]

CONCLUSIONS

For the first time, an international refugee organization was given sufficient funds to engage in a major material assistance program of its own, coordinated with the legal and political protection needed, rather than having to depend primarily on other public and private efforts. Furthermore, the United States supported this body as it had never supported any other international refugee agency. On the other hand, its creators never thought it necessary to make IRO a permanent agency so that it would always be on hand to deal with any refugee problem the moment it arose. It was hustled off stage even before its own limited task was completed. It never had formal authority to do more than make recommendations to national governments, although its ability to make or withhold grants had a powerfully persuasive effect. Finally it was prohibited from aiding more than a fraction of the total number of refugees who needed help.

United Nations Educational, Scientific and Cultural Organization (UNESCO)

" . . . since wars begin in the minds of men, it is in the minds of men that the defences of peace must be constructed. . . ."

This dramatic phrase, which appears in the preamble of the UNESCO constitution, is the famous verbal banner of that new center of international cultural cooperation. While most wartime planners assumed there

[33] René Ristelhueber, "The International Refugee Organization," *International Conciliation*, No. 470 (April 1951), p. 223.
[34] See p. 208.

would be some kind of postwar organization to continue the work of the League cultural bodies, the practical and hard-pressed British took the first concrete step of initiating, in November 1942, periodic meetings of a Council of Allied Ministers of Education (CAME) primarily to help share the immediate burden of rebuilding war-damaged educational facilities. The United States was rather leisurely in associating itself with this effort, sending only an observer in May 1943.

Limited short-range thinking dominated the first CAME draft for a postwar organization which was formulated at a London conference in April 1944 to which the United States sent an able delegation headed by Representative, later Senator, J. William Fulbright. But official opinion soon began to swing towards a more positive long-range point of view, due to the development of UNRRA to handle rehabilitation needs, the rapid conclusion of the war in 1945, and the influence of various private cultural groups, especially in the United States and United Kingdom. This tendency was reinforced during the San Francisco Conference by the success of the Chinese and French in persuading their colleagues to adopt a resolution favoring a permanent UN cultural organization.

Nongovernmental cultural interests also had their day in court, notably American groups which were given the status of consultants to the United States delegation to the San Francisco Conference.[35] The jealousies within and among these interests, which will bedevil UNESCO to its last day, soon raised their heads, particularly in the semantic battle that raged about the naming of the infant organization. The educators insisted that the single word "cultural" was not explicit enough and that "education" must be specifically mentioned. Thereupon the scientists began to clamor for similar recognition and, at a later conference in November 1945, succeeded in wedging "scientific" between "educational" and "cultural." While there was some support for making the agency a subsidiary commission under ECOSOC, most of the private groups felt that it would develop more vigorously as an independent specialized agency, merely affiliated with the UN.

Concurrently with the San Francisco Conference, CAME met for a second drafting conference from April to July 1945 and was much influenced by the forces at work at San Francisco. Finally CAME adopted a United States draft with certain stylistic changes.[36] It was in the venerable hall of the Institute of Civil Engineers in bombed-out London that the final planning conference was held during November 1945. Now that the main lines of the blueprint had been agreed upon by the small CAME group, the project was submitted to a world-wide audience. Of the fifty-one signatories of the UN Charter, all participated except the Soviet Union, the Byelorussian Republic, the Ukrainian Republic, Ethiopia, Costa Rica,

---

[35] Howard E. Wilson, "International Cultural Cooperation," *International Conciliation*, No. 415 (November 1945), pp. 707–721.

[36] For text of United States plan prepared in March 1945 see *Postwar Foreign Policy Preparation . . .* , pp. 649–654.

Honduras and Paraguay. England's new Labor Prime Minister, Mr. Clement Attlee, set the theme of the conference with his phrase, "War begins in the minds of men," subsequently woven into the UNESCO preamble by the American poet-statesman, Archibald MacLeish, and the distinguished French scholar, Etienne Gilson.

CULTURE AND POLITICS

A bird's eye view of the interplay of national interests during the conference reveals a great deal about the fundamental nature of UNESCO. On the issue of the "mass" versus "class" approach, the United States, under the leadership of MacLeish, played a prominent role in insisting that the new organization concern itself far more with mass communications than had the League system. The United States was also foremost in urging the new organization to concentrate its limited resources on projects which would contribute most directly to peace as the prerequisite for cultural relations.

On the question of UNESCO's policing role in promoting the free exchange of information, including strategic scientific intelligence (the first atomic bomb had been exploded only three months before), and in promoting "democratic" education, it was finally agreed that the organization should not have more than a recommendatory role and that its only sanctions would be the glare of publicity and the possibility of referring really explosive situations to the UN security system. It was also decided that states should not be compelled to establish national UNESCO commissions, similar to those created under the League to mobilize and channel nongovernmental opinion, but that states should nevertheless be urged to do so.

Regarding structure, the conference bumped into the familiar dispute as to whether the members of the executive board should be chosen as individuals or governmental representatives. Because the traffic in ideas seemed to the drafters, perhaps mistakenly, more remote from the power struggle than certain other activities, it was agreed that members of the executive board should all be elected by the general conference as individuals with no permanent seats reserved for the great powers (although it was expected that they would always be represented) but with not more than one from any single state. Because the French were adamant that the organization's headquarters be located permanently in Paris, other states, led by the United States and the United Kingdom, were all the more determined that the General Conference be relatively footloose, meeting in various parts of the world. It was also decided that the director-generalship be awarded to a non-Frenchman, a Britisher to begin with. The constitution went into effect in November 1946.

GOALS AND STRUCTURE

The general purposes of UNESCO are:

> to contribute to peace and security by promoting collaboration among the nations through education, science and culture in order to further universal respect for justice, for the rule of law and for the human rights and fundamental freedoms which are affirmed for the peoples of the world, without distinction of race, sex, language or religion, by the Charter of the United Nations.

Membership is open to UN Member states which ratify the UNESCO constitution and to other states recommended by the Executive Board and approved by a two-thirds majority of the General Conference. As of April 1953, there were sixty-eight members. Each state may appoint five delegates to the General Conference, after consultation with a national UNESCO commission or with other educational, cultural or scientific bodies. Each delegation has one vote, and decisions are by simple majority except for draft conventions, which require a two-thirds majority. Members are required to submit all recommendations and draft conventions to their respective competent authorities within a year and to report periodically on action taken. The Executive Board consists of eighteen members elected by the General Conference which is obligated to try to include persons competent in the arts, humanities, sciences, education and diffusion of ideas, and qualified to fulfill the Board's executive duties. The Conference is also directed to strive for a balance of cultures and geographical areas. The term is three years with eligibility for a second term. The Board meets twice a year and makes its decisions by simple majority.

Each member state is also bound to make arrangements "as suit its particular conditions" to associate its principal bodies interested in educational, scientific and cultural matters with the work of the Organization, preferably by the formation of a national commission broadly representative of the government and such bodies. Such commissions or national cooperating bodies are to act in an advisory capacity to their respective delegations to the General Conference and to their governments and are to function "as agencies of liaison in all matters of interest" to the Organization. The Director-General of UNESCO is nominated by the Executive Board and appointed by the General Conference for a six year term, eligible for reappointment. The staff numbers about 800. The annual budget is approximately $8.5 million. The headquarters are in Paris.

CONCLUSIONS

In comparison with the League system, UNESCO represents at least a modest measure of growth. It has a more comprehensive membership with a larger representation of the less developed lands, broader and more

GENERAL CONFERENCE

EXECUTIVE BOARD

SECRETARIAT

DIRECTORATE
DIRECTOR-GENERAL
DEPUTY DIRECTOR-GENERAL

OFFICE OF THE DIRECTOR-GENERAL

BUREAU OF PROGRAMME AND BUDGET

BUREAU OF LEGAL AFFAIRS

BUREAU OF OFFICIAL AND EXTERNAL RELATIONS

BUREAU OF PERSONNEL AND MANAGEMENT

BUREAU OF CONFERENCE PLANNING AND GENERAL SERVICES

BUREAU OF THE COMPTROLLER

DEPARTMENT OF TECHNICAL ASSISTANCE

OFFICE OF LIAISON WITH THE UNITED NATIONS IN NEW YORK

DOCUMENTS AND PUBLICATIONS SERVICE

DEPARTMENT OF MASS COMMUNICATION

DEPARTMENT OF CULTURAL ACTIVITIES

DEPARTMENT OF SOCIAL SCIENCES (Including Statistical Activities)

CO-OPERATION OFFICE IN THE WESTERN HEMISPHERE

DEPARTMENT OF EDUCATION (Including the Exchange of Persons Programme)

DEPARTMENT OF NATURAL SCIENCES

September 1948

intensive activities (particularly in the field of technical assistance), greater financial resources, a larger staff and stronger support from the United States Government. UNESCO's greatest curse is that all the world is its stage. Its jurisdiction encompasses everything that involves any international communication of ideas, an area that, at least in theory, blankets every other UN agency. This makes it extremely difficult for UNESCO to keep its appetite within the bounds of its very limited resources. From this basic frustration flow, to a very large degree, many of the difficulties with which the Organization has wrestled since birth.

The General Conference, lacking the cohesion of consensus, is not willing to confer sufficient leadership responsibility on the Board and Director-General. Its delegations lack continuity. Its budget autopsies have been unduly frequent, detailed and unrelated to available funds. The Board is similarly anarchic and has seldom the time or fortitude to offer real program direction. While the Director-General has urged Board members to remember that they serve as representatives of the entire organization rather than their own countries, there are obvious national affinities which the United States delegation has frankly recognized by proposing that the constitution be amended to make Board members truly national representatives. The staff is also torn by centrifugal interests. There has been more than usual pressure to make appointments on a geographical basis, and the rate of turnover has been disturbingly high. Julian Huxley and Jaime Torres Bodet were exceptionally strong, able and dedicated leaders who were criticized for being too ambitious but whose impatience was understandable and whose courage was commendable. Outside the organization there are still conflicts with other agencies, although this situation has improved, particularly with the development of the Technical Assistance Board (TAB). Relations with member states are hampered by weak national commissions and the fact that most countries place cultural relations near the bottom of their list of priorities.

General Evaluation

Taking a bird's-eye view of all thirteen of the proposed, present and past specialized agencies, one is particularly impressed by the fundamental continuity between the League and United Nations. There is no agency that was not foreshadowed and inspired by some League activity. At the same time, most of the present bodies represent some expansion and strengthening of the League system. Above all, they are the organizational manifestations of certain fundamental shifts in the views of the great powers, especially the United States. After World War II, those powers, with the exception of the Soviet Union, displayed a livelier appreciation, than before the war, of the direct link between world-wide economic and social problems and their own security. They were more willing to use multilateral rather than national or bilateral organizations to deal with such problems. And they wanted to establish these bodies not directly under the UN and its ECOSOC, as the technical committees were under the League Council and Assembly, but as independent self-contained organizations, affiliated with the UN, patterned very much along the lines of the highly regarded ILO.

PATTERN OF GOALS AND ACTIVITIES

Part of the expanded spirit of these agencies is apparent in their purposes and functions. Most of them have been given far more positive and comprehensive objectives than their predecessors. One example of this is the strikingly bold mandate of the WHO. There is also greater emphasis on direct and decentralized "grass roots" operations rather than remote and centralized informational and research work. This trend is perhaps most evident in the ambitious technical assistance program which involves most of the agencies.

Firmer steps are also being taken to promote greater compliance with the organizations' decisions. Many constitutions include the ILO device of requiring member governments to submit such decisions to the proper national authorities and report on the results achieved with supporting explanations. Besides the generally adopted authority to recommend draft conventions, a few organizations, notably ICAO and WHO, have been given limited quasi-legislative authority to approve technical regulations which are binding unless expressly rejected by member governments within a particular time limit, a power possessed by no League body, with the single exception of the affiliated International Commission for Air Navigation. There is also occasional provision for restricted sanctions, usually publicity or withdrawal of privileges, although there is not as much emphasis on this possibility as when the ILO was founded in 1919, especially since the ILO soon discovered that only limited informal rather than ambitious formal sanctions were feasible.[37] In the final analysis the most effective authority of the present agencies stems less from their formal powers than from their ability to persuade, backed by money and able personnel.

In spite of this progress, however, these agencies' mandates are still weak. They have no clear and comprehensive legislative authority similar to that given most national agencies (although many national agencies, especially in the less developed countries, are less influential in actual practice than some of the specialized agencies). And the corollary of this first shortcoming is that these bodies still have no direct authority over the populations they wish to influence, although they do exercise considerable indirect authority working through and with national governments, particularly in connection with the technical assistance program.

[37] See Chap. 20.

STRUCTURAL REFLECTIONS OF NATIONAL INTERESTS

The organizational structures of these agencies show signs of vigorous development since the days of the League. On the whole, they are more integrated units than their recent ancestors, having in many cases absorbed several disparate prewar agencies. The WHO, for example, combined the League Health Committee with the affiliated but independent Paris Office of Public Health. They are also supported and supervised by more regular and widely representative plenary assemblies than were available to most of the League technical committees. Their membership includes many independent Asian and other countries that did not even exist before the war, and the admission of new members is fortunately not hamstrung by the veto, as in the United Nations proper, an asset not generally foreseen when these organizations were created.

Moreover, the composition of both the assemblies and executive councils is more frankly governmental than were many of the League technical bodies since all members of both types of organs are now required to be representatives of governments rather than serve as independent private experts as was the case, at least on paper, in most League technical committees and some plenary conferences. This requirement is modified in some instances, however, when governments are obligated to appoint persons with special qualifications ("most qualified by their technical competence in the field of health" in the case of the WHO). On the whole, the composition of these bodies is not as different in fact, if not in theory, from that of the League bodies as some observers have indicated.[38] Moreover, while there may be some loss in professional independence, there is a gain in maintaining intimate contact with governmental administrations which is the primary channel on which the UN is presently dependent to achieve its objectives.

In most other respects, the executive councils of these organizations are very similar to the League technical committees, although they are not responsible to the UN, as were the latter to the League Council and Assembly, but solely to their own assemblies. As in the League committees, the members of the executive councils are drawn largely from the more influential countries as the guiding forces in each field. In six of the thirteen specialized agencies (IBRD, IMF, ITO, ICAO, IMCO and ILO) formal provision has been made to appoint the major powers in the respective fields, measured by various yardsticks. Nor is it accidental that these six agencies exercise functions closely affecting national financial and trade interests, and two of them (IBRD and IMF) have substantial funds to dispense. Unfortunately, however, the yardsticks are, at best, rather clumsy and have given rise to some controversy and ill will. The constitutions of the other seven agencies have made no such specific provision, but those

[38] A. Loveday, "An Unfortunate Decision," *International Organization*, Vol. 1, No. 2 (June 1947), pp. 279–290.

organizations also invariably elect the great powers as members of their councils.

On the other hand, efforts have been made in all of the agencies to modify great power leadership through various devices favoring the smaller nations. This has been done by requiring some distribution of membership in the executive bodies on other than a power basis, most frequently according to geographic balance but, in the case of UNESCO, according to cultural balance. Provision has also been made in all cases for open election by the assemblies of council members not appointed according to a yardstick. While these efforts help give the organizations a certain democratic flavor, they do not fundamentally alter the fact that the great powers tend to rule the roost as they do in security affairs.

Perhaps the most significant step forward is the more liberal financing and staffing than was the case under the League. Furthermore, these agencies have been given greater access to the "grass roots" through various decentralized subsidiary channels: regional bodies, specialized technical subcommittees and national committees. And yet the specialized agency structures are still obviously inadequate. There is no accurate reflection of real national differences (population, wealth, etc.) built into the policy process as is the case in the representational systems of most national governments. The budgets are still exceedingly meager in relation to the problems that confront the agencies. And the lack of any organic connection among these bodies means that the coordinating process involves the same fumbling that is inherent in any loose alliance of sovereign components as distinguished from a more unified system.

Suggestions for Further Reading

Books

Ascher, Charles S., *Program-Making in UNESCO, 1946–1951* . . . (Chicago: Public Administration Service, 1951).

Brown, William Adams, Jr., *The United States and the Restoration of World Trade* (Washington: Brookings Institution, 1950).

Condliffe, J. B., *Agenda For a Postwar World* (New York: W. W. Norton & Co., Inc., 1942).

Coordination of Economic and Social Activities (New York: Carnegie Endowment for International Peace, 1948).

Corbett, P. W., *Post-War Worlds* (New York: Institute of Pacific Relations, 1942).

Feis, Herbert, *The Sinews of Peace* (New York: Harper & Brothers, 1944).

Goodrich, Leland M., and Hambro, Edvard, *Charter of the United Nations, Commentary and Documents* (Boston: World Peace Foundation, 1949).

Orr, Sir John Boyd, *Fighting for What?* (London: Macmillan & Co., Ltd., 1942).

Staley, Eugene, *World Economy in Transition* (New York: Council on Foreign Relations, 1939).

Van Zandt, J. Parker, *Civil Aviation and Peace* (Washington: Brookings Institution, 1944).

Wilcox, Clair, *A Charter for World Trade* (New York: The Macmillan Company, 1949).

Woodbridge, George, ed., *UNRRA,* 3 Vols. (New York: Columbia University Press, 1950).

Periodicals

American Journal of Public Health, passim for articles on WHO, especially Vols. 35–43.

Allen, Charles E., "World Health and World Politics," *International Organization,* Vol. 4, No. 1 (February 1950).

Ascher, Charles S., "The Development of UNESCO's Program," *International Organization,* Vol. 4, No. 1 (February 1950).

Basch, Antonin, "International Bank for Reconstruction and Development, 1944–1949, *International Conciliation,* No. 455 (November 1949).

Belshaw, H., "The Food and Agriculture Organization of the United Nations," *International Organization,* Vol. 1, No. 2 (June 1947).

Berle, Adolf A., Jr., "Freedoms of the Air," *Harper's Magazine,* Vol. 190, No. 1138 (March 1945).

Black, Eugene R., "The World Bank at Work," *Foreign Affairs,* Vol. 30, No. 3 (April 1952).

Black, John D., "The International Food Movement," *The American Economic Review,* Vol. 33, No. 4 (December 1943).

Cooper, John C., "The Bermuda Plan: World Pattern for Air Transport," *Foreign Affairs,* Vol. 25, No. 1 (October 1946).

Feis, Herbert, "The Conflict Over Trade Ideologies," *Foreign Affairs,* Vol. 25, No. 2 (January 1947).

Flexner, Jean Atherton, "Food Policies of the United Nations," *The American Economic Review,* Vol. 33, No. 4 (December 1943).

Fox, Grace, "The Origins of UNRRA," *Political Science Quarterly,* Vol. 65, No. 4 (December 1950).

Fried, John H. E., "Relations Between the United Nations and the International Labor Organization," *American Political Science Review,* Vol. 41, No. 5 (October 1947).

Goodrich, Carter, "The ILO: A Going Concern," *The Annals of the American Academy of Political and Social Science,* Vol. 246 (July 1946).

Jessup, Philip C., "UNRRA, Sample of World Organization," *Foreign Affairs,* Vol. 22, No. 3 (April 1944).

Johnson, Richard A., "The Origin of the United Nations Educational, Scientific and Cultural Organization," *International Conciliation,* No. 424 (October 1946).

Johnson, Robert H., "International Politics and the Structure of International Organization: The Case of UNRRA," *World Politics,* Vol. 3, No. 4 (July 1951).

Kindleberger, Charles P., "Bretton Woods Reappraised," *International Organization,* Vol. 5, No. 1 (February 1951).

Loveday, A., "Suggestions for the Reform of the United Nations Economic and Social Machinery," *International Organization,* Vol. 7, No. 3 (August 1953).

McDougall, F. L., "International Aspects of Postwar Food and Agriculture," *The Annals of the American Academy of Political and Social Science,* Vol. 225 (January 1943).

Mikesell, Raymond F., "International Monetary Fund, 1944–1949," *International Conciliation,* No. 455 (November 1949).

Mudaliar, Sir Arcot, "World Health Problems," *International Conciliation,* No. 491 (May 1953).

Orr, Sir John Boyd, "Food for All Mankind," *Survey Graphic,* Vol. 36, No. 10 (October 1947).

Riegelman, Carol, "Labor's Bridgehead: The ILO," *Political Science Quarterly,* Vol. 40, No. 2 (June 1945).

Ristelhueber, René, "The International Refugee Organization," *International Conciliation,* No. 470 (April 1951).

Simpson, Smith, "Constitutional Development of the ILO as Affected by the Recent International Labor Conference," *American Political Science Review,* Vol. 38, No. 4 (August 1944).

Viner, Jacob, "Conflicts of Principle in Drafting a Trade Charter," *Foreign Affairs,* Vol. 25, No. 4 (July 1947).

Warner, Edward, "The Chicago Air Conference," *Foreign Affairs,* Vol. 23, No. 3 (April 1945).

White, Harry D., "The Monetary Fund: Some Criticisms Examined," *Foreign Affairs,* Vol. 23, No. 2 (January 1945).

Williams, John H., "Currency Stabilization: American and British Attitudes," *Foreign Affairs,* Vol. 22, No. 2 (January 1944), and other articles in *Foreign Affairs.*

Wilson, Howard E., "International Cultural Cooperation," *International Conciliation,* No. 415 (November 1945).

Winant, John G., "The ILO in Wartime and After," *Foreign Affairs,* Vol. 19, No. 3 (April 1941).

Winslow, Dr. C.-E. A., "[WHO] Program and Accomplishments," *International Conciliation,* No. 437 (March 1948).

Young, John Parke, "Developing Plans for an International Monetary Fund and a World Bank," *Department of State Bulletin,* Vol. 23, No. 593 (November 13, 1950).

Documents

Food and Agriculture Organization, *Annual Reports of the Director-General, Reports of Missions, World Food Survey* and other documents.

International Bank for Reconstruction and Development, *Annual Reports* and other documents.

International Labor Organization, *International Labour Review, Director's Report, Studies and Reports* and other documents.

International Monetary Fund, *Annual Reports* and other documents.

United Nations Educational, Scientific and Cultural Organization, *Reports of the Director General* and other documents.

United Nations Monetary and Financial Conference, *Proceedings and Documents* (Washington: U.S. Government Printing Office, 1948).

United Nations Relief and Rehabilitation Administration, *Reports of the Director-General to the Council, Journal, Operational Analysis Reports 1–53* and other documents.

United States, Congress, *Hearings before the Committee on Foreign Affairs, House of Representatives, 81st Congress, 2nd Session, on H. J. Res. 236, April and May 1950* (ITO Charter).

———, Congress, *Hearings before the Committee on Foreign Relations, United States Senate, 79th Congress, 1st Session, on . . . a Convention on International Civil Aviation . . . February . . . March . . . 1945.*

———, Department of State, *International Civil Aviation, 1945–1948; 1948–1949; 1949–1950.*

———, Department of State, *Postwar Foreign Policy Preparation, 1939–1945,* Department of State Publication 3580, General Foreign Policy Series 15 (Washington: U.S. Government Printing Office, 1950).

———, Department of State, *Proceedings of the International Civil Aviation Conference* (Washington: U.S. Government Printing Office, 1948).

———, Department of State, *Report of the United States Delegation on the International Health Conference,* Department of State Publication 2703, Conference Series 91 (Washington: U.S. Government Printing Office, 1946).

World Health Organization, *Annual Reports of the Director-General, Bulletin, Chronicle* and other documents.

Mandates, Special Areas and Minorities — League

The Mandates System

A LEADING EXPERT on the mandates system, M. William Rappard, first director of the mandates section of the League Secretariat, has described that system not as the product of unsullied idealism but as a "kind of compromise between the proposition advanced by the advocates of annexation and the proposition put forward by those who wished to entrust the colonial territories to international administration." [1] The compromise, moreover, seems to have been weighted heavily on the side of the annexationists. The territorial appetites of all the Allied powers, except the United States, were unmistakably evident at the Paris Peace Conference and were reinforced by various secret commitments, such as the Sykes–Picot Agreement of 1916, that had been negotiated during the war as the basis for carving up the German and Turkish possessions.

Against these pressures there was an array of counterforces that managed to win a greater victory than many observers at Paris originally thought possible. First, there were certain concepts that were the result of long historical evolution and that contributed important ingredients to the modern idea of trusteeship: (1) the device of joint international supervision (*condominium*) of certain controversial areas of interest to two or more powers; (2) British, American and French development of domestic legal provisions for protecting their respective dependent peoples, especially the idea of "trusteeship" which had first been expounded by Edmund Burke to raise the level of British administration in India; and (3) the exercise in Central Africa and Turkey of the collective responsibility of the community of nations, as represented by the Concert of Europe, to conciliate and promote the interests of the European powers in those areas.

More immediate anti-annexationist forces were certain private and governmental interests that conducted a vigorous campaign during and after the war to use the new international organization to help rid the world of colonialism. The private league plans that were heavily legalistic, such as

[1] Permanent Mandates Commission, Minutes, I, 4.

281

the American League to Enforce Peace and the Phillimore projects, made no mention of the colonial problem. The British Independent Labor Party, however, outlined a proposal in August 1917 that contained the seeds of the final mandates system: administration by "individual European States under the supervision of an International Commission." [2] Influenced by this suggestion, the British Foreign Office Memorandum of November 1918 proposed that, "Trusts . . . be drawn up for the various territories . . . [to be] handed over to individual States who would be responsible to the League for the discharge of that mandate." [3]

After receiving this plan, General Smuts of South Africa presented essentially the same proposal to the Imperial War Cabinet, composed of the leaders of the Dominions as well as Great Britain, which accepted the mandatory doctrine, although Australia, New Zealand and South Africa would not agree to apply it to the areas which they were particularly interested in acquiring — the Pacific islands and South West Africa. Then, in December 1918, Smuts published his plan containing a dramatic and persuasive exposition of his concept of the mandatory principle; it included the idea of making the League the successor to the former colonial powers and giving it authority to allocate the mandated territories, thus in fact giving the League title to them. But Smuts insisted that "the German colonies in the Pacific and Africa are inhabited by barbarians, who not only cannot possibly govern themselves but to whom it would be impracticable to apply any idea of political self-determination in the European sense." [4]

DECISIONS AT PARIS

Although President Wilson had for some time urged self-determination for these liberated areas, he had never flatly opposed annexation. Nor did he suggest any positive plan of international supervision until, on December 10, 1918, as he was crossing the Atlantic with the American delegation, he proposed "that the German colonies should be declared the common property of the League of Nations and administered by small nations," [5] an idea which died soon after birth for lack of affection. At the end of December, Prime Minister Lloyd George told President Wilson of the attitude of the Imperial War Cabinet and gave him General Smuts' proposals which Wilson proceeded to graft on to his draft of January 10, 1919, with the important addition that the mandatory system was to apply to all of the former colonies without exception.

Finally, in January 1919, Smuts extracted the sting from this dispute by

[2] *The Times* (London), August 29, 1917, p. 8.

[3] Alfred Zimmern, *The League of Nations and the Rule of Law, 1918–1935* (London: Macmillan, 1936), pp. 196–208.

[4] Jan C. Smuts, *The League of Nations, a Practical Suggestion* (London: Hodder and Stoughton, 1918).

[5] E. M. House, *The Intimate Papers of Colonel House*, edited by Charles Seymour (Boston: Houghton Mifflin, 1928), pp. 281–282.

formulating the compromise which extended the mandate principle to all the territories but at the same time created a "C" class of mandated areas to include those occupied by the three Dominions which would be governed as "integral parts of their territory." [6] The Dominions also won agreement to the principle that they should not be required to observe an "open door" economic policy in the "C" mandated territories and that the Allied and Associated Powers, rather than the League, should receive the territories from the conquered nations and allocate them, more or less in accordance with the secret agreements, to the mandatory powers which would administer them under mandate charters approved and supervised by the League Council. France won the right to recruit native soldiers for defense of the homeland as well as the territories themselves, although this concession was never made clear in the text of Covenant Article 22. In all of this discussion there was no significant support for either joint administration by two or more powers or for direct League administration, largely because of the desire of the interested powers to exercise unrestrained individual administrative authority and because of the general opinion that past experiments in joint control had proved unsuccessful.

The major provisions of Article 22 of the Covenant, as finally approved, are as follows:

1. To those colonies and territories which as a consequence of the late war have ceased to be under the sovereignty of the States which formerly governed them and which are inhabited by peoples not yet able to stand by themselves under the strenuous conditions of the modern world, there should be applied the principle that the well-being and development of such peoples form a sacred trust of civilization and that securities for the performance of this trust should be embodied in this Covenant.

2. The best method of giving practical effect to this principle is that the tutelage of such peoples should be entrusted to advanced nations . . . and that this tutelage should be exercised by them as Mandatories on behalf of the League. . . .

4. Certain communities formerly belonging to the Turkish Empire . . . can be provisionally recognized subject to the rendering of administrative advice and assistance by a Mandatory until such time as they are able to stand alone. The wishes of these communities must be a principal consideration in the selection of the Mandatory.

5. Other peoples, especially those of Central Africa, are at such a stage that the Mandatory must be responsible for the administration of the territory under conditions which will guarantee freedom of conscience and religion, subject only to the maintenance of public order and morals, the prohibition of abuses such as the slave trade, the arms traffic and the liquor traffic, and the prevention of the establishment of fortifications or military and naval bases and of military training of the natives for other than police purposes and the defense of territory, and will also secure equal opportunities for the trade and commerce of other Members of the League.

[6] David Hunter Miller, *The Drafting of the Covenant* (New York and London: Putnam, 1928), Vol. 1, p. 109.

6. There are territories, such as Southwest Africa and certain of the South Pacific islands, which . . . can be best administered under the laws of the Mandatory as integral portions of its territory, subject to the safeguards above mentioned in the interests of the indigenous populations.

7. In every case of mandate, the Mandatory shall render to the Council an annual report in reference to that territory committed to its charge.

8. The degree of authority, control or administration to be exercised by the Mandatory shall, if not previously agreed upon by the Members of the League, be explicitly defined in each case by the Council.

9. A permanent Commission shall be constituted to receive and examine the annual reports of the Mandatories, and to advise the Council on all matters relating to the observance of the mandates.

STRUCTURE OF MANDATES SYSTEM

The pressures which shaped the mandates system were clearly revealed by the fact that the functions of the League Council, advised by the "permanent commission," were to be limited to confirming the original mandate charters, formulated by the mandatory powers themselves, and amendments thereto, taking cognizance of the assignment of mandated territories by the Allied and Associated Powers, and receiving and commenting on the annual reports. The treaties which provided the constitutional foundation for this structure were the Covenant and the mandate charters supplemented by the constitution of the Permanent Mandates Commission and its rules of procedure.

Over-all Supervisory Bodies

The Council was the principal link that connected the League with the mandatories and the mandated territories. Although the Mandates Commission did most of the actual work, the Council was ultimately responsible for exercising the League's official functions in this field. When considering these matters, the Council supplemented its normal membership by inviting the chairman of the Mandates Commission to participate. Representatives of mandatory powers not regularly represented on the Council were also asked to join in its voting as well as discussion on their respective mandated territories. Since these questions were considered matters of substance, rather than procedure, the decisions required unanimity.

The Assembly was an uninvited but vocal guest in the mandates system. Although neither the Covenant nor the mandate charters gave the Assembly any specific authority regarding the mandates system, the members of that ambitious organ, particularly the small noncolonial powers that always comprised a majority of the membership, used the organ as a powerful forum for airing their views on all mandates issues. Occasionally these debates hit their mark with telling effect, as when Assembly criticism of French policy in Syria in 1925 was instrumental in achieving the recall of General Sarrail. During the Assembly's first session, the Council reacted to that body's prying interest regarding the mandates by intimating that the Assembly was roaming rather far afield. But the Council could not deny that the plenary body had the right to discuss and make recommendations (though not "decisions") on mandates as well as any other questions which were "within the sphere of action of the League or affecting the peace of the world" (Covenant Article 3). In spite of this friction, however, the Council normally gave prompt effect to Assembly recommendations.

Permanent Mandates Commission

This Commission was one of two such bodies mentioned specifically in the Covenant; the other was the commission on armaments authorized in Article 9. In the course of its active career the Commission succeeded in winning a remarkable degree of respect for its high standards of impartiality, maturity, continuity and *esprit de corps*.

Membership. After long debate, the Council decided not to bring the mandatory powers into the Mandates Commission as actual members of that body but to have them speak through their "accredited representatives" reporting to the Commission. The membership of the Commission itself was to be composed of nine individual experts with no official governmental connections, a majority to be selected from non-mandatory countries. Although the Secretary-General suggested that the Assembly appoint the Commission members, the Council decided that the spirit, if not the letter, of the Covenant required appointment by the Council. The four individuals who could be chosen from mandatory countries were selected from Great Britain, France, Japan and Belgium. Nationals from the other three mandatory powers (Australia, New Zealand and South Africa) never sat on the Commission. The membership was even more heavily weighted on the colonial side by the decision to select all the non-mandatory members from colonial states also (Italy, Netherlands, Portugal and Spain), with the exception of the lone woman member (first from Sweden, then Norway).

In spite of the obvious effort to isolate Commission members from the corrupting influence of governmental pressure, there remained many unofficial bonds: the consultations with governments, primarily by the Secretary-General, that preceded appointments to the Commission; the careful allocation of members among the various interested states; and the thousand informal and inevitable connections between these experts, most of whom held governmental positions before and after serving on the Commission, and their respective governments. Nevertheless, most of them seem to have bent over backwards to remain as independent as possible. When one British national, Mr. Ormsby-Gore, who had left the Commission to become Colonial Secretary, returned as his country's accredited representative, "he was subjected to critical questions by his successor on the Commission to the general surprise and even amusement of the other members. His acceptance and that of his successor of such questioning as a natural and proper course was not without significance in regard to the judicial attitude which has characterized the Commission."[7] It might be added that Britain has ever been the world's tutor in developing such a "judicial attitude." On the other hand, the nationals of the totalitarian countries, Italy and Japan, clearly responded to the pressures of their governments.

Although the membership was originally set at nine, M. William Rappard was made an "extraordinary member" in 1924, and the official complement was increased to ten in 1926 in order to make room for a German national. Furthermore, the membership developed remarkable continuity. Tenure was not limited, and the average period of service was over seven years; nine members stayed eleven years or more; four stayed fifteen or more; and one (M. Orts of Belgium) stayed eighteen years. To provide liaison with the ILO, a representative of that organization was invited to be present in an advisory capacity during discussions on labor questions.

Voting, Meetings, Officers. Decisions on all questions were made by a majority of the members present, the chair exercising a deciding vote in case of a tie. Meetings were normally held at Geneva twice a year, late June and late October or early November. The chairman, though constitutionally subject to change each year, was always reëlected, largely due to the fact that the chairmanship was given to an Italian, M. Theodoli, as a gesture to help salve Italian resentment at not being assigned a mandated territory. M. Theodoli did not relinquish the post until 1936 when he walked out of the Commission after a heated debate on the application of sanctions against Italy.

The Commission normally kept all its meetings closed to the public except for the first meeting each session. It was said that, since the Commission was advisory to the Council, it should not embarrass the superior body and that greater publicity would not be conducive to a frank exchange of views between the Commission and the accredited representatives. At the same time the Commission did publish and make available to the public slightly condensed minutes, its reports to the Council and the replies which mandatory governments made to Commission questions.

Secretariat Mandates Section

In the final analysis it was a handful of Secretariat officials in the Mandates Section who, together with a few leading figures in the Commission, formed the hard core of the mandates organization. Because of the Secretary-General's policy of not appointing nationals of colonial powers to the Mandates Section, the staff brought only a meager store of expert knowledge with them, but they compensated for this lack through sheer industry and ingenuity. They also found it advantageous to specialize on various territories in order to complement the functional specialization of the Commis-

---

[7] From Lord Lugard manuscript as quoted by H. Duncan Hall, *Mandates, Dependencies, and Trusteeship* (Washington: Carnegie Endowment for International Peace, 1948), p. 180.

sion members. Because the staff was the only full-time personnel working on mandates questions, they became an indispensable center of information which not only analyzed the mandatory reports in advance of each session but also suggested probing questions to be put to the accredited representatives and even engaged in sensitive negotiations to achieve compromises. The accomplishments of this group are all the more remarkable because of their limited numbers — never more than a Director or Chief of Section, two to four senior members, and four to six juniors.

AUTHORITY OF MANDATES SYSTEM

Since the Commission was never authorized to make field investigations, it leaned heavily on the annual mandatory reports. To elicit the fullest possible disclosure, the Commission formulated a questionnaire covering the following subjects: slavery, labor, arms traffic, trade and manufacture of alcohol and drugs, liberty of conscience, military clauses, economic equality, education, public health, land tenure, general welfare, public finances and demographic statistics. In actual practice, the mandatory governments often gave more information than they were asked for, but, when the Commission proposed a more searching questionnaire in 1926, all of them, with the exception of Belgium, prevailed upon the Council not to approve it.

Each accredited representative, who was often the principal administrative officer in the mandated territory, was expected to supply supplementary clarifying information requested by the Commission and to participate freely in the discussion of the report. Furthermore, the Commission members soon developed considerable ability in probing these reports much as members of national parliaments have used their question periods as powerful weapons to make ministers conscious of the ever watchful public eye.

> Only those who have had experience of the internal working of an official administration, in circumstances where there is no organization of public opinion, can appreciate the strength of the influence which can be exerted by publicity of the nature of that involved in the proceedings of the Commission and Council. It is significant that in the earlier days of the legislatures created in the British dependencies, the power of interrogation has been valued more highly than that of passing resolutions or motions, or even of voting on a budget.[8]

After the interrogation and discussion, the representative would withdraw, and the Commission prepared its comments praising signs of progress, often requesting further information (usually as a mild reprimand), and only occasionally engaging in specific recommendations or censure. After the representative had been given an opportunity to reply, the Com-

[8] Lord Hailey, *An African Survey* (New York and London: Oxford University Press, 1938), p. 219.

mission sent its comments with the mandatory reports, its minutes and the representative's comments to the Council, which usually accepted the Commission's recommendations and acted accordingly.

Examination of Petitions

Although it had been assumed by General Smuts, the Imperial War Cabinet and President Wilson that petitions from the peoples in the mandated territories would be accepted by the League, no such provision was included in the Covenant or the mandate charters. When petitions actually began to accumulate in the Commission's mailbox, the Council belatedly accepted a procedure based on a British proposal and on procedures used in connection with the minority agreements and the Saar. Petitions coming directly from the mandated territories were to be submitted to the League via the mandatory powers — a regulation not calculated to encourage excessive frankness on the part of the petitioners. Petitions originating outside the mandated territories went to the League directly, and comments were requested from the interested mandatory powers within six months. If the Commission chose to act on a petition, it sent the mandatory's and its own observations to the Council which then passed judgment on the Commission's observations and usually sent the final answer directly and simultaneously to the petitioner and the mandatory.

It is not surprising, however, that few petitions survived this ordeal, especially since the Commission felt that it should not act on petitions which were directly opposed to the provisions of the Covenant or the mandate charters, or were trivial, anonymous, contained violent or objectionable statements, or attempted to use the Commission as a court of appeal when local courts were competent to deal with the grievance. Nor was any oral petition ever heard by the Commission or the Council since the mandatory powers insisted that such a procedure would imply that the League was a court of law and would uncork serious disturbances in the territories. On the two occasions (1925 and 1932), moreover, when the Commission suggested the possibility of inspection tours, the mandatory powers rose up in arms and blocked the proposal on the grounds that such snooping would be an invitation to rebellion in areas where the administrative authority was already handcuffed by the limitations imposed by the mandates system.

Quasi-legislative Function

The first quasi-legislative function which the League exercised in mandate affairs was the Council's confirmation of the mandate charters. Since those texts also provided that the mandatory powers were to apply appropriate treaty obligations within the mandated territories, the Council and the Commission were responsible for seeing that this provision was implemented, particularly with respect to conventions on the arms and liquor traffic, slavery and various aspects of indigenous labor. The Commission not only helped interpret existing treaties but recommended new ones and helped draft them. Finally, as a sculptor gradually builds up a clay figure around a wire frame, the Commission's policy observations began to construct a body of substantive standards around the skeleton of the Covenant and the mandate charters. Although the Commission recognized the need for a wide variety of approaches to meet the special needs of different territories, it did not hesitate to formulate certain broad principles that provided useful guidance.

CONCLUSIONS

In spite of all its limitations, the League mandates system was a long and important stride in the direction of international supervision of non-self-governing peoples. For the first time, territories torn from vanquished nations were placed under the wing of a permanent international organization and were administered by mandatory powers in behalf of and under conditions approved by that organization. It is true, of course, that the mandatory powers' direct administrative authority was a far stronger influence than the weak and indirect supervisory authority of the League. But it is also true, in spite of the fact that the mandatory powers would have preferred complete and undiluted control of the territories, they felt compelled to accept the principle of international supervision. And, though it remained more principle than practice throughout the interwar period, to have given some institutional expression to that principle was in itself a major achievement.

The greatest assets of the League mandates organization were the Mandates Commission with a membership that displayed remarkable competence, independence and continuity; the devoted industry of a small but able Secretariat staff; and the early development of an annual report procedure that kept the League relatively well informed and the mandatory powers relatively responsible. The greatest weakness was not the organization's failure to exercise its assigned functions but the basic character of the system which enclosed those functions within such confining boundaries. The League was never given clear title to the territories nor authority to issue binding commands, control funds or personnel in the territories, make field investigations, receive petitions directly from the territories or impose sanctions on recalcitrant mandatory powers. Furthermore, the League's observations on the annual reports were formulated six to ten months after the end of the year reviewed. Finally, the fact that all the members of the Mandates Commission, except one, were drawn from colonial nations tended to make its policies excessively cautious. It conscientiously cultivated the small plot assigned it, but it did precious little exploring beyond those narrow limits. Under these circumstances, it is not surprising that the League was more a passive side-line spectator than an active teammate in the administration of the territories.

Supervision of Special Areas

THE SAAR

The interests which prompted the architects of the Versailles settlement to detach the Saar Territory from German sovereignty and place it under the roof of the League were very similar to those which have led to most experiments in international supervision including the mandates system. As the balance of power between two nations shifts, attractive chunks of territory, particularly those studded with lucrative resources, tend to become dislodged from the rim of the descendant power. Whenever outright annexation does not seem quite feasible, a convenient compromise may be to place the area under international supervision — often more mythical than real.

The Saar Territory, as defined by the Versailles Treaty (Part III, Section 4, known as the Saar Statute), was 730 square miles of former German territory, the most densely populated in Europe, rich with industrial plants on top and the third most important European coal field below. France had long cast covetous eyes at this industrial gem, particularly since its coal was a natural complement to the iron resources of the neighboring French Lorraine, and had actually possessed it for brief periods at the end of the seventeenth and the beginning of the nineteenth centuries.[9] At the Paris Peace Conference France originally insisted on outright annexation, chiefly on the ground that she should be allowed to exploit the Saar coal mines in compensation for the apparently deliberate German destruction of the mines in northern France. But the people of the area were so obviously and strongly attached to the German community and culture (only 0.6 per cent of them considered French their native tongue) [10] that Woodrow Wilson favored leaving them under German sovereignty, while Lloyd George proposed a mandate under the League.

The final compromise, drafted with remarkable foresight and precision during a single hectic ten-hour session, was to compel Germany to cede the Territory (composed of parts of Prussia and Bavaria largely according to the location of the coal mines) not to the Allied and Associated Powers, as in the case of the mandated territories, but directly "in favor of the League of Nations in the capacity of trustee" — presumably, but not specifically, on behalf of the signatories of the Versailles Treaty. Through the agency of a special Governing Commission, the League was to administer the area directly, rather than merely "supervising" it from a distance as in the mandates system. This administration was to continue fifteen years, at the end of which the Saarlanders were to decide under what sovereignty they should be placed.

---

[9] Sarah Wambaugh, *The Saar Plebiscite* (Cambridge: Harvard University Press, 1940), Chap. 2.
[10] *Ibid.*, p. 12.

The inhabitants were to retain their nationality, local assemblies, religious liberties, schools and language. Those over twenty, regardless of sex, were to have the right to vote but only for local assemblies. Laws and taxes then in force were to be retained except as modified by the Commission after consulting with local representatives elected in a manner determined by the Commission. France, on the other hand, won full ownership of all coal mines and deposits, plants and equipment, schools and hospitals. The territory was also included within the French customs regime, but during a five-year transitional period there was also to be free trade with Germany.

Structure of Governing Commission

The central link between the League and the Saar Territory was the Governing Commission to which the Versailles Treaty gave all the powers of government within the area that had previously belonged to the German Empire, Prussia and Bavaria. Although the Commission acted only in the name of the League and was to render quarterly reports to the League Council, it was not merely advisory to the Council, as was the Mandates Commission, but had direct administrative authority. Furthermore, when the Council appointed the Commission in February 1920, it agreed not to intervene in the Commission's affairs except for reasons of the highest importance.

Membership. The Versailles Treaty provided that the Commission should be composed of five members: one citizen of France, one native inhabitant of the Saar, not a French citizen, and three from countries other than France and Germany. These members were to be chosen annually by the League Council, although in actual practice they were usually reappointed. One of the fundamental grievances of the local populace was that all of the members first appointed, except the Canadian, were considered excessively pro-French. At the Peace Conference it had been intended that Dr. Charles Homer Haskins, United States member of the Conference Saar Committee, would be the chairman of the Commission, but, when the United States refused to join the League, the Council designated the French member, M. Victor Rault, as the chairman. This was a particularly unfortunate decision, especially since M. Rault spoke no German and was never popular with the Saarlanders. By 1924, however, after the French invasion of the Ruhr and an ensuing crisis in the Saar, there were some changes in the Commission's membership which pleased the inhabitants. Finally in 1926 M. Rault left, and the amiable British-Canadian, G. W. Stephens, who had been a member since 1923, took his place as chairman, but only until 1927. The last two chairmen, Sir Ernest Wilton and G. G. Knox, were British diplomats who never attained the favor which Mr. Stephens had won for himself and the Commission.

Voting, Meetings, Officers. All decisions, including interpretations of the Versailles Treaty which were binding on both France and Germany, were made by majority vote. The Commission had its headquarters at Saarbrucken and usually met twice a week. The chairman was appointed by the League Council.

Authority of the Commission

The legislative authority granted the Governing Commission went far beyond the power given any other League body since it could modify any existing laws or taxes after consulting with, but not necessarily complying with the views of, local representatives elected in accordance with the Commission's own regulations. It is unfortunate, however, that the authors of the Versailles Treaty did not see fit to grant the inhabitants some real legislative authority within the limits of the Versailles framework. Their political impotence was a demoralizing factor that turned them against the League regime.

The Commission was also authorized to appoint and dismiss administrative officials and create such bodies as it deemed necessary. Supervision of the various executive departments was parceled out among the Commission members, the chairman taking the key Departments of Interior, Foreign Affairs, Commerce, Industry and Control of Mines. Existing civil and criminal courts were to remain, but the authority formerly exercised by higher German courts outside the Territory was entrusted to a special supreme court for the Territory. The membership of that body was truly cosmopolitan. The chief justice was Swiss and the other judges were nationals of the Saar, France, Belgium, Czechoslovakia, Luxembourg, the Netherlands and Switzerland.

Conclusions

For the peace of Europe and the world it probably would have been wiser to leave the Saar Territory under German sovereignty as Woodrow Wilson had urged. After the Big Three had decided to detach it, however, the best compromise was undoubtedly to place it under temporary League administration rather than to surrender it entirely to France. It is also interesting that the great powers were willing to place direct and comprehensive governing authority in the hands of an international agency at the very time when they were insisting that such an arrangement was impractical for the mandated territories.

As for the organization of the Saar administration, its record was to demonstrate that it was basically sound and practical. Although the Governing Commission was more cumbersome than a single governor would have been, it had the advantage of being sufficiently representative to assure the inhabitants that no single point of view would prevail unchecked. It is unfortunate, however, that the membership was not made more neutral from the beginning. It would also have been desirable to give the Saarlanders a stronger voice in their own government and to establish more cordial relations with the existing body of civil servants at the outset. Still, the blackest cloud that overshadowed the League regime was not the character of the Commission but the Saarlanders' intense and uncompromising opposition to the basic decision to separate the Saar from Germany, an issue that was to be a constant irritant in European affairs until the Saarlanders were finally able, fifteen years later, to vote themselves back to the fatherland.

DANZIG

Danzig was another example of placing an international "hot potato" under the protection of an "autonomous" regime responsible to an international organization, the League, rather than allowing it to be absorbed by any single claimant power. Danzig had been a bustling trading center, of predominantly German population, with special independent privileges, since its establishment by the Teutonic Knights in 1308. Even when it was officially under Polish suzerainty (1557–1793), it was self-governing and lost its freedom only during the two relatively brief periods under Prussian rule (1793–1807 and 1814 to World War I).

At the Paris Peace Conference, Poland, supported by France, wanted to absorb the city altogether, while the Germans naturally wanted to keep it but were willing at the same time to make it a free port in which Poland would be given certain privileges. Woodrow Wilson and Lloyd George finally prevailed on the French and Poles to accept a compromise making Danzig a free city, protected by the League, with special economic concessions to Poland.

Administrative Framework

The League's responsibilities, as set forth in the Versailles Treaty, the Danzig Poland Treaty of November 1920 and the Danzig Constitution of May 1922, were to protect and guarantee the freedom of the city through the agency of a resident High Commissioner who was to keep a watchful eye on the observance of Danzig's constitution, mediate differences which might arise between Danzig and Poland, and provide for the city's defense through the use of Polish forces. The constitution could not be altered without the League's consent.

Danzig was authorized to frame its own constitution through its elected representatives in agreement with the League High Commissioner, provide protection for its minorities (largely Polish) similar to that set forth in the minority treaties, and contract foreign loans after consulting the Polish Government and the High Commissioner. In 1925 the League Council also granted individual Danzig citizens the right to submit petitions to the High Commissioner who then could decide whether or not to transmit them to the League — a right which many anti-Nazis took advantage of during the thirties.

Poland was to provide military forces to defend the city as called for by the High Commissioner; conduct Danzig's foreign relations subject to consultation with the Danzig Senate before concluding treaties and subject to a veto by the High Commissioner of all treaties incompatible with Danzig's autonomous position; include the city within Poland's customs area; enjoy free use of the Danzig port; control the Vistula and railway system as well as postal, telegraphic and telephonic communications between the port and Poland; and improve waterway, dock and harbor facilities.

Danzig was a unique political animal with four different organizational heads. The League Council exercised the League's authority with respect to the city and appointed the High Commissioner. Danzig's own government consisted of an Assembly (Volkstag) of 120 representatives, elected by universal adult suffrage, and a Senate of 22, elected by the Assembly, which acted as a cabinet and whose President was the unofficial head of state. Poland was represented in Danzig by a Commissioner and a host of lesser officials. Finally a joint Harbor and Waterways Board (five Poles and five Danzigers with the President appointed by both parties or the League Council) was established to administer the port.

Conclusions

As in most other instances of international administration, Danzig was placed under League protection because the balance of power which controlled the decision was such that the territory could not have been granted outright to any single claimant state. Because of Danzig's ancient traditions of relative autonomy, however, its enforced separation from Germany was not as unpopular with the inhabitants as in the case of the Saar, but the special privileges granted to and assumed by Poland tended to force the Danzigers into the arms of the Reich. As for the relationship between the League and Danzig, a far greater degree of self-rule was granted than had been given the Saar with the result that the climate of opinion tended to be more democratic. The High Commissioner device was also a simpler less cumbersome instrument of supervision than was the Saar Governing Commission, and the Commissioner was given ample legal authority to protect Danzig's freedom. Unfortunately, however, the right of appeal from the Commissioner to the League encouraged the parties to beat a wide and well-trod path to Geneva until, in 1925, the Council altered its procedure somewhat in order to reduce the volume of appeals. Another difficulty was the conflict of jurisdiction among the four supervisory authorities. On the whole, however, the administrative structure proved to be sound; it was the fundamental political foundation that was shaky.

Minorities

Wherever there has been an island of Germans in a sea of Frenchmen, Catholics in a sea of Protestants, or some other minority surrounded by a dominant majority, there has invariably been friction, its seriousness depending on the relative tolerance of the peoples involved. Over the centuries this problem has given rise to considerable international conflict, especially when a minority has been supported by another state. Long before World War I a substantial number of experiments in international intervention — some less innocent than others — were attempted for the avowed purpose of protecting such minorities. The Catholic Church has always claimed a right of supervision over its flock in all countries, and the concept of international supervision of minority rights developed largely in connection with the negotiation of treaties in Eastern Europe and Turkey, from the seventeenth century on, pledging states which were absorbing new territories to respect the religious persuasions of the inhabitants.[11] Protection of economic and political rights followed in the wake of these developments. Although this protection seldom went beyond treaty pledges, there were a few more ambitious efforts such as the 1903 intervention by the European powers in Turkey to compel the Sultan to nominate a Christian inspector-general and two civil agents (Russian and Austrian) to help protect persecuted Christians in Macedonia.

Major immediate factors which led to the League-supervised system of minority treaties were Woodrow Wilson's emphasis on the doctrine of national self-determination; the campaign of the Czechs, Poles and other ethnic groups for national independence; the Bolshevik nationality policies; the efforts of various private groups, particularly Jewish, to gain protection for their constituents; and intense dissatisfaction rising out of some of the Paris territorial settlements, particularly German resentment regarding the Polish Corridor, Silesia and the Sudeten Germans included in Czechoslovakia. At the same time, opposition to international supervision came from the East European states that were compelled to sign minority agreements, from many Western leaders who were accustomed to relatively mild minority problems, and particularly from France, whose government gave increasing support to her Balkan neighbors whose good will she valued for security reasons.

MINORITY TREATIES

Although Wilson had originally urged a clause in the Covenant guaranteeing religious freedom, it was finally jettisoned to forestall acceptance of the Japanese-sponsored proposal seeking racial equality which was firmly opposed by the Australians, Americans and others. Nor was there any significant willingness on the part of the designers of the Covenant to apply to themselves the kind of international minorities supervision which they wanted to impose on the Balkan states. Thus the Covenant, as finally approved, contained no mention of the minorities problem.

Instead, the League minorities system was established in accordance with a series of separate agreements which included: (1) five special

[11] C. A. Macartney, *National States and National Minorities* (New York and London: Oxford University Press, 1934), Chap. V.

Minority Treaties between the Principal Allied and Associated Powers and Czechoslovakia, Greece, Poland, Rumania and Yugoslavia; (2) four special chapters inserted in the Treaties of Peace for Austria, Bulgaria, Hungary and Turkey; (3) five Declarations by Albania, Estonia, Finland, Latvia and Lithuania on or after their admission to the League; and (4) two special Conventions — the German-Polish Convention on Upper Silesia and the Convention for the Nemel Territory.

The general rights which were guaranteed included: nationality, life, personal liberty, freedom of worship, equality before the law, equality in civil and political rights, equality of treatment and security in law and in fact, and rights to the use of the minority language. There was to be no discrimination in admission to public employments, functions, honors, or the exercise of professions and industries. Minorities were entitled to maintain and control private charitable, religious, social and educational institutions. They were also assured an equitable share of public funds for educational, religious or charitable purposes. Certain special rights were also granted to minorities in special circumstances such as the Jewish minorities in Greece, Poland and Rumania; the Valachs of Pindus in Greece; the non-Greek monastic communities of Mount Athos; the Moslem minorities in Albania, Greece and Yugoslavia; the Czeckler and Saxon communities in Transylvania; and the Ruthene territory south of the Carpathians in Czechoslovakia.

Finally, all the agreements provided for appeal to the League as the guarantor of these rights. (1) The rights could not be altered without the consent of a majority of the League Council. (2) Any Council member was entitled to bring to the attention of that body any infraction, or danger of infraction, of any of these rights, and the Council was authorized to take such action and give such direction as it might deem proper and effective. (3) Disputes as to law or fact should, if a party demanded, go to the Permanent Court of International Justice whose decision would be final.

SILESIAN EXPERIMENT

Although the Allies had originally decided at Paris to give all of Upper Silesia to their political protégé, Poland, anguished German protests, calling attention to the fact that the overwhelming majority of the population concerned was German in culture and loyalty, persuaded the Council of Four to provide for a plebiscite. The result of the vote, held on March 20, 1921, was a total of 706,000 for Germany and 479,000 for Poland. The pro-Polish French then argued that the division should be made according to the votes in each municipality, rather than treating the total area as a single unit, and in a manner least disturbing to the industrial organization of the area, i.e., giving the important Silesian coal basin to Poland as the foundation for her industrial development. When Britain was equally insistent, however, that the territory should be awarded as a whole, it was decided to transfer the matter to the crowded agenda of the League Council. The final solution, approved by the Council in October 1921, was to favor the French thesis by dividing the territory into German and Polish segments, more or less according to the municipal balloting, and to recommend that Germany and Poland negotiate an agreement to regulate the necessary adjustment, including the protection of the respective minorities, during a fifteen-year transitional period.

The German-Polish convention, which was signed at Geneva on May 15, 1922, provided for the protection of the rights already incorporated in the Polish Minority Treaty with the exception of the nationality article. At the same time this agreement was the most detailed of all the minority arrangements with its six parts divided into 606 articles. Petitions dealing with important grievances against basic provisions of the Convention could go directly to the League Council. All others were to pass through a series of hierarchical sieves: (1) initial complaint to appropriate administrative officials in the first instance; (2) appeal to either of the two Minorities Offices established in the German and Polish areas respectively; (3) appeal to the President of the Upper Silesian Mixed Commission (a body, composed of a Polish member, German member, and a President of another nationality appointed by the League Council, responsible for controlling implementation of the entire Convention); and (4) final appeal to the League Council. All of these opinions were legally no more than recommendations and could not bind the parties to compliance.

LEAGUE STRUCTURE

Although the Council had been designated officially as the League's central stage for dealing with minority problems, most of the bickering was kept in the wings, safely out of general sight and hearing, in "Committees of Three." League members, not regularly represented on the Council, were invited to send representatives to participate in discussions affecting their minorities, and decisions were made by unanimous vote including these specially invited representatives.

The vital centers of the system were the "Committees of Three" (or five in exceptional cases after 1929) composed of the Council President and two (or four) members not connected with the matter under discussion. One such body was appointed for each case that arose. Meetings were held during the sessions of the Council until, in the late year of 1939, they were transferred to the periods between Council sessions to escape the atmosphere of hectic conflict so characteristic of those sessions. These meetings were kept as confidential and informal as possible, with no minutes recorded, in order to foster a conciliatory climate. The most far-reaching proposal for strengthening this structure was that first voiced by Gilbert Murray in 1921: to create a permanent minorities commission (partially inspired by the Permanent Mandates Commission) with greater expertness, independence, time, continuity and staff resources than were characteristic of the Committees of Three. But this plan died after a thorough Council investigation in 1929.

LEAGUE AUTHORITY

Although the minority agreements provided that complaints would be aired by a Council member's calling that body's attention to an infraction of the regulations, it soon became obvious that the League's limited authority scarcely provided the platform for such a bold frontal attack. Few states were anxious to assume the unpopular and delicate role of public prosecutor. Caution, as the better part of the League's valor, led, therefore, to the development of a less direct approach up a series of gradual and tactful steps: (1) A petition could be submitted to the Council by any state or minority individual or group. (2) The Secretary-General decided the receivability of such a petition in accordance with criteria established by the Council in 1923:

> They must not emanate from anonymous or unauthenticated sources; they must not be couched in violent language; they must have in view the protection of minorities in accordance with the Treaties; they must not be submitted in the form of a request for the severance of political relations between a minority and the State; and they must contain information or refer to facts which have not recently been the subject of another petition.[12]

(3) If accepted, the petition was then referred to the accused state with the request that it reply within three weeks as to whether it intended to express any observations (to be submitted within two months). (4) Governmental comments and the petition were then transmitted to the Council members for their information. (5) At the same time, a Committee of Three was formed to deal with the question. These bodies were authorized by the Council in 1920 for the primary purpose of deciding whether or not a Council member should raise the question on the floor of the Council itself. As time went on, however, the Committees of Three handled most of the issues without ever resorting to direct Council consideration. Their duties included examining the information available, requesting further information, negotiating a settlement with the parties involved (usually through the Secretariat Minorities Section), and recommending a final disposition of the case. (6) Only rarely would the petition go on to the Council.

CONCLUSIONS

One can best understand the League's minority organization by realizing that the system was established by the great powers not on a universal

---

[12] League of Nations, *Ten Years of World Cooperation* (Geneva: League Secretariat, 1930), p. 367.

scale but on a very limited scale as a gesture to quiet the fears of those minorities, mainly Jewish and German, who felt particularly vulnerable to persecution, especially in Poland, Rumania and Czechoslovakia. The League system bore an obvious family resemblance to the pre-World War I European interventions in behalf of various minorities. It also represented a substantial step in the direction of stronger international supervision since it provided, unlike the previous efforts, a permanent organization prepared to consider complaints submitted at any time from any source regarding a wide geographical area. But the League's authority to take action was as weak as it was in most other fields. It had no power to initiate an investigation, dispatch an inspection mission, issue binding orders, or wield enforcement sanctions. It was compelled from the beginning, therefore, to pin its hopes to negotiation rather than compulsion. Within these cramped boundaries, it was capable of exerting a mild restraining influence but little more.

Suggestions for Further Reading

Books

de Azcarate, P., *League of Nations and National Minorities* (Washington: Carnegie Endowment for International Peace, 1945).

Bentwich, Norman, *The Mandates System* (London: Longmans, Green and Co., 1930).

Florinsky, Michael T., *The Saar Struggle* (New York: The Macmillan Company, 1934).

Gerig, Benjamin, "Mandates and Colonies," *World Organization* (Washington: American Council on Public Affairs, 1942).

——, *The Open Door and the Mandates System* (London: G. Allen & Unwin, Ltd., 1930).

Gilchrist, Huntington, "Dependent Peoples and Mandates," *Pioneers in World Order* (New York: Columbia University Press, 1944).

Hailey, Lord, *An African Survey: A Study of Problems Arising in Africa South of the Sahara* (London and New York: Oxford University Press, 1938).

Hall, H. Duncan, *Mandates, Dependencies, and Trusteeship* (Washington: Carnegie Endowment for International Peace, 1948).

Kaeckenbeeck, Georges, *The International Experiment of Upper Silesia* (London and New York: Oxford University Press, 1942).

Leonhardt, Hans Leo, *Nazi Conquest of Danzig* (Chicago: University of Chicago Press, 1942).

Macartney, C. A., *National States and National Minorities* (London and New York: Oxford University Press, 1934).

Mason, John Brown, *The Danzig Dilemma* (Stanford: Stanford University Press, 1946).

Reid, Helen Dwight, "Danzig," *World Organization* (Washington: American Council on Public Affairs, 1942).

Robinson, Jacob, "Minorities," *World Organization* (Washington: American Council on Public Affairs, 1942).

Russell, Frank M., *The Saar: Battleground and Pawn* (Stanford: Stanford University Press, 1951).

Stone, Julius, *International Guarantees of Minority Rights* (London and New York: Oxford University Press, 1932).

Wambaugh, Sarah, *The Saar Plebiscite* (Cambridge: Harvard University Press, 1940).

Wright, Quincy, *Mandates Under the League of Nations* (Chicago: University of Chicago Press, 1930).

Documents

League of Nations, Permanent Mandates Commission, *Minutes.*

————, *Ten Years of World Cooperation* (Geneva: League Secretariat, 1930).

————, *The Mandates System: Origins, Principles, Application* (Geneva: League Secretariat, 1945).

Trusteeship and Non-Self-Governing

Peoples — UN

SINCE 1946, United Nations agents have traveled by every manner of conveyance through such exotic and far-flung lands as Eritrea, Tanganyika and Western Samoa, looking, questioning, listening and recommending in order to help the peoples of those territories improve their lot. This is dramatic evidence of the way in which the United Nations has continued and strengthened the League's mandates system and other forms of international supervision of special areas and groups. The United Nations organizations concerned with these matters are analyzed below in two sections: (1) trusteeship and non-self-governing territories systems and (2) supervision of special areas.

While, in one sense, each of these programs goes its own way with some degree of independence, they are also brothers under the skin. They are all efforts to bring to bear the collective views of the United Nations, in which strictly national interests tend to balance each other, upon the administration of certain controversial areas. Moreover, although the San Francisco Conference was separated from the Paris Peace Conference by twenty-six years, the forces which led to the surrender of these areas to international surveillance were approximately the same in both instances. International supervision has long proved a convenient device for escaping the dilemma of deciding how to divide the pie of war booty among several jealous powers. Increasingly vigorous nationalist movements in the dependent territories also find international supervision a useful lever to loosen the bonds of empire. Finally, various humanitarian interests think of international tutelage as the best school to prepare colonies for self-rule.

Trusteeship and Non-Self-Governing Territories

The most striking fact about the United Nations Charter provisions affecting the world's 200 million dependent peoples is not how new those provisions are, but rather how old they are. The League mandates system may be dead, legally, but in its new United Nations clothes, it is more alive than ever. The only significant alterations that give the Charter provisions a "new look" are: (1) a notable strengthening, in Charter Chapter 11, of the long familiar but conveniently vague concept of a nation's international accountability for the welfare of *all* its dependent peoples, and (2) the granting of new powers (inspection, compulsory questionnaire, and direct receipt of petitions, oral as well as written) to the Trusteeship Council (heir to the Permanent Mandates Commission).

NATIONAL PRESSURES

In the vanguard of the anti-colonial battalion during the planning stage stood the United States, congenitally opposed to imperialism though possessed of a solid little empire of its own. And, because of its tremendous influence and strong views on the subject, it became the dominant architect of the United Nations Charter provisions on non-self-governing peoples. The key to United States thinking tended to be its experience with the Philippines, which Secretary of State Cordell Hull liked to cite as his model.[1] Independence was the ultimate, inevitable and only moral goal. United States zeal for unshackling the colonials was tempered, however, by several gnawing concerns of immediate self-interest: chiefly an emotional and strategic interest in the Japanese Pacific islands so dearly won during World War II, as well as an awareness that, as Secretary Hull put it, "we could not alienate . . . [our European allies] in the Orient and expect to work with them in Europe." [2]

Among individuals and private groups in the United States interested in dependent peoples, sentiment during the war was overwhelmingly in favor of a continuation of some form of international trusteeship system with much stronger supervision of all national colonies as well as mandated territories.[3] The first official governmental declaration which touched on this subject was the Atlantic Charter which pledged that the United Nations

> seek no aggrandizement, territorial or other; . . . they desire to see no territorial changes that do not accord with the freely expressed wishes of the peoples concerned; . . . they respect the rights of all peoples to choose the form of government under which they will live. . . .[4]

Surprising as it may seem, it was Winston Churchill, that intrepid Horatius at the bridge of empire, who drafted these words. It seems obvious, how-

---

[1] Cordell Hull, *The Memoirs of Cordell Hull* (New York: Macmillan, 1948), Vol. 2, pp. 1478, 1601.

[2] *Ibid.*, p. 1599. Used by permission of The Macmillan Company.

[3] For representative views see bibliography at end of chapter.

[4] See discussion of circumstances surrounding the drafting of the Atlantic Charter, Sumner Welles, *Where Are We Heading?* (New York: Harper, 1946), pp. 6–18; Winston Churchill, *The Grand Alliance* (Boston: Houghton Mifflin, 1950), pp. 433–444.

ever, that, while he was sincere in seeking no further aggrandizement, he had no intention of holding a plebiscite throughout the British colonies but was aiming this propaganda volley primarily at the European nations that had been subjugated by the Axis powers.

The Department of State, under the leadership of Cordell Hull and Sumner Welles, was determined, in the spirit of liberal United States opinion, to enlarge on the Atlantic Charter commitment as a means of reforming the whole colonial structure. Consequently the State Department began, towards the end of 1942 and the beginning of 1943, by proposing a trusteeship system that would include all colonial territories but soon decided, for what Secretary Hull chose to call "obvious reasons of political feasibility," [5] that it should be restricted to Axis dependencies and former League mandated territories. The State Department was warmly supported by President Roosevelt, who looked to the trusteeship device as a convenient lever to hasten the liquidation of colonialism in such territories as Indo-China, Korea and Hong Kong.[6]

This early thinking, which Hull first discussed in detail with Anthony Eden, in March 1943, reflected the then current emphasis on the regional approach by proposing that trust territories be administered by states, or groups of states, under the supervision of a Regional Council which in turn would be responsible to a universal Council.[7] Both Councils, unlike the League machinery, were to be empowered to inspect territories and receive petitions directly. The earlier effort to apply trusteeship to all dependent peoples now took the form of a broad catechism, foreshadowing the present Chapter 11 of the United Nations Charter, whereby all colonial powers would promise their non-self-governing populations to further their political, economic, social and educational advancement, including the fixing of "dates upon which the colonial peoples would be accorded the status of full independence." [8] To assist in the implementation of these objectives, advisory regional commissions were to be established following the pattern of the much respected Anglo-American Caribbean Commission created in March 1942.

United States Plans Develop

By August 1943, Anthony Eden and his Government had had time to chew on the United States plan, and Eden told Hull frankly that he found it decidedly difficult to digest. While the United States had arrived at its policy via the Philippines, the British had been traveling a different road which had as its ideal goal the Commonwealth relationship of "partnership" rather than independence. But Hull was convinced that the British were wrong and the sooner they saw the light the better. As he describes it,

---

[5] Hull, op. cit., Vol. 2, p. 1638.   [6] Ibid., pp. 1305, 1596.
[7] Ibid., pp. 1235–1236; also Postwar Foreign Policy Preparation, 1939–1945, Department of State Publication 3580 (Washington: Government Printing Office, 1950), pp. 481–482.
[8] Hull, op. cit., Vol. 2, p. 1235.

"Digging my toes in for a lengthy struggle, I brought it up again and again . . . in the months that followed." [9]

Just prior to the Dumbarton Oaks Conference, the State Department's plan [10] had been further developed to include a provision that the United Nations should inherit not only the legal authority of the League in mandate matters but also the authority of the World War I Principal Allied and Associated Powers, primarily to be able to revise the assignment of mandated territories. By that time, the State Department also favored placing ultimate supervisory authority over the trusteeship system in the hands of a "general assembly" to be exercised through a "trusteeship council" composed of "persons of special competence" designated (a) one each by states administering trust territories as continuing members and (b) one each by an equal number of other states named periodically by the assembly. The administering authority might be an "international administration" as well as a state. Regional commissions were now mentioned only as advisory bodies to be created by the assembly.

At this stage, however, the United States Joint Chiefs of Staff, cheered on by Secretary of the Navy James Forrestal, Secretary of the Army Henry Stimson and certain elements of Congress, especially the House Committee on Naval Affairs, insisted that State's trusteeship plan not be discussed at Dumbarton Oaks.[11] These interests were opposed to losing control of strategic Japanese Pacific islands and wanted no dispute over such postwar territorial settlements to jeopardize wartime cooperation with their allies. Although Hull agreed to withhold the trusteeship question, the decision caused him "keen disappointment" and was a thorn in the side of the United States government up to the very eve of the San Francisco Conference.

The first formal agreement among the Big Three on trusteeship did not come until the Yalta Conference, February 1945. When Secretary of State Edward Stettinius began, however, to explain the United States proposal at Yalta, Winston Churchill interrupted with an explosive protest against "the fumbling fingers of forty or fifty nations prying into the life's existence of the British Empire." [12] Stettinius hastily reassured him that the plan was intended to apply primarily to League mandates and Axis territories. But President Roosevelt was inclined to press the British hard on this issue. He had previously told Churchill,

> Winston, this is something which you are just not able to understand. You have 400 years of acquisitive instinct in your blood. . . . A new period has opened in the world's history, and you will have to adjust yourself to it.[13]

[9] Ibid., p. 1238.

[10] Postwar Foreign Policy Preparation . . . , pp. 606–607.

[11] Walter Millis, ed., The Forrestal Diaries (New York: Viking, 1951), pp. 28, 33, 36–38, 44–46, 130–132, 213–216, 233–234; Henry L. Stimson and McGeorge Bundy, On Active Service — In Peace and War (New York: Harper, 1947), pp. 599–605.

[12] Edward R. Stettinius, Jr., Roosevelt and the Russians (New York: Doubleday, 1949), p. 236.

[13] Ibid., p. 237.

Finally Churchill as well as Stalin agreed that the permanent members of the Security Council should consult on the trusteeship question prior to the San Francisco Conference.

On April 10, 1945, just fifteen days before the San Francisco Conference was to convene, President Roosevelt approved a compromise plan whereby the Japanese Pacific islands, as well as other territories, could be administered as "strategic trusts" under the supervision, not of the General Assembly and Trusteeship Council but, of the Security Council, where the United States would be protected by the veto. Two days later President Roosevelt died before discussing the details of this solution with the departments concerned, and the compromise was not sealed by President Truman until April 18, seven days before the Conference began. At that late date there was time for only a brief and partial exchange of views among the Big Five, as pledged at Yalta. Finally, United States personnel, under the able direction of Commander Harold Stassen, drafted, in collaboration with other delegations, especially those of the United Kingdom, U.S.S.R., China and France, a working paper which was adopted as the basis for the Conference negotiations which resulted in Chapters 11, 12 and 13 of the Charter.

Other Anti-Colonial Views

The second most influential anti-colonial power was the Soviet Union, although it was never consulted by the United States as intimately or as extensively as the British. The Russians seem to have been late in recognizing the usefulness of the trusteeship concept as an instrument to further their own special objectives. They indicated no extraordinary interest in the United States trusteeship proposals at Yalta and presented no plan of their own at the beginning of the San Francisco Conference as did the United States, the United Kingdom and France, but tended to adopt the United States pattern. It was only during the ensuing debates at San Francisco and at the later peace treaty conferences that the Russians developed the attitudes which have motivated their actions in this field ever since: that the trusteeship device could be used to undermine already shaky colonial edifices, and, paradoxically enough, that it could also justify extending Soviet control into new territories, notably Tripolitania.[14]

The anti-colonial forces also received vigorous support from Australia and New Zealand, both of which controlled dependent areas. These states were, at the time of the United Nations' birth, under political administrations dominated by labor parties which tended to take the same liberal attitude on colonial questions as their close friends, the British Labor Party. This policy was in marked contrast to the rigidly annexationist views of Australia's Hughes and New Zealand's Massey at Paris in 1919. Although these nations did not believe that independence was the only ideal goal, they urged that extensive and explicit international accountability for

[14] Hull, op. cit., Vol. 2, p. 1466; James Byrnes, Speaking Frankly (New York: Harper, 1947), pp. 94, 96, 220–221.

all dependent peoples be recognized by the colonial powers and that colonial regimes be exposed to public scrutiny through regular and compulsory reporting to an expert advisory body empowered to inspect all dependent territories.[15]

The Chinese Nationalist delegation was motivated by both its age-old resentment against colonial exploitation and its desire to strengthen its bonds with other Asian nationalist forces. China used the San Francisco Conference to strike telling blows for the objective of independence for all dependent territories and for the granting of strong authority, including sanctions, to an international supervisory body. Less influential than China, but no less impatient with imperialism, were those smaller nations that at some period in their history had learned to hate colonialism. These included the more liberal Latin American states, such as Mexico; certain Arab states, especially Egypt; and former mandated territories that had gained their freedom: Iraq, Lebanon and Syria.

Conservative Forces

The United Kingdom was second only to the United States in the degree of influence it exerted upon the development of the trusteeship system. And it used that influence primarily to restrict the supervisory role of the United Nations and to conserve its own freedom of action as much as it could in the face of American pressure. This policy was charted mainly by Colonel Oliver Stanley, Secretary of State for the Colonies, under the watchful eye of Winston Churchill who seems to have taken an even more jaundiced view of international supervision than his Secretary for Foreign Affairs, Anthony Eden. The Churchill–Stanley thesis was considerably more conservative than that advocated by the Labor Party in spite of the fact that certain Labor leaders, including Clement Attlee, Ernest Bevin and Herbert Morrison were members of the War Cabinet. As early as 1940, the Labor Party had insisted that, "In the . . . Colonies . . . the interests of the native population should be paramount and should be safeguarded through an extension and strengthening of the mandate system. . . ."[16]

A fundamental factor in Churchill's thinking was his concern that what was involved was nothing less than the "life's existence of the British Empire," [17] already referred to. Viscount Cranborne put it more plainly as he explained the United Nations Charter to Parliament in June 1945.

> In the earlier stages of this war . . . it was only the existence of our African Colonial Empire, the essential materials which we could draw from it, and

[15] See various Australian and New Zealander papers presented at Institute of Pacific Relations Conference, Mont Tremblant, Quebec, 1942, and Hot Springs, Virginia, 1945; K. H. Bailey, "Dependent Areas of the Pacific: An Australian View," *Foreign Affairs*, Vol. 24, No. 3 (April 1946), pp. 494–512.

[16] British Labour Party, *Labour's Aims in War and Peace* (London: Lincolns-Prager, 1940), p. 92; also see, by the same author, *The Colonies* (London: British Labour Party, 1943) and *The Labour Party's Postwar Policy for the African and Pacific Colonies* (London: British Labour Party, 1943).

[17] Stettinius, *op. cit.*, p. 236.

the reinforcement route to the Middle East across the heart of Africa — it was only these which saved us from defeat. . . . Could we really contemplate . . . the destruction of this machine or its separation into its component parts? [18]

On the eve of the San Francisco Conference, the Churchill–Stanley doctrine rested on the following propositions: (1) self-government for British dependencies should develop primarily *within the Commonwealth;* (2) administration of such territories should be the sole responsibility of Great Britain; (3) international activity should be limited to a proliferation of advisory regional commissions to be concerned with only economic and social, not political, progress; (4) the mandate idea was an outmoded relic of the "old theory of Colonial trusteeship" superseded by "the modern conception of Colonial partnership," [19] an attitude which led at least two competent observers to believe that the British were prepared to abolish the mandate system altogether;[20] and (5) consequently there should be no distinction between mandated territories and all other dependencies, a view which the United States State Department considered "retrogressive." [21] Under the glare of United States displeasure, however, British resistance tended to melt until the United Kingdom accepted a trusteeship system very much along the lines proposed by the United States. This was not such a drastic retreat as it might seem at first glance, however. The trusteeship system would apply to an insignificant proportion of British dependencies. The British were also successful in preventing Chapter 11, which applies to all non-self-governing peoples, from being made as strong a force as many delegations, including the Australians and New Zealanders, wanted to make it.

The French were not actively consulted until San Francisco and then cast a far smaller shadow over the proceedings than they had at Paris in 1919. Since they were committed to the ideal of the French Union, which anticipated integration of dependencies with the mother country, rather than association as in the British Commonwealth, and because of their whole colonial tradition, the French were even less willing than the British to encourage international intervention. Consequently, when they submitted a draft at the beginning of the San Francisco Conference, they included no mention of self-government as an objective, no provision for the voluntary placement of dependencies under the trusteeship system, and no provision for international inspection or direct receipt of petitions.[22]

[18] Louise W. Holborn, *War and Peace Aims of the United Nations* (Boston: World Peace Foundation, 1948), p. 577.

[19] *Ibid.*, p. 556, address by Colonel Stanley before Foreign Policy Association, New York, January 19, 1945; also *ibid.*, pp. 401–404, Colonel Stanley's address to Conservative Association, Oxford, March 5, 1943.

[20] See memorandum transmitted by Leo Pasvolsky to Edward Stettinius, January 23, 1945, *Postwar Foreign Policy Preparation* . . . , pp. 661–663; also Bailey, *op. cit.,* pp. 498–499.

[21] *Ibid.*, Pasvolsky memorandum, p. 662.

[22] UNCIO, III, pp. 604–606.

Even less influential than the French, but fishing in the same pro-colonial stream, were the Netherlands, Belgium and South Africa.

TRUSTEESHIP SYSTEM

Under the impact of these national interests, there was born at San Francisco a trusteeship system whose basic features were recorded in Chapters 12 and 13 of the United Nations Charter. The closely related Chapter 11 regarding all non-self-governing territories is discussed at the end of this section.

Structure

General Supervisory Bodies. A major departure from the League is that the over-all reins of the trusteeship system were placed in the hands of the General Assembly rather than the Security Council, except for "strategic trusts," which are under the Council. While anti-imperialist states tended to welcome this change, the United Kingdom suggested that all trust-administering states and the trusteeship commission report to the Economic and Social Council on non-security matters and to the Security Council on security questions.[23] Finally, the United States plan was adopted and incorporated in Article 85 of the Charter:

> 1. The functions of the United Nations with regard to trusteeship agreements for all areas not designated as strategic, including the approval of the terms of the trusteeship agreements and of their alteration or amendment, shall be exercised by the General Assembly.
> 2. The Trusteeship Council, operating under the authority of the General Assembly, shall assist the General Assembly in carrying out these functions.

While this language seems to tie the Trusteeship Council more closely to the Assembly's apron strings than is the case with the Economic and Social Council, both Councils, in practice, have acted with about equal freedom. Since the League Assembly, though lacking explicit constitutional authority, boldly assumed the right to debate mandate questions, the role assigned the General Assembly is not wholly new but a further development of the League pattern. The fundamental importance of this change is that it is part of an unmistakable trend, the wisdom of which is fiercely debated, towards an ever broader, freer and more anti-colonial scrutiny of trusteeship problems.

The Soviet Union was a willing partner in the United States move to place strategic trusts under the Security Council since the Russians could exert greater influence in the Council than the Assembly. To strengthen the Council's control, the Russians added to the United States' plan a provision that strategic trusts be designated only "on recommendation of the Security Council." [24] The United Kingdom very persuasively opposed

23 *Ibid.,* p. 610.
24 *Ibid.,* p. 619.

the United States view on three grounds: (1) it jeopardized the effective handling of economic and social problems in the strategic areas; (2) it would be difficult "to draw a hard and fast line separating strategic from non-strategic areas"; and (3) great power control of security functions within trust areas could be assured just as effectively by placing those functions, rather than whole geographic areas, under the Security Council's supervision.[25] Australia proposed that administering powers need not report to the United Nations on bases or limited areas which the Assembly, on Security Council recommendation, might declare "of special importance for the maintenance of international peace and security." [26]

The smaller anti-colonial states were understandably opposed to having certain strategic trust territories shrouded in secrecy behind the veto curtain. But, since the United States military-congressional interests were adamant, the opposition, headed by Egypt, concentrated on compelling the Security Council to use the Trusteeship Council to deal with all non-security matters in strategic trust territories. The United States finally retreated to the extent of accepting the language now found in Article 83:

1. All functions of the United Nations relating to strategic areas, including the approval of the terms of the trusteeship agreements and of their alteration or amendment, shall be exercised by the Security Council.

2. The basic objectives set forth in Article 76 [which govern all normal trust territories] shall be applicable to the people of each strategic area.

3. The Security Council shall, subject to the provisions of the trusteeship agreements and without prejudice to security considerations, avail itself of the assistance of the Trusteeship Council to perform those functions of the United Nations under the trusteeship system relating to political, economic, social, and educational matters in the strategic areas.

The British view also left its mark in the form of Article 84:

It shall be the duty of the administering authority to ensure that the trust territory shall play its part in the maintenance of international peace and security. To this end the administering authority may make use of volunteer forces, facilities, and assistance from the trust territory in carrying out the obligations towards the Security Council undertaken in this regard by the administering authority, as well as for local defense and the maintenance of law and order within the trust territory.

Some of the anti-colonial forces, led by Egypt, wanted to subject any use of armed force in the trust territories to "the control of the Security Council," but the amendment was defeated.[27]

The striking difference between the role of the Security Council and that of the League Council in trusteeship matters is that the former is not responsible for supervising the entire trusteeship system, but merely security aspects affecting the maintenance of peace. The Council may exer-

25 *Ibid.*, pp. 612–613.
26 *Ibid.*, p. 549.
27 UNCIO, X, p. 488.

cise this limited authority with regard to either non-strategic trusts, in accordance with the Council's general security responsibilities, or strategic trusts. Over the latter territories the permanent members can wield a veto on *all* questions, including economic and social matters, on the assumption that they are all related to international security. During the United States Senate hearings on the Charter, Senator Tom Connally revealed the United States attitude in plain Texan language:

> We signed the Charter on the theory that our interests in the Pacific and elsewhere were amply protected. . . . When we do agree that . . . [a strategic area] go under trusteeship, we have the right to stipulate the terms . . . we keep the control in our hands.[28]

Trusteeship Council. The United States and United Kingdom began by thinking of the relationship of the Trusteeship Council to the over-all organization in terms of the League pattern, except that the United States wanted the Council placed under the Assembly rather than the Security Council. The anti-colonial climate prevailing at San Francisco, however, led the Conference to bestow upon the Trusteeship Council the same honorific title of "principal organ" that was granted the Assembly, Security Council and ECOSOC, although in all other respects it was left clearly subordinate to the Assembly.

Membership. United States planning regarding the Trusteeship Council's membership set a pattern which was significantly different from that of the League Mandates Commission. The members were to be "specially qualified" state representatives, rather than individual experts without formal governmental connections, and to be divided equally between administering and non-administering states. The most disturbing fly in the ointment was the Soviet Union's insistence that all permanent members of the Security Council, whether administering trust territories or not, be admitted to the charmed circle. The anti-colonial forces wanted the number of non-elected members to be balanced by an equal number of Assembly-elected members. The United States and pro-colonial countries, while bowing to the Soviet proposal, wanted a balance of administering and non-administering powers. The results of these maneuvers were incorporated in Charter Article 86:

> 1. The Trusteeship Council shall consist of the following Members of the United Nations:
> a. those Members administering trust territories;
> b. such of those Members mentioned by name in Article 23 [permanent members of the Security Council] as are not administering trust territories; and
> c. as many other Members elected for three-year terms by the General Assembly as may be necessary to ensure that the total number of members of the Trusteeship Council is equally divided between those Members of

---

[28] *Hearing before the Committee on Foreign Relations on the Charter of the United Nations . . . , July . . . 1945, U. S. Senate, 79th Congress, 1st Session,* pp. 315–316.

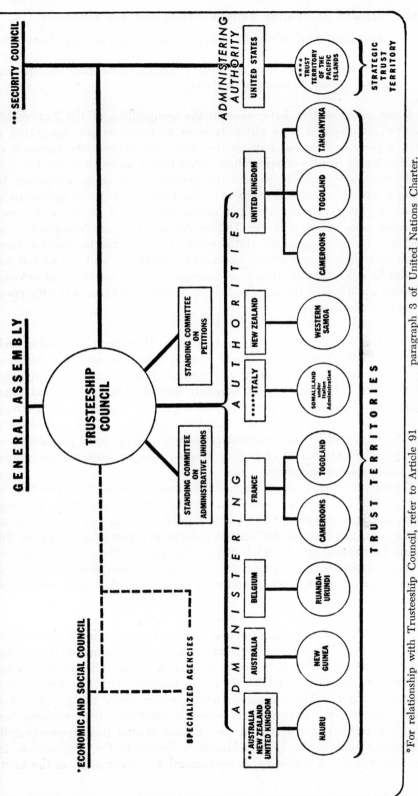

GENERAL ASSEMBLY

SECURITY COUNCIL

ECONOMIC AND SOCIAL COUNCIL

TRUSTEESHIP COUNCIL

SPECIALIZED AGENCIES

STANDING COMMITTEE ON ADMINISTRATIVE UNIONS

STANDING COMMITTEE ON PETITIONS

ADMINISTERING AUTHORITIES

ADMINISTERING AUTHORITY

UNITED STATES

**** TRUST TERRITORY OF THE PACIFIC ISLANDS

STRATEGIC TRUST TERRITORY

UNITED KINGDOM

CAMEROONS   TOGOLAND   TANGANYIKA

NEW ZEALAND

WESTERN SAMOA

*****ITALY

SOMALILAND under Italian Administration

FRANCE

CAMEROONS   TOGOLAND

BELGIUM

RUANDA-URUNDI

AUSTRALIA

NEW GUINEA

** AUSTRALIA NEW ZEALAND UNITED KINGDOM

NAURU

TRUST TERRITORIES

*For relationship with Trusteeship Council, refer to Article 91 of United States Charter.

**Australia exercises full powers of legislation, administration and jurisdiction on behalf of the three governments which jointly constitute the Administering Authority.

***For relationship with Trusteeship Council, refer to Article 83,

paragraph 3 of United Nations Charter.

****Marshalls, the Carolines, and the Marianas (Guam excepted).

*****Italy, as Administering Authority, is aided and advised by a three-member United Nations Advisory Council. Italy participates, without vote, in the deliberations of the Council. The Territory is to become an independent State in 1960.

the United Nations which administer trust territories and those which do not.

2. Each member of the Trusteeship Council shall designate one specially qualified person to represent it therein.

Some commentators have damned the composition of the Trusteeship Council as a retreat from virtue because its members are designated as state representatives, not individual experts, and because the nationals of administering powers comprise half rather than a minority of the Council. This view is excessively pessimistic, however, and needs tempering by several modifying considerations: (1) the League's emphasis on the independent experts always operated under the shadow of many informal national associations; (2) the United Nations Charter compromises by seeking "specially qualified" state representatives, who, in practice, have often been men of considerable specialized experience; and (3) all but one of the members of the Mandates Commission were nationals of colonial powers, while half of the members of the Trusteeship Council usually come from noncolonial states.

Voting, Meetings, Officers. As in the League Mandates Commission, each member of the Trusteeship Council was to have one vote, and decisions were to be made by a majority of the members present and voting. Regular sessions are held twice a year, normally beginning in January and June. Special sessions may be convoked at the request of a majority of the Council's members or of the General Assembly, Security Council or Economic and Social Council. The Trusteeship Council's officers are a president and vice-president elected at each June session, thus far chosen from among the administering members.

Contrary to the League Mandates Commission's habit of meeting in private, the Trusteeship Council and its subsidiary bodies normally hold their meetings in public. The Council publishes summary records of its discussions, the texts of the annual reports, governmental replies to the Council's queries, the texts of non-confidential petitions, the reports of visiting missions and other relevant documents. Consequently the general atmosphere is much more friendly to open discussion than under the League.

Secretariat. The Secretariat's able and influential watchdog in the trusteeship field is the Department of Trusteeship and Information from Non-Self-Governing Territories, presently headed by Assistant Secretary-General Victor Hoo and Principal Director Ralph Bunche. Although the number of trust territories has decreased from fourteen under the League to a modest eleven, the intensity and scope of international supervision has greatly expanded as reflected in the increase in staff from approximately ten professionals in the League Mandates Section to five professionals in the Office of the Assistant Secretary-General and thirty-eight in the Division of Trusteeship.[29] The Trusteeship Division is divided into five sections dealing with: trusteeship agreements, questionnaires and territorial reports, petitions, visits, and territorial research and analysis. As in most other aspects of United Nations work, the Secretariat is one of the most vital cogs, if not the main spring, of the trusteeship machinery. Look at any phase of the job — whether it be weighing the reliability of annual reports, prodding the administering states or roaming through jungles on visiting missions — and you will find the Secretariat staff hard at work and exerting a quiet but powerful influence.

Authority

Objectives. The framers of the trusteeship system staked out much more expansive, but less explicitly defined, objectives than in the case of the League mandates system. Strangely enough, this is attributable to two conflicting pressures. As pro-colonial powers, like the United Kingdom, became resigned to the fact that the tendency was to strengthen rather than weaken the mandates concept, they wanted the framework left as rubbery as possible so as to stretch it to fit their own interests. On the other hand, many anti-colonial powers, like the United States, also wanted flexibility so the trusteeship system and its objectives might grow to meet changing circumstances. Moreover, while the League Covenant provided for three types of mandates, each with its own distinctive set of objectives, there is now only one breed of trusteeship, with only a single set of objectives.

1) *Maintaining International Peace and Security.* In 1919 President Wilson and others could still dream of disarmament, and, in that spirit, mandatory powers were barred, with respect to "B" and "C" territories, from the "establishment of fortifications of military and naval bases" and "military training of the natives for other than police purposes and the defense of territory." Unfortunately virtue's reward was aggression. The Japanese not only armed their Pacific mandates and used them as bases for attack in World War II, but also benefited from the naked condition of the mandated territories in the hands of Australia and New Zealand (New Guinea, Nauru and Western Samoa).

The United States proposed that the first objective of the trusteeship system be "to further international peace and security" which became paragraph "a" of Article 76. The United States also initiated the provision for strategic areas contained in Articles 82 and 83 analyzed above. Australia tended to follow the United States thesis on this question, while the United Kingdom, as we saw above, distinguished between functions rather than areas and was largely responsible for Article 84 obligating administering authorities to ensure that their trust territories play their "part in the maintenance of international peace and security."

[29] UN Doc. A/1812.

2) *Political Advancement.* Although the United States began its trustee-ship planning by waving the banner of "independence," it had, by the time of the San Francisco Conference, compromised sufficiently with the pro-colonial forces to speak in more chastened terms of "political advance-ment" and "progressive development toward self-government." [30] It was the Soviet Union, China and other more radical anti-colonials that wanted "independence" specifically mentioned. The United Kingdom dragged its feet by modifying the term "self-government" with the qualifying phrase, "in forms appropriate to the varying circumstances of each territory." [31]

The final compromise was not to mention "independence" specifically in Chapter 11, dealing with all non-self-governing peoples, but to include it under the trusteeship system in Chapter 12. Thus Article 76(b) reads:

> . . . to promote the political . . . advancement of the inhabitants of the trust territories and their progressive development towards self-government or independence as may be appropriate to the particular circumstances of each territory and its peoples and the freely expressed wishes of the peoples concerned, and as may be provided by the terms of each trusteeship agree-ment. . . .

Under the League mandates system, independence and consideration of the "wishes" of the "communities" were specifically pledged only in the case of the "A" mandates. Neither independence nor self-government was mentioned in the case of "B" and "C" mandates.

3) *Economic and Social Advancement.* The major conflict in this area was between those countries, like the United Kingdom, that wanted this ob-jective left as vague and flexible as possible, and those like Australia, that wanted to transplant in the Charter some of the principles embedded in the League Covenant (freedom of conscience and religion, suppression of traffic in slaves, arms and liquor, etc.), as well as others. Finally, at the behest of the United States, a passage on "human rights" was added, and, at the request of the Soviet Union, "educational advancement" was added. Otherwise the details in the League Covenant were assumed by most of the framers to be implicit in the broader United Nations framework. As adopted, Article 76 (b) and (c) read:

> b. to promote the . . . economic, social, and educational advancement of the inhabitants. . . .
> c. to encourage respect for human rights and for fundamental freedoms for all without distinction as to race, sex, language, or religion, and to encourage recognition of the interdependence of the peoples of the world. . . .

Long a devout proponent, though not always a practitioner, of the "open door" principle as a fundamental tenet of the liberal creed of free trade, the United States began by advocating "nondiscriminatory treatment . . . with respect to the economic and other appropriate civil activities of the

[30] UNCIO, III, p. 599.
[31] *Ibid.*, p. 609.

nationals of all member states." [32] The United Kingdom was opposed to such an explicit and far-reaching commitment on the grounds that it perpetuated, in the case of "B" mandates, a principle that had allowed exploitation of resources that had occasionally been harmful to native interests and would compel "C" mandates to observe a principle which they had not been obliged to do under the League. The Netherlands also emphasized the former point; the Union of South Africa, the latter. The final compromise is embodied in Article 76(d):

> to ensure equal treatment in social, economic, and commercial matters for all Members of the United Nations and their nationals, and also equal treatment for the latter in the administration of justice, without prejudice to the attainment of the foregoing objectives and subject to the provisions of Article 80 [protecting existing rights under the League mandates].

Implementing the Objectives. Not only are the objectives of the trusteeship system more ambitious than those of the League mandates system, but the tools with which to drive them home have been reinforced. These various supervisory powers are wielded primarily by the Trusteeship Council but are also shared with other bodies mentioned above.

1) *Placing Territories under Trusteeship.* Since there was danger that the trusteeship system, though strong on paper, might starve to death for lack of business, two major issues from the beginning were *what kinds of territories* would be subjected to the system and *who would decide.* The most extreme anti-colonial view, first espoused but soon abandoned by United States planners, was that *all* dependent territories should be placed under trusteeship, but there was scarcely a chance of persuading the imperial powers to commit collective suicide. There was, however, a considerable degree of consensus that former mandated territories should continue under trusteeship unless they gained their freedom. There was, nevertheless, some serious opposition on this point from both ends of the colonial spectrum. The extremely conservative Union of South Africa indicated that the best cure for the primitive conditions of mandated South West Africa would be absorption by South Africa. The United States demanded the greatest possible freedom of action in administering the former Japanese mandated Pacific islands as strategic trusts. And the former mandated territories of Iraq, Syria and Lebanon, which were generally recognized as having won their independence, insisted they should not be returned to mandate status, which they considered more a prison than a school for freedom.

In view of the Atlantic Charter pledges against "aggrandizement," "territorial changes that do not accord with the freely expressed wishes of the people concerned," and recognizing "the right of all peoples to choose the form of government under which they will live," there was general accord that ex-enemy territories should not be seized as booty but should either

---

[32] *Ibid.*, p. 599.

be placed under trust or freed. A last category, urged strongly by the United States, was that of other non-self-governing areas that might be voluntarily surrendered to trusteeship. Again opposition came from both the colonial powers, who suspected, correctly, that this was being used as a lever to pry off the manacles of empire, and certain anti-colonial states, such as Guatemala, Ethiopia and Argentina, who feared that certain areas of interest to them might be tossed into the cage of trusteeship.

To the question of *who was to decide* what territories should be made trusts, one of the more radical answers was proposed by Australia: that the General Assembly decide, after considering the recommendations of a conference of the colonial powers.[33] Although the pro-colonial forces succeeded in smothering this alarming idea, the Assembly was given, in Article 85, the authority to approve the trusteeship agreements which implied a correlative authority to exercise a veto by refusing approval. Furthermore, the Council of Foreign Ministers later decided, in 1946, that, if agreement on the disposition of the former Italian colonies could not be reached within a year of the Italian peace treaty's coming into force, the decision was to be made by the General Assembly. Subsequently, in 1949 the Assembly decided that only former Italian Somaliland should be placed under trusteeship.

Some anti-colonial states wanted to make the decision automatic. The Philippines proposed that all dependent territories be surrendered to trusteeship. Egypt urged that *all* mandated territories be turned over. But the United States joined with the United Kingdom and other interested states to form a solid phalanx in favor of the entirely voluntary submission of all territories. The United States was particularly concerned to protect its discretionary power in submitting the Japanese islands to trusteeship. As John Foster Dulles tells it,

> It had been early agreed that trusteeship would not apply automatically to any territory, but that "it will be a matter for subsequent agreement as to which territories . . . will be brought under the trusteeship system. . . ." At the daily meetings of the United States Delegation, Senator Connally and Senator Vandenberg would always put to Commander Stassen this question: "Are you sticking to the 'subsequent agreement' provision?" Commander Stassen would regularly reply in the affirmative. Then the meeting would go on.[34]

Out of this whirlpool of conflicting interests finally emerged the compromises that appear in the Charter:

Article 77

1. The trusteeship system shall apply to such territories in the following categories as may be placed thereunder by means of trusteeships agreements:
   a. territories now held under mandate;

---

[33] *Ibid.*, p. 549.

[34] *War or Peace* (New York: Macmillan, 1950), pp. 79–80. Used by permission of The Macmillan Company.

b. territories which may be detached from enemy states as a result of the Second World War; and

c. territories voluntarily placed under the system by states responsible for their administration.

2. It will be a matter for subsequent agreement as to which territories in the foregoing categories will be brought under the trusteeship system and upon what terms.

Article 78

The trusteeship system shall not apply to territories which have become Members of the United Nations, relationship among which shall be based on respect for the principle of sovereign equality.

Article 80

1. Except as may be agreed upon in individual trusteeship agreements . . . placing each territory under the trusteeship system, and until such agreements have been concluded, nothing in this Chapter shall be construed in or of itself to alter in any manner the rights whatsoever of any states or any peoples or the terms of existing international instruments to which Members of the United Nations may respectively be parties.

2. Paragraph 1 of this Article shall not be interpreted as giving grounds for delay or postponement of the negotiation and conclusion of agreements for placing mandated and other territories under the trusteeship system as provided for in Article 77.

As compared with the mandates system, the basic concept underlying these passages represents very little change. While it is true that the potential scope of trusteeship is widened to include "territories voluntarily placed under the system," in both instances the decisions to submit territories have thus far always been made by the victorious great powers, subject only to recommendations and final ratification by the international organization. The only instance of imposing trusteeship by decision of an international body was the General Assembly's recommendation to place former Italian Somaliland under a ten-year Italian trusteeship. But, of course, it was the great powers who authorized the Assembly to make the decision and agreed in advance that that decision should be accepted as binding.

2) *Formulation of Trusteeship Terms.* The general principles which were to serve as guideposts for the formulation of specific trust agreements are set forth in Charter Article 76, discussed above. Equally important was the question of *who* was to do the formulating. The states likely to be administering authorities naturally sought at San Francisco to protect their freedom of action. The United Kingdom thought the terms should be hammered out between the "state entrusted with . . . administration" (presumably by some earlier agreement) and the international organization. The United States, with France following, thought the terms should be agreed upon by "the states directly concerned" and then approved by the

organization. The Soviet Union, indicating that it wanted to be included in the "states directly concerned," asked that that vague formula be more precisely defined. But the United States and the United Kingdom were not enthusiastic about this idea, and the final language of Article 79 provides that:

> The terms of trusteeship . . . , including any alteration or amendment, shall be agreed upon by the states directly concerned, including the mandatory power in the case of territories held under mandate by a Member of the United Nations, and shall be approved as provided for in Articles 83 and 85.

In the case of the League mandates, it will be remembered that the draft agreements were first negotiated by the Allied and Associated Powers through the Allied Supreme Council, and then examined and approved by the League Council.

Another issue affecting the terms of the trusteeship agreements was the question of the agency to be entrusted with direct administration. There was general agreement that this task could be assigned to a single state or a group of states, although there was less enthusiasm for the second alternative. There was intense difference of opinion, however, over the Chinese-initiated proposal, endorsed by earlier United States plans but dropped before San Francisco, that the international organization itself do the administering. The League practice had been to limit administration to single states. The nations that expected to be administering authorities under the United Nations obviously wanted no one to come between them and their precious trusts. Finally, however, the Chinese proposal was adopted as one of three alternatives in Article 81:

> The trusteeship agreement shall in each case include the terms under which the trust territory will be administered and designate the authority which will exercise the administration of the trust territory. Such authority, hereinafter called the administering authority, may be one or more states or the Organization itself.

3) *Examination of Questionnaires and Reports.* The bright light of publicity was the only real weapon available to the League Mandates Commission, and, to the surprise of many, was a remarkably powerful weapon. At San Francisco there was general agreement that the devices of annual questionnaires and reports should be kept, and primary attention was devoted to strengthening them. The principal innovations, written into Charter Articles 87 and 88, are: (1) the Trusteeship Council is authorized to formulate a questionnaire directly, rather than merely advising the Council as the Mandates Commission did; (2) the questionnaire is specifically authorized in the Charter, as it was not in the Covenant; and (3) the administering authorities are required to reply to the questionnaire, as they were not under the League.

Squeezing the utmost out of this constitutional authority, the Trusteeship

Council has developed a questioning process that is extremely searching. The basic questionnaire was provisionally approved in April 1947 and contains a formidable array of 190 questions, as compared with 60 in the League "B" mandate questionnaire, plus an extensive statistical index. The assembly line process by which individual annual reports are sifted is as follows: (1) a report based upon the questionnaire must be submitted to the United Nations within four months of the end of the year it covers; (2) written questions may then be directed by members of the Trusteeship Council to the administering authority's "special representative"; (3) the Council's oral consideration of the report begins with an opening statement by the special representative; (4) this is followed by questioning; (5) there is a general debate; (6) the views expressed are incorporated in a report prepared by a small *ad hoc* drafting committee; and (7) after this report is finally adopted by the Council it is incorporated in a report for the Assembly.

This questionnaire-and-report system goes far beyond the League process in both coverage and intensity. At the same time, it has been the target of considerable criticism. The administering authorities insist that the questioning is too lengthy and complicated, requires excessive effort on the part of the local administrators, and reveals regrettable lack of understanding of and sympathy for the administering authority's problems. On the other hand, the anti-colonialists complain because the process tends to be superficial, incomplete, uncoordinated with the visiting missions and petitions, and so far behind the pace of events that the Council lacks control of current policies.

4) *Action on Petitions.* The petition has long been a powerful weapon in the fight for democracy. It was the beginning of modern law. In the United Nations trusteeship system, it is a direct wire between the dusty African village and United Nations headquarters in New York. In the League all petitions had to be submitted in writing through the mandatory power. The United States and other anti-colonial interests were largely responsible for writing into the Trusteeship Council's *Rules of Procedure* that the right of petition should be reinforced by allowing complaints to be submitted directly to the United Nations (including visiting missions) and orally as well as in writing. The petitioner may be any interested party, not only a trust territory inhabitant. Petitions must, except in urgent situations, be submitted two months before a Council session, and administering authority observations must be in two weeks before a session. The rules governing the admissibility of petitions are also more lenient than under the League. The only serious prohibition is that they must not be

directed against judgments of competent courts of the Administering Authority or . . . lay before the Council a dispute with which the courts have competence to deal. This rule shall not be interpreted so as to prevent consideration by the Trusteeship Council of petitions against legislation on the grounds of its incompatibility with the provisions of the Charter . . . or of

the Trusteeship agreement, irrespective of whether decisions on cases arising under such legislation have previously been given by the courts of the
Administering Authority.[35]

During each session prior to 1952, the Trusteeship Council appointed an
ad hoc committee (evenly divided between the representatives of administering and non-administering states) to make a preliminary examination of
petitions and make recommendations on their admissibility. The Council
has then proceeded to take action on their substance. The issues revealed
in the petitions have ranged from the complaint about the eighty-year-old
King in the British Cameroons who was keeping a hundred wives (the
Council was cautious on this one) to the request from the people of
Western Samoa for greater political freedom (which resulted in a visiting
mission and significant reforms). There is no doubt that this process has
prepared the ground for a rich harvest of information, as well as protection
of the indigenous peoples, but thus far the Trusteeship Council has not
organized itself so that it could adequately sift the wheat from the chaff.
The tremendous flood of complaints has received relatively superficial
attention. Consequently the Assembly recommended in January 1952 the
creation of a standing Trusteeship Council committee to sift petitions between, as well as during, Council sessions.[36] This plan was adopted by the
Council in March 1953 with the result that petitions are now receiving
more careful consideration than previously. But there is still evidence that
the petition process remains a weak link in the trusteeship system.

5) *Visiting Missions.* The Mandates Commission was chained to Geneva
and never allowed to make on-the-spot inspections. The United States plan,
prior to the San Francisco Conference, authorized the Assembly and Trusteeship Council "to institute investigations." [37] The Chinese agreed, but
the United Kingdom and French drafts omitted such a provision. Later
the French said that

> Power of investigation tends to create the impression that the administer-
> ing authority has precarious authority. Such procedure is not good from the
> point of view of sound administration. It is better to leave this subject to a
> wording sufficiently broad as not to exclude it but which would not specifi-
> cally include it.[38]

Finally a United States compromise draft resulted in the present language
of Article 87:

> The General Assembly and . . . the Trusteeship Council . . . may . . .
> provide for periodic visits to the respective trust territories at times agreed
> upon with the administering authority. . . .

---

[35] UN Doc. T/1/Rev. 1, Rule 81.
[36] General Assembly Resolution 552 (VI).
[37] UNCIO, III, p. 600.
[38] Taken from *The Informal Minutes of Preliminary Consultations on Trusteeship by
Representatives of the Five Powers, Third Meeting.*

On this foundation the Trusteeship Council has built a procedure which greatly enhances its influence. The present plan is to have each trust territory visited approximately once every three years. Everything is done to make these missions as neutral as possible. Representatives of states administering territories to be visited are not normally included, and the mission is to "act only on the basis of the instructions of the Council and shall be responsible to it" (Rule 96). Participation in such missions is also being rotated so as to expose all Council members to the experience. Once the visit is completed, the mission reports to the Council, and this information supplements the picture presented by the annual reports and petitions.

Of the several trusteeship innovations ushered in by the United Nations Charter, the visiting mission probably represents the greatest single stride beyond the mandates system. It means that the United Nations can see trusteeships in operation through its own eyes rather than someone else's. Similarly the United Nations becomes a living reality, rather than a vague myth, in the minds of the indigenous peoples.

> Sometimes the hosts are dressed in toga-like robes, sometimes they carry sceptres and baubles covered with gold leaf, sometimes they are in European dress, sometimes in turbans and garments like the Arabs of Libya betraying their Moslem culture. Sometimes there are drums and dancing, sometimes processions with banners and placards for all the world like a demonstration in any industrial city in Europe or America. But always the faces are expectant, excited under the dignified bearing, deeply stirred at this evidence that a great authority, over-riding even their rulers, is troubling itself over their fate.[39]

And the petitions presented in such scenes have a special poignancy. In Moshi, Tanganyika (British trust), a petition stated:

> We are . . . elated to note the humane considerations which stimulated the hearts of the U.N.O. Trusteeship Council to delegate the Mission to see the existing conditions of the indigenous peoples in the Trusteeship Territories. . . . We all crave for higher and better EDUCATION. . . . We implore . . . the British Government . . . to restore the ex-enemy lands into the native hands, on which the indigenous surplus population can settle.[40]

In Dar-es-Salem, Tanganyika:

> The houses are too close-by. The roads are always incomplete. Avenues percentage is very little. No playing grounds for children. No shade trees isolated in most of these towns. Most of them look like ant-hills in a desert when one sees like a flying-bird. In hospital, social conditions are not good, too.[41]

While the visiting mission represents an important advance, it has also suffered severe birth pangs. Missions have sometimes been dispatched with

[39] John MacLaurin, *The United Nations and Power Politics* (New York: Harper, 1951), p. 336.
[40] *Ibid.*, p. 338.
[41] *Ibid.*, p. 339.

inadequate planning, briefing and staff aid. Moreover, there has never been enough time to make an intensive study of a territory's problems. Persons who have gone on the missions have not always been well qualified nor have they always been members of the Council, with the result that the Council has not benefited fully from the mission's effort. Finally, missions need better coordination with other agencies and more effective utilization of the petition process.[42]

6) *Formulation of Standards.* The seed of law is planted when men begin to generalize from the particular to the universal. As we saw the League Mandates Commission begin the slow process of building general standards, so the United Nations has continued that development. Other than the brief objectives set forth in Article 76, the Charter contains no provision for developing universal trusteeship standards, especially since those familiar with the territories recognize the great differences that make any rigidly uniform approach impractical. And yet emphasis on the unique qualities of certain territories has too frequently been cited as justification for erecting a bamboo curtain between the United Nations and such territories. Champions of the United Nations have wanted to go as far as possible in developing standards, for several reasons: to amplify the objectives set forth in the Charter, to provide some basis for comparing local administrations, to prod the less enlightened administering authorities and to develop goals which will also affect non-trust dependencies.

7) *Sanctions.* The great powers were able to persuade most of the other states that the Security Council should handle trusteeship violations as disturbances to international peace, in spite of the obvious fact that only a rather extreme violation would actually be a real disturbance to the peace. China asked that "any violation" automatically be "brought . . . to the attention of the General Assembly or the Security Council."[43] Egypt, leading the Arab battalion against the British, went furthest by proposing that

> the General Assembly shall have the power to terminate the status of trusteeship, and declare the territory to be fit for full independence. . . . That whenever there is a violation of the terms of the trusteeship . . . , or when the administering power has ceased to be a Member of the United Nations, or has been suspended from membership, the organization shall take the necessary steps for the transfer of the territory under trusteeship to another administering authority. . . .[44]

Opposition to this suggestion, largely by the great powers, was based on several grounds: it would violate the voluntary character of the trust system; the recognition of independence might better be left to individual

---

[42] For recommended improvements, see "Visiting Missions," *International Conciliation,* No. 448 (February 1949); also General Assembly Resolutions 434 (V) and 553 (VI).

[43] UNCIO, III, p. 616.

[44] *Ibid.,* X, p. 547.

agreements; possible transfer was covered under the Security Council's power; and, by way of contradiction, it would be difficult to take away a territory from a state that was not in the mood to surrender it. A subsequent Anglo-American statement explained that

> a Trusteeship State which showed signs of aggressive intentions or had committed an aggression could be dealt with [by the Security Council]. . . . If a State withdraws for reasons which reflect no discredit upon it, and if it declares its willingness to continue to abide by the terms of the trusteeship system, . . . there should be no reason for transferring the trust territory . . . if after ceasing to be a Member . . . , [it] committed violations . . . , any measures provided elsewhere in the Charter . . . could be invoked. . . .

A great gap that remained, however, was what to do about the violation that could not be considered an actual "threat to the peace" under Chapter 7. In such a case even the Security Council could do no more than make recommendations.

Conclusions

The trusteeship system, in essence, is our old friend the mandates system, but with stronger muscles and greater ambitions. The basic similarity between the two is clearly evident in the continued emphasis on the voluntary submission of territories (thus far only ex-enemy areas), direct "administration" by national states (although the United Nations Charter leaves room for international administration), and only "supervision" by the international organization with no power to command, merely to veto, recommend and publicize.

The differences between the new and the old are chiefly in the direction not of narrowing but of expanding the horizons of the trust populations. Giving over-all supervisory authority to the Assembly places trusteeship problems under the wing of a larger and a more anti-colonial forum than the League Council. Making the Trusteeship Council a "principal organ" composed of governmental representatives, rather than independent experts, with strong anti-colonial representation, has made it more authoritative and less conservative than the Mandates Commission. The objectives of the trusteeship system are more vaguely expansive, more committed to independence as the ideal goal and more concerned with general economic and social progress than was the mandates system. Two other changes may or may not benefit the dependent peoples: the new emphasis on compelling the territories to share the burdens of collective security and on modifying the "open door" policy in the interests of these peoples.

There can be no doubt, however, that the new provisions for direct international administration as well as for the submission of other than ex-enemy and former mandated areas to trusteeship are intended to favor the non-self-governing populations. New and stronger instruments are placed in the hands of the international organization in the form of visiting missions, examination of direct and oral petitions, and specific authority to

formulate questionnaires which the administering authority is compelled
to answer. Finally, this yeasty ferment is apparent in the general spirit of
expansion throughout the system. Charter Chapters 12 and 13 are far more
comprehensive than the lean Covenant Article 22. The Trusteeship Council's rules are four times as long as the Mandates Commission's. The new
questionnaire contains three times as many questions as the old one. The
Secretariat trusteeship staff is six times as large as in League days; its
budget, ten times that of its predecessor. This growth is all the more notable in view of the decrease in the number of trust territories from fourteen
to eleven.

The political fact underlying all this expansion is that, since 1919, the
problem of colonialism has become more, rather than less, intense; and the
mood of the international organization more, rather than less, anti-colonial.
The growth of the trusteeship system is both explained and justified by the
fact that its shadow falls far beyond the mere handful of trust territories;
it falls across all dependent lands.

Non-Self-Governing Territories System

It is the 170 million dependent people who live outside the trusteeship
system (as compared with only 20 million covered by that system) who
represent the bulk of the explosive colonial problem. The United Nations'
relationship with these peoples is only a thin thread, but still it is stronger
than under the League. Covenant Article 23 provided merely that League
Members "secure just treatment of . . . native inhabitants" and recognize
a few special responsibilities toward all peoples regarding labor conditions,
traffic in women and children, traffic in drugs and arms, and health. The
United Nations Charter, on the other hand, contains an entire Chapter
(11) which deals exclusively with the Members' obligations towards their
non-self-governing territories in a far wider range of areas and compels the
Members to report regularly to the United Nations on conditions in those
territories.

Chapter 11 is the child of compromise, an especially instructive example
of the harmonization of various national interests with a result that was
not the will of any single state but a mosaic of several. During most of
the planning period, 1943 to 1945, the mood of the United Kingdom, as
expressed chiefly by Colonel Oliver Stanley, was in favor of replacing the
mandates system with a mere pledge accepting the principle of trusteeship
for all dependencies. No international machinery was provided to back it
up other than loose regional commissions to give advice on economic and
social progress. As a stronger variation of this theme, Australia called for a
more detailed pledge and regular reporting to a body like the Mandates
Commission regarding all territories submitted voluntarily or by decision
of the Assembly. The United Kingdom saw only too clearly, however, that
the Australian modification of its plan would be a boomerang that would

spread the mandates system to all British, as well as other, colonial dependencies. To forestall this ironical turn of events, the British, in their plan of May 6, 1945,[45] accepted a revival of the mandates system but limited it to mandated and ex-enemy territories. The general pledge, referring to all non-self-governing territories, would remain but without the teeth (reporting to a commission) suggested by Australia. The final compromise was based on the *Proposed Working Paper* [46] prepared by the United States which accepted the division urged by Britain as well as an anemic version of the Australian reporting plan.

Structure

Seldom before, to rephrase a famous Churchillian formula, has so much organizational activity evolved from so little constitutional authority. Because of the colonial powers' intense opposition to any extensive international prying, Chapter 11 mentions nothing in the way of institutional machinery except that members responsible for non-self-governing territories are to "transmit regularly to the Secretary-General for information purposes" various types of factual material. Nothing is said about what is to be done with that material nor what role other organs should play. The predominantly anti-colonial Assembly was quick, however, to assert its authority, under the umbrella of Article 10, to build machinery to help implement Chapter 11.

The general trend, doggedly opposed at almost every step by the colonial powers, has been the evolution of procedures that ape the trusteeship pattern. The Assembly's Fourth Committee, also responsible for trusteeship, has, from the first session, ridden herd over the provisions of Chapter 11. A shadow "trusteeship council" was also created by the Assembly during the second part of the first session (1946) in the form of a sixteen-member *ad hoc* committee (equally divided between administering and non-administering) states, the latter being elected by the Assembly's Fourth Committee). The Committee's mandate, as revised in 1949, is

> to examine, in the spirit of . . . the Charter, the summaries and analyses of information transmitted under Article 73(e) of the Charter on the economic, social and educational conditions in the Non-Self-Governing Territories, including any papers prepared by the specialized agencies, and any reports or information on measures taken in pursuance of the resolutions adopted by the General Assembly concerning economic, social and educational conditions in the Non-Self-Governing Territories. . . . to submit to the . . . Assembly . . . reports containing such procedural recommendations as it may deem fit and such substantive recommendations as it may deem desirable relating to functional fields generally but not with respect to individual Territories. . . .[47]

45 *Ibid.*, III, pp. 609–611.
46 *Ibid.*, X, pp. 677–683.
47 General Assembly Resolution 332 (IV).

Since the birth of this Committee was opposed by seven of the eight administering Members, including the United States and the United Kingdom (Belgium abstained), there was considerable doubt initially whether the infant would survive. As most of its friends proceeded with caution, however, and as its enemies learned to live with it, the Committee gained strength. After being renewed from year to year, its life was extended in 1949 for a three-year period, a decision endorsed by three of the seven administering Members, and in 1952, for another three years. Although its personnel and discussions have tended to be even more political than its cousin, the Trusteeship Council, it has blazed useful trails and won the support of the great majority of the Members, including some of those who once were its enemies. The major colonial powers, the United Kingdom and France, however, remain sharply critical of what they regard as undue meddling in essentially "domestic" matters.

The Secretariat has also been a strong force in this area, mostly behind the scenes. Leading Secretariat officials, such as Ralph Bunche and Wilfrid Benson, have made no secret of the fact that they favor making Chapter 11 a major instrument for improving present standards of colonial administration.[48] The Secretariat's Division of Information from Non-Self-Governing Territories had, in 1952, a staff of thirty-five, approximately the same as its companion Division of Trusteeship.

Authority

Objectives. The objectives of Chapter 11 are a diluted version of those of the trusteeship system set forth in Chapter 12.

Article 73

Members . . . recognize . . . that the interests of the inhabitants of . . . [non-self-governing] territories are paramount, and accept as a sacred trust the obligation to promote to the utmost, within the system of international peace and security established by the present Charter, the well-being of the inhabitants of these territories, and, to this end:

a. to ensure, with due respect for the culture of the people concerned, their political, economic, social, and educational advancement, their just treatment, and their protection against abuses;

b. to develop self-government, to take due account of the political aspirations of the peoples, and to assist them in the progressive development of their free political institutions, according to the particular circumstances of each territory and its peoples and their varying stages of advancement;

c. to further international peace and security;

d. to promote constructive measures of development, to encourage research, and to cooperate with one another and, when and where appro-

---

[48] R. J. Bunche, "Trusteeship and Non-Self-Governing Territories in the Charter of the UN," *Department of State Bulletin,* Vol. 13, No. 340 (December 30, 1945); Wilfrid Benson, "Non-Self-Governing Territories," *Annual Review of UN Affairs* (New York: New York University Press, 1950), pp. 190–198.

priate, with specialized international bodies with a view to the practical achievement of the social, economic, and scientific purposes set forth in this Article. . . .

Article 74

Members also agree that their policy in respect of the territories . . . must be based on the general principle of good-neighborliness, due account being taken of the interests and well-being of the rest of the world, in social, economic, and commercial matters.

The most intense feeling regarding these objectives centered around the conflict between "independence" and "self-government," already discussed in connection with Chapter 12. "Independence" was finally mentioned specifically in the trusteeship section but not in the non-self-governing territories section. Nevertheless, the United Kingdom, as well as the anti-colonial powers, interpreted Chapter 11 to imply independence as a possible goal for non-self-governing territories.[49] The forward-looking objective concerning "development," "research," and cooperation with specialized agencies is the product of Australian suggestions as modified by the United States *Proposed Working Paper*. Article 74 on "good-neighborliness" incorporates almost verbatim a British proposal that is a counterpart of the "equal treatment" provision in Chapter 12 on trusteeship.

Functions. The Charter is understandably silent on who should decide what territories "have not yet attained a full measure of self-government" and are therefore subject to Chapter 11. When controversy has arisen over this matter because the Soviet Union did not think the Netherlands should report on Indonesia or because the Soviet Union thought the United States should report on the Canal Zone, the Assembly has not hesitated to exert considerable influence by urging that the colonial powers make their decisions according to certain criteria.[50] And in response to Assembly criticism, the United States, the United Kingdom and France have gone to great pains to justify their reasons for not reporting on various territories. Nevertheless, the United Nations cannot legally, though it may in fact, compel a state to report if that state does not wish to.

The function of ferreting out the facts and exposing them to scrutiny is in itself a major force for improving administrative standards. One cannot find in the Charter any authority, paralleling that in the trusteeship system, for a United Nations questionnaire on non-self-governing territories. The Assembly, nonetheless, formulated, as early as its second session (1947), a standard form to be followed by reporting states. That form, as revised in 1951, calls for intensive self-revelation under 105 headings including a searching statistical appendix. But the colonial powers fought so fiercely against United Nations influence on "political" issues, that the four "government" items in the questionnaire were made optional. The reporting

[49] UNCIO, X, p. 562.
[50] General Assembly Resolutions 334 (IV) and 567 (VI).

thus far has been relatively superficial, and the use made of this mass of intelligence has only scratched the surface. But the United Nations is accumulating a growing reservoir of detailed knowledge which, as every reformer knows, can be a powerful weapon for progress. Furthermore, the colonial regimes are subjected to probing questions and recommendations by both the Committee on Information from Non-Self-Governing Territories and the Assembly itself.

Conclusions

At San Francisco, Chapter 11 received far less attention and was clothed with less verbiage than were the trusteeship chapters. Yet Chapter 11 has given rise to more expansive constitutional interpretation and represents a far greater advance beyond the League and a potentially more powerful impact upon the whole problem of colonialism than the trusteeship chapters. Moreover, the United Nations non-self-governing territories program is slowly, almost imperceptibly, following in the footsteps of the mandates and trusteeship systems. This is an evolution, cordially denounced by most colonial powers, which, it should be recalled, follows the plan proposed by the liberal colonial states of Australia and New Zealand. Though partially rejected at San Francisco, this plan has been transformed from theory to reality through the alchemy of practice and interpretation.

The chief strength of this system, which has only begun to develop, is that it provides an unprecedented opportunity to find out the facts about colonial regimes, compare their relative performances and foster their improvement. The chief weaknesses of the system are that it has failed to win adequate support from the chief colonial powers, with the result that the present reporting tends to be incomplete and superficial, and it has failed to make sufficiently effective use of the material which it receives.

Supervision of Special Areas

The age-old device of placing disputed "powder kegs" under the relatively neutral roof of an international organization has also been resorted to by the United Nations, as it was by the League. Although no special regimes were created at San Francisco comparable to the Danzig and Saar arrangements formulated at Paris in 1919, such regimes were anticipated in the provision in Article 77 for supervision under the trusteeship system of "territories voluntarily placed under the system by states responsible for their administration." And such a voluntary surrender to trusteeship may be said to have taken place in the case of the former Italian colony of Somaliland. But colonial powers are notably laggard in placing their own dependencies under trusteeship, and the dependent peoples are equally reluctant to assume a status which they consider a halter far easier to slip on than off.

GENERAL ASSEMBLY AS "CARETAKER"

An alternative means of coping with disputed areas has been to turn to the General Assembly or the Security Council to create temporary non-trusteeship "caretaker" regimes, usually to lead certain territories out of bondage to independence. The Assembly has enjoyed more of this business than the Council for the familiar reason that often the great powers have been unable to settle the destiny of the territory in question among themselves. Under such circumstances, the Assembly has, thus far, created "caretaker" regimes in connection with Palestine, Libya and Eritrea. In each case the great powers wanted to use the Assembly not only to recommend the fate of the disputed areas but actually to help administer them during a transitional period. This scheme proved abortive in the case of Palestine (including Jerusalem) but worked with commendable success in Libya and Eritrea. In all three instances, the Assembly plan was to create an agent, sometimes aided by an advisory council, to work with the local great power administrations to liquidate the existing regimes and help the dependent peoples gird themselves for independence, including the preparation of constitutions. In the Palestine fracas, the Assembly's agents were first the hapless United Nations Palestine Commission of five small state representatives ("five lonely pilgrims") and later the Mediators Folke Bernadotte and Ralph Bunche who, though thought of primarily as peacemakers, did perform "caretaker" functions such as arranging for the provisioning of Jerusalem and protecting "holy sites."

To set Libya free, the Assembly appointed a United Nations Commissioner, Assistant Secretary-General Adrian Pelt, aided and advised by a Council of Ten (representatives nominated by six intimately concerned states, including the United States and the United Kingdom, as well as a representative of the three Libyan provinces and a representative of the Libyan minorities). To help prepare Eritrea as an autonomous unit federated with Ethiopia, the Assembly appointed another United Nations Commissioner, Dr. Eduardo Anze Matienzo, previously Bolivian permanent representative to the United Nations, assisted by experts appointed by the Secretary-General, but with no governmental advisory council.

With respect to minority problems, the United Nations has not attempted to create a separate supervisory system, as was done under the League, but has tended to treat these issues as part of the larger human rights question discussed in Chapters 8 and 21.

SECURITY COUNCIL AND TRIESTE

The only disputed area that has thus far been tossed into the lap of the Security Council is Trieste, the strategic port city lying on the controversial border between Italy and Yugoslavia. After disagreeing violently among themselves, the Big Four (United States, Soviet Union, United Kingdom and France) finally agreed at Paris in 1946, clearly with the League's Danzig experience in mind,[51] that the Security Council should be given the responsibility, without any time limit, for assuring the "integrity and independence" of the "Free Territory of Trieste." The Council was to appoint a Governor, for a five-year term and eligible for reappointment, with authority to take all measures necessary to keep order and defend the independence of the area. Normal legislation and administration were to be left in the hands of a locally-elected government. In spite of certain qualms on the part of Australia and a few other states regarding the constitutionality of assigning the Security Council authority not specifically provided for in the Charter, the Council boldly endorsed the plan in January 1947. Because of increasing East-West conflict, however, the Security Council has been unable to reach a single other positive decision on the Trieste question. Thus a Governor has still not been appointed, after countless attempts, and the "temporary" occupation regime under United States and British forces continues to rule the area.

CONCLUSIONS

In terms of the League experience, these United Nations efforts have been more numerous and more under the direction of the Assembly than the Council, but, with the exception of Trieste, for far shorter periods. A fundamental difference in the type of area involved is that the League was concerned with highly developed self-governing European territories, while the United Nations, again with the exception of Trieste, has dealt with less developed dependent areas. The administrative machinery has been very similar however: a commission or single commissioner under the direction of the international organization. And the United Nations, like the League, has had its resounding failures as well as its heartening successes; neither has been clearly more effective than the other.

Suggestions for Further Reading

Books

British Labour Party, *The Labour Party's Postwar Policy for the African and Pacific Colonies* (London: British Labour Party, 1943).

Corbett, Percy E., *Post-War Worlds* (New York: Institute of Pacific Relations, 1942).

Dulles, John Foster, *War or Peace* (New York: The Macmillan Company, 1950).

Eagleton, Clyde, and Swift, Richard N., eds., *Annual Review of United Nations Affairs, 1949, 1950, 1951, 1952* (New York: New York University Press, 1950, 1951, 1952, 1953).

Goodrich, Leland M., and Hambro, Edvard, *Charter of the United Nations,*

[51] Byrnes, *op. cit.*, p. 147.

Commentary and Documents (Boston: World Peace Foundation, 1949).

Hall, H. Duncan, *Mandates, Dependencies, and Trusteeship* (Washington: Carnegie Endowment for International Peace, 1948).

Hull, Cordell, *The Memoirs of Cordell Hull*, 2 Vols. (New York: The Macmillan Company, 1948).

Institute of Pacific Relations, *Security in the Pacific* (New York: Institute of Pacific Relations, 1945).

————, *War and Peace in the Pacific* (New York: Institute of Pacific Relations, 1943).

Periodicals

Armstrong, Elizabeth H., and Cargo, William I., "The Inauguration of the Trusteeship System of the United Nations," *Department of State Bulletin*, Vol. 16, No. 403 (March 23, 1947).

Bailey, K. H., "Dependent Areas of the Pacific: An Australian View," *Foreign Affairs*, Vol. 24, No. 3 (April 1946).

Bunche, Ralph J., "Trusteeship and Non-Self-Governing Territories in the Charter of the United Nations," *Department of State Bulletin*, Vol. 13, No. 340 (December 30, 1945).

Chieh, Liu, "International Trusteeship System, Visiting Missions," *International Conciliation*, No. 448 (February 1949).

Commission to Study the Organization of Peace, "Reports," *International Conciliation*, Nos. 369 (April 1941), 379 (April 1942), 389 (April 1943), 396 (January 1944), and 403 (September 1944).

Fraser, Peter, "The Work of the Trusteeship Council," *International Conciliation*, No. 445 (November 1948).

Gilchrist, H., "The United Nations: Colonial Questions at the San Francisco Conference," *American Political Science Review*, Vol. 39, No. 5 (October 1945).

Hall, H. D., "The British Commonwealth and Trusteeship," *International Affairs*, Vol. 22, No. 2 (April 1946).

Holland, Sir Robert, "Trusteeship Aspirations," *Foreign Affairs*, Vol. 25, No. 1 (October 1946).

"International Responsibility for Colonial Peoples," *International Conciliation*, No. 458 (February 1950).

Sayre, Francis B., "Advancement of Dependent Peoples," *International Conciliation*, No. 435 (November 1947).

Documents

United Nations, *Documents of the United Nations Conference on International Organization, San Francisco, 1945* (New York and London: United Nations Information Organizations, 1945–1946).

————, Trusteeship Council, *Official Records* and other documents.

United States, Congress, *Hearings Before the Committee on Foreign Relations, on the Charter of the United Nations . . .*, July . . . 1945, U.S. Senate, 79th Congress, 1st Session.

————, Department of State, *Postwar Foreign Policy Preparation 1939–1945*, Department of State Publication 3580, General Foreign Policy Series No. 15 (Washington: U.S. Government Printing Office, 1950).

Courts and Law

> "It seems to me that peace in this world is impossible unless nations
> agree on a definite law to govern their relations with each other and
> also agree that, without any veto power, they will submit their dis-
> putes to adjudication and abide by the decision of an impartial tri-
> bunal. . . . " — ROBERT A. TAFT [1]

FOR CENTURIES MEN IN PURSUIT OF PEACE have sought to subject governments to a common rule of law. Not until 1922, however, was there a
standing international court to which all states could submit their disputes
for judicial settlement. In that year the Permanent Court of International
Justice (PCIJ) opened its doors for business at the Hague in Holland.
While not actually a League body, the "World Court" was an essential part
of the League system.

Although it was interred with appropriate ceremonies by the League
Assembly in 1946, a new court was at the same time rising from the ashes
of the old. Called the International Court of Justice (ICJ) it resembles its
predecessor in every important respect. Its Statute is nearly the same,
word-for-word, even to the point of using the same numeration. The principal difference is that by being created as a "principal organ" of the United
Nations the new court is more closely integrated with the general international system. Its Statute, moreover, is considered to be part of the
Charter.

The establishment of a "World Court" was a reflection of what might be
called the juridical road to peace, a route from which more was expected
at the turn of the century than today. First of all, it was thought that a
standing court would result in the adjudication of more international disputes than had been the case in the past when a special tribunal had to
be established whenever states were prepared to arbitrate. Second, in the
course of its judicial function, it was thought that a court might also further the development of international law. These hopes have been justified

[1] *A Foreign Policy for Americans* (New York: Doubleday, 1951), p. 40.

by any reasonable set of standards.[2] The principal difficulty is that the dangerous disputes are considered "political" by states and therefore not justiciable.

The Court is now one of the stars in the galaxy of international organizations — though not one of the first magnitude. Like other international institutions it has not materialized out of the thin air of mere hopes but in response to practical needs. Whether hostile or friendly in their relations, states find it nearly impossible to exist without some rules or fixed standards of conduct and a court to administer them. These standards vary with circumstances, but so far as they go, they are obeyed to an extent seldom realized by most citizens. Rules regarding privileges and immunities of United Nations officials and delegates, for example, have been followed almost without exception in spite of the pressures of the "cold war." Despite its usefulness, however, a permanent international court was slow in coming.

The Permanent Court of International Justice

Origins

The principal framers of the Covenant paid little attention to proposals for a League Court. A reaction against the legal approach to world order had set in. The Hague Conferences and the Permanent Court of Arbitration had not forestalled the armageddon of 1914–18. Wilson, for example, rejected for a time the idea of a court that was put forward by Colonel House who had been influenced by Elihu Root and the League to Enforce Peace. The Phillimore Plan provided only for arbitration or the submission of disputes to the League conference before states were to be permitted to go to war. Lord Robert Cecil's drafts suggested a court that was described only in general terms, while General Smuts suggested compulsory arbitration for all justiciable disputes. At Paris, however, the members of the League of Nations Commission consulted representatives of thirteen neutral powers who insisted upon a court as an antidote to the "political emphasis" of the Allied and Associated Powers.[3] Since these neutral powers were also small powers their concern for legal protection is understandable.

Finally, the Covenant in Article 14 required the League Council to "formulate and submit to the Members of the League for adoption plans for the establishment of a Permanent Court of International Justice." It was to be "competent to hear and determine any dispute of an international character which the parties thereto submit to it," implying that judicial procedure was voluntary rather than compulsory; and it was em-

[2] Oliver J. Lissitzyn, *The International Court of Justice, Its Role in the Maintenance of International Peace and Security*, United Nations Studies No. 6 (New York: 1951), Carnegie Endowment for International Peace, Chap. II.

[3] C. Howard-Ellis, *The Origin, Structure and Working of the League of Nations* (Boston: Houghton Mifflin, 1928), pp. 79–99 and Chap. XI.

powered to give an "advisory opinion upon any dispute or question referred to it by the Council or by the Assembly."

One of the Council's first acts was to appoint a Committee of Jurists in February 1920, made up of ten experts chosen as individuals from the following countries: Belgium, Brazil, Norway, France, The Netherlands, Great Britain, Italy, Japan, Spain and the United States. With the help of the League Secretariat, this Committee drafted a statute that took as a point of departure the plan for the Permanent Court of Arbitral Justice abandoned at the Second Hague Conference. The council reviewed and modified the draft and transmitted it to the first Assembly which, in December 1920, adopted a resolution calling on the Members to ratify the Statute. The Statute of the Permanent Court of International Justice came into force in September 1921. By 1942 the Statute had been signed by fifty-nine states, ratified by fifty-one; and, of eighteen states that had dropped out of the League, five continued as members of the Court.

Jurisdiction

The Court could assume jurisdiction only over those cases brought to it by states, not necessarily Members of the League. Since individuals were not considered to be subjects of international law, despite some opinion to the contrary, they had to be represented by governments. In this way a Greek subject, in the Mavrommattis Palestine Concessions Case of 1924, sought a judgment against Great Britain through the Greek government for failure of the Palestine Mandate to recognize his utility holdings in Palestine.

The jurisdiction of the Court extended to three types of disputes, sometimes called contentious cases:

> 1. cases voluntarily referred to the Court by both parties;
> 2. cases that could be brought by only one party owing to the provisions of a treaty or convention entered into with one or more other states;
> 3. cases in which one party could bring another to judgment because both had accepted the provisions of Article 36 of the Statute which provided for "compulsory" or "obligatory" jurisdiction in legal cases.

The joker in the pack is that no party could be hailed into court against its will, since every case accepted by the Court depended upon an international agreement accepted by both parties. Either they agreed to go to court when a dispute arose, or the Court's jurisdiction over the dispute in question had already been accepted in a previous agreement. Many of the peace treaties, for example, provided that disputes in connection with the treaties themselves were to be referred to the Court.

Compulsory jurisdiction was the most pressing issue facing the Committee of Jurists in 1920. The jurists were unanimously in favor of it as a guiding principle. In legal cases states, in their view, should be required to appear before the proposed Court even against their will. The jurists' effort to extend judicial procedure was a modest one. They did not say that all international disputes should or could be settled in court. They simply said that those disputes involving questions of law, such as the meaning of a treaty, could best be settled in a court of law. But who was to bell the cat? The League Members were unwilling to be committed to go to court even in legal matters. Court procedure must be a voluntary procedure. So the Council demurred, and the first Assembly compromised. States could voluntarily accept compulsory jurisdiction in advance for certain legal cases by adhering to an "optional clause" placed in Article 36 of the Statute. But they could not be forced to accept the Court's jurisdiction. Lord Balfour and others argued in the Council that acceptance of compulsory jurisdiction even in legal cases would be tantamount to amending the Covenant because Article 12 permitted League Members to submit any dispute between them "either to arbitration or to inquiry by the Council." [4]

It may not surprise the reader to learn that the opposition to the jurists' proposal was led by the big powers and that the compromise "optional" clause was contributed by the Assembly after the smaller powers had protested that, regardless of strength, all states should be on an equal footing in legal disputes at least. Disparities of power, they doubtless thought, would be less consequential in court than in diplomatic negotiations. Time after time the smaller powers worshiped at the altar of "law," "justice" and "courts" in word if not always in deed.

The "optional" clause permitted any party to the Statute to accept the court's jurisdiction "in all legal disputes," which included:

a) the interpretation of a treaty;
b) any question of international law;
c) the existence of any fact which, if established, would constitute a breach of an international obligation;
d) the nature or extent of the reparation to be made for the breach of an international obligation.

States adhered to the optional clause by depositing with the Court a declaration to the effect. Many, particularly the larger powers, attached conditions. Forty-five states accepted the optional clause for varying periods of time.

Organization of the Permanent Court

Fully aware that the second Hague Conference had been unable to decide how to appoint judges to an international court, the Committee of Jurists was able to devise an ingenious compromise between the claims of big and small powers. The Court was to consist of fifteen judges elected jointly by the Council and the Assembly for nine-year terms on the basis of nominations by panels of the Permanent Court of Arbitration.[5] Each national panel was entitled to nominate not more than four judges includ-

---

[4] Howard-Ellis, op. cit., p. 366.
[5] The Court originally had nine judges and four deputy judges. The Statute was amended in 1929 to provide for fifteen judges.

ing not more than two of their own nationality. States not members of the Hague Court had the right to set up similar panels. The League's Secretary-General transmitted the list of nominees to the Council and the Assembly which voted independently by secret ballot. An absolute majority was required for election. This device gave sufficient play to national prestige to gain acceptance. The judges were to be independent and chosen regardless of nationality "from among persons of high moral character, who possess the qualifications required in their respective countries for appointment to the highest judicial offices, or are jurisconsults of recognized competence in international law," and should represent "the main forms of civilization and the principal legal systems of the world." They might not engage in any other occupation while they were members of the Court. Once elected, they had security of tenure. Because every state party to a case before the Court was entitled to have upon the bench a judge of its own nationality, *ad hoc* judges might be appointed by a party to a dispute to serve only during the adjudication of that dispute. This provision was attacked as an unwise concession to national sovereignty and defended as an important means of bringing to the bench the legal point of view of a country involved in adjudication. Although the United States never became a member of the Court three of its nationals were selected in succession to be judges — Charles Evans Hughes, Frank B. Kellogg and Manley O. Hudson.

The court elected its own officers — a President, a Vice-President, a Registrar and staff of the Registry. The Registrar was similar to a secretary-general; he maintained the Court's "General List" of cases before it, communicated with governments, maintained relations with the press, kept the archives and printed the Court's decisions. The seat of the Court was at the Hague where it met in the Peace Palace provided by Andrew Carnegie for the Permanent Court of Arbitration. The League Assembly fixed the judges' salaries and determined the Court's budget, which was part of the League's budget. The judges were entitled to diplomatic privileges and immunities. The Court itself remained permanently in session "except during the judicial vacation."

Procedure of the Court

The Court determined its own rules of procedure. The proceedings consisted of two parts, written and oral. In order to get a case before the Court the parties involved gave written notice to the Registrar. If the case was one of obligatory jurisdiction under a treaty or the optional clause, the application of one party was sufficient. If not, the Registrar had to receive formal notification that a special agreement had been concluded between the parties to submit the case to the Court. If a party failed to appear, the Court could decide against it by default. The parties were represented by "agents" who might or might not be assisted by counsel. The agent had full authority to speak for his government. If counsel presented the case, he acted under the agent's direction. Each government was free to appoint whomever it wished to present its case. There were no "bar exams" to be passed in order to argue a case in this court. The written proceedings consisted of "memorials, counter-memorials, replies and rejoinders," including supporting papers and documents as needed. The Court then heard oral testimony from witnesses, experts, agents, counsel or advocates. Unlike most domestic courts no time limit was set, in deference to national sovereignty. When necessary the Court took provisional measures to preserve the respective rights of either party.

French and English were the official languages of the Court, but any party could be authorized to use another language. The hearings were public unless the Court decided, or the parties requested, otherwise. Decisions were reached by majority vote of the judges present. In case of a tie vote, the President cast the deciding vote. The Court was required to state the reasons for its judgment, read in open court, and give the names of the judges taking part in the decision. Any judge was entitled to state a separate opinion. Judgments were final and without appeal, although revisions could be applied for on the grounds of evidence which was unknown to the Court when the judgment was given. Unless otherwise decided by the Court, each party paid its own share of the costs of litigation.

The Law Applied

In accepting the Statute the League's Members prescribed the standards that should be used in deciding cases. If the parties were agreeable, however, the standards could be flexible. Article 38 of the Statute authorized the Court to apply

> a) international conventions . . . establishing rules recognized by the contesting states;
> b) international custom, as evidence of a general practice accepted as law;
> c) the general principles of law recognized by civilized nations;
> d) judicial decisions and the teachings of the most highly qualified publicists of the various nations, as subsidiary means for the determination of law.

Article 59 limited the fourth point, however, in providing that the decisions of the Court had "no binding force except between the parties and in respect of that particular case." This rule, unlike the Anglo-American doctrine of binding precedent (*stare decisis*), would appear to have inhibited the ability of the Court to contribute to the growth of law. In fact, however, the old Court and the new have given considerable weight to their previous "judicial decisions." [6] Latitude was granted, moreover, not only in permitting the Court to apply general principles of law but also in not prejudicing its power "to decide a case *ex aequo et bono,* if the parties agree thereto" (Article 38, par. 2). This provision may have tempered the

[6] Lissitzyn, *op. cit.,* pp. 9–16.

narrow if not barren doctrine of positivism which developed from an extreme concept of state sovereignty in the nineteenth century. It permitted the Court to apply general principles of justice as well as written law.

Advisory Opinions

In carrying out the Covenant's stipulation in Article 14 that it might give an advisory opinion upon matters referred to it by the Assembly or Council, the Court developed procedures for such opinions that were almost equivalent to those used in regular judgments. Governments and, if appropriate, the Secretary-General were invited to present their views in written and oral briefs. These opinions were prepared and handed down as were the Court's judgments. In an early case, the Eastern Karelia Case of 1923, the Court proclaimed that it could not be *required* to furnish such an opinion. This development occurred when a dispute arose between the Soviet Union and Finland regarding an understanding as to the relationship between Eastern Karelia and the Soviet Union. At Finland's request the League Council called for an advisory opinion on the binding character of the understanding. The Soviet Union, not a member of the Court or the League, denied the authority of both bodies and refused to participate in the Court's proceedings. The Court then stated that "answering the question would be substantially equivalent to deciding the dispute between the parties," which it would not do since the Soviet Union refused to give its consent to the Court's jurisdiction.[7] We shall see that several advisory opinions, including those concerned with the *Nationality Decrees in Tunisia and Morocco* and the *Austro-German Customs Union,* dealt with legal aspects of disputes between states.[8] Six of the Court's advisory opinions actually originated with the Governing Body of the ILO, a circumstance that later influenced the founders of the United Nations to permit the specialized agencies to request such opinions. The drawbacks of advisory opinions were similar to those posed by contentious cases. Since disputes were often involved, states had to give their consent to the Court's jurisdiction, and, though called advisory, some opinions had political overtones that quite overshadowed the legal aspects.

The Permanent Court's Achievement

Although it was not a major instrumentality in keeping the peace, the "World Court" played a useful and busy role. During twenty-two years it considered sixty-five cases, resulting in thirty-two judgments and twenty-seven advisory opinions. None of its judgments was disregarded. Many of its cases involved disputes that, without permanent procedures for adjudication, might have become dangerous running sores. Since its jurisdiction was limited to matters that quarreling states were willing to bring to court,

---

[7] Permanent Court of International Justice, Series B, no. 5 (Advisory Opinion, 1923); and M. O. Hudson, *World Court Reports* (Washington: Carnegie Endowment for International Peace, 1934), Vol. 1, p. 190.

[8] See Chap. 14.

it did not and could not settle the main difficulties that breed wars. Yet it did substantially lessen the burden on diplomacy by providing means of settling some matters in court. Both the Court's Statute and its decisions contributed to the growth of international law. Its stability and the respect it commanded were important steps toward institutionalizing a rule of law. Even when the Court was forced into inactivity by a second World War, governments were so convinced of its utility that the continued existence of some sort of World Court was never in doubt. In nearly six hundred international agreements of various sorts, governments had conferred jurisdiction upon it. Fifty-nine states signed the Statute's Protocol of Signature and fifty-one states actually joined the Court. Among the missing were the United States and the Soviet Union. Despite American leadership in framing the Statute, the counterforces of exaggerated notions of sovereignty, a policy of isolation, shocking misrepresentation of the Court's role and the Senate's rules of procedure combined to block participation which was sought by every President and Secretary of State in office during the Court's existence.[9] So far as the Soviet Union was concerned, international law and the Permanent Court, though useful at times, were fundamentally instruments of oppression of the masses by the controlling classes. The "withering away" of states was expected to render such a court unnecessary.

The International Court of Justice

Old Court or New?

The principal question in the minds of the Charter's framers was not, as after World War I, whether there should be a court, but whether the Permanent Court should be continued or a new court established. The Sponsoring Powers did not answer this question at Dumbarton Oaks, but they were able to agree very quickly on the establishment of an "international court of justice" as "the principal judicial organ of the Organization." Its Statute was to be part of the Charter, and all Members of the Organization were to be its members automatically.[10] Conditions under which non-members of the organization might belong were to be left to the General Assembly acting on the Security Council's recommendation. The sponsors also indicated general satisfaction with the Permanent Court by specifying that its statute should serve for the new court or be "used as a basis" for a new statute.

The League's example was followed when the detailed questions were left to a Committee of Jurists which the Sponsoring Powers invited to

[9] See D. F. Fleming, *The United States and the World Court* (New York: Doubleday, 1945).

[10] For the origins of the ICJ see *Report to the President on the Results of the San Francisco Conference* . . . , Department of State Publication 2349, Conference Series 71 (Washington: Government Printing Office, 1945), Chap. 14; Leland M. Goodrich and Edvard Hambro, *Charter of the United Nations, Commentary and Documents* (Boston: World Peace Foundation, 1949), Chap. 14; and UNCIO, *Report of the Rapporteur of Committee IV*, Doc. 913 IV/1/74 (1), XII, pp. 383 ff.

assemble in Washington soon after the Yalta Conference of February 1945. During April jurists from forty-four of the United Nations, including three judges and a Deputy Registrar of the Permanent Court, prepared a draft statute for submission to the San Francisco Conference. Again the question of continuing the Permanent Court was left open, but the jurists drafted a statute which followed closely the pattern of the old one. In this way the question was left so it could be settled either way.

It was decided at the San Francisco Conference to have a "new court." First, the old statute had no provisions for amendment. How could it be changed so that its provisions would square with those of the Charter? Second, sixteen of the Court's former members, including neutrals and enemy states, were not at the Conference and therefore not eligible to be UN or court members, at least for a while. Third, since the proposed court was to be an integral part of the Organization, it was thought wiser to make it a new if similar court. Equally important, but rarely mentioned, was the fact that neither the United States nor the Soviet Union had joined the Permanent Court. It was thought politically expedient to let sleeping dogs lie by recreating the "old court" as a "new one" in order to cut to a minimum the resistance of the two major powers.

The Conference Committee was careful to explain, however, that its decision did not "break the chain of continuity with the past," and that the "new" International Court of Justice, as it was called, was merely a "revised" court. Article 92 of the Charter, for example, states that the new Statute is based upon the old. The Statute itself provides continuity, since questions that were to be submitted to the Permanent Court by treaties still in force may be referred to the International Court (Article 37).

The few differences between the courts have the effect of making the new one more closely related to UN bodies than its predecessor was to the League. For example, the present Statute is to be amended in the same way as the Charter. United Nations Members are automatically parties to the Statute. Non-members may become parties to the Statute on the basis of conditions laid down by the General Assembly on the recommendation of the Security Council (Charter, Article 93). Switzerland and Liechtenstein joined the Court this way after agreeing to accept the Court's decisions and to recognize the right of the Security Council to make recommendations or to take action giving effect to the Court's decisions. This condition served to place these two non-members of the UN on the same footing as Members, for, under Article 94 of the Charter, the latter are required to comply with the Court's decision in any case to which they are parties. If they do not, the Security Council is empowered to enforce the Court's decision by "recommendations" or "measures to be taken to give effect to the judgment." [11]

This article points up as well as any the difference between the two

---

[11] But the Security Council can act only if it finds a threat to the peace. See *Charter of the United Nations,* Hearings before the Senate Foreign Relations Committee, 79th Congress, 1st session, 1945, p. 287.

courts in their relation to the League and to the United Nations. Under the Charter the judiciary is more closely allied to the security machinery than ever before.

Jurisdiction

The International Court has the same jurisdiction as its predecessor. Again the question of compulsory jurisdiction in legal disputes was warmly debated. The Committee of Jurists could not reach agreement and presented alternate texts, one preserving the optional clause (Article 36) and the other requiring obligatory jurisdiction in the Article's enumerated legal cases. A majority of the San Francisco Conference Committee favored the latter but, owing to opposition led by the United States and the Soviet Union, the old formula was retained. Compulsory jurisdiction was further emasculated when the Conference Committee went on to explain that reservations to the already innocuous optional clause were allowable as they had been under the League.[12] Once again some of the big powers refused even in legal cases to submit to judicial procedure without their consent. But the big powers are not solely to blame for this sad state of affairs. At the end of 1951, only thirty-five states, less than half of the Organization's Membership, had accepted the compulsory jurisdiction of the Court. Among these, many attached reservations the most common of which is reciprocity, whereby one party to a dispute accepts compulsory jurisdiction provided the other parties do likewise.

Although the United States declaration of acceptance of compulsory jurisdiction was deposited promptly with the Court in August 1946, it excluded "disputes with regard to matters which are essentially within the domestic jurisdiction of the United States of America as determined by the United States of America."[13] Although other governments have specified exceptions to the optional clause including similar reservations by France, Mexico and Pakistan,[14] this declaration is an unnecessarily extreme statement of sovereign independence. It appears not to have had the backing of the President, the Secretary of State or the Senate Foreign Relations Committee. It was introduced on the floor of the Senate by Senator Connally as an amendment to a resolution whereby two-thirds of the members of the Senate, present and concurring, were to approve adherence to the optional clause. Without such a reservation, the Senator declared, the Court might invade fields of vital interest to the United States, including the control of the Panama Canal, immigration or tariff policy. Since international law, including the Charter and the Statute, leaves these matters to domestic jurisdiction, the Senator's fears appear to have been unfounded. The Court would assume jurisdiction in such matters only if the fulfillment

---

[12] *Report of the Rapporteur of Committee IV/1*, pp. 390–392.

[13] U.N. Treaty Series, I, pp. 9–13. See also F. O. Wilcox, "The United States Accepts Compulsory Jurisdiction," and Lawrence Preuss, "The International Court of Justice, The Senate, and Matters of Domestic Jurisdiction," *American Journal of International Law*, Vol. 40 (1946), pp. 699–719 and 720–736.

[14] Lissitzyn, *op. cit.*, p. 65, n. 47.

of treaty obligations freely entered into by the United States were in question. Yet the United States is now in the unfortunate position of insisting that it be judge in its own case and that it may deny the Court's jurisdiction even in *legal* matters specified in the Statute. This is an undesirable precedent to establish in view of United States' protestations in favor of a regime of law in world affairs. A legal order is hard to establish if each state reserves to itself the right to decide what the law is and when it may be summoned to court. It is inconsistent with the letter and spirit of the Statute which specifies in paragraph 6 of Article 36 that "In the event of a dispute as to whether the Court has jurisdiction, the matter shall be settled by the decision of the Court."

In contrast, the Members of the Commonwealth of Nations reserved matters of domestic jurisdiction according to international law. The implication is that these states will accept the International Court's decision on the matter. The Permanent Court, for example, refused to adjudicate some matters which it found to be of domestic jurisdiction. When it decided otherwise, the parties to the Statute accepted its decision. This would have been the precedent to follow. Yet, in contrast to its earlier refusal to join the Permanent Court, the United States took a step forward in accepting the optional clause at all. Its declaration of acceptance need not obstruct judicial procedure if used with restraint. The fact is that all states are sensitive to supranational judicial authority on a universal basis. In European regional organizations, however, as we shall see in Part Four, the participating states have more willingly yielded their sovereignty to regional courts. Meanwhile the compulsory jurisdiction of the optional clause has provided the basis for the Court's consideration of two cases — the *Morocco Case* and the *Anglo-Norwegian Fisheries Case.*

The Charter in Article 36, paragraph 3, makes a modest effort to add to the Court's authority. It provides that the Security Council should "take into consideration that legal disputes should as a general rule be referred by the parties to the International Court of Justice. . . ." Whether disputes will be so referred depends upon the policies of the Security Council's members. The United Kingdom sought redress under this article in the Corfu Channel case.

The Organization of the International Court

The organization of the International Court is virtually a carbon copy of that of its predecessor. The judges are elected in the same way, although elections have been staggered to avoid a complete turnover at one time. The Court still meets in the Peace Palace at the Hague. Minor changes include a provision that no two judges of the same nationality may occupy the bench at the same time. A proposal to the Committee of Jurists in Washington, apparently by the Soviet Union, that nominations should be made directly by governments was rejected, and, after further discussion at San Francisco, the old system was retained. The procedure for handling the Permanent Court's budget has been continued with the new court.

In 1953 the members of the Court and the date on which their terms expired were as follows:

Sir Arnold Duncan McNair (U.K.), President	1955
José Gustavo Guerrero (El Salvador), Vice-President	1955
Alejandro Alvarez (Chile)	1955
Green H. Hackworth (U.S.)	1961
Bohdan Winiarski (Poland)	1958
Milovan Zoričič (Yugoslavia)	1958
Jules Basdevant (France)	1955
Helge Klaestad (Norway)	1961
Abdel Hamid Badawi (Egypt)	1958
John E. Read (Canada)	1958
Hsu Mo (China)	1958
Levi Fernandes Carneiro (Brazil)	1955
Sir Benegal N. Rau (India)	1961
E. C. Armand Ugón (Uruguay)	1961
Sergei A. Golunsky (U.S.S.R.)	1961

The Law Applied

The law applied by the International Court is to be the same as that utilized by the Permanent Court, custom and treaty law (Article 38 of the Statute). But international law is slowly growing. The retention of Article 38 in the Statute does not mean that the legal umbrella is incapable of opening further.

Advisory Opinions

Like the Covenant, the Charter empowers the Security Council and the General Assembly to request the Court to give advisory opinions (Article 96). Unlike the Covenant, however, the Charter restricts advisory opinions to *legal* matters. This innovation was deemed wise in view of the League's experience. The Permanent Court's opinion in the Austro-German Customs Union was thought to have been colored by political considerations, and the Court's prestige suffered as a consequence. States are reluctant to seek a judicial remedy for problems which may be settled more to their advantage by a political settlement. This reluctance to go to court has been particularly obvious in the United Nations. Proposals to refer the Indonesian dispute to the International Court for an advisory opinion, for example, failed to gain the requisite support in the Security Council. The same fate was forthcoming in the General Assembly in connection with the questions of Palestine and Indians in South Africa. Another innovation is that the specialized agencies and other bodies of the United Nations also may, with the General Assembly's authorization, request advisory opinions on legal matters within the scope of their activities. In its first five years the International Court handed down six advisory opinions.

It was recognized at San Francisco that the interpretation of the Charter would be a difficult matter, and no single organ of the United Nations was given the general competence to interpret the Charter with binding effect upon all Members and organs. No hard and fast rule could be agreed upon, but a general statement on the problem was included in the Conference record. Ultimately each organ was to "interpret such parts of the Charter as are applicable to its particular functions." [15] In the event of a difference of opinion among the organs or among the Members, the Assembly or the Council might ask the Court for an advisory opinion or set up an *ad hoc* committee of jurists. The International Court was not necessarily expected to be a constitutional umpire as is the United States Supreme Court. But on occasion the Court has played just this role despite the opposition in most instances of the Soviet Union which has denied the competence of the Court to interpret the Charter. In the League, the Council made all the requests for advisory opinions; in the United Nations it has been the General Assembly.

The Admission of a State to the United Nations (1948). Two advisory opinions dealt with the sticky issue of membership in the United Nations.[16] When the General Assembly asked the Court whether, in voting on the admission of a state to the United Nations, a Member was juridically entitled to set conditions not expressly stated in Article 4, the Court answered in the negative.[17] The General Assembly's question arose because the Soviet Union, during Security Council consideration of admissions applications, had blackballed a number of candidates that would otherwise have been elected. The Court's opinion has had no effect whatsoever on the attitude of the Soviet Union, and it is difficult to find any advantage resulting from the Assembly's action in requesting the opinion. Conceivably the opinion might be embarrassing to have on the record if a "package deal" were under consideration whereby several states might be admitted at once in the interest of universality.

Competence of the General Assembly Regarding Admission to the United Nations (1950). A request for an opinion on the General Assembly's competence in admitting new Members also grew out of the deadlock resulting from Soviet vetoes in the Security Council. Could the Assembly admit new Members despite the Security Council deadlock? Argentina and other Latin American states insisted that it could despite the language of Article 4. In November 1949 the question was submitted to the Court which advised in the negative by a vote of 12 to 2 with only the Chilean and Brazilian judges in the minority. The by-products in this opinion were more fruitful than the central issue. In answer to questions that were raised regarding its authority, the Court declared that it could give an opinion on any legal question and within this limit was empowered to interpret the Charter.[18]

---

[15] UNCIO, XIII, Doc. 933, p. 709.
[16] See pp. 104–105.
[17] Advisory Opinion, ICJ *Reports*, 1948, p. 57.
[18] Advisory opinion, ICJ *Reports*, 1950, p. 4.

Reparation for Injuries Suffered in the Service of the United Nations, 1948–49. This advisory opinion confirmed the fact that the United Nations is an international legal personality with authority to bring claims in an international court. When Count Bernadotte, the United Nations Mediator in the Palestine case, was assassinated, the General Assembly decided unanimously in December 1948 to ask the Court whether the United Nations could bring an international claim against the government of a state involving responsibility for injury to a United Nations agent.

The Court decided unanimously that the United Nations could bring a claim against the responsible government for damage to the Organization. By an 11 to 4 decision it held that the Organization could also claim damages to the victim or persons injured through him. In a 10 to 5 decision the Court further decided that there was no conflict between a United Nations claim and similar rights possessed by the victim's state provided the former claim was based upon the breach of obligations due itself.[19] As a result of this opinion the government of Israel paid damages to the United Nations for Count Bernadotte's death. The United States and Soviet judges were in the minority that argued that the United Nations was not competent to advance claims for individuals.

The case is noteworthy in showing that the Court has been unafraid to break new ground in order to serve the developing "need of the community." There was no precedent for reparations claims for damages suffered by the agents of international organizations. Yet the Court agreed unanimously that the United Nations was an international person able to bring claims against states, including non-members:

> Throughout its history, the development of international law has been influenced by the requirements of international life, and the progressive increase in the collective activities of states has already given rise to instances of action upon the international plane by certain entities which are not states.[20]

Peace Treaties with Bulgaria, Hungary and Rumania (1949). When several Members protested the violation of human rights in these three satellites of the Soviet Union, the General Assembly asked for an interpretation of the peace treaties that had been concluded with them. Four questions were submitted to the Court:

1. Did the disputes between the Allied Powers and Bulgaria, Hungary and Rumania involve the interpretation of treaties?

2. If so, were the three governments required to appoint representatives to the treaty commissions envisaged by the treaties?

3. If so, was the Secretary-General empowered to appoint a third member to each commission if the three governments had not appointed their representatives?

19 Advisory Opinion, ICJ *Reports,* 1949, p. 175.
20 *Ibid.,* p. 178.

4. If so, would a commission composed only of one party's representative and a member appointed by the Secretary-General be able to give a binding decision in a dispute?

In March 1950 the Court answered the first two questions affirmatively. In June 1950 the Court, despite the arguments of the United Kingdom and the United States, held that the Secretary-General was authorized to appoint a third member of the commissions only if the parties to the dispute had appointed their members. Since this was not the case, the Secretary-General had no power to proceed, and it was unnecessary to answer the fourth question.

The opinion seems to have been useful because there were specific legal questions at issue. Whether it was useful to bring the political problem to the General Assembly in the first place is not so clear.[21]

The International Status of South-West Africa (1949–50). When the Union of South Africa, hopeful of incorporating the Territory of South-West Africa within its boundaries, balked at placing that Territory under trusteeship, the General Assembly asked the Court for an opinion regarding the Territory's international status.

The Court found that, despite the League's demise, South Africa continued to have international obligations under the Covenant and under the mandate for the area. The responsibility for supervision of the territory now rested with the United Nations, but the Court did not go so far as to require South Africa to submit a trusteeship agreement. (This decision was close, 8 to 6; the others were either unanimous or 12 to 2.) It did hold that South Africa should submit reports to the United Nations, which, in turn, could receive petitions from the territory. Finally, South Africa could not modify the international status of the territory without United Nations consent.

The opinion will probably have little influence on South Africa for some time to come. It was important for the Court to settle the legal problems, however, before the General Assembly took measures to give effect to the opinion. Although it offers no support for United Nations measures to compel South Africa to negotiate a trusteeship agreement, the opinion may have helped to block South Africa's scheme of annexation despite the fact that South Africa has asserted that the opinion is not the same as a judgment and therefore not binding.

Reservations to the Genocide Convention. When some nations expressed doubts regarding the proposed Convention on the Prevention and Punishment of the Crime of Genocide, the General Assembly asked the Court to give an advisory opinion on the legal effects of reservations to the Convention. At the same time the Assembly asked the International Law Commission to study the general question of reservations to multilateral conventions. The specific questions were:

[21] For the Assembly's role in the case see Chap. 15, p. 450.

1. Can a state that accepts the Convention with reservations be regarded as a party to the Convention if the reservations are objected to by one or more of the other parties?
2. If so, what is the reservation's effect on the reserving state and
    a) the parties objecting to the reservation,
    b) those which accept it?
3. What would be the effect of a reservation made:
    a) by a signatory which has not ratified,
    b) by a state entitled to sign or accede but which has not done so?

The Court first disposed of objections that it had no authority to express opinions on these matters. The General Assembly, it noted, was seeking legal guidance on its own actions. The Court then held that no absolute answer could be given to the first question and that the effect of a reservation would depend upon the particular circumstances of each individual case. A reserving state might remain a party to the Convention if its reservations were "compatible with the object and purpose of the Convention." A similar answer was given to the second question. Since no state could be bound by a reservation to which it had not consented, each state must consider on the basis of its individual appraisal whether the reserving state was a party to the Convention. In answer to question 3 an objection to a reservation can have effect only upon ratification by the objecting state. These opinions were adopted by votes of 7 to 5.[22] Undoubtedly it was important for the members of the General Assembly to be advised on these knotty legal questions before they undertook the Convention's obligations. The Court was, therefore, playing a useful role in the difficult task of developing international law.

The Development of International Law

Students of international affairs are prone to argue whether international law is really law. The discussion is apt to be rather sterile. It is clear at the outset that there is no supranational legal order comparable to that of most national states. International law is in a primitive state and, since the middle of the nineteenth century, heavily saturated by the doctrines of the positivists: that no state can be bound without its consent and that treaties, rather than custom or natural law based on "right reason," are the source of law. Those that deny the existence of real international law point out that it is unenforceable. They emphasize law as command rather than obedience. Without a real legislature to make rules and without an executive to enforce them, there can be no real law, in this view.

It is equally clear on the other hand, that, whether one sees through positivist or naturalist glasses, there is a body of international rules which states generally obey and which courts administer. Sometimes states break these rules just as individuals do in their own communities, and often a

[22] Advisory opinion, ICJ *Reports*, 1951, p. 15, and *Yearbook of the United Nations, 1951* (New York: Columbia University Press, 1951), pp. 820–824.

lawbreaker goes unpunished. It is more likely, however, that a state will argue that the law is on its side. The Soviet Union claimed that the Korean War was a civil strife beyond the reach of the Charter's law. The Union of South Africa argued similarly with respect to the treatment of its minorities claiming that its social policies were a matter of domestic jurisdiction. The Court held in the Iranian oil case that it could not assume jurisdiction because the dispute did not fall within existing rules of international law. These examples can be multiplied many times, and they demonstrate that all nations are acutely conscious of international law. From the cases summarized above, it is also clear that there is a judicial process which states are ready to follow in settling many of their difficulties. There is also a complicated structure of rules, embodied in treaties and customary procedure applied by foreign offices and enforced in both national and international courts. One reason for skepticism is that most citizens are almost totally unaware of these rules. But they exist and are generally followed for reasons of utility and tradition. So long as nations consider whether their policies follow legal standards, so long as they justify their actions in legal terms, and so long as they obey some rules and procedures defined and enforced by courts and governments, it is preposterous to deny that international law is really law.

International Legislation

The real difficulty is not that international law is not real law but that it is not sufficiently utilized. Relations between states are only in small measure determined by legal rules. Many of the existing rules, moreover, are vaguely defined, or their meaning is disputed. More important, the international legislative process is tortuous and uncertain owing to the decentralization of the world's power among seventy-odd independent states. This is where the United Nations system comes in. One of its principal purposes is to foster a legislative process through interstate agreement. The work of all the United Nations bodies and the specialized agencies contributes to this end. Even the Security Council influences the legislative process through its control over such matters as regulating the use of force.

It is a relatively inchoate system. Most international legislation, for example, results from agreements worked out by nations multilaterally to be submitted to their respective governments for ratification. At present states consider themselves bound to follow such legislation only if they give their explicit consent. Unlike national law, only some states are bound by some of these agreements. There is no majority rule. The problem is how to gain general acceptance. Would rules ratified by the sixty United Nations Members be acceptable as law to non-members? The chances are that eventually they would be.

Even prior to World War II there was a great body of multilateral conventions that Professor Manley O. Hudson, a former member of the International Court, has gathered together in a nine-volume series entitled *International Legislation*. He asserts on the basis of treaties registered with the

League that 257 legislative items were adopted prior to World War I and 229 after the war.[23] The appropriateness of the term *international legislation* has been questioned since states can usually free themselves of the conventions' obligations in practice if not in law and since all states are not parties to all multilateral conventions. Yet a trend toward a legislative process seems to be developing, although it is anything but dependable.

The experience of the Genocide Convention suggests the difficulties of the international legislative process. With the horrors of Nazi racial persecution in mind the first General Assembly sought ways of stamping out the intentional extermination of large communities of human beings (genocide). For two years the problem was considered by the Economic and Social Council, the Secretariat, an interim body on the codification of international law, an *ad hoc* committee of the Economic and Social Council, and Member governments. In 1948 a draft convention was ready for the General Assembly which approved a resolution asking that it be signed and approved by the membership. Later other states were asked to sign. By 1950 the Secretary-General reported that only five states had ratified the Convention although forty-three of seventy-eight possible states had signed it. Not until January 1951 were the twenty ratifications forthcoming that were necessary to bring the convention into force. Even then the United States and the Soviet Union were among the missing.

The birth pains of the Genocide Convention show that governments are reluctant to yield any of their freedom of action, even though, as in this case, they may unanimously adopt conventions in the General Assembly that seek to establish universal rules of conduct. One feature of the convention that makes governments shy away is that genocide is made a crime in international law for which *individuals* are to be held responsible. States adhering to the Convention are required to pass laws necessary to give it effect.

The failure of the United States to become a party to the convention is particularly hard to condone and is partly due to divergent views between the legislative and executive branches of government. After World War II the United States took the lead in insisting that individuals must be held responsible in international law for violating certain basic rights recognized by civilized communities. The Senate's reluctance is difficult to square with the principles applied in the Nuremberg trials, for example, in which persons were tried for crimes against peace, war crimes and crimes against humanity. These trials were set in motion by an agreement in August 1945 between France, the United Kingdom, the United States and the Soviet Union to establish an International Military Tribunal to try "war criminals" of the Axis Powers. Judges and prosecutors were appointed by the four governments. The Tribunal met at Nuremberg from November 1945 through August 1946 and handed down its judgment a month later. Twenty-two Nazi leaders stood trial as well as six Nazi organizations. All

[23] See Manley O. Hudson, *International Legislation*, 9 Vols. (Washington: Carnegie Endowment for International Peace, 1931–1950).

but three were found guilty; eleven were hanged, and the others received prison sentences. Goering contrived to commit suicide before he could be executed.[24]

The Genocide Convention is precisely in this tradition. Despite the fact that the Convention was even deliberately drawn so that it would not be the "law of the land" but would only call for subsequent legislation, it remains in a Senate pigeon-hole. Sectional differences in America regarding human rights, a "states' rights" tradition and Senate prerogative all played a part in preventing the United States from continuing its role in establishing universal sentiment against race extermination.

The Court's Achievement

The International Court and its predecessors have also contributed to the growth of law. The Court has introduced elements that are important in any legal order — continuity, relative impartiality and precedent. In this way rules have been formulated and clarified. As international legal procedure meets the needs of states, it wins confidence. There have been setbacks to be sure. Iran withdrew her declaration of compulsory jurisdiction in 1951 in a fit of nationalist pique over her petroleum dispute with the United Kingdom, but the increasing volume of the Court's business shows that the stream is beginning to flow the other way. Obviously the Court cannot cope directly with the world's primary sources of conflict such as political, economic and ideological factors. Yet the Court, through its judgments and advisory opinions, is contributing brick and mortar to the structure of world order. But the founders of the United Nations realized that devices other than the Court must be used to develop international law.

International Law Commission

Accordingly the Charter in Article 13 provides that the "General Assembly shall initiate studies and make recommendations for the purpose of . . . encouraging the progressive development of international law and its codification. . . . " In November 1947 the General Assembly established an International Law Commission whose members, like those of the Court, do not serve as representatives of governments but in their individual capacity as experts. Its terms of reference draw a distinction between "codification" and "progressive development." The former refers to the precise formulation of rules of international law in fields where there already has been extensive state practice, precedent and doctrine. The latter refers to preparation of draft conventions on subjects in regard to which the law has not been sufficiently developed in the practice of states.

---

[24] Brig. Gen. Telford Taylor, "Nuremberg Trials: War Crimes and International Law," *International Conciliation*, No. 450 (April 1949); *Nazi Conspiracy and Aggression*, 8 Vols. (Washington: Government Printing Office, 1946); *Trial of the Major War Criminals Before the International Military Tribunal, Nuremberg*, 37 Vols. (Washington: Government Printing Office, 1947–1948).

The Commission was slow in getting under way. In June 1949 the Assembly requested the Commission to codify the law of treaties, including their interpretation and binding force; arbitration procedure; and the regime of the high seas, including the extent of territorial waters and the rights of states on the high seas. These are technical matters on which there is a large body of precedent. The Commission is still at work and may be able to define more precisely the law on these subjects than has been possible in the past. While these matters seem far removed from the arena of war and peace, they are important ingredients in building any cooperative community.

The Commission was also asked to break new ground in formulating the principles of law recognized in the Charter and judgment of the Nuremberg Tribunal, and to prepare a draft code of offences against the peace and security of mankind. By 1950 the Commission had agreed upon seven of the Nuremberg principles which were a distinct departure from practice prior to the Nuremberg Trials themselves. Individuals no less than governments were to be held responsible for three categories of international crimes: "crimes against peace" (planning wars of aggression); "war crimes" (violations of the laws of war regarding captured military and civilian population and property); and "crimes against humanity" (ill-treatment of civil population). Whether many governments would consent to bind themselves to these principles for a long time to come seemed very doubtful.

At its first session the Commission also completed a Draft Declaration on Rights and Duties of states. Basic rights of states were recognized to be independence, equality in law, the exercise of jurisdiction over state territory in accordance with international law and individual or collective self-defense against armed attack. Duties included the peaceful settlement of international disputes and more novel considerations such as respect for human rights and fundamental freedoms of all persons without distinction of sex, language or religion. In 1951 these principles were submitted to governments for their consideration and comment.

The Commission has also considered ways of publicizing customary international law. The Secretariat is considering a publication project to this end. It has considered the perplexing problem of reservations to multilateral conventions. At the instigation of the U.S.S.R. it was asked by the General Assembly to define aggression. Although it has moved cautiously in this direction, the Commission has generally followed the line of thought taken at San Francisco. No definitive enumeration of aggressive acts seems feasible, and the competent organs of the United Nations should not be rigidly held to a list of such acts which is necessarily incomplete. At the request of the General Assembly the Commission has also studied the desirability of establishing an international criminal court for the trial of genocide and other crimes committed by individuals. The Commission reported in 1950 that such a court was both desirable and feasible. A draft statute has been prepared.

While many of these proposals must await the passage of time before they can become crystallized into law, they are not hair-brained schemes. They reflect the efforts of both peoples and governments to bring about a more orderly world. They are evidence of a growing cohesion in the international community. The experience gained in formulating these principles will help governments decide when and how to transform them into law. One thing is certain — international law cannot be developed without procedures for continuing collaboration of this kind.

Suggestions for Further Reading

Books

Carlston, K. S., *The Process of International Arbitration* (New York: Columbia University Press, 1946).

Feller, A. H., *The United Nations and World Community* (Boston: Little, Brown & Company, 1952).

Fleming, D. F., *The United States and the World Court* (New York: Doubleday & Company, Inc., 1945).

Gluck, S., *The Nuremberg Trial and Aggressive War* (New York: Alfred A. Knopf, 1946).

Hudson, M. O., *International Tribunals: Past and Future* (Washington: Carnegie Endowment and Brookings Institution, 1944).

————, *The Permanent Court of International Justice, 1920–1942* (New York: The Macmillan Company, 1943).

————, ed., *World Court Reports*, 4 Vols., a collection of the judgments, orders, and opinions of the Permanent Court of International Justice (Washington: Carnegie Endowment for International Peace, 1934–1943).

————, ed., *International Legislation*, 9 Vols., a collection of the texts of multipartite instruments with the Covenant of the League of Nations (Washington: Carnegie Endowment for International Peace, 1931–1950).

Jackson, R. H., *The Nuremberg Case* (New York: Alfred A. Knopf, 1947).

Jessup, P. C., *A Modern Law of Nations* (New York: The Macmillan Company, 1948).

Lissitzyn, Oliver, "The International Court of Justice: Its Role in the Maintenance of International Peace and Security," *United Nations Studies No. 6* (New York: Carnegie Endowment for International Peace, 1951).

Scott, J. B., ed., *The Hague Court Reports, Second Series* (comprising the awards and other documents of the Permanent Court of Arbitration) (New York: Oxford University Press, 1932).

Periodicals

Gilmore, Grant, "The International Court of Justice," *Yale Law Journal*, Vol. 55, No. 5 (August 1946).

Hudson, M. O., "Twenty-fourth Year of the World Court," *American Journal of International Law*, Vol. 40, No. 1 (January 1946), pp. 1–52. This includes a comparison of the Permanent Court of International Justice with the "new" court, the International Court of Justice. The first issue of this journal each year has an article by Judge Hudson on the work of the Court the preceding year.

Pollux, "The Interpretation of the [United Nations] Charter," *British Yearbook of International Law*, Vol. 23 (1946).

Vulcan, C., "L'Exécution des décisions de la Cour Internationale de Justice d'après la Charte des Nations Unies," *Revue générale de droit internationale public*, Vol. 51, 3rd Series (1947).

Wilcox, F. O., "The United States Accepts Compulsory Jurisdiction," *American Journal of International Law*, Vol. 40, No. 4 (October 1946).

Williams, Sir John Fischer, "Justiciable and Other Disputes," *American Journal of International Law*, Vol. 26, No. 1 (January 1932).

Documents

Historical Survey of Development of International Law and Its Codification by International Conferences, UN Doc. A/AC.10/5, Apr. 29, 1947, reproduced in *American Journal of International Law*, Vol. 41 (1947), Supplement, pp. 29–111.

Report of the International Law Commission, Covering Its Second Session June 5–July 29, 1950, General Assembly, Official Records, Fifth Session, Supplement No. 12. UN Doc. A/1316, Lake Success, N.Y. (1950). The International Law Commission submits similar reports annually to the regular sessions of the General Assembly.

Reports of International Arbitral Awards, 3 vols., seriatim, published by the United Nations.

Treaty Series of the United Nations, 33 vols., seriatim.

The International Court of Justice issues several publications including *Reports of Judgments, Advisory Opinions and Orders; Pleadings, Oral Arguments, Documents; Documents Concerning the Organization of the Court; Yearbooks; Index to the Reports of Judgments, Opinions and Orders.*

International Civil Servants

"I solemnly swear (undertake, affirm, promise) to exercise in all loyalty, discretion and conscience the functions entrusted to me as an international civil servant of the United Nations, to discharge these functions and to regulate my conduct with the interests of the United Nations only in view, and not to seek or accept instructions in regard to the performance of my duties from any government or other authority external to the organization." [1]

BEFORE ACCEPTING ANY APPOINTMENT all members of the staff (Secretariat) of the United Nations must subscribe to the above oath. It is modeled closely on the declaration required of all permanent officials of the League Secretariat beginning in 1932.[2] To several thousand individuals this oath or very similar ones are commonplace because international civil services have now become accepted features of the international landscape. The United Nations proper, not including the affiliated specialized agencies, has employed as many as 4,000 international civil servants including about 2,900 permanent employees and over 1,000 temporary ones. The League Secretariat was small by comparison and never employed much over 700 persons. Now the United Nations Educational and Scientific Organization (UNESCO), a specialized agency, alone employs nearly this number. Regional organizations such as the Organization for European Economic Cooperation (OEEC) and the North Atlantic Treaty Organization (NATO) have employed about 800 and 600 respectively. Naturally the totals fluctuate with the changing workloads of the organizations in question. All together over 10,000 persons may now be in the employ of international secretariats.[3]

[1] *Report of the Secretary-General on Personnel Policy,* UN Doc. A/2364, January 30, 1953. Also Staff Regulation number 2.

[2] Egon F. Ranshofen-Wertheimer, *The International Secretariat, A Great Experiment in International Administration* (Washington: Carnegie Endowment for International Peace, 1945), p. 245.

[3] Walter R. Crocker, "Some Notes on the United Nations Secretariat," *International Organization,* Vol. 4, No. 4 (November 1950), p. 599.

Most governments agree that a declaration of loyalty to an international organization is not the same as an oath of allegiance to a national state. Secretariat officials retain their national citizenship although they must serve the organization with strict impartiality. Governments, in turn, are committed under the United Nations Charter to respect the neutrality of their citizens on the Secretariat.

Secretariat officials are either "seconded" (loaned) by national governments to work for international organizations, as is the case in some wartime collaborative arrangements and some regional security organizations such as NATO, or they are employed as international officials who must shed national service responsibilities and become loyal international civil servants. Officials in a secretariat are not to be confused with the members of the national delegations.

Growth of the Secretariat Idea

International secretariats, as we have seen, did not exist in the modern sense prior to 1919. Some of the early public international unions, however, did have, in addition to a conference or policy-making body and a commission or governing body, a secretariat (bureau) as an administrative and continuing element of the organization. But these bureaus were organized and maintained by one of the smaller neutral states such as Switzerland or Belgium.[4] These bureaus were small, and, although entrusted with international duties, were not international in composition. Bureau officials remained in the pay of their national governments.

A more immediate influence shaping the notion of an international secretariat was the experience of the Inter-Allied Maritime Transport Council of 1917–18 including a permanent staff of administrative officials known as the Allied Maritime Transport Executive. It was composed of British, French, Italian and American civil servants working under the direction of a ministerial council.

The League Secretariat

At the Paris Peace Conference no one doubted the need for a secretariat to service the proposed League of Nations. We have seen that the Smuts Plan for a "League of Nations" published in December 1918 was the first to call for a "permanent secretariat and staff" and included considerable analysis of its role and functions. Thereafter the joint British-American proposals (Cecil–Miller draft) presented to the Conference referred specifically to an international secretariat. Although emphasizing military sanctions the French proposals of Leon Bourgeois also hinted at similar developments described as a "permanent delegation."[5]

[4] See the classic and pioneering study by Paul S. Reinsch, *Public International Unions, Their Work and Organization* (Boston: Ginn, 1911).

[5] See Ranshofen-Wertheimer, *op. cit.*, Chap. II; D. H. Miller, *The Drafting of the Covenant*, Vol. 2 (New York: Putnam, 1928); and F. P. Walters, *A History of the League of Nations*, Vol. 1 (London: Oxford University Press, 1952), Chaps. 5 and 7.

The actual composition and role of the League Secretariat were knottier questions. Article 6 of the Covenant simply stated that at the seat of the League there should be a "permanent secretariat" appointed by a Secretary-General with the approval of the Council. Should the Secretary-General conduct himself like a permanent civil servant or like an international statesman? Should the secretariat be composed of national delegations paid by their respective governments and responsible to them as had been the wartime practice? Or should it be established as a truly international civil service composed of individuals no longer in the service of their home states but dedicated to an international outlook and prepared to furnish impartial advice and service to all Member states? Due largely to the persistence of the League's first Secretary-General, Sir Eric Drummond, the latter view prevailed. Others, including Sir Arthur Salter, secretary to the Transport Executive, and Sir Maurice Hankey of the British Cabinet Secretariat, who reportedly declined an invitation to be the first Secretary-General, favored a staff composed of national components. Although Sir Eric's views were radical for his day they were quickly supported by the League Members. In May 1920 the Council adopted the Balfour Report defining the character of League officials as international civil servants.[6] Later reports in both the League and the United Nations have sustained Sir Eric's concept,[7] but it has been subjected to heavy fire in periods of international tension.

Sir Eric succeeded in building up a fine corps of officials from more than forty different countries, including the United States. Inevitably, League administrative practice drew from the experience of many nations, especially those in Europe. This was to be expected because European countries had developed procedures and standards for the public service at that time unequalled anywhere else.

The League Secretary-General

The first Secretary-General, Sir Eric Drummond, formerly a British civil servant, was selected at Paris before the League was actually a going concern. He was named in Annex 2 of the Covenant itself. No term of office was specified, but, on Sir Eric's resignation in 1933, the Assembly set a ten-year term for the office. M. Joseph Avenol of France was then appointed the second and last Secretary-General by the Council with the Assembly's approval, in accordance with Article 6 of the Covenant.

Some of the League's framers, including Lord Cecil, originally proposed that the League's chief officer should possess wide political authority and carry the impressive title of Chancellor. A preëminent allied statesman,

---

[6] "Staff of the Secretariat; Report Presented by the British Representative, Mr. A. J. Balfour," League of Nations, *Official Journal*, 1920, Vol. 1, pp. 136–139.

[7] See the *Noblemaire Report* of December 1920, on the organization of the Secretariat, League of Nations Documents C.424, M.305. 1921.X and A.140 (a) 1921; *The Report of the Committee of Thirteen*, League of Nations Document A.16. 1930; and *The Report of the Preparatory Commission of the United Nations*, Doc. PC/20, December 23, 1945 (London: H. M. Stationery Office, 1946).

Eleutherios Venizelos, was sounded out for the job. On his refusal, the League framers fell back upon the concept of a career civil servant as exemplified by the permanent under-secretary of a British Ministry.[8] The change was not without significance. It meant that the first officer of the League was an international civil servant rather than an international statesman. This was precisely the role played by Sir Eric. Shunning publicity, he worked anonymously to set high standards of administrative efficiency. To all national delegations he was ever ready with the impartial, judicious advice of the expert. He behaved, in short, as though he were a British permanent secretary advising cabinet ministers on whose shoulders rested the burdens of political responsibility. But, in fact, traditional theories of political responsibility simply could not apply. There was no League "government" or "cabinet" issuing clear policy directives to the civil service. There were only the Assembly and the Council to provide rudimentary and spasmodic guidance. Inevitably in these circumstances Sir Eric's administrative role was influential politically.

Indeed, the position of the Secretary-General has no counterpart in any national government. He must be at once civil servant, cabinet minister and diplomat. In the Sino-Japanese dispute of 1932, for example, the Secretary-General wore all three hats. Yet he could not vote nor directly make proposals to governments in debate. What he could not do before the footlights was by no means, however, the measure of what he could do behind the scenes. It has been argued that Sir Eric was politically influential precisely because he was a nonpolitical figure.

Despite Sir Eric's limited political leadership, many observers concluded that the League would have been better served had its principal officer been an international statesman instead of an international civil servant. Neither of the League Secretaries-General, in this view, exploited to the full the strategic position of his office. This was particularly true of the Secretary-General's seldom-used right to address the Assembly and the Council. In the light of the League's experience, the framers of the Charter sought to give the United Nations Secretary-General the opportunity and authority to seize the reins and crack the whip. But does the Secretary-General really have a whip? Power in international affairs still remains with the states, few of which are prepared to brook any supranational authority.

Another point is that, unlike a cabinet officer in a national government, the Secretary-General must be acceptable to the "opposition." That is to say, he has great difficulty accomplishing his tasks unless he is backed up by at least the most influential members of the organization. Seldom does "government by majority rule" occur in an international organization. Thus Joseph Avenol found his position well-nigh intolerable when he sought to please Italy as well as France and Britain in the Ethiopian crisis of 1936.

Yet it was natural enough to conclude from the League's experience that

[8] There are several sources. See especially, Stephen M. Schwebel, *The Secretary-General of the United Nations* (Cambridge: Harvard University Press, 1952), p. 2, and Viscount Cecil, *A Great Experiment* (London: Oxford University Press, 1941), p. 89.

a more forceful principal officer at the helm had been needed to guide public opinion and governments along the ways of peace. No representative of the organization as a whole had been in the public eye. No one had successfully represented the common public interest in the debates at Geneva. The problem was one of prestige for the organization itself. Rightly or wrongly many students of the League as well as government officials concluded that international order depended on international as well as national statesmen.

Avenol's Resignation. The resignation of M. Avenol in 1940 remains something of a mystery, but even before the Nazi panzer divisions rolled westwards to the English Channel M. Avenol seems to have felt that the League was lost. The following facts regarding his views and resignation have come to light.[9]

First, M. Avenol was convinced that the only future for the League lay in emphasizing the technical aspects of economic and social cooperation. The League's enforcement machinery was unworkable, in his view, and should have been abandoned by Covenant amendment. A "non-political" League might have been able to achieve greater universality of membership.

Second, in contrast to Trygve Lie in 1950, M. Avenol did not take an unqualified stand against aggression. But neither did the great powers. When Avenol undertook diplomatic maneuverings to bring Italy back into the League in 1936, British and French statesmen (Hoare and Laval) had already sought a deal with Italy in the previous December that would have recognized in some measure the latter's claim to Ethiopia.

Third, in the opinion of many League observers Avenol's management of his staff in the face of totalitarian pressure after the Munich crisis of September 1938 left something to be desired. The sudden dismissal of his Chief of Cabinet in December 1938 was criticized as incompatible with his responsibilities as Secretary-General. While he could not avoid dismissing many of his staff after the outbreak of war in September 1939, his retrenchment policy raised doubts whether he really sought to salvage as much of the League's machinery as possible. Although the Secretary-General and the Supervisory Commission had become virtual trustees of the League by Assembly resolution in 1938 and 1939, Avenol acted with little reference to the Commission. Indeed he was sharply criticized by members of both the Council and the Supervisory Commission. When certain League services were to be removed to Princeton, New Jersey, M. Avenol at first objected.

Finally, after the fall of France M. Avenol chose to cast his lot with the Vichy Government rather than with the Free French. His decision to resign as Secretary-General, he tells us, was taken when diplomatic relations be-

[9] The most informative accounts are contained in Ranshofen-Wertheimer, *op. cit.*, pp. 378–381, and Schwebel, *op. cit.*, Appendix. Both sources list the relevant but scanty League documentation.

tween Britain and France were severed following the destruction of the French fleet by the British at Oran in June 1940. Whether Vichy asked him to resign has never been made clear. His simple duty, he declared, lay in "being faithful to my country." [10] He announced his intention of resigning as of September 1, 1940, and at the end of August he journeyed to Vichy. The actual documentation of his resignation remains confused. During the war M. Avenol sought refuge from the Germans in flight to Switzerland. He has remained in seclusion near Geneva since that time. The League's final years were directed by Mr. Sean Lester as Acting Secretary-General under the guidance of the Supervisory Commission.

In sum, it is perhaps fair to say that M. Avenol, like the League, was a victim of circumstances largely beyond his control. While he might well have tried to exert League influence more forcefully, his fate was determined in the foreign offices of the principal powers. There is little likelihood that any Secretary-General could have appreciably altered the flow of events.

Organization of the League Secretariat

In addition to the Secretary-General there were at first four Under-Secretaries-General in the League. In 1922 the post of Deputy Secretary-General was established, and in 1932 a second Deputy was added. These officers and the Directors of Sections comprised the League's "High Directorate" or "Principal Officers." The number of Under-Secretaries varied with the League's membership from two to four and was a constant source of friction and intrigue. In practice the posts of Deputy and Under-Secretary were reserved to the great powers, and, as a matter of practical politics, filled by them. Despite the theory of the Secretariat these officials tended to be national representatives, and, with the deterioration of European politics in the early 1930's, the German and Italian incumbents increasingly sought to control their own nationals on the Secretariat. On occasion confidential information was transmitted to Rome and Berlin. Administratively their functions were little differentiated from the Directors of Sections below them. These offices were evidence of the fact that certain powers, notably Germany and Italy, were unwilling to entrust the direction of the Secretariat to a single official. The work of the Secretariat, in their views, should have been managed by a board of directors with each possessing the right of veto.

Hierarchically the staff was organized in three levels:

First Division: Deputy and under-secretaries-general, directors and chiefs of section, members of section, counsellors, interpreters, translators, etc. — totalling perhaps a quarter of the total of personnel.

Intermediate Division: Secretaries, chief clerks, statisticians, accountants, stenographers and typists — comprising about three-fifths of the staff.

Third Division: Messengers, porters, doormen, caretakers — making up the remainder.

10 Schwebel, *op. cit.,* p. 221.

This organization of personnel provided the basis for differences in such matters as tenure, pay schedules and leaves of absence. Thus for the higher posts, appointments were for a period of seven to ten years with renewals permissible for shorter periods. For the intermediate posts there were seven-year tenures with renewals possible up to the age of retirement. A Committee on Appointments and Promotions advised the Secretary-General on personnel management including staff regulations, pay scales, leaves and disciplinary procedures.

The Secretariat was also organized along substantive (sometimes called "functional") and on service lines.[11] The principal units, known as "Sections," were charged with specific subject matters corresponding to the League's principal activities, such as minorities, mandates and health.

The Service Sections were concerned with the internal administration of the Secretariat, including such matters as personnel, accounts, care of buildings, interpretation, translation, documents, printing, editing and stenographic service. The original eleven sections were finally increased to fifteen, with each serving not only the Assembly and the Council but also other League organs and agencies as needed. In addition to coordination, the Secretariat performed important work in organized publicity through its Information Section for all League activities including communiqués, pamphlets, films and broadcasts from the League's radio station (Radio-Nations).

Although the Covenant was silent on the matter of languages, by administrative rulings English and French were the official languages. Precedent had been established when the Peace Conference of 1919 was the first major diplomatic gathering at which English as well as French became an official language. League communications were drawn up in French and English, and the Secretariat provided official interpretation only from English into French and vice versa. Delegates speaking in other tongues provided their own interpreters. Translation services, however, were sometimes considerably broader.

Within this administrative framework the pattern of work was largely British. Considerable responsibility was delegated throughout the entire staff necessitating almost the teamwork and unity of purpose that have usually characterized British national administration. The system was described as one "in which the work comes up from below."[12] A central Registry distributed nearly all communications to the appropriate sections for action, and only the most important matters were referred to higher authority.

With M. Avenol in charge after 1933 these practices were gradually modified in favor of French administrative procedure. Incoming mail was first examined by the Secretary-General's immediate staff or "cabinet" before routine matters were referred below, often with comments and instruc-

---

[11] An authoritative account is contained in Ranshofen-Wertheimer, op. cit., Chap. VI.
[12] See E. S. Phelan, Yes, and Albert Thomas (London: Cresset Press, 1936), p. 66, and Ranshofen-Wertheimer, op. cit., Chap. IX.

tions attached. Less discretion was thus permitted members of sections. "The current ran downwards and not upwards." As a result personal initiative was somewhat dampened, and many officials felt they had lost caste. For a staff that was far from homogeneous, however, the modified system had some advantages.

The Secretariat's decline in morale and initiative after 1935, however, was by no means due solely to new administrative techniques. Chauvinism and international conflict afforded an unfriendly climate for international officials, many of whom suffered abuse and suspicion. The Secretariat's spirit and effectiveness could be little better than the temper of international politics.

The United Nations Secretariat

The framers of the Charter sought to profit from the vicissitudes of the League's Secretariat. Indeed, once the Big Four had agreed to establish some sort of postwar United Nations Organization, the need for an international secretariat was taken for granted. At both Dumbarton Oaks and San Francisco, agreement on the Secretariat was reached relatively quickly. The Secretariat emerged in Article 7 of the Charter as one of the United Nation's principal organs.

The genesis of this article is quickly traced. In the earliest Charter draft of which there is public record (July 14, 1943) the State Department proposed a "permanent Secretariat" composed of a "General Secretary and such secretaries and staff as may be required." These officials in performing their work were to be exclusively international. They were to declare their loyalty to the proposed international organization and avoid seeking or receiving instructions from any government or other outside authority.[13]

Up to this point the League's example was followed, but a new wrinkle appeared in a later draft (July 18, 1944). For the first time responsibility for maintaining impartial service was to be shared by governments as well as by the Secretariat. Member states were to be required "to impose no obligation upon their nationals who are officials of the international organization that are inconsistent with the performance of their duties." [14] For reasons that have not yet been disclosed the draft that emerged from the four-power Dumbarton Oaks Conference omitted any reference to this loyalty provision. Were the big powers unable to agree on the international character of the Secretariat? In any event, the Sponsoring Powers, under the prodding of other delegations, proposed an amendment that restored the principles of the earlier State Department draft. The final version appears in Article 100 of the Charter. The first paragraph places the burden of

---

[13] See "Draft Constitution of International Organization" in *Postwar Foreign Policy Preparation, 1939–1945*, Department of State Publication 3580 (Washington: Government Printing Office, 1950), p. 476. This draft was prepared prior to discussion at the Moscow conference in October 1943.

[14] *Ibid.*, p. 605.

international loyalty on the Secretary-General and his staff. The second paragraph pledges the Members to "undertake to respect the exclusively international character of the Secretary-General and the staff. . . ."

Canada and New Zealand introduced further amendments to the Dumbarton Oaks Proposals at San Francisco that strengthened the principle of international loyalty. Article 101 places the responsibility for staff appointments squarely on the shoulders of the Secretary-General who acts under regulations established by the General Assembly. "The highest standards of efficiency, competence and integrity" are to be the criteria of appointment. Although the Secretariat need not include nationals of all the Members, recruitment was to be made with "due regard" to the widest possible geographic distribution. This provision implies more than a concern for national prestige. If it is to be effective, an international staff must have first-hand knowledge of the problems, administrative procedures and culture patterns of the different governments represented in the organization.

These principles are repeated and embellished in the Staff Regulations enacted by the General Assembly.[15] An oath or declaration of loyalty is required of all members of the staff. The unauthorized disclosure of information known to the staff by reason of official duty is forbidden. Except for war service, honors, decorations, favors and gifts from governments cannot be accepted. Candidacy for political office is also forbidden.

THE UN SECRETARY-GENERAL

The role of the Secretary-General received particular attention at both Dumbarton Oaks and San Francisco. In the light of League experience, the planners felt that a more forceful figure might gain greater prestige for the new organization so that it would be more influential in harmonizing interstate relations. This would necessitate a political role for the organization's first officer. This has been reported as the view of Franklin Roosevelt, including the shaky rumor that he coveted the post.[16] Early United States drafts prior to Dumbarton Oaks show a line of thought progressing from a "general secretary," to a secretariat responsible to both a "president" (political) and a "secretary-general" (administrative), to a "director-general." The office emerged from the negotiations at Dumbarton Oaks as "Secretary-General" implying nothing more than an administrative role. Yet, despite his title, he is assigned more than management functions, since under Article 99 he has the "right to bring to the attention of the Security Council any matter which in his opinion may threaten international peace and security." We are left to speculate on the arguments at Dumbarton Oaks that led to the seeming inconsistency between the title and the role. Thus the title was to make clear that the Secretariat's head officer was to play a managerial role primarily under the direction of the Member states.

---

[15] See *Yearbook of the United Nations, 1951* (New York: Columbia University Press, 1952), pp. 117–122.

[16] Schwebel, *op. cit.*, p. 18.

His right to bring trouble to the attention of the Security Council, though hailed as a bold departure from the League, should be examined in the light of the rigorous control over UN action which the Sponsoring Powers expected to exercise through the Security Council.

At San Francisco these provisions were included in the Charter as Articles 97–99, almost without change, but not without debate. Some delegations thought the Secretary-General should be able to bring matters endangering peace to the General Assembly as well as the Security Council. Others felt his political prerogative should not be limited to matters threatening international peace and security. The line was held, however. Although in comparison to his League predecessor, the Secretary-General has a bigger role, it was always assumed that so far as coercive action was involved, he would play it under the close direction of the permanent members of the Security Council. The point is emphasized in Article 97. The Secretary-General is appointed by the General Assembly only upon recommendation of the Security Council. This provision nearly resulted in a failure to appoint any Secretary-General at all during the difficult period of 1950–52. Efforts at San Francisco to loosen this aspect of big-power control were of no avail.

On another matter, however, the big powers were forced to yield to small-power indignation. The Sponsoring Powers had offered an amendment to the "Proposals" providing for the election of four Deputy Secretaries-General for a term of three years by the General Assembly upon the recommendation of the Security Council. On two counts this was difficult for the lesser powers to swallow. The big states would doubtless control these positions in addition to the top post, a situation that could be remedied only by Charter amendment requiring big-power unanimity. Moreover, the Secretary-General's control might be weakened and the Secretariat's efficiency lowered by excessive dispersion of high-level authority. Memories of bitter League disputes regarding similar posts were still fresh. As a result the Charter makes no mention of specific officials subordinate to the chief. The problem was left for the organization itself to decide. A similar solution was reached for the length of the Secretary-General's appointment. The Sponsoring Powers sought to amend their own proposals to provide for a three-year term, with reëlection permitted. This suggestion was unceremoniously rejected when the lesser powers discovered that any permanent member of the Security Council could veto this appointment.

Trygve Lie Appointed

The political importance of the office is shown by the concern of the big powers whenever a Secretary-General is appointed. The nomination is surrounded by special precautions, aimed to reduce personal embarrassment and problems of national prestige. The five permanent members meet in private to reach preliminary agreement. The Security Council itself deliberates in closed session, and, following the recommendations of the

Preparatory Commission, transmits only one nomination to the General Assembly which elects by secret ballot. Before the big-power honeymoon ended, these bodies were able to act, and without too much difficulty. Mr. Trygve Lie of Norway became the first Secretary-General in February 1946 by a ballot of 46 to 3.

On reflection the choice seems obvious enough. North America could scarcely have the honor of providing both the Headquarters and the Secretary-General. Europe, moreover, could provide many candidates experienced in international affairs. A representative from a small European power might help to blunt the frequent criticism that the United Nations was principally a big-power affair. In view of the United Nations' origins, a representative from a small country overrun by Hitler was particularly appropriate.

There were other aspects in Lie's favor. He had been Executive Secretary in the Norwegian Labor Party, and, since the new organization embraced all shades of the political spectrum, a non-Communist socialist seemed in 1945 like safe middle ground. He had been a public figure, successful enough to be elected to political office and to be appointed to Cabinet rank. As Norwegian Foreign Minister and as Chairman of his delegation to the San Francisco Conference he had a first-hand knowledge of international affairs.

At San Francisco the term of office had been left for the organization itself to decide. In appointing Mr. Lie the General Assembly set his term of office at five years subject to reappointment and provided a salary of $20,000 sweetened by a representational allowance of equal amount and a handsome residence in Forest Hills, Long Island. Mindful of the first League Secretary-General who on his resignation became Ambassador to Italy, a country soon to flaunt the League, the General Assembly also insisted that, because the Secretary-General was a confidant of many governments, he should not be offered or accept any governmental position immediately upon retirement from the United Nations.

Between East and West

Although a compromise candidate, Lie was thought to be an auspicious choice. As the cold war set in, however, he was inevitably in disfavor with one great power or another. His peace mission in 1950 to close the breach in the United Nations, following the Soviet boycott of the Security Council for its failure to seat the Communist Chinese as representatives of China, caused fuss and fury in the United States.

But the players changed sides abruptly with the North Korean attack in June 1950. Lie was the first to address the hastily convened Security Council, and from the opening gun he insisted that the United Nations must rally to stop aggression. Immediately he became anathema to the Soviet Union and the fair-haired boy of the United States. The former charged he had violated the Charter; the latter insisted that his boldness must be sustained by continuing him in office. Meanwhile, the expiration of his term in February 1951 was fast approaching. Could another compromise candidate be found? Could Lie be continued in office? Six meetings of the Security Council in October 1950 and private big-power consultations produced only a Soviet veto of Lie's renomination and an open threat by the United States to veto anyone else. Stymied, the Security Council could only report to the General Assembly its failure to recommend a candidate. Ambassador Austin of the United States declared that Lie was

> the steadfast advocate and executive of the unity of the fifty-three nations in resisting armed aggression. He has been steadfast in building the principles of the United Nations to stand in place of force. . . . The United States believes that in supporting Mr. Lie it is vindicating the cause for which so many young men and women of the United Nations have given their lives.[17]

The Soviet Union was as vituperative as the United States was laudatory. In the General Assembly Mr. Vyshinsky revealed that although the Soviet Union had not at first objected to Mr. Lie, it later realized he "did not possess the qualifications required of a Secretary-General of the United Nations. . . . He is unobjective, two-faced, and we will have no truck with him." [18]

The politics of the deadlock were complicated by several factors. The United States' extraordinarily vigorous insistence on Lie nourished doubts among those states disposed to question whether Washington was interested in a peaceful settlement. The Soviet Union appeared reasonable to many delgations when it indicated willingness to back various candidates in place of Lie, including Dr. Charles Malik of Lebanon, Sir Benegal Rau of India, Dr. Luis Padilla Nervo of Mexico and General Carlos P. Romulo of the Philippines. Certainly this list included some vigorous anti-Communists. The Indian delegation, echoing the conviction of many that a candidate acceptable to all the permanent members must be found, suggested that the Security Council try a procedure similar to that used in the election of judges to the International Court of Justices and draw up a list of candidates whom no permanent member would veto before proceding to the recommendation. This would, in effect, have eliminated Trygve Lie.

Finally, the General Assembly was convinced that under the circumstances a vote against Lie was a vote against the United Nations. The majority may have been impressed with the United States' argument that the issue was now focused on principles rather than on personalities. The Soviet use of the veto made it impossible to consider new nominations on their merits. India withdrew its suggestion, and joined with fourteen other nations including "Titoist" Yugoslavia to propose to the General Assembly that Lie "be continued in office for a period of three years." Although several governments voiced doubts regarding the procedure's legality, the proposal was carried on November 1, 1950, 46 to 5 with 8 abstentions. Among the abstainers were the Arab bloc, skeptical of legalities

[17] *The New York Times*, October 26, 1950, p. 1.
[18] See UN Doc. A/P.V./296, p. 261 and *The New York Times*, Oct. 31, 1950.

and Lie's role in the birth of Israel, the Nationalist Chinese delegate who could not be expected to support a candidate who felt that the Nationalists no longer represented China, and Australia which indicated "genuine doubts" about the legality of the compromise.

Mr. Lie accepted the prolongation of his Herculean tasks with a deep sense of responsibility:

> I understand your vote to be a reaffirmation . . . of the independence and integrity of the office of Secretary-General of the United Nations. In the present circumstances, I feel that I am under an obligation to the United Nations not to refuse your mandate continuing me in office for a period of three years.[19]

The Soviet Union then announced that after February 1, 1951, it would not recognize Mr. Lie as Secretary-General. Communications, thereafter, would simply be addressed to the Secretariat. Mr. Lie was furious. He felt the Secretariat's integrity was under attack. The governments that voted to keep him in office agreed. The struggle also highlighted the obvious point that in assuming a political role the Secretary-General was a sitting duck in the crossfire of world politics. Did this fact lessen the possibilities of peaceful settlement? Was the primary duty of the General Assembly's members to seek a compromise candidate who might better have been able to guide the Western powers and the Soviet Union toward the reconciliation of their differences at some propitious moment? In answer, it seems clear that no compromise was possible in October 1950. The future of the Organization itself was at stake in the seesaw battles in Korea.

Change of Command

Lie, however, was seeking the proper moment to step down. Such a moment would be at hand when a new Secretary-General, acceptable to both the Soviet Union and the United States, could be elected without sacrificing Charter principles in any way. In November 1952 Mr. Lie felt that such a moment had come and he requested that the appointment of a Secretary-General be added to the Assembly's agenda. There was at least some prospect of success for the truce negotiations in Korea. Meanwhile Mr. Lie's job had become well-nigh intolerable. His personnel policy had come under heavy fire from many quarters. At issue was Lie's action with regard to the refusal of several United States officials on the Secretariat to tell United States authorities whether they were or ever had been members of the Communist Party. This fact coupled with the continued refusal of the U.S.S.R. and four satellites to recognize him as Secretary-General and the improved prospects in Korea seem to have convinced him the time was ripe to change the guard.

In explaining his action to the General Assembly, Lie pulled no punches.

[19] UN Doc. A/P.V./299, pp. 291–292.

He pointed out that for seven years he had exercised and defended the responsibilities of his office. While he had run into opposition from many governments, only the Soviet Union and four allied governments had failed to respect his right as Secretary-General to act and speak as he did on the Korean affair. In his view the behavior of the Soviet Union and its allies was "a policy of the crudest form of pressure, not only against me but against any future Secretary-General who may incur the displeasure of the Soviet Union for doing his duty as he sees it under the Charter." Lie's exasperation was plain to see when he pointed out the irony of a situation in which the Soviets charged that "the Secretariat is dominated by Americans and that they and I are in all respects the obedient tools of Wall Street and Washington," while some in the United States were attacking him for precisely the opposite reason.

While his resignation stemmed in part from the Soviet attitude, Mr. Lie explained his motive to be a desire to permit the office of Secretary-General to receive once more the backing it might derive both from the supporting votes of all five permanent members of the Security Council and recognition as Secretary-General from all the United Nations' Members.[20] To whom was the United Nations to turn? Not until March 1953 did the Security Council meet to consider formally the problem of Lie's successor. For a time another struggle seemed to be brewing. In the end, however, agreement was reached suddenly and rather obviously. On March 31, the Security Council looked once again to the Scandinavian peninsula for a middle way and nominated Dag Hammarskjold of Sweden by a vote of 10 to 0 with 1 abstention (China — presumably because Sweden had recognized the Communist Peoples' Republic). On April 7, the Swedish diplomat was elected by a relieved General Assembly by the convincing vote of 57 to 1 (presumably China again) with one abstention and one Member absent.

Although Dag Hammarskjold was a "dark horse," his appointment seemed as natural to the situation as a glove to the hand. He came from a distinguished Swedish family of long civil service and diplomatic experience. He himself was a professional diplomat and economist serving as Minister of State. Most important, he was a citizen of a country that had remained as neutral as possible. Sweden had eschewed NATO and chosen to contribute hospital services to the United Nations Command in Korea.

Functions of the United Nations Secretary-General

By the time Dag Hammarskjold picked up the reins laid down by his Norwegian predecessor the role of the Secretary-General had been well marked out in theory and practice. This did not mean that it could not be altered. Indeed, Mr. Hammarskjold's background suggested the possibility of a partial return to the administrative rather than the political theory of the office. Hammarskjold had been trained in the ways of civil

---

[20] Lie's views were given to the Assembly in March 1953, and are summarized in *International Organization*, Vol. 7, No. 2 (May 1953), pp. 243–245.

service anonymity and diplomatic niceties rather than in the rough and tumble of trade union politics.

The Charter, as has been noted, goes well beyond the Covenant in its grant of authority to the Secretary-General in what may be called executive discretion. Article 97 prescribes a "Secretary-General and such staff as the Organization may require. . . . He shall be the chief administrative officer of the Organization." The same article implies the political importance of the office in requiring the support of the Security Council's permanent members for the incumbent. The five-year term was prescribed to give a Secretary-General time enough to be influential and not so much time as to remain in office without the Members' confidence.

Article 98 makes the Secretary-General's authority in connection with all United Nations principal bodies quite unambiguous. "The Secretary-General shall act in that capacity at all meetings of the General Assembly, of the Security Council, of the Economic and Social Council, and of the Trusteeship Council. . . ." An opportunity for executive authority is presented by the requirement of Article 98 that the "Secretary-General shall make an annual report to the General Assembly on the work of the Organization."

Article 99 is the chief source of the Secretary-General's executive or political authority. It permits him to "bring to the attention of the Security Council any matter which in his opinion may threaten the maintenance of international peace and security." The Preparatory Commission noted that this was "a special right which goes beyond any power previously accorded to the hand of an international organization." [21]

Mr. Lie is reported to have dubbed Article 99 "an atomic bomb," or at least a "32-inch gun." Formally speaking, he has brought it to bear but once — in the case of Korea. His initiative on that occasion must be considered in the light of the fact that several Members, particularly the United States, were primed to fire their own weapons if the Secretary-General had not used his. But there is no doubt that the spirit of Article 99 has influenced Mr. Lie's behavior on many other issues.

Other United Nations bodies have added to the Secretary-General's authority by delegating specific tasks to him in their rules of procedure. Rule 62 of the General Assembly's Rules of Procedure, in effect, gives him almost as much initiative with regard to the "Town Meeting of the World" as the Security Council. It provides that "The Secretary-General or a member of the Secretariat designated by him as his representative, may at any time make to the General Assembly either oral or written statements concerning any question under consideration by it."

Despite his undoubted preëminence, however, the Secretary-General heads no supranational government. He is more the chief of staff of a loose alliance of sovereign governments than of a government. Yet his influence should not be underplayed. As interpreted by Trygve Lie, the Charter provisions provided an opportunity to exercise the power of public opinion.

[21] *The Report of the Preparatory Commission of the United Nations*, p. 87.

But the warning must be repeated that the Secretary-General's control over public opinion is pretty much on the sufferance of governments.

More specifically, the Secretary-General is influential because of his many key functions. He suggests the priority of items on agendas. Inevitably many governments will be swayed by his arguments as to what is important and what is not. As technical adviser to national delegations he may formulate proposals to meet specific problems. Technical suggestions have been important politically in such matters as the Berlin blockade of 1948 and the seating of representatives of Communist China in 1950. The fact of the matter is that many proposals advanced by national delegations in United Nations conferences are prepared in the name of the Secretary-General by Secretariat officials working discreetly behind the scenes. The reasons are obvious. The Secretariat is a repository of greater technical knowledge than is at the command of many governments. Some of the newer and smaller powers, in particular, depend heavily on the statistical and other facilities of the Secretariat. Because it is charged with developing and defending a global point of view, it may have better perspective than a Member government on the problems and consequences of a particular policy put forward by that government. Its draft reports and working papers are extremely helpful to governments faced with an increasing number of foreign affairs decisions. Its assistance to United Nations missions in the field, including those in Greece, Korea, Palestine and Indonesia, have helped to shape the course of international politics.

The Secretary-General himself carries great prestige. He appoints the members of the Secretariat. Like the Pope of old, he is relatively free of charges of self-interest in mediating international disputes. Time and again Mr. Lie has spoken for the whole international community in advocating health measures, economic development and a peaceful solution for the problems of the cold war. Owing to the ubiquitous nature of his activity through the Secretariat and by means of his own initiative, he is often able to suggest solutions that might have escaped national delegations. His influence is everywhere — at meetings of all the principal organs where he or his personal representative always sits beside the President or Chairman, at dinners, at press conferences, at cocktail parties and last but not least in the corridors. Given any situation save one in which the die has been cast for armed conflict, the Secretary-General stands ready to reconcile conflicting national policies. Clearly, however, incautious use of his political role may do more harm than good.

In several matters Mr. Lie played his political role with considerable boldness. In others, he played it subtly, camouflaging policy with legal opinion. His legal document on the Iranian Case was recognized for what it was, a political move that pleased the Soviet Union and others, while it irritated the United States. In the Palestine Case he made his first large-scale and, as matters turned out, perhaps unwise effort to influence a political problem. The Security Council, he declared, not only can but "will assume its full measure of responsiblity in implementation of the Assem-

bly's [partition] resolution." [22] But the powers that had force to "implement" hung back. [23] The United States and Britain were doubtful of both
the legal and the political aspects of Lie's assertion. But Lie's influence in
the selection of Count Bernadotte as United Nations Mediator and his support of the Count and his successor, Dr. Ralph Bunche, were crucial in
finally putting a stop to the bloodshed.

Lie's Peace Mission

The year 1950 marked Lie's boldest efforts as international statesman.
The United Nations' stock was very low. Regional security arrangements,
particularly NATO, were overshadowing the Charter's security machinery.
The Soviet Union, though still a Member, refused to participate in United
Nations meetings because the People's Republic (Communist) had not
been allowed to replace the Nationalist Government in the United Nations
as the representative of China. Diplomatic discussion between East and
West had virtually ceased. In Lie's view negotiations would have to be renewed if the cold war were not to turn hot, but the dangerous deadlock
could not be relieved "until the Chinese question is settled, so that we may
have present again all nations who have been elected as members of the
different organs." [24]

For six months starting in January 1950 Lie worked unceasingly to break
the stalemate. Accompanied by three Secretariat assistants (Zinchenko of
the U.S.S.R., Laugier of France, and Foote of the U.S.A.) he toured half
the world, including Washington, London, Paris and Moscow. He visited
not only the leaders of the big powers but also those of the non-permanent members of the Security Council whose votes on the seating of the
Chinese Communist delegation would be crucial. To Presidents and Prime
Ministers he personally handed a carefully prepared legal memorandum on
the Chinese question and a twenty-year "peace program." In Paris he discussed his point of view with the heads of ten of the specialized agencies.

With governments Lie resorted to legal means for a political end. With
regard to the Chinese impasse he urged that a distinction be drawn between representation in the United Nations and diplomatic recognition by
sovereign governments. "The people of China have a constitutional right,
under the Charter, to be represented at all times in the United Nations by
the government that has the power to represent them." Representation in
the United Nations, in this view, need not involve diplomatic recognition
by the Members. China was a permanent member of the Security Council
by Charter provision regardless of the nature of her government. Lie suggested that the Security Council investigate which of the two rival Chinese
governments was able to represent the Chinese people and to fulfill the
obligations of membership. His objective seemed clear, since the Nation-

[22] See Schwebel, op. cit., p. 140.
[23] These cases are discussed in Chap. 15.
[24] See Schwebel, op. cit., Chap. 6.

The Herblock Book (*Beacon Press*)

"I'm doing my best to get you in, pal."

alists, recently driven to the island of Formosa, were in no position to control the mainland.

The principal stumbling blocks to Lie's hopes were the Korean War and the United States, where the defeat of the Nationalists had become a burning issue between the executive branch and influential Congressional elements. Although Britain had recognized the Peoples' Republic and France was reported after Lie's trip to be ready to accept the Peiping Government in the Security Council, Washington, even prior to the North Korean attack, was finding it difficult to stomach another Communist power in the United Nations with another, if redundant, veto in the Security Council.

Despite Lie's acceptance of Communist control in China as an ineluctable fact, he had harsh words for Soviet behavior. On his return from his European trip he explained that he did not agree with "the Soviet refusal to attend meetings at which China is represented by the Nationalists. I have made this plain on several occasions here, and I made it plain during my visit to Moscow." Despite this statement Senators Bridges and Knowland of the United States a few days later referred to him as the "Soviet partisan incumbent" and sought to have him replaced as Secretary-General unless he revised his attitude on China "at once." [25] The incident suggests what little chance there was for Lie's proposal. It was never put to the test, however, for just as seven affirmative votes in the Security Council to admit Red China began to take shape, the Korean conflagration broke out.

Lie's "peace mission" culminated in a "Twenty-Year Program for Achieving Peace through the United Nations" which he was able to announce just prior to the Korean outbreak.[26] The program's ten points may be summarized as follows:

> (1) Inauguration of periodic (special high-level) Security Council meetings, attended by foreign ministers or heads of governments to develop means of settling disputes; (2) fresh attempts at the international control of atomic energy; (3) new efforts to control "conventional" armaments; (4) new efforts to make armed forces available to enforce Security Council decisions; (5) universality of United Nations membership including Germany and Japan; (6) increased technical assistance and capital investment for under-developed areas; (7) a bigger role for the specialized agencies and Soviet membership therein; (8) continued development of United Nations' work on human rights; (9) advancement of dependent peoples toward independence by peaceful means; (10) development of international law toward an enforceable world law for a universal society.

The program was ambitious. It was bound to incur the hostility of supernationalists and the skepticism of those who felt that little could be done until the Western powers' rearmament program had redressed the balance of power that tilted so dangerously toward the Communist powers. Mr. Lie found that his reception in Washington, though polite, was chilly in comparison to that received in Paris and Moscow.

The ten-point program received earnest debate in the United Nations. Though somewhat of an anticlimax, the Fifth Assembly in the fall of 1950 by a vote of 51 to 5 commended the Secretary-General for his efforts in preparing the memorandum and referred the various points to the appropriate bodies for study. Because of its scope it was discussed in the Economic and Social Council, the Trusteeship Council, the International Court of Justice, ILO and UNESCO. The Secretary-General reported the results of these discussions to the Sixth Assembly, which in January 1952 instructed that the study be continued.[27]

The Assembly debate on the peace program and the heavy majorities in favor of studying it showed that the majority of the membership approved

[25] *The New York Times,* June 18, 1950, p. 22.
[26] See *United Nations Bulletin,* Vol. 7, No. 12 (June 15, 1950), pp. 509–511.
[27] For a summary see *Yearbook of the United Nations, 1951,* pp. 189–193.

the political role played by Mr. Lie. Only the Soviet Union and the satellites loosed a torrent of abuse on him charging that his behavior was inconsistent with the Charter and that the memorandum had been prepared in the United States Department of State. Lie gained stature by virtue of his dignified refutation of these charges. His stand on Korea had sweetened his relations with Washington while souring them with Moscow.

United Nations Field Service

Lie played a political role in connection with other matters. At times he appeared as an executive proposing bills for a legislature. Outraged by the assassination of Count Folke Bernadotte, United Nations Mediator in Palestine, for example, Lie boldly urged the establishment of a United Nations Guard to furnish military truce observers, to protect UN personnel on field missions and to provide transportation and communication facilities. The occasion for the proposal was a commencement address in 1948 at Harvard University where a year previously Secretary of State Marshall had made his proposals for Europe's economy. Although Lie's proposals were not as compelling as General Marshall's, the General Assembly approved a deflated version of them on November 22, 1949, despite French doubts as to their usefulness and Soviet charges of illegality. The establishment of the modest but useful United Nations Field Service as part of the United Nations Secretariat was due almost entirely to Lie's vigorous leadership.

The Service may not exceed three hundred persons. Its members are authorized to wear a United Nations uniform and to carry side arms on special occasions. (The Field Service is not to be confused with the Secretariat's regular guards, chauffeurs and messengers at United Nations Headquarters.) Training is provided in police work, first aid, shorthand and typing. Perhaps more important is training in the intricacies of the "jeep" in a plant at Toledo, Ohio.

Article 99 in Perspective

Enough has been said to show that the United Nations Secretary-General, with Trygve Lie as incumbent, played a political role that would have been unthinkable in the League. Not everyone will agree that Article 99 is a wise provision, but most will agree that Mr. Lie made a great deal of it. The basic issue is whether the Secretary-General should be a civil servant or a statesman. Do the nature and structure of international society provide any real place for a sort of international president or prime minister? Does the Secretary-General have sufficient power to justify playing a political role? Lie's behavior and the spirit of Article 99 suggest an affirmative answer. Although he had no power in the usual sense of the term and although he was responsible to governments, Lie was very conscious of the fact that the opening words of the Charter's preamble are "We the Peoples of the United Nations determined to save succeeding generations from the scourge of war. . . ." Implied is a loyalty to mankind higher than any exclusive emphasis on national sovereignty. At the very least there is an unstated premise that it is to the interests of governments to seek higher standards of living for all peoples and to conduct their affairs in accordance with universal rules of law. Supporters of Lie's role feel that governments may be compelled increasingly by peoples to adhere to these Charter principles if the Secretary-General stands as a symbol of mankind's common interests. To do this he must appear in the news as a statesman.

Many veterans of foreign affairs, however, will argue differently. Since the Secretary-General's influence, in the last analysis, is dependent on the will of governments, he should emphasize his administrative role and assist governments in reconciling their differences. His first task would then be to win the confidence of as many influential governments as possible. This would necessitate the avoidance of a partisan role or the involvement of the Secretariat in a political tug-of-war. These views apply, of course, to the whole Secretariat which, if it is to have the confidence of governments, must avoid ideological or partisan slants. A political chief may threaten Secretariat impartiality in this view.

The second task would be to win the loyalty and support of the members of the Secretariat. This would necessitate confidence in the Secretary-General's administrative ability. If their chiefs were primarily concerned with their welfare and if he avoided becoming a casualty in a "cold war," the difficult tasks of international officials might be easier. In the present shape of things, it is argued, an unobtrusive role is sounder than an obtrusive one.

The last view seems unwisely restrictive. Efforts in the past to reconcile by peaceful means the inevitably conflicting interests of sovereignties through diplomacy, international conferences and arbitration have never been wholly successful. Governments, therefore, have sought world order through universal institutions under a rule of law. If governments diverge from United Nations principles, human welfare is threatened. There is both room and need for a force such as the Secretary-General and his staff to warn governments when their behavior is contrary to the Charter and when it threatens the common aspirations of mankind.

The Secretary-General as Chief Administrator

Article 97 designates the Secretary-General as the chief administrative officer of the Organization. The task is heavy. He must determine the structure of the Secretariat and appoint its personnel. He must direct its work in servicing the General Assembly, the Councils, and numerous Commissions and Committees. His clients are difficult to please and include not only the United Nations' bodies but national delegations. Mundane matters such as meeting places, world-wide traveling arrangements, typing, translating, documentation, housing and eating facilities are ultimately all his responsibility.

He is responsible for the quality of work performed by his subordinates and for their strict impartiality in carrying out policy decisions of the principal bodies. He must strike a balance between his executive and his administrative function, for Member governments may decide on a course of action contrary to that proposed or preferred by the Secretariat. Under trying circumstances he must maintain both morale and strict discipline amongst a staff of four thousand persons who are anything but homogeneous.

The Secretary-General must also carry important financial responsibilities. Under the General Assembly's direction, he prepares the budget of the United Nations, collects the Members' contributions and controls expenditures. He is now required to develop common fiscal controls, and common administrative and budgetary practices for the specialized agencies.

As administrator, some observers feel Mr. Lie may not have measured up to the standards set by Sir Eric Drummond in the League of Nations. For example, he does not appear to have had the same measure of control and influence over his staff. But his tasks have been many times more difficult. His staff is five times the size of the League itself. Because it is located in New York, it tends to be dominated by United States administrative procedure, unfamiliar to Mr. Lie and to many on the Secretariat. Lie, moreover, owing both to temperament and experience, was less interested in administration. Primarily concerned with the solution of problems themselves, he may not have fully realized the power of administration to shape political, social and economic ends. In any event, Lie's delegation of responsibility in what may be characterized as administrative matters has been greater than in any other areas of his activity. To date an American has always held the post of Assistant Secretary-General for Administration.

The Secretary-General as Coordinator

Coordinating the work of the specialized agencies and that of the main United Nations bodies has proved to be one of the Secretary-General's principal tasks. Although this responsibility is not explicitly stated in the Charter, it falls to the Secretary-General since it is derived from his duties to both the General Assembly and the Economic and Social Council. This coordination process is discussed in Chapter 8.

ORGANIZATION OF THE UNITED NATIONS SECRETARIAT

The Preparatory Commission was faced with two theories of Secretariat organization. One held that it should be organized "organically" — that is, on the basis of the organs to be served. The other held that it should be organized "functionally" — that is, on the basis of the work to be done. A minority view led by the Russians favored the organic theory, but most delegations insisted on a compromise. The present organization is both organic and functional and consists of: eight departments, each headed by an Assistant Secretary-General; an Executive Office of the Secretary-General; and, since 1950, a Technical Assistance Administration with the status of a department and headed by a Director-General. Theoretically, the Secretary-General can call on any department to meet the needs of any United Nations' activities. In fact, the Secretariat tends to be compart-

STRUCTURE OF THE SECRETARIAT *

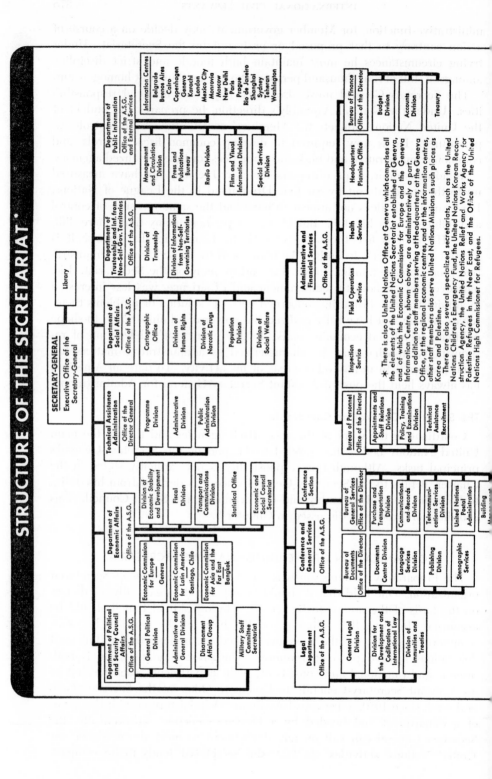

SECRETARY-GENERAL
Executive Office of the Secretary-General

Library

Department of Political and Security Council Affairs
Office of the A.S.G.

- General Political Division
- Administrative and General Division
- Disarmament Affairs Group
- Military Staff Committee Secretariat

Department of Economic Affairs
Office of the A.S.G.

- Economic Commission for Europe Geneva
- Economic Commission for Latin America Santiago, Chile
- Economic Commission for Asia and the Far East Bangkok
- Division of Economic Stability and Development
- Fiscal Division
- Transport and Communications Division
- Statistical Office
- Economic and Social Council Secretariat

Technical Assistance Administration
Office of the Director General

- Programme Division
- Administrative Division
- Public Administration Division

Department of Social Affairs
Office of the A.S.G.

- Cartographic Office
- Division of Human Rights
- Division of Narcotic Drugs
- Population Division
- Division of Social Welfare

Department of Trusteeship and Inf. from Non-Self-Gov. Territories
Office of the A.S.G.

- Division of Trusteeship
- Division of Information from Non-Self-Governing Territories

Department of Public Information
Office of the A.S.G. and External Services

- Management and Circulation Division
- Press and Publications Bureau
- Radio Division
- Films and Visual Information Division
- Special Services Division

Information Centres
Belgrade
Buenos Aires
Cairo
Copenhagen
Geneva
Karachi
London
Mexico City
Monrovia
Moscow
New Delhi
Paris
Prague
Rio de Janeiro
Shanghai
Sydney
Teheran
Washington

Legal Department
Office of the A.S.G.

- General Legal Division
- Division for the Development and Codification of International Law
- Division of Immunities and Treaties

Conference and General Services
Office of the A.S.G.

Conference Section

Bureau of Documents
Office of the Director

- Documents Control Division
- Language Services Division
- Publishing Division
- Stenographic Services

Bureau of General Services
Office of the Director

- Purchase and Transportation Division
- Communications and Records Division
- Telecommunications Services Division
- United Nations Postal Administration
- Building Management

Bureau of Personnel
Office of the Director

- Appointments and Staff Relations Division
- Policy, Training and Examinations Division
- Technical Assistance Recruitment

Administrative and Financial Services
Office of the A.S.G.

- Inspection Service
- Field Operations Service
- Health Service
- Headquarters Planning Office

Bureau of Finance
Office of the Director

- Budget Division
- Accounts Division
- Treasury

★ There is also a United Nations Office at Geneva which comprises all the elements of the United Nations Secretariat established at Geneva, and of which the Economic Commission for Europe and the Geneva Information Centre, shown above, are administratively a part. In addition to staff members serving at Headquarters, at the Geneva Office, at the regional economic centres, and at the information centres, other staff members also serve United Nations Missions in such places as Korea and Palestine.

There are also several specialized secretariats, such as the United Nations Children's Emergency Fund, the United Nations Korean Reconstruction Agency, the United Nations Relief and Works Agency for Palestine Refugees in the Near East, and the Office of the United Nations High Commissioner for Refugees.

mentalized with too little intercommunication. In 1952 the organization of the Secretariat was as follows:

Executive Office of the Secretary-General provides personal staff for the Secretary-General to assist in all his functions including coordination of the Secretariat and Missions abroad. Its chief officer is the Executive Assistant to the Secretary-General. In 1952 its budget allocation was $449,860.

The Department of Political and Security Council Affairs services the Security Council and the First (Political) Committee of the General Assembly. It prepares reports on matters dealing with threats to peace, enforcement, peaceful settlement, armament regulation, security aspects of strategic trusteeships, and the general problems of international political cooperation. Since 1945 it has been headed by a Russian as Assistant Secretary-General, Arkady A. Sobolev succeeded by Konstantin E. Zinchenko. When sanctions were applied in Korea, this officer had to be by-passed in favor of improvised staff and coordinating arrangements among the powers fighting under the United Nations Command. Roughly 110 persons are employed, and in 1952, its budget was $784,040 plus $137,400 for the Military Staff Committee Secretariat.

The Department of Economic Affairs provides services and assistance for the Economic and Social Council, the Assembly's Second (Economic) Committee and for various regional and functional (ECOSOC) commissions in connection with economic and statistical problems. It publishes economic studies and services international economic conferences and furnishes technical assistance chiefly in certain underdeveloped countries. It maintains close relations with the economic specialized agencies. In 1952 it was headed by a British subject as Assistant Secretary-General, David Owen, and employed over 300 persons. Its 1952 budget was $2,281,910.

The Department of Social Affairs staffs the Assembly's Third (Social, Humanitarian and Cultural) Committee and social aspects of the Economic and Social Council's work including among others such matters as human rights, narcotic drugs, health, refugees, and educational and cultural matters. It also services such subsidiary organs as the Commission on Human Rights. It conducts studies and issues publications in the social field and prepares draft agreements and services international social conferences. It maintains close relations with the specialized agencies working in social affairs. In 1952 the Assistant Secretary-General was a French citizen, Guillaume Georges-Picot. It employed about 220 persons. Its 1952 budget was $1,682,910.

The Department of Trusteeship and Information from Non-Self-Governing Territories serves the Trusteeship Council, the Assembly's Fourth Committee (Trusteeship and non-self-governing territories). It assists in studies and documentation including the drafting of trusteeship agreements, formulation of questionnaires and examination of reports from administering authorities. It accepts and examines petitions and participates in official visits and cooperates with the specialized agencies as required. In 1952 the Assistant Secretary-General was a Chinese citizen (Nationalist) Victor Hoo. It employed over 100 persons. Its budget was $926,470.

The Department of Public Information — its various divisions and bureaus work with the specialized agencies to provide information facilities for the United Nations. It maintains nineteen information centers in the principal cities of the world. It provides press services and publications in many languages, broadcasting services (United Nations Radio), film services, photographic services, and maintains liaison with educational groups and non-governmental organizations. It maintains a library and provides facilities for over 1,000 visitors a day at the New York headquarters. It employed over 300 persons in 1952 and its Assistant Secretary-General was Benjamin A. Cohen of Chile. Its 1952 budget was $2,197,550.

The Department of Legal Affairs services other departments of the Secretariat by advising on legal and constitutional questions including the negotiation of agreements on privileges and immunities. It assists in the progressive development and codification of international law and maintains liaison with the International Court of Justice. It prepares draft treaties, resolutions and opinions on interpretations of the Charter and studies national laws of interest to the organization. It assists the Assembly's Sixth (Legal) Committee and the International Law Commission. In 1952 the Assistant Secretary-General in charge was Ivan Kerno of Czechoslovakia, and about fifty persons were employed. Its 1952 budget was $448,670.

The Department of Conferences and General Services provides services and makes arrangements for meetings under United Nations auspices including schedules, translation, interpretation, graphic presentation and publication of journals and official records and maintains archives. It also provides for necessary purchases, transportation and communication requirements, hotel accommodations and custodial arrangements. In 1952 the Assistant Secretary-General in charge was Shamalhadaree Lall of India. The scope and complexity of its responsibilities are shown by the fact that in 1952 it employed well over 1,600 persons and its budget was $9,162,730.

The Department of Administrative and Financial Services provides personnel, budgetary, fiscal and administrative services for the United Nations including conferences and missions. It works closely with the Assembly's Fifth Committee (Administrative and Financial), the Advisory Committee on Administrative and Budgetary Questions and the Committee on Contributions. It advises on organizational aspects of the Secretariat and is responsible for arranging with Member governments for the payment of their contributions. The Assistant Secretary-General in charge is a United States citizen, Byron Price. In 1952 it employed about 275 persons. Its 1952 budget was $1,413,450.

The Technical Assistance Administration is in charge of United Nations technical assistance programs for social welfare, economic development of underdeveloped areas, assistance and training in public administration, and an expanded economic development program financed by voluntary governmental contributions. The expanded program is carried out in conjunction with the specialized agencies and is coordinated by the Technical Assistance Board. It is now one of the permanent departments of the Secretariat. In 1952 its Director-General was Hugh L. Keenleyside of Canada. Its 1952 budget was $1,023,100.

European Office of the United Nations at Geneva — This is the largest overseas organization of the United Nations Secretariat. It utilizes the buildings of the League of Nations. With a staff of more than 800 persons it is the headquarters of the Economic Commission for Europe (Gunnar Myrdal as Executive Secretary) and serves other bodies and specialized agencies as well. In 1952 Wladimir Moderow was the Director Representing the Secretary-General. Its 1952 budget was $4,946,520.

Other field offices include the Economic Commission for Asia and the Far East with headquarters at Bangkok and the Economic Commission for Latin America with headquarters at Santiago, Chile. Their budgets totaled $1,-708,500 in 1952.

The Assistant Secretaries-General are appointed by the Secretary-General for five-year terms. A proposal at San Francisco to have a national from each of the five Sponsoring Powers continuously in these posts was defeated by the smaller powers as too reminiscent of quarrels in the League over similar posts. This same result, however, has been achieved in practice.

A ninth Assistant Secretary-General was appointed in December 1947, for the Executive Office of the Secretary-General and for General Coordination. The first and only incumbent was Mr. R. G. A. Jackson of Australia, who had been service Deputy Director-General of UNRRA. The position was abolished by Mr. Lie as of September 1, 1948. The establishment of this office bore witness to the fact that the Secretary-General needs help at the highest level of the Secretariat both for policy formulation and to administer the directives of policy-making bodies. He must have staff meetings of his top officials to coordinate the organization's work and to get all the views and alternatives that must be presented if wise decisions are to be made. Above all, he needs time to think and a few trusted advisers, free of specialized routine and operations, to help guide his thoughts.

The abrupt termination of the office meant that Lie found it very difficult to deputize his responsibilities or to place anyone between him and his department heads. He preferred to confer directly with his Assistant Secretaries and other high officials and to rely on his able Executive Assistant, Andrew Cordier of the United States, to assist in coordinating his staff.

The appointment of a Deputy Secretary-General has been suggested as a means of help. This office, as we have seen, proved to be a bone of contention in the League with few compensations. It might weaken the Secretariat by injecting national rivalries in its top command. How agree on a Deputy when it is difficult to agree on the Chief? Would not such an appointment increase the problems of prestige among the Members? A Deputy Secretary-General does not appear to be a ready solution.

Another device might be the institution of a Cabinet including the eight Assistant Secretaries-General. But as means of control and coordination such a Cabinet might not fill the bill. The Assistant Secretaries-General are seldom their Chief's choice but are governmental nominees who cannot be removed without giving offense to the Member countries involved. They are not members of a political party devoted to common aims as are the members of a national cabinet. These officials, moreover, are presently more aware of the problems of their particular departments than they are of the organization as a whole. Still, progress might be made if the Secretary-General provided leadership and proper working arrangements including regular meetings, a prepared agenda, staff assistance and the careful recording of decisions.

A final means would be to provide a general staff arrangement for the Secretary-General. Such an arrangement now almost exists in fact. Mr. Lie, for example, was greatly helped by his Executive Office headed since 1945 by his Executive Assistant, Andrew Cordier. More recently W. Martin Hill of the United Kingdom has been Director of Coordination for Specialized Agencies and Economic and Social Matters. There are other personal assistants to help in managing the Secretariat's work. There are both regular staff meetings attended by the Assistant Secretaries-General and a Committee of the Principal Directors of the Departments under the Chairmanship of the Executive Assistant.

In sum, Mr. Lie sought to manage his organization by means of what might be called a "shirt-sleeve Cabinet" composed of his Assistant Secretaries-General and a personal staff under his Executive Assistant. Under the circumstances and due largely to Mr. Cordier, this proved to be a good device. The Secretary-General's principal problem is to obtain help from general counselors rather than being restricted to advice from specialized assistants.[28]

At the end of his first year in office Mr. Hammarskjold laid before the Assembly's Administrative and Budgetary Committee proposals to "streamline" the Secretariat. The ranks of Assistant Secretary-General and Principal Director were to be eliminated in favor of a single echelon of Under Secretaries. Instead, the Secretary-General suggested that he have four administrative aides: an Executive Assistant with policy and coordination responsibilities, a General Counsel, and two other assistants, carrying a new rank of Under Secretary to be in charge of personnel and finance, respectively. The present Department of Administrative and Budgetary Affairs would be divided into two units — personnel and financial. Other departments were to be similarly reorganized and headed by Under Secretaries.[29]

Personnel Policies

Although the Secretary-General is given complete authority to appoint and dismiss Secretariat personnel subject to "staff regulations" established by the General Assembly (Article 101), he has less freedom of action than the Charter implies. Since each Member contributes to the organization's budget and has a special interest in its work, each Member insists on having some of its nationals on the Secretariat. Prestige dictates further that these nationals be placed in positions as high as possible. The most notable exception to the usual over-application for Secretariat employment has been the Soviet Union, which has been content to have only a dozen of its nationals employed. No official reasons have been forthcoming, but evi-

---

[28] See *The United Nations Secretariat*, United Nations Studies #4 (New York: Carnegie Endowment for International Peace, 1950), Chap. VI.

[29] F. R. Scott, "The World's Civil Service," *International Conciliation* (January 1954), p. 275.

dently the Soviet Union adheres to a policy of exposing its citizens to foreign influences as little as possible.

With regard to employment and work conditions, the Charter prescribes two conditions: "the highest standards of efficiency, competence and integrity" and "due regard to . . . as wide a geographic basis as possible." Geography has often rivaled efficiency as Members have urged greater employment of their nationals. Furthermore, the most important posts, including the Assistant Secretary-Generalships, are filled on the nomination or at least the approval of the governments concerned.

Largely because the United Nations is in the United States the Secretariat was quickly oversupplied with Americans, and complaints were registered in the General Assembly. Actually, while United States citizens at the lower levels are as thick as flies around a honey pot, they are relatively rare at high levels.

The standards of work have been surprisingly good, all things considered. Whatever inefficiency there is may have stemmed less from geographic distribution than from hasty recruitment in the early days of the Organization and poor management.[30] At present, geographic distribution applies only to the upper third of the Secretariat's permanent positions which are characterized as "international." According to one recent study the nationals of ten countries hold 74 per cent of these "international" positions in the following proportions: United States, 33.7 per cent; United Kingdom, 11.8 per cent; France, 7.0 per cent; China, 5.5 per cent; Canada, 4.8 per cent; India, 2.5 per cent; Poland, 2.5 per cent; Belgium, 2.1 per cent; Netherlands, 2.1 per cent; and Sweden, 2.0 per cent. All the Latin American countries together total only 7.9 per cent. The Middle East has 3.0 per cent. The Far East including China has 9.6 per cent. This distribution is close to the ratio of budget contributions among the Members.[31]

The members of the Secretariat work under a comprehensive set of "permanent" staff regulations that were finally adopted by the General Assembly in February, 1952. These follow the best civil service practice of a number of states and include the relevant Charter obligations and such matters as classification, salaries, appointments, promotions, leave and disciplinary matters.[32] The regulations are supplemented by "staff rules" promulgated under the Secretary-General's authority.

International personnel administration for several reasons is particularly complex in comparison with national civil service. The future of international organizations often remain uncertain. Many employees travel great distances and must settle in a wholly new cultural environment. Economic hardships must be met, and psychological adjustments made. One difficulty is that the Secretariat is pretty well swallowed up in New York City,

---

[30] For sharp criticism in this respect including reference to neglect of lessons learned from the League experience see Crocker, *op. cit.*

[31] United Nations Secretariat, p. 61. The scale of assessments for the 1953 budget as fixed by the General Assembly may be found on pp. 103–104.

[32] *Yearbook of the United Nations, 1951*, pp. 117–122.

and personal orientation is sometimes more difficult than was the case in the more intimate environment of Geneva.

Adjustments may have been made more difficult by the imposition from the start of administrative procedures similar to those developed by the Bureau of the Budget for the United States. A wiser course might have been to move more slowly so as to evolve procedures best suited to an organization vastly different from a national government. Profit might have been derived from greater study of some aspects of the League experience. The United States dominated the original working concepts of the Secretariat which were presented to the Preparatory Commission by its Advisory Group of Experts on Administrative, Personnel and Budgetary Questions, in March 1946. To some critics it was unfortunate that the influence of Western European countries was not greater. To some Europeans the United States, despite the admirable qualities of many individuals, does not yet possess the tradition of a fully respected civil service, a tradition that has some relevance for an international civil service.

The classification of staff members has been one of the Secretariat's principal headaches. Under United States prodding the Preparatory Commission was induced to abandon the League "caste" system in favor of an allegedly rankless and more flexible American system. We have seen the League's three layers: first, top officials (members of section); second, intermediate (secretarial and administrative staff); and third, clerical and manual (carpenters, chauffeurs and mimeograph machine operators). The first United Nations classification plan, therefore, included a system of grades based instead upon duties and responsibilities performed by the individual. Nineteen different grades were established with a number of steps in each grade leading to salary increases. But new rigidities appeared. It was complicated to administer and sometimes distasteful to those not sophisticated in Washington's administrative procedures. Dubbed impersonal and reminiscent of "American assembly line methods," the system was criticized by the Advisory Committee and a Committee of Experts on Salary, Allowance and Leave Systems. In 1950, the Secretary-General adopted the Committee of Experts' views and adopted a classification scheme based on the following divisions: (1) Directors and Principal Officers, (2) Substantive Service Personnel, (3) Special Service Personnel, (4) General Service Personnel. The last two were responsible for housekeeping and service functions. To some it seemed that the United Nations had at last caught up with the League.

Members of the Secretariat are paid basic salaries that, since tax exempt, are better than those of the civil service of the Member paying the highest salaries. In addition, there are "installation" allowances, dependency allowances, education allowances for children and rent allowances that are designed to ease the adjustment of persons coming from varied national economic and cultural backgrounds. There are liberal provisions for annual leave and sick leave including additional time for travel so Secretariat members may renew home ties. Pay scales are generally fair; some think them too high. But American social and economic standards have presented problems of adjustment; the lack of servants, crowded apartment houses, and the impersonality of an enormous city are conditions that cannot be compensated for by any reasonable salary scales.

The staff regulations (Article IX) give the Secretary-General a good deal of latitude in dismissing employees with either permanent or fixed-term appointments. Yet there are safeguards against capricious action. Although there is no union of Secretariat employees, a Staff Council elected by the members of the Secretariat acts on behalf of the staff in laying its views on personnel matters before the Secretary-General. In addition an Administrative Tribunal of seven members, all independent experts, was created by the General Assembly in 1949. It does not have jurisdiction in disciplinary cases but passes judgment on applications alleging nonobservance of staff members' contracts of employment or of their terms of appointment. In 1951 it met to consider the appeals against the Secretary-General of five staff members whose appointments had been terminated. In two cases the employees were sustained and their dismissals revoked. The Secretary-General had erred in not giving specific reasons for dismissal. The tribunal did not find that his doubts regarding the employees' reliability were sufficient. In the background lurked rumors of Communist activity and Congressional investigations — an issue that was soon to burst into flames. In three cases the Administration was sustained, and the argument of the Staff Council that the dismissals represented "union-busting" were rejected.[33]

In September 1953 the Administrative Tribunal ruled that the dismissal of eleven United States citizens who were employees of the UN was illegal. Four were ordered reinstated with full back salary; seven were awarded financial compensation in lieu of reinstatement. The discharge of nine other UN employees was upheld. The dismissal of these twenty-one UN employees had arisen in connection with a Congressional loyalty investigation. The United States opposed payment and reinstatement on the grounds that the Administrative Tribunal had invaded the discretionary authority of the Secretary-General.[34] The Tribunal's decision is final unless it is overridden by vote of the Assembly.

A Joint Appeals Board and a Joint Disciplinary Committee advise the Secretary-General on discipline cases. The membership is selected jointly by the Secretary-General and the Staff Council. In order to develop a permanent staff the Secretary-General has also reviewed all temporary staff appointments. Hence, a special Selection Committee was appointed under the chairmanship of Mr. F. P. Walters, former Deputy Secretary-General of the League of Nations. Its recommendations were largely followed in both terminating and making appointments. In addition, an International Civil Service Advisory Board reported in 1950 on standards of recruitment to guide the Secretary-General. The United Nations goes further

---

[33] *Yearbook of the United Nations, 1951*, p. 123.
[34] For the Tribunal's ruling see *The New York Times*, September 2, 1953. For the United States' view see *The New York Times*, September 20, 1953.

than the League in providing a career service for the Secretariat's professional members. Present policy is to grant permanent appointments to 70 to 75 per cent of the staff. The League sought the same result by renewing long-term contracts in many cases. In this way able people may be attracted to the staff, secure in the feeling that they may pursue their professional calling free of molestation by governments or anyone else.

Privileges and Immunities

In order to facilitate their tasks, special facilities and immunities are extended to representatives of Members of the United Nations and Secretariat employees. Precedent had been established under the Covenant when Article VII extended "diplomatic immunity" both to representatives of Members of the League and to Secretariat officials. Prior to the League, immunities for international organizations were exceptional.[35]

The Charter retreats from the notion of full diplomatic immunity by providing in Article 105 for "such privileges and immunities as are necessary" for the United Nations to do its work and for representatives and officials in "the independent exercise of their functions." Two treaties define the scope of the organization's privileges and immunities, the Convention of Privileges and Immunities and the Headquarters Agreement between the organization and the United States. (There is a separate convention on privileges for the specialized agencies.) Both are in force, although the United States had not ratified the first as of 1953. The more important provisions are as follows:

> *Representatives of Members* have immunities and privileges only in the exercise of their duties and in traveling to official meetings. These include (1) immunity from arrest "in respect of words . . . and all acts done by them in their capacity as representatives"; (2) inviolability of papers and documents; (3) privileges including among others the right to use codes and pouches; (4) freedom from taxation depending upon residence.
>
> The Headquarters agreement deals with the Representatives' relations to the United States. They have the same privileges and immunities as diplomatic envoys accredited to the United States.
>
> *Officials of the United Nations* (1) are immune from legal process owing to words and acts in connection with their official capacity; (2) are exempt from taxation on income received from the United Nations; (3) are immune from military service and immigrant and alien restrictions; (4) have privileges regarding currency exchange and the importation of household goods.
>
> The Secretary-General and Assistant Secretaries-General and their families have the privileges of diplomatic envoys: a United Nations official may carry a *laissez-passer* as a travel document necessary for certain travel privileges.
>
> The Security Council retains close control of the Secretary-General in these matters for it may waive his immunity. He, in turn, may waive the immunity of any of his officials.

---

[35] Josef L. Kunz, "Privileges and Immunities of International Organizations," *American Journal of International Law*, Vol. 41, No. 4 (1947), pp. 828–836.

These arrangements are generally satisfactory, but an anomalous situation arises from the delay of the United States Senate in approving the Convention on Privileges and Immunities. The United States requires income taxes to be paid by its citizens in the United Nations. Since other countries do not, and because salary scales are arranged on the basis of nonpayment of taxes, special General Assembly action has been necessary to eliminate an obvious inequity. An internal tax fund has been established from which refunds are made to United States nationals. A great deal of complicated bookkeeping and little sense flows from this inactivity of the United States Senate.

The question of immunity gained considerable attention when Valentin A. Gubitchev, a Soviet national and an engineer at United Nations Headquarters, was accused by the United States of conspiracy to commit espionage. When arrested along with Judith Coplon, a United States Government employee, Gubitchev's immunity in connection with the Organization was quickly waived by the Secretary-General. When the pair were found guilty, the State Department in turn refused to recognize Gubitchev's claim to diplomatic immunity. With the fate of Americans in Eastern Europe in mind, Washington then moved to have him deported rather than imprisoned.[36]

The Headquarters

Finding a home for the United Nations has been as ticklish politically as locating a national capital. There were several considerations that for a time defied the efforts of several committees. Most obvious was the fact that the United States in 1945 was the most powerful United Nations Member. A thought held privately by many individuals who remembered the "great betrayal" of 1920 was that the organization should be housed in the United States as a show window to keep up American interest. The United States, moreover, was perhaps the only power after the war really equipped to house and staff a large international organization involving many large conferences at once. Many American groups, from San Francisco to New York and from the Black Hills of South Dakota to the Blue Hills of Massachusetts lobbied for the privilege of playing host. This view, however, was by no means unanimous in the United States.

One of the most obvious places and one favored by many European delegations was the League's Palais des Nations on the outskirts of Geneva in Switzerland. But Switzerland, although she probably would have been a willing host, was a neutral and indicated she would not join the new organization. The Soviet Union, moreover, had bitter memories because it had been given the "gate" at Geneva in 1939 during the Finnish War. The Soviets had quarrels with Switzerland in addition. Equally important, Europe lay in ruins, and the center of political gravity seemed to be shifting toward the New World and the Far East. A headquarters in the United

---

[36] *Department of State Bulletin*, March 20, 1950.

States would symbolize the new state of affairs. In a close vote, therefore, the Assembly decided that the seat of the United Nations should be in the United States with the headquarters in or near New York City.

The organization was then rescued from the dilemma of finding a specific location by a proposed gift of Mr. John D. Rockefeller, Jr., in December 1946, of a site on the East Side of Manhattan. To finance construction the United States sought an agreement to lend the United Nations $65 million. When Congress proved balky, a special session was finally required in 1948 to secure legislative approval of this project. The Rockefeller gift was then accepted.

By 1951 the Secretariat was busily at work in its glass house overlooking the East River. Soon there were handsome and very practical conference halls for all the principal organs. Thousands of visitors are daily impressed with the modern architecture of the Headquarters, enriched by artistic gifts from most of the Members. This aspect of the United Nations is clearly successful. Before this, temporary headquarters were found at Hunter College in New York and later on Long Island at Flushing Meadow and Lake Success, cruelly and crudely dubbed by wits as "neither a lake nor a success."

By agreement with the United States the Headquarters district is placed under United Nations control. Like foreign embassies the District is inviolable, and United States law-enforcement officials enter only with the Secretary-General's permission. In addition, the travel of persons with legitimate business in the organization, including delegates, officials and accredited press representatives, cannot be interfered with. These immunities are accorded on the basis of the Headquarters Agreement and the International Organization Immunities Act of 1945.[37]

The Budget

International organizations are just as dependent on financial resources as any government. The preparation and administration of the budget are among the chief functions of international secretariats, although the decisions of who is to pay, how much and for what purposes are political questions usually left to the Assembly.

Budgets for international organizations are seldom lavish. Without authority to tax, organizations are dependent upon governmental contributions, and budgets are usually subjected to close control both internally by administrative arrangement and externally by the scrutiny of Members. Budgets are usually prepared in the Secretariat and presented by the Secretary-General or Director-General to the political body for approval. On presenting his budget a Secretary-General might well feel like Daniel in the lions' den, but he has no assurance that he will emerge unscathed. Unlike a prime minister or president, he is not assured of the support of a

---

[37] Lawrence Preuss, "The International Organization Immunities Act," *American Journal of International Law,* Vol. 40 (1946), pp. 332–345.

majority party. Instead he is faced with governmental delegates under heavy pressure from the home front to save pennies, especially those spent outside the country. Nor can he, in most instances, appeal to public opinion by pointing to services administered directly by his organization.

One of the League's severest handicaps was that governments continually prodded the Secretary-General to keep down his budget while at the same time they demanded more work of the Secretariat. The two League Secretaries-General devoted much of their energies to the support of the budget in the League's Fourth Committee. They were backed by a Treasurer and his staff in the Secretariat.[38]

The United Nations budget is prepared and approved as follows. The Secretariat's Department of Administrative and Fiscal Services draws up an annual budget for the Secretary-General who publishes it as part of his annual financial report. It is then examined by the appropriate General Assembly committee, and voted in plenary session. The total annual appropriations for the first six years have been in the following amounts.

Year	Amount in dollars
1946	19,390,000
1947	28,616,568
1948	39,285,736
1949	43,204,080
1950	44,520,773
1951	48,925,000
1952	50,547,660
1953	48,327,700

The assessments levied against the members in 1953 are listed in Chapter 4, pages 103–104.

The Secretary-General must collect the contributions and maintain custody of all the funds. He has been delegated the task of consulting with the specialized agencies and developing with them common fiscal controls and common budgetary and financial practices. In order that he may have sufficient resources to do the work required of him if contributions are slow in forthcoming, a $20 million "working capital fund" is established from Members' contributions. It is replenished as soon as the money rolls in.

A three-man Board of Auditors has been appointed by the General Assembly to report on the financial status of the organization.

Characteristics and Problems

International secretariats present their own characteristics and problems. A brief comparison with national civil services is one way to analyze what these problems are. There are both differences and similarities. Perhaps the greatest difference is that there is no binding legislative authority to

[38] For details on the League budget, see Ranshofen-Wertheimer, *op. cit.*, Chap. XIV.

support the work of an international secretariat. Instead of belonging to an executive branch of government closely controlled by a legislative branch, the Secretariat is often the most permanent and positive directing element in an international organization. International administration depends upon decisions reached by diplomatic bodies, bound together by no strong ideological or constitutional bonds.

Another difference is that at least the higher officials in international administration are rather less closely supervised by policy-shaping bodies than are their national counterparts. Their contact with political leadership is generally less frequent, and they often must exercise greater discretion. Supervision of their work is generally less vigorous and informed. No responsible minister or cabinet officer is constantly looking over their shoulders.

Furthermore, the relations of the Secretary-General with the General Assembly or Security Council differ markedly from those of a president or prime minister to a congress or parliament. Neither the Secretary-General nor his top appointees has any direct popular mandate. They are not leaders of the dominant political bloc, as they would be in a parliament. The Secretary-General may not dissolve the Assembly or the Councils and he is not assured of any support comparable to that afforded by a political party. While both are answerable to a "legislative" branch, the Secretary-General has considerably less influence over his than does a prime minister. International officials, moreover, must seek to implement directives indirectly, through national governments, rather than directly.

A more fundamental difference is that international civil servants face special difficulties because they are drawn from many states of differing races, cultures and creeds. Despite differing social customs, languages, and educational background they must learn to work together while at the same time learning to live in an unfamiliar environment. There is a concomitant problem, although observers are not agreed to the extent it really is a problem. International secretariats tend to attract the uprooted, and certainly the "internationalists," who are not typical representatives of the culture and mores of the member states. Given the nature of international organization, a cooperative instrument of different governments and peoples, secretariat officials, it can be argued, should not be unrepresentative of the varied cultures and points of view amongst which the organization must do its work.

In its early days the United Nations Secretariat presented special problems of its own. To staff some 1,600 meetings in 1946, the staff was hastily recruited on an emergency basis by a Bureau of Personnel that was dominated by Americans, many of whom knew little of international organization. In a nine months' period in 1946 the staff jumped from a total of four hundred to twenty-eight hundred.[39] As a result there was inefficiency, overstaffing and overgrading (too high salaries) in many sections of the

[39] *Report of the Secretary-General on Personnel Policy*, Doc. A/2364, January 30, 1953, p. 5.

Secretariat. Some departments at one time had six times the personnel of comparable League sections but whether there was really six times the work to do was open to question. But governments were to blame. As Part III that follows will show, governments were prone to expect miracles in a hurry.

Some personnel, due to careless selection, seemed not fully to understand the nature of their task. Some seemed to be dominated by particular points of view rather than dedicated to impartial service. These difficulties have been largely strained out, however, and the Secretariat compares favorably with national civil services in the efficiency and devotion of its personnel.

Moreover, the differences in public service, national and international, can be exaggerated. Working conditions and methods are in many respects similar. In both instances the official, no matter what his political views, is supposed to carry out with nonpartisan anonymity the directives of policy-making bodies. At the same time the officials in both systems in their capacity as "experts" help shape policy by advising political leaders. An international civil service, like its national prototype, is a career merit system, relatively free of political pressure. In both systems, as in any large private or public hierarchy, there are the pitfalls of impersonality, inertia and inflexibility. The official in both systems is often frustrated by disregard of his work and counsel. Yet there are also the satisfactions in both instances of public service dedicated to the welfare of mankind, and both systems are served by many able men and women.

Secretariats in Action

International secretariats are quite as important in international politics as are national administrative systems in national politics. Their most important function is to provide continuity. While governments and even nations rise and fall and national delegates come and go, the secretariat remains to transform an agency such as the United Nations from a "series of periodic meetings of Assembly and Councils into a permanent and cohesive organization. It is the main centripetal force in the international system." [40] The results of this permanency can scarcely be exaggerated. An international secretariat becomes the repository of technical data, special skills and administrative precedent that nations have accepted for generations in such widely differentiated fields as drug control, international arbitration and international postal regulations. The Secretariat is the only truly international feature of the international system of sovereign states. As such it becomes a separate interested party with its own point of view for which it actively lobbies.

In addition to providing continuity, an international secretariat is the principal agent to provide unity and coordination in international organization. This is particularly true in the highly decentralized United Nations system. Not only must the Secretary-General and his staff serve as the

[40] *The United Nations Secretariat,* p. 8.

principal element of integration among the many international agencies involved, he must also foster coordination of national policies. Thus the Technical Assistance Administration in the United Nations Secretariat promotes teamwork between national technical assistance programs and those of the specialized agencies. A primary function of an international secretariat is, in short, to foster the very purpose of international organization, the close coordination of national policies in fields of mutual concern to the participating states.

There is another and less-well-understood function of an international secretariat. A secretariat official may actually assist the policy organs in negotiating decisions. Hence he turns diplomat on occasion, or, more aptly, mediator in order to reconcile differing national points of view. He may even be encouraged to present his own point of view. Albert Thomas of the ILO insisted on doing just that. In this role the secretariat official must know when to speak up and when to keep quiet. So far as national interests are concerned, his motives must, like Caesar's wife, be above suspicion. The Preparatory Commission summed up the Secretariat's role as follows:

> While the responsibility for the framing and adoption of agreed international policies rests with the organs representative of the Members — the General Assembly, the Security Council, the Economic and Social Council and the Trusteeship Council — the essential tasks of preparing the ground for these decisions and of executing them in cooperation with the Members will devolve largely upon the Secretariat.[41]

Loyalty and the Integrity of the Secretariat

Maintaining the principle of the Secretariat's independence has been a pressing problem for both the League and the United Nations. When national chauvinism runs riot and international relations deteriorate, the principle is sorely beset. It was endangered in the thirties with the rise of the dictators, and it was threatened by the "cold war" in the forties and fifties.

In the League, the German and Italian governments finally challenged the Secretary-General's independent authority directly by seeking to control their nationals on the Secretariat and insisting that they be Fascists or Nazis. An Italian law of 1927, for example, required that Italian nationals should have the permission of the Italian Foreign Office to serve on the Secretariat.[42]

The integrity of the United Nations Secretariat was strained by the harsh circumstances of the "cold war." In addition to the conviction of Gubitchev, another Soviet national on the Secretariat was accused of attempted espionage in the United States and bundled home. Another strain developed when Czechoslovakia and China fell under Communist control. To date non-Communist Czechs and Chinese have been retained on the staff for their competence and loyalty as international civil servants.

[41] UN Doc. PC/20, December 23, 1945, pp. 84–85.
[42] *Leggi usuali d'Italia*, 8th Edition (Milan, 1939), Part I, pp. 677–678.

The most serious problem arose when some United States nationals on the Secretariat were suspected of Communist affiliations past or present. The problem arose when something over two dozen Americans refused to tell a Federal Grand Jury and also a committee of the United States Senate whether they were or ever had been members of the Communist Party on grounds of the protection against self-incrimination allegedly afforded them by the Fifth Amendment of the United States Constitution.[43] The Senate committee reported that as a result of its investigations "a new vista of evidence of subversion on the part of United States citizens opened up to the subcommittee." [44] Of thirty-three witnesses called up by the subcommittee, twenty-six invoked the Constitutional privilege against self-incrimination. Earlier, in December 1952, the Grand Jury made public a "presentment" to a United States District Court stating that there was "infiltration into the United Nations of an overwhelmingly large group of disloyal United States citizens."

In this situation Lie decided to appoint an international commission of jurists to advise him on the problem. This committee was composed of E. S. Herbert of the United Kingdom, W. D. Mitchell of the United States and P. Veldekens of the Netherlands. The committee noted that, since "the United Nations is in no sense a super state," there should be no conflict between a citizen's loyalty to his own state and "the responsibility of such a citizen to the United Nations in respect to work done by him as an officer or employee of the United Nations." Furthermore, the Secretary-General had a special responsibility to see that no one of his staff "engaged in any subversive activities against the host country." The commission went on to say that a staff member who refused on grounds of the Fifth Amendment to tell either whether he was or had been engaged in espionage or whether he was or had been a member of the Communist Party or some other organization declared by the United States to be subversive, was unsuitable for United Nations employment.[45]

While the jurists were deliberating, temporary employees who refused to answer questions on grounds of self-incrimination were dismissed, while those with permanent appointments were placed on compulsory leave. On December 5, 1952, after first giving them an opportunity to change their minds about testifying, and on the basis of the jurists' opinion, Lie dis-

---

[43] *Activities of United States Citizens Employed by the United Nations,* Report of the Subcommittee to Investigate the Administration of the Internal Security Act and other Internal Security Laws, Committee on the Judiciary, United States Senate, 82nd Congress, 2nd Session (Washington: January 2, 1953).

[44] Committee on the Judiciary, *op. cit.,* p. 1. David Weintraub and Irving Kaplan, respected officials in the Secretariat, were the first to be interrogated. The first had had a distinguished record in Federal employment and UNRRA as well as Director of the Secretariat's Division of Economic Stability and Development. The Committee declared he had hired Owen Lattimore, another target of Senate investigation, in connection with the Institute of Pacific Relations, to head a UN Economic Mission to Afghanistan. Weintraub resigned in January 1953 to save the United Nations "embarrassment." Lie accepted the resignation with regret. See *The New York Times,* January 7, 1953.

[45] *Report of the Secretary-General on Personnel Policy,* pp. 9, 11–12, and Annex III.

missed the permanent staff members for violating the fundamental obligations stated in the Staff Regulations. To the General Assembly Lie explained that under the Charter and the Staff Regulations "no staff member should engage in subversive activities against his own government or the government of any Member state." He went on to say that

> With regard to United States Nationals in the Secretariat, I believe that in view of the present laws and regulations of the United States toward the American Communist Party and verdicts of the Courts on the leadership of that party, no United States national who is a member of the American Communist Party and who is, thereby, barred from employment in the service of his own government, should, as a matter of policy, be employed in the Secretariat. A major consideration for such a policy is, of course, the fact that the United States is the host country to the permanent headquarters.[46]

Lie was backed up only in part by the Secretariat's Staff Committee which had b..en badly divided in its views, some members resigning. In a letter to Lie the Staff Committee declared:

> An international civil servant's use of a constitutional privilege in a national enquiry does not automatically, in itself, justify his dismissal. Such an argument denies the principle of the independence of the Secretariat of the United Nations, and its general application would obviously involve serious practical consequences.[47]

In his *Personnel Report* Lie explained that the claim of privilege

> gives rise in practice to an unfavorable inference. . . . It cannot be doubted that a situation of this kind impairs the relationship of mutual confidence and trust which must exist between the international official and the governments of Member States.[48]

Henry Cabot Lodge, Jr., now U.S. Representative to the General Assembly, endorsed Lie's actions and explained that "the privilege against self-incrimination is directed primarily at court proceedings and does not excuse the citizen from his obligation to disclose information to a legislative committee." [49]

Meanwhile Lie announced on January 16, 1953, the appointment of an Advisory Panel, proposed by the Commission of Jurists, to advise him on the handling of future cases of this sort.[50]

Lie also disclosed some past history to the Assembly. Realizing in 1946

[46] *United Nations Bulletin,* Vol. 14, No. 6 (March 15, 1953). The Administrative Tribunal later held that some of these employees should be reinstated or recompensed.

[47] UN Doc. A/2367, March 4, 1953, p. 8.

[48] *Report of the Secretary-General on Personnel Policy,* p. 12.

[49] *Department of State Bulletin,* Vol. 28, No. 722 (April 27, 1953), p. 622.

[50] The chairman of the Panel was Leonard W. Brockington of Canada, in his individual capacity, with the following staff officials as members: Ralph Bunche, Tor Gjesdal, Gustavo Martinez-Cabanas and Constantin Stavropoulos.

that very rapid recruitment of large numbers of staff would be necessary and that the United States would obviously be the principal source for recruitment, he asked Washington for help in finding well-qualified Americans. Secretary of State Byrnes refused so as not to invade the "exclusive responsibilities" of the Secretary-General. While he appreciated the motives involved, Lie said he felt deprived of needed help. In 1949 as the United States became increasingly concerned with Communist subversion generally, some assistance was forthcoming on the suitability of United States nationals for Secretariat employment. But this was unsatisfactory, Lie went on to explain, because Washington simply gave adverse comment on certain individuals — "usually expressed in a single word" — and Lie was left in the dark as to evidence.

Therefore, Lie welcomed a compromise by which the United States sought to protect both the Secretariat and itself by informing the Secretary-General of the background and reliability of United States citizens at work or applying for work in the Secretariat while at the same time leaving to the Secretary-General the final decision to fire or hire. This compromise was established by two executive orders,[51] which apply both to the United Nations and "other public international organizations."

Every United States citizen either holding or applying for a position on the staff of the Secretariat must be investigated. For nationally recruited positions (nonprofessional) held by about 1,300 Americans, only a "name check" is necessary. This involves checking through the files of the Civil Service Commission, FBI and other government department files in addition to nongovernmental checks (educational and employment) to see if there is any derogatory information necessitating a "full field investigation" by the FBI. For the 360 Americans on the "internationally recruited staff" ("professional" category) this field investigation is mandatory. When the investigations are completed, they are transmitted by the State Department to the Secretary-General and include an evaluation as to whether "there is a reasonable doubt as to the loyalty of the person involved to the government of the United States." The standards for establishing such doubt are set forth and in part include sabotage, treason or the advancing thereof, advocacy of revolution or force or violence to alter the constitutional form of government in the United States, unauthorized disclosure of confidential information, serving the interests of another government and membership in organizations designated by the Attorney General as subversive, including, of course, the Communist Party.

From the point of view of Secretariat morale ·the most important innovation has been the establishment of an International Organizations Employees Loyalty Board in the United States Civil Service Commission composed of not less than three members of the Commission. Reports of field

---

51 The first was issued by President Truman on January 9, 1953, as Executive Order 10422. It is included in the Secretary-General's *Report* as Annex V. It was amended on June 2, 1953, by Executive Order 10459 issued by President Eisenhower and is included in the *Department of State Bulletin*, Vol. 28, No. 730 (June 28, 1953), p. 882.

investigations are supplied to the Board, and staff members are given a written statement of the complaints against them, a chance to be heard, and a chance to examine evidence and witnesses. Since some employees felt they had been dismissed by Lie without a chance to defend themselves, the new procedures seemed to be an improvement.

The General Assembly accepted this arrangement as the best way out of a bad situation and, after reviewing the Secretary-General's *Personnel Report*, voted him an expression of confidence on April 1, 1953, by a vote of 41–13–4. Unfortunately a new threat to the Secretariat's integrity appeared over the horizon.

A bill introduced by Senator Pat McCarran was passed by the United States Senate in June 1953 making it a criminal offense punishable by a $10,000 fine or five years in jail for any American to take an appointment with the United Nations without first getting a certificate from the Attorney General stating that his employment would involve no "reasonable probability of danger to the security of the United States." [52] Dag Hammarskjold, the new Secretary-General, saw "considerable difficulties" in reconciling the Charter with the proposed McCarran Bill. With regard to the removal of American Communists on the Secretariat he noted that the Secretary-General must be "entirely independent of any pressure from any member government." [53]

An evaluation of the loyalty fracas should take the following facts into account. First, the principle of Secretariat independence had up to 1953 permitted the retention on the staff of many anti-Communist expatriates from "iron curtain" countries. Could the United States order the removal of Americans it considered unsavory and deny the right of Communist Members to do the same? Was the United States, for example, ready to condone the dismissal of anti-Communist Czechs and Poles? What would happen to the Chinese Nationalists on the staff if the Peoples' Republic were to represent China in the UN?

Second, there were inevitably some red-hot Communists on the Secretariat anyway, since several Members of the organization were Communist powers. It was hard for many delegations to see how the dismissal of over forty United States citizens convicted of no crimes whatsoever and competent specialists to boot was furthering either United States security or the interests of the United Nations. Moreover, in the words of Trygve Lie, "the Secretariat works in a glass house not only physically, but in every respect. It is not a profitable place for spies and saboteurs." National delegations presumably do not circulate confidential documents or whisper strategic secrets to an international staff.

Third, no Secretariat member, with a single exception, had ever been indicted, charged or convicted in any court with regard to *espionage* or any other subversive *activity*, and the single exception (Gubitchev) was

[52] The bill as introduced in the Senate, January 7, 1953, is included in the Secretary-General's *Report* as Annex IV.

[53] *The New York Times*, May 13, 1953.

not a United States national. Thus the issue boiled down to an awkward question: Should United States staff members be dismissed not because they had been proved guilty of subversive *activity* but because the United States government considered them disloyal? Many delegates had grave doubts and voted against approval of the Secretary-General's policy on that account. To many it was sufficient for the staff to comply with the laws and judicial procedure of the host country. Lie had already reminded the staff: "The laws of the United States dealing with the immunities of the United Nations do not provide an immunity from legal process for staff members in regard to their private activities or to their activities prior to employment with the United Nations." [54]

Fourth, the United States, it should be noted, was faced with special problems because of its status as "host country." Since 1949 there was at least some evidence established by judicial procedure of espionage, Communist infiltration into governmental agencies and even treason, although no such evidence was found in connection with Americans on the Secretariat. Suffice it to say, these revelations shocked many Americans unused to the ways of world politics. Allegations that American Communists were on the Secretariat fell upon worried and receptive ears. The United States, moreover, appeared to be at a disadvantage in comparison with other Members who, if they wished, could exert some control by passport rulings over those who sought to travel to the United States to serve on the Secretariat.

Fifth, the merits of individual cases were, at times, dwarfed by political considerations. The loyalty issue in the United Nations was part of the background against which the 1952 Presidential elections were fought. Red-hunting was a source of power to a number of individuals seeking or attempting to hold public office. It was also part of the warp and woof of a campaign by a small but shrilly vocal minority either to drive Communist states out of the United Nations or the organization itself out of the United States.

As a result of these difficulties Secretary-General Hammarskjold in November 1953 requested broader powers to dismiss permanent employees.[55] He sought an explicit prohibition of political activities for staff members, the introduction of "integrity" as a standard for continued employment, and the right to dismiss employees who gave "seriously misleading or incomplete" information on applying for a post at the UN. The right of dismissal for "administrative reasons" was also suggested but not specifically requested at that time. The UN Staff Council unsuccessfully sought postponement of these proposals for further study.

There was no doubt about the results of the loyalty struggle. Morale in the Secretariat was badly shaken. Work almost ceased as roughly sixteen

---

[54] Committee on the Judiciary, *op. cit.*, p. 2.
[55] See "UN Report on Personnel Policy," *The New York Times*, November 4, 1953, and the Secretary-General's remarks before the Administrative and Budgetary Committee, *The New York Times*, November 19, 1953.

hundred Americans lined up in the Secretariat building to be fingerprinted in accordance with the new clearance procedures. Many of the staff felt Lie had failed to maintain the rights of international officials. This was the first order of business facing Mr. Hammarskjold. The United States, moreover, sank very noticeably in the opinion of many other Members as a result of its part in the issue. Yet it is fair to say that, so long as they were properly administered, the final arrangements established between Washington and New York were fair to the individual and consistent with the Charter. The Secretary-General had gained means of access to important information regarding job applicants while retaining his sole right to hire. The tragedy was that the prestige of both the United Nations and the United States had suffered heavily before these arrangements were made. The McCarran bill was a horse of a different color. It would do more than provide information to the Secretary-General. By shifting the effective power of decision to the Attorney-General in Washington, it would challenge the principle of Secretariat independence.

Suggestions for Further Reading

Books

Goodrich, Leland M., and Hambro, E., *Charter of the United Nations, Commentary and Documents* (Boston: World Peace Foundation, 1949).

Hill, Martin, *Immunities and Privileges of International Officials* (Washington: Carnegie Endowment for International Peace, 1947).

Phelan, Edward J., *Yes, and Albert Thomas* (London: The Cresset Press, 1936).

Purves, Chester, *The Internal Administration of an International Secretariat* (London: Royal Institute of International Affairs, 1945).

Ranshofen-Wertheimer, Egon F., *The International Secretariat: A Great Experiment in International Administration* (Washington: Carnegie Endowment for International Peace, 1945).

Royal Institute of International Affairs, *The International Secretariat of the Future: Lessons from Experience by a Group of Former Officials of the League of Nations* (London: Royal Institute of International Affairs, 1944).

Schwebel, Stephen M., *The Secretary-General of the United Nations* (Cambridge: Harvard University Press, 1952).

Periodicals

Boudreau, Frank G., "International Civil Service — The Secretariat of the League of Nations," *Pioneers in World Order*, edited by Harriet E. Davis (New York: Columbia University Press, 1944).

Carnegie Endowment for International Peace, New York:
   Budget of the United Nations, UN Studies No. 1 (September 1947).
   Coordination of Economic and Social Activities, UN Studies No. 2 (July 1948).
   The United Nations Secretariat, UN Studies No. 3 (Autumn 1948).

Crocker, Walter R., "Some Notes on the United Nations Secretariat," *International Organization*, Vol. 4, No. 4 (November 1950).

Hamilton, Thomas J., "The U.N. and Trygve Lie," *Foreign Affairs*, Vol. 29, No. 1 (October 1950).

Jenks, Wilfred C., "Some Problems of an International Civil Service," *Public Administration Review*, Vol. 3, No. 2 (Spring 1943).

Kunz, Josef L., "The Legal Position of the Secretary-General of the United Nations," *American Journal of International Law*, Vol. 40 (1946).

——, "Privileges and Immunities of International Organizations," *American Journal of International Law*, Vol. 41, No. 4 (1947).

Pelt, Adrian, "Peculiar Characteristics of an International Administration," *Public Administration Review*, Vol. 6, No. 2 (Spring 1946).

Preuss, Lawrence, "The International Organization Immunities Act," *American Journal of International Law*, Vol. 40 (1946).

Scott, Frank R., "The World's Civil Service," *International Conciliation*, No. 496 (January 1954).

Stone, Donald C., "Organizing the United Nations," *Public Administration Review*, Vol. 6, No. 2 (Spring 1946).

Documents

Committee of Enquiry on the Organization of the Secretariat, The International Labor Office, and the Registry of the Permanent Court of International Justice (Committee of Thirteen). *Report of the Committee,* League of Nations Doc. A. 16, Geneva, 1930.

Report of the Preparatory Commission of the United Nations, Doc. PC/20, December 23, 1945 (London: H.M. Stationery Office, 1946).

Report of the Secretary-General on Personnel Policy, UN Doc. A/2364, January 30, 1953.

Report to the President on the Results of the San Francisco Conference by the Chairman of the United States Delegation, The Secretary of State, Department of State Publication 2349 (Washington: U.S. Government Printing Office, 1945).

Secretary-General, *Report on the Work of the Organization 1946–1952.*

United Nations Bulletin, passim.

Yearbook of the United Nations.

PART THREE

League and United Nations At Work

 14

The League as Peacemaker

"This is not Peace. It is an Armistice for twenty years."
— MARSHAL FOCH (1919)[1]

IN THE TWO DECADES between the world wars roughly sixty political disputes were handled by the League of Nations, which began business in January 1920. For the same period the Permanent Court of International Justice considered very nearly the same number of legal disputes, handing down thirty-two judgments and twenty-seven advisory opinions.[2]

In the first decade, 1920 to 1930, the League had a substantial measure

[1] Quoted in Georg Schwarzenberger, *Power Politics, A Study of International Society* (New York: F. A. Praeger, 1951), p. 274.
[2] For details see League of Nations, *Ten Years of World Cooperation* (Geneva: League Secretariat, 1930).

of success in settling disputes even though its procedures were not fully developed and in spite of the fact that it had been deserted by the United States which had been largely responsible for its birth. The defection of the United States, in the view of many foreign offices, weakened the League at once and lessened the League's capacity to settle disputes and maintain peace. Yet, by 1930 many political problems had been handled by the League in a generally satisfactory manner.

A number of factors contributed to this success. First, the general optimism which had pervaded the peacemaking at Paris carried over to nourish the League in its early years. In spite of the skepticism of many European leaders, governments were under considerable compulsion to back the League owing to the pressure of public opinion that had been generated by Woodrow Wilson more than by any other leader. After all, had not the holocaust of 1914–18 been a "war to end war"? Had not Immanuel Kant's "eternal peace" dawned on the world now that the "democratic" principle of "self-determination" underlay a League of "fully self-governing" members? Second, the principal powers that had joined the League remained generally united in their foreign policy aims and attitude toward the League, in contrast to the years after 1929. England, France and Italy, for example, managed to iron out many of their differences regarding Germany, and they agreed on the steps that were taken to bring Germany back in the family of nations. This was the period of *rapprochement*, then, between Germany and her former enemies, and it was also a period during which sixty-four nations felt able to renounce war as an instrument of national policy by means of the Kellogg-Briand pact.

Third, in spite of serious difficulties immediately after the war, such as unemployment, the dislocation of traditional trade relations, and the general war destruction, the period of the twenties, particularly after 1924, was, on the surface at least, one of increasing economic prosperity. In sum, there was in Europe, certainly from 1925 to 1929, an era of "good feeling."

In this setting the League was generally well equipped to handle the problems that arose, some of which were legacies of the war involving the settlements attempted in the peace treaties. Not all international disputes by any means, however, came before the League. Many matters were handled by the inter-Allied bodies that remained in operation for a time after the war, such as the Reparations Commissions, the Supreme Council and the Conference of Ambassadors.

The second ten years of the League stand in sharp contrast and must be considered very largely a failure. The cases in that period were less satisfactorily handled and some of them, including the Manchurian episode, the Sino-Japanese dispute, the Italian-Ethiopian crisis and the Spanish civil war, inflicted mortal wounds.

Yet no significant changes had been made in the League itself. It was the political environment that had changed markedly for the worse. No longer did the Allies remain united. Italy openly sought the hand of Germany, and both became "revisionist" powers. Economic and political dis-

© Punch

"SAINT GEORGE'S DUSK"

In this English cartoon The Champion says: "This is humiliating, but I suppose I ought to have had a stronger spear."

content had helped to place in power the Fascists and Nazis, whose avowed purpose was to upset the Versailles apple cart which the League system had been expected to keep in balance.

The problem of settling international disputes is, therefore, part of the wider problem of peaceful change. But the procedures of international relations are rarely adequate to provide for change. The Covenant, to be sure, provided in Article 19 that the Assembly might advise the Members both to reconsider treaties that had become "inapplicable" and to consider "conditions" endangering world peace.

The close connection between territorial and political guarantees (Article 10) with the problem of peaceful change (Article 19) was understood by the framers of the Covenant. Indeed, early drafts made provision for the modification of treaties in the very article extending these guarantees.[3] It was argued, however, that this juxtaposition would undermine the peace settlement, and the matter of treaty revision was carefully placed after the sanctions provision as Article 19. This change was more than a play in a game of musical chairs. It implied a significant change in emphasis. It meant that many League Members, particularly France, wished to relegate any notion of treaty revision as far to the background as possible. It meant also that those directing the affairs of the League were in no way prepared to grant the Assembly the powers of an international legislative body.

Other problems hindered the League's role as peacemaker. Nations were unable to cope with the miseries of the great depression, either by "beggar thy neighbor policies" or by timid cooperative gestures under the auspices of the League. In the deepening shadows of depression amidst the incessant agitation of Hitler and Mussolini and the confusion of British and French foreign policy, confidence in the League steadily deteriorated. The United States did little to correct the situation and hid behind the principles of neutrality which the rest of the world had tried to abandon in favor of the principle of the "hue and cry." While the Soviet Union had been formally accepted into the society of nations, she was an unwelcome partner at best. The Western democracies and the Communist autocracy could not agree to check the Nazi drive for power. By the time they were forced to unite, Russia had already been expelled from the League for her attack on Finland in 1939.

In this discouraging setting the League became less and less of a factor in world affairs. In contrast to the earlier period, the will to settle disputes had largely evaporated.[4]

Some Typical Disputes

Only a few cases before the League and the Permanent Court need be reviewed in order to convey a sense of the difficulties which confronted these organizations. Questions were brought to the League's attention by the action of Members, or as a result of specific treaty provisions on various matters, such as minority questions, or by action of the Supreme Council or Conference of Ambassadors. Interestingly enough, the first case to come before the League Council was, as in the case of the United Nations Security Council, a dispute between the Soviet Union and Persia (now Iran). The problem was of little consequence and was settled by the withdrawal of Russia from the town of Engeli on the Caspian Sea.

The Aaland Islands Dispute, 1920

The first problem of any consequence to come before the League involved

---

[3] D. H. Miller, *Drafting of the Covenant* (New York: Putnam, 1928), Vol. 1, p. 52 and Vol. 2, Doc. 7, p. 65.

[4] For details of the League's dissolution see *International Organization*, Vol. 1, No. 1 (February 1947), p. 141.

a dispute between Finland and Sweden over the control of the Aaland Islands in the Gulf of Bothnia and was handled with conspicuous success. The islands were inhabited by Swedish-speaking people and had been part of the kingdom of Sweden until 1809 when, along with Finland, they were conquered by Russia. When Finland in 1917 declared its independence of Russia, the islanders sought to become Swedish subjects. Finland advanced the legal argument that since she was a sovereign nation, the matter by international law was "solely within the domestic jurisdiction of Finland." Sweden, arguing on political grounds, favored the right of "self-determination" of a linguistic minority and in 1919 asked Finland to hold a plebiscite to determine the future status of the islands. This request was refused.

The case was brought before the Council in June 1920, by a third party, Great Britain, acting under Article 11. Lord Curzon alleged that the problem affected international relations and threatened "to disturb the good understanding between nations upon which peace depends." [5]

The Council, after hearing both parties, decided first to dispose of the legal issue. Since the Permanent Court had not yet been established, a Commission of Three International Jurists was appointed and asked to give an advisory opinion on the question of domestic jurisdiction. The Commission heard arguments for a month and decided that the dispute did "not refer to a question which is left by International Law to the domestic jurisdiction of Finland" since, among other reasons, it arose before Finland was "a definitely constituted State." The Council was therefore competent under Article 15 "to make any recommendations which it deems just and proper in the case."

The Council, excepting the votes of the parties, unanimously accepted the opinion. With the concurrence of the parties it then decided to appoint a Commission of Inquiry (called the Committee of Rapporteurs) of three members, one of whom was a former American diplomat. It was now Sweden's turn to be disappointed. The Commission's report took a conservative view of the right of national self-determination, holding that it "must be applied in a reasonable manner to the relations between states and the minorities they include." On the basis of this report the Council unanimously affirmed Finland's sovereignty but proposed safeguards under the League's guarantee for the Swedish inhabitants of the islands and the conclusion of an agreement for the nonfortification and neutralization of the islands. These conditions were soon incorporated in an international agreement resulting from a conference of Baltic powers. The League was off to an auspicious start. Although feelings ran high, and although the disputants insisted that the problem affected their "vital interests," the dispute was considered, in the words of a Council representative, in relation to the "public interest of Europe."

[5] League of Nations, *Official Journal*, No. 5, 1920, p. 246f. See also Special Supplement Number 3, and the *Aaland Islands Question,* Report by the Commission of Rapporteurs, Council Doc. B. 7, 1921.

The Polish-Lithuanian Dispute, 1920

In the same year, however, there were omens of the future. Although all-out war was averted, the League was unable to bring about a satisfactory settlement of a border dispute between Poland and Lithuania, largely because the security and vital interests of great powers were involved. Poland and Lithuania had had a protracted border squabble since they had broken off from Russia in 1918. Vilna, the capital of ancient Lithuania and also the home of many Poles, was the particular bone of contention. Poland laid the problem before the Council under Article 11. As a result of the Council's mediating efforts, an armistice was signed and a boundary line provisionally agreed upon, leaving Vilna in Lithuanian territory. At this juncture, a Polish general, allegedly acting without orders from Warsaw, seized the city while a League military commission was supervising the cease-fire. Although his action was officially disavowed, Polish troops remained in the city while Council proposals for a plebiscite were unsuccessful. In March 1922 Poland formally annexed the city and soon afterwards the Council provisionally endorsed the Polish frontier claims.

Lithuania, now disenchanted with the League, asked the still extant Conference of Ambassadors to fix a frontier line. The result was a boundary in favor of Poland. In later years Lithuania appealed to both the Assembly and the Council, without success.

An important element contributing to the inability of the League to restrain violence in this case was the attitude of France. Desirous of a strong Poland both to check any possible German drive to the east and to act as a buffer (cordon sanitaire) against Soviet Communist expansion to the west, France was unwilling to apply pressure to her ally, Poland. An alliance system, including the Little Entente (Czechoslovakia, Rumania and Yugoslavia), and military agreements with Poland and Belgium, were France's answer to the weakness of the League and her failure to get a security pact in 1919. Without the hearty cooperation of the great powers, the Covenant's guarantee of territorial integrity and political independence was of little avail.

Further Boundary Disputes, 1921–1930

The League in its first decade successfully contributed to the settlement of several other minor disputes that grew out of the peace treaties. In conjunction with the Council of Ambassadors, the Council settled Albania's frontier dispute with Greece and Yugoslavia (1921–24) and the dispute between Germany and Poland over the administration of Upper Silesia where a plebiscite made the district look much like a Polish-German checkerboard. The Council helped to persuade Lithuania, Poland and Germany to accept an uneasy and largely autonomous regime for the city of Memel until Hitler seized it by a show of force in 1939.

The Permanent Court was instrumental in the settlement of a Polish-Czech dispute in the Jawarzina District and in resolving the Mosul area dispute involving the boundary between Turkey and Britain's mandated territory, Iraq. The Council helped alleviate the Hungarian Optants' dispute (1923–30) involving the property of Hungarians transferred to Rumania by the peace settlement. An agreement was finally effected by the general reparations settlement of 1930.

When there was doubt in these cases regarding the Council's competence, an advisory opinion of the Permanent Court was sought. If found competent to deal with a problem, the Council then usually appointed a commission of inquiry and endeavored to "effect a settlement." Thus in the Mosul case Turkey contended that, under the Treaty of Lausanne, the Council was simply to mediate and had no authority to render an award on the basis of the work of its Commission of Inquiry. The Council then asked for the Court's opinion of the treaty in this respect and was informed that the Council was empowered to make a "decision" regarding the frontier that would be binding on the parties. The issue was subsequently settled between Britain, Turkey and Iraq.

For these minor international disputes, often involving the interpretation of a treaty, the League system of peaceful settlement was usually satisfactory. Judicial procedure and inquiry by the Council proved to be complementary means to a peaceful solution under a rule of law.

The Nationality Decrees in Tunis and Morocco, 1922[6]

In the settlement of certain matters even the great powers have on occasion agreed in advance to abide by the judgment of third parties. Thus Britain and France settled the problem of the status of the Maltese residing in the French Protectorates of Tunis and Morocco who, under British law, were British subjects, on the basis of an advisory opinion of the Permanent Court. Briefly, the facts were that, when certain nationality decrees of November 1921 were applied so as to confer French nationality and liability for military service upon all persons born in these two protectorates, Britain objected to the enforcement of the decrees against persons she regarded as British subjects. When France refused to arbitrate on the grounds that the dispute was not justiciable, Britain appealed to the League Council under Article 15 of the Covenant. France denied the jurisdiction of the Council in the matter since under paragraph 8 of Article 15 the Council could make no recommendations regarding a dispute which it found "by international law [was] solely within the domestic jurisdiction" of one of the parties. In this instance the parties themselves voluntarily carried the dispute to the Court under the auspices of the Council and agreed in advance to accept the Court's advisory opinion.

The Court held that, although nationality questions in general fell within a state's domestic jurisdiction, the British-French dispute over the nationality decrees was not solely such a question. In so doing the Court refused to give "an extensive interpretation" to paragraph 8 of Article 15. While

[6] Publications of the Permanent Court, Series B, Advisory Opinion No. 4.

national sovereignty was not challenged, the specific dispute involved jurisdiction over nationality in "a protected territory" and was a question of international law since "treaties" and international "arrangements" were involved. On the basis of this opinion the parties quickly found ways of reaching a mutually acceptable solution.

The Case of the S. S. Wimbledon [7]

The Permanent Court's first judgment in a dispute between states, as distinguished from an advisory opinion requested by the Council or the Assembly, was closely connected with the fighting between Poland and the Soviet Union after the First World War. The Allies, as we have noted, were vitally concerned to halt the march of communism and sought to aid Poland in various ways. Germany wished to remain strictly neutral. Accordingly, the Kiel Canal authorities in March 1921, acting under a neutrality order of the German government, refused passage through the canal of a British steamship, the *Wimbledon,* chartered by a French company and loaded with munitions for Poland. The British, French, Italian and Japanese governments in January 1923 asked the Court to resolve this tangled issue by ruling that the German refusal was unlawful owing to Article 380 of the Versailles Treaty providing that "the Kiel Canal and its approaches shall be maintained free and open to the vessels of commerce and war of all nations at peace with Germany on terms of entire equality."

The Court concluded that the Canal had "become an international waterway intended to provide under treaty guaranty easier access to the Baltic for the benefit of all nations of the world." Thus Germany's neutrality would not have been imperilled had the *Wimbledon* been allowed to pass because the Canal had become "assimilated to natural straits." Because a treaty had been broken, damages were due the French government acting in behalf of the French firm. Germany, however, was denied permission to make the payment by the Reparations Commission in November of the same year. Nothing more seems to have come of the matter.

The Corfu Case [8]

Where the jurisdiction of the League began and where that of the Conference of Ambassadors left off was by no means certain. When an Italian member of a commission of the Conference of Ambassadors and three assistants were murdered by bandits on Greek soil in 1923 while on a mission to establish the boundary between Greece and Albania, the dilemma came to a sharp focus.

The League was now faced with the expansionist dreams of one of its great powers, dreams that a score of years later were to become a nightmare for the advocates of collective security. Italy, bitterly dissatisfied with the fruits of the Peace Conference, had already seized Fiume in 1919 through the unofficial but tacitly approved military expedition of the poet d'Annunzio, a modern Garibaldi dear to the hearts of Italian nationalists.

[7] Publication of the International Court, Series A, No. 1.
[8] League of Nations, *Ten Years of World Cooperation,* p. 41.

In 1922, after the famous "March on Rome," the Fascists under Mussolini had come to power dedicated to a policy of territorial expansion in the Mediterranean and Africa. Soon Albania, for all practical purposes, was to become a protectorate by the Treaty of Tirana in 1926.

It was not entirely strange, therefore, that Italy took the law into her own hands in this instance. A twenty-four-hour ultimatum incorporating stiff demands was dispatched to Greece, and upon its partial rejection Italy seized the island of Corfu after a bombardment that killed several Greek civilians, including children. Greece appealed simultaneously to the Council of Ambassadors and the League Council under Articles 12 and 15 of the Covenant. Although Mussolini denied the League's competence, the Council sought to act as mediator and forwarded suggestions which were substantially adopted by the Conference of Ambassadors. As a result, Italy was awarded an indemnity for the murders and withdrew her forces from the island.

Although Italy's action may have been induced by the moral condemnation expressed in both the Council and the Assembly, the latter by chance in session at this time, an important restraining factor appears to have been the attitude of Britain and France, neither of which was prepared to see Italy expand her power in the Mediterranean. The League, it was clear, had not changed the fundamental character of international politics. Moreover, it was thought by some to have defaulted pusillanimously to the inter-Allied body. Yet the interaction of the two organs served to restrain a permanent member of the Council and led to a reasonably satisfactory settlement.

The Greco-Bulgarian Dispute [9]

The prestige of the League was never higher than it was two years later when it took vigorous action to settle a border incident involving Greece and Bulgaria that for a brief time threatened to ignite the Balkan powder keg.

On October 22, 1925, a Greek soldier was killed on Bulgarian soil in an exchange of shots fired by frontier guards. When Greek units received orders to advance over the frontier, Bulgaria, in a telegram to the Secretary-General, appealed to the League Council under Articles 10 and 11 of the Covenant. Although the Council was not in session, M. Briand, its president, dispatched from Paris on his own responsibility what amounted to a cease-fire order. Reminding the parties of their obligations under Article 12 of the covenant, he went on to "exhort" them to cease military movements and to withdraw troops "behind their respective frontiers." The Council moved as rapidly as possible, its members managing to assemble by means of plane and train in Geneva two days later. Its first step was to require that the parties report in twenty-four hours on their compliance with the President's orders. In so doing, it refused to consider statements

[9] *Ibid.,* pp. 31–38.

from the parties on the merits of the case without prior assurance of a cessation of hostilities. For this purpose, the French, British and Italian military attachés stationed in Belgrade were asked to establish a military commission to supervise the cease-fire and withdrawal of troops. When the fighting was halted, the Council considered the substance of the case and ordered an on-the-spot investigation of the incident by a commission of inquiry with power to investigate the causes of the dispute, to assign responsibility and determine the reparations due. On the basis of this commission's recommendations, drawn up with the indispensable help of members of the Secretariat, Greece was found to be at fault and was required to pay reparations to Bulgaria. Other recommendations included supervision of frontier patrols by neutrals and ways of settling private property claims arising from an exchange of populations that had occurred in 1919. The parties complied with the Council's measures at all stages.

The satisfactory settlement of the case stood in marked contrast to an earlier Balkan incident at Sarajevo in 1914 that was the spark touching off World War I. The League's reputation was greatly enhanced as a result. The case, moreover, provided a model for future League and United Nations proceedings in handling armed clashes. The fact that the Greek armies, for example, were about to start a general offensive when the cease-fire order arrived emphasized the importance of effecting a cessation of hostilities as soon as possible. The Council's work, it should be added, was greatly helped by having direct reports from its own military commission or "truce" team in the field supervising the cease-fire. But effective procedures were only one reason for the League's success in this instance. There was also the exceptionally energetic leadership of Aristide Briand who, by good fortune, was Council President at the opportune moment and was an earnest advocate of the League's peace system. A widely respected leader, Briand embodied the spirit of the Covenant. His vigorous leadership contributed as much as any other single cause to the League's success in meeting the Greco-Bulgarian challenge. The presidency, unfortunately, did not fall to the lot of such a competent man every month in the year. Moreover, the dispute could be handled effectively because of a climate of good feeling in European politics. This was the period of *rapprochement* between France and Germany and improving economic conditions. There was, in short, a general disposition in the air to encourage the League system. Finally, the dispute involved small powers only. The Soviet Union, often in the midst of Balkan wrangles, was preoccupied with internal problems, and all the big powers seem to have been anxious to have the dispute settled rather than to capitalize on it.

The League and the Western Hemisphere — The Chaco and Leticia Dispute [10]

The League, as we have seen, dealt primarily with European problems, but it did attempt to cope with two disputes involving Latin American

[10] *The Assembly Report on the Dispute between Bolivia and Paraguay,* Monthly Summary of the League of Nations, November 1934.

states. In one, the Gran Chaco dispute between Bolivia and Paraguay, 1928–36, the League's efforts met with very indifferent success. In the other, the Leticia dispute between Peru and Colombia, 1932–34, the League's attempts were more rewarding.

Bolivia and Paraguay had long quarreled bitterly over a large border area known as the Gran Chaco. Intense fighting broke out in December 1928. The League Council intervened on its own initiative and dispatched notes to both parties reminding them of their obligations under the Covenant. The Council felt it could do little, however, because the United States and an Inter-American Conference were also trying to settle the controversy. In 1932 Paraguay, under Articles 10 and 11, appealed to the Council, which sent a commission of inquiry. After a truce had failed, Bolivia appealed under Article 15. The dispute then came before the Assembly, and a munitions embargo against both sides was agreed to. Paraguay then withdrew from the League, and the American Republics, with the Assembly's approval, attempted mediation. A settlement was finally reached in 1936.

The League and the Inter-American Conference system were ineffective in restraining violence in this dispute for several reasons. A contributing factor was, first of all, the fact that the Chaco conflict was in constant danger of falling between two stools — the universal system of the League and the regional system of the American states. There was duplication of effort between the two systems and even on occasion action at cross purposes.

Second and more important, both parties were extremely lax in following the obligations they assumed in joining the League. When, for example, negotiations gave way to hostilities, neither party at first referred the problem to the League. A peaceful solution was quite impossible once the fighting was really under way. Thus Paraguay was understandably reluctant, at the time of the Assembly report, to relinquish gains won in battle.

Third, the attitude of the United States toward the League was a potent factor in contributing to the jurisdictional fumbling that occurred. There seems to be little question that the League's hesitancy stemmed from a general feeling that the dispute was taking place in the backyard of an unduly sensitive and rather uncooperative neighbor.

Finally, one wonders if the dispute ever really engaged the serious attention of the League or even the United States. The dispute must have seemed far away from the mounting problems of depression-ridden Europe with dictatorships adding to its troubles. The United States had its depression worries also, and the remedy for foreign ills was no stronger than nonintervention or, at most, nonrecognition of territorial changes wrought by force. But world law and order required far sterner measures.

In the Leticia dispute the League had a taste of real success. Again a boundary was disputed — this time between Peru and Colombia in the upper Amazon basin, a region then largely unexplored. In 1932 Peruvian troops seized the small Colombian settlement of Leticia. After failing to dislodge the Peruvians, Colombia under Article 15 appealed to the League

Council which, after a cease-fire order by the President and a report by a committee, issued a report asking Peru to withdraw. Upon somewhat belated Peruvian compliance, a League commission was sent to administer the disputed territory until its return to Colombia. Owing largely to the conciliation of the Council's Committee of Three, Peru and Colombia by 1934 had signed a Protocol of Peace, Friendship and Cooperation.

In this instance the League could take full credit for settling a non-European dispute. An important factor in the satisfactory outcome was the absence of any jurisdictional overlapping since the League alone intervened in this instance. It is true, of course, that the dispute never generated the bitterness that marked the Chaco affair. The United States, moreover, lent diplomatic support to the League's efforts.

The Austro-German Customs Union Proposal [11]

In 1931 the League considered one of the most controversial problems of European politics, the celebrated proposal for an Austro-German Customs Union. Ironically enough, the problem arose while the Assembly was considering the studies of its Commission of Inquiry for European Union. This project, of French parentage, was suddenly countered by an Austro-German proposal that seemed to imply union under different auspices. In March 1931 both countries announced that they had signed a treaty providing for a customs union which neighboring countries might join. Political union (*Anschluss*), it should be noted, had been expressly forbidden by the Treaty of Saint Germain, Article 88 of which provided that "the independence of Austria is inalienable otherwise than with the express consent of the Council of the League of Nations." Moreover, the Protocol of 1922 dealing with Austria's financial reconstruction had provided that she must "abstain . . . from any economic or financial engagements calculated directly or indirectly to compromise this independence." The problem, in short, involved the crazy political and economic patchwork that remained after the dissolution of the Austro-Hungarian Empire. In French eyes the project was simply a device to upset the *status quo* of the peace treaties and to subvert French proposals for European union.

The matter was actually laid before the Council by Great Britain which, with France, alleged incompatibility with Austria's previous commitments. Since the interpretation of treaties was involved, the matter, on the surface, appeared to be a clear-cut issue of international law. Accordingly, the Council unanimously availed itself of the opportunity in Article 14 of the Covenant to ask the Permanent Court for an advisory opinion.

Alas, the Court's action quickly revealed the frailties of judicial procedure and the limitations of international law. The root of the problem was the insecurity aroused in the bosoms of France and her friends by the growing might of Germany. For this there was no judicial remedy. In the ensuing confusion, moreover, political considerations seemed to count

11 Permanent Court of International Justice, Series A/B, Advisory Opinion, No. 41.

heavily with the judges. While this was scarcely a new phenomenon in judicial proceedings, it served to lessen confidence in the League system. Thus the Court was badly split. A majority of eight, including the Italian, French, Polish and Rumanian judges, held that the proposed union was illegal owing to the financial protocol of 1922, while seven of these concurring judges wished to go further by ruling that it was also illegal under the provisions of the Treaty of Saint Germain. One judge, Anzillotti, agreed with the majority decision but insisted on stating his reasoning in a separate concurring opinion. The seven dissenters, including the British, American and German judges, held that Austria's independence was not compromised by the mere establishment of a union concluded on the basis of sovereign equality. Independence, in their view, could be threatened only by the consequences of the union. The League and the Court were soon relieved of further responsibility in the matter when, in September 1931, the German and Austrian representatives announced in the Commission of Inquiry for European Union that their project had been dropped.

The case illustrates the inability of the League to cope in any satisfactory manner with the fundamental political and economic problems of Europe. The organization was used by the victorious powers, especially France, to hold the fort of the Versailles settlement. It was given no significant authority or encouragement to effect peaceful changes with respect to such arrangements.

In fairness to France and her allies, it should be said that economic unions between strong and weak states had often led to the political absorption of the latter. Indeed, this was the experience of the *Zollverein* (German customs union) of the nineteenth century. On the other hand, the collapse of the Austro-German negotiations contributed to the downfall of moderate elements in German political life and provided fuel for the Nazis in their ranting against Versailles. In France, moreover, the project, including the surreptitious manner of its negotiation, discredited the moderate elements who had fostered the policy of *rapprochement*.

The Manchurian Affair and the Sino-Japanese War (1931–37) [12]

The League became disastrously embroiled in Far Eastern politics when China, following the seizure of Mukden by Japanese troops during the night of September 18, 1931, appealed to the Council under Article 11. The immediate cause of hostilities was alleged by Japan to have been the blowing up of the tracks of the Japanese-controlled South Manchurian Railway by a detachment of Chinese troops. Later investigations indicated this incident was fabricated. Although Japanese military action quickly spread

[12] For detailed information see Sara S. Smith, *The Manchurian Crisis, A Tragedy in International Relations* (New York: Columbia University Press, 1948); H. L. Stimson, *The Far Eastern Crisis* (New York: Harper, 1936); The Commission of Inquiry (Lytton Commission), League of Nations Publications, Political, Vol. 7, p. 12 (1932); W. W. Willoughby, *The Sino-Japanese Controversy and the League of Nations* (Baltimore: Johns Hopkins Press, 1935).

to include all of Northern Manchuria, Japan claimed to have acted in self-defense, a proposition later rejected by a League of Nations Commission.[13] Reports to the State Department in Washington held the Japanese action was premeditated and systematically carried out. China insisted the Japanese attack on Mukden "was entirely unprovoked and came as a complete surprise." [14]

The underlying cause of the trouble was the clash between rising Chinese nationalism and Japanese imperialism. Since acquiring special rights in Manchuria from Russia in 1905, Japan, for economic and strategic reasons, had sought to widen her control over that area. But Japanese incursions were being increasingly challenged by the Chinese nationalist movement. Boycotts of Japanese goods as reprisals against military interventions in the 1920's had proved damaging. The depression heightened Japan's need for a secure market on the Asiatic mainland. Japanese railways in Manchuria were being paralleled by Chinese railways. It was also clear that the Soviet Union continued to have its own peculiar ambitions in China, especially Manchuria. Furthermore, military elements were gaining control of the Tokyo government.

Both the Council and the Assembly were in session when the Chinese appeal arrived. At first, steps to bring the matter up in the Assembly were considered premature. Criticism of Japan's behavior by a number of small states might sting national pride and make the Council's task of conciliation more difficult. The Council at once called for a cease-fire and sought assurances from the Japanese representative that his country "had no territorial designs on Manchuria. . . ." Both parties were requested to keep the Council informed of future developments. The Japanese, however, continued their advance. The Council, in a second resolution on October 24, then sought to call for the complete withdrawal of Japanese troops by the next Council meeting in November. This step had no legal or practical effect because Japan opposed it. There were no exceptions to the unanimity rule in substantive decisions taken under Article 11. It was now evident that the League had tangled with a major power in a truculent mood. The formula that had worked so well in the Balkan clash a few short years before was found to be of limited usefulness.

Yet a hopeful event now took place. The United States sought to coordinate her efforts to restrain Japan with those of the League. At M. Briand's suggestion, an American representative was invited by the Council to "sit at the Council table but not as a member." The American Consul at Geneva, Prentice Gilbert, was then given the assignment with careful instructions by his government to participate in the proceedings only when American obligations under the Kellogg Pact were involved. Otherwise he was to act solely in the capacity of "observer and auditor." This cautious step was taken despite the vigorous but politely phrased objections of the

[13] Lytton Report, p. 71.
[14] Ibid., p. 69.

delegate of Japan. His approval was unnecessary, however, since the decision to invite the United States representative required only majority support. Japan's request for a study of the constitutional implications of the decision was voted down.[15]

Earlier in October Secretary of State Stimson had announced that the United States was anxious to assist the League in settling the conflict — but by separate diplomatic steps taken on American initiative. On October 20 the United States invoked the Kellogg Pact in notes to both Japan and China. As the Japanese armies continued their undeclared war, the United States went a step further. In diplomatic notes to Japan and China on January 7, 1932, Stimson announced that his government would not recognize any "situation, treaty or agreement which may be brought about by means contrary to the covenants and obligations of the Pact of Paris."

In this fashion the "Stimson doctrine" of nonrecognition was announced to the world. It was intended to make short shrift of any puppet state in Manchuria. It was of little avail, however. One reason was that it was promulgated unilaterally. There had been hope that Britain and France, with vast interests at stake in Asia, would support the doctrine, but both preferred to work with the League, and neither was ready to risk offending Japan. Both seemed to cling to the notion that their interests would not be threatened if Japan found *Lebensraum* in Manchuria.

To continue the story, we must shift back to Geneva. During the preceding December (of 1931) the Council unanimously decided to dispatch to the Far East a five-member Commission of Inquiry headed by an Englishman, Lord Lytton, plus diplomatic officials from France and Italy, a German colonial official and an American general. This proposal was actually initiated by Japan at a time when her armies were rapidly moving forward to subdue all of Manchuria. If delay was the purpose, events could hardly have turned out better. The Commission's report was not received in Geneva until September 1932, nine long months after it had been created.

Japan now threw caution to the winds, and her armies advanced upon Shanghai in an effort to break the Chinese will to resist. The resulting atrocities, in which thousands of civilians were bombed and burned, shocked the civilized world, but no effective reprisals were forthcoming. China, now desperate, abandoned the futile mediatory procedures of Article 11 in favor of Articles 10 and 15. Under the latter she exercised her right of requesting that the conflict be referred to the Assembly. This step marked the first time that the Assembly was called into special session to deal with a dispute under Article 15.

A combination of events now served to coordinate, in some measure at least, the meager efforts of the United States and the League. The Shanghai atrocities led the British and several of the smaller countries to persuade the Assembly to adopt a resolution on March 4, 1932, calling for

---

[15] League of Nations, *Official Journal*, 1931, pp. 2323–2333.

immediate Japanese evacuation of Shanghai. Meanwhile, Stimson had hit upon the notion of protesting to Japan on the basis of the Nine-Power Treaty of 1922, by which the signatories had guaranteed China's territorial integrity, plus his nonrecognition policy. On March 11, 1932, the Assembly unanimously adopted a resolution making this doctrine incumbent upon all League members and establishing a Committee of Nineteen to follow the course of events.

Alas, this step was too little and too late. It was answered in September by Japan's creation of a new state in Manchuria, the "independent Republic of Manchukuo." A Japanese puppet emperor was placed on the throne, and it was announced that the Chinese inhabitants of Manchuria had simply exercised the "power of self-determination"!

In the meantime, the Council continued to grapple with the case. In September it considered the Lytton Report which rejected both the Japanese claim that her military actions were in self-defense and that Manchukuo was an independent state. Yet Japan was said to have certain real grievances against China, including boycotts and the spread of communism. The Commission recommended principally that new treaties be concluded between Japan and China providing first for the definition of their respective rights and responsibilities in Manchuria, which was to be largely autonomous and demilitarized; second, for nonaggression pledges and peaceful procedures for settling disputes between the two countries; and third, for the regulation of their commercial relations.

The Council transmitted these conclusions to the Assembly where they were the basis for a report of February 24, 1933, adopted unanimously save for Japan, a party to the dispute. The only tangible result was the departure of the Japanese delegate from the Assembly Hall. A month later Japan announced her intention of withdrawing from the League. The establishment of a Far Eastern Advisory Committee in the same resolution was the League's final futility.

The reasons for the League's first major debacle are not hard to find, and all of them are interrelated. First, the League was confronted with aggression by a big power. The procedures used in the previous small-power squabbles had been effective to the extent that the great powers had been united in their determination to enforce the peace.

Second, the remaining big states did not close ranks to face Japan with any show of force. The failure of the League was then the failure of the foreign policies of the great powers. Two of them, the United States and the Soviet Union, were not Members of the League. American efforts to back Geneva were fitful and ineffective. Britain and France, as colonial powers, may not have felt that they had clean enough hands to take a strong line against Japan. Britain, in addition, seems to have underestimated the nature of Japan's designs. In addition, a naval insubordination at Invergordon in 1931 did not add to the Lion's sense of well-being.

Third, it was also true from the legal point of view that the elaborate peace machinery of the Peace Pact, the Covenant and the Washington

Treaties did not provide for any sure application of sanctions. Japan correctly assessed that she was taking no great risk.

Fourth, the depression had much to do with the League's disaster. It is doubtful if sufficient popular support could have been aroused in the democracies for an embargo or a show of force in Asia that might have had serious economic repercussions in the west.

Fifth, the governmental system in the United States added to the difficulties. In Mr. Stimson's words, "there was no statutory authority under which the Executive could impose economic sanctions." Congress was concerned primarily with the depression.

A postscript must be added. Japan's forays into China did not end with Manchuria or her withdrawal from Shanghai. Faced with growing opposition in China after the Nationalists and the Communists agreed to cooperate against her, and encouraged by the disintegration and confusion of European politics in the Spanish civil war, Japan renewed her attacks at Liukuchaio in July 1937. China at first appealed to the signatories of the Nine-Power Treaty. On September 12, she turned once more to the League Council under Articles 10, 11 and, because Japan was no longer a League Member, Article 17. The Council merely referred China's appeal to the Far Eastern Committee of the Assembly. This Committee, encouraged by President Roosevelt's "quarantine speech" of October 5 in Chicago, declaring that "peace-loving nations must make a concerted effort" against breakers of the peace, reported to the Assembly that Japan had broken the Pact of Paris and the Nine-Power Treaty. The Assembly approved the report as did the Council. In September 1938 and May 1939 the Council urged all Members to apply individual sanctions under Article 16, scarcely an effective deterrent to aggression.

The Assembly had also recommended a conference of the signatories of the Nine-Power Treaty. In this way the United States might participate directly in any action against Japan. Besides, it was obvious that the League could not apply sanctions as a collective and legally binding measure. The conference came to naught. It met in Brussels and was quickly torpedoed by Italy's joining the Anti-Comintern Pact previously signed by Germany and Japan. There was no possibility of sanctions. Public reaction in the United States was unfavorable to the "quarantine speech." The sinking of the American gunboat, *Panay*, did not incite public opinion to favor American participation in collective measures to restrain Japan. France and Britain were preoccupied with Hitler and Mussolini.

The Italo-Ethiopian Dispute[16]

The background of the Ethiopian war is briefly told. Italy had fallen behind in the imperialist scramble of the nineteenth century. In trying to make off with the scanty remains of the African pie, she was roundly de-

[16] League of Nations, *Official Journal*, 1935; L. Larry Leonard, *International Organization* (New York: McGraw-Hill, 1951), pp. 135–154; Royal Institute of International Affairs, *International Sanctions* (New York: Oxford University Press, 1938).

feated by the Ethiopians at Adowa in 1896. After that time Italy continued to covet the large area which lay between her colonies of Eritrea and Somaliland, which seemed poor by comparison. Yet in 1906 Italy joined Britain and France in signing a tripartite agreement to maintain the territorial and political *status quo* of Ethiopia. Italy sponsored Ethiopia's successful application for League membership, and in 1928 signed a treaty of friendship and nonaggression with the African kingdom. But Italy, it should be remembered, remained disgruntled at the Versailles settlement.

The immediate incident that brought matters to a head was a clash in December 1934 between Italian and Ethiopian military units at Wal Wal, a water source contested by Italy, although it lay over fifty miles within Ethiopia's somewhat indeterminate boundary. Protests were forthcoming from both governments, and Italy demanded compensation and apologies. Ethiopia then suggested arbitration under the 1928 treaty, a proposal that was first summarily rejected by Mussolini. As a result of pressure from France and Britain, however, both desirous of a quick settlement outside the League, the dictator reluctantly agreed to arbitrate the matter.

Ethiopia, meanwhile, had notified the League Secretary-General of the gravity of the situation but did not request specific League action. Nor did any other power exercise its "friendly right" of appealing the case to the League, although it was widely known in diplomatic circles that Italy intended to seize Ethiopia.[17] After serious procrastination by Italy in arbitrating the dispute, Ethiopia finally called for Council action under Article 11 despite the determined efforts of Britain and France to have the matter settled outside the League. A vicious circle of indecisive action now began. Whenever the Council seemed ready to grapple with the problem, Italy would become more amenable to the entreaties of the French and British delegates in the corridors to settle her problems with Ethiopia by arbitration. The Council would then postpone action. At no time, however, did Italy desist from warlike preparations. In May, the Council finally served notice that it would act if a settlement were not reached by arbitration within three months.

In this fashion the famous Wal Wal arbitration began. It came to naught, however. Indeed, Italy took advantage of the time involved to assemble troops and supplies for a drive on the African kingdom. An award was handed down unanimously on September 3, 1935, and exonerated both parties from responsibility in the affair. It was obvious, however, that Italy had no serious intention to abide by the award or to reach a settlement with Ethiopia. On the following day she presented the Council with a memorandum alleging that Ethiopia was a barbarous and uncivilized state and "by her conduct . . . has openly placed herself outside the Covenant of the League. . . ."

Ethiopia now requested Council action under Article 15, whereupon the Italian delegate left the chamber, not deigning to sit as an equal with the

---

[17] For example, see Cordell Hull, *The Memoirs of Cordell Hull* (New York: Macmillan, 1948), Vol. 1, p. 418.

representative of a "barbarous" state. (Italy remained a League member, formally speaking, until her withdrawal in December 1937.) A Committee of Five was next appointed to investigate the problem and to seek a peaceful solution. It included Britain, France, Poland, Turkey and Spain. The Soviet Union, it is interesting to note, refused to serve on this committee, insisting that the step was mere procrastination when stronger medicine was in order.

Events now shifted to the Assembly, which had convened in regular session. Here the British Foreign Secretary for a brief moment raised hopes for stern League action against big-power aggression when he announced that Britain stood four square behind the Covenant and for "collective resistance to all acts of unprovoked aggression." Unfortunately, the speech seems to have been intended largely for domestic consumption. Elections were impending for the British government, and a "peace poll" in Britain had recently disclosed wide public support for the use of sanctions to enforce the Covenant. Hopes were dimmed when the French delegate, M. Laval, took an equivocal stand and chose rather to emphasize friendship for Italy and the importance of continuing conciliation.

The lack of teamwork between Britain and France is understandable if regrettable. The two powers differed on the steps to be taken in the face of German rearmament. Britain, for example, in an agreement of June 1935 endorsed the rebuilding of the German navy up to one-third of the strength of the British fleet. This momentous step was taken without prior agreement with France and without reference to the League. As a result, France was more unwilling than ever to alienate Italy.

Yet both parties agreed on the fundamental point that Germany posed a more immediate threat than Italy. A decisive factor in bringing Britain close to the French point of view in this respect was the reëstablishment of a German air force in March of 1935. With her armaments at a dangerously low level, Britain's cities and civilians seemed helplessly exposed to air attack. Both from the very start of the Ethiopian affair ruled out strong measures that might cement a union between Hitler and Mussolini. But it was difficult to agree even on the halfway measures that were taken to restrain Italy. Would France support the British navy in the Mediterranean in the event of trouble owing to economic sanctions against Italy or the closing of the Suez Canal? Would Britain support France in strong measures to curb German rearmament and the remilitarizing of the Rhineland?

Both Britain and France even went a long way to seek the support of Italy in 1935 against the rising power of Germany. M. Laval conferred with Mussolini for this purpose as early as January 1935, before the Wal Wal incident assumed dangerous proportions. The price of Italian support was quite apparently a free hand in Ethiopia. Britain was soon also helplessly enmeshed in schemes of appeasement. The following April the three powers met at Stresa to consider what measures should be taken in view of German rearmament. The attitude of Britain and France toward Ethi-

"The King of France went up the hill with twenty thousand men —

— The King of France came down the hill and ne'er went up again."

Russell in the Los Angeles Times

THE SANCTIONS SITUATION RECALLS A MEMORABLE RHYME

opia on this occasion was at least equivocal. Italy was apparently permitted to feel that she had "a free hand against Abyssinia." [18] Efforts in July to settle the dispute by internal reforms in Ethiopia and territorial adjustments on the basis of the 1906 tripartite agreement proved futile. Nothing less than all of Ethiopia would placate *Il Duce.*

[18] Winston Churchill, *The Gathering Storm* (Boston: Houghton Mifflin, 1948), p. 134.

Now matters rapidly came to a head. The Committee of Five unsuccessfully proposed that the League should supervise certain reforms in Ethiopia and that Italy's special interest in Ethiopia's development should be recognized. Ethiopia proved amenable to these suggestions while Italy rejected them. A Committee of Thirteen (all members of the Council save Italy) was then appointed to draft the report that was required in paragraph 4 of Article 15. With Britain and France obviously unwilling to take military measures, Italy launched a full-scale attack on Ethiopia including poison gas and aerial bombardment. On October 5, 1935, Ethiopia invoked Article 16, and, on October 7, the Council by adopting the report of yet another committee, a Committee of Six, found that Italy had resorted to war contrary to Article 12. This step brought into play the economic sanctions of Article 16. The Assembly was consequently invited to assist in arranging the application of economic measures against Italy.

For the first time in its history the League had named an aggressor and gone so far as to recommend collective sanctions against a great power. The resulting measures were taken on the initiative of each Member, however, for, as we have already noted, Article 16 had been interpreted as long ago as 1921 to mean that each Member, rather than the Council or the Assembly, was to decide the fact of aggression individually. This technicality made no appreciable difference in the results that followed. The Assembly at once established a Coordination Committee to "facilitate the coordination" of measures taken by individual League Members. This committee, assisted by numerous technical subcommittees, recommended an arms embargo, an embargo on financial help to Italy, an import embargo and a ban on the sale of certain raw materials to Italy. Equally important were measures of mutual support undertaken to lessen the economic plight of League Members applying sanctions.

In the astonishingly short period of a little over a week, all Members approved these steps with the exception of Albania, Austria and Hungary. These states were too close to Italy to feel it prudent to concur in the findings of aggression. Switzerland asked to be excused from applying sanctions on the basis of her traditional policy of neutrality.

The half-hearted attitude of Britain and France became evident when news of the nefarious Hoare–Laval deal leaked to the press in December 1935. Although Italy had been declared an aggressor by the League and in spite of the atrocities of her Ethiopian campaign, Italy was apparently to receive two-thirds of Ethiopia and to exercise effective control over the remaining portion. This was too much for British public opinion. The outburst that followed had to be appeased by the removal of Sir Samuel Hoare from the cabinet in favor of Sir Anthony Eden as Foreign Minister. While the incident furnished a celebrated exception to the British tradition of cabinet solidarity, it did not lead to effective sanctions against Italy. Though severely hurt by the embargoes, Italy completed the rape of Ethiopia by May 1936. In July the Assembly accepted the *fait accompli* by ending the measures taken under Article 16.

The League's first and only attempt to apply economic sanctions ended in failure. Why was this so? Primarily because sanctions were haltingly applied owing to the conflicting foreign policies of the big powers. Britain and France, preoccupied with Germany, refused to consider military sanctions which presumably would have stopped Italy in short order. Even such obvious steps as closing the Suez Canal or placing an embargo on oil were not taken. Other major powers must share the blame. The role of the United States, for example, was of crucial importance. Her trade with Italy, particularly in oil, increased considerably after the outbreak of the Ethiopian affair. These events influenced the attitude of European powers. The enforcement of an oil embargo would have rested chiefly on the British navy. Might not a clash with the United States navy ensue? Freedom of the seas had been a bone of contention between Uncle Sam and John Bull before. Would not American companies capture valuable markets from European competitors if shipment of European oil were halted? When in October 1935 the United States prohibited the export of arms to either belligerent under the provisions of recently enacted neutrality legislation, Ethiopia, the victim, was injured as much as Italy, the aggressor. Neutrality and collective security were mutually exclusive.

Germany, also a major power and now outside the League, was constantly a menacing cloud on the horizon. Her actions were shrewdly timed to exploit the confusion created by Italy. The absurdity of the situation becomes apparent when it is recalled that Britain and France were applying economic sanctions against Italy under the aegis of the League while at the same time wooing Italy as a guarantor of the Franco-German border under the Locarno system. Although the Soviet Union had joined the League, effective collaboration with a Communist dictatorship scarcely seemed the lesser of two evils to Britain and France.

Clearly there was no "concert of powers" within the League. This fact was clearly understood by the smaller powers, some of which sought to escape any entanglement. Belgium sought permission from France and Britain to withdraw from her Locarno obligations into the shell of neutrality. Switzerland and the Scandinavian states behaved similarly by formally repudiating the automatic application of any League sanctions.

Sanctions against Italy failed for other reasons. For one thing, they were not maintained long enough. When they began to pinch, they were lifted. The whole procedure, moreover, was fraught with the gravest technical difficulties and raised problems for governments sensitive to public opinion. Clearly the League Members were reluctant to continue measures that hurt them as well as Italy. Moreover, the Coordination Committee was faced with a herculean task of synchronizing the actions of fifty different nations presenting fifty different combinations of constitutional, political and economic difficulties. Elaborate steps had to be taken to prevent the loss of trade from hurting any one state or group of states. With Italy in control of Ethiopia, moreover, no useful purpose seemed to be served by continuing sanctions. A collapse of the Fascist government, in the view of some states, might lead to the creation of a government that was worse.

The Spanish Civil War[19]

In Spain a civil war broke out in July 1936 between the Rightist forces of General Franco and the republican government in Madrid. Spain simply did not have the stabilizing influence of a prosperous middle class. As a consequence, the struggle was largely between the impoverished masses and a powerfully armed coalition of army, landholders and the church. The character of the strife quickly changed in fact, if not in law, from a "civil" war to a world struggle on a reduced scale. Both Italy and Germany at once saw a golden opportunity to weaken further the position of the democracies. War material and soldiers, officially called "volunteers," were poured into Spain to help Franco. The Soviet Union, in turn, could brook no increase in German and Italian strength and responded by sending quantities of supplies and many technical advisers to assist the republicans.

For Britain and France the alternatives of policy were dreary indeed. Between the Scylla of the Rome-Berlin Axis and the Charybdis of Soviet communism, they hopefully sought to steer a course of "nonintervention." The idea was attractive, but intrinsically worthless when the totalitarians did not play according to the same rules. Domestic factors again influenced the foreign policies of the western powers. A sweeping victory for either side would serve to divide rather than to unite public opinion. Owing to an uneasy balance between Léon Blum's Popular Front government and the parties of the Right, domestic politics in France were particularly sensitive to the struggle. Blum's government could be expected to fall if it aided Madrid. In Britain, the Conservative government seems to have felt that a Fascist Spain was preferable to, or no worse than, a Communist Spain.

Faced with these difficulties, France and Britain sought to limit the spread of the conflagration by a program of "nonintervention" outside the League system. Twenty-seven European states agreed to this program and organized a Nonintervention Committee meeting in London. Its object was to prevent the spread of the conflagration by coordinating measures to prevent the shipment of war materials to either side. While these obligations were scrupulously carried out by France and Britain, they were systematically violated by Germany, Italy and, to a lesser extent, Portugal. Intentionally or unintentionally, obstacles were thus placed in the way of the Madrid government by all concerned. In the United States "nonintervention" had its counterpart in a policy of neutrality which was extended well beyond the requirements of international law. In January 1937 the United States, in view of the "state of civil strife," imposed its own arms embargo. Madrid felt that it had nowhere to turn save Moscow, which was unable to match the contributions of the Axis.

Naturally, the Spanish republicans protested against the policy of nonintervention. Appeals to Britain and France were unsuccessful, and Madrid

[19] N. J. Padelford, *International Law and Diplomacy in the Spanish Civil Strife* (New York: Macmillan, 1939).

desperately resorted to the Council under Article 11. The League's reply was as shopworn as it was useless. In December 1936, nonintervention was endorsed, with the reminder that "every state is under an obligation to refrain from intervening in the internal affairs of another state."

The struggle finally drew to its bloody conclusion. Italy and Germany had officially recognized the Franco government in November 1936. In February 1939, even prior to the fall of Madrid, Britain and France granted *de jure* recognition to the Franco regime. The republican government soon went into exile.

It can be argued that the League did all that could be done under existing rules in taking the attitude that the Spanish war was a domestic matter over which it had no jurisdiction. The Members of the League, however, seemed unduly anxious to take the legal refuge offered when Germany and Italy maintained the fiction but not the practice of civil war and nonintervention. So far as the policies of Britain, France and the United States are concerned, it should be remembered that existing international law would have permitted aid to the republicans and the insurgents but not to the insurgents alone. Madrid could have been supported had these powers desired to adopt such a policy. With respect to the League, it is only fair to say that the preconditions of its functions had vanished long before. The concert of great powers was broken. Indeed, it had not really been established since World War I.

The Expulsion of the Soviet Union

In March 1938 German troops moved into Austria after Britain failed to induce Italy to join in taking steps to oppose Hitler. In an earlier crisis of 1934 *Il Duce* had behaved differently. But no one at this stage thought it worth-while to appeal to the League which many years earlier had been an important means of rescuing Austria financially. Italy now cast her lot irrevocably with Germany and Japan by joining the Anti-Comintern Pact.

The general attitude toward Geneva was doubtless expressed by Lord Halifax in justifying British recognition of the Italian conquest of Ethiopia in return for the withdrawal of Italian "volunteers" from Spain. Britain, the Foreign Secretary told the Assembly, did not feel that the previous action of the League against Italy impaired Britain's freedom of action. When "two ideals are in conflict — on the one hand the ideal of devotion, unflinching but unpractical, to some high purpose; on the other, the ideal of a practical victory for peace — I cannot doubt that the stronger claim is that of peace." [20]

Similarly the League was not involved in the abandonment of Czechoslovakia in September 1938. Chamberlain, in meetings with Hitler at Berchtesgaden and with Hitler, Daladier and Mussolini at Munich, sought "peace in our time" by appeasing Hitler. The fate of Czechoslovakia was decided by the big powers acting outside the League. Czechoslovakia had almost no control of her destiny. The abandonment of the League was

[20] League of Nations, *Official Journal*, May–June 1938, p. 335.

further underscored when the Soviet Union proposed a conference with Britain, France and the United States to plan "collective action" outside Geneva to check aggression. Britain was sympathetic but refused to give prior guarantees to save Czechoslovakia since her "vital interests" were not involved. France would not act without Britain and the United States. The United States avoided Europe like the plague. All three distrusted the Soviet Union. Within six months Germany had taken those parts of Czechoslovakia not handed her at Munich. Within a year German troops crossed the Polish frontier, and France and Britain were at war with Germany. No one sought to place the invasion of Poland before the League.

These events were ominous for future relations between the Soviet Union and the Western powers. The latter, it appeared, were not ready to guarantee Germany's eastern frontier. Indeed, they had been willing to see the industry of Czechoslovakia added to German might without consulting the Soviet Union. On August 23, 1939, eight days prior to the German invasion of Poland, the famous Soviet-German nonaggression pact was signed in Moscow. The work of a belated Anglo-French mission to Moscow went for naught. The Western powers were to receive no help from the east until Hitler invaded Russia.

It was ironic, furthermore, that the League's last gasp was the expulsion of the Soviet Union when nothing had been done to stop Hitler, Mussolini or Franco. On November 30, 1939, Soviet troops began the invasion of Finland. The latter promptly appealed to the League. On December 14, the Council, following debate in the Assembly, found that, in attacking Finland, the U.S.S.R. had placed herself outside the League.

Conclusions

The League's failure to settle disputes in its closing years is due to many causes. The great depression did much to embitter international relations. National governments sought salvation in economic policies that were narrowly nationalistic. The failure of the World Economic Conference at London in 1933 was a signal that international economic cooperation had been consigned to the junk heap. National governments were quick to blame the woes of their citizens on the design of foreigners. Bitterness and xenophobia were eroding the foundations of cooperation.

A similar failure in the disarmament field was another blow to the peaceful settlement of international disputes. The builders of the League system recognized that nations could be expected to reconcile their differences without force of arms only if national armaments were greatly reduced. A reduction in armaments, it was further recognized, was possible only in the event of a dependable collective security system. This, as we have seen, was not forthcoming. The Disarmament Conference of 1932–33 was a failure before it had begun. It was soon followed by intensive rearmament by the dictators and belatedly by the democracies.

The march of the dictators, moreover, confirmed what many had suspected. The League was weak. Japan, through a variety of propitious circumstances, embarked with impunity on a course of aggression. Amid the resulting confusion, other powers soon learned to do even better. All these disasters had a snowballing effect, and the League's fragile peace system was soon demolished.

The first ten years had been different. Then the League was relatively successful in solving disputes. A general air of optimism prevailed. The League, furthermore, was not called upon to handle big-power quarrels. Until the dictators were strong enough to challenge French leadership in Europe, the Geneva system worked. In Asia, with American power nonexistent, Russia was an ineffective counterpoise to Japan. Perhaps that is why the latter was the first major power to challenge the League. Soon the preponderance of power shifted away from France and Britain to those states that wished to alter the shape of things established by the peace treaties. Thus the destiny of the League was closely linked with the prestige of France and Britain. As this declined and the United States remained aloof, the Covenant had inadequate authority to keep the peace.

Yet even in 1935 and 1936 Britain and France were stronger than Germany and Italy. Why were they reluctant to marshal their strength behind the Covenant? One reason advanced was the failure of the United States to join the collective security system. Another was quite obviously the mutual distrust between the Soviet Union and the democracies. Still other reasons were the prevalence of understandably tenacious anti-war sentiments, economic difficulties and the yet undeveloped state of the concept and habit of collective security.

Suggestions for Further Reading

Books

Beer, Max, *The League on Trial,* tr. by W. H. Johnston (Boston: Houghton Mifflin Company, 1933).

Butler, Harold, *The Lost Peace* (New York: Harcourt, Brace & Company, 1942).

Carr, E. H., The *Twenty Years' Crisis, 1919–1939* (New York: The Macmillan Company, 1940).

Cecil (Viscount), *A Great Experiment: An Autobiography* (New York: Oxford University Press, 1941).

Conwell-Evans, T. P., *The League Council in Action* (New York: Oxford University Press, 1929).

Dean, V. M., *Europe in Retreat* (New York: Alfred A. Knopf, 1939).

Dell, Robert, *The Geneva Racket, 1920–1939* (London: Robert Hale, 1941).

Feis, Herbert, *Seen from E. A.* (New York: Alfred A. Knopf, 1947).

Gathorne-Hardy, G. M., *A Short History of International Affairs, 1920–1939* (New York: Oxford University Press, 1942).

Highley, A. E., *The Actions of the States Members of the League of Nations in Application of Sanctions against Italy, 1935–1936* (doctoral thesis) (Geneva: University of Geneva, 1938).

Hindmarsh, A. E., *Force in Peace* (Cambridge: Harvard University Press, 1933).
International Sanctions, a report by a group of members of the Royal Institute of International Affairs (New York: Oxford University Press, 1938).
Morley, Felix, *The Society of Nations* (Washington: Brookings Institution, 1932).
Perkins, E. R., "The Non-application of Sanctions against Japan, 1931–1932," in *Essays in History and International Relations in Honor of George Hubbard Blakeslee* (Worcester: Clark University Press, 1949).
Salter, Sir Arthur, *Security: Can We Retrieve It?* (New York: The Macmillan Company, 1939).
Shotwell, J. T., and Salvin, Marina, *Lessons on Security and Disarmament from the History of the League of Nations* (New York: King's Crown Press, 1949).
Smith, S. S., *The Manchurian Crisis, A Tragedy in International Relations* (New York: Columbia University Press, 1948).
Veronoff, Tatiana, *L'Article 16 de pacte de la société des nations* (Paris: Recueil Sirey, 1937).
Webster, C. K., and Herbert S., *The League of Nations in Theory and Practice* (London: G. Allen and Unwin, Ltd., 1933).

Documents

League of Nations, *Ten Years of World Cooperation* (Geneva: League Secretariat, 1930).
United Nations, *Analysis of Provisions of Pacific Settlement Treaties,* Note by Secretariat, UN Doc. A/AC.18/57, May 6, 1948.
———, *History and Analysis of the General Act for the Pacific Settlement of International Disputes,* September 26, 1928, UN Doc. A/AC.18/56, May 4, 1948.
———, *History and Analysis of the General Convention for Improving the Means of Preventing War and the Regulations for the Execution of Article 4 of This Convention,* Note by Secretariat, UN Doc. A/AC.18/55, May 3, 1948.
———, *Resolutions Adopted by the Assembly of the League of Nations, September 26, 1928, Relating to the Pacific Settlement of International Disputes, Non-aggression and Mutual Assistance,* UN Doc. A/AC.18/43, Mar. 11, 1948.

15

United Nations as Guardian of Peace

> "It is not so difficult to keep unity in time of war since there is a joint aim to defeat the common enemy, which is clear to everyone. The difficult task will come after the war when diverse interests tend to divide the Allies. It is our duty to see that our relations in peacetime are as strong as they have been in war."
> — MARSHAL STALIN, *Yalta, 1945* [1]

THE KINGPIN of the United Nations peace structure was expected to be the continued unity of the big powers of the wartime alliance. For this reason, even more than in the case of the League, world peace would depend on the foreign policies of the major powers. Big-power unity, however, was already dissolving as early as the formal coming into being of the United Nations on October 24, 1945. [2]

Significant changes that weakened the cement of the United Nations wartime alliance had come over the world scene. Deep-rooted hostility between the Communist and non-Communist nations was intensified as the common danger of German and Japanese aggression was removed. Some disputes focused on the struggle between Moscow-dominated communism and the nations of the "free world." Others involved the clash of rising nationalist forces in many places and resulted in tensions between the old colonial areas and their former masters. Britain and France had fallen from the ranks of the great powers. The United States and the U.S.S.R. stood head and shoulders above any other powers and became the focal points of rival coalitions.

Yet the United Nations in its first nine years grappled more or less successfully with about sixteen clearly defined political disputes. Although the Security Council was originally expected to be the principal forum for these questions, the most significant organizational development has been the increasing role of the General Assembly. A few problems required contributions of the Court, the Trusteeship Council and the specialized agencies.

[1] J. F. Byrnes, *Speaking Frankly* (New York: Harper, 1947), p. 44.
[2] *Ibid.*, Chap. 3.

426

Roughly half a dozen other questions affected international peace without becoming specific political "disputes" between two or more states. These, generally, fell to the lot of the General Assembly and included such matters as the disposition of the Italian colonies and the observance of peace treaties in Eastern Europe. Until military sanctions were applied in the Korean affair, no major hostilities took place. At least half a dozen problems were less dangerous following United Nations consideration than before. In other cases, while no substantial change resulted from the events at UN Headquarters, it is fair to say that no deterioration resulted from United Nations action. In short, the organization, through the conciliation and mediation procedures of the Security Council and the General Assembly, in most instances brought some moderating influence to bear and may even have localized conflicts. Yet the debates in the United Nations were often more acrimonious than those of the League. The Soviet Union and its satellites developed name-calling into a major instrument of policy. But the fact that some Members were less involved than others helped to bring a measure of third-party judgment to bear.

As in the League, the early disputes brought to the organization were generally part of the legacy of war which brought violent changes in the world's balance of power. In several early cases, for example, disputes arose as a result of the declining influence of the Western European states in the Middle East and Southeast Asia. More than in the case of the League Council, however, the Security Council was besieged with cases before its practices had become stabilized in accepted rules of procedure. Early disputes in the Council were characterized, therefore, by procedural wrangles which had significant political implications.

The Iranian Complaint Against the Soviet Union [3]

History repeated itself when as in the League's debut Persia, now Iran, was involved in the first case before the United Nations. In a note of January 19, 1946, to the Acting Secretary-General of the United Nations, the Iranian government complained that Soviet troops were interfering in Iran's internal affairs and threatening her territorial integrity. The Soviet Union was further charged with attempting to obtain oil concessions by coercion and with fomenting an independence movement in Azerbaijan. Iran requested that the matter be laid before the Security Council and in March designated it as a dispute.

The Soviet Union contended in turn that, since bilateral negotiations with Iran had been successful in agreeing on a withdrawal date for the following March, there was no dispute likely in fact to endanger peace. Consequently there was no basis for Security Council intervention. The Soviet Union appeared to regard the Iranian action as inspired by the United

[3] For full details of all cases, see the *Official Records* of the Security Council and the General Assembly, the Case Summaries in *International Organization*, the *United Nations Bulletin*, and the *Yearbook of the United Nations*.

States and Britain and retaliated a few days later by bringing to the Council's attention the presence of British troops in Greece.[4]

The case occasioned no surprise among the Big Three. Troops had been stationed in Iran during the war to protect a supply route to Soviet troops on the Eastern front. In 1943 at Teheran the Chiefs of State of the Big Three agreed to withdraw foreign troops soon after the war and to assure Iranian political independence. Negotiations in the Council of Foreign Ministers at Moscow in December, 1945, however, came to an impasse over the continued presence of Soviet troops. American forces had already been ordered to withdraw.[5]

While the Council's discussions were formally limited to procedural aspects of the case, principally whether to include the Iranian complaint on its agenda, there were substantive implications throughout. When, for example, Mr. Gromyko took the first Soviet "walkout" by withdrawing from the Council Chamber when his resolution to postpone discussion until April 10 failed to carry, the Council continued its work and resolved that both parties should report on May 6 "whether all Soviet troops" had been withdrawn from "the whole of Iran." The Security Council also refused Iran's request to withdraw its complaint despite a legal opinion of Secretary-General Trygve Lie. Soviet troops were withdrawn during May. The Council, however, continues its watch over the case which remains at the head of the list of matters of which the Council is "seized."

The case was significant in suggesting the power of mere discussion in the Security Council. Despite the Soviet "walkout" and despite the absence of any substantive finding such as a situation or dispute likely to impair peaceful relations, foreign troops left northern Iran.

The Greek Case[6]

In this same period the United Nations was brought face to face with the turmoil in Greece that followed the war and resulted very largely from the struggle among the great powers for control of the Eastern Mediterranean. This was the first case to show conclusively the weaknesses of the Security Council. As a result the United States sought to strengthen the General Assembly's procedures for handling international conflicts.

First on January 21, 1946, two days after the Iranian complaint, the U.S.S.R. charged that the "presence of British troops in Greece after the termination of the war meant interference in the internal affairs of Greece and caused extraordinary tensions fraught with grave consequences both for the Greek people and the maintenance of peace and security."[7] Again wartime arrangements figured heavily.[8] In October 1944 the United King-

---

[4] Byrnes, however, states that in December he did not want the Iranian matter to come before the General Assembly about to open in January. See *op. cit.*, p. 120.

[5] See Byrnes, *op. cit.*, pp. 118–121 and 303–304.

[6] *The United Nations and the Problem of Greece*, Department of State Publication 2909, Near Eastern Series 9 (Washington: Government Printing Office, 1947).

[7] *Security Council Journal*, No. 2, p. 14.

[8] J. C. Campbell, *The United States in World Affairs, 1945–47* (New York: Council on Foreign Relations, 1947), p. 59.

dom and the Soviet Union had agreed that for military purposes in the war Greece should be part of a British sphere of influence while Bulgaria, Hungary and Rumania were to be in the Soviet sphere. Both powers were to share control over Yugoslavia.[9] The United States, opposed to spheres of influence as a means of organizing the postwar world, concurred in these measures as wartime arrangements on a trial basis for three months. After the war Greece was torn by civil strife between conservative elements and the National Liberation Front (EAM), largely Communist-dominated. Soviet policy sought the removal of British troops which were aiding anti-Communist elements.

Although Bevin for Britain and Gromyko for the U.S.S.R. argued the merits of the case at length, the first phase was brief and inconclusive. Several members indicated that the presence of British troops in Greece was not a threat to the peace and the Greek delegate pointed out that they were on hand by invitation of his government. The matter was temporarily closed on the suggestion of Stettinius of the United States that the President of the Council simply issue a statement taking note of what had happened and declaring the incident closed.

The second phase, equally inconclusive, began on August 24, 1946, when the Ukrainian Republic charged that Greek troops, encouraged by the government, were provoking incidents on the Albanian frontier. The presence of British troops was declared to be the principal factor in the trouble. It was evident that the Greek elections scheduled for September 1946 were an element in the timing of this accusation. Several resolutions now failed. The Soviet Union, which was to cast six vetoes in the case, blocked the establishment of a United States–proposed committee of investigation. Matters were allowed to ride, and the Council simply passed on to its next item of business.

The third and most significant phase of the case opened on December 3, 1946, when the Greek government itself complained to the Council under Articles 34 and 35 that guerrilla warfare was being waged by Albania, Bulgaria and Yugoslavia.[10] Greece and Yugoslavia were invited to the Council table without difficulty. Albania and Bulgaria were not Members of the UN, however, and Article 32 provides for the participation of non-members only if parties to a dispute. The Council contrived, by a resolution that did not pass on the nature of the case, to invite the two states to present their views. Improvisation of this sort is often necessary. Although the debate now descended to levels of vituperation novel in diplomacy, the Council was able by unanimous vote to establish its first commission of inquiry to conduct an on-the-spot investigation. It was composed of representatives of all the Council Members who were assisted by a staff of

[9] Hull, *The Memoirs of Cordell Hull* (New York: Macmillan, 1948), Vol. 2, pp. 1451–1461. Mr. Hull tells us that he was not in favor of "the balance of power or spheres of influence as a means of keeping the peace." The President made this decision without informing the State Department.

[10] UN Doc. S/203, and *Official Records* of the Security Council, 1st year, 2nd Series, Supplement #10, Annex 16.

twenty-seven individuals drawn largely from the Secretariat. When the Committee of Inquiry was ready to withdraw in order to prepare its report, the Council provided that a Subsidiary Group should remain on the scene to report any border violations.

Events outside the UN now bore on the Council's work. On March 12, 1947, the Truman Doctrine was announced by the United States. Faced with the continuing deterioration of the British position in Greece and the Near East, the President announced to Congress that "it must be the policy of the United States to support free peoples who are resisting attempted subjugation by armed minorities or by outside pressure." Congress responded by authorizing the necessary funds for military and economic aid to Greece and Turkey.

What was the relation of this unilateral action to the United Nations? In Washington, Senator Vandenberg sought to fuse "containment" with the American policy of supporting the United Nations. Congress resolved that the aid should cease whenever the Security Council or the General Assembly should by majority vote find that it was "unnecessary or undesirable." On March 28, Ambassador Austin for the United States announced in the Security Council that the policy "was giving momentum to the United Nations." Gromyko of the U.S.S.R. and Lange of Poland, on the other hand, insisted that the doctrine was undermining the organization. Meanwhile the United States, in spite of an important FAO fact-finding mission that had already surveyed Greece, did not attempt to utilize the specialized agencies in the rehabilitation of that unhappy country.

Further Security Council action was hamstrung by big-power disagreement. On May 27, 1947, the Commission made a report to the Security Council in which eight of its members found that Yugoslavia, Albania and Bulgaria were responsible for the border warfare. The Soviet and Polish representatives, however, found Greek "monarcho-fascists" wholly responsible. France, still groping for a middle way, refrained from expressing an opinion on the matter of responsibility. Soviet vetoes now showered upon the Council. Resolutions introduced by the United States incorporating the Commission's findings, establishing a good offices committee and calling for action under Chapter VII were blocked. The United States seemed eager to force more Soviet vetoes for the record. Thus the proposal for action under Chapter VII seemed to have been designed to draw a veto since it closely followed an Australian proposal that had already been vetoed. In one instance the so-called "double veto" was cast.[11] Faced with stalemate, the Council finally adopted by procedural vote a United States proposal to drop the case from its agenda. The way was now clear to lay the problem before the Second Assembly.

From that time until 1951 the General Assembly continued its efforts to settle the problems of Greece. It permitted Bulgaria and Albania to appear

[11] For an explanation see pp. 149–150.

before its First Committee. It passed a series of resolutions that pretty largely followed the pattern of one introduced by the United States in 1947.[12] This called for a peaceful settlement of the problem, the conclusion of frontier agreements, the resumption of diplomatic relations and the cessation of assistance to guerrillas. Most important, the Second Assembly established the United Nations Special Commission on the Balkans (UNSCOB) to assist in carrying out these recommendations. This successor to the Security Council investigation commission was composed of eleven members, including the five big powers and Poland. The latter and the U.S.S.R., however, refused to serve. UNSCOB was soon hampered in other ways. Unlike its predecessor, it was forced to confine its activities to Greece since the boundaries of Albania and Yugoslavia were closed. The "iron curtain" had been rung down at Greece's northern frontier.

The Third Assembly a year later upheld the UNSCOB conclusion that continued support of guerrilla activity by Albania, Yugoslavia and Bulgaria constituted "a threat to the political independence and territorial integrity of Greece and to peace in the Balkans." The Commission was continued by the Third, Fourth and Fifth Assemblies with slight modifications, including resolutions on the repatriation of kidnaped Greek children and soldiers. All these decisions received thumping majority support with the U.S.S.R. and her satellites, usually in a minority of six until reduced to five by the defection of Yugoslavia. The Arab states, however, were prone to abstain.

By 1950 matters had improved — very largely owing to the heresy of Tito in deserting the Cominform. Yugoslavia reëstablished diplomatic relations with Greece and guerrilla activities diminished rapidly. Yet there were other contributing factors. The Truman Doctrine had clearly done much to save Greece from the Communist camp by timely military and economic aid. Patently the work of the organization itself was significant in restraining Greece's northern neighbors. It was, for example, immensely useful to Greece, a small power, to have a multilateral rather than a unilateral Commission, whether from the Security Council or the General Assembly, actually reporting on the scene.[13] In flouting the UNSCOB, moreover, the Soviet Union placed herself and her satellites squarely in the path of majority sentiment at the United Nations. Finally, this issue was the first major question that led the United States to promote an accelerated development of the political role of the General Assembly.

The Syria-Lebanon Case

In a letter to the Secretary-General on February 4, 1946, Syria and Lebanon alleged that the presence of British and French troops was an infringement of their sovereignty and that the terms of withdrawal were inconsistent with the Charter. This case, as has already been noted, mired the Council in procedural confusion. The Council succeeded, however, in

12 UN Doc. A/C.1/9/.
13 See the UNSCOB Report to the Assembly, UN Doc. A/1857.

inviting Syria and Lebanon to participate with the understanding that this action did not constitute a decision by the Council that a dispute did in fact exist. Indeed, the attitude of the British and French representatives at the Council table suggested that there was no dispute of any consequence. Both powers expressed a readiness to withdraw their troops. Both volunteered to abstain from voting whether or not the Council considered the matter a dispute. In spite of a general reaction that, in comparison to other Council debates, these replies were reasonable, the Soviet Union vetoed a United States resolution which would have had the Council merely express confidence in the avowed intentions of withdrawal. The Soviets wished a stronger resolution demanding immediate withdrawal. Consequently the Security Council could agree on nothing. Britain and France acted nevertheless in the spirit of the defeated majority resolution and later reported that the troop withdrawals were completed.

Again wartime arrangements had led to postwar difficulties. Again the Soviet Union sought the removal of Western European troops from strategic areas outside their home territories. Here also was a golden chance for the Soviet Union to play upon the nationalist aspirations of countries in the Middle East. The case was unique in that the Soviet veto had no tangible effect on the outcome.

The Indonesian Case [14]

Affairs in Indonesia gave rise to one of the most important cases to come before the Security Council. Two days after the Japanese surrender in the Pacific in August 1945, a Declaration of Independence was issued by various Indonesian nationalist leaders, some of whom had collaborated with the Japanese. A constitution modeled on that of the United States was soon drafted for the Republic of Indonesia. These events were influenced heavily by the sudden ending of the Pacific war. The first Allied troops under British command, for example, did not arrive to receive the surrender of the Japanese until September 1945. By then the government of the new Republic had been established. Negotiations with the Netherlands in the remainder of 1945 were fruitless since both parties insisted on establishing complete control.

The Security Council became involved when, in January 1946, the Ukrainian Republic complained that the British were using Japanese troops to resist the independence movement in Indonesia. The Ukrainian delegate demanded the appointment of a commission to investigate the trouble and to "establish peace in Indonesia," a proposal supported only by the Soviet Union. The matter was then dropped without further action.

The Netherlands, meanwhile, had found it difficult to reassert authority over the East Indies. In March 1947 the Linggadjati Agreement was signed in which the Netherlands recognized the *de facto* authority of the Repub-

---

[14] J. Foster Collins, "The United Nations and Indonesia," *International Conciliation* No. 459 (March 1950); Charles Wolf, Jr., *The Indonesian Story* (New York: John Day, 1948).

lic over Java, Madura and Sumatra. Both parties agreed further to co-operate in the establishment of a federal state for all of Indonesia to be linked under the Netherlands Crown in a Netherlands-Indonesian union. This proposal was consistent with an earlier wartime declaration of the Crown promising commonwealth status for Indonesia. Efforts to implement the agreement were unsuccessful, however, and in July 1947 Netherlands troops began military operations in what was officially described as "police measures of a strictly limited character."

Where the fault lay need not concern us. Suffice to say the Dutch still felt, in spite of the Linggadjati Agreement, that sovereignty rested with the Netherlands pending a final political settlement. The Indonesians, in turn, were ready to fight for their newly won independence. Neither side trusted the other. India and Australia were now alarmed at the outbreak of hostilities. The former appealed to the Council under Articles 34 and 35 but withdrew in favor of the stronger Australian application which insisted that the hostilities constituted a "breach of the peace" under Article 39. The Council was faced with its first case under Chapter VII of the Charter.

India and the Netherlands and subsequently the Philippines were invited to the Council table as interested parties. The Indonesian Republic, however, was invited only after considerable discussion on several technical problems. Could the Republic be invited to the Council table as a state under the rules of international law? The Council invited representatives of the Republic to its table without deciding the question. Was the whole affair a matter of "domestic jurisdiction" and therefore beyond the Council's competence as claimed by the Netherlands? The other colonial powers on the Council, England, France and Belgium, thought it was. The United States, with one eye on its European friends and the other on Asia, reserved its position on these technical matters but offered its "good offices" to end the fighting. Could the Council take "provisional measures" under Article 40 to stop hostilities without formally deciding that there was a breach of the peace or act of aggression under Article 39? Such a decision could hardly be voted with the colonial powers on the Council generally supporting the Netherlands and the Soviet Union encouraging Indonesian independence.

In this situation the Council displayed a healthy flexibility. Procedural points were not allowed to obstruct its general mandate under the Charter to maintain peace and security. Indonesia, for example, was simply invited to participate by procedural vote. In due course nearly all the states of Southeast Asia were asked to take part in the discussions. Similarly an Australian resolution was softened by a United States amendment so that all references to the Charter were deleted. The Council on August 1 simply called for the immediate cessation of hostilities and the settlement of the problem by arbitration or other peaceful means. A Polish amendment provided that the Council should be kept informed. Although the three colonial powers abstained, the Australian cease-fire resolution was then passed — one day after the problem had come to the Council. Shades of Aristide

Briand! The Council had chosen to make its own interpretation of the Charter rather than to refer the legal problems to the Court, a Belgian suggestion supported only by the United States, France and the United Kingdom.

With hostilities continuing in spite of the cease-fire order, France vetoed a Soviet proposal for the appointment of a commission composed of the entire Council membership to supervise the cease-fire. This was not the first time the U.S.S.R. was to be excluded from UN commissions operating in Indonesia, and elsewhere. Instead the Council established a consular commission, consisting of those members of the Council who had career consuls at Batavia, to report on the progress of the cease-fire order. The Council also established a Committee of Good Offices to promote a political settlement with each party selecting one member and these two selecting the third. Australia, Belgium and the United States were the members of this committee, with Dr. Frank Graham, a university president and an experienced labor conciliator, as the American representative. The colonial powers abstained from voting on the cease-fire decisions and the Soviet Union did likewise when the Consular Commission and the Good Offices Committee were established.

Meanwhile, the Consular Commission had to cover a vast area in Java to report on the cease-fire. It was handicapped by the lack of a trained staff ready to take the field. Consequently, a small group had to be hurriedly recruited from the consular staffs and military services of the members' governments. Its reports, however, led to a further cease-fire order from the Council on November 1, 1947.

During the fighting the Committee of Good Offices was hard at work in Java. Its efforts were rewarded when a truce agreement was finally signed on January 17, 1948, aboard an American naval vessel, the U.S.S. *Renville.* This vessel had been finally chosen as a means of furnishing a neutral site acceptable to both parties. The Renville agreement [15] was subsequently approved by the Council.

The truce broke down, however, during the negotiation of the political principles of the agreement. In December 1948 the Netherlands opened a new offensive against the Republic. A sharp division between the Australian and Belgian members of the Committee of Good Offices had not helped matters. The burden now rested very largely upon a new American representative, Merle Cochran, a veteran foreign service officer, supported by a fresh staff.

The Council then met in emergency session but could agree on only a weak resolution calling for the cessation of hostilities and the release of captured Indonesian leaders. When hostilities continued, the Council on January 28, 1949, adopted a broad resolution sponsored by Cuba, China, Norway and the United States. Besides calling for a cease-fire, the release of Indonesian leaders, and the renewal of political negotiations, the Committee of Good Offices was reestablished as the United Nations Commission

[15] UN Doc. S/649.

for Indonesia. Its authority was broadened to include the power of making recommendations for "the establishment of a federal, independent and sovereign United States of Indonesia."

Outside events were now instrumental in shaping a final settlement. A conference in New Delhi of nineteen Asian, Australasian and Middle Eastern states was called by Nehru of India to consider the situation. Its views were transmitted to the Security Council in January. A change in the composition of the Netherlands government hastened the calling of a round table conference at The Hague which met August 23 to November 2, 1949. The Dutch military action was very costly and far from a complete success. Difficulties were increased when the United States cut off Dutch Marshall Plan aid that was destined for use in Indonesia. Finally, an appeal to the Assembly was threatened by Australia and India.

Meanwhile the Security Council continued to strengthen its grip on the situation. In a resolution of March 13, the Netherlands proposal for a round table conference had been declared consistent with the Council's previous action. During the summer the end of the fighting was reported by UN military observers. At The Hague, the round table conference resulted, by December, in the transference of authority over the Netherland East Indies (exclusive of New Guinea) from the Netherlands to the Republic of the United States of Indonesia. This new republic and the Netherlands were loosely tied in a union under the Netherlands crown. In the Security Council two resolutions approving the Hague agreements, praising the Commission for its work and instructing it to aid in implementing the agreements were defeated by Soviet vetoes in December 1949. The Soviet delegate charged that the Hague Agreement strengthened "in a new-fangled form the old Dutch stranglehold on Indonesia," and was supported by the United States, "anxious as always after the smell of oil, rubber and tin." [16] In the Assembly a resolution commending both the parties and the United Nations Commission was passed the same month by a vote of 44 to 5 with 2 abstentions. No one joined the Soviet bloc in disapproving.

Conclusions. The United Nations and particularly the Security Council derived considerable prestige from the settlement of the Indonesian problem. Its authority had gradually strengthened in the period from the early cease-fire resolutions in 1947 to the Hague Conference in 1949. At that time the United Nations Commission for Indonesia made crucial recommendations that did much to bring the conference to a successful conclusion. United Nations action on various occasions had restrained both the Dutch and the Indonesians. Its task had not been easy, for the dispute entailed the passions of nationalism dashing against the colonial remnants of a previous era. Communism, moreover, was a disconcerting and uncertain element in the situation until the Nationalist forces took measures of their own against the Communist groups.

[16] *The New York Times,* Dec. 14, 1949, and *Records* of the Security Council, 455th meeting.

Would matters have been better without the United Nations intervention? Probably not. Without the intervention of a third party there seemed no way of coping with the mutual suspicions of the Dutch and Indonesians that always threatened to corrode any formal agreements that were reached. In such a situation intervention by a single state or group of states is often unacceptable. Indeed the offer of "good offices" by the United States was rejected. Yet the intervention by the United Nations led to a compromise that was probably the most feasible.

Finally, valuable knowledge was gained on the problems of conciliation and of staff procedures and personnel. The Security Council proved that when its permanent members were not in sharp disagreement, it had considerable strength and surprising flexibility. The United Nations was rapidly being tempered in the fire of experience.

The Spanish Case

Spain was an apple of discord to the United Nations both during and after the war. The Franco government was established with the connivance of the Axis. Although formally remaining neutral, Spanish collaboration with the Axis during the war varied with the fortunes of Mars.[17] Allied sentiment was strongly against Franco. In 1945 Spain was excluded from membership in the United Nations by resolution of the San Francisco Conference "in view of its origin, its nature, its record, and its close association with the aggressor states."

The problem came before the Security Council on April 8, 1946. A note from the Polish government invoked Article 34 and referred to the "international friction" that resulted from the character of the Franco regime. The severance of diplomatic relations was demanded as a sanction under Article 41. France, Mexico and the U.S.S.R. supported Poland. Other members including Britain and the Netherlands expressed doubts as to the Council's jurisdiction. Consequently a subcommittee of three members was appointed to decide whether the matter was a "domestic question" and whether it might lead to international friction or even endanger international peace and security. This step was taken by procedural vote under Article 29 despite the demurral of Ambassador Gromyko, Soviet delegate, who abstained on the question. So began the practice in the United Nations of not considering an abstention a veto.

While it did not find Franco Spain an actual threat to the peace in the sense of Article 39, the subcommittee considered the regime a "potential menace to international peace and security." It was therefore a matter of international concern and not a question of domestic jurisdiction. Further measures were recommended to be taken by the Assembly rather than by the Council. The hand of the committee chairman could be seen in this move. Evatt of Australia was continuing his campaign to defy the great

---

[17] *The Spanish Government and the Axis,* Department of State Publication 2483, European Series 8 (Washington: Government Printing Office, 1946); and Winston Churchill, *Their Finest Hour* (Boston: Houghton Mifflin, 1947), Chap. 11.

powers by building up the General Assembly at the expense of the Security Council. These proposals were not acceptable to the Soviet delegate, who argued that the problems of peace and security were the special responsibilities of the Security Council. Consequently, four Soviet vetoes ensued, including the first "double veto," all of which provoked acrimonious debate regarding the authority of the Four Power Voting Statement. The stalemate was ended when a Polish resolution to shift the problem from the Council to the Assembly received unanimous support. The Soviet delegate had reversed his field.

The General Assembly after considerable debate recommended in December 1946 that Spain be excluded from membership in the specialized agencies, that the members recall Ambassadors and Ministers from Madrid and that the Security Council consider measures to be taken if a representative government were not established within a reasonable time. The recall of Ambassadors had already been anticipated to a large extent and only three Members refused to comply. These measures remained in force until revoked by the Assembly in 1950 when Korean hostilities suggested that totalitarianism on the left seemed of more pressing concern than that on the right.

Coupled with the Indonesian and South African cases, the Spanish case suggested that the "domestic jurisdiction" clause of the Charter was not going to be interpreted rigidly. In showing how cases might be juggled between the Assembly and the Council and that the use of the veto diminished the Council's prestige, the case was suggestive of future events. Substantively, the measures taken seem if anything to have strengthened the Franco regime. Moreover, this was an issue on which the Soviet bloc led the way and won substantial support from many other countries, especially France, at least during the early postwar years while the anti-Axis tradition was still relatively strong.

The Case of the Indian Minority in South Africa

This case has involved only the General Assembly. On June 22, 1946, the Indian government alleged that the Union of South Africa was discriminating against the local Indian population in violation of international agreements, including the Charter, and that the peaceful relations of the two countries were endangered. Debate in a joint committee drawn from the First and Sixth Committees was of particular interest owing to the prestige of the chief protagonists. Mme. Pandit, Indian Ambassador to the United States, presented her country's case while Smuts, the Grand Old Man of the League, now elevated to marshal, was forced by domestic political considerations to argue, ironically enough, that the jurisdiction of the League's successor could not be extended to include consideration of the matter in hand. No clear treaty obligations were involved in his government's view, and the Indians were indisputably South African nationals. Therefore the matter fell within the domestic jurisdiction of South Africa.

Many delegations, including that of the United States, favored an advisory opinion from the International Court. A French-Mexican resolution, however, was finally adopted in the Assembly, which noted that friendly relations between the two states had been impaired and that the Assembly was "of the opinion that the treatment of Indians in the Union should be in conformity with the international obligations under the agreements concluded between the two governments and the relevant provisions of the Charter." Both parties were requested to report on the measures taken to settle the problem. Finally, in 1950, the Assembly recommended the creation of a three-member conciliation commission if the issue were not resolved by a round table conference that had been previously recommended in 1949. Meanwhile, South Africa enacted further discriminatory legislation and defied the United Nations on the issue of Southwest Africa as well.[18] Although the lot of the Indians had not been improved, the matter continued to be discussed at length despite South Africa's protests.

The Case of the Corfu Channel [19]

During 1946 a crisis developed between Communist Albania and the United Kingdom. Involved were an increasing pattern of xenophobia in Communist-controlled countries and resentment at displays of British naval power. In October, two British destroyers were damaged by mines in the Corfu Channel, and forty-four seamen lost their lives. Despite Albanian protests the British, with the permission of an International Central Mine Clearance Board, a wartime agency still in existence, promptly swept the Channel. Twenty-two newly-laid mines of German origin were brought to the surface of the channel, recently certified clear by the Mine Board.

The British then demanded an apology, reparations for the ships and full compensation for the lives lost. On receiving unsatisfactory replies from Albania, the United Kingdom appealed to the Council on January 10, 1947, under Article 35 of the Charter. Albania was invited to the Council and promptly denied any knowledge of the mines. The British sweeping operations in territorial waters, moreover, were challenged as violating Albanian sovereignty. After an examination of the facts by a Council subcommittee appointed under Article 29, a British resolution finding Albania responsible was lost owing to a Soviet veto. The Council then adopted another British suggestion and recommended that the two parties refer the dispute to the International Court where some delegates felt the problem should have been taken in the first place. The Soviet Union acquiesced to the extent of abstaining.

In May 1947 the United Kingdom filed an application with the Court and submitted its case in a "memorial" of October 1. Although protesting the unilateral action of the United Kingdom, Albania agreed in July to appear in Court. In a countermemorial of December 1, however, Albania argued against the Court's jurisdiction because the case had not been sub-

---

[18] See Chap. 10.

[19] International Court of Justice, *Reports of Judgments, Advisory Opinions and Orders*, 1947–48 and 1949, and Security Council, *Official Records*, 1946.

mitted in accordance with a special agreement between the two parties and because Albania had not accepted the compulsory jurisdiction of the Court. Since she had no national on the Court, Albania selected a Czech to be judge *ad hoc.* In a preliminary judgment the Court ruled that Albania had voluntarily accepted its jurisdiction by agreeing to appear before it.

The Court handed down its judgment on April 9, 1949. By eleven votes to five on the first question, Albania was found responsible under international law for the explosions and the resulting damage and loss of life. On the second question, however, the Court unanimously found that Albanian sovereignty had been violated by the British mine-sweeping activities following the explosion. In so doing the Court specifically rejected British arguments that the sweeping was justified under the principles of "self-protection" and "self-help." [20] This was the first occasion on which the International Court or its predecessor had declared the use of force for self help or intervention to be contrary to international law.[21] On December 15, 1949, the Court in a twelve to two decision, the Soviet and Albanian judges dissenting, fixed the amount of reparation due the United Kingdom.

Conclusions. Although Albania has refused to pay the amount awarded, the case was settled in the calm of judicial procedure and was no longer a source of danger to international relations. Since many points of law were involved, including the laws of "territorial waters," "innocent passage," and a Hague Agreement of 1907 on mine-laying, many observers agreed with the Brazilian delegate on the Security Council that the case should have been taken to the Court in the first place. To say, however, that the Court settled the question is to omit an important point. The problem was solved because both parties decided on judicial settlement.

Yet the Court's role must not be slighted. Dependable judicial procedure was at hand when the parties voluntarily decided to make use of it. The Court, moreover, took an important step forward in limiting the use of force by a state seeking redress of its grievances. Weaker states would now appear to have additional protection under law against the strong.

The case was encouraging in that three Communist judges (Soviet, Polish and Yugoslav) joined the majority in sustaining the Court's jurisdiction and two (Polish and Yugoslav) concurred in the assessment of damages. Finally, the Security Council's flexibility in coping with technical problems seems to have been wise. By not standing on legal technicalities the Council seems to have helped the process of peaceful settlement. It did not, for example, find that a situation existed which might endanger peace. Nor did its resolution refer to any specific article of the Charter. Yet a reading of the Charter suggests that such a recommendation should have been taken only after such a finding under Article 34.[22] This, however, would plainly

[20] Corfu Channel Case, judgment of April 9, 1949, ICJ *Reports,* p. 35.
[21] Oliver J. Lissitzyn, *The International Court of Justice,* UN Studies No. 5 (New York: Carnegie Endowment for International Peace, 1951), p. 26.
[22] See the Security Council, *Official Records,* 125th meeting. The United Kingdom delegate referred to Article 36 in submitting his resolution.

have incurred a Soviet veto to protect Albania from the guilt implied by a finding of a situation or threat under Article 34.

The Anglo-Egyptian Case

Anglo-Egyptian relations have occupied the Security Council's attention as one element of the United Nation's embroilment in the social and political upheavals of the Near East. Fundamental factors involved were Britain's decline in power and a growing surge of nationalist resentment in Egypt against foreign influence.

In a letter of July 8, 1947, referring to Articles 35 and 37, Egypt alleged that a dispute existed with the United Kingdom that might endanger peace. The Security Council was asked to direct both the immediate evacuation of British troops from Egypt and the termination of joint Anglo-Egyptian rule over the Sudan under the Condominium of 1899 (Lord Salisbury's famed contribution to international legal arrangements). The presence of British forces constituted an infringement of Egyptian sovereignty and was contrary to the terms of the Charter.

The British delegate argued in his turn that Anglo-Egyptian relations were regulated by treaties dating back to 1899. Specifically, the troops were stationed in Egypt as a matter of right under the terms of a 1936 treaty. After twelve sessions of debate that failed to produce a Council recommendation, the President announced on September 10, 1947, that the question would simply remain on the agenda.

Behind the legal façade lurked problems of grand strategy. Egypt had been an essential military base in defending the Near East during World War II. The Suez Canal and the Sudan remained important links in the naval and air defense of a strategic non-Communist area.

Egypt meanwhile renewed her demands for the withdrawal of troops in November, 1950. On October 15, 1951, the Egyptian Parliament unanimously abrogated the Treaties of 1899 and 1936. The Egyptian government then refused to consider joining a projected four-power Middle East Command composed of Britain, France, the United States and Turkey. Domestic considerations had much to do with the government's action. British Tommies in the Suez area were reinforced and braced themselves against riot and disorder. In early 1954 the Council still remained seized of the matter.

The Palestine Case[23]

In Palestine the United Nations sought to curb an explosive situation. If Jewish forces were largely responsible for the birth of Israel, the United Nations was at least an active midwife. Never before were so many elements of the United Nations peace structure brought to bear on any problem. Before an uneasy settlement was finally achieved, the Palestine case involved five of the principal United Nations organs, several specially

[23] L. Larry Leonard, "The United Nations and Palestine," *International Conciliation*, No. 454 (October 1949).

created commissions and a specialized agency. Most striking, however, was a renewed demonstration of the importance of competence in negotiations. Two United Nations Mediators and an able staff drawn from the Secretariat were indispensable in bringing to bear the restraining influence of the society of nations.

Background. Behind the events of 1947–48 that led to the rise of Israel lay centuries of racial persecution, religious conflict, including the Crusades, and great-power rivalry for control of the strategic Holy Land. Only a few recent events, however, need be recalled. In the struggle against the Central Powers and Turkey in World War I, Great Britain undertook commitments that were inherently contradictory. The Jews were assured in the Balfour Declaration of 1917 that the British government viewed "with favor the establishment in Palestine of a national home for the Jewish people. . . . " For the Arabs there had already been implications during the war of political independence once they were freed with British help from Turkish rule, and in the Balfour Declaration itself was the assertion that "nothing shall be done which may prejudice the civil and religious rights of existing non-Jewish communities in Palestine. . . ." Palestine at once became a matter of international concern. The Paris Peace Conference decided that along with other areas in the Turkish Empire, Palestine should be placed under a League of Nations Mandate. The Supreme Council of the Allied and Associated Powers then assigned the Mandate to Britain.

Tensions between Arab and Jew, not serious up to this point, were multiplied when Nazi persecution and anti-Jewish sentiment in other areas led to an enormous influx of Jewish immigrants into the Promised Land. The Zionists had long sought a home for the Jewish people. Extreme elements now felt that Palestine should be a Jewish state. The efforts of several Royal Commissions proved unavailing in reconciling incompatible policies. Finally, in 1939 Britain sharply curtailed further immigration to placate the Arabs and maintain her Near East position. Violence increased with the continuance of the refugee problem after the war. The Palestine administration, supported by British soldiers, came increasingly under the attack of extremists. The United States now sought to persuade Britain and the Arabs to reopen Palestine to Jewish immigration. In May of 1946 an Anglo-American Committee of Inquiry recommended the immediate entry of 100,000 Jewish refugees and a United Nations trusteeship for Palestine which should be neither Arab nor Jewish but a state protecting Moslems, Christians and Jews alike. These and further proposals proved unattainable.

Special Assembly Session. By now it was clear that no conceivable plan could win the support of both Arabs and Jews. Yet Britain remained unwilling to enforce a policy against the wishes of either side. Consequently, in April 1947 the General Assembly, at the request of the British government, was called into its first special session and asked for recommendations under the authority of Article 10 "concerning the future government of Palestine." The United Kingdom's action coincided with her withdrawal from Greece and was doubtless influenced by the serious financial and economic problems that reached a peak in the hard winter of 1947.

Despite strenuous Arab objections the problem was placed on the Assembly's agenda. Two nongovernmental organizations, the Jewish Agency for Palestine and the Arab Higher Committee, were permitted to appear before the First Committee. In spite of the failure of many earlier commissions to cut the Gordian knot, the Assembly appointed its own United Nations Special Committee on Palestine (UNSCOP) to conduct investigations on the spot and to make recommendations to the Assembly in its regular fall session. The Committee included representatives of eleven states, none of which was a permanent member of the Security Council.[24] The suggestion that it should be composed of individual experts rather than governmental representatives was rejected, but its work depended heavily on a staff drawn from the Secretariat.

UNSCOP. When the Second Assembly met in regular session in September 1947 a majority of the UNSCOP favored the partition of Palestine into an Arab and a Jewish state linked in a United Nations–supervised economic union with Jerusalem as a separate entity. A minority (India, Iran and Yugoslavia) favored a single federated state, a suggestion supported by the Arab states. The Assembly adopted the essentials of the majority plan in November by a vote of 33 to 13 with 10 abstentions. Other provisions included:

> the establishment of a United Nations Commission to assume administrative authority from the United Kingdom not later than August 1, 1943, and to assist in creating the governments; a request that the Security Council take measures to meet any threat to the peace such as an attempt to alter the partition plan by force; responsibility assigned to the Economic and Social Council to assist in effecting economic union; and responsibility assigned to the Trusteeship Council for the administration of Jerusalem.

The new Commission, alas, had little opportunity to accomplish more than acquire the title of the "five lonely pilgrims"[25] and to report heavy fighting between Arab and Jewish forces to the Security Council. The British, reluctant to antagonize the Arabs, refused to permit its entry into Palestine until just prior to the mandate's termination, advanced to May 15, 1948.

The Security Council was now thoroughly perplexed. At the instigation of the United States it retreated from the advanced ground staked out by the Assembly. Between February and April 1948 it concluded that it lacked constitutional authority to enforce a political settlement recommended by the Assembly or even by the Council itself. It could only act to remove a threat to the peace. Accordingly, in April it passed the first of several cease-fire resolutions. The United States had other second thoughts. The

[24] Australia, Canada, Czechoslovakia, India, Guatemala, Iran, The Netherlands, Peru, Sweden, Uruguay and Yugoslavia.
[25] The members were Bolivia, Czechoslovakia, Denmark, Panama and the Philippines.

permanent members should seek a new solution. Perhaps partition should be replaced by a temporary trusteeship arrangement. With this in mind the Council passed the ball back to the Assembly and, under the authority of Article 20, requested it to meet in special session.

The Mediator. With a majority of its members reluctant to discard the partition plan, the Assembly refused to "zig zag" with United States policy. On May 14, one day before the Mandate's demise, a Mediator was appointed in a compromise move to "promote a peaceful adjustment of the future situation of Palestine." On that same day the State of Israel was proclaimed in Palestine, and the United States startled the Assembly by unilaterally granting the new state *de facto* recognition.

The Mediator, Count Folke Bernadotte of Sweden, achieved an initial success when, by skillful use of a Security Council truce resolution of May 28, he achieved a temporary cease-fire. The first steps at mediation failed, however, and on July 15 the Security Council invoked Chapter VII of the Charter for the first time in a resolution finding that "the situation in Palestine constitutes a threat to the peace within the meaning of Article 39 of the Charter." The governments concerned were ordered to "desist from further military action" and the Mediator directed to supervise truce machinery. No other sanctions were imposed, however.

When the Third Assembly met in regular session in the fall of 1948, it had before it recommendations of the Mediator to alter the original partition scheme in favor of the Arabs. Tragically, he was assassinated on September 17 by an armed band in Jewish uniforms. Dr. Ralph Bunche of the Secretariat now skillfully carried on as Acting Mediator. The Assembly next appointed a Conciliation Commission to assume, to the extent necessary, the functions of the Mediator. Yet Dr. Bunche remained hard at work for many more months, a marvel of patience and skill in negotiating armistice agreements. The Island of Rhodes was utilized as a neutral ground for meetings with Arab and Jewish leaders. By the summer of 1949, the necessary armistice agreements had been concluded between Israel and the Arab states and were administered by mixed commissions headed by UN observers. In May Israel became the fifty-ninth Member of the United Nations.

Jerusalem and Refugees. Anything better than an uneasy truce for the next few years, however, was held up by two grave obstacles, the status of Jerusalem and the plight of Arab refugees. The appointment of a Special Municipal Commissioner for Jerusalem, Mr. Harold Evans, an American Quaker, by the United Kingdom on recommendation of the Assembly in 1948 proved futile owing to Arab opposition. To protect the holy places the Assembly instructed the Conciliation Commission and later the Trusteeship Council to prepare a statute to implement their internationalization. The Council finally reported that owing to the consistent opposition of Jordan and Israel, this solution was unworkable. Yet no substitute could

HIGHLIGHTS OF UN ACTION IN PALESTINE

Haifa

GALILEE

Tel Aviv
Jaffa

Jerusalem

Gaza

Beersheba

NEGEB

Neutral
zone

- - -
Partition
line

Area held
by Israel

Aqaba

1947

APRIL, Britain places Palestine
problem before UN
MAY, UN Special Committee
on Palestine created by
Assembly
NOV., Assembly voted for
partition of Palestine

1948

MAY, British mandate ends;
State of Israel proclaimed;
Arab invasion begins;
Assembly special session
decides to send mediator:
Count Bernadotte appointed
JULY, After fighting mars
truce orders, Security Council
passes cease-fire resolution
SEPT., Bernadotte assassinated
Ralph Bunche becomes acting
mediator
DEC., Stanton Griffis appointed
director of UN Relief for
Palestine Refugees; Assembly
establishes a Conciliation
Commission; U.S., France
and Turkey are named as
members

1949

JAN., Armistice talk begins
at Rhodes under Bunche
FEB., Egyptian-Israeli
armistice completed
March-April, Transjordan and
Lebanon sign armistice;
Syria signs cease-fire

GRAPHIC ASSOCIATES

Headline Series, *Foreign Policy Association*

be found to replace this futile policy. UN efforts to aid the 900,000 Arab refugees who fled from Palestine are discussed below in Chapter 18.

Conclusions. A few general conclusions can be drawn from the story of Palestine and the United Nations. First, the armed forces of Israel made the United Nations policy of partition a reality. Yet the organization had done much to restrain a bitter conflict and to supervise what quite clearly after World War II seemed to have been the most feasible solution. Meanwhile the Conciliation Commission, a truce observation group and a relief agency, remained throughout 1950–51 as instruments of the international community nurturing an uneasy peace. Second, it was obvious that the foreign policies of many states, not excluding the United States, were shaped very largely by domestic politics and public opinion. This added immeasurably to the hazards of policy formulation at the United Nations level. It is not without significance that Israel received *de facto* recognition by the United States in an election year. Arab governments, moreover, were quick to direct internal tensions against other governments.

Third, it was obvious that the heroic work of a Mediator and a relatively small staff was not enough. A "guard force" was necessary to protect UN "truce teams."

Fourth, the Assembly proved to be a useful instrument not only in investigating the facts of the problem but also in formulating a settlement that had the support of the great majority of the United Nations, including the United States and the Soviet Union. It was also useful in maintaining the settlement. Although the Assembly made no attempt to apply sanctions directly, it created agencies, principally the Mediator, which were largely responsible for maintaining the armistices. While the Security Council did not follow the Assembly's recommendation to use its authority to enforce the partition plan, it did virtually the same thing by supporting the Mediator and invoking Chapter VII to halt the fighting after partition had been achieved by force of arms.

The Disposal of the Italian Colonies[26]

In one instance the General Assembly was able to solve a problem where the big powers had failed. Under the terms of the Italian Peace Treaty, the Council of Foreign Ministers, composed of France, the United Kingdom, the United States and the Soviet Union, was to dispose of Italy's former colonies. If no agreement were reached by a certain date, the matter was to be laid before the General Assembly, the recommendations of which were to be binding on the four powers.

Unable to agree, the four powers took the problem to the Assembly in September 1948 where it was considered for three successive sessions. Strategic jockeying continued between the United Kingdom and the United States, which had bases in the area, and the Soviet Union, which sought to gain a foothold through a trusteeship arrangement. France wanted to soft-pedal political developments that might threaten her own North African holdings. The Arab states wished early independence for the populations involved, while the Latin American states generally favored Italian interests. These were, in short, the pressure groups at work, and the Assembly took on some of the characteristics of a legislative body. The final arrangements formulated by the Assembly are discussed at the end of Chapter 23.

The Assembly had been authorized for the first time to award an arbitral

[26] Benjamin Rivlin, *Italian Colonies*, United Nations Action Series No. 1 (New York: Carnegie Endowment for International Peace, 1950).

decision accepted in advance by the parties. It provided a useful means by which the great powers could resolve at least one of their differences. In its fourth session the Assembly managed to pass a resolution that satisfied both the anti-colonial and the pro-Italian blocs with something less than each had originally hoped for. Agencies created by the Assembly have helped prepare the areas for self-rule. Thus the Assembly helped to create new political regimes and end sources of friction in the international community. It is widely recognized, of course, that these areas are extremely underdeveloped. Yet prevalent attitudes, within as well as outside these lands, made it difficult to do anything but make them self-governing as quickly as possible. One can only hope that subsequent assistance from the UN and other sources will gradually give them greater strength and stability.

Kashmir: The India-Pakistan Question

Again the chain reaction of events set off by World War II was largely responsible for bringing a case to the Security Council, and once more the decline of British power was a factor leading to difficult political readjustments. After Parliament under Labor leadership passed the India Independence Act in August 1947, two new states, India and Pakistan, were established on the Indian subcontinent. In addition, numerous independent princely states had the option of joining India or Pakistan or, technically speaking, of standing alone. The choice proved troublesome for Kashmir, predominantly a Moslem state with a Hindu ruler. Strife soon broke out between Hindu and Moslem communities. At first an arrangement was sought with Pakistan, but border raids by Moslem tribesmen and economic pressure from Pakistan led the ruler to place Kashmir provisionally under India — apparently as a means of restoring order.

As communal strife and border raids continued, India, on January 1, 1948, complained to the Security Council under Article 35 that the situation was a potential danger to international peace. Both sides presented their views. India charged Pakistan with aggression which Indian troops had barely managed to thwart by quick action. Pakistan charged India with provoking Sikh and Hindu terrorism against the Moslem population.

Between January and April the Council made four important decisions.

1. On January 17, it sustained the President's action in calling upon the parties to improve the situation and to keep the Council informed.

2. A three-member United Nations Commission was established on January 20, with the dual function of investigating the facts under Article 34 and of mediating between the parties.

3. The Council on April 2 finally called for the withdrawal of all foreign troops and nonresident tribesmen. It also established a Plebiscite Administration to hold elections to determine whether the Kashmiri inhabitants wished to join India or Pakistan. The Secretary General was empowered to name an administrator.

4. The membership of the Mediation Commission was increased to five by permitting the Council itself to appoint two members — Belgium and Colombia were added. India, in accordance with the earlier resolution had selected Czechoslovakia, and Pakistan chose Argentina. The last-named chose the United States.

These steps were reaffirmed by a Council vote on June 3, 1948. In July the Commission reached Karachi. The Soviet Union abstained on all these decisions, alleging, as in the Indonesian case, that the membership of the Commission was unsatisfactory and its relation to the Security Council not sufficiently close. Not until March 1949 had sufficient progress been made to warrant the appointment of Admiral Chester Nimitz of the United States as Plebiscite Administrator. Unfortunately that doughty veteran of the Pacific wars could not carry out his new assignment because India and Pakistan, although agreeing to cease hostilities in January 1949, have been unable to agree on the withdrawal of troops or the means of conducting a plebiscite.

In the years 1949–51 the Council changed its tactics. When in December 1949 the Mediation Commission reported failure to achieve demilitarization, the President was instructed to try his hand. Next a suggestion of the Commission itself was adopted, and a single United Nations "representative" was appointed on March 14, 1950, to replace the somewhat cumbersome Commission. Sir Owen Dixon was selected by the Council with the approval of both disputants. In a year's time Sir Owen resigned after failing to secure demilitarization, the crux of the problem. In April 1951 the Council, following its decision of March for demilitarization and arbitration, selected Dr. Frank P. Graham, a distinguished American educator and mediator, to carry on.

Dr. Graham met with representatives of India and Pakistan continuously through 1951 and 1952. The issues separating the parties were narrowed. India still rejected the principle of arbitration and continued to insist on the legality of the Kashmir government's action in joining India. Pakistan relied on the principle of self-determination and favored a strong plebiscite authority.

In August 1952 Dr. Graham reported to the Security Council that both parties had pledged him full cooperation and had expressed their determination to settle the chief remaining obstacle in the way of a settlement: namely, the number and character of forces to be left on each side of a cease-fire line. Discussions on demilitarization were reopened in Geneva on February 4, 1953, but the conference failed to produce any agreement. A plebiscite remained well over the horizon. Yet the intervention of the Security Council had succeeded in bringing an end to the fighting, a not inconsiderable achievement when the strategic importance of the area and the emotional content of the problem are considered. This measure of success for the Council was possible in part because the Kashmir dispute did not involve its permanent members.

The Hyderabad Case

Although the Hyderabad case arose from circumstances similar to those underlying the Kashmir problem, there were some important differences. The ruler of this particular princely state was Moslem and his subjects overwhelmingly Hindu. Hyderabad, moreover, was surrounded by Indian territory and was considered to be the "heart of India" by the Nehru government. Pressure was soon brought to bear upon the Nizam of Hyderabad to join with India.

On August 21, 1948, Hyderabad, although not a Member of the United Nations, complained to the Security Council of Indian intimidation through economic blockade and threats of violence. Not until September, however, after Indian troops had overrun the area, did the Council consider the matter. Even then it did nothing although some members expressed regret at the use of force. Now Hyderabad sought to remove the case. Whether this action was voluntary or the result of pressure was not clear. As in the Iranian case, the Council remained master of its agenda. In October Pakistan sought without avail to quicken Council interest in the matter. Although Hyderabad had been swallowed and evidently digested, and although the Council had done nothing but add an item to its agenda, it remained seized of the matter for several years.

Had the Council ducked its responsibility? Perhaps measures of conciliation or mediation coupled with an admonition against the use of force would have served to strengthen the principles of the Charter. Yet there were many legal uncertainties that bore upon any political measures the Council might take. Was Hyderabad a state? Was the situation a matter of India's domestic jurisdiction? The Council ducked and perhaps wisely.[27] The situation was novel. It had pretty well outstripped the law books. It posed no real danger to international peace. The final result was a foregone conclusion from the very start and seemed sensible in many respects.

The Czechoslovakian Case

Czechoslovakia fell victim to the "cold war" in February 1948. That month, following the development of plans for Western European participation in the Marshall Plan, a Communist coup d'état in Czechoslovakia was successfully carried out. On March 12, Chile requested the Security Council to investigate the events described in a letter dated two days earlier to the Secretary-General from Mr. Papanek, the representative of the old Czech regime. Mr. Papanek argued that the situation should be brought to the Council's attention because the political independence of Czechoslovakia had been violated owing to the threat of force on the part of the Soviet Union. Meanwhile the Communist government was taking steps to

---

[27] For a vigorously asserted counterview see Clyde Eagleton, "The Case of Hyderabad Before the Security Council," *American Journal of International Law* (April 1950), p. 277.

replace Mr. Papanek. This letter was not placed on the Council's provisional agenda because the Secretary-General felt that Mr. Papanek no longer officially represented Czchoslovakia.

The Council discussed the problem in nine meetings despite the protests of the Soviet Union and the Ukraine that the Council could not concern itself with the internal affairs of a country. Chile and Czechoslovakia were invited to the Council table. The latter refused on the ground that the problem was a matter of domestic jurisdiction. Mr. Papanek was invited as an individual under the Council's Rules of Procedure. A futile discussion ensued. A majority proposal to appoint a subcommittee under Article 29 to gather evidence in the case was blocked when the Soviet Union applied the "double veto." So far as any concrete steps to save Czechoslovakia were concerned, it was futile to raise the matter in the first place. The interests of a permanent member were at stake. About all that could be said was that Mr. Papanek revealed a good deal of information regarding the means by which the Soviet Union controlled its near neighbors.

The Berlin Blockade

The problem of Berlin was brought to the Council on September 29, 1948, by France, the United Kingdom and the United States as a threat to the peace under Article 39. The Third Assembly was influential in the disposition of the case although never technically involved. The problem arose under the following circumstances. Pending final peace settlements the Potsdam Agreement of 1945 had provided a four-power rule by the three Western powers and the Soviet Union for all of Germany and for the city of Berlin itself, which was deep in the Soviet occupation zone.

In 1948 the Soviet Union severed nearly all communications to Berlin. The Western occupying authorities were cut off from their respective western zones. Faced with this threat of force, would they evacuate Berlin? The answer was provided by the allied "air lift" and the courage of Berlin's citizens in the western enclaves.

In the Security Council the Soviet delegate cited Article 107 of the Charter to show that the United Nations could have no jurisdiction in the problem since the relations of an enemy state were involved. A majority, however, voted to consider the matter. Ambassador Austin stepped down from the President's chair in favor of Bramuglia of Argentina since the United States was involved in the case. Six "neutral" members under the President's leadership made offers of conciliation. A resolution providing that the lifting of the blockade should coincide with the settlement of a related currency problem in Berlin drew a Soviet veto.

Meanwhile the Assembly had passed a resolution calling upon the great powers to settle their problems generally. Mr. Evatt, the Assembly's President, now joined the Secretary-General in writing a letter to the four occupying powers urging them to cooperate in Mr. Bramuglia's mediation efforts. A committee of experts, including the "neutrals" and Mr. Gunnar

Myrdal, the Secretary of the Economic Commission for Europe, was chosen to find means of establishing a single currency for Berlin.

Eventually the four powers reached an agreement outside the organization. Yet the United Nations continued to prove useful. Mr. Jessup of the United States and Mr. Malik of the Soviet Union, for example, met unobtrusively in the corridors at Lake Success to explore the possibility of a settlement that had been hinted earlier in the Soviet press. The course of debate and recrimination in the Assembly and Council, moreover, did much to convince both sides of the strength and weakness of their positions. The influence of the organization was difficult to measure in tangible terms. It had focused attention on a critical problem, however, and provided informal means for its disposal. On May 4, 1949, the Council was informed that an agreement had been reached that would end the blockade.

Human Rights in Bulgaria, Hungary, Rumania and the U.S.S.R.

In May 1948 the Chilean representative to the General Assembly complained that in preventing Soviet wives of other nationals from leaving their country, the U.S.S.R. was violating fundamental human rights. An Assembly resolution citing the Charter, the Declaration of Human Rights, and resolutions of the Economic and Social Council was carried. It was recommended that the Soviet Union withdraw regulations that contravened such rights. This action had no appreciable effect on the case in hand, which, the Soviet delegate insisted, was a domestic matter.

Since April 1949 the Assembly has been confronted with the problems of human rights arising from the trials of Catholic churchmen in Hungary and Protestant churchmen in Bulgaria. The following autumn Rumania was included in this category of states allegedly disregarding the obligations of the peace treaties which had bound them to assure to all persons "the enjoyment of human rights and of fundamental freedoms." The U.S.S.R. again insisted that the problem was one of domestic concern. The three states also challenged the Assembly's competence and refused to appear before it. A number of non-Communist delegations, including the Belgian, expressed doubts that the treaties empowered the United Nations to intervene in the affairs of the three countries. Since an interpretation of treaties was at issue, the Assembly asked the International Court for an advisory opinion. Were the three states, among other matters, obligated to appoint representatives to commissions to settle disputes arising from the implementation of the treaties? The court answered affirmatively. In 1950, the Assembly condemned the three states for their failure to do so.

Quite obviously the case was pressed as suitable for propaganda against the Soviet bloc. It illustrated incidentally that the organization did not rest on the broad consensus of ethical standards that must be the foundation of a real political community. The Assembly's actions had little success in restoring human rights in the areas concerned.

China, Formosa and Korea[28]

The problem of Korea was left on the doorstep of the General Assembly in September 1947, when the United States chose to widen the responsibility for uniting and rehabilitating that unhappy land. Two years later the Nationalist Government of China complained to the Assembly that its independence was being threatened because the Soviet Union was aiding the Chinese Communists. In 1950 Communist China complained to the Security Council that in sending naval forces to Formosa the United States had committed "armed aggression" against China. These issues were inextricably interwoven and may be considered as a single problem, that of Communist expansion in Asia and the steps taken in the United Nations to cope with it.

Background. This problem, however, must be considered in the light of events that antedate modern communism by a considerable span of time. Korea, for example, had been a cockpit of great-power rivalry long before the Bolshevik Revolution of 1917. Thus in 1895 China was eliminated by Japan as a rival for the control of Korea. Japan and Russia were now the principal competitors — not only for Korea but for Manchuria as well. After the defeat of Russia in 1904–05 Korea became a Japanese protectorate. Outright annexation followed in 1910. The defeat of Japan, in turn, in 1945 brought the United States and Russia face to face for the first time in the Far East. This event was highlighted by the arrangements hastily made in August 1945 for the surrender of Japanese troops. It was agreed that the Japanese north of the 38th parallel would surrender to Russian forces and those south of the parallel to the Americans. Intentionally or not, this agreement fixed the Soviet and American zones of occupation.

Meanwhile, wartime negotiations bore upon the events of 1947–51. At Cairo in December 1943 Chiang Kai-shek, Churchill and Roosevelt agreed that "in due course Korea shall become free and independent." This agreement was incorporated in the Potsdam Declaration of July 26, 1945, which the Soviet Union accepted in declaring war against Japan on August 8. No progress was made, however, by the Soviet and American occupation authorities in setting up a unified administration in Korea. Consequently the Council of Foreign Ministers tackled the problem at Moscow in December 1945. A joint commission was established consisting of representatives of the Soviet and American Commands to assist in the formation of a "provisional Korean democratic government." A four-power trusteeship (China, the United States, the United Kingdom and the U.S.S.R.) was planned to last for a period of up to five years.

These arrangements proved fruitless. Negotiations in the joint commission broke down on the matter of the Korean political groups to be con-

[28] Department of State, *Korea, 1945 to 1948*, Department of State Publication 3305 (Washington: Government Printing Office, 1948), and *United States Policy in the Korean Crisis*, Publication 3922 (1950); George M. McCune, *Korea Today* (Cambridge: Harvard University Press, 1950).

sulted in planning for the provisional government. Each side was striving to unite Korea under a regime friendly to it. Each side feared the loss of the strategic peninsula to the other. In American hands Korea was a threat to the Soviet maritime provinces. In Soviet hands it was a threat to the occupation troops in Japan. Yet Korea was too disorganized politically and economically to be left alone. The Soviets soon planted a ready-made puppet regime in North Korea. The Americans had less success in supporting right-wing groups in the south headed by Syngman Rhee.

The interaction of United States and United Nations policies was evident from this point on. The American forces were now in an unenviable position. Owing to headlong demobilization by the United States after the war, they were weak and dangerously exposed. The occupation burden was heavy economically and embarrassing politically.

In this dilemma the temptation to turn to the United Nations was strong indeed. If the onerous burden were shared with the international organization, cries that the United States had imperialist ambitions might die down. A United Nations Commission in Korea might forestall a Communist coup. Handing Korea over to the Assembly in 1947, moreover, was part of a larger pattern of resistance to Soviet strategy.

The Temporary Commission. In November 1947, by overwhelming vote of the General Assembly, a United Nations Temporary Commission was appointed to observe elections to be held throughout Korea. The "national independence" of Korea was to be established and "all occupying forces then withdrawn at the earliest practicable date." The Soviet Union and its satellites opposed this action. The Ukrainian Republic refused to serve on the temporary commission, which was denied access to North Korea. Beyond this rift, however, there was a significant difference of opinion among the remaining members of the temporary commission (Australia, Canada, China, El Salvador, France, India, Philippines and Syria). The Commonwealth members had doubts regarding the wisdom and legality of holding elections in the south when the Soviets would not cooperate in the north. Such a step, in their view, could do little to bring about Korean unity and independence. It might in fact stiffen Soviet resistance.

The fact that the United Nations was increasingly taking sides in a world struggle was emphasized when the temporary commission was empowered to consult with the Interim Committee, newly created and bitterly opposed by the U.S.S.R. Here a United States resolution was adopted that the Assembly's mandate should be carried out "in such parts of Korea as are accessible to the Commission." This was an important decision. In deciding to observe elections in Southern Korea which were held on May 10, 1948, and in recognizing the government that followed, the United Nations was heavily committed to an anti-Soviet position.

UNCOK. Although able to make spot checks only, the Temporary Commission reported the elections to be a valid expression of the free will of the Korean people. In August the government of the Republic of Korea was established in the southern zone. A 4 to 2 majority of the Commission felt this government had met the standards set by the Assembly, and on December 12, 1948, the Third Assembly declared this to be the only lawful government in South Korea. The General Assembly then appointed a new United Nations Commission on Korea (UNCOK) to report on the transition from occupation to independence and to use its good offices to unite Korea. The second task was manifestly impossible. Meanwhile a "Democratic Peoples' Republic" was established in North Korea. Later UNCOK noted, "the relations between the U.S.S.R. and the United States continue to be the . . . perhaps decisive factor contributing to the growing hardening of relations between north and south." [29]

Matters now went from bad to worse. Moscow stole a march and announced the withdrawal of Soviet occupation forces several months before the evacuation of United States forces was reported to the Commission. Neither Korean government was disposed to negotiate with the other on the matter of unification. The Rhee government adopted an intransigent attitude toward the Commission. Suggestions for internal reform were not welcome. Nor were efforts to initiate discussions with the North Koreans. Tension along the 38th parallel steadily increased. Both sides conducted armed forays into the territory of the other. The Commission warned the Assembly that large-scale military conflict was not improbable and that there was "much military posturing on both sides of the parallel."

It became increasingly evident that if the United Nations was to support the Republic of Korea against armed attack, the backing of the United States would be required. Would this be forthcoming? The Secretary of State announced that the "defense perimeter" of the United States included the Aleutians, Japan, the Ryukyus and the Philippine Islands. Other areas in Asia could not be guaranteed against military attack. "Initial reliance must be on the people attacked to resist it and then upon the commitments of the entire civilized world under the Charter of the United Nations, which so far has not proved a weak reed to lean on by any people who are determined to protect their independence against outside aggression." [30] The United States did, however, conclude a military assistance agreement with Korea in January 1950. The following spring high American civilian and military officials visited Korea. John Foster Dulles, for the Department of State, assured the Korean National Assembly: "You are not alone. You will never be alone so long as you continue to play worthily your part in the great design of human freedom."

Aggression and Sanction. The storm broke on June 25, 1950. North Koreans, well equipped with foreign arms, attacked across the parallel in full force. The reports of the United Nations Commission stated that "the invasion . . . was an act of aggression initiated without warning and with-

[29] *Report of the United Nations Commission on Korea, August 1949,* UN Doc. A/936, Vol. 1, p. 32 ff.

[30] Speech before the National Press Club, Washington, D.C., January 12, 1950.

out provocation in execution of a carefully prepared plan." [31] Without such a report there might not have been such general support in the United Nations for the measures that followed.

In Washington officials of the State and Defense Departments had been roused late at night by reports from the Embassy in Seoul and from Lake Success. The President, after conferring with his principal military and diplomatic advisers, decided that a stand must be taken — under the aegis of the United Nations if possible. Within a few hours after the attack the Security Council was called into session at the request of the United States.

Because the U.S.S.R. continued a boycott of the Council that began in January 1950 as a protest against the continued representation of China in the United Nations by the Nationalist government, the Council was for a time free of the Soviet veto. This fortuity plus vigorous United States leadership gave rise to three grave decisions.

On June 25 the Council found that the armed attack from North Korea was a breach of the peace in the sense of Article 39 under Chapter VII. A cease-fire and the immediate withdrawal of North Korean forces were called for. Members of the United Nations were asked to help in the "execution of this resolution and to refrain from giving assistance to the North Korean authorities." When the Commission reported that the cease-fire had been flouted, the Council on June 27, *recommended* that the United Nations Members furnish such assistance as was necessary to repel the attack and restore peace in the area. Since the agreements for the provision of armed forces and facilities under Article 43 between the Members and the Security Council had never been made, it was not possible for the Council to make a binding decision. Finally, on July 7, the Council recommended further that all military forces and assistance be placed under a "unified command," that the United Nations flag be used, and that the United States name the Supreme Commander. On July 8, President Truman appointed General Douglas MacArthur to this post.

In all these measures the Council followed the lead of the United States. The resolutions adopted were principally American. This was to be expected. Unless the United States bore the main load, effective sanctions could not have been applied. Other forces were simply not available. British and French troops were already engaged heavily in Malaya and Indo-China respectively. Meager forces in Western Europe could not safely be pulled away. A few hours before the Council's resolution on June 27, the President announced that, since the invaders had not heeded the cease-fire order, he had "ordered United States air and sea forces to give the Korean government troops cover and support."

This action, in view of the Council's subsequent recommendations, gave rise to criticism only by the Soviet bloc. Other steps taken by the United States at the same time, however, did not receive such unequivocal support in the anti-Communist coalition and were simply announced to the Council. These included the dispatching of the Seventh Fleet to prevent any attack

[31] Excerpt in *The New York Times* of September 15, 1950.

on the last remaining Nationalist Chinese stronghold of Formosa, and the acceleration of military assistance to the forces of France and the Associated States in Indochina and to the Philippine government. Some members thought that the unilateral action in Formosa might aggravate resentment that already existed in Communist China.

The three votes in the Council were generally strong. That of June 25 was 9 to 0 with the U.S.S.R. absent and only Communist Yugoslavia abstaining. The latter, however, never condoned the North Korean attack as did the U.S.S.R. on its return to the Council. On the recommendations to apply sanctions, however, more significant rifts emerged. The vote on June 27 was 7 to 1. Yugoslavia, preferring mediation, opposed sanctions. India and Egypt abstained, although the former later changed to vote favorably when instructions arrived from New Delhi. Egypt, smarting under United Nations intervention in Palestine, remained opposed to military sanctions. All three abstained on July 7. These votes indicated that India and the Arab world were reluctant to choose between the principal rival blocs in the United Nations.

Meanwhile, the Soviet delegate was scheduled to be the Council's President in August. Mr. Malik assumed the presidency on schedule and succeeded in preventing any further positive action by the Council during the entire month of August while hard-pressed American and South Korean troops fell back before the North Korean onslaught. The Security Council now became the focus of world attention while the Soviet delegate denounced the United Nations action as "imperialist aggression" by the "American bloc" against "the peace-loving peoples of Asia." The Council's actions, he insisted, were illegal for many reasons. The Soviet Union had not participated in the voting. The Nationalist government of China was unlawfully seated at the Council table. The South Koreans had attacked first. The fighting was a "civil war" and of no concern to the Council. He was answered vigorously by such figures as Sir Gladwyn Jebb, Ambassador Austin and others. All appealed to world opinion. Particularly to Americans, watching the propaganda struggle on television, the United Nations suddenly seemed important.

Since the Korean affair was fundamentally a struggle between two of the principal and permanent members of the Security Council, sanctions could not be applied according to the letter of the Charter. The principle of unanimity was abandoned and improvisation was necessary in many respects.

First, military measures were taken without the unanimous support of the Council's permanent members. The great majority of the Members, in responding to the call for military assistance, were prepared to risk steps that amounted to at least indirect coercion of the U.S.S.R.

Secondly, this grave development followed a *recommendation* under Article 39 rather than a *decision* under Articles 42–47 because there were no forces that could be ordered into action under the "strategic direction of the Military Staff Committee." Disagreement among the permanent members had prevented the implementation of Articles 43–47 of the Charter.[32]

Third, the forces made available were placed under the unified command of the United States. With the Military Staff Committee obviously eliminated owing to the membership of the U.S.S.R. and with the United States supplying the great bulk of the forces, this was the most feasible choice.

Finally and most significant, this was the first time, if the action of the great powers in the Concert of Europe is excepted, that military sanctions were initiated by an international organization.

In sum, sanctions were voluntary rather than mandatory. Yet the experiment was fairly heartening. About forty-five nations responded to the call. Of these, sixteen actually provided armed forces while the others contributed important supplies, including food, ambulances and the like. Not all offers were accepted. Thirty-three thousand Nationalist troops remained on Formosa on decision of the Unified Command, ostensibly owing to the threat of Communist attack on the island, but doubtless also owing to the political repercussions throughout the world that would have followed. Twenty governments, principally the Soviet satellites and the Arab bloc, did not offer assistance. Four small Latin American republics were included in that number. Yugoslavia declared her forces were needed at home to resist Cominform activities.

These improvisations gave rise to many problems. The lines of command between Lake Success and the Unified Command were tenuous at best. The conduct of the war was left pretty much in the hands of the Supreme Commander, as is normal in the case of most any theater command. But military operations could never be separated from political problems of the utmost delicacy that constantly threatened the unity of the United Nations coalition. There were varying views, for example, on such matters as the future of Formosa, the recognition of Communist China, the bombing of airfields and staging areas in Manchuria, and the wisdom of crossing the 38th parallel. Matters were scarcely improved when the Supreme Commander gave evidence of acting independently of the authorities in his own country. Representatives of the sixteen nations fighting in the field met regularly at the State Department to be kept informed and to express their views. The arrangement, however, had no formal standing in the chain of command that led from Lake Success to Washington to Korea.

Although feats of valor were performed by military units of many nations — Turkey, Britain, France, the Philippines and the South Koreans themselves — to single out only a few, the United States carried by far the greatest burden of the action. At one time the United States was reported to have 250,000 men in the field while, aside from the South Koreans, the troops from other nations totalled only 26,000. For a long and anxious period a dangerous proportion of American military strength was tied up in Korea, while Europe and other areas were exposed.

Not until September, after a long and bitter retreat, were the United Nations forces able to assume the offensive. A daring landing behind the

[32] See Chap. 16.

U.N. FORCES

AGGRESSION DOESN'T PAY

POINTS NORTH

FERMAN MARTIN

Martin in The Houston Chronicle

"LEARNING HIS LESSONS ON THE RUN"

lines at Inchon in the middle of September turned the tide. Soon the North Koreans were in full flight. Grave decisions now had to be made. At the end of September the foreign minister of Communist China sounded an ominous warning. China would not stand idly by while its neighbors were being invaded by "imperialists" and its own security threatened.

The Resolution of October 7, 1950. Since no further decisions could be reached in the Security Council that did not have Soviet approval, it was necessary to turn to the General Assembly under the terms of the new Uniting for Peace Resolution. Should the United Nations forces be halted at the 38th parallel or should all of Korea be united now that the enemy was on the run? Would the crossing of the parallel provoke attacks by China or the Soviet Union or both? On October 7, 1950, encouraged by military reports from the field, the Assembly had already reaffirmed its previous stand for a "unified, independent, democratic Korea" and recommended that steps be taken to "insure conditions of stability throughout Korea." United Nations forces were to remain only long enough to achieve these objectives, and by a vote of 47 to 5 with 7 abstentions a new United Nations Commission for Unification and Rehabilitation of Korea (UNCURK) was established to assist in carrying out the terms of the resolution. At least tacit approval had been given to the crossing of the 38th parallel.

So far as the United States was concerned, this step seemed to mark a change in policy. Speaking in favor of the resolution, Ambassador Austin declared the parallel to be an "imaginary line" behind which the aggressor might seek refuge for later attacks. Earlier on June 29, however, the Secretary of State had announced that the American support given under the resolutions of June 25 and 27 was "solely for the purpose of restoring the Republic of Korea to its status prior to the invasion from the north and of reëstablishing the peace broken by that aggression." On the basis of reports from her Ambassador in Peking, India now warned of grave consequences if the parallel were crossed. Trying to steer a middle course between East and West, India also sought to have Communist China represented in the United Nations. This step was attempted at the opening session of the Fifth Assembly on September 19, 1950, but failed to receive sufficient votes.

The New War. To understand the events that followed, however, it is necessary to shift our attention back to the Security Council. The Communist People's Republic in China had smarted under President Truman's announcement on June 27 that the Seventh Fleet would "prevent any attack on Formosa." The Chinese cited both the Cairo and the Potsdam Declarations to show that the big powers were committed to the restoration of Formosa "to the Republic of China." Only the United States stood in the way of the final defeat of the Nationalist Government safely ensconced on Formosa. On August 25, Communist China complained to the Security Council that the United States by sending naval forces to Formosa had committed "armed aggression" against China. In addition, American planes attached to the Unified Command were accused of bombing Chinese territory and violating air space over China. Not until November 5, 1950, when the Unified Command reported "meeting a new foe . . . Chinese Communist military units," did the Security Council decide to hear a representative of the People's Republic.

On November 24, the Communist Chinese delegation arrived at the Council table to join the Soviet Union in demanding that the Peoples' Republic replace the Nationalist government as the representative of China, that the United States be condemned as an aggressor for its action on Formosa and its alleged bombing of the Chinese mainland, and that all foreign troops be withdrawn from Korea. Any Chinese troops facing the unified command, they asserted, were "volunteers."

On the same day, despite doubts and warnings previously expressed at Lake Success, General MacArthur ordered a general offensive. This was announced by the Supreme Commander to be the "final assault" of the war which might be over by Christmas. Four days later his forces were reeling before a massive Chinese counteroffensive. On November 28, the Supreme Commander announced to the Security Council that the United Nations was faced with "an entirely new war." Soon his forces were badly split.

Equally ominous, the unity of the United Nations coalition was threatened by the sudden turn of events. In the United States clamor arose to bomb the Communist "sanctuary" in Manchuria. The use of atomic weapons was hinted at in a Presidential press conference. The Europeans, dangerously exposed if a general war should break out, counseled moderation. The British Prime Minister hurried to Washington lest the United States move too fast too soon. Nine members of the Security Council, with India abstaining, voted to call upon the Chinese Communists to withdraw from Korea at once. When the U.S.S.R. vetoed this step, events shifted to the Assembly.

Now the United States pressed for the use of the Assembly's new enforcement machinery. In January 1951 both the House and Senate resolved that the "United Nations should immediately act and declare the Chinese Communist authorities an aggressor in Korea." Other powers, however, including Britain and France, urged restraint. In their view no action should be taken that might lessen the United Nations' chance of mediating in Korea. On December 14, the Assembly, on the suggestion of thirteen Asian and Arab countries led by India, appointed a cease-fire group consisting of India, Canada and Iran. This effort availed nothing. In January the cease-fire group reported that the Communists refused to hold discussions with it. The withdrawal of American aid from Formosa, of foreign troops from Korea and representation for Communist China in the United Nations had to precede any cease-fire, in the Communist view. On February 2, 1951, the Assembly, by a vote of 44 to 7 with 9 abstentions, adopted a United States proposal that Communist China had "engaged in aggression in Korea." The negative votes were cast by the five members of the Soviet bloc and Burma and India. Afghanistan, Egypt, Indonesia, Pakistan, Saudi Arabia, Sweden, Syria, Yemen and Yugoslavia abstained.

Noting that the Security Council could not fulfill its responsibilities, the Assembly's resolution also provided for an Additional Measures Committee and a "good offices" committee composed of the Assembly's President and two persons designated by him. The former was to propose additional means of meeting the aggression in Korea if mediation by the latter failed.

In the meantime, events in the field required new political and military directives. By March, the Chinese forces were being driven back into North Korea. Once more many Members urged restraint and further diplomatic efforts to settle the Korean affairs before any major advance above the 38th parallel. Although apprised of this view, General MacArthur chose another line. He announced publicly that since the Communists could not conquer Korea by force, they must be "painfully aware" that they would be badly beaten if the United Nations carried its military operations to the Chinese mainland itself. The President of the United States then dismissed the General from all his Pacific Commands on two counts. He had disregarded instructions regarding public announcements from the field. He was clearly not in sympathy with the policy of his government. To follow the General's proposals to bomb Manchurian bases, the President declared, would be to risk "starting a general war."[33]

[33] For the facts and controversy on MacArthur's dismissal, see *Military Situation in the Far East,* Hearings before the Committee on Armed Services and the Committee on Foreign Relations, U.S. Senate, 82nd Congress, 2nd Session, May and June, 1951.

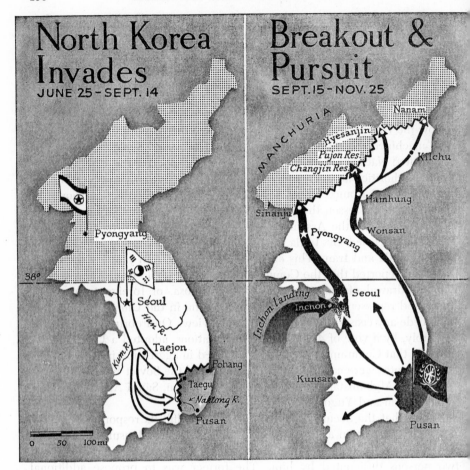

KOREA — 1950

The Communists now launched fresh attacks against United Nations forces under General Matthew B. Ridgway, MacArthur's successor. These failed utterly. Meanwhile the Additional Measures Committee had been hard at work. On May 18, the Assembly accepted its proposal that all the Members of the United Nations apply an embargo on the shipment of war materials to Communist China. At the same time the Good Offices Committee was requested to keep trying. This was the Assembly's first recommendation of economic sanctions on any scale. Prospects for a settlement, however, developed in a different way. On June 23, 1951, Jacob Malik of the Soviet Union declared in a radio broadcast that his people desired peace and that as a first step there should be "discussions . . . between the belligerents for a cease-fire and an armistice providing for the mutual withdrawal of forces from the 38th parallel." The United States, after conferring with

Red China Strikes
NOV. 26 - JAN. 15

MANCHURIA

Changjin trap

Hungnam

★Pyongyang   Wonsan

Seoul ★   Wonju   ● Samchok

Pusan

Seesaw & Stalemate
JAN. 16 - JUNE 25

★ Pyongyang

38°

Seoul ★

TIME Maps by R.M.C.

Time, Inc., 1951

KOREA — 1951

s sixteen fighting allies, instructed General Ridgway to begin cease-fire
scussions with the Communist leaders. The United Nations negotiators
Americans and South Koreans) insisted that an armistice line must con-
rm generally to the existing fighting fronts. On this issue the talks broke
own only to be renewed again in October in the tent city of Panmunjom.
 Finally, it was agreed that prisoner-of-war lists would be exchanged and
reliminary agreements were reached on procedures for a projected armis-
ce to be declared on December 27, 1951. Major disagreements arose,
owever, concerning (1) the manner and timing of the prisoner exchange,
d (2) the terms for armistice enforcement.
 In February the Communists demanded that a political conference be
ld within three months after an armistice to deal with such problems as
ithdrawal of all foreign forces from Korea, peaceful settlement of Korean

questions, and "other questions relating to peace in Korea." The United Nations negotiators accepted the proposals but substituted "et cetera" for the last phrase, an attempt to separate the Korean issue from other issues, like a seat for Red China in the United Nations. They rejected a Communist demand that the Soviet Union be named as a "neutral" armistice inspector. The major disagreements, however, boiled down to the issue of "automatic versus free choice" repatriation of prisoners of war. The Communists refused to accept the United Nations proposal that no prisoner be forced to return against his will.

A turning point was reached in November 1952 when India proposed to the General Assembly a resolution designed to end the conflict. The plan included provisions that no force should be used in repatriating prisoners and that Poland, Czechoslovakia, Switzerland, and Sweden be named as a Commission to administer repatriation. On December 3 this resolution was adopted over the dissenting votes of the Soviet bloc. Although the Communist negotiators at Panmunjom rejected the United Nations proposal, it was a significant event. The fact that it had been presented by India, the leading Asian nation in the United Nations, had an important impact because it showed that the Korean action was truly the concern of the international organization and not just that of the United States. In supporting the Indian resolution the United States rejected the notion of unilateral action which would have threatened the United Nations coalition.

In early 1953 it was suggested by Senator William Knowland that, since there was little prospect for an armistice, the United States blockade Red China and prosecute the war more vigorously, with or without the support of the United Nations allies. Acrimoniously he pointed out that Britain was continuing to trade with China, though the trade was in nonstrategic materials. Secretary of State Dulles and Foreign Secretary Eden met, and an American statement was issued assuring Britain and the United Nations that the United States had no intention of going back on its previous decision to seek a United Nations settlement in Korea.

Beginning in March the peace talks became more productive. The Communists offered to exchange sick and wounded prisoners immediately, and, on April 20, this limited exchange began. On May 25 the United States made a "final" peace offer based on the Indian-sponsored resolution. This was supported by the United Nations allies except South Korea. President Rhee opposed the United Nations compromise which left Korea divided and too many political questions undefined.

On June 8 the United Nations and Communist commands signed an agreement providing for a Neutral Nations Repatriation Commission, composed of Sweden, Switzerland, Poland, Czechoslovakia, with India added as a fifth member. This Commission was to decide repatriation questions on the basis that no prisoner would be returned against his will.

With a truce seemingly ready to sign, the dissatisfied President of South Korea precipitated a crisis by ordering his troops to release 25,000 anti-Red prisoners of war. President Eisenhower and Secretary Dulles repudiated

Rhee's actions and sent a special mission to Seoul. After protracted consultation, Rhee was persuaded not to undermine an armistice. However, the Korean President stated that his acceptance was conditioned on a peace conference being held within ninety days, and further stated that he would walk out if Korean unification were blocked. While these events were taking place, the Communists' biggest offensive in two years was thrown back.

Peace talks were resumed and on July 27, 1953, General William Harrison for the United Nations Command and General Nam Il for the Communists signed an armistice agreement. It was then countersigned by General Mark Clark, who had succeeded Ridgway, and by General Peng Teh-huai and Marshal Kim Il Sung. The agreement recommended that a general peace conference be held within three months and provided for the nonforcible repatriation of prisoners of war under the direction of the neutral nations commission.[34] The rehabilitation efforts of the UN Korean Reconstruction Agency, created by the General Assembly in December 1950, are discussed in Chapter 18.

In anticipation of the recommended political conference, President Pearson called a meeting of the General Assembly for August 17, 1953. It was evident that, although the fighting had been stopped, important political decisions — including the fate of Formosa and a United Nations seat for Communist China — would have to be made before the Korean episode would be concluded. Nonetheless, the United Nations had undertaken an unprecedented action to stop aggression through voluntary military sanctions, had arranged the freeing of prisoners preparatory to a final settlement and had initiated a reconstruction program. This experience revealed, however, how difficult it still was, within the loose UN framework, to mobilize effective collective sanctions, to consummate an effective settlement and to provide adequate rehabilitation.

The United Kingdom's Complaint Against Iran

In 1951 the Iranian drama was reopened, though the powers were cast in roles different from those they had played four years earlier.

On March 7, 1951, the pro-Western premier of Iran, General Razmara, was assassinated by members of a group which sought the liberation of Iran from British influence and nationalization of the oil industry. In April the Shah called the nationalist leader, Mohammed Mossadegh, to form a government. On May 1 the Majlis (Parliament) passed an Oil Nationalization Act, terminating the concessions which had been awarded the Anglo-Iranian Oil Company in 1933 and expropriating the world's largest oil refining plant at Abadan.

A British diplomatic mission to Iran failed to meet with success. President Truman sent a personal representative, W. Averell Harriman, to Teheran and London in an attempt at mediation. He too was ultimately unsuccessful. Despite Mossadegh's insistence that the matter was exclu-

---

[34] See *The New York Times*, July 27, 1953 for complete text of armistice and supplementary agreements.

sively within Iran's domestic jurisdiction, the United Kingdom instituted proceedings in the International Court of Justice. The Court ordered provisional measures to maintain the *status quo* while it considered the question of its competence to decide the issue. Iran immediately withdrew its acceptance of the compulsory jurisdiction of the Court, but the tribunal continued the case.

Boiling with nationalist fervor, Iran forced the evacuation of English personnel from Abadan. British forces in the Middle East were strengthened. The Lion, however, did little but growl. Then, on September 28, the United Kingdom representative requested the Security Council to place the Anglo-Iranian question on its agenda. The British said that they accepted the principle of nationalization, but that Iran's rejection of the International Court's provisional orders and the expulsion of the Oil Company's personnel from Abadan had created a threat to peace and security.

On October 15 Mossadegh, at the Council's invitation, flew to Lake Success to defend his country's action. Playing the great powers against each other, he challenged the competence of the Council and said the only issue was that of compensation to the Oil Company. Two days later the Council adjourned to await the Court's determination. On July 22, that body, in a 9 to 5 decision, found that it had no jurisdiction in the case. The Court held that the agreement signed between the Iranian government and the Oil Company in 1933 was merely a concessionary contract between a government and a foreign corporation and did not regulate relations between the governments of Iran and the United Kingdom.[35]

Iran now had control of its natural riches but lacked the technicians to exploit them. Both Britain and the United States refused to aid her. The flow of oil from Abadan stopped; Iran was on the verge of bankruptcy. Events in 1953 were ominous, as Mossadegh sought to stifle the Shah and the Majlis. As virtual dictator of Iran he played a dangerous game of courting Communist support. Before the year was out, however, the Shah had regained control, and Mossadegh was awaiting trial for treason. There was hope of improved relations between Iran and the West.

Colombian-Peruvian Asylum Cases, 1950–1951

This case was brought before the Court in October 1949 by Colombia, which sought a judgment in its dispute with Peru regarding the interpretation of treaties between the two countries dealing with asylum. The dispute arose when the Colombian Ambassador at Lima, Peru, granted asylum to Victor Raul Haya de la Torre, head of the Peruvian "American People's Revolutionary Alliance," who had failed to effect a revolutionary coup. Colombia sought safe-conduct for him out of Peru. The Peruvian government refused, and the two governments disputed the obligations regarding safe-conduct in the treaties in question. Actually the Court assumed jurisdiction on application of *both* parties because they were unable to draw up a special agreement submitting the case to court. The Court decided in

35 ICJ *Reports*, 1952, p. 115.

favor of Peru stating that asylum had not been granted in accordance with
the treaties and that there was no obligation on Peru to grant safe-conduct
to Haya de la Torre.[36] Colombia immediately asked for an interpretation
of the judgment, a request the Court ruled inadmissible.

When Peru next asked that the revolutionary leader be delivered up,
Colombia asked the Court whether it was bound to comply. Voting 13 to
1 the Court held that Colombia was not bound to deliver Haya de la Torre
to the Peruvian authorities since the treaties did not specify how political
asylum was to be terminated. The Court did its best to please both parties
and suggested that a solution would follow the "good neighborliness" that
characterized relations between the Latin American republics.[37]

The Anglo-Norwegian Fisheries Case, 1949–1951

Once again the unsuspecting cod figured prominently in a case before
an international tribunal. Some of the best fishing grounds lie along Norway's craggy coast and in her breath-taking fjords. Norway sought for
many years to protect her fishery industry by insisting that her territorial
waters extended seaward four miles from a base line along the shore. The
United Kingdom protested against the manner in which the base line was
drawn. In September 1949 the United Kingdom, after a number of British
trawlers were seized and condemned, filed an application with the Court
claiming that Norwegian regulations violated international law. Both parties had filed declarations accepting the Court's compulsory jurisdiction.
The Court held in two votes of 10 to 2 and 8 to 4 that the Norwegian regulations were not contrary to international law. Norway's sharply indented
coast presents special difficulties in establishing a law of territorial waters.[38]

Rights of Nationals of the United States in Morocco, 1950–1952

This case marked a historic occasion as it was not only the first time the
United States was a party before the Court but also the first occasion in
which the United States was involved in compulsory jurisdiction. In October 1950 France instituted proceedings against the United States on the
question of the rights of Americans in Morocco under a number of treaties,
some of which dated from the nineteenth century. Under these treaties
American businessmen claimed special treatment in matters of trade, consular jurisdiction, foreign exchange and taxation. When diplomacy failed,
France invoked the compulsory jurisdiction of the Court. In a series of
decisions in August 1952 the Court managed to find for the United States in
some aspects of the case and for France in others.

Complaints Against France in North Africa

The rise of nationalist movements throughout Africa and the Near and

[36] ICJ *Reports,* 1950, p. 266.
[37] ICJ *Reports,* 1951, pp. 71–84.
[38] ICJ *Reports,* 1951, p. 116.

Far East is one of the most important phenomena of the postwar period. Many of the problems arising from these events have come before the United Nations. Two of them involved France and her North African dependencies, Morocco and Tunisia.

In 1951 there was a series of clashes between Moroccan nationalists and French troops. These incidents led Egypt and the other Arab states to request the General Assembly on October 4 to place on its agenda the question: "Violation of the Principles of the Charter and of the Declaration of Human Rights by France in Morocco."

The problem was discussed by the Assembly's General Committee which considers the agenda. Egypt charged that the French had refused to respect the promises made to the people of Morocco when France assumed a protectorate over that country in 1912. France had then agreed that the Sultan should be independent and the integrity of his dominions respected. The French argued that the General Assembly had no jurisdiction to interfere in a matter regulated by a treaty between France and Morocco. They further stated that reforms were being carried out in Morocco and that United Nations intervention would tend to disrupt progress.

Canada proposed a resolution recommending that consideration of the question of placing the item on the agenda "be postponed for the time being." This proposal was accepted by the Committee by a vote of 6 to 4 with 4 abstentions. The United States and United Kingdom supported postponement; the U.S.S.R. opposed it.

When the General Assembly plenary session considered the Committee's recommendation, the Arab delegates pressed for rejection of the Committee report and for open debate on the Moroccan issue. France's Foreign Minister, M. Schuman, warned that such debate would jeopardize discussions on reforms which were in progress. The Soviet delegate stated that the colonial powers desired to suppress discussion. The United States delegate, Mr. Ernest Gross, felt that discussion should be postponed so that French-Moroccan talks could proceed under favorable conditions. On December 13, the Committee's recommendation to postpone consideration was adopted by a vote of 28 to 23 with 7 abstentions.

Less than two months after the General Assembly had deferred discussion on Morocco, fifteen Arab and Asian countries turned to the Security Council and requested it to consider the problem of Tunisia. They expressed "their deep concern over the alarming news of military intervention and the arrest [by the French authorities] of popular leaders, which actions, in their opinion, constitute a threat to international peace and security."

On April 2, 1952, the Council discussed the procedural issue of placing the item on its agenda. The complaining governments maintained that France had deprived the Bey of Tunis of his sovereign rights and had suppressed the Tunisians in their attempt to gain self-government. France maintained that a dispute no longer existed as the Bey and the French government were negotiating. It was the view of the Chilean representative that a flat rejection of the complainants' request would be "a serious denial of justice."

A draft resolution to include the question on the agenda and one to invite the complaining governments to the Council table were rejected. Chile proposed a compromise resolution to place the item on the agenda with the understanding that such action would not imply any decision regarding the Council's competence to consider the matter and then defer consideration. This compromise, as with the two prior proposals, was rejected. In all three instances the voting showed five (including the Soviet Union) in favor of placing the item on the agenda, two opposed (France and the United Kingdom), and four abstentions (including the United States). Lacking the seven affirmative votes necessary to place an item on the agenda, the matter was, as in the Moroccan case, deferred.

At the opening session of the General Assembly in the fall of 1952, the questions of Morocco and Tunisia were again discussed by the Political and Security Committee of the General Assembly. Despite renewed Arab-Asian demands for strong United Nations action, the Assembly adopted a Latin American resolution which called on the parties to negotiate in accordance with the spirit of the Charter.

These events were significant in many respects. They pointed up the conflicts between colonial powers and native nationalists, between white and colored peoples, and between East and West. They offered the Soviet Union one of its best chances to fish in troubled waters and stir up old resentments. They presented the United States with the dilemma of supporting her western allies, whose aid was necessary for European defense plans, or supporting the awakening peoples of the Near and Far East, whose friendship was necessary for the containment of communism and the maintenance of international harmony.

Conclusions

The Korean affair was of crucial importance in the development of the United Nations. First, it marked the abandonment, for a time at least, of big-power cooperation as the foundation of international order. In meeting Communist aggression in Korea in June 1950, the young organization not only imposed military sanctions for the first time in the history of international organization; it also did so in the face of violent opposition on the part of two major powers, one a permanent member of the Security Council and the other so intended by the Charter's framers. For all practical purposes sanctions were applied against the Soviet Union and China. The organization, therefore, was playing a role very different from that originally intended. Despite the hesitation of India and much of the Moslem world, it had become a rallying ground against the "new imperialism" directed from Moscow. Yet the Korean war remained "limited" by choice of both Communist and non-Communist powers.

Secondly, a major overhauling of the United Nations resulted from the steps taken to meet aggression in Korea. In November 1950 the Assembly assumed a new importance. It was given new machinery and new responsibilities to help it stand in for the veto-ridden Security Council. This development marked no change of direction; it did mark a great speed up in the evolution of the United Nations. Since the Soviet Union could not be counted upon to repeat its absence from the Council of June and July 1950, the Assembly must be retooled so as to be able to cope with aggression. Nothing could be done, of course, to alter its basic authority without an amendment of the Charter. It could not, for example, make binding decisions. But ways were devised to augment its powers of recommendation and persuasion.

Third, in all these developments the influence of the United States was the most important single factor. Yet United States policy itself was modified by the alignment of forces in the Assembly and the Security Council.

Finally, the problems of China and Korea revealed basic differences in attitude regarding the United Nations' role in relation to Communist aggression in Asia. The Assembly's February 1st resolution showed that, in addition to the opposition of the Soviet bloc, the Arab-Asian nations were reluctant to join with the American, European and Commonwealth powers. Indeed, India and Burma actively opposed the United States-sponsored resolution. In calling the People's Republic an aggressor, the Assembly, according to these states, had heightened the conflict by closing the door to any future negotiations a United Nations body might sponsor. In the background lurked distrust of the white man's imperialism. To the great majority of Members, however, the Chinese action was aggression, and the General Assembly was entitled to call it that. It remained the policy of the Assembly that Korea should be united, free and independent.

Prior to Korea it can be said that, while the United Nations had not ushered in the millennium, it had achieved a considerable degree of success in resolving international differences. The new organization had shown an astonishing amount of flexibility in a period of dangerous international tension. Unlike the League in the 1930's it had not been abandoned. This was because all its Members, for one reason or another, felt it was important. In a world of atomic weapons and "super-power" conflict, there seemed to be no safety for the smaller states save in backing a universal organization that might ameliorate the disputes of the mighty and deter aggression. Regional pacts, though a necessary adjunct to a universal collective security organization, were too reminiscent of alliances that had ended in war. Hence, the smaller powers supported the United Nations.

The larger powers, curiously enough, did also. The United States backed the United Nations from the very start as an earnest of its intention to play a cooperative role in world affairs. Even when cooperation gave way to "cold war," the organization continued to be important. It proved to be a useful instrument of "total diplomacy" in a world perpetually threatened by "total war." Some tasks that could not be undertaken by the United States alone might be managed by the United Nations if the United States provided the impetus. The Palestine, Indonesian and Greek problems were cases in point. The organization could intervene where a single powerful state could not. The organization proved, in some measure, to be a rallying ground against communist expansion. Yet at the same time it provided ever-ready means for reaching an agreement when an agreement was desired by the powers concerned.

Paradoxically, the Soviet Union also backed the "political" organs of the United Nations and for much the same reasons. It provided an ever-ready propaganda forum. It was useful even when condemned as a tool of Anglo-American imperialism. Such charges fell on responsive ears in Asia and the Near East. Continued participation in the United Nations was part of the Soviet "peace offensive." Neither the U.S.S.R. nor the United States, in short, could afford not to participate.

For Britain and France the organization was a means of supplementing their declining power. Britain was quick to seek redress of grievances in situations concerning the Corfu Channel, Egypt and Iran. For the Palestine problem, the organization was a way out. France, it is true, was less active in United Nations affairs. Her policy focused more intensively on European regional developments. Yet her permanent membership in the Security Council was one of a diminishing number of reminders of her great-power status.

As disputes increasingly came to involve conflicts between the major powers, the Assembly assumed tasks that, according to the Charter, should have been the lot of the Security Council. It became obvious almost at once that the latter was useful in settling disputes directly in proportion to the extent its permanent members were not involved. The Spanish and Greek cases were the first to suggest the possibilities of an appeal to the Assembly when the Council was unable to act. The Indonesian and Kashmir cases, however, suggested that there was still an important role for the Council to play when the big powers were not directly involved in a matter. In the Palestine case the action of the two bodies was mutually sustaining. It should be noted that the majority of political disputes handled in the Assembly were referred directly to it. The Soviet Union, moreover, has been nearly as active as the Western powers in utilizing the Assembly as a political body. While the United States and the United Kingdom referred such problems as Korea, Greece and Palestine to the Assembly, the U.S.S.R. pressed the Assembly for measures regarding Spain, the complaint of United States aggression against China and the disposal of the Italian colonies.

Did this shift in balance from Council to Assembly actually help to maintain peace and security? It is too soon to answer definitively. The question, however, can be answered tentatively in the affirmative. Even the United States and the Soviet Union were restrained by the balance of forces that emerged from discussion in the "town meeting" of the world. The increasingly influential role of the Assembly, however, presents problems. It should be remembered in this connection that the Security Council veto protects the small as well as the great. It protects the small power against being morally committed to collective action when the big powers are not in agreement. The new role of the Assembly is no cure-all. It would be foolish, for example, for the Assembly to undertake collective measures when a two-thirds majority did not command sufficient power to cope with the aggression. Yet the experience of nine years suggests that lack of big-power unity does not necessarily render collective action ineffective. The test is whether sufficient power can be mobilized against aggression. The Assembly, moreover, because it is the forum for all states and shades of opinion, may be rather more effective in tempering power with justice.

Suggestions for Further Reading

Books

Byrnes, James F., *Speaking Frankly* (New York: Harper & Brothers, 1947).

Chase, E. P., *The United Nations in Action* (New York: McGraw-Hill Book Company, Inc., 1950).

Goodrich, Leland M., and Hambro, Edvard, *Charter of the United Nations, Commentary and Documents*, 2nd ed. (Boston: World Peace Foundation, 1949).

Salomon, A., *L'O.N.U. et la paix: Le Conseil de Securité et le reglement pacifique des differences* (Paris: Editions Internationales, 1948).

Wehl, David, *The Birth of Indonesia* (London: G. Allen & Unwin, Ltd., 1949).

Periodicals

Black, C. E., "Greece and the United Nations," *Political Science Quarterly*, Vol. 63, No. 4 (1948).

Blaisdell, D. C., "Arming the United Nations," *Department of State Bulletin*, Vol. 7, No. 422A (August 3, 1947).

Borchard, Edwin, "The Impracticability of 'Enforcing' Peace," *Yale Law Journal*, Vol. 55 (1946).

Briggs, H. W., "*Rebus sic stantibus* before the Security Council: The Anglo-Egyptian Question," *American Journal of International Law*, Vol. 43 (1949).

Collins, J. F., "The United Nations and Indonesia," *International Conciliation*, No. 459 (March 1950).

Emerson, Rupert, "Reflections on the Indonesian Case," *World Politics*, Vol. 1, No. 1 (October 1948).

Goodrich, Leland M., "Korea," *International Conciliation*, No. 494 (October 1953).

———, "The United Nations: Pacific Settlement of Disputes," *American Political Science Review*, Vol. 39, No. 5 (October 1945).

Hyde, J. N., "Peaceful Settlement: A Survey of Studies in the Interim Committee of the United Nations General Assembly," *International Conciliation*, No. 444 (October 1948).

Leonard, L. Larry, "The United Nations and Palestine," *International Conciliation*, No. 454 (October 1949).

Padelford, Norman, "The Use of the Veto," *International Organization*, Vol 2, No. 2 (June 1948).

Reston, J. B., "Votes and Vetoes," *Foreign Affairs*, Vol. 25, No. 1 (October 1946).

Rivlin, Benjamin, "Italian Colonies," *United Nations Action,* Case Histories: 1 (1950).

Van Wagenen, Richard W., "The Iranian Case 1946," *United Nations Action,* Case Histories: 2 (1952).

Documents

Organization and Procedure of United Nations Commissions, prepared for the Interim Committee of the General Assembly, Subcommittee on International Cooperation in the Political Field (New York: United Nations, 1950).

Preparation of Political and Security Matters Placed before Previous Sessions of the General Assembly, UN Doc. A/AC.18/58, May 14, 1948.

Report of the Security Council to the General Assembly, Covering the Period from 16 July 1949 to 15 July 1950, General Assembly, Official Records, Fifth Session, Supplement No. 2 (A/1361), 1950.

Study of Experience Gained to Date in the Preparation of Political and Security Matters for the General Assembly, UN Doc. A/AC.18/59, May 27, 1948.

Study of the Organizations and Operation of United Nations Commissions, UN Doc. A/AC.18/SC.6/6, July 29, 1949.

United States, *The United Nations and the Problem of Greece,* Department of State Publication 2909, Near Eastern Series 9 (Washington: U.S. Government Printing Office, 1947).

———, *Korea, 1945 to 1948,* Department of State Publication 3305 (Washington: U.S. Government Printing Office, 1948), and *United States Policy in the Korean Crisis,* Department of State Publication 3922 (Washington: U.S. Government Printing Office, 1950).

Use by Organs of the United Nations of Measures and Procedures of Pacific Settlement, UN Doc. A/AC.18/61, June 4, 1948.

Several documents are issued by the UN Secretariat which are of great assistance in following the work of the Security Council, and are short cuts to its deliberations. The *Cumulative Index to the Resolutions of the Security Council to 16 March 1949 (Meetings 1 through 419),* UN Doc. Index Note No. 16/Rev. 2, is useful as a guide to the resolutions only. The *Summary Statement by the Secretary-General of Matters of Which the Security Council is Seized and of the Stage Reached in Their Consideration* is issued weekly.

The student will find useful the summarizations of UN political activities in several sources, notably the *Yearbook of the United Nations, Annual Report of the Secretary-General, The United States and the United Nations,* and *Official Records of the Security Council.*

16

Regulating the Use of Force

> "The fourth is freedom from fear — which, translated into world terms, means a world-wide reduction of armaments to such a point and in such a thorough fashion that no nation will be in a position to commit an act of physical aggression against any neighbor — anywhere in the world.
>
> "That is no vision of a distant millennium. It is a definite basis for a kind of world attainable in our time and generation."
>
> — FRANKLIN D. ROOSEVELT [1]

CONCERN FOR disarmament has increased in proportion to the destructiveness and cost of warfare, amply demonstrated by two World Wars within a single generation. This concern resulted from moral, political, economic, and humanitarian considerations. Although war has always been widely abhorred, the limited wars fought by professional soldiers in the eighteenth century failed to attract attention to the burdens and dangers of armaments. It was the revelations of war conducted by the *levée en masse* (mass citizen armies) during the Napoleonic struggles that led statesmen to ponder the advantages of reducing armament burdens. Many governments began to realize they had neither the material and human resources nor the administrative skill to fight such wars. The backwardness of Russian technology as well as humanitarian and political motivations, for example, influenced the Russian Czar, Nicholas II, to call the First Hague Conference in 1899 in order to seek an "understanding not to increase . . . armed military and naval forces, and . . . the budgets pertaining thereto; and a preliminary examination of the means by which even a reduction might be effected in future in the forces and budgets above mentioned." [2]

Although the First Conference was attended by representatives of twenty-eight nations, including all the major powers, nothing more was accomplished than the passage of two pious resolutions which noted that a lessening of the armaments burden was "extremely desirable for the in-

---

[1] *Annual Message to Congress*, January 6, 1941.
[2] Merze Tate, *The Disarmament Illusion* (New York: Macmillan, 1942), pp. 167 ff.

Crawford, in the Newark News

"THE OBSERVER"

crease of the material and moral welfare of mankind." [3] Despite the fact that the Second Hague Conference was attended by forty-four nations in 1907, it fared no better.[4]

Disarmament lies close to the nerve center of international politics, national insecurity, which paradoxically enough, is a result of the incessant struggle for power waged in a frustrating quest for increasing security. Not only did the Czar and other nineteenth-century leaders seek economy in reducing armaments; they also sought military safety. If nations could agree to limit their armaments to mutually accepted levels, there might be safety for all. Armaments, in short, were thought to be a cause of war rather than

[3] *Ibid.*, p. 285.
[4] *Ibid.*, p. 341.

a symptom of the constant struggle for power in international affairs. Indeed, there was evidence that some nineteenth-century wars were caused by disputes and fears regarding the level of armaments in certain European countries.[5] Was not the steady rise of German naval power, moreover, a cause of Anglo-German rivalry and therefore one of the several causes of the First World War? Until the disillusionment of the League's efforts, therefore, great hopes were pinned on disarmament as a main avenue to peace.

The Regulation of Force Under the League

Disarmament occupied a central place in the League system, more so than was to be the case in the United Nations. Despite the failure of the Hague Conference to make any progress whatsoever, there was a general conviction after the bloodshed of World War I that another try must be made. "The men who knew best how Europe had stumbled helplessly into that fatal catastrophe were convinced that the armaments race which preceded it had been the greatest single element in making disaster inevitable."[6] Obviously, improvements had to be made over the Hague approach. Opportunity came with the Armistice. Disarmament, in the minds of the chief architects of the League, was one element in a triple formula for peace: Arbitration, Security, Disarmament. This structure seemed promising, but which of the three pillars was to be raised first? Did security depend upon disarmament or vice versa? Should improved arbitration be sought before the others? The League never found a satisfactory answer.[7]

Nearly all the League planners sought to reduce or control armaments. Smuts proposed the abolition of compulsory military service, limits on military equipment to be fixed by the proposed Council, and the nationalization and international inspection of arms factories. Wilson's suggestions closely resembled those finally incorporated in the Covenant which are discussed below. For the British Sir Edward Grey warned that a revived "concert" was necessary to control the armaments race, which he predicted would lead either to revolution or war. The French, as we have noted, gave sanctions priority over disarmament and made proposals looking toward an international police force.

A concrete step toward disarmament was taken when German armaments were sharply curtailed by the Treaty of Versailles "in order to render possible the initiation of a general limitation of the armaments of all nations."[8] The Covenant attempted a further step in affirming in Article 8 that "the

---

[5] See Robert Strausz-Hupé and Stefan T. Possony, *International Relations* (New York: McGraw-Hill, 1950), Chap. 20.

[6] F. P. Walters, *A History of the League of Nations* (New York: Oxford University Press, 1952), p. 217.

[7] The reader is reminded of the discussion of collective security under the League in Chap. 5.

[8] Part V of the Treaty of Versailles.

maintenance of peace requires the reduction of national armaments to the lowest point consistent with national safety and the enforcement by common action of international obligations." Nations were not expected to disarm, but to reduce their armaments, which were to be utilized to insure domestic safety and to enforce the collective security provisions of Articles 10 and 16 of the Covenant. What the appropriate armament levels were to be was left for the Council to decide, "taking account of the geographical situation and circumstances of each state. . . ." The same article also expressed a widely held notion "that the manufacture by private enterprise of munitions and implements of war is open to grave objections." The Members were also "to undertake to interchange full and frank information" on their armaments and war industries. The Covenant, in short, expressed a hope, rather than an obligation, that nations should cease to be the sole judges either of the equipment necessary for their arsenals or the use to which it should be put.

Permanent Advisory Commission and Temporary Mixed Commission

Progress was slow. The Covenant had also provided for a permanent Commission to advise the Council on the reduction of armaments "and on military, naval and air questions generally." It was composed of technical experts, that is, representatives of the respective armed forces of the governments on the Council. In 1920, with the embers of war scarcely extinguished, this Commission advised that any reduction of the forces of the League's principal Members would be premature. Perhaps it was impossible to expect any other recommendation from professional soldiers. The First Assembly was dissatisfied and appointed its own body that November to consider the armaments problem in "wider terms." This group was known as the Temporary Mixed Commission and was composed of twenty independent experts instead of governmental representatives. Political, social, and economic expertise was "mixed" with military competence.

The first fruit of the Mixed Commission was the Esher Plan — named for Lord Esher, one of its members. This proposal rested on the shaky but then fashionable premise that armaments cause wars and the corollary, that disarmament in itself can promote security. The scheme called, therefore, for the organization of European armies in units of 30,000 men each, exclusive of colonial contingents. France was to be allotted six units; Italy and Poland, four each; Great Britain, Czechoslovakia, Greece, Yugoslavia, Holland, Rumania and Spain, three each; with other states allotted two or one, as appropriate.

No power seriously rose for this bait, and Lord Esher himself soon suggested that it be withdrawn.[9] To the French, Belgians and Poles it offered no security against a resurgence of German power which depended as much on industrial might and a growing preponderance of skilled manpower as it did on forces in being. The failure of this approach served to identify

9 Walters, op. cit., p. 221.

the problem of security with that of disarmament. Clearly, those powers that feared Germany would not lower their guard until some system was devised to insure that armed attack under any circumstances would not only be illegal, but would be subject to overwhelming punitive action. A resolution of the Assembly in 1922 noted that a reduction in armaments could not be successful unless coupled to "a satisfactory guarantee of the safety of states." The Temporary Mixed Commission, therefore, sought security by means of compulsory arbitration and sanctions as well as disarmament. The ill-fated Draft Treaty of Mutual Assistance and the Geneva Protocol were the result.[10]

The Washington Treaties

It is only fair to say that the proponents of the Esher scheme were influenced by events going on at the same time outside the League that seemed to promise well for disarmament. The United States, although not a League Member, was also bent on disarmament, both to compensate for not joining the League and to reduce the burden of maintaining large armaments. In 1921 President Harding invited the principal naval powers to a Conference in Washington in the hope of halting an onerous naval race already in progress. The resulting naval agreement of February 1922 succeeded in limiting battleships and aircraft carriers by numerical ratio, of $5 : 5 : 3 : 1.75 : 1.75$ among the United States, Great Britain, Japan, Italy and France respectively. Limitations were also placed on the tonnage and armament of these vessels, but no agreement was reached on limiting submarines, destroyers and cruisers.

Unfortunately, the ratio could not be applied to land forces in Europe for several reasons. Most important was the fact that a reduction in naval arms was possible because the Washington naval powers had achieved a measure of security from other treaties of the Conference itself: The Four-Power Treaty pledging the signatories to cooperation and mutual help in the Pacific and the Nine-Power Treaty guaranteeing the independence and integrity of China. Another reason was that large naval vessels were more susceptible to the ratio treatment than were land forces. Both Britain and Japan, moreover, stood to gain if the industrial giant, the United States, could be persuaded to halt its building program. The United States, in turn, found the Washington Treaties to be the best defense of its interests in the Pacific since Congress was reluctant to spend money to fortify Pacific bases. All powers were pleased with the arrangement. But, unfortunately, no machinery or penalties were created to put teeth in this system. Japan lived up to the agreement for only a short time. Moreover, later efforts at the Naval Conference at Geneva in 1927 to limit cruisers, destroyers and submarines were of little or no avail. The surface reason given was that no common yardstick could be devised to measure the divergent interests and commitments of the powers. The London Naval Conference of 1930 had

[10] See Chap. 5.

better luck. The United States, Britain, and Japan at least agreed on limitations for the above three types of vessels. A meeting in 1935 produced a construction holiday between Britain, France and the United States. The saber rattling of Germany and Italy made further progress impossible.

The Preparatory Commission

Having failed to tighten the security machinery of the Covenant, the Temporary Mixed Commission went out of business after 1924. The powers then pursued security outside the League through the Locarno Pacts.[11] With this objective apparently achieved, the Assembly once again called upon the Council in 1925 to tackle the disarmament problem directly by preparing for a disarmament conference. The Council then established a body called the Preparatory Commission for the Disarmament Conference. It was composed of governmental representatives who labored for five long years to recommend means of reducing armaments. Two subcommissions were established to consider military and socio-economic aspects of the problem and to agree on ways of defining and comparing armaments. In 1930 a draft "Convention on the Reduction and Limitation of Armaments" was finally completed for the consideration of governments.[12]

Great hopes were held for the Preparatory Commission, which was the center of attention on the international stage for several years. It included all the States then on the Council and six other League Members plus Germany, the Soviet Union and even the United States. The latter was represented by Hugh Gibson, who was held on a tight rein by his government. The United States never permitted the League Members to forget that she had not subscribed to the full obligations of the Covenant. She felt sympathetic rather than vitally concerned with the pressing problems of disarmament and security.

Two further events augured well for the deliberations, the signing of the Pact of Paris (Kellogg Pact) in 1929, and the adoption by the Assembly of the General Act for the Pacific Settlement of International Disputes in 1928. Yet the Preparatory Commission made little headway. The Draft Convention was as notable for its omissions as for its accomplishments. Agreement on principles of action was nearly impossible to reach owing to the differing strategic interests of the powers. Could a distinction be made between offensive and defensive weapons? How to measure military potential? Could or should there be international supervision of armament industries? What defenses were needed for a given country's defense?

Agreement was finally reached on the following principles: budgetary limitation of war material; time limits on active military service; establishment of a Permanent Disarmament Commission; limitation of effectives in

---

[11] See pp. 127–128.

[12] For the Commission's work, see J. W. Wheeler-Bennett, *Disarmament and Security Since Locarno, 1925–31* (London: Allen & Unwin, 1932); S. de Madariaga, *Disarmament* (New York: Harcourt, Brace, 1929); and F. P. Walters, *A History of the League of Nations*, Chaps, 18, 31, 41, and 44.

land, sea and air forces; limitation of naval weapons by ratio and category in the manner of the 1930 London Conference; and renunciation of chemical and bacteriological warfare. The Commission failed to agree on the abolition of conscription, the problem of how to limit trained reserves, or direct, as opposed to budgetary, limitation of war material.

What were the basic difficulties? There was no lack of memories of horrors of World War I. There was still widespread revulsion against war. The difficulties were really political. The technical obstacles stemmed from the conflicting security policies pursued by the major powers. France continued its insistence on prior consideration of the *security* question and plugged for an elaborate system of armaments inspection. The Germans insisted on *equality* by stressing at first the disarmament promises of the Versailles Treaty. The Draft Convention was unacceptable because it perpetuated the Versailles arrangement. Indeed, it was the shoal of security versus equality on which the Preparatory Commission grounded and on which the Conference itself eventually foundered. Britain and the United States placed their hopes on agreements to reduce armaments rather than on new security obligations or international inspection. After a delayed arrival, the Soviet delegate, Maxim Litvinov, dramatically proposed immediate, total and universal disarmament. This suggestion aroused more apprehension than applause. It would have weakened France in relation to her neighbor, Germany. France and her allies were already suspicious of the collaboration between the Soviet and German general staffs that had begun with the Treaty of Rapallo in 1922. Moreover, there was general distrust of the "danger from the East," especially since the Soviet Union had heaped abuse on the League and on its capitalist clientele. Rebuffed, the Soviet Union later suggested massive reduction of "offensive" weapons. Most alarming was the polarization of forces between the *status quo* powers led by France, which were content with the Versailles Treaty, and the *revisionist* powers, including Germany, Italy, and, for a time, the Soviet Union, which were generally discontent with their lot.

The Geneva World Disarmament Conference, 1932–34

The League Council set February 1932 as the opening date for the full Conference. The great depression had fastened its icy grip on the world's economy. The era of good feeling had evaporated, owing to the Japanese onslaught in Manchuria, the Austro-German Customs Union fiasco, and the increasing belligerence of Germany. Uneasiness and distrust stalked the corridors. Would it have been wiser to postpone the Conference for a time? Governments dared not. Petitions containing millions of signatures and delegations from numerous peace societies descended upon Geneva. Armistice Day in 1931 was the signal for mass disarmament meetings in the United States. It is hard to recapture today the intense faith in disarmament that stirred mankind a quarter of a century ago.

Representatives of fifty-nine of the sixty-four invited states foregathered at Geneva under the Chairmanship of Arther Henderson, whose prestige

© *Low all countries. Reprinted by permission of the artist.*

"THE CONFERENCE EXCUSES ITSELF"

since his appointment by the Council had been dimmed as he was no longer British Foreign Secretary.[13]

The smouldering differences of the Preparatory Commission immediately burst into flame. France, consistent to the end, proposed an ambitious scheme for an international police force under League authority, compulsory arbitration, a clear-cut definition of aggression, and international execution and control of any disarmament convention. Britain, the United States, Germany and Italy hung back. The first two powers resumed the suggestion of defining offensive and defensive weapons and the abolition of the latter by treaty. Chancellor Brüning urged "equality of status" for Germany, whose own disarmament was to be followed by general disarmament. Brüning's political future and the course of German politics depended on the acceptance of this principle. When he failed to score, he was dismissed from office in favor of the less accommodating von Papen, soon to run interference for Hitler. The Soviet Union again urged that the only way to disarm was to disarm.

Stalemate ensued. The gloom was briefly lifted when President Hoover cabled in June a suggestion for an all-round one-third reduction of land forces that were superior in strength to the 100,000-man army allowed Ger-

[13] See J. W. Wheeler-Bennett, *The Pipe Dream of Peace* (New York: Morrow, 1935).

many by the Versailles Treaty. Hoover also included the abolition of certain weapons, including tanks, bombing planes and chemicals. But these seeds fell on inhospitable soil. More promising were overtures made in December by France and the other principal powers when the right of Germany to equality was accepted in principle. But it was too little and too late. This concession might well have been helpful some years earlier. With the advent of Hitler to power in January 1933, however, Germany decisively turned her face towards rearmament. In October the Führer marched Germany out of the Conference and then out of the League.

Other plans failed to relieve the deadlocked Conference, which, its General Commission and Bureau excepted, adjourned for a time to permit bilateral negotiations through traditional diplomatic channels. The smaller powers, helplessly enmeshed in the trials and intrigues of the big powers, exerted unceasing pressure for further efforts. For the British, Prime Minister MacDonald urged armament reduction by stages over a five-year period to specified levels and consultation among the Kellogg Pact signatories in the event of a violation of the Pact. This was a lightly camouflaged effort to associate the United States in sanctions arrangements. In May 1933 Franklin Roosevelt, the new United States President, accepted the outlines of the MacDonald plan and suggested, in addition, a general "solemn and definite pact of nonaggression." His personal representative, Norman H. Davis, went on to explain that the United States was willing "to consult with the other states in case of a threat to peace" and to refrain from interfering with any collective efforts to restore order. Such a proposal in 1935 might have laid to rest the British nightmare of enforcing an embargo on Italy against the United States Navy. In 1933 the proposal was ineffective. All hands now feared that a nonaggression pact was no stronger than a dictator's word.

After the departure of Germany, the Conference ground to a halt. It was adjourned in June 1934, but seems never to have been formally disbanded. Why did it fail? What, if anything, had it achieved?

Most obvious was the ineluctable fact that Germany by 1933 sought rearmament, while the League was committed to disarmament. These objectives were irreconcilable. Had steps been taken earlier to bring about the general disarmament and concomitant equality promised at Versailles, things might have been different. By the time the Conference was under way, a demagogue had risen to power who claimed he could burst the shackles of Versailles. He promptly made good his word, and the psychological consequences were immense. The League could scarcely have suffered a crueler blow. The difficulty was, of course, that it was precisely German equality that France feared. For equality in arms inevitably spelled German industrial and probably political predominance in Europe, which oft-invaded France could not abide. Britain, however, felt less endangered by Germany, and, as a result, she was unable to agree with France on a common German policy.[14]

[14] See Arnold Wolfers, *Britain and France Between Two Wars* (New York: Harcourt, Brace, 1940).

This brings us to the second difficulty. The League, in practice, failed to establish a dependable system of international security. For this the United States must share much of the blame. Her absence, plus that of the Soviet Union until 1934, meant that only part of the peace structure had been erected. Other states were also at fault. The Commonwealth countries were not free of isolationist leanings, and nearly all the powers, as we have seen, were reluctant to accept the security obligations of the Covenant as binding. In this connection we see again how international politics mirror domestic politics. No French premier could remain in office, at least after 1931, on a platform of armaments equality for Germany. Chancellor Brüning, in turn, was doomed unless he achieved immediate agreement on arms equality.

Finally, the Disarmament Conference opened in a period of political and economic turmoil. Germany was pressing for revisionist claims. Until the Nazis came to power, the Russians tended to side with Germany, as did Italy. When the Russians later sought agreement with the democracies, the Conference was already doomed beyond recall. Besides, there never could be a strong bond of trust between the democracies and Communist Russia.

What was accomplished? A decade of intensive study had done much to clarify the *technical* problems, although they were far from solved. At least there was general agreement on the following matters:

1. Supervision and inspection by an international authority are indispensable, including a system of guarantees to prevent infractions.
2. Armament must be limited *qualitatively* by gradually abolishing certain types and *quantitatively* by restricting the number of retained types.
3. There must be agreement on the system and control of national defense expenditure.
4. Air bombardment and both chemical and bacteriological war should be abandoned.
5. The manufacture of arms, private or state, must be supervised.

More important was the *political* lesson: that disarmament was inextricably entwined with security — or, more accurately, insecurity — national and international. This dearly bought experience was the foundation on which the United Nations sought to build. The French thesis, long ridiculed, was at last to be sustained by the theory of the United Nations Charter and the practice of its armaments bodies.

Was international peace helped or hindered by the League's disarmament turmoil? An argument can be made that once the public's attention was riveted on disarmament, "the pipe dream of peace," it became that much more difficult for the democracies to arm themselves against the totalitarian powers. Yet peace must be pursued on all fronts at once. Those who seek guidance solely from the axiom "si vis pacem, para bellum" (if you want peace, prepare for war) sometimes forget that strength in one camp breeds fear in another.

The Regulation of Force Under the United Nations

...for the time being I can only say for myself that I think the atomic bomb has made the United Nations organization more essential to the hopes of humankind than ever before. In whatever degree it may have complicated and darkened the international horizon, by the same token it increasingly becomes an ever sterner necessity if the world is to escape a final cataclysm . . . . Our proper course is clear. It is our task to develop through the United Nations organization a system of complete worldwide inspection which shall guarantee to civilization that no nation (including ourselves) shall use atomic energy for the construction of weapons of war. I know of no other *logical* answer. . . . " — ARTHUR H. VANDENBERG[15]

What the framers of the Charter would have provided in the way of armaments regulation had they known of atomic energy's destructive power will never be known. As the Charter emerged from the optimistic aura of San Francisco, less attention was paid to disarmament than was the case with the Covenant. As a means to world order, the innovations of the Charter rather sought to concentrate authority in one body, the Security Council, which was empowered not only to fix responsibility for aggression, but to curb it as well.[16] Even when armaments are discussed directly, there is a change in emphasis. Article 26, for example, charges the Security Council and its Military Staff Committee with the responsibility of "formulating . . . plans for the establishment of a system of regulation of armaments," while the Covenant, it will be recalled, had specified "reduction of national armaments."

The new accent is on "regulation" rather than "reduction," and this distinction characterizes as well as anything the difference in approach to the security problem between the League and the United Nations. The latter was intended to be superior to the League owing to its ability to enforce its decisions. Much of the French thesis on security was adopted since the Security Council is intended to have forces at its disposal — national contingents rather than a world army, to be sure, but actual military forces "for the purpose of maintaining international peace and security."

Beyond this point sovereign states would not go. Early planning, to be sure, had toyed briefly with the suggestion of a truly international force equipped with international bases. One exploratory State Department memorandum in 1940 dealt with the establishment of an international force including bombing and fighter planes, located at suitable strategic points upon neutral soil, with its personnel recruited from small neutral states. This force was to be under the direction of a Political Body. A permanent Disarmament Commission was to enforce by inspection qualitative and

[15] *The Private Papers of Senator Vandenberg*, edited by Arthur H. Vandenberg, Jr., (Boston: Houghton Mifflin, 1952), pp. 223–224 (letters of Oct. 29 and Nov. 13, 1945).
[16] See Chap. 6.

quantitative disarmament provisions.[17] Long before the Dumbarton Oaks conversations, however, this notion was abandoned as far too radical.

Agreement among the Big Four on the means of regulating force was reached at Dumbarton Oaks without much real difficulty. The Proposals simply provided that the Security Council and the Military Staff Committee were to draw up plans for a "system of regulation of armaments" and "possible disarmament."[18]

These provisions underwent very little change at San Francisco. The smaller powers sought rather to restrict the authority of the big states, first, by attacks on the extent of the veto privilege and, secondly, by efforts to increase the Assembly's authority in matters involving peace and security. But, on the important point that security must precede disarmament, all hands were pretty well agreed. It might be said that the old formulation of Security, Arbitration, and Disarmament was replaced by a new formulation — Security, Peaceful Settlement, and Welfare. Disarmament was given a back seat. Security and economic and social collaboration moved forward. The Conference also agreed to the Sponsoring Powers' proposals that the General Assembly should be limited to the consideration of "principles governing disarmament" while the Security Council was to formulate specific plans.

One important change was made at San Francisco. Canada, supported by the other middle powers, insisted that the provisions of the present Article 44 be included in the Charter. If, in order to halt a threat to the peace, the Security Council calls for the provision of military forces by a United Nations Member not represented on the Security Council, that Member may have a vote (not a veto) on the use of its forces. This, the Canadian delegate wryly noted, was in accord with the cherished American axiom of "no taxation without representation."

ARMED FORCES FOR THE UNITED NATIONS

To enable the Security Council to do its job in maintaining peace and security, all Members of the organization agreed under Article 43 to make available "armed forces assistance, and facilities, including rights of passage. . . . " Special importance is attached to "national air force contingents for combined enforcement action" in Article 45 so that the United Nations may be prepared to take urgent military measures.

These were not intended to be international forces; nor were they really to be United Nations forces. They were to be national forces available to the Security Council by special agreements between the Members or groups of Members and the Security Council itself. These agreements were in-

[17] *Postwar Foreign Policy Preparation, 1939–1945,* Department of State Publication 3850 (Washington: Government Printing Office, 1949), Chap. 5, and the early drafts of the Charter included as appendices, particularly Appendix 5.

[18] *Charter of the United Nations,* Report to the President on the Results of the San Francisco Conference by the Chairman of the United States Delegation, the Secretary of State, Department of State Publication 2349, Conference Series 71 (Washington: Government Printing Office, 1945), Chap. VII.

tended to specify the number and types of forces, their degree of readiness, general location and the nature of facilities and assistance to be provided. Many of the smaller nations, it was thought, would supply equipment or facilities of various sorts instead of troops and guns. Two further stipulations illustrate the care with which national sovereignty is still nurtured. First, each agreement must be ratified in accordance with each Member's constitutional procedure. Second, no Member can be called upon to supply armed forces not provided for in the agreements.[19]

For the United States these principles have been enacted into law by Congress in the United Nations Participation Act of December 1945.[20] The President has been authorized to negotiate a special agreement or agreements with the Security Council on the detailed provision of forces, and Congress must then approve the agreement by legislative enactment or joint resolution. The Act states that it may not be construed as authorizing the President to make forces available to the Security Council beyond those specifically earmarked in the agreements. Thus, the United States has sought to carry out this international obligation of overriding importance through the legislative power rather than through the treaty power, as might have been expected. Since Congress, including both House and Senate, has the power to declare war, to appropriate monies, and to raise and maintain armies, the device is sound. Fulfillment of Charter obligations requires action by the House as well as the Senate. Making United States forces available to the United Nations, moreover, requires close teamwork between the President and Congress, sometimes conspicuous by its absence.

Even if the United Nations should ultimately have weapons at its disposal, there is no assurance, of course, that such weapons will be used in defense of the Charter's principles. No action can be taken by the Security Council unless its permanent members are in agreement. The use of force is prohibited, moreover, except in self-defense (Article 51) or on the authority of the Security Council. It is the general acceptance of the principle that armed force shall be used only under the authority of the organized international community that made possible the development of improvisations that we noted were used to meet aggression in Korea.

Stalemate in the Military Staff Committee[21]

It was left to the Military Staff Committee to recommend the complicated details involved in drawing up the armed forces agreements. In the interim, the Charter, in Article 106, authorized the permanent members of the Council to take "joint action on behalf of the organization" to preserve peace. At its second meeting in January 1946 the Security Council requested the permanent members to initiate Military Staff Committee negotiations. Little was accomplished until the General Assembly in its turn prodded the Security Council in the fall of 1946.

---

19 UNCIO, XII, p. 508, Report of M. Paul Boncour, Rapporteur on Chap. 8, Section B.
20 Public Law 264, 79th Congress, 1st Session.
21 For the establishment and composition of the Military Staff Committee, see Chap. 6.

The political disunity among the permanent members that had already hobbled the Security Council's handling of disputes was no less crippling in the Military Staff Committee. In April 1947 the latter was forced to report to the Security Council that it had been unable to agree on the important aspects regarding the contribution of armed forces by the permanent members who were naturally expected to shoulder most of the burden. Out of a total of forty-one articles governing the principles for arming the United Nations, agreement had been reached on only twenty-five.[22] The areas of agreement, moreover, were relatively unimportant, while matters in disagreement were crucial.

The permanent members were able to agree that the Security Council should have enough forces available to it to be able to take "prompt action" to quell any threat to international peace. This would require that these forces be maintained in specific degrees of readiness. The permanent members also had no trouble agreeing that they should provide most of the armed might and that no member should be required to increase its armaments in order to contribute forces to the organization. Reserves and replacements in personnel and equipment would have to be maintained. Except when operating under the orders of the Security Council, these forces were to remain under the exclusive command of the contributing nations. The national character of the forces was to be retained in such matters as discipline and regulations. When carrying out enforcement provisions, however, these forces might be placed under the command of an over-all supreme commander and were to be based as designated by the Security Council.

On the specific forces the permanent members themselves were to provide, however, there was little agreement. The U.S.S.R. has insisted upon the principle of *equality*, holding that each permanent member should contribute an equal number of units in various categories of arms, such as airborne units, tank units, warships, etc. The other permanent members in turn have refused to recede from their position that the principle of contributing equally to the United Nations would be served best by *comparable* contributions. That is, contributions should be provided in accordance with the varying size and character of the armed forces of each of the permanent members. A member deficient in one category of weapons might make considerable contributions in another. Obviously, each argument supports a national point of view. The Soviets have sought to deëmphasize and limit in this instance, and in concurrent armament discussions, the naval and air superiority of the Western powers, while the latter have sought to maintain their lead in these weapons.

Nor could the Military Staff Committee agree on the location of the armed forces when not actually engaged in enforcement measures. The United States, the United Kingdom and China thought these forces should be stationed wherever the Security Council should decide in the agreements

[22] See D. C. Blaisdell, "Arming the United Nations," *Department of State Bulletin,* Supplement of August 3, 1947.

to be made with the United Nations Members. France thought the Military Staff Committee should make even more specific recommendations. The U.S.S.R. insisted that all forces should remain in their own territories until actually called into action by the Security Council. To do otherwise might jeopardize the friendly relations between states. Nor was agreement reached on the provision of military bases. The French in particular insisted that "facilities" must include bases. The Soviet Union insisted that base rights would afford a means of exerting political pressure against the independence of nations. The Soviet position in these respects is consistent with its general attitude on limiting United Nations authority in favor of its own freedom of action.

A further disagreement cropped up when the Soviet Union insisted that armed forces should be withdrawn after the completion of a mission within a time limit of thirty to ninety days. The other four powers urged that, while armed forces should be withdrawn as soon as possible, withdrawals should be made on decision of the Security Council. There were further differences between the U.S.S.R. and the rest on the availability of national air force contingents and the size of the different categories of forces. Four of the powers were in fairly close agreement on the number of naval vessels, but the Soviet Union, following the principle of equality, made no provision for aircraft carriers or battleships which in 1948 were included in neither the Soviet nor Chinese navy. In comparison with the others, the United States' estimates were lavish in nearly every category. The United States recommended air force contingents three times the size of those suggested by other powers and nearly twice as many ground divisions.[23]

By 1948 the political deadlock in the United Nations terminated serious negotiations in the Military Staff Committee and the Security Council. The Committee has continued the formality of periodic meetings but has had no progress to report. As in other aspects of international security, the General Assembly has endeavored to carry on where the Security Council has failed.

The Assembly and Enforcement

When the Fifth Assembly convened in September 1950, Secretary of State Dean Acheson proposed for the United States a series of recommendations "designed to increase the effectiveness of the United Nations." While the spirit of the proposals was generally infectious, some modifications were to be made to meet the objections of several powers.[24] The widespread acceptance of the plan was not surprising. Many smaller powers had long disparaged the veto-ridden Security Council. The General Assembly had increased its role in security affairs year by year since it had been given

[23] See UN Doc. S/394, June 30, 1947, and figures in the *Yearbook of the United Nations, 1947–1948*, p. 495.

[24] H. Field Haviland, Jr., *The Political Role of the General Assembly*, United Nations Studies, No. 7 (New York: Carnegie Endowment for International Peace, 1951), pp. 156–165.

ACHESON PLAN

1. Assembly meets in 24 hours when Security Council fails to act in emergency

2. Creation of Peace Observation Commission

3. Member states to hold armed force contingents for UN use

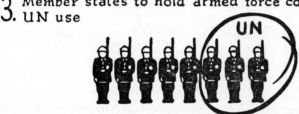

4. Establishment of Collective Measures Committee to study methods of strengthening peace

GRAPHIC ASSOCIATES
Headline Series, *Foreign Policy Association*

charge of the Spanish and Greek cases. Most delegations agreed with the thought expressed by the British that enforcement must not again be left to chance, as had been the case during the previous June and July. A few states warned that hope for big-power unanimity in the Security Council must not be abandoned. Only the U.S.S.R. and its band of followers opposed.

After modifications, the "Acheson Plan" was introduced as a Uniting for Peace Resolution by Canada, France, the Philippines, Turkey, Great Britain,

the United States and Uruguay.[25] Its purpose was to enable the General
Assembly to stand in for the deadlocked Security Council in emergencies.
There were four specific innovations to the Charter's enforcement ma-
chinery.

First, the General Assembly was to recommend collective measures including the use of armed force against aggression if the Security Council
failed to exercise its primary responsibility for the maintenance of international peace and security. If not in session, the General Assembly was to
be summoned on twenty-four hour notice at the request of either the Security
Council, on the vote of any seven of the latter's members, or a majority of
the Members of the United Nations.

Second, a Peace Observation Commission of fourteen members was established with a mandate to observe and report situations anywhere in the
world likely to endanger international peace. It was to have the consent of
the state into whose territory it was to go. It might be utilized by the Assembly or the Security Council.

Third, each member was recommended "to maintain within its national
armed forces" elements formed and organized for services as a United Nations unit on the recommendation of the Security Council or the General
Assembly.

Fourth, a Collective Measures Committee of fourteen members was established to study and report to both the Security Council and the General
Assembly on ways to maintain and strengthen peace and security under the
terms of the Charter.

The Uniting for Peace Resolution was passed on November 2, 1950, by a
vote of 52 to 5 (the Soviet bloc) with 2 abstentions (Argentina and India).
The Peace Observation Commission was called to duty at once. Within a
month the Assembly instructed it to dispatch a subcommittee to continue
the United Nations' watch in the Balkans. The Collective Measures Committee has fared less successfully, but has reported on schedule to the
Sixth and Seventh Assemblies. There the debates have shown some reservations regarding the new peace system on the part of some members of
the Arab-Asian bloc, but only the Soviet bloc has urged its abolition.[26] The
response to the Assembly's appeal for United Nations contingents has been
disheartening, but several nations noted that they had already supplied
similar contingents for duty in Korea. Despite the caution with which it
is being implemented, the importance of the "Peace Plan" can hardly be
overestimated. It formalized the failure to mobilize United Nations force
through joint action of the big powers. Instead, the vast majority of the
Members were now ready to go so far as to attempt to enforce sanctions
against one or more of the great powers themselves. The organization, in
short, was seeking ways to maintain peace in a world as it was instead of
in a world as the Four-Power Voting Statement said it should be.[27]

[25] *Yearbook of the United Nations, 1950*, pp. 193–195.
[26] *Yearbook of the United Nations, 1951*, pp. 181–189.
[27] See Chap. 6.

Of less significance was the fact that the application of military sanctions had to be voluntary, as under the League. There was no formal amendment of the Charter. The Assembly still could not make binding decisions. But a security system in which a sufficiently powerful majority of citizens agrees on the measures to be taken against a lawbreaker is more effective than one in which no one summons the police.

What if a big power should be in the minority in a recommendation to take military action? Would war necessarily follow, as the Four Power Voting Statement implied? Again, Korea affords a case in point. The Soviet Union opposed the United Nations' military action but did not commit its own forces. The war remained limited. Would the United States be morally committed by a two-thirds majority of lesser powers to use its own armed forces against its wish? The answer to that question depends on diplomacy. In assessing the risks, the alternatives must be considered. One is to do nothing in the event of a Security Council stalemate over an act of aggression. The other is to mobilize majority sentiment in support of the Charter's stipulations regarding the use of force.

Is the Uniting for Peace Resolution constitutionally valid? Since the Assembly was given a generous grant of authority under Article 10 to discuss and make recommendations, though not binding decisions, "on any questions or any matters within the scope of the present Charter," the answer is, yes. Nonetheless, the fact cannot be gainsaid that the thinking at Dumbarton Oaks and San Francisco was that the only kind of collective action which would ever be effective would be action that was agreed to and supported unanimously by the great powers. The mobilizing of collective force by mere recommendation seemed neither desirable nor practical in view of the League's experience. While the resolution is within legal limits, it is at the same time a significant modification of the spirit and method, if not the letter, of the Charter, which prescribes that the Security Council should direct the use of collective force. One should not lose sight of the fact, however, that aggression committed or condoned by a great power is unquestionably in defiance of both the Charter's spirit and law.

THE ABSOLUTE WEAPON [28]

When the first atomic bomb exploded over Japan on August 6, 1945, many thought that the Charter had gone up in the smoke of Hiroshima. One observer asked, "Is modern man obsolete?" [29] Eight years later there was still no assurance that the answer was negative. An atomic arms race between the United States and the Soviet Union continued unabated amid warning that there could be no safety for civilization in nuclear warfare.[30]

[28] See Bernard Brodie, ed., *The Absolute Weapon: Atomic Power and World Order* (New York: Harcourt, Brace, 1946).

[29] Norman Cousins, *Modern Man Is Obsolete* (New York: Viking Press, 1945).

[30] J. R. Oppenheimer, "Atomic Weapons and American Policy," *Foreign Affairs*, Vol. 31, No. 4 (May 1953).

Many voices proclaimed that the Charter was obsolete. Some even clamored for world government. But mankind was not yet sufficiently united by a common fear for its safety.

Few governments knew of the existence of atomic weapons during the San Francisco Conference. Indeed, all the delegates appear to have been completely in the dark. One effect of the revelation of atomic energy's destructiveness was a new impetus for disarmament.

Gradually, United States policy unfolded. Three days after the bombing of Hiroshima, President Truman completed the ratification of the Charter. At least there was to be no turning back from the road marked out at San Francisco. A few days later, the President announced to Congress a policy of trusteeship. The atomic bomb was "too dangerous to be loose in a lawless world." Great Britain and the United States did not intend, therefore, to reveal the atomic secret until means were found to "control the bomb so as to protect ourselves and the rest of the world from the danger of total destruction." "We must constitute ourselves trustees of this new force," he told the Congress.[31] As late as October 25, despite considerable public agitation for a policy of international control, he announced again that the United States was holding its knowledge of atomic energy as a "sacred trust." A month later negotiations for the international control of atomic energy were announced. It had become clear that the Charter's security provisions would be meaningless unless steps were taken to curb atomic war. Other nations could scarcely be expected to pin their security on the "sacred trust" of the United States. It was also clear that a short-run monopoly provided only a small margin of safety for the United States. Soon other powers would have the bomb. They, moreover, might be in a position to use it more effectively on the heavily industrialized and democratic United States than vice versa. There remained only a few precious years in which to establish effective international control within the framework of the United Nations.

On November 15, 1945 the President met with British Prime Minister Attlee and Canadian Prime Minister King, and an Agreed Declaration was issued. It was noted that mankind had at its disposal means of destruction hitherto unknown against which there was no adequate military defense and in the employment of which no nation could maintain a monopoly. Safety lay only in the prevention of war and in the maintenance of a rule of law under the United Nations. Therefore, the three governments proposed the establishment of a commission to study the problem of control. It should proceed to work by "separate stages" and make specific proposals:

1. for extending between all nations the exchange of basic scientific information for peaceful ends;

2. for the control of atomic energy to the extent necessary to insure its use only for peaceful purposes;

[31] *The International Control of Atomic Energy: Growth of a Policy,* Department of State Publication 2702 (Washington: Government Printing Office, 1946), p. 11.

3. for the elimination from national armaments of atomic weapons and of all other major weapons adaptable to mass destruction;

4. for effective safeguards by way of inspection and other means to protect complying states against the hazards of violations and evasions.

These principles of action set the guide lines for later action in the United Nations.

In December 1945 the Secretary of State and the Foreign Ministers of the United Kingdom and the Soviet Union met in Moscow and agreed to propose a resolution to establish a United Nations commission on atomic energy. Was the United States about to give up its atomic monopoly prior to "absolute and effective agreement for world-wide inspection and control?" Senator Vandenberg and others thought so because the Moscow communiqué repeated the phrasing of the Agreed Declaration which included the reference to "safeguards" in the fourth and final point. Since he had not been included in the planning for international control, the Senator thought that safeguards would be negotiated at one of the final "stages" after vital information had been shared. Before he was willing to sail for the January meeting of the First Assembly in London, therefore, the Senator wrung assurance from the President and the State Department that adequate security would be part of each stage of disclosure.[32]

The Russians showed very little interest in the matter. The only significant amendment added to the Anglo-American proposals was that, while the General Assembly should establish the proposed commission, the Security Council should issue it directives in matters affecting international peace and security.[33] Meanwhile, France and China, as the two remaining powers on the Security Council, plus Canada, as a contributor to the development of atomic energy, were invited to join in proposing a United Nations atomic energy commission.

The United Nations Atomic Energy Commission

On January 24, 1946 the General Assembly unanimously approved this joint resolution establishing a United Nations Atomic Energy Commission to consist of all governments on the Security Council plus Canada, whether a Security Council member or not. Although created by the General Assembly, the Commission was to report to the Security Council where, as actually proved to be the case, its reports and recommendations could be vetoed. Its terms of reference were precisely those established by the Truman–Attlee–King statement and the Moscow agreement.

Could the United States in good faith make any real proposals to the Commission? A document of classic proportions popularly known as the Acheson–Lilienthal Report provided "a foundation on which to build." [34]

---

[32] Vandenberg, op. cit., pp. 228 and 232–234.

[33] James F. Byrnes, Speaking Frankly (New York: Harper, 1947), p. 267.

[34] A Report on the International Control of Atomic Energy, Department of State Publication 2498 (Washington: Government Printing Office, 1946). Under-Secretary of State Dean Acheson headed a five-member committee which was advised by a Board of Consultants made up of scientists and businessmen under the Chairmanship of David E. Lilienthal, Chairman of the Tennessee Valley Authority.

In simple yet compelling prose it declared that the international control of atomic energy was technically feasible. On June 14, 1946, therefore, the United States presented to the first meeting of the Atomic Energy Commission a plan for the establishment of an international atomic development authority. This proposal was dubbed the Baruch Plan for the United States delegate who proposed it. The Acheson–Lilienthal Report provided the backbone for this plan. It had stated that nations could have no real confidence in inspection (mere "police-like power") or in commitments to "outlaw" the bomb. The problem of "control" was vastly more difficult. Before the United States could yield its head start in atomic weapons, there must be absolute assurance that no nation could prepare to wage atomic war by clandestine means. A principal difficulty was that atomic energy developed for peaceful purposes could easily be directed to military uses. Not until "affirmative powers" were discovered, that could be coupled with inspection, was the control problem reduced to manageable proportions. A helpful factor was the indispensability of uranium, a comparatively rare element, in the manufacture of atomic energy. The United States proposal, therefore, involved a comprehensive and radical control system in which an International Atomic Development Authority would have the power to own, operate, manage, and license all facilities for the production of atomic energy.[35] The outline of the control plan was as follows:

1. An International Atomic Development Authority should conduct continuous surveys of world supplies of uranium and thorium and should control all atomic raw materials. Uranium was the axle around which the control scheme revolved. Its sources were limited and could therefore be centrally controlled all over the globe provided governments would agree. Although the Authority need not own the mines, it would have to be the exclusive owner of the raw materials coming from them.

2. The Authority should control and operate all the plants producing fissionable products in dangerous quantities from uranium and thorium and all plants working with these materials in any significant quantity.

3. The Authority was to possess the exclusive right to conduct research in the field of atomic explosives. Atomic research for peaceful purposes would be conducted by the Authority and by nations under license of the Authority which for this purpose would furnish or license "denatured" materials not suitable for weapons.

4. Dangerous activities of the Authority and its stockpiles should be decentralized and strategically distributed so that no one area might have at its disposal overwhelming sources of power. Protection would then be afforded against the eventuality of sudden seizure by one nation of a stockpile of weapons or atomic plants belonging to the Authority.

5. The Authority was to have freedom to conduct inspections on a continuing basis, including surveys by airplane, without notice to the area inspected, to the extent necessary to enforce the control plan. Since the Authority would own all raw material after it was mined and would operate,

[35] *The International Control of Atomic Energy: Growth of a Policy*, Chap. VI.

if not own, all atomic production facilities, the importance of inspection was considerably reduced though still important.

6. The entire system of international control would be set out in a comprehensive treaty. The Authority should assume its responsibilities and receive information from the United States in a series of "stages" until at the very last it would have control over weapons and the secret data pertaining to them. At this point, national manufacture of atomic weapons would cease and existing weapons would be disposed of according to the treaty.

7. The Authority must have all the power necessary to take prompt and effective action to insure that atomic action was being used solely for peaceful purposes. The Security Council veto must not obstruct the swift punishment of violations of the atomic agreement.[36]

Five days later at the second meeting of the Commission, the Soviet Union presented its own set of proposals (the Gromyko Plan). Envisaged were two international conventions to come into force simultaneously. One would have outlawed atomic weapons; the other would have established a system of control. The Soviet proposals contained the following points:[37]

1. The production or employment of atomic weapons was to be forbidden, and existing stocks of such weapons were to be destroyed within three months after the conventions should come into force.

2. Any violation of the first provision would be "a most serious international crime against humanity."

3. Within six months from the day of the entry into force of the convention each party would enact domestic legislation to punish violations of the international conventions.

4. The convention would be of indefinite duration and would come into force on the approval of the Security Council, including all its permanent members and one-half of the states ratifying the conventions. It would then be binding on all states whether Members of the United Nations or not.

The Soviet delegate also made suggestions for the work of the Atomic Energy Commission. He proposed the establishment of two committees, one to plan the exchange of scientific information and the other to prepare recommendations outlawing and preventing the destructive use of atomic energy.

The two sets of proposals reflect fundamental points of disagreement which have deadlocked the negotiations from that day to this.

First, the Soviets insisted upon the immediate outlawing and destruction of atomic weapons whether the control system were established or not. The United States and soon the majority of both the Commission and the General Assembly were equally insistent that a foolproof control system be established *before* the United States should give up its atomic advantage by destroying weapons or sharing "secrets."

[36] For the U.S. proposals, see *The International Control of Atomic Energy: Growth of a Policy*, Appendix No. 13. Also see speeches by Bernard M. Baruch at the Freedom House Dinner, October 8, 1946 and at the Herald-Tribune Forum, October 29, 1946.
[37] *The International Control of Atomic Energy: Growth of a Policy*, Appendix 22.

Second, the Soviet proposals, in comparison with the Baruch Plan, placed far more stress on national control over the production of atomic energy and national enforcement of the outlaw treaty. Its proposed International Control Commission would have only prescribed supervisory powers instead of complete control and management of the production of atomic energy. In the United States view this proposal would demand the impossible of an inspection system which, therefore, could never provide the requisite security. From their point of view, however, the Russians also felt they were being asked to give up too much. The Soviet delegates stressed repeatedly in the Commission, the Security Council, and the Assembly that the majority plan was a capitalist plot to dominate the Soviet Union by means of an international monopoly in reality controlled by the United States. The rights of sovereign states would be violated by the seizure of atomic production facilities, by unrestricted surveillance from the air, and investigations of industrial installations by international (United States) agents. Where the United States plan called for unlimited authority and right of access for inspection purposes, the minority or Soviet plan insisted on "periodic" and limited inspection.

The third principal difference was more symbolic than real. It involved the question of the veto. For the United States Mr. Baruch in effect proposed an entirely new security and enforcement system. The veto in the Security Council must not be permitted to prevent swift, "condign" punishment in the event of any violation whatsoever of the control arrangements. Mankind, Mr. Baruch announced, was faced with a choice between the "quick and the dead." Since the Soviet Union insisted on retention of the original Charter security system including the principle of big-power unanimity, the result inevitably was a deadlock. This emphasis on punishment was the most marked difference between the Acheson–Lilienthal Report and the Baruch Plan, and appears to have been the product in part of increasing senatorial influence in the atomic energy negotiations.[38]

Some observers felt that this sharp issue, although fundamental, had been introduced too early into the discussions. Would not a violation of the agreement through seizure of facilities or obstruction of international inspection be itself "an instantaneous, dramatic danger signal" that the Consultants had thought would give other nations sufficient time to shift for themselves before weapons could be made? Would not the exercise of the veto itself be a danger signal? The matter boiled down to the question whether the veto itself would really prevent punishment or the taking of security measures by those nations living up to the agreement in the event of violation. Many thought that the control system should at least have been examined further at first in the hope that its possibilities might inspire some measure of mutual confidence among nations. Then the veto problem might recede into the background.

The scope of the United States proposal would have amounted in effect to a considerable measure of world government. The proposed atomic

[38] Vandenberg, op. cit., p. 235.

development authority would have been a source of power and authority unmatched by any other organization on the globe. Mr. Baruch evidently thought it best to come to the heart of the matter at once; hence the veto question from the United States point of view was a test of faith. Were other nations prepared to yield their sovereignty to the extent implied in the majority proposals? If not, the United States would bank its safety on atomic weapons which, in any event, would not be surrendered until the last and final stages in the establishment of the atomic development authority. It is important to remember in this connection that the majority plan is one of the few issues on which nearly all non-Communist members have pretty generally endorsed the United States' position. There was, however, some behind-the-scenes dissatisfaction with American firmness on the veto question.[39]

Obviously, neither the specific veto issue nor the atomic energy problem as a whole can be considered apart from internal politics and governmental procedures. The majority plan and the Soviet proposals were no more soluble than oil and water. Moreover, the fulfillment of the United States proposal depended heavily on action by Congress, which could not be constitutionally bound in advance. Indeed, this latter fact may well explain Baruch's early firmness on the veto issue. The executive could never draw far ahead of its best guess as to what Congress might later approve, and two-thirds of the Senate would have to agree on a control treaty. In addition, the Atomic Energy Act (MacMahon Bill), which became law in August 1946, provided that there should be no international exchange of information regarding the use of atomic energy for industrial purposes "until Congress declares by joint resolution that effective and enforceable international safeguards against the use of atomic energy for destructive purposes have been established."

During the summer of 1946 the Atomic Energy Commission appointed various working committees to consider political as well as scientific and technical aspects of the two proposals. On December 31 the Commission submitted to the Security Council its first report, which it had adopted by a vote of 10 to 0, the U.S.S.R. and Poland abstaining as "unable to be [parties] to any decision on the substance of the United States proposals." This report recommended acceptance of the majority's proposals for the establishment of a comprehensive system of control and inspection under an International Authority. Its specific recommendations followed closely the Baruch Plan already summarized.[40]

The Council considered the Commission's report during February and March 1947 and adopted a resolution instructing it to make further inquiry and report to the Security Council before the next meeting of the General

[39] For an interesting commentary see Frederick Osborn, "Negotiating on Atomic Energy, 1946–47," in R. Dennett and J. E. Johnson, eds., *Negotiating with the Russians* (Boston: World Peace Foundation, 1952).

[40] UN Doc. A/267, December 13, 1946, printed as Appendix IV in *The International Control of Atomic Energy: Policy at the Crossroads*, Department of State Publication 3161 (Washington: Government Printing Office, 1948).

Assembly. Further study during 1947 and 1948 did nothing to break the log jam. In particular, a searching effort was made by several delegations led by the United Kingdom to secure clarification of the Soviet proposals. The replies in regard to such matters as inspection and management were unsatisfactory. A joint report of March 29, 1948 by the United Kingdom, Canada, China and France concluded:

> The Soviet Union proposals are not an acceptable basis for the international control of atomic energy. The United Nations Atomic Energy Commission cannot endorse any scheme which would not prevent the diversion of atomic material, which provides no effective means for the detection of clandestine activities, and which has no provision for prompt and effective enforcement action. The Soviet Union government has not only proposed a scheme that is fundamentally inadequate for the control of atomic energy, but at the same time has made the overriding stipulation they will not agree to establish even such a feeble scheme of control until all atomic weapons have been prohibited and destroyed. It is completely unrealistic to expect any nation to renounce atomic weapons without any assurance that all nations will be prevented from producing them.[41]

In the General Assembly, proposals to suspend the work of the Commission were rejected by the smaller powers, and instead a resolution was passed in November 1948 which:

> 1. requested the Atomic Energy Commission to continue its deliberations;
> 2. asked the six members of the permanent Commission to continue the search for agreements;
> 3. approved the majority proposals (substantially the Baruch Plan) as constituting a basis for establishing an effective system of international control and expressed deep concern at the deadlock in the Commission.

The forced resumption of the Commission's work in 1949 brought no success. News of an atomic explosion in the Soviet Union and the imminent development of super (hydrogen or "fusion") bombs did nothing to relieve the jam. An atomic arms race was under way in earnest.

The Fourth Assembly (1949) sought to keep hope alive by stating its position of the previous year. Special appeals to the Atomic Energy Commission's permanent members by the Assembly's President, Carlos Romulo, were of no avail. Negotiations were suspended in 1950 when the Soviet Union refused to participate in any United Nations meetings with the Nationalist Delegation of China. Meanwhile, the control of atomic weapons became ensnarled with the equally frustrating but less spectacular problem of regulating conventional armaments.

CONVENTIONAL ARMAMENTS — THE 1946 ASSEMBLY RESOLUTION

The United Nations' first attempt to regulate "conventional armaments," as opposed to weapons of "mass destruction," was the result of Soviet initia-

[41] *Yearbook of the United Nations, 1947–48*, p. 470.

tive. In October 1946 Mr. Molotov introduced a resolution in the General Assembly which favored a general reduction of armaments.[42]

The United States, on the other hand, was determined to keep atomic energy discussions separate from other armaments negotiations. For a revolutionary weapon the United States had already advanced a revolutionary control plan which might be weakened if all armaments were considered together. Accordingly, Ambassador Austin advanced a counterproposal which was acceptable to Mr. Molotov. As a result, the General Assembly, on December 14, 1946, unanimously passed a resolution on the "General Principles Governing the Regulation and Reduction of National Armaments." Its provisions included the following points:

1. The Security Council should formulate practical measures for regulating armaments, including a "general progressive and balanced reduction of national armed forces."

2. The Security Council should expedite the work of the Atomic Energy Commission for the prohibition of atomic weapons and the establishment of safeguards for states complying with the prohibition.

3. Agreements regarding armed forces under Article 43 should be completed.

4. Armed forces of Members outside their own territories should be withdrawn as rapidly as possible.

5. An international system of control including regulation, inspection, and reduction of armaments and the special organs to enforce the system should be established within the Security Council's framework.

Three important principles were established by this resolution. First, disarmament was considered in the general setting of regulating the use of force. Second, the control of atomic weapons was separated from the regulation of other weapons. Third, stress was put on international inspection in any regulation system.

Following the Assembly's mandate, the Security Council established a Commission for Conventional Armaments in February 1947 consisting of the governments represented on the Council. On United States insistence, it limited its discussion to armaments other than weapons of mass destruction, which were defined to include atomic, chemical, and biological weapons. The United States, however, failed in its effort to have the Council discuss atomic energy before considering conventional weapons. The new commission in August 1948 agreed on the following principles for regulating arms, by vote of 9 to 2, the Soviet Union opposed:

1. A system to regulate and reduce armaments could be inaugurated only in an atmosphere of international confidence and security.

2. Such a system required the establishment of armed forces under Article 43.

3. A system for the international control of atomic energy would have to be in operation.

[42] *International Control of Atomic Energy: Policy at the Crossroads*, p. 39.

4. Peace treaties with Germany and Japan would have to be concluded.

5. Armaments should then be reduced to the levels required by Articles 43 and 51 (self-defense) of the Charter.

6. Provision must be made for international supervision of the regulation system.

7. Provision must be made for effective enforcement.

The next inning in a game already growing stale was the proposal by Foreign Minister Molotov to the General Assembly in September 1948 that, as a first step, the permanent members of the Security Council should reduce by one-third during one year all existing land, naval, and air forces and that atomic weapons should be prohibited. An international control commission, only vaguely outlined, was to insure compliance. It was a skillful grandstand play. But the Western powers soon had their innings. The Assembly did not adopt the Molotov proposal, but instead resolved in December 1949 that the Commission for Conventional Armaments should study the question and, in addition, propose methods for obtaining and verifying information from Member governments regarding their armed forces and conventional armaments as a first step toward control. The Security Council was to report to the General Assembly on such recommendations. When the Security Council considered this proposal, the Soviet Union vetoed the Commission's suggestion for obtaining information on armaments. The Soviet Union was checkmated since it was unwilling to have information regarding its armed forces disclosed to the world while at the same time it failed to secure approval in the Council (February 1949) for the plan that had already been rejected by the Assembly.

The Fourth Assembly in 1949 approved the Commission's recommendations for disclosure and verification and at the same time noted the lack of unanimity among the big powers. It urged the Security Council to continue its study through its Commission. During the Assembly's discussion the U.S.S.R. charged that the "Anglo-American bloc" had refused to reduce armaments, was maintaining an artificial division between atomic and other weapons, and was extending a system of strategic bases and military alliances. France, Norway, the United Kingdom and the United States replied that arms could not be reduced until the international control of atomic energy was achieved and means of verifying all weapons established.

A Fresh Move

Paradoxically, the next effort for disarmament was taken in the midst of the Korean war, when the Atlantic Pact countries were feverishly rearming in the hope of becoming strong enough to prevent further attack on the non-Communist world. The United States was now ready to yield a point, albeit a small one. In October 1950 President Truman addressed the General Assembly and, among other matters, suggested that it would be useful to explore means of bringing the work of the Atomic Energy Commission and the Commission on Conventional Armaments more closely together "through a new and consolidated disarmament commission." [43] This shift did not mean that the United States was yielding on the point that an atomic control system must operate free of the Security Council veto. It simply meant that agreement on the control plan would require big-power unanimity. After the plan was in effect, it must operate free of the veto. In response, the General Assembly appointed in December 1950 a Committee of Twelve consisting of the Security Council members plus Canada to report on the advisability of establishing such a disarmament commission.

The Disarmament Resolution of January 11, 1952

A recommendation of the Committee of Twelve that a new body, the Commission for the Control of Armaments and Armed Forces, replace the two Commissions on Atomic Energy and Conventional Armaments was adopted by the Sixth Assembly on January 11, 1952. Based on the proposals of France, the United Kingdom and the United States, the resolution was passed 42 to 5 with 7 abstentions.[44] The negative votes were cast by the Soviet bloc. The Soviet Union failed to secure approval of amendments which repeated her previous views. Among those abstaining were some members of the Arab-Asian bloc and Argentina. Egypt said the bomb should have been outlawed. India, Indonesia and Argentina explained their abstentions by saying that the big powers had not agreed on the fundamentals essential to any disarmament proposal. Some of these countries felt that both sides should share the blame for the deadlock. Unlike many of the powers voting with the majority, they did not feel that their security depended to any great extent on the military strength of the West.

The resolution terminated the two previous commissions and established a Disarmament Commission composed of the now-familiar combination of the Security Council members plus Canada. The new commission was directed to prepare a draft treaty concerning:

1. regulation, limitation, and balanced reduction of all armed forces and all armaments;

2. elimination of all major weapons adaptable to mass destruction;

3. effective international control of atomic energy to insure the prohibition of atomic weapons and the use of atomic energy for peaceful purposes only, with the present United Nations plan being used as the basis for the Commission's considerations until a better or no less effective plan were devised;

4. progressive and continuing disclosure and verification of all armed forces and all armaments, including atomic, the implementation of such a scheme being recognized as a first and indispensable step in carrying out the disarmament program;

5. methods of fixing over-all limits and restrictions on all armed forces and armaments, and for determining the allocation within their respective

[43] *Yearbook of the United Nations, 1950,* p. 416.
[44] *Yearbook of the United Nations, 1951,* p. 176.

military establishments of the permitted national armed forces and armaments;

6. the establishment of an international control organ to insure the implementation of the treaty; and

7. an adequate system of safeguards to insure observance of the disarmament program.[45]

The Disarmament Commission

Despite the change of scene, negotiations remained deadlocked. On April 24, 1952, the United States presented a working paper stating the "Essential Principles for a Disarmament Program." [46] Behind this paper, as behind the new United States proposals generally, was the necessity of answering the Soviet charges that the Western powers were not interested in arms reduction since they had spurned the Soviet's one-third reduction proposal and the immediate outlawing of atomic weapons. The principles of the working paper may be summarized as follows:

> First, the goal of disarmament was "to prevent war by relaxing tensions and fears created by armaments and by making war inherently, as it is constitutionally under the Charter, impossible as a means of settling disputes between nations." [47]
>
> Second, armaments must be reduced to levels no higher than necessary for the maintenance of internal order and the fulfillment of security obligations under the Charter.
>
> Third, there must be a "comprehensive and coordinate disarmament program, balanced throughout the process of reduction so as to avoid any disequilibrium of power dangerous to the peace. . . . " This point emphasized the fact that, if the United States had a superior strategic air force, the elimination of strategic bombers would increase the relative strength of the U.S.S.R. The elimination of atomic weapons and a one-third reduction of armaments generally would have the very same effect.
>
> Fourth, effective safeguards must be enforced at all stages of the disarmament program.
>
> Fifth, such safeguards must include an "effective system of progressive and continuing disclosure and verification of all armed forces and armaments, including atomic, to achieve the open world in which alone there can be effective disarmament." This, it will be recalled, had proved a sticking point so far as the Soviet Union was concerned.

Disclosure and Verification

In the United States plan, five stages of disclosure were suggested, proceeding from the less secret to the most secret information, since "no state

---

[45] See *Yearbook of the United Nations, 1951*, pp. 176–177, and the summary in the *Report to the President by the Deputy United States Representative on the United Nations Disarmament Commission*, Department of State press release, January 14, 1953, No. 24.

[46] *Report to the President on Disarmament*, p. 8.

[47] *Ibid.*, p. 9.

would tear the veil of secrecy from its most carefully guarded security arrangements until it could be satisfied that all states are proceeding with the same good faith and the same understanding and at the same pace." First, there would be the disclosure "in breadth, although not in depth, [of] the general contours of the military establishment of all nations." The final stage would provide "detailed disclosure of . . . novel armaments [those not in general use in World War II] themselves and of atomic weapons."

The Soviet delegation characterized the verification proposal as a gigantic intelligence and espionage operation bearing no relation to disarmament. Despite the fact that the United States proposals were now more liberal than they had been in 1946, the Soviets also objected that atomic disclosures were left to a final and indefinite stage.

Ceilings on All Armed Forces

In May 1952 three powers, the United States, the United Kingdom and France, submitted proposals to fix numerical limits on all armed forces. Equal maximum ceilings of between 1,000,000 and 1,500,000 men were to be established for the United States, the U.S.S.R., and China, and between 700,000 and 800,000 for the United Kingdom and France. Ceilings for other powers would be agreed upon later. At all times any dangerous disequilibrium of power was to be avoided. The three governments expressed the hope that a reduction of such magnitude would lessen the likelihood of armed conflict. They noted that an existing imbalance of forces in the world at large was promoting a sense of insecurity. In this way the Western powers met the Soviet challenge of a one-third arms reduction plus prohibition of atomic weapons. The proposals, however, probably represented a greater sacrifice in strength for the Communist powers than they did for the three Western powers. In any event, the Soviets rejected the suggestions as not dealing with the distribution of permitted forces among the various armed services. This is an argument similar to the one advanced in the negotiations dealing with armed forces under Article 43. The Western powers then turned to meet this argument.

Distribution and Limitations on Types and Quantities

In August the Western powers suggested that the permitted armed forces be distributed by agreement among the principal categories of forces and that the types and quantities of armaments permitted be defined. All other weapons were to be eliminated. Regional arrangements were suggested as a means of providing similar limitations on the forces of other powers. Enforcement would involve an international control authority with broad powers. The Soviet Union was not impressed.

Atomic Energy Control

The General Assembly had directed the Disarmament Commission to consider the majority proposals, now called the United Nations Plan, as the basis for its deliberations until a better plan were devised. Although the

HAGUE CONFERENCES 1899-1907

EXPRESSIONS OF
PIOUS HOPE FOR
DISARMAMENT

WORLD WAR I 1914-1918

LEAGUE OF NATIONS 1918

GERMANY WAS DISARMED B
GENERAL DISARMAMENT W
ONLY AN EMPTY PROMISE

PAX

United States said that it did not regard the plan as immutable, no fresh suggestions were forthcoming. The U.S.S.R. continued to object to the ownership and other control features of the majority plan, contending that control should involve only continuous inspection.

The Elimination of Bacteriological Weapons

The discussions on this issue were quickly poisoned by charges and countercharges regarding germ warfare in the Korean war. The Soviets insisted in the very first meeting of the Disarmament Commission that the United States was conducting germ warfare in both Korea and China. This attack had been carried to the Assembly and the Security Council as well. The charges were vigorously denied by the United States and the other nations fighting under the United Nations command in Korea. The United States explained that it had not ratified the Geneva Protocol outlawing germ warfare because that agreement only prohibited such warfare without providing means of enforcing the prohibition. Proposals for impartial Red Cross investigations had been vetoed in the Security Council by the Soviet Union.

"Phantom Proposals"

At the Seventh Assembly in the fall of 1952, Poland, evidently in answer to the Western powers' proposals in the Disarmament Commission and the Assembly, reintroduced the Soviet proposals of the previous year. The United States called them "phantom" or ghost proposals, as they were without real substance, yet prone to reappear at every Assembly session. They included the one-third reduction of forces and the unconditional prohibi-

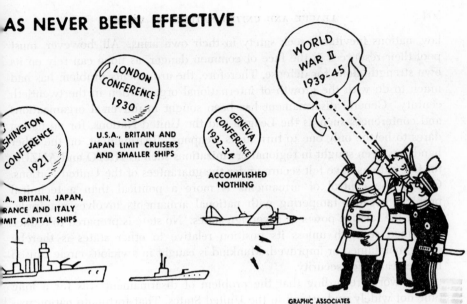

WASHINGTON CONFERENCE 1921

LONDON CONFERENCE 1930

GENEVA CONFERENCE 1932-34

WORLD WAR II 1939-45

U.S.A., BRITAIN AND JAPAN LIMIT CRUISERS AND SMALLER SHIPS

U.S.A., BRITAIN, JAPAN, FRANCE AND ITALY LIMIT CAPITAL SHIPS

ACCOMPLISHED NOTHING

GRAPHIC ASSOCIATES

Headline Series, *Foreign Policy Association*

tion of atomic and other weapons of mass destruction. Enforcement was to be by strict international control and inspection that, however, was not to interfere in the domestic affairs of states. The Western powers continued to emphasize that without international ownership of atomic facilities an unbearable load would be placed on inspection. Detailed questions regarding the Soviet proposals from the British and Canadian delegations brought the answer that there was "some conspiracy among delegations not willing to discuss the question of the prohibition of atomic weapons. . . ."

After fruitless discussion, the Assembly in April 1953 voted to reaffirm its resolution of January 1952 and to ask the Disarmament Commission to keep on trying.[48] It was obvious that the course of the negotiations would be influenced as much by such events as Stalin's death, the Korean truce, and Soviet progress in developing hydrogen bombs as they would be by discussions in the Disarmament Commission. The brightest ray of hope in 1953 was President Eisenhower's proposal, personally presented to the General Assembly on December 8, to explore the creation of a world pool of fissionable material to be utilized for peaceful purposes.

Conclusions

Armaments control is really part of a wider problem — the organization and control of force in the world community. In the absence of effective collective security, which implies a large measure of world government and

[48] *The New York Times*, April 9, 1953.

law, nations inevitably seek safety in their own arms. All, however, must pool their resources in the face of common danger, as none can rely on its own strength alone for defense. Therefore, the armaments problem has had much to do with the growth of international organization in the twentieth century. General disarmament has been sought in universal organizations and conferences such as the League and the United Nations, for no nation dares to be the only one to turn in its weapons. Rearmament, on the other hand, has been sought in regional organizations such as NATO and ANZUS, for few nations have felt secure under the guarantees of the United Nations. Clearly the control of armaments is more a political than a technical problem because tampering with national armaments involves manipulation of the relative power of sovereign states. No state is prepared to reduce its armed strength unless its position relative to other states is thereby either maintained or improved. Mankind is caught in a vicious circle caused by the search for security.

It is worth recording that the problem of disarmament was for a long time not widely understood in the United States. That fortunate nation was able to pursue its own "manifest destiny" somewhat apart from the areas of world conflict. The Canadian-American border has remained demilitarized since 1818 principally because there has been no real struggle for power between the United States and Britain or between the United States and Canada. As a result, armaments were often thought by Americans to be one aspect of a degenerate system of European "power politics" from which the United States was immune.

It should also be noted that the disarmament picture has both a front and a back. While the anxiety attending an armaments race is doubtless a factor that contributed to many wars, unilateral disarmament may encourage war. The natural disinclination of the democracies to arm or to take strong measures in the League period played right into the hands of the dictators. At Munich democratic diplomacy had little power behind it, and ultimately there was no recourse to deal with Hitler but war itself.[49] Therefore, the disarmament discussions in the League and the United Nations inevitably involve "safeguards," "security," and "sanctions." An armament race is evidence that there are values, whether real or fictitious, for which men can be persuaded to fight to the death. It is also evidence that international politics, unlike domestic politics, is a struggle with few governmental or legal restraints.

Although disarmament discussions did involve jockeying for propaganda and military advantage, they were not necessarily advanced in bad faith. A new dimension had been added to the problem — the capacity of man to destroy himself. This, of course, is not really a novel ability. A matter of degree is involved. The change is that man can destroy himself more efficiently than ever before. A concomitant factor is that super-weapons provide larger temptations for the power-crazed and the insecure. There is

[49] See H. J. Morgenthau, *Politics Among Nations, The Struggle for Power and Peace* (New York: Knopf, 1948), Chap. XXI.

WE CAN DISARM WHEN · · · ·

1 OTHER COUNTRIES AGREE TO DISARM

2 INTERNATIONAL INSPECTION IS ACCEPTED

3 COLLECTIVE SECURITY PROTECTS EACH NATION

Headline Series, *Foreign Policy Association*

no doubt that much of the reawakened concern for disarmament stems from the sheer horror with which mankind regards its own handiwork. Although the problem of world order should be attacked on as many fronts as possible, armaments, it should be remembered, are not of themselves the cause of differences and principles for which men are prepared to sacrifice their lives. Disarmament will be possible and, indeed, wise only when there is an effective alternative to the present system of national arms.

Suggestions for Further Reading

Books

Atomic Energy, Its International Implications (New York: Oxford University Press, 1948).

Brodie, Bernard, ed., *The Absolute Weapon: Atomic Power and World Order* (New York: Harcourt, Brace and Company, 1946).

Fox, W. T. R., *The Struggle for Atomic Control,* Public Affairs Pamphlet No. 129 (New York: Public Affairs Comm., Inc., 1947).

Madariaga, Salvador de, *Disarmament* (New York: Coward-McCann, 1929).

Newman, J. R., and Miller, B. S., *The Control of Atomic Energy* (New York: McGraw-Hill Book Company, Inc., 1948).

Smyth, H. D., *Account of the Development of Methods of Using Atomic Energy for Military Purposes* (Princeton: Princeton University Press, 1945).

Tate, M., *The Disarmament Illusion* (New York: The Macmillan Company, 1942).

————, *The United States and Armaments* (Cambridge: Harvard University Press, 1952).

Wheeler-Bennett, J. W., *The Pipe Dream of Peace* (New York: William Morrow & Co., 1935).

————, *Disarmament and Security Since Locarno, 1925–31* (London: G. Allen & Unwin Ltd., 1932).

Woodward, E., *Some Political Consequences of the Atomic Bomb* (London: Oxford University Press, 1946).

Periodicals

Oppenheimer, J. Robert, "Atomic Weapons and American Policy," *Foreign Affairs,* Vol. 31, No. 4 (May 1953).

"The UN Atomic Energy Commission," *International Conciliation,* No. 430 (April 1947).

Urey, H. C., "Atomic Energy in International Politics," *Foreign Policy Reports,* Vol. 22, No. 7 (1946).

Documents

International Control of Atomic Energy: Growth of a Policy, Department of State Publication 2702 (Washington: U.S. Government Printing Office, 1946).

International Control of Atomic Energy: Policy at the Crossroads, Department of State Publication 3161 (Washington: U.S. Government Printing Office, 1948).

International Control of Atomic Energy and the Prohibition of Atomic Weapons, Department of State Publication 3646 (Washington: U.S. Government Printing Office, 1949).

Report on the International Control of Atomic Energy (known as the Acheson–Lilienthal Report), Department of State Publication 2498 (Washington: U.S. Government Printing Office, 1946).

Report to the President by the Deputy United States Representative on the United States Disarmament Commission, Department of State Release No. 24, January 14, 1953.

The Third Report of the United Nations Atomic Energy Commission to the Security Council, UN Doc. AEC/31/Rev. 1, June 27, 1948.

United Nations, Atomic Energy Commission, *Official Records,* 1946–1949.

17

Economic Cooperation — League

ONE OF THE BITTER THESES which John Maynard Keynes, the brilliant and impatient young British economist, "nailed on the door" of the Paris Peace Conference in 1919 was that

> the Treaty includes no provision for the economic rehabilitation of Europe. . . . It is an extraordinary fact that the fundamental economic problem of a Europe starving and disintegrating before their eyes was the one question in which it was impossible to arouse the interest of the [Council of] Four.[1]

While somewhat overheated by the temper of the times, this statement is evidence of the most significant circumstance that cast its shadow over all the League's economic activities: business and governmental leaders of the major countries were not yet willing to sacrifice any appreciable degree of national independence to solve the world's economic problems. While the United States tended to be the most conservative on this score, it is also doubtful whether the British and French were really prepared to surrender much more sovereignty, except in connection with binding up the immediate wounds of wartime destruction and dislocation. Not only was the economic mandate of the Covenant extremely limited, but the League itself, under the leadership of the major powers, was decidedly cautious in undertaking any economic activities except where the benefit to the larger states was obvious and the cost slight. It is also important to understand the general pattern of these interwar activities and recognize their relation to other political, economic and social forces at work in the world at the time before examining specific projects. This experience can be divided roughly into two approximately equal periods: the years of painful but gradual ascent — 1920 to 1929 — and the years of tragic, precipitous decline — 1929 to 1939.[2]

[1] *The Economic Consequences of the Peace* (New York: Harcourt, Brace and Howe, 1920), p. 226.
[2] The best sources on this subject are: Martin Hill, *The Economic and Financial Organization of the League of Nations* (Washington: Carnegie Endowment for International Peace, 1946); H. R. G. Greaves, *The League Committees and World Order*

General Interwar Pattern

Towards Recovery, 1920–29

In 1920 the combatants of World War I were still thoroughly exhausted as a result of their recent struggle. With the outstanding exception of the United States, most of them were starved for want of essential imports which they lacked the means to pay for, bent double with war debts which they had no hope of repaying, wracked by violent economic and political fluctuations both internally and externally, obviously dependent upon each other and yet deeply distrustful. While this sickness was widespread, the most complete paralysis was to be found in Central and Southeastern Europe where national economies were the least self-sufficient and political and economic nationalism the most intense.

Since the United States had refused to participate in any joint relief organization comparable to the Allied system which had existed during the war, major relief and reconstruction efforts remained outside the League in the hands of individual governmental and private agencies.[3] Moreover, the amount of aid furnished by governments was relatively modest (approximately $800 million as compared with $3.7 billion given through the UN Relief and Rehabilitation Administration alone after World War II), and most of it was made available through sales or loans, rather than grants. What the United States was not paid for in dollars, it advanced as loans to the extent of $194 million, 94 per cent of which was later defaulted.[4]

Many observers thought that the debtor countries should have allowed their currencies to depreciate as a means of attracting foreign customers and increasing their exports. But they chose instead, with few exceptions, to erect barriers in order to restrain imports, to conserve scarce exchange, to protect war-built industries, to encourage further industrial development for both military security and the absorption of surplus agricultural populations, to gain bargaining power in negotiations for trade concessions from other countries, and to retaliate against those nations that refused to negotiate.

Contrary to European hopes, the leading postwar creditor nation, the United States, refused to ease the situation by lowering its own barriers in order to enable Europeans to earn the exchange they needed to restock

(London: Oxford University Press, 1931); Michael Heilperin, "Economic and Financial Issues," *World Organization* (Washington: American Council on Public Affairs, 1942); Henry F. Grady, "World Economics," *Pioneers in World Order* (New York: Columbia University Press, 1944); Wallace McClure, *World Prosperity* (New York: Macmillan, 1933); Linden A. Mander, *Foundations of Modern World Society* (Stanford: Stanford University Press, 1947); League of Nations, *Ten Years of World Cooperation* (Geneva: League Secretariat, 1930); and other League documents cited on page 512 below.

[3] See pp. 159–160.

[4] H. W. V. Temperley, ed., *A History of the Peace Conference of Paris* (London: Henry Frowde and Hodder & Stoughton, 1920), Vol. 1, Chap. 8, Part 2; Winifred N. Hadsel, "United States Relief for Europe in World War I," *Foreign Policy Reports*, Vol. 19, No. 1 (March 15, 1943).

their empty larders. On the contrary, the United States infuriated Europe by enacting the protectionist Emergency Tariff of 1921 and the Tariff Act of 1922 because American farmers and industrialists alike were unable to sell at the volume to which they had adjusted their production during the war, and because American leadership in general, long accustomed to thinking in debtor rather than in creditor terms, thought that an export surplus was next to godliness.

Climate of Economic Thought. In order to understand the unhappy road which the League trod, one must recall the basic assumptions with which that road was paved. The most fundamental idea prevalent at the time was that it was both possible and desirable to return to the "normal" prewar economic pattern. A corollary of this was that there should be a minimum of government regulation, national or international. It was assumed that most economic matters lay within the domestic rather than the international sphere and thus outside the League's bailiwick. This resulted in heavy emphasis on "bootstrap thinking" — the doctrine that economic recovery and development would come about almost entirely through self-help on the part of each separate state, largely in the form of monetary and trade reforms.

Conference after conference urged nations to return to the orthodox economic faith: to reduce spending, balance budgets, get back on the gold standard and lower trade barriers. They gave little thought to using international channels to help cushion the impact of the deflationary policies they recommended or assist in capital reconstruction and development. It was assumed that if certain traditional monetary and trade rituals were observed, the world's economic machinery would automatically hum along at a brisk pace. This faith was badly shaken by the great depression, however, when alarming economic, social and political upheavals led the economists to give greater attention to those parts of the machinery which caused the greatest social misery. Only then was the maintenance of a high and stable level of employment placed before balanced budgets and the gold standard.

Activities in the Twenties. Within this environment, the League took its first major step in the economic field at the 1920 Brussels International Financial Conference, the first of four principal conferences that punctuated the League's interwar economic experience. In keeping with the general tendency then prevalent to try to protect "technical" discussions from the blight of politics, and because the conference was intended merely to give advice, its delegates, though appointed by governments, spoke as individual experts rather than as governmental representatives. Unfortunately they did little more than deplore the chaos which they saw about them and urge that each country reaffirm its faith in reason, traditional economics and frugal self-help. Although the world's economic leaders nodded approvingly at the Conference's brave display of orthodox sanity, governments made no major move to implement the recommendations, except to a limited degree in the monetary field.

The second major gathering was the International Economic Conference held at Genoa in April 1922. Although it was organized in close collaboration with the League, it was convoked under the aegis of the Supreme Economic Council in order to facilitate the participation of leading non-League members, particularly the United States, the Soviet Union and Germany. While the supply situation had suddenly changed from famine to feast, most European countries did not have the exchange to buy what they needed. The Conference recommendations implored these nations to restore the prewar freedom and stability of trade relations.

In spite of seemingly insuperable obstacles, however, Europe, with the League's help, was able gradually to get its battered economic machinery moving again during the years 1922 to 1929. League loans were arranged for Austria and Hungary in 1922 and 1924, respectively. A far more important factor in restoring economic vigor was the Dawes Plan of 1924, formulated outside the League framework, to ease the payment of German reparations. This was especially encouraging since it was the first major postwar step taken by the United States to provide positive leadership in world economic matters. About the same time, the European allies finally agreed upon arrangements to pay their war debts to the United States, though on terms which they considered quite unfair. In the wake of these plans, large sums of private credit began to flow across national boundaries, particularly from the United States to Europe. Then Great Britain stabilized its currency in 1925; France, in 1926; and Italy, in 1927. Finally, the formalization of the Locarno treaties in 1925 provided a healthier political climate for this economic recovery.

It was on the crest of this wave that France made its proposal in September 1925, which led eventually to the calling of the third major interwar economic conference, The World Economic Conference, held at Geneva in May 1927. Against a background of relative prosperity and excellent staff preparation, the Conference's expert delegates from fifty countries, the largest gathering of its kind up to that time, met in an atmosphere of cautious optimism and made the same kind of recommendations that had been made before. Not only did influential organizations, such as the International Chamber of Commerce, endorse this program, but France and Germany signed a Commercial Treaty in August 1927 which marked France's return to the most-favored-nation policy. A series of other negotiations, however, failed to produce any startling results.

Collapse and Stagnation, 1929–39

In 1929 the pestilence of the great depression fell upon a world still weak from the ravages of war. As early as the summer of 1928 the net flow of capital from the United States to Europe began to diminish and exchange reservoirs abroad started to shrink. The pinch came first in an excess of supply over demand in agricultural exports during 1929. Then the American boom came to an end with the resounding stock market crash in October 1929. Tariff walls were hastily raised, particularly after the enactment of the extremely protectionist United States Smoot–Hawley Tariff which cast its ominous shadow over the world during all of 1929. although it was not finally passed until 1930. A financial crisis, which began with the virtual failure of the Austrian Kredit-Anstalt Bank in the summer of 1931, led to balance-of-payments difficulties in most European countries, a rash of currency depreciation, and a desperate dosage of exchange controls. At the depth of the depression in 1932, over twenty-five million industrial workers throughout the world were unemployed, demoralized, and willing to try almost any nostrum, political or economic, to regain their security.

In a futile attempt to stem this flood of catastrophe the League called the fourth and last major interwar economic conference, the London Monetary and Economic Conference of 1933. The delegates to this meeting acted as governmental representatives, rather than as independent experts, and the scope of the staff preparation was less extensive than it had been for the previous gatherings. While a determined effort was made at last to view monetary and trade problems as interdependent parts of a single economic structure, the erosion that had already taken place had washed away any real basis for agreement. France wanted monetary stabilization before commercial liberalization, Great Britain wanted commercial liberalization before monetary stabilization, and the United States wanted neither. The Conference finally adjourned without adopting any major conclusions.

In spite of this serious defeat, the League refused to give way entirely. Instead, it changed its tactics. Having found it difficult to persuade large numbers of states to agree upon binding conventions, the League tended, after 1933, to work with smaller groups of nations that were particularly concerned with specific problems. It also began to formulate recommendations not as conventions but as models for bilateral treaties, standards for domestic legislation, or studies to leaven national policies.

Under the impact of the depression, the League also explored new substantive areas: greater emphasis on the interaction rather than the isolation of such economic matters as monetary and trade problems; increased concern with investment and employment in keeping with new developments in economic thinking; an interest in issues particularly related to the depression such as nutrition, housing, and the basic causes of depressions; and a recognition of the direct relationship between domestic and international problems as well as the necessity for dealing with both aspects simultaneously.

In spite of these efforts to hold the fort against total economic anarchy, the League's activities proved to be "too little, too late." One observer described the frustration that permeated Geneva in the last years as follows:

Conferences have been prepared, called, held and adjourned, new advisory bodies have been set up, consulted and dismissed, new inquiries have been instituted and their findings discarded. . . . Strong resolutions have even been voted and promising conventions discussed, sometimes adopted, more seldom ratified, and still less often put in force. But never has it been found possible or expedient to take any firm collective action with a view resolutely to break down those barriers between nations which all are equally unanimous in denouncing in their neighbors and in multiplying and raising at their own frontiers.[5]

Furthermore, economic chaos exacerbated political problems and vice versa. One has only to look at the first major postwar aggression by Japan against Manchuria in 1931 to see the close interaction between depression and aggression. Economic pressures sharpened age-old ambitions to gain new material resources, markets, and populations as the basis for greater political and economic power. At the same time, the depression weakened the strength and morale of the Western powers to resist. And so crisis spawned crisis from Manchuria in 1931 to Poland in 1939.

As the League economic program virtually perished in the flames of World War II, however, a new program was being born, though few people were aware of it at the time. Efforts were quietly being made, between 1939 and 1945, in special research projects undertaken at Geneva, Princeton, Montreal, and other havens of refuge, to study the past in order to build firm foundations for the future. As one reads these reports today — *The Transition from War to Peace Economy;* [6] *Commercial Policy in the Interwar Period;* [7] *Food, Famine, and Relief;* [8] *Economic Stability in the Postwar World;* [9] and *International Currency Experience* [10] — it becomes apparent not only how far the League had travelled since 1919 but also how directly these studies helped to shape the thinking of those who built the United Nations.

Reconstruction and Development

One of the first concerns after World War I was to give credit transfusions to countries which had been especially injured by the war, particularly the Siamese twins, Austria and Hungary, which, having been sawed apart by the Peace Treaty, refused to cooperate economically with each other or with any other neighboring countries in the Balkan jungle. The first financial reconstruction loan, made to Austria in June 1923, was a credit of £26 million raised by public subscription in the markets of ten different countries and guaranteed, not by the League, but by eight European states in varying proportions. In return, Austria promised to establish her currency on a gold basis, organize a central bank of issue under specified con-

---

[5] William E. Rappard, "Post-war Efforts for Freer Trade," *Geneva Studies,* Vol. 9, No. 2 (March 1938), p. 30.
[6] Geneva, 1943, II. Economic and Financial, 1943, II. A. 3.
[7] Geneva, 1942, II. Economic and Financial, 1942, II. A. 6.
[8] Geneva, 1946, II. Economic and Financial, 1946, II. A. 5.
[9] Geneva, 1945, II. Economic and Financial, 1945, II. A. 2.
[10] Geneva, 1944, II. Economic and Financial, 1944, II. A. 4.

ditions, balance her budget, and undertake a long-term program of retrenchment. This was to be done under the supervision and with the advice of a resident League Commissioner General who reported periodically to the Financial Committee. A similar loan was made to Hungary in 1924, and further credits were raised later under League auspices to aid Greece, Bulgaria, Estonia and Danzig.

The fundamental contribution of this loan program was that it provided some credit at reasonable interest rates and helped to provide a limited measure of temporary solvency. It was also a notable pioneering step in multilateral financial assistance. At the same time, it suffered from serious shortcomings — primarily a failure to establish healthy trading relations in Central and Southeast Europe and a reliance on limited monetary reorganization rather than on a broader reform program affecting production, distribution, standards of living and investment.

Technical Assistance and Development

Before the League, economic development was assumed to be the responsibility of each individual nation with credit raised through private channels and a minimum of international governmental cooperation. It was a most significant experiment, therefore, when the Financial Committee combined technical assistance and supervision with the issuance of reconstruction credits. When the depression struck in the thirties, the League placed increasing emphasis on technical assistance, especially since it had no funds to dispense.

> In some cases, what was wanted was an authoritative opinion of experts; in others, evidence on methods and results. The . . . [League] enjoyed the unique advantage of having immediate access to the best sources of information and the ready and voluntary assistance of leading experts from almost every country in the world.[11]

Advice was provided on taxation, central banks, credit control, agricultural credit, nutrition, transportation and housing.

The Economic and Financial Organization also planned a European Conference on the Problems of Rural Life, to be held in October 1939, and based its preparations on the fact that all parts of the world's economic machinery are interrelated.

> Without adequate nutrition or housing accommodation, without suitable education, without an increase in the purchasing power of the poorer classes — itself an immense problem raising questions such as land tenure systems and agrarian reform, land settlement, cooperative systems, and agricultural credit — no great results could be expected from the provision of dispensaries or other services lying within the competence of Ministries of Health.[12]

But World War II broke out in September 1939, and the conference was never held. Still, the League had made progress since 1919. No longer was it content merely to give limited advice in one or two narrowly circumscribed

[11] Hill, *op. cit.*, p. 75.   [12] *Ibid.*, p. 92.

fields in order to return to conditions of the past. At the end of its existence, the League was beginning to promote broad development as well as reconstruction. But still the League never undertook to raise funds itself nor did it initiate any major development of underdeveloped areas. Yet a statement in its 1942 report on *Commercial Policy in the Interwar Period: International Proposals and National Policies* was particularly far-sighted:

> The problem constituted by the multiplicity of small and poor economic units in Central and Eastern Europe . . . was extremely complex and purely economic measures could only have made a partial contribution to its solution. Among such economic measures, however, the primary need was for a constructive plan to facilitate the development of their industries and for help in the execution of that plan. Since no action along these lines was initiated, it is understandable that the agricultural countries were unwilling to take the risk involved in any liberalization of their tariff policies.[13]

Trade

Tariffs

The major characteristics of post-World War I tariff policies, as we have seen above, were the instability and generally high level of tariffs as well as the abandonment of the prewar most-favored-nation treatment. In Europe the core of the protectionist movement lay in the Central and Southeast areas where political and economic foundations were the shakiest. In the conferences of 1920, 1922, and 1927, the League regularly urged a return to the prewar conditions of freer commercial relations.

In the improved political weather of the late twenties, the recommendations of the 1927 Geneva Conference won limited compliance for two years thereafter. The rising tariff level was momentarily retarded, though not arrested, and France and Germany negotiated their 1927 Tariff Agreement reinstating the most-favored-nation clause. Then the dam broke in 1929 and the pace for a catastrophic tariff race was set by the infamous Smoot–Hawley Tariff, a trend which the conciliatory United States Reciprocal Trade Agreements Program of 1934 was only beginning to reverse when war struck again.

The League's positive accomplishments in the tariff field were: the initiation of more thorough and vigorous international study and negotiation than had ever been possible before, the gradual education of the world to accept international action on sensitive tariff questions, the successful promotion of certain positive reforms such as the revival of the most-favored-nation policy, and a limited curtailment of the rising tariff level from 1927 to 1929. The major obstacles were: the uneven economic development and tariff levels among countries, the reluctance of League Members to take a really firm stand on these matters, their failure to deal with tariff problems as an integral part of the total economic setting, their neglect of the problem of

[13] Geneva, 1942, II. A. 6.

THE CIRCUIT OF WORLD TRADE
IN THE TWENTIES

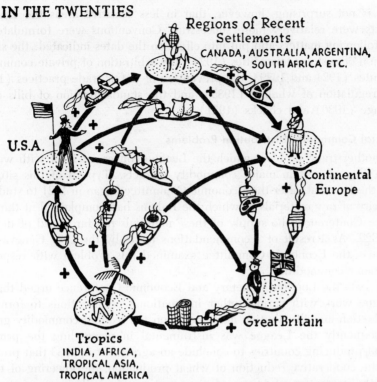

Regions of Recent
Settlements
CANADA, AUSTRALIA, ARGENTINA,
SOUTH AFRICA ETC.

U.S.A.

Continental
Europe

Great Britain

Tropics
INDIA, AFRICA,
TROPICAL ASIA,
TROPICAL AMERICA

✚ signifies "favorable" balances of trade. Thus trade flowed
clockwise. Payments for these could be made because the
circuit was closed. In the thirties, however, some of the
arrows were reversed and the system began to break down

Headline Series, *Foreign Policy Association*

cushioning the short-run shock that would have accompanied any significant reduction of tariffs, and their failure to comprehend the fact that countries were unwilling to expose their economies to the instabilities of *laissez
faire* (or "free trade") policies on the international scene, especially since
such policies had been discredited on the domestic scene.

Other Trade Questions

The League met equally stiff resistance in its efforts to abolish all non-
tariff prohibitions and restrictions. In spite of the Economic Committee's
success in getting twenty-nine countries, including the United States, to
adopt a convention for this purpose in 1927, it was never implemented to
any significant degree. Although it was brought into force in 1930 on a
year-to-year basis by the United States, the United Kingdom, Japan and
four other states, the advent of the depression caused it to be terminated
by the middle of 1934.

It is not surprising, however, that in less sensitive areas the League's efforts were relatively more successful. Conventions were formulated on the following matters and put into effect on the dates indicated: the simplification of customs formalities (1924), the arbitration of private commercial disputes (1924 and 1929), the prevention of unfair trade practices (1925), the regulation of whaling (1935), and the standardization of bills of exchange (1930) and checks (1931).

Special Commodity Distribution Problems

Another trade problem which the League concerned itself with was the instability of certain major commodity markets. Typical of this situation was the fact that, after the Economic Committee began in 1921 to study the scarcity of raw materials of which the Italians had complained at the Paris Peace Conference, the supply of these materials ran far ahead of demand in 1922. As a result of recommendations made by the 1927 Geneva Conference, the Economic Committee examined this problem with respect to six major commodities.

In 1933 the London Monetary and Economic Conference urged that the League work with various other international organizations to formulate production and distribution agreements on ten leading commodity groups. Subsequently the League was instrumental in persuading the principal wheat-producing countries to conclude an agreement in 1933 that provided for the cooperative reduction of wheat production, the lowering of tariffs, and the promotion of increased consumption. A similar sugar agreement was adopted in 1937. There were also active negotiations, but with fewer concrete results, regarding coal, rubber, timber, tin, dairy products, coffee, cocoa, wine and copper. In all of these efforts, however, the results were discouraging since most countries continued to feel that they could do better operating independently. Moreover many important commodities were controlled by private cartel arrangements about which the League did little more than make studies; the most important of these appeared in 1931 under the title of *General Report on the Economic Aspects of International Industrial Agreements.*[14]

Monetary Policy

The League also tried to influence financial and monetary policies. The tone was set by the 1920 Brussels Conference, which called for: an increase in production, reduction of governmental expenditures in relation to revenue, cessation of all subsidies "which conceal from the people the true economic situation," elimination of borrowing for recurrent ordinary expenditure, curbing of all inflationary practices, a return to the manipulation of the interest rate as the "normal" regulator of the volume of credit, an early return to the gold standard, and abandonment of exchange controls.[15] The same policies were warmed over and served up again in much the same form by the Genoa Conference of 1922 and the Geneva Conference of 1927.

[14] E. 736. 1931, II. B. 21.   [15] McClure, *op. cit.*, pp. 477–481.

Special related studies were also carried out under the wing of the Financial Committee. A Gold Delegation of that body prepared a report between 1929 and 1932 which led to the 1933 London Conference agreement that, among other things, exchange stability should be sought on the basis of gold. Another committee reported in 1935 that clearing agreements tended to restrict trade and should not be extended. Still another body urged in 1938 that exchange controls be progressively abandoned. In 1939 a report was published setting forth certain recommended standard procedures in formulating international loan contracts. Monetary and financial factors were also taken into consideration as part of the study undertaken in the thirties on economic depressions. Unfortunately the League was hampered in all of these efforts by two basic obstacles: first, its own hesitancy, except towards the end, to probe to the very roots of economic instability and, second, its Members' unwillingness to surrender their freedom of action.

Stability and Full Employment

As the depression fastened its grip upon the world, the League played a central role in developing the new trend in economic thinking which placed particular emphasis on the maintenance of economic stability and full employment. Undoubtedly one of the major forces behind this movement was the working man's outcry that primary attention should be devoted to those aspects of the economy which affected him most directly. He valued stability and employment above those abstract symbols of economic orthodoxy — free trade, balanced budgets, and the gold standard — which were based on a faith in the "normal" operation of a "natural" economic process which rarely seemed to operate normally or naturally.

The first League studies on the recurrence of depression took the form of two widely influential reports: *Prosperity and Depression; A Theoretical Analysis of Cyclical Movements* by Gottfried von Haberler, published in 1939, and *Statistical Testing of Business Cycle Theories* by J. Tinbergen, published in 1938–39. Then, in 1943, a group of experts, including certain members of the Economic and Financial Committees, known as the Delegation on Economic Depressions, published its first report dealing with the immediate short-range problem of *The Transition from War to Peace Economy*. Not only did this volume receive extraordinary publicity; it also demonstrated the remarkable progress in economic thinking since 1919. The objectives it sought included: (1) "a stable economy and rising standards of living," (2) full employment, (3) satisfaction of the "physiological needs of all classes," (4) spreading the risks of unemployment, (5) "equal educational opportunities," (6) "progressive removal" of trade obstructions, and (7) "courageous international measures of reconstruction and development." [16]

The Delegation's second report, published in 1945, dealt with the long-

[16] Annex 3 of the report.

range problem of *Economic Stability in the Post-War World.* After examining the causes of depression, it came to the following conclusions: (1) General depressions seem to result mainly from fluctuations in investment and employment in industrial countries. (2) These two factors should be kept at a high and stable level through some combination of five sources of demand (private consumption, private investment, current public expenditure, public investment, and net foreign investment).[17] Both of these reports contained a rich harvest of hard-earned wisdom. It remained to be seen whether national governments would heed their advice.

Economic Intelligence

International economic cooperation would soon stall without adequate statistical fuel from each country. Such reporting should be as comprehensive, accurate and comparable as possible. Since the information available during the early twenties scarcely approached this ideal, one of the League's most useful, but less dramatic, accomplishments was the formulation of the 1928 convention on statistical reporting which was subsequently ratified by twenty-six countries. At the same time, the League Council created the Committee of Statistical Experts to develop this work further. Hand in hand with this group, the Secretariat's Economic Intelligence Service compiled a tremendous reservoir of invaluable information and published regular and special reports which were indispensable tools for all national governments. The key importance of this kind of intelligence work in building a cooperative world society is made doubly clear by the refusal of all totalitarian regimes to make such information available.

Transportation and Communications [18]

General Pattern

Since there had been increasing pre-World War I collaboration in strengthening communications bridges among nations, there were strong hopes at the Paris Peace Conference that at last it would be possible to organize a cooperative system that would be sufficiently centralized to harness together the many different forms of communications and sufficiently authoritative to be able to make its decisions stick. As we have seen in Part Two, however, the Peace Treaties authorized no centralized communications organization, entrusted the League with no power to do more than recommend, and included no comprehensive binding conventions

---

[17] Chap. 21 of the report.

[18] The best sources are Jan Hostie, "Communications and Transit," *World Organization*, pp 158–188; Wallace McClure, *op. cit.*, Chaps. 19 and 20; League of Nations, *Ten Years of World Cooperation*, Chap. 6; League of Nations, *Transport Problems which Arose from the War of 1914–1918* (Geneva: League Secretariat, 1945); Mander, *op. cit.*, Chap. 9.

regarding communications. Primary attention was devoted to prying open the doorways leading to the conquered countries without forcing the Allies to make comparable concessions. The only gestures made in the direction of a broad long-range liberalization of communications were Article 23(e) of the Covenant, promising that the signatories would "make provision to secure and maintain freedom of communications and of transit," and the statements in Part XII of the Versailles Treaty indicating that the signatories would formulate certain general conventions in the near future.

When the League began to operate in 1920, an immediate preoccupation of the European countries was the reconstruction of their transportation arteries so that the lifeblood of men and materials could flow again. In keeping with the general climate of opinion at the time, however, the League was hesitant in asserting itself in these reconstruction efforts. Only when the 1922 Genoa Economic and Financial Conference suggested that the League might offer expert assistance, did the Communications and Transit Committee begin to be active in this field, largely through the formulation of conventions and the settlement of disputes under the Peace Treaties.

The effort to achieve progress by convention and peaceful settlement soon stalled, however, as the war-born ardor of collaboration cooled. Thus no major convention was completed after the second General Conference held in 1923. A basic difficulty that was never squarely faced was the fact that the problems of communications, as of most other economic matters, were in such a constant state of flux that even those governments with the most cooperative intentions hesitated to saddle themselves with static conventions that could not be quickly altered when necessary. As it had become apparent on the domestic scene, it soon became clear internationally that such problems could not be dealt with as effectively by inflexible legislation as by flexible and central day-to-day administrative regulation.

The Fourth Conference of 1931 was a decided failure because of both the depression and the League's decision to deploy its major forces on the economic and financial rather than the communications front. In 1935 the League did not even convoke the Fifth General Conference which was to have met that year, but looked instead to the League Assembly which was to perform the functions of the conference, a task for which the Assembly was scarcely equipped. Although the Communications and Transit Committee continued to function, it slowly starved for lack of support.

Maritime Navigation

Since many bipartite treaties had already been negotiated banning discrimination against ships calling at foreign ports, the next important step was the negotiation under League auspices of the multilateral Convention and Statute on the International Regime of Maritime Ports, which was signed in December 1923 and came into force in July 1926. This agreement guaranteed both free use of the maritime ports (those frequented by seagoing vesels) and equal treatment for all ships entering them. But many problems remained unsolved, and one delegate called this agreement no better than "half a loaf." [19]

Inland Transportation

Freedom of Transit. In keeping with the high hopes written into the Versailles Treaty, the League Communications and Transit Committee's first major concern was the formulation of the International Convention and Statute on Freedom of Transit signed at Barcelona in April 1921. While making the usual bow to the need for national regulation in the interest of security, health, and local conditions, this agreement endorsed the principles of complete freedom of transit from one state to another through the territories of the signatories and complete equality of transit conditions. Nevertheless, the concessions to special national requirements still left ample room for many kinds of barriers.

Waterways. Since the Congress of Vienna, there had been wide agreement that freedom and equality of transport should be extended to internal as well as transit traffic on "waterways of international concern" (those accessible to ordinary commercial navigation and providing access to the sea to more than one state). To revise and extend this principle, the First Communications and Transit General Conference adopted a Convention on the Regime of Navigable Waterways of International Concern as well as a broader additional protocol extending free and equal treatment on a reciprocal basis to all national waterways open to navigation from the sea. Unfortunately the opposition of the Netherlands and Switzerland prevented these conventions from being widely ratified.

Still, most of the responsibility for supervising the major inland waterways remained tantalizingly beyond the reach of the League's jurisdiction, and coordination was always difficult. Independent Commissions, several of which had existed prior to the League and all of which had been revised or created under the Treaty of Versailles, controlled the Danube, Rhine, Elbe, and Oder Rivers. None of these was ever brought under League direction in accordance with Covenant Article 24 regarding the supervision of international "bureaus." Nonetheless, the Communications and Transit Organization established a regular exchange of information with these bodies and invited them to send representatives "in an advisory capacity" to various meetings including the General Conferences.

In 1924 the Communications and Transit Committee also decided to jostle the river commissions a bit by appointing Mr. Walker A. Hines, former wartime Director General of Railroads in the United States, to make a thorough study of European inland waterways. His report, delivered in 1925, made numerous observations and recommendations regarding the Danube, the Rhine, and unfair discriminatory railway practices injurious to river transport. Although this report was thoroughly studied, the Committee had no direct authority to implement the suggestions.

[19] Hostie, *op. cit.*, p. 174.

Railroads. While rivers cross state lines smoothly, in spite of political boundaries, the task of linking the spider webs of numerous national railway systems, with their conflicting routes, types of rail and rolling stock, timetables, and rates, is far more complex. Thus one of the League's first concerns was to revise and extend the various pre-World War I railroad agreements. Unfortunately, it proved difficult to achieve broad agreement on this subject, and the Convention on the International Regime of Railways, concluded during the Second General Conference in 1923, was little more than a collection of pious hopes. Nevertheless, it endorsed certain principles of fair and equal treatment regarding rates and conditions of handling passengers, baggage, and freight. The fundamental difficulty lay in the need for a more flexible form of regulation than that provided by a static convention.

Urged on by the Genoa Economic and Financial Conference, the Communications and Transit Committee also interested itself in offering technical assistance to the European railway systems by dispatching General Sir H. Osborne Mance, former President of the Communications Section of the wartime Supreme Economic Council, to examine the situation in the center of transport anarchy, Central and Eastern Europe. General Mance's report recommended certain improvements, but the League attempted no concerted effort to achieve them. It was in order to supplement this report that the Committee asked Mr. Hines to make his study of inland waterways, mentioned above, which pointed to the need for better coordination between rail and river traffic.

As in the waterway situation, much international railway activity lay outside the League's territory and was dealt with by such organizations as the Central Office for International Railway Transport at Berne, Switzerland,[20] none of which was ever brought under the League umbrella in accordance with Article 24 on international "bureaus." Nevertheless the Communications and Transit Committee made arrangements with these bodies for the regular exchange of information and for their representation at League conferences.

Motor Transport. In 1926 a League-sponsored conference revised a European treaty of 1909 regarding international motor traffic. Then, in 1931, the League convoked a more ambitious European Conference on Road Traffic at Geneva which produced two conventions on the standardization of road signals and motor vehicle taxation, respectively, as well as an agreement on lost identification documents ("triptychs").

Technical Assistance

The Communications and Transit Committee's first technical assistance efforts were the studies made by General Mance on railways and Mr. Hines on waterways. In connection with the second study, Poland asked the League's advice on the feasibility of transporting coal and other products

[20] There were six major non-League international railroad associations.

from Upper Silesia to the Baltic partly by means of an artificial waterway through Polish rather than German territory. The Communications and Transit Committee authorized a detailed study of this matter which resulted in a report that recommended the immediate improvement of existing rail and port facilities as well as the gradual development of a system of inland waterways. The Communications and Transit Committee also rendered technical assistance in connection with the League-sponsored financial reconstruction of Austria and Bulgaria.[21]

Aviation[22]

Unlike rail, waterway, and road transportation, international aviation was subject to very little control by the League Communications and Transit Organization. As we saw in Part Two, the 1919 Paris Air Convention gave primary responsibility for this activity to the International Commission for Air Navigation which was officially placed under the "direction" of the League but in practice stood as much aloof as possible. The basic policy guide lines for international aviation were also greatly revised and developed in the Paris Air Convention. Detailed technical rules were incorporated in eight "annexes" to that agreement of which all but the one on customs could be amended by the Commission by special majority vote.

During the interwar years the Commission's principal concern was to keep this body of technical regulations up to date on such problems as standards of airworthiness, marking of aircraft, examination and certification of air personnel, standards for ground organization (airports, ground markings, maps, communications, meteorological services, etc.), traffic and operational rules, log books, and accident investigation. In addition to these activities, the Commission also acted as an information clearing house, a tribunal for settling disputes regarding the technical regulations, and an agency for dispensing expert advice.

The development of international private aviation law was dealt with almost exclusively by the French-sponsored *Comité international technique d'experts juridique aériens* (CITEJA). This body was established in 1926 outside the League's jurisdiction principally to encourage non-League members to participate. Four interwar conferences (1925, 1929, 1933, and 1938) dealt with such topics as air carriers' liabilities, air transport documents, mortgages, collisions, assistance and salvage on sea and land, and relations between aircraft owners and charterers.

In general, one can say that the leading air nations worked relatively well together on technical matters which required cooperation as the price of safety. On other matters, where national interests seemed to block rather than promote collaboration, there was little progress. This was especially true with respect to the efforts that were made to gain free and equal

---

21 See discussion p. 171; also League of Nations, *Transport Problems which Arose from the War of 1914–1918*, pp. 40–42, 45–46.

22 Most useful sources are: Sir Osborne Mance, *International Air Transport* (London: Oxford University Press, 1944); Kenneth W. Colegrove, *International Control of Aviation* (Boston: World Peace Foundation, 1930); Laurence C. Tombs, *International Organization in European Air Transport* (New York: Columbia University Press, 1936).

transit rights, which were not recognized in aviation to the extent they were in rail and water travel. It was also true regarding efforts to win co-operation on customs, rates and the elimination of uneconomic competition among national lines.

Telecommunications[23]

While the telegraph and telephone were well matured before World War I, radio was only a lusty youngster whose growing pains caused most of the major telecommunications difficulties during the interwar period. The center of the stage in these matters, as was discussed in Part Two, was held not by the League but by the independent International Telegraphic and International Radio Telegraphic Unions which combined in 1932 to form the International Telecommunications Union.

The initiative for international cooperation in this field, as in so many other technical activities, came from the Europeans suffering from an excess of competing national services. The giant United States, on the other hand, felt that it had little to fear and much to gain from competition. It never became a party to the telegraph and telephone regulations during the entire interwar period. It did become increasingly concerned, however, about interference in radio broadcasting due to the bargain basement rush that was developing in the scramble for frequencies. Thus the United States took its first major step in the telecommunications field when it convoked the 1927 Washington Radio Conference to make an initial allocation of frequencies and played a leading part at the 1932 Madrid Conference. After this important step, however, there was only one more meeting of the three administrative conferences during the interwar period, in 1938, and progress was discouragingly slow in all the fields.

There were certain problems common to all three of the basic forms of telecommunications. Their rates tended to be complex; their technical development was hampered by national differences; their international accounting was bedeviled by exchange fluctuations; and their consumers suffered from either too much or too little competition. Then there were certain problems peculiar to each of the three fields. In telephony, which seemed to be the least troublesome, there was still all too little collaboration between the American and European continents. In telegraphy, there was intense, often unscrupulous, competition not only among the cable companies themselves but between them and the radio people. In radio, the greatest need was to clean out the Augean stables of unregulated national appropriation of frequencies by establishing an authoritative, centralized, and continuous regulatory system.

Postal Service[24]

In this field, as compared with telecommunications, international collab-

---

[23] Most useful sources are: Sir Osborne Mance, *International Telecommunications* (London: Oxford University Press, 1943); John D. Tomlinson, *International Control of Radio-Communications* (Michigan: J. W. Edwards, 1945).

[24] Best sources: Mander, *op. cit.*, pp. 526–531; John F. Sly, "The Genesis of the Universal Postal Union," *International Conciliation*, No. 233 (October 1927), pp. 51–57;

oration was older than in telephony or radio, more dominated by govern-ments, less complex and more cooperative. During the interwar period the Universal Postal Union Conferences continued to meet every five years much as they did before World War I. At each Conference about 180 dele-gates from nearly all the nations of the world regularly considered be-tween 200 and 2,000 proposals regarding technical regulations for seven different types of postal service. Some of the more important issues con-sidered by the Union included the reduction of transit rates, the protection of neutral rights, and the development of air mail which was the most out-standing technical development in the postal field during the interwar period.

Conclusions

There can be no doubt that these League and affiliated efforts, limited though they were, represented some solid steps towards more effective in-ternational organization in the economic field, as compared with the pre-World War I era. These activities not only encouraged broader and more continuous coordination of various economic and communications func-tions but facilitated wider and more regular consultation among a larger number of countries than ever before. The greatest advances were made, of course, in meeting those needs which seemed most pressing to the major powers — primarily research and recommendations on various phases of international economic relations, modest loans for the reconstruction of a few Southeast European countries, some pioneering technical assistance, feeble and only temporary tariff concessions, and various efforts to gear national communications systems together more effectively.

Still, the League's role was severely limited. Economic activities were planned in terms of a temporary postwar emergency rather than a posi-tive long-range preventive program. The League's Economic and Finan-cial Organization starved along on a pitifully meager budget and staff (never more than seventy officials). There was never sufficient emphasis on the interrelationships among all elements in the economic picture. The Economic Committee, Financial Committee, and International Labor Or-ganization all operated separately with only a minimum of coordination.

League recommendations were usually dominated by the industrially developed nations with little understanding of or sympathy for the prob-lems of the underdeveloped nations. While some assistance was given to the Balkan countries, Asia was scarcely thought of except as the private vineyard of the great colonial powers. In no instance did economic assist-ance in any area take the form of a comprehensive program touching all aspects of a nation's economic life. Obviously the modern concept of tech-

F. H. Williamson, "The International Postal Service and the Universal Postal Union," *Journal of the Royal Institute of International Affairs*, Vol. 9, No. 1 (January 1930), pp. 68–78.

nical assistance to underdeveloped nations was virtually undreamed of until the last few years. League-sponsored financing was arranged entirely on a commercial basis in the form of loans to be secured by adequate assets and repaid with interest. There was no thought of extensive governmental grants such as those which were to be resorted to after World War II. Such gifts were to be made through private channels.

Even within the international sphere some of the most crucial economic problems, such as reparations, were dealt with outside the League, largely under the Supreme Economic Council. Finally, the League seemed to feel that there was no necessity for any great haste. Although the League Secretariat began studying Europe's economic plight in the summer of 1919, and the League Council recommended in March 1920 that a financial conference be held, that conference did not actually meet in Brussels until September 1920. And then it merely told League Members what the problems seemed to be rather than mobilizing direct and immediate governmental action.

Suggestions for Further Reading

Books

Colegrove, Kenneth W., *International Control of Aviation* (Boston: World Peace Foundation, 1930).

Davis, Harriet Eager, ed., *Pioneers in World Order* (New York: Columbia University Press, 1944).

Greaves, H. R. G., *The League Committees and World Order* (London: Oxford University Press, 1931).

Hill, Martin, *The Economic and Financial Organization of the League of Nations* (Washington: Carnegie Endowment for International Peace, 1946).

Keynes, J. M., *The Economic Consequences of the Peace* (New York: Harcourt, Brace and Howe, 1920).

Mance, Sir Osborne, *International Air Transport* (London: Oxford University Press, 1944).

———, *International Telecommunications* (London: Oxford University Press, 1943).

Mander, Linden A., *Foundations of Modern World Society* (Stanford: Stanford University Press, 1947).

McClure, Wallace, *World Prosperity* (New York: The Macmillan Company, 1933).

Myers, Denys P., *Handbook of the League of Nations* (Boston: World Peace Foundation, 1935).

Phelan, Edward J., *Yes, and Albert Thomas* (London: The Cresset Press, 1936).

Ranshofen-Wertheimer, Egon F., *The International Secretariat* (Washington: Carnegie Endowment for International Peace, 1945).

Salter, Arthur, *The Economic Consequences of the League* (London: Europa Publishing Company, 1933).

Symposium, *World Organization* (Washington: American Council on Public Affairs, 1942).

Tombs, Laurence C., *International Organization in European Air Transport* (New York: Columbia University Press, 1936).

Tomlinson, John D., *International Control of Radio-Communications* (Michigan: J. W. Edwards, 1945).

Periodicals

Hadsel, Winifred N., "United States Relief for Europe in World War I," *Foreign Policy Reports*, Vol. 19, No. 1 (March 15, 1943).

McDougall, F. L., "Food and Welfare," *Geneva Studies*, Vol. 9, No. 5 (November 1938).

Rappard, William E., "Postwar Efforts for Freer Trade," *Geneva Studies*, Vol. 9, No. 2 (March 1938).

Sly, John F., "The Genesis of the Universal Postal Union," *International Conciliation*, No. 233 (October 1927).

Sweetser, Arthur, "The Non-Political Achievements of the League," *Foreign Affairs*, Vol. 19, No. 1 (October 1940).

Williamson, F. H., "The International Postal Service and the Universal Postal Union," *Journal of the Royal Institute of International Affairs*, Vol. 9, No. 1 (January 1930).

Documents

League of Nations, *Commercial Policy in the Interwar Period*, Geneva, 1942, II. Economic and Financial, 1942, II.A.6.

——, *Economic Stability in the Postwar World*, Geneva, 1945, II. Economic and Financial, 1945, II.A.2.

——, *Food, Famine, and Relief*, Geneva, 1946, II. Economic and Financial, 1946, II.A.5.

——, *International Currency Experience*, Geneva, 1944, II. Economic and Financial, 1944, II.A.4.

——, *Ten Years of World Cooperation* (Geneva: League Secretariat, 1930).

——, "The Development of International Cooperation in Economic and Social Affairs," *Special Supplement to the Monthly Summary of the League of Nations* (Geneva: August 1939).

——, *The Transition from War to Peace Economy*, Geneva, 1943, II. Economic and Financial, 1943, II.A.3.

18

Reconstruction and Development — UN

EVER SINCE NATIONS began digging themselves out of the rubble of World War II, most governments have devoted a major portion of their time and energy wracking their brains over the problems of increasing their material wealth through relief, reconstruction and development. They realized only too well the decisive effect of these matters on the political and social, as well as material, well-being of their peoples. And, since the long-range trend has been towards increasing economic interdependence among states, it is not surprising that governments have often turned to the UN and its affiliated specialized agencies for help. At the same time enthusiastic internationalists too often forget that these bodies, while sometimes influential beyond their financial resources, have been only part of the picture — a very minor part when measured in terms of the volume of money spent.

As in origin, so in action, the role of these agencies has been determined largely by the interests of the great powers. The dominant fact that has overshadowed their activities is that the United States, by far the greatest source of economic aid, has been willing to channel only a small fraction of its largesse through multilateral channels. Its greatest experiment in a truly international operational program occurred during and immediately after the war while the Big Three alliance was still warm. This was UNRRA, designed solely for the limited task of furnishing relief and "rehabilitation" (preparation for but not actual reconstruction) to liberated countries considered too poor to buy or borrow such aid for themselves. This meant primarily the unoccupied nations of Southern and Eastern, but not Western, Europe. The United States hoped, at least in the beginning, as after World War I, that the needs of Western Europe, notably Britain and France, could be financed by loans rather than outright grants.

The total United States contribution to UNRRA, the largest American donation to any multilateral program before or since, was approximately $2.7 billion. Even during the life of UNRRA, however, the major portion of American assistance was sluiced through bilateral channels: United States armed forces "civilian supply" to militarily administered areas, including occupied territories (over $5 billion between June 1945 and June 1950) and direct loans, following the abrupt termination of wartime Lend-

Lease aid in August 1945, to individual nations, principally the United Kingdom and France (over $10 billion during the same 1945–50 period).[1] The United States insisted, moreover, on terminating UNRRA in March 1947 and relying thereafter almost entirely on bilateral arrangements.

The UN and its affiliated specialized agencies have been used mainly for study and advice, except for modest lending through the International Bank for Reconstruction and Development (to which the United States had paid $635 million as of the end of 1953) and the relatively small operational programs of the International Refugee Organization (to which the United States contributed approximately $41 million a year from 1948 to 1951), the UN International Children's Emergency Fund (to which the United States contributed an average of $14 million a year from 1947 to 1953), and the UN Relief and Works Agency for Palestine Refugees (to which the United States contributed about $20 million a year from 1949 to 1953). After the liquidation of UNRRA, moreover, a series of aggressive Communist moves in Greece, Czechoslovakia, China and elsewhere persuaded the United States to initiate several new major assistance programs outside the UN: the Marshall Plan, begun in 1948 (on which the United States spent $12 billion from 1948 to 1951); the Point Four Program to provide "know-how" to the underdeveloped areas (for which the United States authorized $35 million from 1950 to 1951, $12 million to be channeled through the UN); and the Mutual Defense Assistance Program (for which the United States authorized $7 billion from 1950 to 1951).

The United Kingdom and other recipient countries were not in an advantageous position to contest United States policy, if they had wanted to, and many of them seemed to feel it was more profitable to deal directly with their American benefactor than to merge their requests with those of other countries through a multilateral agency. The Soviet bloc refused to accept the invitation to participate in the Marshall Plan and has persistently damned the United States for economic imperialism and by-passing the UN. The underdeveloped countries have been particularly sensitive to the dangers of political and economic domination by the great powers and have been most insistent that more should be done through the UN.

World Economic Environment, 1945–1954

One cannot understand the course of the UN's economic activities except in terms of the larger world economic setting of which they are a part. In reviewing this experience, three major phases are discernible: 1945 to 1947, the immediate postwar emergency before the Marshall Plan; 1948 to 1949, UN adjustment to the Marshall Plan and the development of limited

---

[1] These and the following U.S. aid figures are taken from *Foreign Aid by the US Government, 1940–51* (Washington: Government Printing Office, 1952). Also see W. A. Brown, Jr., and Redvers Opie, *American Foreign Assistance* (Washington: Brookings Institution, 1953).

technical assistance; and 1950 to 1954, expanded technical assistance and the impact of the Korean conflict.

1945-1947

These were the years of most desperate postwar need, most generous internationally administered relief via UNRRA, and most unfortunate fumbling as UNRRA was terminated. The war damage, caused not only by actual destruction but also by deterioration of equipment and dislocation of former economic relationships, was far more serious than most of the planners estimated at the end of the war — more disastrous than had ever previously befallen mankind. Fortunately the response was quicker, more ample and more truly international than after World War I. But it was halted far short of what the world needed to regain prewar conditions, and there was a disturbing interlude before the geographically more limited Marshall Plan was established.

By 1947 there were approximately 10 per cent more mouths to feed and bodies to clothe and house than in 1937. But production of certain key industrial commodities in most of the world, excluding the United States, was from 4 to 45 per cent below the 1937 level.[2] In the fortunate United States, whose plants had not only escaped direct injury but had grown by leaps and bounds, 1947 industrial production in various major commodities was from 3 to 111 per cent *above* the 1937 level.

The race between population and food was equally precarious. Because of a variety of misfortunes — loss of equipment, slaughter of farm animals, shortages of fertilizers, lack of seeds, and exceptionally cruel European weather in 1946–47 — the world's total food production in 1947–48 was 7 per cent below the 1935–39 average. The deficits of certain areas were even more serious. European production of wheat, rye, barley, oats, maize, and potatoes (excluding the Soviet Union and Albania) was approximately 29 per cent less than the 1934–38 average. United States production, on the other hand, was almost 30 per cent *above* its prewar level.

As a consequence of its fortunate position, the United States had a surplus of exports in goods and services between 1945 and mid-1947 of $16.7 billion. This was the first phase of the postwar "dollar gap." Of this, $6 billion was furnished in the form of outright United States grants ("unilateral transfers"). The rest was financed chiefly through American loans, but United States aid was not sufficient to prevent an alarming erosion of the monetary position of the deficit countries.

The basic all-important fact which emerges from this brief review, and was to dominate the world economy far longer than anyone guessed, is that the prewar circular flow of trade had been seriously dislocated by the war. Most of the world was now a deficit area, and the United States, the

---

[2] The material underlying this analysis is taken largely from *Foreign Aid by the US Government,* and various UN publications, particularly *Economic Report, Salient Features of the World Economic Situation, 1945–47,* UN Sales No.: 1948.II.C.1.

only major power to have experienced a significant net increase in productive capacity, was furnishing large export surpluses to almost all the rest of the world which did not have the goods and services to export in return.

1948–1949

The economic weather improved strikingly during this period, especially in Europe due in large measure to the Marshall Plan (European Recovery Program).[3] 1948 was the most successful postwar year up to that time. The manufacturing and mining index for Europe, excluding the Soviet Union, stood at 90 per cent of 1937, while total world production was 30 per cent above 1937. European agricultural output still remained below prewar levels, but the 1948–49 world supply was 5 per cent above the 1934–38 average and 10 per cent above 1947–48.

Food, raw materials and fuel were so plentiful during 1949 that their prices dipped considerably.[4]   The level of industrial production also dropped, reflecting particularly a weakening of demand in the United States with a consequent short-lived recession. Hence there was increased unemployment in America, Europe and elsewhere. Continued balance-of-payments difficulties also resulted in serious devaluations in the latter part of 1949 led by the British pound. At the same time, certain political events, especially the startling ascent of the Chinese Communists, called attention to the need for greater aid to the underdeveloped countries and led to United States sponsorship of an accelerated technical assistance program administered inside as well as outside the United Nations.

1950–1954

The course of United Nations economic activities during this period shifted almost entirely from postwar reconstruction to new development, and the center of gravity, responding to the trend of political events, moved from Europe towards Asia.[5] The economic issues which absorbed most of the United Nations' attention were the expanded technical assistance program, the financing of development, the impact of the Korean conflict and western rearmament upon the world's economy, and the provision of relief and reconstruction following the termination of that conflict.

While the dollar gap narrowed considerably during the early months of 1950, continued balance of payments problems, especially in Europe, resulted in even stiffer import restrictions. Then the outbreak of the Korean struggle in the summer of 1950 bred a series of misfortunes: inflation, most immediately felt in raw material prices; incipient cuts in the production of consumer goods; and scarcities of capital goods for development

[3] *World Economic Report 1948*, Sales No.: 1949.II.C.3.
[4] *Major Economic Changes in 1949*, UN Doc. E/1601 and Corr. 1.
[5] Principal United Nations economic surveys for this period are: *World Economic Report, 1949–50, 1950–51*, and *1951–52*, UN Sales Nos.: 1951.II.C.1, 1952.II.C.4, and 1953.II.C.2 respectively.

Production Of Rice—Mainstay Of The Asian Diet— Has Not Kept Pace With Population Growth

632 Million   92 Million Tons [1]

763 Million   94 Million Tons [1]

Prewar [2]   Present [3]

[1] Metric tons of rough rice
[2] Population: 1938; production: average for crop years 1935/36 — 1939/40
[3] Population: 1952; production: average for crop years 1950/51 — 1952/53

(Data refer to non-Communist countries of South Asia and the Far East)

Report to Congress on the Mutual Security Program (Washington: U.S. Government Printing Office, 1953), p. 37.

not directly connected with the military effort. This aroused considerable resentment against the rearmament effort initiated by the Korean conflict, especially among the working people of Europe. By early 1951 the underdeveloped countries were alarmed by sudden price declines in some raw materials; price increases in many manufactured goods, transportation, and insurance; and growing scarcity of various capital and consumer goods.

UN studies during 1952 to 1954 emphasized the following problems:

1. While some industrially developed countries, especially the United States, had been able to increase consumption levels, others had had to channel increased production into investment or export.

2. A number of underdeveloped nations had not been able to regain even the low pre-war production and consumption levels.

3. Since the rate of production growth had been greater in the developed than the underdeveloped countries since the end of the war, the gap sep-

arating the "rich" from the "poor" nations was widening rather than narrowing.

4. A relative decrease in the general rate of production growth during 1952 and adjustments following the Korean truce made ECOSOC more concerned than ever about maintaining full employment.

The following analysis gives a bird's-eye view of the evolution of UN and specialized agency activities in the closely intertwined fields of short-term relief and reconstruction, and technical and financial assistance for longer-range development. The major organizations involved are the General Assembly, ECOSOC, Economic and Employment Commission (changed to Economic, Employment, and Development Commission in 1950 and liquidated in 1951), regional commissions, Food and Agriculture Organization, and the International Bank for Reconstruction and Development. One should also keep in mind the interaction between these developments and the fields of trade, monetary and fiscal policy, employment, and transportation and communications which are treated in the following chapter.

Relief and Reconstruction

UNRRA — BOLD BUT BRIEF EXPERIMENT

It is within the environment just reviewed that one must examine the use made of UN and affiliated agencies to provide short-term relief and reconstruction assistance. The first, and last, really large-scale multi-lateral operating program was that of the UN Relief and Rehabilitation Administration (UNRRA), not actually a part of the UN nor a specialized agency, although it was virtually one of the latter. This great humanitarian effort blazed trails which influenced all who followed after.

The forty-four United and Associated Nations met for the first UNRRA Council session at Atlantic City from November 10 to December 1, 1943.

Delegates from war-ravaged lands marveled at the steak and lobster. A top-hatted British food expert gaped as a boardwalk pitchman demonstrated kitchen gadgets and lectured on the vitamins in raw vegetables. . . . Turbans, dark skins, beards, and slant eyes drew the curious glances of similarly-equipped fortune tellers.[6]

On the sensitive issue of determining the scale of national contributions, it was decided that non-occupied countries should make an initial contribution of approximately 1 per cent of their national incomes. The relative size of these contributions was a clear key to relative influence. The United States was to pay $1.5 billion, five times that of the next largest contribution, the United Kingdom's $320 million. Canada came next with $90 million; India, $35 million; and Australia, $32 million.

[6] John Perry, "Why UNRRA Has Failed," *Harper's Magazine*, Vol. 192, No. 1148 (January 1946), p. 83.

After relative inactivity during the rest of 1943 and 1944, the end of the war in 1945 broke the log jam, and UNRRA was forced to sink or swim. Needs were overwhelming; supplies, scarce; transport facilities, jammed and decrepit; and member nations, decidedly sluggish in dropping their contributions into the common till. The major "angel," the United States, promised $1,350 million in March 1944, but a cautious Congress appropriated only $800 million that June, requiring certain sums to be spent on United States cotton and wool. Director-General Herbert Lehman then launched a major lobbying campaign to persuade the American people and their Congress to appropriate the remaining $550 million. Not until a year and a half after the first appropriation, and after Lehman had told the House Foreign Affairs Committee, "We are completely broke . . .," did Congress produce the balance in December 1945.

Mr. Lehman resigned in March 1946, largely in protest against the lack of support from his own Government, which had been laggard not only in the matter of funds but in the maintenance of effective postwar food controls in order to send adequate supplies abroad. He was succeeded by Mr. Fiorello La Guardia (dubbed "Little Flour" by wags of the press), the irrepressible Mayor of New York. In the meantime the United States delegate to the Council, Mr. William Clayton, had endorsed, in August 1945, a second 1 per cent-of-national-income contribution by all uninvaded member nations with the understanding that UNRRA's work would come to an end in March 1947. The United States also insisted that the Central Committee, dominated by the great powers, rather than the plenary Council, approve the Director-General's recommendations for allocating available aid.[7]

Increasing tension between the Soviet bloc and the Western countries first erupted openly in February 1946. Contrary to the previous tradition of unanimity in the Central Committee, the Soviet Union broke with the others when the United States requested trade information from recipient nations, largely due to American suspicions that the Soviet Union was diverting supplies. From then on, the Soviet bloc regularly resisted efforts that seemed to reduce aid to its friends or to encourage refugees who refused to be repatriated.

At the Council meeting in August 1946, just at the crescendo of the UNRRA program, the United States made it clear that it would insist on holding UNRRA to its scheduled liquidation early in 1947. Behind the American attitude lay the tensions mentioned above, the feeling that UNRRA administration had been lax, the desire to continue any further relief as a national program tied more closely to American policies, the expectation of continued economic recovery including a good crop in 1947, and the desire to return to normal trade rather than relief. The United States did not deny that there was need for additional aid but proposed that further requests be handled through national loans or by the Inter-

<hr>

[7] For suggestive analysis of this and other key issues, see Robert H. Johnson, "The Case of UNRRA," World Politics, Vol. 3, No. 4 (July 1951), pp. 520–538.

national Bank or Monetary Fund, although the latter were never intended to administer relief programs. Health, social welfare and refugee operations were to be transferred to various UN bodies. The next two largest contributors to UNRRA, the United Kingdom and Canada, ultimately supported the United States point of view, but the Soviet Union and most of the smaller countries protested that no adequate provision was being made to meet the tremendous needs which still existed.

The liquidation process began as scheduled in 1947, although the European operations were not actually closed out until the summer, and the Far Eastern program was not finished until the end of the year. A noteworthy indication of the wide embrace of UNRRA activities is the surprising number of UN agencies that inherited UNRRA functions (and, in some cases, residual funds): Food and Agriculture Organization ($1.1 million); International Refugee Organization ($3.6 million); World Health Organization ($4 million); UN International Children's Emergency Fund ($34.5 million); and several of the ECOSOC Commissions (but without bequests).

UNRRA's Contribution

Some, though far from all, of UNRRA's impact can be told in figures. Member governments contributed a total of $3.7 billion of which the United States gave 73 per cent; the United Kingdom, 17 per cent; and Canada, 4 per cent.[8] True, this is an insignificant amount compared to what was consumed in the war effort. The United States gave $49 billion in Lend-Lease aid alone. Still UNRRA aid totaled approximately 4.5 times what the Allies spent on World War I relief, and it was also far greater than any other United Nations peacetime budget (the largest of these, the United Nations itself, spends annually only about $47 million). A total of $2.9 billion in relief supplies was shipped to seventeen territories of which the six largest recipients were: China (18 per cent), Poland (16 per cent), Italy (14 per cent), Yugoslavia (14 per cent), and Greece (12 per cent).[9] UNRRA cared for about one million displaced persons.[10] When its staff was largest (June 1946), UNRRA had 27,811 on its rolls (the UN regularly employs approximately 4,000).[11]

What, on balance, were UNRRA's major strengths and weaknesses? At the top of the list of its achievements is the fact that, while UNRRA could never do enough, it was able to prevent some of the catastrophes which followed in the wake of World War I, especially in Eastern and Central Europe.

> The energetic . . . efforts of the [UNRRA] Administration to acquire and distribute trucks, supplemented by the assistance given to the restoration of rail service, permitted the successful internal distribution of essential goods. . . . The work of the Administration . . . helped keep the world free

[8] George Woodbridge, ed., *UNRRA* (New York: Columbia University Press, 1950), Vol. 3, p. 500.

[9] *Ibid.*, p. 428.   [10] *Ibid.*, Vol. 2, p. 496.

[11] *Ibid.*, Vol. I, Part II, Chap. 4.

from devastating epidemics — a remarkable, indeed incredible achievement if viewed in relation to the aftermaths of other great wars. The recovery of agricultural production, even in an internally disturbed country such as Greece, was very considerable. Industrial production did improve with the aid of UNRRA supplies; essential public utility services were made available.[12]

A second strength was its integrated administration as compared with the emphasis on independent national efforts after World War I. A third accomplishment was to organize the relief effort well before the fighting stopped rather than waiting for the armistice as was done in 1918. A fourth contribution was the decision to provide considerably larger resources than after World War I and primarily in the form of grants rather than loans.

Major Liabilities

The greatest weakness was the unwillingness on the part of UNRRA's chief sponsors, especially the United States, to maintain the continuity of the rehabilitation effort. As a British observer put it at the time,

> In a world unriven by ideological hatreds and still able to consider an issue dispassionately, the arguments for maintaining UNRRA for one more year would have seemed unanswerable. The work . . . which UNRRA was pledged to fulfil is still incomplete. . . . [The receiving countries] do not possess sufficient "hard" currency to buy their requirements abroad, nor are the food-providing countries in the New World likely to show much interest in the trickle of goods for export, which the countries in Eastern Europe can now produce. . . . [The] extra time and money needed to round off . . . the work and to secure an orderly transfer of . . . functions . . . are very small. . . . The gap . . . will be accentuated by the fact that so far the international agencies to which . . . [the] many activities are . . . to be transferred are not working realities. . . .[13]

Moreover, the shift from the multilateral to the bilateral approach was the first serious postwar blow struck against broad internationalism in favor of a more limited approach. While some criticisms of UNRRA's administration are valid, as mentioned below, the organization never really went counter to United States policy in any significant respect. To kill it so prematurely seems to have caused more ill will among friends of the United States than was warranted by the advantages gained.

A second liability was the reluctance on the part of UNRRA's sponsors to make any really extraordinary sacrifice for the relief effort. The national contributions were larger than those made after World War I, but they were paltry as compared to the costs of the war and failed to meet even the minimal needs of a limited number of the poorer countries. Furthermore, governments, especially the United States, were too eager to unload

[12] *Ibid.*, p. 539.
[13] "UNRRA and Europe," *The Economist*, Vol. 151, No. 5374 (August 24, 1946), p. 283.

their own special surpluses at advantageous prices and too loath to continue wartime controls so that adequate supplies could be shipped abroad. The richer countries were allowed to procure their own supplies independently of UNRRA, and the final allocation always rested with the Combined Boards controlled chiefly by American and British supply officials.

> The lifting of meat rationing (in September 1945) [in the U.S.] provided a boom market for the packers and made it more profitable for farmers to feed grain to livestock than to sell it for bread. There were bumper crops, and the Department of Agriculture was far more interested in absorbing surpluses through expanded meat production than in providing against hunger abroad. When Governor Lehman . . . said, "The premature removal of food controls in certain countries was, in my judgment, quite unjustified and has contributed greatly to the present tragic position," he meant only one country, the United States. Canada and Britain have intensified their rationing since the war ended.[14]

UNRRA did suffer organizational aches and pains, but most of them can be blamed on the necessary haste with which the agency was organized. It was inevitable that there would be, as there were, too many people with too little to do in some places (notably Cairo) and the reverse in other places. There was inadequate supervision and some misappropriation of relief, but this followed inevitably from the original decision, agreed to by the United States as well as the other sponsors, that distribution would be administered nationally and that UNRRA conditions governing such distribution would be subject to national approval. On the whole the administration seems to have been remarkably effective. "The fact is that supplies were obtained and delivered at a relatively small administrative cost."[15]

Beneath the facts and figures lies the most important measure of UNRRA's work, the solid deposit of practical aid which warmed the hearts as well as the bodies of millions. One glimpse of this humane achievement was reflected in the grateful words of the Byelorussian representative during the sixth and last session of the Council — a statement strikingly free of the "canned" quality of other statements in later years from that quarter:

> . . . it is difficult to express in a few words the great historic importance of this international relief organization, but the outstanding characteristic in this appraisal, in my opinion, is in the gratitude of many millions of ordinary people in many parts of the globe for the assistance which has been given to them by this organization in the most difficult and critical period of their life. The organization existed and functioned in the name of the best human principles. It was at the people's service, and, having achieved great results, has obtained the sympathy of peoples, has written down a remarkable page in the history of friendly relations between peoples and states, for it promoted peace, and strengthened the feeling of friendship between nations.[16]

[14] "Fumbling with Famine," The Nation, Vol. 162, No. 12 (March 23, 1946), pp. 335.
[15] Woodbridge, op. cit., Vol. 2, p. 544; a more critical view is to be found in Marvin Klemme, The Inside Story of UNRRA (New York: Lifetime Editions, 1949).
[16] UNRRA Journal, Sixth Council, p. 33.

FEEDING THE HUNGRY, AFTER UNRRA

The original design in the minds of the principal architects of the post-war international machinery had been that UNRRA should deal with the immediate short-range relief and rehabilitation problems leaving the UN free to concentrate on more long-range issues. But the untimely demise of UNRRA left a gap that the UN had no choice but to try to fill. Since the most desperate relief need was for food, the Food and Agriculture Organization (FAO) assumed the leading role, supported by the General Assembly and ECOSOC. But the major powers never entrusted these agencies with the funds or authority to engage in a directly operational program comparable to that of UNRRA.

Meeting for the first session of its Conference, October to November 1945, FAO gave immediate attention to the food crisis and recommended that governments concentrate on expanding the production and broadening the consumption of basic commodities, making the fullest use of international commodity agreements[17] and expanded trade, and improving nutritional standards. The staff leadership of both the FAO and UNRRA then turned to the General Assembly and were instrumental in persuading that body, during the first months of 1946, to urge all governments to "take immediate and drastic action" to conserve supplies, make known both their resources and needs, and continue contributing to UNRRA. At that time both the United Kingdom and the Soviet Union advocated continuance of UNRRA, but the United States firmly opposed it.

At an FAO-sponsored special Meeting on Urgent Food Problems in Washington, D.C., May 1946, the wartime Combined Food Board (United States, United Kingdom and Canada) was replaced by a broader temporary nineteen-member International Emergency Food Council (IEFC) with authority to continue recommending the allocation of seventeen scarce commodities. Largely at the behest of Director-General Sir John Boyd Orr, the Conference also asked the FAO secretariat to draw up a bolder and more integrated long-term program to deal with present and future food emergencies.

Rise and Fall of a Plan

At the FAO Conference at Copenhagen, Denmark, September 1946, the "Orr plan" seemed to win a great victory as the Conference, with the United States delegation in the lead, approved its general objectives. But the details — calling for a World Food Board with authority to buy and sell on the world market in order to stabilize prices, establish food reserves for emergencies, and subsidize sales to especially needy countries — were referred to a Preparatory Commission on World Food Proposals to formulate concrete recommendations.

[17] For differences between the United States and the United Kingdom on this issue, see pp. 232–233.

When the Preparatory Commission met, however, in Washington, D.C., October 1946 to January 1947, the Orr victory was quickly deflated. The United States and United Kingdom were now unwilling to relinquish any significant operational authority to the proposed supranational World Food Board. All they would agree to was a pledge to foster the Orr objectives through voluntary rather than binding arrangements. They would

> engage in an annual review of the international food situation; promote coordinated industrial as well as agricultural development of the underdeveloped countries; support national and international (emphasis on the IBRD) efforts to finance such development; engage in intergovernmental consultation and action, especially through individual commodity agreements (U.S. answer to the Orr buffer stock idea), with provision for famine reserves, price stabilization reserves, and special sales at special prices to undernourished countries; and, as a mild substitute for the World Food Board, create an advisory World Food Council, composed of eighteen governmental representatives elected by the FAO Conference to replace the original FAO Executive Committee of fifteen experts.

This was a step in the direction of more active international collaboration but without the key ingredients of an integrated approach, binding authority, large-scale funds and immediate action which Orr had wanted.

Even as the Preparatory Commission was meeting, a closely related war was being waged in the UN General Assembly on the issue of continuing UNRRA's work. The delegates were treated to the extraordinary spectacle of Mr. Fiorello LaGuardia, fiery Director-General of UNRRA, proposing, in opposition to his own government, a UN Emergency Food Fund of at least $400 million to fill the food deficit that was expected between the termination of UNRRA and the harvest of 1947. Most of the smaller countries enthusiastically backed the LaGuardia plan, but the United States and United Kingdom, largest potential contributors, opposed it.

The United States argued that the need was less than indicated and should be handled through bilateral and voluntary arrangements, coordinated through informal consultation. The United Kingdom now supported this view. Canada sought to strengthen the UN role by calling for an expert technical committee to advise on minimal import and financial requirements. Norway added the idea of asking individuals and organizations throughout the world to contribute the value of one day's work. Finally, a resolution embodying the United States thesis, as modified by Canada and Norway, was adopted.

The Secretary-General's report on bilateral efforts made to fill the post-UNRRA vacuum was before the General Assembly when it met for its second regular session, September to November 1947. According to that study, assistance planned as of the summer of 1947 covered only 60 to 70 per cent of the total minimal requirements of $583 million as estimated by a Special Technical Committee on Relief Needs After the Termination of UNRRA. The United States was contributing $350 million. The next largest contributions were by the United Kingdom ($40 million), Canada

($18 million) and Australia ($13 million). Twenty-three governments failed to reply to the UN inquiries; twenty-two reported their inability to give aid.

The "Dodd Plan"

A sequel to the "Orr Plan" episode came in 1949. When the economic sun seemed to be shining brightly during the summer of that year, the FAO Council, influenced by the major producing countries, decided to throw away the umbrella created during the stormy period of postwar scarcity, the International Emergency Food Committee, the allocating sub-body which had succeeded the International Emergency Food Council. At the same time the FAO Council turned to the new problem of surpluses, in commodities such as sugar, and asked the Director-General to prepare a report on the matter.

That report, written by a panel of six internationally recognized economists, suggested:

1. maintenance of a high level of production and employment, particularly in the United States;
2. reduction of tariff and other barriers, particularly in the United States;
3. higher productive efficiency;
4. a steady stream of capital investment to the underdeveloped countries;
5. ultimate restoration of multilateral trade and freely convertible currencies.

In addition to these long-range goals the new Director-General — Norris Dodd, formerly of the United States Department of Agriculture — recommended the immediate creation of an International Commodity Clearing House (ICCH, soon nicknamed "itch"), vaguely reminiscent of Lord Orr's ill-fated World Food Board. Its functions were to include:

1. stabilizing prices and encouraging orderly changes in the pattern and scale of production;
2. purchasing, for resale, surpluses occurring in member countries, with sales to be made to buying countries either in their own currencies, at the regular "going price," or at a specially low price in a currency acceptable to the supplying country;
3. facilitating negotiation and administration of commodity agreements;
4. organizing governmental consultation on commodity problems involving the production, distribution and use of primary products.

The fifth FAO Conference, heavily influenced by the views of the United States Treasury Department, rejected this plan in December 1949 on much the same grounds that defeated the "Orr plan." It was held that to pay for food in their own inflated currencies would involve a further accumulation of inconvertible currencies and would encourage the deficit countries to delay balancing their international books in the traditional manner. The plan was also opposed because it would give an international agency too much power. It was alleged that buffer stocks should be held nationally, not internationally, and any international coordination regarding their administration should be on a commodity by commodity, rather than an integrated, basis in accordance with individual intergovernmental agreements. Furthermore such a plan might harm normal trade. Any special financial arrangements should be undertaken by national governments. The Conference then proceeded to endorse these policies and create an FAO Committee on Commodity Problems, composed of fourteen of the chief agricultural exporting and importing nations, including the United States, United Kingdom, France, Canada, Australia, India and Netherlands, to advise on bringing surplus and needy countries together through special intergovernmental agreements.

RECONSTRUCTING FOUNDATIONS OF PRODUCTION

War-damaged nations wanted more, however, than mere relief supplies — food, clothing, fuel, etc. They needed help in reconstructing their basic productive and transportation equipment. The leading UN European powers, especially the Soviet Union, United Kingdom and France, had received much of this kind of assistance through last-minute United States Lend-Lease aid. Most of these countries, but conspicuously not the Soviet Union, also received large postwar United States loans. The occupied territories received minimal reconstruction assistance from the military. But the poorer countries had to depend largely on limited UNRRA "rehabilitation."

The Polish delegation seized the initiative during the first session of the General Assembly, at the beginning of 1946, to ask that the UN itself provide reconstruction assistance. But the United States and United Kingdom were unwilling to go beyond urging individual action by national governments and limited lending by the IBRD. In a resolution incorporating these provisions, the Assembly also recommended the establishment of the first regional commissions, the Economic Commission for Europe (ECE) and Economic Commission for Asia and the Far East (ECAFE), as purely advisory, not lending, agencies.

International Loans

During 1947, the International Bank for Reconstruction and Development (IBRD) at long last broke out of its organizational cocoon and began to give some modest reconstruction assistance. Its total resources, paid in and available for lending, during its first year of operation, were only approximately $1 billion, as compared with the $3.5 billion lending authority of the United States Export-Import Bank and the special $3.75 billion American loan to the United Kingdom. Moreover the Bank's Articles of Agreement obliged it to observe various businesslike requirements, including repayment within a certain period and the charging of interest. During 1947, $497 million — about half the Bank's available resources — were loaned to four European countries — France, Denmark, Luxembourg and the Netherlands — for reconstruction programs that promised the greatest increase in production in the shortest possible time. At this time no loans were made to non-European countries, although the Bank's President, Mr. John J. McCloy, reported that the staff was studying that possibility.

European Coordination

The Economic Commission for Europe (ECE), created by ECOSOC early in 1947, was to take the place of the three existing non-UN European advisory reconstruction agencies (Emergency Economic Committee for Europe — EECE, European Coal Organization — ECO, and European Central Inland Transport Organization — ECITO) and to initiate measures to raise the level of European economic activity. Although the ECE, like other ECOSOC commissions, was born without binding authority and without large operational funds, it was to become a vigorous coordinating center due largely to the trails blazed by its predecessor agencies, the presence of the Big Three, the influential character of the representatives who usually attended, and the competence of the staff headed by the distinguished Swedish social scientist, Gunnar Myrdal.

The concept underlying this, as well as the other, ECOSOC Commissions, is as old as the first nineteenth-century technical "union" and especially characteristic of the allied economic boards during both world wars. It is based on voluntary intergovernmental cooperation through joint planning by national officials possessed of sufficient influence in their home administrations to carry out the projects collectively formulated. This concept works beautifully when hitched to firm and general determination on the part of the participating governments to make it work. Without this force to pull it along, it cannot move an inch.

Fortunately governments were willing to cooperate in many reconstruction efforts, mostly in matters that did not involve large financial sacrifices. During the last months of 1947 and the first of 1948, an elaborate hive of subcommittees, working parties, and expert groups was constructed under the direction of nine main committees. During the first eighteen months of ECE's existence, its sixty subsidiary bodies held 650 meetings attended by some 4,000 representatives. Its principal functions included studying and recommending measures aimed at

> increasing productivity and allocating scarce supplies of coal with the aim of European self-sufficiency; the development of power resources; improving the supply and use of "bottleneck" materials such as fertilizers, ball bearings, high tension insulators, conveyor belts, refractory materials and ceramic insulators; facilitating transportation; expanding the availability of metallurgical coke, scrap, and rich iron ore; preparing economic surveys of Europe; and promoting industrial development and trade, especially east-west exchange impeded by the cold war.

Shadow of the Marshall Plan. The boldest reconstruction move, however, came outside the UN when the United States Secretary of State, George

Marshall, during an address at Harvard University in June 1947, quietly dropped his hint heard 'round the world. The United States, he said, troubled by the increasing deficits of its friends and pressures of its enemies, was ready to consider a major European reconstruction program. The invitation was scarcely uttered before it was eagerly accepted by the British, French and others, not including the Soviet bloc, leading to the enactment by the United States Congress of the Economic Cooperation Act in April 1948, to be administered outside the UN. It is not surprising, therefore, that this unprecedented aid program tended to dominate the economic discussions of the Assembly during the fall of 1947. Poland and Yugoslavia led the Communist attack, criticizing the United States and United Kingdom for ignoring an Assembly recommendation of the previous year that aid be given without political considerations. They pointed out that the UN Special Technical Committee had recognized that Poland, Hungary and Yugoslavia were entitled to aid but had received none.

The U.S. led the counterattack, supported by the United Kingdom, France, Canada, and others, by saying that it was better to have aid outside the UN than none at all, that the Soviet Union had established its own regional aid program without reference to the UN, that the Soviet Union had refused the invitation to participate in the Marshall Plan, and that that program was in harmony with the UN Charter. Finally the Assembly adopted a resolution urging cooperation within the framework of the UN, but nothing was said about post-UNRRA UN reconstruction aid. That, apparently, was a closed chapter.

After frequently denouncing the ECE, and sometimes boycotting it, the Soviet Union, reflecting a new cooperative tactic following the death of Stalin, suddenly smiled on that body and announced during the March 1953 session that it intended to cooperate in various technical committees.

The 1953 edition of the valuable ECE annual surveys of the European economy focused a strong light on the need for greater intraregional collaboration, especially between Eastern and Western Europe, and the problem of the growing gap between prosperous Northwest and poverty-ridden Southeast Europe. This report played a part in the adoption of a resolution, introduced by Greece, Italy, Turkey and Yugoslavia, which invited the Secretariat to study and report on the possibilities of expanding and accelerating the development of the poorer areas, incidentally opening the door wide for cooperation with the Balkan Communist satellite nations.

Regarding the activities of the industry committees, the fields in which the most effective work seems to have been done are coal, electric power, steel, timber, transport and housing. ECE also initiated a determined effort during 1953 to promote greater intraregional collaboration in the field of agriculture, especially aimed at reducing barriers to the exchange of farm commodities. Qualifying these signs of progress, however, was the continuing fundamental antagonism between the Communist and non-Communist nations and the concern of non-European nations about the danger of regional isolationism fortified by various regional preferential arrangements.

RELIEF OPERATIONS

UN Continues Aid for Children

The only trickle of direct UN relief that leaked past the termination of UNRRA, other than the modest amounts involved in the International Refugee Organization program (discussed on pages 656–657), was that of the UN International Children's Emergency Fund (UNICEF).[18] This program was established in 1946 to continue temporarily to give food and other necessities to children in more or less the same countries as those helped by UNRRA. It began by furnishing supplemental foods, which countries otherwise would have had to import, to approximately six million children and mothers, equipment and training to improve the processing of milk, raw materials for children's clothing, and medical supplies.

As of March 1953, the Fund had received a total of $175 million of which 55 per cent, $96 million, had been given by the United States. Since 1950 the program had shifted constantly and radically away from aid to Europe towards the underdeveloped countries. By early 1953 the Fund was providing emergency and long-range food programs for more than a million children and mothers, conducting anti-tuberculosis campaigns covering fourteen million persons and yaws control campaigns affecting five million. In all, supplies and equipment were going out to seventy-five territories in Asia, Latin America, the Eastern Mediterranean and Africa. UNICEF resources also had the effect of extending the work of the specialized agencies. Where the WHO gave technical guidance on malaria, yaws, tuberculosis and other diseases, UNICEF supplied the necessary DDT, penicillin and other supplies. Although UNICEF contributions were also being matched by appropriations by the recipient countries, there continued to be efforts to terminate the program, especially in the United States Congress. Yet the appeal to aid needy children proved very hardy indeed. When the United States House of Representatives tried to eliminate the United States contribution in the summer of 1953, public opinion forced them finally to give as much as the previous year, $9.8 million. Then, in October 1953, the Assembly decided to make UNICEF a permanent organization.

Relief for Palestinian Arabs

Two other sizable UN relief operations have been launched to aid Arab refugees from Palestine and the hapless Korean people who have suffered so much since fighting broke out in their country in 1950. In both cases, the UN has felt a special responsibility to give financial as well as technical aid since the struggles in both areas had been so directly affected by UN policies. The effort in Palestine was initiated in 1948 by Count Folke Bernadotte, the UN Mediator in Palestine, as a means not only of trying to right certain wrongs that had been done but to remove one of the primary obstacles to a permanent peace settlement. While the program began

[14] For organizational description see p. 207.

chiefly as a relief operation, the General Assembly decided in December 1949 that the situation called for bolder and more constructive work projects aimed at the resettlement of the refugees outside of Israel.

The Arab states, however, have generally resisted this move, administered by the UN Relief and Works Agency for Palestine Refugees (UNRWAPR), and UN Member governments in general have been slow and rather tight-fisted in contributing to this operation. The 1951 Assembly approved a longer-range three-year program estimated to cost $250 million for relief and "reintegration." As of the end of 1953, however, progress was still far from satisfactory. The number of refugees under UN care, which had originally been about 900,000, still numbered 870,000, and only $147 million had been contributed.

Binding Up Korea's Wounds

The most recent and potentially most costly United Nations relief program was that created to help rebuild war-torn Korea. When the fighting broke out, ECOSOC asked all governments and agencies, in August 1950, to contribute assistance, and the Secretary-General established makeshift machinery to match offers of assistance against requests from the Unified Command. By the end of 1953, approximately $600 million in cash or kind had been contributed or pledged by fifty-four states.

To provide more long-range direction in such matters the Assembly approved, in the fall of 1950, the creation of a United Nations Commission for the Unification and Rehabilitation of Korea. Later in the session, the Assembly adopted a full-blown reconstruction plan based upon ECOSOC recommendations and strongly influenced by the wishes of the foremost contributor of military force in Korea, the United States:

> 1. Establishment of a United Nations Korean Reconstruction Agency (UNKRA) under direction of a United Nations Agent-General (to be an American, by general understanding) appointed by the Secretary-General and responsible to the General Assembly. The United Nations Commission for the Unification and Rehabilitation of Korea (UNCURK) was to issue binding decisions on where and with what authorities in Korea the UNKRA should operate but merely recommend on other policy questions. The general duties of the Agent-General were to ascertain rehabilitation requirements and provide for procurement and distribution.

> 2. Establishment of an Advisory Committee of five Member states (the Assembly subsequently elected the United States, United Kingdom, Canada, India and Uruguay) to advise the Agent-General on major economic questions.

> 3. Approval of a code of principles to govern the relief and rehabilitation including the objective to "lay the necessary economic foundations for the political unification and independence of the country," the warning that the program must not "serve as means for foreign economic and political interference," a statement that "all classes . . . shall receive their equitable shares . . . without discrimination . . . ," and the proviso that "all authorities in

Korea shall freely permit the personnel of the United Nations to supervise the distribution. . . ."

4. Agreement that contributions were to be voluntary in consultation with a Negotiating Committee of seven member states appointed by the Assembly President (United States, United Kingdom, France, Canada, India, Uruguay and Egypt).

In July 1951 an agreement was reached with the Unified Command whereby the military was to handle all short-term economic aid until military security had been established, confining UNKRA to furnishing technical assistance to the Republic of Korea, planning long-range reconstruction programs and implementing such reconstruction projects which would not interfere with military operations. While the situation was highly "fluid," the military-controlled United Nations Civilian Assistance Command provided the principal external relief amounting to some $300 million from the outset of the fighting to early 1953. Towards the end of that period, however, the front became sufficiently stable for UNKRA to undertake an initial program including the importation of grain, fertilizers and other consumer items as well as the reconstruction of the Taegu Medical College and hospital. The estimated cost for the fiscal year ending June 30, 1953, was $70 million. For its post-truce effort, the first estimate called for $250 million, of which $205 million had been pledged by August 1953, but actual contributions were characteristically feeble.

Technical Assistance for Development

It is said there is nothing new under the sun, and technical assistance is no exception. One study traces its modern antecedents to missionary work early in the nineteenth century.[19] It really began, of course, when the first primitive tribesman gave a neighbor a better seed or hammer. The modest technical efforts of the League of Nations have already been discussed above,[20] and UN agencies were intended from the beginning to render more of the same kind of expert advice. But, during the first year of the UN, 1946, a new concept was born which has ripened into the present far-flung UN Technical Assistance Program.

What is really novel is the greater volume of assistance and emphasis on direct field work by international employees to engage in "show-how," as distinguished from the more traditional League "tell-how." Of course the new approach is more expensive and was not possible until countries were willing to provide the funds. Another change of emphasis is the aiming of technical assistance at a particular group of countries designated as "underdeveloped." While all countries are underdeveloped in comparison with their potential, the delegates and staff of the UN have begun to realize

[19] Walter R. Sharp, *International Technical Assistance* (Chicago: Public Administration Service, 1952), pp. 1–23.
[20] See pp. 513–514.

THE UNDERDEVELOPED AREAS

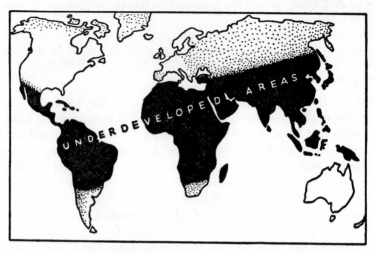

Two-thirds of world population live in the underdeveloped areas

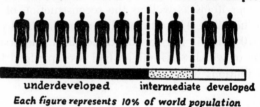

underdeveloped   intermediate   developed

Each figure represents 10% of world population

Headline Series, *Foreign Policy Association*

since the war, as never before, that there is a tremendous gap between the more and less developed, as suggested by the map and chart shown here. Another new factor underlying the UN Technical Assistance Program is the more widespread emphasis among governmental representatives on the relationship of economic development to world peace and the responsibility of the more advanced nations to contribute to that development. Finally, there is greater interest in and understanding of the complex problems involved in the process of economic development.

The seed from which the UN Technical Assistance Program has grown was planted during the General Assembly meetings in the fall of 1946 when the Lebanese delegation, under the leadership of Dr. Charles Malik, suggested the creation of technical "advisory boards" to advise countries needing technical assistance but anxious to avoid "bilateral agreements" which might "endanger . . . [their] economic independence." While Australia, Canada and the Soviet Union warned against overloading ECOSOC at that early date, the Assembly agreed to ask ECOSOC to study this proposal. When that body met at the beginning of 1947, it instructed the Secretary-General to create machinery in the Secretariat to facilitate the furnishing

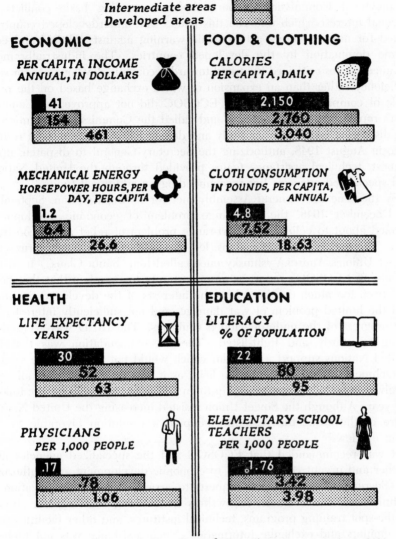

THE BASIC FACTORS

Underdeveloped areas
Intermediate areas
Developed areas

ECONOMIC

PER CAPITA INCOME
ANNUAL, IN DOLLARS

41
154
461

MECHANICAL ENERGY
HORSEPOWER HOURS, PER
DAY, PER CAPITA

1.2
6.4
26.6

FOOD & CLOTHING

CALORIES
PER CAPITA, DAILY

2,150
2,760
3,040

CLOTH CONSUMPTION
IN POUNDS, PER CAPITA,
ANNUAL

4.8
7.52
18.63

HEALTH

LIFE EXPECTANCY
YEARS

30
52
63

PHYSICIANS
PER 1,000 PEOPLE

.17
.78
1.06

EDUCATION

LITERACY
% OF POPULATION

22
60
95

ELEMENTARY SCHOOL
TEACHERS
PER 1,000 PEOPLE

1.76
3.42
3.98

Based on materials prepared by Dept. of State. Figures are mostly for 1939

GRAPHIC ASSOCIATES

Headline Series, *Foreign Policy Association*

of competent technical advice, including services by ECOSOC Commissions
and specialized agencies.

A PLAN IS BORN

More long-range thinking on the problem, including its relation to reconstruction, was stimulated during ECOSOC's fifth session, July to August

1947, as the members aimed some sharp criticism at the Economic and Employment Commission's report, thereby revealing basic conflicts of national interest which underlie this issue. The underdeveloped countries called for more concrete action while warning against political and economic domination by the developed countries. The industrially more advanced states criticized the trend towards economic development for self-sufficiency rather than an expansion of world exchange based on the principle of comparative advantage. ECOSOC did not approve the Commission's report but merely noted it and called the Commission's attention to the discussion. After further study and debate ECOSOC adopted a resolution, in August 1948, authorizing the Secretary-General to dispatch, upon request, technical assistance teams provided through the United Nations and specialized agencies but recommending no additional funds.

By the time the General Assembly met for its third session, September to December 1948, the long-range problem of economic development seemed about to eclipse the short-range problem of relief and reconstruction. The underdeveloped nations, led by Chile's Hernan Santa Cruz (the Soviet Union's Andrei Vyshinsky once called him "Santa Claus") used the debate on ECOSOC's report as an opportunity to complain that that body had been too much dominated by the interests of the developed countries and the limited problem of war damage, and not sufficiently interested in the progress of the underdeveloped countries. The IBRD was accused of being too tardy and tight-fisted. Their recommendation was that the United Nations support a program which would not only pay the salaries of technical experts sent into the field, as it was then doing, but all costs involved in technical assistance, up to an additional $500,000 for the following year. Although the Soviet Union resisted increasing the United Nations share of the costs, the Assembly adopted a resolution favorable to this point of view.

It was recommended that ECOSOC and the specialized agencies give further and urgent consideration to economic development and authorized the Secretary-General, upon request, to arrange for the organization of technical assistance teams, fellowships for training local experts abroad, on-the-spot training programs, technical institutes, and other facilities such as seminars and exchange information. Such assistance was not to be a "means of foreign economic and political interference" nor "accompanied by any considerations of a political nature." It was to be given only to, or through, governments; designed to meet the needs of the country concerned; provided, as far as possible, in the form the requesting country desired; and of high quality and technical competence [Resolution 200 (III)]. But the Assembly appropriated only $288,000 to implement this plan. In another resolution the Assembly, responding to a Brazilian proposal, authorized the Secretary-General to report to ECOSOC on arrangements for an International Center for Training in Public Administration, although the financially hard-pressed British and others thought this a rather expensive luxury. These decisions did not add up to the extensive program the less developed nations had hoped for, but they were all that could be had in the absence of substantial new funds.

Creation of Expanded Program

The Chinese Communists, however, were beginning to press the Nationalist regime to the wall, and, in January 1949, United States President Harry Truman announced, as "point four" in his inaugural address proposals, a "bold new program" to accelerate technical assistance to underdeveloped countries. As part of this campaign, the United States delegation proposed a resolution which ECOSOC adopted, in March 1949, calling on Member governments to promote the expansion of technical assistance, especially through the United Nations and specialized agencies. ECOSOC also requested the Secretary-General to submit a comprehensive plan for expanded technical assistance and, on the initiative of some of the less developed countries, methods of financing economic development. A working party, representing the staff heads of the United Nations and the specialized agencies, then ground out a bulky document which came to be known as the "Gray Book," the virtual "Bible" of the expanded program.[21]

The experts' hope for an initial appropriation of $85 million was pruned considerably when the United States let it be known that $25 million seemed more realistic. This was a particularly bitter pill for the underdeveloped countries that had hoped the United States would support an ambitious technical assistance effort with proportionately generous financial aid. The many arguments for and against this program were to be repeated during the succeeding Assembly session and are discussed below.

The essence of the resolution finally adopted by ECOSOC is as follows:

1. ECOSOC requested the Administrative Committee on Coordination (ACC) to set up a Technical Assistance Board (TAB), composed of the staff heads of the United Nations and specialized agencies participating in the new program, to coordinate these organizations' activities in connection with the program.

2. ECOSOC was to establish a Technical Assistance Committee (TAC), composed of representatives of all members of ECOSOC, to be the latter's agent in giving general direction to TAB and the program as a whole.

3. The General Assembly was asked to authorize the Secretary-General to set up a special account to be nourished by voluntary contributions from Member governments. The first $10 million and 70 per cent of the second $10 million were to be allocated automatically according to the following schedule: UN, 23 per cent; ILO, 11 per cent; FAO, 29 per cent; UNESCO, 14 per cent; ICAO, 1 per cent; WHO, 22 per cent. 30 per cent of the second $10 million and all further contributions were to be allocated by TAB.

4. ECOSOC decided to call a Technical Assistance Conference to negotiate the national contributions and consent to allocation among agencies.

5. It was recommended the program be administered according to An-

---

[21] *Technical Assistance for Economic Development: Plan for an expanded cooperative programme through the United Nations and the specialized agencies.* UN Sales No.: 1949.II.B.1.

nex I, a set of governing principles which included the principles contained in the Assembly's previous resolution on technical assistance [200 (III)] listed above [22] plus others: (a) The objective was to help underdeveloped countries strengthen their economies in order to promote their economic and political independence and insure higher levels of economic and social welfare for their populations; (b) the program should avoid distinctions arising from the political structure of a country or its people's race or religion; (c) experts should have sympathetic understanding of cultural backgrounds and needs of countries, be adaptable to local conditions, understand the broad objectives of the common effort, be open-minded, and not engage in political, commercial, or any activities other than those for which sent; (d) requesting governments should cooperate by defining nature and scope of problem, providing relevant information, creating adequate coordination machinery, giving full and prompt consideration to technical advice received, assuming as much of cost as possible and progressive financial responsibility for administration of projects; (e) agencies should select projects according to goals set forth in Charter and United Nations resolutions, their potential for wide and equitable distribution of benefits as well as increased productivity of resources, the likelihood of quick results, urgency and geographic distribution of national needs, and possibility of adequate financial support.

While bowing to the myth of national sovereignty, ECOSOC was fashioning an instrument that could exert revolutionary influences within the underdeveloped countries.

The Assembly Approves

It was this expanded program which "stole the show" during the General Assembly's economic discussions from September to December 1949. This was the first significant operational program which the United States was largely instrumental in assigning to a United Nations agency since the days of UNRRA. The plan was also strengthened by the fact that it received the unanimous support of the other members of the Assembly including the Soviet Union which was remarkably friendly to it though it never consented to contribute financially to its support until 1953. Still the program was to furnish only advice, not to finance large-scale development, and consequently involved relatively small sums of money (approximately $20 million a year as compared with an average of $915 million a year spent on UNRRA from 1944 to 1947).

During the discussion of the plan, one of the recurring themes voiced by most states was that the program should be governed by ECOSOC's code of governing principles, with particular emphasis on the need for sympathetic understanding of local conditions and avoidance of political and economic interference contrary to the wishes of the requesting governments. The Soviet Union and its satellites urged that the program be kept clear of the contaminating influence of the United States imperialistic

[22] See p. 548.

Point Four Program. Many underdeveloped countries pressed the importance of industrial development as the best way of soaking up surplus population, raising the material standard of living quickly, and freeing themselves from domination by the more developed countries. Others, including industrial powers, thought primary attention should be devoted to increasing the food supply, warned against economic isolation, and urged coordinated development on a regional basis.

Some dissatisfaction was expressed regarding the initial allocation of funds among participating agencies, but it was decided to try the proposed schedule for at least a year. Related to this issue was the Polish-led move to increase the authority of the governmental Technical Assistance Committee (same composition as ECOSOC) over the Technical Assistance Board (staff heads of UN and participating specialized agencies), including the allocation function. But the majority, including the United States and the United Kingdom, decided to leave operating responsibility to the relatively nonpolitical Board. Finally, by one of the Assembly's rare unanimous votes, the ECOSOC plan was adopted on November 16, 1949. Most of the major nations of the world, including the two greatest powers, had worked through the United Nations to launch one of the most constructive acts of international statesmanship since the creation of UNRRA.

TECHNICAL ASSISTANCE OPERATIONS

After the initial "tooling up" during 1950, the "Expanded" Technical Assistance Program began to run at full speed in 1951. By 1953 the UN Secretariat felt the program justified considerably more than the modest annual $20 million previously allowed it. Solid accomplishments in almost all the non-Communist countries of the world were demonstrating the exciting potential of this effort.

> A 51-day stay in Iran was sufficient for a team of UN . . . water resource experts, using aerial photography, to locate 50 sites for wells. Thai farmers, after learning from FAO experts of techniques developed accidentally in the Canary Islands, were able to cultivate pineapple as a year-round crop. . . . In India, the operatives in the Ambica spinning and weaving mills, with the help of an ILO expert in textile production, were able to cut by 50 per cent the number of cones which failed to empty completely and greatly to reduce incidental damage. The output of an iron foundry in Pakistan was increased by 44 per cent . . . , and an FAO expert adviser in workshop practices to the Indian State Government of Uttar Pradish has been able to report remarkable gains in efficiency.[23]

The rapid unfolding of this expanded program is dramatically illustrated in the chart, "The Development of the Expanded Program," on page 552. The distribution of funds by agency and region is illustrated in the bar graph, "Agency Earmarkings and Regional Distributions for 1953," on page 553, showing that Asia and the Far East receive the lion's share, followed

[23] *United Nations Bulletin,* Vol. 15, No. 2 (July 15, 1953), pp. 31, 43.

by Latin America, the Middle East, Europe and Africa, in that order. The charts — "What Four Countries Contributed and Received in 1952" — appear on page 554.

Agricultural Front

FAO was the first and most active technical assistance missionary in the production field. Its trail-blazing ambition, under the driving leadership of Sir John Boyd Orr, was demonstrated remarkably early when it dispatched to Greece, in May 1946, as ECOSOC was just getting itself organized, the first UN-affiliated technical assistance survey mission sent to any country. That group did not limit itself to agricultural problems but recommended, in a report published in March 1947, a comprehensive long-range plan dealing with industry, power, transportation and monetary policy as well as food. It also suggested financing by the IBRD and supervision by a joint mission comprised of representatives from the UN, FAO, IBRD, IMF, and other cooperating agencies. While these proposals did not bear fruit for a long time, due to the immediate pressure of short-term relief and reconstruction needs, they did exert significant influence not only on UN and United States assistance to Greece but also by helping to show the way in the development of the modern technical assistance concept.

Still FAO's anemic budget forced it to stretch its funds as far as possible by resorting to the more traditional device of spreading technical knowl-

NUMBER OF EXPERTS EMPLOYED

1950-1*	7
1952	1(
1953•	2!

NUMBER OF FELLOWSHIPS AWARDED   EACH UNIT REPRESENTS 100 INDIVID(

1950-1*	8
1952	2(
1953•	18

TOTAL OBLIGATIONS INCURRED   EACH UNIT REPRESENTS 1,000,000)

1950-1*	$6,43
1952	$22,96
1953•	$25,30

* *1950-1 Eighteen months*   • *1953 Approved Program*

UN I

THE DEVELOPMENT OF THE EXPANDED PROGRAM

edge through conferences of top experts, usually with influential governmental connections. Most of these meetings, during 1946 and 1947, dealt with broad functional fields: agricultural techniques, animal health, timber, fisheries, nutrition, storage, distribution, and utilization. Other conferences dealt with the problems of specific regions, often in cooperation with the ECOSOC regional commissions. The technical assistance work closest to the "grass roots" was the furnishing of continuing on-the-spot agricultural production advice to Austria, China, Czechoslovakia, Ethiopia, Greece, Hungary, Italy, Poland and Yugoslavia — work inherited from UNRRA in July 1947 together with $600,000 to finance it. Other services included FAO demonstration "schools" for experts on such subjects as artificial insemination, food preservation, soil conservation, and grain storage. In Asia the FAO also sponsored the creation of two permanent bodies to encourage groups of countries to work together cooperatively to help improve production, distribution and utilization in key fields. These were the Indo-Pacific Fisheries Council and the International Rice Commission, both of which first met in March 1949.

From 1950 on, the FAO was able to accelerate its technical assistance efforts, due primarily to the expanded technical assistance program which more than doubled its annual resources. Hence, Director-General Norris Dodd could gladly report at the end of 1952 that there had been greater progress that year than in the previous five years. And yet, reminiscent of the frantic exertions of the Red Queen in *Alice in Wonderland* just to stay

REGIONAL PERCENTAGES

TOTAL	AFRICA	ASIA AND FAR EAST	EUROPE	LATIN AMERICA	MIDDLE EAST	INTER-REGIONAL
$ 5,308,000	4.3%	23.4%	11.2%	29.2%	20.4%	11.5%
$ 6,693,000	11.3%	30.2%	8.4%	22.2%	27.6%	0.3%
$ 2,539,000	6.1%	29.5%	20.5%	34.6%	9.3%	
$ 3,231,000	12.3%	29.1%	5.6%	29.7%	23.3%	
$ 1,052,000	7.0%	36.6%	11.9%	13.6%	30.9%	
$ 5,078,000	3.7%	39.6%	6.5%	24.4%	22.7%	3.1%

100.%

UN Bulletin

AGENCY EARMARKINGS AND REGIONAL DISTRIBUTION FOR 1953

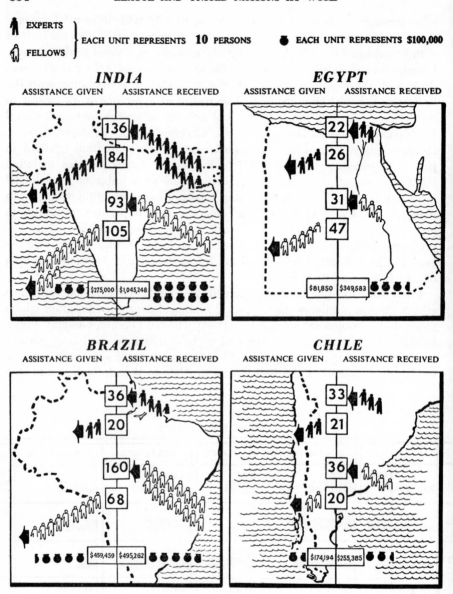

EXPERTS
FELLOWS
} EACH UNIT REPRESENTS **10** PERSONS   EACH UNIT REPRESENTS **$100,000**

INDIA
ASSISTANCE GIVEN   ASSISTANCE RECEIVED

136
84
93
105
$275,000 | $1,045,248

EGYPT
ASSISTANCE GIVEN   ASSISTANCE RECEIVED

22
26
31
47
$81,850 | $349,583

BRAZIL
ASSISTANCE GIVEN   ASSISTANCE RECEIVED

36
20
160
68
$459,459 | $495,262

CHILE
ASSISTANCE GIVEN   ASSISTANCE RECEIVED

33
21
36
20
$174,194 | $255,385

UN Bulletin

WHAT FOUR COUNTRIES CONTRIBUTED AND RECEIVED IN 1952

Showing the Number of Experts and Fellows who Received from and Contributed
to the Program, the Amount Contributed, and the Total Value of Assistance Received.

in the same spot, a 1 per cent world food production increase during 1951–52 had barely kept abreast of the rate of population growth and provided no net improvement. The average food supply per person over large areas of the world, especially in Asia, was still lower than before the war, and the proportion of the world's population with inadequate food supplies had grown appreciably larger. Rearmament, moreover, had pulled productive capacity away from food towards "money crops" of fibers and rubber.[24]

Progress at the "Grass Roots." FAO's activities not only doubled in intensity after 1950 but placed special emphasis on implementing the Assembly's effort to help the poorer farmers and persuading governments to set nutrition and distribution as well as production goals. To finance its technical assistance activities FAO received $6 million from the United Nations expanded program during 1952 as compared with its own regular annual budget of $5.3 million. By the end of 1952 agreements had been concluded with 52 countries calling for 890 experts, of whom 243 had completed their work, 399 were in the field or about to be sent out, leaving 248 still to be recruited.

In the field of "agricultural technology," FAO concentrated on crop production, animal husbandry, management of soil and water, pest and disease control, development of government agricultural "extension" services, accelerating training to overcome bottlenecks of various skills, and fostering cooperatives, credit facilities, land reform, and other rural welfare activities. An intriguing example of one of the hundreds of FAO technical assistance projects can be taken from a mission to Burma, the first under the expanded program.

> There were two interesting elements in the problem: a critical need for modern housing and the existence of large areas of forest containing species hard to process and therefore unmerchantable . . . logs of several . . . species were shipped to Germany for testing. . . . Among other tests, the logs were successfully chipped; the chips, pressed into chip-boards and panels and treated with insect- and decay-preventive chemicals; these panels were designed for assembly into a prefabricated house. Several houses were put together, then taken apart, and are now on the way to Burma. . . .[25]

In the field of "agricultural economics," the FAO gave special attention to improving measures to assist countries suffering from famine. Recent food crises in countries such as India, Pakistan and Yugoslavia had led ECOSOC, during the spring of 1951, to recommend that governments and interested agencies plan in advance coordinated action to meet famine emergencies, that FAO perfect arrangements to foresee such emergencies, and that the Secretary-General act as the central coordinator for private and public relief efforts. FAO also engaged in studies of the crucial importance of encouraging investment in agricultural development, examination

---

[24] See FAO, *Second World Food Survey,* November 1952.
[25] *United Nations Bulletin,* Vol. 14, No. 1 (January 1, 1953), p. 65.

of various balance of payments difficulties, a survey of existing stabilization measures, evaluation of the food and agriculture position in Member states, reviews of general prospects for demand and prices, and technical assistance and analysis regarding agricultural statistics.

"Land Reform" and Politics. The political significance of the agricultural problem was forcibly brought home when the Soviet bloc, during the 1950 General Assembly, supported a Polish resolution aimed at winning the good will of poor farmers. It was proposed that ECOSOC draw up plans to help indigent peasants through land reform, cheap credit, technical assistance, shops to make and repair agricultural machinery, lower taxes, and other welfare measures. A large majority, including the United States and United Kingdom, accepted the challenge by approving the general goals but rejecting elements smacking of Communist theory and administration. The Assembly's resolution recommended that the Secretary-General, in cooperation with FAO and other specialized agencies, submit to ECOSOC an analysis of the degree to which unsatisfactory forms of "agrarian structure," especially land tenure, were impeding economic development. ECOSOC was then to prepare recommendations to the Assembly to improve the conditions of agricultural populations, giving special attention to the problems mentioned by Poland plus rural cooperatives and the general security and welfare of agricultural workers.

A year later, at the end of 1951, the Assembly adopted a set of agricultural objectives that went far beyond those anticipated by the original Polish proposal and promised to be a propaganda boomerang to the Soviet bloc. Its provisions recommended that:

> 1. governments institute appropriate land reforms and other measures such as the promotion of security of land tenure; opportunity to acquire ownership; efficient size of holdings; reasonable credit, rentals, and taxes; cooperative organizations; diversification of production; complementary industries; agricultural workshops; education; improved conditions for agricultural wage laborers.
> 2. specialized agencies and the Secretary-General help regarding these suggestions and check on their implementation.

More to be Done. With all of this hard work, the quest for more of the right kinds of food, better distributed, still stands at the top of the UN's list of first priority problems. We have seen, moreover, that the race between food and population has taken a turn for the worse in many areas as compared with prewar days. Yet leaders in the international agricultural field believe that the world has it within its power to put food supply out ahead of population growth.

Unfortunately, however, nations are not yet taking sufficient measures to win this contest. Far more needs to be done, especially in the following fields: bringing new areas into cultivation (Mexico intends to irrigate two and a half million acres which could make that nation self-sufficient and provide some surplus); soil conservation and the development of better breeds of animals and plants (such as hybrid corn); increasing the supply of fish which is particularly nutritious (the FAO estimates that the yield might be doubled without risk to the world's fish resources); reducing losses through pests and diseases (the annual loss in cereals and oil seeds alone is estimated at 10 per cent of world production); improving the lot of the farmer (through land reform, easier credit, cooperatives, better health measures, and other welfare measures); increasing investment in agricultural improvements (increasing fertilizer production and bringing new land into cultivation are costly enterprises); and organizing more effective international cooperation to help assure adequate and stable world supplies at reasonable prices and to improve distribution to the neediest peoples.[26]

Regional Commissions at Work

Among ECOSOC agencies, the work of ECE, concerned as much with reconstruction as development and overshadowed by the ERP, has been dealt with above. ECAFE and ECLA, created by ECOSOC in March 1947 and February 1948 respectively, are the regional commissions primarily involved in development.

In an area in which needs were vast and its own resources decidedly puny, ECAFE began by concentrating on studies of certain key fields aimed at coordinating national and international development programs, on a regional basis as far as possible. It did not think in terms of building a large staff of its own but of acting chiefly as a go-between, seeking financial and technical aid from other organizations. Its efforts have focused particularly on the following fields:

> iron and steel, coal, electric power, transport, monetary policy, trade, improvement of agriculture through an FAO–ECAFE Joint Working Party, textiles, improving technical training in cooperation with the ILO, economic surveys of Asia and the Far East, and studying flood control.

The latter activity aroused considerable controversy as the result of a Chinese proposal for an independent advisory and operational Bureau of Flood Control to help harness the great Asian rivers. Certain ECOSOC members, clustering around the United States and Canada, opposed committing the United Nations to sponsor a body with such an ambitious and autonomous mandate. Ultimately, in the summer of 1948, ECOSOC approved a purely advisory Bureau to consist of three to five experts, appointed by the Secretary-General, to be attached to the ECAFE staff administratively but independent in its technical advice.

The proposal for an Economic Commission for Latin America had to surmount considerable opposition on the part of some of the more influential powers. The United States, United Kingdom, Canada and others all pointed to the likelihood of overlap with the Inter-American Economic and

[26] For fuller analysis, see Frank L. McDougall, "Food and Population," *International Conciliation*, No. 486 (December 1952).

Social Council. There was also a shaking of heads about encouraging the creation of regional bodies, originally intended solely for emergency reconstruction work, as contrary to the global functional approach. Nonetheless, the Latin Americans won the day.

During 1948 and 1949, the initial work of ECLA was concerned largely with exploratory studies of such fields as agricultural credit; water resources; transportation, storage, distribution and marketing of commodities; and technical training and assistance. By 1950, the Commission began to emerge from its study stage to more active participation in helping to plan and carry out further development in specific fields. Particular emphasis was placed on iron and steel, paper and pulp manufacture, the economic integration of Central America, technical training, programming economic development, financing development, the relation of agriculture to industrialization, and increasing trade.

Not to be outdone, the Middle East countries, under the leadership of Egypt, had also proposed an Economic Commission for the Middle East during the 1947 General Assembly, but the dispute with Israel later persuaded them to postpone that plan indefinitely.

Other Activities

The two specialized agencies, other than the FAO mentioned above, which provide direct technical assistance in the production field are the IBRD and ILO. In connection with particular loan applications the Bank has investigated applicant countries with a fine-tooth comb, studying such matters as:

> economic justification, technical feasibility, financial soundness, prospective market to be served, availability of local capital to meet local costs, labor supply, and availability and quality of management personnel.

So useful did these on-the-spot studies prove in the early years, that the Bank decided to expand this field work, including missions of a broader character to make general surveys and recommendations on the over-all development potential of countries. The experts for these activities have frequently been drawn from other agencies as well as the Bank's own staff. The Bank has also experimented with assigning personnel for longer periods as resident advisers to governments, beginning with Nicaragua. The ILO's technical assistance activities regarding manpower supply and training, labor-management relations, social security systems, health and welfare, and other matters are discussed in Chapter 21. UNESCO assists in educational projects.

Related to these efforts to make better use of the world's resources was the special United Nations Scientific Conference on the Conservation and Utilization of Resources (UNSCCUR) which met at Lake Success, New York, from August to September 1949. The meetings were attended by more than seven hundred experts from over fifty countries. Their major objective was not to make recommendations but to exchange views on the adequacy of resources to meet growing demands. The main issues examined included:

> resource depletion, critical shortages (food, forests, minerals, fuels), interdependence of resources, use and conservation, development of new resources by applied technology, education for conservation, techniques for less-developed countries, and integrated development of river basins.

In spite of all the dark resource dilemmas that confronted them, however, most of these experts seemed confident that the world could, if it would, improve its living standard rather than devour itself.

WEIGHING THE BENEFITS

All these facts and figures tell a remarkable story. Never before has any international program done so much in so many varied fields to improve the lot of so many different peoples all over the world. UNRRA spent more money, but concentrated on only a few war-damaged countries and devoted most of its resources to relief and rehabilitation rather than development. The United States and other individual governments have initiated larger development programs, with more funds for capital investment, but these are bilateral, not multilateral, programs which seldom stimulate as general or whole-hearted cooperation on the part of the recipients as the UN projects.[27] In essence, the unique contribution of the latter is not in the volume of assistance, but in its geographical extent, its fostering of closer truly cooperative links among nations, its avoidance of projects tied to short-term political and strategic considerations, and its giving concrete expression to the United Nations idea at the local level.

The UN program's specific achievements include not only raising the over-all level of material wealth but modestly and gradually beginning to promote a more equitable distribution of that wealth among all classes. It has also influenced governments to improve their administrative processes, especially in comprehensive coordination and long-range planning. Nor is this merely a one-way "hand out." It has stimulated an impressive amount of local self-help in the form of planning, saving, and investing. Each government is obliged to pay as much of the domestic currency costs as possible, e.g., lodging, local travel, office space, local interpreters, and clerks. Of the sixty-four nations contributing experts and the sixty-five pledging financial contributions to the program during 1952, well over half in each case were underdeveloped countries.

Because most of the countries consider themselves real partners in this effort, rather than mere objects of charity, and because the program serves no single national interest, there is less political resistance to it and greater readiness to comply with its demands than is the case with most bilateral projects. The United Nations is also in a position to tap a wider range of

[27] Walter R. Sharp, "The Institutional Framework for Technical Assistance," *International Organization*, Vol. 7, No. 3 (August 1953), pp. 347–348.

Ned White in the Akron Beacon-Journal

RESISTANCE TO BILATERAL AID

"Looking a gift horse in the mouth"

personnel with a broader selection of skills and cultural backgrounds. Frequently an expert from an underdeveloped country can render more appropriate and sympathetic assistance to another somewhat similar country than a person from a far more developed country.

Administrative Improvements

The United Nations administrative machinery has also received dividends from this program. Nothing has done more to knit the various economic and social units of the United Nations and specialized agencies more closely together than the development of the technical assistance coordinating processes. At first the going was rather rough. TAB was a "concert" of sovereign staff heads who originally found it difficult to agree on the allocation of funds — hence the rigid formula for the automatic division of over half the contributions — and were understandably hesitant to interfere very much with each other's projects. Soon, however, especially as demands for assistance outstripped funds, the necessity for firmer coordination became increasingly apparent.

In 1952 ECOSOC approved the Secretary-General's appointment of a full-time Executive Chairman for the TAB authorized to review all proposals and recommend a coordinated program to the Board. Decisions of the Board were also allowed to be by majority, rather than the previous unanimity, to preclude sabotage by a single recalcitrant agency. By this time, moreover, the proportion of funds which could be freely allocated by the Board had increased from the original 30 per cent of the second $10 million to 50 per cent of all contributions. Related to these changes was the tense situation which arose during 1952–53 when the TAB decided to reduce the share of the WHO in favor of other agencies, especially the FAO.

At the local level another significant improvement has been the appointment of resident technical assistance representatives to draw together the strings of all United Nations and specialized agency projects in countries where these bodies are most active. In 1953 these representatives and their senior assistants were stationed in twenty-two countries and drawn from thirteen different nations. They are admirably situated to take a broader and more long-range look at a country's problems than most of the specialized experts. They provide an important element of continuity; are usually well equipped to deal with local leadership; and provide a strategic point of field contact with bilateral projects, especially United States "Point Four" staffs.

The Obstacles

As vigorously as this program has grown, the soil in which it has taken root is far from friendly. Funds are quite inadequate to nourish the host of valid national requests which have sprouted, particularly since 1952. The underdeveloped countries made a determined effort during the 1952 Assembly to set a goal of $40 million rather than the usual $20 million. But this was scaled down to $25 million. Then, in the summer of 1953, the United States Congress cut the Administration's proposed donation to this program from $13.8 million to $9.5 million. It is interesting to compare this with the $118 million voted at the same time for bilateral United States assistance to underdeveloped countries. The American contribution would have been cut even more drastically had not the Soviet Union announced in July 1953 it would give $1 million as its first contribution to the UN program. This was significant recognition of the vigor and widespread influence of the effort among countries whose confidence the Soviet Union wished to win.

The funds have not only been small but they have trickled into the United Nations till at what the *United Nations Bulletin* has called a "leisurely pace." Of the $20 million pledged for 1952, $1.5 million was still unpaid three months after the close of that year. The pledging conference for 1953 was not held until the end of February of that year, thus making life extremely difficult for those responsible for planning the year's projects. And the pledges included services as well as fifty different currencies, the majority of which were inconvertible. Obviously the program would benefit by receiving more funds, sooner, and in convertible currencies.

Other difficulties have their roots in the inherent problems of planning economic and social development. Who should do the planning — experts, politicians, national or international agencies? What goals should be set? How does one weigh the relative importance of health, food, industry, roads and education? Should the plans be made on a national, regional, or global basis? How far ahead is it practical and desirable to try to plan? The United Nations, specialized agencies, and national governments are just beginning to wade into the depths of these questions. Nonetheless there seems to be a mounting consensus that there should be more long-range planning in terms of a broader regional and world framework.

It must also be recognized that some of the UN's objectives are little less than anathema to certain vested interests and have aroused determined opposition. The basic 1949 Assembly resolution on technical assistance stated clearly that one of the program's aims was not only increased productivity but "wide and equitable distribution of the benefits" in order to provide "higher standards of living for the entire population." Some interests favor only increased productivity to benefit their own enterprises but not a spreading of the wealth which would entirely alter the economic, political, and social character of their countries. Hence the United Nations must make some difficult choices. It is obviously limited in the direct pressure it can bring to bear. Undoubtedly it is wiser to concentrate first on getting into a country and then gradually to begin to influence broader questions. Related to this is the tendency, according to the 1953 Secretariat economic survey, for the gap in productivity between the richest and poorest nations to broaden rather than narrow. And it is unlikely that the technical assistance program, operating on its present starvation diet, can do much to reverse this trend.

On the administrative side there is need for further tightening of the coordinating processes among the United Nations and specialized agencies in order to withstand particularistic pressures. No less important but even more difficult is the problem of working more closely with national bilateral activities. In order to assure a supply of the most competent personnel it is also likely that the United Nations will be compelled to offer longer-term contracts, to at least some experts who can be used on that basis, and to pay more liberal compensation to match higher national standards. Operations would also benefit from more thorough advance consultation with and briefing of personnel destined for the field. Finally, there should be better administration, coordination, and follow-up on the part of the recipient governments.

Financing Economic Development

Advice without money has seemed a poor bargain to the underdeveloped countries. Many of them have been surveyed and advised until they never want to see another foreign expert. What they yearn for most of all are funds to put the advice to work. And the clamor for financial assistance to support economic development has increased in direct proportion to the large-scale assistance given by the United States to the developed countries, chiefly since the European Recovery Program was initiated in 1947.

But the financial ambitions of the underdeveloped countries have many handicaps to overcome. Much of the foundation improvement needed — roads, sanitation, irrigation, etc., — is not attractive to private investors. Moreover, there have been unhappy experiences with foreign investment involving exploitation on both sides. Economic penetration has sometimes been the entering wedge for political intervention. The underdeveloped nations have often reacted, copying the practices of some western powers, with excessively protectionist policies. The health of their economies is usually in a delicate state, dependent, as they often are, on only a few primary commodities for export, hampered by a virtual hand-to-mouth existence, with a low volume of savings much of which is frequently siphoned off into foreign investment. Governmental economic policies often suffer from inefficient, if not venal, administration, unrealistic planning, a heritage of abortive national and foreign "plans," and a lack of established contact with influential United States and European banking officials. These factors, plus prosperous conditions in the United States, have tended to keep private investment at home.

Against this gloomy background, the underdeveloped Member governments of the United Nations have hoped to use that organization as a means of irrigating their thirsty economies by tapping substantial financial assistance from the developed countries in addition to technical advice. The only body provided by the major powers for this purpose is the International Bank for Reconstruction and Development (IBRD) which has only modest resources and is obliged to observe certain regulations which, to the poorer countries, have seemed too conservative and hence designed in a way calculated to benefit the more developed countries.

LOANS FOR DEVELOPMENT

In 1948, however, the European Recovery Program made it possible for the IBRD, under United States leadership, to shift markedly from European reconstruction loans to non-European developmental loans. While the over-all volume of its annual lending never rose above $800 million as of the end of 1953, the proportion of financing aimed at non-European development, as distinguished from European reconstruction, grew rapidly as can be seen in the following comparative figures:

Fiscal Year	Developmental Loans No.	Developmental Loans Total Amount	All Loans Total Amount
1947–48	2	$ 16 million	$247 million
1948–49	3	109	137
1949–50	8	134	166
1950–51	21	297	297
1951–52	18	292	299
1952–53	10	179	179

By the end of the calendar year 1953, the total loans granted had reached the substantial total of about $1,664 million.

Besides these quantitative measures, there were other indications that the Bank was making a determined effort to meet the complaints of the underdeveloped countries by liberalizing its policies within the limitations of its Articles of Agreement. To deal with the problem of non-self-liquidating projects, the Bank was willing to base loans on the general capacity of a country to repay a loan, rather than the ability of a particular project to produce the necessary income. In this connection, the Bank was placing increased emphasis on basic agricultural investment (mechanization, land clearance, irrigation, flood control and storage) which had been relatively neglected in the past. The Bank made the most of its authority to lend to private enterprises when guaranteed by governments or sponsored by government-backed development banks and other go-between arrangements. The mobilization of local capital was stimulated through the organization of such development banks and the marketing of domestic securities.

CAMPAIGN TO LOOSEN PURSE STRINGS

But the underdeveloped countries were not content. They particularly wanted more liberal loan terms with respect to repayment time limits and interest rates. They wanted outright grants for "non-self-liquidating" projects. To implement these policies they wanted either to liberalize the authority of the IBRD or create a new agency.

The United Kingdom, France, and other seriously war-damaged countries felt they could afford very little external assistance and wanted to concentrate most of that in their own territories. The United States and Canada, who could afford to give more, were decidedly cool towards the idea of pouring their treasure into what they considered to be a bottomless pit. They did not want to go beyond the IBRD; they stressed self-help, improving the "climate" for private investment, mobilizing domestic savings, increasing production and exports, improving administration, and reducing barriers to imports.

Since 1948, United Nations consideration of the financing question has traveled the ground of these arguments again and again in a protracted tug-of-war between the underdeveloped nations — led by such countries as India, Chile and Brazil — and the developed states — led by the United

States, United Kingdom and Canada. The Soviet bloc has stood on the sidelines cheering the underdeveloped nations, warning them against falling into the vampire embrace of the imperialists, but never offering the UN a single ruble of financial aid. After fruitless discussions in ECOSOC, the Economic and Employment Commission and its Sub-Commission on Economic Development, from the time of the initiation of the Marshall Plan in the summer of 1947 through 1948, the underdeveloped countries succeeded in having the Assembly, at the end of 1948, request the Secretary-General to study methods of financing development. But that report failed to budge ECOSOC off dead center, and again the underdeveloped countries exploded in their favorite forum, the General Assembly, at the end of 1949. Although the United States was willing now to sponsor the expanded technical assistance program, discussed above, it was not willing to promise any further financial assistance through the United Nations. And, again, the Assembly asked ECOSOC to study the matter.

Plans Develop

By the eleventh session of ECOSOC, July to August 1950, a group of independent specialists had recommended, as part of a report on measures to promote full employment, that the IBRD's functions should be expanded, a view supported by Australia, Brazil, Chile, France and others. The Sub-Commission on Economic Development had suggested creating a new United Nations administration to finance development on a more liberal basis. India and Iran were among those endorsing this proposal. The United States and United Kingdom favored the Bank's plan to give increasing attention to the needs of the underdeveloped countries but opposed altering the Bank's constitution. Yet the United Kingdom delegate agreed with the Sub-Commission that much essential development of a "social overhead" nature could not be financed by the Bank and felt that more attention should be given to finding an alternative solution.

The final resolution, drafted chiefly by the United States, United Kingdom, France, Canada, Australia, Brazil, and Chile, was more heavily weighted on the side of the developed than the underdeveloped countries. It recommended that:

1. underdeveloped countries form banking syndicates or development banks to attract and channel foreign investments into essential projects;

2. governments establish conditions to encourage participation of private capital;

3. the more developed countries grant the IBRD permission to use increasing parts of the 18 per cent of their subscriptions pledged in domestic currencies and consider granting permission to the Bank to place its bond issues in their financial markets;

4. governments extend the principle of untied lending to all governmentally controlled or guaranteed lending;

5. the underdeveloped countries do a better job of planning, especially

in the formulation of integrated development programs and projects appropriate for the IBRD;

6. national and international credit organizations consider more effective ways of promoting integrated investment programs, generally accelerating economic development, financing indirect as well as direct foreign costs of development projects, and liberalizing interest rates and amortization periods;

7. the IMF study, in cooperation with the IBRD, the capacity of under-developed countries to service foreign investments;

8. the Secretary-General study the relation of fluctuations of the prices of primary products to the ability of underdeveloped countries to obtain foreign exchange.

The attack redoubled during the Assembly session in the fall of 1950, and the United States and United Kingdom yielded slightly to agree to a resolution recommending that ECOSOC consider and report to the Assembly's sixth session "practical methods, conditions and policies for achieving the adequate expansion and steadier flow of foreign capital . . . and pay special attention to the financing of non-self-liquidating projects. . . . " By the summer of 1951, a further expert report on "full employment" measures carried the fight one step beyond the principles previously approved by ECOSOC to recommend, among other things,

increased IBRD lending to underdeveloped countries to $1 billion annually; creation by the UN of an international development authority to assist in preparing, coordinating, and implementing development plans and to distribute grants-in-aid for specific purposes; and exploration by the UN of the possibility of establishing an international finance corporation to make equity investments and lend to private undertakings.[28]

Much of this thinking was in harmony with a report issued in March 1951 by the United States International Development Advisory Board headed by Nelson Rockefeller.

By the end of 1951, the underdeveloped countries were able to win approval in the Assembly of a resolution requesting ECOSOC to submit to the Assembly's next session detailed plans for establishing a special fund for grants-in-aid and low-interest, long-term loans to underdeveloped countries. This was solidly opposed by most of the major powers including the United States, United Kingdom, France, Canada, Sweden, Australia, Netherlands and Belgium. A less controversial and generally accepted recommendation invited the IBRD to expand its lending to underdeveloped countries.

Debate Continues

As ECOSOC turned once more to the explosive problem, between May and August 1952, it was fortified with two additional reports. The IBRD had transmitted, without approval, a staff report suggesting that the proposed international finance corporation, linked to the Bank and empowered

[28] UN Doc. E/1986.

to make equity investments and nonguaranteed loans to private enterprises, would fill an important gap. It would not be restricted by the Bank's obligation to see that all loans were guaranteed by governments. The capital would be voluntarily subscribed by governments, and the Bank could subsequently approach individual private investors to interest them in taking over the Bank's securities in "good risk" development projects.[29] The Secretary-General had also outlined a series of alternative approaches to financing development, paying special attention to the concept of a separate "special fund," with initial capitalization of $200 to $300 million, to issue grants or loans as partial assistance for economic development projects. The prospective capital-importing countries, led by Pakistan, Cuba and the Philippines, thought that, in addition to the praiseworthy effort to encourage private and public lending, it was likely that most non-self-liquidating projects would have to be financed through very liberal loans or outright grants. The United States, United Kingdom, and France continued to frown on this idea, and the latter two countries indicated that they would be unable to contribute to such an enterprise at that time.

Finally ECOSOC approved three resolutions bearing on the issue:

1. The Bank was commended for its plan, requested to continue developing it, urged to consult with various private and public organizations about it and report to the next Council session.

2. The Fiscal Commission was requested to study and report on the suggestion that income from foreign investments in underdeveloped countries be taxed only in those countries.

3. A special committee of not more than nine persons, serving in their individual capacity, was authorized to prepare a detailed plan for the creation of a special fund as outlined by the Secretary-General.

These decisions were heartily endorsed by the Assembly in the fall of 1952.

By March 1953, the member governments of ECOSOC had received detailed plans for the proposed special fund, prepared by a committee of eight private experts, including Mr. Wayne C. Taylor, former United States Under-Secretary of Commerce and President of the Export-Import Bank. The committee suggested an organization similar to that of a specialized agency but placed directly under the United Nations, like the UNICEF, to be financed by voluntary contributions, initially $250 million, to provide grants or loans with lower interest rates and longer amortization periods than available from the IBRD.

The Bank continued to consider the possibility of establishing the proposed international finance corporation which had become a highly controversial issue in financial circles. Leaders of the underdeveloped countries thought it entirely feasible and desirable. Opinion in the more developed countries was divided. Two governments in the latter group gave their endorsement. Most of the others were cool, if not downright cold, to the idea. Among private financial interests, the United Kingdom National Com-

[29] UN Doc. E/2215, May 1, 1952.

mittee of the International Chamber of Commerce welcomed the proposal as a "desirable development." The strongest business opposition was in the United States with the United States Foreign Trade Council adopting a resolution firmly disapproving. The principal bases for opposition were that the plan was too risky, involved excessive governmental intervention, would not provide enough capital to make much difference, and would compete with private investment. Hence the Bank did not feel that it could go ahead with the proposal.[30] By the end of 1953 the United States still refused to approve either the proposed fund or finance corporation. Nevertheless, the underdeveloped countries won General Assembly adoption of resolutions approving further studies of these plans.

LOOKING BACKWARD AND FORWARD

Financing development abroad is as complex and controversial a problem as financing development at home, only more so. It raises profound questions that go far beyond the scope of this volume such as: what should be financed (industry versus agriculture, etc.), how much can be absorbed by the underdeveloped countries, how much can the wealthier nations afford to give or lend? There are no exact answers to any of these questions, only educated guesses which the United Nations and national governments are beginning to formulate. In examining these problems, it is important to keep in mind that, of the large amount of loans and grants which national governments have provided since World War II, only a very small fraction has been channeled through the United Nations and related agencies.

The chief UN-connected agencies responsible for giving financial assistance for development have been the IBRD, limited to approximately $200 million a year in government-guaranteed loans, and the United Nations with its technical assistance program, providing about $20 million a year in technical advice. The evidence of their achievements, briefly reviewed above, indicates that these agencies have on the whole done a creditable job. The facts suggest that they are not significantly more costly to administer than bilateral programs.[31] They are widely representative in membership and participation and hence are more likely to generate truly international confidence and cooperation than bilateral programs tied closely to certain national policies. The IBRD has gone far beyond the League Council's loan activities;[32] it has engaged in direct international lending, on a far larger scale, with more adequate staff work and some degree of courage and experimentation. The major limitations restraining the Bank are attributable more to its Articles of Agreement, its modest resources, and the world conditions within which it must operate than to any gross inefficiency or lack of imagination on the part of its personnel.

Among the chief drawbacks of the United Nations financing effort is simply the lack of funds. In view of the vast amounts being loaned and

---

[30] UN Doc. E/2441, May 25, 1953.
[31] Sharp, *op. cit.*, pp. 358–360.　　　　　[32] See pp. 512–513.

given away outside the United Nations, it is understandable why many governmental as well as private figures believe it is quite practical as well as desirable to direct more financial assistance through the multilateral agencies. If the major powers adopt such a policy, it is probable that they could win greater friendship and strengthen the international community far more than by giving the same amount of money bilaterally.

At the same time the major powers have a point in feeling that their voices frequently do not carry weight in international decisions commensurate with their financial contributions, especially in the General Assembly, and even ECOSOC. While the basis for weighting votes is a controversial question, it would seem desirable to provide for greater reflection of obvious national differences, similar to that incorporated in the processes of the IBRD and IMF, particularly where financial sacrifice is involved. The Bank also suffers from the reluctance of nations to release the 18 per cent of their capital share in the Bank subscribed in their own currencies as well as resistance to the sale of the Bank's bonds in various domestic markets.

Suggestions for Further Reading

Books

Brown, William Adams, Jr., and Opie, Redvers, *American Foreign Assistance* (Washington: The Brookings Institution, 1953).

Condliffe, John Bell, *The Commerce of Nations* (New York: W. W. Norton & Company, Inc., 1950).

Coordination of Economic and Social Activities (New York: Carnegie Endowment for International Peace, 1948).

Evatt, Herbert Vere, *The Task of Nations* (New York: Duell, Sloan and Pearce, 1949).

Frankel, S. H., *Capital Investment in Africa: Its Course and Effects* (London and New York: Oxford University Press, 1938).

Hoselitz, Berthold Frank, ed., *The Progress of Underdeveloped Areas* (Chicago: University of Chicago Press, 1952).

Klemme, Marvin, *The Inside Story of UNRRA* (New York: Lifetime Editions, 1949).

Levi, Werner, *Fundamentals of World Organization* (Minneapolis: The University of Minnesota Press, 1950).

Mandelbaum, K., *The Industrialization of Backward Areas* (Oxford: B. Blackwell, 1947).

Mikesell, Raymond F., *United States Economic Policy and International Relations* (New York: McGraw-Hill Book Company, Inc., 1952).

Sharp, Walter R., *International Technical Assistance* (Chicago: Public Administration Service, 1952).

Staley, Eugene, *World Economic Development* (Montreal: International Labour Office, 1944).

Woodbridge, George, ed., *UNRRA*, 3 Vols. (New York: Columbia University Press, 1950).

Periodicals

Basch, Antonin, "International Bank for Reconstruction and Development 1944–1949," *International Conciliation*, No. 455 (November 1949).

Belshaw, H., "The Food and Agriculture Organization of the United Nations," *International Organization*, Vol. 1, No. 2 (June 1947).

Black, Eugene R., "The World Bank at Work," *Foreign Affairs*, Vol. 30, No. 3 (April 1952).

Blelloch, David, "Technical Assistance: Programmes and Policies," *International Affairs*, Vol. 28, No. 1 (January 1952).

Franck, Peter G., and Dorothea Seelye, "Implementation of Technical Assistance," *International Conciliation*, No. 468 (February 1951).

Jessup, Philip C., "UNRRA, Sample of World Organization," *Foreign Affairs*, Vol. 22, No. 3 (April 1944).

Kindleberger, Charles P., "Bretton Woods Reappraised," *International Organization*, Vol. 5, No. 1 (February 1951).

Lepawsky, Albert, "The Bolivian Operation," *International Conciliation*, No. 479 (March 1952).

McDougall, Frank L., "Food and Population," *International Conciliation*, No. 486 (December 1952).

Neal, Marian, "United Nations Programs in Haiti," *International Conciliation*, No. 468 (February 1951).

Sharp, Walter R., "The Institutional Framework for Technical Assistance," *International Organization*, Vol. 7, No. 3 (August 1953).

Documents

Food and Agriculture Organization, *Annual Reports of the Director-General, Reports of Missions, World Food Survey,* and other documents.

International Bank for Reconstruction and Development, *Annual Report* and other documents.

United Nations, *Economic Report, . . . 1945–47,* UN Sales No.: 1948, II.C.1,
———, *Major Economic Changes in 1949,* UN Doc. E/1601, Corr. 1.
———, *Technical Assistance . . . : Plan for an expanded cooperative programme . . . ,* UN Sales No.: 1949.II.B.1.
———, *World Economic Report 1948, 1949–50, 1950–51,* and *1951–52,* UN Sales Nos.: 1949.II.C.3.; 1951.II.C.1; 1952.II.C.4; and 1953.II.C.2.

United Nations Relief and Rehabilitation Administration (UNRRA), *Reports of the Director-General to the Council, Journal, Operational Analysis Reports,* and other documents.

United States, Department of Commerce, *Foreign Aid by the United States Government 1940–51* (Washington: U.S. Government Printing Office, 1952).

19

Trade, Monetary and Other Activities — UN

Commerce Among Nations

ONE OF THE MOST striking differences between the economic work of the League and the United Nations is that questions of commercial policy have tended to be elbowed out of the spotlight by the greatly expanded role of governmental operations outside traditional private trade channels. During most of the postwar period trade has been overshadowed by direct governmental aid on a scale never dreamed of in League days. The decisions, and often the administration, that control the flow of goods and services among nations have, to an unprecedented degree, been transferred from private to public hands. Nonetheless, much private trade has continued and has grown increasingly important. In that area the UN's activities have been largely dominated by the efforts of the United States to use the devices of the International Trade Organization (ITO) and General Agreement on Tariffs and Trade (GATT) to promote policies reflecting its own commercial traditions and current productive advantage. Still these plans, as indicated in Part Two, have represented the liberal, rather than the conservative, wing of United States opinion.

The major articles of faith written into these projects are:

1. a general prohibition of quantitative restrictions such as import quotas (never extensively used by the United States except recently to protect agriculture);

2. multilateral negotiation of gradual and reciprocal tariff reductions (in the spirit of the United States reciprocal trade agreements program enacted in 1934 under Cordell Hull's sponsorship);

3. elimination of trade discrimination, aimed particularly against the British Commonwealth preferential system (the United States had not had the regulatory authority nor felt the need to practice discrimination except with respect to a few protected territories such as the Philippines);

4. guaranteeing foreign traders treatment equal to that afforded nationals (representing an old campaign, especially against the British, although the United States had enacted its own "Buy American" legislation);

5. the regulation of commodity agreements, often referred to as "cartels,"

in the interests of consumers as well as producers (inspired by the United States–sponsored 1942 International Wheat Agreement model to prevent arrangements aimed primarily at limited production and high prices).[1]

While this campaign has been moderately successful, using United States concessions as bait, it has been constantly hampered by considerable resistance on the part of most other countries. The latter are less prosperous than the United States and have insisted that they need protection to prevent the spending of their scarce exchange on nonessential imports, to promote "full employment," and to shelter their efforts at economic development. Finally, the United States itself has been schizophrenic on this issue and has become increasingly dominated by protectionist sentiment, particularly as demand has declined and competition increased. While the following analysis concentrates primarily on GATT and separate negotiations regarding commodity agreements, it is well to remember that other activities, especially those of the FAO and ECOSOC regional commissions, dealt with above, were also concerned with trade and commodity issues.

Efforts to Lower Barriers

The first postwar United Nations effort to deal with trade and commodity problems was initiated by the United States, as we have seen in connection with the establishment of the ITO and GATT, and led to ECOSOC's appointment of the Preparatory Committee of the International Conference on Trade and Employment early in 1946. One of that Committee's functions was to sponsor the negotiations, leading to the formulation of the GATT, in which twenty-three states participated from April to October 1947 in Geneva. This was a significant move, engineered chiefly by the United States, to apply for the first time on a streamlined multilateral basis what previously had been done through laborious bilateral tariff bargaining. A total of 123 sets of negotiations were completed, covering some 45,000 items, affecting two-thirds of the import trade of the participating countries and about half of over-all world imports representing a total value in excess of $10 billion (1938 prices). The GATT signatories pledged, moreover, to apply a commercial policy code, similar to that incorporated in the ITO Charter, as far as possible without, however, committing themselves to amend existing legislation or promulgate new legislation.

The first two regular sessions of the GATT contracting parties were held from February to March 1948 (Havana) and from August to September 1948 (Geneva) to review the Agreement in the light of the ITO Charter,

---

[1] For discussion of these issues, see William Adams Brown, Jr., *The United States and the Restoration of World Trade* (Washington: Brookings Institution, 1950); J. B. Condliffe, "International Trade and Economic Nationalism," *International Conciliation*, No. 476 (December 1951); Philip Cortney, *The Economic Munich* (New York: Philosophical Library, 1949); Raymond F. Mikesell, *United States Economic Policy and International Relations* (New York: McGraw-Hill, 1952); National Foreign Trade Council, *Position . . . With Respect to the Havana Charter . . .* (New York: National Foreign Trade Council, 1950); Clair Wilcox, *A Charter for World Trade* (New York: Macmillan, 1949).

which was signed at Havana in March 1948, and to effect certain changes
in the former, including provisions covering the use by underdeveloped or
war-damaged countries of protective measures such as import quotas to
help economic development and reconstruction. Release from or waiver of
certain minor obligations was granted to Ceylon, Pakistan, Brazil and the
United States. In the case of a dispute between the United States and Cuba
over textile import restrictions imposed by the latter, both sides were persuaded to make concessions. The shadow of the East-West conflict also fell
across this sphere. The Soviet Union and its satellites have never participated in any ITO or GATT negotiations.

A second series of GATT tariff negotiations was held at Annecy, France,
April to August 1949, and resulted in the completion of 147 bilateral agreements and the expected accession to the GATT of ten more countries. It
was also decided to incorporate further ITO Charter provisions in the
Agreement. Consultation with the Union of South Africa regarding that
country's recent imposition of import restrictions to safeguard a weak
monetary position resulted in qualified approval of the policy with some
suggestions to soften its impact. Complete or partial permission to maintain
nondiscriminatory protective measures for development or reconstruction
were granted Cuba, India and Ceylon; Chile, Syria-Lebanon and the
United Kingdom withdrew their applications for authorization to employ
such measures. Brazil was also persuaded to amend her import tax law to
insure conformity with GATT obligations.

Holding the Line. Geneva was the scene of the fourth session of the
GATT contracting parties, February to April 1950, when it was agreed
that governments should be urged to adopt certain measures to minimize
the harmful effects of import and export restrictions imposed for balance-
of-payments reasons. Australia was also asked to take action to remove the
competitive inequality between its governmentally subsidized ammonium
sulphate and Chilean nitrate.

During the third series of GATT tariff negotiations held at Torquay,
England, September 1950 to April 1951, 147 bilateral agreements were
negotiated covering some 8,700 items. Moreover the contracting parties
agreed to hold the line of the Geneva and Annecy as well as Torquay concessions, affecting a total of 55,000 tariff rates, until January 1, 1954. During
the fifth session of the GATT contracting parties, while the tariff negotiations were in progress, certain governments, led by the United States,
expressed the view that the narrowing dollar gap justified the progressive
relaxation of import restrictions by the United Kingdom, Australia, New
Zealand, Ceylon and Southern Rhodesia. The International Monetary
Fund (IMF) gave cautious support to this statement. But the countries
involved felt that they were being pushed too hard and too early by their
overoptimistic competitors, particularly in view of the uncertain effects of
the rearmament efforts precipitated by the Korean conflict. During the
same session Chile and Australia announced their agreement on the nitrate

dispute. Other consultations dealt with complaints involving the United States, United Kingdom, France, Belgium, Italy and Czechoslovakia.

A rash of retreats from earlier concessions, symptomatic of an increasing protectionist trend, especially on the part of the United States, broke out during the sixth session of the GATT contracting parties, September to October 1951. The most prominent complaint was that of France, Canada, Australia, Italy, New Zealand and Norway against the recently imposed United States restriction on the importation of dairy products. There were also complaints against Belgian and United Kingdom taxes. The three accused countries were finally granted delays to correct the offending situations. Regarding a United States withdrawal of past concessions on certain hat items, GATT agreed that there seemed to be a temporary need for such a measure but that the United States should keep the question under review and restore the concessions as soon as feasible.

There was no general readiness during the seventh session of the GATT contracting parties at Geneva, October to November 1952, to initiate another round of tariff reductions. It was difficult enough to hold the ground already gained. The United States, moreover, had just experienced a change of political complexion from the Democratic to the Republican Party, long the foe of a liberal trade policy. Nonetheless, the thirty-four participating countries did manage to negotiate the following agreements:

1. granting of specific waivers allowing the six members of the European Coal and Steel Community to discriminate collectively against non-members;

2. although the United States had relaxed quota restrictions on cheese products, the contracting parties urged the United States to continue to try to repeal section 104 (Andresen amendment) of the Defense Production Act and authorized the Netherlands to reduce its imports of wheat flour from the United States;

3. agreement to study effect of United States tariff increases on dried figs and raisin imports complained of by Greece, Italy and Turkey;

4. acceptance of United Kingdom modification of purchase tax in accordance with GATT obligations; and

5. consideration of other complaints against Belgium, Greece, Germany, Brazil and Pakistan.

During the eighth session of the GATT contracting parties, September to October 1953, the United Kingdom was granted only limited authority to impose discriminatory tariffs on agricultural imports and specifically prohibited from forcing any "diversion of trade" away from current suppliers of such shipments, the latter limit to be settled ultimately by the GATT governing body. The member states also agreed to extend the life of the GATT and its carefully spun web of agreements from January 1954 until mid-1955 when, it was hoped, the United States would have reached some definitive decisions regarding its future trade policy. Moreover, the United States led a movement which was successful in making Japan a "provisional associate member" of GATT, although the United Kingdom, Australia, New Zealand and the Union of South Africa, fearful of Japanese competition, refused to extend most-favored-nation treatment to Japan. Finally, France and Greece agreed to discontinue offending trade practices, and strong complaints were lodged against certain United States and Belgian policies.

Commodity Agreements and Business Practices

How to level out the familiar swings from feast to famine in the primary commodity markets was another issue which ran through the planning conferences on the FAO and ITO. Hence ECOSOC was prevailed upon to request, in March 1947, that the Secretary-General appoint an Interim Coordinating Committee for International Commodity Arrangements (ICCICA) to study and report on general and specific commodity market trends, keeping an eagle eye on possible gluts or deficits, and to facilitate intergovernmental consultation in this field. The Committee first met during August and September 1947, and began to issue useful surveys, including annual reviews of the primary commodity situation, and to cooperate in calling occasional commodity conferences.

The twin dangers of surpluses, due to a slackening of the economic tempo during 1949, and deficits, due to the scramble for raw materials such as rubber and tin following the North Korean attack of June 1950, led to accelerated activity on the part of the ICCICA during 1950. As a result, ECOSOC decided in August 1950 to authorize the Secretary-General to convene, on the advice of commodity study groups and ICCICA, intergovernmental conferences to discuss measures to meet special difficulties. The Secretary-General was concurrently to study and report on means of improving this cumbersome procedure for dealing with special commodity problems. Soon thereafter an International Tin Study Group invited the Secretary-General to call a Tin Conference which met in October 1950, but, because of differences among producing and consuming countries, chiefly the United States and United Kingdom, it adjourned without taking positive action.

The matter of improving the commodity arrangements system seemed so complex, however, when ECOSOC met in September 1951, particularly in view of the Korean situation, that it was decided to postpone further discussion of the matter. During the same ECOSOC session the United States also asked that a study be initiated to alleviate restrictive business practices (restraint of competition, limitation of access to markets, and the fostering of monopolistic controls) which were already being dealt with in the European community but needed broader attention. During the debate there was much seesawing over the distinction between "good" governmentally regulated cartels and "bad" unregulated and harmful cartels. The Soviet Union announced that the whole proposal was nothing more than a smoke screen to hide the nefarious machinations of powerful United States monopolies. The final resolution recommended that Member states take measures, based on the ITO Charter principles, to prevent unduly restrictive business practices and decided to establish an *ad hoc* Committee to recommend to ECOSOC measures to help achieve this objective.

In the summer of 1953 the UN sponsored the negotiation of an International Sugar Agreement, announced in August, which was designed to regulate the volume of exports in order to cage the world price of raw sugar between the limits of $3.25 and $4.35 a pound. In December 1953 an expert study, initiated by the General Assembly, favored creating an intergovernmental trade stabilization commission to examine and recommend means of stabilizing primary commodity markets. Such means might include buffer stocks by which international agencies would buy and sell in the world market in order to prevent extreme price fluctuations.

Reviewing the Record

This is a story full of false starts and only modest achievement. With all its pitfalls, however, this is a better record than that of the League. No such substantial and general reduction of trade barriers was ever engineered under League auspices. Moreover, these advances were achieved surprisingly early, under the pressure of United States leadership and enticement of United States concessions. But more recently the campaign has stalled, even fallen back, and the much debated ITO never lived to walk. It is not for lack of machinery, however, that the free trade promotion scheme has been held back. GATT was so reinforced that it has been a workable substitute for the ill-fated ITO. Rather it is the general climate within which the free trade campaign has had to operate.

The greatest immediate obstacles were the wartime destruction and dislocation which left countries incapable of paying for much of their essential imports and intent on husbanding their precious foreign currency resources by all manner of controls. Moreover, protectionism was an old habit, spurred on by the depression and newly encouraged by the rising "full employment" school of national planning. There were also the familiar justifications of protecting "infant" and militarily essential industries as well as maintaining controls useful for economic warfare. Finally, given the best will in the world, there were discomforting doubts about what would happen if nations did drop their protective cloaks, exposing themselves to the unpredictable winds of free trade. Even the United States, apparently most able to afford concessions, showed increasing reluctance to bare its economic anatomy.

The theory of free trade is a persuasive one, championed by liberals since Adam Smith. So was the theory of domestic free trade, *laissez faire*. But nations have erected all kinds of controls to keep their domestic economies within limits set by the interests of business, labor and agriculture. It is unlikely, therefore, that there will be any significant lowering of international barriers until somewhat comparable measures are established to assure a greater degree of security, both political and economic, over a broader area.

But trade barriers continue to block exports

Headline Series, *Foreign Policy Association*

Monetary Policy

The international value of a nation's currency has a tendency, like a private individual's credit, to reflect the balance between resources and liabilities. Monetary policy is, therefore, as much a symptom as a determinant of a nation's basic economic health. Hence the UN's monetary activities, carried on primarily through the affiliated International Monetary Fund (IMF), have been directly affected and largely dominated by other economic programs: chiefly reconstruction and development efforts, both international and bilateral, especially the Marshall Plan. Moreover, because the gap between the requirements and resources of most nations was far greater than had been anticipated, the IMF, created to tide countries over relatively short-term and superficial deficits, found itself over its head in a flood of indebtedness and precarious currencies that it was not designed to handle. During most of the postwar period, therefore, it has been a relatively minor and quiescent figure carried along by a tide that it could help to modify, through advice and very restricted lending, but not reverse.

It is also important to remember that the IMF was shaped, as indicated in Chapter 9, primarily by United States, as distinguished from British, concepts of what was necessary to prevent a recurrence of monetary ills that followed in the wake of World War I. The Americans particularly wanted stability of exchange rates (the British preferred flexibility), firm and continuous IMF control (the British wanted relatively automatic drawing rights on IMF resources), and early convertibility (the British thought this unrealistic).

The infant IMF began to function as its Board of Governors held their

577

inaugural meeting at Savannah, Georgia, in March 1946. The major issues discussed dealt with organizational reflections of the basic policy differences between creditor and debtor nations, symbolized and led by the United States and United Kingdom. The final decisions, moreover, mirrored the economic superiority of the United States. In the contest between the British view that drawing upon IMF resources should be largely automatic and the American view that requests should be carefully regulated by a full-time Board of Executive Directors, the latter emerged victorious. Related to this was the issue of where to locate the headquarters. The British John Maynard Keynes had begun by suggesting London to maintain the financial dominance of that city. When the Americans finally won agreement that it should be in the United States, most Europeans favored New York where

> they would be in the . . . great centre of international finance; they would be sufficiently removed from the politics of Congress and the nationalistic whispering gallery of the Embassies and Legations of Washington; and they would probably be sufficiently near to the seat of UNO to be able to co-operate closely on the economic and statistical side of their work with the Economic and Social Council.[2]

But the United States won the day when

> . . . [Secretary of the Treasury] Mr. [Fred] Vinson told me [Keynes] that the American Delegation had decided that both institutions [IBRD and IMF] should be placed in Washington and that this was a final decision the merits of which they were not prepared to discuss. The United States Administration, he said, was entitled to decide for themselves what location within the United States was to be preferred.[3]

The Fund is Launched

During the first annual meeting of the Board of Governors, September to October 1946, one of the first items of business was to negotiate agreements between individual members and the Fund fixing the initial par values of their currencies before they could be eligible to purchase IMF funds. While many of the current official rates were obviously overvalued, the IMF announced in December 1946 that it would certify thirty-two national par values as they stood in October 1946. The Fund justified this acceptance of the *status quo* on the grounds that, while some rates were undoubtedly too high, they would not seriously handicap exports and that to lower them might aggravate inflationary tendencies. Although there is evidence to indicate that it might have been healthier to deflate some of these rates, there is no doubt that it would have been politically difficult, if not impossible, to force governments to do so.[4]

---

[2] R. F. Harrod, *The Life of John Maynard Keynes* (New York: Harcourt, Brace, 1951), pp. 629–630.

[3] *Ibid.*

[4] Raymond F. Mikesell, "The International Monetary Fund 1944–1949," *International Conciliation*, No. 455 (November 1949), pp. 848–850.

The principal incentive held out to persuade governments to allow their currencies to be pegged was the privilege to purchase IMF funds, chiefly dollars. The first sale of currencies was approved in the spring of 1947: $25 million to France, in exchange for francs, and $12 million, half in dollars and half in British pounds, to the Netherlands, in exchange for guilders. With these sales, there began several significant trends. First, because of the tremendous dollar gap, most countries wanted to purchase dollars. Second, most of the loans were sought in connection with reconstruction and development needs rather than short-term cyclical deficits and thus were not strictly justified under the IMF Articles of Agreement. Most of the Fund's sales were authorized during the first two years of operation, chiefly to Western European governments, and the rate of lending was sharply curtailed when the Marshall Plan became available to assume the major share of the reconstruction burden.

During 1947 there was no appreciable loosening of exchange restrictions which were allowable under the IMF Agreement for a "transitional period" of three to five years and practiced by all but five members (United States, Mexico, Panama, Guatemala and El Salvador). Nonetheless, the Fund urged relaxation of such controls wherever possible. It also spoke out against the efforts to increase the price of gold, especially by gold-producing countries such as South Africa, Canada and Australia. These states justified an increase on the grounds that gold was a commodity as well as a currency and was subject to rising costs with the result that the price freeze, at the level of $35 an ounce, at which the United States had long been committed to buy gold, was stifling production. The Fund reasoned that to increase the price of gold, to which par values of currencies were hitched, would virtually depreciate those currencies, thus causing monetary instability and loss of reserves. This issue was particularly affected by the interests of the United States, which did not want to stimulate the production of gold or increase its price.

European Crisis and Marshall Plan

By December 1947 the IMF also issued a statement discouraging the use of multiple exchange rates, used by about a third of the Fund's members to favor some foreign transactions more than others. Multiple rates have not only been instruments of administrative discrimination against both goods and nations but have greatly complicated negotiations on tariffs and other commercial policy matters. The first serious exchange rate crisis arose at the beginning of 1948 when France asked the Fund to approve a devaluation of the franc with respect to the dollar that the Fund thought excessive and would not approve. France countered by going ahead with the devaluation, whereupon the Fund declared the change unauthorized and France ineligible to make further purchases of IMF resources.

Taking advantage of the launching of the Marshall Plan early in 1948, the IMF announced in April of that year that countries participating in the ERP should request purchase of dollars through the Fund only in "exceptional and unforeseen circumstances." This close tie with United States policies was heavily criticized by the Soviet Union and Byelorussian Republic, during the ECOSOC review of the IMF annual report in August 1948, when it was pointed out that most of the assistance had been given to Western European powers and none to Eastern Europeans.

By September 1949 the balance of payments problem was so serious that the United Kingdom, after hasty "consultation" with the IMF, led a wave of drastic devaluations, including many currencies tied closely to the British pound. The value of the pound with respect to the dollar was reduced from $4.00 to $2.80. The sale of currencies during 1949 was only 23 per cent as much as the previous year, showing a marked decline following the establishment of the Marshall Plan.

Hibernation and Reawakening

The lending spigot was turned off entirely during 1950 with no currency sales whatever. On the other hand, there were some minor "repurchases" (repayment of loans) bringing the total of repurchases since the IMF's establishment to $33 million, only 4 per cent of the total loans of $777.3 million. Technical assistance, through staff missions and studies, dealt with:

> changes in exchange rates; elimination of multiple currency practices; relaxation of exchange controls; modification of monetary, credit and fiscal policies bearing on balance of payments problems; development of institutional machinery such as central banking systems and exchange control administration, improvement of financial statistics; and advice regarding the monetary impact of development programs, levels of monetary reserves, use of Fund resources, gold transactions and subsidies.

Further monetary progress was revealed during the annual ECOSOC survey of IMF activities in February 1951. Mention was made of the beneficial effects of increased production, financial assistance from the United States and other sources, deflationary budget and credit policies, and the 1949 devaluations. At the same time there was apprehension regarding the uncertainties and inflationary effects of the rearmament efforts. While many countries praised the advisory role of the Fund, Chile expressed the views of many underdeveloped nations that the IMF should loosen its purse strings to help meet foreign exchange needs. India and Pakistan thought the Fund's deflationary policy was premature and excessively conservative.

In the wake of these criticisms, the Fund authorized an increasing flow of sales to countries willing to comply with its policies. The purse opened even wider during 1952, and, by early 1954, the cumulative total sold was more than $1 billion.

Balancing the Accounts

In spite of its shortcomings, the IMF is in a fundamentally stronger position than its predecessor, the League Council's Financial Committee. The latter had no funds to lend and no binding authority. The Fund not only has considerable capital but is "backstopped" by many binding obligations pledged by its members in the Articles of Agreement regulating a variety of matters from exchange rates to the price of gold. It is more representative and far more amply staffed. In the course of its activities it has "sold" almost a billion dollars linked to advice which has had some influence on a wide range of national monetary policies.

But this record does not alter the fact that the Fund has not lived up to its parents' expectations. The chief reason, as in the case of most other UN economic bodies, is that the "normal" period for which the IMF was designed was much farther around the corner than was originally thought likely. At the same time, the Fund's policies have on occasion been more cautious than they needed to be, even in the unsettled postwar situation. The IMF must stand ready to bail out countries suffering from genuine short-range difficulties who are willing to follow reasonable advice regarding their monetary policies. Capital resources and country quotas must also be increased if the Fund is to have real stature in the monetary world.

The widespread disease of inconvertibility and other exchange rigidities make it desirable that the Fund should take a hand in organizing multilateral settlement arrangements similar to the European Payments Union, which has been markedly successful. Further efforts should be made to whittle down overvalued exchange rates while leaving room for sufficient flexibility so that governments may adjust to changing circumstances and will not feel compelled to operate outside the Fund. There should also be increasing coordination of monetary with trade and other economic activities. If advances are made along these lines, the IMF's influence in attacking the problems of inconvertibility, multiple exchange rates and other restrictive measures may carry greater weight. Finally, the whole Fund process should be oriented towards more flexible and decentralized negotiation, preferably through encouragement of regional monetary operations.[5]

Employment Policies

The magic words "full employment" have been a prominent theme running through United Nations economic debates from the beginning. Their significance as a central "brave new world" symbol stemmed from the bitter memories of the black depression of the thirties, the determination of organized labor and other groups to avoid a recurrence of such a catastrophe, the development in economic theory of the concept of full employment, the struggle that led to the United Nations Charter pledge to strive towards this goal, and the expectation that there would be a recession

[5] For further discussion of these issues, see Mikesell, "The International Monetary Fund 1944–49," *op. cit.*; Mikesell, *United States Economic Policy and International Relations;* Robert Triffin, "Monetary Reconstruction in Europe," *International Conciliation,* No. 482 (June 1952); Charles P. Kindleberger, "Bretton Woods Reappraised," *International Organization,* Vol. 5, No. 1 (February 1951).

following World War II as there had been after World War I, with particular concern regarding the economic health of that quixotic giant, the United States.

Subsequent United Nations discussions on this issue have been shaped largely by the interests of the great and middle powers and particularly by the conflict of views between the British and Australian Labor Governments on one side and the more conservative United States on the other. Always closely intertwined with this problem have been the issues discussed above: reconstruction and development, trade, and monetary policies. The principal United Nations agencies involved have been the General Assembly, ECOSOC, the Economic and Employment Commission (changed to Economic, Employment and Development Commission in 1950 and terminated in 1951), and the ILO.

Under the leadership of governments particularly sensitive to the interests of organized labor in 1946, such as the United Kingdom, France, Australia, and Norway, the United Nations took its first action on this issue when ECOSOC appointed an Economic and Employment Commission in June 1946 and later asked that body to establish a Sub-Commission on Employment and Economic Stability. After inconclusive debates in all of these bodies, the champions of a bold full employment policy resorted to the United Nations Conference on Trade and Employment, engaged in a marathon struggle over the proposed International Trade Organization, November 1947 to March 1948. As part of the compromises reached during the Conference, the United States agreed with the forces led by the United Kingdom and Australia on a resolution urging ECOSOC to hasten pending studies of the employment issue, develop methods to maintain full employment after the crutch of abnormal postwar demand should be removed, ask Members to report on action they were taking along these lines, and poll the specialized agencies regarding the anticyclical assistance they were prepared to render.

These views gave the full employment campaign considerable impetus, and ECOSOC adopted the essence of the Conference recommendations in March 1948. Approximately a year later the Economic and Employment Commission considered a report by its Sub-Commission on Employment and Economic Stability which it criticized as excessively descriptive, vague and impractical. The Commission finally recommended that the Sub-Commission be abolished and that its work be carried on by the Secretariat, but it had no specific program to submit to ECOSOC.

Labor Applies Pressure

Due to the relative inaction of the United Nations and gathering clouds of a recession in the United States, the ILO General Conference, meeting in June and July 1949, asked its Governing Body to consider instructing the Director-General to prepare a comprehensive report on the subject, and the ILO staff began immediately to gather ammunition.

When ECOSOC met for its ninth session, July and August 1949, it was confronted not only by these events but by an ambitious anti-depression program submitted with much fanfare by the Communist-dominated World Federation of Free Trade Unions (WFTU). After examining the various materials presented to it, ECOSOC adopted a resolution placing the issue on the agenda of the next General Assembly session, welcoming the cooperation of governments, warning against restrictive reactions to deflationary tendencies, asking the Secretary-General to appoint an expert group to report on measures to achieve full employment, and urging governments to plan employment policies so as to assist rather than hinder economic development.

During the subsequent General Assembly consideration of the problem in the fall of 1949, the liberal forces urged stronger international action. The Soviet bloc used the opportunity to advertise the virtues of its own unique panacea which, it was said, had entirely cured the disease of unemployment, and newly Communist-controlled Czechoslovakia introduced a resolution following the lines of the WFTU proposal. The underdeveloped countries pointed out that only basic economic development would absorb their unemployment. The United States stressed the importance of avoiding trade restrictions, while Australia and New Zealand argued that full employment was the prerequisite for removing such restrictions. Finally the Assembly adopted a resolution, introduced by Australia, recommending that each government take action, as the need should arise, to promote and maintain full and productive employment, and requesting that ECOSOC continue to study the problem, especially with respect to underdeveloped countries in such critical fields as agriculture.

Experts Produce Plan

While the Assembly was still meeting, a group of experts appointed by the Secretary-General met from October to December 1949 and prepared a unanimous report, *National and International Measures for Full Employment*.[6] Their recommendations were divided into domestic measures (adoption of full employment targets and comprehensive programs to achieve those targets) and international measures (programs to eliminate structural trade disequilibria, create a high and stable flow of investment, and maintain external disbursements in the face of internal fluctuations).

At ECOSOC's eleventh session, July to August 1950, the United States, United Kingdom and Canada submitted draft resolutions which tended to follow the general pattern of the experts' report. The British called for the boldest and most comprehensive international planning and cooperation, while the United States placed greater emphasis on eliminating obstacles to the free movement of resources. Finally the Council adopted a resolution which merged these different views[7]:

    1. Regarding domestic measures,
       a) governments were requested to publish annual economic objectives

6 UN Sales No.: 1949.II.A.3.   7 ECOSOC Resolution 290 (XI).

(employment, production, consumption, investment, etc.); publish
programs to achieve these goals (steady economic expansion, prevention of recessions, emergency measures to combat unemployment,
curbing of inflation, and promotion of mobility of labor); and furnish
the Secretary-General with full information;

b) the Secretary-General was requested to circulate questionnaires and
submit results to the Economic, Employment and Development Commission as the basis of reports to ECOSOC.

2. Regarding international measures,

a) governments were requested to intensify efforts to achieve balance of
payments at the highest possible level, while avoiding quantitative
and exchange restrictions, reducing other trade barriers, eliminating
discrimination, building normal currency and gold reserves, promoting
a high and stable flow of investment, and avoiding measures injurious
to other countries;

b) the Secretary-General was requested to prepare a survey regarding
these matters and submit it to the Economic, Employment and Development Commission as the basis for reporting to ECOSOC; appoint
a group of three independent experts to assist the Commission; and
appoint another expert group to study alternative ways of reducing
the international impact of recessions;

c) the IBRD and IMF were urged to strive to expand their lending to
offset recessions.

3. The Secretary-General was also requested to appoint an expert group to
give special attention to the employment problems of the underdeveloped
countries.

The General Assembly briefly reviewed this action during its fifth session
in the fall of 1950 and invited governments to cooperate in the program.

During ECOSOC's thirteenth session, August 1951, the Assistant Secretary-General in charge of Economic Affairs, David Owen, reporting on a
Secretariat survey,[8] pointed out that only the United Kingdom had adopted
a full employment standard fully in accordance with the previous ECOSOC
resolution. The United States had established a weaker advisory procedure
to serve as a possible guide for administrative policies. Also before
ECOSOC was the expert report on the problem of unemployment in the
underdeveloped countries which urged as the best antidote various measures to hasten development.[9]

Study Continues

During the debate, the United Kingdom indicated that, while it felt it
could keep its own internal house in order, it was afraid of having everything swept away by an external deluge (eyes towards the United States)
and therefore valued stronger international coordination. The Soviet bloc
and WFTU argued that much current employment in the west was hitched
to nonproductive rearmament which was riding roughshod over the workers' living standards. While the anti-Communist International Confedera-

[8] UN Doc. E/2035 and Add. 1.   [9] UN Sales No.: 1951.II.B.2.

tion of Free Trade Unions (ICFTU) recognized the need for rearming, it also urged greater consideration for the welfare of the workers. The United States, France, Canada, Sweden and India explained that they did not feel that the adoption of rigid numerical full employment goals was technically or economically feasible. ECOSOC finally adopted resolutions giving the Secretary-General greater leeway in carrying out certain employment studies and urging that greater attention be given to the problems of the under-developed countries.

A group of five experts, appointed by the Secretary-General, reported in January 1952 that the principal means of reducing the international impact of recessions lay in the direction of commodity agreements, expanded long-term lending by the IBRD, and larger IMF reserves. On the basis of this and other studies, ECOSOC, during its fourteenth session, May to August 1952, adopted a resolution reiterating some of its past recommendations and also urging the IBRD and IMF to cooperate by liberalizing their policies. In the summer of 1953 ECOSOC debated the matter again, giving special attention to the depressing effect of reduced arms expenditures following the Korean truce, and requested governments and various international agencies to cooperate in helping to maintain a high level of employment.

The net achievement of this give-and-take has been a thorough sifting of the problem so that the world knows more today than ever before about both the nature of the threat and what nations have done and are prepared to do to meet it. The United Nations has also reached a collective agreement among the major Western nations on a voluntary anti-depression plan which at least has the potential of helping to prevent mass unemployment. Under the League this problem was just beginning to be explored. Knowledge and theory were less advanced, and no joint comprehensive plan was ever formulated. But this brief review also demonstrates that there are still differences of opinion among nations on this question and that many governments are not yet ready to enact any binding program either domestically or internationally. Furthermore, the Secretariat staff responsible for this area has been increasingly burdened with peripheral assignments and has not taken full advantage of the opportunity for integrated analysis of national reports and the formulation of recommendations for future action.

Fiscal Policies

The United Nations' "fiscal" activities deal mainly with international aspects of national tax and governmental budgetary matters. A major motivating force is the interest of governments and business groups, especially the International Chamber of Commerce, in reducing external taxes, referred to as the problem of "double taxation" (taxation of a single enterprise by two or more countries). Another factor is the desire of government and business to obtain accurate information about the budgetary health of various countries. Finally there is the desire to render technical assistance to improve national tax and budgetary policies and administration. While these efforts continue the activities of the League of Nations Fiscal Committee, there is much more emphasis now upon direct technical assistance which has been given first priority. The principal agencies concerned are the ECOSOC and its Fiscal Commission which have provided general policy direction and the Secretariat Fiscal Division which has done most of the work.

Technical assistance has been given on such matters as budget administration, technical training, and tax policies and administration. More recently particular attention has been given to advising on tax relief to encourage investment in the underdeveloped countries. And an ambitious publication program has produced periodic information on the financial position of various countries, texts of international tax agreements, budgetary procedures, and the effect of taxation on foreign trade and investment.

Transportation and Communications

No man or word can cross a national boundary without some degree of international cooperation in the companion fields of transportation and communications. The extent of collaboration in these areas has depended, as in other fields, on a weighing of benefits against sacrifices, especially financial, heavily influenced by the interests of the predominant powers. It is not surprising, therefore, that the greatest progress has been made in matters of technical assistance, facilitation of international movement, and standardization of procedures and equipment in the interests of efficiency and safety where the return has seemed greater than the outlay. The greatest resistance has occurred in connection with proposals to regulate rates and volume of business.

The major agencies involved have been ECOSOC, its Transportation and Communications Commission (TCC), the proposed Inter-Governmental Maritime Consultative Organization (IMCO), International Civil Aviation Organization (ICAO), Universal Postal Union (UPU), and International Telecommunication Union (ITU). Reference has already been made above, in the reconstruction and development section, to the closely related activities of the three ECOSOC regional commissions regarding their fostering of cooperation and development in these fields.

General Direction and Coordination

Within the relatively loose-jointed United Nations economic and social system, nothing is more loose-jointed than the collection of programs dealing with transportation and communications, even more so than in League days. To provide at least a gentle shepherd for this rambling flock, ECOSOC created the Transport and Communications Commission (TCC) in June 1946 to provide general assistance in this field; it was to furnish advice on coordinating the work of the specialized agencies, substantive recommendations in fields not covered by any permanent international organization, and suggestions regarding new conventions and machinery where appropriate. As it has evolved, the TCC has tended to concentrate on the gaps where there are no specialized agencies: maritime shipping and inland transport (rail, waterways, motor, and pipelines). By and large, it has not crossed the paths of the specialized agencies except for brief periodic reviews of their activities and consideration of coordination problems.

One of the first interagency issues that the TCC dealt with was the matter of improving coordination among the fields of shipping, aviation, and telecommunications in the interest of greater safety of life at sea. In accordance with suggestions of the TCC and ECOSOC, the United Kingdom sponsored an International Conference of Safety of Life at Sea in London, April to June 1948, which prepared a new convention in this field to replace an outmoded 1929 agreement. It also approved the International Regulations for Preventing Collisions at Sea, 1948, and a number of other recommendations.

Another problem has been the matter of encouraging the reduction of passport and customs barriers. On ECOSOC's initiative, a meeting of experts, held at Geneva in April 1947, produced a series of recommendations to ease passport formalities, abolish visas where possible, reduce visa fees, and simplify other frontier regulations. Governments were something less than enthusiastic, however, about calling further meetings to continue this effort, and ECOSOC considered it sufficient to approve the general tenor of these recommendations and urge bilateral agreements to implement them. In 1950, in response to a recommendation by the International Chamber of Commerce, the TCC recommended that governments take action to facilitate the international movement of goods, pending the establishment of the ITO which would have jurisdiction to deal further with the problem.

By 1951 the Secretary-General reported that eighty-three bilateral agreements had been concluded mutually abolishing visa requirements. The same year the TCC and ECOSOC decided to poll governments regarding the liberalization of customs regulations regarding tourists' automobiles and baggage, on the basis of drafts prepared by the ECE, the World Touring and Automobile Organization, and the International Union of Official Travel Organizations. The Secretariat was also requested to study the transportation of dangerous goods (dynamite, chemicals, etc.), as well as national discrimination in the matter of transportation insurance. At its next session, February 1953, the TCC recommended that the easing of tourism be dealt with at an international conference to be held in 1954, that the movement of dangerous cargoes be examined by a committee of experts, and that the insurance discrimination question be referred to GATT and IMF.

Maritime Shipping

The United Nations' chief function in the maritime sphere has been to act as middleman, facilitating the transition from the temporary postwar United Maritime Consultative Council to the proposed permanent Inter-Governmental Maritime Consultative Organization, the planning of which was discussed in Chapter 9.[10] The smaller nations, however, have been reluctant to ratify the basic agreement because they fear it will saddle them with great-power domination and costly safety, labor, and other regulations. Scandinavian shippers have resisted the United States–supported anti-cartel provisions. Marking time during this extended gestation period, the TCC and ECOSOC have made several substantive sallies in this area regarding proposals for standardized measurement of maritime tonnage and for alleviating the pollution of sea water by ships' oil, but with little success.

Inland Transportation

Under some pressure from the local interests concerned, the TCC decided generally to leave the major problems of coordination and development of inland transportation to the regional commissions, a development scarcely anticipated when the TCC was first planned. In this connection the TCC used its influence to have the ECAFE Inland Transport Committee created. At the same time, the TCC did initiate a conference to revise two 1926 Conventions on Road and Motor Transport and a 1931 Convention on the Unification of Road Signals. This United Nations Conference on Road and Motor Transport, which met in Geneva from August to September 1949, produced a new International Convention on Road Traffic covering all aspects of international road transport. Because of stubborn differences, however, between the American and European schools of road signals, no general agreement could be reached in that area.

The following spring the TCC asked the Secretary-General to appoint a committee of seven experts, representing a wide variety of road signal traditions, to try to cut the Gordian knot. These brave Alexanders returned in 1952 with a compromise draft Convention on a Uniform System of Road Signs and Signals which was approved for signature by the TCC in February 1953. The TCC also recommended in March 1951 that an expert study be launched to achieve greater standardization in the licensing of drivers, although the Soviet Union solemnly declared that this was entirely a matter of domestic jurisdiction. After considering, from 1949 to 1951, the problem of how to coordinate the regulation of all forms of inland transportation, as great an issue internally as internationally, the TCC decided to shove that controversy into the ample laps of the regional commissions.

Aviation

The United Nations' interest in the ever-increasing development of the network of world skyways has been expressed primarily through its affiliate,

[10] See pp. 255–256.

the International Civil Aviation Organization (ICAO), with some peripheral consultation with related organizations such as ECOSOC, TCC,
UPU, ITU, WHO and WMO. The evolution of these activities has continued the pattern of interests revealed during the 1944 Chicago Conference: domination by the great air powers (United States, United Kingdom,
France, Netherlands and Sweden), greatest cooperation in "navigation"
matters (development and standardization of technical equipment and procedures), and slowest progress in the "transport" field (rates, routes, volume, frontier formalities and general financial questions).

Regarding the "freedoms" controversy in the "transport" field, the cause
of so much grief at Chicago, the United States and United Kingdom
reached a bilateral compromise at Bermuda in February 1946, outside
ICAO. There the United States agreed to rate-fixing to satisfy the British,
while the latter abandoned frequency and capacity regulation. Shortly
afterwards the United States concluded similar agreements with France
and Belgium. Further efforts to reach a general agreement led to a special
ICAO conference at Geneva during November 1947, where the controversy
focused on conditions surrounding the fifth freedom. This time the major
air transport countries, led by the United States and United Kingdom,
agreed on the Bermuda pattern with the addition of compulsory arbitration
to settle rate disputes. But the underdeveloped countries blocked a solution by their insistence on additional protection of their own interests,
especially in connection with the fifth freedom. Although there was widespread agreement on some minor issues, this failure on the "freedoms" question put a stop to further intensive efforts to formulate a multilateral accord
and left nations to work out bilateral agreements on routes and rates, chiefly
following the Bermuda model. This leaves the world much farther from
freedom of transportation in the air than on the sea and subject to all kinds
of special bargains, although the influence of the United States–United
Kingdom policy has introduced an element of semi-standardization.[11]

Progress by "Annex." In the technical "navigation" field, ICAO began to
hit its stride during 1948 when the Council approved five technical "annexes" to the ICAO Convention regarding personnel licensing, rules of the
air, meteorological codes, aeronautical charts, and dimensional units to be
used in air-ground communications. These became binding, in accordance
with the ICAO Constitution, when not rejected by a majority of the members within stated time limits. During the subsequent years of 1949 to 1952,
nine more annexes as well as various amendments to previous annexes were
also adopted. Moreover, an ambitious program of regional air navigation
meetings was initiated to plan the development of local facilities and adopt
special procedures where appropriate. Studies were also launched on several problems, such as the simplification of airport formalities and reduction
of costs.

[11] See analysis in Virginia Little, "Control of International Air Transport," *International Organization*, Vol. 3, No. 1 (February 1949), pp. 29–40.

To spread the burden of maintaining navigational facilities in sparsely settled areas, ten member states were engaged by 1948 in a "joint support" project to provide approximately thirty ships to man thirteen "weather stations" in the North Atlantic (reduced to twenty-five and ten, respectively, in 1949) to assist in matters of weather information, navigational aids, communication facilities, and search and rescue. This cooperation, which had begun in 1946, paid early and dramatic dividends when one of these ships, the United States Coast Guard cutter *Bibb* rescued sixty-nine passengers and crew from the United States flying boat *Bermuda Sky Queen*, forced down in the North Atlantic in October 1947. In October, 1953, however, the United States announced its withdrawal from the system on the ground that the cost was not matched by the benefits received, but several aviation and shipping spokesmen were critical of this move. Agreement was reached in 1948 and 1949 to provide joint support for certain facilities in Iceland, Greenland, and the Faeroe Islands. ICAO also adopted in 1948 a Convention on International Recognition of Rights in Aircraft, the conclusion of twenty years of wrangling over the issue. This measure was designed to simplify aircraft financing, thus facilitating the introduction of new equipment.

In 1951, after two years' study and consultation with ECOSOC and the Fiscal Commission, ICAO approved several resolutions aimed at alleviating multiple, discriminatory, and unduly burdensome taxation. The greatest advance in technical assistance activities came with the creation of the UN Expanded Program and an initial allotment to ICAO of $500,000, covering the period June 1950 to December 1951, which provided support for technical advice to ten governments and arranging with twelve countries for the granting of fellowships. ICAO also sponsored a Diplomatic Conference on International Air Law in Rome, September to October 1952, which adopted a new convention to regulate liability for damage caused by foreign aircraft to third parties, replacing an outmoded 1933 Rome convention. During February 1953 ICAO called the first special Air Navigation Conference in Montreal which recommended improvements in simplified air-ground reporting, aids to landing under poor visibility conditions, and radar traffic control requirements. The ICAO Council also happily announced the settlement of an India-Pakistan dispute on non-traffic stops. The parties had agreed to create two twenty-mile wide corridors through Pakistani territory to Afghanistan.

Telecommunications

The startling rapidity with which words, and now pictures, can be flashed around the world has made this a very active field, albeit increasingly incomprehensible to the layman. The United Nations' principal arm in this area has been the ITU, with some consultation with ECOSOC, TCC, UPU, ICAO, and WMO. In reviewing the evolution of these operations, one must be aware that the greatest technical advance, hence the greatest activity, in recent years has been in the radio field where the United States, motivated by commercial as well as governmental interests, has been a major force in the effort to bring order out of chaos in the allocation of radio frequencies.

The year 1947 was devoted chiefly to reorganizing the ITU at the International Telecommunications Conference at Atlantic City, July to October 1947, discussed in Chapter 9.[12] The Administrative Radio Conference, which met at the same time, revised the 1938 Cairo Radio Regulations by extending the world-wide frequency allocation table from 200,000 to 10,500,-000 kilo-cycles. The new allocations were to be recommended by a series of regional and service (broadcasting, maritime, aeronautical, etc.) conferences, and registered by a Provisional Frequency Board (PFB), with the advice of an expert International Frequency Registration Board (IFRB). It was hoped that this vastly complex job would be completed and the PFB dissolved by the end of 1949. Two of ITU's regular technical advisory bodies, the International Telegraphic and Radio Consultative Committees, also met during 1948 to formulate agreements on a multitude of technical questions.

The International Administrative Telegraph and Telephone Conference met at Paris, May to August 1949, to revise the telegraph and telephone regulations last reviewed at Cairo in 1938. A special aim in this connection was to satisfy the United States, Canada, and certain other countries which were not parties to the 1938 regulations. While only minor changes were made in the telephone regulations, several major alterations were made in the telegraphy field in the direction of reducing the categories of telegraph messages, equalizing rates over the same routes, and stabilizing the monetary values of rates in terms of the French gold franc. As part of these arrangements the United States and Canada were also persuaded to join the club.

Although many frequency questions still remained unsolved, the Extraordinary Administrative Radio Conference, twice postponed, was at last held in Geneva, August to December 1951. The compromise worked out was to adopt final allotments for certain sectors of the spectrum, principally below 4,000 kilocycles, and in the still unsettled sectors, chiefly between 3,950 and 27,500 kilocycles, to devise a "process of evolutionary adjustment . . . requiring a period of years." It was also agreed that the IFRB was to ride herd over the whole arrangement, without binding authority but with strong technical competence and advisory influence. The three consultative committees were especially active during 1951, and two of their respective plenary assemblies (telephone and radio) met to approve many technical recommendations on such matters as methods of specifying international telephonic transmission quality and standards of television quality.

Postal Relations

The United Nations affiliate chiefly concerned with international postal affairs is the Universal Postal Union (UPU). Fortunately, this is still a

[12] See pp. 257–258.

sheltered area relatively unruffled by the winds of world politics. As in the case of the ITU, the UPU was principally concerned during 1947 with its basic postwar reorganization during the twelfth Postal Congress at Paris from May to July. There were also changes in various postal regulations facilitating money orders, C.O.D. transactions, the mailing of newspapers and periodicals, and airmail. From that time until the following Congress in 1952, the Executive and Liaison Committee and the Bureau conducted the UPU's business, devoting primary attention to consulting with ICAO and the International Air Transport Association (airlines' association) to reduce airmail costs, facilitating technical advice to postal administrations, standardizing statistics, and simplifying parcel traffic. A Technical Transit Committee also began in 1949 to try to improve and standardize the computation of land and sea rates. The thirteenth UPU Congress met in Brussels, May to July 1952, with the representatives of ninety-one countries present, to consider more than 1,700 proposals for amending the acts of the previous Congress.

Meteorological Activities

The halting of air traffic by storms, interruption of radio communications by lightning, or the artificial inducement of rain — all these are "meteorological" (weather) problems that have concerned the United Nations through its partner agency, the World Meteorological Organization (WMO), in cooperation with other bodies such as the ITU and ICAO. The first WMO Congress did not meet until March to April 1951 in Paris, and most of its attention had to be devoted to administrative matters, especially smoothing the transition from the previous nongovernmental International Meteorological Organization to the new governmental agency. From that time on, WMO's principal activities centered around the preparation of provisional technical regulations, pending approval by the next Congress, to guide national meteorological services in their procedures; preparation of a weather observing manual for aircrews; revision of a 1932 International Cloud Atlas; preparation of world maps on thunderstorm activity in collaboration with the ITU Radio Consultative Committee; provision of technical assistance to develop meteorological services in specific countries; and collaboration with the United Nations to advise on the development of arid zones. As part of this program the WMO regional associations and technical commissions also began to function during 1952.

Statistical Activities

All economic and social progress must be nourished with accurate and comprehensive statistical information. The failure to prevent such catastrophes as depressions and to cure them once they have occurred has been partially due to the lack of such intelligence. The United Nations' chief agent in this field is the ECOSOC Statistical Commission, backed up by the

Secretariat's Statistical Office, in collaboration with other parts of the United Nations and all the specialized agencies.

Since the Statistical Commission met for the first time from January to February 1947, it has been instrumental in achieving considerable improvement and coordination in a field in which every government and agency tends to resist outside encroachment. One of the Commission's primary accomplishments has been to bring about an appreciable increase in the standardization of statistical methods, thus facilitating comparison. Landmarks in this effort are recommended manuals in two basic fields: the International Standard Industrial Classification of Economic Activities, approved in 1948, and the Standard International Trade Classification, approved in 1950. More specialized standards have also been formulated in the areas of population censuses, transport statistics, basic industrial data, industrial production and price indexes, vital statistics, and national income.

Hand in hand with the standardization effort, the Commission has tried to improve the quality of statistical information. Many studies have been prepared in this connection regarding population, industry, national income, vital statistics, and general sampling problems. Beginning in 1949 increasing attention was also given to providing statistical technical assistance to underdeveloped countries.

Within the United Nations system, the Statistical Commission has gradually, and not without some friction, established itself as the coordinating center to eliminate duplication and conflict among the many agencies whose unquenchable thirst for statistics has often harassed national governments. The United Nations' statistical publications provide a remarkably broad and intensive picture of world-wide economic and social activities. These include:

Statistical Yearbook, comprehensive series of all kinds of data; Demographic Yearbook, covering population, vital statistics and migration; National Income Statistics of Various Countries, presenting estimates of national income and its components; Yearbook of International Trade Statistics, giving data on trade by commodity and country of origin and destination; Monthly Bulletin of Statistics, monthly or quarterly data on some 2,000 series; Population and Vital Statistics Reports, quarterly; A Summary of World Trade Statistics, quarterly; Direction of International Trade, quarterly issued jointly by the Statistical Office, IMF, and IBRD.

Reflections on Economic Activities

Measured in ideal terms, the United Nations' economic efforts seem puny and faltering indeed. Judged, however, by the more realistic yardstick of what the world has known in the past, especially during the League era, the United Nations performance seems a heartening chapter in the history of international collaboration. The new emphasis is on building a better world rather than merely protecting and patching the old one. Never did the League think in such positive terms. Never did it take so much direct action through its own personnel regarding so many problems in so many parts of the world. Today it is far truer of the United Nations than of the British Empire to say that the sun never sets on its activities. Nor is it the exclusive club of the Europeans, as the League tended to be. It is now the forum of Asians, Africans, Americans and other peoples never directly represented in the League.

An especially remarkable aspect of this progress is the evolution of the campaign to develop the underdeveloped countries. In League days even the most enlightened observers of the world scene assumed that the gap between rich and poor countries was as much a part of the nature of things as the gap between rich and poor individuals. While the less fortunate nations might climb a bit higher, it was assumed they must do so chiefly by tugging on their own bootstraps. Their economic backwardness was, if not inherent, certainly deeply and firmly rooted in their natures. There was not very much anyone else could do — certainly not the League — to hustle their economic progress.

Today this attitude is fast becoming as extinct as the dodo, chiefly under the impact of United Nations debates and action, centering principally around the technical assistance program. We must recognize, of course, that the major force behind this remarkable effort has not been spontaneous altruism on the part of the developed countries but the recent revolt of the less developed countries themselves, spurred on by the events of World War II, the egalitarian principles of many westerners who have come in contact with them, the leadership of inspiring figures such as Mahatma Gandhi, and the encouragement of the Communists. While the United Nations has not been the recipient of the major portion of national development funds, it has exerted significant influence on national programs and, at the same time, has carried out hundreds of its own projects in most countries of the world. There is no doubt that this has been one of the most revolutionary constructive international forces in history.

The new positive emphasis also reflects an increasing recognition that the problem of war, still thought to be man's principal nemesis, has its roots in a thousand and one contributing causes of tension, including economic difficulties, from burdensome land tenure practices to industrial unemployment. The United Nations' efforts also represent a growing appreciation on the part of most nations, including the greatest, that the multilateral approach has certain practical advantages over the bilateral. Chief among these are the spreading of financial burdens, the availability of a richer variety of cultural and technical resources, and the greater willingness of countries to cooperate with an enterprise in which they have a voice and which represents no single national interest, although one or two may exert strong pressures.

What Has the UN Achieved?

The key question, of course, is: how much has the United Nations really accomplished in the economic field? The first point that emerges from all the evidence presented above is that one would be quite mistaken to assume that the United Nations and the specialized agencies have exercised no real influence merely because they were given no binding legislative authority and only limited funds. While these shortcomings are serious, they are far from insurmountable. These agencies have accomplished much, both directly and indirectly, as the result of a number of informal sources of influence: the weight of the governments supporting their resolutions, especially the great powers; the revealing and analytical qualities of the information which they have harvested and winnowed; the cogency and utility of their recommendations; the ability and prestige of their staffs; and the impact of their limited capacity to control various services, particularly relief and technical assistance. These are the factors that give these agencies actual effectiveness far beyond the apparent limits of their constitutions and budgets.

When one looks back over the broad pattern of concrete achievements, it is scarcely surprising that the principal advances have come where the major powers exerted strong influence, where resistance was weak, and where money and skills were available to meet various national needs. Between 1945 and 1953, approximately $5 billion worth of relief supplies have been furnished to thousands of destitute through UNRRA, IRO, UNICEF, United Nations Relief and Works Agency for Palestine Refugees, and the United Nations Korean Reconstruction Agency. Approximately four hundred different types of technical assistance were being furnished, as of 1953, to most countries of the world through the United Nations and specialized agencies at an annual cost of approximately $20 million. The IBRD has furnished limited financing for reconstruction and development loans totaling $1,664 million through 1953, and the IMF has provided similar financing, totaling $918 million through April 1953. And a vast amount of research, policy formulation, and circulation of information regarding all the economic issues mentioned above has been accomplished at only the cost of staff services and dissemination, something on the order of $20 million a year.

But it would be a patent falsehood to paint only the bright highlights of this picture without adding the shadows. The most debilitating weakness stems from the continued reluctance of nations to surrender their freedom of resources and policy to the direction of international organizations. Most of the smaller nations are just as guilty of this attitude as are the greater states, but the resistance of the latter is more crucial, hence more noticeable, because their resources exert such decisive influence. Yet one should remember that this is a relative, not an absolute, question. No state, not even the greatest, is or can be absolutely independent in actual practice. The mightiest have surrendered considerable freedom of action at some times on some issues. Nonetheless, as indicated above, the resistance to international cooperation, especially on the part of the United States, has seriously hobbled such efforts as maintaining the continuity and providing adequate local supervision of post-World War II relief and rehabilitation,

financing economic development, regulating the production and distribution of various agricultural, industrial, transport and communication
goods and services, and reducing certain trade and monetary barriers.

The reluctance to surrender national independence expresses itself in a
pervasive niggardliness regarding national financial contributions that fundamentally handcuffs all United Nations economic functions. Most striking
evidence of this is that the largest contributor, the United States, has constantly insisted on administering the overwhelming portion of its economic
assistance through non-United Nations channels. Of a total of $30.6 billion
spent by the United States on economic aid from July 1945 through June
1951, only about $4 billion, or 13 per cent, was expended through UNRRA,
the United Nations, and the specialized agencies.[13] While national contributions to the United Nations have been greater than those given the
League, they are still a mere drop in the bucket compared with what is
regularly spent on national administrations. Neither ECOSOC nor its commissions nor the specialized agencies ever have enough funds to do more
than hang on to the tail of the economic bull and cry hopefully for national
action. Nonetheless, one would be mistaken not to appreciate the significance of the trend towards giving greater funds, hence more direct operational scope, to the United Nations as compared with the League.

Essence of United Nations Function

On balance, one must recognize that most of the United Nations' economic activities have taken the form of a flow of substantial "know-how"
and modest grants and loans from the richer to the poorer nations. The
gains to the richer powers have not come primarily in their receipt of
foreign technological and material assistance but in reducing political and
economic tensions injurious to their world-wide interests, developing new
markets, eliminating the competition of lower standards, reducing trade
barriers, improving the "climate" for investment, increasing the knowledge
and understanding of economic forces, fostering healthier monetary conditions, and facilitating transportation and communications, chiefly in terms
of the standards of the more developed countries.

While the major powers have paid a price for these benefits (costs of
financial and technical assistance, lowering their own trade barriers, and
binding themselves to some common standards) their concessions have
been relatively minor, and they have considered the gains well worth the
price. Where this has not been the case, they have not agreed to cooperate.

This is not to say that the smaller nations have not also gained. They
have reaped the many benefits just enumerated. Their position as the battleground in the struggle against communism has greatly enhanced their
bargaining power (reflected in the numerous jokes about aid being allo-

---

[13] *Foreign Aid by the U.S. Government, 1940–51* (Washington: U.S. Government
Printing Office, 1952).

cated in proportion to the numbers of local Communists). But their gains have come primarily where their interests and those of the dominant powers have seemed mutually advantageous, particularly to the latter. It is true, they have forced some concessions, but they have never had the political and economic power to compel the great powers to do anything they firmly resisted. The latter, especially the United States, have always held the upper hand.

This analysis does not prove, however, as is sometimes alleged, that United Nations economic activities are a worthless sham. This system has all the advantages and disadvantages of any loose confederation, as distinguished from a more integrated federation. The domination of the rich and powerful is not fundamentally different from the balance of power within most national governments, including those that allege they operate primarily for the poor and weak, such as the Soviet Union. The principal failing of the United Nations system is that the Member states have refused thus far to surrender any major portion of their freedom of action. Hence the United Nations must speak softly, in recommendations rather than legislative acts. It must depend for its effectiveness more on unpredictable *ad hoc* support than generally accepted and strongly organized administration and enforcement. Nonetheless, the United Nations process does provide an indispensable forum for balancing the interests of the large and small, with the middle powers often playing a strategic mediating role. One must never forget, moreover, that governments' concepts of their self-interest are not static. They have been and are now being enlightened and liberalized by negotiations within these many economic and social bodies.

Suggestions for Further Reading

Books

Brown, William Adams, Jr., *The United States and the Restoration of World Trade* (Washington: Brookings Institution, 1950).

Condliffe, John Bell, *The Commerce of Nations* (New York: W. W. Norton & Company, Inc., 1950).

Cortney, Philip, *The Economic Munich* (New York: Philosophical Library, 1949).

Evatt, Herbert Vere, *The Task of Nations* (New York: Duell, Sloan and Pearce, 1949).

Harrod, R. F., *The Life of John Maynard Keynes* (New York: Harcourt, Brace & Company, 1951).

Kindleberger, Charles P., *The Dollar Shortage* (New York: Massachusetts Institute of Technology Press and Wiley, 1950).

Levi, Werner, *Fundamentals of World Organization* (Minneapolis: The University of Minnesota Press, 1950).

Mikesell, Raymond F., *United States Economic Policy and International Relations* (New York: McGraw-Hill Book Company, Inc., 1952).

Wilcox, Clair, *A Charter for World Trade* (New York: The Macmillan Company, 1949).

Periodicals

Berle, Adolf A., Jr., "Freedoms of the Air," *Harper's Magazine,* Vol. 190, No. 1138 (March 1945).

Condliffe, John Bell, "International Trade and Economic Nationalism," *International Conciliation,* No. 476 (December 1951).

Cooper, John C., "The Bermuda Plan: World Pattern for Air Transport," *Foreign Affairs,* Vol. 25, No. 1 (October 1946).

Feis, Herbert, "The Conflict Over Trade Ideologies," *Foreign Affairs,* Vol. 25, No. 2 (January 1947).

Kindleberger, Charles P., "Bretton Woods Reappraised," *International Organization,* Vol. 5, No. 1 (February 1951).

Little, Virginia, "Control of International Air Transport," *International Organization,* Vol. 3, No. 1 (February 1949).

Loveday, A., "Suggestions for the Reform of the United Nations Economic and Social Machinery," *International Organization,* Vol. 7, No. 3 (August, 1953).

Mikesell, Raymond F., "The International Monetary Fund 1944–1949," *International Conciliation,* No. 455 (November 1949).

Triffin, Robert, "Monetary Reconstruction in Europe," *International Conciliation,* No. 482 (June 1952).

Viner, Jacob, "Conflicts of Principles in Drafting a Trade Charter," *Foreign Affairs,* Vol. 25, No. 4 (July 1947).

Warner, Edward, "The Chicago Air Conference," *Foreign Affairs,* Vol. 23, No. 3 (April 1945).

Documents

International Monetary Fund, *Annual Report, Balance of Payments Yearbook, Staff Papers,* and other documents.

United Nations, General Assembly and ECOSOC, *Official Records* and other documents.

United States, Department of State, *International Civil Aviation, 1945–1948, 1948–1949, 1949–1950.*

20

Social and Cultural Activities — League

Labor

HAVING BUILT UP a tremendous reservoir of political and economic pressure during World War I and at the Paris Peace Conference, organized labor was able during the first few postwar years to push through the sluice gates of the International Labor Organization (ILO) a considerable flood of reform conventions. The way had been carefully prepared for this campaign since the measures adopted dealt with fields in which there was the most obvious need for international cooperation, in which there had already been some international activity, in which there was the most effective organized pressure on the part of labor (largely industrial and maritime, rather than agricultural or commercial), and in which the Peace Conference had recommended action according to the provisions of Part XIII of the Versailles Treaty.

As labor drove ahead, however, its credit was quickly consumed, and employer resistance increased. While the ILO was able to grind out sixteen conventions during its first three years, 1919 to 1921, not a single one was approved during the next three years. And it required an additional eight years to formulate sixteen more conventions. During this painful uphill march, the ILO began to develop a more thorough method of drafting its conventions and recommendations, explore more controversial questions, experiment with a more selective approach through special conferences limited to certain regions or industries, and supplement the traditional progress-by-convention approach with other instruments such as direct technical assistance and the formulation of model statutes. Then, when the depression struck, the Organization concentrated its attention on those problems that seemed most directly connected with that crisis, particularly unemployment. Having glanced at this general pattern of interwar development, it is interesting to look more closely at the particular battle fields where the principal skirmishes took place.

General Conditions of Work

Hours and Wages. For generations laboring men have been primarily concerned with what American workers have traditionally called "pork chops": largely the basic essentials of hours and wages. While the ILO was remarkably active on the hours question from the very beginning, it never got past the front door of the wages problem. During the first ILO Conference, held at Washington in 1919, the workers concentrated their fire in order to win a comprehensive hours convention. The convention which was adopted, the first to be approved by the Organization, provided an eight-hour day and a forty-eight-hour work week in industrial undertakings. Although this measure won a two-thirds majority, it aroused considerable employer alarm and was never ratified by any major industrial state during the interwar period. Nevertheless, all states, including the more advanced, were influenced by its provisions, and many of them subsequently followed them without actually ratifying the convention.[1]

Because of the opposition which confronted labor on this question, it was not until 1930 that the ILO was able to agree to extend the principles of the 1919 convention to commercial employees. Then, in relatively quick succession, other conventions were adopted to limit working hours for particular groups: coal miners, in 1931; sheet-glass workers, in 1934; seamen, in 1936; and road transport workers, in 1939.

A companion effort, in response to the widespread unemployment resulting from the depression, was the campaign to seek even further reduction of hours, not so much to ease labor's load as to spread it among the millions who had no jobs. The Organization adopted a resolution in 1935 approving the principle of the forty-hour week, later extended through conventions to glass bottle works, in 1935; public works, in 1936; and textiles, in 1937.

Another prong in labor's attack upon the hours question was its constant effort to win agreement on guaranteed weekly rest periods and annual holidays-with-pay. During the early period, when conventions were being passed left and right, labor succeeded in obtaining one in 1921 which provided for a weekly rest period of twenty-four consecutive hours in industrial enterprises. A recommendation was also passed the same year proposing the same treatment for commercial employees, but not even a recommendation on the subject could be won for agricultural workers. Then, in 1936, a convention was adopted providing for an annual paid holiday of at least six working days for stipulated industrial and commercial undertakings; at least twelve working days for workers under sixteen years of age. The same year another convention was also approved providing annual paid holidays for seamen, but again nothing was done for farm laborers.

The difficult question of wages not only gave rise to intense differences between labor and management but also required a more sensitive form of regulation than could be provided through the inflexible and cautious medium of conventions. Thus the ILO did little more than prepare numerous studies on the question and adopt a convention in 1928 aimed at providing national minimum wage agencies, particularly for trades and home industries in which there was no effective regulation of wages

[1] By September 1, 1939, eighteen middle and small nations had ratified.

through collective agreements and in which wages were exceptionally low. Organized labor and management in the more advanced countries, who dominated the ILO, tended to support such measures as a means of defending themselves against substandard competitive labor practices but still preferred to arrange their own terms through private bargaining.

Health and Safety. Before the ILO was anything more than a dream, the long campaign to prohibit by international agreement the use of poisonous white phosphorous had dramatized the need for international cooperation to protect workers' health from unscrupulous competitive methods. Consequently it is not surprising that the ILO and particularly its Industrial Hygiene Service have been active in this field from the very beginning. A recommendation was adopted at the first Conference urging all ILO members to adhere to the 1906 Berne convention prohibiting the use of white phosphorus in the manufacture of matches. The same year the ILO also approved a recommendation on disinfection against anthrax, although it was not felt that the disinfection process had been sufficiently developed to warrant a convention. At the same Conference the ILO also recommended that governments establish industrial health services which would coordinate their efforts with the work of the ILO. In 1921, a convention was adopted forbidding the use of white lead except under certain limited circumstances, and in 1925 another was formulated to prohibit night work in bakeries, which had always been the traditional way of providing fresh bread for the world's breakfast. In addition to these measures, the ILO approved other conventions and recommendations dealing specifically with the health of women and children as part of broad programs to give special protection to those groups which are discussed in greater detail below. Although no comprehensive labor health code was ever adopted by the ILO, a proposed code was published by the International Health Office in 1933.

The ILO tried not only to protect workers from disease but also to shield them from accidents which so often and so needlessly rob society of valuable human resources. While European governments had long recognized a responsibility to protect workers from such mishaps, the early doctrine of "safety first" in the United States had placed primary responsibility upon the worker. Then, in the twentieth century, American governmental authorities also became active in this field and began to compel the payment of compensation for injuries caused by certain types of accidents which led employers and insurance companies to initiate an intensive anti-accident campaign. These considerations were among the factors which caused the ILO to adopt a recommendation in 1923 urging the organization of national factory inspection agencies and another recommendation in 1926 calling upon states to establish similar agencies to inspect seamen's conditions of work. Then, in 1929, the ILO wrote its gospel on industrial safety, a recommendation outlining a comprehensive safety program based on both private and public efforts. Other more specific measures included a 1929 recommendation asking countries to prohibit the use of any power-driven machinery without the safety devices prescribed by law, a 1929 recommendation urging states to require the marking of weight on heavy packages to protect seamen and longshoremen, a 1929 convention (revised in 1932) setting forth comprehensive regulations for the protection of workers loading or unloading ships, and a 1937 convention embodying safety provisions for the building industry.

Social Insurance. While the ILO had followed well-blazed trails in its actions on hours and health, it found itself in relatively virgin territory as it began to deal with social insurance. The principal innovator in this field had been no radical reformer but the shrewd, paternalistic "Iron Chancellor" of Germany, Otto von Bismarck, who between 1883 and 1889 had given his country's workmen sickness insurance, accident insurance, invalid insurance, and old-age pensions. Other countries, however, were exceedingly timid in following his example. And, because most of its members found themselves in embarrassing financial straits immediately after World War I, the ILO was inclined to proceed rather cautiously in this field. Not until 1925, under the thawing influence of the Locarno era, did the ILO adopt a convention providing for compensation for industrial accidents; another, for industrial diseases; and a third, for reciprocity of treatment of nationals and foreigners in matters of accident compensation.

In 1927 two more important conventions were approved: one providing sickness insurance in industry and commerce and a similar one for agricultural wage-earners. The greatest advance against social insecurity, however, was made in 1933, under the impact of the depression, with the passage of a spate of six conventions: two establishing old-age insurance (for both agricultural and industry-commerce workers), two on insurance for widows and orphans of workers in agriculture and industry-commerce respectively, and two on invalidity insurance for the same two groups. Then, in 1935, a convention was approved to assure continuity of pension benefits for migrant workers.

Employment and Unemployment. Orthodox economists had long argued that employment should not be artificially regulated but was merely the tail of the economic system which would be wagged up or down according to what was happening to the rest of the animal. But organized labor was never satisfied with this doctrine and was chiefly responsible for the adoption of a 1919 convention which provided that there should be free public employment agencies and that employment information should be sent periodically to the ILO. A recommendation of the same year proposed the abolition of fee-charging employment agencies, agreements on international recruitment, the promotion of unemployment insurance, and the coordination of public works as anti-depression measures. A 1920 convention regarding the employment of seamen stipulated the ultimate abolition of fee-charging agencies and the international coordination of national employment services through the ILO.

With the advent of the depression, the ILO adopted resolutions in 1932 setting forth a trail-blazing "full employment" program including political and financial as well as economic measures. A 1933 convention provided for the abolition of fee-charging agencies within a three-year period, and a 1933 recommendation suggested various policies regarding the administration of public employment agencies. The following year the ILO finally approved a convention providing for the payment of unemployment benefits. Later measures included a 1935 recommendation on the provision of educational and social services for unemployed young people, and two 1937 recommendations on the coordination and planning of public works.

Other General Questions. After the ILO had done all it could to build defenses against some of the major forms of labor insecurity, it turned to other problems that in 1919 had seemed either less pressing or less susceptible to effective international action. One of these questions was the right of association which the founders of the ILO had assumed was generally recognized, especially since the Treaty of Versailles provided for the direct representation of labor in the ILO. When it became apparent, however, that some states (Hungary and Spain were accused specifically) did not recognize such a right, it proved difficult indeed to persuade many management and governmental delegates to adopt any positive measure on the subject. A 1921 convention provided merely that agricultural labor should be granted the same "rights of association and combination" as those given industrial workers, but no convention or recommendation was ever approved regarding industrial workers.

Special Groups

Women. As it pressed forward, the ILO had to juggle two apparently conflicting considerations: the need for maintaining a united labor front in order to exert the greatest possible influence and, at the same time, the need for treating various special groups somewhat differently. What groups should receive special consideration was determined not only by their needs but also by their influence and the pattern of precedents. Women comprised one of these blocs that was accorded extraordinary attention from the very beginning both because of a long history of humanitarian efforts in their behalf and because they had been drawn into factories, farms, and offices during World War I to an unprecedented degree. Yet some of their hardy feminist sisters, especially French and Norwegian contingents, opposed some of these measures as anti-female discrimination. In spite of this resistance, two conventions regarding the rights of women workers were adopted during the 1919 Conference: one providing maternity benefits for women in industry and commerce six weeks before and after childbirth and the other prohibiting night work for women in industry and commerce. For the ladies on the farms the 1921 Conference approved only recommendations suggesting the same rights as those granted their urban sisters. In 1935 another convention provided that no woman should be allowed to perform underground work in mines.

Young People. Children, as well as women, had long been the object of special humanitarian efforts; thus it was only natural that the ILO should carry on this work. A 1919 convention declared that children under 14 (changed to 15 in 1937) were not to be employed in any private or public industrial undertaking, and another of the same year prohibited, with certain exceptions, night work for young people under 18. A 1920 convention provided that children under 14 (changed to 15 in 1936) were not to be employed at sea. The following year, 1921, reform measures regarding children came thick and fast: a convention prohibiting the employment of children under 14 in agriculture except after school hours, a recommendation stipulating the proper period of sleep for children under 14 employed in agriculture, the white lead convention which protected children as well as women, a convention forbidding the employment of young persons under 18 as trimmers or stokers aboard vessels, another convention requiring the employment of young persons under 18 at sea to be subject to annual medical examinations, and a recommendation promoting the development of vocational agricultural education. After this flood of decisions, the ILO did not approve another child labor measure until eleven years later when the depression situation laid its heavy hand on children as well as their parents and gave rise to increased delinquency. A 1932 convention prohibited the employment of children under 14 (changed to 15 in 1937) in nonindustrial enterprises or over that age if they were still required by national law to attend school. A 1935 recommendation urged that all states make 15 the minimum age for leaving school and entering employment and that they require children unable to find employment to continue their education. Two 1939 recommendations also urged improvements in the training of young people: one on vocational education, the other on apprenticeship.

Seamen. Anyone who has strolled along the waterfront of an international port has usually been thrilled by the sight of merchant ships lying side by side flying an assortment of multicolored flags, a sight that dramatizes the constant and direct maritime competition which long ago began to give rise to internationally recognized customs and agreements. The ILO also gave special attention to this field, even to the extent of devoting whole conferences, such as those in 1920, 1926, 1929, 1932, and 1936, primarily to maritime questions. Consequently a considerable structure of agreements was erected — sixteen in all — which came to be known as the International Seamen's Code.

In 1920 four measures were approved in this field: (1) one convention provided that all employment operations be performed through free public agencies managed jointly by owner and seamen associations under a central authority; (2) another convention required owners to pay an unemployment indemnity (two months' wages) to the crew of any ship that was lost or foundered; (3) another convention prohibited the employment of children under 14 (changed to 15 in 1936); and (4) a recommendation urged each member state to formulate a comprehensive seamen's code. In 1921 the two other child labor conventions in this field were adopted: one making employment of those under 18 subject to an annual medical examination, the other fixing 18 as the minimum age for employment as a trimmer or stoker. In 1926 three more measures were accepted: (1) a convention regulating the negotiation of seamen's articles of agreement with the owners, (2) another convention requiring national provision for the repatriation of seamen, and (3) a recommendation concerning the establishment of national inspection services to investigate conditions of maritime labor.

The last spate of measures in this area came in 1936. Five conventions dealt with the following matters: (1) a limit of eight hours a day and fifty-six a week for seamen on vessels over 2,000 tons and not more than eight a day and forty-eight a week for "day workers" on vessels over 700 tons, (2) a provision for holidays with pay, (3) the stipulation that a shipowner is liable for compensation for sickness, injury, and death befalling a seamen in his employ, (4) the establishment of a compulsory sickness insurance scheme for seamen, and (5) the requirement of certificates of competency to be issued officers by central national authorities. The same year a recommendation was approved concerning the policing and regulation of shore fronts in behalf of seamen's welfare while ashore.

Colonial Labor. The ILO entered this field rather gingerly for a number of reasons: the absence of any vigorous organized pressure groups (such as those that fought in behalf of industrial workers and seamen), the frosty attitude of the colonial powers on such delicate questions, and the discouraging magnitude of the job that needed to be done in the colonial area. Not until the League invited the ILO to participate in the temporary Commission on Slavery, created in 1924, did the Organization become actively interested, and it did not adopt a convention in the field until 1930. That measure looked to the suppression of forced labor during a five-year "transitional period." In 1936 another convention was approved to improve colonial recruitment methods. Two more conventions were formulated in 1939: one regulating the negotiation of written contracts governing native labor and the other controlling penal sanctions. The same year a recommendation was also adopted proposing the establishment of labor inspection services in the colonial territories.

Other Special Groups. The problems of migrating laborers have also received special ILO attention in an effort to facilitate the siphoning off of workers from surplus to deficit countries. This difficult question was especially aggravated by the restrictive United States legislation enacted in 1921, 1924 and 1927, and later by the depression. Because states jealously guarded their freedom of action in this area, however, only one convention on migrant labor was adopted during the years 1919 to 1939 and that a relatively minor one in 1926 regulating the inspection of migrating workers. Then, in 1939, three other conventions were approved: one regulating conditions of employment, one dealing with information services, and one ensuring treatment of migrants regarding certain labor rights equal to that accorded nationals. It should also be mentioned that previous conventions on unemployment insurance, accident compensation, sickness insurance, and pensions had incidentally aimed at protecting the interests of migrating workers.

Workers with whiter collars, especially professional and salaried workers, generally received far less attention than the groups discussed above. Nevertheless, the ILO was anxious not to appear to forget them and made several gestures in their direction, including various studies. The salaried employees, moreover, benefited from the conventions and recommendations that dealt with "commercial" workers.

Information

In the ILO's first years the flood of conventions and recommendations did not wait for intensive research by the Organization itself. As the flood subsided, however, and new fields began to be explored, the ILO itself initiated an extensive research program. As the ILO gained experience it also became apparent that, even when no formal action could be agreed upon, the extensive informational irrigation system influenced the daily thoughts and acts of thousands of public and private leaders throughout the world. This clientele was serviced by a network of many channels: the questionnaires and other documents used in the process of formulating specific measures, various special studies, publications (such as *The Labor Review, Industrial and Labor Information, Industrial Safety Survey, Legislative Series, Occupation and Health,* etc.), meetings of experts, periodic national reports on compliance and other matters, and a few technical assistance missions.

Conclusions

An inventory of the ILO's interwar assets and liabilities suggests that its greatest achievement was not as policeman or judge, legislator or executive but as itinerant schoolmaster. It performed the elementary but invaluable function of opening men's eyes not only to the need for and the possibility of improving labor standards but also to the actual methods which were already being developed in the more advanced countries.

The fathers of the ILO had not, of course, expected their offspring to develop in this fashion. They had endowed it with certain semi-legislative and police powers which they wanted used to the utmost. But the formal instruments of conventions and sanctions proved unfortunately awkward and inflexible. A great number of threadbare nations, living under conditions several centuries behind the great powers, found it almost impossible to accept the standards set by their more prosperous neighbors, and, when they did accept them, they were often unable to enforce them. On the other hand, the sleeker nations were frequently unwilling to accept certain measures drafted in the ILO because some of their competitors would not cooperate or because they felt — and rightly so — that conventions could not easily be changed once complex bargains had been built into them, in spite of the fact that changes in the economic and social picture might make such changes desirable. Although many efforts were made to revise the 1919 hours convention, no amendment could ever be agreed upon during the entire interwar period. Furthermore, labor usually thought of conventions as means of pushing ahead into new country, while employers insisted that their principal purpose was merely to make existing boundaries clearer.

As a result not a great many conventions were adopted; those that were adopted represented a rather low common denominator; and ratifications were not only sparse but, because of spotty enforcement, often deceiving. As of September 1939, forty-six conventions were in force supported by 863 ratifications distributed over fifty states. This represented an average of about nineteen ratifications per convention. But bare figures are a poor measure of the Organization's impact. Although none of the industrial powers ratified the 1919 hours convention, almost every one of them followed its general outlines in their domestic policies. And some conventions played a major role in raising the standards of even the more advanced nations. The 1920 convention requiring the payment of up to two months' wages to a seaman unemployed because of shipwreck established a norm well in advance of the law and practice of all the maritime countries with the possible exception of the United States. In September 1939 that convention had been ratified by twenty-six states including Great Britain, France, and Italy. Besides conventions, about sixty recommendations were also approved during the interwar period to deal with certain pressing matters which the states would not swallow in the form of conventions.

Not only did conventions prove to be difficult policy instruments but also sanctions never worked as planned at Paris. The ILO never used its teeth — only its tongue. Although the labor representatives were not afraid of employing economic pressure, employers waxed choleric at the very thought, and governmental representatives were usually reluctant to engage in such an explosive business.

In its various efforts to reinforce the world's labor standards, the ILO did not try to be a pioneer as much as a popularizer. The ILO borrowed ideas from the more advanced nations — primarily Great Britain, Germany, the United States, and France — and peddled them around the world. At the same time, even the industrial leaders benefited from this exchange. The United States, for example, relied heavily on ILO studies as it organized its social security program.

As this work flowed along through the years there were certain shifts in direction. After the reforms which had generally been endorsed at Paris in 1919 had, for the most part, been adopted, the ILO began to branch out beyond the simple questions of hours and wages into broader fields such as social security, education, migration, and hygiene. Then, when the depression struck, the ILO turned its attention to the immediately pressing questions of employment, standards of living, housing and nutrition. The chief forces which directed this whole development were of course those labor groups which were able to mobilize the greatest influence: chiefly industrial and maritime labor. Commercial workers came next; farm laborers were far weaker; and the professionals came last.

In spite of all the pitfalls, however, ILO did a remarkable job when one considers the experience before 1919. In tribute to these achievements one wise and experienced statesman, David Lloyd George, wrote in 1939,

> The transformation which the ILO has brought about in many countries is incredible when one recalls pre- [World War I] conditions . . . China has now worked out a most advanced Factory Act. . . . Millions of workers have benefited by the changes and the country will certainly never go back to the old conditions. . . . It was the insistence shown by the International Labor Office on the appointment of a properly representative workers' delegate at Geneva which brought about the unification of the Japanese workers' movement and the recognition of it by the Government. . . . No organization has ever in the course of nineteen years spared mankind as much misery, torture and degradation which was awaiting it.[2]

Health

The fundamental motivation that led states to cooperate internationally in the health field during the interwar period sprang not so much from general altruism as from their desire to shield their own populations from the incursions of foreign-bred microbes, and their concern that whatever protective regulations might be adopted should not interfere unnecessarily with traffic in goods and persons. The League's first concern in 1920 was an immediate and deathly fear of the epidemics of typhus and relapsing fever, cholera and smallpox which raged violently among the impoverished and war-stricken Eastern European countries. It was only this kind of challenge that could have persuaded the larger powers who dominated the League to initiate that organization's health program with such speed and energy, a program whose major objective during those first years was to disinfect practically everything that moved and breathed in Eastern Europe. To facilitate this campaign the League's Health Organization also promoted the standardization of biological preparations and created special commissions to carry on intensive warfare against particular diseases.

Only gradually did the League's emphasis change from this crisis approach to more positive, preventive, and long-range projects including efforts to help the less developed countries organize their public health services and to probe certain basic social problems such as malnutrition and inadequate housing that provide fertile breeding grounds for disease. A related though separately administered program was the League's anti-

[2] *Memoirs of the Peace Conference* (New Haven: Yale University Press, 1939), Vol. 1, p. 449.

narcotic work that by painfully slow degrees began to dam the flow of this debilitating traffic.

Epidemiological Control

To turn back the threatened invasion of postwar epidemics the alarmed Western powers hastily persuaded the League Council early in 1920 to create a temporary Epidemics Commission, forerunner of the Health Organization, which acted as the general staff of the shock troops of doctors and nurses sent to do battle with the enemy germs in Russia, Greece, Poland, and other eastern countries. When the 1922 Russian famine loosed new floods of disease-ridden refugees, Poland appealed for League assistance. Immediately a League Conference met in Warsaw and agreed on various countermeasures, including a new system of direct and rapid communication of disease reports among various national public health services and the League's Health Organization. This was the first major step in the development of the world-wide epidemiological intelligence system which by 1939 covered areas holding 80 per cent of the world's population and acted as a clearing house for a mass of daily, weekly and monthly reports on the incidence of the chief epidemic diseases. The most important nerve center, other than Geneva, was the Singapore Bureau of the Health Organization, established in 1925 at the request of the Japanese member of the Health Committee, which at its peak in the late thirties was receiving information from 180 major ports and distributing it through wireless stations to 124 public health services. In 1926 a sanitary convention was signed at Paris not only making it obligatory to report five different epidemic diseases but also stipulating many other regulations to prevent such illnesses from crossing national boundaries.

Of the special commissions appointed to deal with particular diseases, the first was the Malaria Sub-Committee of the League Health Committee which was appointed in 1923 and subsequently renamed the Malaria Commission. After devoting its first years to gathering information, this body began an ambitious positive program including the training of malariologists (in special courses and field work in London, Paris, Hamburg, Rome, Singapore, Spain and Yugoslavia), the testing of various antimalarial preparations, and the study and classification of the incidence of malaria in different regions. Other special campaigns were also conducted against smallpox, leprosy, syphilis, sleeping sickness, tuberculosis, cancer and infant mortality.

Biological Standardization

Often lacking standardized biological preparations, doctors using unfamiliar brands of drugs, especially during World War I and after, felt as if they were working blindfolded, and their patients at times suffered the tragic results. As a consequence of the League Health Organization's efforts, begun in 1921, to correct this situation, standard formulae were agreed upon at a series of ten conferences held between 1921 and 1935 dealing with some twenty-seven sera, vaccines, drugs, vitamins and sex hormones. This project was supervised by the Permanent Commission on Biological Standardization created in 1924 and reconstituted in 1935. The two institutions which were used as the principal research and coordinating centers for this work were the Danish State Serum Institute at Copenhagen and the National Institute of Medical Research at Hampstead, England.

Reorganization of National Public Health Services

One of the first major steps in opening the League's door to a more long-range program, now called "technical assistance," was a 1928 Greek request asking the Health Organization to help that government recast its public health service which had been seriously strained by a dengue epidemic. The Health Committee responded by going straight to Greece to make an on-the-spot survey which resulted in a series of recommendations, most of which were subsequently put into effect.

In 1929 a Chinese request for similar assistance led to an even more intensive effort which resulted in the following changes:

> 1. a reorganization of the Chinese port quarantine services satisfying both the Chinese National Government and the various other powers that exercised special privileges in those ports;
> 2. the establishment of a Central Field Health Station as the nucleus of a permanent national health service whose staff was partly trained by League-sponsored study hours;
> 3. the organization of a League study program for medical officers involved in the creation of a national institute for medical instruction;
> 4. the initiation of a concerted League-assisted campaign against smallpox and cholera in Shanghai; and
> 5. the preparation of a League study regarding the reorganization of the entire system of Chinese medical education.

As a result one observer wrote in 1941, "Anyone familiar with recent conditions in China must be astonished at the progress made in organizing the basic health and medical institutions and organizations on the sound lines that characterize them." [3] Other less intensive projects were undertaken in Czechoslovakia, South Africa and several Latin American countries.

Nutrition

The fact that the kind, as distinguished from the quantity, of fuel that goes into one's stomach has a direct bearing on one's physical machinery seems perfectly obvious. But it was not until the late twenties, particularly after the depression emphasized this problem, that the Health Organization devoted a major share of its attention to the relationship of nutrition to health. The first step was taken at the request of Japan when the Health Organization not only dispatched an expert to study that country's food situation but also prepared a report on the general methods to be used in

---

[3] Frank G. Boudreau, "Health, Nutrition and Housing," *World Organization* (Washington: American Council on Public Affairs, 1942), p. 98.

making dietary surveys. Then the big splash came when, as a result of a Chilean request for a similar study, two members of the Secretariat's Health section, Drs. Burent and Aykroid, wrote a report, "Nutrition and Public Health," appearing in the *Health Quarterly* in 1935, which became a virtual best-seller almost overnight.

Albert Thomas, Director of the ILO, took up the theme at the 1935 International Labor Conference, and the League Assembly, that same year, directed a Mixed Commission of agricultural, economic and health experts to prepare a report on the whole question. The Commission's final report, the last of five, which was referred to by the *New York Times* as "the book of the year," aroused a tidal wave of popular interest which resulted in, among other things, the creation of twenty-one national nutrition committees which cooperated with the League in establishing ideal dietary standards. Another offshoot of this campaign was the European Conference on Rural Life, scheduled for 1939, which initiated many important studies regarding assistance to underdeveloped areas but had to be postponed because of World War II.

Narcotics

One of the most insidious scourges of mankind is the traffic in narcotics which, because of fantastic profits and small bulk, slips through weak enforcement systems and fastens upon those unfortunate souls who welcome any means, no matter how debasing, which will help them escape from the reality of this tragic world. When the League's Advisory Committee on Traffic in Opium and Other Dangerous Drugs was appointed in 1921, the first tasks it undertook were to extract from reluctant and badly organized governments certain essential facts about narcotics traffic and to develop a system whereby the flow of these drugs was to be controlled by export and import licenses.[4] Then the Advisory Committee sponsored the negotiation of a new convention in 1925 which provided:

> 1. that the trade and use of narcotics should be limited exclusively "to medical and scientific purposes";
> 2. that the license system should be extended;
> 3. that certain anti-opium measures should be adopted for free ports and zones;
> 4. that heavier penalties should be applied against violators;
> 5. that the kinds of drugs to be regulated should be increased through decisions of the Health Committee; and
> 6. that a Permanent Central Opium Board be created to receive national reports on exports, imports, and seizures and to ask governments to explain any excessive stocks or shipments.

This filled many of the gaps left by the outmoded 1912 convention, but it limited only trade and not manufacture. Thus it was still possible in the

---

[4] For previous regulation efforts, see Bertil A. Renborg, "Narcotic Drugs — International Administration," *World Organization* (Washington: American Council on Public Affairs, 1942), pp. 99–100.

late twenties for a Dutch firm to manufacture and sell four tons of heroin and morphine, an amount equal to four times the needs of the entire world.

Another convention was adopted in 1931 which stipulated that henceforth manufacture itself, as well as trade, would be limited to strictly legitimate needs. These amounts were estimated by each individual country and compiled and reviewed by the Supervisory Body which was created by the same convention. If no estimate was submitted by a particular government, that Body could adopt a figure which was as binding as if it had been submitted by the country in question. If these estimates were exceeded, the Permanent Central Opium Board could use not only its sanction of publicity but also initiate an embargo on further exports to the offending country. Another conference in 1936 produced a convention which stiffened the penalties for violating any of the previous treaties.

Conclusions

The League's health program was remarkable not because it was the first work done in the field — which it was not — nor because it did all that needed to be done — which it did not — but because it made remarkable strides in the direction of international health cooperation. The League's Health Organization and various narcotics bodies distinguished themselves particularly by going beyond the traditional armchair methods of occasional *ad hoc* conferences, studies and conventions. They were permanent vigorous organizations that gave constant attention to rapidly changing conditions. They also went beyond the traditional concept of waiting for epidemics to knock on the door before going into action and developed long-range preventive programs, including extensive specialized assistance to the less developed countries. They also learned, though somewhat late in life, that health is merely one facet of human existence and must be considered as part of the total complex of economic and social conditions. Consequently they began to encourage more coordinated studies such as those related to the projected Conference on Rural Life that was to have been held in 1939. Finally the narcotics bodies achieved a noteworthy reinforcement of the regulatory system in that field.

On the other hand, it would be quite unrealistic not to recognize the basic weaknesses that hobbled these efforts. The financial allotments made to the health program were always severely limited (approximately $190,-000 a year) and had to be supplemented generously by the Rockefeller Foundation (approximately $145,000 a year) and other non-League sources. The new emphasis on positive long-range measures and a more coordinated approach were just beginning to bear fruit when World War II withered the whole program. Nor was there adequate integration of the various international bodies dealing with health matters, particularly the League Health Organization and the Paris International Office of Public Health. Finally, the narcotics apparatus had succeeded in wounding the illicit business and driving it underground but not in killing it altogether.

The most obvious remaining problems were to limit the production of narcotics raw materials, as distinguished from the manufacturing process, and to improve and standardize the treatment of addicts.

Social Questions

Perhaps it is not surprising that the "social question" to which the League devoted most attention throughout the interwar period was an issue which most obviously required international cooperation and which had already received considerable attention prior to World War I — the traffic in women and children. Only by slow degrees did the League's social bodies begin to branch out into related and more positive areas, particularly in connection with general child welfare. Since the League purse yielded very little for this kind of activity, however, the growth of such projects was seriously restricted.

Traffic in Women and Children

To reinforce prewar efforts in this field the League Assembly adopted a new convention in 1921 increasing the age of consent from twenty to twenty-one, making it an offense merely to attempt to procure women, removing conviction as a condition of extradition, prescribing regulations to protect emigrants, providing for an advisory committee in this field, and establishing a better exchange of information. The Council then appointed the Advisory Committee on Traffic in Women and Children (the traditional term "white slaves" was abandoned for the very good reason that not all the victims were white) which met for the first time in June 1922. When the Council decided in 1924 to have the League absorb the intergovernmental activities of the International Association for the Promotion of Child Welfare, formed in Belgium in 1921, a new Committee on Child Welfare was created in 1925, and the two were known as the Advisory Commission for the Protection and Welfare of Children and Young People. In 1936 the Commission was enlarged and became the Advisory Committee on Social Questions.

Largely because of the persuasive arguments of Grace Abbott, the United States national on the Advisory Committee, and the financial support of the American Social Hygiene Bureau, investigators were sent to study the situation in Europe and America in 1924–26 and in the Far East in 1930–32. They returned with first-hand reports of a multimillion dollar business in human exploitation that profoundly shocked the entire world. Partly as a result of these investigations, a 1933 convention abolished the age of consent, which hindered more than it helped regulation. Later a 1937 regional Far East Conference at Bandoeng, Java, recommended the creation of a League bureau in the Far East to facilitate the control system. Another stronger convention was drafted in 1938, but there was never an opportunity to call a diplomatic conference to consider it.

Child Welfare

The odds were always against the League in this aspect of its work owing to the predominant attention given the prostitution problem, the imperfect development of the child welfare field, the attitude of many nations that this was primarily a "domestic question," and the lack of sufficient funds. Nonetheless, a handful of dedicated souls carried on an ambitious research program which touched on the treatment of young offenders, the protection of children born out of wedlock, the placement of children in families, and child health. A Child Welfare Information Center was established in the Secretariat in 1933. Then, in 1935, in keeping with the general trend to broaden the League's economic and social horizons, the Assembly instructed the Committee on Child Welfare to expand the scope of its operations to promote the maximum development of healthy normal children.

Conclusions

While the League's social bodies began by devoting most of their time and money to the traditional issue of the traffic in women and children, it gradually became apparent that this was merely one of many social questions that called for international cooperation. It should also be remembered that even within national governments the entire field of social work was just beginning its rapid development. And the League facilitated this evolution considerably by acting as a major center for the exchange of information. Nevertheless, throughout the interwar period, the League's social program tended to be the ugliest duckling of all — starved for funds, inadequately staffed, and, for lack of these and a clear sense of its own proper mission, restricted within very narrow boundaries.

Population and Migration

One of the factors that accentuated the depression was the absence of adequate outlets to siphon off Europe's surplus population. Before World War I, non-European countries, especially the United States, had absorbed millions of workers, but during and after the war that movement had been shut out. This blow had been softened, however, by the fact that the people of the United States happened to send private capital to Europe during the twenties which helped to maintain the level of employment until the depression stopped that also. To deal with this situation the International Labor Organization began studies which led to a broad research program by the League Committee of Experts on Demographic Problems appointed early in 1939. The following year this work was handed over to the Princeton University Office of Population Research.

Refugees

The story of the League's refugee work is the story of weak and reluctant efforts on the part of the international organization to cope with successive waves of refugees set in motion by a series of political upheavals beginning with World War I. During the early twenties the principal groups that received international assistance were the Russians, Greeks, Bulgars, Turks, Armenians and Syrians. After the relative political and economic calm between 1925 and 1929, the depression, the rise of the Nazis, and other ugly manifestations of man's inhumanity to man started new movements of dispossessed including Germans, Spaniards, Portuguese, Austrians, Czechs and Poles.

As each new wave of disinherited washed across national frontiers, the countries affected turned to the League as well as other governmental and nongovernmental agencies for assistance. But these countries were only a minority of the League membership, and the very governments that were causing the disturbances were often in a position to block or at least retard any positive collective efforts. Furthermore, governments had never taken any extensive cooperative measures to handle refugee movements. Even individually they had usually done very little in the way of direct relief and resettlement; instead they had left the major burden to private individuals and agencies. Consequently the League's activities were stringently limited to securing political and legal protection for refugees, leaving the costly matters of relief and resettlement largely to private organizations. The urge of the good Samaritan was no match for the qualms of the finance minister.

High Commissioner Nansen

The League first dipped a cautious toe into the refugee problem in September 1921 when, in response to an appeal by the Red Cross, the League Council appointed Dr. Fridtjof Nansen, explorer, oceanographer, and humanitarian, to serve as High Commissioner to offer limited international assistance to the Russian refugees who were fleeing the revolution. The principles embodied in the Council's instructions to Dr. Nansen demonstrated clearly the League's reluctance to wade very deeply into such a discouraging morass and established restrictions that were to set the general pattern for all subsequent League refugee efforts: (1) the League accepted responsibility for only political and legal protection of certain specified classes — never all classes — of refugees; (2) such action was to be on a temporary basis; (3) League funds might be spent for only administrative expenses; and (4) the League should coordinate relief and settlement efforts but not provide funds for such purposes.

Nansen tried to compensate for his weak mandate by an extraordinary display of vigor and ingenuity as he set about assisting the approximately one million Russians who had left their homeland by 1921. He interceded with the Russian government to alleviate the conditions of expulsion, attempted to break up the most dangerous congestions of refugees in seriously overcrowded centers, such as Constantinople, arranged for repatriation for a few, sought resettlement for many more, hunted jobs for them, and secured legal protection and freedom of movement largely through the development of a League of Nations passport ("Nansen passport") authorized for Russian refugees by the Geneva "Arrangement" of 1922. The funds for relief and resettlement were contributed by governments and private agencies, raised largely in response to the bold efforts of Nansen, and administered primarily by non-League organizations such as the American Relief Administration and the Red Cross under Nansen's general supervision and coordination.

Another major wave of refugees resulted from the Greco-Turkish Convention of Lausanne (January 1923) whereby approximately 1,300,000 members of the Greek Orthodox Church left Turkey for Greece and nearly 600,000 Moslems went from Greece to Turkey. Then, largely as the result of a Turco-Bulgarian treaty of 1913 and a Greco-Bulgarian treaty of 1919, more than 200,000 Bulgars left neighboring areas to go to postwar Bulgaria. Finally about 300,000 Armenians fled from Turkey between 1919 and 1922 to escape persecution. For each of these categories the League gave separate mandates to Nansen to furnish the same general aid that he gave the Russians plus exceptional forms of assistance in certain cases. For both Greek and Bulgarian refugees, for example, the League Financial Committee was able to arrange for loans to facilitate their resettlement. For the Armenians Nansen labored tirelessly to mobilize political and financial support to reëstablish them in the Soviet Armenian Republic (Erivan), but the League Council refused to endorse this project, largely due to the firm opposition of Great Britain. Thus the scheme was finally abandoned in 1929. Nansen was able, nevertheless, to settle about 125,000 Armenians in Syria and Lebanon where his local representative arranged for loans (provided by the French and local governments, private organizations and the Nansen Office itself) to pay for land, buildings, tools, live stock and other supplies for the poorer refugees.

Because large-scale repatriation had proved hopeless, because there seemed to be a long-range operational job of migration, settlement and employment, because the High Commissioner's task had originally been thought of as temporary, and because by 1924 Nansen was ready to retire, he succeeded, in collaboration with Albert Thomas, Director of the International Labor Office, in transferring the operational tasks to the ILO in 1924, leaving the legal and political functions with the League. While the League Council was delighted to slip this burden off its own shoulders, the ILO Governing Body, in spite of the pressures exerted by Nansen, Thomas and Ramsay MacDonald, was exceedingly reluctant to assume the new and difficult assignment. Thomas was enthusiastic because he had high hopes of performing a major transfusion of refugees from overpopulated Europe to underpopulated Latin America and other inviting Edens, but this vision proved illusory. In fact he never found room in South America for more than 1,000 persons. It is not surprising, therefore, that the ILO decided in 1929 to return the frustrating problem to the League.

Two other events also cast ominous shadows over the refugee program at the beginning of the thirties: the death of Dr. Nansen in May 1930, which left a gap that was never adequately filled, and the incidence of the depression which had a doubly tragic effect — the stimulation of new waves of refugees and the withering of many sources of assistance.

Nansen Office

In this unhappy setting the 1930 Assembly created the "autonomous" International Refugee Office (more commonly known as the "Nansen Office") which was deposited outside the League to raise funds as best it could in order to carry on the High Commissioner's "humanitarian" work. The political and legal functions were officially left with the League and its Secretariat, but in actual practice the field work on these matters was carried on through the Nansen Office's nine local representatives and five correspondents. In 1931 the League set 1938 as the deadline for the completion of the Office's herculean task.

A convention, adopted at Geneva in October 1933, embodied various principles for the protection of refugees, including an undertaking not to expel or refuse admission to them except for reasons of national security and public order. Then, in May 1935, the League Council asked the Office to take under its feeble wings the refugees who were beginning to leave the Saar as a result of the plebiscite held that same year which returned that area to Germany. In this connection the Assembly made a special and emphatically exceptional grant to the Office to resettle about 150 Saarlanders in Paraguay.

High Commissioner for German Refugees

When the foundering Weimar Republic was finally torpedoed by the Nazis in 1933, one of the first repercussions was a new movement of refugees who surged into France and other nearby countries. After the first exodus of approximately 60,000 during 1933 (of which 51,000 were Jews), the tide subsided to an annual flow of about 20,000 to 24,000 until by 1937 approximately 150,000 had fled. Then, with the annexation of Austria in 1938 and with each succeeding loss of territory to Nazi Germany, new groups joined the grim march.

Naturally enough, France, Belgium, Switzerland, the Netherlands and other countries which bore the main brunt of this emergency called on the League for assistance. Thus the High Commissioner for Refugees Coming from Germany was appointed by the League in October 1933 and was made as autonomous as possible so as not to ruffle Germany's sensitive feathers any more than necessary. Secondary reasons for this attitude were the desire of the large private Jewish organizations to have an organization actively interested in their problem and not sentenced to be disbanded in

1938, and the League's traditional feeling that the care of refugees should not be made one of its continuing responsibilities.

During the first two years the High Commissioner, James G. McDonald, labored valiantly, in close collaboration with Viscount Cecil, Chairman of the Commission's Governing Body, and helped to relocate 60,000 out of the 80,000 German refugees who had fled up to that time. This could not have been done, of course, except through the generous and efficient efforts of the large private organizations, most of which were Jewish. Then in 1936 McDonald decided to resign as the best means of calling attention to the need for bringing greater governmental pressure to bear upon the source of the problem — Germany's campaign of racial and political persecution — as well as the need for coordinating all refugee efforts under the direct authority of the League. While this move was instrumental in persuading the League Council to bring the High Commissioner's Office under the League roof, the League's functions continued to be limited to protecting legal status and promoting employment and settlement. Relief was left to private agencies.

The High Commissioner's most important single achievement in the legal and political areas during the next two and a half years was the negotiation of an "Arrangement" on legal status in July 1936 and a convention, following the pattern of the 1933 treaty, which was adopted at Geneva in February 1938. By early 1938 the distribution of German refugees was approximately as follows: Europe, 37 per cent; Palestine, 27 per cent; United States, 17 per cent; South America, 13 per cent; and elsewhere, 6 per cent. In May 1938 Austrian refugees were also placed under the jurisdiction of the High Commissioner and the 1938 Convention.

Reunification

When, in accordance with previous League decisions, the mandates of both the Nansen Office and the High Commissioner were terminated in 1938, the League reluctantly decided to establish a new High Commissioner to deal with all refugees. Although Germany had withdrawn from the League and thus was scarcely in a position to block this action, the Soviet Union was now a member and insisted that the Commissioner should give no aid to White Russians. Like his predecessors, the new Commissioner was also carefully caged in by rigid restrictions. He was to provide only political and legal protection, to superintend the implementation of the 1933 and 1938 conventions, to do no more than facilitate coordination of humanitarian assistance, and to assist non-League organizations to promote emigration and settlement.

The principal non-League governmental effort was initiated by President Franklin Roosevelt, who, apparently without consulting either the League of Nations or the High Commissioner for Refugees Coming from Germany, called a conference which met at Evian, France, in 1938, to discover better ways of dealing with the refugee problem, especially that rising out of the annexation of Austria in March 1938. Although the Intergovernmental Committee, established by that Conference, undertook various negotiations with both the German governments and potential haven governments, it was able to accomplish precious little besides facilitating the settlement of some five hundred refugees in the Dominican Republic.

Conclusions

Although the League refugee program now seems to have been a puny midget in the face of the giant problems which confronted it, it represented substantial progress as compared with what took place before 1919. For the first time, the great majority of nations worked through a permanent international organization to give, on a joint basis, at least political and legal aid to refugees. Although they were never willing in the same manner to engage in large-scale direct assistance for relief and settlement, many states did approach that goal by urging all League Members and private organizations to contribute individually to such efforts, appropriating funds to enable League commissioners to facilitate and coordinate such activities, sponsoring loans for these purposes, and even giving funds directly in exceptional small-scale instances, such as the settlement of the Saarlanders in Paraguay. In spite of these encouraging steps forward, however, the program was always heavily weighted down by the resistance of the majority of these League Members that were not directly involved and that were reluctant to be dragged into any unpredictable and unlimited spending operation.

Cultural Cooperation

The cultural cooperation program was one of the most frustrating and controversial activities of the League of Nations economic and social system. Unlike economic, financial, transportation, and certain other functional matters, cultural activities were not even mentioned in the Covenant. And, once the League had been organized, many nations demonstrated remarkable ingenuity in thinking of reasons for objecting to such activities, especially on the conflicting grounds that they would either exert dangerous pressures on domestic matters, such as education, or they would be so amorphous that they would exert no pressures at all.

The courageous leadership of Senator Henri LaFontaine of Belgium, supported more by the Continental and Latin than by the Anglo-Saxon countries, finally persuaded the Assembly during its first session in 1920 to request the Council to associate itself with efforts to form an organization of intellectual cooperation. Even then, however, the progress of this activity was the slowest of all of the League's functional programs. The Committee on Intellectual Cooperation was not authorized by the Assembly until September 1921 and did not meet until August 1922. Nor did the Committee's staff assistance approach adequate proportions until the Institute of Intellectual Cooperation, established by the French Government in Paris, began to operate in January 1926.

Like many youngsters the Intellectual Organization had a difficult adolescence during which it was compelled to devote much of its attention to the obvious need for postwar rehabilitation of educational and other essential cultural facilities. But, with the invigorating injection in 1926 of the Institute's substantial staff resources, the program began to prosper until, by 1929, it had burgeoned so prodigiously that a study was made to prune it to more manageable proportions. Then, under the twin blights of depression and aggression, special efforts were made to orient the program more directly toward those two crucial problems.

Channels of Communication

Education. In most nations education is the most universal and powerful organized social force for shaping the minds of large masses of people. It was obvious, therefore, that before the Intellectual Organization could hope to create an integrated international cultural community it would have to open the windows and doors of many hitherto tightly closed educational systems. From the very beginning, therefore, the Organization invested substantial amounts of time and effort in an ever-increasing multitude of pedagogical activities: reconstruction of schools; training of teachers; elimination of national bias in textbooks; exchange of ideas among instructors, administrators, and students; promotion of more than forty national pedagogical centers to work with the Intellectual Organization; study of employment problems among educational workers; and, beginning with an ILO request in 1931, development of adult education. Also in 1931, at the request of the League Council, the Institute participated in the general program to render technical assistance to China by making a survey of that country's educational needs, by sending experts to implement the survey's recommendations, and by organizing the exchange of teachers.

Radio, Movies, Libraries and Museums. In 1936 the League convoked a governmental conference which approved a convention prohibiting broadcasts inciting violence or disseminating obviously false statements and encouraging programs that would foster better understanding among nations. But the standards were vague; no machinery was established to interpret or enforce these standards; many democratic states were reluctant to interfere with their traditions of free speech; and the non-democratic nations had no intention of paying anything more than lip service to such a convention. In the movie field, the International Educational Cinematographic Institute in Rome worked closely with the Intellectual Organization. Out of these efforts came many useful developments including a constant exchange of information facilitated by the publication of the *International Review of Educational Cinematography,* beginning in 1929 (renamed *Intercine* in 1935), the negotiation of a convention in 1933 exempting educational films from customs duties and accessory charges, and the convocation of a very productive International Congress of Educational and Instructional Cinematography in 1934 which paved the way for strengthening the Institute's role in coordinating the interests of producers and users of informative films.

The Intellectual Organization also realized that the body of world scholars could not work very effectively without an efficient circulatory system of libraries and museums. Consequently a Committee of Library Experts, formed in 1927, worked with the International Federation of Library Associations and other organizations to facilitate cooperation among libraries, survey and publicize their complementary resources, establish a uniform system of documentation, and study various library administrative problems. The Committee on Intellectual Cooperation also encouraged several bibliographical projects including the publication of a list of *Notable Books*, 1924 to 1929, and the *Index Bibliographicus*, 1925 and 1931. The better utilization of archives was promoted through the publication of an *International Guide to Archives* and a lexicon of archive terminology, the exchange of archivists, and other forms of technical collaboration.

The International Museums Office, created by authority of the League Council in 1926, facilitated cooperation among museums by promoting joint exhibits, publishing the quarterly periodical, *Museion*, beginning in 1927, sponsoring the negotiation of a convention on the protection of national artistic treasures and the restitution of objects taken from national collections, and assisting in the joint solution of other mutual problems.

Substantive Areas

Arts and Letters. One of the most frustrating paradoxes of our times is the fact that, while the industrial revolution has rapidly woven a thick web of cables, wires, and radio waves around the world, national political and cultural differences have cut across these many lines of communication with the result that there is less of a world community of ideas today than there was, at least among the intelligentsia, in past ages that were technologically less advanced. In order to pierce the barriers that separate national cultures, the Intellectual Organization's Committee of Arts and Letters took the initiative in 1932 in organizing a series of annual "conversations" among twenty to thirty of the world's outstanding authorities on such topics as the life and work of Goethe, the future of European culture, art and reality, and the relation of art to the state. A series of "open letters" was also begun in 1932 to make available to the world random essays of leading thinkers on a variety of subjects.

The Committee on Arts and Letters also supervised many other related activities, including the exchange of information among various national literary institutes and encouragement of the translation of national classics. To give further protection to the legal rights of literary workers, the Intellectual Organization played a major role in revising the international Berne Copyright Convention in 1928, in preparing proposals in 1935 for its periodic revision, and in trying to align the Berne Convention with copyright practices in the Western Hemisphere. A conference to complete this latter task was to be held in Brussels in 1940 but had to be postponed because of the war. Finally the Organization helped to facilitate international cooperation in the fields of art and archeology through channels such as the establishment of a Center of Liaison between University Institutes of Archeology and History of Art in Paris in 1933 and the creation of a committee on folk arts which organized a particularly active program.

Exact and Natural Sciences. Since the exact and natural scientists have normally tended to speak the same technical language more than workers in other cultural fields, there had been more international collaboration among them before World War I than in other intellectual areas. Nevertheless there was still great need in 1919 for reinforcement and coordination of the many separate organizations then in existence. After a plan had been formulated in 1925 to coordinate the work of the Intellectual Organization and the independent Council of Scientific Unions, the Committee on Intellectual Cooperation approved a program in 1931 to gear together various overlapping efforts to prepare scientific bibliographies, standardize scientific terminology, survey scientific laboratories, and foster collaboration among scientific museums. In 1932 the international unions of biology, chemistry, geography, physics, and mathematics decided to expedite their committee work by using the Institute of Intellectual Cooperation as their common secretariat. The following year plans were completed for unifying chemical and physical nomenclatures, with biology being included in 1935.

Social Sciences. If anything should have been obvious to those active in the League cultural program it was the fact that they could not progress far without a more profound understanding of men themselves, their psychology, and their myriad relationships. Yet, because the social sciences were not only relatively new but also highly controversial, the League tended to be more laggard in this than in most other areas. The first major social science program, not fully agreed upon until 1927, was aimed at instructing the world's youth on the benefits of international cooperation, especially through the League of Nations. In 1928 the Intellectual Organization created an administrative center to coordinate various national institutes studying international affairs, such as the Royal Institute of International Affairs in London and the Council on Foreign Relations in New York. From these modest beginnings developed the International Studies Conference program, starting with the 1931 Copenhagen meeting and continuing with conferences at two-year intervals, in which more than thirty national committees and institutes participated to discuss such topics as the state and economic life, collective security, peaceful change, and economic policies and the maintenance of peace. Finally, in the late thirties, Dr. James T. Shotwell, American member of the Committee on Intellectual Cooperation, won considerable support for a permanent committee and a department of the Institute to be devoted entirely to the social sciences, but the war prevented this project from being implemented.

Conclusions

One significant measure of the contribution made by the League's cultural program is a comparison of its activities with the situation before World War I. Although various private and governmental cultural organizations had been created before the war to promote their respective special interests, the League Intellectual Organization was the first permanent central agency, with substantial staff assistance, charged with fostering the creation of new organs and the exploration of new fields, greater development of all cultural activities, and coordination of all agencies in these many areas. Yet, when the tensions that produced World War II began to multiply, it soon became obvious that the international cultural community which the Intellectual Organization had striven so hard to build was still more hope than reality. The cultural program had been painfully slow in getting started. Even at its peak it never received adequate financial or substantive support. It tended to dissipate its strength in all directions at once without effective concentration of effort. It placed excessive emphasis on European interests, and aimed most of its activities at the intelligentsia rather than the mass level according to the dubious theory that the new enlightenment would trickle down from top to bottom.

Suggestions for Further Reading

Books

Blelloch, David H., "The International Labor Organization: I," *World Organization* (Washington: American Council on Public Affairs, 1942).

Bonnet, Henri, "Intellectual Cooperation," *World Organization* (Washington: American Council on Public Affairs, 1942).

Boudreau, Frank G., "Health, Nutrition, and Housing," *World Organization* (Washington: American Council on Public Affairs, 1942).

———, "International Health Work," *Pioneers in World Order* (New York: Columbia University Press, 1944).

Butler, Harold, *The Lost Peace* (New York: Harcourt, Brace and Company, 1941).

Castendyck, Elsa, "Social Problems," *Pioneers in World Order* (New York: Columbia University Press, 1944).

———, "Social Questions," *World Organization* (Washington: American Council on Public Affairs, 1942).

Davis, Malcolm, "League of Minds," *Pioneers in World Order* (New York: Columbia University Press, 1944).

Goodrich, Carter, "The International Labor Organization," *Pioneers in World Order* (New York: Columbia University Press, 1944).

Mander, Linden A., *Foundations of Modern World Society* (Stanford: Stanford University Press, 1947).

May, Herbert L., "Dangerous Drugs," *Pioneers in World Order* (New York: Columbia University Press, 1944).

McDonald, James G., "Refugees," *Pioneers in World Order* (New York: Columbia University Press, 1944).

Myers, Denys P., *Handbook of the League of Nations* (Boston: World Peace Foundation, 1935).

Phelan, Edward J., *Yes, and Albert Thomas* (London: The Cresset Press, 1936).

Pierre-Tixier, Andrien, "The International Labor Organization: II," *World Organization* (Washington: American Council on Public Affairs, 1942).

Renborg, Bertil A., *International Drug Control . . .* (Washington: Carnegie Endowment for International Peace, 1947).

————, "Narcotic Drugs — International Administration," *World Organization* (Washington: American Council on Public Affairs, 1942).

Simpson, John Hope, *Refugees* (London: Oxford University Press, 1939).

————, *The Refugee Problem* (London: Oxford University Press, 1939).

Wilson, Francis Graham, *Labor in the League System* (Stanford: Stanford University Press, 1934).

Periodicals

McDougall, F. L., "Food and Welfare," *Geneva Studies*, Vol 9. No. 5 (November 1938).

Olsen, O. E. W., "Post-War Housing Problems," *Geneva Studies*, Vol. 11, No. 6 (October 1940).

Documents

International Labor Office, *The International Labor Code 1939* (Montreal: International Labor Office, 1941).

————, *The International Labor Organization* (London: International Labor Office, 1931).

League of Nations, *La Cooperation Intellectuelle*, 1929–1939.

————, *International Institute of Intellectual Cooperation* (Paris: League of Nations, 1938).

————, *Ten Years of World Cooperation* (Geneva: League Secretariat, 1930)

Social and Cultural Activities — UN

Labor

As NAZI bombs were still blasting the heart of London in December 1943, two top leaders of the British Labor and Conservative Parties met in that city with the Governing Body of the International Labor Organization (ILO) and agreed that improving the lot of the working man should be a principal concern of the United Nations and that the ILO should continue to be the primary channel for this effort. Foreign Minister Anthony Eden "hoped . . . to see the ILO become the main international instrument for giving effect to [the social security provisions] . . . of the Atlantic Charter. . . ." [1] Labor Minister Ernest Bevin hailed the "unparalleled opportunities . . . before the ILO." [2] These sentiments represent a sample of the influential liberal forces within the major democratic nations of the world which have helped make the role of organized labor even stronger, more representative and more ambitious within the United Nations system than it was under the League. The World War II battle of production — and no more crucial battle was ever fought — greatly strengthened labor's hand in government as well as industry. Anti-Axis underground movements depended heavily on the ranks of labor. The development of the "full employment" philosophy and the coming to power of labor governments in such countries as the United Kingdom, Australia and New Zealand gave added impetus. Finally, the fear of postwar unemployment, similar to that which had occurred after World War I, made labor more determined than ever to use all available means, including the ILO, to protect its interests.

The basic pattern of the ILO process has remained fundamentally the same as before the war, although one should keep in mind the limited retooling carried out between 1944 and 1946, which was discussed in Chapter 9. The forces which have molded subsequent ILO decisions are also familiar to the veterans of Geneva. Leadership still lies with the most strongly organized elements of labor and management in the more developed countries of Europe and America. But labor speaks more confidently

---

[1] John G. Winant, "An International Organization That Works," *Saturday Evening Post*, Vol. 216, No. 42 (April 15, 1944), p. 88.

[2] *Ibid.*, p. 90.

than ever before, and the new voices from the less developed lands, especially such leading nations as Japan, India, Pakistan and Indonesia, are gaining greater attention. The Soviet Union, to be sure, has constantly criticized the ILO as the lap dog of capitalism and, though indicating an interest in joining in 1953, had not done so as this volume went to press. On the other hand, the Communist satellite nations of Czechoslovakia, Poland, Hungary and Bulgaria have participated. Yugoslavia has also been a member, both before and after the break with the Cominform. While the ILO is the principal United Nations labor agency, other bodies concerned with this field are ECOSOC, its regional and certain other commissions, FAO, WHO and UNESCO.

"Bread and Butter" Issues

Freedom of Association. The cement of the labor movement is the right to organize and bargain collectively, although it was never possible to adopt a specific agreement on the subject during the interwar period. To sew up this gap, the World Federation of Free Trade Unions (WFTU) and the American Federation of Labor (AFL) seized the initiative early in 1947 by raising the question before the ECOSOC, which tossed it to the ILO. This set in motion an extended chain reaction involving the usual thorough ILO questionnaires, analyses, discussions, resolutions, recommendations and conventions from 1947 to 1952.

The ILO Conference (plenary assembly) began by passing the weakest form of decision, a resolution, in 1947 setting forth the main principles of the freedom of association and right to organize. A painstakingly formulated Freedom of Association Convention was then adopted by the 1948 Conference guaranteeing:

> the right to establish and join organizations of own choice; right to draw up own rules and function freely; right to be dissolved or suspended only by normal judicial procedure; right to join larger federations and international organizations.

The fight was carried further in 1949 by adopting a second convention which set forth specific governmental responsibilities to assure:

> the right to organize adequate protection against anti-union discrimination in employment and freedom from interference for both employers and workers in setting up and operating their respective organizations ("interference" interpreted specifically to include promoting employer-dominated unions or splitting unions).

A further pioneering step to apply a little heat of publicity to melt governmental resistance was taken at the beginning of 1950 when the Governing Body, after long debate, established a Fact-Finding and Conciliation Commission. This body, composed of nine outstanding experts on labor law and industrial relations, is to provide, with the consent of governments accused of violations, an impartial examination of alleged breaches of trade union rights "in an atmosphere free from political prejudice . . . or propaganda in any interests. . . ." Its only sanctions are negotiation, recommendation and publication. To supplement these major landmarks, recommendations were approved laying down guiding principles for collective bargaining machinery (1951), setting standards for voluntary conciliation and arbitration (1951), and cooperation at the plant level between employers and workers regarding matters not covered by collective bargaining (1952).

Ratifications of the basic 1948 and 1949 conventions were relatively rapid. In many countries which have not yet ratified, the agreements are raising the level of national practice, including nations with strong union traditions such as the United Kingdom. But governments have generally refused to give permission to have themselves hauled before the Fact-Finding Commission to have their dirty linen washed in public. To overcome this boycott, the Governing Body itself now conducts "preliminary examinations" and engages in informal negotiations to protect trade union rights. At least one observer has said that these efforts are having "considerable indirect influence." [3]

Social Security. Another basic "bread and butter" problem has been that of providing greater social security for workers. While recommendations and conventions on specialized aspects of this issue had been approved before the war, the first comprehensive agreement, based on a 1944 recommendation, was the 1952 Convention on Minimum Standards of Social Security, the end product of three years of study and consultation. One of its unusual features is its flexible combination of compulsory and optional provisions, born of the difficulty of trying to cut one suit of clothes to fit all countries. Under this compromise, a ratifying state undertakes to comply with:

1. certain general provisions;
2. standards laid down in at least three of the nine parts dealing with medical care, sickness benefits, unemployment benefits, old-age benefits, employment injury benefits, family benefits, maternity benefits, invalid benefits, and survivors' benefits;
3. certain common provisions relevant to the parts selected.

These standards represent at least three major advances: unification of all existing forms of social security in a single pattern, wider coverage of the population, and the establishment of a basic minimum of "social adequacy" as the criterion for the benefits under any part of the program. The ILO has also fostered social security progress in many other ways, such as technical assistance in organizing national programs and furnishing staff for periodic meetings of the International Social Security Association, an independent association of social security institutions.

Since the broad problem of maintaining "full employment" involves far

[3] "The International Labour Organization Since the War," *International Labour Review,* Vol. 67, No. 2 (February 1953), p. 135.

more than just labor policy, the ILO has left that area largely to the United Nations. Nonetheless, alarmed by the 1949 recession in the United States, the ILO initiated a study of the unemployment problem that same year, and, in 1950, the Conference adopted a resolution suggesting far-reaching domestic and international anti-depression measures which exerted some influence on the United Nations effort. Two related agreements were approved by the Conference in 1949. One was a Convention on Labor Clauses in Public Contracts providing that such clauses assure conditions no less favorable than those afforded other workers doing similar labor. The other was a Convention on the Protection of Wages to the effect that wages should be paid directly, promptly, in cash and in full. But the highly explosive questions of hours and wages — the heart of most labor-management disputes — have not proved susceptible of broad universal treatment but have been left primarily to more specific ILO industrial and regional discussions.

Finding Men for the Jobs

Before World War II, the ILO had its hands full trying to defend labor from various abuses. It had little time to think in positive terms of promoting the optimum use of available labor resources. At the end of the war, however, this is exactly what was needed to help meet vast reconstruction and developmental needs. Thus the ILO entered the manpower business to improve the recruitment and training of labor.

One essential step was to help standardize national and international employment practices. The 1948 Employment Service Convention and Recommendation set goals for employment services, in terms of the "full employment" philosophy, which have left their mark on many such systems established since the war. Prewar standards on apprenticeship and training for young people were supplemented by a 1950 recommendation on the training of adults which gave especially useful guidance for the underdeveloped countries. A 1933 convention on fee-charging employment agencies was improved in 1949. That same year the Conference also approved a revised Convention on the treatment of migrants, to facilitate labor mobility, and recommendations on vocational guidance.

The ILO did more than merely recommend. It rolled up its sleeves and went into the field to help survey and meet the labor needs of various areas. It first concentrated on the requirements of Europe, then Asia, Latin America, and more recently the Near and Middle East. Special ILO field offices were set up in India, Brazil and Turkey, and close bonds were established with the ECOSOC regional commissions. Services provided have included: estimates of labor deficits and surpluses, assisting or operating training programs (in approximately twenty-four countries as of 1953), advising on the organization of employment services, technical assistance to increase productivity, and facilitating the migration of workers through all stages from the place of origin to integration in the place of final destination.

The ILO played an especially active part in the latter effort reminiscent of Albert Thomas's prewar migration experiment. A Preliminary Migration Conference at Geneva, April to May 1950, advised a cooperative program but left implementation to separate national efforts. The ILO then called a Special Migration Conference at Naples, October 1951, and submitted its own proposal for direct international operations under an ILO-supervised Migration Administration with the authority, staff and funds to move 1.7 million persons in five years, chiefly from the surplus countries of Germany, Italy and the Netherlands. The United States was the principal opponent, supported by Australia and Canada — all three important potential havens for immigrants. They preferred a more cautious approach based on "informal means." The Conference finally adopted a compromise proposal, sponsored by France, Italy and Belgium, recommending an advisory version of the ILO plan with a "consultative council" to study the problem and recommend cooperative action.

In November 1951 the United States called another meeting at Brussels which set up, outside the United Nations framework, a Provisional Intergovernmental Committee for the Movement of Migrants from Europe along the lines suggested at Naples.[4] Although the ILO did not succeed in carrying out its original project, it was an influential catalyst and is still an important figure in the migration field.

Health, Safety, and Welfare

While ILO efforts in these fields have tended to play second fiddle to other more pressing needs, they have steadily continued to build on the foundations laid during the prewar period. Perhaps the principal advance was the completion in 1949 of a Model Code of Safety Regulations for Industrial Establishments. The ILO Office has also fostered improved health, safety and welfare through various industrial and regional meetings, technical assistance missions, and studies. More concrete action was initiated during the 1952 ILO Conference aimed at the conclusion of a Convention and Recommendation on the Protection of the Health of Workers in Places of Employment.

Help For Special Worker Categories

Protecting women and children is still a task close to the heart of the ILO. It is also subject to a conflict between the desire to lighten the burden of the weak and resistance to jeopardizing the earning and producing capacity of these workers, especially during the immediate postwar reconstruction period. The latter consideration dominated the early revision of certain prewar conventions in order to make restrictions on night work for women and children more flexible. The highly controversial issue of granting equal pay to women for work of equal value collided not only with traditional discrimination in developed as well as underdeveloped countries but also with the depressed economic plight of these nations.

4 For further discussion of activities, see below, p. 658.

After lengthy soul-searching, the 1951 Conference approved a Convention and Recommendation providing for equal remuneration for men and women, and a meeting of experts in December 1951 considered a multitude of measures to improve the laboring status of women. The 1952 Conference then revised the 1919 Maternity Protection Convention by providing more liberal maternity benefits.

The campaign to better the working conditions of young people was carried on primarily with reference to specific industries and geographic areas. For example, the 1952 Conference adopted a thoroughly debated resolution protecting youths laboring in coal mines (minimum age, vocational guidance, vocational training, medical exams, night work, rests and inspection). Regional conferences gave special attention to problems affecting young people. Moreover, the ILO agreed in 1951 to cooperate with the United Nations in a long-range child welfare program.

The ILO has also found itself in the midst of the struggle over non-self-governing territories as it has tried to improve the lot of workers in "non-metropolitan" territories. Before the war primary attention was devoted to prohibiting the worst forms of exploitation of colonial laborers. Then the 1944 Philadelphia Declaration set more positive goals.[5] And the 1947 Conference adopted an impressive series of conventions to achieve those objectives. The most general convention looks towards coordinated development in the fields of health, housing, education, employment, working conditions and social security. Other supporting conventions deal with the rights of association and settlement of labor disputes, limited application of specified ILO conventions, and the length of labor contracts. A host of related efforts are carried on through publications, technical assistance and other agencies such as the Trusteeship Council.

Help for Special Occupations

Shipping. The ILO has penetrated farther and more extensively than ever before into the economic life of nations through the spreading and deepening of its roots in certain leading industries. In this way it has not only adapted its general standards to the peculiar conditions of different fields but has, for the first time, brought top management and labor personnel in these enterprises into direct contact with the ILO.

As before World War II, shipping still receives more ILO attention than any other single industry because of its obvious international character and the strength of the maritime labor organizations. A first and giant postwar step was taken during the 1946 Seattle maritime session of the Conference devoted entirely to shipping questions. A series of conventions and recommendations laid down the following standards:

> a minimum wage fixed on an international basis for the first time; hours of work with a basic eight hour maximum; labor-management machinery for fixing work-loads; paid vacations; social security (incapacity, unemployment,

[5] See p. 260.

old age, retirement, and medical benefits); crew accommodations; medical exams; and certification for employment.

While ratifications have been sluggish, these agreements have already had substantial effect, especially in shaping the policies of "new" maritime countries. For example, a complaint of the Seafarers' Section of the International Transportworkers' Federation in 1948 against ships transferred to the flags of Panama and Honduras used the ILO standards as criteria. This indictment resulted in Panama's requesting the Governing Body to investigate the situation including conditions on board thirty ships in the ports of six different countries. As a result, the Governing Body made certain recommendations; Panama established new machinery to help improve matters; a number of collective agreements were signed between the Seafarers' Section and the owners; and a full-scale boycott was avoided. More recently the ILO has turned its attention to the problems of less well-organized maritime workers: fishermen and Asian seamen.

Other Industries. An entirely postwar innovation has been the development of a small group of "industrial committees" to study and make recommendations regarding the whole spectrum of labor-management problems within certain selected industries.[6] The doughty British labor leader and statesman, Ernest Bevin, first pushed this idea as a means of giving more specialized attention to key industries, particularly to help with postwar reconstruction and to set high standards in the core industries of national economies. There were eight of these bodies as of 1953 covering fields of particular international importance: textiles, mines, petroleum, inland transport, iron and steel, metal trades, building and construction, and chemicals. Each is composed of delegates from countries in which the industry is of some importance. Each national delegation consists of two persons from each of the ILO's basic components: labor, management, and government. These groups first engaged in far-reaching general surveys of all relevant problems and then concentrated on the most pressing issues. While they were slow in arriving at useful conclusions and generating positive national cooperation, one analysis has said, "The action taken nationally to give effect to the conclusions of the committees suggests that these are influencing the course of policy and providing the practical guidance that they are supposed to provide."[7]

Progress in helping agricultural labor still travels at a snail's pace, largely because farm workers, even in the more advanced countries, are still less solidly organized than their city cousins and because of the complexity of enforcing uniform standards in such a decentralized, heterogeneous and traditionally individualistic occupation. Nonetheless the ILO Permanent Agricultural Committee was instrumental in getting approval of a Convention and Recommendation on minimum wage-fixing machinery in agricul-

[6] For thorough survey, see John Price, "Industrial Committees of the ILO," *International Labour Review*, Vol. 65, No. 1 (January 1952), pp. 1–43.
[7] "The ILO Since the War," *op. cit.*, p. 125.

ture (1951) and a convention providing annual holidays with pay in agriculture after a period of continuous service with the same employer (1952). Studies are also going forward to help other "forgotten" occupations that are only weakly organized: white-collar workers, domestic servants and artistic workers.

Regionalism and Technical Assistance

The trend towards closer "grass roots" relations has also been expressed through increased emphasis on regional activities. By 1953 six regional meetings of a general character had been held since World War II — three in Latin America, two in Asia, and one in the Middle East. The field offices and many technical assistance projects also reflect the regional approach. The general effect has been to decentralize ILO efforts even further and to give greater attention to non-European problems.

Allied with this regional emphasis has been the ILO's increasing activity in giving technical assistance to underdeveloped countries as part of the larger United Nations effort along these lines.[8] Although the ILO began immediately after the war to disseminate technical know-how to underdeveloped as well as developed countries, especially through its manpower projects, the major drive did not come until a substantial increase in funds was made available through the United Nations Expanded Program. In 1953 the United Nations gave the ILO approximately $2.3 million. By early 1954 more than three hundred experts had engaged in ILO technical assistance projects in all parts of the world.

Plentiful and accurate information, skillfully analyzed and persuasively interpreted, can be a powerful weapon, even without a police force behind it. The painstakingly thorough Office questionnaires and studies, followed by the sifting of each recommended agreement at least twice by the Governing Body and Conference have paid off in the practical and influential character of ILO decisions. By mid-1953 the Office had prepared at least 150 major studies for the Conference plus 100 more for regional meetings and industrial committees. The ILO is now a prolific world publishing house printing 60,000 pages a year, nearly two normal volumes a day, in three languages. Regular meetings of experts in labor statistics strive to improve the quality, quantity and comparability of labor figures. Annual national reports on compliance with ILO recommendations are more searching and comprehensive than before the war. Investigations of alleged violations of national obligations, such as the one involving Panamanian shipping, exert considerable pressure. "Since the war, far more governments have been examining ILO reports, answering carefully prepared questionnaires, consulting the employers' and workers' organizations, sending delegations to Geneva or elsewhere, and notifying the ILO of the results."[9] Finally, governments, such as those of Greece, Iran and Venezuela, have

---

[8] "The International Labour Organization and Technical Assistance," *International Labour Review*, Vol. 66, Nos. 5–6 (November–December 1952), pp. 391–418.

[9] "The ILO Since the War," *op. cit.*, p. 123.

turned increasingly to the ILO to conduct impartial inquiries in connection with labor issues.

Weighing the Record

Today ILO standards, observed by many leading shipping nations, call for better food and quarters than first class passengers had forty years ago. While the ILO is only one of many forces that have helped foment this revolution of comfort afloat, it has been a central channel for reinforcing and spreading such standards. This and other achievements reveal a pattern of substantial progress since World War II. There have been the formulation of more comprehensive and positive objectives, the livelier appreciation of the relation of labor problems to other economic and social activities, the greater attention devoted to the needs of underdeveloped countries, more emphasis upon direct field work, and greater flexibility in adjusting programs to special regional and occupational conditions.

Concrete effects of this activity can be partially reflected in figures. By early 1953 the International Labor Code included more than a hundred conventions and over ninety recommendations. There had been not only a steady accumulation of ratifications of prewar agreements but relatively quick ratification of several postwar conventions, e.g., ones dealing with freedom of association and the right to organize and bargain collectively. During 1952 alone over a hundred ratifications of forty-nine different conventions were effected by thirty-one countries, more than in any previous year.

> . . . the standards for crew accommodation on board ships being built in many of the most important shipbuilding countries conform to . . . ILO's post-war Convention . . . even though only eight of the governments concerned have . . . ratified. . . . A glance through recent reports . . . shows the slow but cumulative results. . . . This has been the case, to mention but a few examples, in respect of maternity protection or night work for women workers, the machinery of industrial relations, employment services, labour inspection, the minimum age for young people to start to work, and so forth.[10]

But the ILO is still not a true government. It is a useful, continuing and influential forum backed up — nay, pushed ahead — by an able, industrious, ambitious and loyal Director-General and staff. It can question, suggest, negotiate, publicize and persuade but it cannot legally compel any state to do anything. While the trend of national compliance seems better than before the war, it is still lethargic and limited principally to the more developed countries.

Limitations. The direction and pace of ILO activities are still fundamentally conditioned by the gap between the more and less advanced nations, the dominant influence of the major labor and management leaders of the principal powers, and the general state of the world's economy. Within

[10] *Ibid.*, pp. 121–122.

this setting, labor, usually aided and abetted by most of the ILO staff and many governmental delegates, has won adoption of some significant standards. Its success has been aided, of course, not only by its powerful influence rising out of the war situation but by the generally tight labor market since the war. Nonetheless, the resistance of management, never weak, has grown stronger and will probably continue to do so, especially when prosperity falters in some areas and industries. Some say labor has pushed too hard too fast. Certainly it has set goals often well beyond present performance and has ambitions far exceeding the ILO's infinitesimal $6-million-a-year budget. But it is difficult to say that it has pushed too hard compared to the effort needed to improve the lot of the great majority of the world's workers who are living at substandard levels by any civilized criteria.

To take the example of France, usually considered a "developed" country, the general conclusion of scholars is that the French industrial worker has over the years received neither adequate nor fair compensation for his labor. "The real weekly wages of a single worker [in 1949] had declined by perhaps as much as a fifth [since 1938]." [11] While the cost of food in 1950 was 1900 per cent that of 1938 and the cost of clothing 2600 per cent, the hourly wage was only 900 per cent.[12] In 1951 another observer wrote, "A skilled industrial worker [in France] . . . earns about $45 a month . . . but he needs around three times that much to live fairly decently. . . ." [13] The long-range plight of the French worker has been characterized by inadequate real wages and inequitable distribution of income.[14] Multiply this by country after country and you begin to understand why labor has seemed so impatient.

But the ILO does not have the authority, and has not attempted, to set extreme objectives. It has taken its standards not from the thin air of pure idealism but from the current policies of the more advanced countries. It is not so much an inventor as a universalizer, spreading the ideas of the more progressive to the less progressive. The chief benefits accruing to labor in the advanced countries are to reduce the competitive advantage of substandard labor policies, occasionally to improve their own conditions, and generally to foster a more prosperous and stable world economy.

Health

"In Haiti, three patients arrived in a single morning at one of the [WHO] yaws clinics. They were a laborer whose palms were raw with the characteristic blisters, and who had been unable to do any

[11] Donald C. McKay, The United States and France (Cambridge: Harvard University Press, 1951), p. 177.

[12] Ibid., p. 303.

[13] Saul K. Padover, "The Seven-League Boot of France's Economy," United Nations World, Vol. 5, No. 4 (April 1951), p. 50.

[14] McKay, op. cit., p. 178.

work for three years; a small boy who could not stand because the soles of his feet were covered with the sores; and a woman suffering from yaws on her mouth who could not eat solid foods and had kept alive by sucking liquids through a straw. After a single shot of penicillin for each, the man was soon able to take a job, the boy walked again, and the woman was eating normally. The cost of each injection was approximately 15 cents." [15]

This modern miracle is one of many types of services which the World Health Organization (WHO) renders in approximately 115 countries and territories of the world. And, while WHO is the major United Nations affiliate in the health field, there are others busy on related projects that often team up, and sometimes conflict, with WHO, especially UNICEF, FAO, UNESCO, ILO, and the United Nations Secretariat Department of Social Affairs and Narcotic Drugs and Social Commissions.

Because of resistance expressed in the United States House of Representatives, mobilized largely by the American Medical Association, against possible WHO support for "socialized medicine," the United States did not approve the WHO constitution, drafted in the summer of 1946, until two years later. Ratification was also delayed by Latin American pique over the dispute regarding the relation of the Pan American Sanitary Bureau (PASB) to the WHO. The constitution did not come into effect, therefore, until April 1948, and the first regular WHO Assembly did not meet until June of that year. From 1946 to 1948 an Interim Commission chugged along on one cylinder, doing the best it could to continue the health functions of UNRRA, handling only the most urgent reconstruction and emergency problems. Its makeshift subsistence budget was patched together by means of loans from the United Nations ($1.3 million in 1947) and grants from UNRRA ($1.5 million in 1947). A full-scale program could not be launched until 1949, much later than most of the other specialized agencies.

The strategy from the beginning was to concentrate on curing and preventing three of the most widespread communicable diseases: malaria, tuberculosis and treponematoses (syphilis, yaws and bejel). Field operations tended to follow in the footsteps of UNRRA. The greatest postwar shift began in 1950 with the inception of the United Nations Expanded Technical Assistance Program which provided substantial new funds to engage in more direct field work in the underdeveloped countries. Throughout this development leaders from the major powers, possessed of the greatest financial and medical resources, exercised dominant leadership. Nonetheless, some extraordinary contributions were made by men of unique genius from less developed countries, such as Dr. Andrija Stampar of Yugoslavia. While the Soviet Union joined in launching the WHO, its attitude suddenly soured at the June 1948 WHO Assembly because it wanted to show its displeasure against the UN for political reasons and also because some Soviet leaders felt that Russia had received more advice than mate-

15 *The New York Times,* July 3, 1953.

rial aid.[16] In February 1949, the U.S.S.R., Byelorussian S.S.R. and Ukrainian S.S.R. announced their withdrawal. The Balkan satellites lingered longer, presumably because tangible benefits received greatly exceeded their quota contributions, but all withdrew between November 1949 and August 1950.

Fighting Major Health Enemies

The principal weapons brought to bear on the three major public health enemies (malaria, tuberculosis and treponematoses) have included

sending advisers to counsel national authorities; setting up "demonstration teams" to show how to train local personnel and initiate continuing programs; administering concentrated "pilot projects" in selected areas; encouraging and often financing additional advance training either locally or in foreign institutions; promoting the development, standardization, and production of key drugs (DDT for malaria, BCG for tuberculosis, and penicillin for treponematoses); conducting various conferences and seminars; and helping to explore and unify new techniques.

In most of this work UNICEF has provided a major portion of the material aid (equipment and supplies), while the WHO has furnished the technical know-how and medical personnel. A joint WHO/UNICEF malaria control project in the Terai region of northern India had, by early 1953, brought down the infection rate of infants to zero, increased land cultivation by nearly 30,000 acres, expanded food production from 55,000 tons (1947) to 73,500 tons (1950–51), doubled land values, and made possible a population increase in three years from 167,000 to 285,000.

The WHO strategy adopted at the 1948 Assembly also concentrated on three other crucial areas: maternity and child welfare, nutrition, and environmental sanitation. To give human beings a better chance for health as they enter this perilous world, the WHO, again leaning heavily on UNICEF assistance, has concentrated particularly on establishing demonstration and training centers in maternity and child health in about twenty countries. Supplementary efforts have included studies to reduce deaths among premature babies, fellowships, and technical advice to assist in the development of the International Children's Center established in Paris by the French government in cooperation with the UNICEF and WHO.

Other Campaigns

Less time and effort have been devoted to nutrition which is an area tended by various other agencies including FAO, ILO, UNICEF and the United Nations social bodies. Nonetheless, inquiries have been answered, studies prepared, and programs recommended to specific countries, such as Ceylon, Egypt, Yugoslavia, Austria and India. Particular attention has been devoted to the maladies of kwashiorkor (malignant malnutrition) and

[16] Charles E. Allen, "World Health and World Politics," *International Organization*, Vol. 4, No. 1 (February 1950), pp. 40–42.

endemic goiter (counteracted chiefly by iodizing solar-evaporated salt).

In the field of mental health, the WHO has given particular attention to the possible contributions of the science of mental health to the problems of alcoholism, care of homeless children, juvenile delinquency, psychiatric rehabilitation, industrial relations, child guidance, social case work and general mental hygiene. Much of this has been done in cooperation with UNICEF, UNESCO and the United Nations. Less in the forefront but steadily active have been various expert committees fostering progress in the treatment of other diseases that do not seem to warrant priority international attention. Studies have been undertaken, research centers established and aided, field surveys organized, fellowships awarded and technical assistance rendered upon request. These diseases have included: plague, cholera, typhus and other rickettsioses, yellow fever, other parasitic and virus diseases, childhood diseases, trachoma, leprosy, and zoonoses, including brucelosis and rabies.

Stemming Emergency Epidemics

At the end of September 1947 a dread cholera epidemic broke out in Egypt. By October 6 the WHO had agreed with two large United States drug firms to expand their vaccine production. The first shipment was grown, tested, packed and delivered to Cairo within twenty days of the time the order was confirmed. Altogether nineteen governments contributed supplies. WHO also acted as procurement agent for Egypt in purchasing and shipping, mostly by air, more than thirty-two tons of supplies and equipment. On October 20, at the peak of the epidemic, 1,022 new cases were reported with 581 deaths in that one day. During the entire emergency, ten thousand lost their lives. But only three months after the outbreak, on January 23, 1948, Egypt informed the WHO that all port cities and upper provinces were free of cholera. "During the nineteenth century, five different epidemics of cholera used Egypt as a stepping stone to cause havoc in Europe. This did not occur in 1947." [17] Similar assistance, including limited financial grants, has been given such nations as Afghanistan when it suffered a typhus attack and El Salvador when an earthquake left a variety of health problems in its wake.

To give all interested nations quick warning of the outbreak of epidemics, the WHO carries on the epidemiological intelligence service begun by the League and kept alive in skeleton form during the war. The Singapore Bureau of this service is once again the nerve center which receives epidemiological reports from twenty-four sea- and airports covering a wide area bounded by Vladivostok, Egypt, South Africa and New Zealand. Bulletins are disseminated by mail, cable and radio. World-wide reports flow regularly into the Geneva Office where a staff of epidemiologists prepares weekly and monthly summaries. After long and patient negotiation, more-

[17] C.-E. A. Winslow, "World Health Organization — Its Program and Accomplishments," *International Conciliation*, No. 439 (March 1948), p. 135; the above account is also based on Dr. Winslow's description.

over, a set of new quarantine regulations was unanimously adopted by the World Health Assembly in 1951 and became automatically binding except for governments rejecting them within a given period of time.

Technical Assistance and Regionalism

Following the League's pioneer efforts to reorganize the national public health services of Greece and China, the WHO has gone on to expand this service tremendously. Immediately at the end of the war the WHO inherited UNRRA's projects to rebuild the public health programs of liberated countries — especially China, Greece, Ethiopia, Italy and Austria. Subsequent programs in all fields have placed particular emphasis on building skills into continuing local organizations. International meetings on administrative problems have also been held, e.g., the three-day conference in Ceylon, September 1950, attended by thirty directors of Asian national health services. A related function is helping to improve the training of doctors, nurses and other health workers. To implement these and other objectives, the WHO has helped organize training courses in all kinds of subjects, provided medical literature and equipment, and awarded and administered an increasing number of fellowships (approximately seven hundred in 1953).

New frontiers of medical progress are also being explored at various research centers whose work the WHO helps to initiate, direct and coordinate through consultation, exchange of personnel, and occasional grants. These include the Tuberculosis Research Office in Denmark (Copenhagen), International Treponematosis Laboratory Center in the United States (John Hopkins University), the Serological Reference Laboratory in Denmark (Copenhagen), the National Institute for Medical Research in England (London), and many other national cooperating institutions. But the lack of funds cuts this activity to the barest minimum.

The villages of Haiti, India, Libya and many other countries are getting accustomed to the coming and going of WHO personnel on a scale never dreamed of by the more sedentary (and impecunious) prewar international agencies. Special postwar factors that helped produce this expansion of direct field operations have been the precedent set by UNRRA and substantial funds contributed by UNICEF (approximately $6 million in 1951 for health projects in most of which WHO participated) and the United Nations Expanded Technical Assistance Program ($5.7 million given to WHO in 1952). These sums total more than the normal annual WHO budget ($8.5 million in 1953). It is interesting to note parenthetically how UNICEF, begun as a temporary postwar relief program, has injected considerable amounts of money into other United Nations agencies to nourish long-range programs. But in 1953 a shadow fell across all this activity when, because of a shortage in national contributions, the Technical Assistance Board (TAB) cut approximately 27 per cent of WHO's request for funds for that year.

The provision for creating regional "miniature WHO's," built into the constitution primarily to accommodate the Pan American Sanitary Bureau (PASB), was slow in being put into practice. The larger powers tended to resist a move that would add administrative complications and expense, at least in the short run, and headquarters staff chiefs were reluctant to loosen their hold on the reins. But the underdeveloped countries liked the idea of local offices especially responsive to their peculiar problems. Hence, by the summer of 1951, regional committees and offices had been established for six areas: America (Washington), South East Asia (New Delhi), Eastern Mediterranean (Alexandria), West Pacific (Hong Kong), and Africa and Europe (Geneva). The problem of coordinating field and headquarters personnel in the planning process has caused some resentment, especially in the TAB, but these kinks are likely to work out with time and with more long-range planning which is the present trend. Furthermore, the regional centers have already become most vigorous and useful instruments for local planning and coordination.

Standards and Information

When the diabetic American tourist accidentally drops his insulin in the Tiber, it is of some consequence to him that the new supply he buys from a Rome druggist is of the same strength and quality as the old. Hence a Committee on Biological Standardization continues this work of the League Health Organization and has won Assembly approval of new standards for such preparations as Vitamin E, heparin and penicillin and has studied many others. Unlike the League standards, these are now binding on all WHO Members according to the new constitution, unless specifically rejected within a stated time limit. The two world centers for coordinating this work are still the State Serum Institute in Copenhagen and the National Institute for Medical Research in London with their cooperating networks of other national centers. A Committee on the Unification of Pharmacopeias also obtained Assembly adoption of the first International Pharmacopeia in 1950. This is a mountainous compendium giving not only strengths and purities of drugs but also uniform terms and usual and maximum doses.

As part of its information program the WHO has not only tried to reach experts with all the material referred to above but has also devoted much attention, often in conjunction with UNESCO, to educating the general public. It has also tried to improve the quality, quantity, and comparability of a host of health statistics which it publishes in regular *Epidemiological and Vital Statistics Reports*. Other continuing publications include: *Bulletin of the WHO, Chronicle of the WHO, International Digest of Health Legislation*, the *WHO Technical Report Series*, and the *Monograph Series*.

Fighting Narcotics

One night in June 1952 an anti-narcotics squad of the French police raided a lonely villa in a Paris suburb and captured a busy manufacturing center pouring out heroin, most pernicious of all habit-forming drugs. This was one successful skirmish in the world-wide campaign against habit-forming drugs which continues under the United Nations much as it did under the League. The new directing headquarters is the ECOSOC Commission on Narcotic Drugs which takes the place of the League's Advisory Committee on Traffic in Opium and Other Dangerous Drugs. This body, which oversees the whole international system based on nine conventions dating from 1912 to 1948, issues recommendations which are never legally binding but often highly influential. Its partners in this struggle include: the quasi-judicial Permanent Central Opium Board (PCOB) to supervise enforcement of certain prewar conventions; the Drug Supervisory Body (DSB) to check the validity of annual national estimates of needs; WHO, which decides medical questions relating to narcotics; and the Social Commission concerned with the social aspects of addiction.

The basic pattern of the control program remains essentially the same as before the war:

> international conventions require governments to legislate and administer in such a way that the drugs can be used for medical and scientific purposes only, that no unlicensed person . . . may possess the drugs, and that records of all transactions shall be kept, summarized, and sent to an international organization. . . . Enforcement by the international control bodies depends on certain permissible embargoes and on the pressure of public opinion. . . .[18]

Added to all the old problems, however, are some new ones which arose during and after World War II. The prewar controls and League supervision were seriously weakened by the conflict. At least one aggressor, Japan, gave an extra kick to the tottering structure by assisting the opium traffic for revenue and destructive reasons. More recently new synthetic drugs have created serious additional hazards because they can be produced from common raw materials (coal tar and petroleum) and are only belatedly being brought under the prewar conventions. Besides reviving the old controls, the narcotics agencies have given particular attention to regulating the new drugs as well as strengthening and simplifying procedures.

Reinforcing Prewar System. Officially the old system was put back on its feet again when a protocol, signed in December 1946, transferred the League's functions to the United Nations. But the real task of repairing the dikes was not so easy. The general picture since the war has been one of a rising tide of illicit traffic swelled by countless tributaries of synthetics. And the submission of annual estimates and reports of compliance has been exceedingly slow and spotty. Finally in 1951 the returns improved markedly, but the PCOB still reported that the absence of figures from the two most important coca-leaf producing countries made it impossible to estimate a world total for that substance. There was also a disturbing increase of hashish and opium production in Syria and Lebanon. And China was

---

[18] Herbert L. May, "The International Control of Narcotic Drugs," *International Conciliation,* No. 441 (May 1948), p. 304.

reported to be doing a brisk business in the production and sale of narcotics both to gain foreign exchange and create addiction. To plug these and other sources, the Commission on Narcotic Drugs, PCOB and ECOSOC fought back with numerous recommendations aimed at stiffening national enforcement resources, increasing the severity of penalties, reducing allowable production (especially of the deadly heroin), cracking down on shipping personnel (the most notorious traffickers), and developing closer cooperation among national administrations. These efforts began to pay dividends about 1951. For example, Turkey, one of the chief narcotics-producing nations, announced that the traffic in raw opium and heroin had diminished considerably during 1952 and that controls were being greatly tightened.[19]

The most important step to plug new leaks in the regulatory system, particularly synthetic, was approval by the United Nations General Assembly in October 1948 of a convention authorizing the WHO to decide what additional drugs to place under the control of the prewar conventions. This agreement came into force in December 1949, and quick action by the WHO resulted in covering a series of synthetics. A United Nations WHO mission also investigated coca-leaf chewing in Peru and Bolivia at the end of 1949, and their report resulted in a recommendation that immediate steps be taken to limit the supply of coca leaf, the source of cocaine, and prevent its illicit entry into international channels.

To reinforce and streamline the whole system the Commission on Narcotic Drugs directed the Secretariat Division of Narcotic Drugs in August 1948 to prepare a new draft convention which would replace the existing nine treaties as well as strengthen the controls, regulate production of raw materials, prune the machinery, and allow rapid adjustment to changing conditions. These plans, most of which were approved by the Commission in April 1953, are still based on the traditional concept of national administration with only loose supervision by the international agencies. A new international drug board, appointed by ECOSOC, is to replace the PCOB and DSB. But greater friction was generated over the degree to which controls should be stiffened, especially regarding production.

Production and Other Problems. An effort to obtain a temporary accord to limit production of a single drug, opium, at first produced a remarkably bold draft convention approved by representatives of the major producing countries — India, Iran, Turkey and Yugoslavia (the Soviet Union refused to cooperate). Their plan was to establish rigid limitations of production to medical and scientific needs and tight international control through an international opium monopoly which would handle all international transactions. But the major nations that process raw opium refused to sacrifice so much freedom of action. The specific points on which agreement could not be reached were international price regulation, how to prevent competition of substitutes from opium-producing countries, and international in-

[19] *United Nations Bulletin*, Vol. 14, No. 9 (May 1, 1953), p. 330.

spection. As a diluted compromise measure, France proposed that limited control of opium production be applied through the traditional devices already imposed on manufacture and distribution under the 1925 and 1931 conventions: national estimates, licenses, enforcement and reports subject to international review. This plan was finally adopted by a special international conference in June 1953.

Every transaction has two parties, and the Commission, WHO, and Social Commission have also tried to deal with the consumer end. Their major efforts here have been directed at improving the treatment of addicts and attacking the basic economic and social conditions which breed addiction. To clamp down on legalized opium smoking in certain countries, the Commission began in the summer of 1948 by recommending "suppression" of this practice. But the national response was only half-hearted. Thus in April 1953 outright abolition was urged.

The sad truth emerging from this record is that, although the barriers against this debilitating trade are a little higher and a little stronger than before the war, the flood of illegal traffic is proportionately even more powerful. The 1948 convention authorizing the WHO to place new drugs under control and the steps to reorganize the system are significant improvements. Moreover many countries are increasing their enforcement efforts as the threat to their welfare becomes obvious. But governments are still unwilling to allow really strict and direct international regulation. Furthermore, as new drugs spring up, the materials and areas to be patrolled expand tremendously. And the small bulk and high price of the insidious substances make it all the easier for them to slip through the controls to the captive consumers who become more and more desperately dependent on them.[20]

Assets and Liabilities

Governments rarely venture beyond the boundaries of what they conceive to be to their national interest. But national interest is not a static concept. It can retreat or advance. The plain fact is that most states have considered it to their national interest to collaborate more fully on a wider range of problems with the WHO and related agencies than with any previous international health bodies. They have cooperated through the contribution of more money (the WHO budget was $8.5 million in 1953 as compared with approximately $190,000 for the League Health Organization), promotion of more direct field action, support of a wider scope of activities (including the relatively modern fields of mental hygiene and economic and social aspects of health), development of regional planning and coordination, emphasis on a new positive preventive goal of total health, greater integration of international health agencies (such as the Pan American Sanitary Bureau and former Paris International Office of Public Health), and enactment of technical regulations which are binding

[20] For general commentary, see "Narcotic Drug Control," *International Conciliation*, No. 485 (November 1952).

unless specifically rejected within given time limits. These are not mere paper victories. They are concrete achievements.

But the dragon of disease is merely wounded, and the international agencies have little more than wooden swords with which to fight it. Governments are still not willing to contribute more than a small fraction of what they spend on national services. The United States annual grant to WHO is approximately $2 million, only 0.7 per cent of the $300 million it spends on the federal Public Health Service, which is merely supplementary to the state health services. Nor will states give the world bodies binding authority except in limited relatively noncontroversial technical matters.

On all other questions the agencies can merely recommend, and in the more controversial fields, such as birth control and socialized medicine, relatively little progress has been made. There is also the temptation, because of the lack of funds and desire to "sell" WHO through rapid "impact" projects, to undertake quick short-run programs (such as the anti-yaws work) as contrasted with more fundamental and long-run efforts (such as technical training, mass education, and basic economic and social improvement). Some neo-Malthusian critics of the United Nations system have said it is contributing to an explosive population increase which is gobbling up food faster than it can be produced. Others insist that better health is one of the shortest roads to increased food production; they also recognize the need for balanced development.[21]

But, if one is inclined to lose heart on occasion, a bracing antidote is to remember the progress that has been made and to read an occasional tribute from the people the United Nations is trying to help such as the following excerpt published in April 1953 in a leading Indian daily:

> The WHO never attempts to be a fairy godmother. . . . Its assistance is given only when asked . . . and its aim is to afford opportunities for such administrations to help themselves . . . in order to receive about four million dollars worth of technical assistance . . . six nations of this region have spent, or will spend, themselves a sum equal to five to six million . . . there cannot be two opinions about the usefulness of the humanitarian and nation-building activities of bodies like the WHO and the UNICEF.[22]

Human Rights

Traditional international law never recognized the individual as the "subject," only the "object," of that law and had left the definition of individual rights to arrangements among states. The League Covenant contained no mention of human rights. There were only the minority clauses in the peace treaties which had given limited protection to a few groups and had left the handling of appeals to the League Council mainly in the

[21] Abel Wolman, "World Health: the Optimists v. the Pessimists," WHO Newsletter, Vol. 6, No. 8 (September 1953), p. 4.

[22] The Hindu (Madras), April 7, 1953, p. 4.

hands of governments. Then the ruthless oppression and liquidation of masses of peoples during World War II caused a revulsion against such crimes and a movement which led to the writing of a wholly new concept into the Charter. For the first time, a general international, rather than national, bill of rights was to be recognized. For the first time, these standards were to be guaranteed for all people, rather than just some. And, for the first time, these obligations were to be set down in a general treaty, binding all ratifying countries. But, after endless study, drafting and debate, this goal is only partially fulfilled, and, at this writing, a human rights convention has not yet been adopted.

This effort is one that has been carried on in more than one form and by more than one agency. Not only ECOSOC's Commission on Human Rights but also such bodies as the Sub-Commission on Freedom of Information and of the Press, Sub-Commission on Prevention of Discrimination and Protection of Minorities, Commission on the Status of Women, ILO, IRO, UNESCO, and the High Commissioner for Refugees have also joined the struggle. The principal enterprise, however, has been the drafting of a "bill of human rights" chiefly under the supervision of the Commission on Human Rights.

Drafting the Declaration

When it became obvious at the outset that some governments, particularly the United States, wanted only a recommendatory "declaration," while others, including the United Kingdom, wanted a binding convention, a compromise was reached in late 1947 that the "bill of rights" should be comprised of three separate documents: a declaration, a convention and measures of implementation. Since governments were more willing to accept a recommendation than a binding convention, the first agreement produced was the declaration. But the drafting process was a trying one. Were there universal rights decreed by heaven or rooted in man's nature? If there were, it was most difficult to sort them out of a welter of conflicting ideologies.[23]

Buddha had enunciated five social freedoms: from violence, want, exploitation, violation or dishonor, and early death and disease.[24] Islam lists four essential rights: food and clothing, housing, education, and medical and sanitary services.[25] The rights of the individual must be subordinated to society to assure these rights. Chinese ethics accept three universal rights: life, self-expression, and inner satisfaction which requires some leisure time and an atmosphere of toleration.[26] The Communists recog-

---

[23] See F. S. C. Northrop, *The Meeting of East and West* (New York: Macmillan, 1946), for some exploratory thinking on this problem.

[24] S. V. Puntambekar, "The Hindu Concept of Human Rights," *Human Rights: Comments and Interpretations*, A Symposium edited by UNESCO (New York: Columbia University Press, 1949), p. 197.

[25] Humayun Kabir, "Human Rights: The Islamic Tradition and the Problems of the World Today," *ibid.*, p. 192.

[26] Chung-Sho Lo, "Human Rights in the Chinese Tradition," *ibid.*, p. 187.

Universal Declaration of Human Rights

equality before law

freedom of movement

freedom from arbitrary arrest

protection of family

due process of law

right to own property

All human beings are born free and equal ... Everyone is entitled to all the rights .. without distinction of any kind such as race, color, sex, religion, language etc

freedom of expression

right to work

right to rest

freedom of worship

right of assembly

right to adequate living

right to take part in government

right to participate in cultural life

right to organize

right to education

LEGAL RIGHTS

PERSONAL RIGHTS

CIVIL RIGHTS

ECONOMIC RIGHTS

SOCIAL RIGHTS

Headline Series, *Foreign Policy Association*

nize various rights of the working class, with heavy emphasis on economic and social welfare, but demand that the individual be governed by the will of the whole as expressed through the Communist Party. The Anglo-Saxons are united in their defense of traditional western legal and political rights, such as "due process" and free speech, but the United Kingdom and others have been more advanced than the United States in promoting economic and social rights.

If the substance of the declaration required the wisdom of Solomon, the process required the patience of Job. For a year and a half there were widespread consultations with governments, private groups and individuals and long debates in the Commission on Human Rights, ILO, UNESCO, ECOSOC, and the General Assembly. At last, however, in December 1948, a final Declaration of Human Rights was adopted by the General Assembly, 48 to 0 with 8 abstentions (the Soviet bloc, South Africa and Saudi Arabia). The Communist states criticized, among other things, the absence of adequate economic and social rights, a denunciation of fascism and aggression and a listing of duties toward the state. South Africa thought the statement unrealistic. Saudi Arabia complained that it was too western.

The fundamental civil and political rights proclaimed are:

> life, liberty, security of person, free thought, speech and communication; religion and assembly; self-government through free elections; free movement within a state and exit from it; asylum in another state; nationality; non-arbitrary arrest and non-interference with privacy; prohibition of slavery and torture.

The economic and social rights include:

> work, protection against unemployment, trade union membership, adequate standards of living for health and well-being, education, rest and leisure.

All of these are to be guaranteed without distinction as to race, color, sex, language, religion, political or other opinion, property or other status, birth, or national or social origin.

Then began a far-flung effort to carry the word of this revolutionary standard to the ends of the earth to provide a guide and weapon for all oppressed peoples. Since it is officially only a recommendation, the Declaration has no binding authority. Nonetheless it has had substantial influence. Human Rights Day, commemorating the adoption, is observed every December 10 in over eighty states and territories. Declaration articles have been reproduced verbatim in several new national constitutions, national legislation, and treaties. It has also been referred to as a moral standard by the International Court of Justice and a number of national courts.

Conflicts Over Convention

Nations were far more reluctant to sign their names to a binding convention, or "covenant," as it has come to be called. The most crucial dispute arose over whether economic, social, and cultural rights should be combined with political and civil, or be dealt with separately. Some westerners, particularly the United States, thought the economic and social goals too advanced and their nonimplementation would discredit the agreement. Many Anglo-Saxon lawyers thought such standards as "adequate" housing or health too vague to be enforceable in a court of law. Others, especially the Communists and underdeveloped countries, felt that the world's masses were more interested in food, clothing and shelter than the right to voice their opinions atop a soap box.

In 1950 the General Assembly decided that both kinds of rights should be combined in a single package. But the United States and others helped persuade the Assembly to change its mind in 1951 and request the Commission to prepare two separate conventions in time for the 1952 Assembly session. Continued conflicts prevented meeting this deadline, however, and the only relevant action taken in the 1952 session was to adopt a resolution, sponsored by the underdeveloped nations, recommending that Member states: (1) uphold the principle of "self-determination" of peoples and nations, and (2) recognize and promote the realization of such rights of non-self-governing peoples and grant such rights upon demand ascertained by a United Nations-administered plebiscite.

Step by step the two conventions have been shaped by the hard-working Commission on Human Rights. The political and civil draft is obviously the less controversial and follows the general pattern of the Declaration. The more explosive economic, social, and cultural document represents a deflated and much qualified version of the comparable Declaration passages dealing with trade union rights, social security, housing, living standards, health and education. Delegates have come to recognize that rights are never absolute but must be moulded to fit changing conditions according to the interests of society. To quote Oliver Wendell Holmes' classic phrase, "The most stringent protection of free speech would not protect a man in falsely shouting fire in a theatre. . . ." [27] But the circumstances and procedures for governing such limitations of rights are very difficult to tie down.

The demand for self-determination has also opened a Pandora's box of perplexing questions. Who should have the right to self-determination: every neighborhood, city, county or state? Unfortunately some of those who cry loudest for self-determination are those who most relentlessly suppress the self-determinists within their own boundaries. [28] Finally, there is the matter of implementation. Australia led the strong internationalists in 1949, proposing an international court of human rights to which individuals and nongovernmental groups as well as states would have access. The United States and United Kingdom placed primary emphasis on *ad hoc* investigating committees to which states alone could make complaints with room left for eventual reference to the International Court of Justice if necessary. The Soviet Union insisted that all these plans involved serious breaches of domestic jurisdiction.

By 1953 the Commission had adopted the United States–United Kingdom view envisaging a Human Rights Committee composed of nine independent specialists in human rights elected by the International Court of Justice. Complaints could be brought only by states, and the sole sanctions would be investigation, conciliation, recommendation and publicity. No provision was made for reference to the International Court. To enforce economic and social rights the majority favored the western view calling

[27] Schenck *v.* U.S., 249 U.S. 47 (1919).
[28] Clyde Eagleton, "Excesses of Self-Determination," *Foreign Affairs*, Vol. 31, No. 4 (July 1953), pp. 592–604.

for a more lenient plan based on implementation of these more controversial rights by stages and regular national reports to be reviewed by the
United Nations.

Freedom of the Press

The American Society of Newspaper Editors adopted a resolution in
1944 reflecting the international objectives of the wealthiest, strongest and
least regulated publishing nation in the world.

> They wanted barriers to the free flow of news lowered. . . . They wanted the
> right to send newsgatherers anywhere. . . . They wanted what those men
> wrote to be transmitted without censorship and at reasonable cost. . . . They
> wanted to be able to sell and have published in other countries what their
> worldwide organizations gathered. . . . [29]

This led to an attempt to commit the United Nations to such concepts
which was initially "successful beyond expectation." [30] A United Nations
Conference on Freedom of Information met in Geneva, March to April
1948, and succeeded in adopting three draft conventions:

> a convention on the gathering and international transmission of news, pro-
> posed by the United States; a convention on an international right of correc-
> tion, sponsored by France and intended to establish a procedure under which
> governments may obtain publicity for official corrections of allegedly false
> reports which affect their international relations; and a convention on free-
> dom of information submitted by the United Kingdom and intended to pro-
> vide a guaranty to all the nationals of contracting states of freedom of ex-
> pression as well as freedom to seek and receive information from all
> sources.[31]

The first two drafts were then amalgamated as a single convention on the
International Transmission of News and Right of Correction and approved
by the General Assembly in May 1949.

There were intense differences, however, on the freedom of information draft. The extreme "restrictionist" view was that of the Soviet Union
which favored a completely controlled press. The "anti-restrictionist" camp
was led by the United States and generally included the British Commonwealth nations, the Scandinavians, Netherlands, and a few others. Between
these poles there was a large group, including most of the underdeveloped
countries, that wanted to limit freedom of the press to protect private and
national interests (including, at one time, the private life of Egypt's King
Farouk). This latter bloc was numerous enough to adopt another Assembly resolution to the effect that the first convention should not be opened
for signature until the Assembly had taken definite action on the freedom
of information draft.

Further negotiation in the early part of 1951 failed to smooth out these

---

[29] Carroll Binder, "Freedom of Information and the United Nations," *International
Organization*, Vol. 6, No. 2 (May 1952), p. 221.
[30] *Ibid.*, p. 223.   [31] *Ibid.*

differences, and the anti-restrictionist group blocked the calling of a full-dress conference to consider a new freedom of information convention. India, Pakistan and Egypt led an effort to consider this convention in the 1952 Assembly, but the United States and others stopped this move also, with the United Kingdom abstaining. The Assembly then opened for signature the French Convention on the International Right of Correction and noted ECOSOC's appointment of a single *rapporteur*, Salvador Lopez, former editor of the *Philippines Herald*, to study the situation. Mr. Lopez's first report in mid-1953 suggested going ahead with the convention, with only nominal limitations on press freedom, and looking to private press groups for self-regulation.

Protecting Minorities

In the matter of dealing with discrimination and the protection of minorities, there has been far less emphasis in the United Nations on special international supervisory arrangements than there was in the League. There are several reasons behind this change. The post-World War I peace treaty minority provisions gave rise to widespread disillusionment.[32] Today governments are more reluctant than ever to give special recognition and status to minority groups, particularly in view of their use by the Nazis as Trojan horses. The Soviet Union loudly proclaims the ideal of free expression for nationalities but compels them to toe the Communist line and will not hear of the slightest international supervision. Finally, many friends of the minorities believe that the only ultimate solution is to protect such groups by protecting the fundamental rights of all people. This avoids perpetuating their isolation from the rest of the society in which they live.

For all these reasons the problem was assigned to the Commission on Human Rights and its Sub-Commission on Prevention of Discrimination and Protection of Minorities.[33] But this effort has moved no faster than the whole human rights program to which it is hitched. Useful studies have been made. Resolutions have been approved by ECOSOC and the General Assembly urging the fuller use of education and administrative and judicial controls to combat discrimination. And the Sub-Commission has recommended the inclusion of basic minority rights in the human rights convention with provision for a conciliatory body to watch over their implementation.

Genocide and Other Problems

Another reaction to Nazi barbarism was the Genocide Convention approved by the General Assembly in December 1948. This agreement outlawed five kinds of acts aimed at destroying a "national, ethnical, racial or religious group as such," whether committed in time of peace or war:

[32] See Chap. 22.
[33] For commentary on this body see Inis L. Claude, Jr., "The Nature and Status of the Subcommission on Prevention of Discrimination and Protection of Minorities," *International Organization*, Vol. 5, No. 2 (May 1951), pp. 300–312.

killing members of a group; causing them serious physical or mental harm; imposing measures to prevent births; and forcibly transferring children to another group.

Those guilty, whether constitutionally responsible rulers, public officials, or private individuals, are to be tried in the country where the crime was committed or by international tribunals having jurisdiction. This convention came into force in January 1951, but Secretary of State John Foster Dulles announced as late as the first part of 1953 that the United States would not ratify the convention in the foreseeable future.

While ECOSOC has also concerned itself with trade union rights, the ILO has been the leader in this field, as discussed above.[34] To investigate charges against the Soviet Union and other countries of employing forced labor, first initiated by the United States American Federation of Labor, the United Nations and ILO jointly appointed in June 1951 an *ad hoc* Committee on Forced Labor, chaired by Sir Ramaswami Mudaliar of India, to explore and report on the problem. An *ad hoc* Committee of Experts on Slavery was also appointed by the United Nations in 1949 and prepared a study which resulted in an ECOSOC resolution in the spring of 1953 suggesting wider and stricter compliance with the 1926 anti-slavery convention and raising the possibility of a supplementary convention.

The Commission on the Status of Women has been busy studying means of gaining greater equality for women who, except in a few rare matriarchies, are only gradually emerging from male domination in most countries of the world. This labor has produced an impressive series of studies and agreements resulting in the following draft conventions and recommendations which ECOSOC had approved by the summer of 1953:

> a draft Convention on the Political Rights of Women adopted by the General Assembly in December 1952; a recommendation to circulate to governments a draft convention on the nationality of married women; a resolution recommending that governments ensure equal rights and duties of husbands and wives in family matters, right to work and property; a resolution urging equal pay for equal work following the ILO convention; and a resolution recommending the end of discrimination of employment in governmental services.

Reflections on Basic Issues

The struggle over human rights in the United Nations mirrors not only current differences among nations and cultures but also a political, economic and ideological revolution within certain societies, especially in the west, which has largely replaced the concept of *laissez faire* with that of positive governmental assistance. In most nations today, particularly since the depression of the thirties, men demand that governments help to maintain at least a minimal standard of living beneath which, for the good of the whole society, they believe no individual should be allowed to sink.

[34] See pp. 625–634.

Difficulties for International Action

1. Our ideas of Human Rights are different

2. Some say Human Rights are domestic affairs

MIND YOUR
OWN BUSINESS
Sovereign State

HUMAN RIGHTS

3. If UN is to act what powers shall it have?

Headline Series, *Foreign Policy Association*

At the same time, one should ponder carefully the various objections which have been raised, particularly in the United States. It is said that there is insufficient consensus in the world to support such ambitious goals, least of all a legally binding convention. The cold war has made it difficult for opposing sides to be reasonable in formulating such rights. The many qualifications that have been inserted have dulled the force of the drafts. Rights are not given by governments; they are inherent in man's nature. It would be better to have no covenant at all than one that is unrealistically visionary — or, as others say, pusillanimously feeble. To retreat too much

651

from the Declaration will destroy the influence of that document. Economic and social standards are not "rights" and are too vague, unlike political and civil rights, to be enforceable.[35]

True, there is much disagreement in the world about rights, but there is also much consensus, as has been pointed out by authorities representing various cultures.[36] Nor has the lack of uniformity of views prevented common standards from being adopted and legally enforced within states. Exceptions, moreover, are both normal and necessary. They are part of every national bill of rights and do not nullify those rights unless distorted by an undemocratic regime.

It is reasonable enough to warn the United Nations not to establish standards too far in advance of possible implementation. Irresponsible talk about rights can be positively mischievous. This same problem is faced by every national government, but it has not prevented the enactment of goals beyond current practice. Regarding the question of vagueness, the concepts of "adequate" housing or health care are no more vague than the familiar concept in Anglo-Saxon law of what the hypothetical "reasonable man" would think "fair" compensation or a "clear and present danger" to the stability of government. What is "reasonable" or "adequate" can never be exactly defined. On the other hand, approximate criteria can be, and are, devised and enforced every day in national courts.

A swelling chorus argues that the United Nations should not try to tackle the whole problem at once but, like the ILO in the labor field, deal with human rights in stages and issue by issue.[37] This is similar to the new line taken by the United States early in 1953 as part of Secretary of State Dulles' efforts to head off Senator Bricker's constitutional amendment to hobble the President's treaty-making powers.[38] There is no doubt that the ILO make-haste-slowly approach is a good one and should be pushed as far as possible. Nonetheless, one must recognize that rights are related to each other. The effectiveness of political rights is directly linked to economic and social conditions. It is useful, therefore, to have statements that reflect this fact and are comprehensive and advanced. Many nations have adopted just such credos as the cornerstones of their political systems. The very effort to formulate such a statement can be an educating and unifying experience. Hence, the United Nations should not cease trying to devise at least a minimal universal covenant. This is particularly important since so many underdeveloped nations place great store in this effort.[39]

[35] For discussion of some of these objections see Arthur N. Holcombe, *Human Rights in the Modern World* (New York: New York University Press, 1948); Marian Neal, "The United Nations and Human Rights," *International Conciliation*, No. 489 (March 1953).

[36] *Human Rights: Comments and Interpretations;* F. S. C. Northrop, *op. cit.*

[37] P. E. Corbett, *Law and Society in the Relations of States* (New York: Harcourt, Brace, 1951), p. 297; Neal, *op. cit.*, pp. 148–172.

[38] *The New York Times*, April 7, p. 1.

[39] For discussion of a distinguished lawyer's faith in this approach see H. Lauterpacht, *International Law and Human Rights* (New York: F. A. Praeger, 1950).

Social Welfare

Aiding the poor, rehabilitating the physically handicapped, protecting women and children, and improving general family conditions — these are a few of the tasks that fall under the somewhat vague heading, "social" activities. Since this field is so broad, it is traversed by many United Nations and affiliated agencies including the Social Commission, Commission on the Status of Women, Commission on Human Rights, Commission on Narcotic Drugs, the regional commissions, UNICEF, FAO, WHO, ILO and UNESCO. The following paragraphs, however, will concentrate primarily on the work of the Social Commission.

The most immediate postwar task was the rehabilitation of human beings as well as material production. Hence, as UNRRA was coming to an end in 1946 and 1947, the Assembly authorized the Social Commission and the Secretariat's Department of Social Affairs to continue, on a temporary year-to-year basis, various advisory social welfare services developed by UNRRA (technical assistance on social welfare methods, training, advice and instruction in rehabilitation of the physically handicapped, and furnishing social welfare publications). But the need for these and other welfare services was too great throughout the world to stop at that. In 1950 the General Assembly felt compelled to make these services permanent and to strengthen them as part of the Expanded Technical Assistance Program. United Nations functions were broadened to include expert advice, fellowships and scholarships, demonstration projects, technical publications and films, and seminars. Subjects dealt with include all aspects of the social field:

> community, family and child welfare, organization and administration of social welfare services, rehabilitation of the handicapped, social security, crime prevention, housing and town and country planning, and rural welfare services.

Community, Family and Child Welfare

Within this area the United Nations has devoted its greatest efforts to aiding poor, orphaned and physically handicapped children. This emphasis is based, first, on a recognition of the importance of developing sound youth as the foundation of every society, and, second, on the relatively large sums of money which UNICEF was able to provide. As already discussed in the economic relief and health sections, UNICEF has been a means of providing substantial material aid which has been administered in conjunction with the skilled personnel of other related agencies: FAO, WHO, ILO, UNESCO, the United Nations High Commissioner for Refugees, and the Social Commission. By 1953, UNICEF had received approximately $185 million in public and private contributions of which the United States had given approximately 50 per cent. This money provided maternity and child health and welfare training and services (including equipment and supplies for health centers, clinics, laboratories and training child care personnel); mass health programs (supplies and equipment to fight tuberculosis, malaria, syphilis, bejel and other diseases); supplemental food for children and mothers (imported foods and equipment to pasteurize and preserve milk); and raw materials for clothing. Other services in this field have taken the form of a coordinated program to help all handicapped persons; technical assistance by child welfare experts; various studies on child care; annual reports on community, family and child welfare; revision of the 1924 League Declaration of the Rights of the Child; study of the problems of the aged; survey of forty types of governmental supplementation of family income; development of community social welfare centers as the focal points of community organization; and promotion of better housing.

Policing Society

Traffic in persons exploited for profit is still a problem, and the United Nations is continuing the work of the League in this area. Responsibilities regarding such traffic, assigned France by 1904 and 1910 conventions and the League by 1921 and 1933 conventions, were transferred to the United Nations by protocols approved by the General Assembly in 1947 and 1948. Then, in December 1949, the Assembly adopted a new convention which unified the previous conventions with a draft, first prepared under the League in 1937, to outlaw the exploitation of prostitution. This combined convention aimed at eliminating "traffic" and "exploitation" but not the prostitutes themselves. This was based on the philosophy that, as a British representative put it, "man could not be made good by . . . international convention. Higher moral standards were the function of education. But it was possible to strike . . . at the procurer or exploiter . . . " [40] Further action by the Social Commission has centered around reviewing national reports on compliance and considering various means of tightening enforcement including the possibility of a United Nations field bureau, similar to that in the narcotics field, in the Far East where the traffic is most prevalent and least controlled.

The Social Commission has also instituted a "social defence" program in the interest of preventing crime and improving the treatment of offenders. In the fall of 1948 the United Nations called the first postwar international conference of agencies interested in this matter including the independent intergovernmental International Penal and Penitentiary Commission (IPPC). At first the United Nations confined itself to studies, publications and conferences. At the end of 1951, however, it absorbed the IPPC and has accordingly strengthened its activities in this area.

Conclusions

Through careful cultivation, the United Nations' social program is not quite the shrinking violet it tended to be under the League. Besides con-

[40] *United Nations Bulletin*, Vol. 8, No. 1 (January 1, 1950), p. 56.

tinuing certain prewar efforts in child welfare, traffic in persons and aid to the needy, the United Nations has blossomed out with more positive, comprehensive and long-range planning. This reflects the availability of more money and staff as well as new thinking in the social welfare field. But still there is much room for improvement. The multiplicity of agencies busy in the social hive makes coordination particularly difficult. There has been occasional conflict between the Secretariat Departments of Economic Affairs and Social Affairs. This situation has improved, especially through the efforts of the ACC and TAB, but relations should be even closer. There is evidence that some social fields are still not receiving the attention they deserve in the technical assistance program. Moreover, to make the most of an admittedly skimpy budget, the Social Commission needs to go further than it has in developing firm priorities. At the same time, the Commission's critics must recognize that improvement in many social areas depends fundamentally on economic development which requires more large-scale capital investment in addition to the present technical assistance. Finally, the Commission and other United Nations agencies should take fuller advantage of the resources of international and national non-governmental organizations.

Population and Migration

The ECOSOC Population Commission, the principal United Nations authority in this field, has also been affected by the increasing concern with economic development and has devoted much attention to studying the impact of various economic and social policies on population. A significant pilot study has been carried out in India to examine the influence of economic development on population size, composition and distribution. Technical assistance has been rendered to improve the general quality of national and international population studies. And a United Nations *Demographic Yearbook* is published giving comprehensive figures on population, migration and vital statistics for every country and territory for which such statistics are available. To help make populations more fluid, the United Nations and affiliated bodies have tried to facilitate migration so that human resources may move more freely from a population surplus area to a deficit area. This involves a variety of agencies which work through an ACC Technical Working Group on Migration. The Population Commission has studied and recorded migratory movements and their relation to other population problems.

Aiding the Refugee

For the first time in the history of multinational cooperation, the refugee agencies created at the end of World War II had the authority and resources to extend substantial direct material assistance. This was fortunate since the need was vast. By the middle of 1943, the advance of the Nazis and the wholesale transportation of slave labor to Germany had caused the displacement of approximately twenty-one million people. Eight million had been herded to Germany and Austria; another eight million had been shifted within their own countries.

When the United Nations Relief and Rehabilitation Administration (UNRRA) Council convened for its first session in November 1943, it decided its primary refugee task was repatriation. Before UNRRA could get started, however, the military authorities had completed much of that job. Six months after the allied armies had arrived in the conquered Axis nations, five of the ten millions displaced had been repatriated.[41] Further, and perhaps more significantly, it began to be apparent that many refugees had no desire to return to their homelands for fear of oppression. Consequently, UNRRA's efforts required more time, money and energy than had been expected. Great assembly centers had to feed, clothe, house, rehabilitate and finally resettle or repatriate these unfortunates. The military provided the barracks, food and clothing in most cases.

In each center UNRRA endeavored to plant the seeds of democracy by fostering a camp government, with considerable authority, composed of the displaced persons themselves. Under such circumstances, the participating individuals became far more than mere wards. UNRRA also sought to impart new vocational skills, provide adequate medical care and find employment. These laudable aims were not uniformly carried out, but,

> By the end of June, 1947, when UNRRA's mandate came to an end, most displaced persons in most camps and assembly centers were capable of governing themselves with little or no outside supervision. Two years earlier that would not have been possible, nor would it have been possible if UNRRA had pursued a policy of efficient command in the camps.[42]

In the years of its existence, UNRRA supervised the care of 969,000 displaced persons. It was able to secure the repatriation of a total of 1,047,282 [43] but did relatively little in the direction of resettlement.

IRO Takes Over

On June 30, 1947, UNRRA's refugee mantle was assumed by the newly formed International Refugee Organization (IRO) composed of eighteen nations. With a budget for the first year of $155 million and a staff which eventually reached 5,684, the organization was equipped to make major inroads on the problem. The IRO took over the administration of the centers and was able eventually to raise the average food consumption to 2,500 calories per day. Great medical advances were achieved, and the

[41] See René Ristelhueber, "International Refugee Organization," *International Conciliation*, No. 470 (April 1951).

[42] George Woodbridge, ed., *UNRRA* (New York: Columbia University Press, 1950), Vol. 2, p. 525.

[43] *Ibid.*, pp. 496 and 518.

death rate was reduced to a level attained only in the most advanced countries. Legal protection was extended to the refugees to enable them to marry, own property, travel and be generally protected from arbitrary action by national governments.

IRO continued the work of repatriation, but the numbers who would willingly return to their native lands were rapidly diminishing. Only 70,000 were repatriated in three years. Far greater strides were made in resettlement. Various nations, particularly the United States, Australia and Canada, accepted 800,000, screened so as to provide valued skills in farming, industry and the sciences. In order to transport its charges, the IRO maintained the largest private fleet of vessels in the world — thirty-nine ships in all.

But the sponsors of the IRO were unwilling to recognize the need for a continuing operational program, and insisted that the Organization close its doors by September 1951. When the Organization had ceased to perform its functions, it had extended protection to more than 1.5 million refugees. It had resettled 1,046,000 persons, repatriated 74,000, given legal protection to 218,000, and extended various other types of assistance to 263,000. The nations of the world had answered the helpless cry of the refugee in a comprehensive manner unmatched in previous history. Still there remained 400,000 for whom no provision had been made, and 15,000 to 20,000 new refugees appeared each year.

Back to a High Commissioner

In order to meet the continuing problem, the General Assembly returned to the League pattern of a High Commissioner for Refugees, effective January 1, 1951. Dr. G. J. van Heuven Goedhart was chosen to fill the new post. The difficulties which have confronted his activities, however, have been virtually insuperable. He was stripped of all IRO's' operating responsibilities. His position was to be that of providing liason among national governments, voluntary agencies and the refugee. No funds for the care and maintenance of displaced persons were provided. And a meager administrative budget immensely restricted his activity. The Commissioner was permitted $685,000 in 1954, compared to the first year budget of $155 million for IRO. His office currently employs 105 compared to a staff of 5,600 for the IRO. And the problems confronting the Office, particularly considering the unwillingness of many governments to take additional numbers of refugees, are greater than ever.

New legal help for refugees came with the adoption of a Convention Relating to the Status of Refugees by a special conference of twenty-four governments meeting in Geneva during July 1951. This code covers a wide range of minimal rights in such important areas as religion, property rights, commercial enterprise, exercise of liberal professions, juridical status, and the issue of identity papers and travel documents. But there was no adequate international financial assistance. By the end of 1951 the High Commissioner announced he still had 1.5 million refugees under his care with no appreciable resources to help them. He proposed a $3 million fund to provide relief for especially urgent cases, to finance migration or "assimilation" in countries where the refugees were then located, and to establish eleven branch offices to facilitate his labors. The Assembly noted this report but merely authorized him to appeal for voluntary contributions.

A year later, at the end of 1952, he announced that he had collected only $800,000, that there were significant opportunities for assimilation but that it required more financial assistance. The Assembly then "invited" the Commissioner to consult with the International Bank for Reconstruction and Development regarding possible loans that might serve to aid assimilation and further voluntary contributions. In January 1953 the nongovernmental Ford Foundation in the United States contributed $452,000 as well as $658,000 to various private groups assisting in the refugee program, but other gifts continued to be slow and modest. Nonetheless, the High Commissioner carried on, and the General Assembly decided at the end of 1953 that his Office should be continued for another five years.

Other recent United Nations efforts have included the separate program to aid the Arabs who fled from Palestine, presently administered under the United Nations Relief and Works Agency for Palestine Refugees, and aid given Korean refugees through the United Nations Korean Reconstruction Agency — both of these projects supported by sizable direct United Nations contributions as well as non-governmental gifts.[44] There are also many non-United Nations governmental and private efforts including the United States Escapee Program to aid political refugees from the Soviet sphere and the United States–sponsored Intergovernmental Committee for European Migration. The latter is the only significant international resettlement program now in operation. Between its inception in February 1952 and October 1, 1953, the Committee helped 139,000 persons to migrate, chiefly from Germany, Austria, Italy and the Netherlands to the United States, Australia, Brazil and Canada. During 1954 it planned to spend $35 million and move 118,000.[45]

Conclusions

Reviewing the pattern of these international refugee efforts, it becomes clear that the United Nations has made far greater contributions in this respect than the League ever did. The League never authorized any significant direct operational program nor the funds to run one, while UNRRA and IRO were given substantial resources to conduct direct operations which resulted in the repatriation of 1.1 million and the resettlement of 1 million. Then the pressures of the "cold war" and the allegation that the emergency was over and the remaining burden should be borne by governments and private organizations resulted in a return, at the end of 1951, to the League device of a non-operating High Commissioner.

[44] See Chap. 18.
[45] *The New York Times*, October 16, 1953; also see Hugh Gibson, "Migration from Western Europe Under the Intergovernmental Committee for European Migration," *Department of State Bulletin*, Vol. 29, No. 735 (July 27, 1953), pp. 117–121.

But the refugee problem is not solved. It was estimated, as of the end of 1953, that there were still some two million refugees eligible for protection under the High Commissioner. As long as international strife continues, it will squeeze out, to one side or the other, refugees who find their lives made intolerable by the struggle. And it is in the interest of a humane and stable society that new homes and jobs be offered these hapless people as long as they may need them. The question then arises whether they should be cared for under the United Nations or not. In answering this question, one should give thoughtful consideration to the reasons why the United States has recently turned away from the United Nations in this field. It is said that such operations must be protected from the sabotage of those, like the Russians, who do not agree with the underlying assumptions of the refugee program; that the major contributors, like the United States, should be given a stronger voice in the decision-making process than they are afforded in the United Nations; that, once an agency is created by the United Nations, it is almost impossible to end it; and that it is best to work primarily with the European community since that is most important politically, most familiar and sympathetic, and most manageable in its proportions.

While there is some cogency in this reasoning, it also contains certain flaws. The U.S.S.R. was not a member of IRO and does not control a majority in any United Nations economic and social body. While it seems reasonable that the larger contributors should have a commensurate voice in decision-making, there is virtual weighted voting through informal influence in most United Nations bodies, and there is no reason why there could not be formal weighting in any new agency as there now is in the IBRD and IMF. True, it is difficult to terminate a United Nations agency, but this is also a common phenomenon outside the United Nations. One cannot deny that Europe is more familiar and manageable, in Anglo-Saxon eyes, than non-European countries but, as Asia comes of age economically and politically, enlightened self-interest, if not moral considerations, require aid for all refugees everywhere. Moreover, the problem of coordination is eased by working through the most universal international organization, the United Nations. Finally, it has been demonstrated that the major powers win far more international good will for themselves when they work through the United Nations than outside it.

Cultural Relations

In Patzcuaro, Mexico, a small sun-baked fishing village 250 miles west of Mexico City, approximately a hundred instructor-apprentices are learning, with the help of UNESCO and other agencies, to teach reading and writing as part of educating farmers to use a steel plow or to inoculate pigs against cholera. Approximately 75 per cent of the annual cost of this Fundamental Education Center is paid by UNESCO; the rest, by the Organization of

American States (OAS). The FAO, ILO and WHO are contributing faculty members. The head of the school is Lucas Ortiz, former Director of Rural Education in Mexico, who began his career as a rural school teacher in an area where he had to ride to work on horseback. The students are drawn from all parts of Latin America and are being prepared to return home to plant the seeds developed at Patzcuaro.

This is one of many practical expressions of the famed and controversial UNESCO constitutional mandate:

> . . . since wars begin in the minds of men, it is in the minds of men that the defences of peace must be constructed; . . . the wide diffusion of culture and education . . . for justice and liberty and peace are indispensable to the dignity of man and constitute a sacred duty. . . .

UNESCO is not the only toiler in the cultural vineyard. The Patzcuaro project demonstrates how the WHO, FAO and ILO are also involved. Other agencies concerned with this field are ECOSOC commissions, UNICEF and the United Nations Secretariat's Department of Public Information. This section, however, will focus its spotlight primarily on UNESCO as the chief figure in the drama.

Pattern of Development

The evolution of UNESCO's program has been a long series of frustrations and convulsions punctuated by the stormy exits of the first two Directors-General, Julian Huxley of the United Kingdom and Jaime Torres Bodet of Mexico. To understand this conflict one need only contemplate some of the basic questions with which UNESCO has had to grapple. Should school children be educated to look to a loyalty above their national states? Should national bias be removed from textbooks, and how? On what basis should educational and other aid be allocated among various governments, institutions and fields of interest? Can and should a common philosophy be propagated to bind nations together? How valid is the concept of race?

Each interest group and government has had its own pet hates and loves. And the budget has always been too frail to support the mountain of projects heaped upon it. The first Director-General, Mr. Huxley, set the pace by "capturing terrain for international cooperation . . . in all the fields of our competence." [46] He proposed an imaginative, if not cautious, initial array of 147 different projects. The first General Conference approved these and others which were estimated to require $10 million, but only $6 million was contributed by the member governments.

As programs threatened to breech budgetary dikes, it was necessary to make choices and establish priorities, but it was extremely difficult to agree on what they should be. "Political" or "nonpolitical" objectives? Quick or long-range results? Education, or natural science, or social science or arts?

---

[46] Quoted in Charles S. Ascher, "The Development of UNESCO's Program," *International Organization*, Vol. 4, No. 1 (February 1950), p. 18.

Mass or class approach? In one of Mr. Torres Bodet's first pronouncements, he suggested the following yardsticks:

1. Will the project promote the welfare of the masses?
2. Will it enlist the cooperation of intellectual leaders everywhere to work for humanity?
3. Will it produce tangible results quickly? [47]

While Mr. Torres Bodet was willing and eager to establish certain criteria, he had no intention of freezing the budget. The initial funds seemed so puny that he felt there was ample room for judicious expansion. At the end of 1952, therefore, he asked a budget for the next two years that averaged $9.5 million a year. But the United States Congress had demanded a reduction of its quota from the original 44.0 per cent to 33.3 per cent and set an absolute ceiling on its contribution. Thus the Americans led a move, heartily endorsed by the financially hard-pressed British and others, to limit the budget to approximately $8.4 million a year. And Mr. Torres Bodet resigned.

Relief and Reconstruction

Although UNESCO was built to look ahead to long-range problems, it immediately stumbled over the need for postwar reconstruction of schools, laboratories, libraries and other facilities. UNRRA had been designed to do just this, but it was liquidated before the job could be finished. At the same time, the United States and other major sponsors were never willing to grant UNESCO any large reconstruction funds. Hence it was confined to surveying needs and coordinating various non-United Nations relief efforts, including the organization of a voluntary Temporary International Council for Educational Reconstruction (TICER) which managed to scrape together $160 million by the end of 1949.

UNESCO has contributed some of its own funds for relief but only for extraordinary emergencies for which it felt a special responsibility. The annual amount of these grants has varied from $400,000 in 1947–48 to $100,000 in 1951. This money has helped finance thirty-nine schools for Arab refugee children, work camps which rebuilt educational buildings, and the purchase of a high-speed rotary press for printing textbooks in Korea. UNESCO also devised a coupon scheme which provided a clearing arrangement whereby countries without sufficient foreign exchange could pay UNESCO with their own currencies for coupons with which to buy books and other educational materials abroad. UNESCO then redeemed the coupons in the book sellers' currencies. Obviously, this plan is limited by the amount of "soft" currencies UNESCO can absorb and "hard" currencies it can spare, but, by the end of 1952, $3 million worth of coupons had been sold.

---

[47] *Ibid.,* p. 24.

Education

Fifty to seventy-five per cent of the world's population, including ten million in the United States, can neither read nor write.[48] Their ignorance holds them prisoners in their tiny worlds. UNESCO has, from the beginning, considered this one of its principal challenges linked directly to the larger United Nations campaign to raise the living standards of the underdeveloped nations. One of the first efforts was to plant three "pilot projects": in Asia (China), Africa (Tanganyika in conjunction with the anticipated "groundnuts" development scheme) and Latin America (Haiti). This was done, unfortunately, with greater enthusiasm than foresight. The Tanganyika and China experiments had to be jettisoned in 1949 because of technological defeat and civil war respectively. The Haitian experiment has been a classic object lesson in how not to tackle a technical assistance operation.[49]

The location in Haiti, Marbial Valley, was calculated to send the most inveterate optimist into a fit of black despair. It is a steeply mountainous area of fifty square miles containing some thirty thousand illiterate disease-ridden peasants, scratching for a living in eroded and exhausted soil. Their most immediate problem was not how to read but how to stay alive. UNESCO consented to Haiti's request for this project before it had thoroughly explored the situation or arranged with the FAO and WHO to furnish the necessary agricultural and health assistance, and those two organizations have been reluctant, to this day, to give more than limited and temporary aid to bail UNESCO out of a bad plight. What personnel have been made available have rotated with understandable rapidity.

It is scarcely surprising, therefore, that UNESCO tried no more directly operational fundamental education projects but has since concentrated on information, advice and training. An educational clearing house receives approximately five hundred periodicals and six hundred books a month and answers about a hundred requests for information each month. A program of international educational seminars has brought together leaders from various countries to exchange views on such subjects as the training of instructors, teaching geography and the role of libraries in education.

In 1952 alone, UNESCO was asked by member governments to send out twenty-two educational technical assistance missions. The concrete results of such missions were recently reported by Mr. Walter Laves, Chairman of the United States National Commission for UNESCO:

> as a result of the educational mission [to Thailand] . . . a ten-year plan for educational development has been approved and a supplemental scheme is already in operation in one area where all types and grades of . . . activities are being reorganized. The delegate of Burma told me that his government

[48] Earl James McGrath, "The Fight Against Ignorance," *United States National Commission UNESCO News*, Vol. 5, No. 9 (April 1952), p. 3.

[49] Theodore Besterman, *UNESCO* (London: Methuen, 1951), pp. 14–16; Marian Neal, "United Nations Programs in Haiti," *International Conciliation*, No. 468 (February 1951), pp. 102–111.

had doubled its budget for public education and was in the midst of building 1,000 new primary schools, [as] the direct result of the recommendations of a . . . mission. . . . [50]

Adult education is a particularly promising channel for reaching large masses of people. UNESCO sponsored the first international conference on the subject in June 1949, in Denmark, the "home" of the adult education movement; helped establish the International Adult Education Center in Paris in 1952; and has published various studies on the matter. In 1950 the Patzcuaro Fundamental Education Training and Production Center, mentioned above, was established. A similar center was opened in January 1953 at Sirs-el-Layan, forty miles north of Cairo, Egypt, to accommodate approximately fifty teacher-trainees.

To pit education against the sword, UNESCO has held seminars and prepared materials to expand and improve teaching about international cooperation with special emphasis on the activities of the United Nations. A 1950 seminar in Belgium initiated a series of bilateral discussions among European countries to consider ways of correcting national bias in textbooks. At the university level, UNESCO has sponsored various meetings to discuss common problems and the creation of an international association of universities in December 1950. Finally UNESCO has tried to bend the twig in the right direction by giving particular attention to various aspects of child-training, including the problem of maladjustment, and has made special efforts to develop close contacts with youth groups.

Natural and Social Sciences

The sciences were well organized internationally before the war, and UNESCO's efforts have centered primarily around giving modest sums each year ($233,000 in 1951) to help finance meetings, publish reports, and maintain a number of services. For example, UNESCO made it possible for five Europeans and three Asians to attend an international scientific congress of the Pacific in New Zealand in February 1949; otherwise they could not have gone. In the field of research, despite the reluctance to create any direct international operations, two international scientific laboratories were finally established after long debate. The first was the International Computation Center, authorized in November 1951, to be located in Rome. The other is the European Organization for Nuclear Research, authorized in July 1953, to be established in Geneva, Switzerland.

> The aim . . . was . . . an organization in which could be pooled the resources . . . of a group of European countries no one of whom alone could afford to establish an adequate research center. . . . Its purpose is to . . . operate the center in the interests of peaceful developments of atomic energy and make its findings and conclusions available to the public and to other scientists.[51]

[50] "Eight Years of UNESCO Progress," *Department of State Bulletin*, Vol. 28, No. 730 (June 22, 1953), p. 886.

[51] "International Nuclear Research," *United Nations Bulletin*, Vol. 15, No. 3 (August 1, 1953), p. 103.

UNESCO has also sponsored research efforts to study the effect of high altitude and to develop arid zones and the Hylean Amazon area involving nine Latin American countries. Furthermore, UNESCO has surveyed the scientific facilities of various countries and advised on their further development, created four UNESCO Scientific Cooperation Offices in the major areas of the world to encourage regional coordination and development, devoted some attention to improving the quality of scientific teaching, and encouraged the popularization of socially significant scientific work. One distinguished UNESCO scientific field worker wrote,

> At Chiatung one discussed nuclear physics in the family temple within sight of the mountains of Tibet; in the caves of Kuangsi one found large power stations with engineers dying to talk to a technologist from the outside world; and among the aboriginal tribesfolk of Tali, one helped a planktonologist to launch his boat on the lake of Erh-Hai, beneath the Tower of the Five Glories.[52]

The social sciences are Johnny-came-lately's on the international scene, and their development has been considerably more rapid in some areas, notably the United States, than in others. Much of UNESCO's effort, therefore, has been devoted to fostering a network of world ties which took the form of International Sociological, Economic, and Political Science Associations and an International Committee of Comparative Law, all formed by 1949. An International Social Science Council was then created in October 1952 to help bind the others together. Regarding substantive issues UNESCO has been primarily interested in sponsoring studies aimed directly at easing international tensions. These have explored many significant areas:

> (1) the characteristics of some forty cultures, (2) peoples' concepts of their own and other nations, (3) modern methods of affecting attitudes, (4) influences which make for cooperation or aggression, (5) population pressures, and (6) the effect of technology.

Out of these efforts have emerged several suggestive studies including such books as *Tensions That Cause War,* edited by Hadley Cantril.[53] To grease the wheels of international organizations, studies have been undertaken regarding problems involved in international negotiation and administration. Lastly, a *Statement on Race* containing a brief analysis of that concept was issued in 1950, but criticism by British and American scientists led to a revision in 1952.

The Humanities

Philosophy, history and the creative arts tend to be jostled to one side by the "mass" programs. Nonetheless the International Council for Philosophy

---

[52] Besterman, *op. cit.,* pp. 32–33.

[53] (Urbana: University of Illinois Press, 1950); Also see Otto Klineberg, *Tensions Affecting International Understanding* (New York: Social Science Research Council, 1950); and Frederick S. Dunn, *War and the Minds of Men* (New York: Harper for the Council on Foreign Relations, 1950).

and Humanistic Studies has held meetings in cooperation with UNESCO on such subjects as modern languages and literature, folk arts and folklore, and orientalists. In 1950 an international commission of nine eminent scholars was appointed to oversee the preparation of a scientific and cultural history of mankind from earliest times to 1950 — another way of straining national bias out of history by emphasizing interaction rather than divisions among civilizations.

"To get writers and artists together in any one country is difficult enough; on the international plane the task is one to make a strong man blanch. It has in fact made a succession of officials in UNESCO throw in their hands; in no other field has there been so great a turnover of staff."[54] Nonetheless, UNESCO lived to see the formation of an International Theater Institute in 1948 and an International Council for Music in 1949. The first International Conference of Artists was held in the fall of 1952. Through these and other channels UNESCO has encouraged greater exchange of ideas, further development of artistic forms, and a wider availability of art to the general public, especially in the schools.

To improve the quality and circulation of written works UNESCO has set up a central exchange for articles contributing to international understanding, continued publication of the prewar index of translation (*Index Translationum*), and sponsored the translation of lesser known classics beginning with Arabic and Latin American works. Better legal protection for artistic works was sought through the formulation of a universal copyright convention and consideration of an Italian draft convention to safeguard cultural property in time of war. UNESCO also tried to gain wider usefulness for museums and libraries by working in collaboration with associations in those fields to improve their services; encourage a greater exchange of persons, information and materials; and increase free services to the general public. Although a collective catalogue for European libraries, similar to those in the United States, United Kingdom and elsewhere, had to be abandoned as too costly, studies and technical advice regarding bibliographical problems continue.

Circulation of Persons and Ideas

"Primary contacts provide the most important means for developing . . . [a] common framework of thinking."[55] To widen and strengthen these bridges among nations UNESCO has published an annual *Study Abroad — An International Handbook of Fellowships, Scholarships, and Educational Exchange* which in 1951 contained information on 35,000 awards in fifty-five states and territories. In this and other ways it has tried to encourage international study and travel, including the award of its own fellowships (forty-two in 1951) and those contributed by other organizations (twenty-seven in 1951).

To promote the best possible development of "mass communication"

[54] Besterman, *op. cit.*, p. 57.   [55] Dunn, *op. cit.*, p. 102.

(press, film, radio and television), UNESCO recently completed a four-year survey of these facilities in 156 countries and territories. Against this background it has urged action to meet the serious deficit of newsprint; promote uniformity in Braille and certain languages (Ceylon, India and Malaya); improve mass communication techniques; formulate two conventions to lower trade barriers for educational, scientific and cultural materials; lower postal rates; and provide resources to publicize United Nations programs. Its prolific publications program includes periodicals such as the quarterly *Bulletin on Fundamental and Adult Education, Fundamental Education Abstracts, Bulletin for Libraries,* the fellowship handbook mentioned above, monthly *Courier,* fortnightly *UNESCO Features* and a weekly radio script, *World Review.*

Technical assistance activities, like those of other specialized agencies, increased markedly with the development of the United Nations Expanded Technical Assistance Program, and UNESCO received $3 million from the United Nations in 1953. Following in the footsteps of the prewar organizations, UNESCO has done a better job of building cooperating national commissions than any other specialized agency, although they are still spotty and have not prevented some unfortunate opposition, especially in the United States. These groups are particularly important since much implementation of UNESCO recommendations depends on their activities at home. Regional emphasis has not developed as far as in some other agencies, notably the WHO, although it is growing through the efforts of the regional Scientific Cooperation Offices, which are now becoming involved in nonscientific work as well, and regional meetings of national commissions, beginning in Latin America and Asia. UNESCO has, however, gone further than most agencies in strengthening various nongovernmental organizations by giving them grants-in-aid which totaled $456,000 in 1951.

Persistent Issues

It is safe to say that no program has aroused greater hopes and, at the same time, greater frustration than the United Nations cultural work. It should be constantly remembered, however, that much of this disillusionment is inherent in the nature of the animal. In no other field is there greater diversity of interests, greater uncertainty as to objectives, greater lack of commonly accepted truths, and greater difficulty in relating activities to the political goals of the United Nations.

Too many critics have damned UNESCO by standards which that organization never pretended to follow, e.g., promoting certain specific doctrines such as capitalism or communism or attempting to foster all cultural interests for their own sake (known as the "university approach"). On the other hand, there are standards which UNESCO has adopted in its constitution and the yardsticks enunciated by Mr. Torres Bodet by which the organization can and should be judged. These are implied in the following objectives in Article 1 of the UNESCO Constitution:

1. promoting collaboration among the nations through education, science and culture in order to further universal respect for justice, for the rule of law and for . . . human rights and fundamental freedoms . . .
2. advancing the mutual knowledge and understanding of peoples, through all means of mass communication . . .
3. give fresh impulse to popular education and to the spread of culture . . .
4. maintain, increase and diffuse knowledge. . . .

Measured against these goals, UNESCO has accomplished much more than most people give it credit for and has gone considerably beyond the limited achievements of prewar cultural agencies. It has interested itself in a wider range of cultural questions than its predecessors. It has been supported by more money and hence more staff. Its projects are consciously pitched at lower levels to reach far wider audiences in far more countries, especially the underdeveloped areas. There is closer integration of program with related economic, social and political activities of other agencies. The prewar Institute of Intellectual Cooperation had nothing comparable to the fundamental education centers at Patzcuaro and Sirs-el-Layan. There is more direct rubbing of shoulders with people in the field, especially since the development of the United Nations Expanded Technical Assistance Program. There is closer coordination among the myriad governmental and nongovernmental bodies that beat their wings against the alluring cultural light. And the organization has made sincere, though not always effective, attempts to establish a set of priorities by which to control its programmatic appetite.

Culture and Politics

In spite of these impressive advances, however, UNESCO still flounders knee-deep in problems. There is the accusation that it is too "political" — or not "political" enough. It can, of course, scarcely ignore the fact that, without a free political climate, culture suffocates. Yet Julian Huxley undoubtedly went too far too soon in trying to promote unity on the basis of an all-embracing "scientific humanism." More important at this stage is to stress tolerance for all manner of philosophies compatible with democracy. Reinhold Niebuhr is also correct in pointing out that much worth-while cultural activity, such as fundamental education, cannot be guaranteed to produce democracy or peace. That does not mean, however, that all UNESCO efforts aimed at peace are, as he claims, usually "illusory." [56] Activities regarding the teaching of international relations and the alleviation of tensions can make direct and practical contributions in this direction.

The minimal values mentioned may also kindle serious antagonisms. The promotion of human rights and international cooperation has, for example, moved some isolationist fringe elements in the United States to launch

[56] "The Theory and Practice of UNESCO," *International Organization*, Vol. 4, No. 1 (February 1950), p. 6. For a somewhat different view, see Byron Dexter, "Yardstick for UNESCO," *Foreign Affairs*, Vol. 28, No. 1 (October 1949).

vicious attacks against UNESCO.[57] And the general public in the United States, unfortunately, is not armed with sufficient interest or knowledge to withstand such slander. UNESCO must do even more to build grass roots support as it goes, chiefly through its national commissions, but it cannot retreat from the basic values on which it was founded. In this connection it is also well to recall that UNESCO has been able to do precious little to effect a direct reconciliation of the Communist and non-Communist worlds, but no other agency has been able to do much more.

Core of the Problem

Only by seeing UNESCO as part of the larger political scene can one appreciate its true potential and limitations. One can thus understand why it has made more progress in some directions than in others. Where it has offered the most obvious contributions to national welfare and interfered least with established cultural patterns, it has met with some success: for example, in providing basic cultural tools, such as fundamental education and improving the equipment and techniques of mass communication, without emphasizing any controversial content. On the other hand, where it has attempted to reorient basic values without being able to guarantee any significant and certain benefits, it has met the greatest resistance: for example, in its efforts to build moral consensus and allay tensions.

Cultural contact does not automatically produce cooperation. Mr. Vyshinsky and Mr. Dulles have met many times and still do not speak the same language. But Messrs. Everyman in England and the United States, though they may never meet, are relatively close in their thinking. For contact to breed friendship, there must be cultural receptivity, a minimal social bridge anchored in mutual tolerance. When ideological antagonisms, reinforced by the formidable modern apparatus of government and technology, destroy even that narrow bridge, there is little hope for effective cooperation. But one must never give up hope. The best reply to intolerant and unscrupulous aggressiveness, whether Fascist or Communist, is well-informed realism, firm defense of basic democratic values, and perpetual readiness to negotiate feasible compromises which may yet save the world from total destruction.

Another frequent complaint is that too many irons have been thrust into the fire too quickly. Haiti is the classic example, and there is much truth here. But there are other relevant considerations that are frequently ignored. The immediate postwar situation required haste at the expense of some fumbling (though that is no excuse for Haiti). And the judgment as to excessive ambition is usually based on available financial resources. No sane person can claim for an instant that the program is too ambitious in terms of actual need. And who is to say what is a fair budget? There is no easy answer to this question. But the present budget of about $8.5 million seems inordinately modest. The United States contribution of $2.8

---

[57] For statement see *United States National Commission UNESCO News*, Vol. 5, No. 6 (December 1951), p. 7.

million is only 3 per cent of the \$96.3 million spent in 1952 on its own bilateral international information program. All of these frustrations are naturally reflected in various organizational strains and stresses discussed above in Chapter 9.

Suggestions for Further Reading

Books

Ascher, Charles S., *Program-Making in UNESCO, 1946–1951* . . . (Chicago: Public Administration Service, 1951).

Besterman, Theodore, *UNESCO* (London: Methuen & Co., Ltd., 1951).

Cantril, Hadley, ed., *Tensions That Cause War* (Urbana: University of Illinois Press, 1950).

Corbett, Percy E., *Law and Society in the Relations of States* (New York: Harcourt, Brace & Company, 1951).

Dunn, Frederick S., *War and the Minds of Men* (New York: Harper & Brothers for the Council on Foreign Relations, 1950).

Holcombe, Arthur N., *Human Rights in the Modern World* (New York: New York University Press, 1948).

Klineberg, Otto, *Tensions Affecting International Understanding* (New York: Social Science Research Council, 1950).

Lauterpacht, H., *International Law and Human Rights* (New York: F. A. Praeger, Inc., 1950).

Northrop, F. S. C., *The Meeting of East and West* (New York: The Macmillan Company, 1946).

Stoessinger, John, *The Refugee and International Organization*, unpublished dissertation (Cambridge: Harvard University, 1953).

Woodbridge, George, ed., *UNRRA*, 3 Vols. (New York: Columbia University Press, 1950).

Periodicals

Allen, Charles E., "World Health and World Politics," *International Organization*, Vol. 4, No. 1 (February 1950).

Ascher, Charles S., "The Development of UNESCO's Program," *International Organization*, Vol. 4, No. 1 (February 1950).

Binder, Carroll, "Freedom of Information and the United Nations," *International Organization*, Vol. 6, No. 2 (May 1952).

Claude, Inis L., Jr., "The Nature and Status of the Subcommission on Prevention of Discrimination and Protection of Minorities," *International Organization*, Vol. 5, No. 2 (May 1951).

Dexter, Byron, "Yardstick for UNESCO," *Foreign Affairs*, Vol. 28, No. 1 (October 1949).

Eagleton, Clyde, "Excesses of Self-Determination," *Foreign Affairs*, Vol. 31, No. 4 (July 1953).

Laves, Walter, "Eight Years of UNESCO Progress," *Department of State Bulletin*, Vol. 28, No. 730 (June 22, 1953).

May, Herbert L., "The International Control of Narcotic Drugs," *International Conciliation*, No. 441 (May 1948).

Mudaliar, Sir Arcot, "World Health Problems," *International Conciliation,* No. 491 (May 1953).

"Narcotic Drug Control," *International Conciliation,* No. 485 (November 1952).

Neal, Marian, "United Nations Programs in Haiti," *International Conciliation,* No. 468 (February 1951).

Niebuhr, Reinhold, "The Theory and Practice of UNESCO," *International Organization,* Vol. 4, No. 1 (February 1950).

Rees, Elfan, "The Refugee and the UN," *International Conciliation,* No. 492 (June 1953).

Ristelhueber, René, "International Refugee Organization," *International Conciliation,* No. 470 (April 1951).

"The International Labour Organization Since the War," *International Labour Review,* Vol. 67, No. 2 (February 1953).

Winslow, C.-E. A., "World Health Organization–Its Program and Accomplishments," *International Conciliation,* No. 439 (March 1948).

Documents

International Labor Organization, *International Labour Review, Director's Report, Studies and Reports,* and other documents.

United Nations, General Assembly and ECOSOC, *Official Records* and other documents.

UNESCO, *Report of the Director General* and other documents.

———, *Human Rights: Comments and Interpretations* (New York: Columbia University Press, 1949).

United States, *An Appraisal of the United Nations Educational, Scientific and Cultural Organization by the Delegation of the United States . . . to the Second Extraordinary Session of the General Conference of UNESCO . . . ,* Department of State Publication 5209 (Washington: U.S. Government Printing Office, 1953).

World Health Organization, *Annual Report of the Director-General, Bulletin, Chronicle,* and other documents.

League Supervision of Mandates,
Special Areas and Minorities

Mandates System

SINCE THE MANDATORY POWERS had assigned the mandated territories to themselves and had written the mandate charters (subsequently approved by the League Council which they also dominated), and since the Permanent Mandates Commission's membership, with one exception, was composed of nationals drawn from mandatory and other colonial states, it is understandable why the League did not strive to alter the policies of the mandatory powers in any fundamental respect. It tended, rather, to adopt their standards, sift out the better practices developed in various local administrations, and attempt to universalize them, thereby gradually elevating the general level of performance. Although there was widespread agreement within the League that the primary objective of the system was to promote the welfare of the peoples in the territories, and only secondarily the welfare of the mandatory and other states, the implementation of that vague principle was determined largely by the mandatory powers themselves. And, since wheels that don't squeak very loudly get little oil, the mandatory powers provided only meager budgets to improve the lot of the mandated peoples who, generally speaking, were unsophisticated, uninterested in western ways, uneducated, unhealthy and unorganized.

The mandates system got off to a slow start because of delays in the negotiation of the mandate charters. This was due in large measure to the uncooperative attitude of the United States which insisted on halting the negotiations so that it might confer with the Allied Powers directly, rather than through the League, in order to assure its citizens economic equality in the various territories (oil in Iraq was a major concern). The assignment of territories, made by the Allied Supreme Council (Britain, France, Italy, Japan, and, at first, the United States) largely in accordance with the wartime secret agreements mentioned in Chapter 10, was set forth in fourteen mandate charters negotiated between May 1919 and September 1923. They provided for the following distribution:

Mandated Territories	Square Miles	Population	Mandatory
Class "A"			
Iraq	116,600	3,700,000	Great Britain
Syria and Lebanon	77,220	3,650,000	France
Palestine and Trans-Jordan	26,230	1,700,000	Great Britain
Class "B"			
Tanganyika	360,000	5,200,000	Great Britain
Ruanda-Urundi	20,500	3,450,000	Belgium
Togoland (British)	13,041	340,000	Great Britain
Togoland (French)	21,893	750,000	France
Cameroons (British)	34,136	840,000	Great Britain
Cameroons (French)	166,489	2,520,000	France
Class "C"			
Southwest Africa	318,099	300,000	South Africa
New Guinea	93,000	670,000	Australia
North Pacific Islands	960	100,000	Japan
Western Samoa	1,130	60,000	New Zealand
Nauru	9	3,400	Great Britain

Once the "C" mandate charters had been confirmed by the League Council in December 1920, and the texts of the "A" and "B" mandates published, although they were still being negotiated, the Council went ahead to appoint the members of the Permanent Mandates Commission in February 1921, and that body met for its first session in October of the same year. Then the machinery quickly gathered momentum and developed methods and procedures which worked with surprising effectiveness, within the limits imposed on them, until the end of 1939. The greatest strain came with the rise of aggressive forces during the early thirties, particularly with Japan's clandestine violation of its mandatory obligations regarding demilitarization. Finally the Commission ceased to operate after its thirty-seventh session in December 1939.

Politics and Administration

In debating the broad mandates objective set forth in Covenant Article 22 — the "well-being and development" of the mandated peoples — the Commission and Council were soon confronted by the fundamental question: did the framers visualize the territories as self-contained independent areas or did they think of their advancement as integral parts of a mandatory power? In the case of the "A" mandates, independence and native hegemony seemed clearly anticipated. In the case of the "B" and "C" mandates, the issue was not so clear. Sir Frederick Lugard, expressing the general British policy, foresaw eventual though distant self-determination. On the other hand, General Freize d'Andrade, of Portugal, looked for "slow unforced assimilation of weak or inferior communities by strong or more highly developed communities." [1] He believed that, if one tried to preserve

---

[1] Permanent Mandates Commission, Minutes, Session VII, p. 196.

the cultures of the indigenous peoples, one shut them off from modern civilization and thus made it virtually impossible for them ever to govern
themselves under what the Covenant called "the strenuous conditions of
the modern world." These two conflicting philosophies often battled with
each other and were never entirely reconciled.

Just as the mandates organization was being established, this question
arose in a very concrete form with Iraq's bid for freedom. The Arabs of
Mesopotamia had revolted against the British mandate, and Britain had
seen fit to recognize the Kingdom of Iraq with Feisal, son of King Hussein
of Hejaz, as its ruler. In approving the Anglo-Iraq treaty of 1922, negotiated to confirm Britain's mandatory role, the Mandates Commission established the following criteria, among others, that were to govern the granting
of independence to mandated territories:

1. existence of a stable government including the capacity to maintain
territorial integrity and political independence, and
2. the existence of a clear intention to fulfill international responsibilities.[2]

The mandatory powers were by no means prepared to open wide the door
to independence but provided an elastic exit which they could control according to the circumstances. Iraq was the only territory which managed
during the interwar period to slip entirely through the exit when Great
Britain sponsored her admission to the League in 1932 as an "independent"
state (under British protection).

Another troublesome issue was the degree of political participation to
be allowed the indigenous populations. What respect should be given to
local customs and institutions? Should the mandatory's rule be direct, as the
French advocated, or indirect, as the British advocated? Except for the
"A" territories, the mandate charters did not provide specifically for native
participation in government. The Commission urged, nevertheless, increased use of native officials in advisory, or, where practicable, legislative
councils and the appointment of natives to responsible positions in courts
and administrative agencies.

In actual practice, the greatest degree of self-rule was granted where the
local peoples were politically most mature and vocal, largely the inhabitants of the "A" territories. Within those areas, more freedom was allowed
in Iraq and Trans-Jordan than in Syria, where French rule began by being
inflexibly stern, and in Palestine where the Jewish-Arab conflict made self-
rule exceedingly difficult. Even in the case of these two latter territories,
however, the Mandates Commission constantly urged greater independence
for the local peoples, and, when rebellion broke out in Syria in 1925, the
Commission's influence helped to win concessions for the indigenous groups,
including the recall of General Sarrail, the territory's administrator.

In some "B" and "C" territories, native advisory councils were established,
the greatest development of this kind occurring in Western Samoa. The

[2] See discussion in W. H. Ritsher, *Criteria of Capacity for Independence* (Jerusalem:
Syrian Orphanage Press, 1934), Chap. VII.

Commission leveled its strongest criticism against the policies followed in South-West Africa and Tanganyika where the administrations were the most antagonistic to native participation. In general, the lack of any widespread political sophistication among the indigenous peoples and the reluctance of the mandatory powers to let the reins slip from their hands made political advancement painfully slow. Even as late as 1942 no African native sat in a territorial legislature nor held an administrative position with territory-wide authority nor participated in elections to territorial positions.[3]

Economic and Social Issues

The major economic impetus in the territories came from outsiders from the mandatory states and other powers on the basis of the "open door" policy. These individuals were desirous of gaining a maximum return on their somewhat speculative development of local resources, largely mining and other raw material extraction, for a minimum expenditure. Opposed to this pressure was the resistance of the indigenous peoples to all external intervention, particularly to the many devices that were used by the invading carriers of civilization to capture the best land and compel the local people to work it. In an effort to mediate between these conflicting interests, the Commission and the Council were scarcely neutral but tended rather to recommend the more enlightened colonial policies of the day, especially those developed by Great Britain.

Struggle for Land. The traditional colonial land policy had been to grant "the survivors of the defeated tribes such compensation in reserves of land as the embittered feelings of the colonists [would] allow."[4] Although neither the Covenant nor the "A" and "C" mandate charters had laid down any specific land rules, the "B" mandate charters provided that the mandatory power must take into consideration native laws and customs and safeguard native rights and interests, and that the creation of rights over native land in favor of a non-native were to be subject to the mandatory state's prior consent. To enforce these provisions, the Commission made frequent observations that adequate reserves should be provided in all mandated territories and that native ownership should be encouraged. But where land was fertile, climate favorable, and non-natives numerous, control of the land still tended to slip out of the hands of the original inhabitants. In 1928 Raymond Leslie Buell summarized some of the mandatory land policies as follows:

> The natives under the rule of South Africa have been subject to a large number of restrictions. Holding only 8 per cent of the land . . . they have been obliged to seek work in European centers. . . . Moreover the legisla-

---

[3] Rayford W. Logan, *The Operation of the Mandate System in Africa, 1919–1927* (Washington: The Foundation Publishers, 1942), p. 22.

[4] A. H. Snow, *The Question of Aborigines in the Law and Practice of Nations* (Washington: Government Printing Office, 1949), p. 134.

tion forbidding natives to buy land outside the reserves makes the natives' problem of existence more difficult than ever.[5] The Tanganyika Land Ordinance . . . accepts the principle of protecting native rights in land . . . but it does not establish a procedure that will insure that the principle will be applied.[6] While the Cameroons land law is an improvement over the West Africa law . . . it does not appear adequately to safeguard native interests.[7]

Protecting Labor. More difficult questions arose concerning the natives' other major asset, their labor. The Covenant and "C" mandates prohibited the slave *trade* but not *slavery* itself. The St. Germain treaty, negotiated at the same time as the Covenant, went on to "secure the complete suppression of slavery in all its forms." This obligation was also incorporated in the "B" mandates together with two related provisions: (1) the prohibition of all forms of "forced or compulsory labor, except for essential public works and services" (also repeated in the "C" mandates); and (2) "the careful supervision of labor contracts and the recruiting of labor" (omitted in the "C" mandates). Three members of the Mandates Commission sat on the Temporary Slavery Committee which produced the Slavery Convention of 1926 that considerably tightened previous treaties against slavery. As a result of these efforts, most of the situations involving slavery in the mandated territories were cleared up during the first decade of the Mandates Commission's existence.

In spite of the above provisions on forced labor, however, there was less consensus among the colonial powers on this question than on slavery and therefore greater difficulty in regulating it. Finally the ILO, in collaboration with the Mandates Commission, succeeded in formulating the 1930 draft convention which aimed at prohibiting all forced labor after a transitional period (originally five years but extended indefinitely in 1936) during which forced labor on public projects would be allowed under specified conditions which went far beyond the "B" and "C" mandates in protecting native interests. By 1939, the 1930 convention had been ratified by eighteen states including all the major colonial powers. Three other ILO measures also protected the workers in mandated as well as other colonial areas: Recruiting of Indigenous Workers Convention, 1936; Penal Sanctions (Indigenous Workers) Convention, 1939; and Contracts of Employment (Indigenous Workers) Convention, 1939.

Consequently, private forced labor was substantially suppressed, and public forced labor regulated. In the French Cameroons the Commission was able to persuade the mandatory power to liberalize its labor tax far beyond the standards observed in regular French colonies. The Commission's questioning also led to British action to correct abuses in the Cameroons system which provided partial payment in credit to be used in company stores. Aside from the extreme problems of slavery and forced labor, however, the Council and Commission had little success in achieving any

---

[5] *The Native Problem in Africa* (New York: Macmillan, 1928), Vol. 1, p. 86. Used with the permission of The Macmillan Company.
[6] *Ibid.*, p. 490.   [7] *Ibid.*, p. 335.

significant advancement in general labor standards. Since the local workers were largely agricultural, untrained, and unorganized, and since their employers were scarcely eager to encourage such progress, the Commission's most positive act was to appoint a committee which drew up a set of ideal standards on pay, hours, injury compensation, medical care, housing and related matters.

"Open Door" and Economic Development. During most of the interwar period, the "open door" policy ("equal opportunities" for all League Members for "trade and commerce" in the territories) was strongly supported by the great trading nations, primarily Great Britain and the United States, who felt that they had far more to gain by this principle than they could possibly lose. Thus the policy was not only required by the Covenant in the case of "B" mandates, but it was also observed in actual practice in both "A" and "C" territories with few exceptions. Consequently the Commission's remarks on Australian legislation restricting trade with New Guinea to Australian ships resulted in a prompt repeal of the law.

The *laissez faire* school of economics had long insisted that free access to underdeveloped areas would benefit the peoples of those territories as much as it would benefit their more advanced neighbors. It gradually became apparent, however, that this was by no means automatic and that the "open door" policy could very well be part of a pattern of unregulated exploitation of the poor and backward by the rich and advanced. Thus the Commission expressed its concern that the natives be allowed to participate in the economic activity made possible by the "open door" doctrine, but it never succeeded in modifying that doctrine to any appreciable degree for the benefit of the indigenous peoples.

During the interwar years, economic development was exceedingly limited in most of the mandated territories. The reasons for this included the mandatory powers' uncertainty concerning the future status of the areas; their reluctance to foster manufacturing enterprises that would compete with home production; and the relative absence of profitable investment opportunities, local capital, trained labor, and basic transport and communications facilities. As one might expect, most developmental activity took place in the "A" territories through such channels as the oil development in Iraq and various Zionist programs in Palestine. In general Great Britain and Japan invested the largest sums in their mandated territories; Belgium and the Dominions, the next largest; and France, the least.

Education and Health. While the mandatory powers recognized the benefits that would accrue to them through providing useful education and better health care for the local populations, they seldom felt that they could spare as much money on these matters as on economic development which would pay immediate dividends. In the educational field, the Commission opposed policies, often identified with French administration, that would alienate a few Europeanized natives from their own peoples. Instead the Commission suggested greater development of native teachers and native languages, the elimination of nationalistic pro-mandatory propaganda, and a practical curriculum that would make the natives more proficient workers in such fields as agriculture, animal husbandry, arts and crafts, and elementary hygiene. On the whole, therefore, the mandates system did stimulate educational effort but not beyond the standards observed in most comparable colonial areas.

The Commission also urged the adoption of improved methods to combat disease. For example, at its fourth session, the Commission expressed the "hope" that it would be possible for Great Britain to devote larger sums to the improvement of public health in Tanganyika; fortunately, at its eleventh session, it was able to note that the amount had been substantially increased. At the same time a considerable amount of health work was being done by various governmental and private agencies, and the League's role, channeled largely through the Health Organization, was primarily one of coordination, circulation of information and constant encouragement.

Conclusions

Above all, it should be recognized that the principal tensions in the mandated territories resulted from the impingement of modern industrial civilizations upon undeveloped agricultural communities. And no international system created in 1919 could have been expected to alter significantly the accumulated experience of centuries. All the League could reasonably have been expected to do was to support the more liberal colonial policies of its day, and this it did. The League was not, however, the only — nor even the major — reason for the progress that was made. The forces of enlightened self-interest, humanitarianism, and a new school of progressive colonial administration were the major elements that leavened the governing of all dependent areas throughout the world.

The fundamental significance of the mandates system was not that it erased the old-fashioned type of outright unilateral annexation and exploitation but that it superimposed on that system a pattern of indirect supervision exercised by a permanent international organization. It was by no means a revolutionary innovation, merely a more effective and more ambitious application of the familiar concepts of neutralization and trusteeship. Still the effect was more like annexation than internationalization since the mandatory powers dominated it. It was they who wielded direct administrative authority in the territories, and the Council and Mandates Commission were kept at a safe distance in Geneva, reviewing reports and asking questions about events that had long since been embalmed in history.

Feeble as it was, however, the system resulted in certain positive influences which probably would not have materialized had it not existed. Once the mandatory powers, acting through the Council, had created the Mandates Commission, they found their nationals sitting on that body criticizing and comparing the performances of their own territorial administrations and suggesting improvements. The very process of dragging the records of these regimes into the cold light of regular and searching international inquiries was a healthy corrective for narrow national policies. Thus the machinery which the mandatory powers themselves had created began ever so cautiously and gradually to raise the level of their administrations.

The most fundamental weaknesses in the League's supervision of the mandated territories were: that the system was overwhelmingly dominated by the thinking of colonial rather than noncolonial powers; that the private and public interests engaged in exploitation of the territories were the controlling influences; that the "open door" policy was enforced in spite of, and not in behalf of, the interests of the indigenous populations; that political advancement was excessively sluggish except where local pressures, particularly in the "A" territories, forced it; that relatively little money was spent on the territories and what was spent was guided far more by the interests of the mandatories than of the native peoples; and that the feeble influence of the League was greatly muffled by its isolation in terms of authority, space and time.

Special Areas

THE SAAR

In spite of the conscientious efforts of the League Council and the Governing Commission to administer the Saar Territory with impartiality and patience, the basic decision to detach the area from Germany so poisoned the minds and hearts of the inhabitants against the Versailles settlement that the regime was never able to win any significant confidence or cooperation. The sky was darkest during the early twenties, particularly in the period of the Franco-Belgian occupation of the Ruhr. Some rays of optimism broke through during the false sunrise of the Locarno era, but the depression and Herr Hitler blackened the horizon again and created a tragic climate for the plebiscite in 1935.

Political Issues

It is scarcely surprising that one of the first major complaints voiced by the Saarlanders was their lack of any real legislative authority. The Versailles Treaty had provided that the Governing Commission should merely "consult" the inhabitants' representatives in a manner determined by the Commission. But when draft ordinances were submitted to the traditional municipal and district councils (*Kreistage*), which had been newly elected in July 1920, these bodies protested the passive role forced upon them and rejected the draft measures. The Commission then provided for the election of a single Advisory Council (*Landesrat*) of thirty members and the appointment by the Commission of a Technical Committee of eight. The *Landesrat* proved as unfriendly as its predecessors, however, and the Technical Committee, though more tractable, lacked the people's confidence.

For the most part, therefore, the Commission ruled the Saar with no official popular endorsement of its acts.

Another issue that exploded in the Commission's face just as it was getting settled was the German civil servants' outburst against a series of decisions affecting their status: the dismissal of certain of their colleagues, particularly at the higher levels; the importation of seventy-three non-Germans (including forty-three French nationals) to replace the dismissed individuals; and the requirement of an oath of allegiance to the Commission. In August 1920, all state employees decided to strike, and they were supported by a twenty-four-hour sympathy strike of all Saar labor. When the Commission firmly counterattacked, however, by proclaiming a state of siege and expelling the leaders of the demonstration, the rank and file ended their resistance and served thereafter ably and conscientiously. It should also be mentioned that the Governing Commission had agreed from the beginning to retain the great majority of the 8,500 German civil servants, including the heads of the police organization.

The populace was also incensed by the Commission's decision to keep French occupation troops in the area as "garrison" forces. The fact that many of them were Africans seemed to rub salt in the wound. Both the League Council and the Commission recognized that this was not a desirable situation, but the Commission found it difficult to create an adequate police force quickly, particularly in the turbulent early twenties. Thus the agitation did not subside until 1930 when the last French forces were withdrawn at the time of the evacuation of the Rhineland.

All of these separate resentments were concentrated and fanned into a fierce conflagration by the French and Belgian occupation of the Ruhr in 1923. The Saar miners, normally a most restrained and reasonable lot as well as the most important labor group in the Territory, led the revolt by going out on strike in sympathy with their brothers in the Ruhr. The Commission then retaliated with an ordinance that placed such extreme limitations on civil liberties that the League Council ordered an inquiry. As a result of this pressure, the ordinance was replaced with a milder one, and the storm subsided as the Saarlanders saw that the League would protect their basic freedoms.

Hope and Disillusionment. After the conclusion of the Dawes Plan easing German reparations in 1924, the signing of the Locarno treaties in 1925, and the removal of the unpopular French chairman of the Governing Commission in favor of the engaging Mr. Stephens in 1926, the general political atmosphere brightened considerably. In 1929, optimism reached its zenith as Aristide Briand and Gustav Stresemann initiated negotiations to settle the Saar issue before the expiration of the fifteen-year period, presumably by returning the Saar to Germany in exchange for certain economic concessions to France. Unfortunately Stresemann died a month before the negotiations actually began. Neither side proved very conciliatory thereafter, and the conversations fizzled out in July 1930. Then the paralyzing hand of the depression fell upon the Territory, and the rise of Hitler withered all hope of an amicable settlement.

As the fateful hour for the plebiscite approached, the League Council on June 16, 1934, appointed a special Plebiscite Commission composed of three nationals of "neutral" countries (Henry of Switzerland, de Iongh of the Netherlands, and Rodhe of Sweden) plus a technical adviser and deputy member of the Commission (Miss Wambaugh of the United States). While previous to the rise of Hitler there had never been any doubt that the Saar would vote overwhelmingly to return to Germany, the unwholesome odor of the Nazi regime caused some Saarlanders at the eleventh hour to question the wisdom of leaping out of the frying pan so hastily. The leaders of the anti-Nazi and *pro-status quo* movement were the Social Democrats and the Communists who had formed an Anti-Fascist Front late in 1933. But the momentum of the movement to return to the fatherland was too powerful, and the Nazis used every device to hitch their wagon to that movement. The plebiscite which took place on January 13, 1935, was most efficiently organized and executed. A truly international police force, contributed for the occasion by four countries (the United Kingdom, Italy, the Netherlands and Sweden), was a major factor in maintaining relative peace on the fateful day. The results were as follows: [8]

Votes cast	528,105
Union with Germany	477,119
Status quo	46,613
Union with France	2,124
Invalid and blank	2,197

The heart of the Saar's economic anatomy, coal, was in the hands of the French Ministry of Public Works operating through a local administration known as *Mines Domaniales Françaises de la Sarre*. The Governing Commission had relatively little influence in this field except to see that the French administration stayed within the bounds of the Versailles provisions. The general effect of the French operation of the mines was to increase their efficiency without greatly enhancing their profitability.[9] Because of the traditional marriage of Saar coal to Lorraine iron, French interests were not only eager to take advantage of the expropriation of Saar holdings in the recovered Alsace-Lorraine but also began to buy control over Saar steel mills from the financially embarrassed German owners. When the franc fell in 1926, however, and the mark waxed virile, there began to be a retreat of French capital from the Saar which was accelerated as the depression took its toll and the time for the plebiscite approached.

The Saar's trade position was singularly fortunate and symbolic of the Territory's split personality. In accordance with the Versailles Treaty, trade moved freely between the Saar and both Germany and France from

[8] Sarah Wambaugh, *The Saar Plebiscite* (Cambridge: Harvard University Press, 1940), p. 304.

[9] Michael T. Florinsky, *The Saar Struggle* (New York: Macmillan, 1934), pp. 55–62.

1920 to 1925. From 1925 on, the door to France remained open, while that to Germany was only partially closed. Because of the increased French influence, however, the general trend was an increase of Saar exports of coal and steel to France in return for expanded agricultural imports. Still, Germany remained an important customer, especially for metals for which she was the Saar's largest outlet.

Bouquets have frequently been tossed to the Governing Commission for having managed the Territory's finances so efficiently that it was left with a balanced budget and no public debt. But one student of the Territory has pointed out that the Commission was compelled to live conservatively since no one was willing to lend it any money.[10] Furthermore taxation was greatly increased, and the government received, in accordance with the Versailles settlement, large sums from the Reich for social insurance and pension to war veterans. The major financial innovation, moreover, was initiated not by the Commission but by the French government whose payments in francs to all its employees influenced the Territory in 1923 to adopt the franc as its sole legal tender, a move which reinforced French economic and political leadership.

Labor and Education

Saar working people, whose elite were the miners, had traditionally been conservative, stable, and securely rooted in small bucolic villages from which they commuted to the mines and mills. And the Commission and French mines administration tried conscientiously to keep them as contented as possible since it was obvious that the skilled labor force was the Territory's greatest asset. Fortunately the fact that Saar labor received its wages in francs protected it from the worst of the German inflation during the early twenties, and the preferential trade situation helped to shield the area from the depression. Nevertheless labor was in the forefront of the movement to return the Territory to German sovereignty and, contrary to the assumptions of our economic determinists, never allowed economic considerations to obstruct national sentiments.

A particularly fiery social issue was the question of education. The Saarlanders were most incensed by alleged French pressure to persuade them to send their children to the French schools which the Versailles Treaty had provided might be maintained "as incidental to the mines" for the employees and children of the French state. Even in these schools, however, instruction was carried on in both German and French. Furthermore in 1923 only 4,000 German children were attending these schools as compared with 123,000 in the national schools. Nevertheless, the Commission employed a Luxembourg professor to investigate the situation and, after the League Council had debated the question, issued a statement emphasizing the right of all inhabitants to patronize schools of their own free choice.

10 *Ibid.*, p. 158.

Conclusions

Contrary to the dire predictions of those who believed that direct international administration would not be efficient, the Governing Commission performed the functions assigned it with remarkable competence and patience. It provided relatively neutral government, guaranteed the inhabitants' basic rights, maintained order, furnished necessary public services, and fostered the economic and social welfare of the population. Judged even in these limited terms, however, the Commission displayed several weaknesses: a lack of sufficient impartiality in the early years, an unfortunate stiffness towards the people, an inclination to place order above free democratic expression, and an excessively cautious attitude on both political and economic matters. The most fundamental difficulty, of course, was the original decision to separate the Territory from Germany to which the overwhelming majority of the inhabitants were firmly attached by culture and sentiment. This decision prevented the League regime from winning any real popular support so that it was compelled to govern even more undemocratically than had originally been intended. The final lesson of this experiment is that such a callous arrangement constantly exacerbates relations among the interested powers, discredits the international organization given the thankless job of administration, distorts democratic principles, and inflames the local population.

DANZIG

In judging the League's record in supervising the free city of Danzig, it is important to recall that the Peace Conference internationalized Danzig not primarily because of unadulterated altruism but because the balance of power at the Conference made it impossible to grant the city outright to either Poland or Germany. Although Danzig had for centuries enjoyed a substantial degree of autonomy, its people and culture were German, and the special privileges which the peace settlement granted Poland merely served to strengthen the Danzigers' reliance on the Reich. Thus the League was charged with the delicate task of helping Danzig to walk the tightrope of internationally guaranteed autonomy, while Poland and Germany did everything they could to shake the Free City into their own respective power spheres.

Political Tensions

The political history of the Danzig regime was an endless series of altercations between the Danzigers and the Poles rising to an unhappy crescendo with the conquest of the Free City by Hitler's Nazis in September 1939. During the early years there were many disputes centering around conflicting interpretations of the basic laws with a constant stream of appeals to the League Council until the Polish Government finally challenged the High Commissioner's mandate. When the Council gave the Commissioner a strong vote of confidence, the air cleared appreciably. Then, in

June 1925, the extreme Danzig Nationalist Party was replaced by a more conciliatory coalition of Centrists, Liberals and Social Democrats. But the Nationalists returned in the autumn of 1926 to stir the witches' caldron again. Then the coalition came back in January 1928 and retained office until late 1930 when the Nazis began their ominous rise to power.

In 1933 the Nazis won a clear majority, and one of their adherents, H. Rauschning, was made President of the Senate for the first time. The Nazis then followed a temporary policy of conciliation with Poland, but, by 1934, the more extreme Albert Forster forced Rauschning to resign and revealed the mailed fist that had been hidden only momentarily by the policy of collaboration. The constitutional ark of the Free City then began to founder in spite of the League's determined bailing efforts during much of the mid-thirties. The Council issued a stern reprimand in January 1936 which produced at least token concessions on the part of the Nazis, but France and Great Britain were soon cowed by Hitler. Finally, the Nazis were able in September 1939 to pluck the forbidden fruit, safe in the knowledge that the League by that time was little more than a scarecrow.

Life Blood of Commerce

The most fundamental economic issue was the struggle between Poland and Danzig over control of the trade passing between Poland and the Baltic. After Danzig dock workers refused to unload munitions for Poland's use in 1920 against Russia, the Polish Government decided to build Gdynia, only ten miles from Danzig, out of the silt and sand dunes into a rival port, and used it increasingly to take trade away from the Free City. The latter was virtually a dead city by 1933 with 50 percent of its workers unemployed. Danzigers were furious about this development and at the same time resisted Poland's efforts to control the port of Danzig. Although Poland's normal and most profitable trade routes ran east and west, she artificially stimulated maritime traffic via the Baltic, regardless of cost, to support Gdynia and justify retaining the Corridor.

Customs policies were also bedevilled by these conflicting interests. Danzig was small, urban, industrial, technically advanced and accustomed to a high standard of living. She wanted, therefore, to be free to import food, raw materials and capital goods and to export her finished consumer goods. Poland, on the other hand, was large, rural, agricultural, technically backward and poor. To protect her weak industry, reduce her foreign debt, and husband her meager resources, she instituted severe foreign trade controls that cut both imports and exports to a bare minimum. For these reasons Danzig constantly fought the Polish customs administration, which she insisted was trying to strangle her. Other serious economic disputes concerned the administration of the waterways and railway system.

Conclusions

In all fairness, the League's performance should be judged strictly in terms of what the League was asked to do. Under the Versailles Treaty and the subsequent Danzig-Polish agreement and the Danzig constitution, the League was directed to protect the autonomous status of the city and mediate disputes between Poland and Danzig. It performed both of these functions remarkably well, against great pressures, especially from the Nazis, until 1939 when Hitler finally overwhelmed the city. League debates and reprimands were significant forces which helped to hold off the Nazi flood during years when other territories (the Rhineland, Austria and Czechoslovakia) were unable to withstand the tide.

The problem which the League failed to solve had not actually been assigned to it: the establishment of friendly relations between Danzig and Poland and the promotion of sound economic cooperation between the two regimes. These were problems that flowed directly from the basic decisions, made at Paris and not at Geneva, to separate Danzig from Germany, make it an autonomous city under League protection, and give Poland special privileges therein. Although the League Council and its High Commissioner did what they could to implement this settlement, the basic situation was beyond both their authority and capacity to correct.

Protecting Minorities

The course that the League minorities system steered can best be understood by recalling the major political winds that buffeted it. Great Britain was primarily interested in maintaining a peaceful balance of power in Europe; was not closely allied to any particular continental country; and tended to counteract some of France's pressures, especially by defending German interests against Poland contrary to France's pro-Polish tendencies. France, on the other hand, considered herself increasingly dependent on the support of a ring of Eastern European countries (Poland, Czechoslovakia, Rumania and Yugoslavia) and was inclined to side with them against their respective minorities. Germany used its influence to promote the interests of German peoples incorporated within other states, particularly Poland and Czechoslovakia, and, with the rise of Hitler, used this effort as a lever to help pry loose territorial concessions. The minority groups, on the other hand, were usually not as well represented in Geneva as were the national governments except when they had the vigorous support of some power such as Germany.

The general pattern of League action in this field began in an atmosphere highly charged with the doctrine of "self-determination," encouraged and accentuated by the Paris Peace Conference debates. Then, as the newly born East European governments gathered strength, mothered by France, the League became more sensitive to their interests, more cautious in its activities, and less patient with some of the more obstreperous minorities. But the lid was never clamped down altogether, even during the relative calm of the Locarno era. The pro-minority forces, emphasizing the need for a permanent minorities commission, even persuaded the League

Commission to undertake a thorough self-examination (the 1929 Adatci Report) which resulted in a few minor changes, but left the basic system untouched. But the twin scourges of depression and aggression gave rise to increased minority friction, especially in connection with German Jewish and irredentist agitation, until by 1939 the system was little more than a frustrated ghost.

Range of Minorities

The most difficult problem had its source in the presence of approximately a million Germans in Poland — in the Corridor and Polish Upper Silesia. Because these groups were of a higher status and level of sophistication, therefore more vocal, than the Poles in Germany, they tended to give rise to greater disturbances. Another explosive group was the Ukrainian minority of five million in the southern part of the Polish Republic. On the other hand, the three million Jews in Poland seem to have been treated with a considerable measure of wisdom and restraint and never submitted any complaints to the League.

The three million Sudeten Germans in Czechoslovakia (about 21 per cent of the population) were more compactly differentiated from the dominant majority than were the Germans in Poland. Although they were generally well treated and, what is more interesting, largely ignored by the German government until the situation became politically profitable in 1938, this group was always restless and discontented. But again the 350,-000 Jews in Czechoslovakia never felt it necessary to turn to the League for help. The inhabitants of Sub-Carpathian Russia in Czechoslovakia also seem to have been considerately treated with League support and approval. In Rumania it was the 1,500,000 Hungarian bourgeoisie of Transylvania, encouraged by the Hungarian government, who constantly badgered the Rumanian Government, which reciprocated in full measure. The Macedonian minority in Yugoslavia, claimed by Bulgaria, was also a source of frequent petitions to the League. And the 575,000 Germans and 450,000 Hungarians were also used by their home governments to stir up trouble in Yugoslavia. While there were other minority groups protected by international arrangements in Finland, Latvia, Estonia, Lithuania, Greece, Albania, Austria, Bulgaria and Hungary, they were of little significance as compared with those already mentioned.

Roots of Conflict

The basic political issue in the minorities field arose from the fact that the dominant groups in the unstable East European states, many of them newly created, were intensely jealous of their prerogatives and not at all generous about sharing them with minorities. Petitions were thus submitted to the League regarding many varieties of political discrimination, and the League did what it could to win concessions. For example, problems connected with the acquisition of Polish nationality, one of the many complaints in the controversial area of nationality, were settled by German-

Polish negotiations under League Council auspices in 1924. The dominant majorities were also interested in promoting their economic interests, often to the annoyance of the minorities. These matters involved such issues as discrimination in the awarding of governmental contracts, in taxation, in land reform programs, and in compensation and transfer operations connected with territorial adjustments.

The majority governments were also eager to bind the minorities to them by winning their minds through education and propaganda. But minority resistance was particularly uncompromising on these questions and provided a constant flow of grist for the League mill concerning education, religion, and the free use of minority languages. A dispute which consumed prodigious quantities of time, ink and paper arose in Upper Silesia when thousands of Poles tried, for a variety of reasons, to take advantage of the minority schools to have their children taught in German. The Polish Government tried to halt this annoying retreat from Polish enlightenment and thereby initiated a lengthy dispute considered by both the League Council and the Permanent Court of Justice both of which bodies rendered conciliatory decisions but never succeeded in resolving the conflict entirely.

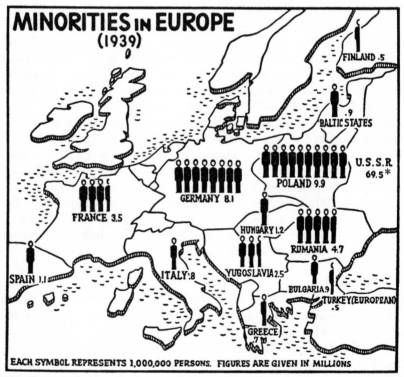

*This figure includes minority population of both Europe and Asiatic autonomous states of the U.S.S.R.

Headline Series, *Foreign Policy Association*

Conclusions

A critical study of the minorities system has called it little more than "a local anaesthetic against certain cases of preventible suffering," but admits that it was "an infinite advance on anything existing before" World War I.[11] It established a permanent and influential forum open to all petitioners and prepared to undertake investigation, negotiation and diplomatic pressure to correct abuses on political, economic and cultural issues. It accomplished most where the great powers cooperated in persuading the parties to compromise, where the treaty states adopted reasonable attitudes, and where the minorities were relatively quiescent. When these auspicious conditions did not exist, the League could do little but stand on one foot and scowl. But the weakness of this system was merely one twig on the branch of the League's general weakness. Furthermore one may well ask whether the basic philosophy underlying the minorities was sound: whether an international organization should attempt to cast its protective mantle over a few special groups, setting them apart from their neighbors, or whether it should devote its efforts to promoting universal minimum human rights for the entire populations of all countries.

Suggestions for Further Reading

See list at end of Chapter 10 together with the following:

Books

Buell, Raymond Leslie, *The Native Problem in Africa*, 2 Vols. (New York: The Macmillan Company, 1928).

Logan, Rayford W., *The Operation of the Mandate System in Africa, 1919–1927* (Washington: The Foundation Publishers, Inc., 1942).

Ritsher, W. H., *Criteria of Capacity for Independence* (Jerusalem: Syrian Orphanage Press, 1934).

[11] C. A. Macartney, *National States and National Minorities* (New York and London: Oxford University Press, 1934), p. 391.

23

UN Supervision of Trust and

Non-Self-Governing Territories

'The noise of the drums rises as the large car approaches, its cloud of dust sweeping up on it and engulfing it for a moment as it draws to a halt. Eight white men climb out, a little unsteady after the long jolting. . . . The rhythm of the drums mounts, it drowns everything as the visitors are led through the great square where musicians, dancers and a thousand spectators turn their eager gaze onto the white men, who have come from the other end of the earth to see them and hear their wishes. . . ."[1]

Trusteeship System at Work

THROUGH SUCH "visiting missions" as the one described above, and in many other ways, the UN trusteeship system is today becoming a living reality to many of the twenty million inhabitants of the eleven trust territories in the Pacific Ocean and Africa that have been placed under its supervision. Since the pattern of interests that has shaped its creation and evolution is fundamentally the same as that which hovered over the League system, one is not surprised to note the fundamental continuity between the UN and League experiences in this field. The administering powers still have the upper hand through their direct administration of the territories. The international organization is restricted to indirect surveillance via annual reports, petitions, oral questioning and discussion, recommendations (and now visiting missions) but not binding commands. On the other hand, the climate has grown markedly more friendly towards the native inhabitants due primarily to the qualified liberalism of the United States (increasingly muted by its involvement in the colonial problems of its allies, especially the United Kingdom and France), the greater influence of Asian and other anti-colonial countries in the international organization (particularly the Assembly), the development of more enlightened policies within the colonial

[1] John MacLaurin, *The United Nations and Power Politics* (New York: Harper, 1951), p. 335.

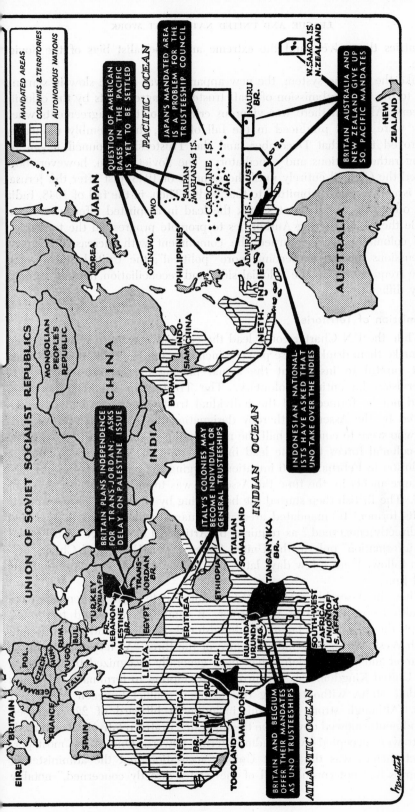

The black areas shown on the map are the mandates created after World War I from former territories of Germany and the Ottoman Empire. Syria and Lebanon had, by 1946, been recognized as independent states. The United Kingdom attempted, without success, to solve the Palestine problem without open hostilities. All the other mandated territories were placed under the trusteeship system, with the exception of South-West Africa which the Union of South Africa hoped to absorb. *(The New York Times, January 20, 1946)*

countries themselves, and the extreme anti-imperialist bias of the Soviet bloc.

Like the League system, the new apparatus was a little slow in starting due to the tardy submission of draft trusteeship agreements by the colonial powers. Although there was vigorous criticism of those agreements when they were finally produced in the fall of 1946, the Assembly ultimately approved them that December, and the Trusteeship Council began by being rather cautious and conciliatory. The Soviet Union, however, boycotted the Council entirely until the summer of 1948, just after the Jerusalem issue had been submitted to that body. Then, in the fall of 1948, India and other anti-colonial states took the lead in a spirited offensive to persuade the Administering Authorities to promote progress in the territories. The colonial powers returned the compliment with increased hostility. Discussions seemed to become more "political"; the United States voted more frequently with the colonial side; and reconciliation became increasingly difficult.

Submission of Territories

While the UN Charter could lead the colonial powers to water, it could not make them drink. Those powers, including the United States, had been most careful to insist that the actual placing of territories under UN supervision be entirely voluntary. The Trusteeship Council, moreover, could not be formed until the individual trust agreements had been approved by the Assembly, thereby designating the Administering Authorities who were to comprise half the membership of the Council. Hence the anti-colonial forces took the lead in persuading the Assembly to adopt a resolution in February 1946 impatiently urging the colonial powers to submit agreements by the time the Assembly was to meet again in the fall of 1946. The British then started the ball rolling by circulating proposed texts for its former "B" mandated areas in January to those states it regarded as "directly concerned," as required by Article 79 of the UN Charter, and "for information" only to the United States, Soviet Union and China. Belgium followed suit a few days later, but France did not circulate its drafts until June.

When the Assembly reconvened in October 1946, eight agreements were submitted covering all of the former "B" and "C" mandated territories, except the previously Japanese-administered Pacific islands, Nauru and South-West Africa. The independence of the three "A" territories — Syria, Lebanon and Trans-Jordan — had been generally recognized by that time. The United Kingdom was concurrently attempting to terminate Palestine's mandate status without giving rise to open conflict between Arabs and Jews. Although strong criticism, including a blizzard of 229 proposed amendments, snowed down upon the suggested drafts, relatively few amendments were accepted by the administering powers. One of the most persistent themes was the Soviet Union's accusation that the administering countries had not consulted all of the "states directly concerned," notably the Soviet Union. The upshot of this dispute was that the Assembly approved the eight agreements in December 1946 without specifying what states were directly concerned and recognizing that no country had waived or prejudiced its right to claim to be such a state. Other issues which agitated this debate and are discussed below in connection with the subsequent evolution of the system included the following: authorization to administer a trust area as an "integral part" of the Administering Authority's territory, consultation with the indigenous inhabitants regarding the trust agreements, international supervision of fortified areas, nationality status of the inhabitants, possibility of direct international administration, desirability and legality of custom unions, and guaranteeing equal rights for all commercial interests. It was because of the allegedly pro-colonial decisions on many of these questions, especially with respect to the "states directly concerned," that the Soviet Union decided not to take its seat in the Trusteeship Council until the summer of 1948.

In accordance with the compromise worked out within the United States Government, the Pacific mandated islands were submitted as "strategic trust territories" to the Security Council, rather than the General Assembly, in February 1947. Although the United States had begun during the war by championing the objectives of independence and commercial equality, it included neither goal in its draft, in deference to Congressional and military opinion. Under pressure from most of the other Security Council members, however, it was finally decided to add independence. The agreement was approved in April 1947. The arrangement for Nauru was delayed by discussions among the three Commonwealth countries involved (Australia, New Zealand and the United Kingdom), particularly over the administration of the main industry, the phosphate works. An agreement was ultimately approved by the Assembly in November 1947.

Problem of South-West Africa. While all other colonial powers have accepted the basic objectives of the trusteeship system, at least officially, and have placed their "B" and "C" mandated territories under that system, the Union of South Africa alone has turned its face in the opposite direction, declaring that "non-Europeans will never have the same political rights as the Europeans," [2] and resolutely refusing to expose the former mandated area of South-West Africa to UN supervision. In the fall of 1946, the South African delegation explained that the native peoples, who had, before the war, engaged in the Bondelswarts and other disturbances, had apparently experienced a change of heart and a majority, speaking through their traditional chieftains, now favored absorption of their lands by the Union. But a majority of the Assembly, led by India's Sir Maharaj Singh, did not believe that the Africans were sufficiently informed on the subject to make a balanced decision. In vain did Field Marshal Smuts quote the quaint sentiments of Chief Kasiki of the Bunja Tribe in Okavango:

[2] *Ibid.*, p. 323.

I want to live under the Union Government. My tribe was poor when the Union Government came here many years ago. I was a man with only a dog. The Union Government has given us bulls. . . . I have spoken to all my people. They only want the Union Government.[3]

The Assembly opposed absorption and "invited" the Union to submit a draft trust agreement in accordance with the Charter. In July 1947 South Africa announced that it would compromise to the extent of maintaining the *status quo* and continuing to make its annual mandatory reports to the UN. Two years later, however, the Union Government, smarting under searching questions and criticism, announced it would discontinue the reports. Then, in November 1949, the Assembly decided to hear a statement by the well-known Reverend Michael Scott, unofficial representative of certain sections of the indigenous population of South-West Africa, who presented evidence of considerable exploitation and discrimination and charged that South Africa had virtually annexed the territory through an act passed in 1949.

The Assembly next asked the International Court of Justice to render an advisory opinion on the situation. In July 1950 the Court decided that the mandate status remained in force, that the Union could not alter that status unilaterally, but neither could the Union be compelled to place the territory under trusteeship. Subsequent negotiations via a special Assembly committee led the Union to offer merely to make a new agreement with France, the United Kingdom and the United States, the "three remaining members of the Principal Allied and Associated Powers" who had made the original allocation after World War I, subject to subsequent ratification by the UN but recognizing no other obligation to that organization. Furthermore, the Union refused to allow any African from South-West Africa to make an oral statement to the UN and barred the Reverend Mr. Scott from returning to the territory.

Stronger Role in Somaliland. In accordance with Article 23 of the Italian Peace Treaty, the Big Four, after failing to agree on the disposition of the former Italian colonies, submitted the question to the General Assembly for final settlement. That body then decided in November 1949 that only Somaliland should be placed under trusteeship. Subsequently the Trusteeship Council and Assembly, rather than the former mandatory powers as in the case of the other trust territories, drafted the trust agreement, and the Assembly adopted it in December 1950. The major differences that distinguished this agreement from the others were the definite time limit (ten years) at the end of which the territory was automatically to gain its freedom, the establishment of a three-government council (Colombia, Egypt and Philippines) to advise the Administering Authority (Italy), and far fuller and more explicit provisions for promoting the welfare of the local inhabitants (thirty-five articles in all as compared with an average of seventeen in the other agreements).

[3] General Assembly, *Official Records*, Doc. A/C.4/41, p. 10.

Trust Territories	Square Miles	Population	Administering Authority
Cameroons (British)	34,136	1,160,000	United Kingdom
Cameroons (French)	166,489	3,000,000	France
New Guinea	93,000	1,000,000	Australia
Nauru	9	3,432	Australia
Pacific Islands	687	55,000	United States
Ruanda-Urundi	20,500	3,960,000	Belgium
Somaliland (formerly Italian)	194,000	1,266,000	Italy
Tanganyika	360,000	7,400,000	United Kingdom
Togoland (British)	13,041	383,600	United Kingdom
Togoland (French)	21,893	999,000	France
Western Samoa	1,130	78,000	New Zealand

Those countries that hoped the trusteeship system would prove an even more influential instrument than its predecessor to improve the lot of dependent peoples have been sorely disappointed that only the above eleven territories with a total population of approximately twenty million had been placed under the system as of early 1954, as compared with sixteen territories with a population of twenty-three million under the League. To extend the reach of the trusteeship device, the Indian delegation proposed as early as 1947, during the second session of the Assembly, that the colonial powers "be requested to submit trusteeship agreements for all or some . . . territories . . . not ready for immediate self-government." While the Soviet Union, China, Brazil, Pakistan and others gladly supported this move, the colonial states, including the United States, were unanimous in their denunciation of it. Finally, by the extraordinary vote of 24 to 24, with one abstention, the proposal failed to win adoption. Nor has there been any implementation of the Charter provision for direct international administration, although it has been advocated by many of the anti-colonial countries and has been approached in non-trust areas such as Libya, Eritrea and Palestine which are discussed at the end of this chapter.

Towards Political Maturity

While the UN is committed to mothering all the interests of the trust territories, there can be little doubt that the "political" area has received the lion's share of attention, especially regarding the central question of the character of the constitutional tissue binding the territories to their respective Administering Authorities. This matter received careful consideration from the very outset when the Soviet Union protested that the draft agreements submitted to the Assembly in the fall of 1946 authorized too intimate an embrace of the trust areas as "integral parts" of the Administering Authorities' territory, a phrase taken directly from the former "B" and "C" mandate charters. Although a slight majority of the Assembly's Fourth Committee supported the Soviet view, all of the administering powers, except New Zealand, rejected the criticism.

Since then, primary attention in this area has been focused on the practice of harnessing seven of the eleven territories (Cameroons, New Guinea, Ruanda-Urundi, Tanganyika and Togolands) to certain neighboring non-trust dependencies in "administrative unions," allegedly for administrative efficiency. Following consideration of the problem in the Trusteeship Council, India, Mexico and Venezuela led a successful campaign in the 1948 session of the Assembly to initiate a thorough study of the question to forestall any development that might jeopardize the advancement of the territories towards the goals of "self-government or independence" stipulated in the Charter. After the Trusteeship Council had appointed a committee to undertake this study, the Assembly passed another resolution in 1951 recommending that the Administering Authorities inform the Trusteeship Council before extending the administrative union device; that separate legislative and judicial organs be maintained in each trust territory involved; that, should adequate separate information on these areas not be made available, the Administering Authorities accept necessary Council supervision over the entire administrative union; and that the indigenous populations be consulted before forming such unions. Needless to say, the administering powers did not welcome this advice.

In July 1950, the Council decided to establish a Standing Committee on Administrative Unions to keep the problem under continuing observation. At the same time, the Council set forth certain guides for the administering powers:

     1. that "clear and precise separate . . . data" be furnished on each territory;
     2. that visiting missions be allowed access to any necessary information;
     3. that the boundaries, separate status, and identity of the trust territories be maintained; and
     4. that expenditures on a territory for a given year equal at least the total public revenue derived from the territory that year.[4]

During its summer session in 1953, the Council broadened these criteria to include consideration of the interests of the inhabitants, terms of the UN Charter and trust agreements, as well as any other relevant factors.

One concrete result of this campaign has been to increase the availability of separate information on many of these territories, but there are still instances where the picture is by no means clear, as evidenced by criticism of the regimes governing the British Cameroons and Togoland. The anti-colonial forces in the Assembly have regularly urged the Trusteeship Council to move faster and more resolutely on this question. But no administrative union has seemed so insidious that either the Assembly or the Council has recommended its actual dissolution. The fact is that this is a most complex issue related to the core problem of the ultimate goal for these areas: absorption, independence or some compromise. While admin-

---

[4] *Yearbook of the United Nations, 1951*, p. 778.

istrative unions may have tended at times to ride rough shod over the separate interests of some territories, it is equally clear that the political progress of the British Cameroons and Togoland would not have been so rapid had their stars not been hitched to the vigorous development of Nigeria and the Gold Coasts respectively. There are also undeniable administrative and economic benefits to be derived thereby, as long as one area is not favored at the expense of the other. One of the surest safeguards against such discrimination is equitable representation for both populations in the central government, which the Trusteeship Council is encouraging.

Another problem rises out of the fact that colonial powers have traditionally carved up dependent territories with relatively little regard for the wishes of the local peoples. One particularly persistent manifestation of this situation has concerned the inhabitants of the British and French Togolands and the Gold Coast. The question first came to the UN in the form of a petition for the unification of the Ewe people who live in all three territories. Concurrent demands were then voiced by other African interests for the unification of the two Togolands without the Gold Coast. Due to differences of opinion among the inhabitants, the obvious reluctance of the Administering Authorities to lose control of their respective dependencies, and the imperfect development of political processes in these lands, it has been impossible to get any clear expression of the "will of the people." After an abortive effort to consult popular opinion through a Consultative Commission for Togoland Affairs, first established in 1948, the British and French won Trusteeship Council approval in July 1951 for the creation of a "joint council" composed of representatives of both Togolands to advise the administrations on matters of common concern to the two peoples. At the same time, the Council and Assembly have placed special emphasis on the importance of doing a better job than previously of consulting with all segments of public opinion.

To gain ultimate independence for the trust territories, the Chinese, Russians and others have strongly urged, particularly during the consideration of the first eight agreements, that a definite time limit be fixed, preferably ten years, at the end of which there would be an automatic review and possible termination of the trust status. Although a majority of the Assembly's Fourth Committee agreed with this proposal, the Administering Authorities were firmly opposed. Then India, the Philippines and Lebanon led an effort which succeeded in persuading the 1951 session of the Assembly to adopt a resolution inviting the Administering Authorities to include in their annual reports information on action taken to help territories achieve self-government or independence and estimates of the time when it was expected such territories would attain one of those goals. But the sole application of this principle thus far has been in the case of the former Italian colony of Somaliland. The second nearest approach was the 1953 pledge of New Zealand that it would give the people of Western Samoa an opportunity by the end of 1954 to decide their own future status.

Popular Participation in Government. The usual governmental pattern in the trust territories follows that of the average non-trust dependency. Power flows from the top, rather than the bottom, through a representative of the administering power (usually a single "governor" or "commissioner"), normally advised by a small executive council (usually appointive, including some measure of indigenous representation). In all of the trust territories now there is also some kind of "legislative council," but the authority is primarily advisory, jurisdiction limited (to "domestic" or "nonpolitical" questions), subject to the governor's veto, representation weighted in favor of the European population (in the French Cameroons, as of 1951, 3,000,000 Africans were represented by 24; 8,980 French, by 16), and, where elections are held, selection by a very restricted electorate, often through indirect representation. The Trusteeship Council has conscientiously tried to take into account differences in political advancement. Nevertheless, the ultimate objectives towards which it constantly strives are: full legislative and executive authority stemming from all the inhabitants of a territory, no discrimination in representation, universal and secret suffrage, direct elections, and emphasis first on local democracy working gradually towards the territorial level. Interestingly enough, there also seems to be a trend, encouraged by many anti-colonial countries, away from the League's reluctance to disturb traditional native procedures, often identified with the British doctrine of "indirect rule." There is strong feeling that that doctrine had the effect, more often than not, of perpetuating a low level of political development as a convenient climate for unrestrained exploitation.

In the ranks of the civil service, indigenous personnel are usually to be found near the bottom of the ladder, and there is sometimes unequal compensation for the same work. Needless to say, the Trusteeship Council has striven to improve the training and status of the non-Europeans. The Council has also urged greater use of indigenous personnel in the courts and the prohibition of corporal punishment, particularly whipping which still survives in such territories as New Guinea, British Togoland and Cameroons, and Tanganyika.

While political development seems to crawl at a snail's pace and is unlikely to travel much faster than the colonial powers tolerate in their non-trust dependencies, there have been some marked advances, occasionally in clear response to UN prodding. For example, the Commissioner of the French Cameroons reported in 1951 that, in accordance with Trusteeship Council recommendations, he was consulting the territorial Representative Assembly more frequently and had created new local governmental units. Australia reported that, following Council suggestions, it was reviewing corporal punishment to see if it could be further restricted. Australia also accepted a Council recommendation that the council of chiefs on the island of Nauru be given greater authority. The most celebrated and far-reaching influence came with the recommendations of the first visiting mission which, in response to a Western Samoan petition, recommended thorough revision of that government which carried great weight in the subsequent reorganization. And Western Samoa, under the extraordinarily enlightened guidance of New Zealand, stands out today as probably the most advanced territory with an assembly which enacts legislation on all domestic matters. The debates of that body are so "keen and intelligent," according to New Zealand authorities, that they are broadcast throughout the island. One wonders how the legislatures of many of our more advanced countries would weather such exposure to public scrutiny.

Improving Economic Conditions

The economic patterns of these territories are basically similar to those of most colonies, and, as in many other dependencies today, there are signs of accelerating development with some limited benefits for the indigenous populations. The productive processes of the trust territories are still over-whelmingly agricultural with the single exception of Nauru which is dominated by the phosphate industry. Much of the agriculture is still of a subsistence nature except for a few major export operations, such as cocoa, bananas, rubber, palm products, coffee, peanuts, copra, cotton and sugar. Major non-agricultural exports are chiefly extractive: phosphates, diamonds, gold, chromite and bauxite. The major export enterprises are still largely in the hands of non-indigenous interests, and the marketing of some key commodities, such as cocoa, is dominated by governmental boards which control prices and often set aside certain reserve funds to help stabilize prices, notoriously unstable in the primary commodity markets. At the same time, some conscious efforts have been made through administrative encouragement, promotion of cooperatives, and mobilization of capital, to enable the indigenous populations to play a more important economic role. For example the French Government gave its Cameroons territory a palm oil processing plant managed by a company 50 per cent of whose stock was reserved for African subscribers. The British Cameroons Development Corporation, which manages 395 square miles of plantation lands, originally established by the pre-World War I German administration, and is the largest plantation enterprise in the Cameroons, is governed by a nine-member board of directors of whom three are Africans. Thirty-two other Africans have been appointed to senior posts in the Corporation staff. The problem of land alienation from the native population does not seem as serious as before the war since most Administering Authorities have stopped transfers to private interests and allow only leases regulated by the central government. Nonetheless, the terms of such leases often seem weighted in favor of the non-indigenous population.

Among the Trusteeship Council's chief concerns have been its efforts to improve the lot of the native populations through increasing their resources of land, tools, credit and technical skills. As part of its general interest in agricultural "reform" and development, the Assembly adopted a resolution in December 1950 initiating such a campaign in connection with the trust territories. The following February the Council appointed a Committee on Rural Economic Development to study and report on the problem. Both the Assembly and Council have also encouraged more long-range and comprehensive economic planning backed by more generous financing, particularly for costly land reclamation, light industries, and expansion of basic transport and communication facilities. Finally, these bodies have prodded the Administering Authorities to make fuller use of the technical assistance resources of the UN and the specialized agencies.

As for the results of these efforts, there is evidence that the Trusteeship Council was a major factor in influencing Australia and the British Phosphate Commissioners on the island of Nauru to increase the royalties paid for the benefit of the local community. It is also apparent that the Council's pressure has been responsible for increases in native participation in certain of the marketing boards.

Trusteeship and Social Welfare

The welfare and security of a people are a direct reflection of their economic and political situation. Since the indigenous populations of the trust territories are at a very low economic and political level, their general social conditions are quite inadequate by the standards of more developed countries. Labor usually takes the form of small-scale tribal or individual effort and is neither organized nor paid as in the more advanced countries. Wartime scarcities and deterioration, moreover, have made it difficult, if not impossible, even to maintain prewar standards. Nevertheless, postwar resuscitation has been remarkably rapid in some territories with consequent benefits for the peoples, as in the British Cameroons, Nauru and Western Samoa. And, where there is wage-labor in connection with major enterprises, such as the British Cameroons Development Corporation, a few workers have become organized and have thus been able to win a little larger slice of the economic pie for themselves. In the Pacific territories there is also the problem of the status and compensation of immigrant Chinese contract labor.

The principal efforts of the Trusteeship Council have been aimed at encouraging cost-of-living studies and wage increases where suggested by those analyses, higher labor standards, including implementation of relevant ILO agreements, elimination of discrimination, and training and promotion of indigenous labor to fill more responsible and lucrative positions. Much of this progress stems from the general economic development of these and other dependent territories, but there is evidence that the character of the progress is often directly attributable to the ministrations of the Trusteeship Council. For example, the Nauruan authorities decided to bow to Council suggestions in allowing some Chinese to bring their families to the island. And various cost-of-living studies and wage increases have stemmed from Council pressure.

Education is the eye of the needle through which the trust peoples must pass if they are to improve their economic, political and social status. But culture costs money — for leisure time as well as teachers and equipment.

Hence the Administering Authorities have not always been generous in financing education. In no territory is there even effective universal primary education, and only limited secondary schooling (none at all in some areas such as New Guinea). Mission schools, whose standards are often inadequately controlled by the central government, provide much of the training. Countless local dialects make communication extraordinarily difficult. And the education that is provided is primarily oriented towards preparing the populations for the less skilled vocations. Finally, much secondary education and most training above that level must be sought outside the territories.

Following various discussions in the Trusteeship Council, the ambitious Assembly session of 1948, under the leadership of India, Mexico, and other anti-colonial countries, took a strong stand urging immediate and marked improvement of trust educational facilities. The Trusteeship Council then initiated a special study on the basis of which it made specific recommendations in the summer of 1949 to Belgium, France and the United Kingdom suggesting what each should do to improve its educational resources, particularly by creating university-level institutions in Ruanda-Urundi, French Cameroons and Togoland, and Tanganyika, and increasing financial support, including aid for schooling outside the territories. The Trusteeship Council and Economic and Social Council have also urged the Administering Authorities to take fuller advantage of UN educational technical assistance resources, including scholarships, particularly in cooperation with UNESCO, but the response has been rather laggard. The Assembly and Trusteeship Council have also been insistent that the administering powers cooperate in the dissemination of information about the UN, again without marked enthusiasm on the part of the administering countries, except in the case of New Zealand. As a result of all of these efforts, Australia announced in 1951, in response to specific Trusteeship Council suggestions, that a training course for Nauruan teachers had finally been initiated to provide the first secondary education on the island. Council influence was also responsible for closer control of mission schools in Western Samoa. And the United States proudly reported doubling the expenditures for education in the Pacific Islands from $168,000 in 1948 to $338,000 in 1949.

Health is another area in which the need seems unlimited and expenditures very modest. Probably the most advanced services are provided in the Pacific Island territories where the United States wants to protect its armed forces and does not hesitate to spend large sums of money ($7.00 per person in 1949 as compared with $1.60 per person expended by Australia in New Guinea). But constant Trusteeship Council reminders have helped to improve medical care in the rural areas as well as urban centers, through the framing of indigenous personnel as well as the importation of outsiders.

Reflections on Basic Issues

One's evaluation of the trusteeship system rests ultimately on one's fundamental assumptions regarding the proper objectives for trust territories.

The following conclusions are based on the premise that a people's interests are never as diligently served by anyone other than themselves and that the indigeneous inhabitants of the trust areas are basically capable of governing themselves. The following observations, therefore, judge the effectiveness of the trusteeship system not by traditional colonial standards nor by impossible Utopian aspirations, but by the standards set forth in Chapters 12 and 13 of the UN Charter.

At the outset, one cannot avoid recognizing the fundamental continuity between the UN and League experiences. One is also conscious, however, of the extent to which the new balance of forces within the international organization, as well as new approaches in thinking about underdeveloped areas in general, have been responsible for some significant advances beyond the League. The principal differences in the political area are the greater emphasis on self-government or independence for all trust territories, not merely "A" mandates as under the League, and more equitable and authoritative participation of the indigenous populations in governmental processes. In the economic sphere there has been noteworthy improvement not only in over-all output but in a broader sharing of productive resources and returns. And these developments have made possible certain advances in labor, educational and health conditions. While it is true that similar movements are afoot in many other dependent areas today, it is also apparent that the exertions of the trusteeship system have both hastened and shaped that progress in specific instances and have also had a leavening effect in various non-trust territories.

At the same time, one must weigh the strong criticism which has been leveled against the system: that it is unrealistically ambitious, lacks necessary consensus, and is a disturbing influence which hinders the Administering Authorities more than it helps them.[5] Whether one believes the UN has attempted too much too soon depends on one's judgment of what is possible. It is obvious that some extreme anti-colonial powers, particularly the Soviet Union, have been overly impatient and, at times, quite unrealistic in their demands. But the great majority of UN Members have urged no more than what many enlightened colonial experts have believed possible.

On the fundamental and complex question of whether these territories should be encouraged to look towards the promised land of complete independence or something short of that, there is no simple answer (certainly not as simple as the Russians or South Africans have suggested). It seems clear, nevertheless, that it would be more efficient economically and administratively for these areas, including Somaliland, to remain allied with a larger community, assuming they would be given an equitable voice in the central government. But relations between most of these areas and their

---

[5] For a discussion of some of these points see Annette Baker Fox, "The United Nations and Colonial Development," *International Organization*, Vol. 4, No. 2 (May 1950), pp. 199–218.

respective Administering Authorities have been so poisoned by past exploitation that there seems little basis for future collaboration. And, because of this unfortunate heritage, other dependencies, which may need some caretaker regime to prepare them for self-government, usually prefer not to be placed in a trusteeship status.

Regarding the question of whether the UN has been an unduly disturbing factor, even the UN's defenders recognize that criticism of the administering states has not always been well-founded nor well-administered. Furthermore the uncertainty of the ultimate destiny of these areas is an unsettling consideration. Then, to have an international body, which is compelled to observe from a distance with neither thorough nor up-to-date information, constantly looking over one's shoulder, and often speaking over one's head to the inhabitants, can be a disconcerting influence. Moreover, the structure of the Assembly gives smaller states a voting influence beyond what their population and resources would seem to warrant. On the other hand, though outside supervision, whether national or international, is always irksome to the administrator on the spot, it is often useful and necessary. In this particular case, there can be little doubt that UN surveillance serves to make the Administering Authorities hew more closely to the line of the Charter than if they were left largely to their own devices. Some writers have suggested that a more restricted regional organization might operate with greater consensus and sympathy regarding the problems of the administering powers. But most anti-colonial countries believe that such an approach would probably be too sensitive to the wishes of the colonial powers, as in the Caribbean Commission, and thus less likely to be as vigorous in its implementation of the Charter.[6]

There are also certain basic economic difficulties which continue to limit the development of these territories. Several of the Administering Authorities, notably the United Kingdom and France, are in no position to increase their investment unless it produces immediate and significant returns, particularly in "hard currencies." The uncertainty of the territories' future status also makes these states hesitant to invest as willingly as in their own dependencies which they believe are more likely to remain in the nest. Moreover, development cannot move very quickly in lands where some farmers refuse to thin out substandard herds because any kind of cow is considered a sign of wealth, where the skills and motivations of the more developed countries are largely lacking, and where hostile natural conditions seriously cripple such schemes as the celebrated, and abortive, groundnuts project in Tanganyika. Although the trusteeship system has had some moderate success in increasing the share of return given the indigenous peoples, it is still difficult to obtain complete information on financial operations and even more difficult to decide what is a fair share for the various parties concerned.

[6] For discussion of Caribbean Commission, see Chap. 27.

Quest for Self-Government

In the spring of 1945, when the San Francisco Conference convened, there were approximately 600 million people in the world who were not fully self-governing. By early 1954 there were only 120 million still in that condition. Between those dates a variety of influences brought about the greatest emancipation movement of all history which resulted in self-government for many lands including India, Pakistan, Indonesia, Jordan, the Philippines, Burma, Ceylon, Israel and Libya. And a significant part of this ferment has been the work of the UN under Chapter 11 of the Charter which commits Members administering non-self-governing territories to "recognize that the interests of the inhabitants . . . are paramount, and . . . promote to the utmost . . . [their] well-being. . . . "

When Is a Territory Non-Self-Governing?

It soon became clear that whether or not a country should be placed under the wing of Chapter 11 was a burning question the answer to which seemed to depend on one's interests in the matter. On August 31, 1953, Mme. Lakshmi N. Menon, representative of India, insisted in the Committee on Information from Non-Self-Governing Territories that the United States should continue to report on Puerto Rico under Chapter 11 since she claimed it was still not entirely self-governing. The United States delegation was equally emphatic in its contention that the Puerto Rican people had freely chosen their own government and decided to remain associated with the United States. In September 1953, Gilberto Concepcion de Gracia, leader of the Puerto Rican Independence Party, agreed with India. Muñoz Marin, head of the Puerto Rican government, sided with the United States.

There are really two questions involved in this issue: (1) who is to decide, and (2) by what criteria? Regarding the first problem, the Assembly began in 1946 by leaving it to the Administering Members to determine voluntarily what areas they would report on. After seventy-four territories had been so designated that first year, only sixty-two were reported on in 1947, sixty-three in 1948. This decrease, which many anti-colonial states felt was not justified, led India, as part of its general campaign against imperialism during the 1948 Assembly session, to propose that the Administering Members be "invited" to communicate to the Secretary-General within six months any relevant information supporting a decision to cease reporting on an area.

The United Kingdom, France and Belgium protested that this implied that the UN had a right to deal with political and constitutional questions, which they denied. The United States, on the other hand, said that it was quite willing to submit such information as long as it was not interpreted as limiting the Administering Member's right to decide for itself the constitutional questions involved. Finally, the Indian resolution was adopted. The general view of the anti-colonial countries seemed to be that the UN could not compel a Member to place a dependency within the boundaries of Chapter 11 but, once a territory had been so declared, the Administering Member did not have sole responsibility for deciding when the territory could be withdrawn. During the 1951 Assembly many countries, including Brazil, Cuba, Egypt, Indonesia and Uruguay, went so far as to claim that the final competence in this matter rested with the UN. But it seems unlikely that this view can be validly supported since the signatories of the Charter have never agreed that any UN organ has the authority to bind them, against their will, in interpreting the Charter concerning such matters.

Regarding the matter of criteria, the 1946 Assembly discussed the issue but finally left it largely to the judgment of the Administering Members. After the lively debate of 1948, however, the 1949 Assembly adopted a resolution, proposed by Egypt and other anti-colonial states, calling for a study of relevant criteria, again vigorously opposed by most of the Administering Members, especially the United Kingdom, France and Belgium. Following recommendations made in October 1951 by the Special Committee on Information Transmitted under Article 73(e) of the Charter, the 1951 Assembly passed a resolution appointing its own Ad Hoc Committee to study the problem further. When the 1952 Assembly failed to reach agreement on that report, it continued the study for another year. Finally, the 1953 Assembly adopted a resolution recommending a variety of criteria including: (1) capacity of a population to decide its future status, (2) existence of a truly democratic system of government, and (3) enjoyment of individual rights. The bitter resistance of one Administering Member was expressed in the words of Lord Hudson, representative of the United Kingdom, who is reported to have said that the list was "a matter of comparative indifference" to his delegation, since "we would never use it, nor in regard to our territories would we expect anyone else to use it."[7]

Part of the complexity arises from the fact that statesmen and political philosophers have, since the time of Socrates, found it difficult to define self-government (or "democracy"), particularly in relation to any federal or dominion relationship. Nonetheless, these deliberations have shed some light, as well as heat, for those countries and delegates open-minded enough to absorb it, and there is no doubt that they have made the colonial powers more conscious than ever of the watchful eye of the UN. At the same time, the final decision on these questions remains in the hands of the administering powers.

Towards Economic and Social Advancement

Like most underdeveloped areas, the economic activities of the non-self-governing territories with which the UN has been concerned are chiefly agricultural and extractive with relatively few industrial operations. While these territories produced 50 per cent of the world's bauxite, as of 1951, they manufactured no aluminum. They produced 54 per cent of the

[7] *The New York Times,* October 9, 1953.

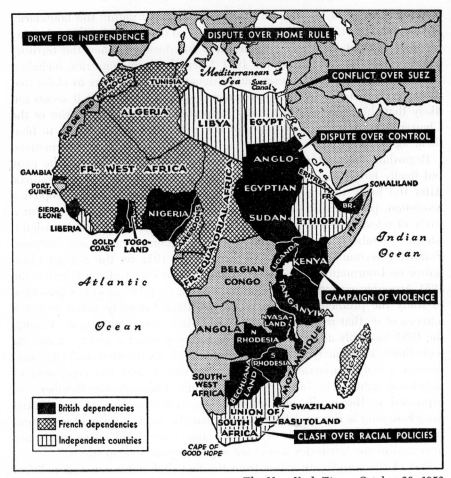

The New York Times, October 26, 1952

AFRICA — SIX AREAS OF TENSION

world's cocoa, but no cocoa powder nor butter. The discussions of the Assembly and its Committee on Information from Non-Self-Governing Territories have, on the other hand, revealed an appreciable acceleration of economic development since the war. The principal goals which these bodies have encouraged have included improvement in production and marketing techniques, expansion of basic transport and communication facilities, development of water and power resources, extension of research and long-term planning, and liberalization of financial assistance. Particular emphasis has been placed on persuading the Administering Members to make greater use of UN and specialized agency technical assistance. While most of the administering powers have not been particularly enthusiastic about these suggestions, the United States delegation, among others, has praised the recommendations as practical and useful. And, very largely as a result of these discussions, the United Kingdom and the Netherlands approached the UN, beginning in 1951, to secure technical assistance for some of their dependent territories.

It is in the broad "social" area that the UN has concentrated most of its attention, both because that field seems less controversial than more frankly "political" questions, at least superficially, and because, at the same time, it can be used as a vantage point from which to survey all aspects of non-self-governing territories. Regarding labor conditions, the Assembly and its Committee on Information from Non-Self-Governing Territories have aimed particularly at persuading the Administering Members to apply appropriate ILO standards, ease the burdens of migrant laborers, expand training programs, and undertake cost-of-living studies as the basis for increasing compensation. These bodies engaged in intensive examination of the educational field during 1949 and 1953, calling attention to the need for more basic education (cooperating with UNESCO and making better use of vernacular languages at the lower levels), further elimination of discrimination, more generous financing, and indigenous participation in educational planning. Beginning in 1950 the Assembly has also requested specific information on the implementation of the Declaration of Human Rights. In 1952 it adopted a resolution which called for abolition of all discriminatory laws and practices contrary to that Declaration, although the United Kingdom, France and Belgium have regularly said that the question of rights was outside UN jurisdiction. Finally, these bodies have urged the same kind of improvement of health care that has been recommended for the trust territories. Although progress is painfully slow in all of these fields, there are some encouraging signs. For example, the UN exertions helped to hasten the termination of educational segregation in French Equatorial Africa. And, in the Federation of Malaya, national schools providing a six-year course of free primary education have been established and opened to all races.

While Chapter 11 of the Charter commits the Administering Members to develop self-government in their dependent territories, it does not compel them to submit information on political questions as it does on economic, social and educational conditions. Nevertheless, the anti-colonial forces have succeeded in including an optional political section in the recommended "standard form" for submitting information and have regularly attempted to use the UN to probe political issues. But, only Australia, Denmark, the Netherlands and the United States have submitted such information; the United Kingdom, France, Belgium and New Zealand have refused. Moreover, when Iraq proposed in 1951 to authorize the Assembly to discuss political questions, France and the United Kingdom virtually threatened to boycott such discussions and succeeded in postponing a vote on the issue.

Conclusions

Judging the effectiveness of these efforts according to the objectives set forth in Chapter 11 of the Charter, the greatest progress seems to have been made in those areas where the most adequate information has been made available and where the Administering Members have been most willing to consider UN advice: education, health, labor standards and economic development. The least advance has come in influencing the Administering Members' political policies. While the advances made do not seem very great nor very rapid, there is at least a formal obligation, subject to constant UN scrutiny, committing all Members to promote the political, economic, and social development of all non-self-governing territories. This did not exist under the League. True, all underdeveloped countries are on the move today, and the greatest benefits tend to go to those peoples who are in the best position, for one reason or another, to compel concessions. Nevertheless, there is evidence that the UN has been an important center for mobilizing pressure to expedite this progress.

At the same time, there are serious difficulties which must be recognized. It is obvious that this system has aroused intense opposition on the part of key colonial powers, particularly the United Kingdom, France and Belgium. This is scarcely surprising since this area has in the past been considered essentially a "domestic" question, the accelerating anti-colonial movement since the war has aroused increasingly defensive attitudes on the part of the imperialist powers, the precarious economic plight of many of those powers makes it all the more difficult for them to be generous financially or politically, and there are still pockets of die-hard imperialist resistance at home. Moreover, the criticism of the anti-colonial states has had to be based on even less information than in the trusteeship system; it has often been unrealistic; and it is based on less Charter authority than in the trusteeship sphere. Naturally such outside interference is repugnant to the colonial powers, but such international interest is by no means a recent invention. As early as the latter part of the nineteenth century, the imperialist states recognized an international responsibility regarding peoples who were not able to defend their own interests. And these peoples would certainly not have progressed as far as they have without international surveillance. While some UN criticism has been far-fetched, much of it has been essentially reasonable, even according to the judgment of certain of the Administering Members such as the United States. While a more regional approach, which some writers have suggested, might be useful, it is doubtful if it would be sufficiently representative to give adequate protection to the interests of the dependent populations. What seems called for, therefore, is not a reversal of this venerable development, but further refinement through more intensive information and study, a more realistic reflection of the relative weight of the participating countries, greater competency on the part of the delegates and a more responsible attitude on the part of all concerned.

Supervision of Special Areas

The hope that the UN might be used to administer directly some territories under the trusteeship system has not yet materialized. But efforts have been made to utilize the UN, as was done with the League, to provide temporary "caretaker" services for certain controversial areas, three of which have been involved in postwar peace treaty negotiations among the "Big Four."

One of these bones of contention is Trieste, the chief port on the north shore of the Adriatic Sea. It has been an important outlet to the Mediterranean for the landlocked nations of Central Europe and an area of considerable strategic significance. Its population is mixed, with the urban section (Trieste and several small cities) largely Italian, and the rural hinterland overwhelmingly Slavic. During the course of the negotiations regarding the Italian peace treaty, the Soviet Union supported Yugoslavia's claim to the area; the United States, Britain and France backed Italy's claim. A compromise solution was finally worked out by which Trieste and a surrounding strip, extending from the Italian border in the north down the western side of the Istrian Peninsula, were to be designated a Free Territory under the supervision of the UN Security Council. Pending implementation of this plan, the area was divided into two zones: the northern one under Anglo-American administration and the southern one under Yugoslavia. The City of Trieste was made a Free Port similar to the Free City of Danzig created after World War I.

Owing to the deterioration of relations among the great powers, however, the Security Council has not been able to establish the Free Territory. Early in 1948, in an attempt to strengthen the election chances of pro-Western elements in Italy, the United States proposed that Trieste be returned to Italy, and Britain and France joined in signing a declaration to that effect. Yugoslavia naturally rejected this proposal, but, after Tito's break with the Soviet Union, his views became more moderate, including acceptance of a substantial degree of international control. Then, after further fruitless negotiations and in another effort to bolster a friendly but sagging Italian government, the United States and Britain announced in October 1953 that they would allow Italian forces to occupy the northern zone. This led to more violent sword-rattling in Yugoslavia than ever. In reviewing this history of frustration, it seems likely that the UN might have provided a relatively neutral regime that could have resolved some of these tensions, but the "veto" has blocked the path entirely.

The East-West conflict also reared its head in the disposition of Italy's threadbare empire. Never a source of significant wealth or prestige, the areas of Libya, Eritrea, and Somaliland were, nonetheless, strategically important, bordering the Mediterranean and Red Sea trade routes. The Soviet Union proposed in 1946 that these territories be made trusteeships, with the U.S.S.R. as either sole or joint trustee. This was unacceptable to Britain and the United States, who were not inclined to give Russia such an advantageous foothold in the Mediterranean and Near East. Finally, the Italian Peace Treaty provided that, if agreement could not be reached within a year, the problem should be submitted to the Assembly. This was done in the spring of 1949, and, by fall, it was decided that Libya should be administered by a UN Commissioner until January 1952 at which time it was to become an independent state. Former Assistant Secretary-General Adrian Pelt was named Commissioner. A ten-year trusteeship was also provided for Somaliland, discussed above. Final action on Eritrea was postponed pending further study by an Eritrean Commission to weigh the rival claims of Ethiopia and Italy and to sound out the wishes of the inhabitants. Following the Commission's report in November 1950, the Assembly decided that Eritrea should be included in a federation with Ethiopia under the latter's crown, the transitional arrangements to be supervised by another UN Commissioner (Eduardo Matienzo of Bolivia).

As the General Assembly had decided, Libya became an independent nation, at least in name, by the end of 1951, with the promulgation of a constitutional monarchy under King Idris I. Among the new nation's first acts was the signing of an agreement with the United States giving that country the right to construct air bases in the Libyan desert. On February 1, 1952, a final report on Libya was presented to the General Assembly. A Soviet resolution calling for the removal of all foreign troops and the liquidation of all foreign military establishments in Libya was rejected as being incompatible with Libyan sovereignty. But the Assembly did adopt resolutions advocating financial and technical assistance for the new country, though no significant funds were provided, and calling for Libya's admission to the UN. Substantial financial and other aid was furnished outside the UN by the United States and United Kingdom. Then, in September 1952, the Ethiopian-Eritrean federation was established. Ethiopia was given control over Eritrea's foreign affairs, currency and trade; all other powers remained with Eritrea.

The UN's chief contributions in these two instances were to devise a definite and workable solution where the great powers had failed, to contribute a substantial amount of technical assistance, to prepare these areas for self-government, and to do all this without giving rise to open conflict. On the other hand, to think that Libya was prepared to stand alone as an independent state after only two years of hasty UN tutelage was manifestly unrealistic. But it is doubtful whether it would have been healthy to leave the territory indefinitely under the wing of one of the colonial powers, and the anti-colonial forces were firmly opposed to such a possibility. What might have been more desirable was a longer period of UN-supervised incubation, but the anti-colonial states also fought that. One must also recognize that Libya is no less prepared for independence than certain other underdeveloped, though "sovereign," states. Furthermore, the UN is capable of aiding Libya as much as if the territory were still advised by a UN Commissioner. The settlement of the Eritrean question seems more reasonable in that it creates a larger and hence more viable community. But it also antagonizes certain interests in Eritrea and may lead to further conflict between the two populations.

The fourth and last special area which the UN has thus far attempted to administer directly is Jerusalem. When the Assembly adopted the Palestine partition plan in November 1947, it also called upon the Trusteeship Council to draft a statute for an international regime for Jerusalem. In April 1948 the Assembly approved the Council's recommendations calling for a neutral Municipal Commissioner. Owing to the breakdown in truce negotiations and the unwillingness of the Arabs to cooperate, however, the Commissioner was never installed. The newly appointed Mediator, Count Folke Bernadotte, was then charged with the task of protecting Jerusalem and the Holy Places.

The City became a center of fighting during the Arab-Israeli War, with the Old City occupied by Jordanian forces and the New City under Israeli control. At the end of 1948 Acting Mediator Ralph Bunche recommended that Jerusalem be accorded special treatment in any settlement. The Assembly accordingly resolved that the City be placed under UN control guaranteeing access to the Holy Places. It requested that the Security Council take steps to insure demilitarization and that the Mediator present proposals for the establishment of an international regime. In the armistice agreements concluded during the spring of 1949, both sides agreed to safeguard the Holy City. In December 1949 the Assembly adopted a resolution restating its intention that the Jerusalem area should be established as an international entity and designating the Trusteeship Council as the Administering Authority. Israel and Jordan reaffirmed their guarantees to safeguard the Holy Places, but opposed internationalization.

The refusal of the two occupying states to cooperate in implementing the UN plan caused the project to wither on the vine. Not wishing to disturb the uneasy peace, the Assembly resolved in January 1952 only to continue the Palestine Commission with headquarters in Jerusalem. The Assembly did, however, request Israel to abandon her plan to move the governmental seat from Tel-Aviv to Jerusalem. Israel replied that the New City was part of its sovereign territory and proceeded to transfer several governmental offices there. Free access to the Holy Places has been allowed, nonetheless, and Israeli troops have protected pilgrims coming to the Christian shrines from the west. The divided city, however, remains a source of tension, a problem which the UN has thus far failed to solve.

Suggestions for Further Reading

Books

Benson, Wilfrid, "Non-Self-Governing Territories," *Annual Review of United Nations Affairs, 1949* (New York: New York University Press, 1950).

Bunche, Ralph J., "Trusteeship," *Annual Review of United Nations Affairs, 1950* (New York: New York University Press, 1951).

Fletcher-Cooke, John, "[Trusteeship] Current Activities," *Annual Review of United Nations Affairs, 1949* (New York: New York University Press, 1950).

Goodrich, Leland, and Hambro, Edvard, *Charter of the United Nations, Commentary and Documents* (Boston: World Peace Foundation, 1949).

Hall, H. Duncan, *Mandates, Dependencies, and Trusteeship* (Washington: Carnegie Endowment for International Peace, 1948).

Hoo, Victor, "Trusteeship and Non-Self-Governing Territories," *Annual Review of United Nations Affairs, 1951* (New York: New York University Press, 1952).

————, "Trusteeship and Non-Self-Governing Territories, Role and Procedure," *Annual Review of United Nations Affairs, 1949* (New York: New York University Press, 1950).

Wieschoff, H. A., "Trusteeship and Non-Self-Governing Territories," *Annual Review of United Nations Affairs, 1952* (New York: New York University Press, 1953).

Periodicals

Armstrong, Elizabeth H., and Cargo, William I., "The Inauguration of the Trusteeship System of the United Nations," *Department of State Bulletin*, Vol. 16, No. 403 (March 23, 1947).

Carr-Gregg, John R. E., "Self-Rule in Africa: Recent Advances in the Gold Coast," *International Conciliation*, No. 473 (September 1951).

Chieh, Liu, "International Trusteeship System, Visiting Missions," *International Conciliation*, No. 448 (February 1949).

Eagleton, Clyde, "Excesses of Self-Determination," *Foreign Affairs*, Vol. 31, No. 4 (July 1953).

Fox, Annette Baker, "The United Nations and Colonial Development," *International Organization*, Vol. 4, No. 2 (May 1950).

Fraser, Peter, "The Work of the Trusteeship Council," *International Conciliation*, No. 445 (November 1948).

Haas, Ernst B., "The Attempt to Terminate Colonialism: Acceptance of the United Nations Trusteeship System," *International Organization*, Vol. 7, No. 1 (February 1953).

"International Responsibility for Colonial Peoples," *International Conciliation*, No. 458 (February 1950).

Isaacs, Harold R., and Ross, Emory, "Africa, New Crises in the Making," *Headline Series*, No. 91 (January-February 1952).

Sayre, Francis B., "Advancement of Dependent Peoples," *International Conciliation*, No. 435 (November 1947).

Documents

United Nations, General Assembly, *Official Records*.

————, Trusteeship Council, *Official Records*.

United States, *United States Participation in the United Nations, Report by the President to the Congress* (Washington: U.S. Government Printing Office, 1947–   ).

PART FOUR

Regional and Other Systems

 24

Atlantic Community — Security

"The twelve nations that compose the North Atlantic Community include some three hundred and thirty-seven million people, about one-sixth of the earth's population. Within this area is the world's greatest concentration of industrial and technical skills. This community of nations is also brought together by a common political experience, the growth of the idea of freedom and the rights of man.

"So geography, political experience, and industrial capacity join to make the North Atlantic Community a natural and a critically important grouping of states. By common action on their mutual problems of defense, economic development, and political cooperation, the North Atlantic states can achieve a substantial increase of their combined strength. In so doing, they increase the strength of the entire free world." — DEAN ACHESON [1]

[1] Address of the Secretary of State before the Civic Federation of Dallas and the Community Course of Southern Methodist University, Dallas, Texas, June 13, 1950. *Department of State Bulletin*, Vol. 22, No. 573 (June 26, 1950), p. 1039.

Background

International organization has reached its highest pitch in the North Atlantic Community. Here, in the years since World War II, states have coordinated their political, economic and military activities to an unprecedented degree. Fourteen nations have pooled a large part of their military strength and adopted a common defense strategy in the North Atlantic Treaty Organization (NATO). By 1954, moreover, there was a possibility that an important element of NATO would be the European Defense Community (EDC) in which six continental nations were seeking to form a regional structure of defense including a European Army with a common budget, procurement program, uniforms and training.

Here also eighteen nations banded together in the Organization for European Economic Cooperation (OEEC) in order to implement the European Recovery Program (ERP) or Marshall Plan, as it was often called in honor of the American Secretary of State who, in 1947, started the ball rolling. Under this arrangement, the European nations were enabled to improve their economic plight by joint planning and mutually agreed import and export programs.

An even more radical development was the effort on the part of six Western European nations to establish under the Schuman Plan a European Coal and Steel Community (ECSC) which would pool the coal-steel resources of France, Western Germany, Belgium, Italy, Luxembourg and the Netherlands. This proposal was intended to provide a single market in coal and steel for the more than 160 million people of these countries. The "political" overtones of this "economic" proposal were obvious since an important sector of European economic life would be operated under the direction of a High Authority with supranational powers.

Finally, the Council of Europe, the most recent of a number of developments for European political integration, was established in 1949. While it remains without direct compulsory authority, its influence is by no means negligible. Indeed the Council's Consultative Assembly has increasingly acted in the spirit of a "Parliament of Europe" and has been the focus of much popular sentiment for closer political integration of Western Continental Europe.

All these developments spawned within a surprisingly short time after the close of the most calamitous war of modern times. The structure of the Atlantic Community was erected bit by bit from the ground up, along "functional" lines rather than created as one integrated whole by a sudden stroke of a political wand.

Although Europe's regional institutions influenced one another and stemmed from a single cause, the inability of the separate European nation-states to meet the needs of their citizens, they originated separately and, for a time, they operated separately. By 1953, however, the different elements were being fused together. Why were these developments moving forward so rapidly?

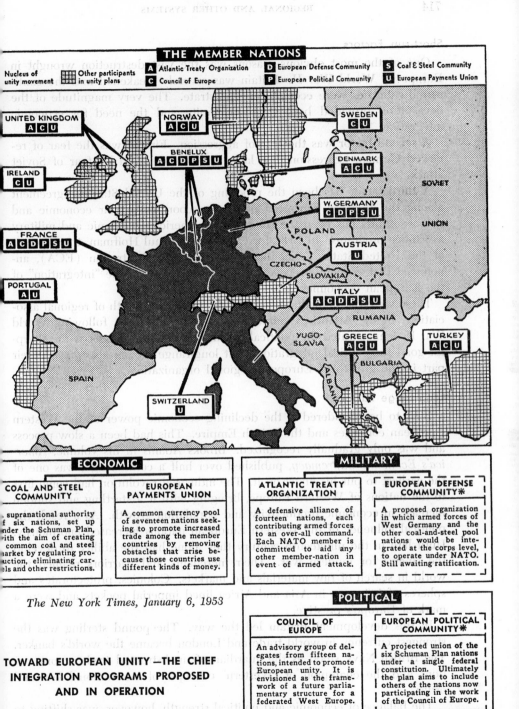

THE MEMBER NATIONS

Nucleus of
unity movement

Other participants
in unity plans

A Atlantic Treaty Organization
C Council of Europe

D European Defense Community
P European Political Community

S Coal & Steel Community
U European Payments Union

UNITED KINGDOM
A C U

IRELAND
C U

FRANCE
A C D P S U

PORTUGAL
A U

SPAIN

NORWAY
A C U

BENELUX
A C D P S U

SWITZERLAND
U

SWEDEN
C U

DENMARK
A C U

W. GERMANY
C D P S U

POLAND

AUSTRIA
U

CZECHO-
SLOVAKIA

ITALY
A C D P S U

RUMANIA

YUGO-
SLAVIA

GREECE
A C U

BULGARIA

ALBANIA

TURKEY
A C U

SOVIET

UNION

ECONOMIC

COAL AND STEEL COMMUNITY

A supranational authority of six nations, set up under the Schuman Plan, with the aim of creating a common coal and steel market by regulating production, eliminating cartels and other restrictions.

EUROPEAN PAYMENTS UNION

A common currency pool of seventeen nations seeking to promote increased trade among the member countries by removing obstacles that arise because those countries use different kinds of money.

MILITARY

ATLANTIC TREATY ORGANIZATION

A defensive alliance of fourteen nations, each contributing armed forces to an over-all command. Each NATO member is committed to aid any other member-nation in event of armed attack.

EUROPEAN DEFENSE COMMUNITY✷

A proposed organization in which armed forces of West Germany and the other coal-and-steel pool nations would be integrated at the corps level, to operate under NATO. Still awaiting ratification.

The New York Times, January 6, 1953

TOWARD EUROPEAN UNITY — THE CHIEF INTEGRATION PROGRAMS PROPOSED AND IN OPERATION

POLITICAL

COUNCIL OF EUROPE

An advisory group of delegates from fifteen nations, intended to promote European unity. It is envisioned as the framework of a future parliamentary structure for a federated West Europe.

EUROPEAN POLITICAL COMMUNITY✷

A projected union of the six Schuman Plan nations under a single federal constitution. Ultimately the plan aims to include others of the nations now participating in the work of the Council of Europe.

✷ *Now in process of formation*

Short-run Factors

One of the most obvious reasons was the vast destruction wrought in Europe by World War II. Britain was severely weakened and the continental countries were economically prostrate. The very magnitude of the devastation provided both the opportunity and the need for economic integration.

A second factor was the fear of aggression. First it was the fear of renewed German aggression, but later this was replaced by fear of Soviet attack.

A third factor has been the prodding of the United States. Agreement among the Western European nations to coordinate their economic and defense efforts has been the condition of American economic and military assistance programs. In 1949, for example, Mr. Paul Hoffman, the Director of the United States Economic Cooperation Administration (ECA), announced that economic recovery was dependent upon the "integration" of the European economies.

These were the immediate factors leading to the growth of regional associations in the Atlantic Community. Events in Europe following World War II demonstrated the political truism that external danger is the sharpest goad for political integration. But long-range factors also played their part in the growth of European regional organization.

Long-range Factors

First to be considered is the declining economic power of the Western European countries and the British Empire. This had been a slow process and was only gradually recognized. Brooks Adams in his volume, *America's Economic Supremacy,* published over half a century ago, was one of the earliest to put his finger on it. The industrial revolution had come first to the nations of Western Europe, bringing with it a startling and sudden increase in economic productivity and population growth. As a result the political influence of the Western European nations increased enormously. Until late in the nineteenth century they alone had the ability to develop the sinews for modern war. Their merchants and warriors roamed the world in search of raw materials and markets. Colonies, protectorates and spheres of influence in Asia and Africa lined imperial pockets and were a mark of Europe's prestige.

In this development Britain led the way. The pound sterling was the strongest currency in world trade and London became the world's banker. The British Navy stood as the guardian of unobstructed trade among nations and the champion of "Western" concepts of international law and order.

The balance of economic and political strength, however, was shifting to two land-secure powers, the United States of America and Czarist Russia. As the frontier was pushed back on the North American continent under the banner of "manifest destiny," a new nation arose including within its frontiers most of the resources, population and markets that are requisite for the economic and political viability of a modern industrial state. By 1900 the United States was indisputably a great power. By 1950 it was a "super-power."

A similar development took place in Russia as vast areas on the Eurasian continent were explored and developed under the Czarist regime. Not until the Bolshevik revolution of 1917, however, did the industrial revolution begin to achieve the rapid development that had occurred earlier in Western Europe and the United States. Within an astonishingly short time the Bolshevik masters, employing the power of the state in ruthless fashion, had done much to overcome the industrial backwardness of the Soviet Union. By 1950 the U.S.S.R. was also a super-power. In comparison, the Western European countries lay weak and ripe for the taking.

Yet only a few years before these nations had maintained large armies. Within a few years after the war, moreover, Western Europe had an annual economic output aproximately twice that of the Soviet Union and a population nearly one-third greater. Why did these nations seem to lie prostrate and mesmerized before the Russian bear? Why did some observers, including ex-President Hoover, feel that the Europeans were not doing all they should to defend themselves?

The answer is due, in large part, to the second long-term factor promoting European integration, the "political collapse of Europe" which has been described by Professor Hajo Holborn and others.[2]

As has already been noted, European diplomatic procedures and institutions such as the policy of the balance of power and the Concert of Europe regularized the relations of the European states after the Napoleonic Wars in the nineteenth century. For nearly a hundred years, in contrast to the eighteenth century, however sharp and frightful European conflicts such as the Franco-Prussian War of 1871 may have been, there were no wars of world-wide scope. Under the double impact of the industrial revolution and the rise of nationalism, however, this regulating mechanism broke down. Two world wars of unprecedented magnitude and the great depression of the 1930's bore witness to the fact that the European state system was utterly inadequate to cope with the political, economic and social problems of the twentieth century. This meant that questions that once could be largely handled as "domestic issues" now assumed global proportions. These difficulties were heightened by political revolutions in Asia and Africa that engulfed many colonial empires in a wave of nationalism.

Another long-term factor underlying the changing structure of Western Europe was the development of a new ethic. Gradually the *laissez faire* notion of justice was displaced by the idea that the state is a fit instrument to ameliorate the lot of the underprivileged. Of course this development is by no means confined to Europe. There is a world-wide "revolution in

---

[2] Hajo Holborn, *The Political Collapse of Europe* (New York: Knopf, 1951).

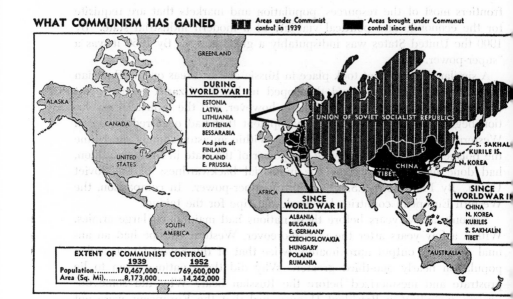

WHAT COMMUNISM HAS GAINED

	Areas under Communist control in 1939
	Areas brought under Communist control since then

DURING WORLD WAR II
ESTONIA
LATVIA
LITHUANIA
RUTHENIA
BESSARABIA
And parts of:
FINLAND
POLAND
E. PRUSSIA

GREENLAND
ALASKA
CANADA
UNITED STATES
SOUTH AMERICA
AFRICA
UNION OF SOVIET SOCIALIST REPUBLICS
S. SAKHALIN
KURILE IS.
N. KOREA
CHINA
TIBET
AUSTRALIA

SINCE WORLD WAR II
ALBANIA
BULGARIA
E. GERMANY
CZECHOSLOVAKIA
HUNGARY
POLAND
RUMANIA

SINCE WORLD WAR II
CHINA
N. KOREA
KURILES
S. SAKHALIN
TIBET

EXTENT OF COMMUNIST CONTROL		
	1939	**1952**
Population	170,467,000	769,600,000
Area (Sq. Mi)	8,173,000	14,242,000

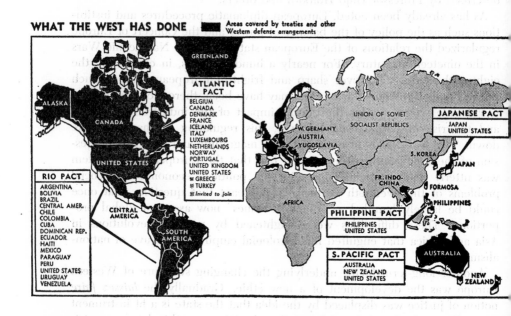

WHAT THE WEST HAS DONE

	Areas covered by treaties and other Western defense arrangements

ATLANTIC PACT
BELGIUM
CANADA
DENMARK
FRANCE
ICELAND
ITALY
LUXEMBOURG
NETHERLANDS
NORWAY
PORTUGAL
UNITED KINGDOM
UNITED STATES
✳ GREECE
✳ TURKEY
✳ Invited to join

RIO PACT
ARGENTINA
BOLIVIA
BRAZIL
CENTRAL AMER.
CHILE
COLOMBIA
CUBA
DOMINICAN REP.
ECUADOR
HAITI
MEXICO
PARAGUAY
PERU
UNITED STATES
URUGUAY
VENEZUELA

JAPANESE PACT
JAPAN
UNITED STATES

PHILIPPINE PACT
PHILIPPINES
UNITED STATES

S. PACIFIC PACT
AUSTRALIA
NEW ZEALAND
UNITED STATES

GREENLAND
ALASKA
CANADA
UNITED STATES
CENTRAL AMERICA
SOUTH AMERICA
UNION OF SOVIET SOCIALIST REPUBLICS
W. GERMANY
AUSTRIA
YUGOSLAVIA
AFRICA
S. KOREA
FR. INDO-CHINA
JAPAN
FORMOSA
PHILIPPINES
AUSTRALIA
NEW ZEALAND

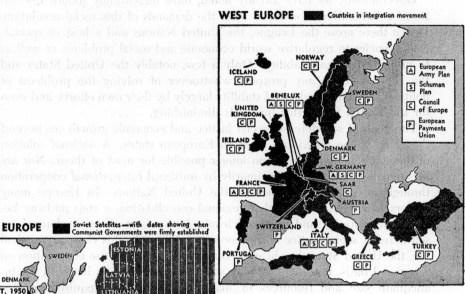

WEST EUROPE ███ Countries in integration movement

NORWAY C P
ICELAND C P
SWEDEN C P
BENELUX A S C P
UNITED KINGDOM C P
IRELAND C P
DENMARK C P
W. GERMANY A S C P
SAAR C
FRANCE A S C P
AUSTRIA P
SWITZERLAND P
ITALY A S C P
PORTUGAL P
GREECE C P
TURKEY C P

A European Army Plan
S Schuman Plan
C Council of Europe
P European Payments Union

T EUROPE ███ Soviet Satellites—with dates showing when Communist Governments were firmly established

SWEDEN
ESTONIA
DENMARK
OCT. 1950
LATVIA
LITHUANIA
NETH.
UNION OF SOVIET SOCIALIST REPUBLICS
WEST GERMANY
PRUSSIA
EAST GERMANY
POLAND
4 JAN. 1947
EB. 1948
CZECHOSLOVAKIA
RUTHENIA
2 NOV. 1946
Occupied by U.S.S.R.
SWITZ.
AUSTRIA
HUNGARY
BESSARABIA
5 MAY 1947
RUMANIA
ITALY
YUGOSLAVIA
BULGARIA
3 NOV. 1946
ALBANIA
1 JAN. 1946
GREECE
TURKEY

TWO WORLDS — THE EXPANSION OF COMMUNISM AND WHAT THE WEST HAS DONE IN DEFENSE

The New York Times, January 6, 1953

expectations," and new institutions are being contrived everywhere to fulfill present-day concepts of social and economic justice.

Governments, we have already noted, have increasingly sought international collaboration in order to meet the demands of this social revolution. Hence there arose the League, the United Nations and a host of specialized agencies to regularize world economic and social problems as well as to promote political stability. Only a few, notably the United States and the U.S.S.R., have any prospect whatsoever of solving the problems of political, economic and social stability largely by their own efforts, and even for the United States this luxury is diminishing.

The goals of self-defense, social justice and economic growth are beyond the grasp of the individual Western European states. A *national* solution of these problems is simply no longer possible for most of them. Nor are these goals being achieved primarily by universal *international* cooperation through an organization such as the United Nations. In Europe many leaders have come to feel that regional consolidation, a step midway between the national and universal levels, is the most effective channel for self-defense, social justice and economic stability. In this view, as we shall see, the United States has heartily concurred. More intense cooperation on a regional basis, it is thought, may solve the contradiction between the inadequate size and resources of many states and the requirements for economic, political and military strength.

To sum up, long-range factors have led to a situation in which world politics are dominated very largely by a rivalry between the United States and the Soviet Union. World War II, which crippled Germany and Japan and weakened the powers of Western Europe, simply accentuated a long-range trend. In this rivalry the fate of Europe itself has been at stake. With a potential of human and material resources that might tip the balance irretrievably either way, Europe has inevitably been a prize in the "cold war" and seemed destined to be the battleground of any future "hot war."

Security Arrangements — NATO

The threat of a Communist-dominated Europe provided the incentive for the establishment of the North Atlantic Treaty Organization. It is a regional organization based on the principle of collective self-defense. Its members, in effect, declare themselves one for all and all for one. This principle is stated in Article 5 of the North Atlantic Treaty whereby the "Parties agree that an armed attack against one or more of them in Europe or North America shall be considered an attack against them all. . . ." While the organization is primarily military in character, the partners, under the terms of Article 2, also undertake to strengthen "their free institutions, by bringing about a better understanding of the principles upon which these

institutions are founded . . . [and to] encourage economic collaboration between any or all of them." In practice military arrangements have increasingly required buttressing by political and economic arrangements.

NATO is quite different in character from either the League or the
United Nations. It is selective (regional) in membership; it is relatively
limited in purpose (primarily defense against aggression); it is intensive
in the field of military cooperation (its international command headquarters has important delegated powers). The ratification of the Treaty by the
United States, together with the military assistance program that followed, marked a revolution in United States foreign policy. No longer was
national security sought in the avoidance of "entangling alliances." For
the first time the United States undertook a peace-time military alliance
with European powers. The New World had truly been called in "to
redress the balance of the Old."

How It Came About

It was soon evident that the establishment of the United Nations could
not make up for the military weakness of Western Europe. At the end of
the war the balance of military power in Europe depended for what
stability it had upon non-European forces, British and American. These
were rapidly withdrawn, however, with the exception of a few divisions
of occupation troops in Germany, then prostrate and disarmed. No forces
remained in Western Europe to balance the Soviet armies stationed a bare
five hundred miles from Paris. Precipitous allied demobilization in contrast
to partial Soviet demobilization and the inability of Western Europe to
spare sufficient resources to equip modern armies contributed to the disequilibrium. Since the war, moreover, the flower of the French officer corps
has been caught up in the Indo-China imbroglio. In these dark days many
agreed with Winston Churchill that United States possession of atomic
weapons was a principal factor in maintaining some sort of military balance between the Communist and non-Communist worlds.

What were the Europeans doing in this period? Their principal concern
was their threadbare economy. Factories, farms and transportation systems
lay in ruins. Soviet power and intentions, by and large, took second place
in their thinking. The task of rehabilitation seemed beyond their powers.
In France existentialism, a philosophy born of despair, held many intellectuals in its grip. Even during 1946, when the wartime unity of the allies
gave way to "cold war," not even Britain and France had a treaty of alliance.
The United Nations Charter had seemed a sufficient security bulwark. Yet
Europe stood in danger of piecemeal subjection by Communist Russia's
nibbling.

The Treaty of Dunkirk

The first step toward regional collective security was the fifty-year Dunkirk Treaty of Alliance and Mutual Assistance signed by Britain and France

on March 4, 1947.[3] From the start this venture had an air of unreality, for it was directed against "any renewal of German aggression" — scarcely the principal European worry at the moment. Moreover, it provided no permanent organization for military planning or the integration of separate defense efforts. It was the brain-child very largely of French foreign policy which sought insurance against renewed German aggression. Under De Gaulle's leadership in 1944 the French Government had hoped to obtain Soviet diplomatic support for these objectives. This was the purpose behind the Franco-Soviet Pact of that year. But these hopes were dashed. France was invited to neither Yalta nor Potsdam. Yet many Frenchmen in 1946 still cherished hopes of leading a "Third Force" and of remaining neutral in the developing struggle between the Western powers and the U.S.S.R.

Western Union

Hopes for a stable Europe soon wilted under the glare of increasing Soviet hostility. When negotiation in the Council of Foreign Ministers collapsed in 1947 on the German peace treaty question, both Secretary of State Marshall and Foreign Minister Bevin feared the loss of Western Europe to Communist control. Evidently the Soviet Union was stalling for time in the Council meetings while drought, winter cold and economic chaos did their work. Military weakness was an additional factor that seemed to invite Soviet intransigence. A dramatic step was necessary to fire European confidence until the Marshall Plan took effect. But any military assistance program might seem too heavy a dose for the American voter, already faced with the cost of the Marshall Plan. Military arrangements would first have to be made by the Europeans themselves. Would they undertake the comprehensive political, economic and military cooperation that both Bevin and Marshall thought essential?

Mr. Bevin took the first step. Before Parliament on January 22, 1948, he declared that the time was "ripe for the consolidation of Western Europe," and he proposed extending the Dunkirk Treaty to include Britain, France and the Benelux countries in a "Western Union." Mr. Bevin referred directly to Soviet expansion, the ruthless communization of Eastern Europe, the development of the "police state" and Soviet hostility to the Marshall Plan. A month later dramatic weight was added to his words when Czechoslovakia fell before a Communist coup. Many agreed with him that the time had come to "organize the kindred souls of the West, just as they [the Communists] have organized kindred souls in the East." [4]

France, smarting under a Soviet rebuff of a proposal for the economic attachment of the Saar to France, approved the notion of Western Union with alacrity. The Benelux Countries (Belgium, the Netherlands and Lux-

---

[3] For the text see *Documents on European Recovery and Defense* (London: Royal Institute of International Affairs, 1949).
[4] The text was printed in *The New York Times*, January 23, 1948.

embourg — first so named in connection with a tripartite customs convention of 1944) also approved. They had long favored a general and wider defense arrangement in place of the Dunkirk Treaty. Accordingly a new treaty was signed at Brussels on March 17, 1948.[5] On the same day President Truman announced to Congress:

> This development deserves our full support. I am confident that the United States will, by appropriate means, extend to the free nations the support which the situation requires. I am sure that the determination of the free countries of Europe to protect themselves will be matched by an equal determination on our part to help them to do so.[6]

This was a harbinger of further developments in the North Atlantic area. Meanwhile, the Marshall Plan was approved by Congress that April.

Scope, Structure and Obligations of Western Union

Although its first three articles dealt with economic, social and cultural collaboration, the Brussels Treaty was intended primarily as a military alliance. It established a Union including Britain, France and the Benelux Countries. Mr. Bevin, however, had referred in January to the necessity of eventually including Italy in his scheme of things. Under Article IV the five Powers undertook to support one another "with all the military and other aid and assistance in their power" in case of aggression against any one of them in Europe no matter what the source of the aggression might be. The obligation was stated to be in accordance with Article 51 of the United Nations Charter. Only German aggression was specifically mentioned. It was to be a matter of consultation under Article VII. Yet the treaty's primary target was known to lie elsewhere.

The most significant difference between the Dunkirk and Brussels Treaties was the establishment of a permanent, continuously operative defense organization including a Consultative Council of Foreign Ministers, a Defense Committee of Defense Ministers, a Chiefs-of-Staff Committee and a Commanders-in-Chief Committee to head "Uniforce," the regional command organization, with Field Marshal Montgomery as Permanent Military Chairman.[7]

This structure was significant for European regional cooperation for several reasons. First, the organization, cumbersome though it was, provided in large part the model for NATO. Indeed, the military organizations, but

[5] The Brussels Treaty of Economic, Social and Cultural Collaboration and Collective Self-Defense. For the text, see *Documents on European Recovery and Defense.*

[6] *Building the Peace,* Foreign Affairs Outline No. 19, Department of State (1949), p. 4.

[7] For details see *Collective Defense under the Brussels and North Atlantic Treaties,* Cmd. 7883 (London: His Majesty's Stationery Office) and *Western Co-operation for Defense* (New York: British Information Service, 1950).

not the political and economic bodies, were soon to be merged into those of NATO. This step was made easier by the assignment in July 1948 of United States and Canadian observers to all committees save the Commanders-in-Chief Committee.

Second, the organization reflected a degree of military cooperation unprecedented among sovereign states in peacetime. The concept of joint defense including the integration of planning, equipment, forces and training, replaced the notion of national self-sufficiency in Western Europe. The concept was more important than the achievement, for the partners had only poverty to share and herculean defense tasks to plan. With the exception of Britain they had only the equipment provided by the United States during the war.

The Vandenberg Resolution

Events abroad combined to stiffen the United States Government's resolve. The European Recovery Program was bitterly denounced by the rival Cominform organization. The Berlin blockade was soon added to the shock of Czechoslovakia's fall. So obvious was the danger that bipartisan support in the United States developed not only for the Marshall Plan, but also for a regional defense pact between the United States and European nations as a means to national security. The spearhead of this program was the Vandenberg Resolution (Senate Resolution 239) adopted on July 11, 1948, by a Republican-controlled Senate with the hearty support of a Democratic President and his Secretary of State. For the first time in history a peacetime alliance with nations *outside* the Western Hemisphere was the principal objective of United States foreign policy. The Senate had advised the President to seek by constitutional process the progressive development of "regional and other collective arrangements for individual and collective self-defense in accordance with" the Charter. Such arrangements were to be supported by "continuous and effective self-help and mutual aid" among like-minded nations.

A dilemma now emerged. Should the United States first lend a helping hand with an arms-aid program or demonstrate its solidarity with the European states by joining them in a mutual defense organization? In the fall the decision was made, largely on the initiative of the United States and Canada, to establish first a regional security system including, in addition to the Brussels powers, the United States, Canada, Iceland, Denmark, Norway, Portugal and Italy. Sweden preferred neutrality, and Spain, at that time, posed too many headaches for inclusion.

NATO Treaty Signed

Delicate negotiations weathered the American elections of 1948, and the President's inaugural address of January 1949 included a pledge "to strengthen freedom-loving nations against the dangers of aggression." On April 4, 1949, the North Atlantic Treaty was signed by the twelve powers in Washington on the day following the State Department announcement that official requests for military assistance had been received from the treaty partners. Within a few months (July 21) the treaty was approved in the American Senate, 82 to 13, one of the largest votes on record, and Congress as a whole had enacted a Mutual Defense Assistance Program to add flesh and blood to the bare bones of the treaty structure. United States insistence on closer military cooperation among the countries of Western Europe had been heeded, and active American participation in the joint effort was now forthcoming. During 1950 the United States concluded bilateral agreements with the other NATO members to provide military assistance of more than one billion dollars. Later, military and economic assistance programs were combined into a single package. Thus the "Mutual Security Program" for the fiscal year ending June 30, 1952, called for $5,240,000,000 in military assistance to "the free countries of Europe," and another $1,650,000,000 in economic aid, primarily to support their expanded defense effort.[8]

These steps, however, were not taken without argument and misgivings in the United States. They provoked the Great Debate of 1950–51 on American foreign policy which was initiated by Republican leaders. Was the United States overextended, as former President Hoover insisted? Should it concentrate its resources on the Western Hemisphere and such strategic outposts as Japan and the British Isles? Or should the United States increase its commitments and mobilize the entire non-Communist world in a wider security system as Governor Dewey seemed to imply?

The main lines of foreign policy, however, held firm during the debate. Indeed they may have been strengthened by it since unusually wide public scrutiny was produced. NATO continued to develop. Four additional divisions were dispatched to Europe in 1951 as earnest of American conviction that Europe could and would be defended.

Similar debates took place in the legislative bodies of other countries. The Communists could be counted on to follow Moscow's lead in condemning the NATO developments as "warmongering." More serious was the cry of Aneurin Bevan's followers in England that rearmament sapped Europe's economic stability and was the wrong weapon to use in the first place. Also serious was the cry of "neutralists" in France and Germany that NATO arrangements unnecessarily provoked the Soviet Union without providing sufficient compensation in military strength.[9] Yet NATO continued to win the support of governments in power. Never could it be forgotten, however, that international organizations depended on the foreign and domestic policies of the participants. And ever-present was the problem noted by an English observer that the need to maintain armaments in peacetime was a

---

[8] *The Mutual Security Program*, Department of State Publication 4236, General Foreign Policy Series 52 (Washington: Government Printing Office, 1951).
[9] For a discussion of the arguments and exponents of neutralism, see Marina Salvin, "Neutralism in France and Germany," *International Conciliation*, No. 472 (June 1951).

"permanent Achilles heel of a democracy in that there are no votes in a forward defense programme." [10]

The Scope of NATO

Originally the North Atlantic Treaty Organization included twelve partners: the United States, Canada, the United Kingdom, Denmark, Iceland, Norway, France, Italy, Portugal and the Benelux Countries. On February 18, 1952, following the recommendation of the North Atlantic Council, Greece and Turkey became full members of the Alliance. Later the same year a momentous step was taken. A Protocol to the Treaty was drawn up providing membership for the German Federal Republic simultaneously with the establishment of the European Defense Community.[11] These additions involved extensive diplomatic negotiations since the unanimous consent of the original partners was required under Article 10 of the Treaty. Again the United States Senate acted with alacrity and even enthusiasm.[12] There was hope that the new Germany would take its place in the organization in the near future.

The principal criterion for membership was a contribution to the "containment" of the Soviet Union. Portugal and Iceland, for example, provided important bases in the Atlantic and elsewhere. The same arguments applied to Eire, but the Dublin government refused to join any arrangement with Britain as long as the partition of the Emerald Isle continued.

Norway and Denmark joined because alone they were defenseless and because membership was the price of United States arms aid. Failing to organize a separate Scandinavian alliance, Sweden chose neutrality. To exclude Italy would have been to risk a Communist victory there. Greece and Turkey were scarcely elements of the Atlantic Community by anyone's definition, but they too were under Soviet pressure and were anxious to join in mutual defense arrangements. To many, particularly the United States, European regional arrangements made little sense without Germany. Western Union, in short, had had a considerable metamorphosis.

But the very scope of the alliance created problems. For a time the United States would be the principal supplier of the necessary military equipment. Would this not be diffused too widely at the same time that commitments under the pact were being expanded? The Brussels countries were reported to feel that this was the case. The United States was, however, very anxious to extend guarantees to other powers that had tempted the Soviet appetite. Had not Greece been saved by a show of firmness in

[10] A. H. Head, "European Defense," *International Affairs*, Vol. 27, No. 1 (January 1951).

[11] See pp. 739–744; and *Department of State Bulletin*, Vol. 27, No. 676 (June 9, 1952).

[12] The United States considers that the accession of new members to the Treaty creates, in effect, a new treaty between that member and the United States. The "advice and consent" of the Senate is therefore sought in regard to each new member. See the authoritative account by R. H. Heindel, T. V. Kalijarvi and F. O. Wilcox, "The North Atlantic Treaty in the U.S. Senate," *The American Journal of International Law*, Vol. 43 (October 1949), pp. 633–665.

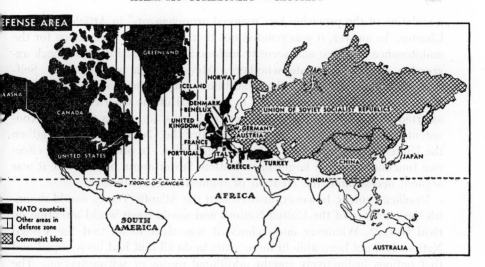

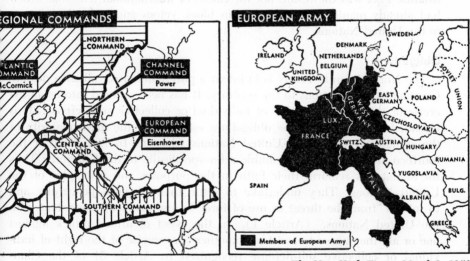

The New York Times, March 9, 1952

THE SET-UP OF THE NORTH ATLANTIC TREATY ORGANIZATION

the United Nations? Had not the Turks firmly opposed Soviet pressure at the Dardanelles as well as in Korea? These factors weighed heavily with American military leaders and Senators.

The decision to join NATO was not an easy one for any of the parties. While all joined in the face of vigorous Soviet protest, Norway was subjected to special pressure and invited to join the Soviet Union in a two-power nonaggression pact. To Oslo this seemed like the kiss of death and the offer was politely but firmly declined. The Soviet Union also protested the inclusion of Italy and Portugal, non-members of the United Nations, as a violation of the provision for "regional arrangements" in Article 52 of the Charter. In answer, it was pointed out that the Charter obligations for the maintenance of peace and security included the responsibility to check aggression against any state whether a Member or a non-member. Self-defense against armed attack, in addition, was an inalienable right of all states and had been incorporated in Article 51 of the Charter. It was even asserted by the United States that regional pacts, so long as they were consistent with the obligation undertaken under the Charter, could strengthen the United Nations itself by deterring aggression. In obstructing the effective functioning of the larger organization, Soviet abuse of the veto, it was argued, necessitated the creation of regional organizations.[13]

Unofficial voices, however, insisted that the Atlantic Treaty would diminish the influence of the United Nations and would focus world attention on rival blocs.[14] Whatever one's views, it was clear to all that the United Nations had not been able in three years to do all that had been hoped and that nations instinctively sought additional means of self-protection. The Atlantic Pact was the result, not the cause, of international tensions, which had already manifested themselves in blocs, vetoes and general acrimony in the United Nations.

Obligations

The North Atlantic Treaty is in intent a purely defensive alliance despite Communist protestations to the contrary. It has been entered into as an exercise of the "inherent right" of individual or collective self-defense. It is intended to square with the obligations incurred by the great majority of the signatories under the United Nations Charter. In fact, four of the fourteen articles and the preamble refer specifically to the Charter.[15] Thus the signatories reaffirm their faith in the purposes and principles of the United Nations. They undertake to settle their disputes peacefully and to refrain "from the threat or use of force in any manner inconsistent with the United Nations." (Article 1). In the event of armed attack against one or all, they agree to assist one another "in exercise of the right of individual or collective self-defense recognized by Article 51 of the Charter. . . ." Any armed attack and the measures taken to meet it are to be reported immediately to the Security Council and are to be terminated if and when the latter restores the peace (Article 5).

The Members are not required to report their defense plans to the Security Council. They must report only the measures taken in self-defense to repel an "armed attack." NATO is not, therefore, a regional arrangement in the sense of Articles 52–54 of the Charter which entail "enforcement action" and other activities wider in scope than the "collective self-defense"

[13] The United States arguments on these points may be found in *North Atlantic Treaty*, Hearings Before the Senate Committee on Foreign Relations (Washington: 1949), Part 1, p. 8ff.

[14] Professor Grayson Kirk expressed these thoughts in 1949. See "The Atlantic Pact and International Security," *International Organization*, Vol. 3, No. 2 (May 1949).

[15] See Appendix *III*.

specified in Article 51.[16] In this respect NATO differs from the Organization of American States (OAS).

The treaty is not to affect "in any way the rights and obligations under the Charter of the Parties which are members of the United Nations, or the primary responsibility of the Security Council for the maintenance of international peace and security." (Article 7). The parties may, after ten years, review the Treaty in light of "universal as well as regional arrangements under the Charter. . . ." (Article 12).

Article 5 contains the principal operative provision of the Treaty and should be examined with care. The parties agree to consider an attack on one or more of them as an attack against all. Each is obligated, in the words of the Senate Foreign Relations Committee Report, "to exercise its honest judgment in deciding upon the measures it will take to help restore and maintain the security of the North Atlantic Area." The "measures" in Article 5 include "such action as [each] deems necessary, including the use of armed force." Thus the military commitment is not as clear cut as that of the Brussels Treaty which required "all the military and other aid and assistance in their power." In the North Atlantic Treaty there is no automatic obligation to take military measures in the event of aggression. This change was due largely to the influence of the American Senate. The Constitution of the United States was said to preclude the automatic military assistance clause of the Brussels Treaty. Despite constitutional niceties, however, events since 1949, including American influence in organizing NATO and the commitment of dollars and GI's in Europe make it clear that any major attack in the Treaty area will find the United States a party to the conflict.

These obligations apply only if an armed attack occurs in the carefully prescribed North Atlantic Area defined in Article 6. It includes the territory of any of the parties in Europe or North America or the Algerian Departments of France and the occupation forces of any Party in Europe. These provisions served to extend the treaty's protection to the Western occupation zones of Austria and Germany and later the Federal Republic prior to its inclusion in NATO. The protocol specifying the inclusion of Greece and Turkey insures that the Mediterranean is included. It refers to "the forces, vessels or aircraft of any of the parties when in or over these territories or any other area in Europe in which occupation forces of any of the parties were stationed on the date when the Treaty entered into force, or the Mediterranean Sea or the Atlantic area. . . ."

Did these guarantees meet the needs of the times? Some commentators thought not. To call a spade a spade, Soviet expansion in Europe since the war did not take the form of an "armed attack." The answer to the question requires a broad view of the situation. Fear and insecurity, stemming from military weakness, were enemies of the Marshall Plan, and the treaty provision promised to replace insecurity with confidence. The obligations

[16] Points made emphatically by Mssrs. Acheson and Bevin before their respective legislative bodies.

undertaken by the NATO countries did much to restore not only military preparedness but the political and economic health of Europe as well.

Most important for the defense of Europe was the fact that the Parties, under Article 4, undertook to "consult together whenever, in the opinion of any of them, the territorial integrity, political independence or security of any of [them] is threatened." In practice, this provision has meant that few aspects of European defense remain outside NATO's purview. Clearly a Communist coup in any country, even if unaided physically from without, would be the subject of NATO consultation. Conceivably aid given to revolutions by outside powers could be considered an "armed attack." The treaty obligations, in short, make possible much of the day-to-day consultation and joint undertakings that are required for Europe's defense. Perhaps the single most effective operative principle in the Treaty is the assurance that the United States linked Europe's safety with its own. This conviction had been lacking between the wars.

Clearly the obligations undertaken in Article 5 would be hollow indeed unless the signatories were able to defend themselves. Their strength could be built up in two ways: first, by individual defense programs and, secondly, by mutual assistance measures including the coordination both of defense plans and military production and the sharing of military supplies. Both means are provided for in Article 3 of the Treaty whereby the parties undertake "separately and jointly, by means of continuous and effective self-help and mutual aid [to] maintain and develop their individual and collective capacity to resist armed attack."

A tremendous enterprise has been authorized by these few words. Under this article $6,000,000,000 worth of military equipment was shipped from the United States to Europe from 1949 to 1953. Similarly contracts amounting to $2,200,000,000 were placed in Europe for "offshore purchases" by the United States during 1952–1953. Finally, a NATO command organization has been established with a Supreme Commander for the allied forces in Europe. Coordinated defense plans have been drawn up and joint maneuvers held.

To effect the "mutual aid" provisions of the Treaty, the Mutual Defense Assistance Act of 1949 and the Mutual Security Act of 1951 were passed by the United States Congress. The latter legislation included both military aid and economic aid. The latter was described as a "defense support" program designed to provide a solid economic foundation for the military program. This legislation was an effort to strike a careful balance between military and economic aid. If rearmament upset Europe's recently revived economy, arms aid would go for naught. On the other hand, rearmament was thought essential to deter possible Soviet aggression through a restoration of some sort of military balance in Europe.

To receive military assistance, the recipient was required to agree to certain stipulations, including "the development and maintenance of its own defensive strength and the defensive strength of the free world." [17]

---

[17] *Mutual Security Act of 1952*, Report of the Committee on Foreign Affairs on H. R. 700 Amending the Mutual Security Act of 1951 (Washington: 1952), p. 70.

Recipients of economic aid, however, were simply required to promote "international understanding and good will." In addition, military assistance was dependent upon approval by the President of the United States of NATO recommendations for an "integrated defense" of the North Atlantic area. In this way American foreign policy sought both to increase the return on every dollar of foreign aid and at the same time to promote European "integration."

While of less immediate concern than Articles 3 and 5, Article 2 has long-run implications. Under it the Parties undertake

> the further development of peaceful and friendly international relations by strengthening their free institutions, by bringing about a better understanding of the principles upon which these institutions are founded, and by promoting conditions of stability and well-being. They will seek to eliminate conflict in their international economic policies and will encourage economic collaboration between any or all of them.

Precedent for these undertakings was contained in Articles 1–3 of the Brussels Treaty. This general statement of intent might cover many things — customs unions or other economic arrangements, cultural and social cooperation or political undertakings such as the closer coordination of the Parties' foreign policies. At the Ottawa meeting of the North Atlantic Council in September 1951, a ministerial committee, composed of the representatives of Belgium, Canada, Italy, the Netherlands and Norway, was instituted to recommend ways of implementing this article.

This committee became known as the Atlantic Community Committee. That its work was not given the highest priority may be divined by the fact that its membership is drawn from the middle and smaller powers of the Organization. It reported to later sessions of the Council on important matters, however, including the need for working out closer relations with the Organization for European Economic Cooperation and the need to improve the mobility of labor among the NATO countries in order to speed up defense production.[18]

Structure

The principal organ in NATO is the Council of Foreign Ministers, modeled after the Consultative Council of the Brussels Treaty. Under Article 9 the Council plans the implementation of the Treaty and may set up any necessary subsidiary bodies. In May 1950 the Council sought to strengthen its organization by appointing a continuously functioning Committee of Deputies with a full-time staff. In the remainder of the organization defense matters were placed under a Committee of Defense Ministers. There were, in addition, a Military Production and Supply Board and a Military Committee composed of the Chiefs-of-Staff of all the members. Both of these units reported to the Defense Committee. Militarily a twelve-power command organization was impossible, however, since it inevitably took on some of the characteristics of a debating society. Accordingly, the real

[18] *Department of State Bulletin,* Vol. 26, No. 663 (March 10, 1952), p. 368.

work of the Military Committee is performed by a continuously functioning Standing Group, representing the Chiefs-of-Staff of the bigger powers, the United States, Britain and France. It was set up because of the need for an efficient military planning group of the Chiefs-of-Staff of those members which had the power to run the show.

Sensible though this unit was, it led at once to the first of several problems that plagued NATO — a measure of resentment on the part of the smaller powers against what seemed to be big-power domination. We have noted the same reaction in regard to the League and the United Nations Councils. The Defense Committee and the Military Committee on which they were represented were largely paper organizations and rarely met. Effective control inevitably remained with the Standing Group which guided the work of five regional planning groups for Northern Europe, Western Europe, Southern Europe and the Western Mediterranean, Canada and the United States, and the North Atlantic Ocean.

A second problem was the need, demonstrated particularly after Korea, for a centralized political authority strong enough to issue and enforce the directives necessary to meet the agreed objectives of the Organization. How was a civilian authority to be set up that would be strong enough to formulate and carry out basic armament and supporting economic policies? How were separate budget estimates to be reviewed and effectively coordinated? There was, in short, no real executive or legislative authority, no party machinery, no Budget Bureau or Treasury as in a national government, to perform these necessary tasks. Nor was there any tradition of cabinet responsibility or legislative accountability to insure that policy decisions were made and carried out. There was, in short, insufficient political authority to compel the efficient pooling of defense efforts deemed necessary by the twelve partners.

Communist aggression in Korea was perhaps the most compelling factor pointing up the need for a simpler organization of fewer committees with clearer lines of authority and more full-time operating agencies. NATO, it now appeared, might be faced with overt military aggression sooner than expected. The Canadian Government proposed a reorganization in the fall of 1950. This was completed the following May and has remained intact in essential details since that time. The principal achievement has been to unify political direction of the alliance by eliminating the three successive layers of ministerial committees. The former separate Committees of Foreign Ministers, Defense Ministers and Finance Ministers have been absorbed into the North Atlantic Council, now the sole ministerial body of the Organization. Member governments may send whichever ministers are most concerned with the problems being discussed. At the Council's Seventh Session at Ottawa in September, 1951, for example, the agenda was so broad that the members were represented by their foreign, defense and finance ministers.[19]

To please the smaller powers a Military Representative Committee was

[19] *Department of State Bulletin*, Vol. 24, No. 620 (May 21, 1951), p. 810.

established including representatives of the full membership. It was to be consulted and kept informed by the big-power Standing Group when the Military Committee was not in session. Finally, the complicated civilian structure was replaced by three permanent civilian agencies: the Council Deputies, July 1950; the Defense Production Board, January 1951; and the Finance and Economic Board, May 1951. All of these had separate international secretariats.

But this civilian structure remained in place only a little over a year. Efficient planning and command required even greater centralization of authority. To solve the pressing problem of meeting the costs of increased armaments and to draw up an Atlantic rearmament balance sheet, an Executive Bureau was also established at the significant Ottawa meeting of the Council in September 1951. The real work was turned over to a Temporary Council Committee composed of W. Averell Harriman of the United States, Hugh Gaitskell (later Sir Edwin Plowden) of the United Kingdom, and Jean Monnet of France.[20]

This group was quickly dubbed the "Three Wise Men." Its task was to devise means of bridging the gap between military goals and economic resources. The "Three Wise Men" were faced with grave tasks. Rearmament in the United States and Europe, following Korea, had upset Europe's economic balance so laboriously fostered by the Marshall Plan. Raw material prices soared, and Europe's standard of living began to slip downward. Europe was plagued with an increased dollar shortage. Nonmilitary production had not prospered sufficiently so that exports were able to pay for imports. Part of the trouble was that Europe's imports were dearer than her exports. This was particularly true after the United States rearmament program sent raw materials prices skyrocketing. Tariff walls were an additional liability. Britain, recently on an even keel and free of Marshall Plan aid, was again heeled over by economic gales. There was danger that the haste of the United States to rearm might undo the good work accomplished by the Marshall Plan.

The Temporary Council Committee grappled with these issues. It estimated and screened the defense needs and capabilities of the Atlantic Allies. In reporting to the Executive Bureau, it kept all partners, large and small, informed of its deliberations. Its recommendations served as the basis for the Council's decisions at its important eighth and ninth meetings in Rome and Lisbon in November 1951 and February 1952, respectively.[21] Here it was decided what forces should be made available to the military commands in 1952. More important, the Council decided how the cost of these forces should be shared by the member countries. A process was emerging, in short, whereby a civilian authority was screening military needs and economic capabilities as the basis for policy recommendations of the most far-reaching sort. The destinies of fourteen nations were spliced

---

[20] *International Organization,* Vol. 5, No. 4 (November 1951), p. 815.
[21] See *International Organization,* Vol. 6, No. 1 (February 1952), and Vol. 6, No. 2 (May 1952).

together in this process. Information on budgets and defense, usually closely guarded secrets of national governments, now formed the basis of collective decisions in the interests of the NATO countries as a whole. After completing its work and establishing a milestone in advancing the concept of collective action, the Temporary Council Committee was terminated by the Council's decision at Lisbon in February 1952. Its work, however, is carried on by the newly established civilian structure of NATO.

After the trail-blazing performance of the "Three Wise Men" in coordinating NATO's military and economic potentialities, the Council readily accepted their recommendation that a Secretary-General be appointed to help prepare and to follow up the Council's decisions. The February 1952 session decided upon a new permanent headquarters in Paris, near the proposed Defense Community and the Supreme Headquarters Allied Powers Europe (described below). This headquarters consists of a Secretary-General and the North Atlantic Council in permanent session with permanent representatives. There are also periodic ministerial sessions of the Council here, to which the Secretary-General reports. As currently organized, the Council and its secretariat perform on a day-to-day basis the work previously done separately by the Council of Deputies, the Defense Production Board, and the Finance and Economic Board. Thus all civilian agencies have been concentrated in a geographical area with other international agencies whose work is closely related to that of NATO and with which close administrative ties were essential for efficiency's sake. The following charts compare NATO's organization before and after the Lisbon meeting of the Council in February 1952.

The NATO Secretary-General (and Vice-Chairman of the Council) appointed at Lisbon was Lord Ismay, British soldier, cabinet Minister and former secretary of the Committee of Imperial Defense, who rates the respect of both military and civilians alike in his delicate international post. Having been empowered to order his own house, Ismay set about cutting down and integrating the previously diversified Council staff. By November 1952 the NATO secretariat was reported as numbering 434 persons, including clerical help. Three Assistant Secretaries-General were appointed to supervise the principal branches of work: Fenoatta, of Italy, for political affairs; R. Sargent, of France, for economic affairs; and D. L. Hopkins, of the United States for defense production. An American and a Dutchman were named as Deputy Secretaries-General.

The functions set out for this permanent international bureaucracy were threefold. First of all, an integrated economic program for NATO as a whole has to be hammered out for the periodic approval of the Council. The Secretariat, with the cooperation of the Permanent Council Representatives, fuses the aggregate of national estimates of needs and capabilities into a common program. The military force and production targets to be set for each member nation have to be reconciled with its politico-economic capabilities, and these in turn must be reviewed periodically. The permanent international staff also seeks out general economies for the Organization through coordinated defense production among the members.

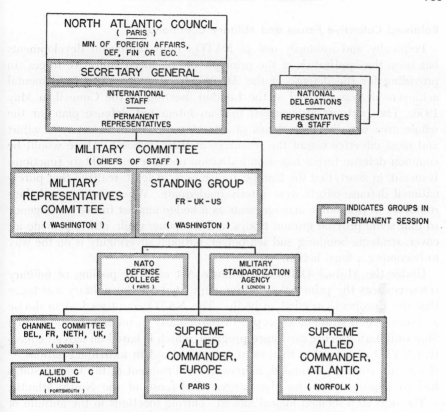

NORTH ATLANTIC COUNCIL
(PARIS)
MIN. OF FOREIGN AFFAIRS,
DEF, FIN OR ECO.

SECRETARY GENERAL

INTERNATIONAL
STAFF

PERMANENT
REPRESENTATIVES

NATIONAL
DELEGATIONS

REPRESENTATIVES
& STAFF

MILITARY   COMMITTEE
(CHIEFS OF STAFF)

MILITARY
REPRESENTATIVES
COMMITTEE
(WASHINGTON)

STANDING GROUP
FR – UK – US
(WASHINGTON)

INDICATES GROUPS IN
PERMANENT SESSION

NATO
DEFENSE
COLLEGE
(PARIS)

MILITARY
STANDARDIZATION
AGENCY
(LONDON)

CHANNEL COMMITTEE
BEL, FR, NETH, UK,
(LONDON)

ALLIED C C
CHANNEL
(PORTSMOUTH)

SUPREME
ALLIED
COMMANDER,
EUROPE
(PARIS)

SUPREME
ALLIED
COMMANDER,
ATLANTIC
(NORFOLK)

NORTH ATLANTIC TREATY ORGANIZATION, APRIL 1, 1952

The second major concern of the Secretariat is to supervise the implementation of programs and to prepare progress reports for the Council. The Secretary-General has ultilized his authority to appoint committees to deal with common problems such as civil defense coordination.

Finally, the civilian staff has the function of solidifying NATO as a permanent institution rather than a mere periodic conference for military cooperation. Lord Ismay has shown a particular concern for promoting NATO public relations, and his staff has given thought to the long-range objectives of the Organization in trade, cultural and social matters beyond the immediate military situation. It remains to be seen how extensive will become the civilian authority which has been developing in the office of the Secretary-General. A continuation of the present evolution could conceivably place the Secretariat ahead of the military chiefs in steering NATO program planning and execution. In any event, the establishment of Permanent Council Representatives and a Secretary-General was a step toward insuring that the pace of defense planning be set not by military but by civilian authority.

Balanced Collective Forces and Military Commands

Politically and militarily one of NATO's most significant developments has been the application of the principle of "balanced collective forces" in providing for the defense of the Atlantic Community. This fundamental achievement was reached at the London meeting of the Council in May 1950. The partners also agreed that an integrated defense plan for the whole area was the best means of attaining maximum economy of effort and most effective use of the resources at their disposal. There would be common defense forces based on a division of labor and military functions. It meant, in short, that the European members, at least, realized that purely national defense efforts were utterly inadequate. When nations pool their resources in peacetime arrangements as a hedge against future contingency so that some provide ground troops and weapons, while others provide air cover, strategic bombing and sea power, national sovereignty is on the way to becoming a legal fiction.

Under the Mutual Defense Assistance Act of 1949, pooling of military resources was the principal condition stipulated for the military assistance that the Europeans needed so badly. The NATO countries had to devise a "fundamental strategic concept . . . particularly in relation to the United States military defense assistance program, which is based on agreed collective NATO plans rather than on unintegrated aid to individual nations."[22] Before aid could be extended, moreover, the President of the United States had to approve plans for the integrated defense of the North Atlantic.

The next step seemed logical indeed. During meetings in the autumn of 1950, the Council and the Defense Committee completed arrangements for an integrated Western European defense force under centralized command. At its Brussels meeting on December 19, 1950, the Council unanimously requested the President of the United States to designate General of the Army Dwight D. Eisenhower for the position of Supreme Allied Commander, Europe (SACEUR).

More than any other individual, General Eisenhower is responsible for NATO's achievements and the revival of hope in Western Europe. This extraordinary man, who had led Allied Armies across the channel to crack the European fortress in World War II, had the confidence of the Europeans. Equally important, he emphasized on every side that he had confidence in them. The result was that they once more believed in themselves.

Before settling down to weld an effective, integrated fighting force, the General conducted a twenty-one day tour of the ten European NATO capitals. The purpose of his trip was to ascertain the resources the European governments were prepared to contribute to the common defense against possible communist aggression. On his return he exuded confidence in Western Europe's military potential which he deemed sufficient with an important proviso. There must be real determination to combine for mutual protection. To the United States Congress he reported in person that he

[22] *Department of State Bulletin,* Vol. 23, No. 585 (September 8, 1950), pp. 468–469.

had found convincing evidence of a "rejuvenation, a growth of determination, a spirit to resist . . . to take the risk." [23] This evidence of morale was to Eisenhower a decisive element in making resistance possible. From the European point of view, however, his visit meant that resistance would be worth while. He convinced Europe that the United States believed its destiny was Europe's destiny. This sense of mutual confidence was driven home by the dispatch of four additional United States divisions in the summer of 1951 to bolster the occupation forces in Germany.

But it was the personality of the Supreme Commander that provided the elixir to instill life in NATO.[24] In Mr. Acheson's words:

> There must be this one dynamic figure to give all of our allies the guidance, the direction, the inspiration which will lead to the translation of papers into people and things and organized people and organized things. General Eisenhower, more than any living soldier, has got the capacity, the prestige, the imagination which can bring that about. His appointment is in itself a great act in Europe. . . .

Fortunately, when Eisenhower laid aside his uniform to toss his hat into the political arena in May 1952, a worthy successor was appointed to fill his shoes. General Matthew Ridgway as United Nations Commander in Korea had also proved a competent leader of an allied coalition and it was important to place an American in charge. The selection of a European might have raised a knotty prestige problem. The American Congress, moreover, had a friendly ear for its military leaders that was often denied its diplomatists. In the spring of 1953, General Alfred Gruenther, who had distinguished himself as Chief-of-Staff to the previous Supreme Commanders, succeeded to that post himself.

SHAPE

After his morale-building tour General Eisenhower set about to mold an effective fighting force from the national units assigned to NATO and to organize an efficient Supreme Headquarters Allied Powers Europe.[25] Unlike his task in World War II as Commander of the Allied Expeditionary Forces, when virtually only two countries needed to be consulted, General Eisenhower had the feelings of twelve and later fourteen nations to consider. For this reason he once declared he was only "one-twelfth" American with eleven-twelfths dedicated to the other nations of NATO. Indeed all staff officers at Supreme Headquarters act in the name of the whole organization, yet no conflict of loyalties has emerged. For American officers, the fact that the North Atlantic Treaty is, under the Constitution, part of the

[23] *The New York Times,* February 2, 1951.

[24] News Conference, December 27, 1950, *Department of State Bulletin,* Vol. 24, No. 600 (January 1, 1951), pp. 3–4.

[25] For an authoritative account, see Colonel Robert J. Wood, "The First Year of SHAPE," in *International Organization,* Vol. 6, No. 2 (May 1952), p. 175.

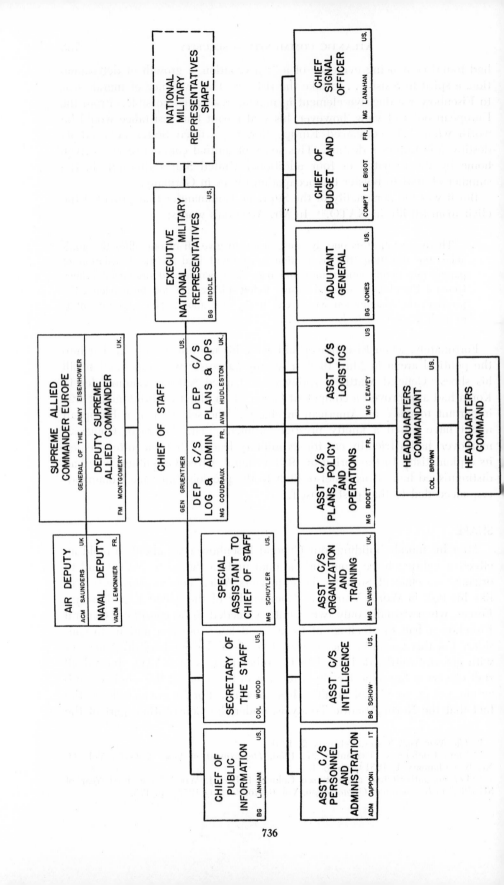

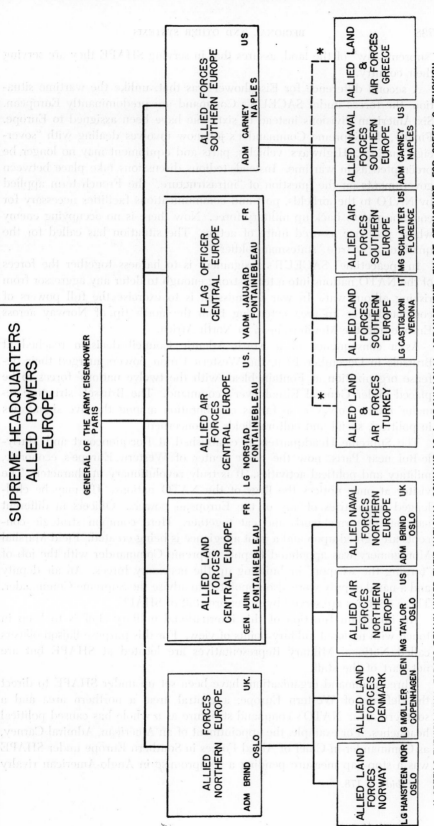

SUPREME HEADQUARTERS
ALLIED POWERS
EUROPE

GENERAL OF THE ARMY EISENHOWER
PARIS

ALLIED FORCES
NORTHERN
EUROPE
U.K.

ADM BRIND OSLO

ALLIED LAND
FORCES
NORWAY
LG HANSTEEN NOR
OSLO

ALLIED LAND
FORCES
DENMARK
LG MØLLER DEN
COPENHAGEN

ALLIED AIR
FORCES
NORTHERN
EUROPE
MG TAYLOR US
OSLO

ALLIED NAVAL
FORCES
NORTHERN
EUROPE
ADM BRIND OSLO
UK

ALLIED LAND
FORCES
CENTRAL
EUROPE
FR
GEN JUIN
FONTAINEBLEAU

ALLIED AIR
FORCES
CENTRAL
EUROPE
U.S.
LG NORSTAD
FONTAINEBLEAU

FLAG OFFICER
CENTRAL EUROPE
FR
VADM JAUJARD
FONTAINEBLEAU

ALLIED FORCES
SOUTHERN EUROPE
US

ADM CARNEY NAPLES

ALLIED LAND
&
AIR FORCES
TURKEY

ALLIED LAND
FORCES
SOUTHERN
EUROPE
IT
LG CASTIGLIONI
VERONA

ALLIED AIR
FORCES
SOUTHERN
EUROPE
US
MG SCHLATTER
FLORENCE

ALLIED NAVAL
FORCES
SOUTHERN
EUROPE
ADM CARNEY US
NAPLES

ALLIED LAND
&
AIR FORCES
GREECE

* GREEK & TURKISH NAVAL FORCES REMAIN UNDER THEIR NATIONAL COMMAND AS A PROVISIONAL ARRANGEMENT. EXACT STRUCTURE FOR GREEK & TURKISH
LAND & AIR FORCES IS NOW IN PROCESS OF DEVELOPMENT.

PRINCIPAL HEADQUARTERS OF ALLIED COMMAND, EUROPE, APRIL 1, 1952 "supreme law" of the land, assures that in serving SHAPE they are serving their country.[26]

A second difference for Eisenhower was that, unlike the wartime situation, the forces under SACEUR's Command are predominantly European. Six American divisions instead of sixty-one have been assigned to Europe. Finally, the Supreme Commander's job now involves dealing with "sovereign" nations. Highways, vehicles, parts and equipment may no longer be preëmpted as in wartime. Instead, tedious discussions take place between governments on the question of "infrastructure," the French term applied by NATO to the airfields, port and communications facilities necessary for common use to back up military force. Now there is no occupying enemy whose presence assured unity of action. The situation has called for the qualities of a true "statesman-soldier."

In "peacetime" SACEUR's assignment is to harness together the forces of the NATO nations into a team strong enough to deter any aggressor from risking all-out war. In war his mission is to exercise the full powers of command over an area extending from the north tip of Norway across Europe and the Mediterranean to North Africa.

As a consequence of a North Atlantic Council decision reached at Brussels in December 1950, the Western Union powers merged their defense organization at Fontainebleau with the twelve nations' forces to be placed under General Eisenhower's command. The Brussels structure remains intact, however, so far as collaboration among the five signatories in political, social and cultural fields is concerned.

The Supreme Headquarters is established at Rocquencourt and Marly-le-Roi near Paris, now the nerve center of Western Europe's economic, military and political activities. It is truly revolutionary in character. The visitor at once notices the flags of the NATO nations. He may be challenged by sentries of any of the European powers. Officers in different national uniforms work and eat together. Here common strategic concepts are agreed upon and a joint allegiance is being created. Field Marshal Montgomery was appointed Deputy Supreme Commander with the job of "forging the weapon" or building up the necessary forces. An air deputy and a naval deputy were also appointed to advise the Supreme Commander. These deputies are served by the entire staff of SHAPE.

An important function of this international military staff is to keep in touch with national military points of view. For this purpose liaison officers called National Military Representatives are located at SHAPE but are not part of the staff.

Three command organizations have been set up under SHAPE to direct the defense of Western Europe, a central area, a northern area and a southern area. NATO's command structure as a whole has caused political headaches. For example, the appointment of an American, Admiral Carney, as Commander-in-Chief of Allied Forces in Southern Europe under SHAPE was a stop-gap measure pending a compromise in Anglo-American rivalry

[26] *Ibid.,* p. 178.

over command of the Mediterranean area as a whole.[27] Another problem was whether there should be a separate Middle East Command including Greece, Turkey and the Arab states as the British preferred. With the inclusion of Greece and Turkey in NATO, the issue was resolved largely in favor of the United States' point of view. In the summer of 1952 the creation of a Greek-Turkish army group headquarters, under SHAPE and under the command of an American officer, was agreed upon by the Council.[28]

The inclusion of a Greek-Turkish Army Group under SHAPE eliminated an opportunity to place a British officer in charge of an important NATO command. A disconcerting problem of prestige arose because a United States officer had already been appointed Supreme Allied Commander Atlantic in January, 1952, the marine counterpart of SHAPE. It meant that the top NATO commands to date had been awarded to the United States. To the British this situation seemed an unwarranted affront. It was bitterly decried both by the Churchill government and by the Labor Opposition.

Other problems facing SHAPE have had less serious political implications. They involved the establishment of an adequate communications system between the fourteen partners, the exchange of confidential information, the standardization of arms and the coordination of the supply efforts of the national forces. Particularly frustrating has been the problem of providing the "infrastructure" mentioned above because ticklish problems in international relations have been involved. French peasants have been denied sorely needed farm land allotted to NATO air forces. Complicated rules have had to be negotiated between the "host" country and the "user" country regarding the responsibility for building runways, hangars, workshops, barracks, mess halls and chapels.

Yet in spite of many difficulties progress at SHAPE has been steady if slow. There was promise that by 1954 Western Europe would be too strong to tempt aggression. One problem remained, however, that dwarfed all the others and threatened NATO's success: what was to be Germany's relation to the growing Atlantic community? Should German military units be included in Europe's defense? One answer to this explosive question was the European Defense Community.

The European Defense Community

The European Defense Community is a "supranational" specialized agency conceived after Communist aggression in Korea in 1950 had made the question of German rearmament the sharpest thorn in NATO's side. It was the more painful because of the abrupt manner with which it was thrust forward by the United States.[29] The problem of Germany was that

[27] See statement by Lieut. Gen. A. M. Gruenther, SHAPE's Chief-of-Staff, in *The New York Times,* June 19, 1951.

[28] *The New York Times,* July 16, 1952.

[29] One journalist considered American haste a "blunder." Drew Middleton, *The Defense of Western Europe* (New York: Appleton-Century-Crofts, 1952), p. 91.

the Western European countries could neither get along with her nor without her. Yet there had been a growing realization on both sides of the Atlantic that a settlement with the Soviet Union of the German problem was as remote as ever. The wisest course, therefore, was to accept a divided Germany for the present and to welcome the West German Republic into the European family.

From the United States point of view German rearmament was urgent for two reasons. The first was that Korea showed that Moscow was ready to turn the cold war into a hot one when the enemy's weakness promised success.[30] The second was the increasing evidence of remilitarization in the Soviet occupation zone in Eastern Germany. Might not satellite troops be used in Europe as they had been in Korea? An additional factor was the apparent conviction of many American leaders that Western Europe could not be defended without German troops and industry. The stage was set for a disagreement that threatened for a time to drive a wedge between the Europeans and the United States.

The subject was broached abruptly in the summer of 1950 when the State Department informed the British and French Foreign Ministers that the United States wished to discuss the question of German rearmament at the September meeting of the Council of Foreign Ministers. On September 5, the United States High Commissioner in Germany, Mr. McCloy, reported that "in some manner the Germans should be enabled if they want to, to defend their own country." [31]

At the Council meeting the United States sought the speedy organization of a limited number of German divisions, ten or twelve, to join the Atlantic defense force. So long as the formation of a German general staff was prohibited, and German units were limited to division strength and placed under a central non-German command such as SHAPE, the United States felt it was safe to arm the former enemy.

Reaction was sharp and sudden. The stiffest resistance was led by the French who were determined, in the words of Mr. René Pleven, the Premier, that there should be "no German divisions, no German general staff, no German minister of war." [32] From the German point of view these were the very conditions of rearmament.

Others also were hesitant to follow the United States for several reasons. Arming Germany might provoke the Soviet Union and intensify rather than reduce the danger of conflict. Germany could be rearmed only at the expense of the Treaty partners who should have prior claim to United States military aid. And finally, many thought that the Federal Republic would not be strong enough to cope with nationalistic forces that would be encouraged by German rearmament. Perhaps the most persuasive influ-

---

[30] The change in United States policy toward Germany may be traced in the words of the Secretary of State in *The Pattern of Responsibility*, edited by McGeorge Bundy (Boston: Houghton Mifflin, 1951), Chap. 5.

[31] *The New York Times*, September 6, 1950.

[32] Speech to the National Assembly, October 24, 1950. Reported in *The New York Times*, October 25, 1950.

ences were the shadows of 1871, 1914 and 1940. It strained the credulity of many Frenchmen, Belgians and others to substitute the Soviet Union for Germany as enemy number one.

Could the problem be solved by diluting German soldiers in a "European Army?" American and British military leaders thought not, at first, but this was the essence of the compromise advanced by Premier Pleven on October 24, 1950. His plan included the creation of a European Army under a European Minister of Defense, who would be responsible to a European authority and who would carry out the directives of a Council of Ministers composed of representatives of the participating countries. This army would be financed by a common budget and would be used to further the obligations of the North Atlantic Treaty. The proposal bore marked resemblance to a resolution submitted by Winston Churchill and passed by the Consultative Assembly of the Council of Europe the preceding August.[33]

The Pleven proposal, backed by the French National Assembly, was then laid before the North Atlantic Defense Committee meeting in Washington, and later before the Council Deputies and the Military Committee. These deliberations led to the announcement of a compromise at the Brussels meeting of the North Atlantic Council that followed the main outline of the French proposals for a European Army rather than adhering to the original British-American preference for a separate German army as a component of NATO.[34] A determining factor at this time was the support rapidly developed in both France and Germany for both the Pleven Plan and for the Schuman Plan to pool French and German iron and coal industries. These two French plans were complementary means of approaching the same goal, Franco-German amity.

Accordingly a European Army Conference of France, Western Germany, Italy, Belgium and Luxembourg met in late 1951 to hammer out specific proposals to implement the Pleven Plan. The Netherlands joined the talks in October 1951. A treaty constituting the European Defense Community (EDC) was signed by representatives of the six powers on May 27, 1952. Nearly two years later there was still doubt whether France would take the plunge even after the meeting of American, British, French and Russian Foreign Ministers at Berlin in January 1954 had failed to produce a settlement of the German question.

Structure

The Treaty provided for a European Defense Force within the political framework of a European Defense Community specifically described in Article 1 as "supranational in character."

> The members will cease to have national armies except for troops that were necessary in "non-European territories" — Indo-China, for example. Instead they will supply troops in units approaching division-size to a com-

[33] It is included in *The New York Times* of August 12, 1950. The Council of Europe is discussed in Chap. 26.
[34] See *The New York Times*, December 14, 1950.

bined and integrated defense force under a Supreme Commander responsible to NATO. This six-nation army is to be financed by a common budget, supplied through common procurement procedures and to have a common uniform. The North Atlantic Command is authorized to allow a member government to withdraw part of its international contingent for use overseas in a crisis. This decision cannot be made unilaterally by a member government, a prohibition resisted by France.

Commissariat

Control is to be exercised by an institution resembling a defense department to be called the Commissariat for the European Defense Community consisting of nine members appointed for six years. The members are not to solicit or accept instructions from any governments and their decisions are binding on all members. They are to elect a President from their number.

Council of Ministers

"To harmonize the actions of the Commissariat with the polices of the member governments," a Council of Ministers is to be established made up of a Cabinet member of each of the member countries. It is to issue directives for the action of the Commissariat, such directives to require unanimous vote. Other decisions require a simple majority except in the case of a tie vote. Then the vote of the members carrying two-thirds of the contributions to the defense force carry the day. This important control body is established so as to function continuously, and, in traditional fashion, the Presidency will be rotated in the alphabetical order of the member states.

Parliamentary Assembly

A Parliamentary Assembly is also provided for in the Treaty and is to be the same body as that established in the European Coal and Steel Treaty (Schuman Plan). It will represent the parliaments of the members and will meet in annual session unless convened in extraordinary session provided for in a number of ways. Representation is to be weighted in this body with eighteen delegates apiece for France, Germany and Italy, ten apiece for Belgium and the Netherlands, and four for Luxembourg. Its functions are to receive annual reports from the Commissariat and make comments thereon. By two-thirds vote it may pass a motion of censure thereby compelling the members of the Commissariat to resign in a body. It is specifically required under Article 38 to study "the creation of an Assembly of the European Defense Community elected on a democratic basis" and consider as a principle that "the definitive organization which will take the place of the present transitional organization should be conceived so as to be capable of constituting one of the elements of an ultimate federal or confederal structure, based upon the principle of the separation of powers and including, particularly, a bicameral representative system." It was also to study means of coordinating the various instruments of European cooperation within the framework of the federal or confederal structure. The Assembly's proposals are then to be forwarded to the Council for transmittal with comments to the member states which undertake to call a conference to examine them. If the Treaty is ratified, the six powers, in short, are committed to hold what might well be a European constitutional convention.

Court of Justice

The Treaty also provides a Court which is to be the same as the Court of Justice of the European Coal and Steel Community. It will "ensure the rule of law in the interpretation and application of the present Treaty and implementing regulations." It will "hear appeals from decisions or recommendations of the Commissariat, by a member state, by the Council or by the Assembly. . . ." The Court's powers are to be extensive and rather similar to those of the United States Supreme Court, for the Commissariat is required to give effect to the annulment of any of its decisions or recommendations by the Court. It may "hear appeals" from decisions of the Council by a member state, by the Commissariat or by the Assembly on legal grounds. It may "annul a decision of the Assembly on the motion of a member state or of the Commissariat." The jurisdiction of the Court may be invoked only on "grounds of lack of legal competence to act or of substantial procedural violations." [35]

The realization of the European Defense Community depended on the establishment of the Federal Republic of Germany as a sovereign and equal partner in the community of nations. This was accomplished in three stages. First, political control of Germany had been relaxed when the Federal Republic was established in 1949. Second, the occupation statute was revised in March 1951, so as to give the new state practically full control of its foreign affairs. An Allied High Commission remained, however, to channel relations between the Federal Government and the Western powers.

Finally, the Federal Republic assumed almost full sovereignty when the occupation ended for all practical purposes with the signing of contractual agreements at Bonn on May 26, 1952, by the Foreign Ministers of France, the United Kingdom and the United States and Chancellor Adenauer of the Federal Republic.[36] In order to insure the defense of Germany in the immediate future, the contractual agreements provided for the continued presence of Allied troops on German soil, with rights and obligations defined.[37] In addition, a protocol to the North Atlantic Treaty extended to the members of the European Defense Community the guarantees of NATO. This was done so that an attack on Germany would henceforth be considered the same as an attack on any Treaty partner. For United States foreign policy the protocol had an added significance. On its signing the Secretary of State, Dean Acheson, declared: "We have seen the beginning of the realization of an ancient dream — the unity of the free people of Western Europe." [38] The Senate, as has already been noted, approved these ar-

[35] Documents relating to the European Defense Community may be found in U.S. 82nd Cong., 2nd Sess., Senate, Executives Q & R, *Convention on Relations with the Federal Republic of Germany and a Protocol to the North Atlantic Treaty — Message from the President of the United States* (Washington: June 2, 1952).

[36] For a summary of the Contractual Agreements see the *Department of State Bulletin,* Vol. 26, No. 676 (June 9, 1952), p. 887.

[37] The protocol and the Convention on Relations Between the Three Powers and the Federal Republic may be found in Senate Document, Executives Q & R, *op. cit.*

[38] Article 5 of the Convention reserves for the Three Powers the right to declare,

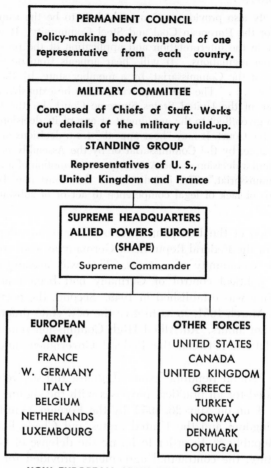

HOW EUROPEAN ARMY FITS INTO NATO

rangements with unusual alacrity. Meanwhile the control of Germany's economy had long since been relaxed so that German industrial power was already making itself felt in the strengthening of Western Europe.

Looking Back

One conclusion to be drawn from NATO and the emerging EDC was that Europe, under the impact of the Soviet threat, was seeking ways to unite. No new alchemy was involved. Self-defense has been the principal

after consultation with the Federal Republic, a state of emergency if the latter or the EDC is unable to deal with: "an attack on the Federal Republic of Berlin, subversion of the Liberal democratic order, a serious disturbance of public order, or a grave threat of any of these events."

force impelling political union since the dawn of history. Because the Italian Government feared that the Community would lack sufficient supranational authority to insure Europe's defense, Article 38 was included in the Treaty. Thereby the six powers pledged themselves to attempt a shift from intergovernmental cooperation to a federal authority. The way ahead, however, promised many dangers. Should the Soviet Union relax its pressure, the United States might not extend the economic and military aid needed to cushion the transition from separatism to federal union.

Equally dubious were the internal politics of the European countries themselves. Neutralists as well as Communists in France had long opposed the Atlantic Pact. The former tended to oppose the EDC as part of a program in which France was unwisely, in their view, choosing sides. The followers of De Gaulle denounced the NATO partnership and particularly the EDC as unworthy of France's former greatness. France in 1953 seemed nearly ready to disown her brain child. In Germany in the elections of 1953, Chancellor Adenauer defeated the Social Democrats who advanced the reunification of Germany as more important than the unification of Western Europe and who felt that a European army would provoke Soviet retaliation. In Italy the weak coalition of center parties was under constant pressure from the Communists and reawakening Fascist groups.

Yet much had already been accomplished under the aegis of NATO even if the European army failed to develop. The North Atlantic Treaty provided the necessary leverage to bring about agreement among Britain, France and the United States on the German question in 1949. The United States at that time sought to woo Germany by relaxing economic controls and by granting her a considerable measure of self government. France, long a fearful neighbor of Germany, balked in the traces. Yet agreement was suddenly achieved in April 1949 on the establishment of the Federal German Republic, control of the Ruhr and the termination of the dismantling of German industry. In the words of the Secretary of State:

> It was not by mere coincidence that these agreements were initiated during the week the North Atlantic Treaty was signed. That historic instrument marks a decisive step toward the creation of a community of democratic nations dedicated to the attainment of peace and determined to insure its preservation by all the material and moral means at their disposal.[39]

France, in brief, was ready to take chances with Germany that she was unwilling to take before the establishment of NATO.

The same framework and the proposed European Defense Community made possible further restoration of German sovereignty and steps toward German rearmament in 1952. While Britain and the United States are not members of the European Defense Community, they include the Community in the obligations they have assumed under the Atlantic Pact. Thus the original European partners have the guarantee against renewed German aggression that was the *sine qua non* of German rearmament.

[39] *Department of State Bulletin*, Vol. 20, No. 514 (May 8, 1949), p. 585.

A measure of NATO's success is that it has provided a cooperative framework that has helped the West to deter Soviet expansion. Military cooperation under NATO and economic cooperation under the Marshall Plan organization have, in comparison with 1947–48, stemmed the growth of communism in Western Europe. Against potential aggressors the Western powers have achieved a united front that was so sadly lacking between the wars.

Was this new regional organization a supranational authority or was it simply another instrument of cooperation? Principally it was the latter. However efficiently the Command organization was established under SHAPE and however great the centralization of civilian authority under the Secretary-General, the fundamental decisions still required the unanimous consent of the national governments represented in the North Atlantic Council. The power of the purse still remained with the individual members. Yet the whole organization was now being served by international military and civilian staffs which constantly coordinated the efforts of national governments to establish jointly a strong defense community. Budgetary and military contributions were planned by joint consultations and consensus. There was promise, therefore, that fewer and fewer disagreements would require negotiation and policy decisions in the Council. The degree of coordination of national policies, foreign and domestic, that has been achieved under the North Atlantic Treaty is clearly unprecedented in peacetime. Moreover, a truly international executive had emerged at SHAPE. Here there was a delegation of command over national forces that was unique in modern history. There was a possibility that a similar delegation of authority was developing on the civilian side under the Secretary-General. The pooling of military resources required the pooling of economic forces, and, as time went by, it became increasingly difficult for any partner to draw apart and make its way alone.

Meanwhile NATO had provided a strong impetus and necessary shelter for a European Union. Under it a common army, common budgets, common assemblies and common courts were taking shape. Yet it could not be forgotten, halfway through the twentieth century, that the fruition of these schemes depended on public understanding and support. Governments still must appeal to electorates. Whether there yet existed the necessary popular support to maintain supranational governmental institutions no one could say for sure.

Suggestions for Further Reading

See list at end of Chapter 26.

25

Atlantic Community — Economic Cooperation

"The mere suggestion of a constructive program of international cooperation, dedicated to reconstruction, recovery and peace, was sufficient to alter the political atmosphere of an entire continent. . . . The sixteen nations which were willing and able to meet together to act upon this suggestion are all still to be counted in the ranks of the democracies. There has been no advance in totalitarianism on the continent of Europe." — DEAN ACHESON [1]

The Organization for European Economic Cooperation

THE ORGANIZATION for European Economic Cooperation (OEEC) is a regional organization established to promote Europe's recovery and defense. It was born of necessity. The Western European powers could not make a go of the economic chaos that followed the Second World War. Their leaders recognized that economic salvation could be achieved only by working together. Their populations were ready for drastic measures to alleviate their problems.

The United States also recognized the danger of economic distress in Europe. That Europe's recovery depended in part on Germany's recovery also seemed obvious to Washington. Both the United States and the Western European governments were convinced that drastic economic steps must be taken to halt the increasing danger of Communist expansion.

But the United States was no longer ready to hand out relief on a piecemeal basis. There must be a new organization of Europe's economy that would provide economic and political stability for the long pull. The Europeans must work together before the United States could be expected to underwrite their recovery.

[1] Statement before the Senate Committee on Foreign Relations and the House Committee on Foreign Affairs, February 8, 1949, Hearings, *Extension of European Recovery*, Senate Committee on Foreign Relations, 81st Congress, 1st Session (Washington: 1949), pp. 16–19.

Origins

Three factors explain the origins of the OEEC. The first was the damage wrought by World War II — damage so vast that it could not be repaired within the confines of old national barriers. Unprecedented cooperation was essential for recovery. But all of Europe's horses and men could not put Humpty Dumpty together again. Colonial empires were gone or going and could not be counted upon to supply needed food and raw materials. Europe's capital equipment was largely obsolete or destroyed. Only the United States could provide the material aid that was required.

The second factor, therefore, was the pressure of United States foreign policy. The price of American aid was an integrated effort by the Europeans to solve their common problems. This price was met through the establishment and work of the OEEC.

But United States policy and the cooperative efforts of the Western European States were influenced by a third factor, the specter of Soviet expansion into Western Europe. Europe's economic debility seemed to invite Communist boldness. The threat spurred both American interest in European reconstruction and the efforts of the European governments to pool their economic resources.

The Department of Economic Affairs of the United Nations Secretariat compiled some telling figures on Europe's economic prostration from 1945 to 1947. The harvest of wheat in Continental Europe was 25,800,000 tons in 1947 against 42,300,000 tons per year before the war. The harvest of potatoes fell by more than 36,000,000 tons in the same period.[2] In 1947 Europe produced only 84 per cent of its prewar coal output and, instead of exporting a surplus, had to import high-cost coal from the United States. In the same year steel production was 63 per cent of the prewar volume necessitating large-scale imports for reconstruction. Many other figures attest the disaster that had befallen Europe. Transportation systems were virtually at a standstill at the war's close. Some of Europe's labor force was in prisoner-of-war camps. Factories and soil had deteriorated from wartime exploitation. Yet there was some initial improvement, and at the end of 1946 reconstruction was proceeding satisfactorily.[3] During the winter of 1946–47, however, economic recovery was stalled by nature. A drought in 1947 threatened crops and reduced industrial power. Then one of the severest winters on record added to Europe's misery and privation.

The monetary barometer of Europe's plight was the "dollar gap." Europe was simply unable to export enough to obtain the dollars necessary to buy essential United States goods which she could get nowhere else. By far the largest portion of Europe's trade deficit was with the United States.

[2] These figures do not include crops of the U.S.S.R. and Albania. *Salient Features of the World Economic Situation, 1943–47,* Economic Report, Department of Economic Affairs, United Nations, January 1948.

[3] *Committee on European Economic Cooperation: General Report,* Department of State Publication 2930, European Series 28 (Washington: Government Printing Office, September 1947), Vol. 1, Chap. 1.

Thus the United States had already furnished $7,800,000,000 of economic assistance in loans and grants, between May 1945 and the fall of 1947 in the British loan ($3,750,000,000 alone), UNRRA, post-UNRRA programs, an "interim-aid program" to France, Italy and Austria, and the distribution of civilian supplies by the armed forces.

By the spring of 1947 it was clear that Europe's recovery required a new approach involving far-reaching cooperation among the European countries themselves. Otherwise further aid programs seemed little better than throwing money down a rat hole.

Accordingly Secretary of State George C. Marshall in the now famous Harvard Commencement Address of June 5, 1947, declared that further

> assistance must not be on a piece-meal basis. Any assistance that this Government may render in the future should provide a cure rather than a mere palliative . . . before the United States Government can proceed much further in its efforts to alleviate the situation and help start the European world on its way to recovery there must be some agreement among the countries of Europe as to the requirements of the situation and the part those countries themselves will take in order to give proper effect to whatever action might be undertaken by this Government.[4]

Without the return of "normal economic health in the world," he declared there could be "no political stability and no assured peace. . . . The American people must understand the situation and steel themselves for further sacrifices, but above all the initiative for an imaginative joint program must come from Europe."

The CEEC Report

The proffered hand was seized with breath-taking haste. Within a fortnight, Foreign Ministers Bevin and Bidault of the United Kingdom and France respectively issued a joint statement welcoming the proposals for "the organization of economic cooperation between the countries of Europe, and the help which the United States of America could envisage to make such cooperation effective." [5]

Because Marshall made it clear that his suggestions applied to "everything west of Asia," Bevin and Bidault invited the Soviet Government to a three-power conference in Paris at the end of June to form a joint program. Mr. Molotov and reportedly over eighty experts arrived in Paris for the opening session on June 27, but withdrew a few days later. The Soviet News Agency, Tass, indicated on June 29 that the Soviet delegation smelled a rat. The United States, it appeared, had drafted the Marshall Plan to make "use of its credit possibilities for expanding its external markets, especially in view of the approaching crisis." It was quite proper (the Russians thought) that the European countries should determine their individual

---

[4] The text is in *Documents on European Recovery and Defense* (London: Royal Institute of International Affairs, 1949), p. 8.
[5] *The New York Times*, June 18, 1947.

needs for American aid but it was very wrong for any conference to focus primarily on an over-all economic program. This would constitute interference in the domestic affairs of countries, which the Soviet Union could never condone.

Bevin and Bidault insisted that the proposed program did not interfere with the rights of states while Molotov alleged that it did. His position, of course, struck at the very heart of the Marshall proposal: the principle that the economic life of Europe must be organized on a new cooperative basis. On July 3, Bevin and Bidault faced the fact of Soviet hostility to their scheme and invited all the European countries except Russia, Germany and Spain to attend a conference in Paris on July 12 to discuss the Marshall proposals.

Sixteen countries attended in all — in addition to the United Kingdom and France, there were Austria, Belgium, Denmark, Greece, Iceland, Ireland, Italy, Luxembourg, the Netherlands, Norway, Portugal, Sweden, Switzerland and Turkey. The Soviets' eight close neighbors, Albania, Bulgaria, Czechoslovakia, Finland, Hungary, Poland, Rumania and Yugoslavia, declined on the ground that the United States proposals would "establish an American economic domination of Europe endangering the independence and sovereignty of the European States." [6] Poland and Czechoslovakia, after accepting the invitation to attend the conference, were forced to withdraw.

The conference, free of Communist obstructions, made great headway. In four days it adjourned after setting up a Committee of European Economic Cooperation (CEEC) to prepare a report on the economic needs and capabilities of Europe as a whole including requirements for outside help.[7] The conference also established four Technical Committees to collect data on the needs and assets of the sixteen nations in food and agriculture, fuel and power, iron and steel, and transport.

The CEEC Report, which grew out of these committees' work, furnished a program to expand Europe's agricultural and industrial output by, first of all, a coordinated productive effort by the European countries themselves and, second, by economic aid from outside sources, principally the United States. By 1951 the sixteen nations hoped to produce enough to meet their essential needs, including necessary imports without depending on "handouts" from overseas. Financial stability in each country, economic cooperation and the reduction of trade barriers were cited as steps the Europeans could and would take to help themselves.[8]

A detailed estimate of the four-year program including outside assistance was carefully screened by the United States and was the basis of the President's recommendation to Congress for legislation authorizing the appropriation of $17 billion from April 1948 to January 1952.

[6] Report from Albania quoted in *The New York Times*, July 12, 1947.

[7] Its organization and terms of reference are included in Appendix A of the *CEEC General Report*.

[8] See *CEEC General Report*, passim.

The European Recovery Program

Uncle Sam, sometimes called Uncle Shylock after World War I, met the challenge. A first-year installment of the European Recovery Program was forthcoming with the passage of the Foreign Assistance Act of 1948 which provided $4,300,000,000 in grants and $1,000,000,000 in loans.[9]

Structure. Two weeks after Congress passed the Foreign Assistance Act of 1948, the sixteen European nations signed on April 16, 1948, a Convention establishing the Organization for European Economic Cooperation.[10] Organizational machinery was now provided to continue the close cooperation that made possible both the CEEC Report and United States assistance. The Parties recognized that "their economic systems are interrelated and that the prosperity of each of them depends on the prosperity of all." They pledged cooperation in raising trade and production and in lowering tariff barriers. To hasten the attainment of these objectives, they agreed to make a "study of customs unions or analogous arrangements, such as free trade areas. . . ."

Council. The Organization includes a Council comprising delegates of all the OEEC members which finally came to eighteen: Austria, Belgium, Denmark, France, The German Federal Republic, Greece, Iceland, Ireland, Italy, Luxembourg, Netherlands, Norway, Portugal, Sweden, Switzerland, Turkey, United Kingdom and the Anglo-American Zone of the Free Territory of Trieste. The Council met every two months, to decide on the division of aid allocated by the United States Economic Cooperation Administration (ECA) and to coordinate their own efforts at recovery. Decisions require the common agreement of all the members. It now plans for Europe's long-term economic and financial stability. A Chairman and two Vice-Chairmen are designated annually. Members are usually represented at the Ministerial level.

An *Executive Committee* consists of seven members chosen annually by the Council. It is in permanent session and, having no authority of its own, carries out the instructions of the Council. It is, in effect, the active center of the organization. It examines all questions to be submitted to the Council. The Council elects annually a Chairman and a Vice-Chairman. Inevitably it tends to be dominated by the larger powers, especially the United Kingdom and France. For four consecutive years it was ably chaired by a representative of the former. Any member, however, not represented on the Executive Committee, may participate in its discussion and decisions where affairs affecting its interests are at issue. The Committee keeps the entire membership informed of its proceedings.

A *Secretariat* comprises a staff that reached a peak of nearly one thousand individuals during the European Recovery Program. After 1952 it was reduced to about seven hundred international civil servants responsible solely to the Organization. The staff is headed by a Secretary-General and a first

---

[9] Public Law 472, 80th Congress, 2nd Session.

[10] Convention for European Economic Cooperation in *Documents on European Recovery and Defense,* p. 69.

and second Deputy Secretary-General appointed by the Council and under its instructions. M. Robert Marjolin of France was the first incumbent of the top post.

Technical Committees and Other Bodies have been established by the Council to handle the volume of work required of the Organization. They are composed of representatives of the member countries most directly interested in their activities. They are termed either "vertical" or "horizontal" according to the nature of their work. The former specialize in some specific branch of economic activity such as coal, oil, etc. The latter, four in number, are more general and deal with Economic Matters, Trade, Intra-European Payments and Manpower. A special Overseas Affairs Committee deals with colonies.

There are, in addition, *national delegations* representing each member country and usually headed by a Minister. Each member maintains a permanent mission in Paris, the Headquarters of the Organization.[11]

The *U.S. Economic Cooperation Administration* (ECA), later the Mutual Security Administration (MSA), and still later the Foreign Operations Administration (FOA), also has an office in Paris and is headed by a Special Representative and a Deputy. Since 1952 the Special Representative has also been Chief United States Delegate to the NATO Council. MSA was represented by observers at most meetings of the Technical Committees, Council and Executive Committee. Special MSA Missions were established in each member country to promote local implementation of the European Recovery Program.

OEEC maintains close relations with other international organizations which pursue similar objectives, including among others the International Monetary Fund, the International Labor Organization, the Food and Agriculture Organization, the UN Economic Commission for Europe and the Council of Europe.

Functions and Authority. With respect to its powers, the Organization "may take decisions for implementation by Members." Its authority is very similar to that of the wartime structures of economic cooperation such as the Combined Boards of World War II. Ministerial representatives of governments in power reach decisions by common agreement. The OEEC, in short, is a cooperative instrument rather than a supranational authority. Yet its procedures inevitably shape to a large extent the economic policies of its members. It may also make recommendations to the United States, other non-member governments, and to international organizations.

Its functions are broad and include the formulation of measures to achieve "a sound European economy through the economic cooperation of its members." This objective is long-term. The "success of the European recovery program" was its first "immediate task."[12] When the European Recovery Program was complete, the OEEC continued its efforts to build a sound economy.

---

[11] *The OEEC, Two Years of Economic Cooperation* (Paris: 1950), *passim.*
[12] See Articles 11 and 12 of the Convention.

One of its most important accomplishments has been to decide how to cut the pie of United States assistance. At first United States aid was allocated on the basis of nationally prepared "requirements" programs which were then examined by the Organization to determine the total dollar aid for each year. This was a difficult process. It involved cutting down each member's request for aid until the total amount was shrunk within the limits set by the United States. The visualization of Europe's economy as a whole was difficult. In the last two years of the European Recovery Program the Organization followed in large measure an estimate made by ECA as to the needs of Europe as a whole. Each member then received the same proportionate share of American aid that it had obtained in the first two years. This change eliminated some friction and also focused attention on the means of integrating Europe's economy more closely.[13]

In any event, the distribution of Marshall Plan dollars was a significant achievement. The behavior of the participating countries was almost without precedent in the relations of sovereign states. They submitted national economic programs to the prying eyes of the Organization's membership. Ministers and technical experts worked in closer relationship with their opposite numbers in other countries than had ever before been possible except in war.

Coordination and increased production were achieved in such industries as oil-refining and steel-making. The limited supply of shipping available was allocated to transport American coal in the winter of 1950. Collective action in restricting the use of scarce materials such as copper has been initiated. Production and use of electric power including the construction of new transmission lines to link national power systems have been successfully promoted.[14] Less successful have been the efforts of OEEC to increase productivity by improving the mobility of European labor. Italy's two million unemployed remain unharnessed to industry as do labor surpluses in Greece and other countries. British coal unions were unwilling in 1952 to have Italian miners dig British coal although increased coal production held the key to many of Britain's economic problems.

In order to build up intra-European trade, the OEEC also busies itself with the internal affairs of all the members. It has helped to restore the internal financial stability of many, by restraining the ups and downs of inflation and deflation, to promote multilateral trading in Europe in place of the postwar stagnation. In this way larger markets have become possible and have led to increased production. Annual questionnaires are sent to each member, and the replies are analyzed by a committee of international ex-

---

[13] This process is described in the Second Report of the Organization for European Economic Cooperation, *European Economic Recovery Programme* (Paris: 1950), pp. 81–84. See also Howard S. Ellis, *The Economics of Freedom, The Progress of Future Aid to Europe* (New York: Council on Foreign Relations and Harper, 1950), p. 375.

[14] These accomplishments are described in *European Economic Cooperation*, Survey prepared by the Organization for European Economic Cooperation (Paris: May 1951), (hereafter referred to as OEEC Survey.)

perts who publish reports and recommendations for the improvement of the separate economies.[15]

Further steps to liberalize trade through the reduction of tariff barriers and the establishment of customs unions have been halting despite professions of good intent. The OEEC Convention favored customs unions in principle and the OEEC cooperated with and has benefited from the General Agreement on Tariffs and Trade (GATT) which came into effect on January 1, 1948.[16]

European economic cooperation has also been sought through regional economic unions smaller than the area represented in the OEEC. The first of these was the Belgian-Netherlands-Luxembourg (Benelux) Customs and Economic Union, the convention for which had been signed in London on September 5, 1944.[17] On coming into effect two years later the Union abolished all entry duties among the three countries and set up a uniform rate of duties on imports from other countries.

Progress toward a full economic union of the Benelux countries, however, has been slow and painful. So far the three countries have been unable to equalize wages, prices, taxes, subsidies, social welfare burdens and economic controls. The problem derives from the fact that the Dutch economy suffered more than the other Benelux economies in the war and its aftermath when Indonesia burst its colonial ties. Also two of the partners pursued divergent economic policies.[18] Belgium, because of her export surplus, has been able to relax controls and import large quantities of consumers' goods while the Netherlands, because of its export deficit, has felt constrained to retain wage and price controls and to restrict imports.

The adjustments required for full economic union even in an area as small as Benelux are enormous when national economies have for many decades evolved separately. Yet Benelux has been the most successful of the regional economic groupings in Western Europe. A fruitless attempt was the amalgamation of the French, Italian and Benelux economies in a union known in the modern alphabetical language as FINEBEL. Similarly abortive was a proposed French-Italian customs union. Although a treaty was signed on March 26, 1949, it has not been ratified by either party.[19]

The work of the OEEC has been both encouraging and disappointing. In reviving Europe's economy the mutual efforts of the countries working together in OEEC have been astounding. But in establishing more integrated patterns for the long haul, difficulties have overshadowed successes. Yet European economic integration was clearly an objective of United States foreign policy. In October 1949 Paul Hoffman, ECA Director, flew to Paris and addressed the Council of the OEEC in strong terms. In the remaining years of the recovery program, he said, Europe must balance its

---

[15] OEEC Survey, *op. cit.*, pp. 36–37.
[16] See Chap. 19.
[17] For the text see *Documents on European Recovery and Defense*, pp. 1–4.
[18] Ellis, *op. cit.*, p. 383.
[19] *Documents on European Recovery and Defense*, p. 131.

dollar accounts which meant increased exports and control of inflation. But the accomplishment of this task

> will not be meaningful unless we have come to grips with our second task — the building of an expanding economy in Western Europe through economic integration. The substance of such integration would be the formulation of a single large market within which quantitative restrictions on the movement of goods, monetary barriers to the flow of payments, and eventually all tariffs are permanently swept away.[20]

Only two years remained, he warned, during which American aid could be counted on to cushion the "inevitable shortrun dislocations" of integration.

Mr. Hoffman's appeal brought a ready response. Two days later the Council of the OEEC passed a resolution recognizing "the need to form a single large market in Europe in which goods and services could move freely," and providing for the removal of quantitative restrictions on at least 50 per cent of their imports from all other OEEC countries by December 1949.[21] This was a change from prewar European commercial policy. On January 31, 1950, the Council resolved that as soon as a multilateral payments scheme had come into effect, quantitative restrictions would be removed, first, on at least 60 per cent and, later, on 75 per cent of imports on private account from other member countries taken as a group.[22]

The "multilateral payments scheme" became the European Payments Union. On coming into force in September 1950, it made possible the removal of some quantitative restrictions as the OEEC Members had agreed. In addition, they now agreed to accept as a code the Council Decisions on the Liberalization of Trade.[23] While some OEEC partners have applied for relief under the safeguard clauses of the code, liberalization measures made some progress.

The European Payments Union

Unless the reduction of quota restrictions and tariffs were accompanied by a European exchange system that allowed participating countries to convert currencies freely, little could be done to liberalize trade. It was for this reason that the OEEC Council made the 75 per cent reduction of quota restrictions on the import of goods among member countries subject to the formation of a European Payments Union (EPU). According to ECA, the EPU was "the most important advance" that the Western European nations have made toward economic integration since they formed the OEEC.[24] Now a multilateral settlement of balances arising from current

---

[20] *The New York Times,* November 1, 1949.

[21] *The New York Times,* November 3, 1949, and Second Report of the OEEC, p. 224.

[22] *Ibid.,* pp. 226–227.

[23] The text may be found in the *Ninth Report to the Congress of the Economic Cooperation Administration,* Supplement, 81st Congress, 2nd Session, House Document No. 713, Part 2, p. 48.

[24] *Tenth Report to Congress of the Economic Cooperation Administration,* 82nd Congress, 1st Session, House Document No. 52, p. 28.

intra-European trade is provided for by permitting the participating countries to cancel their total deficits against their total surpluses by means of a credit clearing house that was at first supported by a working fund of ECA dollars to provide short-term loans. No longer does each country have to keep its payments in balance with every other individually. Each participating country may now concentrate on its balance with the group as a whole. This means that two countries whose trading accounts are out of balance may nonetheless continue to trade. The result has been an increased volume of intra-European trade. The Bank of International Settlements in Basle acts as agent for the EPU. The operations of the latter are under the direction of a Managing Board. The major threats to the success of this system are the persisting trade advantages of countries such as Belgium or Portugal relative to the other members and the unequal strain and intensifying effects of rearmament.

Looking Back

The European Recovery Program phase of the OEEC experience was highly successful. Production and trade throughout Western Europe rose spectacularly. Industrial production increased 45 per cent between 1947 and 1950, bringing annual production to about 25 per cent above the 1938 level.[25] Toward the end of 1950 the Western European countries reached the production targets originally set for 1952.[26] Apparently all would have been well but for the Korean invasion of June 1950, which necessitated increased production since part of Europe's output had to be diverted to defense programs. In addition, Europe's export prices could not keep pace with the price of sorely needed imports which mounted steadily in a new inflationary wave.

It is fair to say, nonetheless, that the European Recovery Program accomplished its mission and on schedule. The further economic aid that has been forthcoming since 1950 was necessitated by the rearmament programs that seemed essential lest military weakness invite further Communist aggression.

Whether a fuller economic union in Western Europe will come to pass in the near future is hard to say. Meanwhile the OEEC has provided a new constructive element in the life of Western Europe. It has done much to promote "a European way of thinking." Actually the boldest step in this direction was related only indirectly to the OEEC. It was the Schuman Plan announced on May 9, 1950, by M. Robert Schuman on behalf of the French government. Ostensibly it was another step toward the "functional integration" of Europe. But actually a political purpose was its guiding star — to make armed conflict between France and Germany "not only unthinkable, but materially impossible." [27]

[25] This progress is summarized in detail in the *Eleventh Report to Congress of the Economic Cooperation Administration*, May 1951, and *Economic Progress and Problems of Western Europe*, Third Annual Report of the Organization for European Economic Cooperation, Paris, June 1951.
[26] Third OEEC Report, p. 51.
[27] M. Robert Schuman, *The New York Times*, May 11, 1950.

The European Coal and Steel Community — Schuman Plan

> "We are here together, French and Germans, members of the same community; vital interests of Germany and France are under the control of an authority that is no longer either French or German, but European. . . .
>
> "We will perform our duties with complete independence in the general interest of the community. For the performance of our duties we will neither request nor accept instructions from any government or organization." [28]

Foreign Minister Schuman's proposal for a unified six-nation coal, iron and steel community was put forward primarily as a solution to the German problem. Ever since the Second World War, France had sought to hobble her powerful neighbor by removing West German coal and steel

Alexander in the Philadelphia Bulletin

EUROPEAN UNITY

"Beginning to take shape."

[28] M. Jean Monnet, President of the High Authority of the European Coal and Steel Community on the occasion of its opening session, Luxembourg, August 10, 1952. Reported in *The New York Times*, August 11, 1952.

production from the control of any future German government. The Schuman plan marked the abandonment of the French postwar policy designed at first to gain permanent control of West German coal and steel producing areas, and later reduced to separating the Ruhr and the Rhineland from Germany by incorporating them in a new state under international control. The first effort was blocked by the three other powers, Britain, the United States and the Soviet Union. The second resulted in both the creation of the Ruhr Authority (the United States, the United Kingdom, France and the Benelux countries in December 1948) to control the allocation of German coal by consumption and export quotas, and the establishment of the Saar as an autonomous region under French economic control for a fifty-year period.

Neither of these measures afforded permanent solutions to allay French fears. As the cold war settled in, the Western powers increasingly wooed the Germans. Production restrictions on steel and coal were gradually liberalized and increased political freedom was granted. By 1949 the Federal Republic was established and made a partner of the OEEC in order to bolster Europe's economy. In the same year German steel production exceeded France's. These steps were designed to save Germany for the West, but to the French the reëstablishment of a sovereign German state that soon might be free to use its industrial capacity as it wished spelled only danger. The United States, however, was particularly insistent on the restoration of a large measure of German economic and political potential. The problem from the French point of view was to allow such a restoration with a minimum of risk. The Schuman Plan was advanced as the answer.

The Plan was announced in May 1950 after Franco-German relations had been exacerbated by the French "legitimization" of the economic annexation of the Saar by means of the General Convention of March 3, 1950, signed in Paris by Foreign Minister Schuman and Herr Hoffman, Prime Minister of the Saar.[29] German public opinion was as severely antagonized by this step as French public opinion was pleased. It was now clearly incumbent on the French authorities to mollify German resentment by showing that they were not attempting to bind Germany hand and foot forever.

The striking proposals in the Schuman Plan had wider implications than peace between France and Germany. The unification of Western Europe was the ultimate aim. In this way Franco-German rivalry might become less of a danger to world peace. French Prime Minister Schuman declared:

> A united Europe will not be achieved all at once, nor in a single framework; it will be formed by concrete measures which first of all create a solidarity in fact. . . . By pooling basic production and by creating a new high authority whose decisions will be binding on France, Germany and other countries who may subsequently join, this proposal will create the first concrete foundation for a European federation which is so indispensable for the preservation of peace.[30]

[29] See *Chronology of International Events and Documents* (London: Royal Institute of International Affairs, March 1950), p. 163.

[30] The text of M. Schuman's statement is in *The New York Times*, May 11, 1950.

Here, then, was a pragmatic approach to the German problem and European union along "functional" lines. Let the European nations establish European institutions to manage such segments of their international life as they were willing to yield to supranational control. In this way a sense of community would be encouraged and a more comprehensive political union would become possible.

This is sometimes called the "sector" approach to Western European integration. It has been suggested by the French in other fields of activity such as agriculture (The Pflimlin Plan). It became politically fashionable because it was politically feasible. When, as we shall see, efforts in the Council of Europe to unite Europe by direct action failed, largely owing to British opposition, unification hopes were transferred to the functional approach. The Schuman Plan became both a symbol of unification and a first step.

On this basis, M. Schuman proposed that the steel and coal industries of France and Germany, and of any others in Europe who cared to join, should be unified under a single authority. All comers would have equal rights, and the authority would work not for any one nation but for the interests of all. The invitation was quickly taken up by Belgium, Germany, Italy, Luxembourg and, with some hesitation at first, the Netherlands. Negotiations began on June 20, 1950.

Britain was conspicuous by her absence, and many for a time wondered if the Plan would be stillborn for this resaon. Without British production thrown in the balance, would not Germany rule the industrial roost? Britain's attitude was shaped by the Labor Government. For a while the British Government held the door ajar, but on June 13 the National Executive Committee of the Labor Party slammed it shut. A policy statement entitled *European Unity* was issued: "European peoples do not want a supranational authority to impose agreements." [31] Cooperation between responsible governments was held to be the proper course. Partisan tones rang loud in the allegation that a supra-European authority "would have a permanently anti-socialist majority and would arouse the hostility of European workers." "Vital British interests" were advanced as reasons for rejection since Britain's ties to the Commonwealth were stronger than bonds with Europe.

> Finally the Labour Party cannot see European unity as an overriding end in itself. Britain is not just a small crowded island off the western coast of Continental Europe. She is the nerve center of a world-wide Commonwealth which extends into every continent.[32]

For his Government, Mr. Attlee announced in the House of Commons that there was a vast difference between surrendering sovereignty to institutions such as the OEEC, which were responsible through ministerial

---

[31] *European Unity*, Labor Publications Department (London: Transport House, 1950), p. 6.
[32] *Ibid.*, p. 4.

representatives to national legislatures, and handing over vital economic forces to an independent supranational authority responsible to nobody. Moreover, many Britains distrusted the less stable governments of some continental countries. Finally, Britain had ties with the United States closer than those of any other European power. She had received special treatment from Washington through the postwar British loan. She was still an equal partner in the Combined Chiefs of Staff. Perhaps she would fare better remaining somewhat aloof from Europe.

The six continental powers, however, had set their course and were determined to steam ahead. After year-long negotiations, a Treaty Constituting the European Coal and Steel Community was signed on April 18, 1951, by the Foreign Ministers of France, the German Federal Republic, Italy, Belgium, the Netherlands and Luxembourg.[33] In May of 1951 the Consultative Assembly of the Council of Europe did all in its power to hasten events by voting 80 to 7 to urge the participating powers to speed ratification and the other powers to cooperate with the plan. It was subsequently ratified by the respective national parliaments and entered into force on August 10, 1952. By May 1, 1953, common markets for coal, steel and scrap iron had become operative as tariffs, quotas and exchange controls on these materials were swept away.

Organization Under Treaty

Structure. The Community has a federal-type organization with authority divided between institutions representing the Community and institutions representing the states.

The High Authority. It is composed of nine members designated for six years and chosen for their general competence. They are not responsible to their national governments; they neither report to them, nor do they receive instructions from them. Each state, in turn, agrees to respect their "supranational character." It is similar in character to the Commissariat of the EDC. The governments or the member states designate eight members by agreement among themselves. These eight then elect a ninth member by a majority of five votes. A President and a Vice President of the High Authority are designated by a similar procedure. M. Jean Monnet, actually the architect of the proposals put forward by M. Schuman, became the first President. The High Authority acts by majority vote. It issues decisions, recommendations, and opinions, and its decisions are "binding in all their details." It is the Community's executive agent.

A *Consultative Committee* is "attached to the High Authority," consisting of between thirty and fifty-one members selected in their individual capacity from the ranks of "producers, workers and consumers and dealers in equal numbers." The members are appointed by the Council (described below). The High Authority may consult the Consultative Committee on any matter and is required to do so in the case of recommendations or decisions relating to the principal objectives of the treaty regarding production, marketing, pricing and employment.

[33] See Treaty text in Senate Document, Executives Q and R, *op. cit.,* pp. 255–328.

The Assembly. It is composed of "representatives of the peoples of the member States of the Community" selected by the parliaments of each member state from their own membership once a year or by "direct universal suffrage, according to the procedure determined by each respective High Contracting Party." Germany, France and Italy have eighteen delegates each; Belgium and the Netherlands, ten each; and Luxembourg, four. It designates a President and other officers from its membership. It meets in annual session to review the work of the Authority — specifically the general report which the latter submits to it. It may submit questions to the High Authority and, by a two-thirds vote of the members present and voting, representing a majority of the total membership, it may censure the Authority and compel its members to resign. The High Authority, is, therefore, in large measure responsible to this representative body. The treaty establishing the European Defense Community provides that this Assembly shall be common to both Communities.

The Council. This is more of a conventional diplomatic-type body added to the orginal French proposals on the insistence of the Belgians. It is composed of one minister from each of the six participating countries. It is similar, therefore, to the Council of the European Defense Community but comprises ministers other than Defense Ministers. Its purpose is to harmonize "the action of the High Authority and that of the governments, which are responsible for the general economic policy of their countries." The Council has considerable authority. On the most important matters covered in the Treaty the High Authority is required to consult the Council. The latter has the right to advance proposals to the High Authority, and, since it approves much of the critical work of the Authority, such as the fixing of prices or allocations to meet a shortage situation, it has the whip hand. Some of the Authority's actions require the unanimous decision of the Council and some require a weighted majority based on a percentage of the total value of coal and steel produced in the Community (Article 28). In crucial matters, the age-old principle of unanimity based on the principle of one-state-one-vote still obtains. Specifically the Council must be consulted by the Authority before loans are granted to carry out investment programs and before measures are taken to offset adverse economic effects caused by steel or coal production shifts. Yet there is a great deal the High Authority may do even in the absence of Council unanimity on certain matters. For much of the Community's work the Council and the Authority are simply required to "consult together and exchange information." The Authority, therefore, appears to have greater discretion than the proposed Defense Community's Commissariat.

The Court. Judicial functions are carried out by a court comprising seven judges, appointed for six years by agreement among the member governments "from among persons of recognized independence and competence." It is also the Court of Justice of the European Defense Community. It has the right to nullify the decisions of the other institutions in much the same manner that United States courts may declare laws unconstitutional. If one of its decisions or recommendations is annulled by the Court, for example, the High Authority must give effect to the annulment. It may consider complaints brought before it by member governments, companies and individuals.

Relationship to the Council of Europe. The Community uses the seat of the Council of Europe for its meetings. Other arrangements link the two organizations. The Governments represented in the Community appoint representatives to the Council of Europe's Consultative Assembly. The Coal and Steel Assembly is required by formal agreement to submit annual reports to the Committee of Ministers of the Council of Europe.

Functions

The Treaty establishes a "European Coal and Steel Community, based on a common market, common objectives and common institutions." This single market serves over 160 million people in Western Europe and pools the coal and steel resources of the six participating nations. According to Article 2,

> The mission of the . . . Community is to contribute to economic expansion, the development of employment and the improvement of the standard of living in the participating countries through the institution, . . . of a common market. . . .

Article 4 would seem to dispose of the notion that the Community is a super-cartel. Quantitative restrictions on the movement of coal and steel, including import and export duties "or charges with an equivalent effect," are prohibited. Discrimination among producers, buyers or consumers is forbidden as are subsidies or state assistance or "restrictive practices tending towards the division of markets or the exploitation of the consumer."

The High Authority does not own a coal mine or operate a steel mill. It has no direct power to close inefficient factories or shift workers from one location to another. But it has wide authority to develop free competition in a single market. The result should be a reorganization of the European coal and steel industries in an economically efficient manner. It should also make it impossible for any single partner to monopolize Western Europe's war-making potential.

The Community, through its High Authority, polices both the member states and the coal and steel industries. Against the states it will enforce the provisions of Articles 3 and 4 looking to a "common market." State action is not permitted that will benefit one partner at the expense of another. Vital policies regarding the production and marketing of steel are left in the hands of a "European body" executing what is, in effect, an organic law of a European Community. With respect to the industries, the High Authority will enforce the treaty provisions designed to achieve a free, competitive market. Yet in accordance with Article 83, "the establishment of the Community does not in any way prejudice the regime of ownership of the enterprises subject to the provisions of the present Treaty." In other words coal and steel may be nationalized or left to unregulated free enterprise so far as national governments are concerned. But all enterprises, however owned, must conform to the Treaty provisions regarding a single market operating under free competitive conditions in the Community as a whole. National boundaries, in short, will have little effect on the conditions attending the marketing of coal and steel.

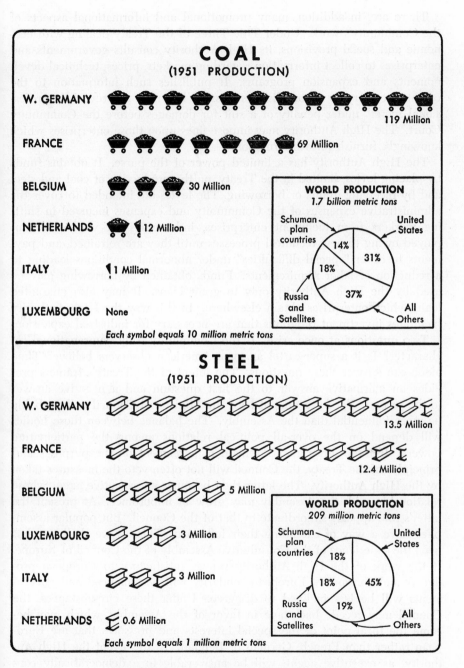

COAL
(1951 PRODUCTION)

W. GERMANY — 119 Million

FRANCE — 69 Million

BELGIUM — 30 Million

NETHERLANDS — 12 Million

ITALY — 1 Million

LUXEMBOURG — None

Each symbol equals 10 million metric tons

WORLD PRODUCTION
1.7 billion metric tons

Schuman plan countries 14%
United States 31%
Russia and Satellites 18%
All Others 37%

STEEL
(1951 PRODUCTION)

W. GERMANY — 13.5 Million

FRANCE — 12.4 Million

BELGIUM — 5 Million

LUXEMBOURG — 3 Million

ITALY — 3 Million

NETHERLANDS — 0.6 Million

Each symbol equals 1 million metric tons

WORLD PRODUCTION
209 million metric tons

Schuman plan countries 18%
United States 45%
Russia and Satellites 18%
All Others 19%

PRODUCTION OF SCHUMAN PLAN COUNTRIES

There are, in addition, many promotional and informational aspects of the Community's work. Under Title Three of the Treaty dealing with economic and social provisions, its High Authority consults governments and enterprises to collect information regarding markets, prices, technical developments and expansion programs. It publishes such information to the extent necessary to accomplish its mission but may not reveal "a professional secret" under penalty of a suit for damages before the Community Court. The High Authority may impose fines upon those enterprises which knowingly furnish false information.

The High Authority has a limited power of the purse. It obtains funds by placing levies, limited in the Treaty, on the production of coal and steel and by receiving grants or borrowing. The levies are intended to cover the administrative expenses of the Community and expenses incurred in shifting workers from inefficient enterprises, indemnities for workers unemployed owing to new technical processes until they are retrained, and payments to cover "special difficulties" under abnormal conditions leading to a reduction of labor requirements. Funds obtained by borrowing may be used by the High Authority only to grant loans. It may also guarantee loans which enterprises obtain elsewhere. In this way the High Authority facilitates investment programs that are necessary for industrial expansion.

Two questions at once arise. Is the Community truly "supranational" in character? Is it a super-cartel as some American observers believe? Time alone can answer these questions. The intent of the Treaty's framers provides an affirmative answer to the first question and a negative answer to the second. Yet for a time at least the Ministerial Council will probably be more influential than the Assembly. The balance between these bodies will depend on the over-all political relations among the participating powers. If these governments remain in agreement on the purposes and principles of the Treaty, the Council will not often veto the measures taken by the High Authority. The latter then becomes an executive agent whose relationship with the Assembly may grow in importance. At present the latter's role appears subordinate to that of the Council. But popular assemblies have a way of extending their influence. This, as we shall see, has been the experience of the Consultative Assembly of the Council of Europe. If the work of the High Authority proves satisfactory to European producers and consumers, European solidarity will be enhanced and governments will be less inclined to disagree. Under these circumstances, the Council may recede backstage in favor of the Assembly, which may become the focal point of the special interests and pressures that are European rather than French, German or Belgian. In this event the High Authority, as executive agent, will be answerable to a democratically controlled and politically responsible body.

Moreover, regulatory and technical bodies like popular assemblies also have a way of developing considerable influence. The High Authority, in its day-to-day business, may well develop a wide latitude of discretion in its regulatory functions by the very nature of its operations. It has some of the attributes of a United States regulatory commission. It will be the source of much technical information difficult for popularly elected representatives or appointed ministers to fathom. It will make important decisions affecting the lives of many Europeans. It inevitably will attract the attention of consumers, managers and workers who seek special favors. It has the capacity to become a vital European institution politically and economically.

It is the powers of the High Authority in abnormal periods of stress and strain which arouse suspicions in the United States that a new type of cartel may be in the making although the expressed objective of the Treaty is to fashion a single market free of restrictive practices in restraint of trade. In the first place, a five-year transitional period is permitted following the creation of the common markets. During this period many tortuous adjustments will have to be made. High-cost Belgian coal, for example, will have to be protected until workers shift to other industries or more efficient production methods are introduced. The same general condition exists with respect to Italian steel production which, for a time, will require protective measures to avoid disturbing hardships.

In the second place, exceptions to the general rules of the Treaty may be made in periods of abnormal stress. Article 58 provides, for example:

> In case of a decline in demand, if the High Authority deems that the Community is faced with a period of manifest crisis . . . , it shall, after consulting the Consultative Committee and with the concurrence of the Council, establish a system of production quotas . . . [and] may in particular regulate the rate of operation of the enterprises by appropriate levies on tonnages exceeding a reference level defined by a general decision.

Here governmental arrangements in restraint of trade are clearly permitted. Here is authority to regulate a free competitive market in times of stress. Yet the over-all objectives of the Treaty remained clearly pointed in the opposite direction. There is a world of difference, moreover, between price fixing and production quotas fixed by private companies in a cartel and such arrangements made by public authority with institutions established to direct its work in the public interest. The High Authority officially operates under standards set by the Assembly with the guidance of Council and Consultative Committees. These officials may be censured and even compelled to resign by the Assembly. Redress of grievances may be sought in the Court of Justice, which may nullify decisions of the Coal and Steel Community if such decisions do not square with the Community's fundamental law. A system of public law and administration and political accountability is developing that is analogous to a national legislative and administrative process. The path taken by the Community will depend on circumstances largely beyond its control, world economic conditions and the character of international relations. If the Coal and Steel Community is faced with difficulties such as low-cost production in Asia or higher industrial efficiency in the United States, the High Authority will be ready to coordinate the policies of all Western European steel producers. If economic agreements with non-European powers are necessary the Authority will be in a position to enforce them. The Community may well lessen rather than emphasize the drawbacks of cartels.

More important is the possibility that the Community may provide an avenue to the nirvana of friendly Franco-German relations. For example, the Ruhr Authority established after World War II to control German industrial might was more willingly abandoned by the French as the Coal and Steel Community prepared to take hold. The Community, in short, seemed to be a most promising step toward federation and a solution of the Franco-German problem. A real doubt, however, was whether the Community could accomplish its task in the last analysis without a more fully developed European political authority to enforce its will.

Suggestions for Further Reading

See list at end of Chapter 26.

✿ **26**

The Council of Europe

> "Our constant aim must be to build and fortify the strength of the United Nations. Under and within that world concept we must re-create the European family in a regional structure called, it may be, the United States of Europe. The first step is to form a Council of Europe. . . . In all this urgent work, France and Germany must take the lead together. Great Britain, the British Commonwealth of Nations, mighty America, and I trust Soviet Russia — for then indeed all would be well — must be the friends and sponsors of the new Europe and must champion its right to live and shine."
>
> — Winston Churchill [1]

THE PAGES OF HISTORY are strewn with proposals to unify Europe. The Council of Europe is the most recent and the most likely of the developments in this direction. Yet its establishment in 1949 has revealed serious differences within its ranks. "It is at once a goal, a stepping stone, and a foil." [2] Broadly speaking, there are two schools of thought regarding the Council. One, led principally by French and Belgian statesmen, has sought from the beginning to transform the Council into a European Federal government. Another, led principally by the British, feels that to follow such a course would be to move too fast too soon. But these views cannot be categorized nationally. There are differences of opinion regarding the means and desirability of uniting Europe among all European leaders. The supporters of the Council are agreed, however, that its task is to foster a closer unity of the European nations. The means, timing and degree are subjects of sharp debate.

Yet from its opening session the Council of Europe has been a significant factor in European politics. No European government, in framing national policies, foreign or domestic, can afford to disregard the Consultative As-

---

[1] Speech at Zurich, September 1946. The text is reproduced as Appendix B in Andrew and Frances Boyd, *Western Union* (Washington: The Public Affairs Press, 1949).

[2] Alan de Rusett, *Strengthening the Framework of Peace* (London: Royal Institute of International Affairs, 1950), p. 115.

767

Yardley in the Baltimore

"YOU NEED A YOUNGER MAN"

sembly's resolutions or the temper of its debates. One reason is that the notion of European union has a long, honorable and popular tradition. Today it fires the imagination of many leaders and ordinary citizens.

How It Came About

The roots of European union lie deep in history's soil. The conquest of Julius Caesar in the first century B.C. linked the areas of present-day France, England and the Low Countries to the older Roman territories of Italy, Spain and the Balkans. The Christian Church arose from the ashes of the Roman Empire to preserve a Christian and European cultural and spiritual unity that remained firm for centuries. Furthermore after the Empire declined and fell, a semblance of unity was restored when Charlemagne, king of the Franks, was crowned Emperor of Rome by Pope Leo III in St. Peter's on Christmas Day, 800 A.D. Although Charlemagne's empire fell apart with the quarrelling of his heirs, the notion of a "Holy Roman Empire" persisted in the eastern or German section until officially interred by Napoleon in 1806. A union of the peoples of Europe remained the ideal of many thinkers including Dante, Pierre Dubois, the Duc de Sully, William Penn and Jean Jacques Rousseau.[3]

[3] See Chap. 2.

The peace plans of Jeremy Bentham (1793) and Immanuel Kant (1795) marked a turning point after which European unification was no longer thought of as the key to world peace. Their concern was with the entire world including colonies, international trade and world armaments. Their thinking led ultimately to the League of Nations and the United Nations rather than to European federation. Yet the ideal of European unity was fanned in the nineteenth century by the writings of Victor Hugo, the conquests of Napoleon and the "Young Europe Movement" led by Giuseppe Mazzini. But Napoleon's and Mazzini's projects boomeranged. Both stimulated nationalist sentiments that in the end collided with the ideal of European federation.

A new stimulus was provided by the agonies of 1914–18, and in 1923 the Pan-Europe Movement was initiated by Count Richard N. Coudenhove-Kalergi. Its aim was "the creation of a European Confederation in which sovereignty and equality would be preserved." [4] All continental countries were to be included save, prophetically enough, Britain and the Soviet Union. The former was held to have overseas interests that would weaken Europe's cohesion. The latter was thought to menace Europe's peace. The movement attracted the support of many statesmen, including Edouard Herriot, Aristide Briand and Ernest Bevin. Its high-water mark was reached when Foreign Minister Briand informally presented some suggestions at a luncheon meeting during the 1929 session of the League Assembly. On May 17, 1930, the Briand Memorandum on European Federal Union was sent to the twenty-six other European members of the League.[5] Unhappily the project was talked to death until the rise of National Socialism in Germany, changes of government in France and England, and the fiasco of the proposed Austro-German Customs Union ended the Locarno era of good feeling.[6] In the face of depression and rising international animosities, a special "League Commission for European Union" made negligible progress.

Actually M. Briand drew no revolutionary rabbits from his silk hat. He did not envisage a real federal union since his proposals were in no way to affect "any of the sovereign rights of the states which are members of such an association." Its object was

> a federation based on the idea of union and not of unity — that is to say, a federation elastic enough to respect the independence and the national sovereignty of each State while guaranteeing to all the benefits of collective solidarity in the settlement of the political questions affecting the destiny of the European commonwealth. . . .

It was not to rival the League but to supplement it. Its machinery was to include a European Conference, a Secretariat and a Permanent Political

[4] Quoted in *European Movement and the Council of Europe* (London and New York: Hutchinson for the European Movement, 1949), p. 28.
[5] *Memorandum on the Organization of a System of European Federal Union* — a translation is included as Appendix A in Andrew and Frances Boyd, *op. cit.*
[6] See Chap. 5.

Committee. It was to consider economic and cultural cooperation. It was, in short, to be a loose association, *entente* or, at the most, confederation of European states within the global framework of the League.

The European Movement

Once more, after World War II, further progress was stimulated by horrible destruction, waste and suffering. The common experience of many countries in the Nazi occupation, in the Resistance movement and in the Allied liberation had psychological consequences favoring postwar collaboration. Cooperative programs, including Benelux among others, developed in London among governments in exile. But the war was not enough. Winston Churchill's plea for union with France during the military disasters of June 1940 was hopelessly late. Nor did further results obtain from a secret memorandum of October 1942 in which Churchill told the British War Cabinet that a "United States of Europe" would be necessary to stem Russian barbarism; nor from his appeal in a world-wide broadcast on March 22, 1943, "that under a world institution embodying or representing the United Nations there should come into being a Council of Europe."[7] Another danger that forced Europe's proud nations to huddle together about the warming fire of proposed union was the blast of the cold war precipitated by Soviet expansionism. Finally the moral encouragement of the United States strengthened the impetus that launched a new and more promising "European Movement."

When Mr. Churchill spoke at Zurich University on September 19, 1948, he found a more receptive audience for the United Europe idea than he had during the war. He asserted that there was only one path which the European nations could follow.

> It is to create the European family, or as much of it as we can, and provide it with a structure under which it can dwell in peace and safety and freedom. We must build a kind of United States of Europe.

He recalled the suffering and privations of Europe's citizens and the decline in prestige of the European states acting at cross purposes.

The speech provided welcome propaganda ammunition for a number of new organizations that soon sprang up, including among others:

> The European Union of Federalists, founded by Dr. Henry Brugmans, which held Congresses in Amsterdam in 1947, in Montreux in 1947, and in Rome in 1948;
> The Economic League for European Cooperation under Paul Van Zeeland, former Prime Minister of Belgium;
> The French Council for United Europe, headed by Raoul Dautry and Edouard Herriot:

[7] Both incidents are described by Professor F. L. Schuman in "The Council of Europe," *The American Political Science Review*, Vol. 45, No. 3 (September 1951), pp. 725–726. Mr. Churchill asserted that the Council "must eventually embrace the whole of Europe. . . ."

Nouvelles Equipes Internationales under Robert Bichet, a former French Minister;

The Socialist Movement for United States of Europe, headed by Michel Rasquin;

The European Parliamentary Union, led by Coudenhove-Kalergi; and

The United Europe Movement, founded by Winston Churchill himself in 1947 with Duncan Sandys as Chairman.

To avoid duplication and needless confusion many of these organizations were spliced together in December 1947 into an International Committee of Movements of European Unity with Duncan Sandys as Executive Chairman and Dr. J. H. Retinger as Secretary-General. Not only were they agreed on the need for Europe to unite; many also hoped eventually for world government. The Committee's first Congress was held at The Hague, May 7–10, 1948. The meeting was a direct ancestor of the Council of Europe.[8] Eight hundred Europeans attended, including distinguished public figures such as Princess Juliana, who delivered the welcoming address in the Netherlands Parliament Building. Discussions were conducted in three separate committees dealing with the political, economic and social, and cultural aspects of union. Many resolutions were adopted unanimously by the Congress which declared:

> Human dignity is Europe's finest achievement, freedom her true strength. Both are at stake in the struggle. The union of our Continent is now needed, not only for the salvation of the liberties we have won, but also for the expansion of their benefits to all mankind. Upon this union depend Europe's destiny and the world's peace.[9]

The Congress declared that the European nations must "transfer and merge some portion of their sovereign rights," that a European Assembly and a Court of Justice should be established and a Charter of Human Rights put into force.

By October 1948 the International Committee instituted the "European Movement" on a permanent basis with Winston Churchill, Léon Blum, Alcide de Gasperi and Paul-Henri Spaak as Honorary Presidents. Its structure was organized in February 1949 at a Second Congress in Brussels. An Executive Committee of the European Movement was established which forwarded proposals for a European Assembly to the Brussels Pact powers.

Diplomatic Steps

The next steps were taken by the diplomatists as governments responded to public opinion on both sides of the Atlantic. Events already described, such as the Czech coup, the Berlin Blockade, the Truman Doctrine and the Marshall Plan riveted public attention on Europe's weakness and travails. Developments that led to the Brussels and Atlantic Pacts and the

[8] The story of this organization is told in Paul Reynaud, *Unite or Perish* (New York: Simon and Schuster, 1951), pp. 191–192 and *European Movement and the Council of Europe*, pp. 33–34.

[9] See Andrew and Frances Boyd, *op. cit.*, Appendix H.

OEEC also gave rise to the Council of Europe. Leaders such as Premier Spaak of Belgium, Count Sforza of Italy and Georges Bidault of France were emphatic that Europe must unite. Echoes came from British leaders of both parties but were rather faint when anything more than intergovernmental collaboration was proposed.

As early as July 1947 Georges Bidault had proposed that the Permanent Commission of the Brussels Pact Council investigate the establishment of a European Assembly.[10] In October the Brussels Consultative Council established a "Committee for the Study of European Unity." The Committee was confronted with two points of view. The French and Belgians indicated they really sought European unity by proposing a European Assembly. The British countered with a Council of Ministers to be appointed by Cabinets and to be held in close check, so that while it might discuss "all matters of common concern" it could not discuss matters of defense or economic problems that fell within the scope of OEEC. The British government at that time preferred to restrict European unity to intergovernmental cooperation while the French, Belgians, and to some extent the Dutch governments sought supranational institutions. Until he got a green light from the Commonwealth Conference of October 1948, Ernest Bevin stoutly maintained that until "Governments have settled the issue of defense, economic cooperation, and the political developments which must follow . . ." the creation of a European Assembly would be like "putting on the roof before building the house."[11] An obvious compromise was reached when the Committee proposed that both a Council and an Assembly be established.

On January 28, 1949, the Brussels Consultative Council announced that five Western Union powers were ready to accept the compromise to establish "a Council of Europe consisting of a ministerial committee meeting in private and a consultative body meeting in public." Since they had been unable to agree on the composition of the latter, a further compromise provided that the delegates were to be chosen by whatever method each country might prefer. Later agreements stated that the Consultative Assembly would be purely advisory, would meet only once a year and must not discuss defense matters.

In March other powers — Sweden, Denmark, Norway, Italy and Eire — joined the Brussels powers' discussion. The European Movement was regularly consulted and in April held a non-governmental European Economic Conference which advocated full economic union. On May 5, 1949, the ten European Foreign Ministers signed the Statute of the Council of Europe[12] which received sufficient ratifications to come into force on August 3, 1949.

The Council of Europe, it should be noted at once, was born of a union between public opinion and governmental action. Public support for closer

10 Reynaud, *op. cit.*, p. 195.
11 *The New York Times*, September 16, 1948.
12 See *Documents on European Recovery and Defense* (London: Royal Institute of International Affairs, 1949), p. 140.

relationship among the European states came to a head in the unofficial European Movement whose propaganda did much to prompt governments to take the necessary constituent measures. The child, moreover, displayed characteristics inherited from both parents. There was some promise of a true European governing body that would be sustained by a European point of view. There were also unmistakable signs of a traditional inter-governmental diplomatic body. It would take time to form the offspring's final character.

Structure

Membership. Under Article 4 of the Statute any European state may be a member on invitation of the Committee of Ministers by a two-thirds vote (Article 20, par. c.) which leaves this important element of control in the hands of gov-ernmental delegates. The Committee, however, agreed under some pressure in November 1949 to "consult" the Assembly before inviting new states to member-ship.

Every member, under Article 3, "must accept the principles of the rule of law and the enjoyment by all, within the Council's jurisdiction, of human rights and fundamental freedom, and collaborate sincerely and effectively in the realization of the aim of the Council as specified in Chapter I." This Chapter states the aim to be the achievement of "a greater unity between its Members" by discussion and agreement on matters of common concern in economic, social, cultural, scien-tific, legal and administrative matters.

Article 5 provides for associate members which are entitled to be represented only in the Consultative Assembly. Greece, Turkey and Iceland were admitted as full members in August 1949. In March 1950 Western Germany and the Saar were invited to become associate members, and the former became a full member on May 2, 1951. Only five European countries that are not Soviet satellites remain outside the Council's membership: Austria (still occupied), Yugoslavia, Portugal, Spain and Switzerland. Article 7 makes provision for the withdrawal of members; and Article 8, for expulsion for violation of the principles specified in Article 3. By 1952 there were fourteen full members and one associate.

The Committee of Ministers. It consists of the foreign ministers of the mem-ber countries, each having one vote. Alternates from a member's government may be designated. It represents the governmental element in the Council of Europe and, under the statute, guides the work of the Assembly. Article 15 provides that "on the recommendation of the Consultative Assembly or on its own initiative, [the Committee] shall consider the action required to further the aim of the Council of Europe, including the conclusion of conventions or agreements and the adoption by governments of a common policy with regard to particular mat-ters." Its conclusions are forwarded to members by the Secretary-General. It may make recommendations to "Governments of members;" it may request such Governments to report on the action taken on such recommendations.

Under Article 16 the Committee shall, subject to the right of the Assembly to manage its own affairs within the limits of its authority, "decide with binding effect all matters relating to the internal organization and arrangements of the Council of Europe . . . , " including financial and administrative regulations.

Resolutions of the Committee, under Article 20, "require the unanimous vote of the representatives casting a vote, and of a majority of the representatives

Council of Europe ··· Infant Union?

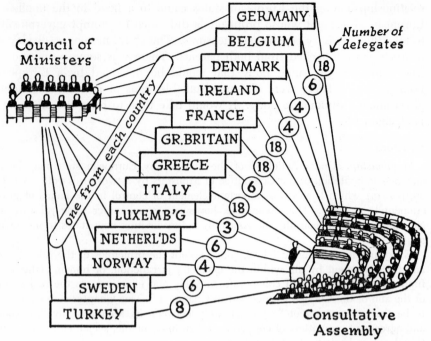

Council of Ministers

Number of ✓delegates

one from each country

GERMANY	
BELGIUM	
DENMARK	18
IRELAND	6
FRANCE	4
GR.BRITAIN	4
GREECE	18
ITALY	18
LUXEMB'G	6
NETHERL'DS	18
NORWAY	3
SWEDEN	6
TURKEY	4
	6
	8

Consultative Assembly

Headline Series, *Foreign Policy Association*

entitled to sit on the Committee." (This permits abstentions that do not constitute a veto, up to a point.) Procedural matters are decided by simple majority. Voting has been a bone of contention. The British have insisted on unanimity, but a change in its rules of procedure on August 2, 1951, permitted the Council to reach decisions by "partial agreement" so that some members could proceed with a project while others stood aside. But the suitability of a partial agreement must be upheld by all the ministers voting.[13]

Unless it decides otherwise the Committee meets privately in Strasbourg before each session of the Consultative Assembly and at such other times as it may decide (Article 21). The Presidency is rotated among the member states.

The Consultative Assembly. Article 22 declares it to be "the deliberative organ of the Council of Europe. It shall debate matters within its competence under this Statute and present its conclusions, in the form of recommendations, to the Committee of Ministers." Article 23 states that its agenda must be approved by the Committee of Ministers.

Representatives and their substitutes are, under Article 25, "appointed in such manner as the government of [each] member shall decide." All must be nationals of their states and none can at the same time be a member of the Committee of Ministers. Some have been appointed by Cabinets (British, German, Benelux, and the Scandinavian countries) and others elected by parliaments (French and Italian). Election has been the rule since 1951, and in practice all have been parliamentarians chosen in proportion to the voting strength of the parties of

[13] *The New York Times,* August 3, 1951.

which they are members. Communists, however, are excluded by common agreement under the requirements of Article 1 that all members must accept the rule of law and fundamental human rights and freedoms.

In 1952 it had 132 members appointed according to population among the member states. Since an agreement reached in September 1949, Britain, France, Germany and Italy each have eighteen representatives; Turkey ten; Belgium, Greece, the Netherlands and Sweden have six each; Denmark, Eire and Norway four each; and Iceland, Luxembourg and the Saar have three each. These representatives are seated neither by parties, as in a national legislature, nor by countries, as would be the case in a traditional diplomatic body, but in alphabetical order of their names. They speak and vote as individuals.

The Consultative Assembly, under Article 28, adopts its own rules of procedure and elects a President each session, who controls its proceedings but "shall not take part in the debate or vote." Paul-Henri Spaak was elected first President in August 1949 following his resignation as Belgian Premier and Foreign Minister and his withdrawal from the Committee of Ministers. Reelected in 1950 and 1951 this vigorous champion of European unity chafed at the Council's snail-like progress and lack of harmony. He resigned in December 1951 to trumpet at the walls of Jericho from the outside. The President and six Vice-Presidents are elected by majority vote in secret ballot. They comprise the Assembly's "Bureau" which, within the limits of the agenda, manages the Assembly's daily work.

The Assembly decides the date and length of its sessions but may not meet for a period in excess of one month each year unless the Committee of Ministers agrees to an extension (Article 32). Its meetings are held in Strasbourg, the seat of the Council of Europe, in the *Maison de l'Europe*, a prefabricated semi-permanent structure, functional in character and appearance and intended to serve as a temporary headquarters for perhaps ten years. All acts of the Assembly, save those relating to "internal procedure" require a two-thirds majority of the representatives casting a vote (Articles 29 and 30). These include "recommendations" to the Committee of Ministers, "resolutions" directed at its own committees and "declarations" for world-wide consumption.

The Assembly's work is done principally in six general committees that bear marks of both national and international practice: General Affairs (political), Rules of Procedure and Privileges, Economic Questions, Social Questions, Cultural and Scientific Questions, and Legal and Administrative Questions. Unlike the United Nations General Assembly each committee usually has twenty or more deputies distributed among the member states in close proportion to their Assembly representation. Committee membership is proposed by the Bureau and approved by the Assembly. Each elects a Chairman and two Vice-Chairmen. A *Rapporteur* is selected for each subject under consideration. Reports and minority reports may be made. The Committees have no power to summon witnesses *sub poena*.

There is, in addition, a *Standing Committee,* comprising the President, the six Vice-Presidents, the Six Chairmen of the general committees *ex officio* and fifteen other representatives. It meets at least four times a year between the Assembly's sessions to facilitate the latter's work by coordinating reports, resolutions and recommendations.

A Joint Committee, established in August 1950, consists of five members of the Committee of Ministers and seven members of the Assembly, including its President. It acts "to maintain good relations between the two bodies and to coordinate their activities." [14] A Credentials Committee includes twenty members chosen by lot.

The Secretariat: Articles 36 and 37 provide for a Secretary-General and a Deputy Secretary-General appointed by the Assembly on the recommendation of the Committee of Ministers. Jacques-Camille Paris was the first to hold the top post. The staff, appointed by the Secretary-General, numbers roughly two hundred persons, who solemnly affirm that they will serve the Council conscientiously "uninfluenced by any national considerations." They may not hold any other salaried post nor be a member of the Assembly or of any national legislature. While the Secretariat works for both the Assembly and the Committee of Ministers, the Secretary-General is responsible to the latter "for the work of the Secretariat," a safeguard against independent action by the Assembly. The cost of the Secretariat and other common expenses "are shared between all members" on the basis of population (Article 38). The annual budget is prepared by the Secretary-General and approved by the Committee of Ministers. Each member pays the expenses of its own Representatives and Ministers.

The seat of the Council of Europe is at Strasbourg. Its official languages are English and French. Other languages may be used under circumstances specified by the Assembly and Committee of Ministers.

Functions and Performance

The aim of the Council of Europe is "to achieve a greater unity between its Members" in order to safeguard the spiritual and moral values common to their heritage including individual freedom, political liberty and the rule of law. The members agree in principle that economic and social progress is desirable and can be achieved only by closer unity between them. Implicit is a common understanding that the "Western" way of life is endangered by totalitarian philosophy.

How to achieve closer unity has not been agreed upon. The dilemma has emerged in a conflict between the Committee of Ministers and the Consultative Assembly, a conflict that has been the most persistent of the Council's troubles and is perhaps inevitable owing to the fundamental differences in the character of the two component bodies. M. Paul Reynaud has said that one is for Europe and the other is against it.[15] One is responsible directly to national governments and is therefore prone to be conservative, slow and secretive in its business. The other, in contrast, is inclined to be bold, perhaps overly hasty and, because its members in the main are champions of change in search of public support, anything but secretive. The Assembly is responsible not to governments but largely to the individual consciences of its members. While the delegates tend to represent national party points of view, they have, in their capacity as Assembly delegates, no direct electoral relationship to the citizens at home. To some critics this is tantamount to being responsible to no one.

Other differences are also evident. Differences in national point of view

[14] See T. G. B. Cocks, *Procedure of the Consultative Assembly* (Strasbourg: 1951), pp. 43–81.

[15] Paul Reynaud, *op. cit.*, pp. 196–197.

and in party points of view emerge in both bodies. Some European socialists, including figures such as André Philip of France and Paul-Henri Spaak of Belgium, have been anxious to take strong measures towards unity at once. But French Socialist Guy Mollet, the German Socialists (SPD) and the British Laborites have hung back. In fact neither major British party has been ready to take the plunge of full political union with the European countries or to weaken commonwealth ties. The split within the Assembly itself is often described as "federalist" versus "functionalist."

The quarrel between Assembly and Council came to a head almost at once. There has been nothing in the way of party discipline, cabinet responsibility or national traditions to bind the two together.[16] In August 1949 the Assembly, encouraged by the leadership of Winston Churchill and others, challenged the Committee of Ministers' right to determine its agenda. Owing largely to the influence and skill of President Spaak, the Committee of Ministers was persuaded to liberalize its procedures in some respects and to approve several new agenda items.[17] The Assembly, however, has continued to be restless in its subordinate role as an advisory and consultative body. It has complained that its advice, in the form of numerous resolutions and recommendations, was unheeded by the Committee of Ministers or shunted off to other bodies such as the OEEC for further study. In 1950 these complaints forced the establishment of the "Joint Committee" to improve liaison between the two bodies. The Assembly's efforts to call the tune have been resisted by the Ministers on the ground that to grant the Assembly the dominant role would be to give it a measure of control over the policy of member governments.

In fact both bodies have been forced to compromise. Although there has been no amendment to the Statute, the balance between them does not rest so strongly with the Council as formerly. Projects advanced by the Assembly, in turn, have been turned aside or blunted by the Committee. For example, the Assembly has abandoned for a time the "federalist" conception of European unity in favor of the "functional approach" which the Committee felt able to accept. On September 5, 1949, the Assembly approved 88 to 2 a motion by R. W. G. Mackay, British Labor M.P., seconded by André Philip, a French Socialist, that the Assembly consider its goal to be "the creation of a European political authority with limited functions but real powers." [18] The goal proved difficult to achieve. Most of the British delegates, and soon the Scandinavian and Benelux representatives, balked at any genuine supranational or federal authority. The French then felt unable to stomach a continental federation without the British and the Scandinavians for fear of Germany, while the Germans alleged that a European union would be loaded in France's favor. In November the

16 Prof. F. L. Schuman feels that the roles of the two bodies approximate in some respects those of independent branches of government under the American principle of the separation of powers, *op. cit.*, p. 734.

17 See *Report on the Proceedings of the First Session of the Council of Europe,* Cmd. No. 7807 (London: HMSO, 1949), pp. 4–5.

18 Schuman, *op. cit.*, p. 735.

Council of Ministers poured cold water on the project. As a consequence the Assembly changed direction and did not back up its General Affairs Committee which had been assigned the task of defining an authority with "limited functions but real powers" and, in the close vote of 11 to 10 on November 19, 1950, had gone on record in favor of a federation with or without Britain. When the British and Scandinavian members admitted that their governments were unprepared to yield any sovereignty though prepared to see others do so if they wished, the Assembly on November 23, 1950, voted 82 to 19 with 16 abstentions to approve a report endorsing "functionalism" as the way to union. Specialized authorities were to be established by intergovernmental agreements to deal with specialized matters such as transportation, agriculture, etc.

A sop was thrown to the federalists, however. Resolution Number 54 was passed on the same day, 73–7–16, recommending both the fusion of the Brussels Treaty Organization and the OEEC with the Council of Europe and the acceptance of the "Mackay Plan," so named for the Laborite M.P. who proposed it. Under this plan the Assembly would become a lower chamber with authority to initiate and pass bills establishing specialized authorities while the Committee of Ministers would become an upper chamber retaining its unanimity rule with power to accept or reject bills. An executive council of Ministers chosen from the lower house would be responsible to both chambers. Measures approved by both bodies would become part of the "law of the land" of each member of the Council of Europe superseding conflicting national legislation. In this way the Council of Europe would derive its authority by passing legislation and federation might be achieved by stages. Individuals in the member countries would be bound by Council legislation that was supplemental to their national laws.[19]

Governments were not ready to accept the competition to their authority implicit in this compromise. On May 5, 1951, the Committee of Ministers refused to endorse the Mackay Plan noting that "it would be inadvisable, if they wished to preserve solidarity amongst the free countries of Europe, to pursue plans which by some are considered too ambitious and premature."

Nevertheless, the two bodies have collaborated to some extent and reached agreement on a number of matters. One result of the work in the Council of Europe has been the "Convention for the Protection of Human Rights and Fundamental Freedoms" which was signed in Rome on November 14, 1950, by the representatives of the fifteen countries. Envisaged is a European Commission of Human Rights, elected by the Committee of Ministers on nomination of the Consultative Assembly, to investigate complaints from governments, groups and individuals after national remedies have been exhausted and to provide for the conciliation of disputes. A European

---

[19] The text of the Mackay proposal may be found in the *Compilation of Recommendations and Resolutions Adopted by the Consultative Assembly during the Second Session* (Strasbourg: The Council of Europe, 1950).

Court of Human Rights is to judge cases where conciliation proves impossible. The Convention defers to national sovereignty since neither the Court nor the Commission can exercise its functions until the parties recognize its competence. While the seeds were sown by the European Movement at the Hague Conference, the project actually took root in Treaty form in the Council of Europe. It is perhaps the Council's first "legislation." [20]

The Assembly, moreover, is not a voice unheeded. National policies are influenced by events at Strasbourg. Although specifically excluded from discussing methods of defense, the Assembly at its 1950 session went on record in favor of a "unified European Army." Its committees have discussed European economic integration, the Schuman Plan, a European passport, uinform social security laws and the like.

The Eden Plan

The year 1951 marked a turning point for the Council of Europe. The Assembly and the Committee of Ministers became more compatible because the initiative for European unity shifted away from the Council, which gradually found it had a more readily agreed-upon role to play. The principal steps may be sketched briefly.

At the second part of the Consultative Assembly's third session the British seemed to jeopardize the proposed Schuman Plan and European Army by announcing they could join neither. When the Assembly then rejected in a close vote a proposal to summon a constitutional convention for the six Schuman Plan nations, its President, Paul-Henri Spaak, promptly resigned. Declaring that the Assembly had accomplished little in three years and was "played out," [21] he assumed the Chairmanship of the European Movement and spurred the drafting of a constitution by the Schuman Plan countries. "Little Europe" was now the gleam in the eye of European federalists.

Yet the Council of Europe was thought to be too important to let go by the board. How was Germany to be rearmed as the United States insisted? How could a European Army be accepted as the price of German rearmament as the French demanded? How could the United Kingdom exert some influence over the "functional communities" which, despite her aloofness, were being established by the European powers? The United Kingdom, in particular, realized that the Council might provide administrative arrangements to solve these policy riddles, and she suddenly shifted her field to become the Council's ardent champion.

Thus France, the United Kingdom and the United States announced at Washington in September 1951 their acceptance in principle of a European Army and the inclusion of Germany as an equal in the continental European

---

[20] See *The European Convention on Human Rights* (Strasbourg: Council of Europe, 1952).

[21] American Committee on United Europe, *The Council of Europe: Consultative Assembly, Report on Third Session, Part II*, pp. 15–16.

Reprinted by courtesy of the Daily Dispatch, Manchester

A BRITISH VIEWPOINT

Community which would be closely associated with the United States and Britain in all stages of its development.

British ardor for the Council of Europe as a link between the Schuman Plan Members and the other members of the Council was announced by Mr. Anthony Eden, Secretary of State for Foreign Affairs, at a meeting of the Committee of Ministers in March, 1952. The "Eden Plan," as it came to be called, was discussed and approved by the Assembly in its two sessions the following May and September. But Britain's voice in Europe's future was not to be too loud. While the Assembly expressed satisfaction that the United Kingdom in this way felt able to associate itself with the "specialized authorities" or "communities," it warned that such association "must not hamper in any way the normal functioning or development of the communities, especially of a Political Community." [22]

A Constitution for "Little Europe"

When the Assembly of the Coal and Steel Community held its first session in Strasbourg in September 1952, it was given a mandate by the six Foreign Ministers concerned to draw up a constitution for Europe. Because this task had been entrusted to the still unborn Assembly of the European Defence Community, it was necessary to create an Assembly *ad hoc*

[22] *Council of Europe News* (Strasbourg: Directorate of Information, June 1952), pp. 3–4.

(Spaak's suggestion) as a constituent body. It worked closely with a committee of the Council of Europe, including a Jurists' Committee and a Study Commission for a European Constitution of the European Movement. A draft constitution was presented to the Assembly *ad hoc* in March 1953.[23] Thus the preparatory work for the creation of a federal authority was done both by the European Movement and the Council of Europe.

In the September 1952 meeting of the Consultative Assembly, Foreign Minister Eden praised this effort but warned that "wider achievements embracing Western Europe as a whole . . . must not be forgotten." [24] For military and economic cooperation, intergovernmental agencies such as OEEC and NATO were essential. Freedom in the West, he cautioned, "rests on the conjunction, in harmony and strength, of the British Commonwealth, Europe and the United States."

Conclusions

Thus the Council was not, for a time, to become a political authority binding all fifteen members. It was rather to bridge the gap between the six European nations seriously considering federation and the other members who, despite their skepticism of political union, realized that their safety lay in association. On this point the Consultative Assembly and the Committee of Ministers could agree.

Inevitably the horizons of national parliaments have been widened as delegates have returned from Strasbourg where fundamental and perennial problems of mankind are discussed as they affect Europeans. The gap between talking and acting, and between planning and policy is not as wide as might appear. Ministers and parliamentary delegates accredited to the Council of Europe are used to governing. While some seek to preserve freedom of action for their home governments, most are seeking new solutions to old problems and new ways of organizing Europe's political relationships. Its chief role at present is to serve as an informational and educative organ for the "European" point of view. Its activities carry weight, moreover, because the Council was set up by treaty among European governments.

Nor has this experience been entirely limited to Europeans. On May 12, 1951, the Consultative Assembly unanimously resolved that problems of common interest should be discussed by delegates of the two Houses of the United States Congress and of the Consultative Assembly. In November fourteen members of Congress met in Strasbourg with eighteen members of the Assembly to compare notes on union and on the social and economic ramifications of Europe's rearmament effort.[25] Neither delegation

[23] See European Movement, *Europe Today and Tomorrow*, Nos. 18–19 (September-October 1952), and Council of Europe, Directorate of Information, *Introductory Report of the Committee of Jurists on the Problem of a European Political Community*, No. 2 (September 13, 1952).

[24] Consultative Assembly, Fourth Session II, *Official Report*, September 15, 1952, Doc. As(4) C.R.10, pp. 9 and 14.

[25] See *The Council of Europe*, Department of State Publication 4492 (Washington: Government Printing Office, 1952), p. 6 and *The Union of Europe, Its Progress, Problems, Prospects, and Place in the Western World*, 82nd Congress, 2nd Session, Senate Doc. 90.

NORWAY
1 **3** **4**

SWEDEN
3 **4**

UNITED KINGDOM
1 **3** **4**

DENMARK
1 **3** **4**

IRELAND
3 **4**

BENELUX
1 **2** **3** **4**

Atlantic

Ocean

E. GER.

POLA

WEST GERMANY
2 **3** **4**

CZECHOSLOVAK

FRANCE
1 **2** **3** **4**

SWITZ.
4

AUSTRIA
4

HUNGA

YUGOSLAV

PORTUGAL
1 **4**

SPAIN

Mediterranean

ITALY
1 **2** **3** **4**

Sea

Unity plans now operating:		Membership of the four plans:	
1 North Atlantic Treaty Organization	**3** Council of Europe	Members of all four plans	Members of two plans
2 Coal and Steel Community	**4** European Payments Union	Members of three plans	Members of one plan

The New York Times, February 22,

PROGRESS ON EUROPEAN U

782

HAT HAS BEEN DONE

MILITARILY: Nine West European nations have contributed forces to over-all command of the North Atlantic Treaty Organization, with pledge to aid each other in event of attack.

ECONOMICALLY: Six have formed Coal and Steel Community to create a free market in these commodities. Fourteen belong to Payments Union, a currency pool facilitating trade.

POLITICALLY: Fifteen send delegates to the Council of Europe, an advisory group envisioned as the framework of a future parliamentary structure for a federated Europe.

HAT REMAINS TO BE DONE

MILITARILY: The agreement signed by six nations to bring vital West German forces into an integrated Defense Community has yet to be ratified by the national parliaments.

ECONOMICALLY: In many fields tariff obstacles, discriminatory practices and cartels persist, restricting production and flow of goods, thus keeping living standards depressed.

POLITICALLY: The proposed federation of the Coal and Steel Community nations, plus others now in the Council of Europe, is only in paper stage, with many obstacles remaining.

HE RESOURCES   *How Western Europe compares with major world powers*

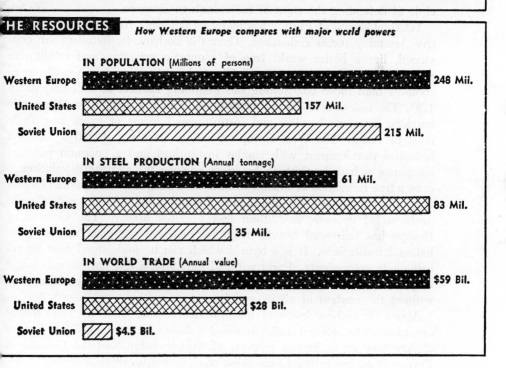

IN POPULATION (Millions of persons)

Western Europe — 248 Mil.
United States — 157 Mil.
Soviet Union — 215 Mil.

IN STEEL PRODUCTION (Annual tonnage)

Western Europe — 61 Mil.
United States — 83 Mil.
Soviet Union — 35 Mil.

IN WORLD TRADE (Annual value)

Western Europe — $59 Bil.
United States — $28 Bil.
Soviet Union — $4.5 Bil.

GOALS THAT HAVE YET TO BE REACHED

Chart on comparative resources is based on latest figures and — in the case of the Soviet Union — on current estimates.

had any official authority. The meetings were simply exploratory of common interests. The Americans were disappointed at the European reluctance or inability to unite in a hurry and found the British chiefly to blame. The Europeans, in turn, asked embarrassing questions about United States' tariff policy and aid for NATO.

The climate of opinion at Strasbourg is more European than national. We have seen that delegates are seated alphabetically rather than as state delegates. National rivalries to date have had little play although the revival of German power and the Frenchman's continued obsession for *sécurité* provide a potential source of national friction. There is no philosophy represented at Strasbourg that is alien or dangerous to Western liberalism. The Council of Europe is a camp of free men seeking to preserve, indeed to strengthen, their heritage. While there are advocates both of socialism and free enterprise all hands are agreed on the fundamental principle of defending the right of individuals to disagree.

Yet the Council of Europe has many weaknesses. At times its Consultative Assembly seems rudderless. Over the horizon, its founders are convinced, lies a better world free of economic privation and totalitarian pressure. But what is the course? The tasks at Strasbourg are vastly more complex than those confronting the Founding Fathers at Philadelphia in 1787. The task of creation in Europe is also a task of demolition. Economic barriers, language barriers and institutional barriers of great magnitude must be razed. The West European nations have not shared a common historical development with similar institutions and a common political allegiance as had the thirteen American colonies prior to the Revolution.

So a true federation of European states will take time. Meanwhile human ingenuity has devised new techniques of social cooperation to tackle the old problems of defense, destitution and personal liberty. The Council of Europe has borrowed heavily from international organization and from national institutions. It is a hybrid which can be understood best by recalling its antecedents. Early national parliaments did not have full and unquestioned authority to govern and the League of Nations could not act without the consent of all its members.

Above all, nothing is immutable in human affairs. The shift from feudal organization to national status involved a change in men's loyalties. Such a change may be in motion in parts of Europe today, and the Council of Europe is an institutional expression of changing loyalties.

Its growth seems predestined, because Europe's political and economic patchwork has long been out of date. Certainly the plethora of European institutions that have grown in piecemeal fashion since 1945 cry for coordination. The Council has addressed itself to that problem. It has served to focus attention on common problems growing daily more pressing to all Europeans in an age of advanced technology and clashing ideologies. It may prove able to keep alive the sparks of hope and idealism that remain in Europe. One wonders if it is not the most promising answer to totalitarianism.

Suggestions for Further Reading

Books

American Committee on United Europe, *A Statement of Progress* (New York: American Committee on United Europe, 1952).

Aron, R., and Marc, A., *Principes du Federalisme* (Paris: le Portulan, 1948).

Boyd, Andrew and Frances, *Western Union* (Washington: Public Affairs Press, 1949).

British Labour Party, National Executive Committee, *European Unity* (London: The Labour Party, 1950).

Commission to Study the Organization of Peace, *The Security of the United States and Western Europe* (New York: American Association for the United Nations, 1949).

Coudenhove-Kalergi, R. N., *Crusade for Pan-Europe* (New York: G. P. Putnam's Sons, 1943).

Diebold, William, Jr., *Trade and Payments in Western Europe: A Study in Economic Cooperation, 1947–1951* (New York: Council of Foreign Relations, 1952).

Ellis, Howard S., *The Economics of Freedom: The Progress and Future of Aid to Europe* (New York: Council on Foreign Relations and Harper & Brothers, 1950).

European Movement and the Council of Europe (London: Published on behalf of the European Movement by Hutchinson & Co., 1949).

Friedrich, Carl J., *Inevitable Peace* (Cambridge: Harvard University Press, 1948).

Hawtrey, R. G., *Western European Union: Implications for the United Kingdom* (London: Royal Institute of International Affairs, 1949).

Herriot, Edouard, *The United States of Europe* (New York: Viking Press, 1930).

Hoffman, Paul G., *Peace Can Be Won* (New York: Doubleday & Company, Inc., 1951).

MacKay, R. W. G., *Federal Europe* (London: Michael Joseph, Ltd., 1940).

Middleton, D., *The Defense of Western Europe* (New York: Appleton-Century-Crofts, Inc., 1952).

Philip, André, *The Schuman Plan: Nucleus of a European Community* (New York: European Movement, June 1951).

Reynaud, Paul, *Unite or Perish* (New York: Simon and Schuster, 1951).

Royal Institute of International Affairs, *Atlantic Alliance — NATO's Role in the Free World* (London and New York: Royal Institute of International Affairs, 1952).

———, *Defence in the Cold War* (London: Royal Institute of International Affairs, A Chatham House Study Group Report, 1950).

———, *Documents on European Recovery and Defense, March 1947–April 1949* (London: Royal Institute of International Affairs, 1949).

de Rusett, Alan, *Strengthening the Framework of Peace* (London and New York: Royal Institute of International Affairs, 1950).

Streit, C. K., *Union Now* (New York: Harper & Brothers, 1949).

Ward, Barbara, *Policy for the West* (New York: W. W. Norton & Company, 1951).

———, *The West at Bay* (New York: W. W. Norton & Company, 1948).

Periodicals

Goormaghtigh, John, "European Integration," *International Conciliation,* No. 488 (February 1953).

Loewenstein, K., "The Union of Western Europe: Illusion and Reality," *Columbia Law Review,* Vol. 52 (January–February, 1952).

Schuman, F. L., "The Council of Europe," *American Political Science Review,* Vol. 45, No. 3 (September 1951).

Stone, D. C., "The Impact of U. S. Assistance Programs on the Political and Economic Integration of Western Europe," *American Political Science Review,* Vol. 46, No. 4 (December 1952).

Vernon, Raymond, "The Schuman Plan: Sovereign Powers of the European Coal and Steel Community," *American Journal of International Law,* Vol. 47, No. 2 (April 1953).

Documents

COUNCIL OF EUROPE

Balance Sheet of the Work of the Consultative Assembly, August 1949–August 1952 (Strasbourg: Directorate of Information, 1952).

Council of Europe News, First, second and third years (Strasbourg: 1951–1953).

European Assembly, Summary of the Debates in the Consultative Assembly of the Council of Europe, Vol. 1, Second Ordinary Session, August 7–28, 1950.

European Convention on Human Rights (Strasbourg: 1952).

GREAT BRITAIN

Report on the Proceedings of the First Session of the Council of Europe (with related documents), Cmd. 7807 (London: Her Majesty's Stationery Office, 1949).

Report on the Proceedings of the Second Session of the Committee of Ministers and of the Second Meeting of the Standing Committee of the Council of Europe, Cmd. 7838 (London: Her Majesty's Stationery Office, 1949).

ORGANIZATION FOR EUROPEAN ECONOMIC COOPERATION

Economic Progress and Problems of Western Europe, Third Annual Report (June 1951).

European Economic Cooperation, Survey Prepared for the Organization for European Economic Cooperation (May 1951).

UNITED NATIONS

Economic Survey of Europe (Annual).

UNITED STATES

Congress, *Mutual Defense Assistance Act of 1949,* Public Law 329, 81st Congress, 1st Session.

Department of State, *An Analysis of the Schuman Plan,* Department of State Publication 4176 (Washington: U.S. Government Printing Office, April 1951).

———, *Collective Security in the Atlantic Area,* Publication 3377 (January 1949).

———, *Convention for European Economic Cooperation with Related Documents, Paris, April 16, 1948,* Publication 3145 (1948).

————, *General Report of the Committee of European Economic Cooperation*, Publication 2930, European Series 28 (September 21, 1947).

————, *The Mutual Security Program: Message on Foreign Aid Transmitted by the President to the Congress on May 24, 1951*, Publication 4236, General Foreign Policy Series 52 (1951).

————, *The Schuman Plan Constituting a European Coal and Steel Community*, Publication 4173 (April 1951).

————, *Strengthening the Forces of Freedom (Supplement, May–June 1950)*, Publication 3852a (1950).

Economic Cooperation Administration, *Report to Congress* (Quarterly).

President, *First Semiannual Report on the Mutual Defense Assistance Program*, H. Doc. 613, 81st Congress, 2nd Session (1950).

————, *Second Semiannual Report to the Congress on the Mutual Defense Assistance Program (April 6–October 6, 1950)*, H. Doc. 119, 82nd Congress, 1st Session (May 1951).

27

Commonwealth, American and Other Systems

> "Equality of status and freedom of association combined to ensure the effective independence of the Dominions; common allegiance, the unity of the Commonwealth." — NICHOLAS MANSERGH[1]

The Commonwealth

THE BRITISH COMMONWEALTH represents that rare phenomenon — a brood of dependencies which have attained maturity without bursting the family bonds. It is, of course, more a world-wide than a regional organization. The eight states — Australia, Canada, Ceylon, India, Pakistan, New Zealand, the United Kingdom and the Union of South Africa — which make up the Commonwealth are located in every part of the globe, and each is an independent, self-governing entity. The legal thread on which these jewels are strung is almost indefinable. The Commonwealth is composed of states which differ from each other in culture, religion, language and governmental structure. Yet it has in many ways become a symbol of international understanding and cooperation at its best.

The Commonwealth is not an "organization" in the same sense as the Arab League and the Organization of American States. It was not "established"; nor does it have a constitution or formal administrative machinery. Indeed, the very term "Commonwealth" has never been officially or legally adopted. The Commonwealth of Nations is, rather, the result of a slow, evolutionary process by which the former British Empire, ruled from the United Kingdom, has been transformed into a free association of equal member states bound together by a common allegiance to certain principles symbolized by the British Crown. That the Commonwealth may have been "forced" on Great Britain as her Dominions and Colonies became too powerful to dominate, or that Britain encouraged the formulation of the Commonwealth idea in an attempt to "salvage" as much of her empire as she could, is relatively unimportant in view of the fact that the process of

[1] "The Commonwealth at the Queen's Accession," *International Affairs*, Vol. 29, No. 3 (July 1953), p. 278.

Commonwealth development has been remarkably peaceful and that the result has been an effective example of international collaboration.

Origins

As with so many British institutions, the Commonwealth seems to have evolved almost by accident. The germ of the idea grew out of the system of Imperial Conferences — a series of meetings which were themselves not formally planned or instituted — which began in 1887 when leaders of the Dominions and Colonies came together in London to celebrate Victoria's Golden Jubilee. For the next fifteen years the leading statesmen of the Empire met in the British capital whenever a great event brought them together. Conferences were held in 1897, the Diamond Jubilee year, and in 1902, when Edward VII was crowned. Then, at a conference called in 1907 to review the status of the Dominions and colonial areas, it was resolved:

> That it will be to the advantage of the Empire if a Conference, to be called the Imperial Conference, is held every four years, at which questions of common interest may be discussed and considered as between His Majesty's Government and his Governments of the self-governing Dominions beyond the seas. The Prime Minister of the United Kingdom will be *ex officio* President, and the Prime Ministers of the self-governing Dominions *ex officio* members of the Conference.[2]

The Imperial Conference system operated during the First World War, when India was first represented, and was supplemented at that time by an Imperial War Cabinet, meeting in London under the British Prime Minister and charged with the task of coordinating the Commonwealth war effort with that of the mother country. This Cabinet was not an attempt to supplant the British parliamentary system with an enlarged imperial parliament and cabinet; it was, in effect, a council of allies, and did not meet after 1919.

In 1923 an Imperial Conference was convened, and an Imperial Economic Conference was held concurrently. The Irish Free State, newest member of the Commonwealth, attended. The Conference of 1926 was a landmark. The Union of South Africa and the Irish Free State, the most nationalist elements in the Commonwealth, requested that the Conference define the relations of the Commonwealth members. The ensuing *Balfour Report* defined the relationship in terms of complete autonomy and equality combined with cooperation. This *Report* was circulated at the 1930 Conference, approved by the members of the Commonwealth, and used as the basis for the United Kingdom act of 1931, entitled the Statute of Westminster. As much as any one document, this Statute could be considered the "constitution" of the Commonwealth. Its preamble stated that "the

---

[2] *Minutes of Proceedings of the Colonial Conference, 1907*, Cmd. 3523 (London: Eyre & Spottiswoode for HMSO, 1907), p. 82. Papers laid before the Conference are printed separately in Cmd. 3524.

Crown is the Symbol of the free association of the members of the British Commonwealth of Nations . . . ," and its provisions clarified the complete legal independence of the seven members then involved.[3]

The world economic depression brought the Commonwealth nations together in 1932 at Ottawa, Canada, where, on the initiative of the Dominions, it was agreed to set up an imperial preferential trading system to combat their common economic difficulties. The coronation of George VI in 1937 marked the last Imperial Conference, as World War II and its aftermath necessitated new changes in the Commonwealth concept.

Each of the Commonwealth members entered the war of its own choice, but this time no Commonwealth War Cabinet was established. Nevertheless, there was close coordination which motivated several proposals that the Commonwealth be formalized as a model international organization which could be the nucleus for wider international collaboration. There was also a consciousness of the changing world position of Britain in relation to the United States and the Soviet Union and of the role which the Commonwealth might play in the postwar world. In 1943 Field Marshal Jan Smuts of South Africa, who had long been a Commonwealth leader, suggested that new regional relationships be formed within the Commonwealth. Each regional arrangement would remain part of the continuing Commonwealth, while the United Kingdom would be able to bind itself more closely to the western European democracies. Smuts anticipated that the resultant West European area, supplemented by the Commonwealth, would form a "third force" capable of balancing the postwar bipolarity of power and thus of maintaining world peace.[4]

This idea was carried further in 1944 by Lord Halifax, who stated that the war's end would find four great powers — the United States, the Soviet Union, China and Britain. But, he added, the fourth power must include the British Commonwealth. Halifax advocated that the Commonwealth's unity of ideals be translated into a "unity of policy," emphasizing that this did not imply any retreat from the Statute of Westminster.[5] These "Smuts–Halifax proposals" were severely criticized in Canada on the ground that they implied an unsuitable rivalry between the two focal powers and ran counter to the establishment of global security.[6] However, the idea of regional arrangements within the Commonwealth was applauded by Australia and New Zealand, which had already signed a regional cooperation pact (ANZAC Pact).

Meanwhile, in preparation for the United Nations Conference scheduled to open in San Francisco on April 21, 1945, a meeting of the Commonwealth Prime Ministers was arranged. There had been no Commonwealth-wide meetings since before the war, when the last Imperial Conference had convened, but the Prime Ministers' meeting in May 1944 was not an attempt to

[3] 22 Geo. V, c. 4 (London: HMSO, 1931).

[4] *The New York Times*, December 12, 1943.

[5] *The New York Times*, January 25, 1944.

[6] See speech by Prime Minister Mackenzie King in House of Commons, *The New York Times*, February 1, 1944.

revive that institution, which would not have been acceptable to the member states. It was, rather, an *ad hoc* gathering which had no formal agenda and issued no final statement. The purpose of the conference was to allow the United Kingdom Government to report to the other Commonwealth Governments on the events which had transpired at Yalta and Dumbarton Oaks relating particularly to the United Nations Organization.

The role of the Commonwealth in the United Nations became an issue of some import in 1945. The U.S.S.R. had indicated that it would ask for United Nations representation for two of its Republics, the Ukrainian S.S.R. and the Byelorussian S.S.R., claiming that the Commonwealth's unity would give Britain and the United States a disproportionately large representation. This charge was also hurled at Britain by segments of the American press. In April 1945 the Prime Ministers' conference issued statements designed to refute these allegations. They read in part: "It is . . . quite possible both to be a citizen of the world and a member of a family. . . . The nations of the British Commonwealth will not go to San Francisco as a bloc bent on concerting their votes in opposition to those of others . . . . participation in the San Francisco Conference . . . will be as autonomous nations, each participating in its own right." [7]

At the San Francisco Conference, Australia became a leader of the "small nations," Canada and New Zealand were instrumental in drafting some of the final Security Council provisions of the Charter, and India provided the chairman of a technical committee. All six of the Commonwealth nations represented at San Francisco (Australia, Canada, India, New Zealand, United Kingdom and Union of South Africa) ratified the Charter in their own manner, and they have participated in all United Nations activities as independent states.

Organization and Functions

The Prime Ministers met again in London in 1946 to exchange views on such matters as drafting the peace treaties, the future of Germany, arrangements for military liaison, and economic cooperation in the South Pacific and Southeast Asia. At the end of these meetings, a statement was issued which affirmed the worth of the existing flexible method of consultation and pointed out "that the methods now practised are preferable to any rigid centralized machinery . . . [which] might even hamper the combination of autonomy and unity which is characteristic of the British Commonwealth and is one of their great achievements." The statement concluded with a declaration of support for the United Nations. [8]

In August 1947 the new Dominions of India and Pakistan were established. The birth of an independent India had been long in coming, and a good deal of bitterness had been engendered during the years of British domination of the subcontinent. Because of this background, Indian na-

[7] *Manchester Guardian*, April 5, 1945.
[8] *The New York Times*, May 24, 1946.

tionalists rejected the idea of Dominion status (as did the Moslem nationalists of Pakistan) and demanded that India be proclaimed a republic.

A conference of Prime Ministers met in London on April 21, 1949, to consider this problem. The final decision was that India would remain a member of the Commonwealth. Being a republic, however, it would accept the British monarch only as "Head of the Commonwealth," with no implication of allegiance or obligation to the Crown. This relationship defied legal definition, but the fact that India had decided to remain in the Commonwealth was an event of great significance. Since allegiance no longer constituted a requirement of membership, Pakistan also decided to remain within the Commonwealth. Unlike her neighbors, Burma chose to break the family ties and, in September 1947, proclaimed herself a "Sovereign, Independent Republic to be known as the Union of Burma." In February 1948, the independent Government of Ceylon, formed after elections in 1947, was admitted as the ninth Commonwealth member nation. The number of Commonwealth nations was reduced to eight in 1949, however, when Ireland, after twenty-five years of tenuous membership, culminated its nationalist aspirations by withdrawing from all association with the Commonwealth and proclaiming itself the Republic of Ireland or Eire.

The next meeting of the Commonwealth Prime Ministers was held in London in January 1951. Southern Rhodesia, which had been invited to attend several previous meetings, joined the conference. A peace treaty with Japan and the Near East situation were discussed. The United Kingdom and Canada explained their obligations under the North Atlantic Treaty, which they had signed in 1949. This Treaty and the North Atlantic Treaty Organization (NATO) established by it were viewed as a regional security arrangement compatible with Commonwealth principles as well as with Article 52 of the United Nations Charter.

Conferences and Other Instruments

The Prime Ministers' Conference, although not formally established as an organ of the Commonwealth and having no regular place or time of meeting, has become, in effect, the most important political body representing Commonwealth affairs. In addition to these periodic top-level conferences, other Commonwealth meetings have been held with increasing frequency since the end of World War II. They have been on a regional as well as all-Commonwealth basis. In 1949 a meeting of Finance Ministers discussed steps to reduce the drain on sterling reserves and secure a stable relationship between the sterling and dollar areas. In 1947 a regional conference was held in Canberra, Australia, to discuss the terms of the Japanese peace treaty, and in October 1948 an important conference was held in Colombo, Ceylon, to discuss the economic and political problems of Southeast Asia. This conference established a pattern of convening a meeting of financial experts concurrently with the political meeting. The Colombo Plan for agricultural and industrial development to aid the Southeast Asian

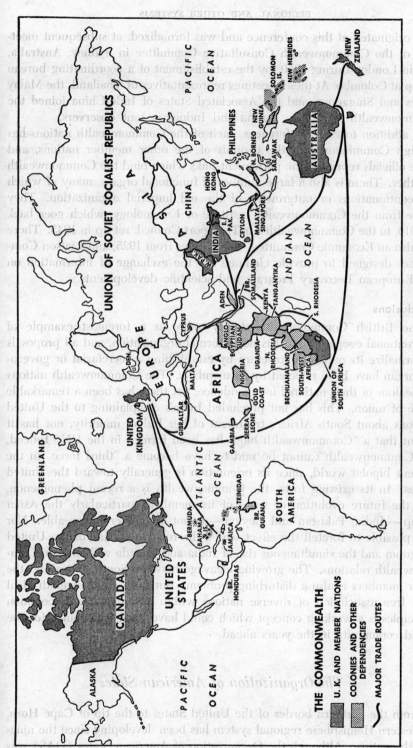

area originated at this conference and was formalized, at subsequent meetings of the Commonwealth Consultative Committee in Sydney, Australia, and in London during 1950, by the establishment of a coordinating bureau set up at Colombo. At these meetings representatives of Thailand, the Malay States and Singapore, and the Associated States of Indo-China joined the Commonwealth members. Burma and Indonesia sent observers.

In addition to such conferences, each of the Commonwealth nations has a High Commissioner in the capitals of the other member nations, and these officials represent the permanent links which bind the Commonwealth together. There is also a large number of functional organs, many of which are continuations or outgrowths of the old imperial organization. They range from the Commonwealth Institute of Entomology, which goes back to 1910, to the Commonwealth Air Transport Council, set up in 1945. There are also an Economic Committee, which dates from 1925, and Liaison Committees designed to provide channels for the exchange of information on the European Recovery Program and scientific developments.

Conclusions

The British Commonwealth stands today as a foremost example of international cooperation. It is not a formal organization, and all proposals to formalize its nebulous structure by establishing a secretariat or governing organ have been rejected by its members. The Commonwealth nations are jealous of their national independence; yet there has been a remarkable sense of union. This has not precluded India's complaining to the United Nations about South Africa's treatment of her Indian minority, nor has it meant that a "Commonwealth bloc" has been formed in the UN. Indeed, the Commonwealth cannot be said to have become a "third force" in the present bipolar world, since its orientation is generally toward the United States. In its existing form, the Commonwealth is a recent phenomenon, and the future evolution of some of its members, particularly the Asian group — India, Pakistan and Ceylon — is not altogether foreseeable. Nor is it possible to foretell the effect which the relative decline of the United Kingdom and the simultaneous rise of India and Canada will have on Commonwealth relations. The growing cleavage between South Africa and the other members is also a disturbing problem. But the Commonwealth ideal of a free association of diverse nations within a framework of common principles is a working concept which could have great importance for the world community in the years ahead.

The Organization of American States

From the northern border of the United States to the tip of Cape Horn, a Western Hemisphere regional system has been developing since the nineteenth century. Although the Organization of American States (OAS) was formally established as recently as 1948, it has its roots in a series of Inter-

American Conferences which date back to 1890. Indeed, the present organization is, in many ways, the old Inter-American System "writ large." [9] The long effort to promote Pan-American cooperation forms a pattern of responses to the changing political and economic relationships among the American states themselves and between the Western Hemisphere and the rest of the world.

At the turn of the last century the United States replaced Britain as the great naval power in the hemisphere. Because of this power ascendancy, Uncle Sam often exercised an unrestrained influence over his Latin neighbors. But, largely through the instrumentalities of the Inter-American System, this unequal relationship has been gradually modified in fact as well as in theory. In place of the former unilateralism and predominance of Washington, Inter-American institutions now exist which seek to promote more coordinated, mutually beneficial relations among the American states. But the United States is still *primus inter pares*.

Background

A few *ad hoc* international conferences were held in South America during the nineteenth century, but it was not until 1890 that the first Inter-American Conference was called. The meetings in Washington resulted in the establishment of the International Union of American Republics and the creation of a standing Commercial Bureau. This first Conference recommended methods for the peaceful settlement of disputes, and, on United States' initiative, sought ways to strengthen commercial relations within the hemisphere. Conditions during the succeeding years were favorable to this latter aim, and, by resolution of the Third Inter-American Conference (1910), the original commercial office became the Pan-American Union.[10] The new organization served, in effect, as a permanent secretariat, with responsibilities relating to cultural as well as commercial and archival matters. The Governing Board of the Union was composed of diplomatic representatives of the American republics accredited to Washington. Two Latin American complaints were met by the Fifth Conference (1923) which resolved that persons other than diplomats in Washington might be appointed to the Board and that its presidency and vice-presidency should no longer be designated by the United States Secretary of State but should be elective.

Institutions were created throughout the life of the Inter-American System which have continued to operate. In 1902 a Pan-American Sanitary Bureau was established, and in 1906 the International Conference of American Jurists came into being. During this same period, special technical conferences on commerce, agriculture, communications and other problems were called periodically. In the twenties, two notable institutions were

[9] Arthur P. Whitaker, "Development of American Regionalism: The Organization of American States," *International Conciliation*, No. 469 (March 1951), p. 124.

[10] In 1903 the Commercial Bureau had become the International Bureau of the American States.

formed: the Institutes for the Protection of Children (1924) and for Geography and History (1929). In addition, numerous Pan-American Conferences were held to deal with social and economic problems, and, during the Great Depression of the thirties, Inter-American Conferences and Commissions began to deal seriously with these problems.[11] At the same time, the "Good Neighbor Policy" — dramatized, though not originated, by Franklin Roosevelt — was aimed at easing Latin American resentment against encroachment from the North. The policy of periodic interventions by the United States (such as in Mexico in the 1860's, Venezuela in 1895 and 1901, and elsewhere somewhat less violently) had been formalized by the Platt Amendment to the Army Appropriation Bill of 1901 (subsequently made part of the United States–Cuba Treaty of 1903) and given the earmarks of a political philosophy by the Roosevelt corollary to the Monroe Doctrine in 1904. This policy was finally laid to rest when the United States delegates to the Inter-American Conferences of 1933, 1936 and 1938 accepted anti-intervention resolutions.[12]

The advent of World War II stimulated efforts to insure Pan-American solidarity against aggression from outside the hemisphere. The Lima Conference in 1938 agreed to provide for formal consultation in the event of war or threat of war. Consultation was to be carried on by means of Meetings of the Foreign Ministers of the American Republics. The American governments had already declared at the special Buenos Aires Peace Conference (1936), attended by President Roosevelt, that ". . . every act susceptible of disturbing the peace of America affects each and every one of them. . . ."[13] Three Meetings of the Foreign Ministers of the American Republics took place during World War II. They developed in scope beyond mere "consultation" to include coordination of hemisphere defense and the breaking off of diplomatic relations with the Axis powers. In 1942 the Third Meeting created an Inter-American Defense Board to carry out the former task.

Foundations of New System

Early in 1945, decisive steps toward a new American system were taken at the Chapultepec Conference (Mexico City Conference on Problems of War and Peace). Inter-American unity was restored, at least superficially, when Argentina agreed to accept the policy of common action against the Axis. The Act of Chapultepec announced that after the war's end the American states desired to conclude a permanent treaty of mutual defense and consolidate the diverse inter-American treaties for peaceful settlement of disputes. It also envisaged an Inter-American System bound together under a permanent charter. On these points the Act was in conflict with the

[11] A useful summary of the nonpolitical Inter-American Conferences is given by M. Margaret Ball, *The Problem of Inter-American Organization* (Stanford: Stanford University Press, 1944), Chap. III.

[12] See Edward O. Guerrant, *Roosevelt's Good Neighbor Policy* (Albuquerque: University of New Mexico Press, 1950), Chap. 1.

[13] See M. Margaret Ball, *op. cit.*, p. 54 and *passim*.

Dumbarton Oaks Proposals of 1944, which would have limited the role of regional groupings, in the settlement of disputes, to enforcement action only with the prior authorization of the Security Council. But the American states presented a united front on this issue at the San Francisco Conference and succeeded, under the leadership of Senator Vandenberg, in having Article 51 inserted in the United Nations Charter. This crucial Article authorizes individual or collective self-defense against aggression pending appropriate action by the Security Council.

Achievement of the projects anticipated by the Act of Chapultepec was unexpectedly delayed until 1947 and 1948 because of the deterioration in relations between Argentina and her neighbors. The United States State Department's publication of a "Blue Book" on Argentina's wartime relations with the Axis and the proposal of Uruguay that multilateral intervention be used to protect democratic institutions in the Americas reflected the tension within the hemisphere.

But the frigid winds of the "cold war" induced nineteen of the twenty-one republics[14] to meet at Rio de Janeiro in September 1947 where they signed the Inter-American Treaty of Reciprocal Assistance. The Rio Treaty (subsequently ratified by all twenty-one nations) provides for mutual assistance in the event of any aggression or threat of aggression, whether from within or without the Western Hemisphere defense area (defined as including both poles and Greenland). Argentina proposed that intra-continental disputes be left for solution by consultation only and that unanimous approval be required for collective action, but she lost the day to the stiffer United States-sponsored proposals. The Treaty stipulates (Article 3) that an armed attack on any state shall be deemed to be an attack on all, and each of the contracting parties undertakes to assist in meeting any attack as an exercise of the inherent right of self-defense recognized by the United Nations Charter.

An Organ of Consultation (meetings of Foreign Ministers) is to gather "without delay," in case of an armed attack, and "immediately," if the integrity or political independence of any American state should be affected (1) by an aggression which is not an armed attack or (2) by " . . . any other fact or situation that might endanger the peace of America . . ." (Article 6). This Organ is to decide, by two-thirds vote, "the measures which must be taken in the case of an aggression" or upon measures for common defense. A majority vote suffices for procedural matters. Decisions are binding upon all signatories, except that no state can be required to use armed force without its consent. Article 10 specifically subordinates these procedures to the rights and obligations with regard to self-defense set out in the United Nations Charter.[15] This regional defense arrangement within the framework of the United Nations Charter was a momentous

---

[14] Nicaragua's coup d'état government had not yet been recognized; Ecuador withdrew because of a revolution at home.

[15] "Inter-American Treaty of Reciprocal Assistance," *Department of State Bulletin,* Vol. 17, No. 429 (September 21, 1947), pp. 565–567.

precedent which was to be copied nine months later by the North Atlantic powers.

Organization

The political edifice which was erected on the Rio Treaty followed one-half year later when, at the Ninth Inter-American Conference held in March-April 1948 at Bogotá, Colombia, the Inter-American System was converted into the Organization of American States. This long-delayed conference produced the Charter or Organic Pact of the OAS and the American Treaty of Pacific Settlement (Pact of Bogotá). Other agreements were also reached, including an economic agreement, a Charter of Social Guarantees, and a Declaration of the Rights and Duties of Man. The Charter incorporated many of the proposals submitted at Mexico City in 1945 as well as the views of certain states, led by Mexico, pertaining to the duties of governments in relation to the economic, social and cultural welfare of their people. The Pact is also designed to consolidate former treaties for the peaceful settlement of disputes by providing a system of uniform acceptance of procedures — good offices, mediation, investigation, conciliation, and judicial or arbitral decision.

The supreme organ of the OAS is the Inter-American Conference, which meets every five years. The OAS Council is the permanent executive and also serves as the Provisional Organ of Consultation (pending a Meeting of Foreign Ministers in case of attack on the hemisphere). It is composed of one delegate from each of the twenty-one member nations. Under the Council's supervision are an Economic and Social Council, Council of Jurists and Cultural Council. The specialized agencies which have been in existence since the beginning of the century have also been incorporated into the new system and continue to function. The Pan-American Union has been elevated to the position of central permanent organ and General Secretariat of the new system. Its Director is Secretary-General of the OAS, chosen for a ten-year term by the Conference and not eligible to succeed himself.

Foreign Ministers' Meetings constitute another instrumentality of the new system and are closely related to the OAS Council. The Council is charged with convening such meetings "to consider problems of an urgent nature. . . . " In the event of an armed attack, the Council Chairman must call a meeting; in other cases, a request by any member is sufficient. To advise the Council and the Foreign Ministers in matters of defense, the Charter has provided an Advisory Defense Committee, composed of the military chiefs of all the states. It can be seen that the new organization incorporates those institutions which were part of the old Inter-American System and also many structural features of the United Nations, although some of its agencies — like the Foreign Ministers' Consultative Meeting — have no UN counterpart.

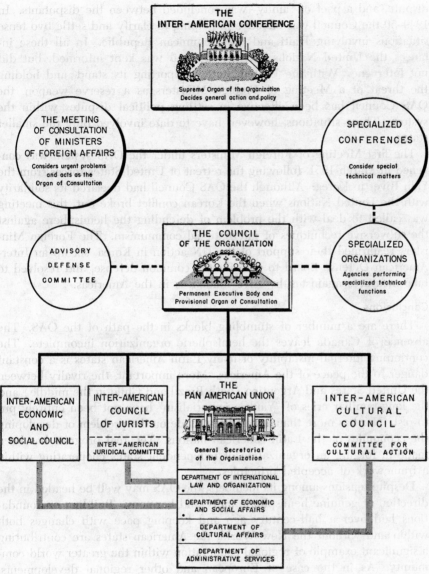

THE
INTER-AMERICAN CONFERENCE

Supreme Organ of the Organization
Decides general action and policy

THE MEETING
OF CONSULTATION
OF MINISTERS
OF FOREIGN AFFAIRS

Considers urgent problems
and acts as the
Organ of Consultation

SPECIALIZED
CONFERENCES

Consider special
technical matters

ADVISORY
DEFENSE
COMMITTEE

THE COUNCIL
OF THE ORGANIZATION

Permanent Executive Body and
Provisional Organ of Consultation

SPECIALIZED
ORGANIZATIONS

Agencies performing
specialized technical
functions

INTER-AMERICAN
ECONOMIC
AND
SOCIAL COUNCIL

INTER-AMERICAN
COUNCIL
OF JURISTS

INTER-AMERICAN
JURIDICAL COMMITTEE

THE
PAN AMERICAN UNION

General Secretariat
of the Organization

DEPARTMENT OF INTERNATIONAL
LAW AND ORGANIZATION

DEPARTMENT OF ECONOMIC
AND SOCIAL AFFAIRS

DEPARTMENT OF
CULTURAL AFFAIRS

DEPARTMENT OF
ADMINISTRATIVE SERVICES

INTER-AMERICAN
CULTURAL
COUNCIL

COMMITTEE FOR
CULTURAL ACTION

* The Directors of these Departments are the
Executive Secretaries of the respective Councils

Américas, Pan American Union

ORGANIZATION OF AMERICAN STATES

Settlement of Disputes

Thus far, the Organization's efforts to maintain peace within the American hemisphere have been relatively successful. It was faced almost at once with an emergency situation when Costa Rica complained to the Council that Nicaraguan forces had entered its territory. The Council immediately sent an investigating committee to the area. Finding both sides at fault, the Council (with strong United States backing) aided in settling the dispute, and a pact of "amity" was concluded between the disputants. In 1949–50 the Council was effective in helping to clarify and settle two tense situations involving Haiti and the Dominican Republic. In all these intances the United Nations Security Council was kept informed, but did not intervene. With the United States supporting its stand, and holding the threat of a Meeting of Foreign Ministers as a reserve weapon, the OAS Council has been effective in settling political disputes within the system. These situations, however, have to date involved only the smaller states.

The first Meeting of Foreign Ministers under the OAS system was convened in March 1951, following the retreat of United States forces from the Yalu River in Korea. Although the OAS Council had declared its solidarity with the United Nations when the Korean conflict broke out, this meeting was called to deal with the problem of defending the hemisphere against the subversive techniques of international communism. The Foreign Ministers reaffirmed their support of the UN action in Korea, set up an Inter-American Defense Board to plan for the common defense, and resolved to take measures against subversive influences in the Americas.

Conclusions

There are a number of stumbling blocks in the path of the OAS. The absence of Canada leaves the hemispheric organization incomplete. The continuing internal instability of many Latin American states is a constant danger to the peace of the Americas. More important, the rivalry between the United States and Argentina (with Brazil and Chile in the middle) and the long-familiar cries of "Yankee imperialism" have not been entirely put to rest. Nor has more than a start been made on the problem of developing the economies of the Latin American nations. Yet, real progress has been made in forging an organization of independent states cooperating within a framework of accepted principles.

Despite tensions among its members, the OAS may well be headed in the direction of genuine hemispheric unity and harmony. Building on foundations laid over a half-century ago and keeping pace with changes both within and without the New World, the American states are contributing a significant example of regional cooperation within the greater world community. As in the case of European and other regional developments, external threats more than any other factor have goaded independent states into formalizing and institutionalizing cooperative relationships.

The Arab League

The Arab League — comprising the seven Arab states of Egypt, Lebanon, Iraq, Trans-Jordan, Saudi Arabia, Syria and Yemen — was established in March 1945 as a "regional arrangement" within the definition about to be established in Article 52 of the United Nations Charter. The Pact that established the League states that its purpose is to "strengthen the ties between the participating States, to coordinate their political programs in such a way as to effect a real collaboration between them, to preserve their independence and sovereignty, and to consider in general the affairs and interests of the Arab countries." [16] Two major compulsions lay behind this attempt to unify the Arab world: the desire to rid the area of foreign influences and the desire to present a united Arab front against Zionism.

Unity Out of Conflict

The League had its origin in the Pan-Arab movement which captured the imagination of the Arab peoples during the interwar period and was a manifestation of growing Arab nationalism. In 1931 nationalist leaders met in Jerusalem and drew up an Arab Covenant in the name of the "Arab nations" pledged to the goal of "complete independence." Although Great Britain was the major target of Arab nationalism, British policy was quickly reoriented in an attempt to control and guide its course. It was largely the result of British encouragement that closer inter-Arab cooperation was attained. There are deep and serious intra-Arab factional disputes, however, which have a long history and have become the major stumbling blocks in the path of Arab League unity. These disputes center around three protagonists — the Hashimites of Jordan and Iraq, Ibn Saud of Arabia, and the Egyptians — and are related to British attempts to capture Arab nationalism.

During the First World War, Britain made an agreement with Sherif Hussein of the Hejaz and Mecca which promised Arab independence under Hashimite rule. This plan was thwarted, however, by Ibn Saud, ruler of the Wahhabi Arab Moslems of the Nejd. He defeated the Hashimite forces under the command of Hussein's son, Abdullah, in 1919, and in 1924 captured Mecca. Hussein abdicated, and the Hashimites were left in control of two North Arab areas which had been given them by the British. Abdullah accepted the Emirate of Transjordan in 1921, when his younger brother, Faisal, was placed on the throne of Iraq.

But Abdullah made it clear to the British that he expected their support in gaining his dream of a Greater Syria, which would include all of the North Arab lands from the Mediterranean to the Persian Gulf, following the ancient Fertile Crescent, and would be ruled by the House of Hashim. Britain's inability to convince the French (who administered the Syria-Lebanon mandate) of the merits of this idea, and the growth of Egyptian and Saudi Arabian power during the interwar period prevented the fulfillment of the Greater Syria scheme.

But the rise of Egypt and her attempts to gain recognition as the leader of the Arab world have given rise to the principal point of contention. While the Hashimites still long for Arab unity under their House, the Egyptians, with a wealthy ally in Ibn Saud, have opposed any attempt which would frustrate the Egyptian desire to lead the Pan-Arab movement. Britain has not looked with favor on Egyptian aspirations, however, largely because of the deterioration in Anglo-Egyptian relations since the interwar

[16] Article I, Pact of the League of Arab States.

period. The Egyptian attitude, moreover, has shown some changes in the
direction of moderation since the republican regime of Premier Naguib
was established in 1952. In 1936 an Iraqi-Saudi Arabian Treaty of Brotherhood and Alliance was concluded, with Yemen acceding later. In the
same year, Egypt and Saudi Arabia signed a Treaty of Friendship.

World War II then brought the Near East into the spotlight and gave
the Arab unity idea its greatest bargaining power. As Nazi designs on the
area and its strategic military position astride the routes to oil and the
Soviet Union made the Near East more important than ever, Arab nationalists pressed for complete independence and Arab unity. Britain continued
to bid for Arab friendship by announcing in 1941 that "His Majesty's Government for their part will give their full support to any scheme that commands general approval." [17] This act of encouragement was exploited
when, in 1943, the Foreign Minister of Iraq, Nuri es-Said, proposed that a
North Arab federation be set up as a first step toward the establishment of
an Arab League. Egypt and Saudi Arabia viewed this proposal as an
attempt to further Hashimite dynastic ambitions and opposed the scheme.
Instead Prime Minister Nahas Pasha of Egypt suggested that Arab leaders
meet in Alexandria to discuss the establishment of an Arab League. The
questions of Syria-Lebanon independence and Zionism provided areas of
common agreement. A draft pact was circulated in 1944, and it was formally signed in Cairo on March 22, 1945. The Pact was immediately communicated to the Secretariat of the United Nations Conference, then meeting in San Francisco, as a "regional arrangement" under the Charter.

Organization

As its organization demonstrates, the League was designed to be a loose
confederation of sovereign states. Although its members were to coordinate
their domestic and foreign policies, settle their internal disputes without
recourse to arms and submit inter-Arab disputes to the League Council,
whose decision would be binding (Article IV, Pact of the League of Arab
States), the actual powers of the League were limited by the provision that
in order to commit all members a decision had to be made unanimously
(Article VII). Decisions taken by majority vote were to bind only those
who had accepted them.

Economic and social agencies were also established, and a "functional"
approach to the problems of the Near East was outlined. Committees were
set up to draft agreements and make recommendations concerning health,
finances, and a variety of other economic, social, and cultural matters.
These Committees are supervised and assisted by the League Secretariat
and report to the League Council, which can then consider the reports and
recommend their implementation to the member states.

The Secretariat, with headquarters in Cairo, is the administrative organ
of the League. Its powers were not closely defined in the Pact, but it has
come to play an influential and often independent role. This is largely the

[17] Foreign Secretary Anthony Eden quoted in *The Times* (London), May 30, 1941.

result of the efforts and personality of the first Secretary-General, Abdul Rahman Azzam Pasha, who was formerly Egyptian Minister of Arab Affairs and whose anti-imperialist attitude was feared by the League's British sponsors.

Stresses in Action

The League was held together at its inception by its two principal goals: the desire to oust foreign influences and resist Zionist aspirations for a Jewish state in Palestine. The first goal was substantially achieved when Syria and Lebanon were freed from French and then British domination immediately after the war. But the goal of an Arab Palestine not only failed of achievement; it became a source of friction between the competing factions within the League.

The Arab states formed a bloc in the United Nations during the 1947 debate on Palestine, but their attempts to prevent a decision which would set up a Jewish state were fruitless, largely because of United States–Soviet Union agreement in support of a partition plan.[18] When the State of Israel was proclaimed on May 14, 1948, the members of the Arab League immediately attacked the new Jewish state. But there was no coordination among the various Arab armies. This lack of unity, coupled with the resulting defeat of the Arab forces, dealt a hard blow to the League.

The split between Hashimite Jordanians and Egyptians was made doubly clear when the latter sponsored an all-Palestine government in September 1948, after Eastern Palestine had already been annexed by Jordan. This inter-Arab conflict continued after armistice agreements with Israel were concluded. On April 1, 1950, at the instance of Egypt, all members of the League voted to expel any member making a separate peace with Israel, and the League was empowered to take punitive measures against any member that did so. This decision was clearly aimed at Jordan. Then, on May 15, the League condemned Jordan for her unilateral annexation of Eastern Palestine; and Egypt, Saudi Arabia, Syria and Lebanon voted to expel Jordan from the League. Only the opposition of Iraq and Yemen prevented this action.

In June 1950 an Egyptian-sponsored Arab collective security pact was signed by five of the seven League members. This pact was also aimed against Jordanian expansion and was presented to a League session from which Jordan was absent. Because of this fact, Iraq refused to sign. She later adhered to a revised agreement, which meant that only Jordan remained outside the new arrangement. The collective security pact provided that aggression against any signatory should be deemed aggression against them all. It established a Joint Defense Council, composed of each state's Foreign and Defense Ministers, and a permanent Military Staff Committee, composed of all chiefs of staff.

In the summer of 1951, King Abdullah of Jordan, recognized head of the Hashimite House, was assassinated by a follower of the ex-Grand Mufti of

[18] See the Palestine Case, Chap. 15.

Jerusalem, Haj Amin el-Husseini, whom the Egyptians had supported as head of the proposed all-Palestine government of 1948. This event weakened Jordan's position and left Iraq as the Hashimite center opposed to Egyptian ascendancy in the Arab world. However, Egypt's attempt to keep the League out of the United Nations' Korean action in 1950 as a sign of Arab dissatisfaction with the United States' stand on Palestine ended in failure, as one by one the other Arab states supported some of the UN measures. Moreover, recent Egyptian disagreements with Britain over the Suez and Sudan have resulted in a loss of British support for an Egyptian-dominated Arab League.

The history of the Arab League's functional agencies is somewhat brighter than its history of political disputes and dissensions. There has been considerable cultural and technical cooperation, all-Arab conferences in a variety of fields have been held, and draft agreements pertaining to aviation and commerce have been drafted.

The over-all impression one has of the Arab League is that it is a highly volatile alliance born more of reaction against external pressures than of internal consensus. It has been a convenient, though not always effective, instrument for combatting the colonial powers and Zionists. It has helped the Arab nations exercise, as a bloc in the United Nations, more influence than probably would have been the case without it. In alliance with the Latin Americans, the Arab group was able to secure significant concessions from Britain and France. But, despite limited political, economic and social successes, the League's professed goal of unifying the Arab world is still very far from realization.

Soviet Regional Organizations

The Soviet Union and its Communist neighbors have developed their own brand of regional organization. In answer to the Organization of European Economic Cooperation (OEEC) and the Marshall Plan, these governments have established the Cominform (Communist Information Bureau) and the Molotov Plan. Neither is typical of the international cooperative institutions that have developed in the last century or so among truly independent states. Like its prewar predecessor, the Comintern (Third Communist International), the Cominform resembles more a general and his staff than a team of partners. It regiments the activities of several national Communist parties that carry out policies determined centrally by the Communist leaders in Moscow. Little is known of its activities or organization.

The Soviet Union has also fashioned its own regional security system. Since 1948, mutual assistance arrangements have been created, linking Moscow with each of its satellites. A treaty with Bulgaria, signed on March 18, 1948, is an example. It provides mutual protection against aggression by Germany "or any other state which may . . . join Germany in its policy of

aggression. . . . " Each party is obligated to render unqualified assistance
if the other is attacked. Since the governments concerned are, for all intents and purposes, the same, these pacts can be expected to be honored.
Similar agreements have been concluded among the satellite states themselves, presumably at the behest of Moscow. Furthermore, these treaties
state that their provisions are "in accordance with the principles of the
Charter of the United Nations Organization." That unhappy document has
been used to provide a legal fig leaf for the most incompatible of rival
regional systems. Nevertheless, the Soviet acknowledgment of the propaganda value of such a protestation is significant in itself.

Cominform

Like its North Atlantic and Western European counterparts, the Cominform grew out of the harsh circumstances of the war and its aftermath. In
1943, as a gesture of good will toward the Western Allies during the war
against the Nazis, the Comintern was dissolved. For the next four years
there was no formal organ of international communism. Then, in September 1947, three months after the Marshall Plan had been announced, representatives of the Communist Parties of the U.S.S.R., Yugoslavia, Poland,
Hungary, Rumania, Bulgaria, Czechoslovakia, Italy and France met near
Warsaw to establish the Cominform.

On hand to act as midwives at the delivery of the new organization were
Soviet leaders Zhdanov and Malenkov. There was a conscious effort, however, to give the meeting an appearance of independence from Moscow.
The Cominform sought to profit from the mistakes of the Comintern. The
latter had had its seat in Moscow; its organization was centralized; and its
policies were directed from the Kremlin. Its guiding principle was communism as a truly international movement, spreading from the nucleus of
the only established and functioning Communist state. Largely because
the nationalist sentiments in Europe and in the non-Russian Communist
parties of the Continent were not sufficiently taken into account, the Comintern proved rather ineffective during the crises of the interwar period.
With the end of World War II and the establishment of Communist governments in Eastern Europe, the opportunity for a new policy was presented.

The Cominform was organized along national lines, with the Soviet
Union ostensibly in the position of *primus inter pares*. This principle was
enunciated by Zhdanov in his speech to the Cominform's first plenary session: "The Soviet Union unswervingly holds the position that political and
economic relations between states must be built exclusively on the basis of
equality of the parties and mutual respect for their sovereign rights." [19] To
demonstrate this new principle, the Cominform's first headquarters was,
ironically enough, established in Belgrade, the future capital of "Titoism."
Its major function was announced as being the exchange of information
rather than policy-planning, and, in accord with this function, it publishes

[19] *For a Lasting Peace, For a People's Democracy*, November 10, 1947.

a weekly propaganda organ entitled *For a Lasting Peace, For a People's Democracy*. That the Cominform would not actually be an organization of equal members, however, was made evident by Zhdanov in the very same speech. In saying that the Communist world would "bend every effort" to doom the Marshall Plan to failure, he did not present an issue to the conference for discussion, but authoritatively declared what Cominform policy would be. This statement was also a clue to the "economic coordination" of the satellites with the Soviet system which was to come later with the "Molotov Plan."

Titoism

That the Soviet fears of "nationalist Communism," which were primarily responsible for the Cominform's scheme of organization, were well founded became clear in the summer of 1948 when the "Tito heresy" rocked the Communist world to its foundations. The Yugoslav Communist Party (CPY), led by Tito, was unique among Communist parties of Eastern Europe. It had developed an attitude of independence and national spirit during the war when its members formed the core of Partisan resistance to the Nazis. There were among Yugoslav Communists a spirit of common endeavor and a personal devotion to their leader of Partisan days, Tito, rather than to Stalin. Moreover, Yugoslavia, alone among the nations of Eastern Europe, had not been "liberated" by the Red Army. This last fact also meant that the Yugoslav Communist Party was not taken over after the war by officials dispatched from Moscow.

All of these factors bore on the Soviet and Cominform decision to brand Tito a "deviationist" and a "traitor to Marxism." The struggle began in 1947 with a series of letters from Moscow to the Communist Party of Yugoslavia rebuking the Yugoslavs for "hiding behind a national front" and "appeasing the middle-class." The climax came in June 1948 when the Cominform met in Bucharest, and Rumania denounced the CPY and "invited" it to replace Tito and three of his closest associates. In July, the Cominform's headquarters were hastily moved from Belgrade to Bucharest. Tito was faced with a hard decision. He had either to give in completely to Moscow and lose control of his national party or defy the Soviet Union. With reluctance, the Yugoslav Communists chose the latter alternative.[20]

The Yugoslav defection revealed both the strategy underlying the establishment of the Cominform and its difficulty in coping with the problem of nationalism within the satellite area. Although the Cominform was organized primarily to channel the dynamic force of nationalism into the stream of international communism, its major function became the battle against "Titoism." The purges of 1949–51 in Poland, Rumania, Bulgaria and Czechoslovakia brought to trial many leading Communists on charges of "Titoism," "chauvinism," "Zionism," and "deviationism." These trials demonstrate that the Cominform, despite its failure to avert the debacle in Yugo-

[20] See Adam Ulam, *Titoism and the Cominform* (Cambridge: Harvard University Press, 1952), pp. 124–134.

slavia, continues to be a major instrument of both Soviet policy and international communism.

The Molotov Plan

Although its timing indicated a Soviet attempt to combat the Marshall Plan, the "Molotov Plan" was directly related to the larger Soviet strategy of integrating the satellite areas with the Soviet Union. The Cominform was designed to accomplish this purpose in the political sphere; the Molotov Plan was its economic counterpart. The descent of the "iron curtain" had very serious effects on the economy of Eastern Europe. The chief markets of Poland and Czechoslovakia had always been in the West — England, Germany and France. Trade between Eastern and Western Europe in 1949 had declined by more than 50 per cent from its prewar level. Many of the economic problems of Europe as a whole are traceable to this decline in East-West trade, and there have been many attempts made to revive it. In 1948 and 1949 France and England concluded trade agreements with Poland, and the United Nations Economic Commission for Europe (ECE) has investigated the possibilities of reviving and expanding such trade. The problem has, of course, serious implications. While the United States has agreed in principle to a revival of East-West trade, it has in fact attached conditions to its economic and military assistance programs which are aimed at curtailing any trade which would tend to strengthen the economies and governments of the Communist satellite states.

The aim of the Soviet Union has been to isolate the satellites from the West, economically as well as politically. That some sort of Soviet economic plan was necessary if this were to be accomplished became clear in 1947 when Poland and Czechoslovakia toyed with the idea of requesting inclusion in the Marshall Plan. But, as Zhdanov had declared at the first meeting of the Cominform, one goal of Soviet economic policy was to doom the Marshall Plan to failure. The primary purpose of the Molotov Plan — a term which came to be used in 1948 after the satellites had been warned to look eastward, not westward, for economic aid — was the economic integration of Eastern Europe into the Communist system. By developing its own trade with Eastern Europe and by increasing trade among the satellites, the Soviets have sought to accomplish this purpose. The U.S.S.R. has signed trade pacts with all the satellites, has aided in the development of the Danube Basin, and has helped to build Czechoslovakia and Poland into a new industrial base for the East European economy. The Molotov Plan was formalized in January 1949 when a Council for Mutual Economic Assistance was established ostensibly to coordinate the economic development of Eastern Europe. Its real purpose seems to be to tie the satellite economies to the Soviet Union. This would tend to make the countries of Eastern Europe economic, if not political, provinces of the U.S.S.R.

The Cominform together with the Molotov Plan can be viewed as instruments of Soviet policy designed to create an integrated political and economic region out of the Communist nations of Eastern Europe and the

Soviet Union. It is the Soviet answer to NATO, the Marshall Plan, the Schuman Plan and the Council of Europe. This is a development of great import for the future, as the satellite area is both a bridge and a barrier between Western Europe and the Soviet Union. If the Soviet policy is successful, Europe may be divided by a barricade more difficult to penetrate than the present "iron curtain." Soviet success would further weaken the position of democratic elements in the region, and would make Titoist defection even more difficult. However, the uprisings in East Germany in 1953, signs of strain elsewhere behind the "iron curtain," and the Soviet reaction to them indicate that the attempt to isolate Eastern Europe from the West is still far from being successful.

Caribbean Commission

World War II was responsible for the establishment of a number of regional arrangements. The first of these was the Caribbean Commission. This example of working regionalism had its origin in discussions between the United States and the United Kingdom in early 1942 concerning the economic development and military security of the islands of the Caribbean area. On March 9, 1942, the two governments announced the establishment of an Anglo-American Caribbean Commission. It was to be an advisory group designated to deal with social and economic matters. The Commission was composed of six members (three from each of the two participating governments, each appointing a co-chairman) and was organized in two sections, one working through the British Colonial Office; the other, through the United States State Department.

The outbreak of serious enemy submarine warfare in the Caribbean compelled the Commission to concentrate on the immediate problems of military security. A number of projects were undertaken by the Commission in the first year of its operation, the most successful of which was the Land-Water Highway, by which cargoes were shipped from and to the United States over a route which crossed Cuba, Haiti, the Dominican Republic and Puerto Rico. This plan reduced the danger of losses to subs considerably by eliminating eight hundred miles of open sea traffic.

When the submarine danger was ended in late 1943, the Anglo-American Commission turned to the major purposes for which it had been organized. Two subsidiary advisory agencies were added to the regional arrangement, the West Indian Conference and the Caribbean Research Council. This latter organ was established to supervise scientific and technological research in the area. Designed as a start toward an inclusive regional organization, the Research Council included representatives of the Netherlands. It was to consist of not fewer than seven nor more than fifteen members appointed by the Commission with the consent of the three participating governments. The Council's first meeting was held in 1947 in Port-of-Spain, Trinidad. Haiti, Cuba and the Dominican Republic were invited to cooperate in a program of agricultural, educational and trade development outlined at the meeting.

The West Indian Conference provides a plenary forum for representatives of the territories in the area. It was established in 1944 by the United States and Great Britain and is composed of two delegates from each of the territories. It has no executive powers other than those conferred by the two governments. When the first Conference was held at Barbados in 1944, France, the Netherlands and Canada were invited to observe. The recommendations of the Conference, dealing with social and economic development, received approval in both Washington and London, but in vague and general terms only. Despite the initial disappointing lack of specific support, the Conference has continued to meet biennially. At the third Conference, held at Guadeloupe in 1948, nine committees submitted recommendations ranging from proposals to improve educational facilities to plans for the development of tourist trade. In addition to delegates from the territories, observers were present from Canada, Cuba, the Dominican Republic, Haiti, the International Labor Office and the United Nations.

Commission Broadened

In 1945 the two original participating governments invited France and the Netherlands to join the Commission, thus bringing within the regional organization all the governments with dependencies in the area. A formal agreement signed at Washington on October 30, 1946, established the Caribbean Commission. Like its predecessor, the new Commission was only an advisory body, but it was given the power to recommend policies and to approach the local territorial governments directly in formulating those policies. The Commission operates under the unanimity role on substantive matters. The Research Council and the West Indian Conference were continued as subsidiary advisory bodies.

The four-power agreement provided that the Commission and its subsidiary agencies should cooperate as fully as possible with the United Nations and its specialized agencies. Informal liaison was set up with the United Nations Secretariat and several specialized agencies, including the ILO. Since 1950 the Caribbean Commission has participated, along with other intergovernmental organizations, in the sessions of the United Nations Economic Commission for Latin America. A Commission secretariat was established in 1946 at Trinidad with Lawrence Cramer, former Governor of the United States' Virgin Islands, as first Secretary-General. A Working Committee, which meets every two months, does the preliminary planning for the Commission, advises the Secretary-General on policy, and coordinates the work of the three bodies which comprise the regional organization.

The Commission has been limited by the fact that it is merely an economic and social advisory body that must make its recommendations by unanimous consent. The United States was primarily responsible for this rule, as it feared being out-voted by the European delegates. However, real progress has been made in the exchange of trade data, developing tourist interest, and vocational education. The experience gained from the Caribbean Commission was drawn upon in establishing a South Pacific Commission, and from these experiments important lessons have been learned regarding regional international cooperation.

Regionalism in the Pacific

Regional security arrangements in the Pacific area have grown as the result, first, of Japanese expansionism and, after World War II, the threat of international communism. As early as 1937, Australia and New Zealand indicated at a British Imperial Conference that they would favor security agreements within the Commonwealth and League of Nations, designed to frustrate the Japanese appetite for empire. No regional arrangement had been formulated, however, when the war engulfed the Pacific area in 1941. The war made it clear to the Commonwealth members in the area that they had to look across the Pacific to the colossus of North America rather than to the mother country.

In 1944 a Pacific War Council was set up in Washington to coordinate the Allied war effort in the Pacific. Concomitantly, Australia and New Zealand signed an agreement (the ANZAC Pact, or Canberra Agreement) providing for the establishment of a regional zone of defense within the framework of a general system of global security, close military collaboration, common foreign policy in matters of common concern, joint administration of dependent territories within the zone, and a common immigration policy. In addition, the Pact proposed that a South Seas Regional Commission be established to advance the interests of native peoples, and it set up machinery for collaboration and consultation. The major organs of this regional system are a biennial ministerial conference and an Australian-New Zealand Affairs Secretariat meeting both in Canberra and Wellington. The two countries extended an invitation to other nations interested in the Pacific area to cooperate with them.

After the war, the Australian and New Zealand Governments organized a South Seas Conference, attended also by the United States, United Kingdom, France and the Netherlands. The Conference resulted in the establishment of the South Pacific Commission (largely modeled on the Caribbean Commission) "to encourage and strengthen international cooperation in promoting the economic and social welfare and advancement of the peoples of the non-self-governing territories in the South Pacific region administered by them." It also provided for two subsidiary bodies — a Research Council and a South Pacific Conference. The Commission is an advisory and consultative organization, administered through a secretariat permanently located at Noumea in French New Caledonia and headed by W. D. Forsyth, of Australia. Several sessions of the Commission have been held, and, on April 24, 1950, the first South Pacific Conference convened at Suva, on the Island of Fiji.

Security Pacts

Meanwhile, on July 4, 1946, the independent Republic of the Philippines was proclaimed. Two treaties were concluded between the new government and the United States, permitting the latter to maintain naval, air and ground forces in the Philippines. On August 30, 1951, the United States and the Philippines signed a mutual Defense Treaty which provided that an attack on either party would be deemed an attack on both and reiterated the two nations' unity concerning matters of collective regional security.

Two days after this treaty was signed, the United States concluded another security treaty with Australia and New Zealand. This tripartite agreement (the ANZUS Pact) was phrased in the same language as the United States–Philippine Treaty. The result of these two agreements was to establish a regional security system for the South Pacific area, with the United States as the binding link between the two Commonwealth partners of Australia and the Philippine Republic.

On September 8, 1951, all the non-Communist powers which had joined in the war against Japan met in San Francisco to sign the Japanese Peace Treaty. The treaty provided that security agreements might supplement it, and, on the same day, a security treaty between the United States and Japan was concluded. It gave the United States the right to maintain land, sea, and air forces in and about Japan for the security of Japan "against armed attack from without, including assistance given at the express request of the Japanese Government to put down large-scale internal riots and disturbances in Japan, caused through instigation or intervention by an outside power or powers." [21]

The Japanese Treaty was obviously aimed against the Soviet Union and international communism. With the other three agreements already in force, it extended the regional defense system to include the entire Pacific area. It is a system built upon a series of mutual defense and security agreements in which the United States plays the central unifying role. The arrangements did not apply to the Korean action, but all the signatories (except Japan, which is not a United Nations Member) were engaged in the Korean conflict as Members of the United Nations and (again except Japan) were nominated to participate in the Korean Conference. In addition to these various treaties, Asian conferences have been held since 1946 on matters of special concern to the nations of the East. The most important of these was the Delhi Conference of 1949, at which the Indonesian problem was discussed by nineteen Asian nations, including those members of the British Commonwealth which are signatories of the treaties discussed above.

Regional harmony in the Asia-Pacific area is still hampered, however, by old antagonisms. The new nations of the East are distrustful of their former colonial masters, and the color issue is a constant source of irritation. These tensions, along with economic and cultural factors, are largely re-

[21] Article I, Security Treaty between United States and Japan, September 8, 1951.

sponsible for the Asian tendency toward neutralism in the present world situation. Intense national pride and a desire to preserve and give expression to their newly won independence characterize the nations of the East and the leaders who speak for them, such as Nehru. There are, moreover, significant tensions among Asian governments themselves, as in the case of India and Pakistan. Because of these considerations, regionalism is necessarily secondary to nationalism at present. Nonetheless, an interlocking system of regional cooperation has been inaugurated in the Asia-Pacific area which could make this most important area a pillar of future world peace.

Suggestions for Further Reading

Books

Antonius, George, The Arab Awakening (Philadelphia: J. B. Lippincott Co., 1939).

Ball, M. Margaret, The Problem of Inter-American Organization (Stanford: Stanford University Press, 1944).

Elliott, William Y., The New British Empire (New York: McGraw-Hill Book Company, Inc., 1932).

Fox, A. B., Freedom and Welfare in the Caribbean (New York: Harcourt, Brace & Company, 1949).

Frye, Richard, ed., The Near East and the Great Powers (Cambridge: Harvard University Press, 1951).

Guerrant, Edward O., Roosevelt's Good Neighbor Policy (Albuquerque: University of New Mexico Press, 1950).

Harvey, Heather J., Consultation and Cooperation in the Commonwealth (New York: Oxford University Press, 1952).

Lenczowski, George, The Middle East in World Affairs (Ithaca: Cornell University Press, 1952).

Scott, James B., ed., The International Conferences of American States, 1889–1928 (New York: Oxford University Press, 1931).

———, ed., The International Conferences of American States, First Supplement, 1933–1940 (New York: Carnegie Endowment for International Peace, 1940).

Stewart, Robert B., Treaty Relations of the British Commonwealth of Nations (New York: The Macmillan Company, 1939).

Ulam, Adam B., Titoism and the Cominform (Cambridge: Harvard University Press, 1952).

Periodicals

Black, C. E., "Soviet Policy in Eastern Europe," The Annals of the American Academy of Political and Social Science, Vol. 263 (May 1949).

Bough, James A., "The Caribbean Commission," International Organization, Vol. 3, No. 4 (November 1949).

For a Lasting Peace, For a People's Democracy, 1948–

Harvey, Heather J., "The British Commonwealth," International Conciliation, No. 487 (January 1953).

"Inter-American Treaty of Reciprocal Assistance," *Department of State Bulletin,* Vol. 17, No. 429 (September 21, 1947).

Lleras, Alberto, "The American Regional System," *Bulletin of the Pan American Union,* Vol. 81, No. 8 (August 1947).

Mansergh, Nicholas, "The Commonwealth at the Queen's Accession," *International Affairs,* Vol. 29, No. 3 (July 1953).

"Report on the South Sea Conference with an Analysis of the Agreement Establishing the South Pacific Commission," *Department of State Bulletin,* Vol. 16, No. 402 (March 16, 1947).

Sanders, William, "Bogota Conference: Ninth International Conference of American States," *International Conciliation,* No. 442 (June 1948).

Seabury, Paul, "The League of Arab States: Debacle of a Regional Arrangement," *International Organization,* Vol. 3, No. 4 (November 1949).

Whitaker, Arthur P., "Development of American Regionalism: The Organization of American States," *International Conciliation,* No. 469 (March 1951).

Wood, F. L. W., "The ANZAC Dilemma," *International Affairs,* Vol. 29, No. 2 (April 1953).

Documents

Anglo-American Caribbean Commission, *Reports* (1942–1946).

Caribbean Commission, *Reports* (1946–   ).

United Nations, Economic Commission for Latin America (ECLA), *Annual Report* and other documents.

PART FIVE

Fundamental Issues

28

The New Diplomacy and World Order

"As you have no doubt surmised, I see the most serious fault of our past policy formulation to lie in something that I might call the legalistic-moralistic approach to international problems. This approach runs like a red skein through our foreign policy of the last fifty years. It has in it something of the old emphasis on arbitration treaties, something of the Hague Conferences and schemes for universal disarmament, something of the more ambitious American concepts of the role of international law, something of the League of Nations and the United Nations, something of the Kellogg Pact, something of the idea of a universal 'Article 51' pact, something of the belief in World Law and World Government." — GEORGE F. KENNAN [1]

THE TURMOIL OF EVENTS since World War II has cast sombre shadows over the UN. Many Americans have an uneasy feeling that the concepts, if not

[1] George F. Kennan, *American Diplomacy, 1900–1950* (Chicago: University of Chicago Press, 1951), p. 95.

the institutions, of universal international organization are faulty. Have these concepts encouraged dangerous misapprehensions regarding the nature of international politics? Has a reasonable settlement of "the awkward conflicts of national interest" been impeded at times by unwise use of international organization, as Ambassador Kennan suggests? Does United States support of international organization connote a legalistic-moralistic approach to world affairs that works against the "forgotten art of diplomacy"?

We do not think so. International organization is, at least for the present, primarily a new diplomatic technique devised to meet changing conditions in world affairs. The question is not whether international organization works at cross-purposes with diplomacy, but whether the new diplomatic technique has been correctly conceived and wisely utilized.

How to Evaluate International Organization?

The measurement of international organizations' accomplishments is an extremely difficult task. Has the UN been an important force for peace? Have NATO and OEEC promoted political stability and economic improvement in Europe? If the answers seem to be affirmative, the question remains whether similar or better results might have been achieved by other means. The issue is a real one since nearly all countries are presently reexamining their commitments in both the UN and various regional affiliations.[2] Since international organizations do not have governmental authority equal to that of most states, the fate of the former rests with the latter. Inevitably governments consider whether, in accepting the aims and obligations of international organizations, they have not subjected their freedom of action to undesirable limitations.

The Problem of Peace

The avowed purposes of the UN are not only the prevention of aggression, but the promotion of the "good life," the most difficult and complex goal conceivable. As a consequence, the Charter includes so many possible avenues to peace that nearly every aspect of international relations has been touched upon by the UN. On the basis of past experience, the approach laid down in the Charter seems sound. The fullest development of mankind's potential requires world-wide coordination of political, economic and social affairs. The authority of individual states does not extend far enough to regulate the many matters which now affect the well-being of their populations. International cooperation cannot be limited to armament regulation or a world police force. It must attack sources of tension, including economic and social problems.

At present, however, there is no strong central government with authority to regulate human affairs, and an international organization as comprehensive and as weak as the UN is a hotbed of frustrations. Members may find that they are confronted, by virtue of their Charter obligations, with contradictions of policy. Some nations, for example, find that policies

[2] See UN Charter, Article 109, for provisions regarding review of the Charter.

designed to achieve the purpose of "collective measures for the prevention . . . of acts of aggression" do not square with the principles of "equal rights and self-determination of peoples. . . ." The United States finds that it cannot pursue its policy of collective security in the UN without risking less welcome debates on economic and social matters. Some Americans feel that commitments under the North Atlantic Treaty are unwise limitations on the United States' freedom of action. Doubts of this order in the United States have given rise to proposals for amending the Constitution to limit the treaty power and the President's discretion in foreign affairs.[3] It is very important, therefore, to find means of evaluating international organization.

Planning

All governments in this age are characterized by a high degree of central planning and regulation. The complex interdependence of industrial society makes such a development inevitable. Planning on solely a national basis, moreover, has been inadequate to meet the responsibilities of national governments. President Eisenhower, in his inaugural address, put the matter this way:

> No free people can for long cling to any privilege or enjoy any safety in economic solitude. . . . This basic law of interdependence, so manifest in the commerce of peace, applies with thousandfold intensity in the event of war.[4]

Governments, then, have been forced to extend planning and coordination to the international level. And this requires a framework of organization or, in many cases, an express statement in a charter or fundamental law of the objectives and methods of planning. Neither citizens nor governments will buy a pig in a poke. In the United States these objectives and procedures were expressly stated in a written Constitution before the component states would agree to plan jointly for the general welfare in a federal government. Although the British Constitution has not been formalized by a single stroke of the pen, it exists nonetheless, and no British government dares depart from it.

In international relations, planning on a continuous basis was long felt to be unnecessary. Joint policies were arrived at in *ad hoc* conferences and applied for specific purposes and for limited periods of time. Continuing organizational machinery was not considered essential. As international planning and coordination of foreign policies on a continuing basis have become recognized as necessary, however, international charters have been ratified and international organizations established.

The prevalence of policy coordination among governments also explains the opposition of many individuals, Americans not excepted, to international organization. Central supervision, national or international, is considered to involve unfortunate limitations on the freedom of individuals

[3] See Arthur H. Dean, "The Bricker Amendment and Authority Over Foreign Affairs," *Foreign Affairs*, Vol. 32, No. 1 (October 1953).
[4] *The New York Times*, January 21, 1953.

and private associations. Membership in NATO or UN implies increased governmental activity, which is resented in some quarters. A root assumption of the UN Charter is that collective security, to be successful, must be fortified by the peaceful settlement of political problems and the alleviation of economic and social distress the world over. This aspiration runs head-on into the barrier of "domestic jurisdiction" behind which most countries seek refuge, including France, South Africa, the United States and the U.S.S.R., to name only a few. This is a misfortune since the stated objectives and principles of organizations such as the UN and NATO will not be achieved unless governments coordinate their military, economic and social policies.

Indeed, a strong case can be made for the argument that international planning may enhance rather than lessen the dignity of the individual. To the extent that governments by their own efforts cannot meet the rising level of human expectations, international cooperation is the answer. There is no other avenue of escape from human misery and insecurity. Time and again, governments have been forced to recognize that their national interests require a broad concept of the public interest embracing more than merely their own inhabitants.

Coordination or planning at the international level implies two things: strong, stable national governments as members of international organizations and a considerable degree of consensus as to basic civil rights and social needs among peoples of many nations. These factors suggest that an evaluation of international organizations should take into account their role as instruments of national foreign policy and their achievements in establishing a sense of community at the world and regional levels. An appraisal of international organization must include, therefore, an analysis of multilateral diplomacy. Yet their success as diplomatic instruments is by no means the only criterion by which to judge international organization. The recent proliferation of international agencies reflects a widely held and deep-seated desire in many parts of the world for a stronger and more integrated world community. Although many aspects of human nature and behavior are suggestive of the jungle, man has the capacity of aspiration. It is of little importance whether the UN Charter's preamble is binding or not. The fact of the matter is that governments were constrained to affirm at San Francisco that the "peoples of the United Nations" were determined

> . . . to save succeeding generations from the scourge of war . . . ,
> to reaffirm faith in fundamental human rights, in the dignity and worth of the human person, in the equal rights of men and women and of nations large and small . . . ,
> to establish conditions under which justice and respect for . . . international law can be maintained, . . . to promote social progress and better standards of life in larger freedom. . . .

The Charter, then, affords evidence of at least an embryonic sense of community and shared aspirations among peoples of different nations. On the regional level, the North Atlantic Treaty is evidence of a far more highly integrated community. The question whether the purposes of the UN to maintain international peace and security and to achieve international cooperation in economic, social and cultural affairs can be realized depends on the Organization's ability to prevent armed conflict and to foster consensus among peoples of widely differing cultures, political traditions and economic development. The basic force which has given rise to international organization has been the ceaseless quest for protection from economic, social, political and military insecurity.

The New Diplomacy

The most significant development in the relations among states in the last fifty years has been the increase of multilateral as distinguished from bilateral diplomacy. Yet individual national states still control greater resources and authority than any international organization. That is why such organizations, despite some exceptions, are still more instruments of multilateral diplomacy than supranational governments.

Inevitably, states act in their own self-interest. Need such a state of affairs doom mankind forever to international anarchy? Not inevitably. International organization can serve to enlighten self-interest. The nineteenth-century notion of a harmony of interests need not necessarily be abandoned. The problem is to provide means of developing a harmony. International organization is such a means. During the twentieth century the stake of peoples and governments in international cooperation and world peace is increasing steadily. The general public consciousness can be made more aware of this stake by the activities of the UN and other organizations. Where there is conflict instead of harmony, the UN — and, indeed, regional organizations as well — offer means of mobilizing support to withstand aggression and to propose settlements. Could the United States, for example, have countered Communist aggression in Korea without the sanction of the UN or the conviction among most nations that all had a common interest in suppressing aggression? The memory of the white man's imperialism and the goal of collective security loomed too large for the United States to apply military sanctions unilaterally. Indeed, the removal of General MacArthur from his UN Command in 1951 was in part due to the fact that the United States Government felt that the better part of wisdom was to exercise military power with as wide backing among the United Nations as possible. Even the United States, moreover, has neither the manpower nor the raw materials to achieve security without the support of other powers.

International organization, then, does not end the politics of the balance of power. Nor does it eliminate national interests or the need for diplomacy. It does provide means of applying balance-of-power principles intelligently and pacifically. And it offers a ready means of gauging the international feasibility and acceptability of a given definition of the national interest. Politics remains the art of the possible. The effect of a given course of action on nearly the entire international community is more readily ascertainable if advanced in the councils of the UN. The record shows that the foreign policies of all states have been modified and restrained by events in the United Nations. Without such restraints, international politics would resemble even more than is now the case the fumbling of arsonists in a powder magazine. International organization, therefore, can foster enlightened self-interest. It permits negotiations and compromise on the wide range of complex issues that bear on current international relations. It facilitates cooperative action on the problems common to mankind.

Multilateral diplomacy, however, has its pitfalls. Because it is very largely open diplomacy, delegates are very often tempted to advance policies in order to influence the course of domestic politics. Multilateral diplomacy then runs the danger of becoming a means of manipulating home elections. The reader may recall the discussions in the United States of the war in Korea and Communist China's representation in the UN. This is too dangerous a game to play. Positions taken in the glare of publicity, moreover, cannot be discarded easily, and, as a result, diplomacy by conference can be dangerously rigid. Private negotiations can often foster a settlement that an inflamed public opinion might prevent. But these pitfalls do not necessitate the abandonment of the multilateral technique. Rather they demand an understanding of the vices as well as the virtues of multilateralism. International organization is an instrument to be used with diplomatic skill and understanding. It is no substitute for wise foreign policy, and it need not interfere with the time-honored techniques of diplomacy. Private conversations and bilateral diplomacy, for example, are constantly carried on within the halls of the UN or NATO.

Multilateral diplomacy presents other difficulties. International organizations offer a chance to fish in troubled waters as well as to foster international good will. The international forum is a powerful instrument which can and has been used for mischievous as well as constructive purposes. Moreover, the complexity of the new diplomacy makes the problem of coordination, within as well as among governments, increasingly difficult and time-consuming. It is a hardship for many small countries to train large staffs to attend many meetings occurring during increasingly long sessions. Paraguay tried to cover the meetings of the Eighth General Assembly with three delegates dashing from one committee room to another.[5] The big powers also have their problems. Immense preparation is required of all states to cover the agenda items of a UN meeting.

Inevitably, there are those who long for the days when the private lives of countries were not constantly up for debate and public scrutiny. In spite of these and other difficulties, however, international organization is worth the price. NATO did not create the need for allies. It is the result of that need. The UN did not originate anti-colonial sentiments or spark the fires

[5] *The New York Times*, November 1, 1953, p. 19.

of nationalism or create new economic and social expectations among the world's depressed billions. These forces have long been at work. Because they affect the whole world, multilateral procedures must be devised to cope with them. The embarrassment of airing dirty linen in public should not blind one to the advantages of having a continuing forum in which to reconcile international differences.

The Way Ahead

The proper study of international relations involves not only a consideration of what men do but also of what great humanitarians have said men ought to do. Since man has the capacity to will and carry out the improvement of his lot, the Sermon on the Mount is as relevant in international affairs as Machiavelli's *Prince*. Although bitter struggles for power swirl about international organizations, so do many humanitarian proposals which governments cannot afford to neglect. The UN has become a means of raising men's sights and of establishing world-wide norms of behavior without which no world governmental structure can exist. At the same time, human welfare requires a stronger international mechanism. Many will argue that existing international organizations are weak reeds against man's propensity toward self-destruction. With the atomic age, the Charter may have been obsolete before it was ratified. But it remains to be demonstrated how the hearts and minds of men can be turned toward a broader community. How, for example, can the UN be strengthened?

Amendment or Interpretation?

Any number of world constitutions, charters and plans can be and have been drawn up. The problem is to gain acceptability. What may be acceptable to one people and government will not be acceptable to others. Any blueprint for world order, of necessity, implies loss of power for some ruling group, and power is not readily relinquished. Plans for a non-Communist world federal union, for example, have little attraction for the ruling élite of the Soviet Union. In fact, Soviet rulers seem to derive personal advantage from external danger and pressure, real or imagined.

Any proposal that might be acceptable to governments at this time would be too weak to provide a framework for world government. It is hard to see how governments that refuse the UN armaments proposals as interfering with their sovereign rights can be persuaded to accept world federalism or any important Charter amendment. The real problem is that the great powers cannot agree on any Charter amendment that would alter the world's present balance of power in any fundamental way. World peace, it is said, requires a world-wide organization of police power and universally accepted rules of law. The Charter already permits such developments if and when governments really follow its principles. The problem is to foster a sense of community in the world at large. Although constitution-making is part of the process of creating consensus, a constitution requires at least a minimum sense of community.

The realistic idealist in search of peace must depend primarily upon the short-run device of Charter interpretation. Here lies the best chance for the building of consensus in social, economic, political and psychological terms. Surely the history of the United Nations shows that its Charter is a flexible document. Interpretation already has permitted radical changes such as the alteration in the balance between Security Council and General Assembly, and, despite the veto — and despite most expectations in 1945 — the application of sanctions against one great power, China, and indirectly against another, the U.S.S.R. Domestic jurisdiction did not stand against rising nationalism in Indonesia. Insistence on amendments not acceptable to all the major powers might well break up the UN or cause important powers to withdraw. Interpretation seems less likely to run this risk.

The most readily available means of forging a world community is the United Nations. If the organization is used with wisdom and restraint, it may inspire confidence so that in time a stronger governmental frame can be provided for a commonwealth of man. The Charter's potentialities for fostering a universal rule of law have by no means been adequately developed. It is important to recall that the Draft Declaration of Human Rights represents as much moral consensus as can be expected from even the free nations of the world. The Communist powers do not and cannot accede to any genuine conception of civil liberties, which is as convincing evidence as there can be of the foundations that must be built before there can be anything like world government.

Suggestions for Further Reading

See list at end of Chapter 29.

29

The Future of International Organization

> "Constitutional experts who have studied the history of the United Nations believe that there is nothing in history to match the speed and effectiveness with which the United Nations developed in time of trial." [1]

IN PONDERING the future course of international organization, the first question to be answered is: should international organization really be encouraged or not, and why?

In reply to this query, one can say immediately that the dominant desire of most of mankind today and the strongest motive for closer international cooperation is not sheer idealism, but an understandable anxiety to avoid annihilation in another world war. In reaction to this danger, some men call for immediate world government, while others merely recognize that the inadequacy of individual national resources for self-defense requires broader alliances. But, as men realize that isolated economies are no longer efficient for producing guns, many have also come to realize that they are equally inefficient in producing butter. Then there are moral aspects of the question. Those who believe in the ideal of the brotherhood of all men believe that the more extensive the community, the more it achieves their goal. A more utilitarian point of view is that the fullest development of the world's human resources, like its economic resources, requires the fullest measure of social collaboration. All these considerations cry for the unity and strengthening of the international community to the maximum degree possible.

At the same time, one must clearly recognize the multitude of obstacles that stand in the way of these efforts: the vested interests of various national governmental and nongovernmental groups, vast differences in cultural mores, antagonistic political systems, different capacities and achievements

[1] A. M. Rosenthal, *The United Nations, Its Record and Prospects,* prepared for the Carnegie Endowment for International Peace (New York: Manhattan Publishing Company, 1953), p. 15.

in economic development, inertia, and the awesome complexities involved in running a mammoth world society. The following observations deal with the most fundamental issues that will have to be faced by those who seriously try to improve existing institutions. In the course of this analysis, special emphasis is placed on an appraisal of what might be accomplished in a possible reorganization of the UN.

Domestic Jurisdiction

A great deal of printer's ink has been spilled on this issue. France insists that the unrest in Tunisia and Morocco is her own concern. The U.S.S.R. rejects the UN plan for armaments control as impinging on her sovereignty. The United Kingdom insists that the Central Africa Federation is neither the Reverend Michael Scott's nor the UN's business. Iran insists that her oil is no affair of the United Kingdom or the International Court of Justice.

The most pernicious development of all, however, threatens to take place in the United States. Despite the fact already noted that the UN is not authorized "to intervene in matters which are essentially within the domestic jurisdiction of any state," (Charter Article 2, par. 7), certain elements, including some of the more vocal members of the American Bar Association, are seeking further ways of hobbling United States participation in the UN. Fearful that the President and Senate will bargain away American liberties at the conference table, because treaties are the "supreme law of the land," (Article VI of the Constitution), the Senate barely defeated, in February 1954, a resolution to amend the Constitution's treaty provisions.[2] The aim of the proposed amendment was to limit drastically the capacity of the United States to enter international commitments. It would have altered the balance between Congress and the President in conducting foreign affairs so as to give Congress as a whole a voice the

[2] On June 15, 1953, the Senate Committee on the Judiciary reported favorably (9–5) the following Constitutional amendment, generally known as the Bricker amendment.

1. A provision of a treaty which conflicts with this Constitution shall not be of any force or effect.

2. A treaty shall become effective as internal law in the United States only through legislation which would be valid in the absence of a treaty.

3. Congress shall have power to regulate all executive and other agreements with any foreign power or international organization. All such agreements shall be subject to the limitations imposed on treaties by this article.

4. The Congress shall have power to enforce this article by appropriate legislation.

5. This article shall be inoperative unless it shall have been ratified as an amendment to the Constitution by the legislature of three fourths of the several states within seven years from the date of its submission.

For comment, see Arthur H. Dean, "The Bricker Amendment and Authority over Foreign Affairs," Foreign Affairs, Vol. 32, No. 1 (October 1953), p. 1; A. E. Sutherland, Jr., "Restricting the Treaty Power," Harvard Law Review, Vol. 65, No. 8 (June 1952), p. 1306; Henry Steele Commager, "The Perilous Folly of Senator Bricker," The Reporter, Vol. 9, No. 6 (October 13, 1953), p. 12; and Treaties and Executive Agreements, Hearings before a subcommittee of the Committee on the Judiciary on S. J. Resolution 130, 82nd Congress, 2nd Session, May–June 1952.

Founding Fathers insisted it was not qualified to have. It would have altered the federal system in favor of the states, thereby weakening federal authority in foreign affairs at a time in history when national safety demands that such authority be strengthened. It would, in short, very nearly have turned the clock back to the Articles of Confederation.

The fears of the amendment's sponsors are almost wholly groundless. Some Americans are particularly anxious lest the Draft Conventions on Human Rights or the Genocide Convention become the opening through which the UN camel will enter the American tent. But such conventions or declarations will not be enforced against the will of Congress since Congress, in the Supreme Court's view, can effectively annul a treaty by subsequent legislation. UN treaties on sensitive economic and social issues, moreover, are now specifically drawn so that they will not be "self-executing" until supporting legislation is passed. That is, they are unenforceable in the courts without implementing legislation. Such treaties now also include safeguards specifying that they have no power to upset federal relationships specified in any Member's constitution.

The amendment would have greatly strengthened the domestic jurisdiction limitation. It is one aspect of a campaign to limit American participation in NATO and the UN. The significant thing about the domestic jurisdiction controversy is that powerful groups in many countries still value freedom of action more than international collaboration, and national sovereignty more than standards of the common public interest. The controversy illustrates the difficulties of correcting unfounded misapprehensions regarding international organizations. Many Americans, for example, have been persuaded by certain pressure groups and their spokesmen in the press that international organizations are supergovernments threatening basic liberties. Nothing could be further from the truth, but the truth is not easy to come by. Actually, many of the senators who favored the Bricker amendment were also on record in favor of amending the Charter so as to strengthen the UN. Either they did not fully understand the nature of the Bricker proposals or, so far as public opinion is concerned, they felt it important to cover both sides of the street.

The controversy also shows how narrow is the range of agreement in the international sphere. Few governments are prepared to be criticized for their social policies, in general, and racial policies, in particular. One commentator summarizes the problem as follows:

> The community on the state level stresses . . . differences in order to justify its existence since they are what set it apart from others. Emphasis upon the essential equality of all human beings would be a step toward the elimination of the state. No people insisting upon the maintenance of the sovereign independence of the state can therefore ever fully live up to any doctrine preaching the brotherhood of man. If, on the other hand, a world community is the goal, such doctrines must be elevated to the pedestal now occupied by nationalism.[3]

[3] Werner Levi, *Fundamentals of World Organization* (Minneapolis: University of Minnesota Press, 1950), p. 19.

So far as amendment of the Charter's domestic jurisdiction clause is concerned, it is inconceivable that either the United States or the U.S.S.R., without mentioning others, would consent to any liberalization of this provision. The greatest danger is that some states may attempt to raise the domestic jurisdiction barrier even higher. To do so would be disastrous. To the argument that it would inspire more confidence in the UN among Members, the answer is that the Organization would be emasculated. Surely the record shows that peace is not served by states being sole judges of their actions that affect international relations or by reducing international obligations. The decision regarding domestic jurisdiction should rest with the international community and not with individual states. As it now stands, domestic jurisdiction can bar UN interference in everything but the application of sanctions against aggression. The immediate problem is to hold ground already gained. The long-range problem is to build a broader sense of community so that national barriers will gradually be lowered to facilitate the solution of international problems. This would necessitate not only liberalizing the definition of "domestic jurisdiction" but giving international organizations more authority to control the interpretation of such a definition.

Regional Systems

Below the universal level there are various regional bodies that can be stout limbs or Achilles' heels of the world organization. The fact is that, while an area like Europe is not so integrated a community as Belgium, it is more integrated than the world as a whole. Contrary to the glum prophecy that regionalism will be the death knell of universalism, regional organizations can be a constructive step towards a broader amalgamation. Regional affinities should be utilized to accomplish tasks for which there is yet no basis at a more universal level. The Tennessee Valley Authority is an example in the United States; the European Coal and Steel Community is an example among the states of Europe.

The threat of military aggression from the Soviet Union must be recognized as the principal impetus behind the strongest of all contemporary regional systems, the North Atlantic Community. As a result, the agencies of that system are mainly preoccupied with defense problems. While defense has been widely criticized as an excessively narrow focus, it is no more limited than the initial integrating motivation which led to most modern federations, including the United States. Nonetheless, it would seem desirable to broaden as well as to strengthen the functions of this and other regional arrangements discussed in previous chapters. And, at the same time, it is essential that we keep our eyes on the goal of an ultimate world community.

It might be argued that, since one of the basic assumptions of the UN, big-power unity, has expired in the frigid climate of the cold war, the organization should be abandoned. Regional emphasis was carefully considered in World War II, it will be recalled, and, largely on United States' insistence, superseded by a policy in favor of universal organization. Security, economic and social problems were held to be global in scope. Within three or four crowded, disillusioning years, however, the United States became the leading champion of regional organizations — NATO, ANZUS and the like.

The United States never abandoned the UN, however, despite the revolutionary changes in American security policy. The Vandenberg resolution of June 1948, the sensational harbinger of the North Atlantic Treaty, was equally concerned to strengthen the UN Charter. Not only were NATO and other developments held to square with the letter of the Charter; they were pictured as strengthening it. The future of the UN depends upon the maintenance of peace. The paralysis of the Charter collective security provisions due to the cold war and the aggressive policies of the Soviet Union convinced most Western nations that a regional alliance was essential to compensate for the UN's weakness.

In the case of Western Europe, regional organizations may coalesce into a federal government that might be more rigorous in its support of Charter principles than the present separate units can be. Thus, it is not unreasonable to argue that most regional developments have supported the world organization. This is not the same as arguing, however, that regionalism should be the sole or primary emphasis. There are several reasons for arguing that the world organization should be the major long-term concern. First, the major problems of peace and security are world-wide problems. The struggles in Korea and Southeast Asia impinge heavily on the security interests of the United States, the Soviet Union and most other states. No major regional bloc could put its faith in its own armaments control scheme unless it were part of a globally coordinated and enforced plan. Neither Italy nor Europe alone can at the moment solve Italy's overpopulation and unemployment problems. So it goes; the world simply cannot be divided into self-contained regions.

Second, geographic proximity does not always breed friendship. Culturally, parts of Latin America have more in common with certain European countries than with the United States. The Commonwealth is a political, economic and cultural community, but not on a "regional" basis. And within many of the usually defined regions some of the bloodiest wars have been fought and the highest tariff walls created — witness Franco-German relations.

Nonetheless, there are solid grounds for regional developments. World trade and development may benefit from strong regional coordination. While armaments regulation must be on a global plan, it might be implemented through regional groupings. These and other problems of defense and economic well-being can be handled best in certain regional organizations because the partners are prepared to go further in coordinating their policies than would be the case with the members of a wider association.

Finally, regional associations may serve to restrain the tensions between the United States and the Soviet Union. If regional associations do in fact acquire some measure of power and stability, they are less likely to be pawns in a global struggle for power. For some time to come regional and world organizations will develop simultaneously.

Collective Security and Peaceful Change

The theory and practice of collective security under various organizations, including the League and UN, have already been examined in some detail. Collective security is an attempt to overcome the weaknesses of the international community in which there is as yet no certain centralized system of law enforcement. The system requires that the security of each state shall be the concern of all states so that, if one is in danger, all others will act as though their own security were threatened. The traditional rules of "self-help" and neutrality must be abandoned. The system has for its object both the elimination of force in settling international disputes and the development of a sense of mutual security among states. The reduction and regulation of national armaments should be a concomitant step. This state of affairs has proved possible between a limited number of states. The United States–Canadian border remains unfortified, and disputes between the United States and Canada and between the United States and Britain have long been settled by nonviolent methods.

Collective security under both the Covenant and the Charter, however, has been based on the assumption that a peaceful world cannot be established until similar conditions prevail in the relations among at least all the principal powers. Practice has always lagged far behind theory, however, and, for many reasons, it must as long as the state system exists in its present form. The reason is that the essential requirement of collective security cannot be achieved: the mustering of overwhelming strength against any aggressor or would-be aggressor. Such strength can be assembled only if the vast majority of states want international peace more than they want national objectives that can be obtained only by sacrificing peace. Strength to counter aggression requires: (1) some agreed definition of aggression; (2) some agreed body to apply that definition by majority vote; (3) advance pledges by states to provide resources to back up such decisions.

The fact of the matter is that states have conflicting interests which prevent their acting in harmony. While collective security rests on the implicit assumption that at least all the most powerful states are satisfied with the established order, some inevitably wish to change the *status quo,* and, if necessary, may go so far as to adopt violent measures to do so. Therefore, the preconditions of international peace through collective security have never come to pass. Sufficient strength to enforce collective security could never be assembled under the League, for example. The United States refused to link its security with the League system, relying, instead, on its own strength, its isolated position and policies of neutrality. Germany, Japan and Italy sought to change the Versailles system, which France and, to a lesser extent, Britain sought to maintain. These conflicting national interests prevented the application of any sanctions against Japan and the application of sufficient strength against Italy.

Since World War II, the United States has become the outstanding champion of collective security. Presidents, secretaries of state, congressmen, and senators have asserted repeatedly that collective security is the way to peace. Yet the strength of the United States and the U.S.S.R. works against collective security. The first order of business for each power is to weaken the other. Contemplating each other's might, each feels insecure, despite the Charter, and each woos other powers to its side. One unfortunate result of this situation is that other powers, less strong, sometimes tend to favor neutralist policies, forgetting that the major struggle is not just between the U.S.S.R. and the United States but one in which the U.S.S.R. has challenged the free world. The more insecure powers feel, the less they follow the precepts of collective security, and the weaker the system becomes. All states are caught in a vicious circle. The UN command in Korea, instead of having overwhelming force at its disposal, was on two occasions nearly pushed into the sea. Sanctions had to be applied against one great power and indirectly against two. Sufficient force was, however, finally assembled to throw back the aggressors in most convincing fashion.

It seems quite clear that future conflicts will approximate this situation, wherever they may be. The framers of the Charter realized that the best security system that could be devised depended upon the cooperation of the principal powers. This they could only leave to diplomacy, for there was no way of bringing the big states to heel and no way of insuring that they would not pursue conflicting foreign policies.

As a result, the concept of collective security has been severely criticized. India, for example, argues with great logic that the UN was not expected to apply sanctions against a major power and that, in a big-power conflict, the UN ought to be an agent of conciliation and mediation rather than of enforcement. Shrewd observers such as Hans Morgenthau, Robert L. Schuman and Walter Lippmann have concluded that the concept of collective security is positively a danger to peace, because an overwhelming superiority of force can never be achieved in a conflict under present circumstances. Its greatest danger is held to be the maximization rather than the limitation of war. Thus, many countries, in this view, have been drawn into the Korean conflict owing to their collective security obligations.

The argument is quite persuasive. Nonetheless, one must ask, first, whether the objective of the UN — i.e., international peace — did not require meeting force with force in Korea; and, second, whether that force could have been assembled but for the UN. How, for example, after the Chinese entered the Korean war, could the United Kingdom have participated in the UN action in the light of her recognition of red China? True, the United States could doubtless have fought the Korean War alone, but it would have been fought at a price — the failure of the UN system to meet the challenge of aggression and great resentment in Asia.

It is doubtless true that the theoretical model of collective security can never be duplicated in real life. It is nonetheless useful as a model. International peace and security depend at the very least on *collective action*, even if *collective security* lies beyond reach. The UN offers an essential means to collective action. Far from maximizing war, the UN deters aggression by enhancing the likelihood of strong counteraction under obligations of the Charter. Furthermore, it seems preferable in terms of building an orderly world community to keep such counteraction within the framework of UN principles and objectives, weak though that framework may be at present, rather than to force such action outside the UN.

Meanwhile, collective security must be considered in broad perspective. To the extent that the international community can devise means of effecting peaceful change, the burden on the security system may be reduced. The UN shows possibilities in these respects. Since the Charter was drafted, one quarter of the world's population has won independence and self-government without a world-wide conflagration. Although severe international conflicts will continue to threaten peace, there are grounds for hoping that these conflicts need not erupt into large-scale, devastating war. Since aggression was checked in Korea, no power feels that it can disregard all its UN obligations with impunity. This is a marked change from the League. The UN is a restraining influence in the struggle for power.

Economic and Social Cooperation

How can Asia grow more rice and see that it gets to all the peoples who need it? How can steel be more efficiently produced and distributed in Europe? How can the development of the Hylean Amazon area, which involves six different Latin American countries, be coordinated most effectively? These are the kinds of challenges which have given rise to the network of international economic and social agencies which circle the globe today. They mirror the obvious fact that maximum development of the world's economic and social potential requires world-wide planning and mobility of resources surmounting national barriers.

The following observations are based on the assumption that the broad economic and social goals of mankind should be: (1) the most efficient output (measured in human as well as material costs) of goods and services to satisfy men's freely expressed wants, and (2) the fullest satisfaction of men's psychological and social needs consonant with a democratic ethic. These goals go beyond mere maintenance of peace and mere *laissez faire* economics. The eighteenth- and nineteenth-century assumption that the main task was to remove incumbrances that prevented the "normal" operation of a "natural order" has not proved adequate to satisfy men's needs. There is a necessity for positive planning and building of the kind of world we want to live in. We have learned that it will not plan and build itself.

Measuring Progress Thus Far

Scanning the broad horizon of the development traced in this volume from nineteenth-century river commissions to the twentieth-century ECSC (European Coal and Steel Community), several conclusions emerge. First, it is apparent that that the parade has marched in step to the tunes called by the great powers. Activities which have prospered are those that seemed to offer the greatest benefits to those powers with the least sacrifice in freedom and treasure. But, at times, the great powers endured considerable sacrifice when the need seemed most pressing, particularly in wartime. This highlights the fact that what a country's "national interest" has seemed to require at any particular moment has not been a static concept, as some writers have tended to imply, but has changed according to a variety of material and ideological considerations. Nor has this evolution been unilinear. Rather, it has changed pace and direction in a number of cyclical fluctuations, although the long-run trend seems generally to have been towards greater international collaboration.

It has by no means been easier to gain cooperation in all "functional" or "technical" activities than in "political" matters. While, under the pressure of war, cooperation has been great among allies, it has decreased precipitously once the fighting has stopped. In general, the inclination has been to cooperate most in informational activities which give substantial benefits in terms of keeping track of what other countries are doing, and of learning new techniques at relatively low cost. In international, as in national, activities, moreover, informational programs normally pave the way for operational functions. Other things being equal, the great powers have been reluctant to undertake more ambitious activities whose costs are greater and tend to be financed by the rich for the benefit of the poor.

Regarding specific functional areas, international cooperation in postwar relief and reconstruction was greater after World War II than World War I, but the principal programs in both instances were largely bilateral. Remarkable progress has been made in the concept of developing underdeveloped countries since World War II, but the aid has, for the most part, taken the form of technical assistance with only modest, though increasing, financing through the International Bank for Reconstruction and Development. Concrete concessions in the reduction of tariffs and other trade barriers have also been greater since World War II, through a variety of international bodies, but they fall far short of what the planners of the postwar world had hoped for. International regulation of monetary policies has been seriously frustrated by the vast problems left in the wake of two world wars and a depression, as well as stubborn resistance on the part of national financial interests.

Substantial advances have been made in thinking about the questions of employment and stability, but the "full employment" program is still in its informational swaddling clothes. International cooperation in transportation and communications is among the most essential prerequisites for any kind of intercourse among nations and is considered to involve relatively slight sacrifices. Even in these areas, however, national interests have vigorously opposed regulation in such sensitive matters as traffic and rates. The most strongly organized labor groups have been quite successful in using the ILO and other agencies to study labor problems, recommend improved standards, and influence governments to enforce them, although the weaker labor interests and less developed countries still suffer from grossly inadequate working conditions. The more advanced countries have done a great deal internationally to eradicate diseases which threaten their welfare and are now undertaking more positive and long-range health activities. Yet the funds and authority given international health bodies are still woefully meager. Because aiding refugees and other migrants to find new homes normally involves at least two, and usually more, countries, it is essentially an international task which nations have supported more generously since World War II than previously. But still they have placed severe time, functional and financial limitations on such efforts. In the field of cultural exchange, League and UN agencies have been supported in improving the means of communication (education, literature, art, libraries, etc.), but the substantive content of such exchange has naturally stirred the caldron of conflict since there is no commonly accepted standard by which to judge the validity of such content.

Is Functionalism the Answer?

Among the prophets who have emphasized the importance of economic and social problems in international relations, one of the earliest in modern times was the "mercantilist" school which advocated the robber-baron philosophy that the object should be to take as much physical wealth as possible from other countries and give as little in return as one could get away with — all regulated under a paternalistic government. The clear rational light of Liberalism then dawned during the eighteenth and nineteenth centuries to illumine the way for the new industrial entrepreneurs who wanted to escape the strait jacket of governments largely dominated by landed nobility. They felt they could hold their own in open competition and therefore preached *laissez faire* both internationally and domestically. Many of the high priests of this crusade also agreed with Richard Cobden that "Free Trade would have the tendency to unite mankind in the bonds of peace." [4] Unfortunately, the aberrations that were explained as mere sand in the wheels of the "natural order" turned out to be more "normal" than that order itself. Unregulated self-interest did not, it was discovered, automatically produce the greatest happiness for the greatest number.

The rudest shocks to the liberal philosophy came in the form of various depressions, a number of wars, including two of world-wide scope, and the increased economic and political power of the "masses," who began to ask for the security and comforts of the upper classes. "Keynesian" and

[4] John Bright and James E. Thorold Rogers, *Speeches on Questions of Public Policy* (London: Macmillan, 1870), Vol. 2, p. 421.

socialist thinkers reacted by calling for more conscious planning and regulation of international as well as national economic and social relations. A more threatening challenge has been the Communist thesis which sees history as a cart drawn by the horse of dialectical materialism and wars as the inevitable by-product of national and class struggle. While it is true, of course, that the quest for economic wealth has been a central element in the struggle for power among nations, it is also obvious that this virus has infected Communist as well as non-Communist regimes.

One of the more recent refinements of liberalism is the "functionalist" school, which suggests that the surest road to an integrated world community is through "nonpolitical," "functional," or "technical" cooperation.[5] It is alleged that one should not try to enter immediately through the front door of world government, but approach the objective indirectly through the back door of less dramatic "practical and continuous association in everyday affairs."[6] This seems a most level-headed antidote for excessive idealism. It recognizes that thousands of nongovernmental associations among businessmen, scientists, labor leaders, teachers, and bankers have been responsible for much of the limited consensus already created among nations. And, where there is a body of demonstrable truth which is commonly accepted throughout much of the world, as in medicine, there is a basis for technical agreement, which governmental interests sometimes obstruct.

On the other hand, governments are involved in more and more human affairs — not because of any diabolical plot, but largely in response to the growing complexity of our highly specialized society in which the greater opportunity for interpersonal conflict requires greater facilities for mediation. Moreover, governments have been responsible for *promoting* technical cooperation as well as being the *product* of circumstances arising in connection with it. Just as the United States Federal Government has created new channels for technical cooperation (e.g., the Public Health Service and TVA), so a world federation could have the same effect. The centralization of administration within national governments, moreover, can make implementation of international agreements far easier than if private groups are entirely relied upon. There have also been occasions when government leadership has sponsored international technical cooperation and private interests have wrecked it, as in the case of the proposed International Trade Organization.

Another difficulty with the functionalist thesis is that many obstacles arise in functional fields that are not caused by governmental politics, but by scientific vested interests, honest disagreements on scientific theories, or ethical questions regarding scientific matters. Finally, although functional-

---

[5] See James Avery Joyce, ed., *World Organization — Federal or Functional* (London: Watts, 1945); David Mitrany, *A Working Peace System* (London: The National Peace Council, 1946).

[6] From the pamphlet "World Unity and the Nations," by David Mitrany and Maxwell Garnett, *Towards World Government*, No. 3 (London: The National Peace Council, 1945).

ists tend to say that ideological agreement follows technical cooperation, they seldom emphasize the fact that a basically cooperative ethic is a prerequisite for technical collaboration. Certainly the functional approach has frequently been blocked by the ideological chasm that divides the Communist and non-Communist worlds.

Besides these schools of thought which tend to stress the importance of economic and social questions, though they agree on little else, there are those philosophies which tend to look at these issues through the other end of the telescope. First, there is the "fire brigade" contingent who, on the basis of the familiar and misleading adage, "First things come first," believe that international organization is primarily an emergency apparatus to be trotted out to deal only with the most obvious and extreme threat to mankind: an actual outbreak of war. One modern expression of this thesis is the world federalist view that the first task is to muzzle the most dangerous weapons of destruction.[7] There are others who emphasize that all states are driven by basically the same motivation — the quest for power — and that international economic and social activities will not fundamentally alter that pattern. A related thesis is that economic and social problems are more the effect than the cause of political problems. Hitler's determination to lead Germany to world conquest, it is said, was far more the reason for German aggression than the hackneyed talk of *Lebensraum* and raw materials, and that aggression caused many economic and social problems which could be solved only by stopping Hitler. Finally, there are the strong nationalists who dislike international interference in economic and social affairs and insist that such matters are essentially "domestic" questions.

In weighing all of these arguments, it becomes abundantly apparent that part of the problem is semantic. The concepts "political," "economic," and "social" overlap and interact. The single problem of labor standards is commonly classified under all three headings. Every cause of tension, whatever one may call it, is a potential serpent in the garden, but obviously the greatest threats are those which are likely to unleash large-scale military struggles. Many men of good will, therefore, have concentrated on extracting the sting directly by attempting to abolish armaments and their masters, the nation-states. But this has proved a most discouraging task since governments consider such efforts as invitations to extinction. Hence, many prophets of peace have been forced to retreat to the functionalist back door. And here one becomes involved in every economic and social problem — from tariffs to neuroses. Evidently, no single approach is likely to be sufficient by itself. All must be pursued to the utmost. But there is no question that, within the economic and social realm, greater over-all planning and direction would result in more efficient development of world resources — human and material. Such planning requires more international authority and money.

[7] Cord Meyer, *Peace or Anarchy?* (Boston: Little, Brown, 1947); Grenville Clark and Louis B. Sohn, *Peace Through Disarmament and Charter Revision,* Preliminary Print (Dublin, N.H.: 1953).

Supervision of Special Areas and Peoples

Not from the calm deliberations of social reformers, but from the strident clash of national ambitions, has arisen the device of international supervision. Describing the environment which gave rise to the mandate and trusteeship systems, for example, one writer has said that, "The European diplomacy of the . . . half-century [before World War I] was almost continuously occupied in preventing the friction generated by the partition of Africa from bursting into the flames of a European war. . . ." [8] As the struggle over various territorial carcasses has grown increasingly ferocious, the victims have often been placed under some kind of international protection, at least temporarily. And it must be admitted that, while national interests continue to be the dominant forces, this solution is certainly a more enlightened alternative than going to war over such spoils. In the following reflections on the past and future evolution of such supervision, the underlying assumption is that mankind's goal in this area should be to help the peoples placed under international protection achieve the same political and welfare objectives set forth above for the rest of humanity and to do this as rapidly as the integrated development of world resources will allow.

Colonial Territories

In spite of all their shortcomings, the League and UN systems for supervising various mandated and trust territories have proved useful instruments for raising the level of colonial administration through the prohibition of unilateral disposal of such areas and through regular international surveillance. If those systems had made no contribution other than the periodic exchanges of views among distinguished individuals who were influential in determining their countries' colonial policies, such as Britain's Frederick Lugard and Alan Burns, they would have been well worth the effort. But they have done much more. They have dredged up more and more revealing information, sometimes forcing the national authorities to expand their own knowledge of their colonial charges. And this is not an unimportant achievement since progress depends so directly on accurate and current information. Wages cannot be raised without knowing a good deal about the financial condition of major enterprises and the general cost of living. Moreover, this intelligence has been critically sifted each year and judged in accordance with broad standards which have evolved over the years and have tended to influence national authorities to re-examine their own performances in terms of the same criteria. Finally, all colonial powers which are Members of the UN have bound themselves, under Chapter 11 of the UN Charter, to promote similar objectives in all of their

---

[8] G. L. Beer, *African Questions at the Paris Peace Conference, with Papers on Egypt, Mesopotamia, and the Colonial Settlement* (New York: Macmillan, 1923), p. 193.

dependencies. While these many efforts have not been the only influences at work, they have helped to accelerate and guide the humanizing of colonial policies generally.

But the development of these territories still lies directly in the hands of the colonial powers and cannot move much faster than the resources and policies of those powers allow. Other frequent shortcomings have been inadequate information, expertise, impartiality, and continuity among those who have served on the international bodies concerned with these problems. Progress, nevertheless, has been remarkably rapid during just the past ten years, as compared with the previous hundred years.

Further experiments in international supervision have dealt with the powder-keg territories of the Saar, Danzig, Libya and Eritrea, and certain minorities under various post-World War I agreements. In all of these areas, the League and UN have been used to good advantage to temper national domination with varying degrees of international guardianship. In supervising territories, international regimes have proved themselves capable of providing relatively satisfactory government, within limits imposed by certain national interests, contrary to the dire prophecies that international administration simply would not work.

On the other hand, the League was unable to subdue the basic international tensions that had given rise to the establishment of the Saar and Danzig regimes, but it would have been an impressive miracle to calm such age-old passions. In the case of the Saar, the League was saddled with the thankless task of maintaining a basically unjust arrangement dictated by the French appetite for reparations, but it managed to soften that injustice a bit with the passage of time. The device of a commission composed of the nationals of various interested countries proved a more awkward and less neutral channel as used in the Saar than the single internationally appointed commissioners, advised by national representatives, assigned to Danzig, Libya and Eritrea. The wisdom of pretending that Libya was prepared for independence after such inadequate preparation may be questioned, although perhaps this was the most enlightened solution possible under the circumstances. The League minorities experience demonstrated how difficult it was for a weak international supervisory system to intervene to protect a small island of inhabitants living under an indifferent, or hostile, government smarting under obviously discriminatory commitments. The concept of universal human rights, to be enforced in all societies, seems more hopeful as an ideal, but thus far has not been very effective in practice.

Looking towards the future, all of this development of international supervision should not be abandoned but should be strengthened as a means of balancing one national interest against another. The goals should continue to aim towards the promotion of democratic procedures and broadly based social welfare. The administrative apparatus should not discard direct governmental representation altogether, but modify it through striving for greater information, specialized competence and continuity.

Membership

Membership is the gateway that controls the character of any organization. One of the first problems to be faced regarding the membership of the UN or any other universal organization is whether its Members should be governments or delegates elected directly by the people according to party affiliations, as in most national legislatures. Some European organizations are moving toward the popular election of delegates. This is an alternative which would reflect different points of view surmounting national boundaries, and it seems more conducive to the development of a democratic world community than membership by governments, which mirrors, for the most part, the views of the parties in power and tends to perpetuate organization along national lines. In any revision of the UN, however, it is unlikely that the great powers would approve a change to popular representation, but it would seem desirable to encourage the practice which some states have experimented with of including minority representation in their delegations.

Then there is the question of weighted voting. The great powers are constantly reluctant to appeal to the General Assembly on many questions, and the small powers exert an undue influence in that body because of the obviously unrealistic provision that assigns one vote to all states regardless of population and other differences. It is patently inequitable for Lebanon, with a population of 1.2 million, to have the same voting strength as India with 300 million. The distinguished representative of one small country, Paul-Henri Spaak of Belgium, has said,

> I do not think that Belgium plays the same role in international politics as the United States. I do not think that an organization such as that of the United Nations will really be able to function well if it is based upon a system that is clearly unreal. For myself, I can quite well conceive of establishing some sort of qualified vote and quantitative vote, and of having each nation in the General Assembly and later in the Security Council vote in a manner that might be described as "weighted." [9]

The major obstacles to any change in this matter are the reluctance on the part of some small countries to surrender their present favored position, the uncertainty among the great powers as to the effect of any change on their relative influence, and the difficulty of devising a satisfactory formula. While many writers have recommended some combination of economic and population factors (some people even seem to be weighing culture in the present debate over American materialism versus everyone else's non-materialism), it would undoubtedly be simpler and more in keeping with usual democratic procedures to reflect only differences in population with perhaps an upper and lower limit. One plan proposes allowing one representative for each five million population, or major fraction thereof, with

[9] "The Role of the General Assembly," *International Conciliation*, No. 445 (November 1948), p. 601.

no state to have more than thirty representatives and every state above 100,000 in population to have at least one.[10] According to this proposal, the United States, Canada, non-Communist Europe, and the Commonwealth countries would have 184; the Soviet Union, Communist China, and the rest of the Soviet bloc, 74; non-Communist Asia (excluding Commonwealth countries), 60; Latin America, 39; Middle East, 19; and Africa, 8.

Finally, there is the question of automatic versus selective admission. A basic assumption of the UN Charter and this volume has been that the ultimate objective should be a community of democratic nations. But it is abundantly clear that not all of the present Members of the UN are democratic. The central question is: Should one seek democracy through forcing applicants to remain outside the gates until they can convince the right Members that they are pure in heart — thus raising the difficult question of how to decide when a country has actually been converted — or admit all countries in the expectation that their constant relations with the UN may be a stronger influence for democracy and international cooperation than total exclusion? This is a difficult choice, but it would seem that the latter is the preferable alternative.

Authority

No government can expect to be very effective without authority to deal directly with the people it serves and to exert full legislative and executive power. Obviously, the UN and NATO fall far short of this goal, since they must deal with peoples through the filter of their governments, which may or may not represent them equitably. The ECSC, however, does have direct, binding authority. While governments are still reluctant to encourage international organizations to by-pass them, it is desirable and possible to strengthen certain direct contacts between international organizations and the peoples of the world. For example, extensive field work, particularly in connection with the technical assistance program, gives UN personnel excellent opportunities to meet the public face to face. Another useful development is the organization of nongovernmental commissions, such as the national UNESCO commissions, to serve as direct links between international organizations and various national leadership groups.

Once in contact with people, international organizations, like national governments, operate through three major functions: research, decision-making, and implementation. Since the UN has already made great strides in obtaining more plentiful, accurate, current and comparable information, no radical change is needed here, but primarily an extension of what has already been done. Decision-making centers around the voting process, which has been improved in the UN, as compared with the League, by making greater use of various majority rules. The most flexible procedure is to rely on a simple majority for all decisions, but the UN Members, espe-

[10] Grenville Clark and Louis B. Sohn, *op. cit.*, pp. 17–24.

cially the great powers, have been reluctant to go that far, particularly since the representational system has been so unrealistic. But the adoption of weighted voting in more international organizations might pave the way for greater use of the simple majority, reserving two-thirds or larger majorities for only the most basic questions, such as constitutional amendments.

Finally, there is the need for more effective implementation of decisions. The goal should be binding authority on all matters entrusted to the international organization, but it is unrealistic to expect such authority to be given an international organization at this stage except within a very limited jurisdiction and, in some instances, like the European Coal and Steel Community, involving only a few like-minded nations. The ideal should be to extend international authority to those matters that seem essential for the survival and welfare of mankind, such as governing the use of force, a federal system of law and courts, and interstate commerce. Those familiar with the history of the United States will note that this follows the pattern of the transition from the Articles of Confederation to the present federal system. For all the talk about the inapplicability of this analogy to the world scene, the difference is one of degree rather than of kind. It seems clear, however, that world peace will, for a long time to come, depend on the play of national forces, only loosely coordinated through such bodies as the UN and NATO.

When law is flouted, however, dependable police support should be close at hand. While the UN now has the authority to recommend all forms of sanctions, binding decisions, subject to the veto, are restricted to controlling national contingents, which have never been agreed upon, and are authorized merely to maintain peace and not to enforce any particular settlement favored by the UN. It is highly doubtful that the great powers will agree to any significant formal amendment of the Charter in this respect, but it is possible through interpretation to pursue further the efforts which have already been made, especially under the Uniting for Peace Resolution (Acheson Plan), to arrange in advance for voluntary compliance with a UN recommendation for enforcement action. Much more can be done along these lines than most people suspect and than states are willing to bind themselves to in formal agreements. Witness the NATO system, which legally depends on only voluntary cooperation. The crucial prerequisite is to provide in advance for a sure and quick preponderance of power to counteract any threat or act of aggression. The more pooling of resources and authority there is, the more effective the system will be.

Assembly and Executive Bodies

Because of the unrealistic tradition of equal representation for all states, the Assembly in both the League and UN has been championed by the smaller nations and distrusted by the larger powers, which have thought of the political Council, in which they have held weighted positions, as their favorite instrument. Nevertheless, there has been an unmistakable trend in both systems for the great as well as small powers to turn to the Assembly, not only because of stalemates in the Council, but to gain broader support than that represented in the smaller body. Contrary to current misconceptions in some quarters, this has been as true of Communist as non-Communist governments. And, with the weighted voting and wider use of the simple majority recommended above, the Assembly could be a more realistic and useful organ than at present. But, even if these changes were achieved, the Assembly would continue to be hampered by its unwieldy proportions, lack of integrating party affiliations, and vast cultural, political, and economic differences dividing its members. It should, therefore, leave to other smaller and more specialized bodies the tasks of drafting complex policy decisions (as in connection with the human rights convention), technical research, and hearing statements by various petitioners (as in the case of the Italian colonies issue). Rather, it should concentrate on those functions for which it is best equipped: the general review of past performances and the formulation of broad policy statements to guide future programs. At the same time, the fact should be recognized that some national legislatures find it equally difficult to exercise such self-restraint.

As for the executive branch, the UN has, not one cabinet, but three (Security Council, Economic and Social Council, and Trusteeship Council), as well as a combination chief minister and permanent undersecretary (the Secretary-General). Of these four agents, only the latter three are expected to comply with Assembly recommendations. The ideal would be a single cabinet, under a chief executive, selected by all Members of the UN. In the present atmosphere, however, it is questionable whether the great powers would agree to any fundamental rearrangement of the present machinery, especially affecting the Security Council. And, until the suggested recommendations regarding representation, voting, and implementation are accepted, it is doubtful whether any shuffling of these bodies would be very meaningful.

The Security Council represents a clumsy reflection of the obvious power superiority of the great powers, plus a polite gesture towards France and China and participation by lesser states on a rotating basis. Because of the cold war, however, the usefulness of that body, hobbled by the Big Five veto, has been greatly circumscribed. The Council's control over police action should be brought under the more representative guidance of the Assembly if the composition of that body can be made more realistic, as proposed above. The Economic and Social Council's composition has been relatively satisfactory since it has habitually contained, not only the great powers, but an equitable distribution of lesser states. And its simple majority rule for all decisions has made its policy process quite flexible. Its chief drawbacks have stemmed from the vitriolic sabotage of the Soviet bloc and the lack of time, money, and support given it as well as the inadequate expertise and continuity of some of the national delegates. Another major problem is the matter of holding the reins of the numerous agencies, specialized and other, at work in the economic and social fields. For the time being, this matter can be dealt with through further program integration via the technical assistance program. Eventually, however, all important independent agencies should be made more integral partners of the central organization. The composition of the Trusteeship Council is an improvement over the League Mandates Commission, thanks to the increase in the representation of noncolonial powers, and it also enjoys the ease of simple majority decisions. The fact that all of these bodies are composed of governmental representatives is by no means a fatal defect. Such representation provides direct access to influential governmental policy-makers. At the same time, the decisions of such men must be tempered by greater continuity and experience as well as good staff work.

The position of the Secretary-General — half politician and half civil servant — is especially ticklish. Ideally, it would be preferable to have the "S-G" as a strong but nonpolitical permanent undersecretary working in close conjunction with a political chief executive at the head of the single cabinet mentioned above. But, since the consensus for such a framework is lacking at present, the Secretary-General must continue to be the source of some degree of over-all political leadership, somewhat apart from individual national interests. Furthermore, it is high time that the Member governments gave him maximum leeway in building a truly international staff, unrestricted by national pressures except where absolutely necessary to protect the host country from a "clear and present danger" of sabotage.

Creating a Sense of Community

From these reflections, certain methodological conclusions emerge. It now seems clear that no single road leads to the promised land. A major battle in this connection still rages between federalists and functionalists; each school insists that its way is best. But, in fact, both approaches, as well as others, must be explored as far as possible. As we have said before, functional cooperation helps create the foundations for a stronger governmental superstructure, but that structure can greatly facilitate functional cooperation. Reflection on one's own "backyard" within the nation-state helps to clarify the ingredients necessary to produce a more integrated community. No single factor is responsible for our domestic communities, but a multitude of considerations, including physical proximity, cultural bonds, economic relations, common political allegiance enforced by binding authority and police power, and reaction against outside interference. While all of these factors must be explored fully, it is clear that they are less effective, at present, in the world at large than in regional or national communities. Although it is nigh impossible to say which factor is most important, it seems clear that the general objective of closer world cooperation is best for the welfare of all mankind.

Suggestions for Further Reading

Books

Almond, Gabriel, *The American People and Foreign Policy* (New York: Harcourt, Brace & Company, 1950).

Bentwich, Norman, and Martin, Andrew, *A Commentary on the Charter of the United Nations* (London: Macmillan and Co., Ltd., 1950).

Brinton, Crane, *From Many One* (Cambridge: Harvard University Press, 1948).

Bryson, Lyman, and others, *Foundations of World Organization: A Political and Cultural Appraisal* (New York: Harper & Brothers, 1952).

Clark, Grenville, and Sohn, Louis B., *Peace Through Disarmament and Charter Revision — Detailed Proposals for Revision of the United Nations Charter.* Preliminary print (Dublin, New Hampshire: July 1953).

Corbett, Percy E., *Law and Society in the Relations of States* (New York: Harcourt, Brace & Company, 1951).

———, *The Individual and World Society* (Princeton: Center for Research on World Political Institutions, 1953).

DeHuszar, G. B., ed., *Persistent International Issues* (New York: Harper & Brothers, 1947).

Deutsch, Karl W., *Nationalism and Social Communication* (New York: The Technology Press of the Massachusetts Institute of Technology and John Wiley and Sons, Inc., 1953).

Dunn, F. S., *War and the Minds of Men* (New York: Harper and Brothers, for the Council on Foreign Relations, 1950).

Eagleton, Clyde, *International Government* (New York: Ronald Press, 1948).

Geiger, Theodore, and Cleveland, H., *Making Western Europe Defensible*, Planning Pamphlet No. 74 (Washington: National Planning Association, August 1951).

Goodrich, Leland M., and Hambro, Edvard, *Charter of the United Nations, Commentary and Documents* (Boston: World Peace Foundation, 1949).

Holcombe, Arthur N., *Our More Perfect Union* (Cambridge: Harvard University Press, 1950).

Jessup, Philip, *A Modern Law of Nations* (New York: The Macmillan Company, 1948).

Joyce, James Avery, ed., *World Organization — Federal or Functional* (London: Watts and Company, 1945).

Klineberg, Otto, *Tensions Affecting International Understanding* (New York: Social Science Research Council, 1950).

Leonard, L. Larry, *International Organization* (New York: McGraw-Hill Book Company, Inc., 1951).

Levi, Werner, *Fundamentals of World Organization* (Minneapolis: University of Minnesota Press, 1950).

MacIver, R. M., *Society* (New York: Farrar, Rinehart, 1937).

———, *The Web of Government* (New York: The Macmillan Company, 1947).

Mander, Linden A., *Foundations of Modern World Society* (Stanford: Stanford University Press, 1947).

Mangone, Gerard J., *The Idea and Practice of World Government* (New York: Columbia University Press, 1951).

————, *A Short History of International Organization* (New York: McGraw-Hill Book Company, Inc., 1954).

Meyer, Cord, Jr., *Peace or Anarchy?* (Boston: Little, Brown & Company, 1947).

Mitrany, David, *A Working Peace System* (London: Royal Institute of International Affairs, 1943).

Morgenthau, Hans, *Politics Among Nations* (New York: Alfred A. Knopf, 1948).

Murphy, Gardner, ed., *Human Nature and Enduring Peace* (Boston: Houghton Mifflin Company, 1945).

Nef, John U., *War and Human Progress* (Cambridge: Harvard University Press, 1950).

Northrop, F. S. C., *The Taming of the Nations* (New York: The Macmillan Company, 1952).

Orr, Lord Boyd, *Food — The Foundation of World Unity* (London: National Peace Council, 1948).

Pool, I. de S., Laswell, H. D., and Lerner, Daniel, *Symbols of Internationalism* (Stanford: Stanford University Press, 1951).

Potter, Pitman B., *An Introduction to the Study of International Organization* (New York: Appleton-Century-Crofts, Inc., 1948).

Reves, Emery, *The Anatomy of Peace* (New York: Harper & Brothers, 1945).

Rusett, Alan de, *Strengthening of the Framework of Peace* (London: Royal Institute of International Affairs, 1950).

Schuman, Frederick L., *The Commonwealth of Man* (New York: Alfred A. Knopf, 1952).

Streit, Clarence, *Union Now* (New York: Harper & Brothers, 1939).

Van Wagenen, Richard W., *Research in the International Organization Field* (Princeton: Center for Research on World Political Institutions, 1952).

Weber, Max, *The Theory of Social and Economic Organization*, trans. by A. M. Henderson and Talcott Parsons (New York: Oxford University Press, 1947).

Woodward, E. L., and others, *Foundations for World Order* (Denver: University of Denver Press, 1949).

Wright, Quincy, *A Study of War*, 2 vols. (Chicago: University of Chicago Press, 1942).

————, ed., *The World Community* (Chicago: University of Chicago Press, 1948).

Periodicals

Cheever, D. S., "The Role of the United Nations in the Conduct of United States Foreign Policy," *World Politics*, Vol. 2, No. 3 (April 1950).

Cohen, Benjamin V., "The Impact of the United Nations on United States Foreign Policy," *International Organization*, Vol. 5, No. 2 (May 1951).

Fox, William T. R., "The United Nations in the Era of Total Diplomacy," *International Organization*, Vol. 5, No. 2 (May 1951).

Goodrich, Leland, "The United Nations and Domestic Jurisdiction," *International Organization*, Vol. 3, No. 1 (February 1949).

Hutchins, Robert M., "Preliminary Draft of a World Constitution," *Common Sense*, Vol. 1, No. 9 (March 1948).

International Social Science Bulletin, "International Congress of Sociology, International Congress of Political Science," Vol. 3, No. 2 (Summer 1951).

Mitrany, David, "The Functional Approach to World Government," *International Affairs*, Vol. 24, No. 3 (July 1948).

Potter, Pitman B., "Universalism versus Regionalism in International Organization," *American Political Science Review*, Vol. 37, No. 5 (October 1943).

Rothwell, Charles Easton, "International Organization and World Politics," *International Organization*, Vol. 3, No. 4 (November 1949).

Rudzinski, Alexander W., "The Influence of the United Nations on Soviet Policy," *International Organization*, Vol. 5, No. 2 (May 1951).

Toynbee, Arnold, "The International Outlook," *International Affairs*, Vol. 23, No. 4 (October 1947).

The Covenant of the League of Nations¹

THE HIGH CONTRACTING PARTIES,

In order to promote international co-operation and to achieve international peace and security
> by the acceptance of obligations not to resort to war,
> by the prescription of open, just and honourable relations between nations,
> by the firm establishment of the understandings of international law as the actual rule of conduct among Governments,
> and by the maintenance of justice and a scrupulous respect for all treaty obligations in the dealings of organised peoples with one another,

Agree to this Covenant of the League of Nations.

Article 1

1. The original Members of the League of Nations shall be those of the Signatories which are named in the Annex to this Covenant and also such of those other States named in the Annex as shall accede without reservation to this Covenant. Such accession shall be effected by a Declaration deposited with the Secretariat within two months of the coming into force of the Covenant. Notice thereof shall be sent to all other Members of the League.

2. Any fully self-governing State, Dominion or Colony not named in the Annex may become a Member of the League if its admission is agreed to by two-thirds of the Assembly, provided that it shall give effective guarantees of its sincere intention to observe its international obligations, and shall accept such regulations as may be prescribed by the League in regard to its military, naval and air forces and armaments.

3. Any Member of the League may, after two years' notice of its intention so to do, withdraw from the League, provided that all its international obligations and all its obligations under this Covenant shall have been fulfilled at the time of its withdrawal.

¹ Text numbered in conformity with the resolution adopted by the seventh ordinary session of the Assembly on September 16th, 1926, and containing Article 6 as amended, in force since August 13th, 1924, Articles 12, 13 and 15 as amended, in force since September 26th, 1924, and Article 4 as amended, in force since July 29th, 1926. The texts printed in italics indicate the amendments.

Article 2

The action of the League under this Covenant shall be effected through the instrumentality of an Assembly and of a Council, with a permanent Secretariat.

Article 3

1. The Assembly shall consist of Representatives of the Members of the League.

2. The Assembly shall meet at stated intervals and from time to time as occasion may require at the Seat of the League or at such other place as may be decided upon.

3. The Assembly may deal at its meetings with any matter within the sphere of action of the League or affecting the peace of the world.

4. At meetings of the Assembly, each Member of the League shall have one vote, and may have not more than three Representatives.

Article 4

1. The Council shall consist of Representatives of the Principal Allied and Associated Powers, together with Representatives of four other Members of the League. These four Members of the League shall be selected by the Assembly from time to time in its discretion. Until the appointment of the Representatives of the four Members of the League first selected by the Assembly, Representatives of Belgium, Brazil, Spain and Greece shall be members of the Council.

2. With the approval of the majority of the Assembly, the Council may name additional Members of the League whose Representatives shall always be Members of the Council; the Council with like approval may increase the number of Members of the League to be selected by the Assembly for representation on the Council.

2. *bis. The Assembly shall fix by a two-thirds majority the rules dealing with the election of the non-permanent Members of the Council, and particularly such regulations as relate to their term of office and the conditions of re-eligibility.*

3. The Council shall meet from time to time as occasion may require, and at least once a year, at the Seat of the League, or at such other place as may be decided upon.

4. The Council may deal at its meetings with any matter within the sphere of action of the League or affecting the peace of the world.

5. Any Member of the League not represented on the Council shall be invited to send a Representative to sit as a member at any meeting of the Council during the consideration of matters specially affecting the interests of that Member of the League.

6. At meetings of the Council, each Member of the League represented on the Council shall have one vote, and may have not more than one Representative.

Article 5

1. Except where otherwise expressly provided in this Covenant or by the terms of the present Treaty, decisions at any meeting of the Assembly or of the Council

shall require the agreement of all the Members of the League represented at the meeting.

2. All matters of procedure at meetings of the Assembly or of the Council, including the appointment of Committees to investigate particular matters, shall be regulated by the Assembly or by the Council and may be decided by a majority of the Members of the League represented at the meeting.

3. The first meeting of the Assembly and the first meeting of the Council shall be summoned by the President of the United States of America.

Article 6

1. The permanent Secretariat shall be established at the Seat of the League. The Secretariat shall comprise a Secretary-General and such secretaries and staff as may be required.

2. The first Secretary-General shall be the person named in the Annex; thereafter the Secretary-General shall be appointed by the Council with the approval of the majority of the Assembly.

3. The secretaries and staff of the Secretariat shall be appointed by the Secretary-General with the approval of the Council.

4. The Secretary-General shall act in that capacity at all meetings of the Assembly and of the Council.

5. *The expenses of the League shall be borne by the Members of the League in the proportion decided by the Assembly.*

Article 7

1. The Seat of the League is established at Geneva.

2. The Council may at any time decide that the Seat of the League shall be established elsewhere.

3. All positions under or in connection with the League, including the Secretariat, shall be open equally to men and women.

4. Representatives of the Members of the League and officials of the League when engaged on the business of the League shall enjoy diplomatic privileges and immunities.

5. The buildings and other property occupied by the League or its officials or by Representatives attending its meetings shall be inviolable.

Article 8

1. The Members of the League recognise that the maintenance of peace requires the reduction of national armaments to the lowest point consistent with national safety and the enforcement by common action of international obligations.

2. The Council, taking account of the geographical situation and circumstances of each State, shall formulate plans for such reduction for the consideration and action of the several Governments.

3. Such plans shall be subject to reconsideration and revision at least every ten years.

4. After these plans have been adopted by the several Governments, the limits of armaments therein fixed shall not be exceeded without the concurrence of the Council.

5. The Members of the League agree that the manufacture by private enterprise of munitions and implements of war is open to grave objections. The Council shall advise how the evil effects attendant upon such manufacture can be prevented, due regard being had to the necessities of those Members of the League which are not able to manufacture the munitions and implements of war necessary for their safety.

6. The Members of the League undertake to interchange full and frank information as to the scale of their armaments, their military, naval and air programmes and the condition of such of their industries as are adaptable to warlike purposes.

Article 9

A permanent Commission shall be constituted to advise the Council on the execution of the provisions of Articles 1 and 8 and on military, naval and air questions generally.

Article 10

The Members of the League undertake to respect and preserve as against external aggression the territorial integrity and existing political independence of all Members of the League. In case of any such aggression or in case of any threat or danger of such aggression, the Council shall advise upon the means by which this obligation shall be fulfilled.

Article 11

1. Any war or threat of war, whether immediately affecting any of the Members of the League or not, is hereby declared a matter of concern to the whole League, and the League shall take any action that may be deemed wise and effectual to safeguard the peace of nations. In case any such emergency should arise, the Secretary-General shall, on the request of any Member of the League, forthwith summon a meeting of the Council.

2. It is also declared to be the friendly right of each Member of the League to bring to the attention of the Assembly or of the Council any circumstance whatever affecting international relations which threatens to disturb international peace or the good understanding between nations upon which peace depends.

Article 12

1. The Members of the League agree that if there should arise between them any dispute likely to lead to a rupture they will submit the matter either to arbitration *or judicial settlement* or to enquiry by the Council, and they agree in no case to resort to war until three months after the award by the arbitrators *or the judicial decision* or the report by the Council.

2. In any case under this Article the award of the arbitrators *or the judicial decision* shall be made within a reasonable time, and the report of the Council shall be made within six months after the submission of the dispute.

Article 13

1. The Members of the League agree that whenever any dispute shall arise between them which they recognise to be suitable for submission to arbitration *or judicial settlement,* and which cannot be satisfactorily settled by diplomacy, they will submit the whole subject-matter to arbitration *or judicial settlement.*

2. Disputes as to the interpretation of a treaty, as to any question of international law, as to the existence of any fact which, if established, would constitute a breach of any international obligation, or as to the extent and nature of the reparation to be made for any such breach, are declared to be among those which are generally suitable for submission to arbitration *or judicial settlement.*

3. *For the consideration of any such dispute, the court to which the case is referred shall be the Permanent Court of International Justice, established in accordance with Article 14, or any tribunal agreed on by the parties to the dispute or stipulated in any convention existing between them.*

4. The Members of the League agree that they will carry out in full good faith any award *or decision* that may be rendered, and that they will not resort to war against a Member of the League which complies therewith. In the event of any failure to carry out such an award *or decision,* the Council shall propose what steps should be taken to give effect thereto.

Article 14

The Council shall formulate and submit to the Members of the League for adoption plans for the establishment of a Permanent Court of International Justice. The Court shall be competent to hear and determine any dispute of an international character which the parties thereto submit to it. The Court may also give an advisory opinion upon any dispute or question referred to it by the Council or by the Assembly.

Article 15

1. If there should arise between Members of the League any dispute likely to lead to a rupture, which is not submitted to arbitration *or judicial settlement* in accordance with Article 13, the Members of the League agree that they will submit the matter to the Council. Any party to the dispute may effect such submission by giving notice of the existence of the dispute to the Secretary-General, who will make all necessary arrangements for a full investigation and consideration thereof.

2. For this purpose, the parties to the dispute will communicate to the Secretary-General, as promptly as possible, statements of their case with all the relevant facts and papers, and the Council may forthwith direct the publication thereof.

3. The Council shall endeavour to effect a settlement of the dispute, and, if such efforts are successful, a statement shall be made public giving such facts and explanations regarding the dispute and the terms of settlement thereof as the Council may deem appropriate.

4. If the dispute is not thus settled, the Council either unanimously or by a majority vote shall make and publish a report containing a statement of the facts of the dispute and the recommendations which are deemed just and proper in regard thereto.

5. Any Member of the League represented on the Council may make public a statement of the facts of the dispute and of its conclusions regarding the same.

6. If a report by the Council is unanimously agreed to by the members thereof other than the Representatives of one or more of the parties to the dispute, the Members of the League agree that they will not go to war with any party to the dispute which complies with the recommendations of the report.

7. If the Council fails to reach a report which is unanimously agreed to by the members thereof, other than the Representatives of one or more of the parties to the dispute, the Members of the League reserve to themselves the right to take such action as they shall consider necessary for the maintenance of right and justice.

8. If the dispute between the parties is claimed by one of them, and is found by the Council, to arise out of a matter which by international law is solely within the domestic jurisdiction of that party, the Council shall so report, and shall make no recommendation as to its settlement.

9. The Council may in any case under this Article refer the dispute to the Assembly. The dispute shall be so referred at the request of either party to the dispute provided that such request be made within fourteen days after the submission of the dispute to the Council.

10. In any case referred to the Assembly, all the provisions of this Article and of Article 12 relating to the action and powers of the Council shall apply to the action and powers of the Assembly, provided that a report made by the Assembly, if concurred in by the Representatives of those Members of the League represented on the Council and of a majority of the other Members of the League, exclusive in each case of the Representatives of the parties to the dispute, shall have the same force as a report by the Council concurred in by all the members thereof other than the Representatives of one or more of the parties to the dispute.

Article 16

1. Should any Member of the League resort to war in disregard of its covenants under Articles 12, 13 or 15, it shall *ipso facto* be deemed to have committed an act of war against all other Members of the League, which hereby undertake immediately to subject it to the severance of all trade or financial relations, the prohibition of all intercourse between their nationals and the nationals of the covenant-breaking State, and the prevention of all financial, commercial or personal intercourse between the nationals of the covenant-breaking State and the nationals of any other State, whether a Member of the League or not.

2. It shall be the duty of the Council in such case to recommend to the several Governments concerned what effective military, naval or air force the Members of the League shall severally contribute to the armed forces to be used to protect the covenants of the League.

3. The Members of the League agree, further, that they will mutually support one another in the financial and economic measures which are taken under this Article, in order to minimise the loss and inconvenience resulting from the above measures, and that they will mutually support one another in resisting any special measures aimed at one of their number by the covenant-breaking State,

and that they will take the necessary steps to afford passage through their territory to the forces of any of the Members of the League which are co-operating to protect the covenants of the League.

4. Any Member of the League which has violated any covenant of the League may be declared to be no longer a Member of the League by a vote of the Council concurred in by the Representatives of all the other Members of the League represented thereon.

Article 17

1. In the event of a dispute between a Member of the League and a State which is not a Member of the League, or between States not Members of the League, the State or States not Members of the League shall be invited to accept the obligations of membership in the League for the purposes of such dispute, upon such conditions as the Council may deem just. If such invitation is accepted, the provisions of Articles 12 to 16 inclusive shall be applied with such modifications as may be deemed necessary by the Council.

2. Upon such invitation being given, the Council shall immediately institute an enquiry into the circumstances of the dispute and recommend such action as may seem best and most effectual in the circumstances.

3. If a State so invited shall refuse to accept the obligations of membership in the League for the purposes of such dispute, and shall resort to war against a Member of the League, the provisions of Article 16 shall be applicable as against the State taking such action.

4. If both parties to the dispute when so invited refuse to accept the obligations of membership in the League for the purposes of such dispute, the Council may take such measures and make such recommendations as will prevent hostilities and will result in the settlement of the dispute.

Article 18

Every treaty or international engagement entered into hereafter by any Member of the League shall be forthwith registered with the Secretariat and shall as soon as possible be published by it. No such treaty or international engagement shall be binding until so registered.

Article 19

The Assembly may from time to time advise the reconsideration by Members of the League of treaties which have become inapplicable and the consideration of international conditions whose continuance might endanger the peace of the world.

Article 20

1. The Members of the League severally agree that this Covenant is accepted as abrogating all obligations or understandings *inter se* which are inconsistent with the terms thereof, and solemnly undertake that they will not hereafter enter into any engagements inconsistent with the terms thereof.

2. In case any Member of the League shall, before becoming a Member of the League, have undertaken any obligations inconsistent with the terms of this Cove-

nant, it shall be the duty of such Member to take immediate steps to procure its release from such obligations.

Article 21

Nothing in this Covenant shall be deemed to affect the validity of international engagements, such as treaties of arbitration or regional understandings like the Monroe doctrine, for securing the maintenance of peace.

Article 22

1. To those colonies and territories which as a consequence of the late war have ceased to be under the sovereignty of the States which formerly governed them and which are inhabited by peoples not yet able to stand by themselves under the strenuous conditions of the modern world, there should be applied the principle that the well-being and development of such peoples form a sacred trust of civilisation and that securities for the performance of this trust should be embodied in this Covenant.

2. The best method of giving practical effect to this principle is that the tutelage of such peoples should be entrusted to advanced nations who, by reason of their resources, their experience or their geographical position, can best undertake this responsibility, and who are willing to accept it, and that this tutelage should be exercised by them as Mandatories on behalf of the League.

3. The character of the mandate must differ according to the stage of the development of the people, the geographical situation of the territory, its economic conditions and other similar circumstances.

4. Certain communities formerly belonging to the Turkish Empire have reached a stage of development where their existence as independent nations can be provisionally recognised subject to the rendering of administrative advice and assistance by a Mandatory until such times as they are able to stand alone. The wishes of these communities must be a principal consideration in the selection of the Mandatory.

5. Other peoples, especially those of Central Africa, are at such a stage that the Mandatory must be responsible for the administration of the territory under conditions which will guarantee freedom of conscience and religion, subject only to the maintenance of public order and morals, the prohibition of abuses such as the slave trade, the arms traffic and the liquor traffic, and the prevention of the establishment of fortifications or military and naval bases and of military training of the natives for other than police purposes and the defence of territory, and will also secure equal opportunities for the trade and commerce of other Members of the League.

6. There are territories, such as South West Africa and certain of the South Pacific Islands, which, owing to the sparseness of their population, or their small size, or their remoteness from the centres of civilisation, or their geographical contiguity to the territory of the Mandatory, and other circumstances, can be best administered under the laws of the Mandatory as integral portions of its territory, subject to the safeguards above mentioned in the interests of the indigenous population.

7. In every case of mandate, the Mandatory shall render to the Council an annual report in reference to the territory committed to its charge.

8. The degree of authority, control or administration to be exercised by the Mandatory shall, if not previously agreed upon by the Members of the League, be explicitly defined in each case by the Council.

9. A permanent Commission shall be constituted to receive and examine the annual reports of the Mandatories and to advise the Council on all matters relating to the observance of the mandates.

Article 23

Subject to and in accordance with the provisions of international conventions existing or hereafter to be agreed upon, the Members of the League:

(a) will endeavour to secure and maintain fair and humane conditions of labour for men, women and children, both in their own countries and in all countries to which their commercial and industrial relations extend, and for that purpose will establish and maintain the necessary international organisations;

(b) undertake to secure just treatment of the native inhabitants of territories under their control;

(c) will entrust the League with the general supervision over the execution of agreements with regard to the traffic in women and children, and the traffic in opium and other dangerous drugs;

(d) will entrust the League with the general supervision of the trade in arms and ammunition with the countries in which the control of this traffic is necessary in the common interest;

(e) will make provision to secure and maintain freedom of communications and of transit and equitable treatment for the commerce of all Members of the League. In this connection, the special necessities of the regions devastated during the war of 1914–1918 shall be borne in mind;

(f) will endeavour to take steps in matters of international concern for the prevention and control of disease.

Article 24

1. There shall be placed under the direction of the League the international bureaux already established by general treaties if the parties to such treaties consent. All such international bureaux and all commissions for the regulation of matters of international interest hereafter constituted shall be placed under the direction of the League.

2. In all matters of international interest which are regulated by general conventions but which are not placed under the control of international bureaux or commissions, the Secretariat of the League shall, subject to the consent of the Council and if desired by the parties, collect and distribute all relevant information and shall render any other assistance which may be necessary or desirable.

3. The Council may include as part of the expenses of the Secretariat the expenses of any bureau or commission which is placed under the direction of the League.

Article 25

The Members of the League agree to encourage and promote the establishment and co-operation of duly authorized voluntary national Red Cross organisations having as purposes the improvement of health, the prevention of disease and the mitigation of suffering throughout the world.

Article 26

1. Amendments to this Covenant will take effect when ratified by the Members of the League whose Representatives compose the Council and by a majority of the Members of the League whose Representatives compose the Assembly.

2. No such amendments shall bind any Member of the League which signifies its dissent therefrom, but in that case it shall cease to be a Member of the League.

Charter of the United Nations[2]

WE THE PEOPLES OF THE UNITED NATIONS DETERMINED

to save succeeding generations from the scourge of war, which twice in our lifetime has brought untold sorrow to mankind, and
to reaffirm faith in fundamental human rights, in the dignity and worth of the human person, in the equal rights of men and women and of nations large and small, and
to establish conditions under which justice and respect for the obligations arising from treaties and other sources of international law can be maintained, and
to promote social progress and better standards of life in larger freedom,

AND FOR THESE ENDS

to practice tolerance and live together in peace with one another as good neighbors, and
to unite our strength to maintain international peace and security, and
to ensure, by the acceptance of principles and the institution of methods, that armed force shall not be used, save in the common interest, and
to employ international machinery for the promotion of the economic and social advancement of all peoples,

HAVE RESOLVED TO COMBINE OUR EFFORTS TO ACCOMPLISH THESE AIMS.

Accordingly, our respective Governments, through representatives assembled in the city of San Francisco, who have exhibited their full powers found to be in good and due form, have agreed to the present Charter of the United Nations and do hereby establish an international organization to be known as the United Nations.

CHAPTER I

PURPOSES AND PRINCIPLES

Article 1

The Purposes of the United Nations are:
1. To maintain international peace and security, and to that end: to take effective collective measures for the prevention and removal of threats to the peace, and for the suppression of acts of aggression or other breaches of the

2 United States, Department of State, Publication 2368, Conference Series 76.

peace, and to bring about by peaceful means, and in conformity with the principles of justice and international law, adjustment or settlement of international disputes or situations which might lead to a breach of the peace;

2. To develop friendly relations among nations based on respect for the principle of equal rights and self-determination of peoples, and to take other appropriate measures to strengthen universal peace;

3. To achieve international cooperation in solving international problems of an economic, social, cultural, or humanitarian character, and in promoting and encouraging respect for human rights and for fundamental freedoms for all without distinction as to race, sex, language, or religion; and

4. To be a center for harmonizing the actions of nations in the attainment of these common ends.

Article 2

The Organization and its Members, in pursuit of the Purposes stated in Article 1, shall act in accordance with the following Principles.

1. The Organization is based on the principle of the sovereign equality of all its Members.

2. All Members, in order to ensure to all of them the rights and benefits resulting from membership, shall fulfil in good faith the obligations assumed by them in accordance with the present Charter.

3. All Members shall settle their international disputes by peaceful means in such a manner that international peace and security, and justice, are not endangered.

4. All Members shall refrain in their international relations from the threat or use of force against the territorial integrity or political independence of any state, or in any other manner inconsistent with the Purposes of the United Nations.

5. All Members shall give the United Nations every assistance in any action it takes in accordance with the present Charter, and shall refrain from giving assistance to any state against which the United Nations is taking preventive or enforcement action.

6. The Organization shall ensure that states which are not Members of the United Nations act in accordance with these Principles so far as may be necessary for the maintenance of international peace and security.

7. Nothing contained in the present Charter shall authorize the United Nations to intervene in matters which are essentially within the domestic jurisdiction of any state or shall require the Members to submit such matters to settlement under the present Charter; but this principle shall not prejudice the application of enforcement measures under Chapter VII.

CHAPTER II

MEMBERSHIP

Article 3

The original Members of the United Nations shall be the states which, having participated in the United Nations Conference on International Organization at San Francisco, or having previously signed the Declaration by the United Nations of January 1, 1942, sign the present Charter and ratify it in accordance with Article 110.

Article 4

1. Membership in the United Nations is open to all other peace-loving states which accept the obligations contained in the present Charter and, in the judgment of the Organization, are able and willing to carry out these obligations.

2. The admission of any such state to membership in the United Nations will be effected by a decision of the General Assembly upon the recommendation of the Security Council.

Article 5

A Member of the United Nations against which preventive or enforcement action has been taken by the Security Council may be suspended from the exercise of the rights and privileges of membership by the General Assembly upon the recommendation of the Security Council. The exercise of these rights and privileges may be restored by the Security Council.

Article 6

A Member of the United Nations which has persistently violated the Principles contained in the present Charter may be expelled from the Organization by the General Assembly upon the recommendation of the Security Council.

CHAPTER III

ORGANS

Article 7

1. There are established as the principal organs of the United Nations: a General Assembly, a Security Council, an Economic and Social Council, a Trusteeship Council, an International Court of Justice, and a Secretariat.

2. Such subsidiary organs as may be found necessary may be established in accordance with the present Charter.

Article 8

The United Nations shall place no restrictions on the eligibility of men and women to participate in any capacity and under conditions of equality in its principal and subsidiary organs.

CHAPTER IV

THE GENERAL ASSEMBLY

Composition

Article 9

1. The General Assembly shall consist of all the Members of the United Nations.

2. Each Member shall have not more than five representatives in the General Assembly.

Functions and Powers

Article 10

The General Assembly may discuss any questions or any matters within the scope of the present Charter or relating to the powers and functions of any organs provided for in the present Charter, and, except as provided in Article 12, may make recommendations to the Members of the United Nations or to the Security Council or to both on any such questions or matters.

Article 11

1. The General Assembly may consider the general principles of cooperation in the maintenance of international peace and security, including the principles governing disarmament and the regulation of armaments, and may make recommendations with regard to such principles to the Members or to the Security Council or to both.

2. The General Assembly may discuss any questions relating to the maintenance of international peace and security brought before it by any Member of the United Nations, or by the Security Council, or by a state which is not a Member of the United Nations in accordance with Article 35, paragraph 2, and, except as provided in Article 12, may make recommendations with regard to any such questions to the state or states concerned or to the Security Council or to both. Any such question on which action is necessary shall be referred to the Security Council by the General Assembly either before or after discussion.

3. The General Assembly may call the attention of the Security Council to situations which are likely to endanger international peace and security.

4. The powers of the General Assembly set forth in this Article shall not limit the general scope of Article 10.

Article 12

1. While the Security Council is exercising in respect of any dispute or situation the functions assigned to it in the present Charter, the General Assembly shall not make any recommendation with regard to that dispute or situation unless the Security Council so requests.

2. The Secretary-General, with the consent of the Security Council, shall notify the General Assembly at each session of any matters relative to the maintenance of international peace and security which are being dealt with by the Security Council and shall similarly notify the General Assembly, or the Members of the United Nations if the General Assembly is not in session, immediately the Security Council ceases to deal with such matters.

Article 13

1. The General Assembly shall initiate studies and make recommendations for the purpose of:

a. promoting international cooperation in the political field and encouraging the progressive development of international law and its codification;

b. promoting international cooperation in the economic, social, cultural, educational, and health fields, and assisting in the realization of human rights and fundamental freedoms for all without distinction as to race, sex, language, or religion.

2. The further responsibilities, functions, and powers of the General Assembly with respect to matters mentioned in paragraph 1 (b) above are set forth in Chapters IX and X.

Article 14

Subject to the provisions of Article 12, the General Assembly may recommend measures for the peaceful adjustment of any situation, regardless of origin, which it deems likely to impair the general welfare or friendly relations among nations, including situations resulting from a violation of the provisions of the present Charter setting forth the Purposes and Principles of the United Nations.

Article 15

1. The General Assembly shall receive and consider annual and special reports from the Security Council; these reports shall include an account of the measures that the Security Council has decided upon or taken to maintain international peace and security.

2. The General Assembly shall receive and consider reports from the other organs of the United Nations.

Article 16

The General Assembly shall perform such functions with respect to the international trusteeship system as are assigned to it under Chapters XII and XIII, including the approval of the trusteeship agreements for areas not designated as strategic.

Article 17

1. The General Assembly shall consider and approve the budget of the Organization.

2. The expenses of the Organization shall be borne by the Members as apportioned by the General Assembly.

3. The General Assembly shall consider and approve any financial and budgetary arrangements with specialized agencies referred to in Article 57 and shall examine the administrative budgets of such specialized agencies with a view to making recommendations to the agencies concerned.

Voting

Article 18

1. Each member of the General Assembly shall have one vote.

2. Decisions of the General Assembly on important questions shall be made by a two-thirds majority of the members present and voting. These questions shall include: recommendations with respect to the maintenance of international peace and security, the election of the non-permanent members of the Security Council, the election of the members of the Economic and Social Council, the election of members of the Trusteeship Council in accordance with paragraph 1 (c) of Article 86, the admission of new Members to the United Nations, the suspension of the rights and privileges of membership, the expulsion of Members, questions relating to the operation of the trusteeship system, and budgetary questions.

3. Decisions on other questions, including the determination of additional categories of questions to be decided by a two-thirds majority, shall be made by a majority of the members present and voting.

Article 19

A member of the United Nations which is in arrears in the payment of its financial contributions to the Organization shall have no vote in the General Assembly if the amount of its arrears equals or exceeds the amount of the contributions due from it for the preceding two full years. The General Assembly may, nevertheless, permit such a Member to vote if it is satisfied that the failure to pay is due to conditions beyond the control of the Member.

Procedure

Article 20

The General Assembly shall meet in regular annual sessions and in such special sessions as occasion may require. Special sessions shall be convoked by the Secretary-General at the request of the Security Council or of a majority of the Members of the United Nations.

Article 21

The General Assembly shall adopt its own rules of procedure. It shall elect its President for each session.

Article 22

The General Assembly may establish such subsidiary organs as it deems necessary for the performance of its functions.

CHAPTER V

THE SECURITY COUNCIL

Composition

Article 23

1. The Security Council shall consist of eleven Members of the United Nations. The Republic of China, France, the Union of Soviet Socialist Republics, the United Kingdom of Great Britain and Northern Ireland, and the United States of America shall be permanent members of the Security Council. The General Assembly shall elect six other Members of the United Nations to be non-permanent members of the Security Council, due regard being specially paid, in the first instance to the contribution of Members of the United Nations to the maintenance of international peace and security and to the other purposes of the Organization, and also to equitable geographical distribution.

2. The non-permanent members of the Security Council shall be elected for a term of two years. In the first election of the non-permanent members, however, three shall be chosen for a term of one year. A retiring member shall not be eligible for immediate re-election.

3. Each member of the Security Council shall have one representative.

Functions and Powers

Article 24

1. In order to ensure prompt and effective action by the United Nations, its Members confer on the Security Council primary responsibility for the maintenance of international peace and security, and agree that in carrying out its duties under this responsibility the Security Council acts on their behalf.

2. In discharging these duties the Security Council shall act in accordance with the Purposes and Principles of the United Nations. The specific powers granted to the Security Council for the discharge of these duties are laid down in Chapters VI, VII, VIII, and XII.

3. The Security Council shall submit annual and, when necessary, special reports to the General Assembly for its consideration.

Article 25

The Members of the United Nations agree to accept and carry out the decisions of the Security Council in accordance with the present Charter.

Article 26

In order to promote the establishment and maintenance of international peace and security with the least diversion for armaments of the world's human and economic resources, the Security Council shall be responsible for formulating, with the assistance of the Military Staff Committee referred to in Article 47, plans to be submitted to the Members of the United Nations for the establishment of a system for the regulation of armaments.

Voting

Article 27

1. Each member of the Security Council shall have one vote.

2. Decisions of the Security Council on procedural matters shall be made by an affirmative vote of seven members.

3. Decisions of the Security Council on all other matters shall be made by an affirmative vote of seven members including the concurring votes of the permanent members; provided that, in decisions under Chapter VI, and under paragraph 3 of Article 52, a party to a dispute shall abstain from voting.

Procedure

Article 28

1. The Security Council shall be so organized as to be able to function continuously. Each member of the Security Council shall for this purpose be represented at all times at the seat of the Organization.

2. The Security Council shall hold periodic meetings at which each of its members may, if it so desires, be represented by a member of the government or by some other specially designated representative.

3. The Security Council may hold meetings at such places other than the seat of the Organization as in its judgment will best facilitate its work.

Article 29

The Security Council may establish such subsidiary organs as it deems necessary for the performance of its functions.

Article 30

The Security Council shall adopt its own rules of procedure, including the method of selecting its President.

Article 31

Any Member of the United Nations which is not a member of the Security Council may participate, without vote, in the discussion of any question brought before the Security Council whenever the latter considers that the interests of that Member are specially affected.

Article 32

Any Member of the United Nations which is not a member of the Security Council or any state which is not a Member of the United Nations, if it is a party to a dispute under consideration by the Security Council, shall be invited to participate, without vote, in the discussion relating to the dispute. The Security Council shall lay down such conditions as it deems just for the participation of a state which is not a Member of the United Nations.

CHAPTER VI

PACIFIC SETTLEMENT OF DISPUTES

Article 33

1. The parties to any dispute, the continuance of which is likely to endanger the maintenance of international peace and security, shall, first of all, seek a solution by negotiation, enquiry, mediation, conciliation, arbitration, judicial settlement, resort to regional agencies or arrangements, or other peaceful means of their own choice.

2. The Security Council shall, when it deems necessary, call upon the parties to settle their dispute by such means.

Article 34

The Security Council may investigate any dispute, or any situation which might lead to international friction or give rise to a dispute, in order to determine whether the continuance of the dispute or situation is likely to endanger the maintenance of international peace and security.

Article 35

1. Any Member of the United Nations may bring any dispute, or any situation of the nature referred to in Article 34, to the attention of the Security Council or of the General Assembly.

2. A state which is not a Member of the United Nations may bring to the attention of the Security Council or of the General Assembly any dispute to which it is a party if it accepts in advance, for the purposes of the dispute, the obligations of pacific settlement provided in the present Charter.

3. The proceedings of the General Assembly in respect of matters brought to its attention under this Article will be subject to the provisions of Articles 11 and 12.

Article 36

1. The Security Council may, at any stage of a dispute of the nature referred to in Article 33 or of a situation of like nature, recommend appropriate procedures or methods of adjustment.

2. The Security Council should take into consideration any procedures for the settlement of the dispute which have already been adopted by the parties.

3. In making recommendations under this Article the Security Council should also take into consideration that legal disputes should as a general rule be referred by the parties to the International Court of Justice in accordance with the provisions of the Statute of the Court.

Article 37

1. Should the parties to a dispute of the nature referred to in Article 33 fail to settle it by means indicated in that Article, they shall refer it to the Security Council.

2. If the Security Council deems that the continuance of the dispute is in fact likely to endanger the maintenance of international peace and security, it shall decide whether to take action under Article 36 or to recommend such terms of settlement as it may consider appropriate.

Article 38

Without prejudice to the provisions of Articles 33 to 37, the Security Council may, if all the parties to any dispute so request, make recommendations to the parties with a view to a pacific settlement of the dispute.

CHAPTER VII

ACTION WITH RESPECT TO THREATS TO THE PEACE, BREACHES OF THE PEACE, AND ACTS OF AGGRESSION

Article 39

The Security Council shall determine the existence of any threat to the peace, breach of the peace, or act of aggression and shall make recommendations, or decide what measures shall be taken in accordance with Articles 41 and 42, to maintain or restore international peace and security.

Article 40

In order to prevent an aggravation of the situation, the Security Council may, before making the recommendations or deciding upon the measures provided for in Article 39, call upon the parties concerned to comply with such provisional measures as it deems necessary or desirable. Such provisional measures shall be without prejudice to the rights, claims, or position of the parties concerned. The Security Council shall duly take account of failure to comply with such provisional measures.

Article 41

The Security Council may decide what measures not involving the use of armed force are to be employed to give effect to its decisions, and it may call upon the Members of the United Nations to apply such measures. These may include complete or partial interruption of economic relations and of rail, sea, air, postal, telegraphic, radio, and other means of communication, and the severance of diplomatic relations.

Article 42

Should the Security Council consider that measures provided for in Article 41 would be inadequate or have proved to be inadequate, it may take such action by air, sea, or land forces as may be necessary to maintain or restore international peace and security. Such action may include demonstrations, blockade, and other operations by air, sea, or land forces of Members of the United Nations.

Article 43

1. All Members of the United Nations, in order to contribute to the maintenance of international peace and security, undertake to make available to the Security Council, on its call and in accordance with a special agreement or agreements, armed forces, assistance, and facilities, including rights of passage, necessary for the purpose of maintaining international peace and security.

2. Such agreement or agreements shall govern the numbers and types of forces, their degree of readiness and general location, and the nature of the facilities and assistance to be provided.

3. The agreement or agreements shall be negotiated as soon as possible on the initiative of the Security Council. They shall be concluded between the Security Council and Members or between the Security Council and groups of Members and shall be subject to ratification by the signatory states in accordance with their respective constitutional processes.

Article 44

When the Security Council has decided to use force it shall, before calling upon a Member not represented on it to provide armed forces in fulfillment of the obligations assumed under Article 43, invite that Member, if the Member so desires, to participate in the decisions of the Security Council concerning the employment of contingents of that Member's armed forces.

Article 45

In order to enable the United Nations to take urgent military measures, Members shall hold immediately available national air-force contingents for combined international enforcement action. The strength and degree of readiness of these contingents and plans for their combined action shall be determined, within the limits laid down in the special agreement or agreements referred to in Article 43, by the Security Council with the assistance of the Military Staff Committee.

Article 46

Plans for the application of armed force shall be made by the Security Council with the assistance of the Military Staff Committee.

Article 47

1. There shall be established a Military Staff Committee to advise and assist the Security Council on all questions relating to the Security Council's military requirements for the maintenance of international peace and security, the employment and command of forces placed at its disposal, the regulation of armaments, and possible disarmament.

2. The Military Staff Committee shall consist of the Chiefs of Staff of the permanent members of the Security Council or their representatives. Any Mem-

ber of the United Nations not permanently represented on the Committee shall be invited by the Committee to be associated with it when the efficient discharge of the Committee's responsibilities requires the participation of that Member in its work.

3. The Military Staff Committee shall be responsible under the Security Council for the strategic direction of any armed forces placed at the disposal of the Security Council. Questions relating to the command of such forces shall be worked out subsequently.

4. The Military Staff Committee, with the authorization of the Security Council and after consultation with appropriate regional agencies, may establish regional subcommittees.

Article 48

1. The action required to carry out the decisions of the Security Council for the maintenance of international peace and security shall be taken by all the Members of the United Nations or by some of them, as the Security Council may determine.

2. Such decisions shall be carried out by the Members of the United Nations directly and through their action in the appropriate international agencies of which they are members.

Article 49

The Members of the United Nations shall join in affording mutual assistance in carrying out the measures decided upon by the Security Council.

Article 50

If preventive or enforcement measures against any state are taken by the Security Council, any other state, whether a Member of the United Nations or not, which finds itself confronted with special economic problems arising from the carrying out of those measures shall have the right to consult the Security Council with regard to a solution of those problems.

Article 51

Nothing in the present Charter shall impair the inherent right of individual or collective self-defense if an armed attack occurs against a Member of the United Nations, until the Security Council has taken the measures necessary to maintain international peace and security. Measures taken by Members in the exercise of this right of self-defense shall be immediately reported to the Security Council and shall not in any way affect the authority and responsibility of the Security Council under the present Charter to take at any time such action as it deems necessary in order to maintain or restore international peace and security.

CHAPTER VIII

REGIONAL ARRANGEMENTS

Article 52

1. Nothing in the present Charter precludes the existence of regional arrangements or agencies for dealing with such matters relating to the maintenance of international peace and security as are appropriate for regional action, provided

that such arrangements or agencies and their activities are consistent with the Purposes and Principles of the United Nations.

2. The Members of the United Nations entering into such arrangements or constituting such agencies shall make every effort to achieve pacific settlement of local disputes through such regional arrangements or by such regional agencies before referring them to the Security Council.

3. The Security Council shall encourage the development of pacific settlement of local disputes through such regional arrangements or by such regional agencies either on the initiative of the states concerned or by reference from the Security Council.

4. This Article in no way impairs the application of Articles 34 and 35.

Article 53

1. The Security Council shall, where appropriate, utilize such regional arrangements or agencies for enforcement action under its authority. But no enforcement action shall be taken under regional arrangements or by regional agencies without the authorization of the Security Council, with the exception of measures against any enemy state, as defined in paragraph 2 of this Article, provided for pursuant to Article 107 or in regional arrangements directed against renewal of aggressive policy on the part of any such state, until such time as the Organization may, on request of the Governments concerned, be charged with the responsibility for preventing further aggression by such a state.

2. The term enemy state as used in paragraph 1 of this Article applies to any state which during the Second World War has been an enemy of any signatory of the present Charter.

Article 54

The Security Council shall at all times be kept fully informed of activities undertaken or in contemplation under regional arrangements or by regional agencies for the maintenance of international peace and security.

CHAPTER IX

INTERNATIONAL ECONOMIC AND SOCIAL COOPERATION

Article 55

With a view to the creation of conditions of stability and well-being which are necessary for peaceful and friendly relations among nations based on respect for the principle of equal rights and self-determination of peoples, the United Nations shall promote:

a. higher standards of living, full employment, and conditions of economic and social progress and development;

b. solutions of international economic, social, health, and related problems; and international cultural and educational cooperation; and

c. universal respect for, and observance of, human rights and fundamental freedoms for all without distinction as to race, sex, language, or religion.

Article 56

All Members pledge themselves to take joint and separate action in cooperation with the Organization for the achievement of the purposes set forth in Article 55.

Article 57

1. The various specialized agencies, established by intergovernmental agreement and having wide international responsibilities, as defined in their basic instruments, in economic, social, cultural, educational, health, and related fields, shall be brought into relationship with the United Nations in accordance with the provisions of Article 63.

2. Such agencies thus brought into relationship with the United Nations are hereinafter referred to as specialized agencies.

Article 58

The Organization shall make recommendations for the coordination of the policies and activities of the specialized agencies.

Article 59

The Organization shall, where appropriate, initiate negotiations among the states concerned for the creation of any new specialized agencies required for the accomplishment of the purposes set forth in Article 55.

Article 60

Responsibility for the discharge of the functions of the Organization set forth in this Chapter shall be vested in the General Assembly and, under the authority of the General Assembly, in the Economic and Social Council, which shall have for this purpose the powers set forth in Chapter X.

CHAPTER X

THE ECONOMIC AND SOCIAL COUNCIL

Composition

Article 61

1. The Economic and Social Council shall consist of eighteen Members of the United Nations elected by the General Assembly.

2. Subject to the provisions of paragraph 3, six members of the Economic and Social Council shall be elected each year for a term of three years. A retiring member shall be eligible for immediate re-election.

3. At the first election, eighteen members of the Economic and Social Council shall be chosen. The term of office of six members so chosen shall expire at the end of one year, and of six other members at the end of two years, in accordance with arrangements made by the General Assembly.

4. Each member of the Economic and Social Council shall have one representative.

Functions and Powers

Article 62

1. The Economic and Social Council may make or initiate studies and reports with respect to international economic, social, cultural, educational, health, and related matters and may make recommendations with respect to any such matters to the General Assembly, to the Members of the United Nations, and to the specialized agencies concerned.

2. It may make recommendations for the purpose of promoting respect for, and observance of, human rights and fundamental freedoms for all.

3. It may prepare draft conventions for submission to the General Assembly, with respect to matters falling within its competence.

4. It may call, in accordance with the rules prescribed by the United Nations, international conferences on matters falling within its competence.

Article 63

1. The Economic and Social Council may enter into agreements with any of the agencies referred to in Article 57, defining the terms on which the agency concerned shall be brought into relationship with the United Nations. Such agreements shall be subject to approval by the General Assembly.

2. It may coordinate the activities of the specialized agencies through consultation with and recommendations to such agencies and through recommendations to the General Assembly and to the Members of the United Nations.

Article 64

1. The Economic and Social Council may take appropriate steps to obtain regular reports from the specialized agencies. It may make arrangements with the Members of the United Nations and with the specialized agencies to obtain reports on the steps taken to give effect to its own recommendations and to recommendations on matters falling within its competence made by the General Assembly.

2. It may communicate its observations on these reports to the General Assembly.

Article 65

The Economic and Social Council may furnish information to the Security Council and shall assist the Security Council upon its request.

Article 66

1. The Economic and Social Council shall perform such functions as fall within its competence in connection with the carrying out of the recommendations of the General Assembly.

2. It may, with the approval of the General Assembly, perform services at the request of Members of the United Nations and at the request of specialized agencies.

3. It shall perform such other functions as are specified elsewhere in the present Charter or as may be assigned to it by the General Assembly.

Voting

Article 67

1. Each member of the Economic and Social Council shall have one vote.

2. Decisions of the Economic and Social Council shall be made by a majority of the members present and voting.

Procedure

Article 68

The Economic and Social Council shall set up commissions in economic and social fields and for the promotion of human rights, and such other commissions as may be required for the performance of its functions.

Article 69

The Economic and Social Council shall invite any Member of the United Nations to participate, without vote, in its deliberations on any matter of particular concern to that Member.

Article 70

The Economic and Social Council may make arrangements for representatives of the specialized agencies to participate, without vote, in its deliberations and in those of the commissions established by it, and for its representatives to participate in the deliberations of the specialized agencies.

Article 71

The Economic and Social Council may make suitable arrangements for consultation with non-governmental organizations which are concerned with matters within its competence. Such arrangements may be made with international organizations and, where appropriate, with national organizations after consultation with the Member of the United Nations concerned.

Article 72

1. The Economic and Social Council shall adopt its own rules of procedure, including the method of selecting its President.

2. The Economic and Social Council shall meet as required in accordance with its rules, which shall include provision for the convening of meetings on the request of a majority of its members.

CHAPTER XI

DECLARATION REGARDING NON-SELF-GOVERNING TERRITORIES

Article 73

Members of the United Nations which have or assume responsibilities for the administration of territories whose peoples have not yet attained a full measure of self-government recognize the principle that the interests of the inhabitants of these territories are paramount, and accept as a sacred trust the obligation to promote to the utmost, within the system of international peace and security established by the present Charter, the well-being of the inhabitants of these territories, and, to this end:

    a. to ensure, with due respect for the culture of the peoples concerned, their political, economic, social, and educational advancement, their just treatment, and their protection against abuses;

    b. to develop self-government, to take due account of the political aspirations of the peoples, and to assist them in the progressive development of their free political institutions, according to the particular circumstances of each territory and its peoples and their varying stages of advancement;

    c. to further international peace and security;

    d. to promote constructive measures of development, to encourage research, and to cooperate with one another and, when and where appropriate, with specialized international bodies with a view to the practical achievement of the social, economic, and scientific purposes set forth in this Article; and

e. to transmit regularly to the Secretary-General for information purposes, subject to such limitation as security and constitutional considerations may require, statistical and other information of a technical nature relating to economic, social, and educational conditions in the territories for which they are respectively responsible other than those territories to which Chapters XII and XIII apply.

Article 74

Members of the United Nations also agree that their policy in respect of the territories to which this Chapter applies, no less than in respect of their metropolitan areas, must be based on the general principle of good-neighborliness, due account being taken of the interests and well-being of the rest of the world, in social, economic, and commercial matters.

Chapter XII

INTERNATIONAL TRUSTEESHIP SYSTEM

Article 75

The United Nations shall etsablish under its authority an international trusteeship system for the administration and supervision of such territories as may be placed thereunder by subsequent individual agreements. These territories are hereinafter referred to as trust territories.

Article 76

The basic objectives of the trusteeship system, in accordance with the Purposes of the United Nations laid down in Article 1 of the present Charter, shall be:

a. to further international peace and security;

b. to promote the political, economic, social, and educational advancement of the inhabitants of the trust territories, and their progressive development towards self-government or independence as may be appropriate to the particular circumstances of each territory and its peoples and the freely expressed wishes of the peoples concerned, and as may be provided by the terms of each trusteeship agreement;

c. to encourage respect for human rights and for fundamental freedoms for all without distinction as to race, sex, language, or religion, and to encourage recognition of the interdependence of the peoples of the world; and

d. to ensure equal treatment in social, economic, and commercial matters for all Members of the United Nations and their nationals, and also equal treatment for the latter in the administration of justice, without prejudice to the attainment of the foregoing objectives and subject to the provisions of Article 80.

Article 77

1. The trusteeship system shall apply to such territories in the following categories as may be placed thereunder by means of trusteeship agreements:

a. territories now held under mandate;

b. territories which may be detached from enemy states as a result of the Second World War; and

c. territories voluntarily placed under the system by states responsible for their administration.

2. It will be a matter for subsequent agreement as to which territories in the foregoing categories will be brought under the trusteeship system and upon what terms.

Article 78

The trusteeship system shall not apply to territories which have become Members of the United Nations, relationship among which shall be based on respect for the principle of sovereign equality.

Article 79

The terms of trusteeship for each territory to be placed under the trusteeship system, including any alteration or amendment, shall be agreed upon by the states directly concerned, including the mandatory power in the case of territories held under mandate by a Member of the United Nations, and shall be approved as provided for in Articles 83 and 85.

Article 80

1. Except as may be agreed upon in individual trusteeship agreements, made under Articles 77, 79, and 81, placing each territory under the trusteeship system, and until such agreements have been concluded, nothing in this Chapter shall be construed in or of itself to alter in any manner the rights whatsoever of any states or any peoples or the terms of existing international instruments to which Members of the United Nations may respectively be parties.

2. Paragraph 1 of this Article shall not be interpreted as giving grounds for delay or postponement of the negotiation and conclusion of agreements for placing mandated and other territories under the trusteeship system as provided for in Article 77.

Article 81

The trusteeship agreement shall in each case include the terms under which the trust territory will be administered and designate the authority which will exercise the administration of the trust territory. Such authority, hereinafter called the administering authority, may be one or more states or the Organization itself.

Article 82

There may be designated, in any trusteeship agreement, a strategic area or areas which may include part or all of the trust territory to which the agreement applies, without prejudice to any special agreement or agreements made under Article 43.

Article 83

1. All functions of the United Nations relating to strategic areas, including the approval of the terms of the trusteeship agreements and of their alteration or amendment, shall be exercised by the Security Council.

2. The basic objectives set forth in Article 76 shall be applicable to the people of each strategic area.

3. The Security Council shall, subject to the provisions of the trusteeship

agreements and without prejudice to security considerations, avail itself of the assistance of the Trusteeship Council to perform those functions of the United Nations under the trusteeship system relating to political, economic, social, and educational matters in the strategic areas.

Article 84

It shall be the duty of the administering authority to ensure that the trust territory shall play its part in the maintenance of international peace and security. To this end the administering authority may make use of volunteer forces, facilities, and assistance from the trust territory in carrying out the obligations towards the Security Council undertaken in this regard by the administering authority, as well as for local defense and the maintenance of law and order within the trust territory.

Article 85

1. The functions of the United Nations with regard to trusteeship agreements for all areas not designated as strategic, including the approval of the terms of the trusteeship agreements and of their alteration or amendment, shall be exercised by the General Assembly.

2. The Trusteeship Council, operating under the authority of the General Assembly, shall assist the General Assembly in carrying out these functions.

CHAPTER XIII

THE TRUSTEESHIP COUNCIL

Composition

Article 86

1. The Trusteeship Council shall consist of the following Members of the United Nations:

    a. those Members administering trust territories;

    b. such of those Members mentioned by name in Article 23 as are not administering trust territories; and

    c. as many other Members elected for three-year terms by the General Assembly as may be necessary to ensure that the total number of members of the Trusteeship Council is equally divided between those Members of the United Nations which administer trust territories and those which do not.

2. Each member of the Trusteeship Council shall designate one specially qualified person to represent it therein.

Functions and Powers

Article 87

The General Assembly and, under its authority, the Trusteeship Council, in carrying out their functions, may:

    a. consider reports submitted by the administering authority;

    b. accept petitions and examine them in consultation with the administering authority;

    c. provide for periodic visits to the respective trust territories at times agreed upon with the administering authority; and

    d. take these and other actions in conformity with the terms of the trusteeship agreements.

Article 88

The Trusteeship Council shall formulate a questionnaire on the political, economic, social, and educational advancement of the inhabitants of each trust territory, and the administering authority for each trust territory within the competence of the General Assembly shall make an annual report to the General Assembly upon the basis of such questionnaire.

Voting

Article 89

1. Each member of the Trusteeship Council shall have one vote.
2. Decisions of the Trusteeship Council shall be made by a majority of the members present and voting.

Procedure

Article 90

1. The Trusteeship Council shall adopt its own rules of procedure, including the method of selecting its President.
2. The Trusteeship Council shall meet as required in accordance with its rules, which shall include provision for the convening of meetings on the request of a majority of its members.

Article 91

The Trusteeship Council shall, when appropriate, avail itself of the assistance of the Economic and Social Council and of the specialized agencies in regard to matters with which they are respectively concerned.

CHAPTER XIV

THE INTERNATIONAL COURT OF JUSTICE

Article 92

The International Court of Justice shall be the principal judicial organ of the United Nations. It shall function in accordance with the annexed Statute, which is based upon the Statute of the Permanent Court of International Justice and forms an integral part of the present Charter.

Article 93

1. All Members of the United Nations are *ipso facto* parties to the Statute of the International Court of Justice.
2. A state which is not a Member of the United Nations may become a party to the Statute of the International Court of Justice on conditions to be determined in each case by the General Assembly upon the recommendation of the Security Council.

Article 94

1. Each Member of the United Nations undertakes to comply with the decision of the International Court of Justice in any case to which it is a party.
2. If any party to a case fails to perform the obligations incumbent upon it under a judgment rendered by the Court, the other party may have recourse to

the Security Council, which may, if it deems necessary, make recommendations or decide upon measures to be taken to give effect to the judgment.

Article 95

Nothing in the present Charter shall prevent Members of the United Nations from entrusting the solution of their differences to other tribunals by virtue of agreements already in existence or which may be concluded in the future.

Article 96

1. The General Assembly or the Security Council may request the International Court of Justice to give an advisory opinion on any legal question.

2. Other organs of the United Nations and specialized agencies, which may at any time be so authorized by the General Assembly, may also request advisory opinions of the Court on legal questions arising within the scope of their activities.

Chapter XV

THE SECRETARIAT

Article 97

The Secretariat shall comprise a Secretary-General and such staff as the Organization may require. The Secretary-General shall be appointed by the General Assembly upon the recommendation of the Security Council. He shall be the chief administrative officer of the Organization.

Article 98

The Secretary-General shall act in that capacity in all meetings of the General Assembly, of the Security Council, of the Economic and Social Council, and of the Trusteeship Council, and shall perform such other functions as are entrusted to him by these organs. The Secretary-General shall make an annual report to the General Assembly on the work of the Organization.

Article 99

The Secretary-General may bring to the attention of the Security Council any matter which in his opinion may threaten the maintenance of international peace and security.

Article 100

1. In the performance of their duties the Secretary-General and the staff shall not seek or receive instructions from any government or from any other authority external to the Organization. They shall refrain from any action which might reflect on their position as international officials responsible only to the Organization.

2. Each Member of the United Nations undertakes to respect the exclusively international character of the responsibilities of the Secretary-General and the staff and not to seek to influence them in the discharge of their responsibilities.

Article 101

1. The staff shall be appointed by the Secretary-General under regulations established by the General Assembly.

2. Appropriate staffs shall be permanently assigned to the Economic and Social Council, the Trusteeship Council, and, as required, to other organs of the United Nations. These staffs shall form a part of the Secretariat.

3. The paramount consideration in the employment of the staff and in the determination of the conditions of service shall be the necessity of securing the highest standards of efficiency, competence, and integrity. Due regard shall be paid to the importance of recruiting the staff on as wide a geographical basis as possible.

CHAPTER XVI

MISCELLANEOUS PROVISIONS

Article 102

1. Every treaty and every international agreement entered into by any Member of the United Nations after the present Charter comes into force shall as soon as possible be registered with the Secretariat and published by it.

2. No party to any such treaty or international agreement which has not been registered in accordance with the provisions of paragraph 1 of this Article may invoke that treaty or agreement before any organ of the United Nations.

Article 103

In the event of a conflict between the obligations of the Members of the United Nations under the present Charter and their obligations under any other international agreement, their obligations under the present Charter shall prevail.

Article 104

The Organization shall enjoy in the territory of each of its Members such legal capacity as may be necessary for the exercise of its functions and the fulfillment of its purposes.

Article 105

1. The Organization shall enjoy in the territory of each of its Members such privileges and immunities as are necessary for the fulfillment of its purposes.

2. Representatives of the Members of the United Nations and officials of the Organization shall similarly enjoy such privileges and immunities as are necessary for the independent exercise of their functions in connection with the Organization.

3. The General Assembly may make recommendations with a view to determining the details of the application of paragraphs 1 and 2 of this Article or may propose conventions to the Members of the United Nations for this purpose.

CHAPTER XVII

TRANSITIONAL SECURITY ARRANGEMENTS

Article 106

Pending the coming into force of such special agreements referred to in Article 43 as in the opinion of the Security Council enable it to begin the exercise of its responsibilities under Article 42, the parties to the Four-Nation Declaration, signed at Moscow, October 30, 1943, and France, shall, in accordance with the provisions of paragraph 5 of that Declaration, consult with one another and as occasion requires with other Members of the United Nations with a view to such joint action on behalf of the Organization as may be necessary for the purpose of maintaining international peace and security.

Article 107

Nothing in the present Charter shall invalidate or preclude action, in relation to any state which during the Second World War has been an enemy of any signatory to the present Charter, taken or authorized as a result of that war by the Governments having responsibility for such action.

CHAPTER XVIII

AMENDMENTS

Article 108

Amendments to the present Charter shall come into force for all Members of the United Nations when they have been adopted by a vote of two thirds of the members of the General Assembly and ratified in accordance with their respective constitutional processes by two thirds of the Members of the United Nations, including all the permanent members of the Security Council.

Article 109

1. A General Conference of the Members of the United Nations for the purpose of reviewing the present Charter may be held at a date and place to be fixed by a two-thirds vote of the members of the General Assembly and by a vote of any seven members of the Security Council. Each Member of the United Nations shall have one vote in the conference.

2. Any alteration of the present Charter recommended by a two-thirds vote of the conference shall take effect when ratified in accordance with their respective constitutional processes by two-thirds of the Members of the United Nations including all the permanent members of the Security Council.

3. If such a conference has not been held before the tenth annual session of the General Assembly following the coming into force of the present Charter, the proposal to call such a conference shall be placed on the agenda of that session of the General Assembly, and the conference shall be held if so decided by a majority vote of the members of the General Assembly and by a vote of any seven members of the Security Council.

CHAPTER XIX

RATIFICATION AND SIGNATURE

Article 110

1. The present Charter shall be ratified by the signatory states in accordance with their respective constitutional processes.

2. The ratifications shall be deposited with the Government of the United States of America, which shall notify all the signatory states of each deposit as well as the Secretary-General of the Organization when he has been appointed.

3. The present Charter shall come into force upon the deposit of ratifications by the Republic of China, France, the Union of Soviet Socialist Republics, the United Kingdom of Great Britain and Northern Ireland, and the United States

of America, and by a majority of the other signatory states. A protocol of the ratifications deposited shall thereupon be drawn up by the Government of the United States of America which shall communicate copies thereof to all the signatory states.

4. The states signatory to the present Charter which ratify it after it has come into force will become original Members of the United Nations on the date of the deposit of their respective ratifications.

Article 111

The present Charter, of which the Chinese, French, Russian, English, and Spanish texts are equally authentic, shall remain deposited in the archives of the Government of the United States of America. Duly certified copies thereof shall be transmitted by that Government to the Governments of the other signatory states.

IN FAITH WHEREOF the representatives of the Governments of the United Nations have signed the present Charter.

DONE at the city of San Francisco the twenty-sixth day of June, one thousand nine hundred and forty-five.

APPENDIX III

Members of the United Nations and Specialized Agencies
(As of 31 December 1952)

	UN	ILO	FAO	UNESCO	ICAO	BANK	FUND	WHO[4]	UPU[6]	ITU[8]	WMO[11]	IMCO	IC.ITO[13]
AFGHANISTAN													
ALBANIA								5					
ARGENTINA													
AUSTRALIA												12	
AUSTRIA													
BELGIUM												12	
BOLIVIA													
BRAZIL													
BULGARIA								5					
BURMA												12	
BYELORUSSIAN SSR								5					
*CAMBODIA											★	12	
CANADA													
CEYLON													
CHILE													
CHINA								5					
COLOMBIA													
COSTA RICA													
CUBA													
CZECHOSLOVAKIA								5					
DENMARK													
DOMINICAN REPUBLIC													
ECUADOR													
EGYPT													
EL SALVADOR													
ETHIOPIA													
FINLAND													
FRANCE												12	
GERMANY		1	1	1		1	1	1	7	1			
GREECE													
GUATEMALA												12	
HAITI													
HONDURAS													
HUNGARY								5					
ICELAND													
INDIA													

(To designate certain of the members listed in the following notes, the nomenclature in use by the specialized agency concerned has been used. This in some cases differs from the official nomenclature of the United Nations.)

1. Refers to Federal Republic of Germany.

2. Refers to Republic of Korea.

3. Czechoslovakia, Hungary and Poland notified UNESCO they no longer consider themselves members. Spain, Nepal and Libya were admitted to membership in UNESCO by the General Conference at its seventh session (November-December 1952), but had not by the end of the year deposited their instruments of acceptance of UNESCO's Constitution.

4. WHO has three associate members: the French Protectorate of Morocco, Southern Rhodesia and Tunisia.

5. The Governments of Bulgaria, the Byelorussian SSR, the Ukrainian SSR, and the USSR in 1949, the Nationalist Government of China and the Governments of Albania, Czechoslovakia, Hungary, Poland and Romania in 1950, notified WHO that they no longer consider themselves Members of that organization.

6. In addition to members listed, UPU'S total of 93 Members, excluding Germany, includes: Algeria; Belgian Congo; French Morocco; French Overseas Territories and Territories administered as such; Netherlands Antilles and Surinam; Portuguese Colonies of West Africa; Portuguese Colonies of East Africa, Asia and Oceania; Spanish Colonies; Spanish Morocco; Tunisia; United Kingdom Overseas Colonies, Protectorates and Territories under Trusteeship; and United States Possessions.

7. Germany is temporarily prevented from

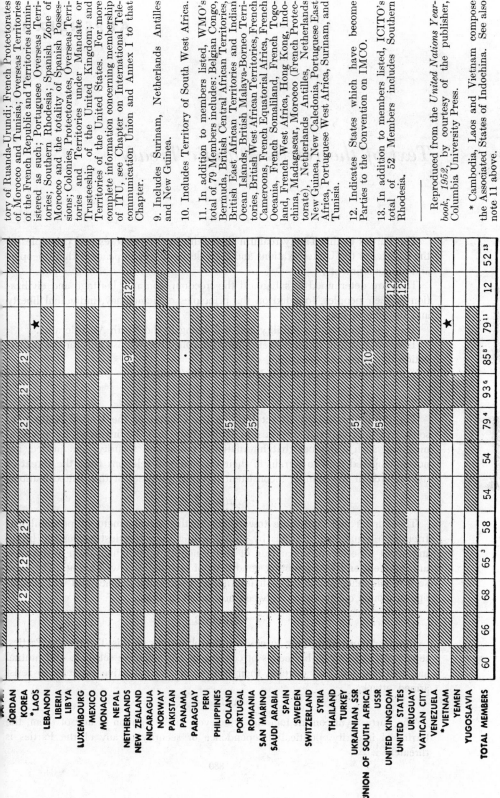

tory of Ruanda-Urundi; French Protectorates of Morocco and Tunisia; Overseas Territories of the French Republic and Territories administered as such; Portuguese Overseas Territories; Southern Rhodesia; Spanish Zone of Morocco and the totality of Spanish Possessions; Colonies, Protectorates, Overseas Territories and Territories under Mandate or Trusteeship of the United Kingdom; and Territories of the United States. For more complete information concerning membership of ITU, see Chapter on International Telecommunication Union and Annex I to that Chapter.

9. Includes Surinam, Netherlands Antilles and New Guinea.

10. Includes Territory of South West Africa.

11. In addition to members listed, WMO's total of 79 Members includes: Belgian Congo, Bermuda, British Central African Territories, British East African Territories and Indian Ocean Islands, British Malaya-Borneo Territories, British West African Territories, French Cameroons, French Equatorial Africa, French Oceania, French Somaliland, French Togoland, French West Africa, Hong Kong, Indochina, Madagascar, Morocco (French Protectorate), Netherlands Antilles, Netherlands New Guinea, New Caledonia, Portuguese East Africa, Portuguese West Africa, Surinam, and Tunisia.

12. Indicates States which have become Parties to the Convention on IMCO.

13. In addition to members listed, ICITO's total of 52 Members includes Southern Rhodesia.

Reproduced from the *United Nations Yearbook, 1952,* by courtesy of the publisher, Columbia University Press.

* Cambodia, Laos and Vietnam compose the Associated States of Indochina. See also note 11 above.

Text of the North Atlantic Treaty

The Parties to this Treaty reaffirm their faith in the purposes and principles of the Charter of the United Nations and their desire to live in peace with all peoples and all governments.

They are determined to safeguard the freedom, common heritage and civilization of their peoples, founded on the principles of democracy, individual liberty and the rule of law.

They seek to promote stability and well-being in the North Atlantic area.

They are resolved to unite their efforts for collective defense and for the preservation of peace and security.

They therefore agree to this North Atlantic Treaty:

Article 1

The Parties undertake, as set forth in the Charter of the United Nations, to settle any international disputes in which they may be involved by peaceful means in such a manner that international peace and security, and justice, are not endangered, and to refrain in their international relations from the threat or use of force in any manner inconsistent with the purposes of the United Nations.

Article 2

The Parties will contribute toward the further development of peaceful and friendly international relations by strengthening their free institutions, by bringing about a better understanding of the principles upon which these institutions are founded, and by promoting conditions of stability and well-being. They will seek to eliminate conflict in their international economic policies and will encourage economic collaboration between any or all of them.

Article 3

In order more effectively to achieve the objectives of this Treaty, the Parties, separately and jointly, by means of continuous and effective self-help and mutual aid, will maintain and develop their individual and collective capacity to resist armed attack.

Article 4

The Parties will consult together whenever, in the opinion of any of them, the territorial integrity, political independence or security of any of the Parties is threatened.

Article 5

The Parties agree that an armed attack against one or more of them in Europe or North America shall be considered an attack against them all; and consequently they agree that, if such an armed attack occurs, each of them, in exercise of the right of individual or collective self-defense recognized by Article 51 of the Charter of the United Nations, will assist the Party or Parties so attacked by taking forthwith, individually and in concert with the other Parties, such action as it deems necessary, including the use of armed force, to restore and maintain the security of the North Atlantic area.

Any such armed attack and all measures taken as a result thereof shall immediately be reported to the Security Council. Such measures shall be terminated when the Security Council has taken the measures necessary to restore and maintain international peace and security.

Article 6

For the purpose of Article 5 an armed attack on one or more of the Parties is deemed to include an armed attack on the territory of any of the Parties in Europe or North America, on the Algerian departments of France, on the occupation forces of any Party in Europe, on the islands under the jurisdiction of any Party in the North Atlantic area north of the Tropic of Cancer or on the vessels or aircraft in this area of any of the Parties.

Article 7

This Treaty does not affect, and shall not be interpreted as affecting, in any way the rights and obligations under the Charter of the Parties which are members of the United Nations, or the primary responsibility of the Security Council for the maintenance of international peace and security.

Article 8

Each Party declares that none of the international engagements now in force between it and any other of the Parties or any third state is in conflict with the provisions of this Treaty, and undertakes not to enter into any international engagement in conflict with this Treaty.

Article 9

The Parties hereby establish a council, on which each of them shall be represented, to consider matters concerning the implementation of this Treaty. The council shall be so organized as to be able to meet promptly at any time. The council shall set up such subsidiary bodies as may be necessary; in particular it shall establish immediately a defense committee which shall recommend measures for the implementation of Articles 3 and 5.

Article 10

The Parties may, by unanimous agreement, invite any other European state in a position to further the principles of this Treaty and to contribute to the security of the North Atlantic area to accede to this Treaty. Any state so invited may become a party to the Treaty by depositing its instrument of accession with the Government of the United States of America. The Government of the United

States of America will inform each of the Parties of the deposit of each such instrument of accession.

Article 11

This Treaty shall be ratified and its provisions carried out by the Parties in accordance with their respective constitutional processes. The instruments of ratification shall be deposited as soon as possible with the Government of the United States of America, which will notify all the other signatories of each deposit. The Treaty shall enter into force between the states which have ratified it as soon as the ratifications of the majority of the signatories, including the ratifications of Belgium, Canada, France, Luxembourg, the Netherlands, the United Kingdom and the United States, have been deposited and shall come into effect with respect to other states on the date of the deposit of their ratifications.

Article 12

After the Treaty has been in force for ten years, or at any time thereafter, the Parties shall, if any of them so requests, consult together for the purpose of reviewing the Treaty, having regard for the factors then affecting peace and security in the North Atlantic area, including the development of universal as well as regional arrangements under the Charter of the United Nations for the maintenance of international peace and security.

Article 13

After the Treaty has been in force for twenty years, any Party may cease to be a party one year after its notice of denunciation has been given to the Government of the United States of America, which will inform the Governments of the other Parties of the deposit of each notice of denunciation.

Article 14

This Treaty, of which the English and French texts are equally authentic, shall be deposited in the archives of the Government of the United States of America. Duly certified copies thereof will be transmitted by that Government to the Governments of the other signatories.

C·J57

345–346, 349–351, 372, 450, 779; need for enforcement of, 80, 99, 126, 275, 347–349, 595, 839; war crimes, 349–351. *See also* International Court of Justice, International Law Commission, Permanent Court of International Justice

International Law Commission, UN, 94, 96, 346–347, 350–351, 378; codification of international law, 350–351; Declaration on Rights and Duties of States, 351; Nuremberg Trials, on, 351

International Meteorological Organization, (IMO), 256. *See also* World Meteorological Organization (WMO)

International Military Tribunal (Nuremberg Trials), 349–350

International Monetary Fund (IMF), 25, 62, 191, 194, 202, 220–221, 236–245, 249, 255, 276, 534, 552, 566, 569, 573, 577–581, 584–585, 587, 593, 595, 659, 752; Board of Governors, 239–241, 577–578; budget, 221, 241; conditions regulating access to, 238, 249; currencies, on par value of, 578–581; establishment, 62, 191, 236–241, 577; functions, 238–239, 577; gold, upholding value of, 239; import restrictions, on, 573; interest rate on loans, 238–239; ITO, relationship with, 249; membership in, 238–239, 242; purpose of loans, 238; resources available, 239, 245, 581, 585; structure, 239–241; subscription quotas, 239, 241, 569, 581; technical assistance of, 580–581; UN supervision, question of, 220–221; voting procedures, 238–241, 659

International Museums Office, 621

International Office for Refugees, League of Nations, 182–183, 617–618

International Office of Public Health, Paris, 41, 177–179, 263–265, 276, 601, 612, 642; General Advisory Health Council, 178–179, 180, 264

International Opium Commission, 41

international organization — definition of, and functions of, 6–15, 816–841; early development of (prior to League of Nations), 18–42

International Organization Immunities Act of 1945, 386

International Organization of Employers, 201

International Penal and Penitentiary Commission, 654

International Pharmacopeia, 639

International Prize Court, 40

International Radio Telegraphic Union, 170, 171, 523

International Refugee Organization (IRO), 202, 208, 267–269, 528, 534, 543, 595, 644, 656–659; budget, 269, 656–657; constitution, 268; dissolution of, 269; ECOSOC recommendation of plan for, 268; establishment, 267–268; evaluation, 267, 269; Inter-Governmental Committee on Refugees, assumption of responsibilities of, 268; Preparatory Commission, 268; services to refugees, 268, 656–657; UNRRA, assuming responsibilities of, 268

International Regulation for Preventing Collisions at Sea (1948), 587

International Rice Commission, FAO, 234, 553

International Sanitary Convention for Aerial Navigation (1933), 264

International Seamen's Code, 604–605

International Seismological Association, 161

International Social Science Council, 664

International Social Security Association, 627

International Standard Industrial Classification of Economic Activities, 593

International Studies Conference, 622

International Sugar Agreement (1953), 576

International Sugar Union, 41–42

International Telecommunication Union (ITU), 170–172, 194, 221, 257–258, 523, 586, 589–592; Administrative Radio Conference, 258; Administrative Telegraph and Telephone Conference, 258; budget, 221, 258; functions, 257–258; International Frequency Registration Board, 258; membership of, 258; Radio Consultative Committee, 258; Telegraph Consultative Committee, 258; Telephone Consultative Committee, 258; voting procedures, 258

international tension, *see* "Cold War"

International Theater Institute, 665

International Tin Study Group, 575

International Trade Organization (ITO), proposed, 66, 207–208, 233, 245–250, 571–576, 582, 833; charter, 572–573, 575; commercial policy code, 572; commodity agreements, 233, 248–249; Conference on Trade and Employment, 248; employment, 248; FAO, relationship with, 233; IMF, relationship with, 249; Interim Commission, 208, 249, 276; monopolies, 249; quotas, import, 248–249; structure, 249; subsidies, 249; tariffs, 248; trade, 248; voting procedures, 249

international transmission of news and right of correction, 648

International Transport Workers' Federation, 631

International Treponematosis Laboratory Center, U.S., 638

International Union of American Republics, 795

International Union of Official Travel Organizations, 587

international unions, public, 41–42

International Wheat Council, 55, 228, 233, 246, 516, 572

Inter-Parliamentary Union, 201

investment, international problems of private and public, 513, 518, 563–569, 584, 586, 596, 614, 676, 702, 764. *See also* economic development, finance, IBRD, loans

Iran — expropriation of British oil refineries in, 463–464, 469; United Nations: — participation in, 65, 104, 459, 464, 551; — International Court of Justice on case of petroleum dispute with United Kingdom, 348, 350, 464, 469, 824; — Soviet Union, dispute with, 137–138, 151, 156, 369, 402, 427–428, 448; — technical assistance, 551

Iraq — Arab League, participation in, 800–804; League of Nations: — on dispute involving boundary of, 405; — mandated territory of, 672–673; United Nations: — participation in, 104, 306, 315, 705; — Trusteeship Council, participation in, 306, 315

Irish Free State, Commonwealth, British, member of, 789–792

IRO, *see* International Refugee Organization

"Iron Curtain," 36, 431, 807–808. *See also* "Cold War"

irrigation, international problems of, 556, 564. *See also* food